The NEW STRONG'S GUIDE TO BIBLE WORDS

*An English Index to
Hebrew and Greek Words*

KEYED TO STRONG'S
NUMBERING SYSTEM

JAMES STRONG, LL.D., S.T.D.

THOMAS NELSON PUBLISHERS
Nashville • Atlanta • London • Vancouver

Published in Nashville, Tennessee, by Thomas Nelson, Inc. Distributed in Canada by Nelson/Word Inc.

The publisher wishes to acknowledge the editorial and composition services of John R. Kohlenberger III and Multnomah Graphics.

Library of Congress Cataloging-in-Publication Data

Strong, James, 1822–1894.
   The new Strong's guide to Bible words / James Strong.
     p. cm.
   ISBN: 978-1-4185-3218-5
   1. Bible—Concordances, English. 2. Hebrew language—Dictionaries—English. 3. Aramaic language—Dictionaries—English. 4. Greek language, Biblical—Dictionaries—English. 5. Bible. O.T.—Dictionaries—Hebrew. 6. Bible. O.T.—Dictionaries—Aramaic. 7. Bible. N.T.—Dictionaries—Greek. I. Strong, James, 1822–1894. New exhaustive concordance of the Bible. II. Strong, James, 1822–1894. New Strong's complete dictionary of Bible words. III. Strong, James, 1822–1894. New Strong's Hebrew and Aramaic dictionary. IV. Strong, James, 1822–1894. New Strong's Greek dictionary. V. Title.
BS425.S85   1997
220.5′2033—dc20
                                                   96–36197
                                                   CIP

Printed in the United States of America
1 2 3 4 5 6 7 8 9 10 — 01 00 99 98 97 96

How to Use the English Index to Hebrew and Greek Words

What the Index Is

The English Index to Hebrew and Greek words contains every major word in the *KJV* with a list of every Hebrew, Aramaic, and Greek word that each English word translates. Words that are omitted from this list include words that appear in the Appendix of Articles in the original *Strong's Exhaustive Concordance* (such as "a," "and," and "the") and words that do not directly translate a Hebrew, Aramaic, or Greek word (such as "aileth," "letting," and "shouldest"). English words are listed in alphabetical order, exactly as they are spelled in the *KJV*.

Under each English entry is a listing of every Hebrew, Aramaic, and Greek word that the English word translates. These lists are organized in alphabetical order (which is also *Strong's* number order): Old Testament words first, then New Testament words. Each line has four elements: (1) *Strong's* number, (2) the original language word in transliteration, (3) the total number of times the word is so translated, and (4) a brief definition. (See the example on the following page.)

(1) If *Strong's* number is not italicized, it refers to an original word in the *Hebrew and Aramaic Dictionary*. If Strong's number and the transliterated word are *italicized*, it refers to an original word in the *Greek Dictionary*.

(2) Words are transliterated exactly as in the *Dictionaries*. If more than one Strong's number is listed on an entry line (**4672 + 1767** under "able," for example), in the interest of saving space, only the first word is transliterated. The additional word(s) are transliterated in the *Dictionaries*.

(3) The total number of occurrences is given to show patterns of *KJV* usage and in case you wish to study the original language words in the order of their frequency. For example, Greek word *25 (agapaō)* is translated "love" 70 times in the *KJV* and may be a more significant or interesting word than *2309 (thelō)*, which is translated as "love" only once.

(4) The brief definition summarizes *Strong's* fuller dictionary entries. These definitions actually function as a dictionary to the vocabulary of the *KJV*, informing you that a "habergeon" is a "coat of mail" or that "unction" is a "special endowment of the Holy Spirit." Sometimes these definitions update the scholarship of the *KJV*, as in the case of "unicorn," which is defined as "wild bull." As is the case of the occurrences statistics, the definition may also point out a key Hebrew, Aramaic, or Greek word that you may want to study in more detail by referring to the *Dictionaries*.

Using the Index with *The New Strong's™ Exhaustive Concordance*

The English Index provides a quick and easily used summary of the hundreds of thousands of contexts in *The New Strong's™ Exhaustive Concordance*, while the *Concordance* lists every context for every word of the *KJV*. This allows you to study the use of the word in the Bible itself, which is the most important way to understand how a specific word is used in a specific context. Although *Strong's Hebrew and Aramaic* and *Greek Dictionaries* offer definitions for each word of the original languages, these words do not have the sum total of every definition in every context. Greek word *26 (agapē)*, for example, cannot mean "affection" *and* "love-feast" every time it occurs. It means "affection" in such contexts as Philemon 7 and "love-feast" in Jude 12. Similarly, the historical or etymological materials that *Strong's Dictionaries* often present at the beginning of an entry may show something of the origin of a word, but are not necessarily its *definition* in every biblical context. For example, when Greek word *314 (anaginōskō)* is used in the New Testament, it means "to read," rather than "to know again," as *Strong's Dictionary* describes its origin.

Because the Index lists every Hebrew, Aramaic, and Greek word that is translated by any English word of the *KJV*, it functions as a concise dictionary and thesaurus of the biblical languages. Quickly scanning the entry for the word "love" shows that the word is used of general positive affection, deep compassion, fraternal affection, love for husbands, love for children, and greedy love of money. Reading the appropriate *Dictionary* entries will enlarge on these definitions. Again, if a *Strong's* number is not italicized (e.g., **157**), consult the *Hebrew and Aramaic Dictionary*. If a *Strong's* number is italicized (e.g., *26*), consult the *Greek Dictionary*. Each entry in the *Dictionaries* also provides a complete list of *KJV* words that translate the original language word, following the :— symbol. Greek word *26 (agapē)*, for example, lists four English words: charitably, charity, dear, and love. This shows the range of meaning the *KJV* translators assigned to *agapē*. By returning to the Index and looking up each of these English words, you find even more original language words to study.

In short, the wealth of materials contained in *The New Strong's™ Guide to Bible Words* is truly maximized in conjunction with *The New Strong's™ Exhaustive Concordance* when carefully applied to the study of God's Word.

An Example
from the English Index

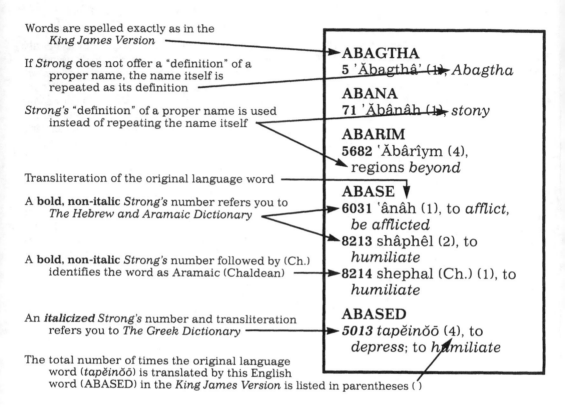

Words are spelled exactly as in the *King James Version*

ABAGTHA
5 'Ăbagthâ' (1), *Abagtha*

If *Strong* does not offer a "definition" of a proper name, the name itself is repeated as its definition

ABANA
71 'Ăbânâh (1), *stony*

Strong's "definition" of a proper name is used instead of repeating the name itself

ABARIM
5682 'Ăbârîym (4), regions *beyond*

Transliteration of the original language word

ABASE
A **bold, non-italic** *Strong's* number refers you to *The Hebrew and Aramaic Dictionary*

6031 'ânâh (1), to *afflict, be afflicted*

8213 shâphêl (2), to *humiliate*

A **bold, non-italic** *Strong's* number followed by (Ch.) identifies the word as Aramaic (Chaldean)

8214 shephal (Ch.) (1), to *humiliate*

An *italicized* *Strong's* number and transliteration refers you to *The Greek Dictionary*

ABASED
5013 tapĕinŏō (4), to depress; to *humiliate*

The total number of times the original language word (*tapĕinŏō*) is translated by this English word (ABASED) in the *King James Version* is listed in parentheses ( )

Words Omitted from the English Index

a	coloured	hers	one's	sunder	unperfect
about	condition	herself	onward	surely	unweighed
agone	counting	him	or	taker	unto
ailed	cunningly	himself	our	tapestry	up
aileth	dealer	his	ours	tend	upon
also	dealers	hurling	ourselves	tendeth	us
am	dealing	I	out	than	venomous
amounting	deals	in	parties	that	was
an	dearly	into	pertain	the	waxen
and	deputed	infallible	playedst	thee	we
apace	description	inflicted	playeth	thee-ward	weighing
appertained	deserve	its	practices	their	were
appertaineth	deserveth	itself	provokedst	theirs	what
are	determine	is	purposing	them	whatsoever
art	direction	it	quantity	themselves	which
as	dost	karnaim	ragged	then	who
battering	doth	letting	rests	thence	whom
be	drewest	liers	rovers	thenceforth	whom
became	duties	lign	sap	therefrom	whomsoever
becamest	easily	masteries	seatward	these	whose
become	ed	me	self	they	whoso
becometh	employment	meanest	selfsame	thine	whosoever
been	entreateth	mightest	selves	things'	with
belongest	estates	mine	shall	this	witty
belonging	exploits	mixt	shalt	those	ye
bestead	extendeth	my	she	thou	you
busied	folks	myself	so	though	your
but	for	no	soever	thus	yours
by	from	none	shouldest	thy	yourselves
caring	guiding	nor	slave	thyself	you-ward
cases	guilt	not	soundeth	titles	
causest	hadst	O	strongly	to	
causing	he	of	such	too	
closer	her	on	suits	toward	

ENGLISH INDEX TO THE BIBLICAL LANGUAGES

AARON
175 'Ahărôwn (315),
Aharon
2 Aarṓn (4), Aaron

AARON'S
175 'Ahărôwn (30),
Aharon
2 Aarṓn (1), Aaron

AARONITES
175 'Ahărôwn (2),
Aharon

ABADDON
3 Abaddṓn (1),
destroying angel

ABAGTHA
5 'Ăbagthâ' (1), Abagtha

ABANA
71 'Ăbânâh (1), stony

ABARIM
5682 'Ăbârîym (4),
regions beyond

ABASE
6031 'ânâh (1), to afflict,
be afflicted
8213 shâphêl (2), to
humiliate
8214 shᵉphal (Ch.) (1), to
humiliate

ABASED
5013 tapĕinŏō (4), to
depress; to humiliate

ABASING
5013 tapĕinŏō (1), to
depress; to humiliate

ABATED
1639 gâra' (1), to
remove, lessen,
withhold
2637 châçêr (1), to lack;
to fail, want, make less
5127 nûwç (1), to vanish
away, flee
7043 qâlal (2), to be,
make light
7503 râphâh (1), to
slacken

ABBA
5 Abba (3), father

ABDA
5653 'Abdâ' (2), work

ABDEEL
5655 'Abdᵉ'êl (1), serving
God

ABDI
5660 'Abdîy (3),
serviceable

ABDIEL
5661 'Abdîy'êl (1),
servant of God

ABDON
5658 'Abdôwn (8),
servitude

ABED-NEGO
5664 'Ăbêd Nᵉgôw (1),
servant of -Nego
5665 'Ăbêd Nᵉgôw' (Ch.)
(14), servant of -Nego

ABEL
59 'Âbêl (2), meadow

62 'Âbêl Bêyth-Mă'akâh
(2), meadow of
Beth-Maakah
1893 Hebel (8),
emptiness or vanity
6 Abĕl (4), emptiness or
vanity

ABEL-BETH-MAACHAH
62 'Âbêl Bêyth-Mă'akâh
(2), meadow of
Beth-Maakah

ABEL-MAIM
66 'Âbêl Mayim (1),
meadow of water

ABEL-MEHOLAH
65 'Âbêl Mᵉchôwlâh (3),
meadow of dancing

ABEL-MIZRAIM
67 'Âbêl Mitsrayim (1),
meadow of Egypt

ABEL-SHITTIM
63 'Âbêl hash-Shittîym
(1), meadow of the
acacias

ABEZ
77 'Ebets (1), Ebets

ABHOR
887 bâ'ash (1), to be a
moral stench
1602 gâ'al (4), to detest;
to reject; to fail
2194 zâ'am (1), to be
enraged
3988 mâ'aç (1), to spurn;
to disappear
5006 nâ'ats (1), to scorn
8374 tâ'ab (1), to loathe
8581 tâ'ab (9), to loathe,
i.e. detest
655 apŏstugĕō (1), to
detest utterly, hate

ABHORRED
887 bâ'ash (2), to be a
moral stench
973 bâchal (1), to loathe,
detest
1602 gâ'al (1), to detest;
to reject; to fail
2194 zâ'am (1), to be
enraged
3988 mâ'aç (2), to spurn;
to disappear
5006 nâ'ats (2), to scorn
5010 nâ'ar (1), to reject
6973 qûwts (2), to be,
make disgusted
8262 shâqats (1), to
loathe, pollute
8581 tâ'ab (3), to loathe,
i.e. detest

ABHORREST
6973 qûwts (1), to be,
make disgusted
948 bdĕlussō (1), to
detest, abhor

ABHORRETH
2092 zâham (1), to
loathe, make loatheful
3988 mâ'aç (1), to spurn;
to disappear
5006 nâ'ats (1), to scorn

8581 tâ'ab (2), to loathe,
i.e. detest

ABHORRING
1860 dᵉrâ'ôwn (1),
aversion, loathing

ABI
21 'Ăbîy (1), fatherly

ABI-ALBON
45 'Ăbîy-'albôwn (1),
valiant, strong

ABI-EZER
44 'Ăbîy'ezer (2), helpful

ABI-EZRITE
33 'Abîy hâ-'Ezrîy (1),
father of the Ezrite

ABI-EZRITES
33 'Abîy hâ-'Ezrîy (2),
father of the Ezrite

ABIA
29 'Ăbîyâh (1),
worshipper of Jehovah
7 Abia (3), knowing

ABIAH
29 'Ăbîyâh (4),
worshipper of Jehovah

ABIASAPH
23 'Ăbîy'âçâph (1),
gatherer

ABIATHAR
54 'Ebyâthâr (29),
· abundant, liberal
8 Abiathar (1),
abundant, liberal

ABIATHAR'S
54 'Ebyâthâr (1),
abundant, liberal

ABIB
24 'âbîyb (6), head of
grain; month of Abib

ABIDA
28 'Ăbîydâ' (1), knowing

ABIDAH
28 'Ăbîydâ' (1), knowing

ABIDAN
27 'Ăbîydân (5), judge

ABIDE
935 bôw' (1), to go or
come
1481 gûwr (2), to sojourn,
live as an alien
1692 dâbaq (1), to cling
or adhere
2342 chûwl (1), to wait
2583 chânâh (1), to
encamp for abode
3427 yâshab (31), to
dwell, remain; to settle
3557 kûwl (3), to keep in;
to maintain
3867 lâvâh (1), to unite;
to remain
3885 lûwn (5), to be
obstinate
5975 'âmad (2), to stand
6965 qûwm (1), to rise
7937 shâkar (1), to
become tipsy, to satiate
1961 ĕpimĕnō (3), to
remain; to persevere

3306 mĕnō (27), to stay,
remain
3887 paramĕnō (1), to be
permanent, persevere
4357 prŏsmĕnō (1), to
remain; to adhere to

ABIDETH
935 bôw' (1), to go or
come
3427 yâshab (4), to dwell,
to remain; to settle
3885 lûwn (3), to be
obstinate
5975 'âmad (2), to stand
3306 mĕnō (20), to stay,
remain

ABIDING
3427 yâshab (2), to dwell,
to remain; to settle
4723 miqveh (1),
confidence; collection
5596 çâphach (1), to
associate; be united
7931 shâkan (1), to reside
63 agraulĕō (1), to camp
out, live outdoors
1304 diatribō (1), to
remain, stay
3306 mĕnō (2), to stay,
remain

ABIEL
22 'Ăbîy'êl (3), possessor
of God

ABIEZER
44 'Ăbîy'ezer (5), helpful

ABIGAIL
26 'Ăbîygayil (17), source
of joy

ABIHAIL
32 'Ăbîyhayil (6),
possessor of might

ABIHU
30 'Ăbîyhûw' (12),
worshipper of Him

ABIHUD
31 'Ăbîyhûwd (1),
possessor of renown

ABIJAH
29 'Ăbîyâh (20),
worshipper of Jehovah

ABIJAM
38 'Ăbîyâm (5), seaman

ABILENE
9 Abilēnē (1), Abilene

ABILITY
1767 day (1), enough,
sufficient
3581 kôach (2), force,
might; strength
5381 nâsag (1), to reach
1411 dunamis (1), force,
power, miracle
2141 ĕupŏrĕō (1), to have
means, have ability
2479 ischus (1),
forcefulness, power

ABIMAEL
39 'Ăbîymâ'êl (2), father
of Mael

ABIMELECH
40 'Ăbîymelek (65),
father of the king

ABIMELECH'S
40 'Ăbîymelek (2), father
of the king

ABINADAB
41 'Ăbîynâdâb (13),
generous, i.e. liberal

ABINOAM
42 'Ăbîynô'am (4),
gracious

ABIRAM
48 'Ăbîyrâm (11), lofty,
high

ABISHAG
49 'Ăbîyshag (5),
blundering

ABISHAI
52 'Ăbîyshay (25), (poss.)
generous

ABISHALOM
53 'Ăbîyshâlôwm (2),
friendly

ABISHUA
50 'Ăbîyshûwa' (5),
prosperous

ABISHUR
51 'Ăbîyshûwr (2), (poss.)
mason

ABITAL
37 'Ăbîyṭal (2), fresh

ABITUB
36 'Ăbîyṭûwb (1), good

ABIUD
10 Abioud (2), possessor
of renown

ABJECTS
5222 nêkeh (1), smiter;
attacker

ABLE
2296 châgar (1), to gird
on a belt; put on armor
2428 chayil (4), army;
wealth; virtue; strength
3201 yâkôl (44), to be able
3202 yᵉkêl (Ch.) (4), to be
able
3318 yâtsâ' (15), to go,
bring out
3320 yâtsab (3), to
station, offer, continue
3546 kᵉhal (Ch.) (2), to be
able
3581 kôach (1), force,
might; strength
4672+1767 mâtsâ' (2), to
find or acquire
4979+3027 mattânâh (1),
present; offering; bribe
4991+3027 mattâth (2),
present
5060+1767 nâga' (1), to
strike
5375 nâsâ' (2), to lift up
5381 nâsag (6), to reach
5975 'âmad (1), to stand
6113 'âtsar (1), to hold
back; to maintain
6113+3581 'âtsar (2), to
hold back; to maintain
7272 regel (1), foot; step
1410 dunamai (41), to be
able or possible

1415 dunatŏs (10),
powerful or capable
1840 ĕxischuŏ (1), to be
entirely competent
2192 ĕchō (1), to have;
hold; keep
2425 hikanŏs (1), ample;
fit
2427 hikanŏō (1), to
make competent
2480 ischuō (6), to have
or exercise force

ABNER
74 'Abnêr (62),
enlightening

ABNER'S
74 'Abnêr (1),
enlightening

ABOARD
1910 ĕpibainō (1), to
mount, embark, arrive

ABODE
1961 hâyâh (2), to exist,
i.e. be or become
2583 chânâh (3), to
encamp
3427 yâshab (33), to
dwell, remain; to settle
5975 'âmad (1), to stand
7931 shâkan (6), to reside
390 anastrĕphō (1), to
remain, to live
835 aulizŏmai (1), to
pass the night
1304 diatribō (4), to
remain, stay
1961 ĕpimĕnō (1), to
remain; to persevere
2476 histĕmi (1), to
stand, establish
2650 katamĕnō (1), to
reside, stay, live
3306 mĕnō (12), to stay,
remain
3438 monē (1), residence,
dwelling place
4160 pŏiĕō (1), to make
or do
5278 hupŏmĕnō (1), to
undergo (trials)

ABODEST
3427 yâshab (1), to dwell,
to remain; to settle

ABOLISH
2498 châlaph (1), to
hasten away

ABOLISHED
2865 châthath (1), to
break down
4229 mâchâh (1), to erase
2673 katargĕō (3), to be,
render entirely useless

ABOMINABLE
2194 zâ'am (1), to be
enraged
6292 piggûwl (3),
unclean, fetid
8251 shiqqûwts (2),
disgusting idol
8262 shâqats (2), to
loathe, pollute
8263 sheqets (2), filthy
idolatrous object
8441 tôw'êbâh (4),
something disgusting
8581 tâ'ab (6), to loathe

111 athĕmitŏs (1),
illegal; detestable
947 bdĕluktŏs (1),
detestable, abominable
948 bdĕlussō (1), to
detest, abhor

ABOMINABLY
8581 tâ'ab (1), to loathe

ABOMINATION
887 bâ'ash (1), to be a
moral stench
6292 piggûwl (1),
unclean, fetid
8251 shiqqûwts (7),
disgusting idol
8262 shâqats (2), to
loathe, pollute
8263 sheqets (9), filthy
idolatrous object
8441 tôw'êbâh (52),
something disgusting
946 bdĕlugma (1),
detestable, abominable

ABOMINATIONS
8251 shiqqûwts (13),
disgusting idol
8441 tôw'êbâh (61),
something disgusting
946 bdĕlugma (2),
detestable, abominable

ABOUND
7227 rab (1), great
4052 pĕrissĕuō (12), to
superabound
4121 plĕŏnazō (4), to
superabound
4129 plĕthunō (1), to
increase in numbers
5248 hupĕrpĕrissĕuō (1),
to superabound

ABOUNDED
4052 pĕrissĕuō (4), to
superabound
4121 plĕŏnazō (1), to
superabound

ABOUNDETH
7227 rab (1), great
4052 pĕrissĕuō (1), to
superabound
4121 plĕŏnazō (1), to
superabound

ABOUNDING
3513 kâbad (1), to be
rich, glorious
4052 pĕrissĕuō (2), to
superabound

ABOVE
4480 min (2), from, out of
4605 ma'al (55), upward,
above, overhead
4791 mârôwm (7),
elevation; elation
5921 'al (67), above, over,
upon, or against
5922 'al (Ch.) (1), above,
over, upon, or against
507 anō (5), upward or
on the top, heavenward
509 anōthĕn (5), from
above; from the first
511 anōtĕrŏs (1), upper
part; former part
1883 ĕpanō (2), over or on
1909 ĕpi (5), on, upon
3844 para (4), from; with;
besides; on account of

4012 pĕri (1), about;
around
4117 plĕgma (1), plait or
braid of hair
4253 prŏ (4), before in
time or space
5228 hupĕr (13), over;
above; beyond
5231 hupĕranō (2),
above, upward

ABRAHAM
85 'Abrâhâm (160),
father of a multitude
11 Abraam (68), father of
a multitude

ABRAHAM'S
85 'Abrâhâm (14), father
of a multitude
11 Abraam (5), father of
a multitude

ABRAM
87 'Abrâm (54), high
father

ABRAM'S
87 'Abrâm (7), high
father

ABROAD
1980 hâlak (1), to walk;
live a certain way
2351 chûwts (21),
outside, outdoors
3318 yâtsâ' (1), to go,
bring out
5074 nâdad (1), to rove,
flee; to drive away
5203 nâtash (1), to
disperse; to thrust off
5310 nâphats (1), to dash
to pieces; to scatter
6327 pûwts (4), to dash
in pieces; to disperse
6340 pâzar (1), to scatter
6504 pârad (1), to spread
6524 pârach (1), to break
forth; to bloom
6527 pâraṭ (5), to scatter
words, i.e. prate
6555 pârats (3), to break
out
6566 pâras (5), to break
apart, disperse, scatter
6581 pâsâh (3), to spread
6584 pâshaṭ (1), to strip
7350 râchôwq (1),
remote, far
7554 râqa' (2), to pound
7849 shâṭach (1), to
expand
864 aphiknĕŏmai (1), to
go forth by rumor
1096+5456 ginŏmai (1),
to be, become
1232 diagnŏrizō (1), to
tell abroad
1255 dialalĕō (1), to
converse, discuss
1287 diaskŏrpizō (2), to
scatter; to squander
1289 diaspĕirō (3), to
scatter like seed
1290 diaspŏra (1),
dispersion
1310 diaphĕmizō (1), to
spread news
1330 diĕrchŏmai (1), to
traverse, travel through

1519+1096 ĕis (1), *to or into*
1519+5318 ĕis (2), *to or into*
1632 ĕkchĕō (1), to *pour forth;* to *bestow*
1831 ĕxĕrchŏmai (4), to *issue;* to *leave*
4496 rhiptō (1), to *fling, toss;* to *lay out*
4650 skŏrpizō (2), to *dissipate, be liberal*

ABSALOM
53 'Ăbîyshâlôwm (102), *friendly*

ABSALOM'S
53 'Ăbîyshâlôwm (5), *friendly*

ABSENCE
666 apŏusia (1), *being away, absence*
817 atĕr (1), *apart* from, *without*

ABSENT
5641 çâthar (1), to *hide by covering*
548 apĕimi (7), to *be away, be absent*
553 apĕkdĕchŏmai (3), to *expect fully, await*

ABSTAIN
567 apĕchŏmai (6), to *hold oneself off*

ABSTINENCE
776 asitia (1), state of food *fasting*

ABUNDANCE
369+4557 'ayin (1), *there is no, none*
1995 hâmôwn (3), *noise, tumult; many, crowd*
2123 zîyz (1), *fulness of the breast*
3502 yithrâh (1), *wealth, abundance*
4342 makbîyr (1), *plenty*
6109 'otsmâh (1), *numerousness*
6283 'ăthereth (1), *copiousness*
7227 rab (1), *great*
7230 rôb (35), *abundance*
7235 râbâh (2), to *increase*
7647 sâbâ' (1), *copiousness*
7962 shalvâh (1), *security, ease*
8228 shepha' (1), *abundance*
8229 shiph'âh (3), *copiousness*
8317 shârats (1), to *swarm,* or *abound*
100 hadrŏtēs (1), *liberality*
1411 dunamis (1), *force, power, miracle*
4050 pĕrissĕia (2), *superabundance*
4051 pĕrissĕuma (4), *superabundance*
4052 pĕrissĕuō (5), to *superabound*
5236 hupĕrbŏlē (1), *supereminence*

ABUNDANT
1419 gâdôwl (1), *great*
7227 rab (2), *great*
4052 pĕrissĕuō (2), to *superabound*
4055 pĕrissŏtĕrŏs (3), *more superabundant*
4056 pĕrissŏtĕrōs (2), *more superabundantly*
4121 plĕŏnazō (1), o *superabound*
4183 pŏlus (1), *much*
5250 hupĕrplĕŏnazō (1), to *superabound*

ABUNDANTLY
1288 bârak (1), to *bless*
3381 yârad (1), to *descend*
5042 nâba' (1), to *gush forth;* to *utter*
6524 pârach (1), to *break forth;* to *flourish*
7227 rab (2), *great*
7230 rôb (4), *abundance*
7235 râbâh (1), to *increase*
7301 râvâh (2), to *slake thirst or appetites*
7937 shâkar (1), to *become tipsy, to satiate*
8317 shârats (6), to *swarm,* or *abound*
1519+4050 ĕis (1), *to or into*
1537+4053 ĕk (1), *out of*
4053 pĕrissŏs (1), *superabundant*
4054 pĕrissŏtĕrŏn (2), *superabundant way*
4056 pĕrissŏtĕrōs (4), *more superabundantly*
4146 plŏusiōs (2), *copiously, abundantly*

ABUSE
5953 'âlal (2), to *glean;* to *overdo*
2710 katachraŏmai (1), to *overuse*

ABUSED
5953 'âlal (1), to *glean;* to *overdo*

ABUSERS
733 arsĕnŏkŏitēs (1), *sodomite*

ABUSING
2710 katachraŏmai (1), to *overuse*

ACCAD
390 'Akkad (1), *Accad*

ACCEPT
1878 dâshên (1), to *be fat, thrive;* to *satisfy*
3947 lâqach (1), to *take*
5375 nâsâ' (8), to *lift up*
7306 rûwach (1), to *smell* or *perceive*
7521 râtsâh (13), to *be pleased with;* to *satisfy*
588 apŏdĕchŏmai (1), *welcome persons*

ACCEPTABLE
977 bâchar (1), *select, chose, prefer*
2656 chêphets (1), *pleasure; desire*
7522 râtsôwn (9), *delight*

ABUNDANT (col 3 start)
8232 shephar (Ch.) (1), to *be beautiful*
587 apŏdĕktŏs (2), *agreeable, pleasant*
1184 dĕktŏs (2), *approved, favorable*
2101 ĕuarĕstŏs (4), *fully agreeable, pleasing*
2144 ĕuprŏsdĕktŏs (2), *approved, favorable*
5285 hupŏpnĕō (1), to *breathe gently*

ACCEPTABLY
2102 ĕuarĕstōs (1), *quite agreeably*

ACCEPTANCE
7522 râtsôwn (1), *delight*

ACCEPTATION
594 apŏdŏchē (2), *acceptance, approval*

ACCEPTED
3190 yâṭab (2), to *be, make well*
5307 nâphal (2), to *fall*
5375 nâsâ' (3), to *lift up*
7521 râtsâh (7), to *be pleased with;* to *satisfy*
7522 râtsôwn (4), *delight*
7613 sᵉ'êth (1), *elevation; swelling* leprous *scab*
1184 dĕktŏs (3), *approved, favorable*
1209 dĕchŏmai (2), to *receive, welcome*
2101 ĕuarĕstŏs (1), *fully agreeable, pleasing*
2144 ĕuprŏsdĕktŏs (3), *approved, favorable*
5487 charitŏō (1), one *highly favored*

ACCEPTEST
2983 lambanō (1), to *take, receive*

ACCEPTETH
5375 nâsâ' (1), to *lift up*
7521 râtsâh (2), to *be pleased with;* to *satisfy*
2983 lambanō (1), to *take, receive*

ACCEPTING
4327 prŏsdĕchŏmai (1), to *receive;* to *await for*

ACCESS
4318 prŏsagōgē (3), *admission, access*

ACCHO
5910 'Akkôw (1), to *hem in*

ACCOMPANIED
2064+4862 ĕrchŏmai (1), to *go or come*
4311 prŏpĕmpō (1), to *escort* or *aid in travel*
4902 sunĕpŏmai (1), to *travel* in company *with*
4905 sunĕrchŏmai (1), to *go with*

ACCOMPANY
2192 ĕchō (1), to *have; hold; keep*

ACCOMPANYING
5973 'îm (1), *with*

ACCOMPLISH
3615 kâlâh (5), to *complete, prepare*

ACCORDING (col 4)
4390 mâlê' (1), to *fill*
6213 'âsâh (2), to *do* or *make*
6381 pâlâ' (1), to *be, make great, difficult*
6965 qûwm (1), to *rise*
7521 râtsâh (1), to *be pleased with;* to *satisfy*
8552 tâmam (1), to *complete, finish*
4137 plĕrŏō (1), to *fill, make complete*

ACCOMPLISHED
1961 hâyâh (1), to *exist,* i.e. *be* or *become*
3615 kâlâh (7), to *complete, prepare*
4390 mâlê' (6), to *fill*
8552 tâmam (1), to *complete, finish*
1822 ĕxartizō (1), to *finish out;* to *equip fully*
2005 ĕpitĕlĕō (1), to *terminate;* to *undergo*
4130 plēthō (4), to *fulfill, complete*
5055 tĕlĕō (4), to *end,* i.e. *complete, execute*

ACCOMPLISHING
2005 ĕpitĕlĕō (1), to *terminate;* to *undergo*

ACCOMPLISHMENT
1604 ĕkplērōsis (1), *completion, end*

ACCORD
5599 çâphîyach (1), *self-sown* crop; *freshet*
6310 peh (1), *mouth; opening*
830 authairĕtŏs (1), *self-chosen*
844 autŏmatŏs (1), *spontaneous, by itself*
3661 hŏmŏthumadŏn (11), *in togetherness*
4861 sumpsuchŏs (1), *united in spirit*

ACCORDING
413 'êl (2), *to, toward*
834 'ăsher (1), *because, in order that*
1767 day (1), *enough, sufficient*
3605 kôl (1), *all, any*
3644 kᵉmôw (2), *like, as*
3651 kên (1), *just; right, correct*
4481 min (Ch.) (1), *from* or *out of*
5921 'al (39), *above, over, upon,* or *against*
6310 peh (21), *mouth; opening*
6903 qᵉbêl (Ch.) (1), *on account of, so as, since*
7272 regel (1), *foot; step*
2526 kathŏ (2), *precisely as, in proportion as*
2530 kathŏti (1), *as far* or *inasmuch as*
2531 kathōs (5), *just* or *inasmuch as, that*
2596 kata (109), *down; according to*
4314 prŏs (3), *for; on, at; to, toward; against*
5613 hōs (2), *which, how*

ACCORDINGLY
5922 'al (Ch.) (1), *above,
over, upon,* or *against*

ACCOUNT
2803 châshab (1), *to
think, regard; to value*
2808 cheshbôwn (1),
contrivance; plan
4557 miçpâr (1), *number*
6030 'ânâh (1), *to
respond, answer*
6486 pᵉquddâh (1),
visitation; punishment
1677 ĕllŏgĕŏ (1), *to
charge to one's account*
2233 hēgĕŏmai (1), *to
deem, i.e. consider*
3049 lŏgizŏmai (1), *to
credit; to think, regard*
3056 lŏgŏs (8), *word,
matter, thing; Word*

ACCOUNTED
2803 châshab (5), *to
think, regard; to value*
5608 çâphar (1), *to
enumerate; to recount*
1380 dŏkĕŏ (2), *to think,
regard, seem good*
2661 kataxiŏŏ (2), *to
deem entirely deserving*
3049 lŏgizŏmai (2), *to
credit; to think, regard*

ACCOUNTING
3049 lŏgizŏmai (1), *to
credit; to think, regard*

ACCOUNTS
2941 ṭa'am (Ch.) (1),
sentence, command

ACCURSED
2763 charam (1), *to
devote to destruction*
2764 chêrem (13),
doomed object
7043 qâlal (1), *to be easy,
trifling, vile*
7045 qᵉlâlâh (1),
vilification
331 anathĕma (4),
excommunicated

ACCUSATION
7855 siṭnâh (1),
opposition
156 aitia (3), *logical
reason; legal crime*
2724 katĕgŏria (3), *legal
criminal charge*
2920 krisis (2), *decision;
tribunal; justice*
4811 sukŏphantĕŏ (1), *to
exact unlawfully, extort*

ACCUSE
3960 lâshan (1), *to
calumniate, malign*
1908 ĕpĕrĕazŏ (1), *to
insult, slander*
2722 katĕchŏ (11), *to
hold down fast*
2723 katĕgŏrĕŏ (2), *to
bring a charge*
4811 sukŏphantĕŏ (1), *to
exact unlawfully, extort*

ACCUSED
399+7170 'âkal (Ch.) (2),
to eat
1225 diaballŏ (1), *to
malign by accusation*

1458 ĕgkalĕŏ (4), *to
charge, criminate*
1722+2724 ĕn (1), *in;
during; because of*
2722 katĕchŏ (4), *to hold
down fast*
2723 katĕgŏrĕŏ (2), *to
bring a charge*

ACCUSER
2723 katĕgŏrĕŏ (1), *to
bring a charge*

ACCUSERS
1228 diabŏlŏs (2),
traducer, i.e. Satan
2723 katĕgŏrĕŏ (6), *to
bring a charge*

ACCUSETH
2723 katĕgŏrĕŏ (1) *to
bring a charge*

ACCUSING
2722 katĕchŏ (1), *to hold
down fast*

ACCUSTOMED
3928 limmûwd (1),
instructed one

ACELDAMA
184 Akeldama (1), *field
of blood*

ACHAIA
882 Achaïa (11), *Greece*

ACHAICUS
883 Achaïkŏs (1),
Achaïan

ACHAN
5912 'Âkân (6),
troublesome

ACHAR
5917 'Âkâr (1),
troublesome

ACHAZ
881 Achaz (2), *possessor*

ACHBOR
5907 'Akbôwr (7), *Akbor*

ACHIM
885 Achĕim (2), cf.
Jehovah will raise

ACHISH
397 'Âkîysh (21), *Akish*

ACHMETHA
307 'Achmᵉthâ' (1),
Ecbatana

ACHOR
5911 'Âlôwr (5), *troubled*

ACHSA
5915 'Akçâh (1), *anklet*

ACHSAH
5915 'Akçâh (2), *anklet*
5919 'akshûwb (2), *asp,
coiling serpent*

ACHSHAPH
407 'Akshâph (3),
fascination

ACHZIB
392 'Akzîyb (4), *deceitful*

ACKNOWLEDGE
3045 yâda' (5), *to know*
5234 nâkar (6), *to
acknowledge*
1921 ĕpiginŏskŏ (4), *to
acknowledge*

ACKNOWLEDGED
3045 yâda' (1), *to know*

5234 nâkar (1), *to
acknowledge*
1922 ĕpignŏsis (1),
acknowledgement

ACKNOWLEDGEMENT
1922 ĕpignŏsis (1),
acknowledgement

ACKNOWLEDGING
1922 ĕpignŏsis (3),
acknowledgement

ACQUAINT
5532 çâkan (1), *to be
familiar with*

ACQUAINTANCE
3045 yâda' (6), *to know*
4378 makkâr (2),
acquaintance
1110 gnōstŏs (2),
well-known
2398 idiŏs (1), *private or
separate*

ACQUAINTED
3045 yâda' (1), *to know*
5532 çâkan (1), *to be
familiar with*

ACQUAINTING
5090 nâhag (1), *to drive
forth; to lead*

ACQUIT
5352 nâqâh (2), *to be,
make clean*

ACRE
4618 ma'ănâh (1),
furrow, plow path

ACRES
6776 tsemed (1), *acre
(i.e. a day's plowing)*

ACT
5556 çol'âm (1),
destructive locust kind
6467 pô'al (1), *act or
work, deed*
1888 ĕpautŏphōrōᵢ (1), *in
actual crime*

ACTIONS
5949 'ălîylâh (1),
opportunity, action

ACTIVITY
2428 chayil (1), *wealth;
virtue; valor; strength*

ACTS
1697 dâbâr (51), *word;
matter; thing*
4640 Ma'say (4),
operative
5949 'ălîylâh (1),
opportunity, action
6467 pô'al (2), *act or
work, deed*

ADADAH
5735 'Ăd'âdâh (1),
festival

ADAH
5711 'Âdâh (8), *ornament*

ADAIAH
5718 'Ădâyâh (9),
Jehovah has adorned

ADALIA
118 'Ădalyâ' (1), *Adalja*

ADAM
120 'âdâm (14), *human
being; mankind*
121 'Âdâm (8), *Adam*

76 Adam (8), *first man*

ADAM'S
76 Adam (1), *first man*

ADAMAH
128 'Ădâmâh (1), *soil;
land*

ADAMANT
8068 shâmîyr (2), *thorn;
(poss.) diamond*

ADAMI
129 'Ădâmîy (1), *earthy*

ADAR
143 'Ădâr (8), (poss.) *fire;
Adar*
144 'Ădâr (Ch.) (1),
(poss.) *fire; Adar*
146 'Addâr (1), *ample*

ADBEEL
110 'Adbᵉ'êl (2),
chastised of God

ADD
3254 yâçaph (22), *to add
or augment*
5414 nâthan (2), *to give*
5595 çâphâh (3), *to
accumulate; to remove*
2007 ĕpitithēmi (2), *to
impose*
2018 ĕpiphĕrō (1), *to
inflict, bring upon*
2023 ĕpichŏrēgĕŏ (1), *to
fully supply*
4369 prŏstithēmi (2), *to
lay beside, annex*

ADDAN
135 'Addân (1), *firm*

ADDAR
146 'Addâr (1), *ample*

ADDED
3254 yâçaph (4), *to add
or augment*
3255 yᵉçaph (Ch.) (1), *to
add or augment*
4323 prŏsanatithēmi (1),
to add; to impart
4369 prŏstithēmi (9), *to
lay beside, annex,
repeat*

ADDER
6620 pethen (2), *asp*
6848 tsepha' (1), *viper*
8207 shᵉphîyphôn (1),
cerastes or adder

ADDERS'
5919 'akshûwb (1), *asp,
coiling serpent*

ADDETH
3254 yâçaph (3), *to add
or augment*
1928 ĕpidiatassŏmai (1),
to supplement

ADDI
78 Addi (1), *finery*

ADDICTED
5021 tassŏ (1), *to arrange*

ADDITION
3914 lôyâh (1), *wreath*

ADDITIONS
3914 lôyâh (2), *wreath*

ADDON
114 'Addôwn (1),
powerful

ADER
5738 'Eder (1), arrangement

ADIEL
5717 'Ădîy'êl (3), ornament of God

ADIN
5720 'Ādîyn (4), voluptuous

ADINA
5721 'Ădîynâ' (1), effeminacy

ADINO
5722 'ădîynôw (1), his spear

ADITHAIM
5723 'Ădîythayim (1), double prey

ADJURE
7650 shâba' (2), to swear
1844 ĕxŏrkizŏ (1), to charge under oath
3726 hŏrkizŏ (2), to solemnly enjoin

ADJURED
422 'âlâh (1), imprecate, utter a curse
7650 shâba' (1), to swear

ADLAI
5724 'Adlay (1), Adlai

ADMAH
126 'Admâh (5), earthy

ADMATHA
133 'Admâthâ' (1), Admatha

ADMINISTERED
1247 diakŏnĕŏ (2), to act as a deacon

ADMINISTRATION
1248 diakŏnia (1), attendance, aid, service

ADMINISTRATIONS
1248 diakŏnia (1), attendance, aid, service

ADMIRATION
2295 thauma (1), wonder, marvel
2296 thaumazŏ (1), to wonder; to admire

ADMIRED
2296 thaumazŏ (1), to wonder; to admire

ADMONISH
3560 nŏuthĕtĕŏ (3), to caution or reprove

ADMONISHED
2094 zâhar (2), to enlighten
5749 'ûwd (1), to protest, testify; to restore
3867 parainĕŏ (1), to recommend or advise
5537 chrēmatizŏ (1), to utter an oracle

ADMONISHING
3560 nŏuthĕtĕŏ (1), to caution or reprove

ADMONITION
3559 nŏuthĕsia (3), mild rebuke or warning

ADNA
5733 'Adnâ' (2), pleasure

ADNAH
5734 'Adnâh (2), pleasure

ADO
2350 thŏrubĕŏ (1), to disturb; clamor

ADONI-BEZEK
137 'Ădônîy-Bezeq (3), lord of Bezek

ADONI-ZEDEK
139 'Ădônîy-Tsedeq (2), lord of justice

ADONIJAH
138 'Ădônîyâh (25), worshipper of Jehovah

ADONIKAM
140 'Ădônîyqâm (3), high, lofty

ADONIRAM
141 'Ădônîyrâm (2), lord of height

ADOPTION
5206 huiŏthĕsia (5), adoption

ADORAIM
115 'Ădôwrayim (1), double mound

ADORAM
151 'Ădôrâm (2), Adoram

ADORN
2885 kŏsmĕŏ (2), to decorate; to snuff

ADORNED
5710 'âdâh (1), to remove; to bedeck
2885 kŏsmĕŏ (3), to decorate; to snuff

ADORNETH
5710 'âdâh (1), to remove; to bedeck

ADORNING
2889 kŏsmŏs (2), world

ADRAMMELECH
152 'Adrammelek (3), splendor of (the) king

ADRAMYTTIUM
98 Adramuttēnŏs (1), Adramyttene

ADRIA
99 Adrias (1), Adriatic Sea

ADRIEL
5741 'Adrîy'êl (2), flock of God

ADULLAM
5725 'Ădullâm (8), Adullam

ADULLAMITE
5726 'Ădullâmîy (3), Adullamite

ADULTERER
5003 nâ'aph (3), to commit adultery

ADULTERERS
5003 nâ'aph (5), to commit adultery
3432 mŏichŏs (4), male paramour

ADULTERESS
802+376 'ishshâh (1), woman, wife
5003 nâ'aph (2), to commit adultery

3428 mŏichalis (2), adulteress

ADULTERESSES
5003 nâ'aph (2), to commit adultery
3428 mŏichalis (1), adulteress

ADULTERIES
5004 nî'ûph (2), adultery
5005 na'ăphûwph (1), adultery
3430 mŏichĕia (2), adultery

ADULTEROUS
5003 nâ'aph (1), to commit adultery
3428 mŏichalis (3), adulteress

ADULTERY
5003 nâ'aph (17), to commit adultery
3428 mŏichalis (1), adulteress
3429 mŏichaŏ (6), to commit adultery
3430 mŏichĕia (2), adultery
3431 mŏichĕuŏ (14), to commit adultery

ADUMMIM
131 'Ădummîym (2), red spots

ADVANCED
1431 gâdal (1), to be great, make great
5375 nâsâ' (2), to lift up
6213 'âsâh (1), to do or make

ADVANTAGE
5532 çâkan (1), to be serviceable to
4053 pĕrissŏs (1), superabundant
4122 plĕŏnĕktĕŏ (1), to be covetous
5622 ŏphĕlĕia (1), value, advantage

ADVANTAGED
5623 ŏphĕlĕŏ (1), to benefit, be of use

ADVANTAGETH
3786 ŏphĕlŏs (1), accumulate or benefit

ADVENTURE
5254 nâçâh (1), to test, attempt
1325 didōmi (1), to give

ADVENTURED
7993 shâlak (1), to throw out, down or away

ADVERSARIES
6696 tsûwr (1), to cramp, i.e. confine; to harass
6862 tsar (21), trouble; opponent
6887 tsârar (2), to cramp
7378 rîyb (1), to hold a controversy; to defend
7853 sâtan (5), to attack by accusation
7854 sâtân (1), opponent
480 antikĕimai (4), be adverse to
5227 hupĕnantiŏs (1), opposed; opponent

ADVERSARY
376+7379 'îysh (1), man; male; someone
1166+4941 bâ'al (1), to be master; to marry
6862 tsar (6), trouble; opponent
6869 tsârâh (1), trouble; rival-wife
6887 tsârar (1), to cramp
7854 sâtân (6), opponent
476 antidikŏs (5), opponent
480 antikĕimai (1), be adverse to

ADVERSITIES
6869 tsârâh (1), trouble; rival-wife
7451 ra' (1), bad; evil

ADVERSITY
6761 tsela' (1), limping
6862 tsar (1), trouble; opponent
6869 tsârâh (4), trouble; rival-wife
7451 ra' (3), bad; evil
2558 kakŏuchĕŏ (1), to maltreat; to torment

ADVERTISE
1540+241 gâlâh (1), to denude; to reveal
3289 yâ'ats (1), to advise

ADVICE
1697 dâbâr (2), word; matter; thing
2940 ţa'am (1), intelligence; mandate
3289 yâ'ats (2), to advise
5779 'ûwts (1), to consult
6098 'êtsâh (1), advice; plan; prudence
8458 tachbûlâh (1), guidance; plan
1106 gnōmē (1), cognition, opinion

ADVISE
3045 yâda' (1), to know
3289 yâ'ats (1), to advise
7200 râ'âh (1), to see

ADVISED
3289 yâ'ats (1), to advise
1012+5087 bŏulē (1), purpose, plan, decision

ADVISEMENT
6098 'êtsâh (1), advice; plan; prudence

ADVOCATE
3875 paraklētŏs (1), intercessor, consoler

AENEAS
132 Ainĕas (2), (poss.) praise

AENON
137 Ainōn (1), springs

AFAR
4801 merchâq (3), distant place; from afar
7350 râchôwq (29), remote, far
7368 râchaq (1), to recede; remove
3112 makran (2), at a distance, far away
3113 makrŏthĕn (13), from a distance or afar

467 muŏpazŏ (1), to *see indistinctly, be myopic*
4207 pŏrrhŏthĕn (2), *distantly, at a distance*

AFFAIRS
1697 dâbâr (2), *word; matter; thing*
5673 'ăbîydâh (Ch.) (2), *labor or business*
2596 kata (1), *down; according to*
4012 pĕri (2), *about; around*
4230 pragmatĕia (1), *transaction*

AFFECT
2206 zēlŏŏ (2), to *have warmth of feeling for*

AFFECTED
2206 zēlŏŏ (1), to *have warmth of feeling for*
2559 kakŏŏ (1), to *injure; to oppress; to embitter*

AFFECTETH
5953 'âlal (1), to *glean; to overdo*

AFFECTION
7521 râtsâh (1), to *be pleased with; to satisfy*
794 astŏrgŏs (2), *hard-hearted*
3806 pathŏs (1), *passion, concupiscence*
4698 splagchnŏn (1), *intestine; affection, pity*
5426 phrŏnĕŏ (1), to *be mentally disposed*

AFFECTIONATELY
2442 himĕirŏmai (1), to *long for, desire*

AFFECTIONED
5387 philŏstŏrgŏs (1), *lovingly devoted*

AFFECTIONS
3804 pathēma (1), *passion; suffering*
3806 pathŏs (1), *passion, concupiscence*

AFFINITY
2859 châthan (3), to *become related*

AFFIRM
1226 diabĕbaiŏŏmai (2), to *confirm thoroughly*
5346 phēmi (1), to *speak or say*

AFFIRMED
1340 diïschurizŏmai (2), to *asseverate*
5335 phaskŏ (1), to *assert a claim*

AFFLICT
3013 yâgâh (1), to *grieve; to torment*
3513 kâbad (1), to *be heavy, severe, dull*
3905 lâchats (1), to *press; to distress*
6031 'ânâh (28), to *afflict, be afflicted*
6887 tsârar (2), to *cramp*
7489 râ'a' (2), to *break to pieces*

AFFLICTED
1790 dak (1), *injured, oppressed*
3013 yâgâh (3), to *grieve; to torment*
4523 mâç (1), *disconsolate*
6031 'ânâh (21), to *afflict, be afflicted*
6040 'ŏnîy (1), *depression, i.e. misery*
6041 'ânîy (15), *depressed*
6862 tsar (1), *trouble; opponent*
6887 tsârar (2), to *cramp*
7043 qâlal (1), to *be easy, trifling, vile*
7489 râ'a' (3), to *break to pieces*
2346 thlibō (3), to *crowd, press, trouble*
2347 thlipsis (1), *pressure, trouble*
2553 kakŏpathĕō (1), to *undergo hardship*
5003 talaipōrĕŏ (1), to *be wretched*

AFFLICTEST
6031 'ânâh (1), to *afflict, be afflicted*

AFFLICTION
205 'âven (3), *trouble, vanity, wickedness*
3905 lâchats (3), to *press; to distress*
4157 mûw'âqâh (1), *pressure; distress*
6039 'ĕnûwth (1), *affliction*
6040 'ŏnîy (33), *depression, i.e. misery*
6862 tsar (3), *trouble; opponent*
6869 tsârâh (7), *trouble; rival-wife*
6887 tsârar (1), to *cramp*
7451 ra' (5), *bad; evil*
7667 sheber (2), *fracture; ruin*
2347 thlipsis (11), *pressure, trouble*
2552 kakŏpathĕia (1), *hardship, suffering*
2561 kakōsis (1), *maltreatment*
4797 sugchĕō (1), to *throw into disorder*

AFFLICTIONS
6031 'ânâh (1), to *afflict, be afflicted*
7451 ra' (1), *bad; evil*
2347 thlipsis (6), *pressure, trouble*
2553 kakŏpathĕō (1), to *undergo hardship*
3804 pathēma (3), *passion; suffering*
4777 sugkakŏpathĕō (1), to *suffer hardship*

AFFORDING
6329 pûwq (1), to *issue; to furnish; to secure*

AFFRIGHT
3372 yârê' (1), to *fear; to revere*

AFFRIGHTED
270+8178 'âchaz (1), to *seize, grasp; possess*
926 bâhal (1), to *tremble; be, make agitated*
1204 bâ'ath (1), to *fear*
2865 châthath (1), to *break down*
6206 'ârats (1), to *awe; to dread; to harass*
1568 ĕkthambĕŏ (2), to *astonish utterly*
1719 ĕmphŏbŏs (2), *alarmed, terrified*

AFOOT
3978 pĕzĕuŏ (1), to *travel by land, i.e. on foot*
3979 pĕzĕ₁ (1), *on foot*

AFORE
3808 lô' (1), *no, not*
6440 pânîym (2), *face; front*
6924 qedem (1), *before, anciently*
4270 prŏgraphō (1), to *write previously*
4279 prŏĕpaggĕllŏmai (1), to *promise from before*
4282 prŏĕtŏimazŏ (1), to *fit up in advance*

AFOREHAND
4301 prŏlambanŏ (1), to *take before*

AFORETIME
4481+6928+1836 min (Ch.) (1), *from or out of*
6440 pânîym (2), *face; front*
6924 qedem (1), *before, anciently*
7223 rî'shôwn (1), *first, in place, time or rank*
4218 pŏtĕ (1), *at some time, ever*
4270 prŏgraphō (1), to *write previously*

AFRAID
926 bâhal (3), to *tremble; be, make agitated; hasten, hurry anxiously*
1204 bâ'ath (10), to *fear*
1481 gûwr (6), to *sojourn, live as an alien*
1672 dâ'ag (3), *be anxious, be afraid*
1763 deᶜchal (Ch.) (1), to *fear; be formidable*
2119 zâchal (1), to *crawl; glide*
2296 châgar (1), to *gird on a belt; put on armor*
2342 chûwl (1), to *dance, whirl; to writhe*
2727 chârag (1), to *be dismayed, tremble*
2729 chârad (20), to *shudder with terror*
2730 chârêd (1), *fearful*
2865 châthath (6), to *break down, either by violence, or by fear*
3025 yâgôr (5), to *fear*
3372 yârê' (78), to *fear; to revere*
3373 yârê' (3), *fearing; reverent*

AFRIGHTED
6206 'ârats (3), to *awe; to dread; to harass*
6342 pâchad (9), to *be startled; to fear*
7264 râgaz (1), to *quiver*
7297 râhâh (1), to *fear*
7493 râ'ash (1), to *undulate, quake*
8175 sâ'ar (3), to *storm; to shiver, i.e. fear*
1168 dĕiliaŏ (1), to *be timid, cowardly*
1630 ĕkphŏbŏs (1), *frightened out of one's wits*
1719 ĕmphŏbŏs (3), *alarmed, terrified*
5141 trĕmō (1), to *tremble or fear*
5399 phŏbĕŏ (29), to *fear, be frightened*

AFRESH
388 anastaurŏŏ (1), to *re-crucify*

AFTER
167 'âhal (1), to *pitch a tent*
310 'achar (492), *after*
311 'achar (Ch.) (3), *after*
314 'achărôwn (5), *late or last; behind; western*
413 'êl (4), *to, toward*
834 'ăsher (2), *because, in order that*
870 'âthar (Ch.) (3), *after*
1767 day (2), *enough, sufficient*
1863 dardar (1), *thorn*
3602 kâkâh (4), *just so*
4480 min (1), *from, out of*
4481 min (Ch.) (1), *from or out of*
5921 'al (18), *above, over, upon, or against*
6256 'êth (1), *time*
6310 peh (1), *mouth; opening*
7093 qêts (10), *extremity; after*
7097 qâtseh (1), *extremity*
7272 regel (4), *foot; step*
516 axiōs (1), *appropriately, suitable*
1207 dĕutĕrŏprōtŏs (1), *second-first*
1223 dia (3), *through, by means of; because of*
1230 diaginŏmai (1), to *have time elapse*
1377 diōkŏ (1), to *pursue; to persecute*
1534 ĕita (3), *then, moreover*
1567 ĕkzĕtĕŏ (2), to *seek out*
1722 ĕn (1), *in; during; because of*
1836 hĕxēs (1), *successive, next*
1872 ĕpakŏlŏuthĕō (1), to *accompany, follow*
1887 ĕpauriŏn (1), *to-morrow*
1894 ĕpĕidē (1), *when, whereas*
1899 ĕpĕita (3), *thereafter, afterward*
1905 ĕpĕrōtaŏ (1), to *inquire, seek*

1909 ĕpi (3), *on, upon*
1934 ĕpizētĕō (4), *to search (inquire) for*
1938 ĕpithumētēs (1), *craver*
1971 ĕpipŏthĕō (3), *intensely crave*
2089 ĕti (1), *yet, still*
2517 kathĕxēs (1), *in a sequence*
2569 kalŏpŏiĕō (3), *to do well*
2596 kata (58), *down; according to*
2614 katadiōkō (1), *to search for, look for*
2628 katakŏlŏuthĕō (1), *to accompany closely*
3195 mĕllō (2), *to intend,* i.e. *be about to be*
3326 mĕta (96), *with, among; after, later*
3693 ŏpisthĕn (2), *at the back; after*
3694 ŏpisō (22), *behind, after, following*
3753 hŏtĕ (3), *when; as*
3765 ŏukĕti (1), *not yet, no longer*
3779 hŏutō (2), *in this way; likewise*
4023 pĕriĕchō (1), *to clasp; to encircle*
4137 plĕrŏō (1), *to fill, make complete*
4329 prŏsdŏkia (1), *apprehension*
4459 pōs (1), *in what way?; how?; how* much!
5225 huparchō (1), *to come into existence*
5613 hōs (3), *which, how,* i.e. *in that manner*
5615 hōsautōs (1), *in the same way*
5618 hōspĕr (1), *exactly like*

AFTERNOON
5186+3117 nâṭâh (1), *to stretch* or *spread out*

AFTERWARD
310 'achar (21), *after*
314 'achărôwn (2), *late* or *last; behind; western*
1208 dĕutĕrŏs (1), *second; secondly*
1534 ĕita (1), *then, moreover*
1899 ĕpĕita (2), *thereafter, afterward*
2517 kathĕxēs (1), *in a sequence*
2547 kakĕithĕn (1), *from that place* (or *time*)
3347 mĕtĕpĕita (1), *thereafter*
5305 hustĕrŏn (7), *more lately,* i.e. *eventually*

AFTERWARDS
268 'âchôwr (1), *behind, backward; west*
310 'achar (5), *after*
310+3651 'achar (2), *after*
314 'achărôwn (1), *late* or *last; behind; western*
1899 ĕpĕita (1), *thereafter, afterward*

5305 hustĕrŏn (1), *more lately,* i.e. *eventually*

AGABUS
13 Agabŏs (2), *locust*

AGAG
90 'Ăgag (8), *flame*

AGAGITE
91 'Ăgâgîy (5), *Agagite*

AGAIN
310 'achar (1), *after*
322 'âchôrannîyth (1), *by turning around*
1571 gam (2), *also; even*
1906 hêd (1), *shout of joy*
1946 hûwk (Ch.) (1), *to go, come*
3138 yôwreh (2), *autumn rain showers*
3254 yâçaph (49), *to add* or *augment*
3284 ya'ănâh (1), *ostrich*
5437 çâbab (1), *to surround*
5750 'ôwd (51), *again; repeatedly; still; more*
7725 shûwb (246), *to turn back; to return*
7999 shâlam (3), *to reciprocate*
8138 shânâh (1), *to fold; to transmute*
8145 shênîy (7), *second; again*
8579 tinyânûwth (Ch.) (1), *second time*
313 anagĕnnaō (2), *to beget* or *bear again*
321 anagō (2), *to lead up; to bring out*
326 anazaō (3), *to recover life, live again*
330 anathallō (1), *to flourish; to revive*
344 anakamptō (1), *to turn back, come back*
364 anamnēsis (1), *recollection*
375 anapĕmpō (2), *to send up* or *back*
386 anastasis (2), *resurrection* from death
450 anistēmi (15), *to come back to life*
456 anŏikŏdŏmĕō (2), *to rebuild*
467 antapŏdidōmi (2), *to requite good or evil*
470 antapŏkrinŏmai (1), *to contradict* or *dispute*
479 antikalĕō (1), *to reciprocate*
483 antilĕgō (1), *to dispute, refuse*
486 antilŏidŏrĕō (1), *to rail in reply, retaliate*
488 antimĕtrĕō (2), *to measure in return*
509 anōthĕn (2), *from the first; anew*
518 apaggĕllō (2), *to announce, proclaim*
523 apaitĕō (1), *to demand back*
560 apĕlpizō (1), *to fully expect in return*
591 apŏdidōmi (2), *to give away*

600 apŏkathistēmi (1), *to reconstitute*
618 apŏlambanō (1), *to receive; be repaid*
654 apŏstrĕphō (2), *to turn away or back*
1208 dĕutĕrŏs (3), *second; secondly*
1364 dis (2), *twice*
1453 ĕgĕirō (8), *to waken,* i.e. *rouse*
1458 ĕgkalĕō (1), *to charge*
1515 ĕirēnē (1), *peace; health; prosperity*
1880 ĕpanĕrchŏmai (1), *return home*
1994 ĕpistrĕphō (5), *to revert, turn back to*
3326 mĕta (1), *with, among; after, later*
3825 palin (141), *anew,* i.e. *back; once more*
4388 prŏtithĕmai (2), *to place before*
4762 strĕphō (2), *to turn around or reverse*
5290 hupŏstrĕphō (6), *to return*

AGAINST
413 'êl (144), *to, toward*
431 'ălûw (Ch.) (1), *lo!*
834 'âsher (1), *because, in order that*
4136 mûwl (19), *in front of, opposite*
4775 mârad (1), *to rebel*
5048 neged (33), *over against or before*
5227 nôkach (11), *opposite, in front of*
5704 'ad (3), *as far (long) as; during; while; until*
5921 'al (525), *above, over, upon,* or *against*
5922 'al (Ch.) (7), *above, over, upon,* or *against*
5971 'am (1), *people; tribe; troops*
5973 'îm (35), *with*
5978 'immâd (1), *along with*
5980 'ummâh (26), *near, beside, along with*
6440 pânîym (11), *face; front*
6640 tsᵉbûw (Ch.) (1), *affair; matter of determination*
6655 tsad (Ch.) (1), *at or upon the side of; against*
6903 qᵉbêl (Ch.) (1), *in front of, before*
6965 qûwm (1), *to rise*
7125 qîr'âh (41), *to encounter, to happen*
210 akōn (1), *unwilling*
368 anantirrhētŏs (1), *indisputable*
470 antapŏkrinŏmai (1), *to contradict* or *dispute*
471 antĕpō (1), *to refute*
481 antikru (1), *opposite*
483 antilĕgō (5), *to dispute, refuse*
495 antipĕran (1), *on the opposite side*

497 antistratĕuŏmai (1), *to wage war against*
561 apĕnanti (2), *before or against*
1519 ĕis (24), *to or into*
1690 ĕmbrimaŏmai (1), *to blame, warn sternly*
1693 ĕmmainŏmai (1), *to rage at*
1715 ĕmprŏsthĕn (1), *in front of*
1722 ĕn (1), *in; during*
1727 ĕnantiŏs (1), *opposite*
1909 ĕpi (38), *on, upon*
2018 ĕpiphĕrō (1), *to inflict, bring upon*
2019 ĕpiphōnĕō (1), *to exclaim, shout*
2596 kata (59), *down; according to*
2620 katakauchaŏmai (2), *to exult against*
2649 katamarturĕō (1), *to testify against*
2691 katastrēniaō (1), *to be voluptuous against*
2702 kataphĕrō (1), *to bear down*
2713 katĕnanti (4), *directly opposite*
2729 katischuŏ (1), *to overpower, prevail*
3326 mĕta (4), *with, among; after, later*
3844 para (2), *from; with; besides; on account of*
4012 pĕri (2), *around*
4314 prŏs (23), *for; on, at; to, toward; against*
4366 prŏsrēgnumi (1), *to burst upon*
5396 phluarĕō (1), *to berate*

AGAR
28 Agar (2), *Hagar*

AGATE
3539 kadkôd (1), (poss.) *sparkling ruby*
7618 shᵉbûw (2), *agate*

AGATES
3539 kadkôd (1), (poss.) *sparkling ruby*

AGE
582 'ĕnôwsh (1), *man; person, human*
1121 bên (3), *son, descendant; people*
1755 dôwr (2), *dwelling*
2207 zôqen (1), *old age*
2209 ziqnâh (1), *old age*
2465 cheled (2), *fleeting time; this* world
3117 yôwm (6), *day; time period*
3485 Yissâˢkâr (1), *he will bring a reward*
3624 kelach (2), *maturity*
7869 sêyb (1), *old age*
7872 sêybâh (6), *old age*
2244 hēlikia (1), *maturity*
2250 hēmĕra (1), *day; period of time*
5046 tĕlĕiŏs (1), *complete; mature*
5230 hupĕrakmŏs (1), *past the prime of youth*

AGED
2204 zâqên (1), to be old
2205 zâqên (4), old
3453 yâshîysh (1), old man
4246 prĕsbutēs (2), old man
4247 prĕsbutis (1), old woman

AGEE
89 'Âgê' (1), Agee

AGES
165 aiōn (2), perpetuity, ever; world
1074 gĕnĕa (2), generation; age

AGO
3117 yôwm (1), day; time period
6928 qadmâh (Ch.) (1), former time; formerly
7350 râchôwq (3), remote, far
575 apŏ (4), from, away
3819 palai (2), formerly; sometime since
4253 prŏ (1), before in time or space

AGONY
74 agōnia (1), anguish, anxiety

AGREE
1526 ĕisi (1), they are
2132 ĕunŏĕŏ (1), to reconcile
2470 isŏs (1), similar
4160+3391+1106 pŏiĕŏ (1), to make or do
4856 sumphōnĕŏ (3), to be harmonious

AGREED
3259 yâ'ad (1), to meet; to summon; to direct
800 asumphōnŏs (1), disagreeable
2470 isŏs (1), similar
3982 pĕithō (1), to pacify or conciliate
4856 sumphōnĕŏ (2), to be harmonious
4934 suntithĕmai (2), to consent, concur, agree

AGREEMENT
2374 chôzeh (1), beholder in vision
2380 châzûwth (1), revelation; compact
4339 mêyshâr (1), straightness; rectitude
4783 sugkatathĕsis (1), accord with

AGREETH
3662 hŏmŏiazō (1), to resemble, be like
4856 sumphōnĕŏ (1), to be harmonious

AGRIPPA
67 Agrippas (12), wild-horse tamer

AGROUND
2027 ĕpŏkĕllō (1), to beach a ship vessel

AGUE
6920 qaddachath (1), inflammation

AGUR
94 'Âgûwr (1), one received

AH
162 'ăhâhh (8), Oh!, Alas!, Woe!
253 'âch (2), Oh!; Alas!
1945 hôwy (7), oh!, woe!
3758 ŏua (1), ah!; so!

AHA
253 'âch (7), Oh!; Alas!

AHAB
256 'Ach'âb (90), friend of (his) father

AHAB'S
256 'Ach'âb (2), friend of (his) father

AHARAH
315 'Achrach (1), after (his) brother

AHARHEL
316 'Acharchêl (1), safe

AHASAI
273 'Achzay (1), seizer

AHASBAI
308 'Achaçbay (1), Achasbai

AHASUERUS
325 'Ăchashvêrôwsh (30), Xerxes

AHASUERUS'
325 'Ăchashvêrôwsh (1), Xerxes

AHAVA
163 'Ahăvâ' (3), Ahava

AHAZ
271 'Âchâz (41), possessor

AHAZIAH
274 'Ăchazyâh (37), Jehovah has seized

AHBAN
257 'Achbân (1), one who understands

AHER
313 'Achêr (1), Acher

AHI
277 'Achîy (2), brotherly

AHIAH
281 'Ăchîyâh (4), worshipper of Jehovah

AHIAM
279 'Ăchîy'âm (2), uncle

AHIAN
291 'Achyân (1), brotherly

AHIEZER
295 'Ăchîy'ezer (6), brother of help

AHIHUD
282 'Ăchîyhûwd (1), possessor of renown
284 'Ăchîychûd (1), mysterious

AHIJAH
281 'Ăchiyâh (20), worshipper of Jehovah

AHIKAM
296 'Ăchîyqâm (20), high, exalted

AHILUD
286 'Ăchîylûwd (5), brother of one born

AHIMAAZ
290 'Ăchîyma'ats (15), brother of anger

AHIMAN
289 'Ăchîyman (4), gift

AHIMELECH
288 'Ăchîymelek (16), brother of (the) king

AHIMELECH'S
288 'Ăchîymelek (1), brother of (the) king

AHIMOTH
287 'Ăchîymôwth (1), brother of death

AHINADAB
292 'Ăchîynâdâb (1), brother of liberality

AHINOAM
293 'Ăchîynô'am (7), brother of pleasantness

AHIO
283 'Achyôw (6), brotherly

AHIRA
299 'Ăchîyra' (5), brother of wrong

AHIRAM
297 'Ăchîyrâm (1), high, exalted

AHIRAMITES
298 'Ăchîyrâmîy (1), Achiramite

AHISAMACH
294 'Ăchîyçâmâk (3), brother of support

AHISHAHAR
300 'Achîyshachar (1), brother of (the) dawn

AHISHAR
301 'Ăchîyshâr (1), brother of (the) singer

AHITHOPHEL
302 'Ăchîythôphel (20), brother of folly

AHITUB
285 'Ăchîyţûwb (15), brother of goodness

AHLAB
303 'Achlâb (1), fertile

AHLAI
304 'Achlay (2), wishful

AHOAH
265 'Ăchôwach (1), brotherly

AHOHITE
266 'Ăchôwchîy (4), Achochite
1121+266 bên (1), son, descendant; people

AHOLAH
170 'Ohŏlâh (5), her tent (idolatrous sanctuary)

AHOLIAB
171 'Ohŏlîy'âb (5), tent of (his) father

AHOLIBAH
172 'Ohŏlîybâh (6), my tent (is) in her

AHOLIBAMAH
173 'Ohŏlîybâmâh (8), tent of (the) height

AHUMAI
267 'Ăchûwmay (1), neighbor of water

AHUZAM
275 'Ăchuzzâm (1), seizure

AHUZZATH
276 'Ăchuzzath (1), possession

AI
5857 'Ay (34), ruin
5892 'îyr (1), city, town, unwalled-village

AIAH
345 'Ayâh (5), hawk

AIATH
5857 'Ay (1), ruin

AIDED
2388+3027 châzaq (1), to be strong; courageous

AIJA
5857 'Ay (1), ruin

AIJALON
357 'Ayâlôwn (7), deer-field

AIJELETH
365 'ayeleth (1), doe deer

AIN
5871 'Ayin (5), fountain

AIR
7307 rûwach (1), breath; wind; life-spirit
8064 shâmayim (21), sky; unseen celestial places
109 aēr (7), air, sky
3772 ŏuranŏs (10), sky; air; heaven

AJAH
345 'Ayâh (1), hawk

AJALON
357 'Ayâlôwn (3), deer-field

AKAN
6130 'Ăqân (1), crooked

AKKUB
6126 'Aqqûwb (8), insidious

AKRABBIM
6137 'aqrâb (2), scorpion

ALABASTER
211 alabastrŏn (3), alabaster

ALAMETH
5964 'Âlemeth (1), covering

ALAMMELECH
487 'Allammelek (1), oak of (the) king

ALAMOTH
5961 'Âlâmôwth (2), soprano

ALARM
7321 rûwa' (4), to shout for alarm or joy
8643 tᵉrûw'âh (6), battle-cry; clangor

ALAS
160 'ahăbâh (7), affection, love
188 'ôwy (1), Oh!, Woe!
253 'âch (1), Oh!; Alas!
994 bîy (1), Oh that!
1930 hôw (1), oh! ah!
1945 hôwy (2), oh!, woe!
3758 ŏua (5), ah!; so!

ALBEIT
2443 hina (1), in order that

ALEMETH
5964 'Âlemeth (3), covering

ALEXANDER
223 Alĕxandrŏs (5), man-defender

ALEXANDRIA
221 Alĕxandrĕus (3), of Alexandria

ALEXANDRIANS
221 Alĕxandrĕus (1), of Alexandria

ALGUM
418 'algûwmmîym (3), Algum-wood

ALIAH
5933 'Alvâh (1), moral perverseness

ALIAN
5935 'Alvân (1), lofty

ALIEN
1616 gêr (1), foreigner
5236 nêkâr (1), foreigner
5237 nokrîy (3), foreign; non-relative

ALIENATE
5674 'âbar (1), to cross over; to transition

ALIENATED
3363 yâqa' (2), to be dislocated
5361 nâqa (3), to feel aversion
526 apallŏtriŏō (2), to be excluded

ALIENS
5237 nokrîy (1), foreign; non-relative
245 allŏtriŏs (1), not one's own
526 apallŏtriŏō (1), to be excluded

ALIKE
259 'echâd (1), first
834 'ăsher (1), who, which, what, that
1571 gam (1), also; even
3162 yachad (5), unitedly
7737 shâvâh (1), to equalize; to resemble

ALIVE
2416 chay (30), alive; raw; fresh; life
2418 chăyâ' (Ch.) (1), to live
2421 châyâh (34), to live; to revive
8300 sârîyd (1), survivor; remainder
326 anazaō (2), to recover life, live again
98 zaō (15), to live

2227 zōŏpŏiĕō (1), to (re-) vitalize, give life

ALL
622 'âçaph (1), to gather, collect
1571 gam (1), also; even
3162 yachad (1), unitedly
3605 kôl (4194), all, any
3606 kôl (Ch.) (50), all, any or every
3632 kâlîyl (2), whole, entire; complete; whole
3885 lûwn (14), to be obstinate with
4393 m°lô' (9), fulness
4557 miçpâr (3), number
5973 'îm (2), with
7230 rôb (1), abundance
8552 tâmam (2), to complete, finish
537 hapas (39), all, every one, whole
1273 dianuktĕrĕuō (1), to pass, spend the night
2178 ĕphapax (1), once for all
2527 kathŏlŏu (1), entirely, completely
3122 malista (1), in the greatest degree
3364 ŏu mē (7), not at all, absolutely not
3367 mēdĕis (1), not even one
3650 hŏlŏs (62), whole or all, i.e. complete
3654 hŏlōs (2), completely
3745 hŏsŏs (6), as much as
3762 ŏudĕis (4), none, nobody, nothing
3779 hŏutō (1), in this way; likewise
3829 pandŏchĕiŏn (1), public lodging-place
3832 panŏiki (1), with the whole family
3833 panŏplia (1), full armor
3837 pantachŏu (1), universally, everywhere
3843 pantōs (2), entirely; at all events
3956 pas (947), all, any, every, whole
4219 pŏtĕ (1), at what time?
4561 sarx (1), flesh

ALLEGING
3908 paratithēmi (1), to present something

ALLEGORY
238 allēgŏrĕō (1), to allegorize

ALLELUIA
239 allēlŏuïa (4), praise Jehovah!

ALLIED
7138 qârôwb (1), near, close

ALLON
438 'Allôwn (2), oak

ALLON-BACHUTH
439 'Allôwn Bâkûwth (1), oak of weeping

ALLOW
1097 ginōskō (1), to know
4327 prŏsdĕchŏmai (1), to receive; to await for
4909 sunĕudŏkĕō (1), to assent to, feel gratified

ALLOWANCE
737 'ărûchâh (1), ration, portion of food

ALLOWED
1381 dŏkimazō (1), to test; to approve

ALLOWETH
1381 dŏkimazō (1), to test; to approve

ALLURE
6601 pâthâh (1), to be, make simple; to delude
1185 dĕlĕazō (1), to delude, seduce

ALMIGHTY
7706 Shadday (48), the Almighty God
3841 pantŏkratōr (9), Absolute sovereign

ALMODAD
486 'Almôwdâd (2), Almodad

ALMON
5960 'Almôwn (1), hidden

ALMON-DIBLATHAIM
5963 'Almôn Diblâthây°mâh (2), Almon toward Diblathajim

ALMOND
8247 shâqêd (2), almond tree or nut

ALMONDS
8246 shâqad (6), to be, almond-shaped
8247 shâqêd (2), almond tree or nut

ALMOST
4592 m°'aṭ (5), little or few
3195 mĕllō (1), to intend, i.e. be about to be
4975 schĕdŏn (3), nigh, i.e. nearly

ALMS
1654 ĕlĕĕmŏsunē (13), benefaction

ALMSDEEDS
1654 ĕlĕĕmŏsunē (1), benefaction

ALMUG
484 'almuggiym (3), Almug-wood

ALOES
174 'ăhâlîym (4), aloe-wood sticks
250 alŏē (1), aloes

ALONE
259 'echâd (4), first
905 bad (42), apart, only, besides
909 bâdad (9), to be solitary, be alone
2308 châdal (2), to desist, stop; be fat
4422 mâlaṭ (1), to escape as if by slipperiness

ALLOW (right column continued)
7503 râphâh (4), to slacken
7662 sh°baq (Ch.) (1), t allow to remain
7896 shîyth (1), to place, put
863 aphiēmi (6), to leave; to pardon, forgive
1439 ĕaō (3), to let be, i.e. permit or leave alone
2651 katamŏnas (2), separately, alone
3440 mŏnŏn (3), merely, just
3441 mŏnŏs (21), single, only; by oneself

ALONG
1980 hâlak (3), to walk, live a certain way

ALOOF
5048 neged (1), over against or before

ALOTH
1175 B°'âlôwth (1), mistresses

ALOUD
1419+3605 gâdôwl (1), great
1627 gârôwn (1), throat
1993 hâmâh (1), to be in great commotion
2429 chayil (Ch.) (3), strength; loud sound
5414+854+6963 nâthan (1), to give
6670 tsâhal (2), to be cheerful; to sound
6963+1419 qôwl (1), voice or sound
7311+1419 rûwm (1), to be high; to rise or raise
7321 rûwa' (1), to shout for alarm or joy
7442 rânan (5), to shout for joy
7452 rêa' (1), crash; noise; shout
7768 shâva' (1), to halloo, call for help
310 anabŏaō (1), to cry out

ALPHA
1 A (4), first

ALPHAEUS
256 Alphaiŏs (5), Alphæus

ALREADY
3528 k°bâr (5), long ago, formerly, hitherto
2235 ēdē (18), even now
4258 prŏamartanō (1), to sin previously
5348 phthanō (1), to be beforehand

ALTAR
741 'ărî'êyl (3), altar
4056 madbach (Ch.) (1), sacrificial altar
4196 mizbêach (347), altar
1041 bōmŏs (1), altar
2379 thusiastēriŏn (21), altar

ALTARS
4196 mizbêach (52), altar

‑9 thusiastērion (1),
‑tar

ALTASCHITH
16 'Al tashchêth (4),
"Thou must not
destroy"

ALTER
2498 châlaph (1), to
hasten away; to pass
8133 sh^enâ' (Ch.) (2), to
alter, change
8138 shânâh (1), to
transmute

ALTERED
5674 'âbar (1), to cross
over; to transition
1096+2087 ginŏmai (1),
to be, become

ALTERETH
5709 'ădâ' (Ch.) (2), to
pass on or continue

ALTHOUGH
272 'ăchuzzâh (2),
possession
3588 kîy (7), for, that
because
2543 kaitŏi (1),
nevertheless

ALTOGETHER
259 'echâd (1), first
1571 gam (1), also; even
3162 yachad (5), unitedly
3605 kôl (4), all, any
3617 kâlâh (3), complete
destruction
3650 hŏlŏs (1), whole or
all, i.e. complete
3843 pantōs (2), entirely;
at all events

ALUSH
442 'Âlûwsh (2), Alush

ALVAH
5933 'Alvâh (1), moral
perverseness

ALVAN
5935 'Alvân (1), lofty

ALWAY
3605+3117 kôl (4), all,
any or every
5331 netsach (1),
splendor; lasting
5769 'ôwlâm (2), eternity;
ancient; always
8548 tâmîyd (4),
constantly, regularly
104 aĕi (8), ever, always
1275 diapantŏs (2),
constantly, continually
3842 pantŏtĕ (1), at all
times
3956+2250 pas (1), all,
any, every, whole

ALWAYS
3605+3117 kôl (4), all,
any or every
3605+6256 kôl (4), all,
any or every
5331 netsach (2),
splendor; lasting
5769 'ôwlâm (2), eternity;
ancient; always
8548 tâmîyd (6),
constantly, regularly
104 aĕi (3), ever, always

1223+3956 dia (3),
through, by means of
1275 diapantŏs (3),
constantly, continually
1539 hĕkastŏtĕ (1), at
every time
1722+3956+2540 ĕn (2),
in; during; because of
3839 pantē (1), wholly
3842 pantŏtĕ (29), at all
times

AMAD
6008 'Am'âd (1), people
of time

AMAL
6000 'Âmâl (1), wearing
effort; worry

AMALEK
6002 'Ămâlêq (24),
Amalek

AMALEKITE
6003 'Ămâlêqîy (3),
Amalekite

AMALEKITES
6003 'Ămâlêqîy (24),
Amalekite

AMAM
538 'Ămâm (1),
gathering-spot

AMANA
549 'Ămânâh (1),
covenant

AMARIAH
568 'Ămaryâh (14),
Jehovah has promised

AMASA
6021 'Ămâsâ' (16),
burden

AMASAI
6022 'Ămâsay (5),
burdensome

AMASHAI
6023 'Ămashçay (1),
burdensome

AMASIAH
6007 'Ămaçyâh (1),
Jehovah has loaded

AMAZED
926 bâhal (2), to tremble;
be, make agitated
2865 châthath (1), to
break down
8074 shâmêm (1), to
devastate; to stupefy
8539 tâmahh (1), to be
astounded
1096+2285 ginŏmai (1),
to be, become
1568 ĕkthambĕō (2), to
astonish utterly
1605 ĕkplēssō (3), to
astonish
1611 ĕkstasis (1),
astonishment
1611+2983 ĕkstasis (1),
astonishment
1839 ĕxistēmi (6), to
become astounded
2284 thambĕō (2), to
astound, be amazed

AMAZEMENT
1611 ĕkstasis (1),
astonishment

4423 ptŏēsis (1),
something alarm

AMAZIAH
558 'Ămatsyâh (40),
strength of Jehovah

AMBASSADOR
6735 tsîyr (3), hinge;
herald or errand-doer
4243 prĕsbĕuō (1), to act
as a representative

AMBASSADORS
3887 lûwts (1), to scoff; to
interpret; to intercede
4397 mal'âk (4),
messenger
6735 tsîyr (2), hinge;
herald or errand-doer
4243 prĕsbĕuō (1), to act
as a representative

AMBASSAGE
4242 prĕsbĕia (1),
ambassadors

AMBER
2830 chashmal (3),
bronze

AMBUSH
693 'ârab (7), to ambush,
lie in wait

AMBUSHES
693 'ârab (1), to ambush,
lie in wait

AMBUSHMENT
3993 ma'ărâb (2),
ambuscade, ambush

AMBUSHMENTS
693 'ârab (1), to ambush,
lie in wait

AMEN
543 'âmên (22), truly,
"may it be so!"
281 amēn (51), surely; so
be it

AMEND
2388 châzaq (1), to
fasten upon; to seize
3190 yâţab (4), to be,
make well
2192+2866 ĕchō (1), to
have; hold; keep

AMENDS
7999 shâlam (1), to be
friendly; to reciprocate

AMERCE
6064 'ânash (1), to inflict
a penalty, to fine

AMETHYST
306 'achlâmâh (2),
amethyst
271 amĕthustŏs (1),
amethyst

AMI
532 'Âmîy (1), skilled
craftsman

AMIABLE
3039 y^edîyd (1), loved

AMINADAB
284 Aminadab (3),
people of liberality

AMISS
5753 'âvâh (1), to be
crooked
7955 shâlâh (Ch.) (1),
wrong

824 atŏpŏs (1), improper;
injurious; wicked
2560 kakōs (1), badly;
wrongly; ill

AMITTAI
573 'Ămittay (2),
veracious

AMMAH
522 'Ammâh (1), cubit

AMMI
5971 'am (1), people

AMMI-NADIB
5993 'Ammîy Nâdîyb (1),
my people (are) liberal

AMMIEL
5988 'Ammîy'êl (6),
people of God

AMMIHUD
5989 'Ammîyhûwd (10),
people of splendor

AMMINADAB
5992 'Ammîynâdâb (13),
people of liberality

AMMISHADDAI
5996 'Ammîyshadday
(5), people of (the)
Almighty

AMMIZABAD
5990 'Ammîyzâbâd (1),
people of endowment

AMMON
5983 'Ammôwn (91),
inbred

AMMONITE
5984 'Ammôwnîy (9),
Ammonite

AMMONITES
1121+5984 bên (7), son,
descendant; people
5984 'Ammôwnîy (16),
Ammonite

AMMONITESS
5984 'Ammôwnîy (4),
Ammonite

AMNON
550 'Amnôwn (25),
faithful

AMNON'S
550 'Amnôwn (3), faithful

AMOK
5987 'Âmôwq (2), deep

AMON
526 'Âmôwn (17), skilled
craftsman
300 Amŏn (2), skilled
craftsman

AMONG
413 'êl (7), to, toward
854 'êth (8), with; among
996 bêyn (33), between
997 bêyn (Ch.) (1),
between; "either...or"
1460 gêv (1), middle,
inside, in, on, etc.
1767 day (1), enough,
sufficient
4480 min (4), from, out of
5921 'al (7), above, over,
upon, or against
5973 'îm (8), with
7130 qereb (74), nearest
part, i.e. the center

7310 reٔvâyâh (1),
satisfaction
8432 tâvek (142), center,
middle
575 apŏ (1), from, away
1223 dia (1), through, by
means of; because of
1519 ĕis (18), to or into
1537 ĕk (5), out, out of
1722 ĕn (115), in; during;
because of
1909 ĕpi (4), on, upon
2596 kata (2), down;
according to
3319 mĕsŏs (7), middle
3326 mĕta (5), with,
among; after, later
3844 para (2), from; with;
besides; on account of
4045 pĕripiptō (1), to fall
into the hands of
4314 prŏs (19), for; on, at;
to, toward; against
4315 prŏsabbatŏn (1),
Sabbath-eve
5259 hupŏ (1), under; by
means of; at

AMONGST
8432 tâvek (2), center,
middle

AMORITE
567 'Ĕmôrîy (14),
mountaineer

AMORITES
567 'Ĕmôrîy (73),
mountaineer

AMOS
5986 'Âmôwç (7),
burdensome
301 Amŏs (1), strong

AMOZ
531 'Âmôwts (13), strong

AMPHIPOLIS
295 Amphipŏlis (1), city
surrounded by a river

AMPLIAS
291 Amplias (1), enlarged

AMRAM
2566 Chamrân (1), red
6019 'Amrâm (13), high
people

AMRAM'S
6019 'Amrâm (1), high
people

AMRAMITES
6020 'Amrâmîy (2),
Amramite

AMRAPHEL
569 'Amrâphel (2),
Amraphel

AMZI
557 'Amtsîy (2), strong

ANAB
6024 'Ănâb (2), fruit

ANAH
6034 'Ănâh (12), answer

ANAHARATH
588 'Ănâchărâth (1),
gorge or narrow pass

ANAIAH
6043 'Ănâyâh (2),
Jehovah has answered

ANAK
6061 'Ânâq (9), necklace
chain

ANAKIMS
6062 'Ănâqîy (9), Anakite

ANAMIM
6047 'Ănâmîm (2),
Anamim

ANAMMELECH
6048 'Ănammelek (1),
Anammelek

ANAN
6052 'Ânân (1), cloud

ANANI
6054 'Ănânîy (1), cloudy

ANANIAH
6055 'Ănanyâh (2),
Jehovah has covered

ANANIAS
367 Ananias (11),
Jehovah has favored

ANATH
6067 'Ănâth (2), answer

ANATHEMA
331 anathĕma (1),
excommunicated

ANATHOTH
6068 'Ănâthôwth (16),
answers

ANCESTORS
7223 rî'shôwn (1), first, in
place, time or rank

ANCHOR
45 agkura (1), anchor

ANCHORS
45 agkura (2), anchor

ANCIENT
2204 zâqên (6), to be old,
venerated
3453 yâshîysh (1), old
man
5769 'ôwlâm (6), eternity;
ancient; always
6267 'attîyq (1), weaned;
antique
6268 'attîyq (Ch.) (3),
venerable, old
6917 qâdûwm (1),
pristine hero
6924 qedem (8), East,
eastern; antiquity;
before, anciently

ANCIENTS
2204 zâqên (9), to be old,
venerated
6931 qadmôwnîy (1),
anterior time; oriental

ANCLE
4974 sphurŏn (1), ankle

ANCLES
657 'epheç (1), end; no
further

ANDREW
406 Andrĕas (13), manly

ANDRONICUS
408 Andrŏnikŏs (1), man
of victory

ANEM
6046 'Ânêm (1), two
fountains

ANER
6063 'Ânêr (3), Aner

ANETHOTHITE
6069 'Anthôthîy (1),
Antothite

ANETOTHITE
6069 'Anthôthîy (1),
Antothite

ANGEL
4397 mal'âk (100),
messenger
4398 mal'ak (Ch.) (2),
messenger
32 aggĕlŏs (95),
messenger; angel

ANGEL'S
32 aggĕlŏs (2),
messenger; angel

ANGELS
430 'ĕlôhîym (1), the true
God; gods; great ones
4397 mal'âk (10),
messenger
8136 shin'ân (1), change,
i.e. repetition
32 aggĕlŏs (80),
messenger; angel
2465 isaggĕlŏs (1),
angelic, like an angel

ANGELS'
47 'abbîyr (1), mighty

ANGER
639 'aph (173), nose or
nostril; face; person
2195 za'am (1), fury,
anger
2534 chêmâh (1), heat;
anger; poison
3707 kâ'aç (42), to grieve,
rage, be indignant
3708 ka'aç (2), vexation,
grief
5006 nâ'ats (1), to scorn
5674 'âbar (1), to cross
over; to transition
5678 'ebrâh (1), outburst
of passion
6440 pânîym (3), face;
front
7307 rûwach (1), breath;
wind; life-spirit
3709 ŏrgē (3), ire;
punishment
3949 parŏrgizō (1), to
enrage, exasperate

ANGERED
7107 qâtsaph (1), to burst
out in rage

ANGLE
2443 chakkâh (2), fish
hook

ANGRY
599 'ânaph (13), be
enraged, be angry
639 'aph (4), nose or
nostril; face; person
1149 beٔnaç (Ch.) (1), to
be enraged, be angry
2194 zâ'am (2), to be
enraged
2734 chârâh (10), to
blaze up
3707 kâ'aç (2), to grieve,
rage, be indignant
3708 ka'aç (1), vexation,
grief
4751+5315 mar (1), bitter;
bitterness; bitterly

ANGUISH
2342 chûwl (1), to dance,
whirl; to writhe in pain
4689 mâtsôwq (1),
confinement; disability
4691 meٔtsûwqâh (1),
trouble, anguish
6695 tsôwq (3), distress
6862 tsar (1), trouble;
opponent
6869 tsârâh (5), trouble;
rival-wife
7115 qôtser (1),
shortness (of spirit)
7661 shâbâts (1),
intanglement
2347 thlipsis (1),
pressure, trouble
4730 stĕnŏchôria (1),
calamity, distress
4928 sunŏchē (1),
anxiety, distress

ANIAM
593 'Ănîy'âm (1),
groaning of (the) people

ANIM
6044 'Ănîym (1),
fountains

ANISE
432 anēthŏn (1), dill
seed for seasoning

ANNA
451 Anna (1), favored

ANNAS
452 Annas (4), Jehovah
has favored

ANOINT
4886 mâshach (25), to
rub or smear
5480 çûwk (5), to smear
218 alĕiphō (3), to oil
with perfume, anoint
1472 ĕgchriō (1), to
besmear, anoint
3462 murizō (1), to apply
perfumed unguent to

ANOINTED
1101 bâlal (1), to mix
1121+3323 bên (1), son,
descendant; people
4473 mimshach (1), with
outstretched wings
4886 mâshach (43), to
rub or smear with oil
4888 mishchâh (1),
unction; gift
4899 mâshîyach (37),
consecrated person;
Messiah
5480 çûwk (2), to smear
218 alĕiphō (5), to oil
with perfume, anoint
2025 ĕpichriō (1), to
smear over, anoint

2025+1909 ĕpichriō (1), to
smear over, anoint
5548 chriō (5), to smear
or rub with oil

ANOINTEDST
4886 mâshach (1), to rub
or smear with oil

ANOINTEST
1878 dâshên (1), to
anoint; to satisfy

ANOINTING
4888 mishchâh (24),
unction; gift
8081 shemen (1), olive
218 alĕiphō (1), to oil
with perfume, anoint
5545 chrisma (2), special
endowment

ANON
2112 ĕuthĕŏs (1), at once
or soon
2117 ĕuthus (1), at once,
immediately

ANOTHER
250 'Ezrâchîy (22),
Ezrachite
251 'âch (1), brother;
relative
259 'echâd (35), first
269 'achôwth (6), sister
312 'achêr (58), other,
another, different; next
317 'ochŏrîy (Ch.) (5),
other, another
321 'ochŏrân (Ch.) (1),
other, another
376 'îysh (5), man; male;
someone
1668 dâ' (Ch.) (2), this
1836 dên (Ch.) (1), this
2088 zeh (10), this or that
2090 zôh (1), this or that
2114 zûwr (3), to be
foreign, strange
3671 kânâph (1), edge or
extremity; wing
5234 nâkar (2), to treat
as a foreigner
5997 'âmîyth (2),
comrade or kindred
7453 rêa' (20), associate
7468 rᵉ'ûwth (2), female
associate
8145 shênîy (7), second;
again
8264 shâqaq (1), to seek
greedily
240 allēlôn (70), one
another
243 allŏs (60), different,
other
245 allŏtriŏs (4), not
one's own
246 allŏphulŏs (1),
Gentile, foreigner
1438 hĕautŏu (7),
himself, herself, itself
1520 hĕis (2), one
2087 hĕtĕrŏs (44), other
or different
3588 hŏ (1), "the," i.e. the
definite article
3739 hŏs (6), who, which
4299 prŏkrima (1),
prejudgment
4835 sumpathēs (1),
commiserative

ANOTHER'S
7453 rêa' (2), associate;
one close
240 allēlôn (2), one
another
2087 hĕtĕrŏs (1), other or
different

ANSWER
559 'âmar (9), to say,
speak
1696 dâbar (1), to speak,
say; to subdue
1697 dâbâr (7), word;
matter; thing
3045 yâda' (1), to know
4405 millâh (1), word;
discourse; speech
4617 ma'ăneh (7), reply,
answer
6030 'ânâh (60), to
respond, answer;
6600 pithgâm (Ch.) (2),
decree; report
7725 shûwb (12), to turn
back; to return
8421 tûwb (Ch.) (2), to
reply, answer
470 antapŏkrinŏmai (1),
to contradict or dispute
611 apŏkrinŏmai (12), to
respond
612 apŏkrisis (3),
response
626 apŏlŏgĕŏmai (4), to
give an account of self
627 apŏlŏgia (4), plea or
verbal defense
1906 ĕpĕrōtēma (1),
inquiry
2036 ĕpō (1), to speak
5538 chrēmatismŏs (1),
divine response

ANSWERABLE
5980 'ummâh (1), near,
beside, along with

ANSWERED
559 'âmar (90), to say,
speak
1697 dâbâr (4), word;
matter; thing
6030 'ânâh (175), to
respond, answer
6032 'ănâh (Ch.) (16), to
respond, answer
6039 'ĕnûwth (1),
affliction
7725 shûwb (2), to turn
back; to return
8421 tûwb (Ch.) (1), to
reply, answer
611 apŏkrinŏmai (201),
to respond
626 apŏlŏgĕŏmai (2), to
give an account of self

ANSWEREDST
6030 'ânâh (2), to
respond, answer

ANSWEREST
6030 'ânâh (2), to
respond, answer
611 apŏkrinŏmai (4), to
respond

ANSWERETH
6030 'ânâh (6), to
respond, answer
7725 shûwb (1), to turn
back; to return

611 apŏkrinŏmai (4), to
respond
4960 sustŏichĕŏ (1), to
correspond to

ANSWERING
488 antimĕtrĕŏ (1), to
measure in return
611 apŏkrinŏmai (29), to
respond
5274 hupŏlambanō (1),
to take up, i.e. continue

ANSWERS
8666 tᵉshûwbâh (2), reply
612 apŏkrisis (1),
response

ANT
5244 nᵉmâlâh (1), ant

ANTICHRIST
500 antichristŏs (4),
opponent of Messiah

ANTICHRISTS
500 antichristŏs (1),
opponent of Messiah

ANTIOCH
490 Antiŏchĕia (18),
Antiochia
491 Antiŏchĕus (1),
inhabitant of Antiochia

ANTIPAS
493 Antipas (1), instead
of father

ANTIPATRIS
494 Antipatris (1),
Antipatris

ANTIQUITY
6927 qadmâh (1), priority
in time; before; past

ANTOTHIJAH
6070 'Anthôthîyâh (1),
answers of Jehovah

ANTOTHITE
6069 'Anthôthîy (2),
Antothite

ANTS
5244 nᵉmâlâh (1), ant

ANUB
6036 'Ânûwb (1), borne

ANVIL
6471 pa'am (1), time;
step; occurence

ANY
259 'echâd (18), first
376 'îysh (25), man
1697 dâbâr (2), thing
1991 hêm (1), wealth
3254 yâçaph (2), to add
3605 kôl (175), all, any
3606 kôl (Ch.) (8), all,
any or every
3792 kᵉthâb (Ch.) (1),
writing, record or book
3972 mᵉ'ûwmâh (12),
something; anything
4310 mîy (1), who?
5315 nephesh (3), life;
breath; soul; wind
5750 'ôwd (9), again;
repeatedly; still; more
5769 'ôwlâm (1), eternity;
ancient; always
1520 hĕis (2), one
1535 ĕitĕ (1), if too
1536 ĕi tis (52), if any
1538 hĕkastŏs (1), each

2089 ĕti (10), yet, still
3361 mē (1), not; lest
3362 ĕan mē (2), if not
3364 ŏu mē (2), not at all
3367 mēdĕis (5), not even
one
3370 Mēdŏs (2),
inhabitant of Media
3379 mēpŏtĕ (7), not
ever; if, or lest ever
3381 mēpōs (4), lest
somehow
3387 mētis (6), whether
any
3588 hŏ (1), "the," i.e. the
definite article
3762 ŏudĕis (12), none,
nobody, nothing
3763 ŏudĕpŏtĕ (2), never
at all
3765 ŏukĕti (4), not yet,
no longer
3956 pas (9), all, any,
every, whole
4218 pŏtĕ (4), at some
time, ever
4455 pōpŏtĕ (3), at no
time
4458 -pōs (4), particle
used in composition
5100 tis (122), some or
any person or object
5150 trimēnŏn (1), three
months' space

APART
905 bad (6), apart, only,
besides
5079 niddâh (3), time of
menstrual impurity
5674 'âbar (1), to cross
over; to transition
6395 pâlâh (1), to
distinguish
659 apŏtithēmi (1), to put
away; get rid of
2596 kata (7), down;
according to

APELLES
559 Apĕllēs (1), Apelles

APES
6971 qôwph (2), ape or
monkey

APHARSACHITES
671 'Äpharçᵉkay (Ch.)
(2), Apharsekite

APHARSATHCHITES
671 'Äpharçᵉkay (Ch.)
(1), Apharsekite

APHARSITES
670 'Äphârᵉçay (Ch.) (1),
Apharesite

APHEK
663 'Äphêq (8), fortress

APHEKAH
664 'Äphêqâh (1), fortress

APHIAH
647 'Äphîyach (1), breeze

APHIK
663 'Äphêq (1), fortress

APHRAH
1036 Bêyth lᵉ-'Aphrâh
(1), house of dust

APHSES
6483 Pitstsêts (1),
dispersive

APIECE
259 'echâd (1), *first*
5982+259 'ammûwd (1), *column, pillar*
303 ana (2), *each; in turn; among*

APOLLONIA
624 Apŏllōnia (1), *sun*

APOLLOS
625 Apŏllōs (10), *sun*

APOLLYON
623 Apŏlluōn (1), *Destroyer*

APOSTLE
652 apŏstŏlŏs (19), *commissioner of Christ*

APOSTLES
652 apŏstŏlŏs (53), *commissioner of Christ*
5570 psĕudapŏstŏlŏs (1), *pretended preacher*

APOSTLES'
652 apŏstŏlŏs (5), *commissioner of Christ*

APOSTLESHIP
651 apŏstŏlē (4), *office of apostle*

APOTHECARIES
7543 râqach (1), to *perfume, blend spice*

APOTHECARIES'
4842 mirqachath (1), *unguent; unguent-pot*

APOTHECARY
7543 râqach (4), to *perfume, blend spice*

APPAIM
649 'Appayim (2), *two nostrils*

APPAREL
899 beged (4), *clothing; treachery or pillage*
1264 bᵉrôwm (1), *damask*
3830 lᵉbûwsh (8), *garment; wife*
3847 lâbash (1), to *clothe*
4254 machălâtsâh (1), *mantle, garment*
4403 malbûwsh (4), *garment, clothing*
8071 simlâh (2), *dress, mantle*
2066 ĕsthēs (3), to *clothe; dress*
2440 himatiŏn (1), to *put on clothes*
2441 himatismŏs (1), *clothing*
2689 katastŏlē (1), *costume or apparel*

APPARELLED
3847 lâbash (1), to *clothe*
2441 himatismŏs (1), *clothing*

APPARENTLY
4758 mar'eh (1), *appearance; vision*

APPEAL
1941 ĕpikalĕŏmai (2), to *invoke*

APPEALED
1941 ĕpikalĕŏmai (4), to *invoke*

APPEAR
1540 gâlâh (1), to *denude; uncover*
1570 gâlash (2), to *caper*
4286 machsôph (1), *peeling, baring*
6524 pârach (1), to *break forth; to bloom; to fly*
7200 râ'âh (24), to *see*
82 adēlŏs (1), *indistinct, not clear*
398 anaphainō (1), to *appear*
1718 ĕmphanizō (1), to *show forth*
2064 ĕrchŏmai (1), to *go or come*
3700 ŏptanŏmai (2), to *appear*
5316 phainō (9), to *show; to appear, be visible*
5318+5600 phanĕrŏs (1), *apparent, visible, clear*
5319 phanĕrŏō (9), to *render apparent*

APPEARANCE
4758 mar'eh (30), *appearance; vision*
5869 'ayin (1), *eye; sight; fountain*
1491 ĕidŏs (1), *form, appearance, sight*
3799 ŏpsis (1), *face; appearance*
4383 prŏsōpŏn (2), *face, presence*

APPEARANCES
4758 mar'eh (2), *appearance; vision*

APPEARED
1540 gâlâh (1), to *denude; uncover*
3318 yâtsâ' (1), to *go, bring out*
6437 pânâh (1), to *turn, to face*
7200 râ'âh (39), to *see*
1718 ĕmphanizō (1), to *show forth*
2014 ĕpiphainō (3), to *become visible*
3700 ŏptanŏmai (15), to *appear*
5316 phainō (5), to *show; to appear, be visible*
5319 phanĕrŏō (3), to *render apparent*

APPEARETH
1540 gâlâh (1), to *denude; uncover*
4758 mar'eh (1), *appearance; vision*
7200 râ'âh (3), to *see*
8259 shâqaph (1), to *peep or gaze*
5316 phainō (3), to *show; to appear, be visible*

APPEARING
602 apŏkalupsis (1), *disclosure, revelation*
2015 ĕpiphanĕia (5), *manifestation*

APPEASE
3722+6440 kâphar (1), to *cover; to expiate*

APPEASED
7918 shâkak (1), to *lay a trap; to allay*
2687 katastĕllō (1), to *quell, quiet*

APPEASETH
8252 shâqaṭ (1), to *repose*

APPERTAIN
2969 yâ'âh (1), to *be suitable, proper*

APPETITE
2416 chay (1), *alive; raw; fresh; life*
5315 nephesh (2), *life; breath; soul; wind*
8264 shâqaq (1), to *seek greedily*

APPHIA
682 Apphia (1), *Apphia*

APPII
675 'Appiŏs (1), *Appius*

APPLE
380 'îyshôwn (2), *pupil, eyeball*
380+1323 'îyshôwn (1), *pupil, eyeball*
892 bâbâh (1), *pupil of the eye*
1323 bath (1), *daughter, descendant, woman*
8598 tappûwach (3), *apple*

APPLES
8598 tappûwach (3), *apple*

APPLIED
5414 nâthan (2), to *give*
5437 çâbab (1), to *surround*

APPLY
935 bôw' (2), to *go, come*
5186 nâṭâh (1), to *stretch or spread out*
7896 shîyth (1), to *place, put*

APPOINT
559 'âmar (1), to *say, speak*
977 bâchar (1), *select, chose, prefer*
3259 yâ'ad (2), to *meet; to summon; to direct*
5344 nâqab (1), to *specify, designate, libel*
5414 nâthan (4), to *give*
5975 'âmad (2), to *stand*
6485 pâqad (10), to *visit, care for, count*
6680 tsâvâh (1), to *constitute, enjoin*
7136 qârâh (1), to *bring about; to impose*
7760 sûwm (11), to *put*
7896 shîyth (2), to *place*
7971 shâlach (1), to *send away*
1303 diatithĕmai (1), to *put apart, i.e. dispose*
2525 kathistĕmi (1), to *designate, constitute*
5087 tithēmi (2), to *place, put*

APPOINTED
559 'âmar (2), to *say*

APPEASED ... 561 'ēmer (1), *something said*
1121 bên (3), *son, people of a class or kind*
1696 dâbar (1), to *speak, say; to subdue*
2163 zâman (3), to *fix a time*
2296 châgar (3), to *gird on a belt; put on armor*
2706 chôq (1), *appointment; allotment*
2708 chuqqâh (1), to *delineate*
2710 châqaq (1), to *enact laws; to prescribe*
2764 chêrem (1), *doomed object*
3045 yâda' (1), to *know*
3198 yâkach (2), to *decide, justify*
3245 yâçad (1), *settle, consult, establish*
3259 yâ'ad (3), to *meet; to summon; to direct*
3677 keçe' (2), *full moon*
4150 môw'êd (20), *assembly, congregation*
4151 môw'âd (1), *ranking of troop*
4152 mûw'âdâh (1), *appointed place*
4487 mânâh (4), to *allot; to enumerate or enroll*
4662 miphqâd (1), *designated spot; census*
5324 nâtsab (1), to *station*
5414 nâthan (7), to *give*
5567 çâman (1), to *designate*
5975 'âmad (10), to *stand*
6213 'âsâh (2), to *do or make*
6485 pâqad (4), to *visit, care for, count*
6635 tsâbâ' (3), *army, military host*
6680 tsâvâh (4), to *constitute, enjoin*
6942 qâdâsh (1), to *be, make clean*
7760 sûwm (8), to *put*
7896 shîyth (1), to *place*
322 anadĕiknumi (1), to *indicate, appoint*
606 apŏkĕimai (1), to *be reserved; to await*
1299 diatassō (4), to *institute, prescribe*
1303 diatithĕmai (1), to *put apart, i.e. dispose*
1476 hĕdraiŏs (1), *immovable; steadfast*
1935 ĕpithanatiŏs (1), *doomed to death*
2476 histēmi (1), to *stand, establish*
2749 kĕimai (1), to *lie outstretched*
4160 pŏiĕō (1), to *do*
4287 prŏthĕsmiŏs (1), *designated day or time*
4384 prŏtassō (1), to *prescribe beforehand*
4929 suntassō (2), to *direct, instruct*
5021 tassō (3), to *assign or dispose*

5081 tēlaugōs (1), in a
far-shining manner
5087 tithēmi (3), to put

APPOINTETH
6966 qûwm (Ch.) (1), to
rise

APPOINTMENT
3259 yâ'ad (1), to meet;
to summon; to direct
3883 lûwl (1), spiral step
6310 peh (2), mouth;
opening

APPREHEND
2638 katalambanō (1), to
seize; to understand
4084 piazō (1), to seize,
arrest, or capture

APPREHENDED
2638 katalambanō (2), to
seize; to possess; to
understand
4084 piazō (1), to seize,
arrest, or capture

APPROACH
5066 nâgash (5), to be,
come, bring near
7126 qârab (12), to
approach, bring near
7138 qârôwb (1), near,
close
676 aprŏsitŏs (1),
unapproachable

APPROACHED
5066 nâgash (1), to be,
come, bring near
7126 qârab (1), to
approach, bring near

APPROACHETH
1448 ĕggizō (1), to
approach

APPROACHING
7132 qᵉrâbâh (1),
approach
1448 ĕggizō (1), to
approach

APPROVE
7520 râtsad (1), to look
askant; to be jealous
1381 dŏkimazō (2), to
test; to approve

APPROVED
584 apŏdĕiknumi (1), to
accredit
1384 dŏkimŏs (6),
acceptable, approved
4921 sunistaō (1), to
introduce (favorably)

APPROVEST
1381 dŏkimazō (1), to
test; to approve

APPROVETH
7200 râ'âh (1), to see

APPROVING
4921 sunistaō (1), to
introduce (favorably)

APRONS
2290 chăgôwr (1), belt
for the waist
4612 simikinthiŏn (1),
narrow apron

APT
6213 'âsâh (1), to do
1317 didaktikŏs (2),
instructive

AQUILA
207 Akulas (6), eagle

AR
6144 'Âr (6), city

ARA
690 'Ărâ' (1), lion

ARAB
694 'Ărâb (1), ambush

ARABAH
6160 'ărâbâh (2), desert,
wasteland

ARABIA
6152 'Ărâb (6), Arabia
688 Arabia (2), Arabia

ARABIAN
6153 'ereb (1), dusk
6163 'Ărâbîy (3), Arabian

ARABIANS
6163 'Ărâbîy (5), Arabian
690 'Araps (1), native of
Arabia

ARAD
6166 'Ărâd (5), fugitive

ARAH
733 'Ărach (4),
way-faring

ARAM
758 'Ărâm (7), highland
689 Aram (3), high

ARAM-NAHARAIM
763 'Ăram Năhărayim
(1), Aram of (the) two
rivers

ARAM-ZOBAH
760 'Ăram Tsôwbâh (1),
Aram of Coele-Syria

ARAMITESS
761 'Ărammîy (1),
Aramite

ARAN
765 'Ărân (2), stridulous

ARARAT
780 'Ărâraṭ (2), Ararat

ARAUNAH
728 'Ăravnâh (9),
Aravnah or Ornah

ARBA
704 'Arba' (2), four

ARBAH
704 'Arba' (1), four

ARBATHITE
6164 'Arbâthîy (2),
Arbathite

ARBITE
701 'Arbîy (1), Arbite

ARCHANGEL
743 archaggĕlŏs (2),
chief angel

ARCHELAUS
745 Archĕlaŏs (1),
people-ruling

ARCHER
1869 dârak (1), to walk,
lead; to string a bow
7198 qesheth (1), bow;
rainbow

ARCHERS
1167+2671 ba'al (1),
master; husband
1869+7198 dârak (1), to
walk; to string a bow

2686 châtsats (1), to
distribute into ranks
3384 yârâh (3), to throw,
shoot an arrow
3384+376+7198 yârâh (1),
to shoot an arrow
3384+7198 yârâh (1), to
throw, shoot an arrow;
to point; to teach
7198 qesheth (2), bow;
rainbow
7228 rab (2), archer

ARCHES
361 'êylâm (15), portico,
porch

ARCHEVITES
756 'Arkᵉvay (Ch.) (1),
Arkevite

ARCHI
757 'Arkîy (1), Arkite

ARCHIPPUS
751 Archippŏs (2),
horse-ruler

ARCHITE
757 'Arkîy (5), Arkite

ARCTURUS
5906 'Ayish (2), Great
Bear constellation

ARD
714 'Ard (3), fugitive

ARDITES
716 'Ardîy (1), Ardite

ARDON
715 'Ardôwn (1), roaming

ARELI
692 'Ar'êlîy (2), heroic

ARELITES
692 'Ar'êlîy (1), heroic

AREOPAGITE
698 Arĕŏpagitēs (1),
Areopagite

AREOPAGUS
697 Arĕiŏs Pagŏs (1),
rock of Ares

ARETAS
702 Arĕtas (1), Aretas

ARGOB
709 'Argôb (5), stony

ARGUING
3198 yâkach (1), to be
correct; to argue

ARGUMENTS
8433 tôwkêchâh (1),
correction, refutation

ARIDAI
742 'Ărîyday (1), Aridai

ARIDATHA
743 'Ărîydâthâ' (1),
Aridatha

ARIEH
745 'Aryêh (1), lion

ARIEL
740 'Ărî'êl (5), Lion of
God

ARIGHT
3190 yâṭab (1), to be,
make well
3559 kûwn (1), to render
sure, proper
3651 kên (1), just; right,
correct

4339 mêyshâr (1),
straightness; rectitude

ARIMATHAEA
707 Arimathaia (4),
height

ARIOCH
746 'Ăryôwk (7), Arjok

ARISAI
747 'Ăriyçay (1), Arisai

ARISE
2224 zârach (3), to rise;
to be bright
5782 'ûwr (1), to awake
5927 'âlâh (2), to ascend,
be high, mount
5975 'âmad (1), to stand
6965 qûwm (106), to rise
6966 qûwm (Ch.) (3), to
rise
6974 qûwts (1), to awake
7721 sôw' (1), rising
305 anabainō (1), to go
up, rise
393 anatĕllō (1), to cause
to arise
450 anistēmi (14), to
stand up; to come back
to life
1453 ĕgĕirō (13), to
waken, i.e. rouse

ARISETH
2224 zârach (4), to rise;
to be bright
5927 'âlâh (1), to ascend,
be high, mount
6965 qûwm (2), to rise
450 anistēmi (1), to
stand up; to come back
to life
1096 ginŏmai (2), to be,
become
1453 ĕgĕirō (1), to
waken, i.e. rouse

ARISING
6965 qûwm (1), to rise

ARISTARCHUS
708 Aristarchŏs (5), best
ruling

ARISTOBULUS'
711 Aristŏbŏulŏs (1), best
counselling

ARK
727 'ârôwn (194), box
8392 têbâh (28), box,
basket
2787 kibōtŏs (6), ark;
chest or box

ARKITE
6208 'Arqîy (2), tush

ARM
248 'ezrôwa (2), arm
2220 zᵉrôwa (59), arm;
foreleg; force, power
2502 châlats (1), to
depart; to equip
3802 kâthêph (1),
side-piece
1023 brachiōn (3), arm
3695 hŏplizō (1), to equip

ARMAGEDDON
717 Armagĕddōn (1), hill
of the rendezvous

ARMED
2502 châlats (16), to
equip; to present

ARMENIA

2571 châmûsh (3),
able bodied *soldiers*
3847 lâbash (3), to *clothe*
4043 mâgên (2), small
shield (buckler)
5401 nâshaq (3), to *kiss;*
to *equip* with weapons
5402 nesheq (1), military
arms, arsenal
7324 rûwq (1), to *pour*
out, i.e. *empty*
2528 kathŏplizō (1), to
equip fully with armor

ARMENIA

780 'Ărâraṭ (2), *Ararat*

ARMHOLES

679+3027 'atstsîyl (2),
joint of the hand

ARMIES

1416 gᵉdûwd (1), *band of*
soldiers
2428 chayil (4), *army;*
wealth; virtue; valor
4264 machăneh (4),
encampment
4630 ma'ărâh (1), *open*
spot
4634 ma'ărâkâh (6), *row;*
pile; military array
6635 tsâbâ' (22), *army,*
military host
3925 parĕmbŏlē (1),
battle-array
4753 stratĕuma (3), body
of *troops*
4760 stratŏpĕdŏn (1),
body of troops

ARMONI

764 'Armônîy (1), *palatial*

ARMOUR

2185 zônôwth (1), *harlots*
2290 chăgôwr (1), *belt*
for the waist
2488 chălîytsâh (1), *spoil,*
booty of the dead
3627 kᵉlîy (11),
implement, thing
4055 mad (2), *vesture,*
garment; carpet
5402 nesheq (3), military
arms, arsenal
3696 hŏplŏn (2),
implement, or *utensil*
or *tool*
3833 panŏplia (3), *full*
armor

ARMOURBEARER

5375+3627 nâsâ' (18), to
lift up

ARMOURY

214 'ôwtsâr (1),
depository
5402 nesheq (1), military
arms, arsenal
8530 talpîyâh (1),
something *tall*

ARMS

1672 dâ'ag (1), *be*
anxious, be afraid
2220 zᵉrôwa' (24), *arm;*
foreleg; force, power
2684 chôtsen (1), *bosom*
43 agkalē (1), *arm*
1723 ĕnagkalizŏmai (2),
to *take into one's arms*

ARMY

1416 gᵉdûwd (4), *band of*
soldiers
2426 chêyl (1), *rampart,*
battlement
2426+6635 chêyl (1),
rampart, battlement
2428 chayil (52), *army;*
wealth; virtue; valor
2429 chayil (Ch.) (2),
army; strength
2502 châlats (1), to
deliver, equip
4634 ma'ărâkâh (7), *row;*
pile; military array
4675 matstsâbâh (1),
military guard
6635 tsâbâ' (7), *army,*
military host
4753 stratĕuma (3), body
of *troops*

ARNAN

770 'Arnân (1), *noisy*

ARNON

769 'Arnôwn (25),
brawling stream

AROD

720 'Ărôwd (1), *fugitive*

ARODI

722 'Ărôwdîy (1), *Arodite*

ARODITES

722 'Ărôwdîy (1), *Arodite*

AROER

6177 'Ărô'êr (16),
nudity of situation

AROERITE

6200 'Ărô'êrîy (1),
Aroërite

AROSE

2224 zârach (2), to *rise;*
to *be bright*
5927 'âlâh (2), to *ascend,*
be high, mount
5975 'âmad (1), to *stand*
6965 qûwm (107), to *rise*
6966 qûwm (Ch.) (1), to
rise
7925 shâkam (7), to *start*
early in the morning
305 anabainō (1), to *go*
up, rise
450 anistēmi (24), to
stand up; to *come back*
to life
906 ballō (1), to *throw*
1096 ginŏmai (11), to *be,*
become
1326 diĕgĕirō (2), to
arouse, stimulate
1453 ĕgĕirō (13), to
waken, i.e. *rouse*
1525 ĕisĕrchŏmai (1), to
enter

ARPAD

774 'Arpâd (4), *spread*
out

ARPHAD

774 'Arpâd (2), *spread*
out

ARPHAXAD

775 'Arpakshad (9),
Arpakshad
742 *Arphaxad* (1),
Arphaxad

ARRAY

631 'âçar (1), to *fasten;* to
join battle
3847 lâbash (2), to *clothe*
5844 'âṭâh (1), to *wrap,*
i.e. *cover, veil, clothe*
6186 'ârak (26), to set in
a *row*, i.e. *arrange,*
7896 shîyth (1), to *place*
2441 himatismŏs (1),
clothing

ARRAYED

3847 lâbash (4), to *clothe*
1746 ĕnduō (1), to *invest*
with clothing
4016 pĕriballō (6), to
wrap around, clothe

ARRIVED

2668 kataplĕō (1), to *sail*
down
3846 paraballō (1), to
reach a place; to *liken*

ARROGANCY

1347 gâ'ôwn (3),
ascending; majesty
6277 'âthâq (1), *impudent*

ARROW

1121+7198 bên (1),
people of a class or kind
2671 chêts (11), *arrow;*
shaft of a spear
2678 chitstsîy (4), *arrow*

ARROWS

1121 bên (1), *people* of a
class or kind
2671 chêts (36), *arrow;*
wound; shaft of a spear
2678 chitstsîy (1), *arrow*
2687 châtsâts (1), *gravel,*
grit
7565 resheph (1), *flame*

ARTAXERXES

783 'Artachshastâ' (Ch.)
(14), *Artaxerxes*

ARTAXERXES'

783 'Artachshastâ' (Ch.)
(1), *Artaxerxes*

ARTEMAS

734 Artĕmas (1), *gift of*
Artemis

ARTIFICER

2794 chôrêsh (1), skilled
fabricator worker
2796 chârâsh (1), skilled
fabricator or worker

ARTIFICERS

2796 chârâsh (2), skilled
fabricator or worker

ARTILLERY

3627 kᵉlîy (1),
implement, thing

ARTS

4021 pĕrіĕrgŏs (1),
magic, sorcery

ARUBOTH

700 'Ărubbôwth (1),
Arubboth

ARUMAH

725 'Ărûwmâh (1), *height*

ARVAD

719 'Arvad (2), *refuge for*
the *roving*

ARVADITE

721 'Arvâdîy (2), *Arvadite*

ARZA

777 'artsâ' (1), *earthiness*

ASA

609 'Âçâ' (57), *Asa*
760 Asa (2), *Asa*

ASA'S

609 'Âçâ' (1), *Asa*

ASAHEL

760 'Ăram Tsôwbâh (1),
Aram of Coele-Syria
6214 'Ăsâh'êl (17), *God*
has made

ASAHIAH

6222 'Ăsâyâh (2),
Jehovah has made

ASAIAH

6222 'Ăsâyâh (6),
Jehovah has made

ASAPH

623 'Âçâph (44), *collector*

ASAPH'S

623 'Âçâph (1), *collector*

ASAREEL

840 'Ăsar'êl (1), *right of*
God

ASARELAH

841 'Ăsar'êlâh (1), *right*
toward God

ASCEND

5927 'âlâh (9), to *ascend,*
be high, mount
305 anabainō (4), to *go*
up, rise

ASCENDED

5927 'âlâh (10), to
ascend, be high, mount
305 anabainō (9), to *go*
up, rise

ASCENDETH

305 anabainō (2), to *go*
up, rise

ASCENDING

5927 'âlâh (2), to *ascend,*
be high, mount
305 anabainō (3), to *go*
up, rise

ASCENT

4608 ma'ăleh (2),
elevation; platform
5930 'ôlâh (1), *sacrifice*
wholly consumed in fire
5944 'ălîyâh (1), *upper*
things; second-story

ASCRIBE

3051 yâhab (1), to *give*
5414 nâthan (2), to *give*

ASCRIBED

5414 nâthan (2), to *give*

ASENATH

621 'Âçᵉnath (3), *Asenath*

ASER

768 Asēr (2), *happy*

ASH

766 'ôren (1), *ash* tree

ASHAMED

954 bûwsh (79), to be
ashamed; disappointed
1322 bôsheth (1), *shame*
2659 châphêr (4), to be
ashamed, disappointed
3637 kâlam (12), to *taunt*
or *insult*

153 aischunŏmai (5), to
feel shame for oneself
422 anĕpaischuntŏs (1),
unashamed
1788 ĕntrĕpō (2), to
respect; to confound
1870 ĕpaischunŏmai
(11), to feel shame
2617 kataischunō (7), to
disgrace or shame

ASHAN
6228 'Âshân (4), smoke

ASHBEA
791 'Ashbêa' (1), adjurer

ASHBEL
788 'Ashbêl (3), flowing

ASHBELITES
789 'Ashbêlîy (1),
Ashbelite

ASHCHENAZ
813 'Ashkᵉnaz (2),
Ashkenaz

ASHDOD
795 'Ashdôwd (21),
ravager

ASHDODITES
796 'Ashdôwdîy (1),
Ashdodite

ASHDOTH-PISGAH
798+6449 'Ashdôwth
hap-Piçgâh (3), ravines
of the Pisgah

ASHDOTHITES
796 'Ashdôwdîy (1),
Ashdodite

ASHER
836 'Âshêr (42), happy

ASHERITES
843 'Âshêrîy (1), Asherite

ASHES
665 'êpher (24), ashes
1878 dâshên (2), to be
fat, thrive; to fatten
1880 deshen (8), fat;
fatness, ashes
6083 'âphâr (2), dust,
earth, mud; clay,
6368 pîyach (2), powder
dust or ashes
4700 spŏdŏs (3), ashes
5077 tĕphrŏŏ (1), to
incinerate

ASHIMA
807 'Ăshîymâ' (1),
Ashima

ASHKELON
831 'Ashqᵉlôwn (9),
Ashkelon

ASHKENAZ
813 'Ashkᵉnaz (1),
Ashkenaz

ASHNAH
823 'Ashnâh (2), Ashnah

ASHPENAZ
828 'Ashpᵉnaz (1),
Ashpenaz

ASHRIEL
845 'Asrî'êlîy (1), Asrielite

ASHTAROTH
6252 'Ashtârôwth (11),
increases

ASHTERATHITE
6254 'Ashtᵉrâthîy (1),
Ashterathite

ASHTEROTH
6255 'Ashtᵉrôth
Qarnayim (1),
Ashtaroth of (the)
double horns

ASHTORETH
6252 'Ashtârôwth (3),
increases

ASHUR
804 'Ashshûwr (2),
successful

ASHURITES
843 'Âshêrîy (2), Asherite

ASHVATH
6220 'Ashvâth (1), bright

ASIA
773 Asia (20), Asia Minor
775 Asiarchēs (1), ruler
in Asia

ASIDE
2015 hâphak (1), to turn
about or over
3943 lâphath (1), to
clasp; to turn aside
5186 nâţâh (16), to
stretch or spread out
5265 nâça' (1), start on a
journey
5437 çâbab (2), to
surround
5493 çûwr (4), to turn off
5844 'âţâh (1), to wrap,
i.e. cover, veil, clothe
6437 pânâh (1), to turn,
to face
7750 sûwţ (1), become
derelict
7847 sâţâh (5), to deviate
from duty, go astray
402 anachôrĕŏ (3), to
retire, withdraw
565 apĕrchŏmai (1), to
go off, i.e. depart
659 apŏtîthēmi (2), to put
away; get rid of
863 aphiēmi (1), to leave;
to pardon, forgive
1824 ĕxautēs (2),
instantly, at once
2596 kata (1), down;
according to
5087 tithēmi (1), to
place, put
5298 hupŏchôrĕŏ (1), to
vacate down, i.e. retire

ASIEL
6221 'Ăsîy'êl (1), made of
God

ASK
1156 bᵉ'â' (Ch.) (2), to
seek or ask
1245 bâqash (1), to
search out
1875 dârash (1), to
pursue or search
7592 shâ'al (41), to ask
154 aitĕŏ (38), to ask for
523 apaitĕŏ (1), to
demand back
1833 ĕxĕtazō (1), to
ascertain or interrogate
1905 ĕpĕrōtaō (8), to
inquire, seek

2065 ĕrōtaō (11), to
interrogate; to request
4441 punthanŏmai (2), to
ask for information

ASKED
1156 bᵉ'â' (Ch.) (1), to
seek or ask
1245 bâqash (1), to
search out
7592 shâ'al (49), to ask
7593 shᵉ'êl (Ch.) (3), to
ask
154 aitĕŏ (4), to ask for
1905 ĕpĕrōtaō (45), to
inquire, seek
2065 ĕrōtaō (11), to
interrogate; to request
3004 lĕgō (1), to say
4441 punthanŏmai (4), to
ask for information

ASKELON
831 'Ashqᵉlôwn (3),
Ashkelon

ASKEST
7592 shâ'al (1), to ask
154 aitĕŏ (1), to ask for
1905 ĕpĕrōtaō (1), to
inquire, seek

ASKETH
7592 shâ'al (5), to ask
154 aitĕŏ (5), to ask for
2065 ĕrōtaō (1), to
interrogate; to request

ASKING
7592 shâ'al (3), to ask
350 anakrinō (2), to
interrogate, determine
1905 ĕpĕrōtaō (1), to
inquire, seek
2065 ĕrōtaō (1), to
interrogate; to request

ASLEEP
3463 yâshên (2), sleepy
7290 râdam (2), to
stupefy
879 aphupnŏŏ (1), to
drop (off) in slumber
2518 kathĕudō (5), to fall
asleep
2837 kŏimaō (6), to
slumber; to decease

ASNAH
619 'Açnâh (1), Asnah

ASNAPPER
620 'Oçnappar (Ch.) (1),
Osnappar

ASP
6620 pethen (1), asp

ASPATHA
630 'Açpâthâ' (1),
Aspatha

ASPS
6620 pethen (3), asp
785 aspis (1), serpent,
(poss.) asp

ASRIEL
844 'Asrîy'êl (2), right of
God

ASRIELITES
845 'Asrî'êlîy (1), Asrielite

ASS
860 'âthôwn (16), female
donkey, ass

2543 chămôwr (55), male
donkey or ass
5601 çappîyr (1),
sapphire
5895 'ayîr (2), young
robust donkey or ass
6171 'ârôwd (1), onager
or wild donkey
6501 pere' (3), onager,
wild donkey
3678 ŏnariŏn (1), little
donkey
3688 ŏnŏs (5), donkey
5268 hupŏzugiŏn (2),
donkey

ASS'S
860 'âthôwn (1), female
donkey, ass
2543 chămôwr (1), male
donkey or ass
6501 pere' (1), onager,
wild donkey
3688 ŏnŏs (1), donkey

ASSAULT
6696 tsûwr (1), to cramp,
i.e. confine; to harass
3730 hŏrmē (1), violent
impulse, i.e. onset

ASSAULTED
2186 ĕphistēmi (1), to be
present; to approach

ASSAY
5254 nâçâh (1), to test,
attempt

ASSAYED
2974 yâ'al (1), to assent;
to undertake, begin
5254 nâçâh (1), to test,
attempt
3985 pĕirazō (1), to
endeavor, scrutinize,
entice, discipline
3987 pĕiraō (1), to
attempt, try

ASSAYING
3984+2983 pĕira (1),
attempt, experience

ASSEMBLE
622 'âçaph (10), to
gather, collect
1481 gûwr (1), to sojourn,
live as an alien
2199 zâ'aq (2), to call
out, convene publicly
3259 yâ'ad (1), to meet;
to summon; to direct
5789 'ûwsh (1), to hasten
6908 qâbats (5), to
collect, assemble

ASSEMBLED
622 'âçaph (4), to gather,
collect
662 'âphaq (1), to abstain
1413 gâdad (1), to gash,
slash oneself
2199 zâ'aq (1), to call
out, convene publicly
3259 yâ'ad (3), to meet;
to summon; to direct
6633 tsâbâ' (1), to mass
an army or servants
6638 tsâbâh (1), to array
an army against
6908 qâbats (1), to
collect, assemble

ASSEMBLIES

6950 qâhal (11), to convoke, gather
7284 r^egash (Ch.) (3), to gather tumultuously
1096 ginŏmai (1), to be, become
4863 sunagō (6), to gather together
4871 sunalizō (1), to accumulate
4905 sunĕrchŏmai (1), to gather together

ASSEMBLIES

627 'àçuppâh (1), collection of sayings
4150 môw'êd (1), assembly, congregation
4744 miqrâ' (2), public meeting
5712 'êdâh (1), assemblage; family
6116 'àtsârâh (1), assembly

ASSEMBLING

6633 tsâbâ' (1), to mass an army or servants
1997 ĕpisunagōgē (1), meeting, gathering

ASSEMBLY

4150 môw'êd (3), assembly, congregation
4186 môwshâb (1), seat; site; abode
5475 çôwd (5), intimacy; consultation; secret
5712 'êdâh (8), assemblage; family
6116 'àtsârâh (9), assembly
6951 qâhâl (17), assemblage
6952 q^ehillâh (1), assemblage
1577 ĕkklēsia (3), congregation
3831 panēguris (1), mass-meeting
4864 sunagōgē (1), assemblage

ASSENT

6310 peh (1), mouth; opening

ASSENTED

4934 suntithĕmai (1), to place jointly

ASSES

860 'âthôwn (17), female donkey, ass
2543 chămôwr (40), male donkey or ass
5895 'ayîr (2), young robust donkey or ass
6167 'àrâd (Ch.) (1), onager or wild donkey
6501 pere' (4), onager, wild donkey

ASSHUR

804 'Ashshûwr (8), successful

ASSHURIM

805 'Àshûwrîy (1), Ashurite

ASSIGNED

5414 nâthan (2), to give

ASSIR

617 'Aççîyr (5), prisoner

ASSIST

3936 paristēmi (1), to stand beside, present

ASSOCIATE

7489 râ'a' (1), to break to pieces; to make

ASSOS

789 Assŏs (2), Assus

ASSUR

804 'Ashshûwr (2), successful

ASSURANCE

539 'âman (1), to be firm, faithful, true; to trust
983 betach (1), safety, security, trust
4102 pistis (1), faithfulness; faith, belief
4136 plērŏphŏria (4), full assurance

ASSURE

3983 pĕinaō (1), to famish; to crave

ASSURED

571 'emeth (1), certainty, truth, trustworthiness
6966 qùwm (Ch.) (1), to rise
4104 pistŏō (1), to assure

ASSUREDLY

571 'emeth (1), certainty, truth, trustworthiness
3045 yâda' (1), to know
3318 yâtsâ' (1), to go, bring out
3588 kîy (3), for, that because
8354 shâthâh (1), to drink, imbibe
806 asphalōs (1), securely
4822 sumbibazō (1), to unite; to infer, show

ASSWAGE

2820 châsak (1), to refuse, spare, preserve

ASSWAGED

2820 châsak (1), to refuse, spare, preserve
7918 shâkak (1), to lay a trap; to allay

ASSYRIA

804 'Ashshûwr (118), successful

ASSYRIAN

804 'Ashshûwr (13), successful

ASSYRIANS

804 'Ashshûwr (10), successful

ASTAROTH

6252 'Ashtârôwth (1), increases

ASTONIED

1724 dâham (1), to be astounded
7672 sh^ebash (Ch.) (1), to perplex, be baffled
8074 shâmêm (6), to devastate; to stupefy
8075 sh^emam (Ch.) (1), to devastate; to stupefy
8429 t^evahh (Ch.) (1), to amaze, take alarm

ASTONISHED

8074 shâmêm (14), to devastate; to stupefy
8539 tâmahh (1), to be astounded
1605 ĕkplēssō (10), to astonish
1839 ĕxistēmi (6), to become astounded
2284 thambĕō (2), to astound, be amazed
4023+2285 pĕriĕchō (1), to clasp; to encircle

ASTONISHMENT

8047 shammâh (14), ruin; consternation
8074 shâmêm (1), to devastate; to stupefy
8078 shimmâmôwn (2), stupefaction, despair
8541 timmâhôwn (2), consternation, panic
8653 tar'êlâh (1), reeling, staggering
1611 ĕkstasis (1), bewilderment, ecstasy, astonishment

ASTRAY

5080 nâdach (1), to push off, scattered
7683 shâgag (1), to stray
7686 shâgâh (2), to stray
8582 tâ'âh (13), to vacillate, stray
4105 planaō (5), to roam, wander from safety

ASTROLOGER

826 'ashshâph (Ch.) (1), conjurer, enchanter

ASTROLOGERS

825 'ashshâph (2), conjurer, enchanter
826 'ashshâph (Ch.) (5), conjurer, enchanter
1895+8064 hâbar (1), to be a horoscopist

ASUNDER

996 bêyn (1), between
673 apŏchōrizō (1), to rend apart; to separate
1288 diaspaō (1), to sever or dismember
1371 dichŏtŏmĕō (1), to flog severely
2997 laschō (1), to crack open
4249 prizō (1), to saw in two
5563 chōrizō (2), to place room between

ASUPPIM

624 'àçûph (2), stores of goods

ASYNCRITUS

799 Asugkritŏs (1), incomparable

ATAD

329 'âţâd (2), buckthorn tree

ATARAH

5851 'Àţârâh (1), crown

ATAROTH

5852 'Àţrôwth (5), crowns

ATAROTH-ADAR

5853 'Àţrôwth 'Addâr (1), crowns of Addar

ATAROTH-ADDAR

5853 'Àţrôwth 'Addâr (1), crowns of Addar

ATE

398 'âkal (2), to eat
2719 katĕsthiō (1), to devour

ATER

333 'Âţêr (5), maimed

ATHACH

6269 'Àthâk (1), lodging

ATHAIAH

6265 'Àthâyâh (1), Jehovah has helped

ATHALIAH

6271 'Àthalyâh (17), Jehovah has constrained

ATHENIANS

117 Athēnaiŏs (1), inhabitant of Athenæ

ATHENS

116 Athēnai (6), city Athenæ
117 Athēnaiŏs (1), inhabitant of Athenæ

ATHIRST

6770 tsâmê' (2), to thirst
1372 dipsaō (3), to thirst for

ATHLAI

6270 'Athlay (1), compressed

ATONEMENT

3722 kâphar (73), to cover; to expiate
3725 kippûr (7), expiation
2643 katallagē (1), restoration

ATONEMENTS

3725 kippûr (1), expiation

ATROTH

5855 'Àţrôwth Shôwphân (1), crowns of Shophan

ATTAI

6262 'Attay (4), timely

ATTAIN

3201 yâkôl (1), to be able
5381 nâsag (1), to reach
7069 qânâh (1), to create; to procure
2658 katantaō (2), to attain or reach

ATTAINED

935 bôw' (4), to go or come
5381 nâsag (1), to reach
2638 katalambanō (1), to seize; to possess
2983 lambanō (1), to take, receive
3877 parakŏlouthĕō (1), to attend; trace out
5348 phthanō (2), to anticipate or precede

ATTALIA

825 Attalĕia (1), Attaleia

ATTEND
6440 pânîym (1), *face; front*
7181 qâshab (9), to *prick up the ears*
2145 *ĕuprŏsĕdrŏs* (1), *diligent service*

ATTENDANCE
4612 ma'ămâd (2), *position; attendant*
4337 *prŏsĕchō* (2), to *pay attention to*

ATTENDED
995 bîyn (1), to *understand; discern*
7181 qâshab (1), to *prick up the ears*
4337 *prŏsĕchō* (1), to *pay attention to*

ATTENDING
4343 *prŏskartĕrĕsis* (1), *persistency*

ATTENT
7183 qashshâb (2), *hearkening*

ATTENTIVE
7183 qashshâb (3), *hearkening*
1582 *ĕkkrĕmamai* (1), to *listen closely*

ATTENTIVELY
8085 shâma' (1), to *hear* intelligently

ATTIRE
2871 ṭâbûwl (1), *turban*
7196 qishshûr (1), *girdle* or *sash* for women
7897 shîyth (1), *garment*

ATTIRED
6801 tsânaph (1), to *wrap*, i.e. *roll* or *dress*

AUDIENCE
241 'ôzen (7), *ear*
189 akŏĕ (1), *hearing; thing heard*
191 akŏuō (4), to *hear; obey*

AUGMENT
5595 çâphâh (1), to *scrape*; to *accumulate*

AUGUSTUS
828 Augŏustŏs (3), *revered one*

AUGUSTUS'
828 Augŏustŏs (1), *revered one*

AUL
4836 martsêa' (2), *awl* for *piercing*

AUNT
1733 dôwdâh (1), *aunt*

AUSTERE
840 austĕrŏs (2), *severe, harsh; exacting*

AUTHOR
159 aitiŏs (1), *causer*
747 archĕgŏs (1), *chief leader; founder*

AUTHORITIES
1849 ĕxŏusia (1), *authority, power, right*

AUTHORITY
7235 râbâh (1), to *increase*
8633 tôqeph (1), *might*
831 authĕntĕō (1), to *have authority*
1413 dunastēs (1), *ruler* or *officer*
1849 ĕxŏusia (28), *authority, power, right*
1850 ĕxŏusiazō (1), to *control, master another*
2003 ĕpitagē (1), *injunction or decree*
2715 katĕxŏusiazō (2), to *wield full privilege over*
5247 hupĕrŏchē (1), *superiority*

AVA
5755 'Ivvâh (1), *overthrow, ruin*

AVAILETH
7737 shâvâh (1), to *level; to resemble; to adjust*
2480 ischuō (3), to *have or exercise force*

AVEN
206 'Âven (3), *idolatry*

AVENGE
5358 nâqam (8), to *avenge or punish*
5358+5360 nâqam (1), to *avenge or punish*
5414+5360 nâthan (1), to *give*
6485 pâqad (1), to *visit, care for, count*
1556 ĕkdikĕō (4), to *vindicate; retaliate*
4160+3588+1557 pŏiĕō (2), to *make or do*

AVENGED
3467 yâsha' (1), to *make safe, free*
5358 nâqam (9), to *avenge or punish*
5414+5360 nâthan (1), to *give*
8199 shâphaṭ (2), to *judge*
1556 ĕkdikĕō (1), to *vindicate; retaliate*
2919+3588+2917 krinō (1), to *decide; to try*

AVENGER
1350 gâ'al (6), to *redeem; to be the next of kin*
5358 nâqam (2), to *avenge or punish*
1558 ĕkdikŏs (1), *punisher, avenger*

AVENGETH
5414+5360 nâthan (2), to *give*

AVENGING
3467 yâsha' (2), to *make safe, free*
6544+6546 pâra' (1), to *absolve, begin*

AVERSE
7725 shûwb (1), to *turn back; to return*

AVIM
5761 'Avvîym (1), *Avvim*

AVIMS
5757 'Avvîy (1), *Avvite*

AVITES
5757 'Avvîy (2), *Avvite*

AVITH
5762 'Ăvîyth (2), *ruin*

AVOID
6544 pâra' (1), to *loosen; to expose, dismiss*
1223 dia (1), *through*, by means of; *because* of
1578 ĕkklinō (1), to *shun; to decline*
3868 paraitĕŏmai (1), to *deprecate, decline*
4026 pĕriistēmi (1), to *stand around; to avoid*

AVOIDED
5437 çâbab (1), to *surround*

AVOIDING
1624 ĕktrĕpō (1), to *turn away*
4724 stĕllō (1), to *repress, abstain* from

AVOUCHED
559 'âmar (2), to *say, speak*

AWAIT
1917 ĕpibŏulē (1), *plot, plan*

AWAKE
5782 'ûwr (20), to *awake*
6974 qûwts (11), to *awake*
1235 diagrēgŏrĕō (1), to *waken thoroughly*
1326 diĕgĕirō (1), to *arouse, stimulate*
1453 ĕgĕirō (2), to *waken*, i.e. *rouse*
1594 ĕknēphō (1), to *rouse* (oneself) *out*
1852 ĕxupnizō (1), to *waken, rouse*

AWAKED
3364 yâqats (4), to *awake*
6974 qûwts (4), to *awake*

AWAKEST
5782 'ûwr (1), to *awake*
6974 qûwts (1), to *awake*

AWAKETH
6974 qûwts (3), to *awake*

AWAKING
1096+1853 ginŏmai (1), to *be, become*

AWARE
3045 yâda' (2), to *know*
1097 ginōskō (2), to *know*
1492 ĕidō (1), to *know*

AWAY
310 'achar (1), *after*
1197 bâ'ar (16), to *be brutish, be senseless*
1272 bârach (1), to *flee suddenly*
1473 gôwlâh (7), *exile; captive*
1497 gâzal (4), to *rob*
1540 gâlâh (17), to *denude; uncover*
1541 gᵉlâh (Ch.) (1), to *reveal mysteries*
1546 gâlûwth (4), *captivity; exiles*
1589 gânab (1), to *thieve; to deceive*

1639 gâra' (1), to *shave, remove, lessen*
1870 derek (1), *road; course of life*
1898 hâgâh (2), to *remove, expel*
1920 hâdaph (1), to *push away or down; drive out*
2219 zârâh (1), to *toss about; to diffuse*
2763 charam (1), to *devote to destruction*
2846 châthâh (1), to *lay hold of; to take away*
2862 châthaph (1), to *clutch, snatch*
3212 yâlak (4), to *walk; to live; to carry*
3318 yâtsâ' (4), to *go, bring out*
3988 mâ'aç (1), to *spurn; to disappear*
4422 mâlaṭ (1), to *escape as if by slipperiness*
5074 nâdad (1), to *rove, flee; to drive away*
5077 nâdâh (1), to *exclude, i.e. banish*
5111 nûwd (Ch.) (1), to *flee*
5186 nâṭâh (1), to *stretch or spread out*
5265 nâça' (3), *start* on a *journey*
5493 çûwr (70), to *turn off*
5496 çûwth (1), to *stimulate; to seduce*
5674 'âbar (7), to *cross over; to transition*
5709 'ădâ' (Ch.) (3), to *remove; to bedeck*
5710 'âdâh (1), to *pass on or continue; to remove*
7311 rûwm (2), to *be high; to rise or raise*
7368 râchaq (3), to *recede; remove*
7617 shâbâh (7), to *transport into captivity*
7628 shᵉbîy (1), *exile; booty*
7673 shâbath (1), to *repose; to desist* from
7726 shôwbâb (1), *apostate*, i.e. *idolatrous*
7953 shâlâh (1), to *draw out or off*, i.e. *remove*
115 athĕtēsis (1), *cancellation*
142 airō (12), to *lift, to take up*
337 anairĕō (1), to *take away*, i.e. *abolish*
343 anakaluptō (1), to *unveil*
520 apagō (12), to *take away*
522 apairō (1), to *remove, take away*
565 apĕrchŏmai (15), to *go off*, i.e. *depart*
577 apŏballō (2), to *throw off*; fig. to *lose*
580 apŏbŏlē (1), *rejection, loss*
595 apŏthĕsis (1), *laying aside*
617 apŏkuliō (3), to *roll away, roll back*

628 apŏlŏuŏ (1), to *wash fully*
630 apŏluŏ (27), to *relieve, release*
645 apŏspaŏ (1), to *withdraw* with force
646 apŏstasia (1), *defection from truth*
649 apŏstĕllŏ (4), to *send out* on a mission
654 apŏstrĕphŏ (6), to *turn away or back*
657 apŏtassŏmai (1), to *say adieu; to renounce*
659 apŏtithĕmi (1), to *put away; get rid of*
665 apŏtrĕpŏ (1), to *deflect, avoid*
667 apŏhĕrŏ (3), to *bear off, carry away*
683 apŏthĕŏmai (4), to *push off; to reject*
726 harpazŏ (2), to *seize*
851 aphairĕŏ (8), to *remove, cut off*
863 aphiĕmi (4), to *leave; to pardon, forgive*
868 aphistĕmi (2), *instigate* to revolt
1294 diastrĕphŏ (1), to *distort*
1544 ĕkballŏ (1), to *throw out*
1593 ĕknĕuŏ (1), to *quietly withdraw*
1599 ĕkpĕmpŏ (1), to *despatch, send out*
1601 ĕkpiptŏ (1), to *drop away*
1602 ĕkplĕŏ (1), to *depart by ship*
1808 ĕxairŏ (1), to *remove, drive away*
1813 ĕxalĕiphŏ (2), to *obliterate*
1821 ĕxapŏstĕllŏ (4), to *despatch, or to dismiss*
1831 ĕxĕrchŏmai (1), to *issue; to leave*
1854 ĕxŏ (1), *out, outside*
2210 zēmiŏŏ (1), to *experience detriment*
2673 katargĕŏ (6), to *be, render entirely useless*
3179 mĕthistĕmi (1), to *move*
3334 mĕtakinĕŏ (1), to *be removed, shifted from*
3350 mĕtŏikĕsia (3), *expatriation, exile*
3351 mĕtŏikizŏ (1), to *transfer as a settler or captive*
3895 parapiptŏ (1), to *apostatize, fall away*
3911 paraphĕrŏ (1), to *carry off; to avert*
3928 parĕrchŏmai (5), to *go by; to perish*
4014 pĕriairĕŏ (3), to *cast off anchor; to expiate*
4879 sunapagŏ (2), to *take off together*
5217 hupagŏ (3), to *withdraw or retire*

AWE
1481 gûwr (1), to *sojourn, live as an alien*

6342 pâchad (1), to *be startled; to fear*
7264 râgaz (1), to *quiver*

AWOKE
3364 yâqats (6), to *awake*
1326 diĕgĕirŏ (1), to *arouse, stimulate*
1453 ĕgĕirŏ (1), to *waken, i.e. rouse*

AX
1270 barzel (1), *iron; iron implement*
1631 garzen (2), *axe*
4601 Ma'ăkâh (1), *depression*
4621 ma'ătsâd (1), *axe*
7134 qardôm (1), *axe*
513 axinē (1), *axe*

AXE
1631 garzen (2), *axe*
7134 qardôm (1), *axe*
513 axinē (1), *axe*

AXES
2719 chereb (1), *knife, sword*
3781 kashshîyl (1), *axe*
4037 magzêrâh (1), *cutting blade, ax*
4050 mᵉgêrâh (1), *stone cutting saw*
7134 qardôm (3), *axe*

AXLETREES
3027 yâd (2), *hand; power*

AZAL
682 'Âtsêl (1), *noble*

AZALIAH
683 'Ătsalyâhûw (2), *Jehovah has reserved*

AZANIAH
245 'Ăzanyâh (1), *heard by Jehovah*

AZARAEL
5832 'Ăzar'êl (1), *God has helped*

AZAREEL
5832 'Ăzar'êl (5), *God has helped*

AZARIAH
5838 'Ăzaryâh (47), *Jehovah has helped*
5839 'Ăzaryâh (Ch.) (1), *Jehovah has helped*

AZAZ
5811 'Ăzâz (1), *strong*

AZAZIAH
5812 'Ăzazyâhûw (3), *Jehovah has strengthened*

AZBUK
5802 'Azbûwq (1), *stern depopulator*

AZEKAH
5825 'Ăzêqâh (7), *tilled*

AZEL
682 'Âtsêl (6), *noble*

AZEM
6107 'Etsem (2), *bone*

AZGAD
5803 'Azgâd (4), *stern troop*

AZIEL
5815 'Ăzîy'êl (1), *strengthened of God*

AZIZA
5819 'Ăzîyzâ' (1), *strengthfulness*

AZMAVETH
5820 'Azmâveth (8), *strong (one) of death*

AZMON
6111 'Atsmôwn (3), *bone-like*

AZNOTH-TABOR
243 'Aznôwth Tâbôwr (1), *flats of Tabor*

AZOR
107 Azōr (2), *helpful*

AZOTUS
108 Azōtŏs (1), *Azotus, i.e. Ashdod*

AZRIEL
5837 'Azrîy'êl (3), *help of God*

AZRIKAM
5840 'Azrîyqâm (6), *help of an enemy*

AZUBAH
5806 'Ăzûwbâh (4), *forsaking*

AZUR
5809 'Azzûwr (2), *helpful*

AZZAH
5804 'Azzâh (3), *strong*

AZZAN
5821 'Azzân (1), *strong one*

AZZUR
5809 'Azzûwr (1), *helpful*

BAAL
1168 Ba'al (61), *master*
896 Baal (1), *master*

BAAL'S
1168 Ba'al (1), *master*

BAAL-BERITH
1170 Ba'al Bᵉrîyth (2), *Baal of (the) covenant*

BAAL-GAD
1171 Ba'al Gâd (3), *Baal of Fortune*

BAAL-HAMON
1174 Ba'al Hâmôwn (1), *possessor of a multitude*

BAAL-HANAN
1177 Ba'al Chânân (5), *possessor of grace*

BAAL-HAZOR
1178 Ba'al Châtsôwr (1), *possessor of a village*

BAAL-HERMON
1179 Ba'al Chermôwn (2), *possessor of Hermon*

BAAL-MEON
1186 Ba'al Mᵉ'ôwn (3), *Baal of (the) habitation*

BAAL-PEOR
1187 Ba'al Pᵉ'ôwr (6), *Baal of Peor*

BAAL-PERAZIM
1188 Ba'al Pᵉ'râtsîym (4), *possessor of breaches*

BAAL-SHALISHA
1190 Ba'al Shâlîshâh (1), *Baal of Shalishah*

BAAL-TAMAR
1193 Ba'al Tâmâr (1), *possessor of (the) palm-tree*

BAAL-ZEBUB
1176 Ba'al Zᵉbûwb (4), *Baal of (the) Fly*

BAAL-ZEPHON
1189 Ba'al Tsᵉphôwn (3), *Baal of winter*

BAALAH
1173 Ba'ălâh (5), *mistress*

BAALATH
1191 Ba'ălâth (3), *office of mistress*

BAALATH-BEER
1192 Ba'ălath Bᵉ'êr (1), *mistress of a well*

BAALE
1184 Ba'ălêy Yᵉhûwdâh (1), *masters of Judah*

BAALI
1180 Ba'ălîy (1), *my master*

BAALIM
1168 Ba'al (18), *master*

BAALIS
1185 Ba'ălîç (1), *in exultation*

BAANA
1195 Ba'ănâ' (2), *in affliction*

BAANAH
1195 Ba'ănâ' (10), *in affliction*

BAARA
1199 Bâ'ărâ' (1), *brutish*

BAASEIAH
1202 Ba'ăsêyâh (1), *in (the) work of Jehovah*

BAASHA
1201 Ba'shâ' (28), *offensiveness*

BABBLER
1167+3956 ba'al (1), *master; husband*
4691 spĕrmŏlŏgŏs (1), *gossip or trifler in talk*

BABBLING
7879 sîyach (1), *uttered contemplation*

BABBLINGS
2757 kĕnŏphōnia (2), *fruitless discussion*

BABE
5288 na'ar (1), *male child; servant*
1025 brĕphŏs (4), *infant*
3516 nēpiŏs (1), *infant; simple-minded* person

BABEL
894 Bâbel (2), *confusion*

BABES
5768 'ôwlêl (2), *suckling child*
8586 ta'ălûwl (1), *caprice (as a fit coming on)*
1025 brĕphŏs (1), *infant*

3516 nēpĭŏs (5), *infant; simple-minded* person

BABYLON
894 Bâbel (247), *confusion*
895 Bâbel (Ch.) (25), *confusion*
897 Babulōn (12), *Babylon*

BABYLON'S
894 Bâbel (8), *confusion*

BABYLONIANS
896 Bablîy (Ch.) (1), *Babylonian*
1121+894 bên (3), *people* of a class or kind

BABYLONISH
8152 Shin'âr (1), *Shinar*

BACA
1056 Bâkâ' (1), *Baca*

BACHRITES
1076 Bakrîy (1), *Bakrite*

BACK
268 'âchôwr (16), *behind, backward; west*
310 'achar (1), *after*
322 'ăchôrannîyth (1), *backwardly, by turning*
1354 gab (1), *mounded or rounded: top or rim*
1355 gab (Ch.) (1), *back*
1458 gav (7), *back*
1639 gâra' (1), to *shave, remove, lessen*
1973 hâlᵉâh (1), *far away; thus far*
2015 hâphak (2), to *turn about or over*
2820 châsak (4), to *restrain or refrain*
3607 kâlâ' (1), to *hold back or in; to prohibit*
4185 mûwsh (1), to *withdraw*
4513 mâna' (4), to *deny, refuse*
5253 nâçag (1), to *retreat*
5437 çâbab (1), to *surround*
5472 çûwg (3), to *go back, to retreat*
5493 çûwr (2), to *turn off*
5637 çârar (1), to be *refractory, stubborn*
6203 'ôreph (4), *nape or back of the neck*
6437 pânâh (6), to *turn, to face*
6544 pâra' (1), to *loosen; to expose, dismiss*
7725 shûwb (70), to *turn back; to return*
7926 shᵉkem (2), *neck; spur* of a hill
617 apŏkuliō (2), to *roll away, roll back*
650 apŏstĕrĕō (1), to *deprive; to despoil*
3557 nŏsphizŏmai (2), to *sequestrate*
3577 nōtŏs (1), *back*
3694 ŏpisō (5), *behind, after, following*
4762 strĕphō (1), to *turn quite around or reverse*
5288 hupŏstĕllō (2), to *cower or shrink*

5289 hupŏstŏlē (1), *shrinkage, timidity*
5290 hupŏstrĕphō (3), to *turn under, behind*

BACKBITERS
2637 katalalŏs (1), *slanderer*

BACKBITETH
7270 râgal (1), to *reconnoiter; to slander*

BACKBITING
5643 çêther (1), *cover, shelter*

BACKBITINGS
2636 katalalia (1), *defamation, slander*

BACKBONE
6096 'âtseh (1), *spine*

BACKS
268 'âchôwr (1), *behind, backward; west*
1354 gab (1), *mounded or rounded: top or rim*
1458 gav (1), *back*
6203 'ôreph (4), *nape of the neck*

BACKSIDE
268 'âchôwr (1), *behind, backward; west*
310 'achar (1), *after*
3693 ŏpisthĕn (1), *at the back; after*

BACKSLIDER
5472 çûwg (1), to *go back, to apostatize*

BACKSLIDING
4878 mᵉshûwbâh (7), *apostasy*
5637 çârar (1), to be *refractory, stubborn*
7726 shôwbâb (2), *apostate, i.e. idolatrous*
7728 shôwbêb (2), *apostate, heathenish*

BACKSLIDINGS
4878 mᵉshûwbâh (4), *apostasy*

BACKWARD
268 'âchôwr (11), *behind, backward; west*
322 'ăchôrannîyth (6), *backwardly, by turning*
1519+3588+3694 ĕis (1), to *or into*

BAD
873 bî'ûwsh (Ch.) (1), *wicked, evil*
7451 ra' (13), *bad; evil*
2556 kakŏs (1), *bad, evil*
4190 pŏnērŏs (1), *malice, wicked, bad; crime*
4550 saprŏs (1), *rotten, i.e. worthless*

BADE
559 'âmar (6), to *say, speak*
1696 dâbar (1), to *speak, say; to subdue*
6680 tsâvâh (3), to *constitute, enjoin*
657 apŏtassŏmai (1), to *say adieu; to renounce*
2036 ĕpō (3), to *speak*
2564 kalĕō (4), to *call*

BADEST
1696 dâbar (1), to *speak, say; to subdue*

BADGERS'
8476 tachash (14), (poss.) *antelope*

BADNESS
7455 rôa' (1), *badness*

BAG
3599 kîyç (4), *cup; utility bag*
3627 kᵉlîy (2), *implement, thing*
6872 tsᵉrôwr (3), *parcel; kernel or particle*
1101 glōssŏkŏmŏn (2), *money purse*

BAGS
2754 chârîyt (1), *pocket*
6696 tsûwr (1), to *cramp, i.e. confine; to harass*
905 balantiŏn (1), *money pouch*

BAHARUMITE
978 Bachărûwmîy (1), *Bacharumite*

BAHURIM
980 Bachûrîym (5), *young men*

BAJITH
1006 Bayith (1), *house; temple; family, tribe*

BAKBAKKAR
1230 Baqbaqqar (1), *searcher*

BAKBUK
1227 Baqbûwq (2), *bottle*

BAKBUKIAH
1229 Baqbuqyâh (3), *wasting of Jehovah*

BAKE
644 'âphâh (6), to *bake*
1310 bâshal (1), to *boil up, cook; to ripen*
5746 'ûwg (1), to *bake*

BAKED
644 'âphâh (2), to *bake*
1310 bâshal (1), to *boil up, cook; to ripen*

BAKEMEATS
3978+4639+644 ma'ăkâl (1), *food*

BAKEN
644 'âphâh (4), to *bake*
7246 râbak (1), to *soak* bread in oil
8601 tûphîyn (1), *baked cake*

BAKER
644 'âphâh (8), to *bake*

BAKERS
644 'âphâh (2), to *bake*

BAKERS'
644 'âphâh (1), to *bake*

BAKETH
644 'âphâh (1), to *bake*

BALAAM
1109 Bil'âm (57), *foreigner*
903 Balaam (3), *foreigner*

BALAAM'S
1109 Bil'âm (3), *foreigner*

BALAC
904 Balak (1), *waster*

BALADAN
1081 Bal'ădân (2), *Bel* (is his) *lord*

BALAH
1088 Bâlâh (1), *failure*

BALAK
1111 Bâlâq (42), *waster*

BALAK'S
1111 Bâlâq (1), *waster*

BALANCE
3976 mô'zên (7), *pair of balance scales*
7070 qâneh (1), *reed*

BALANCES
3976 mô'zên (8), *pair of balance scales*
3977 mô'zên (Ch.) (1), *pair of balance scales*

BALANCINGS
4657 miphlâs (1), *poising*

BALD
1371 gibbêach (1), *bald forehead*
1372 gabbachath (3), *baldness on forehead*
5556 çol'âm (1), *destructive locust kind*
7139 qârach (4), to *depilate, shave*
7142 qêrêach (3), *bald on the back of the head*
7144 qorchâh (1), *baldness*
7146 qârachath (1), *bald spot; threadbare spot*

BALDNESS
7144 qorchâh (9), *baldness*

BALL
1754 dûwr (1), *circle; ball*

BALM
6875 tsᵉrîy (6), *balsam*

BAMAH
1117 Bâmâh (1), *elevation, high place*

BAMOTH
1120 Bâmôwth (2), *heights*

BAMOTH-BAAL
1120 Bâmôwth (1), *heights of Baal*

BAND
613 'ĕçûwr (Ch.) (2), *manacles, chains*
1416 gᵉdûwd (5), *band of soldiers*
2428 chayil (2), *army; wealth; virtue; valor*
5688 'ăbôth (1), *entwined things: a string, wreath*
8193 sâphâh (1), *lip, language, speech*
4686 spĕira (7), *tenth of a Roman Legion*

BANDED
4160+4963 pŏiĕō (1), to *make or do*

BANDS
102 'aggâph (7), *crowds of troops*

BANI
612 'êçûwr (2),
manacles, chains
631 'âçar (1), to fasten; to
join battle
1416 gᵉdûwd (8), band of
soldiers
2256 chebel (3),
company, band
2683 chêtsen (1), bosom
2784 chartsubbâh (2),
fetter; pain
4133 môwṭâh (2), pole;
ox-bow; yoke
4147 môwçêr (6), halter;
restraint
4189 môwshᵉkâh (1),
cord, band
4264 machăneh (2),
encampment
5688 'ăbôth (3), entwined
things: a string, wreath
7218 rô'sh (2), head
1199 dĕsmŏn (3),
shackle; impediment
2202 zĕuktêria (1),
tiller-rope, band
4886 sundĕsmŏs (1),
ligament; control

BANI
1137 Bânîy (15), built

BANISHED
5080 nâdach (2), to push
off, scattered

BANISHMENT
4065 maddûwach (1),
seduction, misleading
8331 sharshâh (1), chain

BANK
5550 çôlᵉlâh (3), siege
mound, i.e. rampart
8193 sâphâh (10), lip;
edge, margin
5132 trapĕza (1), table or
stool

BANKS
1415 gâdâh (3), border,
bank of a river
1428 gidyâh (1), border,
bank of a river

BANNER
1714 degel (1), flag,
standard, banner
5251 nêç (2), flag; signal;
token

BANNERS
1713 dâgal (3), to be
conspicuous

BANQUET
3738 kârâh (1), to dig; to
plot; to bore, hew
4797 mirzach (1), cry of
joy; revel or feast
4960 mishteh (10), drink;
banquet or feast
4961 mishteh (Ch.) (1),
drink; banquet or feast
8354 shâthâh (1), to
drink, imbibe

BANQUETING
3196 yayin (1), wine;
intoxication

BANQUETINGS
4224 pŏtŏs (1),
drinking-bout

BAPTISM
908 baptisma (22),
baptism

BAPTISMS
909 baptismŏs (1),
baptism

BAPTIST
907 baptizō (1), baptize
910 Baptistēs (13),
baptizer

BAPTIST'S
910 Baptistēs (1),
baptizer

BAPTIZE
907 baptizō (9), baptize

BAPTIZED
907 baptizō (57), baptize

BAPTIZEST
907 baptizō (1), baptize

BAPTIZETH
907 baptizō (2), baptize

BAPTIZING
907 baptizō (4), baptize

BAR
270 'âchaz (1), to seize,
grasp; possess
1280 bᵉrîyach (4), bolt;
cross-bar of a door
4132 môwṭ (2), pole; yoke

BAR-JESUS
919 Bariēsŏus (1), son of
Joshua

BAR-JONA
920 Bariōnas (1), son of
Jonah

BARABBAS
912 Barabbas (11), son of
Abba

BARACHEL
1292 Bârak'êl (2), God
has blessed

BARACHIAS
914 Barachias (1),
blessing of Jehovah

BARAK
1301 Bârâq (13), (flash
of) lightning
913 Barak (1), (flash of)
lightning

BARBARIAN
915 barbarŏs (3),
foreigner, non-Greek

BARBARIANS
915 barbarŏs (2),
foreigner, non-Greek

BARBAROUS
915 barbarŏs (1),
foreigner, non-Greek

BARBED
7905 sukkâh (1), dart,
harpoon

BARBER'S
1532 gallâb (1), barber

BARE
2029 hârâh (1), to
conceive, be pregnant
2308 châdal (1), to desist,
stop; be fat
2342 chûwl (1), to dance,
whirl; to writhe in pain
2554 châmaç (1), to be
violent; to maltreat

BARE
2834 châsaph (4), to
drain away or bail up
3205 yâlad (110), to bear
young; to father a child
4910 mâshal (1), to rule
5190 nâṭal (1), to lift; to
impose
5375 nâsâ' (34), to lift up
6181 'eryâh (4), nudity
6209 'ârar (1), to bare; to
demolish
6544 pâra' (1), to loosen;
to expose, dismiss
7146 qârachath (1), bald
spot; threadbare spot
7287 râdâh (2), to
subjugate; to crumble
7980 shâlaṭ (1), to
dominate, i.e. to govern
399 anaphĕrō (1), to take
up; to lead up
941 bastazō (4), to lift,
bear
1080 gĕnnaō (1), to
procreate, regenerate
1131 gumnŏs (1), nude
or not well clothed
3140 marturĕō (9), to
testify; to commend
4160 pŏiĕō (2), to make
or do
5342 phĕrō (1), to bear or
carry
5576 psĕudŏmarturĕō
(2), to offer false
evidence

BAREFOOT
3182 yâchêph (4), not
wearing sandals

BAREST
4910 mâshal (1), to rule
5375 nâsâ' (1), to lift up
3140 marturĕō (1), to
testify; to commend

BARHUMITE
1273 Barchûmîy (1),
Barchumite

BARIAH
1282 Bârîyach (1),
Bariach

BARK
5024 nâbach (1), to bark

BARKED
7111 qᵉtsâphâh (1),
fragment

BARKOS
1302 Barqôwç (2), Barkos

BARLEY
8184 sᵉ'ôrâh (33), barley
2915 krithē (1), barley
2916 krithinŏs (2),
consisting of barley

BARN
1637 gôren (1), open area
4035 mᵉgûwrâh (1),
fright; granary
596 apŏthēkē (2),
granary, grain barn

BARNABAS
921 Barnabas (29), son of
prophecy

BARNFLOOR
1637 gôren (1), open area

BARNS
618 'âçâm (1), barn

BARREL
3537 kad (3), jar, pitcher

BARRELS
3537 kad (1), jar, pitcher

BARREN
4420 mᵉlêchâh (1),
salted land, i.e. a desert
6115 'ôtser (1), closure;
constraint
6135 'âqâr (11), sterile,
barren
6723 tsîyâh (1), arid
desert
7909 shakkuwl (2),
bereaved
7921 shâkôl (2), to
miscarry
692 argŏs (1), lazy;
useless
4722 stĕgō (4), to endure
patiently

BARRENNESS
4420 mᵉlêchâh (1),
salted land, i.e. a desert

BARS
905 bad (1), limb,
member; bar; chief
1280 bᵉrîyach (35), bolt;
cross-bar of a door
4800 merchâb (1), open
space; liberty

BARSABAS
923 Barsabas (2), son of
Sabas

BARTHOLOMEW
918 Barthŏlŏmaiŏs (4),
son of Tolmai

BARTIMAEUS
924 Bartimaiŏs (1), son
of the unclean

BARUCH
1263 Bârûwk (26),
blessed

BARZILLAI
1271 Barzillay (12),
iron-hearted

BASE
1097+8034 bᵉlîy (1),
without, not yet
3653 kên (2), pedestal or
station of a basin
4350 mᵉkôwnâh (7),
pedestal; spot or place
4369 mᵉkûnâh (1), spot
7034 qâlâh (1), to be light
8217 shâphâl (4),
depressed, low
36 agĕnēs (1), ignoble,
lowly
5011 tapĕinŏs (1),
humiliated, lowly

BASER
60 agŏraiŏs (1), people
of the market place

BASES
4350 mᵉkôwnâh (13),
pedestal; spot or place
4369 mᵉkûnâh (1), spot

BASEST
8215 sh⁰phal (Ch.) (1), *low*
8217 shâphâl (1), *depressed, low*

BASHAN
1316 Bâshân (59), *Bashan*

BASHAN-HAVOTH-JAIR
1316+2334 Bâshân (1), *Bashan*

BASHEMATH
1315 Bosmath (6), *fragrance*

BASKET
1731 dûwd (2), *pot, kettle; basket*
2935 ṭene' (4), *basket*
3619 k⁰lûwb (2), *bird-trap; basket*
5536 çal (12), *basket*
4553 sarganē (1), *wicker basket*
4711 spuris (1), *hamper or lunch-receptacle*

BASKETS
1731 dûwd (1), *pot, kettle; basket*
1736 dûwday (1), *basket*
5536 çal (2), *basket*
5552 çalçillâh (1), *twig*
2894 kŏphinŏs (6), *small basket*
4711 spuris (4), *hamper or lunch-receptacle*

BASMATH
1315 Bosmath (1), *fragrance*

BASON
3713 k⁰phôwr (2), *bowl; white frost*
5592 çaph (2), *dish*
3537 niptēr (1), *basin for washing*

BASONS
101 'aggân (1), *bowl*
3713 k⁰phôwr (3), *bowl; white frost*
4219 mîzrâq (11), *bowl for sprinkling*
5592 çaph (2), *dish*

BASTARD
4464 mamzêr (2), *mongrel*

BASTARDS
3541 nŏthŏs (1), *spurious or illegitimate son*

BAT
5847 'ăṭallêph (2), *mammal, bat*

BATH
1324 bath (6), *liquid measure*

BATH-RABBIM
1337 Bath Rabbîym (1), *city of Rabbah*

BATH-SHEBA
1339 Bath-Sheba' (11), *daughter of an oath*

BATH-SHUA
1340 Bath-Shûwa' (1), *daughter of wealth*

BATHE
7364 râchats (18), to *lave, bathe*

BATHED
7301 râvâh (1), to *slake thirst or appetites*

BATHS
1324 bath (8), *liquid measure*
1325 bath (Ch.) (1), *liquid measure*

BATS
5847 'ăṭallêph (1), *bat*

BATTERED
7843 shâchath (1), to *decay; to ruin*

BATTLE
3593 kîydôwr (1), (poss.) *tumult, battle*
4221 môach (1), *bone marrow*
4264 machăneh (1), *encampment*
4421 milchâmâh (143), *battle; war; fighting*
4661 mappêts (1), *war-club*
5402 nesheq (1), *military arms, arsenal*
5430 çe'ôwn (1), *military boot*
6635 tsâbâ' (5), *army, military host*
6635+4421 tsâbâ' (1), *army, military host*
7128 q⁰râb (5), *hostile encounter*
4171 pŏlĕmŏs (5), *warfare; battle; fight*

BATTLEMENT
4624 ma'ăqeh (1), *parapet*

BATTLEMENTS
5189 n⁰ṭîyshâh (1), *tendril plant shoot*

BATTLES
4421 milchâmâh (6), *battle; war; fighting*

BAVAI
942 Bavvay (1), *Bavvai*

BAY
249 'ezrâch (1), *native born*
554 'âmôts (2), *red*
3956 lâshôwn (3), *tongue; tongue-shaped*

BAZLITH
1213 Batslûwth (1), *peeling*

BAZLUTH
1213 Batslûwth (1), *peeling*

BDELLIUM
916 b⁰dôlach (2), *bdellium, amber; pearl*

BEACON
8650 tôren (1), *mast pole; flag-staff pole*

BEALIAH
1183 B⁰'alyâh (1), *Jehovah (is) master*

BEALOTH
1175 B⁰'âlôwth (1), *mistresses*

BEAM
708 'ereg (1), *weaving; braid; also shuttle*

3714 kâphîyç (1), *girder, beam*
4500 mânôwr (4), *frame of a loom*
5646 'âb (1), *architrave*
6982 qôwrâh (2), *rafter; roof*
1385 dŏkŏs (6), *stick or plank*

BEAMS
1356 gêb (1), *well, cistern*
3773 kârûthâh (3), *hewn timber beams*
6763 tsêlâ' (1), *side of a person or thing*
6982 qôwrâh (2), *rafter; roof*
7136 qârâh (4), to *bring about; to impose*

BEANS
6321 pôwl (2), *beans*

BEAR
1319 bâsar (4), to *announce (good news)*
1677 dôb (10), *bear*
1678 dôb (Ch.) (1), *bear*
2398 châṭâ' (2), to *sin*
3205 yâlad (16), to *bear young; to father a child*
3212 yâlak (1), to *walk; to live; to carry*
3318 yâtsâ' (1), to *go, bring out*
3557 kûwl (1), to *keep in; to measure*
4910 mâshal (1), to *rule*
5187 n⁰ṭîyl (1), *laden*
5201 nâṭar (1), to *guard; to cherish anger*
5375 nâsâ' (100), to *lift up*
5445 çâbal (3), to *carry*
5749 'ûwd (1), to *protest, testify; to encompass*
6030 'ânâh (2), to *respond, answer*
6213 'âsâh (4), to *do*
7287 râdâh (1), to *subjugate; to crumble*
7981 sh⁰lêṭ (Ch.) (1), to *dominate, i.e. govern*
8323 sârar (1), to *have, exercise, get dominion*
8382 tâ'am (1), to *be twinned, i.e. duplicate*
8505 tâkan (1), to *balance, i.e. measure*
142 airō (4), to *lift, to take up*
399 anaphērō (1), to *take up; to lead up*
430 anĕchŏmai (4), *put up with, endure*
503 antŏphthalmĕō (1), to *face into the wind*
715 arktŏs (1), *bear (animal)*
941 bastazō (11), to *lift, bear*
1080 gĕnnaō (1), to *procreate, regenerate*
3114 makrŏthumĕō (1), to *be forbearing, patient*
3140 marturĕō (21), to *testify; to commend*
4160 pŏiĕō (2), to *do*
5041 tĕknŏgŏnĕō (1), to *be a child bearer*

5297 hupŏphĕrō (1), to *bear from underneath*
5342 phĕrō (4), to *bear*
5409 phŏrĕō (1), to *wear*
5576 psĕudŏmarturĕō (4), to offer *falsehood in evidence*

BEARD
2206 zâqân (14), *beard*
8222 sâphâm (1), *beard*

BEARDS
2206 zâqân (4), *beard*

BEARERS
5449 çabbâl (3), *porter, carrier*

BEAREST
3205 yâlad (1), to *bear young; to father a child*
941 bastazō (1), to *lift, bear*
3140 marturĕō (1), to *testify; to commend*
5088 tiktō (1), to *produce from seed*

BEARETH
3205 yâlad (2), to *bear young; to father a child*
4910 mâshal (1), to *rule*
5375 nâsâ' (7), to *lift up*
6030 'ânâh (2), to *respond, answer*
6509 pârâh (1), to *bear fruit*
6779 tsâmach (1), to *sprout*
8382 tâ'am (1), to *be twinned, i.e. duplicate*
1627 ĕkphĕrō (1), to *bear out; to produce*
2592 karpŏphŏrĕō (1), to *be fertile*
3140 marturĕō (3), to *testify; to commend*
4722 stĕgō (1), to *endure patiently*
4828 summarturĕō (1), to *testify jointly*
5342 phĕrō (2), to *bear or carry*
5409 phŏrĕō (1), to *wear*

BEARING
2232 zâra' (1), to *sow seed; to disseminate*
3205 yâlad (3), to *bear young; to father a child*
5375 nâsâ' (10), to *lift up*
941 bastazō (3), to *lift, bear*
4064 pĕriphĕrō (1), to *transport*
4828 summarturĕō (2), to *testify jointly*
4901 sunĕpimarturĕō (1), to *testify further jointly*
5342 phĕrō (1), to *bear or carry*

BEARS
1677 dôb (2), *bear*

BEAST
929 b⁰hêmâh (83), *animal, beast*
1165 b⁰'îyr (1), *cattle, livestock*
2123 zîyz (1), *moving creature*

B

2416 chay (34), *alive;
raw; fresh; life*
2423 chêyvâ' (Ch.) (6),
wild *animal; monster*
5038 neʰbêlâh (1), *carcase
or carrion*
5315 nephesh (1), *life;
breath; soul; wind*
5315+929 nephesh (1),
life; breath; soul; wind
7409 rekesh (1), *relay of
animals*
2226 zôŏn (7), *living
animal*
2342 thēriŏn (40),
dangerous animal
2934 ktēnŏs (1),
domestic animal

BEAST'S
2423 chêyvâ' (Ch.) (1),
wild *animal; monster*

BEASTS
338 'îy (3), *solitary wild
creature that howls*
929 beʰhêmâh (51),
animal, beast
1165 beʰîyr (3), *cattle,
livestock*
2123 zîyz (1), *moving
creature*
2416 chay (42), *alive;
raw; fresh; life*
2423 chêyvâ' (Ch.) (13),
wild *animal; monster*
2874 ṭebach (1), *butchery*
2966 ṭeʰrêphâh (5), *torn
prey*
3753 karkârâh (1),
cow-camel
4806 meʰrîy' (2), *stall-fed
animal*
6728 tsîyîy (3), wild *beast*
2226 zôŏn (16), *living
animal*
2341 thēriŏmachĕŏ (1),
to be a beast fighter
2342 thēriŏn (6),
dangerous animal
2934 ktēnŏs (3),
domestic animal
4968 sphagiŏn (1),
offering for slaughter
5074 tĕtrapŏus (2),
quadruped animal

BEAT
1743 dûwk (1), *to
pulverize in a mortar*
1792 dâkâ' (1), *to
pulverize; be contrite*
1849 dâphaq (1), *to
knock; to press severely*
1854 dâqaq (2), *to crush*
2040 hâraç (1), *to pull
down; break, destroy*
2251 châbaṭ (2), *to knock
out or off, thresh a tree*
3807 kâthath (4), *to
bruise or strike, beat*
5221 nâkâh (4), *to strike,
kill*
5422 nâthats (3), *to tear
down*
7554 râqa' (1), *to pound*
7833 shâchaq (3), *to
grind or wear away*
1194 dĕrŏ (5), *to flay, i.e.
to scourge or thrash*

1911 ĕpiballŏ (1), *to
throw upon*
4350 prŏskŏptŏ (1), *to
trip up; to strike*
4363 prŏspiptŏ (1), *to
beat or strike*
4366 prŏsrēgnumi (2), *to
burst upon*
4463 rhabdizŏ (1), *to
strike with a stick*
5180 tuptŏ (2), *to strike,
beat, wound*

BEATEN
1643 geres (2), *grain*
1851 daq (1), *crushed;
small or thin*
1986 hâlam (1), *to strike,
beat, stamp, conquer*
2251 châbaṭ (1), *to knock
out or off, thresh a tree*
2865 châthath (1), *to
break down*
3795 kâthîyth (4), *pure
oil from beaten olives*
3807 kâthath (3), *to
bruise or strike, beat*
4347 makkâh (1), *blow;
wound; pestilence*
4749 miqshâh (8), *work
molded by hammering*
5060 nâga' (1), *to strike*
5062 nâgaph (1), *to strike*
5221 nâkâh (4), *to strike,
kill*
5310 nâphats (1), *to dash
to pieces; to scatter*
7820 shâchaṭ (5), *to
hammer out*
1194 dĕrŏ (5), *to flay, i.e.
to scourge or thrash*
4463 rhabdizŏ (1), *to
strike with a stick*

BEATEST
2251 châbaṭ (1), *to knock
out or off, thresh a tree*
5221 nâkâh (1), *to strike,
kill*

BEATETH
1194 dĕrŏ (1), *to flay, i.e.
to scourge or thrash*

BEATING
1986 hâlam (1), *to strike,
beat, stamp, conquer*
1194 dĕrŏ (1), *to flay, i.e.
to scourge or thrash*
5180 tuptŏ (1), *to strike,
beat, wound*

BEAUTIES
1926 hâdâr (1),
magnificence

BEAUTIFUL
2896 ṭôwb (1), *good; well*
2896+4758 tôwb (1),
good; well
3303 yâpheh (7),
beautiful; handsome
3303+8389 yâpheh (2),
beautiful; handsome
4998 nâ'âh (1), *to be
pleasant, i.e. beautiful*
6643 tseʰbîy (1),
conspicuous splendor
8597 tiph'ârâh (6),
ornament
5611 hŏraiŏs (4),
flourishing, beauteous

BEAUTIFY
6286 pâ'ar (3), *to shake a
tree*

BEAUTY
1926 hâdâr (3),
magnificence
1927 hădârâh (4),
decoration, ornament
1935 hôwd (1), *grandeur,
majesty*
2530 châmad (1), *to
delight in; lust for*
3308 yŏphîy (20), *beauty*
4758 mar'eh (1),
appearance; vision
5276 nâ'êm (1), *to be
agreeable*
5278 no'am (4), *delight,
suitableness*
6287 peʰ'êr (1), *fancy
head-dress*
6643 tseʰbîy (2),
conspicuous splendor
6736 tsîyr (1), *carved
idolatrous image*
8597 tiph'ârâh (10),
ornament

BEBAI
893 Bêbay (6), *Bebai*

BECAUSE
413 'êl (3), *to, toward*
834 'âsher (42), *because,
in order that*
1115 biltîy (3), *except,
without, unless, besides*
1558 gâlâl (4), *on
account of, because of*
1697 dâbâr (1), *word;
matter; thing*
1768 dîy (Ch.) (2), *that; of*
1870 derek (1), *road;
course of life*
3027 yâd (2), *hand; power*
3282 ya'an (59), *because,
for this reason*
3588 kîy (455), *for, that
because*
3605 kôl (1), *all, any*
4480 min (2), *from, out of*
4481 min (Ch.) (1), *from
or out of*
4616 ma'an (11), *on
account of*
5668 'âbûwr (7), *on
account of*
5921 'al (45), *above, over,
upon, or against*
6118 'êqeb (2), *unto the
end; for ever*
6119 'âqêb (1), *track,
footprint*
6440 pânîym (67), *face;
front*
6448 pâçag (1), *to
contemplate*
8478 tachath (1), *bottom;
underneath; in lieu of*
575 apŏ (1), *from, away*
1063 gar (5), *for, indeed,
but, because*
1223 dia (54), *through,
by means of; because of*
1360 diŏti (13), *on the
very account that*
1537 ĕk (2), *out, out of*
1722 ĕn (3), *in; during;
because of*
1893 ĕpĕi (7), *since*

1894 ĕpĕidĕ (2), *when,
whereas*
1909 ĕpi (1), *on, upon*
2443 hina (1), *in order
that*
2530 kathŏti (2), *as far
or inasmuch as*
3704 hŏpŏs (1), *in the
manner that*
3754 hŏti (184), *that;
because; since*
4314 prŏs (2), *for; on, at;
to, toward; against*
5484 charin (2), *on
account of, because of*

BECHER
1071 Beker (5), *young
bull camel*

BECHORATH
1064 Beʰkôwrath (1),
primogeniture

BECKONED
1269 dianĕuŏ (1), *to nod
or express by signs*
2656 katanĕuŏ (1), *to
make a sign or signal*
2678 katasĕiŏ (2), *to
motion a signal or sign*
3506 nĕuŏ (2), *nod, i.e.
signal*

BECKONING
2678 katasĕiŏ (2), *to
motion a signal or sign*

BED
3326 yâtsûwa' (3), *bed;
wing or lean-to*
3331 yâtsa' (1), *to strew*
4296 miṭṭâh (23), *bed;
sofa, litter or bier*
4702 matstsâ' (1), *couch*
4903 mishkab (Ch.) (6),
bed
4904 mishkâb (29), *bed;
sleep; intercourse*
6170 'ărûwgâh (1),
parterre, kind of garden
6210 'eres (4), *canopy
couch*
6210+3326 'eres (1),
canopy couch
2825 klinē (8), *couch*
2845 kŏitē (2), *couch;
conception*
2895 krabbatŏs (10),
sleeping mat
4766 strŏnnumi (1), *to
spread a couch*

BED'S
4296 miṭṭâh (1), *bed;
sofa, litter or bier*

BEDAD
911 Beʰdad (2), *separation*

BEDAN
917 Beʰdân (2), *servile*

BEDCHAMBER
2315+4296 cheder (3),
apartment, chamber
2315+4904 cheder (3),
apartment, chamber

BEDEIAH
912 Bêdeʰyâh (1), *servant
of Jehovah*

BEDS
4296 miṭṭâh (2), *bed;
sofa, litter or bier*

4904 mishkâb (5), *bed; sleep; intercourse*
6170 'ărûwgâh (1), *parterre, kind of garden*
2825 klinĕ (1), *couch*
2895 krabbatŏs (1), *sleeping mat*

BEDSTEAD
6210 'eres (1), *canopy couch*

BEE
1682 dᵉbôwrâh (1), *bee*

BEELIADA
1182 Bᵉ'elyâdâ' (1), *Baal has known*

BEELZEBUB
954 Bĕĕlzĕbŏul (7), *dung-god*

BEER
876 Bᵉ'êr (2), *well, cistern*

BEER-ELIM
879 Bᵉ'êr 'Êlîym (1), *well of heroes*

BEER-LAHAI-ROI
883 Bᵉ'êr la-Chay Rô'îy (1), *well of a living (One) my seer*

BEER-SHEBA
884 Bᵉ'êr Sheba' (34), *well of an oath*

BEERA
878 Bᵉ'êrâ' (1), *well*

BEERAH
880 Bᵉ'êrâh (1), *well*

BEERI
882 Bᵉ'êrîy (2), *fountain*

BEEROTH
881 Bᵉ'êrôwth (6), *wells*

BEEROTHITE
886 Bᵉ'êrôthîy (4), *Beërothite*

BEEROTHITES
886 Bᵉ'êrôthîy (1), *Beërothite*

BEES
1682 dᵉbôwrâh (3), *bee*

BEESH-TERAH
1203 Bᵉ'eshtᵉrâh (1), *with Ashtoreth*

BEETLE
2728 chargôl (1), *leaping insect*

BEEVES
1241 bâqâr (7), *plowing ox; herd*

BEFALL
579 'ânâh (1), *to meet, to happen*
4672 mâtsâ' (1), *to find or acquire; to occur, meet or be present*
7122 qârâ' (4), *to encounter, to happen*
7136 qârâh (2), *to bring about; to impose*
4876 sunantaŏ (1), *meet with; to occur*

BEFALLEN
4672 mâtsâ' (3), *to find or acquire; to occur*
4745 miqreh (1), *accident or fortune*

7122 qârâ' (1), *to encounter, to happen*
7136 qârâh (1), *to bring about; to impose*
4876 sunantaŏ (1), *to meet with; to occur*

BEFALLETH
4745 miqreh (2), *accident or fortune*

BEFELL
935 bôw' (1), *to go, come*
4672 mâtsâ' (1), *to find or acquire; to occur*
7136 qârâh (1), *to bring about; to impose*
1096 ginŏmai (1), *to be, become*
4819 sumbainŏ (1), *to concur, happen*

BEFORE
413 'êl (8), *to, toward*
639 'aph (2), *nose or nostril; face; person*
854 'êth (4), *with; by; at*
865 'ethmôwl (1), *heretofore, formerly*
2958 ţᵉrôwm (1), *not yet, before*
2962 ţerem (41), *not yet or before*
3808 lô' (2), *no, not*
3942 liphnay (1), *anterior, in front of*
4136 mûwl (1), *in front of, opposite*
4551 maççâ' (1), *stone quarry; projectile*
4608 ma'ăleh (1), *elevation; platform*
5048 neged (70), *over against or before*
5084 nâdân (1), *sheath*
5226 nêkach (1), *opposite*
5227 nôkach (9), *opposite, in front of*
5703 'ad (1), *perpetuity; ancient*
5704 'ad (1), *as far (long) as; during; while; until*
5869 'ayin (8), *eye; sight; fountain*
5921 'al (12), *above, over, upon, or against*
5973 'îm (5), *with*
6440 pânîym (1110), *face; front*
6471 pa'am (1), *time; step; occurence*
6903 qᵉbêl (Ch.) (3), *in front of, before*
6905 qâbâl (1), *in front of*
6924 qedem (10), *before, anciently*
6925 qŏdâm (Ch.) (29), *before*
6931 qadmôwnîy (1), *anterior time*
7130 qereb (1), *nearest part, i.e. the center*
7223 rî'shôwn (1), *first, in place, time or rank*
561 apĕnanti (2), *opposite, before*
575 apŏ (2), *from, away*
1519 ĕis (2), *to or into*
1715 ĕmprŏsthĕn (41), *in front of*

1722 ĕn (1), *in; during; because of*
1725 ĕnanti (1), *before, in presence of*
1726 ĕnantiŏn (4), *in the presence of*
1773 ĕnnuchŏn (1), *by night*
1799 ĕnŏpiŏn (63), *in the face of, before*
1909 ĕpi (17), *on, upon*
2596 kata (2), *down; according to*
2713 katĕnanti (1), *directly opposite*
2714 katĕnôpiŏn (3), *directly in front of*
3319 mĕsŏs (1), *middle*
3764 ŏudĕpō (1), *not even yet*
3844 para (3), *from; with; besides; on account of*
3908 paratithēmi (9), *to present something*
3936 paristĕmi (2), *to stand beside, present*
4250 prin (7), *prior, sooner, before*
4253 prŏ (43), *before in time or space*
4254 prŏagŏ (15), *to lead forward; to precede*
4256 prŏaitiaŏmai (1), *to previously charge*
4257 prŏakŏuŏ (1), *to hear beforehand*
4264 prŏbibazŏ (1), *to bring to the front*
4267 prŏginŏskŏ (1), *to know beforehand*
4270 prŏgraphō (1), *to write previously*
4275 prŏĕidō (1), *to foresee*
4277 prŏĕpō (1), *to say already, to predict*
4278 prŏĕnarchŏmai (1), *to commence already*
4280 prŏĕrĕŏ (8), *to say already, predict*
4281 prŏĕrchŏmai (4), *to go onward, precede*
4282 prŏĕtŏimazŏ (1), *to fit up in advance*
4283 prŏĕuaggĕlizŏmai (1), *to announce in advance*
4293 prŏkataggĕllō (3), *to predict, promise, foretell*
4295 prŏkĕimai (3), *to be present to the mind*
4296 prŏkĕrussŏ (1), *to proclaim in advance*
4299 prŏkrima (1), *prejudgment*
4300 prŏkurŏō (1), *to ratify previously*
4301 prŏlambanŏ (1), *to take before*
4302 prŏlĕgō (2), *to predict, forewarn*
4304 prŏmĕlĕtaŏ (1), *to premeditate*
4308 prŏŏraŏ (1), *to notice previously*
4309 prŏŏrizŏ (1), *to predetermine*

4310 prŏpaschŏ (1), *to undergo previously*
4313 prŏpŏrĕuŏmai (1), *to precede as guide*
4314 prŏs (2), *for; on, at; to, toward; against*
4315 prŏsabbatŏn (1), *Sabbath-eve*
4363 prŏspiptō (5), *to prostrate oneself*
4384 prŏtassŏ (1), *to prescribe beforehand*
4386 prŏtĕrŏn (4), *previously*
4391 prŏüparchō (1), *to be or do previously*
4401 prŏchĕirŏtŏnĕŏ (1), *to elect in advance*
4412 prŏtŏn (1), *firstly*
4413 prŏtŏs (2), *foremost*

BEFOREHAND
4271 prŏdēlŏs (2), *obvious, evident*
4294 prŏkatartizŏ (1), *to prepare in advance*
4303 prŏmarturŏmai (1), *to witness beforehand*
4305 prŏmĕrimnaŏ (1), *to care in advance*

BEFORETIME
865+832 'ethmôwl (1), *heretofore, formerly*
6440 pânîym (5), *face; front*
7223 rî'shôwn (1), *first, in place, time or rank*
8543+8032 tᵉmôwl (2), *yesterday*
4391 prŏüparchō (1), *to be or do previously*

BEG
7592 shâ'al (2), *to ask*
1871 ĕpaitĕŏ (1), *to ask for, beg*

BEGAN
2490 châlal (34), *to profane, defile*
2974 yâ'al (1), *to assent; to undertake, begin*
3246 yᵉçûd (1), *foundation; beginning)*
5927 'âlâh (1), *to ascend, be high, mount*
6751 tsâlal (1), *to shade; to grow dark*
8271 shᵉrê' (Ch.) (1), *unravel, commence*
756 archŏmai (64), *to begin*
2020 ĕpiphōskŏ (1), *to grow light*
2192 ĕchŏ (1), *to have; hold; keep*

BEGAT
3205 yâlad (176), *to bear young; to father a child*
616 apŏkuĕŏ (1), *to generate, bring to being*
1080 gĕnnaŏ (43), *to procreate, regenerate*

BEGET
3205 yâlad (10), *to bear young; to father a child*

BEGETTEST
3205 yâlad (2), *to bear young; to father a child*

B

BEGETTETH
3205 yâlad (3), to *bear young*; to *father a child*

BEGGAR
34 'ebyôwn (1), *destitute; poor*
4434 ptôchŏs (2), *pauper, beggar*

BEGGARLY
4434 ptôchŏs (1), *pauper, beggar*

BEGGED
154 aitĕō (2), to *ask for*
4319 prŏsaitĕō (1), to *solicit, beg*

BEGGING
1245 bâqash (1), to *search*; to *strive after*
4319 prŏsaitĕō (2), to *solicit, beg*

BEGIN
2490 châlal (12), to *profane, defile*
8462 tᵉchillâh (1), *original; originally*
756 archŏmai (11), to *begin*
3195 mĕllō (1), to *intend*, i.e. *be about to be*

BEGINNEST
2490 châlal (1), to *profane, defile*

BEGINNING
227 'âz (3), *at that time or place; therefore*
1931 hûw' (2), *he, she, it; this or that*
5769 'ôwlâm (1), *eternity; ancient; always*
7218 rô'sh (12), *head*
7223 rî'shôwn (4), *first*
7225 rê'shîyth (18), *first*
8462 tᵉchillâh (14), *original; originally*
509 anōthĕn (1), *from above; from the first*
746 archē (39), *first in rank; first in time*
756 archŏmai (8), to *begin*
4412 prŏtŏn (1), *firstly*
4413 prŏtŏs (1), *foremost*

BEGINNINGS
7218 rô'sh (2), *head*
7221 rî'shâh (1), *beginning*
746 archē (1), *first*

BEGOTTEN
3205 yâlad (7), to *bear young*; to *father a child*
3318 yâtsâ' (1), to *go, bring out*
4138 môwledeth (1), *lineage, offspring*
313 anagĕnnaō (1), to *beget or bear again*
1080 gĕnnaō (7), to *procreate, regenerate*
3439 mŏnŏgĕnēs (6), *sole, one and only*
4416 prōtŏtŏkŏs (1), *first-born*

BEGUILE
2603 katabrabĕuō (1), to *award a price against*

BEGUILED
3884 paralŏgizŏmai (1), to *delude, deceive*

BEGUILED
5230 nâkal (1), to *act treacherously*
5377 nâshâ' (1), to *lead astray, to delude*
7411 râmâh (2), to *hurl; to shoot; to delude*
1818 ĕxapataō (1), to *seduce wholly, deceive*

BEGUILING
1185 dĕlĕazō (1), to *delude, seduce*

BEGUN
2490 châlal (6), to *profane, defile*
756 archŏmai (1), to *begin*
1728 ĕnarchŏmai (2), to *commence on, begin*
2691 katastrēniaō (1), to *be voluptuous against*
4278 prŏĕnarchŏmai (2), to *commence already*

BEHALF
854 'êth (1), *with; by; at*
5973 'îm (1), *with*
8478 tachath (1), *bottom; underneath; in lieu of*
1909 ĕpi (1), *on, upon*
3313 mĕrŏs (2), *division or share*
4012 pĕri (1), *about; around*
5228 hupĕr (4), *over; in behalf of*

BEHAVE
2388 châzaq (1), to *fasten upon; to seize*
5234 nâkar (1), to *care for, respect, revere*
7292 râhab (1), to *urge severely*
7919 sâkal (1), to *be circumspect*
390 anastrĕphō (1), to *remain, to live*
807 aschēmŏnĕō (1), to *be, act unbecoming*

BEHAVED
1980 hâlak (1), to *walk; live a certain way*
7489 râ'a' (1), to *be good for nothing*
7737 shâvâh (1), to *level*, i.e. *equalize*
7919 sâkal (4), to *be circumspect*
812 ataktĕō (1), to *be, act irregular*
1096 ginŏmai (1), to *be, become*

BEHAVETH
807 aschēmŏnĕō (1), to *be, act unbecoming*

BEHAVIOUR
2940 ṭa'am (2), *taste; perception*
2688 katastēma (1), *demeanor*
2887 kŏsmiŏs (1), *orderly*

BEHEADED
5493+7218 çûwr (1), to *turn off*

BEHEADED
6202 'âraph (1), to *break the neck, to destroy*
607 apŏkĕphalizō (4), to *decapitate*
3990 pĕlĕkizō (1), to *remove the head*

BEHELD
2370+934 chăzâ' (Ch.) (6), to *gaze upon*
5027 nâbaṭ (2), to *scan; to regard* with favor
7200 râ'âh (23), to *see*
333 anathĕŏrĕō (1), to *look again*
991 blĕpō (2), to *look at*
1492 ĕidō (10), to *know*
1689 ĕmblĕpō (3), to *observe; to discern*
2300 thĕaŏmai (2), to *look closely at*
2334 thĕŏrĕō (4), to *see; to discern*

BEHEMOTH
930 bᵉhêmôwth (1), *hippopotamus*

BEHIND
268 'âchôwr (5), *behind, backward; west*
310 'achar (49), *after*
3498 yâthar (1), to *remain or be left*
5975 'âmad (1), to *stand*
2641 katalĕipō (1), to *abandon*
3693 ŏpisthĕn (4), *at the back; after*
3694 ŏpisō (6), *behind, after, following*
5278 hupŏmĕnō (1), to *undergo (trials)*
5302 hustĕrĕō (4), to *be inferior; to fall short*

BEHOLD
431 'ălûw (Ch.) (5), *lo!*
718 'ărûw (Ch.) (4), *lo!, behold!*
1887 hê' (1), *Lo!, Look!*
2005 hên (237), *lo!; if!*
2009 hinnêh (770), *lo!; Look!*
2205 zâqên (2), *old, venerated*
2209 ziqnâh (1), *old age*
2372 châzâh (7), to *gaze at; to perceive*
5027 nâbaṭ (9), to *scan; to regard* with favor
6822 tsâphâh (1), to *peer into the distance*
7200 râ'âh (58), to *see*
7789 shûwr (5), to *spy out, survey*
7891 shîyr (1), to *sing*
816 atĕnizō (1), to *gaze intently*
991 blĕpō (3), to *look at*
1492 ĕidō (5), to *know*
1689 ĕmblĕpō (1), to *observe; to discern*
1896 ĕpĕidŏn (1), to *regard*
2029 ĕpŏptĕuō (2), to *watch, observe*
2334 thĕŏrĕō (3), to *see; to discern*
2396 idĕ (24), *surprise!, lo!, look!*

BEHOLD
2400 idŏu (180), *lo!, note!, see!*
2657 katanŏĕō (2), to *observe fully*

BEHOLDEST
5027 nâbaṭ (1), to *scan; to regard* with favor
991 blĕpō (3), to *look at*

BEHOLDETH
6437 pânâh (1), to *turn, to face*
7200 râ'âh (2), to *see*
2657 katanŏĕō (1), to *observe fully*

BEHOLDING
6822 tsâphâh (1), to *peer; to observe, await*
7200 râ'âh (2), to *see*
816 atĕnizō (2), to *gaze intently*
991 blĕpō (2), to *look at*
1689 ĕmblĕpō (1), to *observe; to discern*
2334 thĕŏrĕō (4), to *see; to discern*
2657 katanŏĕō (1), to *observe fully*
2734 katŏptrizŏmai (1), to *see reflected*
3708 hŏraō (1), to *stare, see clearly*

BEHOVED
1163 dĕi (1), *it is (was) necessary*
3784 ŏphĕilō (1), to *owe; to be under obligation*

BEING
1961 hâyâh (4), to *exist*, i.e. *be or become*
5750 'ôwd (2), *again; repeatedly; still; more*
1096 ginŏmai (5), to *be, become*
1909 ĕpi (1), *on, upon*
2070 ĕsmĕn (1), *we are*
2192 ĕchō (1), to *have; hold; keep*
5225 huparchō (13), to *come into existence*
5605 ōdinō (1), to *experience labor pains*
5607 ōn (35), *being, existence*

BEKAH
1235 beqa' (1), *half shekel*

BEL
1078 Bêl (3), *Bel (Baal)*

BELA
1106 Bela' (13), *gulp; destruction*

BELAH
1106 Bela' (1), *gulp; destruction*

BELAITES
1108 Bal'îy (1), *Belaite*

BELCH
5042 nâba' (1), to *gush forth; emit a foul odor*

BELIAL
1100 bᵉlîya'al (16), *wickedness, trouble*
955 Bĕlial (1), *worthlessness*

BELIED
3584 kâchash (1), to *lie,
disown;* to *disappoint*

BELIEF
4102 pistis (1), *faith,
belief; conviction*

BELIEVE
539 'âman (19), to *be
firm, faithful, true*
544 apĕithĕō (1), to
disbelieve
569 apistĕō (2), to
disbelieve, disobey
571 apistŏs (4), *without
faith; untrustworthy*
4100 pistĕuō (109), to
have faith, i.e. *credit;* to
entrust
4100+1722 pistĕuō (1), to
have faith, i.e. *credit*
4100+1909 pistĕuō (1), to
have faith, i.e. *credit*
4102 pistis (1), *faith,
belief; conviction*
4103 pistŏs (2), *trustful;
reliable*

BELIEVED
539 'âman (21), to *be
firm, faithful, true*
540 'âman (Ch.) (1), to *be
firm, faithful, true*
544 apĕithĕō (6), to
disbelieve
569 apistĕō (3), to
disbelieve, disobey
569+4100 apistĕō (1), to
disbelieve, disobey
3982 pĕithō (3), to *rely* by
inward certainty
4100 pistĕuō (76), to *have
faith,* i.e. *credit*
4103 pistŏs (2),
trustworthy; reliable
4135 plĕrŏphŏrĕō (1), to
assure or *convince*

BELIEVERS
4100 pistĕuō (1), to *have
faith,* i.e. *credit*
4103 pistŏs (1),
trustworthy; reliable

BELIEVEST
4100 pistĕuō (8), to *have
faith,* i.e. *credit*

BELIEVETH
539 'âman (4), to *be firm,
faithful, true;* to *trust*
544 apĕithĕō (1), to
disbelieve
569 apistĕō (1), to
disbelieve, disobey
571 apistŏs (3), *without
faith; untrustworthy*
1537+4102 ĕk (1), *out of*
4100 pistĕuō (33), to *have
faith,* i.e. *credit*
4103 pistŏs (2),
trustworthy; reliable

BELIEVING
4100 pistĕuō (6), to *have
faith,* i.e. *credit*
4103 pistŏs (2),
trustworthy; reliable

BELL
6472 pa'ămôn (3), *bell*

BELLIES
1064 gastĕr (1), *stomach;
womb; gourmand*

BELLOW
6670 tsâhal (1), to *be
cheerful;* to *sound*

BELLOWS
4647 mappûach (1),
bellows

BELLS
4698 mᵉtsillâh (1), *small
bell*
6472 pa'ămôn (3), *bell*

BELLY
990 beṭen (30), *belly;
womb; body*
1512 gâchôwn (2), *belly*
3770 kᵉrês (1), *paunch*
4577 mᵉ'a'(Ch.) (1),
bowels, belly
4578 mê'âh (3), *viscera;
anguish, tenderness*
6897 qôbâh (1), *abdomen*
2836 kŏilia (10),
abdomen, womb, heart

BELONG
1510 ĕimi (1), I *exist,* I *am*

BELONGED
4490 mânâh (1), *ration;
lot* or *portion*
1510 ĕimi (1), I *exist,* I *am*

BELONGETH
1510 ĕimi (1), I *exist,* I *am*

BELOVED
157 'âhab (6), to *have
affection, love*
1730 dôwd (29), *beloved,
friend; relative*
2530 châmad (3), to
delight in; lust for
3033 yᵉdîdûwth (1),
darling object
3039 yᵉdîyd (5), *loved*
4261 machmâd (1),
object of affection or
desire
25 agapaō (5), to *love*
27 agapētŏs (57), *beloved*

BELOVED'S
1730 dôwd (2), *beloved,
friend; relative*

BELSHAZZAR
1113 Bêlsha'tstsar (Ch.)
(8), *Belshatstsar*

BELTESHAZZAR
1095 Bêlṭᵉsha'tstsar (2),
Belteshatstsar
1096 Bêlṭᵉsha'tstsar
(Ch.) (8), *Belteshatstsar*

BEMOAN
5110 nûwd (5), to
deplore; to *taunt*

BEMOANED
5110 nûwd (1), to
deplore; to *taunt*

BEMOANING
5110 nûwd (1), to
deplore; to *taunt*

BEN
1122 Bên (1), *son*

BEN-AMMI
1151 Ben-'Ammîy (1),
son of my people

BEN-HADAD
1130 Ben-Hădad (18),
son of Hadad
1131 Binnûwy (7), *built*

BEN-HAIL
1134 Ben-Chayil (1), *son
of might*

BEN-HANAN
1135 Ben-Chânân (1),
son of Chanan

BEN-ONI
1126 Ben-'Ôwnîy (1), *son
of my sorrow*

BEN-ZOHETH
1132 Ben-Zôwchêth (1),
son of Zocheth

BENAIAH
1141 Bᵉnâyâh (42),
Jehovah has built

BENCHES
7175 qeresh (1), *slab* or
plank; deck of a ship

BEND
1869 dârak (7), to *tread,
trample;* to *string* a bow
3719 kâphan (1), to *bend*

BENDETH
1869 dârak (2), to *walk,
lead;* to *string* a bow

BENDING
7817 shâchach (1), to
sink or *depress*

BENE-BERAK
1138 Bunnîy (1), *built*

BENE-JAAKAN
1142 Bᵉnêy Ya'ăqân (2),
sons of Yaakan

BENEATH
4295 maṭṭâh (7), *below*
or *beneath*
8478 tachath (17),
bottom; underneath
2736 katō (3), *downwards*

BENEFACTORS
2110 ĕuĕrgĕtēs (1),
philanthropist

BENEFIT
1576 gᵉmûwl (1), *act;
service; reward*
3190 yâṭab (1), to *be,
make well*
18 agathŏs (1), *good*
2108 ĕuĕrgĕsia (1),
beneficence
5485 charis (1),
gratitude; benefit given

BENEFITS
1576 gᵉmûwl (1), *act;
service; reward*
8408 tagmûwl (1),
bestowment

BENEVOLENCE
2133 ĕunŏia (1), *eagerly,
with a whole heart*

BENINU
1148 Bᵉnînûw (1), *our
son*

BENJAMIN
1144 Binyâmîyn (158),
son of (the) *right hand*
953 bĕbĕlŏō (4), to
desecrate, profane

BENJAMIN'S
1144 Binyâmîyn (4), *son
of* (the) *right hand*

BENJAMITE
1145 Ben-yᵉmîynîy (9),
son of (the) *right hand*

BENJAMITES
1145 Ben-yᵉmîynîy (8),
son of (the) *right hand*

BENO
1121 bên (2), *son,
descendant; people*

BENT
1869 dârak (7), to *walk,
lead;* to *string* a bow
8511 tâlâ' (1), to *suspend;*
to *be uncertain*

BEON
1194 Bᵉ'ôn (1), *Beon*

BEOR
1160 Bᵉ'ôwr (10), *lamp*

BERA
1298 Bera' (1), *Bera*

BERACHAH
1294 Bᵉrâkâh (3),
benediction, blessing

BERACHIAH
1296 Berekyâh (1),
blessing of Jehovah

BERAIAH
1256 Bᵉrâ'yâh (1),
Jehovah has created

BEREA
960 Bĕrŏia (3), *region
beyond the coast-line*

BEREAVE
2637 châcêr (1), to *lack;*
to *fail, want, make less*
3782+(7921) kâshal (1), to
totter, waver; to *falter*
7921 shâkôl (4), to
miscarry

BEREAVED
7909 shakkuwl (2),
bereaved
7921 shâkôl (3), to
miscarry

BEREAVETH
7921 shâkôl (1), to
miscarry

BERECHIAH
1296 Berekyâh (10),
blessing of Jehovah

BERED
1260 Bered (2), *hail*

BERI
1275 Bêrîy (1), *Beri*

BERIAH
1283 Bᵉrîy'âh (11), *in
trouble*

BERIITES
1284 Bᵉrîy'îy (1), *Beriite*

BERITES
1276 Bêrîy (1), *Berites*

BERITH
1286 Bᵉrîyth (1), *Berith*

BERNICE
959 Bĕrnikē (3),
victorious

BERODACH-BALADAN
1255 Bᵉrô'dak Bal'ădân (1), *Berodak-Baladan*

BEROTHAH
1268 Bêrôthâh (1), *cypress-like*

BEROTHAI
1268 Bêrôwthâh (1), *cypress-like*

BEROTHITE
1307 Bêrôthîy (1), *Berothite*

BERRIES
1620 gargar (1), *berry*
1636 ĕlaia (1), *olive*

BERYL
8658 tarshîysh (7), (poss.) *topaz*
969 bĕrullŏs (1), *beryl*

BESAI
1153 Bᵉçay (2), *domineering*

BESEECH
577 'ânnâ' (8), *I ask you!*
2470+6440 châlâh (1), *to be weak, sick, afflicted*
4994 nâ' (26), *I pray!, please!, I beg you!*
1189 dĕŏmai (6), *to beg, petition, ask*
2065 ĕrōtaō (4), *to interrogate; to request*
3870 parakalĕō (20), *to call, invite*

BESEECHING
2065 ĕrōtaō (1), *to interrogate; to request*
3870 parakalĕō (2), *to call, invite*

BESET
3803 kâthar (1), *to enclose, besiege; to wait*
5437 çâbab (3), *to surround*
6696 tsûwr (1), *to cramp, i.e. confine; to harass*
2139 ĕupĕristatŏs (1), *entangling, obstructing*

BESIDE
310 'achar (1), *after*
413 'êl (2), *to, toward*
657 'ephec (3), *end; no further*
681 'êtsel (12), *side; near*
854 'êth (2), *with; by; at; among*
905 bad (45), *apart, only, besides*
1107 bil'ădêy (7), *except, without, besides*
1115 biltîy (3), *except, without, unless, besides*
2108 zûwlâh (6), *except; apart from; besides*
3027 yâd (1), *hand; power*
5921 'al (17), *above, over, upon, or against*
5973 'îm (4), *with*
5980 'ummâh (2), *near, beside, along with*
6654 tsad (3), *side; adversary*
846 autŏs (1), *he, she, it*
1839 ĕxistēmi (2), *to astound*
1909 ĕpi (3), *on, upon*

3105 mainŏmai (1), *to rave as a maniac*
4862 sun (1), *with or together*
5565 chōris (3), *separately, apart* from

BESIDES
905 bad (1), *apart, only, besides*
2108 zûwlâh (1), *except; apart from; besides*
5750 'ôwd (4), *again; repeatedly; still; more*
5921 'al (1), *above, over, upon, or against*
3063 lŏipŏn (1), *something remaining; finally*
4359 prŏsŏphĕilō (1), *to be indebted*

BESIEGE
6696 tsûwr (8), *to cramp, i.e. confine; to harass*
6887 tsârar (3), *to cramp*

BESIEGED
935+4692 bôw' (3), *to go or come*
4692 mâtsôwr (1), *siege-mound; distress*
4693 mâtsôwr (2), *limit, border*
5341 nâtsar (2), *to guard, protect, maintain*
5437 çâbab (1), *to surround*
6696 tsûwr (14), *to cramp, i.e. confine*

BESODEIAH
1152 Bᵉçôwdᵉyâh (1), *in (the) counsel of Jehovah*

BESOM
4292 maṭ'ăṭê' (1), *broom*

BESOR
1308 Bᵉsôwr (3), *cheerful*

BESOUGHT
1245 bâqash (2), *to search out*
2470 châlâh (5), *to be weak, sick, afflicted*
2603 chânan (4), *to implore*
1189 dĕŏmai (3), *to beg, petition, ask*
2065 ĕrōtaō (9), *to interrogate; to request*
3870 parakalĕō (21), *to call, invite*

BEST
2173 zimrâh (1), *choice*
2459 cheleb (5), *fat; choice* part
2896 tôwb (8), *good; well*
3190 yâṭab (1), *to be, make well*
4315 mêyṭâb (6), *best*
5324 nâtsab (1), *to station*
6338 pâzaz (1), *to refine* gold
2909 krĕittŏn (1), *stronger, i.e. nobler*
4413 prŏtŏs (1), *foremost*

BESTIR
2782 chârats (1), *to be alert, to decide*

BESTOW
5414 nâthan (2), *to give*

5415 nᵉthan (Ch.) (2), *to give*
6213 'âsâh (1), *to do or make*
4060 pĕritithēmi (1), *to present*
4863 sunagō (2), *to gather together*
5595 psōmizō (1), *to nourish, feed*

BESTOWED
1580 gâmal (2), *to benefit or requite; to wean*
3240 yânach (2), *to allow to stay*
5414 nâthan (2), *to give*
6485 pâqad (1), *to visit, care for, count*
1325 didōmi (2), *to give*
2872 kŏpiaō (3), *to feel fatigue; to work hard*

BETAH
984 Beṭach (1), *safety, security, trust*

BETEN
991 Beṭen (1), *belly; womb; body*

BETH-ANATH
1043 Bêyth 'Ănâth (3), *house of replies*

BETH-ANOTH
1042 Bêyth 'Ănôwth (1), *house of replies*

BETH-ARABAH
1026 Bêyth hâ-'Ărâbâh (3), *house of the desert*

BETH-ARAM
1027 Bêyth hâ-Râm (1), *house of the height*

BETH-ARBEL
1009 Bêyth 'Arbê'l (1), *house of God's ambush*

BETH-AVEN
1007 Bêyth 'Âven (7), *house of vanity*

BETH-AZMAVETH
1041 Bêyth 'Azmâveth (1), *house of Azmaveth*

BETH-BAAL-MEON
1010 Bêyth Ba'al Mᵉ'ôwn (1), *house of Baal of (the) habitation*

BETH-BARAH
1012 Bêyth Bârâh (2), *house of (the) river ford*

BETH-BIREI
1011 Bêyth Bir'îy (1), *house of a creative one*

BETH-CAR
1033 Bêyth Kar (1), *house of pasture*

BETH-DAGON
1016 Bêyth-Dâgôwn (2), *house of Dagon*

BETH-DIBLATHAIM
1015 Bêyth Diblâthayim (1), *house of (the) two figcakes*

BETH-EL
1008 Bêyth-'Êl (66), *house of God*

BETH-ELITE
1017 Bêyth hâ-'Êlîy (1), *Beth-elite*

BETH-EMEK
1025 Bêyth hâ-'Êmeq (1), *house of the valley*

BETH-EZEL
1018 Bêyth hâ-'Êtsel (1), *house of the side*

BETH-GADER
1013 Bêyth-Gâdêr (1), *house of (the) wall*

BETH-GAMUL
1014 Bêyth Gâmûwl (1), *house of (the) weaned*

BETH-HACCEREM
1021 Bêyth hak-Kerem (2), *house of the vineyard*

BETH-HARAN
1028 Bêyth hâ-Rân (1), *house of the height*

BETH-HOGLA
1031 Bêyth Choglâh (1), *house of a partridge*

BETH-HOGLAH
1031 Bêyth Choglâh (2), *house of a partridge*

BETH-HORON
1032 Bêyth Chôwrôwn (14), *house of hollowness*

BETH-JESHIMOTH
1020 Bêyth ha-Yᵉshîy-môwth (3), *house of the deserts*

BETH-JESIMOTH
1020 Bêyth ha-Yᵉshîy-môwth (1), *house of the deserts*

BETH-LEBAOTH
1034 Bêyth Lᵉbâ'ôwth (1), *house of lionesses*

BETH-LEHEM
1035 Bêyth Lechem (30), *house of bread*

BETH-LEHEM-JUDAH
1035 Bêyth Lechem (10), *house of bread*

BETH-LEHEMITE
1022 Bêyth hal-Lachmîy (4), *Beth-lechemite*

BETH-MAACHAH
1038 Bêyth Ma'ăkâh (2), *house of Maakah*

BETH-MARCABOTH
1024 Bêyth ham-Markâbôwth (2), *place of (the) chariots*

BETH-MEON
1010 Bêyth Ba'al Mᵉ'ôwn (1), *house of Baal of (the) habitation*

BETH-NIMRAH
1039 Bêyth Nimrâh (2), *house of (the) leopard*

BETH-PALET
1046 Bêyth Peleṭ (1), *house of escape*

BETH-PAZZEZ
1048 Bêyth Patstsêts (1), *house of dispersion*

BETH-PEOR
1047 Bêyth Pᵉ'ôwr (4),
house of Peor

BETH-PHELET
1046 Bêyth Peleṭ (1),
house of escape

BETH-RAPHA
1051 Bêyth Râphâ' (1),
house of (the) giant

BETH-REHOB
1050 Bêyth Rᵉchôwb (2),
house of (the) street

BETH-SHAN
1052 Bêyth Shᵉ'ân (3),
house of ease

BETH-SHEAN
1052 Bêyth Shᵉ'ân (6),
house of ease

BETH-SHEMESH
1053 Bêyth Shemesh
(21), house of (the) sun

BETH-SHEMITE
1030 Bêyth
hash-Shimshîy (2),
Beth-shimshite

BETH-SHITTAH
1029 Bêyth hash-Shiṭṭâh
(1), house of the acacia

BETH-TAPPUAH
1054 Bêyth Tappûwach
(1), house of (the) apple

BETH-ZUR
1049 Bêyth Tsûwr (4),
house of (the) rock

BETHABARA
962 Bēthabara (1),
ferry-house

BETHANY
963 Bēthania (11),
date-house

BETHER
1336 Bether (1), section

BETHESDA
964 Bēthĕsda (1), house
of kindness

BETHINK
7725+413+3820 shûwb
(2), to turn back

BETHLEHEM
1035 Bêyth Lechem (1),
house of bread
965 Bēthlĕĕm (8), house
of bread

BETHPHAGE
967 Bēthphagē (3),
fig-house

BETHSAIDA
966 Bēthsaïda (7),
fishing-house

BETHUEL
1328 Bᵉthûw'êl (10),
destroyed of God

BETHUL
1329 Bᵉthûwl (1), Bethuel

BETIMES
7836 shâchar (3), to
search for
7925 shâkam (2), to load
up, i.e. to start early

BETONIM
993 Bᵉṭônîym (1), hollows

BETRAY
7411 râmâh (1), to hurl;
to shoot; to delude
3860 paradidōmi (17), to
hand over

BETRAYED
3860 paradidōmi (18), to
hand over

BETRAYERS
4273 prŏdŏtēs (1),
betraying

BETRAYEST
3860 paradidōmi (1), to
hand over

BETRAYETH
3860 paradidōmi (3), to
hand over

BETROTH
781 'âras (4), to engage
for matrimony, betroth

BETROTHED
781 'âras (6), to engage
for matrimony, betroth
2778 châraph (1), to
spend the winter
3259 yâ'ad (2), to engage
for marriage

BETTER
2896 ṭôwb (75), good; well
3027 yâd (1), hand; power
3148 yôwthêr (1),
moreover; rest; gain
3190 yâṭab (4), to be,
make well
3504 yithrôwn (1),
preeminence, gain
1308 diaphĕrō (3), to
differ; to surpass
2570 kalŏs (5), good;
beautiful; valuable
2573 kalōs (1), well
2909 krĕittōn (18),
stronger, i.e. nobler
3081 lusitĕlĕi (1), it is
advantageous
4052 pĕrissĕuō (1), to
superabound
4284 prŏĕchŏmai (1), to
excel
4851 sumphĕrō (1), to
collect; advantage
5242 hupĕrĕchō (1), to
excel; superior
5543 chrēstŏs (1),
employed, i.e. useful

BETTERED
5623 ōphĕlĕō (1), to
benefit, be of use

BETWEEN
996 bêyn (190), between
997 bêyn (Ch.) (1),
between; "either...or"
5921 'al (1), upon, against
5973 'îm (2), with
8432 tâvek (3), center,
middle
1722 ĕn (1), in; during;
because of
3307 mĕrizō (1), to
apportion, bestow
3342 mĕtaxu (6), betwixt
4314 prŏs (2), for; on, at;
to, toward; against

BETWIXT
996 bêyn (13), between
6293 pâga' (1), to impinge

1537 ĕk (1), out, out of

BEULAH
1166 bâ'al (1), to be
master; to marry

BEWAIL
1058 bâkâh (4), to weep,
moan
2799 klaiō (1), to sob,
wail
3996 pĕnthĕō (1), to
grieve

BEWAILED
1058 bâkâh (1), to weep,
moan
2875 kŏptō (2), to beat
the breast

BEWAILETH
3306 yâphach (1), to
breathe hard, gasp

BEWARE
6191 'âram (1), to be
cunning; be prudent
8104 shâmar (9), to
watch
991 blĕpō (6), to look at
4337 prŏsĕchō (7), to pay
attention to
5442 phulassō (2), to
watch, i.e. be on guard

BEWITCHED
940 baskainō (1), to
fascinate, bewitch
1839 ĕxistēmi (2), to
astound; to be insane

BEWRAY
1540 gâlâh (1), to
denude; uncover

BEWRAYETH
5046 nâgad (1), to
announce
7121 qârâ' (1), to call out
1212+4160 dēlŏs (1),
clear, plain, evident

BEYOND
1973 hâlᵉâh (5), far
away; thus far
5674 'âbar (4), to cross
over; to transition
5675 'ăbar (Ch.) (7),
region across
5676 'êber (21), opposite
side; east
5921 'al (2), above, over
1900 ĕpĕkĕina (1), on the
further side of, beyond
4008 pĕran (7), across,
beyond
5228 hupĕr (1), over;
above; beyond
5233 hupĕrbainō (1), to
transcend
5238 hupĕrĕkĕina (1),
beyond, still farther
5239 hupĕrĕktĕinō (1), to
overreach
5249 hupĕrpĕrissōs (1),
exceedingly

BEZAI
1209 Bêtsay (3), Betsai

BEZALEEL
1212 Bᵉtsal'êl (9), in (the)
protection of God

BEZEK
966 Bezeq (3), lightning

BEZER
1221 Betser (5),
inaccessible spot

BICHRI
1075 Bikrîy (8), youthful

BID
559 'âmar (6), to say
1696 dâbar (2), to speak,
say; to subdue
6942 qâdâsh (1), to be,
make clean
479 antikalĕō (1), to
invite in return
657 apŏtassŏmai (1), to
say adieu; to renounce
2036 ĕpō (2), to speak
2564 kalĕō (2), to call
2753 kĕlĕuō (1), to order
3004 lĕgō (1), to say

BIDDEN
559 'âmar (1), to say
7121 qârâ' (2), to call out
2564 kalĕō (10), to call
4367 prŏstassō (1), to
arrange towards

BIDDETH
3004 lĕgō (1), to say

BIDDING
4928 mishma'ath (1),
royal court; obedience

BIDKAR
920 Bidqar (1), stabbing
assassin

BIER
4296 miṭṭâh (1), bed;
sofa, litter or bier
4673 sŏrŏs (1), funeral
bier

BIGTHA
903 Bigthâ' (1), Bigtha

BIGTHAN
904 Bigthân (1), Bigthan

BIGTHANA
904 Bigthân (1), Bigthana

BIGVAI
902 Bigvay (6), Bigvai

BILDAD
1085 Bildad (5), Bildad

BILEAM
1109 Bil'âm (1), foreigner

BILGAH
1083 Bilgâh (3),
desistance

BILGAI
1084 Bilgay (1), desistant

BILHAH
1090 Bilhâh (11), timid

BILHAN
1092 Bilhân (4), timid

BILL
5612 çêpher (4), writing
975 bibliŏn (1), scroll;
certificate
1121 gramma (2),
writing; education

BILLOWS
1530 gal (1), heap; ruins
4867 mishbâr (1), breaker

BILSHAN
1114 Bilshân (2), Bilshan

BIMHAL
1118 Bimhâl (1), *with pruning*

BIND
631 'âçar (13), to *fasten; to join* battle
2280 châbash (6), to *wrap firmly, bind*
3729 kᵉphath (Ch.) (1), to *fetter, bind*
6029 'ânad (1), to *lace fast, bind*
6887 tsârar (3), to *cramp*
7164 qâraç (1), to *hunch*
7194 qâshar (10), to *tie, bind*
7405 râkaç (2), to *tie, bind*
7573 râtham (1), to *yoke*
1195 dĕsmĕuŏ (1), to *enchain, tie on*
1210 dĕŏ (9), to *bind*
5265 hupŏdĕŏ (1), to *put on shoes or sandals*

BINDETH
247 'âzar (1), to *belt*
631 'âçar (1), to *fasten; to join* battle
2280 châbash (4), to *wrap firmly, bind*
6014 'âmar (1), to *gather grain into sheaves*
6887 tsârar (2), to *cramp*

BINDING
481 'âlam (1), to be *tongue-tied, be silent*
632 'êçâr (1), *obligation, vow, pledge*
681 'êtsel (1), *side; near*
8193 sâphâh (1), *lip, edge, margin*
1195 dĕsmĕuŏ (1), to *enchain, tie on*

BINEA
1150 Bin'â' (2), *Bina*

BINNUI
1131 Binnûwy (7), *built*

BIRD
1167+3671 ba'al (1), *master; owner; citizen*
5775 'ôwph (3), *bird*
5861 'ayiţ (2), bird of prey (poss.) *hawk*
6833 tsippôwr (21), *little hopping bird*
3732 ŏrnĕŏn (1), *bird*

BIRD'S
6833 tsippôwr (1), *little hopping bird*

BIRDS
5775 'ôwph (6), *winged bird*
5861 'ayiţ (1), bird of prey (poss.) *hawk*
6833 tsippôwr (10), *little hopping bird*
4071 pĕteinŏn (5), *bird which flies*
4421 ptĕnŏn (1), *bird*

BIRDS'
6853 tsᵉphar (Ch.) (1), *bird*

BIRSHA
1306 Birsha' (1), *with wickedness*

BIRTH
3205 yâlad (2), to *bear young; to father a child*
4351 mᵉkûwrâh (1), *origin*
4866 mishbêr (2), *vaginal opening*
5309 nephel (3), *abortive miscarriage*
7665 shâbar (1), to *burst*
8435 tôwlᵉdâh (1), *family descent; family record*
1079 gĕnĕtĕ (1), *birth*
1083 gĕnnĕsis (2), *nativity*
5605 ŏdinŏ (2), to *experience labor pains*

BIRTHDAY
3117+3205 yôwm (1), *day; time period*
1077 gĕnĕsia (2), *birthday* ceremonies

BIRTHRIGHT
1062 bᵉkôwrâh (9), *state of, rights of first born*
4415 prôtŏtŏkia (1), *primogeniture* rights

BIRZAVITH
1269 Birzôwth (1), *holes*

BISHLAM
1312 Bishlâm (1), *Bishlam*

BISHOP
1984 ĕpiskŏpē (1), *episcopate*
1985 ĕpiskŏpŏs (5), *overseer, supervisor*

BISHOPRICK
1984 ĕpiskŏpē (1), *episcopate*

BISHOPS
1985 ĕpiskŏpŏs (1), *overseer, supervisor*

BIT
4964 metheg (1), *bit*
5391 nâshak (2), to *strike; to oppress*

BITE
5391 nâshak (6), to *strike; to oppress*
1143 daknŏ (1), to *bite*

BITETH
5391 nâshak (2), to *strike; to oppress*

BITHIAH
1332 Bithyâh (1), *worshipper of Jehovah*

BITHRON
1338 Bithrôwn (1), *craggy* spot

BITHYNIA
978 Bithunia (2), *Bithynia*

BITS
5469 chalinŏs (1), *curb or head-stall, i.e. bit*

BITTEN
5391 nâshak (2), to *strike; to oppress*

BITTER
4751 mar (20), *bitter; bitterness; bitterly*
4784 mârâh (1), to *rebel or resist; to provoke*

4805 mᵉrîy (1), *rebellion, rebellious*
4815 mᵉrîyrîy (1), *bitter, i.e. poisonous*
4843 mârar (2), to *be, make bitter*
4844 mᵉrôr (2), *bitter herb*
4846 mᵉrôrâh (2), *bitter bile; venom of a serpent*
8563 tamrûwr (2), *bitterness*
4087 pikrainŏ (4), to *embitter, turn sour*
4089 pikrŏs (2), *sharp, pungent, i.e. bitter*

BITTERLY
779 'ârar (1), to *execrate, place a curse*
4751 mar (3), *bitter; bitterness; bitterly*
4843 mârar (1), to *be, make bitter*
8563 tamrûwr (1), *bitterness*
4090 pikrŏs (2), *bitterly, i.e. violently*

BITTERN
7090 qippôwd (3), *bittern*

BITTERNESS
4470 memer (1), *sorrow*
4472 mamrôr (1), *bitterness, misery*
4751 mar (10), *bitter; bitterness; bitterly*
4814 mᵉrîyrûwth (1), *bitterness*
4843 mârar (4), to *be, make bitter*
4844 mᵉrôr (1), *bitter herb*
4088 pikria (4), *acridity, bitterness*

BIZJOTHJAH
964 bizyôwthᵉyâh (1), *contempts of Jehovah*

BIZTHA
968 Biztâ' (1), *Biztha*

BLACK
380 'îyshôwn (1), *pupil, eyeball; middle*
3648 kâmar (1), to *shrivel with heat*
5508 çôchereth (1), (poss.) black *tile*
6937 qâdar (4), to be *dark-colored*
7835 shâchar (1), to be *dim or dark in color*
7838 shâchôr (6), *dusky, jet black*
7840 shᵉcharchôreth (1), *swarthy, dark*
3189 mĕlas (3), *black*

BLACKER
2821 châshak (1), to be *dark; to darken*

BLACKISH
6937 qâdar (1), to be *dark-colored*

BLACKNESS
3650 kimrîyr (1), *obscuration, eclipse*
6289 pâ'rûwr (2), *flush of anxiety*

6940 qadrûwth (1), *duskiness*
1105 gnŏphŏs (1), *gloom as of a storm, darkness*
2217 zŏphŏs (1), *gloom*

BLADE
3851 lahab (2), *flame of fire; flash of a blade*
7929 shikmâh (1), *shoulder-bone*
5528 chŏrtŏs (2), *pasture, herbage or vegetation*

BLAINS
76 'âba'bû'âh (2), *pustule, skin eruption*

BLAME
2398 châţâ' (2), to *sin*
299 amômŏs (1), *unblemished, blameless*
3469 mômaŏmai (1), to *carp at, i.e. to censure*

BLAMED
2607 kataginŏskŏ (1), to *find fault with*
3469 mômaŏmai (1), to *carp at, i.e. to censure*

BLAMELESS
5352 nâqâh (1), to be, *make clean; to be bare*
5355 nâqîy (2), *innocent*
273 amĕmptŏs (3), *irreproachable*
274 amĕmptōs (1), *faultlessly*
298 amômētŏs (1), *unblamable*
338 anaitiŏs (1), *innocent*
410 anĕgklētŏs (4), *irreproachable*
423 anĕpilēptŏs (2), *not open to blame*

BLASPHEME
1288 bârak (2), to *bless*
5006 nâ'ats (2), to *scorn*
987 blasphēmĕŏ (6), to *speak impiously*

BLASPHEMED
1442 gâdaph (5), to *revile, blaspheme*
2778 châraph (1), to *spend the winter*
5006 nâ'ats (2), to *scorn*
5344 nâqab (1), to *specify, designate, libel*
987 blasphēmĕŏ (7), to *speak impiously*

BLASPHEMER
989 blasphēmŏs (1), *slanderous*

BLASPHEMERS
987 blasphēmĕŏ (1), to *speak impiously*
989 blasphēmŏs (1), *slanderous*

BLASPHEMEST
987 blasphēmĕŏ (1), to *speak impiously*

BLASPHEMETH
1442 gâdaph (1), to *revile, blaspheme*
5344 nâqab (1), to *specify, designate, libel*
987 blasphēmĕŏ (2), to *speak impiously*

BLASPHEMIES
5007 neʾâtsâh (1), *scorn; to bloom*
988 blasphēmia (5), *impious speech*

BLASPHEMING
987 blasphēmĕō (1), *to speak impiously*

BLASPHEMOUS
989 blasphēmŏs (2), *slanderous*

BLASPHEMOUSLY
987 blasphēmĕō (1), *to speak impiously*

BLASPHEMY
5007 neʾâtsâh (2), *scorn; to bloom*
987 blasphēmĕō (1), *to speak impiously*
988 blasphēmia (11), *impious speech*

BLAST
5397 neshâmâh (3), *breath, life*
7307 rûwach (4), *breath; wind; life*-spirit

BLASTED
7709 shedêmâh (1), *cultivated field*
7710 shâdaph (3), *to scorch*
7711 shedêphâh (1), *blight; scorching*

BLASTING
7711 shedêphâh (5), *blight; scorching*

BLASTUS
986 Blastŏs (1), (poss.) to *yield fruit*

BLAZE
1310 diaphēmizō (1), *to spread news*

BLEATING
6963 qôwl (1), *voice or sound*

BLEATINGS
8292 sherûwqâh (1), *whistling; scorn*

BLEMISH
3971 m'ûwm (15), *blemish; fault*
8400 teballûl (1), *cataract in the eye*
8549 tâmîym (44), *entire, complete; integrity*
299 amōmŏs (2), *unblemished, blameless*

BLEMISHES
3971 m'ûwm (1), *blemish; fault*
3470 mōmŏs (1), *flaw or blot*

BLESS
1288 bârak (115), *to bless*
2127 ĕulŏgĕō (10), *to invoke a benediction*

BLESSED
833 'âshar (7), *to be honest, prosper*
835 'esher (27), *how happy!*
1288 bârak (175), *to bless*
1289 berak (Ch.) (4), *to bless*

1293 berâkâh (3), *benediction, blessing*
1757 ĕnĕulŏgĕō (2), *to confer a benefit, bless*
2127 ĕulŏgĕō (30), *to invoke a benediction*
2128 ĕulŏgētŏs (8), *adorable, praised*
3106 makarizō (1), *to pronounce fortunate*
3107 makariŏs (43), *fortunate, well off*

BLESSEDNESS
3108 makarismŏs (3), *fortunate*

BLESSEST
1288 bârak (3), *to bless*

BLESSETH
1288 bârak (8), *to bless*

BLESSING
1288 bârak (1), *to bless*
1293 berâkâh (51), *benediction, blessing*
2127 ĕulŏgĕō (1), *to invoke a benediction*
2129 ĕulŏgia (12), *benediction*

BLESSINGS
1293 berâkâh (11), *benediction, blessing*
2129 ĕulŏgia (1), *benediction*

BLEW
8628 tâqa' (18), *to clatter, slap, drive, clasp*
1920 ĕpiginŏmai (1), *to come up, happen*
4154 pnĕō (3), *to breeze*
5285 hupŏpnĕō (1), *to breathe gently*

BLIND
5786 'âvar (1), *to blind*
5787 'ivvêr (26), *blind*
5788 'ivvârôwn (1), *blindness*
5956 'âlam (1), *to veil from sight, i.e. conceal*
5185 tuphlŏs (52), *blindness; blind person*

BLINDED
4456 pōrŏō (2), *to render stupid or callous*
5186 tuphlŏō (3), *to cause blindness*

BLINDETH
5786 'âvar (1), *to blind*

BLINDFOLDED
4028 pĕrikaluptō (1), *cover eyes*

BLINDNESS
5575 çanvêr (3), *blindness*
5788 'ivvârôwn (2), *blindness*
4457 pōrōsis (2), *stupidity or callousness*

BLOOD
1818 dâm (337), *blood; juice; life*
5332 nêtsach (1), *blood (as if red juice)*
129 haima (97), *blood*
130 haimatĕkchusia (1), *pouring of blood*

131 haimŏrrhĕō (1), *to have a hemorrhage*

BLOODGUILTINESS
1818 dâm (1), *blood; juice; life*

BLOODTHIRSTY
582+1818 'ênôwsh (1), *man; person, human*

BLOODY
1818 dâm (15), *blood; juice; life*
1420 dusĕntĕria (1), *dysentery*

BLOOMED
6692 tsûwts (1), *to blossom, flourish*

BLOSSOM
6524 pârach (4), *to bloom; to fly; to flourish*
6525 perach (1), *calyx flower; bloom*
6692 tsûwts (1), *to blossom, flourish*

BLOSSOMED
6692 tsûwts (1), *to blossom, flourish*

BLOSSOMS
5322 nêts (1), *flower*
6731 tsîyts (1), *burnished plate; bright flower*

BLOT
3971 m'ûwm (2), *blemish; fault*
4229 mâchâh (10), *to erase; to grease*
1813 ĕxalĕiphō (1), *to obliterate*

BLOTTED
4229 mâchâh (5), *to erase; to grease*
1813 ĕxalĕiphō (1), *to obliterate*

BLOTTETH
4229 mâchâh (1), *to erase; to grease*

BLOTTING
1813 ĕxalĕiphō (1), *to obliterate*

BLOW
2690 châtsar (1), *to blow the trumpet*
4347 makkâh (1), *blow; wound; pestilence*
5265 nâça' (1), *start on a journey*
5301 nâphach (3), *to inflate, blow hard*
5380 nâshab (1), *to blow; to disperse*
5398 nâshaph (2), *breeze as the wind*
6315 pûwach (2), *to blow, to fan, kindle; to utter*
7321 rûwa' (1), *to shout*
8409 tigrâh (1), *strife, i.e. infliction*
8628 tâqa' (23), *to clatter, slap, drive, clasp*
8643 terûw'âh (1), *battle-cry; clangor*
4154 pnĕō (2), *to breeze*

BLOWETH
5301 nâphach (1), *to inflate, blow hard*

5380 nâshab (1), *to blow; to disperse*
8628 tâqa' (1), *to clatter, slap, drive, clasp*
4154 pnĕō (1), *to breeze*

BLOWING
8628 tâqa' (2), *to clatter, slap, drive, clasp*
8643 terûw'âh (2), *battle-cry; clangor*

BLOWN
5301 nâphach (1), *to inflate, blow hard*
8628 tâqa' (3), *to clatter, slap, drive, clasp*

BLUE
8504 tekêleth (50), *color violet*

BLUENESS
2250 chabbûwrâh (1), *weal, bruise*

BLUNT
6949 qâhâh (1), *to be dull; be blunt*

BLUSH
3637 kâlam (3), *to taunt or insult*

BOANERGES
993 Bŏanĕrgĕs (1), *sons of commotion*

BOAR
2386 chăzîyr (1), *hog, boar*

BOARD
7175 qeresh (17), *slab or plank; deck of a ship*

BOARDS
3871 lûwach (4), *tablet*
6763 tsêlâ' (2), *side*
7175 qeresh (33), *slab*
7713 sedêrâh (1), *row, i.e. rank of soldiers*
4548 sanis (1), *planked timber, board*

BOAST
559 'âmar (1), *to say*
1984 hâlal (6), *to boast*
3235 yâmar (1), *to exchange*
3513 kâbad (1), *to be heavy, severe, dull*
6286 pâ'ar (1), *to shake a tree*
2620 katakauchaŏmai (1), *to exult against*
2744 kauchaŏmai (8), *to glory in; to boast*

BOASTED
1431 gâdal (1), *to be great, make great*
2744 kauchaŏmai (1), *to glory in; to boast*

BOASTERS
213 alazōn (2), *braggart*

BOASTEST
1984 hâlal (1), *to boast*

BOASTETH
1984 hâlal (3), *to boast*
3166 mĕgalauchĕō (1), *to be arrogant, egotistic*

BOASTING
2744 kauchaŏmai (1), *to glory in; to boast*

2745 *kauchēma* (1), boast; brag
2746 *kauchēsis* (6), boasting; bragging
3004 *lĕgō* (1), to *say*

BOASTINGS
212 *alazŏnēia* (1), boasting

BOAT
5679 *'ăbârâh* (1), crossing-place
4142 *plŏiariŏn* (2), small boat
4627 *skaphē* (3), *skiff* or *yawl*, i.e. life boat

BOATS
4142 *plŏiariŏn* (1), small boat

BOAZ
1162 *Bô'az* (24), *Boaz*

BOCHERU
1074 *Bôk*ᵉ*rûw* (2), first-born

BOCHIM
1066 *Bôkîym* (2), *weepers*

BODIES
1354 *gab* (1), mounded or rounded: top or rim
1472 *g*ᵉ*vîyâh* (7), dead body
1480 *gûwphâh* (1), corpse
1655 *geshem* (Ch.) (2), body
5038 *n*ᵉ*bêlâh* (2), carcase or carrion
6297 *peger* (6), carcase; corpse
4430 *ptōma* (3), corpse, carrion
4983 *sōma* (11), body

BODILY
4983 *sōma* (1), body
4984 *sōmatikŏs* (2), corporeal or physical
4985 *sōmatikōs* (1), corporeally

BODY
990 *beṭen* (8), belly; womb; body
1320 *bâsâr* (2), flesh; body; person
1460 *gêv* (1), middle, inside, in, on, etc.
1465 *gêvâh* (1), back
1472 *g*ᵉ*vîyâh* (3), dead body
1480 *gûwphâh* (1), corpse
1655 *geshem* (Ch.) (3), body
3409 *yârêk* (1), leg or shank, flank; side
5038 *n*ᵉ*bêlâh* (4), carcase or carrion
5085 *nidneh* (Ch.) (1), sheath; body
5315 *nephesh* (9), life; breath; soul; wind
6106 *'etsem* (2), bone; body; substance
7607 *sh*ᵉ*'êr* (1), flesh, meat; kindred by blood
4954 *sussōmŏs* (1), fellow-member
4983 *sōma* (131), body
5559 *chrōs* (1), skin

BODY'S
4983 *sōma* (1), body

BOHAN
932 *Bôhan* (2), thumb

BOIL
1158 *bâ'âh* (1), to *ask*; be bulging, swelling
1310 *bâshal* (4), to *boil* up, cook; to *ripen*
7570 *râthach* (2), to *boil*, churn
7822 *sh*ᵉ*chîyn* (9), inflammation, ulcer

BOILED
1310 *bâshal* (2), to *boil*
7570 *râthach* (1), to *boil*, churn

BOILING
4018 *m*ᵉ*bashsh*ᵉ*lâh* (1), cooking hearth

BOILS
7822 *sh*ᵉ*chîyn* (2), inflammation, ulcer

BOISTEROUS
2478 *ischurŏs* (1), forcible, powerful

BOLD
982 *bâṭach* (1), to *trust*, be confident or sure
662 *apŏtŏlmaō* (1), to bring forth boldly
2292 *tharrhĕō* (2), to be bold
3954 *parrhēsia* (1), frankness, boldness
3955 *parrhēsiazŏmai* (2), to be frank, confident
5111 *tŏlmaō* (4), to be bold, courageous

BOLDLY
983 *beṭach* (1), safety, security, trust
2292 *tharrhĕō* (1), to be bold
3954 *parrhēsia* (3), frankness, boldness
3955 *parrhēsiazŏmai* (6), to be frank, confident
5111 *tŏlmaō* (1), to be bold, courageous
5112 *tŏlmērŏtĕrŏn* (1), with greater confidence

BOLDNESS
5797 *'ôz* (1), strength
3954 *parrhēsia* (9), frankness, boldness

BOLLED
1392 *gib'ôl* (1), calyx

BOLSTER
4763 *m*ᵉ*ra'ăshâh* (6), headpiece; head-rest

BOLT
5274 *nâ'al* (1), to *fasten* up, lock

BOLTED
5274 *nâ'al* (1), to *fasten* up, lock

BOND
632 *'ĕçâr* (7), obligation, vow, pledge
4148 *mûwçâr* (1), reproof, warning
4562 *mâçôreth* (1), band

1199 *dĕsmŏn* (1), shackle; impediment
1401 *dŏulŏs* (6), slave, servant
4886 *sundĕsmŏs* (3), ligament; control

BONDAGE
3533 *kâbash* (2), to conquer, subjugate
5647 *'âbad* (1), to do, work, serve
5650 *'ebed* (10), servant
5656 *'ăbôdâh* (8), work
5659 *'abdûwth* (3), servitude
1397 *dŏulĕia* (5), slavery, bondage
1398 *dŏulĕuō* (4), to serve as a slave
1402 *dŏulŏō* (4), to enslave
2615 *katadŏulŏō* (2), to enslave utterly

BONDMAID
8198 *shiphchâh* (1), household female slave
3814 *paidiskē* (1), female slave or servant

BONDMAIDS
519 *'âmâh* (2), female servant or slave

BONDMAN
5650 *'ebed* (5), servant
1401 *dŏulŏs* (1), slave, servant

BONDMEN
5647 *'âbad* (1), to do, work, serve
5650 *'ebed* (16), servant

BONDS
632 *'ĕçâr* (3), obligation, vow, pledge
4147 *môwçêr* (5), halter; restraint
254 *halusis* (1), fetter or manacle
1198 *dĕsmiŏs* (2), bound captive; one arrested
1199 *dĕsmŏn* (14), shackle; impediment or disability
1210 *dĕō* (1), to bind

BONDSERVANT
5656+5650 *'ăbôdâh* (1), work of any kind

BONDSERVICE
5647 *'âbad* (1), to do, work, serve

BONDWOMAN
519 *'âmâh* (4), maid-servant or female slave
3814 *paidiskē* (4), female slave or servant

BONDWOMEN
8198 *shiphchâh* (3), household female slave

BONE
1634 *gerem* (1), bone; self
6106 *'etsem* (14), bone; body; substance
7070 *qâneh* (1), reed
3747 *ŏstĕŏn* (1), bone

BONES
1633 *gâram* (1), to crunch the bones
1634 *gerem* (2), bone; self
1635 *gerem* (Ch.) (1), bone
6106 *'etsem* (89), bone; body; substance
3747 *ŏstĕŏn* (4), bone
4974 *sphurŏn* (1), ankle

BONNETS
4021 *migbâ'âh* (4), cap wrapped around head
6287 *p*ᵉ*'êr* (2), fancy head-dress

BOOK
1697 *dâbâr* (7), word; matter; thing
5609 *ç*ᵉ*phar* (Ch.) (3), book
5612 *çêpher* (136), writing
974 *bibliaridiŏn* (4), little scroll
975 *bibliŏn* (23), scroll; certificate
976 *biblŏs* (15), scroll

BOOKS
5609 *ç*ᵉ*phar* (Ch.) (1), book
5612 *çêpher* (2), writing
975 *bibliŏn* (4), scroll; certificate
976 *biblŏs* (1), scroll of writing

BOOTH
5521 *çukkâh* (2), tabernacle; shelter

BOOTHS
5521 *çukkâh* (8), tabernacle; shelter

BOOTIES
4933 *m*ᵉ*shiççâh* (1), plunder

BOOTY
957 *baz* (1), plunder, loot
4455 *malqôwach* (1), spoil, plunder
4953 *mashrôwqîy* (Ch.) (1), musical *pipe*

BOOZ
1003 *Bŏŏz* (3), *Boöz*

BORDER
1366 *g*ᵉ*bûwl* (136), boundary, border
1379 *gâbal* (2), to set a boundary line, limit
3027 *yâd* (1), hand; power
3411 *y*ᵉ*rêkâh* (1), recesses, far away
4526 *miçgeret* (6), margin; stronghold
7093 *qêts* (2), extremity; after
7097 *qâtseh* (2), extremity
8193 *sâphâh* (3), lip; edge, margin
2899 *kraspĕdŏn* (2), margin

BORDERS
1366 *g*ᵉ*bûwl* (20), boundary, border
1367 *g*ᵉ*bûwlâh* (1), boundary marker
1552 *g*ᵉ*lîylâh* (3), circuit or region

3027 yâd (1), *hand; power*
3671 kânâph (2), *edge or extremity; wing*
4526 miçgereth (7), *margin; stronghold*
5299 nâphâh (1), *height*
7093 qêts (1), *extremity*
7097 qâtseh (1), *extremity*
8444 tôwtsâ'âh (1), *exit,* i.e. *boundary*
8447 tôwr (1), *succession, order*
2899 kraspĕdŏn (1), *margin*
3181 mĕthŏriŏs (1), *frontier region*
3725 hŏriŏn (1), *region, area, vicinity*

BORE
5344 nâqab (1), *to puncture, perforate*
7527 râtsa' (1), *to pierce*

BORED
5344 nâqab (1), *to puncture, perforate*

BORN
249 'ezrâch (11), *native born*
990 beţen (1), *belly; womb; body*
1121 bên (2), *son, descendant*
3205 yâlad (80), *to bear young; to father a child*
3209 yillôwd (4), *born*
3211 yâlîyd (6), *born; descendants*
4138 môwledeth (2), *offspring, family*
313 anagĕnnaō (1), *to beget or bear again*
1080 gĕnnaō (39), *to procreate, regenerate*
1084 gĕnnētŏs (2), *pertaining to birth*
1085 gĕnŏs (2), *kin, offspring in kind*
1626 ĕktrōma (1), *untimely birth*
5088 tiktō (3), *to produce from seed*

BORNE
3205 yâlad (3), *to bear young; to father a child*
5190 nâţal (1), *to lift; to impose*
5375 nâsâ' (14), *to lift up*
5445 çâbal (1), *to carry*
5564 çâmak (1), *to lean upon; take hold of*
6006 'âmaç (1), *to impose a burden*
142 airō (1), *to lift, to take up*
941 bastazō (4), *to lift, bear*
1418 dus- (2), *hard,* i.e. *with difficulty*
5409 phŏrĕō (1), *to wear*

BORROW
3867 lâvâh (1), *to borrow; to lend*
5670 'âbaţ (1), *to pawn; to lend; to entangle*
7592 shâ'al (4), *to ask*
1155 danĕizō (1), *to loan on interest; to borrow*

BORROWED
3867 lâvâh (1), *to borrow; to lend*
7592 shâ'al (2), *to ask*

BORROWER
3867 lâvâh (2), *to borrow; to lend*

BORROWETH
3867 lâvâh (1), *to borrow; to lend*

BOSCATH
1218 Botsqath (1), *swell of ground*

BOSOM
2243 chôb (1), *bosom*
2436 chêyq (32), *bosom, heart*
2683 chêtsen (1), *bosom*
6747 tsallachath (2), *bosom*
2859 kŏlpŏs (5), *lap area*

BOSOR
1007 Bŏsŏr (1), *lamp*

BOSSES
1354 gab (1), *mounded or rounded: top or rim*

BOTCH
7822 sheehîyn (2), *inflammation, ulcer*

BOTH
413 'êl (1), *to, toward*
1571 gam (30), *also; even; "both...and"*
3162 yachad (1), *unitedly*
8147 sheenayim (78), *two-fold*
8174 Sha'aph (2), *fluctuation*
297 amphŏtĕrŏs (14), *both*
1417 duŏ (2), *two*
1538 hĕkastŏs (1), *each or every*
2532 kai (45), *and; or; even; also*
5037 tĕ (39), *both or also*

BOTTLE
1228 baqbûk (2), *bottle*
2573 chêmeth (4), skin *bottle*
4997 nô'd (4), skin *bag*
5035 nebel (5), skin *bag*

BOTTLES
178 'ôwb (1), *wineskin; necromancer, medium*
2573 chêmeth (1), skin *bottle*
4997 nô'd (2), skin *bag*
5035 nebel (3), skin *bag*
779 askŏs (12), *leather bottle or bag*

BOTTOM
773 'ar'îyth (Ch.) (1), *bottom, dirt floor*
2436 chêyq (2), *bosom, heart*
3247 yeeçôwd (10), *foundation*
4688 meetsôwlâh (1), *deep place*
4699 meetsullâh (1), *shade, deep*
7172 qarqa' (1), *floor*
7507 reephîydâh (1), *railing*

8328 sheresh (1), *root*
2736 katō (2), *downwards*

BOTTOMLESS
12 abussŏs (7), *deep place, abyss*

BOTTOMS
7095 qetseb (1), *shape; base*

BOUGH
534 'âmîyr (1), *top*
1121 bên (2), *son, descendant; people*
2793 chôresh (1), *wooded forest*
6288 pe'ôrâh (1), *foliage, branches*
7754 sôwk (2), *branch*

BOUGHS
5577 çançîn (1), *twig*
5589 çe'appâh (2), *twig*
5634 çar'appâh (1), *twig*
5688 'ăbôth (3), *entwined things: foliage*
6056 'ănaph (Ch.) (1), *bough, branch*
6057 'ânâph (3), *twig*
6288 pe'ôrâh (2), *foliage, branches*
6529 peerîy (1), *fruit*
7105 qâtsîyr (3), *harvest; limb of a tree*
7730 sôwbek (1), *thicket*

BOUGHT
3739 kârâh (1), *to purchase by bargaining*
4736 miqnâh (7), *acquisition*
7069 qânâh (21), *to create; to procure*
7666 shâbar (7), *to deal in cereal grain*
59 agŏrazō (13), *to purchase; to redeem*
5608 ōnĕŏmai (1), *to purchase, buy*

BOUND
615 'âçîyr (2), *captive, prisoner*
631 'âçar (33), *to fasten; to join battle*
640 'âphad (1), *to fasten, gird*
1366 geebûwl (4), *boundary, border*
2280 châbash (4), *to wrap firmly, bind*
3256 yâçar (1), *to chastise; to instruct*
3729 keephath (Ch.) (3), *to fetter, bind*
4205 mâzôwr (1), *sore needing a bandage*
6123 'âqad (1), *to tie the feet with thongs*
6616 pâthîyl (1), *twine, cord*
6887 tsârar (7), *to cramp*
7194 qâshar (4), *to tie, bind*
7576 râthaq (1), *to fasten, bind*
8244 sâqad (1), *to fasten, bind*
8379 ta'ăvâh (1), *limit,* i.e. *full extent*
332 anathĕmatizō (3), *to declare or vow an oath*

1196 dĕsmĕō (1), *shackle; bind*
1210 dĕō (28), *to bind*
2611 katadĕō (1), *to bandage a wound*
3784 ŏphĕilō (2), *to owe; to be under obligation*
4019 pĕridĕō (1), *to wrap around*
4029 pĕrikĕimai (1), *to enclose, encircle*
4385 prŏtĕinō (1), *to tie prostrate for scourging*
4887 sundĕō (1), *to be a fellow-prisoner*

BOUNDS
1366 geebûwl (1), *boundary, border*
1367 geebûwlâh (2), *boundary marker*
1379 gâbal (2), *to set a boundary*
2706 chôq (2), *appointment; allotment*
3734 hŏrŏthĕsia (1), *boundary-line*

BOUNTIFUL
2896 ţôwb (1), *good; well*
7771 shôwa' (1), *noble,* i.e. *liberal; opulent*

BOUNTIFULLY
1580 gâmal (4), *to benefit or requite; to wean*
2129 ĕulŏgia (1), *benediction*

BOUNTIFULNESS
572 haplŏtēs (1), *sincerity; generosity*

BOUNTY
3027 yâd (1), *hand; power*
2129 ĕulŏgia (2), *benediction*

BOW
86 'abrêk (1), *kneel*
3721 kâphaph (2), *to curve, bow*
3766 kâra' (9), *to prostrate*
5186 nâţâh (6), *to stretch or spread out*
5791 'âvath (1), *to wrest, twist*
7198 qesheth (55), *bow, rainbow*
7812 shâchâh (17), *to prostrate in homage*
7817 shâchach (2), *to sink or depress*
2578 kamptō (3), *to bend*
4781 sugkamptō (1), *to afflict*
5115 tŏxŏn (1), *bow*

BOWED
3721 kâphaph (3), *to curve, bow*
3766 kâra' (11), *to prostrate; to make miserable*
5186 nâţâh (5), *to stretch or spread out*
5791 'âvath (1), *to wrest, twist*
6915 qâdad (13), *to bend*
7743 shûwach (1), *to sink*
7812 shâchâh (35), *to prostrate in homage*

B

7817 shâchach (4), to
sink or depress
1120 gŏnupĕtĕō (1), to
fall on the knee, kneel
2578 kamptō (1), to bend
2827 klinō (2), to slant or
slope
4794 sugkuptō (1), to be
completely overcome

BOWELS
4578 mê'âh (26), viscera;
anguish, tenderness
7130 qereb (1), nearest
part, i.e. the center
7358 rechem (2), womb
4698 splagchnŏn (9),
intestine; affection, pity

BOWETH
3766 kâra' (2), to
prostrate
7817 shâchach (1), to
sink or depress

BOWING
5186 nâṭâh (2), to stretch
or spread out
5087 tithēmi (1), to put

BOWL
1543 gullâh (3), fountain;
bowl or globe
4219 mîzrâq (13), bowl
for sprinkling
5602 cêphel (1), basin,
bowl

BOWLS
1375 gᵉbîya' (8), goblet;
bowl
1543 gullâh (3), fountain;
bowl or globe
4219 mîzrâq (8), bowl for
sprinkling
4518 mᵉnaqqîyth (3),
sacrificial basin
5592 çaph (2), dish

BOWMEN
7411+7198 râmâh (1), to
hurl; to shoot

BOWS
7198 qesheth (13), bow,
rainbow

BOWSHOT
2909+7198 ṭâchâh (1), to
stretch a bow

BOX
6378 pak (2), flask, jug
8391 tᵉ'ashshûwr (2),
cedar
211 alabastrŏn (4),
alabaster, vase

BOY
3206 yeled (1), young
male

BOYS
3206 yeled (1), young
male
5288 na'ar (1), male
child; servant

BOZEZ
949 Bôwtsêts (1), shining

BOZKATH
1218 Botsqath (1), swell
of ground

BOZRAH
1224 Botsrâh (9),
sheep-fold, animal pen

BRACELET
685 'ets'âdâh (1), bracelet

BRACELETS
2397 châch (1), ring for
the nose or lips
6616 pâthîyl (2), twine,
cord
6781 tsâmîyd (6),
bracelet; lid
8285 shêrâh (1),
wrist-band

BRAKE
1234 bâqa' (3), to cleave,
break, tear open
1518 gîyach (1), to issue
forth; to burst forth
1855 dᵉqaq (Ch.) (5), to
crumble; crush
1961 hâyâh (1), to exist,
i.e. be or become
3807 kâthath (1), to
bruise or strike, beat
5310 nâphats (1), to dash
to pieces; to scatter
5422 nâthats (12), to tear
down
5423 nâthaq (3), to tear
off
6555 pârats (4), to break
out
6561 pâraq (1), to break
off or crunch; to deliver
6565 pârar (2), to break
up; to violate, frustrate
7323 rûwts (1), to run
7533 râtsats (1), to crack
in pieces, smash
7665 shâbar (20), to burst
1284 diarrhēssō (2), to
tear asunder
2608 katagnumi (2), to
crack apart
2622 kataklaō (2), to
divide in pieces
2806 klaō (9), to break
bread
4937 suntribō (1), to
crush completely

BRAKEST
7533 râtsats (1), to crack
in pieces, smash
7665 shâbar (4), to burst

BRAMBLE
329 'âṭâd (3), buckthorn
942 batŏs (1), brier

BRAMBLES
2336 chôwach (1), thorn;
hook; ring for the nose

BRANCH
534 'âmîyr (1), top
1121 bên (1), son,
descendant; people
2156 zᵉmôwrâh (3), twig,
vine branch
2158 zâmîyr (1), song
3127 yôwneqeth (1),
sprout, new shoot
3712 kippâh (3), leaf
5342 nêtser (4), shoot of
a plant; descendant
5929 'âleh (1), leaf;
foliage
6057 'ânâph (1), twig
6780 tsemach (5), sprout,
branch
6788 tsammereth (2),
foliage

7070 qâneh (5), reed
7105 qâtsîyr (2), harvest;
limb of a tree
2798 kladŏs (2), twig or
bough
2814 klēma (3), limb or
shoot

BRANCHES
905 bad (3), limb,
member; bar; chief
1121 bên (1), son,
descendant; people
1808 dâlîyâh (8), bough,
branch
2156 zᵉmôwrâh (1),
pruned twig, branch
3127 yôwneqeth (3),
sprout, new shoot
3709 kaph (1), hollow of
hand; paw; sole
5189 nᵉṭîyshâh (1),
tendril plant shoot
5585 çâ'îyph (2), fissure
of rocks; bough
5688 'ăbôth (1), entwined
things: string or foliage
5929 'âleh (3), leaf;
foliage
6056 'ănaph (Ch.) (3),
bough, branch
6057 'ânâph (3), twig
6058 'ânêph (1),
branching
6073 'ŏphe' (1), bough
6288 pᵉ'ôrâh (4), foliage,
branches
7070 qâneh (19), reed
7641 shibbôl (1), stream;
ear of grain
7976 shilluchâh (1),
shoot of a vine
8299 sârîyg (3),
entwining tendril
902 baïŏn (1), palm twig
2798 kladŏs (9), twig or
bough
2814 klēma (1), limb or
shoot
4746 stŏibas (1), bough
of a tree so employed

BRAND
181 'ûwd (1), poker stick
for a fire

BRANDISH
5774 'ûwph (1), to cover,
to fly; to faint

BRANDS
3940 lappîyd (1), flaming
torch, lamp or flame

BRASEN
5178 nᵉchôsheth (27),
copper; bronze
5473 chalkiŏn (1), copper
dish or kettle

BRASS
5153 nâchûwsh (1),
coppery, i.e. hard
5154 nᵉchûwshâh (7),
copper; bronze
5174 nᵉchâsh (Ch.) (9),
copper
5178 nᵉchôsheth (102),
copper; bronze
5470 chalkĕŏs (1), copper
5474 chalkŏlibanŏn (2),
burnished copper
5475 chalkŏs (3), copper

BRAVERY
8597 tiph'ârâh (1),
ornament

BRAWLER
269 amachŏs (1), not
quarrelsome

BRAWLERS
269 amachŏs (1), not
quarrelsome

BRAWLING
4090 mᵉdân (2), contest
or quarrel

BRAY
3806 kâthash (1), to
pound in a mortar
5101 nâhaq (1), to bray;
to scream from hunger

BRAYED
5101 nâhaq (1), to bray;
to scream from hunger

BREACH
919 bedeq (1), gap
1234 bâqa' (2), to cleave,
break, tear open
6555 pârats (1), to break
out
6556 perets (10), break,
gap
7667 sheber (5), fracture;
ruin
8569 tᵉnûw'âh (1), enmity

BREACHES
919 bedeq (7), gap
1233 bᵉqîya' (1), fissure,
breach
4664 miphrâts (1),
haven, cove
6555 pârats (1), to break
out
6556 perets (3), break,
gap
7447 râçîyç (1), ruin;
dew-drop
7667 sheber (1), fracture;
ruin

BREAD
3899 lechem (236), food,
bread
740 artos (72), loaf of
bread

BREADTH
2947 ṭêphach (1),
palm-breadth
2948 ṭôphach (3),
palm-breadth
4800 merchâb (1), open
space; liberty
6613 pᵉthay (Ch.) (2),
width
7338 rachab (1), width,
expanse
7341 rôchab (75), width
4114 platŏs (4), width

BREAK
215 'ôwr (1), to be
luminous
1234 bâqa' (3), to cleave,
break, tear open
1633 gâram (2), to
crunch the bones
1758 dûwsh (1), to
trample or thresh
1792 dâkâ' (3), to
pulverize; be contrite
1854 dâqaq (3), to crush;
crumble

1986 hâlam (1), to *strike, beat, stamp, conquer*
2000 hâmam (1), to *disturb, drive, destroy*
2040 hâraç (7), to *pull* down; *break, destroy*
2490 châlal (3), to *profane, defile*
3318 yâtsâ' (1), to *go, bring out*
5003 nâ'aph (1), to *commit adultery*
5106 nûw' (1), to *refuse, forbid, dissuade*
5214 nîyr (2), to *till* the soil
5310 nâphats (10), to *dash* to pieces
5422 nâthats (6), to *tear* down
5423 nâthaq (2), to *tear* off
5670 'âbaṭ (1), to *pawn;* to *lend;* to *entangle*
6202 'âraph (3), to *break* the neck, to *destroy*
6206 'ârats (1), to *awe;* to *dread;* to *harass*
6315 pûwach (2), to *blow,* to *fan, kindle;* to *utter*
6476 pâtsach (6), to *break* out in sound
6524 pârach (2), to *break* forth; to *bloom;* to *fly*
6555 pârats (7), to *break* out
6561 pâraq (3), to *break* off or *crunch;* to *deliver*
6562 peraq (Ch.) (1), to *discontinue, stop*
6565 pârar (14), to *break* up; to *violate, frustrate*
6605 pâthach (1), to *open* wide; to *loosen, begin*
6743 tsâlach (1), to *push* forward
6746 tselôchîyth (1), *vial* or *salt-cellar*
7489 râ'a' (3), to *break* to pieces
7533 râtsats (1), to *crack* in pieces, *smash*
7665 shâbar (33), to *burst*
7702 sâdad (2), to *break* ground
827 augē (1), *radiance, dawn*
1358 diŏrussō (2), to *penetrate* burglariously
2608 katagnumi (1), to *crack apart*
2806 klaō (2), to *break* bread
3089 luō (1), to *loosen*
4486 rhēgnumi (2), to *break, burst forth*
4919 sunthruptō (1), to *crush together*

BREAKER
6555 pârats (1), to *break* out
3848 parabatēs (1), *violator, lawbreaker*

BREAKEST
7665 shâbar (1), to *burst*

BREAKETH
1234 bâqa' (1), to *cleave, break, tear open*

1638 gâraç (1), to *crush, break;* to *dissolve*
1855 deqaq (Ch.) (1), to *crumble; crush*
2040 hâraç (1), to *pull* down; *break, destroy*
5927 'âlâh (1), to *ascend, be high, mount*
6327 pûwts (1), to *dash* in pieces; to *disperse*
6555 pârats (3), to *break* out
6566 pâras (1), to *break* apart, *disperse, scatter*
7665 shâbar (5), to *burst*
7779 shûwph (1), to *gape,* i.e. *snap* at
7940 Sâkar (1), *recompense*

BREAKING
4290 machtereth (1), *burglary*
4866 mishbêr (1), vaginal *opening*
5927 'âlâh (1), to *ascend, be high, mount*
6524 pârach (2), to *break* forth; to *bloom;* to *fly*
6556 perets (3), *break, gap*
6565 pârar (2), to *break* up; to *violate, frustrate*
6979 qûwr (1), to *throw* forth; to *wall up*
7667 sheber (2), *fracture; ruin*
7670 shibrôwn (1), *ruin*
2800 klasis (2), *fracturing*
2806 klaō (1), to *break* bread
3847 parabasis (1), *violation, breaking*

BREAKINGS
7667 sheber (1), *fracture; ruin*

BREAST
2306 chădîy (Ch.) (1), *breast*
2373 châzeh (11), animal *breast* meat
7699 shad (3), female *breast*
4738 stēthŏs (3), area of the human *chest*

BREASTPLATE
2833 chôshen (25), *gorget*
8302 shiryôwn (1), *corslet, coat of mail*
2382 thōrax (2), *corslet, chest*

BREASTPLATES
2382 thōrax (3), *corslet, chest*

BREASTS
1717 dad (2), female *breast* or *bosom*
2373 châzeh (2), animal *breast* meat
3824 lêbâb (1), *heart*
5845 'ăṭîyn (1), *receptacle* for milk
7699 shad (19), female *breast*
4738 stēthŏs (2), area of the human *chest*

BREATH
5315 nephesh (1), *life; breath; soul; wind*
5396 nishmâ' (Ch.) (1), *breath, life*
5397 neshâmâh (12), *breath, life*
7307 rûwach (27), *breath; wind; life-*spirit
4157 pnŏē (1), *breeze; breath*

BREATHE
3307 yâphêach (1), *puffing; breathing* out
5301 nâphach (1), to *inflate, blow* hard
5397 neshâmâh (2), *breath, life*

BREATHED
5301 nâphach (1), to *inflate, blow* hard
5397 neshâmâh (2), *breath, life*
1720 ĕmphusaō (1), to *blow at* or *on*

BREATHETH
5397 neshâmâh (1), *breath, life*

BREATHING
7309 revâchâh (1), *relief*
1709 ĕmpnĕō (1), to *be animated by*

BRED
7311 rûwm (1), to *be high;* to *rise* or *raise*

BREECHES
4370 miknâç (5), *drawers* concealing the privates

BREED
1121 bên (1), *people* of a class or kind
8317 shârats (1), to *swarm,* or *abound*

BREEDING
4476 mimshâq (1), *possession*

BRETHREN
251 'âch (329), *brother; relative; member*
252 'ach (Ch.) (1), *brother; relative*
80 adĕlphŏs (225), *brother*
81 adĕlphŏtēs (1), *fraternity, brotherhood*
5360 philadĕlphia (1), *fraternal affection*
5361 philadĕlphŏs (1), *fraternal*
5569 psĕudadĕlphŏs (2), *pretended associate*

BRETHREN'S
251 'âch (1), *brother; relative; member*

BRIBE
3724 kôpher (2), *redemption-*price

BRIBERY
7810 shachad (1), to *bribe; gift*

BRIBES
7810 shachad (3), to *bribe; gift*

BRICK
3835 lâban (3), to *make* bricks
3843 lebênâh (4), *brick*

BRICKKILN
4404 malbên (3), *brick-kiln*

BRICKS
3843 lebênâh (4), *brick*

BRIDE
3618 kallâh (9), *bride; son's wife*
3565 numphē (5), young *married* woman

BRIDECHAMBER
3567 numphôn (3), *bridal* room

BRIDEGROOM
2860 châthân (8), *bridegroom*
3566 numphiŏs (15), *bridegroom*

BRIDEGROOM'S
3566 numphiŏs (1), *bridegroom*

BRIDLE
4269 machçôwm (1), *muzzle*
4964 metheg (3), *bit*
7448 reçen (4), *jaw* restraint of a horse
5469 chalinŏs (1), *bit* or *bridle*

BRIDLES
5469 chalinŏs (1), *bit* or *bridle*

BRIDLETH
5468 chalinagōgĕō (1), to *curb, hold in check*

BRIEFLY
346 anakĕphalaiŏmai (1), to *sum up*
1223+3641 dia (1), *through,* by means of

BRIER
2312 chêdeq (1), *prickly* plant
5544 çillôwn (1), *prickle*
5636 çarpâd (1), *stinging nettle*

BRIERS
1303 barqân (2), *thorn, biers*
5621 çârâb (1), *thistle*
8068 shâmîyr (8), *thorn;* (poss.) *diamond*
5146 tribŏlŏs (1), *thorny caltrop* plant

BRIGANDINE
5630 çiyrôn (1), *coat of mail,* scale armor

BRIGANDINES
5630 çiyrôn (1), *coat of mail,* scale armor

BRIGHT
216 'ôwr (1), *luminary; lightning; happiness*
925 bâhîyr (1), *shining, bright*
934 bôhereth (11), *whitish, bright* spot
1300 bârâq (1), *lightning; flash of lightning*

BRIGHTNESS

1305 bârar (1), to *brighten; purify*
2385 châzîyz (1), *flash of lightning*
3851 lahab (1), *flame of fire; flash of a blade*
3974 mâ'ôwr (1), *luminary, light source*
4803 mârat (1), to *polish; to make bald*
4838 mâraq (1), to *polish; to sharpen; to rinse*
5051 nôgahh (1), *brilliancy*
6219 'âshôwth (1), *polished*
6247 'esheth (1), *fabric*
7043 qâlal (1), to *be, make light*
796 astrapē (1), *lightning; light's glare*
2986 lamprŏs (2), *radiant; clear*
5460 phōtĕinŏs (1), *well-illuminated*

BRIGHTNESS

2096 zôhar (2), *brilliancy, shining*
2122 zîyv (Ch.) (2), *cheerfulness*
3314 yiph'âh (2), *splendor, beauty*
3368 yâqâr (1), *valuable*
5051 nôgahh (11), *brilliancy*
5054 nᵉgôhâh (1), *splendor, luster*
541 apaugasma (1), *effulgence, radiance*
2015 ĕpiphanĕia (1), *manisfestation*
2987 lamprŏtēs (1), *brilliancy*

BRIM

7097 qâtseh (1), *extremity*
8193 sâphâh (7), *lip; edge, margin*
507 anō (1), *upward or on the top, heavenward*

BRIMSTONE

1614 gophrîyth (7), *sulphur*
2303 thĕiŏn (7), *sulphur*
2306 thĕiōdēs (1), *sulphurous yellow*

BRING

338 'îy (1), *solitary wild creature that howls*
503 'âlaph (1), *increase by thousands*
622 'âçaph (2), to *gather, collect*
858 'âthâh (Ch.) (2), to *arrive; go*
935 bôw' (248), to *go or come*
1069 bâkar (1), to *give the birthright*
1431 gâdal (1), to *be great, make great*
1518 gîyach (1), to *issue forth; to burst forth*
1876 dâshâ' (1), to *sprout new plants*
1980 hâlak (1), to *walk; live a certain way*
2142 zâkar (2), to *remember; to mention*

2342 chûwl (1), to *dance, whirl; to writhe* in pain
2381 Chăzîy'êl (1), *seen of God*
2986 yâbal (5), to *bring*
3051 yâhab (2), to *give*
3205 yâlad (17), to *bear young; to father a child*
3212 yâlak (3), to *walk; to live; to carry*
3254 yâçaph (1), to *add or augment*
3318 yâtsâ' (73), to *go, bring out*
3381 yârad (24), to *descend*
3513 kâbad (1), to *be heavy, severe, dull*
3533 kâbash (1), to *conquer, subjugate*
3665 kâna' (3), to *humiliate, vanquish*
3947 lâqach (17), to *take*
4608 ma'âleh (1), *elevation; platform*
4672 mâtsâ' (2), to *find or acquire; to occur*
5060 nâga' (3), to *strike*
5066 nâgash (14), to *be, come, bring near*
5080 nâdach (1), to *push off, scattered*
5107 nûwb (1), to *(make) flourish; to utter*
5375 nâsâ' (10), to *lift up*
5381 nâsag (1), to *reach*
5414 nâthan (11), to *give*
5437 çâbab (2), to *surround*
5647 'âbad (1), to *do, work, serve*
5674 'âbar (1), to *cross over; to transition*
5924 'êllâ' (Ch.) (3), *above*
5927 'âlâh (35), to *ascend, be high, mount*
6049 'ânan (1), to *cover, becloud; to act covertly*
6213 'âsâh (9), to *do or make*
6315 pûwach (1), to *blow, to fan, kindle; to utter*
6398 pâlach (1), to *slice; to break open; to pierce*
6509 pârâh (2), to *bear fruit*
6779 tsâmach (1), to *sprout*
6805 tsâ'ad (1), to *pace, step regularly*
7034 qâlâh (1), to *hold in contempt*
7126 qârab (36), to *approach, bring near*
7311 rûwm (1), to *be high; to rise or raise*
7392 râkab (1), to *ride*
7665 shâbar (1), to *burst*
7725 shûwb (72), to *turn back; to return*
7760 sûwm (1), to *put, place*
7817 shâchach (1), to *sink or depress*
7896 shîyth (1), to *place*
7971 shâlach (1), to *send away*
8045 shâmad (1), to *desolate*

8074 shâmêm (2), to *devastate; to stupefy*
8213 shâphêl (4), to *humiliate*
8317 shârats (3), to *wriggle, swarm*
71 agō (14), to *lead; to bring, drive; to weigh*
114 athĕtĕō (1), to *disesteem, neutralize*
321 anagō (2), to *lead up; to bring out; to sail*
363 anamimnĕskō (1), to *remind; to recollect*
518 apaggĕllō (2), to *announce, proclaim*
520 apagō (1), to *take away*
667 apŏhĕrō (1), to *bear off, carry away*
1295 diasōzō (1), to *cure, preserve, rescue*
1396 dŏulagōgĕō (1), to *enslave, subdue*
1402 dŏulŏō (1), to *enslave*
1521 ĕisagō (1), to *lead into*
1533 ĕisphĕrō (2), to *carry inward*
1625 ĕktrĕphō (1), to *cherish or train*
1627 ĕkphĕrō (1), to *bear out; to produce*
1863 ĕpagō (2), *inflict; charge*
2018 ĕpiphĕrō (1), to *inflict, bring upon*
2036 ĕpō (1), to *speak or say*
2097 ĕuaggĕlizō (2), to *announce good news*
2592 karpŏphŏrĕō (4), to *be fertile*
2609 katagō (3), to *lead down; to moor a vessel*
2615 katadŏulŏō (2), to *enslave utterly*
2673 katargĕō (1), to *be, render entirely useless*
3919 parĕisagō (1), to *lead in aside*
4160 pŏiĕō (6), to *do*
4311 prŏpĕmpō (3), to *send forward*
4317 prŏsagō (2), to *bring near*
4374 prŏsphĕrō (2), to *present to; to treat as*
5062 tĕssarakŏnta (1), *forty*
5088 tiktō (3), to *produce from seed*
5179 tupŏs (1), *shape, i.e. statue or resemblance*
5342 phĕrō (17), to *bear or carry*
5461 phōtizō (1), to *shine or to brighten up*

BRINGERS

539 'âman (1), to *be firm, faithful, true; to trust*

BRINGEST

935 bôw' (1), to *go, come*
1319 bâsar (3), to *announce (good news)*
1533 ĕisphĕrō (1), to *carry inward*

BRINGETH

935 bôw' (6), to *go or come*
1069 bâkar (1), to *give the birthright*
1319 bâsar (5), to *announce (good news)*
2142 zâkar (1), to *remember*
2659 châphêr (1), to *shame, reproach*
3318 yâtsâ' (18), to *go, bring out*
3381 yârad (2), to *descend*
3615 kâlâh (1), to *complete, prepare*
5060 nâga' (1), to *strike*
5107 nûwb (1), to *(make) flourish; to utter*
5148 nâchâh (3), to *guide*
5414 nâthan (3), to *give*
5927 'âlâh (3), to *ascend, be high, mount*
6213 'âsâh (1), to *do or make*
6331 pûwr (1), to *crush*
6445 pânaq (1), to *enervate, reduce vigor*
6779 tsâmach (1), to *sprout*
7725 shûwb (3), to *turn back; to return*
7737 shâvâh (1), to *level, equalize; to resemble*
7817 shâchach (1), to *sink or depress*
8213 shâphêl (1), to *humiliate*
399 anaphĕrō (1), to *take up; to lead up*
616 apŏkuĕō (1), to *bring into being*
1521 ĕisagō (1), to *lead into*
1544 ĕkballō (3), to *throw out*
2592 karpŏphŏrĕō (2), to *be fertile*
4160 pŏiĕō (7), to *do*
4393 prŏphĕrō (2), to *bear forward*
4992 sōtēriŏn (1), *defender or defence*
5088 tiktō (2), to *produce from seed*
5342 phĕrō (2), to *bear or carry*

BRINGING

935 bôw' (6), to *go, come*
2142 zâkar (1), to *remember; to mention*
3318 yâtsâ' (3), to *go, bring out*
5375 nâsâ' (3), to *lift up*
7725 shûwb (2), to *turn back; to return*
71 agō (1), to *lead; to bring, drive; to weigh*
163 aichmalōtizō (2), to *make captive*
1863 ĕpagō (1), *inflict; charge*
1898 ĕpĕisagōgē (1), *introduction*
4160 pŏiĕō (1), to *do*
5342 phĕrō (3), to *bear or carry*

BRINK
7097 qâtseh (1), *extremity*
8193 sâphâh (5), *lip; edge, margin*

BROAD
7338 rachab (1), *width, expanse*
7338+3027 rachab (1), *width, expanse*
7339 rᵉchôb (3), *myriad*
7341 rôchab (21), *width*
7342 râchâb (5), *roomy, spacious*
7554 râqa' (1), *to pound*
7555 riqqûa' (1), *thin metallic plate*
2149 ĕuruchŏrŏs (1), *spacious, wide*
4115 platunŏ (1), *to widen*

BROADER
7342 râchâb (1), *roomy, spacious*

BROIDED
4117 plĕgma (1), *plait or braid* of hair

BROIDERED
7553 riqmâh (7), *embroidery*
8665 tashbêts (1), *checkered* stuff

BROILED
3702 ŏptŏs (1), *roasted, broiled*

BROKEN
6 'âbad (1), *perish; destroy*
1234 bâqa' (6), *to cleave, break, tear open*
1638 gâraç (1), *to crush, break; to dissolve*
1792 dâkâ' (3), *to pulverize; be contrite*
1794 dâkâh (3), *to collapse; contrite*
1854 dâqaq (1), *to crush; crumble*
1986 hâlam (2), *to strike, beat, stamp, conquer*
2040 hâraç (4), *to pull down; break, destroy*
2490 châlal (1), *to profane, defile*
2844 chath (6), *terror*
2865 châthath (6), *to break down*
3807 kâthath (1), *to bruise or strike*
4535 maççâch (1), *cordon; barrier; in turn*
4790 mᵉrôwach (1), *bruised, pounded*
5181 nâchath (2), *to sink, descend; to press*
5218 nâkê' (3), *smitten; afflicted*
5310 nâphats (1), *to dash to pieces; to scatter*
5421 nâtha' (1), *to tear out*
5422 nâthats (5), *to tear down*
5423 nâthaq (7), *to tear off*
5927 'âlâh (1), *to ascend, be high, mount*

BRINK
6105 'âtsam (1), *to be, make powerful*
6209 'ârar (1), *to bare; to demolish*
6331 pûwr (1), *to crush*
6480 pâtsam (1), *to rend, tear* by earthquake
6524 pârach (2), *to break forth; to bloom*
6531 perek (1), *severity*
6555 pârats (12), *to break out*
6565 pârar (9), *to break up; to violate, frustrate*
7280 râga' (1), *to stir up*
7462 râ'âh (1), *to tend a flock, i.e. pasture it*
7465 rô'âh (1), *breakage*
7489 râ'a' (2), *to break to pieces*
7533 râtsats (4), *to crack in pieces, smash*
7616 shâbâb (1), *fragment, i.e. ruin*
7665 shâbar (65), *to burst*
8406 tᵉbar (Ch.) (1), *to be fragile*
1358 diŏrussŏ (2), *to penetrate* burglariously
1575 ĕkklaŏ (3), *to exscind, cut off*
1846 ĕxŏrussŏ (1), *to dig out*
2608 katagnumi (1), *to crack apart*
2801 klasma (2), *piece, bit*
2806 klaŏ (3), *to break bread*
3089 luŏ (6), *to loosen*
4917 sunthlaŏ (2), *to dash together, shatter*
4937 suntribŏ (3), *to crush completely*
4977 schizŏ (1), *to split or sever*

BROKENFOOTED
7667+7272 sheber (1), *fracture; ruin*

BROKENHANDED
7667+3027 sheber (1), *fracture; ruin*

BROKENHEARTED
7665+3820 shâbar (1), *to burst*
4937+2588 suntribŏ (1), *to crush completely*

BROOD
3555 nŏssia (1), hen's *brood*

BROOK
4323 mîykâl (1), *brook*
5158 nachal (37), *valley, ravine;* mine *shaft*
5493 chĕimarrhŏs (1), *winter-torrent*

BROOKS
650 'âphîyq (1), *valley; stream; mighty, strong*
2975 yᵉ'ôr (4), Nile *River;* Tigris *River*
5158 nachal (9), *valley, ravine;* mine *shaft*

BROTH
4839 mârâq (2), *soup-broth*

BRINK
6564 pârâq (1), *fragments* in soup

BROTHER
251 'âch (244), *brother; relative; member*
1730 dôwd (1), *beloved, friend; relative*
2992 yâbam (2), *to marry* a brother's widow
2993 yâbâm (2), *husband's brother*
7453 rêa' (1), *associate; one close*
80 adĕlphŏs (109), *brother*

BROTHER'S
251 'âch (25), *brother; relative; member*
2994 yᵉbêmeth (3), dead brother's widow, i.e. *sister-in-law*
80 adĕlphŏs (7), *brother*

BROTHERHOOD
264 'achăvâh (1), *fraternity; brotherhood*
81 adĕlphŏtēs (1), *fraternity, brotherhood*

BROTHERLY
251 'âch (1), *brother; relative; member*
5360 philadĕlphia (5), *fraternal affection*

BROTHERS'
1730 dôwd (1), *beloved, friend; relative*

BROUGHT
539 'âman (5), *to be firm, faithful, true; to trust*
622 'âçaph (3), *to gather, collect*
656 'âphêç (1), *to cease*
857 'âthâh (1), *to arrive; go*
858 'âthâh (Ch.) (7), *to arrive; go*
935 bôw' (264), *to go or come*
1197 bâ'ar (1), *to be brutish, be senseless*
1310 bâshal (1), *to boil up, cook; to ripen*
1319 bâsar (2), *to announce* (good news)
1431 gâdal (6), *to be great, make great*
1468 gûwz (1), *to pass rapidly*
1540 gâlâh (1), *to denude; uncover*
1541 gᵉlâh (Ch.) (1), *to reveal mysteries*
1589 gânab (1), *to thieve; to deceive*
1809 dâlal (3), *to slacken, dangle*
1820 dâmâh (2), *to be silent; to fail, cease*
1946 hûwk (Ch.) (1), *to go, come*
1961 hâyâh (2), *to exist, i.e. be or become*
2254 châbal (2), *to bind* by a pledge; *to pervert*
2342 chûwl (3), *to dance, whirl; to writhe* in pain
2659 châphêr (3), *to be ashamed, disappointed*

BROUGHT
2986 yâbal (7), *to bring*
2987 yᵉbal (Ch.) (2), *to bring*
3205 yâlad (12), *to bear young; to father a child*
3212 yâlak (8), *to walk; to live; to carry*
3218 yekeq (1), *young locust*
3318 yâtsâ' (127), *to go, bring out*
3381 yârad (17), *to descend*
3467 yâsha' (2), *to make safe, free*
3474 yâshar (1), *to be straight; to make right*
3533 kâbash (2), *to conquer, subjugate*
3665 kâna' (4), *to humiliate, vanquish*
3766 kâra' (2), *to make miserable*
3947 lâqach (8), *to take*
4161 môwtsâ' (2), *going forth*
4355 mâkak (2), *to tumble; to perish*
4551 maççâ' (1), *stone quarry; projectile*
5060 nâga' (1), *to strike*
5066 nâgash (13), *to be, come, bring near*
5090 nâhag (4), *to drive forth; to carry away*
5148 nâchâh (2), *to guide*
5265 nâça' (3), *start* on a journey
5375 nâsâ' (13), *to lift up*
5414 nâthan (3), *to give*
5437 çâbab (1), *to surround*
5493 çûwr (1), *to turn off*
5674 'âbar (6), *to cross over; to transition*
5927 'âlâh (65), *to ascend, be high, mount*
5954 'ălal (Ch.) (4), *to go in; to lead in*
6030 'ânâh (1), *to respond, answer*
6213 'âsâh (3), *to do or make*
6565 pârar (1), *to break up; to violate, frustrate*
6819 tsâ'ar (1), *to be small; be trivial*
6908 qâbats (1), *to collect, assemble*
7126 qârab (27), *to approach, bring near*
7127 qᵉrêb (Ch.) (1), *to approach, bring near*
7136 qârâh (1), *to bring about; to impose*
7235 râbâh (1), *to increase*
7311 rûwm (1), *to be high; to rise or raise*
7323 rûwts (1), *to run*
7392 râkab (1), *to ride*
7617 shâbâh (1), *to transport* into captivity
7725 shûwb (39), *to turn back; to return*
7760 sûwm (4), *to put, place*
7817 shâchach (3), *to sink or depress*

7971 shâlach (1), to *send away*
8213 shâphêl (3), to *humiliate*
8239 shâphath (1), to *place* or *put*
8317 shârats (2), to *swarm*, or *abound*
71 agō (32), to *lead; to bring, drive; to weigh*
321 anagō (4), to *lead up; to bring out; to sail*
397 anatrĕphō (1), to *rear, care for*
654 apŏstrĕphō (1), to *turn away* or *back*
985 blastanō (1), to *yield fruit*
1080 gĕnnaō (1), to *procreate, regenerate*
1096 ginŏmai (2), to *be, become*
1325 didōmi (1), to *give*
1402 dŏulŏō (1), to *enslave*
1521 ĕisagō (7), to *lead into*
1533 ĕisphĕrō (2), to *carry inward*
1627 ĕkphĕrō (1), to *bear out; to produce*
1806 ĕxagō (6), to *lead forth, escort*
1850 ĕxŏusiazō (1), to *control, master another*
2018 ĕpiphĕrō (2), to *inflict, bring upon*
2049 ĕrēmŏō (2), to *lay waste*
2064 ĕrchŏmai (1), to *go*
2097 ĕuaggĕlizō (1), to *announce good news*
2164 ĕuphŏrĕō (1), to *be fertile, produce a crop*
2476 histēmi (1), to *stand, establish*
2601 katabibazō (1), to *cause to bring down*
2609 katagō (4), to *lead down; to moor a vessel*
2865 kŏmizō (1), to *provide* for
2989 lampō (1), to *radiate brilliancy*
3350 mĕtŏikĕsia (1), *exile, deportation*
3860 paradidōmi (1), to *hand over*
3920 parĕisaktŏs (1), *smuggled in, infiltrated*
3930 parĕchō (2), to *hold near, i.e. to present*
3936 paristēmi (2), to *stand beside, present*
4160 pŏiĕō (1), to *make*
4254 prŏagō (3), to *lead forward; to precede*
4311 prŏpĕmpō (4), to *send forward*
4317 prŏsagō (1), to *bring near*
4374 prŏsphĕrō (15), to *present to; to treat as*
4851 sumphĕrō (1), to *collect; to conduce*
4939 suntrŏphŏs (1), *one brought up with*
5013 tapĕinŏō (1), to *depress; to humiliate*

5044 tĕknŏtrŏphĕō (1), to *be a child-rearer*
5088 tiktō (4), to *produce from seed*
5142 trĕphō (1), to *nurse, feed, care for*
5342 phĕrō (17), to *bear* or *carry*
5461 phōtizō (1), to *shine* or to *brighten* up

BROUGHTEST
935 bŏw' (4), to *go* or *come*
3318 yâtsâ' (7), to *go, bring out*
5927 'âlâh (2), to *ascend, be high, mount*

BROW
4696 mêtsach (1), *forehead*
3790 ŏphrus (1), *eye-brow*

BROWN
2345 chûwm (4), *sunburnt* or *swarthy*

BRUISE
1792 dâkâ' (1), to *pulverize; be contrite*
1854 dâqaq (1), to *crush; crumble*
7490 rᵉ'a' (Ch.) (1), to *shatter, dash to pieces*
7667 sheber (2), *fracture; ruin*
7779 shûwph (2), to *gape, i.e. snap at*
4937 suntribō (1), to *crush completely*

BRUISED
1792 dâkâ' (1), to *pulverize; be contrite*
1854 dâqaq (1), to *crush; crumble*
4600 mâ'ak (1), to *press, to pierce, emasculate*
6213 'âsâh (2), to *do* or *make*
7533 râtsats (2), to *crack in pieces, smash*
2352 thrauō (1), to *crush*
4937 suntribō (1), to *crush completely*

BRUISES
2250 chabbûwrâh (1), *weal, bruise*

BRUISING
6213 'âsâh (1), to *do* or *make*
4937 suntribō (1), to *crush completely*

BRUIT
8052 shᵉmûw'âh (1), *announcement*
8088 shêma' (1), *something heard*

BRUTE
249 alŏgŏs (2), *irrational, not reasonable*

BRUTISH
1197 bâ'ar (11), to *be brutish, be senseless*

BUCKET
1805 dᵉlîy (1), *pail, bucket*

BUCKETS
1805 dᵉlîy (1), *pail, bucket*

BUCKLER
4043 mâgên (6), *small shield (buckler); skin*
5507 çôchêrâh (1), *surrounding shield*
6793 tsinnâh (3), *large shield; piercing cold*
7420 rômach (1), *iron pointed spear*

BUCKLERS
4043 mâgên (3), *small shield (buckler); skin*
6793 tsinnâh (2), *large shield; piercing cold*

BUD
4161 môwtsâ' (1), *going forth*
5132 nûwts (1), to *fly away, leave*
6524 pârach (2), to *break forth; to bloom*
6525 perach (1), *calyx flower; bloom*
6779 tsâmach (6), to *sprout*

BUDDED
5132 nûwts (1), to *fly away, leave*
6524 pârach (3), to *break forth; to bloom*
985 blastanō (1), to *yield fruit*

BUDS
6525 perach (1), *calyx flower; bloom*

BUFFET
2852 kŏlaphizō (2), to *strike*

BUFFETED
2852 kŏlaphizō (3), to *strike*

BUILD
1124 bᵉnâ' (Ch.) (6), to *build*
1129 bânâh (140), to *build; to establish*
456 anŏikŏdŏmĕō (2), to *rebuild*
2026 ĕpŏikŏdŏmĕō (2), to *rear up, build up*
3618 ŏikŏdŏmĕō (12), *construct; edification*

BUILDED
1124 bᵉnâ' (Ch.) (10), to *build*
1129 bânâh (36), to *build; to establish*
2680 kataskĕuazō (2), to *construct; to arrange*
3618 ŏikŏdŏmĕō (1), *construct; edification*
4925 sunŏikŏdŏmĕō (1), to *construct*

BUILDEDST
1129 bânâh (1), to *build; to establish*

BUILDER
5079 tĕchnitēs (1), *artisan, craftsman*

BUILDERS
1129 bânâh (9), to *build; to establish*
3618 ŏikŏdŏmĕō (5), *construct; edification*

BUILDEST
1129 bânâh (3), to *build; to establish*
3618 ŏikŏdŏmĕō (2), *construct; edification*

BUILDETH
1129 bânâh (7), to *build; to establish*
2026 ĕpŏikŏdŏmĕō (2), to *rear up, build up*

BUILDING
1124 bᵉnâ' (Ch.) (3), to *build*
1129 bânâh (15), to *build; to establish*
1140 binyâh (1), *structure*
1146 binyân (7), *edifice, building*
1147 binyân (Ch.) (1), *edifice, building*
4746 mᵉqâreh (1), *frame of timbers*
1739 ĕndōmēsis (1), *structure*
2026 ĕpŏikŏdŏmĕō (1), to *rear up, build up*
2937 ktisis (1), *formation*
3618 ŏikŏdŏmĕō (1), *construct; edification*
3619 ŏikŏdŏmē (3), *structure; edification*

BUILDINGS
3619 ŏikŏdŏmē (3), *structure; edification*

BUILT
1124 bᵉnâ' (Ch.) (1), to *build*
1129 bânâh (155), to *build; to establish*
2026 ĕpŏikŏdŏmĕō (3), to *rear up, build up*
2680 kataskĕuazō (1), to *construct; to arrange*
3618 ŏikŏdŏmĕō (10), *construct; edification*

BUKKI
1231 Buqqîy (5), *wasteful*

BUKKIAH
1232 Buqqîyâh (2), *wasting of Jehovah*

BUL
945 Bûwl (1), *rain*

BULL
7794 shôwr (1), *bullock*
8377 tᵉ'ôw (1), *antelope*

BULLOCK
1121+1241 bên (3), *son, descendant*
1241 bâqâr (1), *plowing ox; herd*
5695 'êgel (1), *bull-calf*
6499 par (89), *bullock*
7794 shôwr (10), *bullock*

BULLOCK'S
6499 par (3), *bullock*

BULLOCKS
1241 bâqâr (4), *plowing ox; herd*
5695 'êgel (1), *bull-calf*
6499 par (36), *bullock*
7794 shôwr (1), *bullock*
8450 tôwr (Ch.) (3), *bull*

BULLS
47 'abbîyr (4), *mighty*

1241 bâqâr (1), *plowing ox; herd*
6499 par (2), *bullock*
5022 taurŏs (2), *bullock, ox*

BULRUSH
100 'agmôwn (1), *rush; rope of rushes*

BULRUSHES
1573 gôme' (2), *papyrus plant*

BULWARKS
2426 chêyl (1), *entrenchment, rampart*
2430 chêylâh (1), *entrenchment, rampart*
4685 mâtsôwd (1), *net or snare; besieging tower*
4692 mâtsôwr (1), *siege-mound; distress*
6438 pinnâh (1), *pinnacle; chieftain*

BUNAH
946 Bûwnâh (1), *discretion*

BUNCH
92 'ăguddâh (1), *band; bundle; knot; arch*

BUNCHES
1707 dabbesheth (1), *hump of a camel*
6778 tsammûwq (2), *lump of dried grapes*

BUNDLE
6872 tse rôwr (3), *parcel; kernel or particle*
4128 plēthŏs (1), *large number, throng*

BUNDLES
6872 tse rôwr (1), *parcel; kernel or particle*
1197 dĕsmĕ (1), *bundle*

BUNNI
1137 Bânîy (3), *built*

BURDEN
3053 ye hâb (1), *lot given*
4853 massâ' (52), *burden, utterance*
4858 massâ'âh (1), *conflagration from the rising of smoke*
4864 mas'êth (1), *raising; beacon; present*
5445 çâbal (1), to *carry*
5448 çôbel (3), *load, burden*
5449 çabbâl (1), *porter, carrier*
6006 'âmaç (1), to *impose* a burden
922 barŏs (3), *load, abundance, authority*
1117 gŏmŏs (1), *cargo, wares or freight*
2599 katabarĕŏ (1), to *be* a burden
5413 phŏrtiŏn (2), *burden, task or service*

BURDENED
916 barĕŏ (1), to *weigh* down, *cause pressure*
2347 thlipsis (1), *pressure, trouble*

BURDENS
92 'ăguddâh (1), *band; bundle; knot; arch*
4853 massâ' (5), *burden, utterance*
4864 mas'êth (2), *raising; beacon; present*
4942 mishpâth (1), *pair of stalls for cattle*
5447 çêbel (1), *load; forced labor*
5449 çabbâl (5), *porter, carrier*
5450 çe bâlâh (6), *porterage; forced labor*
922 barŏs (1), *load, abundance, authority*
5413 phŏrtiŏn (3), *burden, task or service*

BURDENSOME
4614 ma'ămâçâh (1), *burdensomeness*
4 abarēs (1), *not burdensome*
1722+922 ĕn (1), *in; during; because of*
2655 katanarkaŏ (2), to *be a burden*

BURIAL
6900 qe bûwrâh (4), *sepulchre*
1779 ĕntaphiazŏ (1), to *enswathe for burial*

BURIED
6912 qâbar (96), to *inter, pile up*
2290 thaptŏ (7), to *celebrate funeral rites*
4916 sunthaptŏ (2), to *be buried with*

BURIERS
6912 qâbar (1), to *inter, pile up*

BURN
1197 bâ'ar (19), to *be brutish, be senseless*
1754 dûwr (1), *circle; ball; pile*
2734 chârâh (1), to *blaze*
2787 chârar (1), to *melt, burn, dry* up
3344 yâqad (3), to *burn*
3857 lâhaţ (1), to *blaze*
4729 miqtâr (1), *hearth*
5400 nâsaq (1), to *catch* fire
5927 'âlâh (2), to *ascend, be high, mount*
6702 tsûwth (1), to *blaze, set on fire*
6999 qâţar (59), to *turn into fragrance* by fire
8313 sâraph (40), to *be, set on fire*
2370 thumiaŏ (1), to *offer aromatic fumes*
2545 kaiŏ (1), to *set on fire*
2618 katakaiŏ (4), to *consume wholly* by burning
4448 purŏŏ (2), to *be ignited, glow; inflamed*

BURNED
1197 bâ'ar (8), to *be brutish, be senseless*

2787 chârar (7), to *melt, burn, dry* up
3341 yâtsath (9), to *burn* or *set on fire*
3554 kâvâh (2), to *blister, be scorched*
3857 lâhaţ (2), to *blaze*
5375 nâsâ' (2), to *lift up*
6866 tsârab (1), to *burn*
6999 qâţar (19), to *turn into fragrance* by fire
8313 sâraph (33), to *be, set on fire*
8314 sârâph (1), *poisonous serpent*
8316 se rêphâh (1), *cremation*
1572 ĕkkaiŏ (1), to *inflame deeply*
1714 ĕmprēthŏ (1), to *burn, set on fire*
2545 kaiŏ (3), to *set on fire*
2618 katakaiŏ (6), to *consume wholly* by burning
2740 kausis (1), act of burning
4448 purŏŏ (1), to *be ignited, glow; inflamed*

BURNETH
1197 bâ'ar (4), to *be brutish, be senseless*
2142 zâkar (1), to *remember; to mention*
3344 yâqad (1), to *burn*
3857 lâhaţ (2), to *blaze*
4348 mikvâh (1), *burn*
5635 çâraph (1), to *cremate*
6919 qâdach (1), to *inflame*
6999 qâţar (2), to *turn into fragrance* by fire
8313 sâraph (4), to *be, set on fire*
2545 kaiŏ (1), to *set on fire*

BURNING
784 'êsh (3), *fire*
1197 bâ'ar (6), to *be brutish, be senseless*
1513 gechel (1), *ember, hot coal*
1814 dâlaq (1), to *flame; to pursue*
1815 de laq (Ch.) (1), to *flame, burn*
2746 charchûr (1), *hot fever*
3344 yâqad (3), to *burn*
3345 ye qad (Ch.) (10), to *burn*
3346 ye qêdâ' (Ch.) (1), *consuming fire*
3350 ye qôwd (1), *burning, blazing*
3555 ke vîyâh (1), *branding, scar*
3587 kîy (1), *brand or scar*
3940 lappîyd (1), *flaming torch, lamp or flame*
4169 môwq e dâh (1), *fuel*
4348 mikvâh (4), *burn*
6867 tsârebeth (2), *conflagration*
6920 qaddachath (1), *inflammation*

6999 qâţar (1), to *turn into fragrance* by fire
7565 resheph (1), *flame*
8316 se rêphâh (9), *cremation*
2545 kaiŏ (6), to *set on fire*
2742 kausŏn (1), *burning heat, hot day*
4451 purŏsis (2), *ignition; conflagration, calamity*

BURNINGS
4168 môwqêd (1), *conflagration, burning*
4955 misrâphâh (2), *cremation*

BURNISHED
7044 qâlâl (1), *brightened, polished*

BURNT
398 'âkal (1), to *eat*
1197 bâ'ar (6), to *be brutish, be senseless*
3632 kâlîyl (1), *whole, entire; complete; whole*
4198 mâzeh (1), *exhausted, empty*
5927 'âlâh (1), to *ascend, be high, mount*
5928 'ălâh (Ch.) (1), *wholly consumed in fire*
5930 'ôlâh (284), *sacrifice wholly consumed in fire*
6999 qâţar (24), to *turn into fragrance* by fire
8313 sâraph (36), to *be, set on fire*
8316 se rêphâh (2), *cremation*
2618 katakaiŏ (2), to *consume wholly* by burning
3646 hŏlŏkautōma (3), *wholly-consumed*

BURST
1234 bâqa' (1), to *cleave, break, tear open*
5423 nâthaq (4), to *tear off*
6555 pârats (1), to *break out*
2997 laschŏ (1), to *crack open*
4486 rhēgnumi (2), to *break, burst forth*

BURSTING
4386 me kittâh (1), *fracture*

BURY
6912 qâbar (33), to *inter, pile up*
1779 ĕntaphiazŏ (1), to *enswathe for burial*
2290 thaptŏ (4), to *celebrate funeral rites*
5027 taphē (1), *burial*

BURYING
6912 qâbar (2), to *inter, pile up*
1780 ĕntaphiasmŏs (2), *preparation for burial*

BURYINGPLACE
6913 qeber (7), *sepulchre*

BUSH
5572 çe neh (6), *bramble*
942 batŏs (5), *brier*

BUSHEL
3426 mŏdiŏs (3), dry measure of volume

BUSHES
5097 nahălôl (1), pasture
7880 sîyach (2), shrubbery

BUSHY
8534 taltal (1), wavy

BUSINESS
1697 dâbâr (8), word; matter; thing
4399 mᵉlâ'kâh (12), work; property
4639 ma'ăseh (1), action; labor
6045 'inyân (2), employment, labor
2398 idiŏs (1), private or separate
4229 pragma (1), matter, deed, affair
4710 spŏudē (1), despatch; eagerness
5532 chrĕia (1), affair; occasion, demand

BUSY
6213 'âsâh (1), to do or make

BUSYBODIES
4020 pĕriĕrgazŏmai (1), to meddle
4021 pĕriĕrgŏs (1), busybody; magic

BUSYBODY
244 allotriĕpiskŏpŏs (1), meddler, busybody

BUTLER
4945 mashqeh (8), butler; drink; well-watered

BUTLERS
4945 mashqeh (1), butler; drink; well-watered

BUTLERSHIP
4945 mashqeh (1), butler; drink; well-watered

BUTTER
2529 chem'âh (10), curds, milk or cheese
4260 machămâ'âh (1), buttery; flattery

BUTTOCKS
4667 miphsâ'âh (1), crotch area
8357 shêthâh (2), seat i.e. buttock

BUY
3739 kârâh (1), to purchase by bargaining
3947 lâqach (2), to take
7066 qᵉnâ' (Ch.) (1), to purchase
7069 qânâh (24), to create; to procure
7666 shâbar (14), to deal in cereal grain
59 agŏrazō (13), to purchase; to redeem
1710 ĕmpŏrĕuŏmai (1), to trade, do business

BUYER
7069 qânâh (3), to create; to procure

BUYEST
7069 qânâh (2), to create; to procure

BUYETH
3947 lâqach (1), to take
59 agŏrazō (2), to purchase; to redeem

BUZ
938 Bûwz (3), disrespect, scorn

BUZI
941 Bûwzîy (1), Buzi

BUZITE
940 Bûwzîy (2), Buzite

BYWAYS
734+6128 'ôrach (1), well-traveled road

BYWORD
4405 millâh (1), word; discourse; speech
4912 mâshâl (1), pithy maxim; taunt
4914 mᵉshôl (1), satire
8148 shᵉnîynâh (3), gibe, verbal taunt

CAB
6894 qab (1), dry measure of volume

CABBON
3522 Kabbôwn (1), hilly

CABINS
2588 chânûwth (1), vault or cell

CABUL
3521 Kâbûwl (2), sterile

CAESAR
2541 Kaisar (21), Cæsar

CAESAR'S
2541 Kaisar (9), Cæsar

CAESAREA
2542 Kaisarĕia (17), of Cæsar

CAGE
3619 kᵉlûwb (1), bird-trap; basket
5438 phulakē (1), guarding or guard

CAIAPHAS
2533 Kaïaphas (9), dell

CAIN
7014 Qayin (17), lance
2535 Kaïn (3), lance

CAINAN
7018 Qêynân (5), fixed
2536 Kaïnan (2), fixed

CAKE
1690 dᵉbêlâh (1), cake of pressed figs
2471 challâh (7), cake shaped as a ring
4580 mâ'ôwg (1), cake of bread, provision
5692 'uggâh (3), round-cake
6742 tsᵉlûwl (1), round or flattened cake

CAKES
1690 dᵉbêlâh (2), cake of pressed figs
2471 challâh (8), cake shaped as a ring
3561 kavvân (2), sacrificial wafer

3823 lâbab (1), to make cakes
3834 lâbîybâh (3), fried or turned cake
4682 matstsâh (4), unfermented cake
5692 'uggâh (4), round-cake
7550 râqîyq (1), thin cake, wafer

CALAH
3625 Kelach (2), maturity

CALAMITIES
343 'êyd (1), misfortune, ruin, disaster
1942 havvâh (1), desire; craving
7451 ra' (1), bad; evil

CALAMITY
343 'êyd (16), misfortune, ruin, disaster
1942 havvâh (3), desire; craving

CALAMUS
7070 qâneh (3), reed

CALCOL
3633 Kalkôl (1), sustenance

CALDRON
100 'agmôwn (1), rush; rope of rushes
5518 çîyr (3), thorn; hook
7037 qallachath (2), kettle

CALDRONS
1731 dûwd (1), pot, kettle; basket
5518 çîyr (2), thorn; hook

CALEB
3612 Kâlêb (32), forcible

CALEB'S
3612 Kâlêb (4), forcible

CALEB-EPHRATAH
3613 Kâlêb 'Ephrâthâh (1), Caleb-Ephrathah

CALF
1121+1241 bên (2), son, descendant
5695 'êgel (21), calf
3447 mŏschŏpŏiĕō (1), to fabricate a bullock-idol
3448 mŏschŏs (4), young bullock

CALF'S
5695 'êgel (1), calf

CALKERS
2388+919 châzaq (2), to fasten upon; to seize

CALL
559 'âmar (2), to say, speak
833 'âshar (5), to go forward; guide
2142 zâkar (3), to remember; to mention
5493 çûwr (1), to turn off
5749 'ûwd (3), to duplicate or repeat
7121 qârâ' (131), to call out
7725 shûwb (1), to turn back; to return
8085 shâma' (2), to hear intelligently

363 anamimnēskō (1), to remind; to recollect
1941 ĕpikalĕŏmai (9), to invoke
2564 kalĕō (17), to call
2840 kŏinŏō (2), to make profane
2983 lambanō (1), to take, receive
3004 lĕgō (4), to say
3106 makarizō (1), to pronounce fortunate
3333 mĕtakalĕō (2), to summon for, call for
3343 mĕtapĕmpō (2), to summon or invite
3687 ŏnŏmazō (1), to give a name
4341 prŏskalĕŏmai (2), to call toward oneself
4779 sugkalĕō (1), to convoke, call together
5455 phōnĕō (4), to emit a sound

CALLED
559 'âmar (4), to say, speak
935 bôw' (1), to go or come
2199 zâ'aq (3), to call out, announce
6817 tsâ'aq (2), to shriek; to proclaim
7121 qârâ' (380), to call out
7123 qᵉrâ' (Ch.) (1), to call out
7760 sûwm (1), to put, place
8085 shâma' (1), to hear intelligently
154 aitĕō (1), to ask for
363 anamimnēskō (1), to remind; to recollect
1458 ĕgkalĕō (1), to charge, criminate
1528 ĕiskalĕō (1), to invite in
1941 ĕpikalĕŏmai (4), to invoke
1951 ĕpilĕgŏmai (1), to surname, select
2028 ĕpŏnŏmazō (1), to be called, denominate
2036 ĕpō (1), to speak
2046 ĕrĕō (1), to utter
2564 kalĕō (103), to call
2822 klētŏs (11), appointed, invited
2919 krinō (2), to decide; to try, condemn, punish
3004 lĕgō (36), to say
3044 Linŏs (1), (poss.) flax linen
3333 mĕtakalĕō (2), to summon for, call for
3686 ŏnŏma (4), name
3687 ŏnŏmazō (1), to give a name
3739+2076 hŏs (1), who, which, what, that
3870 parakalĕō (1), to call, invite
4316 prŏsagŏrĕuō (1), to designate a name
4341 prŏskalĕŏmai (25), to call toward oneself
4377 prŏsphōnĕō (2), to address, exclaim

4779 sugkalĕō (5), to convoke, call together
4867 sunathrŏizō (1), to convene
5455 phōnĕō (16), to emit a sound
5537 chrēmatizō (2), to utter an oracle
5581 pseŭdōnumŏs (1), untruly named

CALLEDST
6485 pāqad (1), to visit, care for, count
7121 qârâ' (3), to call out

CALLEST
3004 lĕgō (3), to say

CALLETH
7121 qârâ' (13), to call out
2564 kalĕō (6), to call
3004 lĕgō (4), to say
4341 prŏskalĕŏmai (1), to call toward oneself
4779 sugkalĕō (2), to convoke, call together
5455 phōnĕō (4), to emit a sound

CALLING
2142 zākar (1), to remember; to mention
4744 miqrâ' (1), public meeting
7121 qârâ' (3), to call out
363 anamimnēskō (1), to remind; to recollect
1941 ĕpikalĕŏmai (2), to invoke
2564 kalĕō (1), to call
2821 klēsis (10), invitation; station in life
4341 prŏskalĕŏmai (2), to call toward oneself
4377 prŏsphōnĕō (2), to address, exclaim
5455 phōnĕō (1), to emit a sound

CALM
1827 dᵉmâmâh (1), quiet
8367 shâthaq (2), to subside
1055 galēnē (3), tranquillity, calm

CALNEH
3641 Kalneh (2), Calneh or Calno

CALNO
3641 Kalneh (1), Calneh or Calno

CALVARY
2898 kraniŏn (1), skull

CALVE
2342 chûwl (2), to dance, whirl; to writhe in pain

CALVED
3205 yâlad (1), to bear young; to father a child

CALVES
1121 bên (2), son, descendant
1121+1241 bên (1), son, descendant
5695 'êgel (10), bull calf
5697 'eglâh (2), cow calf
6499 par (1), bullock

3448 mŏschŏs (2), young bullock

CALVETH
6403 pâlaṭ (1), to slip out, i.e. escape; to deliver

CAME
857 'âthâh (4), to arrive; go
858 'âthâh (Ch.) (3), to arrive; go
935 bôw' (668), to go or come
1061 bikkûwr (1), first-fruits of the crop
1518 gîyach (1), to issue forth; to burst forth
1691 Diblayim (1), two cakes
1916 hădôm (2), foot-stool
1946 hûwk (Ch.) (1), to go, come
1961 hâyâh (527), to exist, i.e. be or become
1980 hâlak (7), to walk; live a certain way
2015 hâphak (1), to turn about or over
3212 yâlak (6), to walk; to live; to carry
3318 yâtsâ' (106), to go, bring out
3329 yâtsîy' (1), issue forth, i.e. offspring
3381 yârad (42), to descend
3847 lâbash (3), to clothe
3996 mâbôw' (1), entrance; sunset; west
4161 môwtsâ' (1), going forth
4291 mᵉṭâ' (Ch.) (4), to arrive, to extend
4672 mâtsâ' (2), to find or acquire; to occur
5060 nâga' (5), to strike
5066 nâgash (27), to be, come, bring near
5182 nᵉchath (Ch.) (1), to descend; to depose
5312 nᵉphaq (Ch.) (3), to issue forth; to bring out
5437 çâbab (1), to surround
5559 çᵉlîq (Ch.) (5), to ascend, go up
5674 'âbar (4), to cross over; to transition
5927 'âlâh (82), to ascend, be high, mount
5954 'ălal (Ch.) (4), to go in; to lead in
5957 'âlam (Ch.) (1), forever
6293 pâga' (1), to impinge
6473 pâ'ar (1), to open wide
6555 pârats (1), to break out
6743 tsâlach (5), to push forward
7122 qârâ' (1), to encounter, to happen
7126 qârab (20), to approach, bring near
7127 qᵉrêb (Ch.) (5), to approach, bring near
7131 qârêb (1), near

7725 shûwb (16), to turn back; to return
191 akŏuō (1), to hear; obey
305 anabainō (3), to go up, rise
565 apĕrchŏmai (1), to go off, i.e. depart
1096 ginŏmai (88), to be, become
1237 diadĕchŏmai (1), succeed, receive in turn
1448 ĕggizō (3), to approach
1525 ĕisĕrchŏmai (10), to enter
1531 ĕispŏrĕuŏmai (1), to enter
1607 ĕkpŏrĕuŏmai (1), to depart, be discharged
1831 ĕxĕrchŏmai (38), to issue; to leave
1904 ĕpĕrchŏmai (1), to supervene
1910 ĕpibainō (1), to mount, ascend
1994 ĕpistrĕphō (1), to revert, turn back to
1998 ĕpisuntrĕchō (1), to hasten together upon
2064 ĕrchŏmai (199), to go or come
2113 ĕuthudrŏmĕō (1), to sail direct
2186 ĕphistēmi (7), to be present; to approach
2240 hēkō (3), to arrive, i.e. be present
2597 katabainō (16), to descend
2658 katantaō (8), to arrive at; to attain
2718 katĕrchŏmai (6), to go, come down
2944 kuklŏō (1), to surround, encircle
2983 lambanō (1), to take, receive
3415 mnaŏmai (1), to bear in mind
3719 ŏrthrizō (1), to get up early in the morning
3854 paraginŏmai (16), to arrive; to appear
3918 parĕimi (1), to be present; to have come
3922 parĕisĕrchŏmai (1), to supervene
3928 parĕrchŏmai (1), to go by; to perish
4130 plēthō (1), to fulfill, complete
4334 prŏsĕrchŏmai (65), to come near, visit
4370 prŏstrĕchō (1), to hasten by running
4836 sumparaginŏmai (1), to convene
4863 sunagō (6), to gather together
4872 sunanabainō (2), to ascend in company
4905 sunĕrchŏmai (8), to gather together
5342 phĕrō (3), to bear or carry

CAMEL
1581 gâmâl (5), camel
2574 kamēlŏs (4), camel

CAMEL'S
1581 gâmâl (1), camel
2574 kamēlŏs (2), camel

CAMELS
327 'âchastârân (2), mule
1581 gâmâl (44), camel

CAMELS'
1581 gâmâl (3), camel

CAMEST
935 bôw' (8), to go, come
1518 gîyach (1), to issue forth; to burst forth
1980 hâlak (3), to walk; live a certain way
3318 yâtsâ' (7), to go, bring out
3381 yârad (3), to descend
7126 qârab (1), to approach, bring near
7725 shûwb (1), to turn back; to return
1096 ginŏmai (1), to be, become
1525 ĕisĕrchŏmai (1), to enter
1831 ĕxĕrchŏmai (1), to issue; to leave
2064 ĕrchŏmai (1), to go or come

CAMON
7056 Qâmôwn (1), elevation

CAMP
2583 chânâh (3), to encamp
4264 machăneh (127), encampment
8466 tachănâh (1), encampment
3925 parĕmbŏlē (3), encampment

CAMPED
2583 chânâh (1), to encamp

CAMPHIRE
3724 kôpher (2), village; bitumen; henna

CAMPS
4264 machăneh (7), encampment

CAN
3045 yâda' (1), to know
3201 yâkôl (18), to be able
3202 yᵉkêl (Ch.) (2), to be able
1097 ginŏskō (1), to know
1410 dunamai (65), to be able or possible
1492 ĕidō (2), to know
2480 ischuō (1), to have or exercise force

CANA
2580 Kana (4), Cana

CANAAN
3667 Kᵉna'an (90), humiliated
5478 Chanaanaiŏs (1), Kenaanite

CANAANITE
3669 Kᵉna'ănîy (12), Kenaanite; merchant
2581 Kananîtēs (2), zealous

CANAANITES
3669 Kᵉna'ăniy (55), Kenaanite; merchant

CANAANITESS
3669 Kᵉna'ăniy (1), Kenaanite; merchant

CANAANITISH
3669 Kᵉna'ăniy (2), Kenaanite; merchant

CANDACE
2582 Kandakē (1), Candacë

CANDLE
5216 nîyr (8), lamp; lamplight
3088 luchnŏs (8), portable lamp

CANDLES
5216 nîyr (1), lamp; lamplight

CANDLESTICK
4501 mᵉnôwrâh (34), chandelier, lamp-stand
5043 nebrᵉshâ' (Ch.) (1), lamp-stand
3087 luchnia (6), lamp-stand

CANDLESTICKS
4501 mᵉnôwrâh (6), chandelier, lamp-stand
3087 luchnia (6), lamp-stand

CANE
7070 qâneh (2), reed

CANKER
1044 gaggraina (1), ulcer, i.e. gangrene

CANKERED
2728 katiŏŏ (1), to corrode, tarnish

CANKERWORM
3218 yekeq (6), young locust

CANNEH
3656 Kanneh (1), Canneh

CANNOT
369 'ayin (1), there is no, i.e., not exist, none
408 'al (2), not; nothing
518 'îm (1), whether?; if, although; Oh that!
1077 bal (2), nothing; not at all; lest
1097 bᵉlîy (1), without, not yet; lacking;
1115 biltîy (1), not, except, without, unless
3201 yâkôl (3), to be able
3308 yŏphîy (2), beauty
3808 lô' (57), no, not
176 akatagnōstŏs (1), unblamable
180 akatapaustŏs (1), unrefraining, unceasing
215 alalētŏs (1), unspeakable
368 anantirrhētŏs (1), indisputable
551 apĕirastŏs (1), not temptable
761 asalĕutŏs (1), immovable, fixed
893 apsĕudēs (1), veracious, free of deceit
1492 ĕidō (2), to know

CANST
3201 yâkôl (6), to be able
3202 yᵉkêl (Ch.) (2), to be able
1097 ginōskō (1), to know
1410 dunamai (9), to be able or possible
1492 ĕidō (1), to know

CAPERNAUM
2584 Kapĕrnaŏum (16), walled village which is comfortable

CAPHTHORIM
3732 Kaphtôrîy (1), Caphtorite

CAPHTOR
3731 Kaphtôr (3), wreath-shaped island

CAPHTORIM
3732 Kaphtôrîy (1), Caphtorite

CAPHTORIMS
3732 Kaphtôrîy (1), Caphtorite

CAPPADOCIA
2587 Kappadŏkia (2), Cappadocia

CAPTAIN
1167 ba'al (1), master; husband; owner; citizen
2951 ṭiphçar (1), military governor
5057 nâgîyd (5), commander, official
5387 nâsîy' (12), leader; rising mist, fog
5921 'al (1), above, over, upon, or against
6346 pechâh (2), prefect, officer
7101 qâtsîyn (2), magistrate
7218 rô'sh (4), head
7227 rab (23), great
7229 rab (Ch.) (1), great
7990 shallîyṭ (Ch.) (1), premier, sovereign
7991 shâlîysh (2), officer; of the third rank
8269 sar (51), head person, ruler
747 archēgŏs (1), chief leader; founder
4755 stratēgŏs (3), military governor
4759 stratŏpĕdarchēs (1), military commander
5506 chiliarchŏs (18), colonel

CAPTAINS
441 'allûwph (1), friend, one familiar; chieftain
2951 ṭiphçar (1), military governor
3733 kar (1), ram sheep; battering ram
3746 kârîy (2), life-guardsman
5057 nâgîyd (1), commander, official
6346 pechâh (7), prefect, officer

6347 pechâh (Ch.) (4), prefect, officer
7101 qâtsîyn (1), magistrate
7218 rô'sh (6), head
7991 shâlîysh (9), officer; of the third rank
8269 sar (80), head person, ruler
4755 stratēgŏs (2), military governor
5506 chiliarchŏs (4), colonel

CAPTIVE
1473 gôwlâh (4), exile; captive
1540 gâlâh (24), to denude; uncover
1546 gâlûwth (2), captivity; exiles
6808 tsâ'âh (1), to depopulate; imprison
7617 shâbâh (21), to transport into captivity
7628 shᵉbîy (3), exile; booty
162 aichmalōtĕuō (2), to capture
163 aichmalōtizō (1), to make captive
2221 zōgrĕō (1), to capture or ensnare

CAPTIVES
1123+1547 bên (Ch.) (1), son
1473 gôwlâh (3), exile; captive
1540 gâlâh (3), to denude; uncover
1546 gâlûwth (3), captivity; exiles
7617 shâbâh (16), to transport into captivity
7628 shᵉbîy (8), exile; booty
7633 shibyâh (8), exile; captive
164 aichmalōtŏs (1), captive

CAPTIVITY
1473 gôwlâh (28), exile; captive
1540 gâlâh (9), to denude; uncover
1546 gâlûwth (11), captivity; exiles
1547 gâlûwth (Ch.) (3), captivity; exiles
2925 ṭalṭêlâh (1), overthrow or rejection
7622 shᵉbûwth (31), exile; prisoners
7628 shᵉbîy (30), exile; booty
7633 shibyâh (6), exile; captive
161 aichmalōsia (2), captivity
163 aichmalōtizō (2), to make captive

CARBUNCLE
1304 bârᵉqath (3), flashing gem (poss.) emerald

CARBUNCLES
68+688 'eben (1), stone

CARCAS
3752 Karkaç (1), Karkas

CARCASE
1472 gᵉvîyâh (2), dead body
4658 mappeleth (1), down-fall; ruin; carcase
5038 nᵉbêlâh (29), carcase or carrion
6297 peger (1), carcase; corpse
4430 ptōma (1), corpse, carrion

CARCASES
5038 nᵉbêlâh (7), carcase or carrion
6297 peger (13), carcase; corpse
2966 kōlŏn (1), corpse

CARCHEMISH
3751 Karkᵉmîysh (2), Karkemish

CARE
983 beṭach (1), safety, security, trust
1674 dᵉâgâh (1), anxiety
1697 dâbâr (1), word; matter; thing
2731 chărâdâh (1), fear, anxiety
7760+3820 sûwm (2), to put, place
1959 ĕpimĕlĕŏmai (3), to care for
3199 mĕlō (3), it is a care or concern
3308 mĕrimna (3), solicitude; worry
3309 mĕrimnaō (2), to be anxious about
4710 spŏudē (2), despatch; eagerness
5426 phrŏnĕō (1), to be mentally disposed

CAREAH
7143 Qârêach (1), bald

CARED
1875 dârash (1), to pursue or search
3199 mĕlō (2), it is a care or concern

CAREFUL
1672 dâ'ag (1), be anxious, be afraid
2729 chârad (1), to hasten with anxiety
2818 chăshach (Ch.) (1), to need
3309 mĕrimnaō (2), to be anxious about
5426 phrŏnĕō (1), to be mentally disposed
5431 phrŏntizō (1), be anxious; to be careful

CAREFULLY
2470 châlâh (1), to be weak, sick, afflicted
8085 shâma' (1), to hear intelligently
1567 ĕkzētĕō (1), to seek out
4708 spŏudaiŏtĕrŏs (1), more speedily

CAREFULNESS
1674 dᵉâgâh (2), anxiety

275 amĕrimnŏs (1), *not anxious, free of care*
4710 spŏudē (1), *despatch; eagerness*

CARELESS
982 bâṭach (3), *to trust, be confident or sure*
983 beṭach (2), *safety, security, trust*

CARELESSLY
983 beṭach (3), *safety, security, trust*

CARES
3303 mĕn (3), *not translated*

CAREST
3199 mĕlō (3), *it is a care or concern*

CARETH
1875 dârash (1), *to pursue or search*
3199 mĕlō (2), *it is a care or concern*
3309 mĕrimnaō (4), *to be anxious about*

CARMEL
3760 Karmel (26), *planted field; garden*

CARMELITE
3761 Karmᵉlîy (5), *Karmelite*

CARMELITESS
3762 Karmᵉlîyth (2), *Karmelitess*

CARMI
3756 Karmîy (8), *gardener*

CARMITES
3757 Karmîy (1), *Karmite*

CARNAL
4559 sarkikŏs (9), *pertaining to flesh*
4561 sarx (2), *flesh*

CARNALLY
7902+2233 shᵉkâbâh (2), *lying down*
7903+2233 shᵉkôbeth (1), *sexual lying down with*
4561 sarx (1), *flesh*

CARPENTER
2796 chârâsh (1), *skilled fabricator or worker*
2796+6086 chârâsh (1), *skilled fabricator*
5045 tĕktōn (1), *craftsman in wood*

CARPENTER'S
5045 tĕktōn (1), *craftsman in wood*

CARPENTERS
2796 chârâsh (6), *skilled fabricator or worker*
2796+6086 chârâsh (2), *skilled fabricator*
6086 'êts (1), *wood, things made of wood*

CARPUS
2591 Karpŏs (1), (poss.) *fruit*

CARRIAGE
3520 kᵉbûwddâh (1), *magnificence, wealth*

3627 kᵉlîy (2), *implement, thing*

CARRIAGES
3627 kᵉlîy (1), *implement, thing*
5385 nᵉsûw'âh (1), *load, burden*
643 apŏskĕuazō (1), *to pack up baggage*

CARRIED
935 bôw' (10), *to go, come*
1473 gôwlâh (10), *exile; captive*
1540 gâlâh (35), *to denude; uncover*
1541 gᵉlâh (Ch.) (1), *to reveal mysteries*
1546 gâlûwth (3), *captivity; exiles*
1980 hâlak (1), *to walk; live a certain way*
2986 yâbal (3), *to bring*
3212 yâlak (1), *to walk; to live; to carry*
3318 yâtsâ' (3), *to go, bring out*
3947 lâqach (3), *to take*
4116 mâhar (1), *to hurry; promptly*
4131 môwṭ (1), *to slip, shake, fall*
5090 nâhag (3), *to drive; to lead, carry away*
5095 nâhal (1), *to conduct; to protect*
5186 nâṭâh (2), *to stretch or spread out*
5375 nâsâ' (15), *to lift up*
5376 nᵉsâ' (Ch.) (1), *to lift up*
5437 çâbab (3), *to surround*
5445 çâbal (1), *to carry*
5674 'âbar (1), *to cross over; to transition*
5927 'âlâh (3), *to ascend, be high, mount*
7392 râkab (3), *to ride*
7617 shâbâh (18), *transport into captivity*
7725 shûwb (2), *to turn back; to return*
71 agō (1), *to lead; to bring, drive; to weigh*
339 anakathizō (1), *to sit up*
520 apagō (1), *to take away*
667 apŏhĕrō (4), *to bear off, carry away*
941 bastazō (1), *to lift, bear*
1580 ĕkkŏmizō (1), *to bear forth to burial*
1627 ĕkphĕrō (1), *to bear out; to produce*
1643 ĕlaunō (1), *to push*
3346 mĕtatithēmi (1), *to transport; to exchange*
3350 mĕtŏikĕsia (1), *exile, deportation*
4064 pĕriphĕrō (3), *to transport*
4216 pŏtamŏphŏrētŏs (1), *overwhelmed by a stream*
4792 sugkŏmizō (1), *to convey together*

4879 sunapagō (1), *to take off together*

CARRIEST
2229 zâram (1), *to gush water, pour forth*

CARRIETH
1589 gânab (1), *to thieve; to deceive*
5375 nâsâ' (1), *to lift up*
941 bastazō (1), *to lift, bear*

CARRY
935 bôw' (7), *to go or come*
1319 bâsar (1), *to announce* (good news)
1540 gâlâh (5), *to denude; uncover*
1980 hâlak (1), *to walk; live a certain way*
2904 ṭûwl (1), *to cast down or out, hurl*
2986 yâbal (1), *to bring*
2987 yᵉbal (Ch.) (1), *to bring*
3212 yâlak (3), *to walk; to live; to carry*
3318 yâtsâ' (18), *to go, bring out*
3381 yârad (2), *to descend*
3947 lâqach (2), *to take*
4853 massâ' (1), *burden, utterance*
5182 nᵉchath (Ch.) (1), *to descend; to depose*
5375 nâsâ' (18), *to lift up*
5445 çâbal (3), *to carry*
5674 'âbar (2), *to cross over; to transition*
5927 'âlâh (3), *to ascend, be high, mount*
6403 pâlaṭ (1), *to slip out, i.e. escape; to deliver*
7400 râkîyl (1), *scandal-monger*
7617 shâbâh (5), *to transport into captivity*
7725 shûwb (4), *to turn back; to return*
142 airō (1), *to lift, to take up*
941 bastazō (1), *to lift, bear*
1308 diaphĕrō (1), *to bear, carry; to differ*
1627 ĕkphĕrō (2), *to bear out; to produce*
3351 mĕtŏikizō (1), *to transfer as a captive*
4046 pĕripŏiĕŏmai (1), *to acquire; to gain*
5342 phĕrō (1), *to bear or carry*

CARRYING
1540 gâlâh (1), *to denude; uncover*
5375 nâsâ' (3), *to lift up*
7411 râmâh (1), *to hurl; to shoot; to delude*
1627 ĕkphĕrō (1), *to bear out; to produce*
3350 mĕtŏikĕsia (2), *exile, deportation*

CARSHENA
3771 Karshᵉnâ' (1), *Karshena*

CART
5699 'ăgâlâh (15), *wheeled vehicle*

CARVED
2405 châṭûbâh (1), *tapestry*
2707 châqah (1), *to carve; to delineate*
4734 miqla'ath (1), *bas-relief sculpture*
6456 pᵉçîyl (3), *idol*
6459 peçel (2), *idol*
6603 pittûwach (2), *sculpture; engraving*
7049 qâla' (3), *to sling a stone; to carve*

CARVING
2799 chărôsheth (2), *skilled work*

CARVINGS
4734 miqla'ath (1), *bas-relief sculpture*

CASE
1697 dâbâr (1), *word; matter; thing*
3602 kâkâh (1), *just so*
7725 shûwb (2), *to turn back; to return*
156 aitia (1), *logical reason; legal crime*
3364 ŏu mē (1), *not at all, absolutely not*

CASEMENT
822 'eshnâb (1), *latticed window*

CASIPHIA
3703 Kâçiphyâ' (2), *silvery*

CASLUHIM
3695 Kaçlûchîym (2), *Casluchim*

CASSIA
6916 qiddâh (2), *cassia*
7102 qᵉtsîy'âh (1), *cassia*

CAST
1299 bâraq (1), *to flash lightning*
1457 gâhar (1), *to prostrate oneself*
1602 gâ'al (1), *to detest; to reject; to fail*
1644 gârash (9), *to drive out; to expatriate*
1740 dûwach (1), *to rinse clean, wash*
1760 dâchâh (1), *to push down; to totter*
1920 hâdaph (2), *to push away or down; drive out*
1972 hâlâ' (1), *to remove or be remote*
2186 zânach (17), *to reject, forsake, fail*
2219 zârâh (1), *to toss about; to diffuse*
2490 châlal (1), *to profane, defile*
2904 ṭûwl (12), *to cast down or out, hurl*
3032 yâdad (3), *to throw lots*
3034 yâdâh (2), *to throw; to revere or worship*
3240 yânach (1), *to allow to stay*

834 'ăsher (1), *because,
in order that*
1697 dâbâr (6), *word;
matter; thing*
1700 dibrâh (1), *because,
on account of*
1779 dîyn (7), *judge;
judgment; law suit*
1961 hâyâh (1), *to exist,
i.e. be or become*
2600 chinnâm (15),
gratis, free
3651 kên (1), *just; right,
correct*
4616 ma'an (1), *on
account of*
4941 mishpâṭ (12),
verdict; formal decree
5252 nᵉçibbâh (1), *turn of
affairs*
5414 nâthan (5), *to give*
5438 çibbâh (1), *turn of
affairs*
5668 'âbûwr (1), *on
account of*
7379 rîyb (23), *contest,
personal or legal*
7387 rêyqâm (2), *emptily;
ineffectually*
7945 shel (1), *on account
of; whatsoever*
8267 sheqer (1), *untruth;
sham*
156 aitia (9), *logical
reason; legal crime*
158 aitiōn (2), *reason,
basis; crime*
846 autŏs (1), *he, she, it*
873 aphŏrizō (1), *to limit,
exclude, appoint*
1223 dia (13), *because of,
for the sake of*
1352 diŏ (2),
consequently, therefore
1432 dōrĕan (1),
gratuitously, freely
1500 ĕikē (1), *idly, i.e.
without reason or effect*
1752 hĕnĕka (4), *on
account of*
2289 thanatŏō (3), *to kill*
3056 lŏgŏs (1), *word,
matter, thing*
4160 pŏiĕō (3), *to do*
5484 charin (3), *on
account of, because of*

CAUSED
1961 hâyâh (1), *to exist,
i.e. be or become*
5414 nâthan (7), *to give*
3076 lupĕō (1), *to
distress; to be sad*
4160 pŏiĕō (2), *to do*

CAUSELESS
2600 chinnâm (2), *gratis,
free*

CAUSES
182 'ôwdôwth (1), *on
account of; because*
1697 dâbâr (2), *word;
matter; thing*
7379 rîyb (1), *contest,
personal or legal*
1752 hĕnĕka (1), *on
account of*

CAUSETH
5414 nâthan (1), *to give*

2358 thriambĕuō (1), *to
lead in triumphal
procession*
2716 katĕrgazŏmai (1),
to finish; to accomplish
4160 pŏiĕō (3), *to do*

CAUSEWAY
4546 mᵉçillâh (2), *main
thoroughfare; viaduct*

CAVE
4631 mᵉ'ârâh (32), *dark
cavern*
4693 spēlaiŏn (1),
cavern; hiding-place

CAVE'S
4631 mᵉ'ârâh (1), *dark
cavern*

CAVES
2356 chôwr (1), *cavity,
socket, den*
4247 mᵉchillâh (1),
cavern, hole
4631 mᵉ'ârâh (3), *dark
cavern*
3692 ŏpē (1), *hole, i.e.
cavern; spring of water*

CEASE
988 bâṭêl (1), *to desist
from labor, cease*
989 bᵉṭêl (Ch.) (3), *to stop*
1820 dâmâh (1), *to be
silent; to fail, cease*
1826 dâmam (1), *to stop,
cease; to perish*
2308 châdal (12), *to
desist, stop; be fat*
2790 chârash (1), *to be
silent; to be deaf*
3254 yâçaph (1), *to add
or augment*
3615 kâlâh (1), *to
complete, consume*
4185 mûwsh (1), *to
withdraw*
6565 pârar (1), *to break
up; to violate, frustrate*
7503 râphâh (1), *to
slacken*
7647 sâbâ' (1),
copiousness
7673 shâbath (37), *to
repose; to desist*
7725 shûwb (1), *to turn
back; to return*
7918 shâkak (1), *to lay a
trap; to allay*
8552 tâmam (1), *to
complete, finish*
180 akatapaustŏs (1),
unrefraining, unceasing
3973 pauō (4), *to stop,
i.e. restrain, quit*

CEASED
989 bᵉṭêl (Ch.) (1), *to stop*
1826 dâmam (1), *to stop,
cease; to perish*
1934+989 hăvâ' (Ch.) (1),
to be, to exist
2308 châdal (6), *to desist,
stop; be fat*
5117 nûwach (1), *to rest;
to settle down*
5307 nâphal (1), *to fall*
5975 'âmad (1), *to stand*
6313 pûwg (1), *to be
sluggish; be numb*

7673 shâbath (6), *to
repose; to desist*
1257 dialĕipō (1), *to
intermit, stop*
2270 hēsuchazō (1), *to
refrain*
2664 katapauō (1), *to
cause to desist*
2673 katargĕō (1), *to be,
render entirely useless*
2869 kŏpazō (3), *to tire,
i.e. to relax*
3973 pauō (7), *to stop,
i.e. restrain, quit*

CEASETH
1584 gâmar (1), *to end;
to complete; to fail*
1820 dâmâh (1), *to be
silent; to fail, cease*
2308 châdal (1), *to desist,
stop; be fat*
3615 kâlâh (1), *to cease,
be finished, perish*
7673 shâbath (4), *to
repose; to desist*
8367 shâthaq (1), *to
subside*
3973 pauō (1), *to stop,
i.e. restrain, quit*

CEASING
2308 châdal (1), *to desist,
stop; be fat*
83 adēlŏtēs (1),
uncertainty
89 adialĕiptōs (4),
without omission
1618 ĕktĕnēs (1), *intent,
earnest*

CEDAR
729 'âraz (1), *of cedar*
730 'erez (49), *cedar tree*
731 'arzâh (1), *cedar
paneling*

CEDARS
730 'erez (24), *cedar tree*

CEDRON
2748 Kĕdrōn (1), *dusky
place*

CELEBRATE
1984 hâlal (1), *to speak
words of thankfulness*
2278 chăbereth (1),
consort, companion
7673 shâbath (1), *to
repose*

CELESTIAL
2032 ĕpŏuraniŏs (2),
above the sky, celestial

CELLARS
214 'ôwtsâr (2),
depository

CENCHREA
2747 Kĕgchrĕai (2), *millet*

CENSER
4289 machtâh (7), *pan
for live coals*
4730 miqtereth (1),
incense coal-pan
2369 thumiastēriŏn (1),
altar of incense
3031 libanōtŏs (2),
censer for incense

CENSERS
4289 machtâh (8), *pan
for live coals*

CENTURION
1543 hĕkatŏntarchēs
(17), *captain of a
hundred*
2760 kĕnturiōn (3),
captain of a hundred

CENTURION'S
1543 hĕkatŏntarchēs (1),
captain of a hundred

CENTURIONS
1543 hĕkatŏntarchēs (3),
captain of a hundred

CEPHAS
2786 Kēphas (6), *rock*

CEREMONIES
4941 mishpâṭ (1), *verdict;
formal decree; justice*

CERTAIN
259 'echâd (9), *first*
376 'îysh (4), *man; male;
someone*
582 'ĕnôwsh (8), *man;
person, human*
592 'ănîyâh (2), *groaning*
1400 gᵉbar (Ch.) (2),
person; someone
1697 dâbâr (2), *word;
matter; thing*
3045 yâda' (3), *to know*
3330 yatstsîyb (Ch.) (1),
fixed, sure
3559 kûwn (2), *to render
sure, proper*
6256 'êth (1), *time*
6422 palmôwnîy (1), *a
certain one*
444 anthrōpŏs (2),
human being; mankind
444+5100 anthrōpŏs (1),
human being; mankind
790 astatĕō (1),
homeless, vagabond
804 asphalēs (1), *secure;
certain*
1212 dēlŏs (1), *clear,
plain, evident*
1520 hĕis (5), *one*
4225 pŏu (2), *somewhere,
i.e. nearly*
5100 tis (112), *some or
any person or object*

CERTAINLY
389 'ak (1), *surely; only;
however*
403 'âkên (1), *surely!,
truly!; but*
3588 kîy (1), *for, that
because*
3689 ŏntōs (1), *really,
certainly*

CERTAINTY
3330 yatstsîyb (Ch.) (1),
fixed, sure
3559 kûwn (1), *to render
sure, proper*
7189 qôsheṭ (1), *reality*
803 asphalĕia (1),
security; certainty
804 asphalēs (2), *secure;
certain*

CERTIFIED
559 'âmar (1), *to say*
3064 Yᵉhûwdîy (1),
Jehudite

C

CERTIFY
3046 yᵉda' (Ch.) (3), to
know
5046 nâgad (1), to
announce
1107 gnôrizō (1), to
make known, reveal

CHAFED
4751 mar (1), *bitter;*
bitterness; bitterly

CHAFF
2842 châshash (2), *dry*
grass, chaff
4671 môts (8), *chaff*
5784 'ûwr (Ch.) (1), *chaff*
8401 teben (1), *threshed*
stalks of cereal grain
892 achurŏn (2), *chaff* of
grain

CHAIN
2002 hamnîyk (Ch.) (3),
necklace
5178 nᵉchôsheth (1),
copper; bronze
6059 'ânaq (1), to *collar;*
to *fit out*
6060 'ânâq (1), *necklace*
chain
7242 râbîyd (2), *collar*
spread around the neck
7659 shib'âthayim (1),
seven-fold
8333 sharshᵉrâh (1),
chain
254 halusis (3), *fetter* or
manacle

CHAINS
246 'ăziqqîym (2),
manacles, chains
685 'ets'âdâh (1), *bracelet*
2131 zîyqâh (3), *burning*
arrow; bond, fetter
2397 châch (2), *ring* for
the nose or lips
2737 chârûwz (1), strung
beads
3574 kôwshârâh (1),
prosperity
5178 nᵉchôsheth (2),
copper; bronze
5188 nᵉṭîyphâh (1),
pendant for the ears
5688 'ăbôth (3), *entwined*
things: string, wreath
6060 'ânâq (2), *necklace*
chain
7569 rattôwq (2), *chain*
8333 sharshᵉrâh (6),
chain
8337 shêsh (1), *six; sixth*
254 halusis (7), *fetter* or
manacle
1199 dĕsmŏn (1),
shackle; impediment
4577 sĕira (1), *chain*, as
binding or *drawing*

CHALCEDONY
5472 chalkēdōn (1),
copper-like, chalcedony

CHALCOL
3633 Kalkôl (1),
sustenance

CHALDAEANS
5466 Chaldaiŏs (1),
native or *the region of*
the lower Euphrates

CHALDEA
3778 Kasdîy (7),
astrologer

CHALDEAN
3777 Kesed (2), *Kesed*

CHALDEANS
3778 Kasdîy (48),
astrologer
3779 Kasday (Ch.) (17),
magian or *astrologer*

CHALDEANS'
3778 Kasdîy (1),
astrologer

CHALDEES
3778 Kasdîy (13),
astrologer

CHALDEES'
3778 Kasdîy (1),
astrologer

CHALKSTONES
68+1615 'eben (1), *stone*

CHALLENGETH
559 'âmar (1), to *say*

CHAMBER
2315 cheder (15),
apartment, chamber
2646 chuppâh (1), *canopy*
3326 yâtsûwa' (1), *bed;*
wing or *lean-to*
3957 lishkâh (14), *room*
5393 nishkâh (2), *room,*
cell
5944 'ălîyâh (6),
second-story room
5952 'allîyth (Ch.) (1),
second-story room
6763 tsêlâ' (3), *side* of a
person or thing
8372 tâ' (4), *room*
5253 hupĕrŏ₁ŏn (3), *third*
story apartment

CHAMBERING
2845 kŏitē (1), *couch;*
conception

CHAMBERLAIN
5631 çârîyç (4), *eunuch;*
official of state
1909+3588+2846 ĕpi (1),
on, upon
3623 ŏikŏnŏmŏs (1),
overseer, manager

CHAMBERLAINS
5631 çârîyç (9), *eunuch;*
official of state

CHAMBERS
2315 cheder (8),
apartment, chamber
3326 yâtsûwa' (2), *bed;*
wing or *lean-to* of a
building
3957 lishkâh (31), *room*
in a building
5393 nishkâh (1), *room,*
cell
5944 'ălîyâh (6), *upper*
things; *second-story*
room
6763 tsêlâ' (8), *side* of a
person or thing
8372 tâ' (9), *room*
5009 tamĕiŏn (1), *room*

CHAMELEON
3581 kôach (1), large
lizard

CHAMOIS
2169 zemer (1), *gazelle*

CHAMPAIGN
6160 'ărâbâh (1), *desert,*
wasteland

CHAMPION
376+1143 'îysh (2), *man;*
male; someone
1368 gibbôwr (1),
powerful; great *warrior*

CHANAAN
5477 Chanaan (2),
humiliated

CHANCE
4745 miqreh (1),
accident or *fortune*
6294 pega' (1), casual
impact
7122 qârâ' (2), to
encounter, to *happen*
4795 sugkuria (1),
chance occurrence
5177 tugchanŏ (1), to
happen; perhaps

CHANCELLOR
1169+2942 bᵉ'êl (Ch.) (3),
master

CHANCETH
4745 miqreh (1),
accident or *fortune*

CHANGE
2015 hâphak (1), to
change, overturn
2487 chălîyphâh (4),
alternation, change
2498 châlaph (4), to
pierce; to *change*
4171 mûwr (5), to *alter;*
to *barter*, to *dispose of*
4254 machălâtsâh (1),
mantle, garment
7760 sûwm (1), to *put,*
place
8133 shᵉnâ' (Ch.) (1), to
alter, change
8138 shânâh (3), to *fold,*
i.e. *duplicate;* to
transmute
8545 tᵉmûwrâh (1),
barter, compensation
236 allassō (2), to *make*
different, change
3331 mĕtathĕsis (1),
transferral,
disestablishment
3337 mĕtallassō (1), to
exchange
3345 mĕtaschĕmatizō
(1), to *transfigure* or
disguise; to *apply*

CHANGEABLE
4254 machălâtsâh (1),
mantle, garment

CHANGED
2015 hâphak (2), to
change, overturn
2498 châlaph (6), to *pass*
on; to *change*
2664 châphas (1), to
seek; to *mask*
4171 mûwr (6), to *alter;*
to *barter*, to *dispose of*
5437 çâbab (2), to
surround
8132 shânâ' (3), to *alter,*
change

CHANGERS
2773 kᵉrmatistēs (1),
money-broker

CHANGERS'
2855 kŏllubistēs (1),
coin-dealer

CHANGES
2487 chălîyphâh (7),
alternation, change

CHANGEST
8138 shânâh (1), to *fold,*
to *transmute*

CHANGETH
4171 mûwr (1), to *alter;*
to *barter*, to *dispose of*
8133 shᵉnâ' (Ch.) (1), to
alter, change

CHANGING
8545 tᵉmûwrâh (1),
barter, compensation

CHANNEL
7641 shibbôl (1), *stream;*
ear of grain

CHANNELS
650 'âphîyq (3), *valley;*
stream; mighty, strong

CHANT
6527 pâraṭ (1), to *scatter*
words, i.e. *prate*

CHAPEL
4720 miqdâsh (1),
sanctuary of deity

CHAPITER
3805 kôthereth (12),
capital of a column
6858 tsepheth (1),
capital of a column

CHAPITERS
3805 kôthereth (12),
capital of a column
7218 rô'sh (4), *head*

CHAPMEN
582+8846 'ĕnôwsh (1),
man; person, human

CHAPT
2865 châthath (1), to
break down

CHARASHIM
2798 Chărâshîym (1),
skilled worker

CHARCHEMISH
3751 Karkᵉmîysh (1),
Karkemish

CHARGE
3027 yâd (1), *hand; power*
4931 mishmereth (46),
watch, sentry, post

4941 mishpâṭ (1), *verdict;* formal *decree; justice*
5414 nâthan (1), *to give*
5447 çêbel (1), *load; forced labor*
5749 'ûwd (1), *to protest, testify*
5921 'al (3), *above, over, upon, or against*
6213 'âsâh (1), *to do or make*
6485 pâqad (1), *to visit, care for, count*
6486 pᵉquddâh (2), *visitation; punishment*
6496 pâqîyd (1), *superintendent, officer*
6680 tsâvâh (16), *to constitute, enjoin*
7130 qereb (1), *nearest part, i.e. the center*
7592 shâ'al (1), *to ask*
7650 shâba' (7), *to swear*
77 adapanŏs (1), *free of charge*
1263 diamarturŏmai (2), *to attest or protest*
1458+2596 ĕgkalĕŏ (1), *to charge, criminate*
1462 ĕgklēma (1), *accusation*
1781 ĕntĕllŏmai (2), *to enjoin, give orders*
1909 ĕpi (1), *on, upon*
2004 ĕpitassŏ (1), *to order, command*
2476 histēmi (1), *to stand, establish*
3049 lŏgizŏmai (1), *to take an inventory*
3726 hŏrkizŏ (1), *to solemnly enjoin*
3852 paraggĕlia (2), *mandate, order*
3853 paraggĕllŏ (4), *to enjoin; to instruct*

CHARGEABLE
3513 kâbad (2), *to be rich, glorious*
1912 ĕpibarĕŏ (2), *to be severe toward*
2655 katanarkaŏ (1), *to be a burden*

CHARGED
559 'âmar (1), *to say*
5414 nâthan (1), *to give*
5674+5921 'âbar (1), *to cross over; to transition*
6485 pâqad (3), *to visit, care for, count*
6680 tsâvâh (23), *to constitute, enjoin*
7650 shâba' (2), *to swear*
7760 sûwm (1), *to put, place*
916 barĕŏ (1), *to weigh down, cause pressure*
1291 diastĕllŏmai (6), *to distinguish*
1690 ĕmbrimaŏmai (2), *to blame, warn sternly*
1781 ĕntĕllŏmai (1), *to enjoin, give orders*
2008 ĕpitimaŏ (5), *to rebuke, warn, forbid*
3146 mastigŏŏ (1), *to punish by flogging*
3853 paraggĕllŏ (3), *to enjoin; to instruct*

CHARGEDST
5749 'ûwd (1), *to protest, testify; to encompass*

CHARGER
7086 qeʿârâh (13), *bowl*
4094 pinax (4), *plate, platter, dish*

CHARGERS
105 'ăgarṭâl (2), *basin*
7086 qeʿârâh (1), *bowl*

CHARGES
4931 mishmereth (4), *watch, sentry, post*
1159 dapanaŏ (1), *to incur cost; to waste*
3800 ŏpsŏniŏn (1), *rations, stipend or pay*

CHARGEST
6485 pâqad (1), *to visit, care for, count*

CHARGING
1263 diamarturŏmai (1), *to attest or protest*
3853 paraggĕllŏ (1), *to enjoin; to instruct*

CHARIOT
668 'appiryŏwn (1), *palanquin, carriage*
4818 merkâbâh (23), *chariot*
5699 'ăgâlâh (1), *wheeled vehicle*
7393 rekeb (28), *vehicle for riding*
7395 rakkâb (2), *charioteer*
7398 rᵉkûwb (1), *vehicle ridden on*
716 harma (3), *chariot, carriage*

CHARIOTS
2021 hôtsen (1), *weapon*
4817 merkâb (1), *chariot; seat in chariot*
4818 merkâbâh (20), *chariot*
7393 rekeb (87), *vehicle for riding*
7396 rikbâh (1), *chariot*
716 harma (1), *chariot, carriage*
4480 rhêda (1), *wagon for riding*

CHARITABLY
2596+26 kata (1), *down; according to*

CHARITY
26 agapē (28), *love; love-feast*

CHARMED
3908 lachash (1), *incantation; amulet*

CHARMER
2266+2267 châbar (1), *to fascinate by spells*

CHARMERS
328 'aṭ (1), *gently, softly*
3907 lâchash (1), *to whisper a magic spell*

CHARMING
2266+2267 châbar (1), *to fascinate by spells*

CHARRAN
5488 Charrhan (2), *parched*

CHASE
1760 dâchâh (1), *to push down; to totter*
7291 râdaph (5), *to run after with hostility*

CHASED
1272 bârach (1), *to flee suddenly*
5074 nâdad (2), *to rove, flee; to drive away*
5080 nâdach (1), *to push off, scattered*
6679 tsûwd (1), *to lie in wait; to catch*
7291 râdaph (8), *to run after with hostility*

CHASETH
1272 bârach (1), *to flee suddenly*

CHASING
1814 dâlaq (1), *to flame; to pursue*

CHASTE
53 hagnŏs (3), *innocent, modest, perfect, pure*

CHASTEN
3198 yâkach (1), *to decide, justify, convict*
3256 yâçar (3), *to chastise; to instruct*
6031 'ânâh (1), *to afflict, be afflicted*
3811 paidĕuŏ (1), *to educate or discipline*

CHASTENED
3198 yâkach (1), *to decide, justify, convict*
3256 yâçar (2), *to chastise; to instruct*
8433 tôwkêchâh (1), *chastisement*
3811 paidĕuŏ (3), *to educate or discipline*

CHASTENEST
3256 yâçar (1), *to chastise; to instruct*

CHASTENETH
3256 yâçar (2), *to chastise; to instruct*
4148 mûwçâr (1), *reproof, warning*
3811 paidĕuŏ (2), *to educate or discipline*

CHASTENING
4148 mûwçâr (3), *reproof, warning*
3809 paidĕia (3), *disciplinary correction*

CHASTISE
3256 yâçar (6), *to chastise; to instruct*
3811 paidĕuŏ (2), *to educate or discipline*

CHASTISED
3256 yâçar (5), *to chastise; to instruct*

CHASTISEMENT
4148 mûwçâr (3), *reproof, warning*
3809 paidĕia (1), *disciplinary correction*

CHASTISETH
3256 yâçar (1), *to chastise; to instruct*

CHATTER
6850 tsâphaph (1), *to coo or chirp as a bird*

CHEBAR
3529 Kᵉbâr (8), *length*

CHECK
4148 mûwçâr (1), *reproof, warning*

CHECKER
7639 sᵉbâkâh (1), *net-work balustrade*

CHEDORLAOMER
3540 Kᵉdorlâ'ômer (5), *Kedorlaomer*

CHEEK
3895 lᵉchîy (6), *jaw; area of the jaw*
4973 mᵉthallᵉ'âh (1), *tooth*
4600 siagŏn (2), *cheek*

CHEEKS
3895 lᵉchîy (5), *jaw; area of the jaw*

CHEER
3190 yâṭab (1), *to be, make well*
8055 sâmach (1), *to be, make gleesome*
2114 ĕuthumĕŏ (3), *to be cheerful*
2293 tharsĕŏ (5), *to have courage; take heart!*

CHEERETH
8055 sâmach (1), *to be, make gleesome*

CHEERFUL
2896 tôwb (1), *good; well*
3190 yâṭab (1), *to be, make well*
5107 nûwb (1), *to (make) flourish; to utter*
2431 hilarŏs (1), *prompt or willing*

CHEERFULLY
2115 ĕuthumŏs (1), *cheerful, encouraged*

CHEERFULNESS
2432 hilarŏtēs (1), *cheerful readiness*

CHEESE
1385 gᵉbînah (1), *curdled milk*
8194 shâphâh (1), *cheese*

CHEESES
2757+2461 chârîyts (1), *slice, portion*

CHELAL
3636 Kᵉlâl (1), *complete*

CHELLUH
3622 Kᵉlûwhay (1), *completed*

CHELUB
3620 Kᵉlûwb (2), *bird-trap; basket*

CHELUBAI
3621 Kᵉlûwbay (1), *forcible*

CHEMARIMS
3649 kâmâr (1), *pagan priest*

CHEMOSH
3645 Kᵉmôwsh (8), powerful

CHENAANAH
3668 Kᵉna'ănâh (5), humiliated

CHENANI
3662 Kᵉnânîy (1), planted

CHENANIAH
3663 Kᵉnanyâh (3), Jehovah has planted

CHEPHAR-HAAMMONAI
3726 Kᵉphar hâ-'Ammôwnîy (1), village of the Ammonite

CHEPHIRAH
3716 Kᵉphîyrâh (4), village

CHERAN
3763 Kᵉrân (2), Keran

CHERETHIMS
3774 Kᵉrêthîy (1), executioner

CHERETHITES
3746 kârîy (1), life-guardsman
3774 Kᵉrêthîy (8), executioner

CHERISH
5532 çâkan (1), to be familiar with

CHERISHED
5532 çâkan (1), to be familiar with

CHERISHETH
2282 thalpô (2), to foster, care for

CHERITH
3747 Kᵉrîyth (2), cut

CHERUB
3742 kᵉrûwb (26), cherub
3743 Kᵉrûwb (2), cherub

CHERUBIM
3742 kᵉrûwb (2), cherub

CHERUBIMS
3742 kᵉrûwb (61), cherub
5502 chĕrŏubim (1), cherubs or kerubim

CHERUBIMS'
3742 kᵉrûwb (1), cherub

CHESALON
3693 Kᵉçâlôwn (1), fertile

CHESED
3777 Kesed (1), Kesed

CHESIL
3686 Kᵉçîyl (1), stupid or silly

CHESNUT
6196 'armôwn (2), plane tree

CHEST
727 'ârôwn (6), box

CHESTS
1595 genez (1), treasury coffer

CHESULLOTH
3694 Kᵉçullôwth (1), fattened

CHEW
5927 'âlâh (3), to ascend, be high, mount

CHEWED
3772 kârath (1), to cut (off, down or asunder)

CHEWETH
1641 gârar (1), to chew
5927 'âlâh (6), to ascend, be high, mount

CHEZIB
3580 Kᵉzîyb (1), falsified

CHICKENS
3556 nŏssiŏn (1), birdling, chick-bird

CHIDE
7378 rîyb (4), to hold a controversy; to defend

CHIDING
7379 rîyb (1), contest, personal or legal

CHIDON
3592 Kîydôwn (1), dart, javelin

CHIEF
1 'âb (3), father
441 'allûwph (1), friend, chieftain, leader
678 'âtsîyl (1), extremity; noble
1167 ba'al (1), master; husband; owner; citizen
1368 gibbôwr (1), powerful; great warrior
3548 kôhên (2), one officiating as a priest
5051 nôgahh (1), brilliancy
5057 nâgîyd (1), commander, official
5059 nâgan (1), to play; to make music
5329 nâtsach (55), i.e. to be eminent
5387 nâsîy' (8), leader; rising mist, fog
6260 'attûwd (1), he-goats; leaders of the people
6438 pinnâh (2), pinnacle; chieftain
7217 rê'sh (Ch.) (1), head
7218 rô'sh (97), head
7223 rî'shôwn (3), first
7225 rê'shîyth (5), first
7229 rab (Ch.) (1), great
7725 shûwb (3), to turn back; to return
8269 sar (33), head person, ruler
204 akrŏgōniaiŏs (2), corner, cornerstone
749 archiĕrĕus (65), high-priest, chief priest
750 archipŏimĕn (1), head shepherd
752 archisunagōgŏs (2), director of the synagogue services
754 architĕlōnēs (1), chief tax-gatherer
758 archōn (3), first in rank or power
775 Asiarchēs (1), ruler in Asia
2233 hēgĕŏmai (3), to lead, i.e. command
4410 prōtŏkathĕdria (2), place of pre-eminence

4411 prōtŏklisia (2), pre-eminence at meals
4413 prōtŏs (10), foremost
5506 chiliarchŏs (19), colonel

CHIEFEST
47 'abbîyr (1), mighty
1713 dâgal (1), to be conspicuous
4608 ma'ăleh (1), elevation; platform
7218 rô'sh (1), head
7225 rê'shîyth (1), first
3390 mētrŏpŏlis (1), main city
4413 prōtŏs (1), foremost
5228+3029 hupĕr (2), over; above; beyond

CHIEFLY
3122 malista (2), in the greatest degree
4412 prōtŏn (1), firstly

CHILD
1121 bên (10), son, descendant
2029 hârâh (2), to conceive, be pregnant
2030 hâreh (12), pregnant
2056 vâlâd (1), boy
2233 zera' (2), seed; fruit
3173 yâchîyd (1), only son; alone; beloved
3205 yâlad (5), to bear young; to father a child
3206 yeled (39), young male
4392 mâlê' (1), full; filling; fulness; fully
5288 na'ar (44), male child; servant
5290 nô'ar (1), boyhood
5768 'ôwlêl (1), suckling child
1025 brĕphŏs (1), infant
1471 ĕgkuŏs (1), pregnant
1722+1064+2192 ĕn (7), in; during; because of
3439 mŏnŏgĕnēs (1), sole, one and only
3516 nēpiŏs (4), infant; simple-minded person
3812 paidiŏthēn (1), from infancy
3813 paidiŏn (28), child: immature
3816 pais (5), child; slave or servant
5043 tĕknŏn (5), child
5088 tiktō (1), to produce from seed
5207 huiŏs (3), son

CHILD'S
3206 yeled (2), young male
5290 nô'ar (1), boyhood
3813 paidiŏn (1), child: immature

CHILDBEARING
5042 tĕknŏgŏnia (1), maternity, childbearing

CHILDHOOD
3208 yaldûwth (1), boyhood or girlhood
5271 nâ'ûwr (1), youth; juvenility; young people

CHILDISH
3516 nēpiŏs (1), infant; simple-minded person

CHILDLESS
6185 'ărîyrîy (4), barren of child
7921 shâkôl (2), to miscarry
815 atĕknŏs (1), childless

CHILDREN
1121 bên (1523), son, descendant
1123 bên (Ch.) (4), son
1129 bânâh (2), to build; to establish
2945 taph (12), family of children and women
3205 yâlad (1), to bear young; to father a child
3206 yeled (31), young male
3211 yâlîyd (4), born; descendants
5288 na'ar (7), male child; servant
5768 'ôwlêl (12), suckling child
6768 Tseleq (1), fissure
815 atĕknŏs (2), childless
1025 brĕphŏs (1), infant
3515 nēpiazō (1), to act as a baby
3516 nēpiŏs (2), infant; simple-minded person
3808 paidariŏn (1), little boy
3813 paidiŏn (17), child: immature
3816 pais (2), child; slave or servant
5027 taphē (2), act of burial
5040 tĕkniŏn (9), infant; i.e. a darling
5041 tĕknŏgŏnĕō (1), to be a child bearer
5043 tĕknŏn (70), child
5044 tĕknŏtrŏphĕō (1), to be a child-rearer
5206 huiŏthĕsia (1), adoption
5207 huiŏs (44), son
5388 philŏtĕknŏs (1), loving one's child(ren)

CHILDREN'S
1121 bên (16), son, descendant
3813 paidiŏn (1), child: immature Christian
5043 tĕknŏn (2), child

CHILEAB
3609 Kil'âb (1), restraint of (his) father

CHILION
3630 Kilyôwn (2), pining, destruction

CHILION'S
3630 Kilyôwn (1), pining, destruction

CHILMAD
3638 Kilmâd (1), Kilmad

CHIMHAM
3643 Kimhâm (4), pining

CHIMNEY
699 'ărubbâh (1), window; chimney

CHINNERETH
3672 Kinnᵉrôwth (4),
(poss.) harp-shaped

CHINNEROTH
3672 Kinnᵉrôwth (2),
(poss.) harp-shaped

CHIOS
5508 Chiŏs (1), Chios

CHISLEU
3691 Kiçlêv (2), Hebrew
month

CHISLON
3692 Kiçlôwn (1), hopeful

CHISLOTH-TABOR
3696 Kiçlôth Tâbôr (1),
flanks of Tabor

CHITTIM
3794 Kittîy (6), islander

CHIUN
3594 Kîyûwn (1), deity
(poss.) Priapus or
Baal-peor

CHLOE
5514 Chlŏē (1), green

CHODE
7378 rîyb (2), to hold a
controversy; to defend

CHOICE
970 bâchûwr (3), male
youth; bridegroom
977 bâchar (4), select,
chose, prefer
1249 bar (1), beloved;
pure; empty
1305 bârar (2), to
examine; select
4005 mibchâr (9), select
8321 sôrêq (1), choice
vine stock
1586 ĕklĕgŏmai (1), to
select, choose, pick out

CHOICEST
4055 mad (1), vesture,
garment; carpet
8321 sôrêq (1), choice
vine stock

CHOKE
4846 sumpnigō (2), to
drown; to crowd

CHOKED
638 apŏpnigō (3), to stifle
or choke
4155 pnigō (1), to throttle
or strangle; to drown
4846 sumpnigō (2), to
drown; to crowd

CHOLER
4843 mârar (2), to be,
make bitter

CHOOSE
972 bâchîyr (1), selected
one
977 bâchar (53), select,
chose, prefer
1254 bârâ' (2), to create;
fashion
1262 bârâh (1), to feed
6901 qâbal (1), to take
138 hairĕŏmai (1), to
prefer, choose

CHOOSEST
977 bâchar (2), select,
chose, prefer

CHOOSETH
977 bâchar (3), select,
chose, prefer

CHOOSING
138 hairĕŏmai (1), to
prefer, choose

CHOP
6566 pâras (1), to break
apart, disperse, scatter

CHOR-ASHAN
3565 Kôwr 'Âshân (1),
furnace of smoke

CHORAZIN
5523 Chŏrazin (2),
Chorazin

CHOSE
977 bâchar (24), select,
chose, prefer
1586 ĕklĕgŏmai (4), to
select, choose, pick out
1951 ĕpilĕgŏmai (1), to
surname, select

CHOSEN
970 bâchûwr (21), male
youth; bridegroom
972 bâchîyr (8), selected
one
977 bâchar (58), select,
chose, prefer
1305 bârar (2), to
examine; select
4005 mibchâr (4), select
138 hairĕŏmai (1), to
prefer, choose
140 hairĕtizō (1), to
make a choice
1586 ĕklĕgŏmai (15), to
select, choose, pick out
1588 ĕklĕktŏs (7),
selected; chosen
1589 ĕklŏgē (1),
selection, choice
4400 prŏchĕirizŏmai (1),
to purpose
4401 prŏchĕirŏtŏnĕŏ (1),
to elect in advance
4758 stratŏlŏgĕŏ (1), to
enlist in the army
5500 chĕirŏtŏnĕŏ (1), to
select or appoint

CHOZEBA
3578 Kôzᵉbâ' (1),
fallacious

CHRIST
5477 Chanaan (1),
humiliated
5547 Christŏs (551),
Anointed One

CHRIST'S
5547 Christŏs (15),
Anointed One

CHRISTIAN
5546 Christianŏs (2),
follower of Christ

CHRISTIANS
5546 Christianŏs (1),
follower of Christ

CHRISTS
5580 psĕudŏchristŏs (2),
spurious Messiah

CHRONICLES
1697+3117 dâbâr (38),
word; matter; thing

CHRYSOLITE
5555 chrusŏlithŏs (1),
yellow chrysolite

CHRYSOPRASUS
5556 chrusŏprasŏs (1),
greenish-yellow
chrysoprase

CHUB
3552 Kûwb (1), Kub

CHUN
3560 Kûwn (1),
established

CHURCH
1577 ĕkklēsia (80),
congregation

CHURCHES
1577 ĕkklēsia (36),
congregation
2417 hiĕrŏsulŏs (1),
temple-despoiler

CHURL
3596 kîylay (2),
begrudging

CHURLISH
7186 qâsheh (1), severe

CHURNING
4330 mîyts (1), pressure

CHUSHAN-RISHATHAIM
3573 Kûwshan
Rish'âthâyim (4),
Cushan of double
wickedness

CHUZA
5529 Chŏuzas (1),
Chuzas

CIELED
2645 châphâh (1), to
cover; to veil, to encase
5603 çâphan (2), to hide
by covering; to roof
7824 shâchîyph (1),
board, panel

CIELING
5604 çippûn (1),
wainscot, paneling

CILICIA
2791 Kilikia (8), Cilicia

CINNAMON
7076 qinnâmôwn (3),
cinnamon spice
2792 kinamōmŏn (1),
cinnamon

CINNEROTH
3672 Kinnᵉrôwth (1),
(poss.) harp-shaped

CIRCLE
2329 chûwg (1), circle

CIRCUIT
2329 chûwg (1), circle
5437 çâbab (1), to
surround
8622 tᵉqûwphâh (1),
revolution, course

CIRCUITS
5439 çâbîyb (1), circle;
neighbor; environs

CIRCUMCISE
4135 mûwl (5), to
circumcise
5243 nâmal (1), to be
circumcised
4059 pĕritĕmnō (4), to
circumcise

CIRCUMCISED
4135 mûwl (23), to
circumcise
203 akrŏbustia (1),
uncircumcised
4059 pĕritĕmnō (13), to
circumcise
4061 pĕritŏmē (1),
circumcision; Jews

CIRCUMCISING
4135 mûwl (1), to
circumcise
4059 pĕritĕmnō (1), to
circumcise

CIRCUMCISION
4139 mûwlâh (1),
circumcision
4061 pĕritŏmē (35),
circumcision; Jews

CIRCUMSPECT
8104 shâmar (1), to
watch

CIRCUMSPECTLY
199 akribŏs (1), exactly,
carefully

CIS
2797 Kis (1), bow

CISTERN
953 bôwr (4), pit hole,
cistern, well

CISTERNS
877 bô'r (1), well, cistern

CITIES
5892 'îyr (419), city, town,
unwalled-village
7141 Qôrach (1), ice
8179 sha'ar (2), opening,
i.e. door or gate
4172 pŏlis (19), town

CITIZEN
4177 pŏlitēs (2), citizen

CITIZENS
4177 pŏlitēs (1), citizen

CITY
4062 madhêbâh (1), gold
making
5892 'îyr (650), city, town,
unwalled-village
5982 'ammûwd (1),
column, pillar
7149 qiryâ' (Ch.) (6), city
7151 qiryâh (32), city
7176 qereth (5), city
7179 qash (1), dry straw
8179 sha'ar (1), opening,
i.e. door or gate
3390 mĕtrŏpŏlis (1),
main city
4172 pŏlis (143), town
4173 pŏlitarchēs (2),
magistrate, city official

CLAD
3680 kâçâh (1), to cover
5844 'âţâh (1), to wrap,
i.e. cover, veil, clothe

CLAMOROUS
1993 hâmâh (1), to be in
great commotion

CLAMOUR
2906 kraugē (1), outcry

CLAP
4222 mâchâ' (2), to strike
the hands together

CLAPPED
5606 çâphaq (2), to *clap* the hands
8628 tâqa' (2), to *clatter, slap, drive, clasp*

CLAPPED
4222 mâchâ' (1), to *strike* the hands together
5221 nâkâh (1), to *strike, kill*

CLAPPETH
5606 çâphaq (1), to *clap* the hands

CLAUDA
2802 Klaudē (1), *Claude*

CLAUDIA
2803 Klaudia (1), *Claudia*

CLAUDIUS
2804 Klaudiŏs (3), *Claudius*

CLAVE
1234 bâqa' (6), to *cleave, break, tear open*
1692 dâbaq (6), to *cling* or *adhere*
2388 châzaq (1), to *fasten* upon; to *seize*; to *be strong; courageous*
2853 kŏllaō (1), to *glue together*

CLAWS
6541 parçâh (2), split *hoof*

CLAY
2563 chômer (11), *clay; dry measure*
2635 chăçaph (Ch.) (9), *clay*
2916 ţîyţ (3), *mud or clay*
4423 meleţ (1), smooth clay *cement floor*
4568 ma'ăbeh (2), *compact* part of soil
5671 'abţîyţ (1), something *pledged*, i.e. (collect.) *pawned* goods
4081 pēlŏs (6), lump of *clay*

CLEAN
656 'âphêç (1), to *cease*
1249 bar (3), *beloved; pure; empty*
1305 bârar (1), to *brighten; purify*
2134 zak (2), *pure; clear*
2135 zâkâh (4), to *be translucent*
2141 zâkak (2), to *be transparent; clean, pure*
2548 châmîyts (1), *salted* provender or fodder
2889 ţâhôwr (49), *pure, clean, flawless*
2891 ţâhêr (41), to *be pure, unadulterated*
5355 nâqîy (1), *innocent*
6565 pârar (1), to *break up*; to *violate, frustrate*
8552 tâmam (3), to *complete, finish*
2511 katharizō (5), to *cleanse*
2513 katharŏs (10), *clean, pure*
2889 kŏsmŏs (3), *world*
3689 ŏntōs (1), *really, certainly*

CLEANNESS
1252 bôr (4), *purity, cleanness*
5356 niqqâyôwn (1), *clearness; cleanness*

CLEANSE
1305 bârar (1), to *brighten; purify*
2135 zâkâh (1), to *be translucent*
2398 châţâ' (7), to *sin*
2891 ţâhêr (15), to *be pure, unadulterated*
5352 nâqâh (5), to *be, make clean; to be bare*
2511 katharizō (6), to *cleanse*

CLEANSED
2135 zâkâh (1), to *be translucent*
2891 ţâhêr (23), to *be pure, unadulterated*
2893 ţohŏrâh (1), *purification; purity*
3722 kâphar (1), to *cover; to expiate*
5352 nâqâh (1), to *be, make clean; to be bare*
6663 tsâdaq (1), to *be, make right*
2511 katharizō (9), to *cleanse*

CLEANSETH
2891 ţâhêr (1), to *be pure, unadulterated*
8562 tamrûwq (1), *scouring*, i.e. *soap*
2511 katharizō (1), to *cleanse*

CLEANSING
2893 ţohŏrâh (8), *purification; purity*
2512 katharismŏs (2), *ablution; expiation*

CLEAR
216 'ôwr (1), *luminary; lightning; happiness*
1249 bar (1), *beloved; pure; empty*
2135 zâkâh (1), to *be translucent*
3368 yâqâr (1), *valuable*
5352 nâqâh (3), to *be, make clean; to be bare*
5355 nâqîy (1), *innocent*
6663 tsâdaq (1), to *be, make right*
6703 tsach (1), *dazzling*, i.e. *sunny, bright*
53 hagnŏs (1), *innocent, modest, perfect, pure*
2513 katharŏs (1), *clean, pure*
2929 krustallizō (1), to *appear as ice*
2986 lamprŏs (1), *radiant; clear*

CLEARER
6965 qûwm (1), to *rise*

CLEARING
5352 nâqâh (1), to *be, make clean; to be bare*
627 apŏlŏgia (1), *plea* or verbal *defense*

CLEARLY
1305 bârar (1), to *brighten; purify*
1227 diablĕpō (2), see *clearly*
2529 kathŏraō (1), to *distinctly apprehend*
5081 tēlaugōs (1), *plainly*

CLEARNESS
2892 ţôhar (1), *brightness; purification*

CLEAVE
1234 bâqa' (3), to *cleave, break, tear open*
1692 dâbaq (18), to *cling* or *adhere*; to *catch*
1693 dĕbaq (Ch.) (1), to *stick*; to *be united*
1695 dâbêq (1), *adhering, sticking to*
3867 lâvâh (1), to *unite*
5596 çâphach (1), to *associate; be united*
8156 shâça' (1), to *split* or *tear*; to *upbraid*
2853 kŏllaō (1), to *glue together*
4347 prŏskŏllaō (3), to *glue to*, i.e. *to adhere*

CLEAVED
1692 dâbaq (3), to *cling* or *adhere*; to *catch*

CLEAVETH
1234 bâqa' (2), to *cleave, break, tear open*
1692 dâbaq (6), to *cling* or *adhere*; to *catch*
3332 yâtsaq (1), to *pour out*
6398 pâlach (1), to *slice*; to *break* open; to *pierce*
6821 tsâphad (1), to *adhere, join*
8157 sheça' (1), *fissure, split*
2853 kŏllaō (1), to *glue together*

CLEFT
1234 bâqa' (1), to *cleave, break, tear open*
8156 shâça' (1), to *split* or *tear*; to *upbraid*

CLEFTS
1233 bĕqîya' (1), *fissure, breach*
2288 chăgâv (3), *rift, cleft* in rocks
5366 nᵉqârâh (1), *fissure*

CLEMENCY
1932 ĕpiĕikĕia (1), *mildness, gentleness*

CLEMENT
2815 Klēmēs (1), *merciful*

CLEOPAS
2810 Klĕŏpas (1), *renown father*

CLEOPHAS
2832 Klōpas (1), cf. *friend* of (his) *father*

CLIFF
4608 ma'ăleh (1), *elevation; platform*

CLIFFS
6178 'ârûwts (1), *feared; horrible* place or *chasm*

CLIFT
5366 nᵉqârâh (1), *fissure*

CLIFTS
5585 çâ'îyph (1), *fissure* of rocks; *bough*

CLIMB
5927 'âlâh (4), to *ascend, be high, mount*

CLIMBED
5927 'âlâh (1), to *ascend, be high, mount*
305 anabainō (1), to *go up, rise*

CLIMBETH
305 anabainō (1), to *go up, rise*

CLIPPED
1639 gâra' (1), to *shave, remove, lessen*

CLODS
1487 gûwsh (1), *mass* of earth, dirt *clod*
4053 migrâphâh (1), *clod* of cultivated dirt
7263 regeb (2), *lump* of clay
7702 sâdad (2), to *harrow* a field

CLOKE
4598 mᵉ'îyl (1), outer *garment* or *robe*
1942 ĕpikaluma (1), *pretext, covering*
2440 himatiŏn (2), to *put* on *clothes*
4392 prŏphasis (2), *pretext, excuse*
5341 phĕlŏnēs (1), outer *garment, mantle, cloak*

CLOSE
681 'êtsel (1), *side; near*
1443 gâdar (1), to *build a* stone *wall*
1692 dâbaq (1), to *cling* or *adhere*; to *catch*
4526 miçgereth (2), *margin; stronghold*
5641 çâthar (1), to *hide* by covering
5956 'âlam (1), to *veil* from sight, i.e. *conceal*
6113 'âtsar (1), to *hold* back; to *maintain*
6862 tsar (1), *trouble; opponent*
788 assŏn (1), *more nearly*, i.e. *very near*
4601 sigaō (1), to *keep silent*

CLOSED
2115 zûwr (1), to *press together, tighten*
3680 kâçâh (1), to *cover*
5437 çâbab (1), to *surround*
5462 çâgar (2), to *shut up*; to *surrender*
5640 çâtham (1), to *stop up*; to *keep secret*
6105 'âtsam (1), to *be, make powerful*
6113 'âtsar (1), to *hold* back; to *maintain*
2576 kammuō (2), to *close* or *shut* the eyes

4428 ptussō (1), to *fold,*
i.e. *furl* or *roll* a scroll

CLOSEST
8474 tachârâh (1), to *vie*
with a rival

CLOSET
2646 chuppâh (1), *canopy*
5009 tamĕiŏn (1), *room*

CLOSETS
5009 tamĕiŏn (1), *room*

CLOTH
899 beged (9), *clothing;*
treachery or *pillage*
4346 makbâr (1),
netted-cloth
8071 simlâh (2), *dress,*
mantle
4470 rhakŏs (2), *piece* of
cloth
4616 sindōn (3), *byssos,*
i.e. bleached *linen*

CLOTHE
3847 lâbash (12), to
clothe
294 amphiĕnnumi (2), to
enrobe, clothe

CLOTHED
3680 kâçâh (1), to *cover*
3736 karbêl (1), to *gird*
or *clothe*
3830 lᵉbûwsh (1),
garment; wife
3847 lâbash (39), to
clothe
3848 lᵉbash (Ch.) (3), to
clothe
294 amphiĕnnumi (2), to
enrobe, clothe
1463 ĕgkŏmbŏŏmai (1),
to *wear, be clothed*
1737 ĕndiduskō (1), to
clothe
1746 ĕnduō (6), to *invest*
with clothing, i.e. to
dress
1902 ĕpĕnduŏmai (2), to
clothe
2439 himatizō (2), to
dress, clothe
4016 pĕriballō (14), to
wrap around, clothe

CLOTHES
899 beged (69), *clothing;*
treachery or *pillage*
1545 gᵉlôwm (1),
clothing, fabric
4055 mad (1), *vesture,*
garment; carpet
5497 çûwth (1), *clothing*
8008 salmâh (3), *clothing*
8071 simlâh (6), *dress,*
mantle
2440 himatiŏn (12), to
put on clothes
3608 ŏthŏniŏn (5), strips
of linen *bandage*
4683 sparganŏō (2), to
wrap with cloth
5509 chitōn (1), *tunic* or
shirt

CLOTHEST
3847 lâbash (1), to *clothe*

CLOTHING
899 beged (1), *clothing;*
treachery or *pillage*

3830 lᵉbûwsh (9),
garment; wife
4374 mᵉkaççeh (1),
covering
8071 simlâh (2), *dress,*
mantle
8516 talbôsheth (1),
garment
1742 ĕnduma (1),
apparel, outer *robe*
2066 ĕsthēs (2), to *clothe*
4749 stŏlē (1),
long-fitting *gown*

CLOTHS
899 beged (4), *clothing;*
treachery or *pillage*

CLOUD
5645 'âb (9), *thick*
clouds; thicket
5743 'ûwb (1), to darkly
becloud
6051 'ânân (75), *nimbus*
cloud
6053 'ănânâh (1),
cloudiness
6205 'ărâphel (1), *gloom,*
darkness
3507 nĕphĕlē (18), *cloud*
3509 nĕphŏs (1), *cloud*

CLOUDS
2385 chăzîyz (1), *flash* of
lightning
3709 kaph (1), hollow of
hand; paw; sole of foot
5387 nâsîy' (1), *leader;*
rising *mist, fog*
5645 'âb (20), *thick*
clouds; thicket
6050 'ănan (Ch.) (1),
nimbus cloud
6051 'ânân (5), *nimbus*
cloud
6053 'ănânâh (1),
cloudiness
7834 shachaq (11),
firmament, clouds
3507 nĕphĕlē (8), *cloud*

CLOUDY
6051 'ânân (6), *nimbus*
cloud

CLOUTED
2921 țâlâ' (1), to be
spotted or *variegated*

CLOUTS
5499 çᵉchâbâh (2), *rag*

CLOVEN
8156 shâça' (1), to *split*
or *tear;* to *upbraid*
1266 diamĕrizō (1), to
distribute

CLOVENFOOTED
8156+8157 shâça' (1), to
split or *tear;* to *upbraid*
8156+8157+6541 shâça'
(2), to *split* or *tear*

CLUSTER
811 'eshkôwl (5), *bunch*
of grapes

CLUSTERS
811 'eshkôwl (4), *bunch*
of grapes
6778 tsammûwq (2),
lump of *dried* grapes
1009 bŏtrus (1), *bunch,*
cluster of grapes

CNIDUS
2834 Knidŏs (1), *Cnidus*

COAL
1513 gechel (2), *ember,*
hot *coal*
7531 ritspâh (1), hot
stone; pavement
7815 shᵉchôwr (1), *soot*

COALS
1513 gechel (16), *ember,*
hot *coal*
6352 pechâm (3), black
coal, charcoal
7529 retseph (1), red-hot
stone for baking
7565 resheph (2), *flame*
439 anthrakia (2), *fire*
bed of burning *coals*
440 anthrax (1), live *coal*

COAST
1366 gᵉbûwl (47),
boundary, border
2256 chebel (4),
company, band
2348 chôwph (1), *cove,*
sheltered bay
3027 yâd (5), *hand; power*
5299 nâphâh (1), *height;*
sieve
7097 qâtseh (1), *extremity*
3864 parathalassiŏs (1),
by the lake
3882 paraliŏs (1),
maritime; seacoast

COASTS
1366 gᵉbûwl (23),
boundary, border
1367 gᵉbûwlâh (5), *region*
1552 gᵉlîylâh (1), *circuit*
or *region*
2348 chôwph (1), *cove,*
sheltered bay
3027 yâd (1), *hand; power*
3411 yᵉrêkâh (3), *far*
away places
7097 qâtseh (1), *extremity*
7098 qâtsâh (1),
termination; fringe
3313 mĕrŏs (3), *division*
or *share*
3725 hŏriŏn (10), *region,*
area, vicinity
5117 tŏpŏs (1), *place*
5561 chōra (1), *territory*

COAT
3801 kᵉthôneth (16),
garment that *covers*
4598 mᵉ'îyl (1), outer
garment or *robe*
8302 shiryôwn (3),
corslet, coat of mail
1903 ĕpĕndutēs (1), outer
garment, coat
5509 chitōn (4), *tunic* or
shirt

COATS
3801 kᵉthôneth (7),
garment that *covers*
5622 çarbal (Ch.) (2),
cloak
5509 chitōn (5), *tunic* or
shirt

COCK
220 alĕktōr (12), *rooster*

COCKATRICE
6848 tsepha' (1), *hissing*
viper

COCKATRICES
6848 tsepha' (1), *hissing*
viper

COCKCROWING
219 alektŏrŏphōnia (1),
rooster-crowing

COCKLE
890 bo'shâh (1), *weed*

COFFER
712 'argâz (3), *box, chest*

COFFIN
727 'ârôwn (1), *box*

COGITATIONS
7476 ra'yôwn (Ch.) (1),
mental *conception*

COLD
2779 chôreph (1),
autumn (and winter)
6793 tsinnâh (1), *large*
shield; piercing cold
7119 qar (2), *cool; quiet;*
cool-headed
7120 qôr (1), *cold*
7135 qârâh (5), *coolness,*
cold
5592 psuchŏs (3),
coolness, cold
5593 psuchrŏs (4), *chilly,*
cold
5594 psuchō (1), to *chill,*
grow cold

COLHOZEH
3626 Kol-Chôzeh (2),
every seer

COLLAR
6310 peh (1), *mouth;*
opening

COLLARS
5188 nᵉțîyphâh (1),
pendant for the ears

COLLECTION
4864 mas'êth (2), *raising;*
beacon; present
3048 lŏgia (1),
contribution, collection

COLLEGE
4932 mishneh (2),
duplicate copy; double

COLLOPS
6371 pîymâh (1), *obesity*

COLONY
2862 kŏlōnia (1), *colony*

COLORS
6320 pûwk (1), *stibium*

COLOSSE
2857 Kŏlŏssai (1),
colossal

COLOSSIANS
2858 Kŏlŏssaĕus (1),
inhabitant of Colossæ

COLOUR
5869 'ayin (11), *eye;*
sight; fountain
4392 prŏphasis (1),
pretext, excuse

COLOURS
2921 țâlâ' (1), to be
spotted or *variegated*
6446 paç (5), *long*
-sleeved tunic

COLT

6648 tseba' (3), *dye*

7553 riqmâh (2), *variegation* of color

COLT

1121 bên (1), *son, descendant*

5895 'ayîr (2), young robust donkey or *ass*

4454 pôlŏs (12), *young donkey*

COLTS

1121 bên (1), *son, descendant*

5895 'ayîr (2), young robust donkey or *ass*

COME

270 'âchaz (1), to *seize, grasp; possess*

314 'achărôwn (8), *late* or *last; behind; western*

635 'Eçtêr (1), *Esther*

835 'esher (3), how *happy!*

857 'âthâh (12), to *arrive*

858 'âthâh (Ch.) (3), to *arrive; go*

935 bôw' (681), to *go, come*

1869 dârak (1), to *walk, lead;* to *string* a bow

1934 hăvâ' (Ch.) (3), to *be,* to *exist*

1961 hâyâh (131), to *exist,* i.e. *be* or *become*

1980 hâlak (7), to *walk; live a certain way*

3045 yâda' (3), to *know*

3051 yâhab (1), to *give*

3205 yâlad (1), to *bear young;* to *father a child*

3212 yâlak (72), to *walk;* to *live;* to *carry*

3318 yâtsâ' (84), to *go, bring out*

3381 yârad (57), to *descend*

4279 mâchar (8), *tomorrow; hereafter*

4291 mᵉṭâ' (Ch.) (1), to *arrive;* to *extend*

4609 ma'ălâh (1), *thought* arising

4672 mâtsâ' (8), to *find* or *acquire;* to *occur*

5060 nâga' (13), to *strike*

5066 nâgash (28), to *be, come, bring near*

5181 nâchath (2), to *sink, descend*

5185 nâchêth (1), *descending*

5312 nᵉphaq (Ch.) (1), to *issue forth;* to *bring out*

5506 çᵉchôrâh (1), *traffic*

5674 'âbar (14), to *cross over;* to *transition*

5927 'âlâh (104), to *ascend, be high, mount*

6213 'âsâh (1), to *do or make*

6264 'âthîyd (1), *prepared; treasure*

6631 tse'ĕtsâ' (1), *produce, children*

6743 tsâlach (1), to *push forward*

6923 qâdam (5), to *anticipate, hasten*

7122 qârâ' (4), to *encounter,* to *happen*

7125 qir'âh (1), to *encounter,* to *happen*

7126 qârab (33), to *approach, bring near*

7131 qârêb (2), *near*

7136 qârâh (2), to *bring about;* to *impose*

7138 qârôwb (1), *near, close*

7725 shûwb (30), to *turn back;* to *return*

8175 sâ'ar (1), to *storm;* to *shiver,* i.e. *fear*

8622 tᵉqûwphâh (1), *revolution, course*

191 akŏuō (1), to *hear; obey*

305 anabainō (7), to *go up, rise*

565 apĕrchŏmai (3), to *go off,* i.e. *depart*

576 apŏbainō (1), to *eventuate, become*

864 aphiknĕŏmai (1), to *go forth* by rumor

1096 ginŏmai (43), to *be, become*

1204 dĕurŏ (8), *hither!; hitherto*

1205 dĕutĕ (12), *come hither!*

1224 diabainō (1), to *pass by, over, across*

1330 diĕrchŏmai (1), to *traverse, travel through*

1448 ĕggizō (9), to *approach*

1511 ĕinai (8), to *exist*

1525 ĕisĕrchŏmai (18), to *enter*

1531 ĕispŏrĕuŏmai (1), to *enter*

1607 ĕkpŏrĕuŏmai (3), to *depart, be discharged*

1684 ĕmbainō (2), to *embark;* to *reach*

1764 ĕnistēmi (1), to *be present*

1831 ĕxĕrchŏmai (24), to *issue;* to *leave*

1834 ĕxēgĕŏmai (1), to *tell, relate again*

1880 ĕpanĕrchŏmai (1), *return* home

1904 ĕpĕrchŏmai (8), to *supervene*

1910 ĕpibainō (1), to *ascend, embark, arrive*

1975 ĕpipŏrĕuŏmai (1), to *go, come to*

2049 ĕrēmŏō (1), to *lay waste*

2064 ĕrchŏmai (290), to *go or come*

2186 ĕphistēmi (2), to *be present;* to *approach*

2240 hēkō (24), to *arrive,* i.e. *be present*

2597 katabainō (20), to *descend*

2638 katalambanō (1), to *seize;* to *possess*

2647 kataluō (1), to *halt* for the night

2658 katantaō (3), to *arrive* at; to *attain*

2673 katargĕō (1), to *be, render entirely useless*

2718 katĕrchŏmai (2), to *go, come down*

3195 mĕllō (16), to *intend,* i.e. *be about* to

3854 paraginŏmai (15), to *arrive;* to *appear*

3918 parĕimi (6), to *be present;* to *have come*

3928 parĕrchŏmai (1), to *go by;* to *perish*

3936 paristēmi (1), to *stand beside, present*

4137 plērŏō (1), to *fill, make complete*

4301 prŏlambanŏ (1), to *take before*

4331 prŏsĕggizō (1), to *approach near*

4334 prŏsĕrchŏmai (6), to *come near, visit*

4365 prŏspŏrĕuŏmai (1), to *come towards*

4845 sumplērŏō (2), to *be complete, fulfill*

4905 sunĕrchŏmai (14), to *go with*

4940 suntugchanō (1), to *come together*

5290 hupŏstrĕphō (1), to *turn under, behind*

5302 hustĕrĕō (3), to *be inferior;* to *fall short*

5348 phthanō (4), to *be anticipate or precede*

5562 chōrĕō (1), to *pass, enter;* to *hold, admit*

COMELINESS

1926 hâdâr (3), *magnificence*

1935 hôwd (1), *grandeur, majesty*

2157 ĕuschēmŏsunē (1), *decorousness*

COMELY

2433 chîyn (1), graceful *beauty*

3190 yâṭab (1), to *be, make well*

3303 yâpheh (1), *beautiful; handsome*

4998 nâ'âh (1), to *be pleasant or suitable*

5000 nâ'veh (7), *suitable* or *beautiful*

8389 tô'ar (1), *outline, figure or appearance*

8597 tiph'ârâh (1), *ornament*

2158 ĕuschēmōn (2), *decorous, proper; noble*

4241 prĕpō (1), to *be suitable or proper*

COMERS

4334 prŏsĕrchŏmai (1), to *come near, visit*

COMEST

935 bôw' (22), to *go or come*

2199 zâ'aq (1), to *call out, announce*

7126 qârab (2), to *approach, bring near*

2064 ĕrchŏmai (3), to *go or come*

COMETH

857 'âthâh (3), to *arrive*

935 bôw' (89), to *go, come*

1961 hâyâh (1), to *exist,* i.e. *be* or *become*

1980 hâlak (2), to *walk; live a certain way*

3318 yâtsâ' (19), to *go, bring out*

3381 yârad (1), to *descend*

4672 mâtsâ' (1), to *occur, meet or be present*

5034 nâbêl (1), to *wilt;* to *fall away*

5060 nâga' (1), to *strike*

5414 nâthan (1), to *give*

5674 'âbar (1), to *cross over;* to *transition*

5927 'âlâh (10), to *ascend, be high, mount*

6293 pâga' (1), to *impinge*

6437 pânâh (1), to *turn,* to *face*

6627 tsâ'âh (2), human *excrement*

6631 tse'ĕtsâ' (1), *produce, children*

7131 qârêb (5), *near*

7698 sheger (1), what *comes forth*

7725 shûwb (3), to *turn back;* to *return*

305 anabainō (1), to *go up, rise*

1096 ginŏmai (2), to *be, become*

1511 ĕinai (1), to *exist*

1607 ĕkpŏrĕuŏmai (2), to *depart, be discharged*

1831 ĕxĕrchŏmai (1), to *issue;* to *leave*

1999 ĕpisustasis (1), *insurrection*

2064 ĕrchŏmai (97), to *go or come*

2186 ĕphistēmi (1), to *be present;* to *approach*

2591 Karpŏs (1), (poss.) *fruit*

2597 katabainō (3), to *descend*

3854 paraginŏmai (3), to *arrive;* to *appear*

4334 prŏsĕrchŏmai (1), to *come near, visit*

4905 sunĕrchŏmai (1), to *gather together*

COMFORT

1082 bâlag (2), to *be comforted*

4010 mablîygîyth (1), *desolation*

5162 nâcham (33), to *be sorry;* to *pity, console*

5165 nechâmâh (1), *consolation*

5582 çâ'ad (3), to *support*

7502 râphad (1), to *spread a bed;* to *refresh*

2174 ĕupsuchĕō (1), to *feel encouraged*

2293 tharsĕō (3), to *have courage; take heart!*

3870 parakalĕō (9), to *call, invite*

3874 paraklēsis (6), *imploring, exhortation*

3888 paramuthĕŏmai (2), to *console*
3889 paramuthia (1), *consolation*
3890 paramuthiŏn (1), *consolation*
3931 parēgŏria (1), *consolation, comfort*

COMFORTABLE
4496 mᵉnûwchâh (1), *peacefully; consolation*
5150 nichûwm (1), *consoled; solace*

COMFORTABLY
5921+3820 'al (4), *above, over, upon, or against*
5921+3824 'al (1), *above, over, upon, or against*

COMFORTED
5162 nâcham (20), to *be sorry; to pity, console*
3870 parakaleō (13), to *call, invite*
3888 paramuthĕŏmai (2), to *console*
4837 sumparakalĕō (1), to *console jointly*

COMFORTEDST
5162 nâcham (1), to *be sorry; to pity, console*

COMFORTER
5162 nâcham (3), to *be sorry; to pity, console*
3875 paraklētŏs (4), *intercessor, consoler*

COMFORTERS
5162 nâcham (5), to *be sorry; to pity, console*

COMFORTETH
5162 nâcham (3), to *be sorry; to pity, console*
3870 parakalĕō (2), to *call, invite*

COMFORTLESS
3737 ŏrphanŏs (1), *parentless, orphaned*

COMFORTS
5150 nichûwm (1), *consoled; solace*
8575 tanchûwm (1), *compassion, solace*

COMING
857 'âthâh (1), to *arrive*
935 bôw' (19), to *go,* come
1980 hâlak (1), to *walk; live a certain way*
3318 yâtsâ' (2), to *go, bring out*
3381 yârad (2), to *descend*
3996 mâbôw' (1), *entrance; sunset; west*
4126 môwbâ' (1), *entrance*
5182 nᵉchath (Ch.) (1), to *descend; to depose*
5674 'âbar (1), to *cross over; to transition*
7122 qârâ' (1), to *encounter, to happen*
7272 regel (1), *foot; step*
305 anabainō (2), to *go up, rise*
602 apŏkalupsis (1), *disclosure, revelation*

1525 ĕisĕrchŏmai (3), to *enter*
1529 ĕisŏdŏs (1), *entrance*
1531 ĕispŏrĕuŏmai (1), to *enter*
1660 ĕlĕusis (1), *advent, coming*
1831 ĕxĕrchŏmai (1), to *issue; to leave*
1904 ĕpĕrchŏmai (1), to *supervene*
2064 ĕrchŏmai (27), to *go or come*
2186 ĕphistēmi (1), to *be present; to approach*
2597 katabainō (1), to *descend*
3854 paraginŏmai (1), to *arrive; to appear*
3952 parŏusia (22), *advent, coming*
4334 prŏsĕrchŏmai (3), to *come near, visit*

COMINGS
4126 môwbâ' (1), *entrance*

COMMAND
559 'âmar (2), to *say*
6310 peh (1), *mouth; opening*
6680 tsâvâh (84), to *constitute, enjoin*
1781 ĕntĕllŏmai (4), to *enjoin, give orders*
2004 ĕpitassō (1), to *order, command*
2036 ĕpō (3), to *speak*
2753 kĕlĕuō (1), to *order, direct*
3853 paraggĕllō (8), to *enjoin; to instruct*

COMMANDED
559 'âmar (25), to *say*
560 'ămar (Ch.) (12), to *say,* speak
1696 dâbar (4), to *speak, say; to subdue*
4480+2941 min (1), *from or out of*
4687 mitsvâh (2), *command*
6680 tsâvâh (333), to *constitute, enjoin*
7761+2942 sûwm (Ch.) (3), to *put, place*
1291 diastĕllŏmai (1), to *enjoin*
1299 diatassō (6), to *institute, prescribe*
1781 ĕntĕllŏmai (6), to *enjoin, give orders*
2004 ĕpitassō (4), to *order, command*
2036 ĕpō (5), to *speak*
2750 kĕiria (1), *swathe of cloth*
2753 kĕlĕuō (20), to *order, direct*
3853 paraggĕllō (11), to *enjoin; to give instruction*
4367 prŏstassō (6), to *enjoin*
4483 rhĕō (1), to *utter,* i.e. *speak or say*

COMMANDEDST
6680 tsâvâh (4), to *constitute, enjoin*

COMMANDER
6680 tsâvâh (1), to *constitute, enjoin*

COMMANDEST
6680 tsâvâh (2), to *constitute, enjoin*
2753 kĕlĕuō (1), to *order, direct*

COMMANDETH
559 'âmar (3), to *say, speak*
6680 tsâvâh (6), to *constitute, enjoin*
2004 ĕpitassō (3), to *order, command*
3853 paraggĕllō (1), to *enjoin; to instruct*

COMMANDING
6680 tsâvâh (1), to *constitute, enjoin*
1299 diatassō (1), to *institute, prescribe*
2753 kĕlĕuō (1), to *order, direct*

COMMANDMENT
559 'âmar (2), to *say*
565 'imrâh (1), *something said*
1697 dâbâr (15), *word; matter; thing*
1881 dâth (2), *royal edict or statute*
2941 ţa'am (Ch.) (2), *sentence, command*
2942 ţᵉ'êm (Ch.) (2), *judgment; account*
3318 yâtsâ' (1), to *go, bring out*
3982 ma'ămar (2), *edict, command*
4406 millâh (Ch.) (1), *word, command*
4662 miphqâd (1), *appointment*
4687 mitsvâh (43), *command*
6310 peh (37), *mouth; opening*
6673 tsav (1), *injunction*
6680 tsâvâh (9), to *constitute, enjoin*
1291 diastĕllŏmai (1), to *enjoin*
1297 diatagma (1), *authoritative edict*
1781 ĕntĕllŏmai (2), to *enjoin, give orders*
1785 ĕntŏlē (42), *prescription, regulation*
2003 ĕpitagē (6), *injunction or decree*
2753 kĕlĕuō (2), to *order, direct*
3852 paraggĕlia (1), *mandate, order*
3853 paraggĕllō (1), to *enjoin; to instruct*

COMMANDMENTS
1697 dâbâr (5), *word; matter; thing*
2706 chôq (1), *appointment; allotment*
4687 mitsvâh (130), *command*

6490 piqqûwd (2), *mandate of God, Law*
1778 ĕntalma (3), *precept, command*
1781 ĕntĕllŏmai (1), to *enjoin, give orders*
1785 ĕntŏlē (27), *prescription, regulation*
3852 paraggĕlia (1), *mandate, order*

COMMEND
3908 paratithēmi (2), to *present something*
4921 sunistaō (5), to *set together*

COMMENDATION
4956 sustatikŏs (2), *recommendatory*

COMMENDED
1984 hâlal (2), to *speak words of thankfulness*
7623 shâbach (1), to *address in a loud tone*
1867 ĕpainĕō (1), to *applaud, commend*
3908 paratithēmi (1), to *present something*
4921 sunistaō (1), to *set together*

COMMENDETH
3936 paristēmi (1), to *stand beside, present*
4921 sunistaō (3), to *set together*

COMMENDING
4921 sunistaō (1), to *set together*

COMMISSION
2011 ĕpitrŏpē (1), *permission*

COMMISSIONS
1881 dâth (1), *royal edict or statute*

COMMIT
1556 gâlal (2), to *roll; to commit*
2181 zânâh (11), to *commit adultery*
4560 mâçar (1), to *set apart; apostatize*
4603 mâ'al (4), to *act treacherously*
5003 nâ'aph (6), to *commit adultery*
5414 nâthan (1), to *give*
5753 'âvâh (2), to *be crooked*
6213 'âsâh (14), to *do or make*
6313 pûwg (1), to *be sluggish; be numb*
6466 pâ'al (1), to *do, make or practice*
6485 pâqad (2), to *visit, care for, count*
7760 sûwm (1), to *put, place*
2038 ĕrgazŏmai (1), to *toil*
2416 hiĕrŏsulĕō (1), to *be a temple-robber*
3429 mŏichaō (2), to *commit adultery*
3431 mŏichĕuō (10), to *commit adultery*

3908 paratithēmi (3), to present something
4100 pisteuō (2), to have faith, to entrust
4160 pŏiĕō (2), to make
4203 pŏrnĕuō (3), to indulge unlawful *lust*
4238 prassō (2), to execute, accomplish

COMMITTED
1961 hâyâh (2), to exist, i.e. be or become
2181 zânâh (5), to commit adultery
2398 châṭâ' (6), to sin
4600 mâ'ak (6), to pierce, emasculate, handle
5003 nâ'aph (5), to commit adultery
5414 nâthan (5), to give
5753 'âvâh (2), to be crooked
6213 'âsâh (28), to do or make
6485 pâqad (4), to visit, care for, count
7561 râsha' (1), to be, do, declare wrong
8581 tâ'ab (1), to loathe, i.e. detest
764 asĕbĕō (1), to be, act impious or wicked
1325 didōmi (1), to give
1439 ĕaō (1), to let be, i.e. permit or leave alone
3431 mŏichĕuō (1), to commit adultery
3860 paradidōmi (2), to hand over
3866 parathēkē (1), trust, deposit entrusted
3872 parakatathēkē (2), deposit, trust
3908 paratithēmi (1), to present something
4100 pisteuō (5), to have faith; to entrust
4160 pŏiĕō (4), to make
4203 pŏrnĕuō (4), to indulge unlawful *lust*
4238 prassō (3), to execute, accomplish
5087 tithēmi (1), to place

COMMITTEST
2181 zânâh (1), to commit adultery

COMMITTETH
5003 nâ'aph (4), to commit adultery
5800 'âzab (1), to loosen; relinquish; permit
6213 'âsâh (4), to do or make
3429 mŏichaō (4), to commit adultery
3431 mŏichĕuō (2), to commit adultery
4160 pŏiĕō (3), to make or do
4203 pŏrnĕuō (1), to indulge unlawful *lust*

COMMITTING
5003 nâ'aph (1), to commit adultery
6213 'âsâh (1), to do or make

COMMODIOUS
428 anĕuthĕtŏs (1), inconvenient

COMMON
776 'erets (1), earth, land, soil; country
1121 bên (1), people of a class or kind
2455 chôl (2), profane, common, not holy
2490 châlal (1), to profane, defile
7227 rab (1), great
7230 rôb (1), abundance
442 anthrōpinŏs (1), human
1219 dēmŏsiŏs (1), public; in public
2839 kŏinŏs (8), common, i.e. profane
2840 kŏinŏō (1), to make profane
4183 pŏlus (1), much, many
4232 praitōriŏn (1), governor's court-room

COMMONLY
1310 diaphēmizō (1), to spread news
3654 hŏlōs (1), altogether

COMMONWEALTH
4174 pŏlitĕia (1), citizenship

COMMOTION
7494 ra'ash (1), bounding, uproar

COMMOTIONS
181 akatastasia (1), disorder, riot

COMMUNE
559 'âmar (1), to say
1696 dâbar (4), to speak, say; to subdue
1697 dâbâr (1), word; matter; thing
5608 çâphar (1), to enumerate; to recount
7878 sîyach (1), to ponder, muse aloud

COMMUNED
1696 dâbar (14), to speak, say; to subdue
1255 dialalĕō (1), to converse, discuss
3656 hŏmilĕō (2), to converse, talk
4814 sullalĕō (1), to talk together, i.e. converse

COMMUNICATE
2841 kŏinōnĕō (1), to share or participate
2842 kŏinōnia (1), benefaction; sharing
2843 kŏinōnikŏs (1), liberal
4790 sugkŏinōnĕō (1), to co-participate in

COMMUNICATED
394 anatithĕmai (1), propound, set forth
2841 kŏinōnĕō (1), to share or participate

COMMUNICATION
1697 dâbâr (1), word; matter; thing

7879 sîyach (1), uttered contemplation
148 aischrŏlŏgia (1), vile conversation
2842 kŏinōnia (1), benefaction; sharing
3056 lŏgŏs (2), word, matter, thing; Word

COMMUNICATIONS
3056 lŏgŏs (1), word, matter, thing
3657 hŏmilia (1), associations

COMMUNING
1696 dâbar (2), to speak, say; to subdue

COMMUNION
2842 kŏinōnia (4), benefaction; sharing

COMPACT
2266 châbar (1), to fascinate by spells

COMPACTED
4822 sumbibazō (1), to drive together

COMPANIED
4905 sunĕrchŏmai (1), to gather together

COMPANIES
736 'ŏr°châh (1), caravan
1416 g°dûwd (1), band of soldiers
1979 hălîykâh (1), walking; procession
4256 machălŏqeth (1), section or division
4264 machăneh (1), encampment
6951 qâhâl (1), assemblage
7218 rô'sh (7), head
4849 sumpŏsiŏn (1), group

COMPANION
2270 châbêr (2), associate, friend
2278 chăbereth (1), consort, companion
4828 mêrêa' (3), close friend
7453 rêa' (3), associate; one close
7462 râ'âh (2), to associate as a friend
4791 sugkŏinōnŏs (1), co-participant
4904 sunĕrgŏs (1), fellow-worker

COMPANIONS
2269 chăbar (Ch.) (1), associate, friend
2270 châbêr (5), associate, friend
2271 chabbâr (1), partner
3675 k°nâth (Ch.) (8), colleague
4828 mêrêa' (1), close friend
7453 rêa' (1), associate; one close
7464 rê'âh (2), female associate
2844 kŏinōnŏs (1), associate, partner
4898 sunĕkdēmŏs (1), fellow-traveller

COMPANIONS'
7453 rêa' (1), associate; one close

COMPANY
736 'ŏr°châh (1), caravan
1323 bath (1), daughter, descendant, woman
1416 g°dûwd (3), band of soldiers
1995 hâmôwn (1), noise, tumult; many, crowd
2199 zâ'aq (1), to convene publicly
2256 chebel (2), company, band
2267 cheber (1), society, group; magic spell;
2274 chebrâh (1), association
2416 chay (1), alive; raw; fresh; life
2428 chayil (1), army; wealth; virtue; valor; strength
3862 lahăqâh (1), assembly
4246 m°chôwlâh (1), round-dance
4264 machăneh (5), encampment
5712 'êdâh (13), assemblage; crowd
6635 tsâbâ' (1), army, military host
6951 qâhâl (16), assemblage
7218 rô'sh (5), head
7285 regesh (1), tumultuous crowd
7462 râ'âh (1), to associate as a friend
8229 shiph'âh (2), copiousness
2398 idiŏs (1), private or separate
2828 klisia (1), party or group
2853 kŏllaō (1), to glue together
3461 murias (1), ten-thousand
3588+4012 hŏ (1), "the"
3658 hŏmilŏs (1), multitude
3792 ŏchlŏpŏiĕō (1), to raise a disturbance
3793 ŏchlŏs (7), throng
4012 peri (1), about; around
4128 plēthŏs (1), large number, throng
4874 sunanamignumi (3), to associate with
4923 sunŏdia (1), traveling company

COMPARABLE
5577 çançin (1), twig

COMPARE
4911 mâshal (1), to use figurative language
6186 'ârak (1), to set in a row, i.e. arrange,
3846 paraballō (1), to reach a place; to liken
4793 sugkrinō (1), to combine

COMPARED
1819 dâmâh (1), to resemble, liken
6186 'ârak (1), to set in a row, i.e. arrange,
7737 shâvâh (2), to resemble; to adjust

COMPARING
4793 sugkrinō (2), to combine

COMPARISON
3644 kᵉmôw (1), like, as; for; with
3850 parabŏlē (1), fictitious narrative

COMPASS
247 'âzar (1), to belt
2329 chûwg (1), circle
3749 karkôb (2), rim, ledge, or top margin
3803 kâthar (2), to enclose, besiege; to wait
4230 mᵉchûwgâh (1), compass
4524 mêçab (1), around, surround
5362 nâqaph (3), to surround or circulate
5437 çâbab (22), to surround
5439 çâbîyb (2), circle; environs; around
5849 'âṭar (1), to encircle, enclose in; to crown
4013 pĕriagō (1), to walk around
4022 pĕriĕrchŏmai (1), to stroll, vacillate, veer
4033 pĕrikuklŏō (1), to blockade completely

COMPASSED
661 'âphaph (5), to surround
2328 chûwg (1), to describe a circle
5362 nâqaph (4), to surround or circulate
5437 çâbab (28), to surround
5849 'âṭar (1), to encircle, enclose in; to crown
2944 kuklŏō (3), to surround, encircle
4029 pĕrikĕimai (2), to enclose, encircle

COMPASSEST
2219 zârâh (1), to toss about; to diffuse

COMPASSETH
5437 çâbab (4), to surround
6059 'ânaq (1), to collar; to fit out

COMPASSING
5362 nâqaph (2), to surround or circulate
5437 çâbab (1), to surround

COMPASSION
2550 châmal (5), to spare, have pity on
7349 rachûwm (5), compassionate
7355 râcham (8), to be compassionate

7356 racham (2), compassion; womb
1653 ĕlĕĕŏ (3), to give out compassion
3356 mĕtriŏpathĕō (1), to deal gently
3627 ŏiktĕirō (1), to exercise pity
4697 splagchnizŏmai (12), to feel sympathy
4834 sumpathĕō (1), to commiserate
4835 sumpathēs (1), commiserative

COMPASSIONS
7355 râcham (1), to be compassionate
7356 racham (1), compassion; womb

COMPEL
597 'ânaç (1), to insist, compel
5647 'âbad (1), to do, work, serve
29 aggarĕuō (2), to press into public service
315 anagkazō (1), to necessitate, compel

COMPELLED
5080 nâdach (1), to push off, scattered
6555 pârats (1), to break out
29 aggarĕuō (1), to press into public service
315 anagkazō (3), to necessitate, compel

COMPELLEST
315 anagkazō (1), to necessitate, compel

COMPLAIN
596 'ânan (1), complain
1058 bâkâh (1), to weep, moan
7378 rîyb (1), to hold a controversy; to defend
7878 sîyach (1), to ponder, muse aloud

COMPLAINED
596 'ânan (1), complain
7878 sîyach (1), to ponder, muse aloud

COMPLAINERS
3202 mĕmpsimŏirŏs (1), discontented

COMPLAINING
6682 tsᵉvâchâh (1), screech of anguish

COMPLAINT
7878 sîyach (9), to ponder, muse aloud

COMPLAINTS
157 aitiama (1), thing charged

COMPLETE
8549 tâmîym (1), entire, complete; integrity
4137 plērŏō (2), to fill, make complete

COMPOSITION
4971 mathkôneth (2), proportion

COMPOUND
4842 mirqachath (1), unguent; unguent-pot

COMPOUNDETH
7543 râqach (1), to perfume, blend spice

COMPREHEND
3045 yâda' (1), to know
2638 katalambanō (1), to possess; to understand

COMPREHENDED
3557 kûwl (1), to measure; to maintain
346 anakĕphalaiŏmai (1), to sum up
2638 katalambanō (1), to possess; to understand

CONANIAH
3562 Kôwnanyâhûw (1), Jehovah has sustained

CONCEAL
2790 chârash (1), to be silent; to be deaf
3582 kâchad (2), to destroy; to hide
3680 kâçâh (2), to cover
5641 çâthar (1), to hide

CONCEALED
3582 kâchad (2), to destroy; to hide

CONCEALETH
3680 kâçâh (2), to cover

CONCEIT
4906 maskìyth (1), carved figure
5869 'ayin (4), eye; sight; fountain

CONCEITS
3844+1438 para (2), from; with; besides

CONCEIVE
2029 hârâh (3), to conceive, be pregnant
2030 hâreh (4), pregnant
2232 zâra' (1), to sow seed; to disseminate
3179 yâcham (4), to conceive
2602 katabŏlē (1), conception, beginning
4815 sullambanō (1), to conceive; to aid

CONCEIVED
2029 hârâh (1), to conceive, be pregnant
2030 hâreh (33), pregnant
2232 zâra' (1), to sow seed; to disseminate
2803 châshab (1), to plot; to think, regard
3179 yâcham (2), to conceive
3254 yâçaph (1), to add or augment
1080 gĕnnaō (1), to procreate, regenerate
2845+2192 kŏitē (1), couch; conception
4815 sullambanō (4), to conceive; to aid
5087 tithēmi (1), to place

CONCEIVING
2030 hâreh (1), pregnant

CONCEPTION
2032 hêrôwn (3), pregnancy

CONCERN
4012 pĕri (2), about; around

CONCERNETH
1157 bᵉ'ad (1), at, beside, among, behind, for

CONCERNING
413 'êl (15), to, toward
854 'êth (1), with; by; at; among
5921 'al (78), above, over, upon, or against
5922 'al (Ch.) (6), above, over, upon, or against
6655 tsad (Ch.) (1), at the side of; against
1519 ĕis (5), to or into
2596 kata (5), down; according to
3754 hŏti (1), that; because; since
4012 pĕri (44), about; around
4314 prŏs (1), for; on, at; to, toward; against
5228 hupĕr (1), over; above; beyond

CONCISION
2699 katatŏmē (1), mutilation, cutting

CONCLUDE
3049 lŏgizŏmai (1), to credit; to think, regard

CONCLUDED
2919 krinō (1), to decide; to try, condemn, punish
4788 sugklĕiō (2), to net fish; to lock up persons

CONCLUSION
5490 çôwph (1), termination; end

CONCORD
4857 sumphōnēsis (1), accordance, agreement

CONCOURSE
1993 hâmâh (1), to be in great commotion
4963 sustrŏphē (1), riotous crowd

CONCUBINE
6370 pîylegesh (22), concubine

CONCUBINES
3904 lᵉchênâh (Ch.) (3), concubine
6370 pîylegesh (14), concubine

CONCUPISCENCE
1939 ĕpithumia (3), longing

CONDEMN
7561 râsha' (11), to be, do, declare wrong
8199 shâphaṭ (1), to judge
2607 kataginōskō (2), to condemn
2618 katakaiō (1), to consume wholly by burning
2632 katakrinō (7), to judge against
2633 katakrisis (1), act of sentencing adversely
2919 krinō (1), to decide; to try, condemn, punish

CONDEMNATION
2631 katakrima (3), adverse sentence
2633 katakrisis (1), act of sentencing adversely
2917 krima (5), decision
2920 krisis (2), decision; tribunal; justice
5272 hupŏkrisis (1), deceit, hypocrisy

CONDEMNED
3318+7563 yâtsâ' (1), to go, bring out
6064 'ânash (2), to inflict a penalty, to fine
7561 râsha' (1), to be, do, declare wrong
176 akatagnŏstŏs (1), unblamable
843 autŏkatakritŏs (1), self-condemned
1519+2917 ĕis (1), to or into
2613 katadikazō (4), to condemn
2632 katakrinō (8), to judge against
2919 krinō (2), to decide; to try, condemn, punish

CONDEMNEST
2632 katakrinō (1), to judge against

CONDEMNETH
7561 râsha' (2), to be, do, declare wrong
2632 katakrinō (1), to judge against
4314 prŏs (1), for; on, at; to, toward; against

CONDEMNING
7561 râsha' (1), to be, do, declare wrong
2919 krinō (1), to decide; to try, condemn, punish

CONDESCEND
4879 sunapagō (1), to take off together

CONDITIONS
4314 prŏs (1), for; on, at; to, toward; against

CONDUCT
5674 'âbar (1), to cross over; to transition
7971 shâlach (1), to send away
4311 prŏpĕmpō (1), to send forward

CONDUCTED
5674 'âbar (1), to cross over; to transition
2525 kathistēmi (1), to designate, constitute

CONDUIT
8585 tᵉ'âlâh (4), irrigation channel; bandage or plaster

CONEY
8227 shâphân (2), rock-rabbit, (poss.) hyrax

CONFECTION
7545 rôqach (1), aromatic, fragrance

CONFECTIONARIES
7543 râqach (1), to perfume, blend spice

CONFEDERACY
1285 bᵉrîyth (1), compact, agreement
7195 qesher (2), unlawful alliance

CONFEDERATE
1167+1285 ba'al (1), master; owner; citizen
1285+3772 bᵉrîyth (1), compact, agreement
5117 nûwach (1), to rest; to settle down

CONFERENCE
4323 prŏsanatithēmi (1), to add; to consult

CONFERRED
1961+1697 hâyâh (1), to exist, i.e. be or become
4323 prŏsanatithēmi (1), to add; to consult
4814 sullalĕō (1), to talk together, i.e. converse
4820 sumballō (1), converse, consult

CONFESS
3034 yâdâh (11), to revere or worship
1843 ĕxŏmŏlŏgĕō (5), to acknowledge or agree
3670 hŏmŏlŏgĕō (12), to acknowledge, agree

CONFESSED
3034 yâdâh (3), to throw; to revere or worship
1843 ĕxŏmŏlŏgĕō (1), to acknowledge or agree
3670 hŏmŏlŏgĕō (3), to acknowledge, agree

CONFESSETH
3034 yâdâh (1), to throw; to revere or worship
3670 hŏmŏlŏgĕō (2), to acknowledge, agree

CONFESSING
3034 yâdâh (1), to throw; to revere or worship
1843 ĕxŏmŏlŏgĕō (2), to acknowledge or agree

CONFESSION
3034 yâdâh (1), to throw; to revere or worship
8426 tôwdâh (2), expressions of thanks
3670 hŏmŏlŏgĕō (1), to acknowledge, agree
3671 hŏmŏlŏgia (1), confession

CONFIDENCE
982 bâṭach (4), to trust, be confident or sure
983 beṭach (1), safety, security; trust
985 biṭchâh (1), trust
986 biṭṭâchôwn (2), trust
3689 keçel (1), loin; back; viscera; trust
3690 kiçlâh (1), trust
4009 mibṭâch (8), security; assurance
2292 tharrhĕō (1), to exercise courage
3954 parrhēsia (6), frankness, boldness
3982 pĕithō (6), to rely
4006 pĕpŏithēsis (5), reliance, trust

CONFIDENCES
4009 mibṭâch (1), security; assurance

CONFIDENT
982 bâṭach (2), to trust, be confident or sure
2292 tharrhĕō (2), to exercise courage
3982 pĕithō (3), to rely
5287 hupŏstasis (1), essence; assurance

CONFIDENTLY
1340 diïschurizŏmai (1), to asseverate

CONFIRM
553 'âmats (1), to be strong; be courageous
1396 gâbar (1), to be strong; to prevail
2388 châzaq (2), to bind, restrain, conquer
3559 kûwn (1), to set up; establish, fix, prepare
4390 mâlê' (1), to fill; be full
6965 qûwm (4), to rise
950 bĕbaiŏō (2), to stabilitate, keep strong
2964 kurŏō (1), to ratify, validate a treaty

CONFIRMATION
951 bĕbaiōsis (2), confirmation

CONFIRMED
2388 châzaq (1), to bind, restrain, conquer
3559 kûwn (2), to render sure, proper or prosperous
5975 'âmad (2), to stand
6965 qûwm (2), to rise
950 bĕbaiŏō (2), to stabilitate, keep strong
1991 ĕpistērizō (1), to re-establish, strengthen
2964 kurŏō (1), to ratify, validate a treaty
3315 mĕsitĕuō (1), to ratify as surety, confirm
4300 prŏkurŏō (1), to ratify previously

CONFIRMETH
6965 qûwm (3), to rise

CONFIRMING
950 bĕbaiŏō (1), to stabilitate, keep strong
1991 ĕpistērizō (1), to re-establish, strengthen

CONFISCATION
6065 'ănash (Ch.) (1), fine, penalty, mulct

CONFLICT
73 agōn (2), contest, struggle

CONFORMABLE
4832 summŏrphŏs (1), similar, conformed to

CONFORMED
4832 summŏrphŏs (1), similar, conformed to
4964 suschēmatizō (1), to conform

CONFOUND
1101 bâlal (2), to mix; confuse
2865 châthath (1), to break down
2617 kataischunō (2), to disgrace or shame

CONFOUNDED
954 bûwsh (21), be ashamed; disappointed
2659 châphêr (6), to be ashamed, disappointed
3001 yâbêsh (9), to dry up; to wither
3637 kâlam (11), to taunt or insult
2617 kataischunō (1), to disgrace or shame
4797 sugchĕō (2), to throw into disorder

CONFUSED
7494 ra'ash (1), bounding, uproar
4797 sugchĕō (1), to throw into disorder

CONFUSION
954 bûwsh (1), be ashamed, disappointed
1322 bôsheth (7), shame
2659 châphêr (2), to be ashamed, disappointed
3637 kâlam (1), to taunt or insult
3639 kᵉlimmâh (6), disgrace, scorn
7036 qâlôwn (1), disgrace
8397 tebel (2), confused mixture
8414 tôhûw (3), waste, desolation, formless
181 akatastasia (2), disorder, riot
4799 sugchusis (1), riotous disturbance

CONGEALED
7087 qâphâ' (1), to thicken, congeal

CONGRATULATE
1288 bârak (1), to bless

CONGREGATION
482 'êlem (1), silence
2416 chay (2), alive; raw; fresh; life
4150 môw'êd (147), assembly, congregation
5712 'êdâh (123), assemblage; crowd
6951 qâhâl (85), assemblage
6952 qᵉhillâh (1), assemblage
4865 sunagōnizŏmai (1), to be a partner

CONGREGATIONS
4150 môw'êd (1), assembly, congregation
4721 maqhêl (2), assembly

CONIAH
3659 Konyâhûw (3), Jehovah will establish

CONIES
8226 sâphan (2), to conceal

CONONIAH
3562 Kôwnanyâhûw (2),
Jehovah has sustained

CONQUER
3528 nikaō (1), to
subdue, conquer

CONQUERING
3528 nikaō (1), to
subdue, conquer

CONQUERORS
5245 hupĕrnikaō (1), to
gain a decisive victory

CONSCIENCE
4893 sunĕidēsis (31),
moral consciousness

CONSCIENCES
4893 sunĕidēsis (1),
moral consciousness

CONSECRATE
2763 charam (1), to
devote to destruction
4390+3027 mâlê' (10), to
fill; be full
5144 nâzar (1), to devote
6942 qâdâsh (2), to be,
make clean

CONSECRATED
4390+3027 mâlê' (7), to
fill; be full
6942 qâdâsh (4), to be,
make clean
6944 qôdesh (1), sacred
place or thing
1457 ĕgkainizō (1), to
inaugurate
5048 tĕlĕiŏō (1), to
perfect, complete

CONSECRATION
4394 millû' (7), fulfilling;
setting; consecration
5145 nezer (2), set apart;
dedication

CONSECRATIONS
4394 millû' (4), fulfilling;
setting; consecration

CONSENT
14 'âbâh (4), to be
acquiescent
225 'ûwth (3), to assent
376 'îysh (1), man; male
3820 lêb (1), heart
7926 shᵉkem (2), neck;
spur of a hill
4334 prŏsĕrchŏmai (1),
to assent to
4852 sumphēmi (1), to
assent to
4859 sumphōnŏs (1),
agreeing; agreement

CONSENTED
225 'ûwth (1), to assent;
agree
8085 shâma' (1), to hear
1962 ĕpinĕuō (1), to
assent, give consent
4784 sugkatatithĕmai
(1), to accord with

CONSENTEDST
7521 râtsâh (1), to be
pleased with; to satisfy

CONSENTING
4909 sunĕudŏkĕō (2), to
assent to, feel gratified

CONSIDER
559 'âmar (1), to say
995 bîyn (20), to
understand; discern
3045 yâda' (4), to know
5027 nâbaṭ (5), to scan;
to regard with favor
6448 pâçag (1), to
contemplate
7200 râ'âh (15), to see
7725 shûwb (1), to turn
back; to return
7760 sûwm (2), to put
7760+3820 sûwm (4), to
put, place
7760+3820+5921 sûwm
(2), to put, place
7919 sâkal (2), to be or
act circumspect
357 analŏgizŏmai (1), to
contemplate
1260 dialŏgizŏmai (1), to
deliberate
1492 ĕidō (1), to know
2334 thĕōrĕō (1), to see;
to discern
2648 katamanthanō (1),
to note carefully
2657 katanŏĕō (4), to
observe fully
3539 nŏiĕō (1), to
exercise the mind

CONSIDERED
995 bîyn (1), to
understand; discern
2803 châshab (1), to
think, regard; to value
5414 nâthan (1), to give
7200 râ'âh (4), to see
7760+3820 sûwm (2), to
put, place
7896+3820 shîyth (1), to
place, put
7920 sᵉkal (Ch.) (1), to be
or act circumspect
8085 shâma' (1), to hear
2657 katanŏĕō (2), to
observe fully
4894 sunĕidō (1), to
understand
4920 suniēmi (1), to
comprehend

CONSIDEREST
7200 râ'âh (1), to see
2657 katanŏĕō (1), to
observe fully

CONSIDERETH
995 bîyn (1), to
understand; discern
2161 zâmam (1), to plan
3045 yâda' (2), to know
7200 râ'âh (2), to see
7725 shûwb (1), to turn
back; to return
7919 sâkal (2), to be or
act circumspect

CONSIDERING
995 bîyn (2), to
understand; discern
333 anathĕōrĕō (1), to
look again
4648 skŏpĕō (1), to watch
out for, i.e. to regard

CONSIST
4921 sunistaō (1), to set
together

CONSISTETH
2076 ĕsti (1), he (she or
it) is; they are

CONSOLATION
8575 tanchûwm (1),
compassion, solace
3874 paraklēsis (14),
imploring, solace

CONSOLATIONS
8575 tanchûwm (3),
compassion, solace

CONSORTED
4845 sumplērŏō (1), to be
complete, fulfill

CONSPIRACY
7195 qesher (9), unlawful
alliance
4945 sunōmŏsia (1), plot,
conspiracy

CONSPIRATORS
7194 qâshar (1), to tie,
bind

CONSPIRED
5320 Naphtûchîym (1),
Naphtuchim
7194 qâshar (18), to tie,
bind

CONSTANT
2388 châzaq (1), to
fasten upon; to seize

CONSTANTLY
5331 netsach (1),
splendor; lasting
1226 diabĕbaiŏŏmai (1),
to confirm thoroughly
1340 diïschurizŏmai (1),
to asseverate

CONSTELLATIONS
3685 Kᵉçîyl (1),
constellation Orion

CONSTRAIN
315 anagkazō (1), to
necessitate, compel

CONSTRAINED
2388 châzaq (1), to
fasten upon; to seize
315 anagkazō (3), to
necessitate, compel
3849 parabiazŏmai (2),
to compel by entreaty

CONSTRAINETH
6693 tsûwq (1), to
oppress, distress
4912 sunĕchō (1), to hold
together

CONSTRAINT
317 anagkastōs (1),
compulsorily

CONSULT
3289 yâ'ats (1), to advise

CONSULTATION
4824 sumbŏuliŏn (1),
advisement

CONSULTED
3272 yᵉ'aṭ (Ch.) (1), to
counsel
3289 yâ'ats (8), to advise
4427 mâlak (1), to reign
as king
7592 shâ'al (1), to ask
1011 bŏulĕuō (1), to
deliberate; to resolve
4823 sumbŏulĕuō (1), to
recommend, deliberate

CONSULTER
7592 shâ'al (1), to ask

CONSULTETH
1011 bŏulĕuō (1), to
deliberate; to resolve

CONSUME
398 'âkal (9), to eat
402 'oklâh (1), food
1086 bâlâh (1), to wear
out, decay; consume
1497 gâzal (1), to rob
2000 hâmam (1), to
disturb, drive, destroy
2628 châçal (1), to eat
off, consume
3423 yârash (1), to
inherit; to impoverish
3615 kâlâh (23), to
complete, consume
4529 mâçâh (1), to
dissolve, melt
4743 mâqaq (4), to melt;
to flow, dwindle, vanish
5486 çûwph (4), to
terminate
5487 çûwph (Ch.) (1), to
come to an end
5595 çâphâh (1), to
scrape; to accumulate
8046 shᵉmad (Ch.) (1), to
desolate
8552 tâmam (2), to
complete, finish
355 analiskō (2), destroy
1159 dapanaō (1), to
incur cost; to waste

CONSUMED
398 'âkal (21), to eat
622 'âçaph (1), to gather
1846 dâ'ak (1), to be
extinguished; to expire
3615 kâlâh (37), to
complete, consume
4127 mûwg (1), to soften,
flow down, disappear
5486 çûwph (1), to
terminate
5595 çâphâh (5), to
scrape; to accumulate
6244 'âshêsh (3), to fail
6789 tsâmath (1), to
extirpate, root out
8552 tâmam (24), to
complete, finish
355 analiskō (1), destroy

CONSUMETH
398 'âkal (2), to eat
1086 bâlâh (1), to wear
out, decay; consume
7503 râphâh (1), to
slacken

CONSUMING
398 'âkal (2), to eat
2654 katanaliskō (1), to
consume utterly

CONSUMMATION
3617 kâlâh (1), complete
destruction

CONSUMPTION
3617 kâlâh (2), complete
destruction
3631 killâyôwn (1),
pining, destruction
7829 shachepheth (2),
wasting disease

C

CONTAIN
1004 bayith (1), *house;*
temple; family, tribe
3557 kûwl (3), *to keep in;*
to maintain
5375 nâsâ' (1), *to lift up*
1467 ĕgkratĕuŏmai (1),
to exercise self-restraint
5562 chŏrĕō (1), *to pass,*
enter; to hold, admit

CONTAINED
3557 kûwl (2), *to keep in;*
to maintain
4023 pĕriĕchō (1), *to*
encircle; to contain

CONTAINETH
3557 kûwl (1), *to keep in;*
to maintain

CONTAINING
5562 chŏrĕō (1), *to pass,*
enter; to hold, admit

CONTEMN
3988 mâ'aç (1), *to spurn;*
to disappear
5006 nâ'ats (1), *to scorn*

CONTEMNED
936 bûwz (1), *to*
disrespect, scorn
959 bâzâh (1), *to*
disesteem, ridicule
5006 nâ'ats (1), *to scorn*
7034 qâlâh (1), *to hold in*
contempt

CONTEMNETH
3988 mâ'aç (1), *to spurn;*
to disappear

CONTEMPT
937 bûwz (7), *disrespect,*
scorn
963 bizzâyôwn (1),
disesteem, disrespect
1860 dᵉrâ'ôwn (1), *object*
of loathing
7043 qâlal (1), *to be easy,*
trifling, vile

CONTEMPTIBLE
959 bâzâh (3), *to*
disesteem, ridicule
1848 ĕxŏuthĕnĕō (1), *to*
treat with contempt

CONTEMPTUOUSLY
937 bûwz (1), *disrespect*

CONTEND
1624 gârâh (3), *to*
provoke to anger
1777 dîyn (1), *to judge; to*
strive or contend for
3401 yârîyb (1),
contentious; adversary
7378 rîyb (7), *to hold a*
controversy; to defend
8474 tachârâh (1), *to vie*
with a rival
1864 ĕpagōnizŏmai (1),
to struggle for, fight for

CONTENDED
4695 matstsûwth (1),
quarrel, contention
7378 rîyb (4), *to hold a*
controversy; to defend
1252 diakrinō (1), *to*
decide; to hesitate

CONTENDEST
7378 rîyb (1), *to hold a*
controversy; to defend

CONTENDETH
3401 yârîyb (1),
contentious; adversary
7378 rîyb (1), *to hold a*
controversy; to defend
8199 shâphaṭ (1), *to judge*

CONTENDING
1252 diakrinō (1), *to*
decide; to hesitate

CONTENT
14 'âbâh (1), *to be*
acquiescent
2974 yâ'al (7), *to assent;*
to undertake, begin
3190+5869 yâṭab (1), *to*
be, make well
8085 shâma' (1), *to hear*
intelligently
714 arkĕō (4), *to avail; be*
satisfactory
842 autarkēs (1),
contented
2425+3588+4160 hikanŏs
(1), *ample; fit*

CONTENTION
4066 mâdôwn (3),
contest or quarrel
4683 matstsâh (1),
quarrel
7379 rîyb (2), *contest,*
personal or legal
73 agōn (1), *contest,*
struggle
2052 ĕrithĕia (1), *faction,*
strife, selfish ambition
3948 parŏxusmŏs (1),
incitement; dispute

CONTENTIONS
4079 midyân (4), *contest*
or quarrel
2054 ĕris (2), *quarrel, i.e.*
wrangling

CONTENTIOUS
4066 mâdôwn (3),
contest or quarrel
1537+2052 ĕk (1), *out of*
5380 philŏnĕikŏs (1),
disputatious

CONTENTMENT
841 autarkeia (1),
contentedness

CONTINUAL
1115+5627 biltîy (1), *not,*
except, without, unless
2956 ṭârad (1), *to drive on*
8548 tâmîyd (27),
constantly, regularly
88 adialĕiptŏs (1),
permanent, constant
1519+5056 ĕis (1), *to or*
into

CONTINUALLY
1980 hâlak (3), *to walk;*
live a certain way
1980+7725 hâlak (1), *to*
walk; live a certain way
3605+3117 kôl (10), *all,*
any or every
6256 'êth (1), *time*
8411 tᵉdîyrâ' (Ch.) (2),
constantly, faithfully
8544 tᵉmûwnâh (1),
something fashioned
8548 tâmîyd (52),
constantly, regularly

CONTINUANCE
539 'âman (2), *to be firm;*
to be permanent
3117 yôwm (1), *day; time*
period
5769 'ôwlâm (1), *eternity;*
ancient; always
5281 hupŏmŏnē (1),
endurance, constancy

CONTINUE
309 'âchar (1), *to remain;*
to delay
1961 hâyâh (2), *to exist,*
i.e. be or become
3427 yâshab (2), *to dwell,*
to remain; to settle
3885 lûwn (1), *to be*
obstinate
4900 mâshak (1), *to draw*
out; to be tall
5975 'âmad (4), *to stand*
6965 qûwm (3), *to rise*
7931 shâkan (1), *to reside*
1265 diamĕnō (2), *to stay*
constantly
1696 ĕmmĕnō (1), *to*
remain; to persevere
1961 ĕpimĕnō (5), *to*
remain; to persevere
2476 histēmi (1), *to*
stand, establish
3306 mĕnō (7), *to stay,*
remain
3887 paramĕnō (1), *to be*
permanent, persevere
4160 pŏiĕō (2), *to do*
4342 prŏskartĕrĕō (1), *to*
persevere
4357 prŏsmĕnō (1), *to*
remain; to adhere to
4839 sumparamĕnō (1),
to remain in company

CONTINUED
1961 hâyâh (3), *to exist,*
i.e. be or become
2388 châzaq (1), *to*
fasten upon; to seize
3254 yâçaph (2), *to add*
or augment
3427 yâshab (3), *to dwell,*
to remain; to settle
5125 nûwn (1), *to be*
perpetual
5975 'âmad (1), *to stand*
7235 râbâh (1), *to*
increase
1096 ginŏmai (1), *to be,*
become
1265 diamĕnō (1), *to stay*
constantly
1273 dianuktĕrĕuō (1), *to*
pass, spend the night
1300 diatĕlĕō (1), *to*
persist, continue
1304 diatribō (2), *to*
remain, stay
1696 ĕmmĕnō (1), *to*
remain; to persevere
1961 ĕpimĕnō (2), *to*
remain; to persevere

CONTINUANCE
1275 diapantŏs (1),
constantly, continually
1519+1336 ĕis (2), *to or*
into
1725 ĕnanti (1), *before, in*
presence of
4342 prŏskartĕrĕō (3), *to*
be constantly diligent

CONTINUETH
5975 'âmad (1), *to stand*
1696 ĕmmĕnō (1), *to*
remain; to persevere
3306 mĕnō (1), *to stay,*
remain
3887 paramĕnō (1), *to be*
permanent, persevere
4357 prŏsmĕnō (1), *to*
remain; to adhere to

CONTINUING
1641 gârar (1), *to*
ruminate; to saw
3306 mĕnō (1), *to stay,*
remain
4342 prŏskartĕrĕō (2), *to*
persevere; to adhere

CONTRADICTING
483 antilĕgō (1), *to*
dispute, refuse

CONTRADICTION
485 antilŏgia (2),
dispute, disobedience

CONTRARIWISE
5121 tŏunantiŏn (3), *on*
the contrary

CONTRARY
2016 hephek (2), *reverse,*
perversion
7147 qᵉrîy (7), *hostile*
encounter
480 antikĕimai (2), *be*
adverse to
561 apĕnanti (1),
opposite, against
1727 ĕnantiŏs (6),
opposite
3844 para (3), *from; with;*
besides; on account of
3891 paranŏmĕō (1), *to*
transgress, violate law
5227 hupĕnantiŏs (1),
opposed; opponent

CONTRIBUTION
2842 kŏinōnia (1),
benefaction; sharing

CONTRITE
1792 dâkâ' (1), *to be*
contrite, be humbled
1793 dakkâ' (2), *contrite,*
humbled
1794 dâkâh (1), *to*
collapse; contrite
5223 nâkeh (1), *maimed;*
dejected

CONTROVERSIES
7379 rîyb (1), *contest,*
personal or legal

CONTROVERSY
7379 rîyb (12), *contest,*
personal or legal
3672 hŏmŏlŏgŏumĕnōs
(1), *confessedly*

CONVENIENT
2706 chôq (1),
appointment; allotment
3477 yâshâr (2), *straight*

433 anēkŏ (2), *be proper, fitting*
2119 ĕukairĕō (1), *to have opportunity*
2121 ĕukairŏs (1), *opportune, suitable*
2520 kathēkō (1), *becoming, proper*
2540 kairŏs (1), *occasion, set or proper*

CONVENIENTLY
2122 ĕukairŏs (1), *opportunely*

CONVERSANT
1980 hâlak (2), *to walk; live a certain way*

CONVERSATION
1870 derek (2), *road; course of life*
390 anastrĕphō (2), *to remain, to live*
391 anastrŏphē (13), *behavior*
4175 pŏlitĕuma (1), *citizenship*
4176 pŏlitĕuŏmai (1), *to behave as a citizen*
5158 trŏpŏs (1), *deportment, character*

CONVERSION
1995 ĕpistrŏphē (1), *moral revolution*

CONVERT
7725 shûwb (1), *to turn back; to return*
1994 ĕpistrĕphō (1), *to revert, turn back to*

CONVERTED
2015 hâphak (1), *to turn about or over*
7725 shûwb (1), *to turn back; to return*
1994 ĕpistrĕphō (6), *to revert, turn back to*
4762 strĕphō (1), *to turn around or reverse*

CONVERTETH
1994 ĕpistrĕphō (1), *to revert, turn back to*

CONVERTING
7725 shûwb (1), *to turn back; to return*

CONVERTS
7725 shûwb (1), *to turn back; to return*

CONVEY
5674 'âbar (1), *to cross over; to transition*
7760 sûwm (1), *to put*

CONVEYED
1593 ĕknĕuō (1), *to quietly withdraw*

CONVICTED
1651 ĕlĕgchō (1), *to confute, admonish*

CONVINCE
1651 ĕlĕgchō (1), *to confute, admonish*
1827 ĕxĕlĕgchō (1), *to punish*

CONVINCED
3198 yâkach (1), *to be correct; to argue*

1246 diakatĕlĕgchŏmai (1), *to prove downright*
1651 ĕlĕgchō (2), *to confute, admonish, rebuke*

CONVINCETH
1651 ĕlĕgchō (1), *to confute, admonish*

CONVOCATION
4744 miqrâ' (15), *public meeting*

CONVOCATIONS
4744 miqrâ' (3), *public meeting*

COOK
2876 ṭabbâch (2), *butcher, cook*

COOKS
2876 ṭabbâch (1), *butcher, cook*

COOL
7307 rûwach (1), *breath; wind; life-spirit*
2711 katapsuchō (1), *to refresh, cool off*

COOS
2972 Kōs (1), *Cos*

COPIED
6275 'âthaq (1), *to grow old; to transcribe*

COPING
2947 ṭêphach (1), *palm-breadth*

COPPER
5178 nᵉchôsheth (1), *copper; bronze*

COPPERSMITH
5471 chalkĕus (1), *copper-worker*

COPULATION
7902 shᵉkâbâh (3), *lying down*

COPY
4932 mishneh (2), *duplicate copy; double*
6572 parshegen (3), *transcript*
6573 parshegen (Ch.) (4), *transcript*

COR
3734 kôr (1), *dry measure*

CORAL
7215 râ'mâh (2), *high in value, (poss.) coral*

CORBAN
2878 kŏrban (1), *votive offering or gift*

CORD
2256 chebel (4), *company, band*
2339 chûwṭ (1), *string; measuring tape; line*
3499 yether (1), *remainder; small rope*

CORDS
2256 chebel (12), *company, band*
4340 mêythâr (8), *tent-cord; bow-string*
5688 'ăbôth (5), *entwined things*
4979 schŏiniŏn (1), *rushlet, i.e. grass-withe*

CORE
2879 Kŏrĕ (1), *ice*

CORIANDER
1407 gad (2), *coriander*

CORINTH
2882 Kŏrinthŏs (6), *Corinthus*

CORINTHIANS
2881 Kŏrinthiŏs (4), *inhabitant of Corinth*

CORINTHUS
2882 Kŏrinthŏs (1), *Corinthus*

CORMORANT
6893 qâ'ath (2), *pelican*
7994 shâlâk (2), *bird of prey (poss.) pelican*

CORN
1098 bᵉlîyl (1), *feed, fodder*
1121 bên (1), *son, descendant*
1250 bâr (9), *cereal grain*
1637 gôren (1), *open area*
1643 geres (2), *grain*
1715 dâgân (37), *grain*
3759 karmel (1), *planted field; garden produce*
5669 'âbûwr (2), *kept over; stored grain*
6194 'ârêm (1), *heap, mound; sheaf*
7054 qâmâh (7), *stalk of cereal grain*
7383 rîyphâh (1), *grits cereal*
7668 sheber (7), *grain*
7688 shâgach (1), *to glance sharply at*
2848 kŏkkŏs (1), *kernel*
4621 sitŏs (2), *grain, especially wheat*
4702 spŏrimŏs (3), *field planted with seed*
4719 stachus (3), *head of grain*

CORNELIUS
2883 Kŏrnēliŏs (10), *Cornelius*

CORNER
2106 zâvîyth (1), *angle, corner (as projecting)*
3671 kânâph (1), *edge or extremity; wing*
3802 kâthêph (2), *shoulder-piece; wall*
4742 mᵉquts'âh (1), *angle*
6285 pê'âh (5), *direction; region; extremity*
6434 pên (1), *angle*
6437 pânâh (1), *to turn, to face*
6438 pinnâh (17), *pinnacle; chieftain*
204 akrŏgōniaiŏs (2), *corner, cornerstone*
1137 gōnia (6), *angle; cornerstone*

CORNERS
2106 zâvîyth (1), *angle, corner (as projecting)*
3671 kânâph (2), *edge or extremity; wing*
4740 maqtsôwa' (1), *angle*
4742 mᵉquts'âh (6), *angle*

6284 pâ'âh (1), *to blow away*
6285 pê'âh (11), *region; extremity*
6438 pinnâh (6), *pinnacle; chieftain*
6471 pa'am (3), *time; step; occurence*
6763 tsêlâ' (2), *side*
7098 qâtsâh (1), *termination; fringe*
7106 qâtsa' (1), *to strip off, i.e. (partially) scrape*
746 archē (2), *first in rank; first in time*
1137 gōnia (2), *angle; cornerstone*

CORNET
7162 qeren (Ch.) (4), *horn*
7782 shôwphâr (3), *curved ram's horn*

CORNETS
4517 mᵉna'na' (1), *rattling instrument*
7782 shôwphâr (1), *curved ram's horn*

CORNFLOOR
1637+1715 gôren (1), *open area*

CORPSE
4430 ptōma (1), *corpse, carrion*

CORPSES
1472 gᵉvîyâh (2), *dead body*
6297 peger (2), *carcase; corpse*

CORRECT
3198 yâkach (1), *to be correct; to argue*
3256 yâçar (6), *to chastise; to instruct*

CORRECTED
3256 yâçar (1), *to chastise; to instruct*
3810 paidĕutēs (1), *teacher or discipliner*

CORRECTETH
3198 yâkach (2), *to be correct; to argue*

CORRECTION
3198 yâkach (1), *to be correct; to argue*
4148 mûwçâr (8), *reproof, warning*
7626 shêbeṭ (1), *stick; clan, family*
8433 tôwkêchâh (1), *correction*
1882 ĕpanŏrthōsis (1), *rectification, correction*

CORRUPT
1605 gâ'ar (1), *to chide, reprimand*
2254 châbal (1), *to bind by a pledge; to pervert*
2610 chânêph (1), *to soil, be defiled*
4167 mûwq (1), *to blaspheme, scoff*
4743 mâqaq (1), *to melt; to flow, dwindle, vanish*
7843 shâchath (11), *to decay; to ruin*
7844 shᵉchath (Ch.) (1), *to decay; to ruin*

853 aphanizō (2), to consume (becloud)
1311 diaphthĕirō (1), to ruin, to pervert
2585 kapēlĕuō (1), to retail, i.e. to adulterate
2704 kataphthĕirō (1), to spoil entirely
4550 saprŏs (6), rotten, i.e. worthless
5351 phthĕirō (4), to spoil; to deprave

CORRUPTED
7843 shâchath (11), to decay; to ruin
4595 sēpō (1), to putrefy, rot
5351 phthĕirō (2), to spoil; to deprave

CORRUPTERS
7843 shâchath (2), to decay; to ruin

CORRUPTETH
1311 diaphthĕirō (1), to ruin, to pervert

CORRUPTIBLE
862 aphthartŏs (1), undecaying, immortal
5349 phthartŏs (6), perishable, not lasting

CORRUPTING
7843 shâchath (1), to decay; to ruin

CORRUPTION
1097 b^{e}lîy (1), without, not yet; lacking;
4889 mashchîyth (2), destruction; corruption
4893 mishchâth (1), disfigurement
7845 shachath (4), pit; destruction
1312 diaphthŏra (6), decay, corruption
5356 phthŏra (7), ruin; depravity, corruption

CORRUPTLY
2254 châbal (1), to bind by a pledge; to pervert
7843 shâchath (1), to decay; to ruin

COSAM
2973 Kōsam (1), Cosam

COST
2600 chinnâm (2), free
1160 dapanē (1), expense, cost

COSTLINESS
5094 timiŏtēs (1), expensiveness

COSTLY
3368 yâqâr (4), valuable
4185 pŏlutĕlēs (1), extremely expensive
4186 pŏlutimŏs (1), extremely valuable

COTES
220 'ăvêrâh (1), stall, pen

COTTAGE
4412 m^{e}lûwnâh (1), hut
5521 çukkâh (1), tabernacle; shelter

COTTAGES
3741 kârâh (1), meadow

COUCH
3326 yâtsûwa' (1), bed; wing or lean-to
4904 mishkâb (1), bed; sleep
6210 'eres (2), canopy couch
7742 sûwach (1), to muse pensively
2826 klinidiŏn (2), pallet or little couch

COUCHED
3766 kâra' (1), to prostrate
7257 râbats (1), to recline, repose, brood

COUCHES
6210 'eres (1), canopy couch
2895 krabbatŏs (1), sleeping mat

COUCHETH
7257 râbats (1), to recline, repose, brood

COUCHING
7257 râbats (1), to recline, repose, brood

COUCHINGPLACE
4769 marbêts (1), resting place

COULD
3045 yâda' (2), to know
3201 yâkôl (46), to be able
3202 y^{e}kêl (Ch.) (1), to be able
3546 k^{e}hal (Ch.) (1), to be able
5074 nâdad (1), to rove, flee; to drive away
5234 nâkar (1), to acknowledge
5346 Neqeb (1), dell
102 adunatŏs (1), weak; impossible
1410 dunamai (29), to be able or possible
1415 dunatŏs (1), powerful or capable
2192 ĕchō (3), to have; hold; keep
2480 ischuō (7), to have or exercise force
2489 Iōanna (1), Jehovah-favored
5342 phĕrō (1), to bear or carry

COULDEST
3201 yâkôl (1), to be able
2480 ischuō (1), to have or exercise force

COULDST
3202 y^{e}kêl (Ch.) (1), to be able

COULTER
855 'êth (1), digging implement

COULTERS
855 'êth (1), digging implement

COUNCIL
7277 rigmâh (1), throng
4824 sumbŏuliŏn (2), deliberative body
4892 sunĕdriŏn (20), tribunal

COUNCILS
4891 sunĕgĕirō (2), to raise up with

COUNSEL
1697 dâbâr (1), word; matter; thing
3245 yâçad (2), settle, consult
3289 yâ'ats (21), to advise
4431 m^{e}lak (Ch.) (1), counsel, advice
5475 çôwd (6), intimacy; consultation; secret
5843 'êṭâ' (Ch.) (1), prudence
6098 'êtsâh (80), advice; plan; prudence
8458 tachbûlâh (2), guidance; plan
1011 bŏulĕuō (1), to deliberate; to resolve
1012 bŏulē (9), purpose, plan, decision
4823 sumbŏulĕuō (4), to recommend, deliberate
4824 sumbŏuliŏn (5), deliberative body

COUNSELED
3289 yâ'ats (1), to advise

COUNSELLED
3289 yâ'ats (3), to advise

COUNSELLOR
3289 yâ'ats (10), to advise
6098 'êtsâh (1), advice; plan; prudence
1010 bŏulĕutēs (2), adviser, councillor
4825 sumbŏulŏs (1), adviser

COUNSELLORS
1884 d^{e}thâbâr (Ch.) (2), skilled in law; judge
1907 haddâbâr (Ch.) (4), vizier, high official
3272 y^{e}'aṭ (Ch.) (2), to counsel
3289 yâ'ats (12), to advise
6098 'êtsâh (1), advice; plan; prudence

COUNSELS
4156 môw'êtsâh (6), purpose, plan
6098 'êtsâh (2), advice; plan; prudence
8458 tachbûlâh (3), guidance; plan
1012 bŏulē (1), purpose, plan, decision

COUNT
1961 hâyâh (1), to exist, i.e. be or become
2803 châshab (3), to think; to compute
3699 kâçaç (1), to estimate, determine
4487 mânâh (1), to allot; to enumerate or enroll
5414 nâthan (1), to give
5608 çâphar (4), to inscribe; to enumerate
515 axiŏō (1), to deem entitled or fit, worthy
2192 ĕchō (2), to have; hold; keep
2233 hēgĕŏmai (7), to deem, i.e. consider
3049 lŏgizŏmai (1), to credit; to think, regard
3106 makarizō (1), to esteem fortunate
5585 psēphizō (1), to compute, estimate

COUNTED
2803 châshab (18), to think; to compute
5608 çâphar (2), to inscribe; to enumerate
6485 pâqad (3), to visit, care for, count
515 axiŏō (2), to deem entitled or fit, worthy
1075 gĕnĕalŏgĕō (1), trace in genealogy
2192 ĕchō (2), to have; hold; keep
2233 hēgĕŏmai (3), to deem, i.e. consider
2661 kataxiŏō (2), to deem entirely deserving
3049 lŏgizŏmai (4), to credit; to think, regard
4860 sumpsēphizō (1), to compute jointly

COUNTENANCE
639 'aph (1), nose or nostril; face; person
1921 hâdar (1), to favor or honor; to be proud
2122 zîyv (Ch.) (4), cheerfulness
4758 mar'eh (8), appearance; vision
5869 'ayin (1), eye; sight; fountain
6440 pânîym (30), face
8389 tô'ar (1), outline, figure or appearance
2397 idĕa (1), sight
3799 ŏpsis (1), face; appearance
4383 prŏsōpŏn (3), face, presence
4659 skuthrōpŏs (1), gloomy or mournful

COUNTENANCES
4758 mar'eh (2), appearance; vision

COUNTERVAIL
7737 shâvâh (1), to resemble; to adjust

COUNTETH
2803 châshab (2), to think; to compute
5585 psēphizō (1), to compute, estimate

COUNTRIES
776 'erets (48), earth, land, soil; country
5316 nepheth (1), height
5561 chōra (1), space of territory

COUNTRY
127 'ădâmâh (1), soil; land
249 'ezrâch (5), native born
339 'îy (1), dry land; coast; island
776 'erets (91), earth, land, soil; country
1552 g^{e}lîylâh (1), circuit or region

2256 chebel (1), *company, band*
4725 mâqôwm (1), *general locality, place*
6521 pᵉrâzîy (1), *rustic*
7704 sâdeh (17), *field*
68 agrŏs (8), *farm*land, *countryside*
589 apŏdēmēŏ (4), *visit a foreign land*
1085 gĕnŏs (1), *kin, offspring in kind*
1093 gē (2), *soil, region, whole earth*
3968 patris (8), *hometown*
4066 pĕrichŏrŏs (4), *surrounding country*
5561 chōra (15), *space of territory*

COUNTRYMEN
1085 gĕnŏs (1), *kin, offspring in kind*
4853 sumphulētēs (1), *of the same country*

COUPLE
2266 châbar (5), *to fascinate by spells*
6776 tsemed (4), *paired yoke*
8147 shᵉnayim (1), *two-fold*

COUPLED
2266 châbar (7), *to fascinate by spells*
8382 tâ'am (2), *to be twinned, i.e. duplicate*
8535 tâm (2), *morally pious; gentle, dear*

COUPLETH
2279 chôbereth (2), *joint*

COUPLING
2279 chôbereth (2), *joint*
4225 machbereth (8), *junction*

COUPLINGS
4226 mᵉchabbᵉrâh (1), *joiner*

COURAGE
553 'âmats (9), *to be strong; be courageous*
2388 châzaq (8), *to be strong; courageous*
3824 lêbâb (1), *heart*
7307 rûwach (1), *breath; wind; life-spirit*
2294 tharsŏs (1), *boldness, courage*

COURAGEOUS
533+3820 'ammîyts (1), *strong; mighty; brave*
553 'âmats (2), *to be strong; be courageous*
2388 châzaq (2), *to be strong; courageous*

COURAGEOUSLY
2388 châzaq (1), *to be strong; courageous*

COURSE
4131 môwt (1), *to slip, shake, fall*
4256 machălŏqeth (19), *section or division*
4794 mᵉrûwtsâh (2), *race*
165 aiōn (1), *perpetuity, ever; world*

1408 drŏmŏs (3), *career, course of life*
2113 ĕuthudrŏmēŏ (1), *to sail direct*
2183 ĕphēmĕria (2), *rotation or class*
3313 mĕrŏs (1), *division or share*
4144 plŏŏs (2), *navigation, voyage*
5143 trĕchō (1), *to run or walk hastily; to strive*
5164 trŏchŏs (1), *wheel; circuitous course of life*

COURSES
2487 chălîyphâh (1), *alternation, change*
2988 yâbâl (1), *stream*
4255 machlᵉqâh (Ch.) (1), *section or division*
4256 machălŏqeth (14), *section or division*
4546 mᵉçillâh (1), *main thoroughfare; viaduct*

COURT
1004 bayith (1), *house; temple; family, tribe*
2681 châtsîyr (1), *court or abode*
2691 châtsêr (114), *enclosed yard*
5835 'ăzârâh (2), *enclosure; border*
5892 'îyr (1), *city, town, unwalled-village*
833 aulē (1), *palace; house; courtyard*

COURTEOUS
5391 philŏphrŏn (1), *kind, well-disposed*

COURTEOUSLY
5364 philanthrōpōs (1), *fondly to mankind*
5390 philŏphrŏnōs (1), *friendliness of mind*

COURTS
2691 châtsêr (24), *enclosed yard*

COUSIN
4773 suggĕnēs (1), *relative; countryman*

COUSINS
4773 suggĕnēs (1), *relative; countryman*

COVENANT
1285 bᵉrîyth (264), *compact, agreement*
1242 diathēkē (17), *contract; devisory will*

COVENANTBREAKERS
802 asunthĕtŏs (1), *untrustworthy*

COVENANTED
3772 kârath (2), *to make an agreement*
2476 histēmi (1), *to stand, establish*
4934 suntithēmai (1), *to consent, concur, agree*

COVENANTS
1242 diathēkē (3), *contract; devisory will*

COVER
2645 châphâh (1), *to cover; to veil, to encase*

3680 kâçâh (50), *to cover*
4374 mᵉkaççeh (1), *covering*
5258 nâçak (4), *to pour a libation; to anoint*
5526 çâkak (5), *to fence in; cover over; protect*
5844 'âţâh (5), *to wrap, i.e. cover, veil, clothe*
7159 qâram (1), *to cover*
7779 shûwph (1), *to gape, to overwhelm*
2572 kaluptō (2), *to cover*
2619 katakaluptō (1), *cover with a veil*
4028 pĕrikaluptō (1), *to cover eyes*

COVERED
1104 bâla' (1), *to swallow; to destroy*
2645 châphâh (7), *to cover; to veil, to encase*
2926 ţâlal (1), *to cover, roof*
3271 yâ'aţ (1), *to clothe, cover*
3680 kâçâh (61), *to cover*
3728 kâphash (1), *to tread down*
3780 kâsâh (1), *to grow fat*
3813 lâ'aţ (1), *to muffle, cover*
4374 mᵉkaççeh (1), *covering*
5526 çâkak (8), *to fence in; cover over; protect*
5603 çâphan (3), *to hide by covering; to roof*
5743 'ûwb (1), *to darkly becloud*
5844 'âţâh (3), *to wrap, i.e. cover, veil, clothe*
5848 'âţaph (1), *to shroud, clothe*
6632 tsâb (1), *covered cart*
6823 tsâphâh (5), *to sheet over with metal*
7159 qâram (1), *to cover*
1943 ĕpikaluptō (1), *to forgive*
2572 kaluptō (2), *to cover*
2596 kata (1), *down*
2619 katakaluptō (2), *cover with a veil*
4780 sugkaluptō (1), *to conceal altogether*

COVEREDST
3680 kâçâh (1), *to cover*

COVEREST
3680 kâçâh (1), *to cover*
5844 'âţâh (1), *to wrap, i.e. cover, veil, clothe*

COVERETH
3680 kâçâh (20), *to cover*
4374 mᵉkaççeh (2), *covering*
5526 çâkak (2), *to fence in; cover over; protect*
5844 'âţâh (1), *to wrap, i.e. cover, veil, clothe*
5848 'âţaph (1), *to shroud, i.e. clothe*
2572 kaluptō (1), *to cover*

COVERING
168 'ôhel (1), *tent*

3680 kâçâh (2), *to cover*
3681 kâçûwy (2), *covering*
3682 kᵉçûwth (6), *cover; veiling*
3875 lôwţ (1), *veil*
4372 mikçeh (16), *covering*
4539 mâçâk (7), *veil; shield*
4540 mᵉçukkâh (1), *covering*
4541 maççêkâh (2), *cast image); woven coverlet*
4817 merkâb (1), *chariot; seat in chariot*
5526 çâkak (2), *to fence in; cover over; protect*
5643 çêther (1), *cover, shelter*
5844 'âţâh (1), *to wrap, i.e. cover, veil, clothe*
6781 tsâmîyd (1), *bracelet; lid*
6826 tsippûwy (3), *encasement with metal*
4018 pĕribŏlaiŏn (1), *mantle, veil*

COVERINGS
4765 marbad (2), *coverlet, covering*

COVERS
7184 qâsâh (3), *jug*

COVERT
4329 mêyçâk (1), *covered portico*
4563 miçtôwr (1), *refuge, hiding place*
5520 çôk (1), *hut of entwined boughs; lair*
5521 çukkâh (1), *tabernacle; shelter*
5643 çêther (5), *cover, shelter*

COVET
183 'âvâh (1), *to wish for, desire*
2530 châmad (3), *to delight in; lust for*
1937 ĕpithumĕŏ (2), *to long for*
2206 zēlŏŏ (2), *to have warmth of feeling for*

COVETED
2530 châmad (1), *to delight in; lust for*
1937 ĕpithumĕŏ (1), *to long for*
3713 ŏrĕgŏmai (1), *to reach out after, long for*

COVETETH
183 'âvâh (1), *to wish for, desire*
1214 bâtsa' (1), *to plunder; to finish*

COVETOUS
1214 bâtsa' (1), *to plunder; to finish*
866 aphilargurŏs (1), *not greedy*
4123 plĕŏnĕktēs (4), *eager for gain, greedy*
4124 plĕŏnĕxia (1), *fraudulence, extortion*
5366 philargurŏs (2), *avaricious*

COVETOUSNESS
1215 betsa' (10), plunder;
unjust gain
866 aphilarguròs (1), not
greedy
4124 plĕŏnĕxia (8),
fraudulence, avarice

COVOCATION
4744 miqrâ' (1), public
meeting

COW
5697 'eglâh (1), cow calf
6510 pârâh (2), heifer
7794 shôwr (2), bullock

COW'S
1241 bâqâr (1), plowing
ox; herd

COZ
6976 Qôwts (1), thorns

COZBI
3579 Kozbîy (2), false

CRACKLING
6963 qôwl (1), voice or
sound

CRACKNELS
5350 niqqud (1), crumb,
morsel; biscuit

CRAFT
4820 mirmâh (1), fraud
1388 dŏlŏs (1), wile,
deceit, trickery
2039 ĕrgasia (1),
occupation; profit
3313 mĕrŏs (1), division
or share
3673 hŏmŏtĕchnŏs (1),
fellow-artificer
5078 tĕchnĕ (1), trade,
craft; skill

CRAFTINESS
6193 'ôrem (1),
stratagem, craftiness
3834 panŏurgia (4),
trickery or sophistry

CRAFTSMAN
2976 yâ'ash (1), to
despond, despair
5079 tĕchnitĕs (1),
skilled craftsman

CRAFTSMEN
2796 chârâsh (5), skilled
fabricator or worker
5079 tĕchnitĕs (2),
skilled craftsman

CRAFTY
6175 'ârûwm (2),
cunning; clever
6191 'âram (1), to be
cunning; be prudent
3835 panŏurgŏs (1),
shrewd, clever

CRAG
8127 shên (1), tooth;
ivory; cliff

CRANE
5483 çûwç (2), horse;
bird swallow

CRASHING
7667 sheber (1), fracture;
ruin

CRAVED
154 aitĕŏ (1), to ask for

CRAVETH
404 'âkaph (1), to urge

CREATE
1254 bârâ' (8), to create;
fashion

CREATED
1254 bârâ' (33), to create;
fashion
2936 ktizŏ (12), to
fabricate, create

CREATETH
1254 bârâ' (1), to create;
fashion

CREATION
2937 ktisis (6), formation

CREATOR
1254 bârâ' (3), to create;
fashion
2936 ktizo (1), to
fabricate, create
2939 ktistĕs (1), founder

CREATURE
2416 chay (6), alive; raw;
fresh; life
5315 nephesh (9), life;
breath; soul; wind
8318 sherets (1), swarm,
teeming mass
2937 ktisis (11),
formation
2938 ktisma (2), created
product

CREATURES
255 'ôach (1), creature
that howls;
2416 chay (9), alive; raw;
fresh; life
2938 ktisma (2), created
product

CREDITOR
1167+4874+3027 ba'al (1),
master; owner; citizen
5383 nâshâh (1), to lend
or borrow
1157 danĕistĕs (1),
money lender

CREDITORS
5383 nâshâh (1), to lend
or borrow

CREEK
2859 kŏlpŏs (1), lap area;
bay

CREEP
7430 râmas (2), to glide
swiftly, i.e. crawl
8317 shârats (2), to
wriggle, swarm
8318 sherets (2), swarm,
teeming mass
1744+1519 ĕndunŏ (1), to
sneak in, creep in

CREEPETH
7430 râmas (9), to glide
swiftly, i.e. crawl
7431 remes (1), any
rapidly moving animal
8317 shârats (4), to
wriggle, swarm

CREEPING
7431 remes (15), any
rapidly moving animal
8318 sherets (11),
swarm, teeming mass
2062 hĕrpĕtŏn (3), reptile

CREPT
3921 parĕisdunŏ (1), to
slip in secretly

CRESCENS
2913 Krĕskĕs (1), growing

CRETE
2914 Krĕtĕ (5), Cretĕ

CRETES
2912 Krĕs (1), inhabitant
of Crete

CRETIANS
2912 Krĕs (2), inhabitant
of Crete

CREW
5455 phŏnĕŏ (5), to emit
a sound

CRIB
18 'ĕbûwç (3), manger or
stall

CRIED
2199 zâ'aq (31), to call
out, announce
2200 zeʿîq (Ch.) (1), to
make an outcry, shout
2980 yábab (1), to bawl,
cry out
5414 nâthan (1), to give
6817 tsâ'aq (29), to
shriek; to proclaim
7121 qârâ' (54), to call
out
7123 qeʿrâ' (Ch.) (3), to
call out
7321 rûwa' (2), to shout
for alarm or joy
7768 shâva' (10), to
halloo, call for help
310 anabŏaŏ (2), to cry
out
349 anakrazŏ (5), to
scream aloud
863 aphiĕmi (1), to leave;
to pardon, forgive
994 bŏaŏ (3), to shout for
help
2019 ĕpiphŏnĕŏ (2), to
exclaim, shout
2896 krazŏ (43), to call
aloud
2905 kraugazŏ (6), to
clamor, shout
5455 phŏnĕŏ (5), to emit
a sound

CRIES
995 bŏĕ (1), to call for aid

CRIEST
2199 zâ'aq (2), to call
out, announce
6817 tsâ'aq (1), to shriek;
to proclaim
7121 qârâ' (2), to call out

CRIETH
2199 zâ'aq (1), to call
out, announce
5414+6963 nâthan (1), to
give
6817 tsâ'aq (2), to shriek;
to proclaim
7121 qârâ' (4), to call out
7442 rânan (3), to shout
for joy
7768 shâva' (2), to
halloo, call for help
2896 krazŏ (4), to call
aloud

CRIME
2154 zimmâh (1), bad
plan
1462 ĕgklĕma (1),
accusation

CRIMES
4941 mishpâṭ (1), verdict;
formal decree; justice
156 aitia (1), logical
reason; legal crime

CRIMSON
3758 karmîyl (3),
carmine, deep red
8144 shânîy (1), crimson
dyed stuffs
8438 tôwlâ' (1), maggot
worm; crimson-grub

CRIPPLE
5560 chŏlŏs (1), limping,
crippled

CRISPING
2754 chârîyṭ (1), pocket

CRISPUS
2921 Krispŏs (2), crisp

CROOKBACKT
1384 gibbên (1),
hunch-backed

CROOKED
1281 bârîyach (1),
fleeing, gliding serpent
1921 hâdar (1), to favor
or honor; to be high
4625 ma'ăqâsh (1), crook
in a road
5753 'âvâh (1), to be
crooked
5791 'âvath (2), to wrest,
twist
6121 'âqôb (1),
fraudulent; tracked
6128 'ăqalqal (1), crooked
6129 'ăqallâthôwn (1),
crooked
6140 'âqash (1), to knot
or distort; to pervert
6141 'iqqêsh (1),
distorted, warped, false
6618 peʿthaltôl (1),
tortuous, perverse
4646 skŏliŏs (2), crooked;
perverse

CROP
4760 mur'âh (1), craw or
crop of a bird
6998 qâṭaph (1), to strip
off, pick off

CROPPED
6998 qâṭaph (1), to strip
off, pick off

CROSS
4716 staurŏs (28), pole or
cross

CROSSWAY
6563 pereq (1), rapine;
fork in roads

CROUCH
7812 shâchâh (1), to
prostrate in homage

CROUCHETH
1794 dâkâh (1), to
collapse; contrite

CROW
5455 phŏnĕŏ (7), to emit
a sound

CROWN
2213 zêr (10), border molding on a building
3804 kether (3), royal headdress
5145 nezer (11), royal chaplet
5850 'ăṭârâh (20), crown
6936 qodqôd (7), crown of the head
4735 stěphanŏs (15), chaplet, wreath

CROWNED
3803 kâthar (1), to enclose, besiege; to wait
4502 minnᵉzâr (1), prince
5849 'âṭar (2), to encircle, enclose in; to crown
4737 stephanŏō (2), to adorn with a wreath

CROWNEDST
4737 stephanŏō (1), to adorn with a wreath

CROWNEST
5849 'âṭar (1), to encircle, enclose in; to crown

CROWNETH
5849 'âṭar (1), to encircle, enclose in; to crown

CROWNING
5849 'âṭar (1), to encircle, enclose in; to crown

CROWNS
5850 'ăṭârâh (3), crown
1238 diadēma (3), crown or diadem
4735 stěphanŏs (3), chaplet, wreath

CRUCIFIED
4362 prŏspēgnumi (1), to fasten to a cross
4717 staurŏō (31), to crucify
4957 sustaurŏō (5), to crucify with

CRUCIFY
388 anastaurŏō (1), to re-crucify
4717 staurŏō (13), to crucify

CRUEL
393 'akzâr (3), violent, deadly; brave
394 'akzârîy (8), terrible, cruel
395 'akzᵉrîyûwth (1), fierceness, cruelty
2555 châmâç (1), violence; malice
2556 châmêts (1), to be fermented; be soured
7185 qâshâh (2), to be tough or severe
7186 qâsheh (1), severe

CRUELLY
6233 'ôsheq (1), injury; fraud; distress

CRUELTY
2555 châmâç (4), violence; malice
6531 perek (1), severity

CRUMBS
5589 psichiŏn (3), little bit or morsel

CRUSE
1228 baqbûk (1), bottle
6746 tsᵉlôchîyth (1), vial or salt-cellar
6835 tsappachath (7), flat saucer

CRUSH
1792 dâkâ' (1), to pulverize; be contrite
2115 zûwr (1), to press together, tighten
7533 râtsats (1), to crack in pieces, smash
7665 shâbar (1), to burst

CRUSHED
1792 dâkâ' (2), to pulverize; be contrite
2000 hâmam (1), to disturb, drive, destroy
2116 zûwreh (1), trodden on
3807 kâthath (1), to bruise, strike, beat
3905 lâchats (1), to press; to distress
7533 râtsats (1), to crack in pieces, smash

CRY
602 'ânaq (3), to shriek, cry out in groaning
1993 hâmâh (1), to be in great commotion
2199 zâ'aq (25), to call out, announce
2201 za'aq (18), shriek, outcry, lament
5414+6963 nâthan (1), to give
6030 'ânâh (2), to respond, answer
6165 'ârag (1), to long for, pant for
6463 pâ'âh (1), to scream in childbirth
6670 tsâhal (3), to be cheerful; to sound
6682 tsᵉvâchâh (2), screech of anguish
6817 tsâ'aq (15), to shriek; to proclaim
6818 tsa'âqâh (19), shriek, wail
6873 tsârach (1), to whoop
6963 qôwl (1), voice or sound
7121 qârâ' (37), to call out
7321 rûwa' (5), to shout for alarm or joy
7440 rinnâh (12), shout
7442 rânan (1), to shout for joy
7768 shâva' (8), to call for help
7769 shûwa' (1), call
7773 sheva' (1), call
7775 shav'âh (11), call
8173 shâ'a' (1), to fondle, please or amuse (self)
994 bŏaō (2), to shout for help
2896 krazō (3), to call
2905 kraugazō (1), to clamor, shout
2906 kraugē (3), outcry

CRYING
603 'ănâqâh (1), shrieking, groaning
2201 za'aq (2), shriek, outcry, lament
4191 mûwth (1), to die; to kill
6682 tsᵉvâchâh (1), screech of anguish
6818 tsa'âqâh (2), shriek, wail
7121 qârâ' (1), to call out
7771 shôwa' (1), call
8663 tᵉshû'âh (1), crashing or clamor
310 anabŏaō (1), to cry out
994 bŏaō (6), to shout for help
1916 ĕpibŏaō (1), to cry out loudly
2896 krazō (9), to call
2906 kraugē (2), outcry

CRYSTAL
2137 zᵉkûwkîyth (1), transparent glass
7140 qerach (1), ice; hail; rock crystal
2929 krustallizō (1), to appear as ice
2930 krustallŏs (2), rock crystal

CUBIT
520 'ammâh (35), cubit
1574 gômed (1), measurement of length
4083 pēchus (2), measure of time or length

CUBITS
520 'ammâh (197), cubit
521 'ammâh (Ch.) (4), cubit
4088 pikria (2), acridity, bitterness

CUCKOW
7828 shachaph (2), gull

CUCUMBERS
4750 miqshâh (1), cucumber field
7180 qishshû' (1), cucumber

CUD
1625 gêrâh (11), cud

CUMBERED
4049 pĕrispaō (1), to be distracted

CUMBERETH
2673 katargĕō (1), to be, render entirely useless

CUMBRANCE
2960 ṭôrach (1), burden

CUMI
2891 kŏumi (1), rise!

CUMMIN
3646 kammôn (3), cummin
2951 kuminŏn (1), dill or fennel

CUNNING
542 'âmân (1), expert artisan, craftsman
995 bîyn (1), to understand; discern
1847 da'ath (1), understanding

CURSE
2450 châkâm (10), wise, intelligent, skillful
2803 châshab (11), to plot; to think, regard
3045 yâda' (4), to know
4284 machăshâbâh (3), contrivance; plan

CUP
1375 gᵉbîya' (4), goblet; bowl
3563 kôwç (29), cup; (poss.) owl
3599 kîyç (1), cup; utility bag
5592 çaph (1), dish
4221 pŏtēriŏn (31), drinking-vessel

CUPBEARER
4945 mashqeh (1), butler; drink; well-watered

CUPBEARERS
4945 mashqeh (2), butler; drink; well-watered

CUPS
101 'aggân (1), bowl
3563 kôwç (1), cup
4518 mᵉnaqqîyth (1), sacrificial basin
7184 qâsâh (1), jug
4221 pŏtēriŏn (2), drinking-vessel

CURDLED
7087 qâphâ' (1), to thicken, congeal

CURE
1455 gâhâh (1), to heal
7495 râphâ' (1), to cure, heal
2323 thĕrapĕuō (2), to relieve disease

CURED
8585 tᵉ'âlâh (1), bandage or plaster
2323 thĕrapĕuō (3), to relieve disease

CURES
2392 iasis (1), curing

CURIOUS
4284 machăshâbâh (1), contrivance; plan
4021 pĕriĕrgŏs (1), meddlesome, busybody

CURIOUSLY
7551 râqam (1), variegation; embroider

CURRENT
5674 'âbar (1), to cross over; to transition

CURSE
423 'âlâh (9), imprecation; curse
779 'ârar (15), to execrate, place a curse
1288 bârak (3), to bless
2764 chêrem (4), doomed object
3994 mᵉ'êrâh (4), execration, curse
5344 nâqab (4), to specify, designate, libel
6895 qâbab (7), to stab with words
7043 qâlal (17), to be easy, trifling, vile

CURSED
7045 qᵉlâlâh (24), vilification
7621 shᵉbûw'âh (1), sworn oath
8381 ta'âlâh (1), imprecation
332 anathĕmatizō (3), to declare or vow an oath
2652 katanathĕma (1), imprecation
2653 katanathĕmatizō (1), to imprecate
2671 katara (3), imprecation, execration
2672 kataraŏmai (4), to execrate, curse

CURSED
779 'ârar (44), to execrate, place a curse
1288 bârak (1), to bless
2764 chĕrem (3), doomed object
5344 nâqab (1), to specify, designate, libel
6895 qâbab (1), to stab with words
7043 qâlal (17), to be easy, trifling, vile
1944 ĕpikataratŏs (3), execrable, cursed
2671 katara (1), imprecation, execration
2672 kataraŏmai (1), to execrate, curse

CURSEDST
422 'âlâh (1), imprecate, utter a curse
2672 kataraŏmai (1), to execrate, curse

CURSES
423 'âlâh (5), imprecation: curse
7045 qᵉlâlâh (3), vilification

CURSEST
779 'ârar (1), to execrate, place a curse

CURSETH
779 'ârar (2), to execrate, place a curse
7043 qâlal (6), to be easy, trifling, vile
2551 kakŏlŏgĕō (2), to revile, curse

CURSING
423 'âlâh (4), imprecation: curse
3994 mᵉ'êrâh (1), execration, curse
7045 qᵉlâlâh (4), vilification
685 ara (1), imprecation, curse
2671 katara (2), imprecation, execration

CURSINGS
7045 qᵉlâlâh (1), vilification

CURTAIN
1852 dôq (1), fine, thin cloth
3407 yᵉrîy'âh (23), drapery
4539 mâçâk (1), veil; shield

CURTAINS
3407 yᵉrîy'âh (31), drapery

CUSH
3568 Kûwsh (8), Cush

CUSHAN
3572 Kûwshân (1), Cushan

CUSHI
3569 Kûwshîy (10), Cushite

CUSTODY
3027 yâd (4), hand; power
6486 pᵉquddâh (1), visitation; punishment

CUSTOM
1870 derek (1), road; mode of action
1983 hălâk (Ch.) (3), toll, duty on goods at a road
2706 chôq (2), appointment; allotment
4941 mishpâṭ (2), verdict; formal decree; justice
1480 ĕthizō (1), customary, required
1485 ĕthŏs (2), usage
3588+1486 hŏ (1), "the" i.e. the definite article
4914 sunētheia (2), usage, custom
5056 tĕlŏs (2), conclusion of an act or state
5058 tĕlōniŏn (3), tax-gatherer's booth

CUSTOMS
2708 chuqqâh (2), to delineate
1485 ĕthŏs (5), usage

CUT
1214 bâtsa' (3), to plunder; to finish
1219 bâtsar (1), to be inaccessible
1254 bârâ' (2), to create; fashion
1413 gâdad (5), to gash, slash oneself
1438 gâda' (21), to fell a tree; to destroy
1494 gâzaz (2), to shear; shave; destroy
1504 gâzar (8), to cut down; to destroy
1505 gᵉzar (Ch.) (2), to quarry rock
1629 gâraz (1), to cut off
1820 dâmâh (5), to be silent; to fail, cease
1826 dâmam (5), to stop, cease; to perish
2404 châṭab (1), to chop or carve wood
2498 châlaph (1), to pierce; to change
2672 châtsab (1), to cut stone or carve wood
2686 châtsats (1), to curtail
3582 kâchad (10), to destroy; to hide
3683 kâçach (2), to cut off
3772 kârath (175), to cut (off, down or asunder)
4135 mûwl (2), to circumcise

5243 nâmal (4), to be circumcised
5352 nâqâh (2), to be, make clean; to be bare
5362 nâqaph (1), to strike; to surround
5408 nâthach (7), to dismember, cut up
5648 'âbad (Ch.) (2), to do, work, serve
5927 'âlâh (1), to ascend, be high, mount
6780 tsemach (1), sprout, branch
6789 tsâmath (7), to extirpate, destroy
6990 qâṭaṭ (1), to destroy
6998 qâṭaph (2), to strip off, pick off
7059 qâmaṭ (1), to pluck, i.e. destroy
7082 qâçaç (1), to lop off
7088 qâphad (1), to roll together
7094 qâtsab (1), to clip, or chop
7096 qâtsâh (1), to cut off; to destroy
7112 qâtsats (10), to chop off; to separate
7113 qᵉtsats (Ch.) (1), to chop off, lop off
7167 qâra' (1), to rend
7787 sûwr (1), to saw
8295 sâraṭ (1), to gash oneself
8456 tâzaz (1), to lop off
581 apŏgĕnŏmĕnŏs (1), deceased
609 apŏkŏptō (6), mutilate the genitals
851 aphairĕō (1), to remove, cut off
1282 diapriō (2), to be furious
1371 dichŏtŏmĕō (2), to flog severely
1581 ĕkkŏptō (7), to cut off; to frustrate
2875 kŏptō (2), to beat the breast
4932 suntĕmnō (1), to cut short, i.e. do speedily

CUTH
3575 Kûwth (1), Cuth or Cuthah

CUTHAH
3575 Kûwth (1), Cuth or Cuthah

CUTTEST
7114 qâtsar (1), to curtail, cut short

CUTTETH
1234 bâqa' (1), to cleave, break, tear open
3772 kârath (1), to cut (off, down or asunder)
6398 pâlach (1), to slice; to break open; to pierce
7096 qâtsâh (1), to cut off; to destroy
7112 qâtsats (1), to chop off; to separate
7167 qâra' (1), to rend

CUTTING
1824 dᵉmîy (1), quiet, peacefulness

2799 chărôsheth (2), skilled work
7096 qâtsâh (1), to cut off; to destroy
2629 katakŏptō (1), to mangle, cut up

CUTTINGS
1417 gᵉdûwd (1), furrow ridge
8296 sereṭ (2), incision

CYMBAL
2950 kumbalŏn (1), cymbal

CYMBALS
4700 mᵉtsêleth (13), pair of cymbals
6767 tsᵉlâtsal (3), whirring

CYPRESS
8645 tirzâh (1), (poss.) cypress

CYPRUS
2954 Kuprŏs (8), Cyprus

CYRENE
2957 Kurēnē (4), Cyrenë

CYRENIAN
2956 Kurēnaiŏs (2), inhabitant of Cyrene

CYRENIANS
2956 Kurēnaiŏs (1), inhabitant of Cyrene

CYRENIUS
2958 Kurēniŏs (1), Quirinus

CYRUS
3566 Kôwresh (15), Koresh
3567 Kôwresh (Ch.) (8), Koresh

DABAREH
1705 Dâbᵉrath (1), Daberath

DABBASHETH
1708 Dabbesheth (1), hump of a camel

DABERATH
1705 Dâbᵉrath (2), Daberath

DAGGER
2719 chereb (3), knife, sword

DAGON
1712 Dâgôwn (11), fish-god

DAGON'S
1712 Dâgôwn (1), fish-god

DAILY
3117 yôwm (20), day; time period
3117+259 yôwm (1), day; time period
3119 yôwmâm (2), daily
3605+3117 kôl (11), all, any or every
8548 tâmîyd (7), constantly, regularly
1967 ĕpiŏusiŏs (2), for subsistence, i.e. needful
2184 ĕphēmĕrŏs (1), diurnal, i.e. daily
2522 kathēmĕrinŏs (1), quotidian, i.e. daily

2596+1538+2250 *kata* (1), down; according to
2596+2250 *kata* (15), down; according to
2596+3956+2250 *kata* (1), down; according to
3956+2250 *pas* (1), all, any, every, whole

DAINTIES
4303 maṭ'am (1), *delicacy*
4516 man'am (1), *delicacy eaten*
4574 ma'ădân (1), *delicacy; pleasure*

DAINTY
4303 maṭ'am (1), *delicacy*
8378 ta'ăvâh (1), *longing; delight*
3045 liparŏs (1), *costly, rich*

DALAIAH
1806 D^elâyâh (1), *Jehovah has delivered*

DALE
6010 'êmeq (2), *broad depression* or *valley*

DALMANUTHA
1148 Dalmanŏutha (1), *Dalmanutha*

DALMATIA
1149 Dalmatia (1), *Dalmatia*

DALPHON
1813 Dalphôwn (1), *dripping*

DAM
517 'êm (5), *mother*

DAMAGE
2257 chăbal (Ch.) (1), *harm, wound*
2555 châmâç (1), *violence; malice*
5142 n^ezaq (Ch.) (1), to *suffer, inflict loss*
5143 nêzeq (1), *injure, loss*
2209 zēmia (1), *detriment; loss*
2210 zēmiŏō (1), to *experience detriment*

DAMARIS
1152 Damaris (1), *gentle*

DAMASCENES
1159 dapanaō (1), to *incur cost; to waste*

DAMASCUS
1833 d^emesheq (1), *damask* fabric
1834 Dammeseq (44), *Damascus*
1154 Damaskŏs (15), *Damascus*

DAMNABLE
684 apŏlĕia (1), *ruin* or *loss*

DAMNATION
684 apŏlĕia (1), *ruin* or *loss*
2917 krima (7), *decision*
2920 krisis (3), *decision; tribunal; justice*

DAMNED
2632 katakrinō (2), to *judge against*

2919 krinō (1), to *decide; to try, condemn, punish*

DAMSEL
3207 yaldâh (1), *young female*
5291 na'ărâh (24), *female child; servant*
7356 racham (1), *womb; maiden*
2877 kŏrasiŏn (6), *little girl*
3813 paidiŏn (4), *child: boy* or *girl; immature*
3814 paidiskĕ (4), *female slave* or *servant*

DAMSEL'S
5291 na'ărâh (8), *female child; servant*

DAMSELS
5291 na'ărâh (2), *female child; servant*
5959 'almâh (1), *lass, young woman*

DAN
1835 Dân (71), *judge*

DAN-JAAN
1842 Dân Ya'an (1), *judge of purpose*

DANCE
2342 chûwl (1), to *dance, whirl; to writhe*
4234 mâchôwl (4), (round) *dance*
7540 râqad (3), to *spring about wildly* or *for joy*

DANCED
2342 chûwl (1), to *dance, whirl; to writhe* in pain; to *wait; to pervert*
3769 kârar (1), to *dance in whirling motion*
3738 ŏrchĕŏmai (4), to *dance*

DANCES
4246 m^echôwlâh (5), round-*dance*

DANCING
2287 châgag (1), to *observe* a festival
3769 kârar (1), to *dance in whirling motion*
4234 mâchôwl (1), (round) *dance*
4246 m^echôwlâh (2), round-*dance*
7540 râqad (1), to *spring about wildly* or *for joy*
5525 chŏrŏs (1), round *dance; dancing*

DANDLED
8173 shâ'a' (1), to *fondle, please* or *amuse* (self)

DANGER
1777 ĕnŏchŏs (5), *liable*
2793 kindunĕuō (2), to *undergo peril*

DANGEROUS
2000 ĕpisphalēs (1), *insecure, unsafe*

DANIEL
1840 Dânîyê'l (29), *judge of God*
1841 Dânîyê'l (Ch.) (50), *judge of God*

1158 Daniël (2), *judge of God*

DANITES
1839 Dânîy (4), *Danite*

DANNAH
1837 Dannâh (1), *Dannah*

DARA
1873 Dâra' (1), *Dara*

DARDA
1862 Darda' (1), *pearl of knowledge*

DARE
5111 tŏlmaŏ (4), to be *bold; to dare*

DARIUS
1867 Dâr^eyâvêsh (10), *Darejavesh*
1868 Dâr^eyâvêsh (Ch.) (15), *Darejavesh*

DARK
651 'âphêl (1), *dusky, dark*
653 'ăphêlâh (1), *duskiness, darkness*
2420 chîydâh (5), *puzzle; conundrum; maxim*
2821 châshak (5), to be *dark; to darken*
2822 chôshek (7), *darkness; misery*
2824 cheshkâh (1), *darkness, dark*
2841 chashrâh (1), *gathering of clouds*
3544 kêheh (5), *feeble; obscure*
4285 machshâk (3), *darkness; dark place*
5399 nesheph (1), *dusk, dawn*
5939 'ălâṭâh (1), *dusk*
6205 'ărâphel (2), *gloom, darkness*
6751 tsâlal (1), to *shade; to grow dark*
6937 qâdar (4), to be *dark-colored*
7087 qâphâ' (1), to *thicken, congeal*
850 auchmĕrŏs (1), *obscure, dark*
4652 skŏtĕinŏs (1), *dark, very dark*
4653 skŏtia (2), *dimness*

DARKEN
2821 châshak (1), to be *dark; to darken*

DARKENED
2821 châshak (7), to be *dark; to darken*
3543 kâhâh (1), to *grow dull, fade; to be faint*
6150 'ârab (1), to *grow dusky* at sundown
6272 'âtham (1), be *desolated* by scorching
6937 qâdar (1), to be *dark-colored*
4654 skŏtizō (8), to be, *become dark*

DARKENETH
2821 châshak (1), to be *dark; to darken*

DARKISH
3544 kêheh (1), *feeble; obscure*

DARKLY
1722+135 ĕn (1), *in; during; because of*

DARKNESS
652 'ôphel (6), *dusk, darkness*
653 'ăphêlâh (6), *duskiness, darkness*
2816 chăshôwk (Ch.) (1), *dark, darkness*
2821 châshak (1), to be *dark; to darken*
2822 chôshek (69), *darkness; misery*
2825 chăshêkâh (5), *darkness; misery*
3990 ma'ăphêl (1), *opaque, dark*
3991 ma'phêl^eyâh (1), *opaqueness, darkness*
4285 machshâk (4), *darkness; dark place*
5890 'êyphâh (2), *covering of darkness*
6205 'ărâphel (13), *gloom, darkness*
2217 zŏphŏs (2), *gloom*
4652 skŏtĕinŏs (2), *dark, very dark*
4653 skŏtia (13), *dimness*
4655 skŏtŏs (31), *darkness*
4656 skŏtŏō (1), to *make dark, i.e. blind*

DARKON
1874 Darqôwn (2), *Darkon*

DARLING
3173 yâchîyd (2), *only son; alone; beloved*

DART
2671 chêts (1), *arrow; wound; shaft* of a spear
4551 maççâ' (1), *stone quarry; projectile*
1002 bŏlis (1), *javelin, projectile*

DARTS
7626 shêbeṭ (1), *stick; clan, family*
7973 shelach (1), *spear; shoot* of growth
8455 tôwthâch (1), *stout club*
956 bĕlŏs (1), *spear* or *arrow*

DASH
5062 nâgaph (1), to *strike*
5310 nâphats (2), to *dash* to pieces; to *scatter*
7376 râṭash (2), to *dash* down
4350 prŏskŏptō (2), to *trip up; to strike*

DASHED
7376 râṭash (4), to *dash* down
7492 râ'ats (1), to *break* in pieces; to *harass*

DASHETH
5310 nâphats (1), to *dash* to pieces; to *scatter*

6327 pûwts (1), to *dash in pieces; to disperse*

DATHAN
1885 Dâthân (10), *Dathan*

DAUB
2902 ṭûwach (1), to *whitewash*

DAUBED
2560 châmar (1), to *glow; to smear*
2902 ṭûwach (6), to *whitewash*

DAUBING
2915 ṭîyach (1), *plaster, whitewash coating*

DAUGHTER
1004 bayith (1), *house; temple; family, tribe*
1121 bên (1), *son, descendant*
1323 bath (270), *daughter, descendant*
3618 kallâh (13), *bride; son's wife*
2364 thugatēr (24), *female child*
2365 thugatriŏn (2), *little daughter*
3565 numphē (3), *young married woman*

DAUGHTER'S
1323 bath (3), *daughter, descendant, woman*

DAUGHTERS
1121 bên (244), *son, descendant*
3618 kallâh (3), *bride*
2364 thugatēr (5), *female child, or descendant*
5043 tĕknŏn (1), *child*

DAVID
1732 Dâvîd (1019), *loving*
1138 Dabid (58), *loving*

DAVID'S
1732 Dâvîd (53), *loving*
1138 Dabid (1), *loving*

DAWN
1306 diaugazō (1), to *dawn, shine through*
2020 ĕpiphōskō (1), to *grow light*

DAWNING
5399 nesheph (2), *dusk, dawn*
5927 'âlâh (1), to *ascend, be high, mount*
6079 'aph'aph (1), *morning ray*
6437 pânâh (1), to *turn, to face*

DAY
215 'ôwr (1), to *be luminous*
216 'ôwr (1), *luminary; lightning; happiness*
1242 bôqer (4), *morning*
3117 yôwm (1250), *day; time period*
3118 yôwm (Ch.) (4), *day; time period*
3119 yôwmâm (53), *daily*
4283 mochŏrâth (2), *tomorrow, next day*
5399 nesheph (1), *dusk, dawn*

7837 shachar (6), *dawn*
737 arti (1), *just now; at once*
827 augē (1), *radiance, dawn*
839 auriŏn (1), *to-morrow*
1773 ĕnnuchŏn (1), *by night*
1887 ĕpauriŏn (8), *to-morrow*
2250 hēmĕra (200), *day; period of time*
3574 nuchthēmĕrŏn (1), *full day*
3588+2596+2250 hŏ (2), *"the," definite article*
4594 sēmĕrŏn (38), *this day, today, now*
4594+2250 sēmĕrŏn (1), *this day, today, now*
4595 sēpō (1), to *putrefy, rot*
5459 phôsphŏrŏs (1), *morning-star*
5610 hōra (1), *hour, i.e. a unit of time*

DAY'S
3117 yôwm (6), *day; time period*
2250 hēmĕra (1), *day; period of time*
4594 sēmĕrŏn (1), *this day, today, now*

DAYS
3117 yôwm (665), *day; time period*
3118 yôwm (Ch.) (9), *day; time period*
8543 tᵉmôwl (1), *(day before) yesterday*
1909 ĕpi (2), *on, upon*
2250 hēmĕra (154), *day; period of time*
5066 tĕtartaiŏs (1), of the *fourth day*

DAYS'
3117 yôwm (13), *day; time period*

DAYSMAN
3198 yâkach (1), to *decide, justify, convict*

DAYSPRING
7837 shachar (1), *dawn*
395 anatŏlē (1), *dawn of sun; east*

DAYTIME
3119 yôwmâm (8), *daily*

DEACON
1247 diakŏnĕō (2), to *act as a deacon*

DEACONS
1249 diakŏnŏs (3), *attendant, deacon(-ess)*

DEAD
1472 gᵉvîyâh (1), *dead body*
1478 gâva' (1), to *expire, die*
4191 mûwth (136), to *die; to kill*
4194 mâveth (7), *death; dead*
5038 nᵉbêlâh (7), *carcase or carrion*
5315 nephesh (8), *life; breath; soul; wind*

6297 peger (6), *carcase; corpse*
7496 râphâ' (7), *dead*
7703 shâdad (1), to *ravage*
581 apŏgĕnŏmĕnŏs (1), *deceased*
599 apŏthnēskō (29), to *die off*
2258 ēn (1), *I was*
2289 thanatŏō (1), to *kill*
2348 thnēskō (12), to *die, be dead*
2837 kŏimaō (1), to *slumber; to decease*
3498 nĕkrŏs (130), *corpse; dead*
3499 nĕkrŏō (2), to *deaden, i.e. to subdue*
4430 ptōma (3), *corpse, carrion*
4880 sunapŏthnēskō (1), to *decease with*
5053 tĕlĕutaō (3), to *finish life, i.e. expire*

DEADLY
4194 mâveth (1), *death; dead*
5315 nephesh (1), *life; breath; soul; wind*
2286 thanasimŏs (1), *poisonous, deadly*
2287 thanatēphŏrŏs (1), *fatal, i.e. bringing death*
2288 thanatŏs (2), *death*

DEADNESS
3500 nĕkrōsis (1), *death, deadness*

DEAF
2790 chârash (1), to *be silent; to be deaf*
2795 chêrêsh (9), *deaf*
2974 kōphŏs (5), *deaf or silent*

DEAL
1580 gâmal (2), to *benefit or requite; to wean*
6213 'âsâh (26), to *do*
6536 pâraç (1), to *split, distribute*
4054 pĕrissŏtĕrŏn (1), *more superabundantly*

DEALEST
6213 'âsâh (1), to *do*

DEALETH
6213 'âsâh (7), to *do*
4374 prŏsphĕrō (1), to *present to; to treat as*

DEALINGS
1697 dâbâr (1), *word; matter; thing*
4798 sugchraŏmai (1), to *have dealings with*

DEALT
1580 gâmal (2), to *benefit or requite; to wean*
2505 châlaq (2), to *be smooth; be slippery*
6213 'âsâh (18), to *do or make*
1793 ĕntugchanō (1), to *entreat, petition*
2686 katasŏphizŏmai (1), to *be crafty against*
3307 mĕrizō (1), to *apportion, bestow*

4160 pŏiĕō (2), to *do*

DEAR
3357 yaqqîyr (1), *precious*
26 agapē (1), *love*
27 agapētŏs (3), *beloved*
1784 ĕntimŏs (1), *valued, considered precious*
5093 timiŏs (1), *honored, esteemed, or beloved*

DEARTH
1226 batstsôreth (1), *drought*
7458 râ'âb (5), *hunger*
3042 limŏs (2), *scarcity, famine*

DEATH
4191 mûwth (82), to *die; to kill*
4192 Mûwth (1), *"To die for the son"*
4193 môwth (Ch.) (1), *death*
4194 mâveth (126), *death; dead*
6757 tsalmâveth (18), *shade of death*
7523 râtsach (1), to *murder*
8546 tᵉmûwthâh (1), *execution, death*
336 anairĕsis (5), *act of killing*
337 anairĕō (2), to *take away, i.e. abolish, murder*
520 apagō (1), to *take away*
599 apŏthnēskō (1), to *die off*
615 apŏktĕinō (6), to *kill outright; to destroy*
1935 ĕpithanatiŏs (1), *doomed to death*
2079 ĕschatŏs (1), *finally, i.e. at the extremity*
2288 thanatŏs (113), *death*
2289 thanatŏō (7), to *kill*
5054 tĕlĕutē (1), *deceasedness, death*

DEATHS
4194 mâveth (1), *death; dead*
4463 mâmôwth (2), *mortal disease, death*
2288 thanatŏs (1), *death*

DEBASE
8213 shâphêl (1), to *humiliate*

DEBATE
4683 matstsâh (1), *quarrel*
7378 rîyb (2), to *hold a controversy; to defend*
2054 ĕris (1), *quarrel, i.e. wrangling*

DEBATES
2054 ĕris (1), *quarrel, i.e. wrangling*

DEBIR
1688 Dᵉbîyr (14), *inmost part of the sanctuary*

DEBORAH
1683 Dᵉbôwrâh (10), *bee*

DEBT
3027 yâd (1), *hand; power*

5378 nâshâ' (1), to *lend* on interest
5386 nᵉshîy (1), *debt*
1156 danĕiŏn (1), *loan; debt*
3782 ŏphĕilĕ (1), *sum owed; obligation*
3783 ŏphĕilĕma (1), *due; moral fault*
3784 ŏphĕilŏ (1), to *owe; to be under obligation*

DEBTOR
2326 chôwb (1), *debt*
3781 ŏphĕilĕtēs (2), person *indebted*
3784 ŏphĕilŏ (1), to *owe; to be under obligation*

DEBTORS
3781 ŏphĕilĕtēs (3), person *indebted*
5533 chrĕŏphĕilĕtēs (2), *indebted* person

DEBTS
4859 mashshâ'âh (1), secured *loan*
3783 ŏphĕilĕma (1), *due; moral fault*

DECAPOLIS
1179 Dĕkapŏlis (3), *ten-city* region

DECAY
4131 môwṭ (1), to *slip, shake, fall*

DECAYED
2723 chorbâh (1), *desolation, dry* desert
3782 kâshal (1), to *totter, waver; to falter*

DECAYETH
2717 chârab (1), to *parch; desolate, destroy*
4355 mâkak (1), to *tumble in ruins*
3822 palaiŏŏ (1), to *become worn out*

DECEASE
1841 ĕxŏdŏs (2), *exit*, i.e. *death*

DECEASED
7496 râphâ' (1), *dead*
5053 tĕlĕutaŏ (1), to *finish life*, i.e. *expire*

DECEIT
4820 mirmâh (19), *fraud*
4860 mashshâ'ôwn (1), *dissimulation*
7423 rᵉmîyâh (2), *remissness; treachery*
8267 sheqer (1), *untruth*
8496 tôk (2), *oppression*
8649 tormâh (4), *fraud*
539 apatē (1), *delusion*
1387 dŏliŏŏ (1), to *practice deceit*
1388 dŏlŏs (2), *wile, deceit, trickery*
4106 planĕ (1), *fraudulence; straying*

DECEITFUL
3577 kâzâb (1), *falsehood; idol*
4820 mirmâh (8), *fraud*
6121 'âqôb (1), *fraudulent; tracked*

6280 'âthar (1), to *be, make abundant*
7423 rᵉmîyâh (4), *remissness; treachery*
8267 sheqer (2), *untruth; sham*
8501 tâkâk (1), to *dissever*, i.e. *crush*
8649 tormâh (1), *fraud*
539 apatē (1), *delusion*
1386 dŏliŏs (1), *guileful, tricky*

DECEITFULLY
898 bâgad (2), to *act covertly*
2048 hâthal (1), to *deride, mock*
4820 mirmâh (3), *fraud*
6231 'âshaq (1), to *oppress; to defraud*
7423 rᵉmîyâh (3), *remissness; treachery*
1389 dŏlŏŏ (1), to *adulterate, falsify*

DECEITFULNESS
539 apatē (3), *delusion*

DECEITS
4123 mahăthallâh (1), *delusion*
4820 mirmâh (1), *fraud*

DECEIVABLENESS
539 apatē (1), *delusion*

DECEIVE
2048 hâthal (1), to *deride, mock*
3884 lûwlê' (1), *if not*
5377 nâshâ' (7), to *lead astray*, to *delude*
6601 pâthâh (2), to *be, make simple;* to *delude*
7952 shâlâh (1), to *mislead*
538 apataŏ (1), to *cheat, delude*
1818 ĕxapataŏ (3), to *seduce wholly, deceive*
4105 planaŏ (10), to *wander; to deceive*
4106 planĕ (1), *fraudulence; straying*

DECEIVED
2048 hâthal (2), to *deride, mock*
5377 nâshâ' (5), to *lead astray*, to *delude*
6231 'âshaq (1), to *oppress; to defraud*
6601 pâthâh (6), to *be, make simple;* to *delude*
7411 râmâh (4), to *hurl;* to *shoot;* to *delude*
7683 shâgag (1), to *stray;* to *sin*
7686 shâgâh (1), to *stray, wander; to transgress*
8582 tâ'âh (1), to *vacillate, reel or stray*
538 apataŏ (2), to *cheat, delude*
1818 ĕxapataŏ (1), to *seduce wholly, deceive*
4105 planaŏ (10), to *wander; to deceive*

DECEIVER
5230 nâkal (1), to *act treacherously*

7686 shâgâh (1), to *stray, wander; to transgress*
8591 tâ'a' (1), to *cheat;* to *maltreat*
4108 planŏs (2), *roving; impostor* or *misleader*

DECEIVERS
4108 planŏs (2), *roving; impostor* or *misleader*
5423 phrĕnapatēs (1), *seducer, misleader*

DECEIVETH
7411 râmah (1), to *hurl;* to *shoot;* to *delude*
538 apataŏ (1), to *cheat, delude*
4105 planaŏ (3), to *roam, wander; to deceive*
5422 phrĕnapataŏ (1), to *delude, deceive*

DECEIVING
3884 paralŏgizŏmai (1), to *delude, deceive*
4105 planaŏ (1), to *roam, wander; to deceive*

DECEIVINGS
539 apatē (1), *delusion*

DECENTLY
2156 ĕuschēmŏnōs (1), *fittingly, properly*

DECIDED
2782 chârats (1), to *be alert*, to *decide*

DECISION
2742 chârûwts (2), *diligent, earnest*

DECK
3302 yâphâh (1), to *be beautiful*
5710 'âdâh (1), to *remove;* to *bedeck*

DECKED
5710 'âdâh (3), to *remove;* to *bedeck*
7234 râbad (1), to *spread*
5558 chrusŏŏ (2), to *guild, bespangle*

DECKEDST
5710 'âdâh (1), to *remove;* to *bedeck*
6213 'âsâh (1), to *do*

DECKEST
5710 'âdâh (1), to *remove;* to *bedeck*

DECKETH
3547 kâhan (1), to *officiate* as a priest

DECLARATION
262 'achvâh (1), *utterance*
6575 pârâshâh (1), *exposition*
1335 diēgĕsis (1), *recital, written account*

DECLARE
560 'âmar (Ch.) (1), to *say, speak*
874 bâ'ar (1), to *explain*
952 bûwr (1), to *examine*
1696 dâbar (1), to *speak, say;* to *subdue*
3045 yâda' (3), to *know*
5046 nâgad (46), to *announce*

5608 çâphar (20), to *enumerate;* to *recount*
7878 sîyach (1), to *ponder, muse aloud*
8085 shâma' (1), to *hear intelligently*
312 anaggĕllō (2), to *announce, report*
518 apaggĕllō (2), to *announce, proclaim*
1107 gnōrizō (3), to *make known, reveal*
1213 dēlŏō (1), to *make plain by words*
1334 diĕgĕŏmai (1), to *relate fully, describe*
1555 ĕkdiĕgĕŏmai (1), to *narrate through wholly*
1718 ĕmphanizō (1), to *show forth*
1732 ĕndĕixis (2), *demonstration*
2097 ĕuaggĕlizō (1), to *announce good news*
2605 kataggĕllō (1), to *proclaim, promulgate*
3853 paraggĕllō (1), to *enjoin;* to *instruct*
5419 phrazō (2), to *indicate, to expound*

DECLARED
559 'âmar (1), to *say, speak*
1696 dâbar (1), to *speak, say;* to *subdue*
3045 yâda' (3), to *know*
5046 nâgad (13), to *announce*
5608 çâphar (4), to *enumerate;* to *recount*
6567 pârash (1), to *separate;* to *specify*
8085 shâma' (1), to *hear intelligently*
312 anaggĕllō (1), to *announce, report*
394 anatithĕmai (1), to *set forth a declaration*
518 apaggĕllō (1), to *announce, proclaim*
1107 gnōrizō (1), to *make known, reveal*
1213 dēlŏō (2), to *make plain by words*
1229 diaggĕllō (1), to *herald thoroughly*
1334 diĕgĕŏmai (2), to *relate fully, describe*
1834 ĕxēgĕŏmai (4), to *tell, relate again*
2097 ĕuaggĕlizō (1), to *announce good news*
3724 hŏrizō (1), to *appoint, decree, specify*
5319 phanĕrŏŏ (1), to *render apparent*

DECLARETH
5046 nâgad (4), to *announce*

DECLARING
5046 nâgad (1), to *announce*
1555 ĕkdiĕgĕŏmai (1), to *narrate through wholly*
1834 ĕxēgĕŏmai (1), to *tell, relate again*
2605 kataggĕllō (1), to *proclaim, promulgate*

DECLINE
5186 nâṭâh (3), to *stretch* or spread out
5493 çûwr (1), to *turn* off
7847 sâṭâh (1), to *deviate* from duty, *go astray*

DECLINED
5186 nâṭâh (3), to *stretch* or spread out
5493 çûwr (1), to *turn* off

DECLINETH
5186 nâṭâh (2), to *stretch* or spread out

DECREASE
4591 mâ'aṭ (1), to *be, make small* or *few*
1642 ĕlattŏō (1), to *lessen*

DECREASED
2637 châçêr (1), to *lack; to fail, want, make less*

DECREE
633 'ĕçâr (Ch.) (7), *edict, decree*
1504 gâzar (1), to *exclude; decide*
1510 gᵉzêrâh (Ch.) (2), *decree, decision*
1697 dâbâr (1), *word; matter; thing*
1881 dâth (9), royal *edict* or *statute*
1882 dâth (Ch.) (3), *Law;* royal *edict* or *statute*
2706 chôq (7), *appointment; allotment*
2710 châqaq (2), to *engrave; to enact* laws
2940 ṭa'am (1), *taste; intelligence; mandate*
2942 ṭeˈêm (Ch.) (13), *judgment; account*
3982 ma'ămar (1), *edict, command*
6599 pithgâm (1), judicial *sentence; edict*
1378 dŏgma (1), *law*

DECREED
1504 gâzar (1), to *destroy, exclude; decide*
2706 chôq (1), *appointment; allotment*
2782 chârats (1), to *be alert, to decide*
6965 qûwm (1), to *rise*
2919 krinō (1), to *decide; to try, condemn, punish*

DECREES
2711 chêqeq (1), *enactment, resolution*
1378 dŏgma (2), *law*

DEDAN
1719 Dᵉdân (11), *Dedan*

DEDANIM
1720 Dᵉdânîym (1), *Dedanites*

DEDICATE
2596 chânak (1), to *initiate* or *discipline*
6942 qâdâsh (3), to *be, make clean*

DEDICATED
2596 chânak (3), to *initiate* or *discipline*
2764 chêrem (1), *doomed* object

DEDICATING
2598 chănukkâh (2), *dedication*

DEDICATION
2597 chănukkâ' (Ch.) (4), *dedication*
2598 chănukkâh (6), *dedication*
1456 ĕgkainia (1), Feast of *Dedication*

DEED
199 'ûwlâm (2), *however* or *on the contrary*
1697 dâbâr (3), *word; matter; thing*
3559 kûwn (1), to *set up; establish, fix, prepare*
4639 ma'âseh (1), *action; labor*
2041 ĕrgŏn (6), *work*
2108 ĕuĕrgĕsia (1), *beneficence*
4162 pŏiēsis (1), *action,* i.e. *performance*
4334 prŏsĕrchŏmai (1), to *come near, visit*

DEEDS
1578 gᵉmûwlâh (1), *act; service; reward*
1697 dâbâr (2), *word; matter; thing*
4639 ma'âseh (2), *action; labor*
5949 'ălîylâh (2), *opportunity, action*
6467 pô'al (2), *act* or *work, deed*
1411 dunamis (1), *force, power, miracle*
2041 ĕrgŏn (16), *work*
2735 katŏrthōma (1), *made fully upright*
3739+4238 hŏs (1), *who, which, what, that*
4234 praxis (3), *act; function*

DEEMED
5282 hupŏnŏĕō (1), to *think; to expect*

DEEP
4113 mahămôrâh (1), (poss.) *abyss, pits*
4278 mechqâr (1), *recess, unexplored* place
4615 ma'ămâq (2), *deep* place
4688 mᵉtsôwlâh (5), *deep* place
4950 mishqâ' (1), clear pond with *settled* water
5994 'ămîyq (Ch.) (1), *profound, unsearchable*
6009 'âmaq (5), to *be, make deep*
6013 'âmôq (8), *deep, profound*
6683 tsûwlâh (1), *watery abyss*
7290 râdam (2), to *stupefy*

6942 qâdâsh (7), to *be, make clean*
6944 qôdesh (12), *sacred* place or thing
1457 ĕgkainizō (1), to *inaugurate*

DEDICATING
2598 chănukkâh (2), *dedication*

DEDICATION
2597 chănukkâ' (Ch.) (4), *dedication*
2598 chănukkâh (6), *dedication*
1456 ĕgkainia (1), Feast of *Dedication*

8257 shâqa' (1), to *be overflowed; to cease*
8328 sheresh (1), *root*
8415 tᵉhôwm (20), *abyss* of the sea, i.e. the *deep*
8639 tardêmâh (7), *trance, deep sleep*
12 abussŏs (2), *deep place, abyss*
899 bathŏs (3), *extent; mystery,* i.e. *deep*
901 bathus (2), *deep, profound*
1037 buthŏs (1), *deep* sea
2532+900 kai (1), *and; or; even; also*

DEEPER
6012 'âmêq (1), *deep, obscure*
6013 'âmôq (8), *deep, profound*

DEEPLY
6009 'âmaq (2), to *be, make deep*
389 anastĕnazō (1), to *sigh deeply*

DEEPNESS
899 bathŏs (1), *extent; mystery,* i.e. *deep*

DEEPS
4688 mᵉtsôwlâh (3), *deep* place
8415 tᵉhôwm (1), *abyss* of the sea, i.e. the *deep*

DEER
3180 yachmûwr (1), *deer*

DEFAMED
987 blasphēmĕō (1), to *speak impiously*

DEFAMING
1681 dibbâh (1), *slander, bad report*

DEFEAT
6565 pârar (2), to *break up; to violate, frustrate*

DEFENCE
1220 betser (1), *gold*
2646 chuppâh (1), *canopy*
4043 mâgên (2), small *shield (buckler);* animal *skin*
4686 mâtsûwd (1), *net* or *capture; fastness*
4692 mâtsôwr (2), *siege-mound; distress*
4869 misgâb (7), *refuge*
5526 çâkak (1), to *fence in; cover over; protect*
6738 tsêl (3), *shade; protection*
626 apŏlŏgĕŏmai (1), to *give an account*
627 apŏlŏgia (3), *plea* or *verbal defense*

DEFENCED
1219 bâtsar (5), to *be inaccessible*
4013 mibtsâr (4), *fortification; defender*

DEFEND
1598 gânan (7), to *protect*
3467 yâsha' (1), to *make safe, free*
7682 sâgab (2), to *be, make lofty; be safe*

8199 shâphaṭ (1), to *judge*

DEFENDED
5337 nâtsal (1), to *deliver*
292 amunŏmai (1), to *protect, help*

DEFENDEST
5526 çâkak (1), to *fence in; cover over; protect*

DEFENDING
1598 gânan (1), to *protect*

DEFER
309 'âchar (2), to *remain; to delay*
748 'ârak (1), to *be, make long*

DEFERRED
309 'âchar (1), to *remain; to delay*
4900 mâshak (1), to *draw out; to be tall*
306 anaballŏmai (1), to *put off, adjourn*

DEFERRETH
748 'ârak (1), to *be, make long*

DEFIED
2194 zâ'am (1), to *be enraged*
2778 châraph (5), to *spend the winter*

DEFILE
1351 gâ'al (2), to *soil, stain; desecrate*
2490 châlal (2), to *profane, defile*
2930 ṭâmê' (25), to *be morally contaminated*
2936 ṭânaph (1), to *soil, make dirty*
733 arsĕnŏkŏitĕs (1), *sodomite*
2840 kŏinŏō (6), to *make profane*
3392 miainō (1), to *contaminate*
5351 phthĕirō (1), to *spoil, ruin; to deprave*

DEFILED
1351 gâ'al (2), to *soil, stain; desecrate*
2490 châlal (5), to *profane, defile*
2610 chânêph (3), to *soil, be defiled*
2930 ṭâmê' (44), to *be morally contaminated*
2931 ṭâmê' (5), *foul; ceremonially impure*
2933 ṭâmâh (1), to *be ceremonially impure*
5953 'âlal (1), to *glean; to overdo*
6031 'ânâh (1), to *afflict, be afflicted*
6942 qâdâsh (1), to *be, make clean*
2839 kŏinŏs (1), *common,* i.e. *profane*
3392 miainō (4), to *contaminate*
3435 mŏlunō (3), to *soil, make impure*

DEFILEDST
2490 châlal (1), to *profane, defile*

DEFILETH
2490 châlal (1), to profane, defile
2610 chânêph (1), to soil, be defiled
2930 ṭâmê' (1), to be foul; be morally contaminated
2840 kŏinŏŏ (5), to make profane
4695 spilŏŏ (1), to stain or soil

DEFRAUD
6231 'âshaq (1), to oppress; to defraud
650 apŏstĕrĕŏ (3), to despoil or defraud
4122 plĕŏnĕktĕŏ (1), to be covetous

DEFRAUDED
6231 'âshaq (2), to oppress; to defraud
650 apŏstĕrĕŏ (1), to despoil or defraud
4122 plĕŏnĕktĕŏ (1), to be covetous

DEFY
2194 zâ'am (2), to be enraged
2778 châraph (3), to spend the winter

DEGENERATE
5494 çûwr (1), turned off; deteriorated

DEGREE
898 bathmŏs (1), grade of dignity
5011 tapĕinŏs (2), humiliated, lowly

DEGREES
4609 ma'ălâh (24), thought arising

DEHAVITES
1723 Dahăvâ' (Ch.) (1), Dahava

DEKAR
1857 Deqer (1), stab

DELAIAH
1806 Dᵉlâyâh (6), Jehovah has delivered

DELAY
309 'âchar (1), to remain; to delay; to procrastinate
311 anabŏlē (1), putting off, delay
3635 ŏknĕŏ (1), to be slow, delay

DELAYED
954 bûwsh (1), to be disappointed; delayed
4102 mâhahh (1), to be reluctant

DELAYETH
5549 chrŏnizŏ (2), to take time, i.e. linger

DELECTABLE
2530 châmad (1), delight in; lust for

DELICACIES
4764 strēnŏs (1), luxury, sensuality

DELICATE
6026 'ânag (1), to be soft or pliable
6028 'ânôg (3), luxurious
8588 ta'ănûwg (1), luxury; delight

DELICATELY
4574 ma'ădân (2), delicacy; pleasure
6445 pânaq (1), to enervate, reduce vigor
5172 truphē (1), luxury or debauchery

DELICATENESS
6026 'ânag (1), to be soft or pliable

DELICATES
5730 'êden (1), pleasure

DELICIOUSLY
4763 strēniaŏ (2), to be luxurious, live sensually

DELIGHT
1523 gîyl (1), rejoice
2530 châmad (1), to delight in; lust for
2531 chemed (1), delight
2654 châphêts (17), to be pleased with, desire
2655 châphêts (1), pleased with
2656 chêphets (3), pleasure; desire
2836 châshaq (1), to join; to love, delight
4574 ma'ădân (1), delicacy; pleasure
5276 nâ'êm (1), to be agreeable
6026 'ânag (6), to be soft or pliable
6027 'ôneg (1), luxury
7521 râtsâh (2), to be pleased with
7522 râtsôwn (5), delight
8173 shâ'a' (4), to fondle, please or amuse (self) dismay, i.e. stare
8191 sha'shûa' (4), enjoyment
8588 ta'ănûwg (1), luxury; delight
4913 sunēdŏmai (1), to rejoice in with oneself

DELIGHTED
2654 châphêts (10), to be pleased with, desire
5727 'âdan (1), to be soft or pleasant
6026 'ânag (1), to be soft or pliable

DELIGHTEST
7521 râtsâh (1), to be pleased with

DELIGHTETH
2654 châphêts (12), to be pleased with, desire
7521 râtsâh (2), to be pleased with

DELIGHTS
5730 'êden (1), pleasure
8191 sha'shûa (3), enjoyment
8588 ta'ănûwg (2), luxury; delight

DELIGHTSOME
2656 chêphets (1), pleasure; desire

DELILAH
1807 Dᵉlîylâh (6), languishing

DELIVER
579 'ânâh (1), to meet, to happen
1350 gâ'al (1), to redeem; to be the next of kin
2502 châlats (5), to depart; to deliver
3467 yâsha' (3), to make safe, free
4042 mâgan (2), to rescue, to surrender
4422 mâlaṭ (17), to be delivered; be smooth
4672 mâtsâ' (1), to find or acquire; to occur
5186 nâṭâh (1), to stretch or spread out
5337 nâtsal (115), to deliver
5338 nᵉtsal (Ch.) (2), to extricate, deliver
5414 nâthan (78), to give
5462 çâgar (10), to shut up; to surrender
6299 pâdâh (3), to ransom; to release
6308 pâda' (1), to retrieve
6403 pâlaṭ (11), to escape; to deliver
6561 pâraq (1), to break off or crunch; to deliver
7725 shûwb (5), to turn back; to return
7804 shᵉzab (Ch.) (6), to leave; to free
8000 shᵉlam (Ch.) (1), to restore; be safe
8199 shâphaṭ (1), to judge
525 apallassŏ (1), to release; be reconciled
1325 didŏmi (1), to give
1807 ĕxairĕŏ (2), to tear out; to select; to release
3860 paradidŏmi (15), to hand over
4506 rhuŏmai (8), to rescue
5483 charizŏmai (2), to grant as a favor, rescue

DELIVERANCE
2020 hatstsâlâh (1), rescue, deliverance
3444 yᵉshûw'âh (2), deliverance; aid
6405 pallêṭ (1), escape
6413 pᵉlêyṭâh (5), escaped portion
8668 tᵉshûw'âh (5), rescue, deliverance
629 apŏlutrōsis (1), ransom in full
859 aphĕsis (1), pardon, freedom

DELIVERANCES
3444 yᵉshûw'âh (1), deliverance; aid

DELIVERED
2502 châlats (9), to depart; to deliver
3052 yᵉhab (Ch.) (1), to give

3205 yâlad (6), to bear young; to father a child
3467 yâsha' (8), to make safe, free
4042 mâgan (1), to rescue, to surrender
4422 mâlaṭ (16), to be delivered; be smooth
4560 mâçar (1), to set apart; apostatize
4672 mâtsâ' (1), to find or acquire; to occur
5234 nâkar (1), to acknowledge, care for
5337 nâtsal (58), to deliver
5414 nâthan (98), to give
5462 çâgar (6), to shut up; to surrender
5674 'âbar (1), to cross over; to transition
6299 pâdâh (2), to ransom; to release
6403 pâlaṭ (3), to slip out, i.e. escape; to deliver
6487 piqqâdôwn (2), deposit
7804 shᵉzab (Ch.) (2), to leave; to free
325 anadidŏmi (1), to hand over, deliver
525 apallassŏ (1), to release; be reconciled
591 apŏdidŏmi (2), to give away
1080 gĕnnaŏ (1), to procreate, regenerate
1325 didŏmi (2), to give
1560 ĕkdŏtŏs (1), surrendered
1659 ĕlĕuthĕrŏŏ (1), to exempt, liberate
1807 ĕxairĕŏ (2), to tear out; to select; to release
1825 ĕxĕgĕirŏ (1), to resuscitate; release
1929 ĕpididŏmi (2), to give over
2673 katargĕŏ (1), to be, render entirely useless
3860 paradidŏmi (44), to hand over
4506 rhuŏmai (9), to rescue
5088 tiktŏ (5), to produce from seed

DELIVEREDST
5414 nâthan (1), to give
3860 paradidŏmi (2), to hand over

DELIVERER
3467 yâsha' (2), to make safe, free
5337 nâtsal (1), to deliver
6403 pâlaṭ (5), to slip out, i.e. escape; to deliver
3086 lutrōtēs (1), redeemer, deliverer
4506 rhuŏmai (1), to rescue

DELIVEREST
5337 nâtsal (1), to deliver
6403 pâlaṭ (1), to slip out, i.e. escape; to deliver

DELIVERETH
2502 châlats (2), to depart; to deliver
5337 nâtsal (7), to deliver

DELIVERING
5414 nâthan (1), to *give*
6403 pâlaṭ (1), to *slip* out,
i.e. *escape; to deliver*
6475 pâtsâh (1), to *rend*,
i.e. *open*
7804 sheʿzab (Ch.) (1), to
leave; to free

DELIVERING
1807 ĕxairĕō (1), to *tear*
out; to select; to release
3860 paradidōmi (2), to
hand over

DELIVERY
3205 yâlad (1), to *bear*
young; to *father a child*

DELUSION
4106 planē (1),
fraudulence; straying

DELUSIONS
8586 taʿălûwl (1), *caprice*
(as a fit *coming on*)

DEMAND
7592 shâʿal (3), to *ask*
7595 sheʿêlâ' (Ch.) (1),
judicial *decision*

DEMANDED
559 'âmar (1), to *say*
7592 shâʿal (1), to *ask*
7593 sheʿêl (Ch.) (1), to
ask
1905 ĕpĕrōtaō (2), to
inquire, seek
4441 punthanŏmai (2), to
ask for information

DEMAS
1214 Dēmas (3), *Demas*

DEMETRIUS
1216 Dēmētriŏs (3),
Demetrius

DEMONSTRATION
585 apŏdĕixis (1),
manifestation, proof

DEN
1358 gôb (Ch.) (10), lion
pit
3975 meʿûwrâh (1),
serpent's *hole* or *den*
4583 mâʿôwn (2), *retreat*
or asylum *dwelling*
4585 meʿôwnâh (1), *abode*
4631 meʿârâh (1), dark
cavern
5520 çôk (1), *hut* of
entwined boughs
4693 spēlaiŏn (3),
cavern; hiding-place

DENIED
3584 kâchash (2), to *lie,
disown; to disappoint*
4513 mâna' (1), to *deny,
refuse*
533 aparnĕŏmai (2),
disown, deny
720 arnĕŏmai (14), to
disavow, reject

DENIETH
720 arnĕŏmai (4), to
disavow, reject

DENOUNCE
5046 nâgad (1), to
announce

DENS
695 'ereb (1), *hiding
place; lair*

4492 minhârâh (1),
cavern, fissure
4585 meʿôwnâh (4), *abode*
4631 meʿârâh (1), dark
cavern
4693 spēlaiŏn (2),
cavern; hiding-place

DENY
3584 kâchash (3), to *lie,
disown; to disappoint,
cringe*
4513 mâna' (1), to *deny,
refuse*
7725 shûwb (1), to *turn
back; to return*
483 antilĕgō (1), to
dispute, refuse
533 aparnĕŏmai (11),
disown, deny
720 arnĕŏmai (7), to
disavow, reject

DENYING
720 arnĕŏmai (4), to
disavow, reject

DEPART
1540 gâlâh (1), to
denude; uncover
1980 hâlak (3), to *walk;
live a certain way*
3212 yâlak (15), to *walk;
to live; to carry*
3249 yâçûwr (1),
departing
3318 yâtsâ' (3), to *go,
bring out*
3363 yâqa' (1), to *be
dislocated*
3868 lûwz (2), to *depart;
to be perverse*
4185 mûwsh (8), to
withdraw
5493 çûwr (42), to *turn* off
5927 'âlâh (2), to *ascend,
be high, mount*
6852 tsâphar (1), to
return
7971 shâlach (4), to *send
away*
8159 shâʿâh (1), to *be
nonplussed, bewildered*
321 anagō (1), to *lead
up; to bring out; to sail*
360 analuō (1), to *depart*
565 apĕrchŏmai (4), to
go off, i.e. depart
630 apŏluō (2), to *relieve,
release*
672 apŏchōrĕō (1), to *go
away, leave*
868 aphistēmi (4), to
desist, desert
1607 ĕkpŏrĕuŏmai (2), to
depart, be discharged
1633 ĕkchōrĕō (1), to
depart, go away
1826 ĕxĕimi (1), *leave;
escape*
1831 ĕxĕrchŏmai (7), to
issue; to leave
3327 mĕtabainō (3), to
depart, move from
4198 pŏrĕuŏmai (5), to
go, come; to travel
5217 hupagō (1), to
withdraw or retire
5562 chōrĕō (6), to *pass,
enter; to hold, admit*

DEPARTED
935 bôw' (1), to *go, come*
1540 gâlâh (3), to
denude; uncover
1980 hâlak (3), to *walk;
live a certain way*
3212 yâlak (47), to *walk;
to live; to carry*
3318 yâtsâ' (10), to *go,
bring out*
4185 mûwsh (2), to
withdraw
5074 nâdad (1), to *rove,
flee; to drive* away
5265 nâça' (30), *start* on
a *journey*
5493 çûwr (31), to *turn* off
5709 'ădâ' (Ch.) (1), to
pass on or *continue*
5927 'âlâh (1), to *ascend,
be high, mount*
321 anagō (2), to *lead
up; to bring out; to sail*
402 anachōrĕō (8), to
retire, withdraw
525 apallassō (1), to
release; be reconciled
565 apĕrchŏmai (24), to
go off, i.e. depart
630 apŏluō (1), to *relieve,
release; to let die,
pardon or divorce*
673 apŏchōrizō (2), to
rend apart; to separate
868 aphistēmi (6), to
desist, desert
1316 diachōrizŏmai (1),
to *remove* (oneself)
1330 diĕrchŏmai (1), to
traverse, travel through
1607 ĕkpŏrĕuŏmai (1), to
depart, be discharged
1826 ĕxĕimi (1), *leave;
escape*
1831 ĕxĕrchŏmai (22), to
issue; to leave
2718 katĕrchŏmai (1), to
go, come down
3327 mĕtabainō (3), to
depart, move from
3332 mĕtairō (2), to
move on, leave
3855 paragō (1), to *go
along or away*
4198 pŏrĕuŏmai (6), to
go, come; to travel
5562 chōrĕō (1), to *pass,
enter; to hold, admit*
5563 chōrizō (1), to *part;
to go away*

DEPARTETH
3212 yâlak (2), to *walk;
to live; to carry*
4185 mûwsh (1), to
withdraw
5493 çûwr (3), to *turn* off
672 apŏchōrĕō (1), to *go
away, leave*

DEPARTING
3318 yâtsâ' (2), to *go,
bring out*
5253 nâçag (1), to *retreat*
5493 çûwr (2), to *turn* off
672 apŏchōrĕō (1), to *go
away, leave*
867 aphixis (1),
departure, leaving
868 aphistēmi (1), to
desist, desert

1831 ĕxĕrchŏmai (1), to
issue; to leave
1841 ĕxŏdŏs (1), *exit*, i.e.
death
5217 hupagō (1), to
withdraw or retire

DEPARTURE
3318 yâtsâ' (1), to *go,
bring out*
359 analusis (1),
departure

DEPOSED
5182 neʿchath (Ch.) (1), to
descend; to depose

DEPRIVED
5382 nâshâh (1), to *forget*
6485 pâqad (1), to *visit,
care for, count*
7921 shâkôl (1), to
miscarry

DEPTH
6009 'âmaq (1), to *be,
make deep*
6012 'âmêq (1), *deep,
obscure*
8415 tehôwm (5), *abyss*
of the sea, i.e. the *deep*
899 bathŏs (4), *extent;
mystery*, i.e. *deep*
3989 pĕlagŏs (1), deep or
open sea

DEPTHS
4615 maʿămâq (3), *deep
place*
4688 metsôwlâh (2), *deep
place*
6010 'êmeq (1), broad
depression or *valley*
8415 tehôwm (10), *abyss*
of the sea, i.e. the *deep*
899 bathŏs (1), *extent;
mystery*, i.e. *deep*

DEPUTIES
6346 pechâh (2), *prefect,
officer*
446 anthupatŏs (1),
Roman *proconsul*

DEPUTY
5324 nâtsab (1), to *station*
446 anthupatŏs (4),
Roman *proconsul*

DERBE
1191 Dĕrbē (4), *Derbe*

DERIDE
7832 sâchaq (1), to
laugh; to scorn; to play

DERIDED
1592 ĕkmuktĕrizō (2), to
sneer at, ridicule

DERISION
3887 lûwts (1), to *scoff; to
interpret; to intercede*
3932 lâʿag (5), to *deride;
to speak unintelligibly*
7047 qeleç (3),
laughing-stock
7814 seʿchôwq (5),
laughter; scorn
7832 sâchaq (1), to
laugh; to scorn; to play

DESCEND
3381 yârad (6), to
descend
2597 katabainō (4), to
descend

DESCENDED
3381 yârad (12), to descend
2597 katabainō (7), to descend

DESCENDETH
2718 katĕrchŏmai (1), to go, come down

DESCENDING
3381 yârad (1), to descend
2597 katabainō (7), to descend

DESCENT
35 agĕnĕalŏgētŏs (1), unregistered as to birth
1075 gĕnĕalŏgĕō (1), trace in genealogy
2600 katabasis (1), declivity, slope

DESCRIBE
3789 kâthab (4), to write

DESCRIBED
3789 kâthab (2), to write

DESCRIBETH
1125 graphō (1), to write
3004 lĕgō (1), to say

DESCRY
8446 tûwr (1), to wander, meander for trade

DESERT
1576 gᵉmûwl (1), act; service; reward
2723 chorbâh (1), desolation, dry desert
3452 yᵉshîymôwn (4), desolation
4057 midbâr (13), desert; also speech; mouth
6160 'ărâbâh (8), desert, wasteland
6728 tsîyîy (3), desert-dweller; beast
2048 ĕrēmŏs (12), remote place, deserted place

DESERTS
2723 chorbâh (2), desolation, dry desert
4941 mishpâṭ (1), verdict; formal decree; justice
6160 'ărâbâh (1), desert, wasteland
2047 ĕrēmia (1), place of solitude, remoteness
2048 ĕrēmŏs (1), remote place, deserted place

DESERVING
1576 gᵉmûwl (1), act; service; reward

DESIRABLE
2531 chemed (3), delight

DESIRE
15 'âbeh (1), longing
35 'abîyôwnâh (1), caper-berry
183 'âvâh (7), to wish for, desire
1156 bᵉ'â' (Ch.) (1), to seek or ask
1245 bâqash (1), to search out; to strive
2530 châmad (4), to delight in; lust for
2532 chemdâh (3), delight

2654 châphêts (6), to be pleased with, desire
2655 châphêts (2), pleased with
2656 chêphets (9), pleasure; desire
2836 châshaq (1), to join; to love, delight
2837 chêsheq (1), delight, desired thing
3700 kâçaph (1), to pine after; to fear
4261 machmâd (3), object of desire
5315 nephesh (3), life; breath; soul; wind
5375+5315 nâsâ' (2), to lift up
7522 râtsôwn (3), delight
7592 shâ'al (3), to ask
7602 shâ'aph (1), to be angry; to hasten
8378 ta'ăvâh (14), longing; delight
8420 tâv (1), mark, signature
8669 tᵉshûwqâh (3), longing
154 aitĕō (5), to ask for
515 axiŏō (1), to deem entitled or fit, worthy
1934 ĕpizētĕō (2), to demand, to crave
1937 ĕpithumĕō (4), to long for
1939 ĕpithumia (3), longing
1971 ĕpipŏthĕō (1), intensely crave
1972 ĕpipŏthēsis (2), longing for
1974 ĕpipŏthia (1), intense longing
2065 ĕrōtaō (1), to interrogate; to request
2107 ĕudŏkia (1), delight, kindness, wish
2206 zēlŏō (2), to have warmth of feeling for
2309 thĕlō (9), to will; to desire; to choose
3713 ŏrĕgŏmai (2), to reach out after, long for

DESIRED
183 'âvâh (5), to wish for, desire
559 'âmar (1), to say, speak
1156 bᵉ'â' (Ch.) (2), to seek or ask
2530 châmad (5), to delight in; lust for
2532 chemdâh (1), delight
2654 châphêts (1), to be pleased with, desire
2656 chêphets (2), pleasure; desire
2836 châshaq (2), to join; to love, delight
3700 kâçaph (1), to pine after; to fear
7592 shâ'al (4), to ask
154 aitĕō (10), to ask for
1809 ĕxaitĕŏmai (1), to demand
1905 ĕpĕrōtaō (1), to inquire, seek

1934 ĕpizētĕō (1), to demand, to crave
1937 ĕpithumĕō (1), to long for
1939 ĕpithumia (1), longing
2065 ĕrōtaō (4), to interrogate; to request
2212 zētĕō (1), to seek
2309 thĕlō (1), to will; to desire; to choose
3870 parakalĕō (5), to call, invite

DESIREDST
7592 shâ'al (1), to ask
3870 parakalĕō (1), to call, invite

DESIRES
3970 ma'ăvay (1), desire
4862 mish'âlâh (1), request
2307 thĕlēma (1), purpose; inclination

DESIREST
2654 châphêts (2), to be pleased with, desire

DESIRETH
183 'âvâh (4), to wish for, desire
559 'âmar (1), to say, speak
2530 châmad (2), to delight in; lust for
2655 châphêts (1), pleased with
2656 chêphets (1), pleasure; desire
7592 shâ'al (1), to ask
7602 shâ'aph (1), to be angry; to hasten
8378 ta'ăvâh (3), longing; delight
1937 ĕpithumĕō (1), to long for
2065 ĕrōtaō (1), to interrogate; to request
2309 thĕlō (1), to will; to desire; to choose

DESIRING
154 aitĕō (2), to ask for
1937 ĕpithumĕō (1), to long for
1971 ĕpipŏthĕō (3), intensely crave
2212 zētĕō (2), to seek
2309 thĕlō (2), to will; to desire; to choose
3870 parakalĕō (2), to call, invite

DESIROUS
183 'âvâh (1), to wish for, desire
2309 thĕlō (3), to will; to desire; to choose
2442 himĕirŏmai (1), to long for, desire
2755 kĕnŏdŏxŏs (1), self-conceited

DESOLATE
490 'almânâh (2), widow
816 'âsham (6), to be guilty; to be punished
820 'ashmân (1), uninhabited places
910 bâdâd (1), separate, alone

1327 battâh (1), area of desolation
1565 galmûwd (2), sterile, barren, desolate
2717 chârab (5), to parch through drought; desolate, destroy
2723 chorbâh (7), desolation, dry desert
3173 yâchîyd (1), only son; alone; beloved
3341 yâtsath (1), to burn or set on fire
3456 yâsham (4), to lie waste
3582 kâchad (1), to destroy; to hide
4923 mᵉshammâh (2), waste; object of horror
5352 nâqâh (1), to be, make clean; to be bare
7722 shôw' (2), tempest; devastation
8047 shammâh (11), ruin; consternation
8074 shâmêm (43), to devastate; to stupefy
8076 shâmêm (8), ruined, deserted
8077 shᵉmâmâh (42), devastation
2048 ĕrēmŏs (4), remote place, deserted place
2049 ĕrēmŏō (2), to lay waste
3443 mŏnŏō (1), to isolate, i.e. bereave

DESOLATION
2721 chôreb (1), ruined; desolate
2723 chorbâh (5), desolation, dry desert
4875 mᵉshôw'âh (1), ruin
7584 sha'ăvâh (1), rushing tempest
7612 shē'th (1), devastation
7701 shôd (2), violence, ravage, destruction
7722 shôw' (4), tempest; devastation
8047 shammâh (12), ruin; consternation
8074 shâmêm (3), to devastate; to stupefy
8077 shᵉmâmâh (11), devastation
2049 ĕrēmŏō (2), to lay waste
2050 ĕrēmōsis (3), despoliation, desolation

DESOLATIONS
2723 chorbâh (3), desolation, dry desert
4876 mashshûw'âh (1), ruin
8047 shammâh (1), ruin; consternation
8074 shâmêm (4), to devastate; to stupefy
8077 shᵉmâmâh (2), devastation

DESPAIR
2976 yâ'ash (2), to despond, despair
1820 ĕxapŏrĕŏmai (1), to be utterly at a loss

DESPAIRED
1820 ĕxapŏrĕŏmai (1), to
be utterly at a loss
DESPERATE
605 'ānash (1), to be frail,
feeble
2976 yā'ash (1), to
despond, despair
DESPERATELY
605 'ānash (1), to be frail,
feeble
DESPISE
936 bûwz (4), to
disrespect, scorn
959 bāzâh (6), to ridicule,
scorn
2107 zûwl (1), to treat
lightly
3988 mâ'aç (9), to spurn;
to disappear
5006 nâ'ats (1), to scorn
7043 qālal (1), to be easy,
trifling, vile
7590 shā't (2), reject by
maligning
114 athĕtĕŏ (1), to
disesteem, neutralize
1848 ĕxŏuthĕnĕŏ (3), to
treat with contempt
2706 kataphrŏnĕŏ (7), to
disesteem, despise
3643 ŏligŏrĕŏ (1), to
disesteem, despise
4065 pĕriphrŏnĕŏ (1), to
depreciate, contemn
DESPISED
937 bûwz (4), disrespect,
scorn
939 bûwzâh (1),
something scorned
959 bāzâh (26), to
ridicule, scorn
3988 mâ'aç (12), to
spurn; to disappear
5006 nâ'ats (6), to scorn
7034 qālâh (1), to be,
hold in contempt
7043 qālal (2), to be easy,
trifling, vile
7590 shā't (1), reject by
maligning
114 athĕtĕŏ (1), to
disesteem, set aside
818 atimazŏ (1), to
maltreat, dishonor
820 atimŏs (1), without
honor
1519+3762+3049 ĕis (1),
to or into
1848 ĕxŏuthĕnĕŏ (3), to
treat with contempt
DESPISERS
865 aphilagathŏs (1),
hostile to virtue
2707 kataphrŏntēs (1),
contemner, scoffer
DESPISEST
2706 kataphrŏnĕŏ (1), to
disesteem, despise
DESPISETH
936 bûwz (4), to
disrespect, scorn
959 bāzâh (4), to ridicule,
scorn
960 bāzôh (1), scorned
3988 mâ'aç (3), to spurn;
to disappear

5006 nâ'ats (1), to scorn
114 athĕtĕŏ (3), to
disesteem, set aside
DESPISING
2706 kataphrŏnĕŏ (1), to
disesteem, despise
DESPITE
7589 shᵉ'âṭ (1), contempt
1796 ĕnubrizŏ (1), to
insult
DESPITEFUL
7589 shᵉ'âṭ (2), contempt
5197 hubristēs (1),
maltreater
DESPITEFULLY
1908 ĕpĕrĕazŏ (2), to
insult, slander
5195 hubrizŏ (1), to
exercise violence
DESTITUTE
2638 châçêr (1), lacking
5800 'āzab (1), to loosen;
relinquish; permit
6168 'ārâh (1), to empty,
pour out; demolish
6199 'ar'âr (1), naked;
poor
8047 shammâh (1), ruin;
consternation
650 apŏstĕrĕŏ (1), to
deprive; to despoil
3007 lĕipŏ (1), to fail or
be absent
5302 hustĕrĕŏ (1), to be
inferior; to fall short
DESTROY
6 'âbad (38), perish;
destroy
7 'âbad (Ch.) (4), perish;
destroy
9 'ăbêdâh (1), destruction
622 'âçaph (1), to gather,
collect
816 'âsham (1), to be
guilty; to be punished
1104 bâla' (7), to
swallow; to destroy
1641 gârar (1), to
ruminate; to saw
1792 dâkâ' (1), to be
contrite, be humbled
1820 dâmâh (1), to be
silent; to fail, cease
1949 hûwm (1), to make
an uproar; agitate
2000 hâmam (3), to
disturb, drive, destroy
2040 hâraç (1), to pull
down; break, destroy
2254 châbal (5), to
pervert, destroy
2255 chăbal (Ch.) (2), to
ruin, destroy
2763 charam (14), to
devote to destruction
3238 yânâh (1), to rage
or be violent
3423 yârash (1), to
inherit; to impoverish
3615 kâlâh (1), to
complete, consume
3772 kârath (2), to cut
(off, down or asunder)
4049 mᵉgar (Ch.) (1), to
overthrow, depose
4135 mûwl (3), to
circumcise

5006 nâ'ats (1), to scorn
114 athĕtĕŏ (3), to
disesteem, set aside
DESPISING
2706 kataphrŏnĕŏ (1), to
disesteem, despise
DESPITE
7589 shᵉ'âṭ (1), contempt
1796 ĕnubrizŏ (1), to
insult
DESPITEFUL
7589 shᵉ'âṭ (2), contempt
5197 hubristēs (1),
maltreater

4191 mûwth (1), to die; to
kill
4229 mâchâh (2), to
erase; to grease
4889 mashchîyth (4),
destruction; corruption
5255 nâçach (1), to tear
away
5362 nâqaph (1), to
strike; to surround
5395 nâsham (1), to
destroy
5422 nâthats (4), to tear
down
5595 çâphâh (3), to
scrape; to remove
6789 tsâmath (4), to
extirpate, destroy
6979 qûwr (1), to throw
forth; to wall up
7665 shâbar (2), to burst
7703 shâdad (1), to
ravage
7722 shôw' (1), tempest;
devastation
7843 shâchath (68), to
decay; to ruin
7921 shâkôl (1), to
miscarry
8045 shâmad (40), to
desolate
8074 shâmêm (2), to
devastate; to stupefy
622 apŏllumi (19), to
destroy fully; to perish
1311 diaphthĕirŏ (1), to
ruin, to decay
2647 kataluŏ (6), to
demolish; to halt
2673 katargĕŏ (3), to be,
render entirely useless
3089 luŏ (2), to loosen
5351 phthĕirŏ (1), to
spoil, ruin; to deprave
DESTROYED
6 'âbad (17), perish;
destroy
7 'âbad (Ch.) (1), perish;
destroy
1104 bâla' (1), to
swallow; to destroy
1792 dâkâ' (1), to
pulverize; be contrite
1820 dâmâh (1), to be
silent; to fail, cease
1822 dummâh (1),
desolation
2026 hârag (1), to kill,
slaughter
2040 hâraç (3), to pull
down; break, destroy
2254 châbal (2), to
pervert, destroy
2255 chăbal (Ch.) (3), to
ruin, destroy
2717 chârab (1), to
desolate, destroy
2718 chărab (Ch.) (1), to
demolish
2763 charam (23), to
devote to destruction
2764 chêrem (1),
extermination
3615 kâlâh (1), to cease,
be finished, perish
3772 kârath (2), to cut
(off, down or asunder)

3807 kâthath (3), to
bruise, strike, beat
4229 mâchâh (3), to
erase; to grease
5422 nâthats (1), to tear
down
5428 nâthash (1), to tear
away, be uprooted
5595 çâphâh (2), to
scrape; to remove
5642 çᵉthar (Ch.) (1), to
demolish
6658 tsâdâh (1), to
desolate
6789 tsâmath (1), to
extirpate, destroy
7321 rûwa' (1), to shout
7665 shâbar (7), to burst
7703 shâdad (1), to
ravage
7843 shâchath (21), to
decay; to ruin
8045 shâmad (43), to
desolate
8074 shâmêm (1), to
devastate; to stupefy
622 apŏllumi (7), to
destroy fully; to perish
1311 diaphthĕirŏ (1), to
ruin, to pervert
1842 ĕxŏlŏthrĕuŏ (1), to
extirpate
2507 kathairĕŏ (2), to
lower, or demolish
2647 kataluŏ (1), to
demolish; to halt
2673 katargĕŏ (2), to be,
render entirely useless
3645 ŏlŏthrĕuŏ (1), to
slay, destroy
4199 pŏrthĕŏ (2), to
ravage, pillage
5356 phthŏra (1), ruin;
depravity, corruption

DESTROYER
2717 chârab (1), to
desolate, destroy
6530 pᵉrîyts (1), violent,
i.e. a tyrant
7703 shâdad (1), to
ravage
7843 shâchath (3), to
decay; to ruin
3644 ŏlŏthrĕutēs (1),
serpent which destroys

DESTROYERS
2040 hâraç (1), to pull
down; break, destroy
4191 mûwth (1), to die; to
kill
7843 shâchath (1), to
decay; to ruin
8154 shâçâh (1), to
plunder

DESTROYEST
6 'âbad (1), perish;
destroy
7843 shâchath (1), to
decay; to ruin
2647 kataluŏ (2), to
demolish; to halt

DESTROYETH
6 'âbad (4), perish;
destroy
3615 kâlâh (1), to
complete, consume
4229 mâchâh (1), to
erase; to grease

7843 shâchath (2), to
decay; to ruin

DESTROYING
1104 bâla' (1), to
swallow; to destroy
2763 charam (5), to
devote to destruction
4889 mashchîyth (1),
destruction; corruption
4892 mashchêth (1),
destruction
6986 qeţeb (1), *ruin*
7843 shâchath (5), to
decay; to ruin

DESTRUCTION
6 'âbad (1), *perish;
destroy*
10 'ăbaddôh (1),
perishing
11 'ăbaddôwn (5),
perishing
12 'abdân (1), *perishing*
13 'obdân (1), *perishing*
343 'êyd (7), *misfortune,
ruin, disaster*
1793 dakkâ' (1), *crushed,
destroyed; contrite*
2035 hărîyçûwth (1),
demolition, destruction
2041 hereç (1),
demolition, destruction
2256 chebel (1),
company, band
2475 chălôwph (1),
destitute orphans
2764 chêrem (2),
extermination
3589 kîyd (1), *calamity,
destruction*
4103 mᵉhûwmâh (3),
confusion or uproar
4288 mᵉchittâh (7), *ruin;
consternation*
4876 mashshûw'âh (1),
ruin
4889 mashchîyth (2),
destruction; corruption
6365 pîyd (2), *misfortune*
6986 qeţeb (2), *ruin*
6987 qôţeb (1),
extermination
7089 qᵉphâdâh (1), *terror*
7171 qerets (1),
extirpation
7591 shᵉ'îyâh (1),
desolation
7667 sheber (20),
fracture; ruin
7670 shibrôwn (1), *ruin*
7701 shôd (7), *violence,
ravage, destruction*
7722 shôw' (2), *tempest;
devastation*
7843 shâchath (1), to
decay; to ruin
7845 shachath (2), *pit;
destruction*
8045 shâmad (1), to
desolate
8395 tᵉbûwçâh (1), *ruin*
8399 tablîyth (1),
consumption
684 apôlĕia (5), *ruin or
loss*
2506 kathairĕsis (2),
demolition
3639 ŏlĕthrŏs (4), *death,
punishment*

4938 *suntrimma* (1),
complete ruin

DESTRUCTIONS
2723 chorbâh (1),
desolation, dry desert
7722 shôw' (1), *tempest;
devastation*
7825 shᵉchîyth (1), *pit*-fall

DETAIN
6113 'âtsar (2), to *hold
back; to maintain*

DETAINED
6113 'âtsar (1), to *hold
back; to maintain*

DETERMINATE
3724 hŏrizō (1), to
appoint, decree, specify

DETERMINATION
4941 mishpâţ (1), *verdict;
formal decree; justice*

DETERMINED
559 'âmar (1), to *say*
2782 chârats (6), to *be
alert, to decide*
2852 châthak (1), to
decree
3289 yâ'ats (2), to *advise*
3615 kâlâh (5), to *cease,
be finished, perish*
7760 sûwm (1), to *put,
place*
1011 bŏulĕuō (1), to
deliberate; to resolve
1956 ĕpiluō (1), to
explain; to decide
2919 krinō (7), to *decide;
to try, condemn, punish*
3724 hŏrizō (3), to
appoint, decree, specify
4309 prŏŏrizō (1), to
predetermine
5021 tassō (1), to *assign
or dispose*

DETEST
8262 shâqats (1), to
loathe, pollute

DETESTABLE
8251 shiqqûwts (6),
disgusting idol

DEUEL
1845 Dᵉ'ûw'êl (4), *known
of God*

DEVICE
1902 higgâyôwn (1),
musical notation
2808 cheshbôwn (1),
contrivance; plan
4209 mᵉzimmâh (1),
plan; sagacity
4284 machăshâbâh (4),
contrivance; plan
1761 ĕnthumĕsis (1),
deliberation; idea

DEVICES
2154 zimmâh (1), *bad
plan*
4156 môw'êtsâh (1),
purpose, plan
4209 mᵉzimmâh (5),
plan; sagacity
4284 machăshâbâh (8),
contrivance; plan
3540 nŏēma (1),
perception, purpose

DEVIL
1139 daimŏnizŏmai (7),
to *be demonized*
1140 daimŏniŏn (18),
demonic being
1142 daimōn (1), *evil
supernatural spirit*
1228 diabŏlŏs (35),
traducer, i.e. *Satan*

DEVILISH
1141 daimŏniŏdēs (1),
demon-like, of the devil

DEVILS
7700 shêd (2), *demon*
8163 sâ'îyr (2), *shaggy;
he-goat; goat idol*
1139 daimŏnizŏmai (6),
to *be demonized*
1140 daimŏniŏn (40),
demonic being
1142 daimōn (4), *evil
supernatural spirit*

DEVISE
2790 chârash (3), to
engrave; to plow
2803 châshab (13), to
weave, fabricate

DEVISED
908 bâdâ' (1), to *invent;
to choose*
1819 dâmâh (1), to
resemble, liken
2161 zâmam (3), to *plan*
2803 châshab (5), to *plot;
to think, regard*
4284 machăshâbâh (1),
contrivance; plan
4679 sŏphizō (1), to
make wise

DEVISETH
2790 chârash (2), to
engrave; to plow
2803 châshab (4), to *plot;
to think, regard*
3289 yâ'ats (2), to *advise*

DEVOTE
2763 charam (1), to
devote to destruction

DEVOTED
2763 charam (1), to
devote to destruction
2764 chêrem (5),
doomed object

DEVOTIONS
4574 sĕbasma (1), *object
of worship*

DEVOUR
398 'âkal (57), to *eat*
399 'ăkal (Ch.) (2), to *eat*
402 'oklâh (2), *food*
7462 râ'âh (1), to *tend a
flock*, i.e. *pasture it*
7602 shâ'aph (1), to *be
angry; to hasten*
2068 ĕsthiō (1), to *eat*
2666 katapinō (1), to
devour by swallowing
2719 katĕsthiō (6), to
devour

DEVOURED
398 'âkal (42), to *eat*
399 'ăkal (Ch.) (2), to *eat*
402 'oklâh (1), *food*
1104 bâla' (2), to
swallow; to destroy

DEVIL
3898 lâcham (1), to *fight
a battle*, i.e. *consume*
2719 katĕsthiō (5), to
devour

DEVOURER
398 'âkal (1), to *eat*

DEVOUREST
398 'âkal (1), to *eat*

DEVOURETH
398 'âkal (6), to *eat*
1104 bâla' (2), to
swallow; to destroy
3216 yâla' (1), to *blurt or
utter inconsiderately*
2719 katĕsthiō (1), to
devour

DEVOURING
398 'âkal (5), to *eat*
1105 bela' (1), *gulp;
destruction*

DEVOUT
2126 ĕulabēs (3),
circumspect, pious
2152 ĕusĕbēs (3), *pious*
4576 sĕbŏmai (3), to
revere, i.e. *adore*

DEW
2919 ţal (30), *dew,
morning mist*
2920 ţal (Ch.) (5), *dew,
morning mist*

DIADEM
4701 mitsnepheth (1),
turban
6797 tsânîyph (2),
head-dress, turban
6843 tsᵉphîyrâh (1),
encircling crown

DIAL
4609 ma'ălâh (2),
thought arising

DIAMOND
3095 yahălôm (3), (poss.)
onyx
8068 shâmîyr (1), *thorn;
(poss.) diamond*

DIANA
735 Artĕmis (5), *prompt*

DIBLAIM
1691 Diblayim (1), *two
cakes*

DIBLATH
1689 Diblâh (1), *Diblah*

DIBON
1769 Dîybôwn (9), *pining*

DIBON-GAD
1769 Dîybôwn (2), *pining*

DIBRI
1704 Dibrîy (1), *wordy*

DID
1580 gâmal (2), to *benefit
or requite; to wean*
1961 hâyâh (1), to *exist*,
i.e. *be or become*
2052 Vâhêb (1), *Vaheb*
5648 'ăbad (Ch.) (1), to
do, work, serve
6213 'âsâh (327), to *do or
make*
6313 pûwg (1), to *be
sluggish; be numb*
7965 shâlôwm (2), *safe;
well; health, prosperity*

15 agathŏpŏiĕŏ (1), *to be a well-doer*
91 adikĕŏ (1), *to do wrong*
1·731 ĕndĕiknumi (1), *to show, display*
3000 latrĕuŏ (1), *to minister to God*
4160 pŏiĕŏ (54), *to make or do*
4238 prassŏ (1), *to execute, accomplish*

DIDDEST
387 anastatŏŏ (1), *to disturb, cause trouble*

DIDST
6213 'âsâh (14), *to do or make*
6466 pâ'al (1), *to do, make or practice*

DIDYMUS
1324 Didumŏs (3), *twin*

DIE
1478 gâva' (8), *to expire, die*
4191 mûwth (255), *to die; to kill*
4194 mâveth (7), *death; dead*
8546 tᵉmûwthâh (1), *execution, death*
599 apŏthnĕskŏ (40), *to die off*
622 apŏllumi (1), *to destroy fully; to perish*
684 apŏlĕia (1), *ruin or loss*
4880 sunapŏthnĕskŏ (2), *to decease with*
5053 tĕlĕutaŏ (3), *finish life, i.e. expire*

DIED
1478 gâva' (3), *to expire, die*
4191 mûwth (154), *to die; to kill*
4194 mâveth (7), *death; dead*
5038 nᵉbêlâh (1), *carcase or carrion*
5307 nâphal (1), *to fall*
599 apŏthnĕskŏ (32), *to die off*
5053 tĕlĕutaŏ (2), *finish life, i.e. expire*

DIEST
4191 mûwth (1), *to die; to kill*

DIET
737 'ărûchâh (2), *ration, portion of food*

DIETH
4191 mûwth (16), *to die; to kill*
4194 mâveth (4), *death; dead*
5038 nᵉbêlâh (4), *carcase or carrion*
599 apŏthnĕskŏ (2), *to die off*
5053 tĕlĕutaŏ (3), *finish life, i.e. expire*

DIFFER
1252 diakrinŏ (1), *decide; to hesitate*

DIFFERENCE
914 bâdal (3), *to divide, separate, distinguish*
6395 pâlâh (1), *to distinguish*
1252 diakrinŏ (2), *to decide; to hesitate*
1293 diastŏlē (2), *variation, distinction*
3307 mĕrizŏ (1), *to disunite, differ*

DIFFERENCES
1243 diairĕsis (1), *distinction or variety*

DIFFERETH
1308 diaphĕrŏ (2), *to bear, carry; to differ*

DIFFERING
1313 diaphŏrŏs (1), *varying; surpassing*

DIG
2658 châphar (3), *to delve, to explore*
2672 châtsab (1), *to cut stone or carve wood*
2864 châthar (5), *to break or dig into*
3738 kârâh (2), *to dig; to plot; to bore, hew*
4626 skaptŏ (2), *to dig*

DIGGED
2658 châphar (13), *to delve, to explore*
2672 châtsab (3), *to cut stone or carve wood*
2864 châthar (2), *to break or dig into*
3738 kârâh (8), *to dig; to plot; to bore, hew*
5365 nâqar (3), *to bore; to gouge*
5737 'âdar (2), *to hoe a vineyard*
6131 'âqar (1), *to pluck up; to hamstring*
2679 kataskaptŏ (1), *to destroy, be ruined*
3736 ŏrussŏ (3), *to burrow, i.e. dig out*
4626 skaptŏ (1), *to dig*

DIGGEDST
2672 châtsab (1), *to cut stone or carve wood*

DIGGETH
2658 châphar (1), *to delve, to explore*
3738 kârâh (2), *to dig; to plot; to bore, hew*

DIGNITIES
1891 Ĕpaphrŏditŏs (2), *devoted to Venus*

DIGNITY
1420 gᵉdûwlâh (1), *greatness, grandeur*
4791 mârôwm (1), *elevation; haughtiness*
7613 sᵉ'êth (2), *elevation; swelling scab*

DIKLAH
1853 Diqlâh (2), *Diklah*

DILEAN
1810 Dil'ân (1), *Dilan*

DILIGENCE
4929 mishmâr (1), *guard; deposit; usage; example*

2039 ĕrgasia (1), *occupation; profit*
4704 spŏudazŏ (2), *to make effort*
4710 spŏudē (6), *despatch; eagerness*

DILIGENT
2742 chârûwts (5), *diligent, earnest*
3190 yâṭab (1), *to be, make well*
3966 mᵉ'ôd (1), *very, utterly*
4106 mâhîyr (1), *skillful*
4704 spŏudazŏ (2), *to make effort*
4705 spŏudaiŏs (1), *prompt, energetic*
4707 spŏudaiŏtĕrŏs (1), *more earnest*

DILIGENTLY
149 'adrazdâ' (Ch.) (1), *carefully, diligently*
995 bîyn (1), *to understand; discern*
3190 yâṭab (2), *to be, make well*
3966 mᵉ'ôd (4), *very, utterly*
5172 nâchash (1), *to prognosticate*
7182 qesheb (1), *hearkening*
7836 shâchar (2), *to search for*
8150 shânan (1), *to pierce; to inculcate*
199 akribōs (2), *exactly, carefully*
1567 ĕkzētĕŏ (1), *to seek out*
1960 ĕpimĕlōs (1), *carefully, diligently*
4706 spŏudaiŏtĕrŏn (1), *more earnestly*
4709 spŏudaiŏs (1), *earnestly, promptly*

DIM
2821 châshak (1), *to be dark; to darken*
3513 kâbad (1), *to be heavy, severe, dull*
3543 kâhâh (3), *to grow dull, fade; to be faint*
3544 kêheh (1), *feeble; obscure*
6004 'âmam (1), *to overshadow*
6965 qûwm (1), *to rise*
8159 shâ'âh (1), *to inspect, consider*

DIMINISH
1639 gâra' (6), *to shave, remove, lessen*
4591 mâ'aṭ (2), *to be, make small or few*

DIMINISHED
1639 gâra' (2), *to shave, remove, lessen*
4591 mâ'aṭ (3), *to be, make small or few*

DIMINISHING
2275 hēttēma (1), *failure or loss*

DIMNAH
1829 Dimnâh (1), *dung-heap*

DIMNESS
4155 mûw'âph (1), *obscurity; distress*
4588 mâ'ûwph (1), *darkness, gloom*

DIMON
1775 Dîymôwn (2), *Dimon*

D

DIMONAH
1776 Dîymôwnâh (1), *Dimonah*

DINAH
1783 Dîynâh (7), *justice*

DINAH'S
1783 Dîynâh (1), *justice*

DINAITES
1784 Dîynay (Ch.) (1), *Dinaite*

DINE
398 'âkal (1), *to eat*
709 aristaŏ (2), *to eat a meal*

DINED
709 aristaŏ (1), *to eat a meal*

DINHABAH
1838 Dinhâbâh (2), *Dinhabah*

DINNER
737 'ărûchâh (1), *ration, portion of food*
712 aristŏn (3), *breakfast or lunch; feast*

DIONYSIUS
1354 Diŏnusiŏs (1), *reveller*

DIOTREPHES
1361 Diŏtrĕphēs (1), *Zeus-nourished*

DIP
2881 ṭâbal (9), *to dip*
911 baptŏ (1), *to overwhelm, cover*

DIPPED
2881 ṭâbal (6), *to dip*
4272 mâchats (1), *to crush; to subdue*
911 baptŏ (1), *to overwhelm, cover*
1686 ĕmbaptŏ (1), *to wet*

DIPPETH
1686 ĕmbaptŏ (2), *to wet*

DIRECT
3384 yârâh (1), *to point; to teach*
3474 yâshar (3), *to be straight; to make right*
3559 kûwn (1), *to set up: establish, fix, prepare*
3787 kâshêr (1), *to be straight or right*
5414 nâthan (1), *to give*
6186 'ârak (1), *to set in a row, i.e. arrange,*
2720 katĕuthunŏ (2), *to direct, lead, direct*

DIRECTED
3559 kûwn (1), *to set up: establish, fix, prepare*
6186 'ârak (1), *to set in a row, i.e. arrange,*
8505 tâkan (1), *to balance, i.e. measure*

DIRECTETH
3474 yâshar (1), to be
straight; to make right
3559 kûwn (2), to set up:
establish, fix, prepare

DIRECTLY
413+5227 'êl (1), to,
toward
1903 hâgîyn (1), (poss.)
suitable or turning

DIRT
2916 tîyt (2), mud or clay
6574 parsh°dôn (1),
crotch or anus

DISALLOW
5106 nûw' (1), to refuse,
forbid, dissuade

DISALLOWED
5106 nûw' (3), to refuse,
forbid, dissuade
593 apŏdŏkimazō (2), to
repudiate, reject

DISANNUL
6565 pârar (2), to break
up; to violate, frustrate
208 akurŏō (1), to
invalidate, nullify

DISANNULLED
3722 kâphar (1), to
placate or cancel

DISANNULLETH
114 athětěō (1), to
neutralize or set aside

DISANNULLING
115 athětěsis (1),
cancellation

DISAPPOINT
6923 qâdam (1), to
anticipate, hasten

DISAPPOINTED
6565 pârar (1), to break
up; to violate, frustrate

DISAPPOINTETH
6565 pârar (1), to break
up; to violate, frustrate

DISCERN
995 bîyn (2), to
understand; discern
3045 yâda' (3), to know
5234 nâkar (4), to
acknowledge
7200 râ'âh (1), to see
8085 shâma' (2), to hear
intelligently
1252 diakrinō (1), to
decide; to hesitate
1253 diakrisis (1),
estimation
1381 dŏkimazō (1), to
test; to approve

DISCERNED
995 bîyn (1), to
understand; discern
5234 nâkar (2), to
acknowledge
350 anakrinō (1), to
interrogate, determine

DISCERNER
2924 kritikŏs (1),
discriminative

DISCERNETH
3045 yâda' (1), to know

DISCERNING
1252 diakrinō (1), to
decide; to hesitate
1253 diakrisis (1),
estimation

DISCHARGE
4917 mishlachath (1),
mission; release; army

DISCHARGED
5310 nâphats (1), to dash
to pieces; to scatter

DISCIPLE
3100 mathētěuō (1), to
become a student
3101 mathētěs (27),
pupil, student
3102 mathētria (1),
female pupil, student

DISCIPLES
3928 limmûwd (1),
instructed one
3101 mathētěs (240),
pupil, student

DISCIPLES'
3101 mathētěs (1), pupil,
student

DISCIPLINE
4148 mûwçâr (1),
reproof, warning

DISCLOSE
1540 gâlâh (1), to
denude; uncover

DISCOMFITED
1949 hûwm (3), to make
an uproar; agitate
2000 hâmam (2), to put
in commotion
2522 châlash (1), to
prostrate, lay low
2729 chârad (1), to
shudder with terror
3807 kâthath (1), to
bruise, strike, beat
4522 maç (1), forced
labor

DISCOMFITURE
4103 m°hûwmâh (1),
confusion or uproar

DISCONTENTED
4751+5315 mar (1), bitter;
bitterness; bitterly

DISCONTINUE
8058 shâmat (1), to let
alone, desist, remit

DISCORD
4066 mâdôwn (1),
contest or quarrel
4090 m°dân (1), contest
or quarrel

DISCOURAGE
5106 nûw' (1), to refuse,
forbid, dissuade

DISCOURAGED
2865 châthath (1), to
break down
4549 mâçaç (1), to waste;
to faint
5106 nûw' (1), to refuse,
forbid, dissuade
7114 qâtsar (1), to
curtail, cut short
7533 râtsats (1), to crack
in pieces, smash

120 athumĕō (1), to be
disheartened

DISCOVER
1540 gâlâh (10), to
denude; uncover
2834 châsaph (1), to
drain away or bail up
6168 'ârâh (1), to be,
make bare; to empty

DISCOVERED
1540 gâlâh (18), to
denude; uncover
3045 yâda' (1), to know
6168 'ârâh (1), to be,
make bare; to empty
398 anaphainō (1), to
appear
2657 katanŏĕō (1), to
observe fully

DISCOVERETH
1540 gâlâh (1), to
denude; uncover
2834 châsaph (1), to
drain away or bail up

DISCOVERING
6168 'ârâh (1), to be,
make bare; to empty

DISCREET
995 bîyn (2), to
understand; discern
4998 sōphrōn (1),
self-controlled

DISCREETLY
3562 nŏunĕchōs (1),
prudently

DISCRETION
2940 ta'am (1), taste;
intelligence; mandate
4209 m°zimmâh (4),
plan; sagacity
4941 mishpât (2), verdict;
formal decree; justice
7922 sekel (1),
intelligence; success
8394 tâbûwn (1),
intelligence; argument

DISDAINED
959 bâzâh (1), to ridicule,
scorn
3988 mâ'aç (1), to spurn;
to disappear

DISEASE
1697 dâbâr (1), word;
matter; thing
2483 chŏlîy (7), malady;
anxiety; calamity
4245 machăleh (1),
sickness
3119 malakia (3),
enervation, debility
3553 nŏsĕma (1),
ailment, disease

DISEASED
2456 châlâ' (2), to be sick
2470 châlâh (2), to be
weak, sick, afflicted
770 asthĕnĕō (1), to be
feeble
2560+2192 kakōs (2),
badly; wrongly; ill

DISEASES
4064 madveh (2),
sickness
4245 machăleh (1),
sickness

4251 machlûy (1), disease
8463 tachălûw' (2),
malady, disease
769 asthĕnĕia (1),
feebleness of body
3554 nŏsŏs (6), malady,
disease

DISFIGURE
853 aphanizō (1), to
consume (becloud)

DISGRACE
5034 nâbêl (1), to be
foolish or wicked

DISGUISE
2664 châphas (2), to let
be sought; to mask
8138 shânâh (1), to
transmute

DISGUISED
2664 châphas (5), to let
be sought; to mask

DISGUISETH
5643 çêther (1), cover,
shelter

DISH
5602 çêphel (1), basin,
bowl
6747 tsallachath (1), bowl
5165 trubliŏn (2), bowl

DISHAN
1789 Dîyshân (5),
antelope

DISHES
7086 q°'ârâh (3), bowl

DISHON
1788 dîyshôn (7),
antelope

DISHONEST
1215 betsa' (2), plunder;
unjust gain

DISHONESTY
152 aischunē (1), shame
or disgrace

DISHONOUR
3639 k°limmâh (3),
disgrace, scorn
6173 'arvâh (Ch.) (1),
nakedness
7036 qâlôwn (1), disgrace
818 atimazō (2), to
maltreat, dishonor
819 atimia (4), disgrace

DISHONOUREST
818 atimazō (1), to
maltreat, dishonor

DISHONOURETH
5034 nâbêl (1), to wilt; to
be foolish or wicked
2617 kataischunō (2), to
disgrace or shame

DISINHERIT
3423 yârash (1), to
inherit; to impoverish

DISMAYED
926 bâhal (1), to tremble;
hurry anxiously
2844 chath (1), terror
2865 châthath (26), to
break down
8159 shâ'âh (2), to be
bewildered

DISMAYING
4288 m°chittâh (1), *ruin; consternation*

DISMISSED
6362 pâṭar (1), to *burst through*; to *emit*
630 apŏluō (2), to *relieve, release*; to *divorce*

DISOBEDIENCE
543 apĕithĕia (3), *disbelief*
3876 parakŏē (3), *disobedience*

DISOBEDIENT
4784 mârâh (2), to *rebel or resist*; to *provoke*
506 anupŏtaktŏs (1), *insubordinate*
544 apĕithĕō (4), to *disbelieve*
545 apĕithēs (6), *willful disobedience*

DISOBEYED
4784 mârâh (1), to *rebel or resist*; to *provoke*

DISORDERLY
812 ataktĕō (1), to *be, act irregular*
814 ataktōs (2), *morally irregularly*

DISPATCH
1254 bârâ' (1), to *create; fashion*

DISPENSATION
3622 ŏikŏnŏmia (4), *administration*

DISPERSE
2219 zârâh (7), to *toss about*; to *diffuse*
6327 pûwts (1), to *dash in pieces*; to *disperse*

DISPERSED
2219 zârâh (1), to *toss about*; to *diffuse*
5310 nâphats (1), to *dash to pieces*; to *scatter*
6327 pûwts (2), to *dash in pieces*; to *disperse*
6340 pâzar (1), to *scatter*
6504 pârad (1), to *spread or separate*
6555 pârats (1), to *break out*
1287 diaskŏrpizō (1), to *scatter*; to *squander*
1290 diaspŏra (1), *dispersion*
4650 skŏrpizō (1), to *dissipate*

DISPERSIONS
8600 t°phôwtsâh (1), *dispersal*

DISPLAYED
5127 nûwç (1), to *vanish away, flee*

DISPLEASE
2734 chârâh (1), to *blaze up*
6213+7451+5869 'âsâh (1), to *do or make*
7489+5869 râ'a' (3), to *be good for nothing*

DISPLEASED
599 'ânaph (1), *be enraged, be angry*

DISQUIET
888 b°'êsh (Ch.) (1), to *be displeased*
2198 zâ'êph (2), *angry, raging*
2734 chârâh (3), to *blaze up*
3415+5869 yâra' (1), to *fear*
6087 'âtsab (1), to *worry, have pain or anger*
7107 qâtsaph (3), to *burst out in rage*
7451+241 ra' (1), *bad; evil*
7489+5869 râ'a' (7), to *be good for nothing*
23 aganaktĕō (3), to *be indignant*
2371 thumŏmachĕō (1), to *be exasperated*

DISPLEASURE
2534 chêmâh (3), *heat; anger; poison*
2740 chârôwn (1), *burning of anger*
7451 ra' (1), *bad; evil*

DISPOSED
7760 sûwm (2), to *put, place*
1014 bŏulŏmai (1), to *be willing, desire*
2309 thĕlō (1), to *will*; to *desire; to choose*

DISPOSING
4941 mishpâṭ (1), *verdict; formal decree; justice*

DISPOSITION
1296 diatagē (1), *putting into effect*

DISPOSSESS
3423 yârash (2), to *inherit*; to *impoverish*

DISPOSSESSED
3423 yârash (2), to *inherit*; to *impoverish*

DISPUTATION
4803 suzētēsis (1), *discussion, dispute*

DISPUTATIONS
1253 diakrisis (1), *estimation*

DISPUTE
3198 yâkach (1), to *be correct*; to *argue*

DISPUTED
1256 dialĕgŏmai (3), to *discuss*
1260 dialŏgizŏmai (1), to *deliberate*
4802 suzētĕō (1), to *discuss, controvert*

DISPUTER
4804 suzētētēs (1), *sophist*

DISPUTING
1256 dialĕgŏmai (3), to *discuss*
4802 suzētĕō (1), to *discuss, controvert*
4803 suzētēsis (1), *discussion, dispute*

DISPUTINGS
1261 dialŏgismŏs (1), *consideration; debate*
3859 paradiatribē (1), *meddlesomeness*

DISQUIET
7264 râgaz (1), to *quiver*

DISQUIETED
1993 hâmâh (4), to *be in great commotion*
7264 râgaz (2), to *quiver*

DISQUIETNESS
5100 n°hâmâh (1), *snarling, growling*

DISSEMBLED
3584 kâchash (1), to *lie, disown*; to *disappoint*
8582 tâ'âh (1), to *vacillate, reel or stray*
4942 sunupŏkrinŏmai (1), to *act hypocritically*

DISSEMBLERS
5956 'âlam (1), to *veil from sight, i.e. conceal*

DISSEMBLETH
5234 nâkar (1), to *treat as a foreigner*

DISSENSION
4714 stasis (3), one *leading an uprising*

DISSIMULATION
505 anupŏkritŏs (1), *sincere, genuine*
5272 hupŏkrisis (1), *deceit, hypocrisy*

DISSOLVE
8271 sh°rê' (Ch.) (1), to *unravel, commence*

DISSOLVED
4127 mûwg (3), to *soften, flow down, disappear*
4743 mâqaq (1), to *melt; to flow, dwindle, vanish*
6565 pârar (1), to *break up*; to *violate, frustrate*
2647 kataluō (1), to *demolish*; to *halt*
3089 luō (2), to *loosen*

DISSOLVEST
4127 mûwg (1), to *soften, flow down, disappear*

DISSOLVING
8271 sh°rê' (Ch.) (1), to *free, separate*

DISTAFF
6418 pelek (1), *spindle-whorl; crutch*

DISTANT
7947 shâlab (1), to *make equidistant*

DISTIL
5140 nâzal (1), to *drip, or shed by trickling*
7491 râ'aph (1), to *drip*

DISTINCTION
1293 diastŏlē (1), *variation, distinction*

DISTINCTLY
6567 pârash (1), to *separate; to specify*

DISTRACTED
6323 pûwn (1), to *be perplexed*

DISTRACTION
563 apĕrispastŏs (1), *undistractedly*

DISTRESS
4689 mâtsôwq (1), *confinement; disability*
4691 m°tsûwqâh (1), *trouble, anguish*
4712 mêtsar (1), *trouble*
6693 tsûwq (5), to *oppress, distress*
6696 tsûwr (2), to *cramp, i.e. confine*; to *harass*
6862 tsar (4), *trouble; opponent*
6869 tsârâh (8), *trouble; rival-wife*
6887 tsârar (5), to *cramp*
7451 ra' (1), *bad; evil*
318 anagkē (3), *constraint; distress*
4730 stĕnŏchōria (1), *calamity, distress*
4928 sunŏchē (1), *anxiety, distress*

DISTRESSED
3334 yâtsar (4), to *be in distress*
5065 nâgas (2), to *exploit; to tax, harass*
6696 tsûwr (1), to *cramp, i.e. confine*; to *harass*
6887 tsârar (2), to *cramp*
6973 qûwts (1), to *be, make disgusted*
4729 stĕnŏchōrĕō (1), to *hem in closely*

DISTRESSES
4691 m°tsûwqâh (5), *trouble, anguish*
6862 tsar (1), *trouble; opponent*
4730 stĕnŏchōria (2), *calamity, distress*

DISTRIBUTE
2505 châlaq (1), to *be smooth; be slippery*
5157 nâchal (1), to *inherit*
5414 nâthan (1), to *give*
1239 diadidōmi (1), to *divide up, distribute*
2130 ĕumĕtadŏtŏs (1), *liberal, generous*

DISTRIBUTED
2505 châlaq (2), to *be smooth; be slippery*
5157 nâchal (1), to *inherit*
1239 diadidōmi (1), to *divide up, distribute*
3307 mĕrizō (2), to *apportion, bestow*

DISTRIBUTETH
2505 châlaq (1), to *be smooth; be slippery*

DISTRIBUTING
2841 kŏinōnĕō (1), to *share or participate*

DISTRIBUTION
1239 diadidōmi (1), to *divide up, distribute*
2842 kŏinōnia (1), *benefaction; sharing*

DITCH
4724 miqvâh (1), *water reservoir*
7745 shûwchâh (1), *chasm*
7845 shachath (2), *pit; destruction*

999 bŏthunŏs (2), *cistern, pit-hole*

DITCHES
1356 gêb (1), *well, cistern; pit*

DIVERS
582 'ĕnôwsh (1), *man; person, human*
2921 ţâlâ' (1), *to be spotted or variegated*
3610 kil'ayim (1), *two different kinds of thing*
6446 paç (2), *long -sleeved tunic*
6648 tseba' (3), *dye*
7553 riqmâh (2), *variegation of color*
8162 sha'aţnêz (1), *linen and woolen*
1313 diaphŏrŏs (1), *varying; surpassing*
4164 pŏikilŏs (8), *various in character or kind*
4187 pŏlutrŏpŏs (1), *in many ways*
5100 tis (2), *some or any*

DIVERSE
3610 kil'ayim (1), *two different kinds of thing*
8133 shᵉnâ' (Ch.) (5), *to alter, change*
8138 shânâh (2), *to duplicate; to transmute*

DIVERSITIES
1085 gĕnŏs (1), *kin, offspring in kind*
1243 diairĕsis (2), *distinction or variety*

DIVIDE
914 bâdal (5), *to divide, separate, distinguish*
1234 bâqa' (2), *to cleave, break, tear open*
1504 gâzar (2), *to destroy, divide*
2505 châlaq (17), *to be smooth; be slippery*
2673 châtsâh (3), *to cut or split in two; to halve*
5157 nâchal (3), *to inherit*
5307 nâphal (4), *to fall*
5312 nᵉphaq (Ch.) (2), *to issue forth; to bring out*
6385 pâlag (1), *to split*
6536 pâraç (4), *to break in pieces; to split*
6565 pârar (1), *to break up; to violate, frustrate*
1266 diamĕrizō (1), *distribute*
3307 mĕrizō (1), *to apportion, bestow*

DIVIDED
914 bâdal (2), *to divide, separate, distinguish*
1234 bâqa' (2), *to cleave, break, tear open*
1334 bâthar (2), *to chop up, cut up*
1504 gâzar (1), *to destroy, divide*
2505 châlaq (21), *to be smooth; be slippery*
2673 châtsâh (8), *to cut or split in two; to halve*
5307 nâphal (2), *to fall*

5408 nâthach (1), *to dismember, cut up*
5504 çachar (1), *profit from trade*
6385 pâlag (3), *to split*
6386 pᵉlag (Ch.) (1), *dis-united*
6504 pârad (2), *to spread or separate*
6537 pᵉraç (Ch.) (1), *to split up*
7280 râga' (1), *to settle, to stir up*
7323 rûwts (1), *to run*
1096 ginŏmai (1), *to be, become*
1244 diairĕō (1), *distribute, apportion*
1266 diamĕrizō (4), *to distribute*
2624 kataklērŏdŏtĕō (1), *to apportion an estate*
3307 mĕrizō (8), *to apportion, bestow*
4977 schizō (2), *to split or sever*

DIVIDER
3312 mĕristĕs (1), *apportioner*

DIVIDETH
2672 châtsab (1), *to cut stone or carve wood*
6536 pâraç (5), *to break; to split, distribute*
7280 râga' (2), *to settle, to stir up*
873 aphŏrizō (1), *to limit, exclude, appoint*
1239 diadidōmi (1), *to divide up, distribute*

DIVIDING
1234 bâqa' (1), *to cleave, break, tear open*
2505 châlaq (1), *to be smooth; be slippery*
6387 pᵉlag (Ch.) (1), *half-time unit*
1244 diairĕō (1), *distribute, apportion*
3311 mĕrismŏs (1), *separation, distribution*
3718 ŏrthŏtŏmĕō (1), *to expound correctly*

DIVINATION
4738 miqçâm (2), *augury, divination*
7080 qâçam (1), *to divine magic*
7081 qeçem (8), *divination*
4436 Puthōn (1), *inspiration in soothsaying*

DIVINATIONS
7081 qeçem (1), *divination*

DIVINE
5172 nâchash (1), *to prognosticate*
7080 qâçam (5), *to divine magic*
7081 qeçem (1), *divination*
7181 qâshab (1), *to prick up the ears*
2304 thĕiŏs (2), *divinity*
2999 latrĕia (1), *worship, ministry service*

DIVINERS
7080 qâçam (7), *to divine magic*

DIVINETH
5172 nâchash (1), *to prognosticate*

DIVINING
7080 qâçam (1), *to divine magic*

DIVISION
2515 châluqqâh (1), *distribution, portion*
6304 pᵉdûwth (1), *distinction; deliverance*
1267 diamĕrismŏs (1), *disunion*
4978 schisma (3), *dissension, i.e. schism*

DIVISIONS
4256 machălôqeth (8), *section or division*
4653 miphlaggâh (1), *classification, division*
6391 pᵉluggâh (3), *section*
6392 pᵉluggâh (Ch.) (1), *section*
1370 dichŏstasia (2), *dissension*
4978 schisma (2), *dissension, i.e. schism*

DIVORCE
3748 kᵉrîythûwth (1), *divorce*

DIVORCED
1644 gârash (3), *to drive out; to divorce*
630 apŏluō (1), *to relieve, release; to divorce*

DIVORCEMENT
3748 kᵉrîythûwth (3), *divorce*
647 apŏstasiŏn (3), *marriage divorce*

DIZAHAB
1774 Dîy zâhâb (1), *of gold*

DO
1167 ba'al (1), *master; husband; owner; citizen*
1580 gâmal (1), *to benefit or requite; to wean*
3190 yâţab (2), *to be, make well*
3318 yâtsâ' (1), *to go, bring out*
4640 Ma'say (1), *operative*
5647 'âbad (17), *to do, work, serve*
5648 'âbad (Ch.) (5), *to do, work, serve*
5674 'âbar (1), *to cross over; to transition*
5953 'âlal (2), *to glean; to overdo*
6213 'âsâh (617), *to do*
6466 pâ'al (6), *to do*
6467 pô'al (1), *act or work, deed*
14 agathŏĕrgĕō (1), *to do good work*
15 agathŏpŏiĕō (6), *to be a well-doer*
17 agathŏpŏiŏs (1), *virtuous one*

91 adikĕō (2), *to do wrong*
1107 gnōrizō (1), *to make known, reveal*
1286 diasĕiō (1), *to intimidate*
1398 dŏulĕuō (1), *to serve as a slave*
1754 ĕnĕrgĕō (1), *to be active, efficient, work*
2005 ĕpitĕlĕō (1), *to terminate; to undergo*
2038 ĕrgazŏmai (2), *to toil*
2140 ĕupŏïïa (1), *beneficence, doing good*
2192 ĕchō (1), *to have; hold; keep*
2480 ischuō (1), *to have or exercise force*
2554 kakŏpŏiĕō (2), *to injure; to sin, do wrong*
2698 katatithĕmi (1), *to place down*
2716 katĕrgazŏmai (3), *to finish; to accomplish*
3930 parĕchō (1), *to hold near, i.e. to present*
4160 pŏiĕō (199), *to do*
4238 prassō (15), *to execute, accomplish*
4704 spŏudazō (2), *to make effort*
4982 sōzō (1), *to deliver; to protect*

DOCTOR
3547 nŏmŏdidaskalŏs (1), *Rabbi*

DOCTORS
1320 didaskalŏs (1), *instructor*
3547 nŏmŏdidaskalŏs (1), *Rabbi*

DOCTRINE
3948 leqach (4), *instruction*
4148 mûwçâr (1), *reproof, warning*
8052 shᵉmûw'âh (1), *announcement*
1319 didaskalia (15), *instruction*
1322 didachĕ (28), *instruction*
3056 lŏgŏs (1), *word, matter, thing*

DOCTRINES
1319 didaskalia (4), *instruction*
1322 didachĕ (1), *instruction*

DODAI
1739 dâveh (1), *menstrual; fainting*

DODANIM
1721 Dôdânîym (2), *Dodanites*

DODAVAH
1735 Dôwdâvâhûw (1), *love of Jehovah*

DODO
1734 Dôwdôw (5), *loving*

DOEG
1673 Dô'êg (6), *anxious*

DOER
6218 'âsôwr (3), group of ten
2557 kakŏurgŏs (1), criminal, evildoer
4163 pŏiētēs (3), performer; poet

DOERS
6213 'âsâh (2), to do or make
6466 pâ'al (1), to do, make or practice
4163 pŏiētēs (2), performer; poet

DOEST
5648 'ăbad (Ch.) (1), to do, work, serve
6213 'âsâh (18), to do or make
6466 pâ'al (1), to do, make or practice
7965 shâlwm (1), safe; well; health, prosperity
4160 pŏiĕō (14), to do
4238 prassō (1), to execute, accomplish

DOETH
1580 gâmal (1), to benefit or requite; to wean
5648 'ăbad (Ch.) (1), to do, work, serve
6213 'âsâh (44), to do
7760 sûwm (1), to put, place
15 agathŏpŏiĕō (1), to be a well-doer
91 adikĕō (1), to do wrong
2554 kakŏpŏiĕō (1), to injure; to sin, do wrong
4160 pŏiĕō (34), to do
4238 prassō (3), to execute, accomplish
4374 prŏsphĕrō (1), to present to; to treat as

DOG
3611 keleb (14), dog; male prostitute
2965 kuŏn (1), dog

DOG'S
3611 keleb (2), dog; male prostitute

DOGS
3611 keleb (16), dog; male prostitute
2952 kunariŏn (4), small dog
2965 kuŏn (4), dog

DOING
854 'êth (1), with; by; at; among
4640 Ma'say (1), operative
5949 'ălîylâh (1), opportunity, action
6213 'âsâh (14), to do or make
15 agathŏpŏiĕō (2), to be a well-doer
16 agathŏpŏiïa (1), virtue, doing good
92 adikĕma (1), wrong done
1096 ginŏmai (2), to be, become
1398 dŏulĕuō (1), to serve as a slave

2041 ĕrgŏn (1), work
2109 ĕuĕrgĕtĕō (1), to be philanthropic
2554 kakŏpŏiĕō (1), to injure; to sin, do wrong
2569 kalŏpŏiĕō (1), to do well
4160 pŏiĕō (8), to do

DOINGS
4611 ma'ălâl (35), act, deed
4640 Ma'say (3), operative
5949 'ălîylâh (13), opportunity, action

DOLEFUL
255 'ôach (1), creature that howls;
5093 nihyâh (1), lamentation

DOMINION
1166 bâ'al (1), to be master; to marry
1196 Ba'ănâh (1), in affliction
3027 yâd (2), hand; power
4474 mimshâl (2), ruler; dominion, rule
4475 memshâlâh (10), rule; realm or a ruler
4896 mishṭâr (1), jurisdiction, rule
4910 mâshal (7), to rule
4915 môshel (2), empire; parallel
7287 râdâh (9), to subjugate
7300 rûwd (1), to ramble free or disconsolate
7980 shâlaṭ (1), to dominate, i.e. govern
7985 sholṭân (Ch.) (11), official
2634 katakuriĕuō (1), to control, subjugate
2904 kratŏs (4), vigor, strength
2961 kuriĕuō (4), to rule, be master of
2963 kuriŏtēs (2), rulers; masters

DOMINIONS
7985 sholṭân (Ch.) (1), official
2963 kuriŏtēs (1), rulers; masters

DONE
466 'Ĕlîyphᵉlêhûw (1), God of his distinction
1254 bârâ' (1), to create; fashion
1580 gâmal (1), to benefit or requite; to wean
1639 gâra' (1), to shave, remove, lessen
1697 dâbâr (1), word; matter; thing
1961 hâyâh (2), to exist, i.e. be or become
3254 yâçaph (1), to add or augment
3615 kâlâh (9), to complete, prepare
5414 nâthan (1), to give
5647 'âbad (1), to do, work, serve

5648 'ăbad (Ch.) (4), to do, work, serve
5953 'âlal (3), to glean; to overdo
6213 'âsâh (318), to do or make
6466 pâ'al (21), to do, make or practice
7760 sûwm (1), to put, place
8552 tâmam (2), to complete, finish
91 adikĕō (3), to do wrong
1096 ginŏmai (61), to be, become
1796 ĕnubrizō (1), to insult
2673 katargĕō (4), to be, render entirely useless
2716 katĕrgazŏmai (2), to finish; to accomplish
4160 pŏiĕō (52), to do
4238 prassō (6), to execute, accomplish

DOOR
1004 bayith (1), house; temple; family, tribe
1817 deleth (21), door; gate
4201 mᵉzûwzâh (2), door-post
4947 mashqôwph (1), lintel
5592 çaph (11), dish
6607 pethach (114), opening; door
6907 qubba'ath (2), goblet, cup
8179 sha'ar (1), opening, i.e. door or gate
2374 thura (28), entrance, i.e. door, gate
2377 thurōrŏs (2), doorkeeper

DOORKEEPER
5605 çâphaph (1), to wait at (the) threshold

DOORKEEPERS
7778 shôw'êr (2), janitor, door-keeper

DOORS
1817 deleth (48), door; gate
5592 çaph (2), dish
6607 pethach (11), opening; door
8179 sha'ar (1), opening, i.e. door or gate
2374 thura (9), entrance, i.e. door, gate

DOPHKAH
1850 Dophqâh (2), knock

DOR
1756 Dôwr (6), dwelling

DORCAS
1393 Dŏrkas (2), gazelle

DOTE
2973 yâ'al (1), to be or act foolish

DOTED
5689 'ăgab (6), to lust sensually

DOTHAN
1886 Dôthân (3), Dothan

DOTING
3552 nŏsĕō (1), to be sick, be ill

DOUBLE
3717 kâphal (2), to fold together; to repeat
3718 kephel (3), duplicate, double
4932 mishneh (8), duplicate copy; double
8147 shᵉnayim (5), two-fold
1362 diplŏus (2), two-fold
1374 dipsuchŏs (2), vacillating
3588+1362 hŏ (1), "the," i.e. the definite article

DOUBLED
3717 kâphal (3), to fold together; to repeat
8138 shânâh (1), to fold, i.e. duplicate

DOUBLETONGUED
1351 dilŏgŏs (1), insincere

DOUBT
551 'omnâm (1), verily, indeed, truly
142+5590 airō (1), to lift, to take up
639 apŏrĕō (1), be at a mental loss, be puzzled
686 ara (1), then, so, therefore
1063 gar (1), for, indeed, but, because
1252 diakrinō (2), to decide; to hesitate
1280 diapŏrĕō (1), to be thoroughly puzzled
1365 distazō (1), to waver in opinion
3843 pantōs (1), at all events; in no event

DOUBTED
639 apŏrĕō (1), be at a mental loss, be puzzled
1280 diapŏrĕō (2), to be thoroughly puzzled
1365 distazō (1), to waver in opinion

DOUBTETH
1252 diakrinō (1), to decide; to hesitate

DOUBTFUL
1261 dialŏgismŏs (1), consideration; debate
3349 mĕtĕōrizō (1), to be anxious

DOUBTING
639 apŏrĕō (1), be at a mental loss, be puzzled
1252 diakrinō (2), to decide; to hesitate
1261 dialŏgismŏs (1), consideration; debate

DOUBTLESS
518 'im (1), whether?; if, although; Oh that!
3588 kîy (1), for, that because
1065 gĕ (1), particle of emphasis
1211 dē (1), now, then; indeed, therefore

D

3304 mĕnŏungĕ (1), *so then at least*

DOUBTS
7001 qᵉṭar (Ch.) (2), *riddle*

DOUGH
1217 bâtsêq (4), *fermenting dough*
6182 'ărîyçâh (4), *ground-up meal*

DOVE
3123 yôwnâh (14), *dove*
4058 pĕristĕra (4), *pigeon, dove*

DOVE'S
1686 dibyôwn (1), (poss.) *vegetable or root*

DOVES
3123 yôwnâh (5), *dove*
4058 pĕristĕra (5), *pigeon, dove*

DOVES'
3123 yôwnâh (2), *dove*

DOWN
935 bôw' (11), *to go or come*
1288 bârak (1), *to bless*
1438 gâda' (9), *to fell a tree; to destroy*
1457 gâhar (1), *to prostrate, bow down*
1760 dâchâh (1), *to push down; to totter*
2040 hâraç (22), *to pull down; break, destroy*
2904 ṭûwl (2), *to cast down or out, hurl*
3212 yâlak (1), *to walk; to live; to carry*
3281 Ya'lâm (1), *occult*
3332 yâtsaq (1), *to pour out*
3381 yârad (339), *to descend*
3665 kâna' (3), *to humiliate, vanquish*
3766 kâra' (9), *to prostrate*
3782 kâshal (4), *to totter, waver, stumble*
3996 mâbôw' (2), *entrance; sunset; west; towards*
4174 môwrâd (3), *descent, slope*
4295 maṭṭâh (1), *below or beneath*
4535 maççâch (1), *cordon; military barrier*
4606 mê'al (Ch.) (1), *setting of the sun*
4769 marbêts (2), *resting place*
5117 nûwach (1), *to rest; to settle down*
5128 nûwa' (1), *to waver*
5181 nâchath (4), *to sink, descend; to lead down*
5182 nᵉchath (Ch.) (2), *to descend; to depose*
5183 nachath (1), *descent; quiet*
5186 nâṭâh (8), *to stretch or spread out*
5242 Nᵉmûw'êlîy (2), *Nemuelite*

5243 nâmal (1), *to be circumcised*
5307 nâphal (9), *to fall*
5422 nâthats (29), *to tear down*
5456 çâgad (4), *to prostrate oneself*
5493 çûwr (1), *to turn off*
6131 'âqar (1), *to pluck up; to hamstring*
6201 'âraph (1), *to drip*
6915 qâdad (5), *to bend*
7250 râba' (2), *to lay down*
7252 reba' (1), *prostration for sleep*
7257 râbats (13), *to recline, repose, brood*
7323 rûwts (1), *to run*
7491 râ'aph (1), *to drip*
7503 râphâh (2), *to slacken*
7665 shâbar (1), *to burst*
7673 shâbath (1), *to repose; to desist*
7743 shûwach (1), *to sink*
7812 shâchâh (20), *to prostrate in homage*
7817 shâchach (12), *to sink or depress*
7821 shᵉchîyṭâh (1), *slaughter*
7901 shâkab (40), *to lie down*
7971 shâlach (2), *to send away*
8045 shâmad (2), *to desolate*
8058 shâmaṭ (2), *to jostle; to let alone*
8213 shâphêl (7), *to humiliate*
8214 shᵉphal (Ch.) (1), *to humiliate*
8231 shâphar (1), *to be, make fair*
8257 shâqa' (1), *to be overflowed; to cease*
8497 tâkâh (1), *to strew, i.e. encamp*
345 anakĕimai (2), *to recline at a meal*
347 anaklinō (7), *to lean back, recline*
377 anapiptō (10), *lie down, lean back*
387 anastatŏō (1), *to disturb, cause trouble*
1308 diaphĕrō (1), *to bear, carry; to differ*
1581 ĕkkŏptō (5), *to cut off; to frustrate*
1931 ĕpiduō (1), *to set*
2504 kagō (1), *and also*
2506 kathairĕsis (1), *demolition*
2507 kathairĕō (6), *to lower, or demolish*
2521 kathēmai (4), *to sit down; to remain, reside*
2523 kathizō (14), *to seat down, dwell*
2524 kathiĕmi (4), *to lower, let down*
2596 kata (3), *down; according to*
2597 katabainō (64), *to descend*

2598 kataballō (2), *to throw down*
2601 katabibazō (2), *to cause to bring down*
2609 katagō (5), *to lead down; to moor a vessel*
2621 katakĕimai (1), *to lie down; to recline*
2625 kataklinō (2), *to take a place at table*
2630 katakrēmnizō (1), *to precipitate down*
2647 kataluō (3), *to halt for the night*
2662 katapatĕō (1), *to trample down; to reject*
2667 katapiptō (1), *to fall down*
2673 katargĕō (1), *to be, render entirely useless*
2679 kataskaptō (1), *to destroy, be ruined*
2701 katatrĕchō (1), *to hasten, run*
2718 katĕrchŏmai (6), *to go, come down*
2736 katō (5), *downwards*
2778 kēnsŏs (1), *enrollment*
2875 kŏptō (2), *to beat the breast*
3879 parakuptō (3), *to lean over*
3935 pariēmi (1), *to neglect; to be weakened*
4098 piptō (2), *to fall*
4496 rhiptō (2), *to fling, toss; to lay out*
4776 sugkathizō (1), *to give, take a seat with*
4781 sugkamptō (1), *to afflict*
4782 sugkatabainō (1), *to descend with*
5011 tapĕinŏs (1), *humiliated, lowly*
5294 hupŏtithēmi (1), *to hazard; to suggest*
5465 chalaō (5), *to lower as into a void*

DOWNSITTING
3427 yâshab (1), *to dwell, to remain; to settle*

DOWNWARD
4295 maṭṭâh (5), *below or beneath*

DOWRY
2065 zebed (1), *gift*
4119 môhar (3), *wife-price*

DRAG
4365 mikmereth (2), *fishing-net*

DRAGGING
4951 surō (1), *to trail, drag, sweep*

DRAGON
8577 tannîyn (6), *sea-serpent; jackal*
1404 drakōn (13), *fabulous kind of serpent*

DRAGONS
8568 tannâh (1), *female jackal*
8577 tannîyn (15), *sea-serpent; jackal*

DRAMS
150 'ădarkôn (2), *daric*
1871 darkᵉmôwn (4), *coin*

DRANK
4960 mishteh (2), *drink; banquet or feast*
8354 shâthâh (8), *to drink, imbibe*
8355 shᵉthâh (Ch.) (3), *to drink, imbibe*
4095 pinō (5), *to imbibe, drink*

DRAUGHT
4280 machărâ'âh (1), *privy sink, latrine*
61 agra (2), *haul of fish in a net*
856 aphĕdrōn (2), *privy or latrine*

DRAVE
1644 gârash (3), *to drive out; to expatriate*
3423 yârash (2), *to impoverish; to ruin*
5071 nᵉdâbâh (1), *abundant gift*
5090 nâhag (4), *to drive forth; to lead*
5394 nâshal (1), *to divest, eject, or drop*
556 apĕlaunō (1), *to dismiss, eject*
1856 ĕxōthĕō (1), *to expel; to propel*

DRAW
748 'ârak (1), *to be, make long*
1518 gîyach (1), *to issue forth; to burst forth*
1802 dâlâh (1), *to draw out water); to deliver*
2502 châlats (1), *to pull off; to strip; to depart*
2834 châsaph (1), *to drain away or bail up*
3318 yâtsâ' (1), *to go, bring out*
4900 mâshak (11), *to draw out; to be tall*
5423 nâthaq (1), *to tear off*
5498 çâchab (3), *to trail along*
6329 pûwq (1), *to issue; to furnish; to secure*
7324 rûwq (8), *to pour out, i.e. empty*
7579 shâ'ab (9), *to bale up water*
8025 shâlaph (4), *to pull out, up or off*
501 antlĕō (3), *dip water*
502 antlēma (1), *bucket for drawing water*
645 apŏspaō (1), *unsheathe a sword*
1670 hĕlkuō (4), *to drag, draw, pull in*
4334 prŏsĕrchŏmai (1), *to come near, visit*
5288 hupŏstĕllō (1), *to cower or shrink*
5289 hupŏstŏlē (1), *shrinkage, timidity*

DRAWER
7579 shâ'ab (1), *to bale up water*

DRAWERS
7579 shâ'ab (3), to *bale* up water

DRAWETH
4900 mâshak (2), to *draw* out; to *be tall*
7503 râphâh (1), to *slacken*

DRAWING
4857 mash'âb (1), water trough for cattle
1096 ginŏmai (1), to *be, become*

DRAWN
3318 yâtsâ' (1), to *go, bring out*
3947 lâqach (1), to *take*
4900 mâshak (2), to *draw* out; to *be tall*
5080 nâdach (1), to *push* off, *scattered*
5203 nâtash (1), to *disperse*; to *thrust* off
5423 nâthaq (3), to *tear* off
5498 çâchab (1), to *trail* along
6267 'attîyq (1), *weaned; antique*
6605 pâthach (2), to *open* wide; to *loosen, begin*
6609 pᵉthîchâh (1), *drawn* sword
7579 shâ'ab (1), to *bale* up water
7725 shûwb (1), to *turn* back; to *return*
8025 shâlaph (5), to *pull* out, up or off
8388 tâ'ar (5), to *delineate*; to *extend*
385 anaspaŏ (1), to *take* up or *extricate*
1828 ĕxĕlkō (1), to *drag away*, i.e. *entice*

DREAD
367 'êymâh (1), *fright*
2844 chath (1), *terror*
3372 yârê' (1), to *fear*; to *revere*
4172 môwrâ' (1), *fearful*
6206 'ârats (2), to *awe*; to *dread*; to *harass*
6343 pachad (3), *sudden alarm, fear*

DREADFUL
1763 dᵉchal (Ch.) (2), to *fear*; *be formidable, awesome*
3372 yârê' (5), to *fear*; to *revere*
3374 yir'âh (1), *fear; reverence*
6343 pachad (1), *sudden alarm, fear*

DREAM
2472 chălôwm (44), *dream; dreamer*
2492 châlam (1), to *dream*
2493 chêlem (Ch.) (21), *dream*
1798 ĕnupniŏn (1), *dream, vision*
3677 ŏnar (6), *dream*

DREAMED
2492 châlam (19), to *dream*

DREAMER
1167+2472 ba'al (1), *master; owner; citizen*
2492 châlam (3), to *dream*

DREAMERS
2492 châlam (1), to *dream*
1797 ĕnupniazŏmai (1), to *dream*

DREAMETH
2492 châlam (2), to *dream*

DREAMS
2472 chălôwm (19), *dream; dreamer*
2493 chêlem (Ch.) (1), *dream*
1797 ĕnupniazŏmai (1), to *dream*

DREGS
6907 qubba'ath (2), *goblet, cup*
8105 shemer (1), *settlings* of wine, *dregs*

DRESS
5647 'âbad (2), to *do, work, serve*
6213 'âsâh (7), to *do* or *make*

DRESSED
6213 'âsâh (6), to *do* or *make*
1090 gĕŏrgĕō (1), to *till* the soil

DRESSER
289 ampĕlŏurgŏs (1), *vineyard caretaker*

DRESSERS
3755 kôrêm (1), *vinedresser*

DRESSETH
3190 yâṭab (1), to *be, make well*

DREW
748 'ârak (2), to *be, make long*
1802 dâlâh (2), to *draw* out water); to *deliver*
1869 dârak (1), to *walk, lead*; to *string* a bow
3318 yâtsâ' (1), to *go, bring out*
4871 mâshâh (3), to *pull* out
4900 mâshak (6), to *draw* out; to *be tall*
7579 shâ'ab (4), to *bale* up water
7725 shûwb (2), to *turn* back; to *return*
8025 shâlaph (15), to *pull* out, up or off
307 anabibazō (1), haul up a net
501 antlĕō (1), *dip* water
645 apŏspaō (1), *unsheathe* a sword
868 aphistēmi (1), to *desist, desert*
1670 hĕlkuō (4), to *drag, draw, pull in*

DRIED
1809 dâlal (1), to *slacken, dangle*
2717 chârab (9), to *parch; desolate, destroy*
2787 chârar (1), to *melt, burn, dry up*
3001 yâbêsh (22), to *dry* up; to *wither*
3002 yâbêsh (1), *dry*
6704 tsîcheh (1), *parched*
7033 qâlâh (1), to *toast, scorch*
3583 xĕrainō (3), to *shrivel*, to *mature*

DRIEDST
3001 yâbêsh (1), to *dry* up; to *wither*

DRIETH
3001 yâbêsh (3), to *dry* up; to *wither*

DRINK
1572 gâmâ' (1), to *swallow*
4469 mamçâk (1), *mixed*-wine
4945 mashqeh (2), *butler; drink; well-watered*
4960 mishteh (3), *drink; banquet* or feast
5257 nᵉçîyk (1), *libation; molten image; prince*
5261 nᵉçak (Ch.) (1), *libation*
5262 neçek (59), *libation; cast idol*
5435 çôbe' (1), *wine*
7937 shâkar (2), to *become tipsy, to satiate*
7941 shêkâr (21), *liquor*
8248 shâqâh (42), to *quaff*, i.e. to *irrigate*
8249 shiqqûv (1), *draught, drink*
8250 shiqqûwy (1), *beverage; refreshment*
8353 shêth (Ch.) (1), *six; sixth*
8354 shâthâh (161), to *drink, imbibe*
8355 shᵉthâh (Ch.) (1), to *drink, imbibe*
4095 pinō (50), to *imbibe, drink*
4188 pŏma (1), *beverage, drink*
4213 pŏsis (3), *draught, drink*
4222 pŏtizō (9), to *furnish drink, irrigate*
4608 sikĕra (1), *intoxicant*
4844 sumpinō (1), to *partake a beverage*

DRIED (column 3)

2020 ĕpiphōskō (1), to *grow light*
4264 prŏbibazō (1), to *bring to the front*
4317 prŏsagō (1), to *bring near*
4334 prŏsĕrchŏmai (1), to *come near, visit*
4358 prŏsŏrmizō (1), to *moor to*, i.e. *land at*
4685 spaō (2), to *draw* a sword
4951 surō (3), to *trail, drag, sweep*

DRINKERS
8354 shâthâh (1), to *drink, imbibe*

DRINKETH
6231 'âshaq (1), to *overflow*
8354 shâthâh (8), to *drink, imbibe*
4095 pinō (7), to *imbibe, drink*

DRINKING
4945 mashqeh (2), *butler; drink; well-watered*
8354 shâthâh (12), to *drink, imbibe*
8360 shᵉthîyâh (1), *manner of drinking*
4095 pinō (6), to *imbibe, drink*

DRINKS
4188 pŏma (1), *beverage, drink*

DRIVE
1644 gârash (12), to *drive* out; to *divorce*
1920 hâdaph (2), to *push* away or down; *drive out*
2957 ṭᵉrad (Ch.) (2), to *expel, drive on*
3423 yârash (30), to *impoverish; to ruin*
5080 nâdach (5), to *push* off, *scattered*
5086 nâdaph (1), to *disperse, be windblown*
5090 nâhag (2), to *drive* forth; to *carry away*
6327 pûwts (1), to *dash* in pieces; to *disperse*
1929 ĕpididōmi (1), to *give over*

DRIVEN
1644 gârash (5), to *drive* out; to *divorce*
1760 dâchâh (2), to *push* down; to *totter*
1920 hâdaph (1), to *push* away or down; *drive out*
2957 ṭᵉrad (Ch.) (2), to *expel, drive on*
3423 yârash (2), to *impoverish; to ruin*
5080 nâdach (23), to *push* off, *scattered*
5086 nâdaph (4), to *disperse, be windblown*
5437 çâbab (2), to *surround*
5472 çûwg (1), to *go* back, to *retreat*
5590 çâ'ar (1), to *rush* upon; to *toss* about
7617 shâbâh (1), to *transport* into captivity
416 anemizō (1), to *toss* with the wind
1308 diaphĕrō (1), to *bear, carry*; to *differ*
1643 ĕlaunō (2), to *push*
5342 phĕrō (1), to *bear* or *carry*

DRIVER
5065 nâgas (1), to *exploit*; to *tax, harass*

7395 rakkâb (1), *charioteer*

DRIVETH
2342 chûwl (1), to *dance, whirl;* to *writhe*
5086 nâdaph (1), to *disperse, be windblown*
5090 nâhag (1), to *drive forth;* to *carry away*
1544 ĕkballō (1), to *throw out*

DRIVING
1644 gârash (1), to *drive out;* to *divorce*
3423 yârash (2), to *impoverish;* to *ruin*
4491 minhâg (2), *chariot-driving*

DROMEDARIES
1070 beker (1), *young bull camel*
7409 rekesh (1), *relay of animals on a post-route*
7424 rammâk (1), *brood mare*

DROMEDARY
1072 bikrâh (1), *young she-camel*

DROP
4752 mar (1), *drop in a bucket*
5140 nâzal (1), to *drip,* or *shed* by trickling
5197 nâṭaph (7), to *fall in drops*
6201 'âraph (2), to *drip*
7491 râ'aph (4), to *drip*

DROPPED
1982 hêlek (1), *wayfarer, visitor; flowing*
5197 nâṭaph (5), to *fall in drops*
5413 nâthak (1), to *flow forth, pour* out

DROPPETH
1811 dâlaph (1), to *drip*

DROPPING
1812 deleph (2), *dripping*
5197 nâṭaph (1), to *fall in drops*

DROPS
96 'egel (1), *reservoir*
5197 nâṭaph (1), to *fall in drops*
7447 râçîyç (1), *ruin; dew-drop*
2361 thrŏmbŏs (1), *clot of blood*

DROPSY
5203 hudrōpikŏs (1), to *suffer edema*

DROSS
5509 çîyg (8), *refuse, scoria*

DROUGHT
1226 batstsôreth (1), *drought*
2721 chôreb (3), *parched; ruined*
2725 chărâbôwn (1), *parching heat*
6710 tsachtsâchâh (1), *dry desert* place
6723 tsîyâh (2), *arid desert*

6774 tsimmâ'ôwn (1), *desert*
8514 tal'ûwbâh (1), *dehydration*

DROVE
1272 bârach (1), to *flee suddenly*
1644 gârash (3), to *drive out;* to *divorce*
3423 yârash (2), to *impoverish;* to *ruin*
4264 machăneh (1), *encampment*
5380 nâshab (1), to *blow;* to *disperse*
5425 nâthar (1), to *jump;* to *terrify; shake* off
5739 'êder (3), *muster, flock*
1544 ĕkballō (1), to *throw out*

DROVES
5739 'êder (1), *muster, flock*

DROWN
7857 shâṭaph (1), to *gush;* to *inundate*
1036 buthizō (1), to *sink;* to *plunge*

DROWNED
2823 châshôk (1), *obscure*
8248 shâqâh (2), to *quaff,* i.e. to *irrigate*
2666 katapinō (1), to *devour by swallowing*
2670 katapŏntizō (1), to *submerge, be drowned*

DROWSINESS
5124 nûwmâh (1), *sleepiness*

DRUNK
7301 râvâh (1), to *slake* thirst or appetites
7910 shikkôwr (2), *intoxicated*
7937 shâkar (4), to *become tipsy,* to *satiate*
8354 shâthâh (15), to *drink, imbibe*
8355 shᵉthâh (Ch.) (1), to *drink, imbibe*
3182 mĕthuskō (2), to *become drunk*
3184 mĕthuō (1), to *get drunk*
4095 pinō (2), to *imbibe, drink*

DRUNKARD
5435 çôbe' (2), *wine*
7910 shikkôwr (2), *intoxicated*
3183 mĕthusŏs (1), *drunkard*

DRUNKARDS
5435 çôbe' (1), *wine*
7910 shikkôwr (3), *intoxicated*
8354+7941 shâthâh (1), to *drink, imbibe*
3183 mĕthusŏs (1), *drunkard*

DRUNKEN
5435 çôbe' (1), *wine*
7301 râvâh (1), to *slake* thirst or appetites

7910 shikkôwr (6), *intoxicated*
7937 shâkar (13), to *become tipsy,* to *satiate*
7943 shikkârôwn (2), *intoxication*
8354 shâthâh (3), to *drink, imbibe*
3182 mĕthuskō (1), to *become drunk*
3184 mĕthuō (5), to *get drunk*
4095 pinō (1), to *imbibe, drink*

DRUNKENNESS
7302 râveh (1), *sated, full* with drink
7943 shikkârôwn (2), *intoxication*
8358 shᵉthîy (1), *intoxication*
3178 mĕthē (3), *intoxication*

DRUSILLA
1409 Drŏusilla (1), *Drusilla*

DRY
954 bûwsh (1), be *ashamed; disappointed*
2717 chârab (3), to *parch, desolate, destroy*
2720 chârêb (3), *parched; ruined*
2721 chôreb (3), *parched; ruined*
2724 chârâbâh (8), *desert, dry* land
3001 yâbêsh (9), to *dry* up; to *wither*
3002 yâbêsh (7), *dry*
3004 yabbâshâh (14), *dry ground*
3006 yabbesheth (2), *dry ground*
5424 netheq (1), *scurf,* i.e. *diseased skin*
6703 tsach (1), *dazzling,* i.e. *sunny, bright*
6707 tsᵉchîychâh (1), *parched desert* region
6723 tsîyâh (10), *arid desert*
6724 tsîyôwn (2), *desert*
6774 tsimmâ'ôwn (1), *desert*
6784 tsâmaq (1), to *dry* up, *shrivel* up
504 anudrŏs (2), *dry, arid*
3584 xērŏs (2), *scorched; arid; withered*

DRYSHOD
5275 na'al (1), *sandal*

DUE
1167 ba'al (1), *master; husband; owner; citizen*
1697 dâbâr (1), *word; matter; thing*
2706 chôq (2), *appointment; allotment*
4941 mishpâṭ (1), *verdict; formal decree; justice*
514 axiŏs (1), *deserving, comparable* or *suitable*
2398 idiŏs (3), *private* or *separate*
3784 ŏphĕilō (2), to *owe;* to *be under obligation*

DUES
3782 ŏphĕilē (1), *sum owed; obligation*

DUKE
441 'allûwph (20), *friend, one familiar; chieftain*

DUKES
441 'allûwph (13), *friend, one familiar; chieftain*
5257 nᵉçîyk (1), *libation; molten image; prince*

DULCIMER
5481 çûwmpôwnᵉyâh (Ch.) (3), *bagpipe*

DULL
917 barĕŏs (2), *heavily, with difficulty*
3576 nōthrŏs (1), *lazy; stupid*

DUMAH
1746 Dûwmâh (4), *silence; death*

DUMB
481 'âlam (7), to be *tongue-tied, be silent*
483 'illêm (6), *speechless*
1748 dûwmâm (1), *silently*
216 alalŏs (3), *mute, not able to speak*
880 aphōnŏs (3), *mute, silent; unmeaning*
2974 kōphŏs (8), *deaf* or *silent*
4623 siōpaō (1), to *be quiet*

DUNG
830 'ashpôth (4), *heap of rubbish; Dung gate*
1557 gâlâl (1), *dung pellets*
1561 gêlel (4), *dung; dung* pellets
1828 dômen (6), *manure, dung*
2716+(6675) chere' (2), *excrement*
2755 chărêy-yôwnîym (1), *excrements of doves* or a *vegetable*
6569 peresh (7), *excrement*
6832 tsᵉphûwa' (1), *excrement*
906+2874 ballō (1), to *throw*
4657 skubalŏn (1), *what is thrown to the dogs*

DUNGEON
953 bôwr (13), *pit hole, cistern, well; prison*

DUNGHILL
830 'ashpôth (2), *heap of rubbish; Dung gate*
4087 madmênâh (1), *dunghill*
5122 nᵉvâlûw (Ch.) (3), to *be foul; sink*
2874 kŏpria (1), *manure* or *rubbish pile*

DUNGHILLS
830 'ashpôth (1), *heap of rubbish; Dung gate*

DURA
1757 Dûwrâ' (Ch.) (1), *circle* or *dwelling*

DURABLE
6266 'âthîyq (1), *venerable* or *splendid*
6276 'âthêq (1), *enduring value*

DURETH
2076 ĕsti (1), he (she or it) *is*; they *are*

DURST
3372 yârê' (1), to *fear*; to *revere*
5111 tŏlmaō (7), to be *bold*; to *dare*

DUST
80 'âbâq (5), *fine dust*; *cosmetic powder*
1854 dâqaq (1), to *crush*; *crumble*
6083 'âphâr (91), *dust, earth, mud*; *clay*,
7834 shachaq (1), *firmament, clouds*
2868 kŏniŏrtŏs (5), *blown dust*
5522 chŏŏs (2), loose *dirt*

DUTY
1697 dâbâr (2), *word*; *matter*; *thing*
3784 ŏphĕilō (2), to *owe*; to *fail* in duty

DWARF
1851 daq (1), *crushed*; *small* or *thin*

DWELL
1481 gûwr (11), to *sojourn, live as an alien*
1752 dûwr (1), *remain*
1753 dûwr (Ch.) (3), to *reside, live in*
2073 zᵉbûwl (1), *residence, dwelling*
2082 zâbal (1), to *reside*
3427 yâshab (210), to *dwell, to remain*
3488 yᵉthîb (Ch.) (1), to *sit* or *dwell*
3885 lûwn (1), to be *obstinate*
4186 môwshâb (1), *seat*; *site*; *abode*
5975 'âmad (1), to *stand*
7931 shâkan (69), to *reside*
7932 shᵉkan (Ch.) (1), to *reside*
1774 ĕnŏikĕō (2), to *inhabit, live with*
2521 kathēmai (1), to *sit down*; to *remain, reside*
2730 katŏikĕō (19), to *reside, live in*
3306 mĕnō (2), to *stay, remain*
3611 ŏikĕō (4), to *reside, inhabit, remain*
4637 skēnŏō (4), to *occupy*; to *reside*
4924 sunŏikĕō (1), to *reside together* as a family

DWELLED
3427 yâshab (6), to *dwell, to remain*; to *settle*

DWELLERS
7931 shâkan (1), to *reside*
2730 katŏikĕō (2), to *reside, live in*

DWELLEST
3427 yâshab (14), to *dwell, to remain*
7931 shâkan (3), to *reside*
2730 katŏikĕō (1), to *reside, live in*
3306 mĕnō (1), to *stay, remain*

DWELLETH
1481 gûwr (1), to *sojourn, live as an alien*
3427 yâshab (20), to *dwell, to remain*
4908 mishkân (1), *residence*
7931 shâkan (9), to *reside*
8271 shᵉrê' (Ch.) (1), to *free, separate*; to *reside*
1774 ĕnŏikĕō (2), to *inhabit, live with*
2730 katŏikĕō (7), to *reside, live in*
3306 mĕnō (9), to *stay, remain*
3611 ŏikĕō (4), to *reside, inhabit, remain*

DWELLING
168 'ôhel (3), *tent*
2073 zᵉbûwl (1), *residence, dwelling*
3427 yâshab (17), to *dwell, to remain*
4070 mᵉdôwr (Ch.) (4), *dwelling*
4186 môwshâb (5), *seat*; *site*; *abode*
4349 mâkôwn (2), *basis*; *place*
4583 mâ'ôwn (6), *retreat* or asylum *dwelling*
4585 mᵉ'ôwnâh (1), *abode*
4908 mishkân (4), *residence*
5116 nâveh (3), *at home*; *lovely*; *home*
7931 shâkan (1), to *reside*
1460 ĕgkatŏikĕō (1), *reside, live among*
2730 katŏikĕō (3), to *reside, live in*
2731 katŏikēsis (1), *residence*
3611 ŏikĕō (1), to *reside, inhabit, remain*

DWELLINGPLACE
4186 môwshâb (1), *seat*; *site*; *abode*
790 astatĕō (1), *homeless, vagabond*

DWELLINGPLACES
4186 môwshâb (2), *seat*; *site*; *abode*
4908 mishkân (3), *residence*

DWELLINGS
4033 mâgûwr (2), *abode*
4186 môwshâb (8), *seat*; *site*; *abode*
4908 mishkân (6), *residence*
5116 nâveh (1), *at home*; *lovely*; *home*

DWELT
1753 dûwr (Ch.) (2), to *reside, live in*
2583 chânâh (2), to *encamp*
3427 yâshab (189), to *dwell, to remain*
4186 môwshâb (2), *seat*; *site*; *abode*
7931 shâkan (11), to *reside*
1774 ĕnŏikĕō (1), to *inhabit, live with*
2730 katŏikĕō (12), to *reside, live in*
3306 mĕnō (2), to *stay, remain*
3940 parŏikia (1), *foreign residence*
4039 pĕriŏikĕō (1), to be *a neighbor*
4637 skēnŏō (1), to *occupy*; to *reside*

DYED
2556 châmêts (1), to be *fermented*; *be soured*
2871 ṭâbûwl (1), *turban*

DYING
1478 gâva' (1), to *expire, die*
599 apŏthnēskō (4), to *die off*
3500 nĕkrōsis (1), *death, deadness*

EACH
259 'echâd (10), *first*
376 'îysh (5), *man*; *male*; *someone*
802 'ishshâh (2), *woman, wife*; *women, wives*
905 bad (1), *limb, member*; *bar*; *chief*
240 allēlōn (2), *one another*
303 ana (1), *each*; in *turn*; among
1538 hĕkastŏs (2), *each* or *every*

EAGLE
5404 nesher (19), large *bird of prey*
7360 râchâm (2), *kind of vulture*
105 aĕtŏs (2), *eagle, vulture*

EAGLE'S
5403 nᵉshar (Ch.) (1), large *bird of prey*
5404 nesher (1), large *bird of prey*

EAGLES
5404 nesher (5), large *bird of prey*
105 aĕtŏs (2), *eagle, vulture*

EAGLES'
5403 nᵉshar (Ch.) (1), large *bird of prey*
5404 nesher (1), large *bird of prey*

EAR
24 'âbîyb (1), *head of grain*; *month of Abib*
238 'âzan (33), to *listen*
241 'ôzen (63), *ear*

2790 chârash (1), to be *silent*; to be *deaf*
5647 'âbad (1), to do, *work, serve*
8085 shâma' (1), to *hear intelligently*
3775 ŏus (13), *ear*; *listening*
4719 stachus (2), *head* of grain
5621 ōtiŏn (5), *earlet, ear (-lobe)*

E

EARED
5647 'âbad (1), to do, *work, serve*

EARING
2758 chârîysh (2), *plowing*; *plowing season*

EARLY
1242 bôqer (3), *morning*
6852 tsâphar (1), to *return*
7836 shâchar (6), to *search* for
7837 shachar (2), *dawn*
7925 shâkam (62), to *start early*
8238 shᵉpharphar (Ch.) (1), *dawn*
260+4404 hama (1), at *the same time, together*
3719 ŏrthrizō (1), to *get up early in the morning*
3721 ŏrthriŏs (1), up *at day-break*
3722 ŏrthrŏs (3), *dawn, daybreak*
4404 prōï (3), *at dawn*; *day-break* watch
4405 prōïa (1), *day-dawn, early morn*
4406 prōïmŏs (1), *autumnal* showering

EARNEST
603 apŏkaradŏkia (2), *intense anticipation*
728 arrhabōn (3), *pledge, security*
1972 ĕpipŏthēsis (1), *longing for*
4056 pĕrissŏtĕrōs (1), *more superabundantly*
4710 spŏudē (1), *eagerness, earnestness*

EARNESTLY
2734 chârâh (1), to *blaze* up
3190 yâṭab (1), to *be, make well*
816 atĕnizō (3), to *gaze intently*
1617 ĕktĕnĕstĕrŏn (1), *more earnest*
1864 ĕpagōnizŏmai (1), to *struggle for, fight for*
1971 ĕpipŏthĕō (1), *intensely crave*
2206 zēlŏō (1), to *have warmth* of feeling for
4335 prŏsĕuchē (1), *prayer*; *prayer chapel*

EARNETH
7936 sâkar (1), to *hire*

EARRING
5141 nezem (5), *nose-ring*

EARRINGS
3908 lachash (1),
incantation; amulet
5141 nezem (9),
nose-ring
5694 'âgîyl (2), ear-ring

EARS
24 'âbîyb (1), head of
grain; month of Abib
241 'ôzen (100), ear
3759 karmel (3), planted
field; garden produce
4425 mᵉlîylâh (1), cut-off
head of cereal grain
7641 shibbôl (13),
stream; ear of grain
189 akŏĕ (4), hearing;
thing heard
191 akŏuō (1), to hear;
obey
3775 ŏus (24), ear;
listening
4719 stachus (3), head of
grain

EARTH
127 'ădâmâh (52), soil;
land
772 'ăra' (Ch.) (20),
earth, ground, land
776 'erets (710), earth,
land, soil; country
778 'ăraq (Ch.) (1), earth
2789 cheres (1), piece of
earthenware pottery
3007 yabbesheth (Ch.)
(1), dry land
6083 'âphâr (7), dust,
earth, mud; clay
1093 gē (186), soil,
region, whole earth
1919 ĕpigĕiŏs (1),
worldly, earthly
2709 katachthŏniŏs (1),
infernal
3625 ŏikŏumĕnē (1),
Roman empire
3749 ŏstrakinŏs (1),
made of clay

EARTHEN
2789 cheres (8), piece of
earthenware pottery
3335 yâtsar (1), to form;
potter; to determine
3749 ŏstrakinŏs (1),
made of clay

EARTHLY
1537+3588+1093 ĕk (1),
out, out of
1919 ĕpigĕiŏs (4),
worldly, earthly

EARTHQUAKE
7494 ra'ash (6),
vibration, uproar
4578 sĕismŏs (10), gale
storm; earthquake

EARTHQUAKES
4578 sĕismŏs (3), gale
storm; earthquake

EARTHY
5517 chŏikŏs (4), dusty,
dirty, i.e. terrene

EASE
2896 tôwb (1), good; well
3427 yâshab (1), to dwell,
to remain; to settle

4496 mᵉnûwchâh (1),
peacefully; consolation
5162 nâcham (1), to be
sorry; to pity, console
5375 nâsâ' (1), to lift up
7043 qâlal (2), to be easy,
trifling, vile
7280 râga' (1), to settle,
i.e. quiet; to wink
7599 shâ'an (2), to loll,
i.e. be peaceful
7600 sha'ănân (6),
secure; haughty
7946 shal'ănân (1),
tranquil
7961 shâlêv (2), carefree;
security, at ease
373 anapauō (1), to
repose; to refresh

EASED
1980 hâlak (1), to walk;
live a certain way
425 anĕsis (1),
relaxation; relief

EASIER
7043 qâlal (1), to be easy,
trifling, vile
2123 ĕukŏpŏtĕrŏs (7),
better for toil

EAST
2777 charçûwth (1),
pottery
4161 môwtsâ' (1), going
forth
4217 mizrâch (33), place
of sunrise; east
4217+8121 mizrâch (2),
place of sunrise; east
6921 qâdîym (61), east;
eastward; east wind
6924 qedem (42), east,
eastern; antiquity
6926 qidmâh (3), east; on
the east, in front
6930 qadmôwn (1),
eastern
6931 qadmôwnîy (4),
oriental, eastern
395 anatŏlē (9), dawn of
sun; east

EASTER
3957 pascha (1),
Passover events

EASTWARD
1870+6921 derek (1),
road; course of life
4217 mizrâch (19), place
of sunrise; east
4217+8121 mizrâch (1),
place of sunrise; east
6921 qâdîym (7), East;
eastward; east wind
6924 qedem (11), east,
eastern; antiquity
6926 qidmâh (1), east; on
the east, in front

EASY
7043 qâlal (1), to be easy,
trifling, vile
2138 ĕupĕithēs (1),
compliant, submissive
2154 ĕusēmŏs (1),
significant
5543 chrēstŏs (1),
employed, i.e. useful

EAT
398 'âkal (497), to eat

399 'ăkal (Ch.) (1), to eat
402 'oklâh (2), food
1262 bârâh (4), to feed
2490 châlal (1), to
profane, defile
2939 tᵉ'am (Ch.) (2), to
feed
3898 lâcham (5), to fight
a battle, i.e. consume
3899 lechem (1), food,
bread
6310 peh (1), mouth;
opening
7462 râ'âh (2), to tend a
flock, i.e. pasture it
1089 gĕuŏmai (1), to
taste; to eat
2068 ĕsthiō (39), to eat
2719 katĕsthiō (1), to
devour
3335 mĕtalambanō (1),
to participate
3542+2192 nŏmē (1),
pasture, feeding
4906 sunĕsthiō (4), to
take food with
5315 phagō (88), to eat

EATEN
398 'âkal (86), to eat
935+413+7130 bôw' (2), to
go or come
1197 bâ'ar (2), to be
brutish, be senseless
2490 châlal (1), to
profane, defile
7462 râ'âh (1), to tend a
flock, i.e. pasture it
977 bibrōskō (1), to eat
1089 gĕuŏmai (2), to
taste; to eat
2068 ĕsthiō (1), to eat
2719 katĕsthiō (1), to
devour
2880 kŏrĕnnumi (1), to
cram, i.e. glut or sate
4662 skōlēkŏbrōtŏs (1),
diseased with maggots
5315 phagō (5), to eat

EATER
398 'âkal (3), to eat

EATERS
2151 zâlal (1), to be loose
morally, worthless

EATEST
398 'âkal (3), to eat

EATETH
398 'âkal (31), to eat
1104 bâla' (1), to
swallow; to destroy
2068 ĕsthiō (13), to eat
4906 sunĕsthiō (1), to
take food with
5176 trōgō (5), to gnaw
or chew, i.e. to eat

EATING
398 'âkal (13), to eat
400 'ôkel (4), food
3894 lâchûwm (1), flesh
as food
1035 brōsis (1), food;
rusting corrosion
2068 ĕsthiō (6), to eat
5176 trōgō (1), to gnaw
or chew, i.e. to eat
5315 phagō (1), to eat

EBAL
5858 'Êybâl (8), bare, bald

EBED
5651 'Ebed (6), servant

EBED-MELECH
5663 'Ebed Melek (6),
servant of a king

EBEN-EZER
72 'Eben hâ-'êzer (3),
stone of the help

EBER
5677 'Êber (13), regions
beyond

EBIASAPH
43 'Ebyâçâph (3),
Ebjasaph

EBONY
1894 hôben (1), ebony

EBRONAH
5684 'Ebrônâh (2),
Ebronah

EDAR
5740 'Êder (1), flock

EDEN
5731 'Êden (20), pleasure

EDER
5740 'Êder (3), flock

EDGE
5310 nâphats (1), to dash
to pieces; to scatter
6310 peh (34), mouth;
opening
6440 pânîym (1), face;
front
6697 tsûwr (1), rock
6949 qâhâh (3), to be
dull; be blunt
7097 qâtseh (8), extremity
8193 sâphâh (5), lip;
edge, margin
4750 stŏma (2), mouth;
edge

EDGES
6366 pêyâh (1), edge
7098 qâtsâh (1),
termination; fringe
7099 qetsev (1), limit,
borders
1366 distŏmŏs (1),
double-edged

EDIFICATION
3619 ŏikŏdŏmē (4),
edification

EDIFIED
3618 ŏikŏdŏmĕō (2), to
construct, edify

EDIFIETH
3618 ŏikŏdŏmĕō (3), to
construct, edify

EDIFY
3618 ŏikŏdŏmĕō (2), to
construct, edify
3619 ŏikŏdŏmē (1),
edification

EDIFYING
3618 ŏikŏdŏmĕō (1), to
construct, edify
3619 ŏikŏdŏmē (7),
edification

EDOM
123 'Ĕdôm (87), red

EDOMITE
130 'Ĕdômîy (6), Edomite

EDOMITES
130 'Ědômîy (12), *Edomite*

EDREI
154 'edre'îy (8), *mighty*

EFFECT
1697 dâbâr (1), *word; matter; thing*
5106 nûw' (1), *to refuse, forbid, dissuade*
5656 'ăbôdâh (1), *work of any kind*
6213 'âsâh (1), *to do or make*
6565 pârar (1), *to break up; to violate, frustrate*
208 akuroō (2), *to invalidate, nullify*
1601 ěkpiptō (1), *to drop away*
2673 katargěō (4), *to be, render entirely useless*
2758 kěnόō (1), *to make empty*

EFFECTED
6743 tsâlach (1), *to push forward*

EFFECTUAL
1753 ěněrgěia (2), *efficiency, energy*
1754 ěněrgěō (2), *to be active, efficient, work*
1756 ěněrgěs (2), *active, operative*

EFFECTUALLY
1754 ěněrgěō (2). *to be active, efficient, work*

EFFEMINATE
3120 malakŏs (1), *soft; catamite homosexual*

EGG
2495 challâmûwth (1), *(poss.) purslain plant*
5609 ôŏn (1), *egg*

EGGS
1000 bêytsâh (6), *egg*

EGLAH
5698 'Eglâh (2), *heifer*

EGLAIM
97 'Eglayim (1), *double pond*

EGLON
5700 'Eglôwn (13), *vituline*

EGYPT
4713 Mitsrîy (1), *Mitsrite*
4714 Mitsrayim (585), *double border*
125 Aiguptŏs (24), *Ægyptus*

EGYPTIAN
4713 Mitsrîy (18), *Mitsrite*
4714 Mitsrayim (2), *double border*
124 Aiguptiŏs (3), *inhabitant of Ægyptus*

EGYPTIAN'S
4713 Mitsrîy (4), *Mitsrite*

EGYPTIANS
4713 Mitsrîy (7), *Mitsrite*
4714 Mitsrayim (88), *double border*
124 Aiguptiŏs (2), *inhabitant of Ægyptus*

EHI
278 'Êchîy (1), *Echi*

EHUD
261 'Êchûwd (10), *united*

EIGHT
8083 shᵉmôneh (74), *eight; eighth*
3638 ŏktō (6), *eight*

EIGHTEEN
7239+8083 ribbôw (1), *myriad*
8083+6240 shᵉmôneh (18), *eight; eighth*
1176+2532+3638 děka (3), *ten*

EIGHTEENTH
8083+6240 shᵉmôneh (11), *eight; eighth*

EIGHTH
8066 shᵉmîynîy (28), *eight, eighth*
8083 shᵉmôneh (4), *eight; eighth*
3590 ŏgdŏŏs (5), *eighth*
3637 ŏktaěměrŏs (1), *eighth-day*

EIGHTIETH
'084 shᵉmônîym (1), *eighty; eightieth*

EIGHTY
8084 shᵉmônîym (3), *eighty; eightieth*

EITHER
176 'ôw (7), *or, whether; desire*
376 'îysh (3), *man; male; someone*
518 'îm (1), *whether?; if, although; Oh that!*
1571 gam (1), *also; even; "both...and"*
3588 kîy (1), *for, that because*
8145 shênîy (1), *second; again*
2228 ē (9), *or; than*

EKER
6134 'Êqer (1), *naturalized citizen*

EKRON
6138 'Eqrôwn (22), *eradication*

EKRONITES
6139 'Eqrôwnîy (2), *Ekronite*

EL-BETH-EL
416 'Êl Bêyth-'Êl (1), *God of Bethel*

EL-ELOHE-ISRAEL
415 'Êl 'ĕlôhêy Yisrâ'êl (1), *mighty God of Israel*

EL-PARAN
364 'Êyl Pâ'rân (1), *oak of Paran*

ELADAH
497 'El'âdâh (1), *God has decked*

ELAH
425 'Êlâh (17), *oak*

ELAM
5867 'Êylâm (28), *distant*

ELAMITES
5962 'Almîy (Ch.) (1), *Elamite*
1639 Élamîtěs (1), *distant ones*

ELASAH
501 'El'âsâh (2), *God has made*

ELATH
359 'Êylôwth (5), *grove (of palms)*

ELDAAH
420 'Eldâ'âh (2), *God of knowledge*

ELDAD
419 'Eldâd (2), *God has loved*

ELDER
1419 gâdôwl (8), *great*
2205+3117 zâqên (1), *old, venerated*
7227 rab (1), *great*
3187 měizōn (1), *larger, greater*
4245 prěsbutěrŏs (7), *elderly; older; presbyter*
4850 sumprěsbutěrŏs (1), *co-presbyter*

ELDERS
2205 zâqên (113), *old, venerated*
7868 sîyb (Ch.) (5), *to become aged*
4244 prěsbutěriŏn (2), *order of elders*
4245 prěsbutěrŏs (58), *elderly; older; presbyter*

ELDEST
1060 bᵉkôwr (5), *firstborn, i.e. oldest son*
1419 gâdôwl (6), *great*
2205 zâqên (1), *old, venerated*
7223 rî'shôwn (1), *first, in place, time or rank*
4245 prěsbutěrŏs (1), *elderly; older; presbyter*

ELEAD
496 'El'âd (1), *God has testified*

ELEALEH
500 'El'âlê (5), *God (is) going up*

ELEASAH
501 'El'âsâh (4), *God has made*

ELEAZAR
499 'El'âzâr (71), *God (is) helper*
1648 Élěazar (2), *God (is) helper*

ELECT
972 bâchîyr (4), *selected one*
1588 ěklěktŏs (13), *selected; chosen*

ELECT'S
1588 ěklěktŏs (3), *selected; chosen*

ELECTED
4899 suněklěktŏs (1), *co-elected*

ELECTION
1589 ěklŏgē (6), *selection, choice*

ELEMENTS
4747 stŏichěiŏn (4), *elements, elementary*

ELEPH
507 'Eleph (1), *thousand*

ELEVEN
259+6240 'echâd (9), *first*
505+3967 'eleph (3), *thousand*
6249+6240 'ashtêy (6), *eleven; eleventh*
1733 hěnděka (6), *eleven*

ELEVENTH
259+6240 'echâd (4), *first*
6249+6240 'ashtêy (12), *eleven; eleventh*
1734 hěnděkatŏs (3), *eleventh*

ELHANAN
445 'Elchânân (4), *God (is) gracious*

ELI
5941 'Êlîy (32), *lofty*
2241 ēli (1), *my God*

ELI'S
5941 'Êlîy (1), *lofty*

ELIAB
446 'Ĕlîy'âb (20), *God of (his) father*

ELIAB'S
446 'Ĕlîy'âb (1), *God of (his) father*

ELIADA
450 'Elyâdâ' (3), *God (is) knowing*

ELIADAH
450 'Elyâdâ' (1), *God (is) knowing*

ELIAH
452 'Ĕlîyâh (2), *God of Jehovah*

ELIAHBA
455 'Elyachbâ' (2), *God will hide*

ELIAKIM
471 'Elyâqîym (12), *God of raising*
1662 Éliakřim (3), *God of raising*

ELIAM
463 'Ĕlîy'âm (2), *God of (the) people*

ELIAS
2243 Hēlias (30), *God of Jehovah*

ELIASAPH
460 'Ĕlyâçâph (6), *God (is) gatherer*

ELIASHIB
475 'Elyâshîyb (17), *God will restore*

ELIATHAH
448 'Ĕlîy'âthâh (2), *God of (his) consent*

ELIDAD
449 'Ĕlîydâd (1), *God of (his) love*

E

ELIEL
447 'Ĕlîy'êl (10), God of (his) God

ELIENAI
462 'Ĕlîy'êynay (1), Elienai

ELIEZER
461 'Ĕlîy'ezer (14), God of help
1663 Ĕlîĕzĕr (1), God of help

ELIHOENAI
454 'Ely^eĥôw'êynay (1), toward Jehovah (are) my eyes

ELIHOREPH
456 'Ĕlîychôreph (1), God of autumn

ELIHU
453 'Ĕlîyhûw (11), God of him

ELIJAH
452 'Ĕlîyâh (69), God of Jehovah

ELIKA
470 'Ĕlîyqâ' (1), God of rejection

ELIM
362 'Êylîm (6), palm-trees

ELIMELECH
458 'Ĕlîymelek (4), God of (the) king

ELIMELECH'S
458 'Ĕlîymelek (2), God of (the) king

ELIOENAI
454 'Ely^eĥôw'êynay (8), toward Jehovah (are) my eyes

ELIPHAL
465 'Ĕlîyphâl (1), God of judgment

ELIPHALET
467 'Ĕlîyphelet (2), God of deliverance

ELIPHAZ
464 'Ĕlîyphaz (15), God of gold

ELIPHELEH
466 'Ĕlîyph^elêhûw (2), God of his distinction

ELIPHELET
467 'Ĕlîyphelet (6), God of deliverance

ELISABETH
1665 Ĕlisabĕt (8), God of (the) oath

ELISABETH'S
1665 Ĕlisabĕt (1), God of (the) oath

ELISEUS
1666 Ĕlissaiŏs (1), Elisha

ELISHA
477 'Ĕlîyshâ' (58), Elisha

ELISHAH
473 'Ĕlîyshâh (3), Elishah

ELISHAMA
476 'Ĕlîyshâmâ' (17), God of hearing

ELISHAPHAT
478 'Ĕlîyshâphât (1), God of judgment

ELISHEBA
472 'Ĕlîysheba' (1), God of (the) oath

ELISHUA
474 'Ĕlîyshûwa' (2), God of supplication (or of riches)

ELIUD
1664 Ĕlioud (2), God of majesty

ELIZAPHAN
469 'Ĕlîytsâphân (4), God of treasure

ELIZUR
468 'Ĕlîytsûwr (5), God of (the) rock

ELKANAH
511 'Elqânâh (20), God has obtained

ELKOSHITE
512 'Elqôshîy (1), Elkoshite

ELLASAR
495 'Ellâçâr (2), Ellasar

ELMODAM
1678 Ĕlmŏdam (1), Elmodam

ELMS
424 'êlâh (1), oak

ELNAAM
493 'Elna'am (1), God (is his) delight

ELNATHAN
494 'Elnâthân (7), God (is the) giver

ELOI
1682 ĕlōï (1), my God

ELON
356 'Êylôwn (7), oak-grove

ELON-BETH-HANAN
358 'Êylôwn Bêyth Chânân (1), oak-grove of (the) house of favor

ELONITES
440 'Êlôwnîy (1), Elonite

ELOQUENT
376+1697 'îysh (1), man; male; someone
995 bîyn (1), to understand; discern
3052 lŏgiŏs (1), fluent, i.e. an orator

ELOTH
359 'Êylôwth (3), grove (of palms)

ELPAAL
508 'Elpa'al (3), God (is) act

ELPALET
467 'Ĕlîyphelet (1), God of deliverance

ELSE
369 'ayin (1), there is no, i.e., not exist, none
518 'îm (1), whether?; if, although; Oh that!
3588 kîy (3), for, that because

5750 'ôwd (13), again; repeatedly; still; more
1490 ĕi dĕ mē(gĕ) (8), but if not
1893 ĕpĕi (2), since
2087 hĕtĕrŏs (1), other or different
2532 kai (1), and; or; even; also

ELTEKEH
514 'Elt^eqê' (2), Eltekeh

ELTEKON
515 'Elt^eqôn (1), God (is) straight

ELTOLAD
513 'Eltôwlad (2), God (is) generator

ELUL
435 'Ĕlûwl (1), Elul

ELUZAI
498 'El'ûwzay (1), God (is) defensive

ELYMAS
1681 Ĕlumas (1), Elymas

ELZABAD
443 'Elzâbâd (2), God has bestowed

ELZAPHAN
469 'Ĕlîytsâphân (2), God of treasure

EMBALM
2590 chânat (1), to embalm; to ripen

EMBALMED
2590 chânat (3), to embalm; to ripen

EMBOLDENED
3618 ŏikŏdŏmĕŏ (1), to construct, edify

EMBOLDENETH
4834 mârats (1), to be pungent or vehement

EMBRACE
2263 châbaq (8), to clasp the hands, embrace

EMBRACED
2263 châbaq (3), to clasp the hands, embrace
782 aspazŏmai (2), to salute; welcome

EMBRACING
2263 châbaq (1), to clasp the hands, embrace
4843 sumpĕrilambanō (1), to embrace

EMBROIDER
7660 shâbats (1), to interweave

EMBROIDERER
7551 râqam (2), variegation; embroider

EMERALD
5306 nôphek (3), (poss.) garnet
4664 smaragdinŏs (1), of emerald
4665 smaragdŏs (1), green emerald

EMERALDS
5306 nôphek (1), (poss.) garnet

EMERODS
2914 t^echôr (2), piles, tumor
6076 'ôphel (6), tumor; fortress

EMIMS
368 'Êymîym (3), terrors

EMINENT
1354 gab (3), mounded or rounded: top or rim
8524 tâlal (1), to elevate

EMMANUEL
1694 Ĕmmanŏuĕl (1), God with us

EMMAUS
1695 Ĕmmaŏus (1), Emmaüs

EMMOR
1697 Ĕmmŏr (1), male donkey or ass

EMPIRE
4438 malkûwth (1), rule; dominion

EMPLOY
935+6440 bôw' (1), to go or come

EMPLOYED
5921 'al (1), above, over, upon, or against
5975 'âmad (1), to stand

EMPTIED
1238 bâqaq (2), to depopulate, ruin
1809 dâlal (1), to slacken, dangle
6168 'ârâh (2), to be, make bare; to empty
7324 rûwq (2), to pour out, i.e. empty
7386 rêyq (1), empty; worthless

EMPTIERS
1238 bâqaq (1), to depopulate, ruin

EMPTINESS
922 bôhûw (1), ruin, desolation

EMPTY
950 bûwqâh (1), empty, pillaged
1238 bâqaq (3), to depopulate, ruin
6437 pânâh (1), to turn, to face
6485 pâqad (3), to visit, care for, count
7324 rûwq (5), to pour out, i.e. empty
7385 rîyq (5), emptiness; worthless thing; in vain
7386 rêyq (2), empty; worthless
7387 rêyqâm (12), emptily; ineffectually
8414 tôhûw (1), waste, desolation, formless
2756 kĕnŏs (4), empty; vain; useless
4980 schŏlazō (1), to take a holiday

EMULATION
3863 parazēlŏō (1), to excite to rivalry

EMULATIONS
2205 zēlŏs (1), *zeal,
ardor; jealousy, malice*

EN-DOR
5874 'Êyn-Dô'r (3),
fountain of dwelling

EN-EGLAIM
5882 'Êyn 'Eglayim (1),
fountain of two calves

EN-GANNIM
5873 'Êyn Gannîym (3),
fountain of gardens

EN-GEDI
5872 'Êyn Gedîy (6),
fountain of a kid

EN-HADDAH
5876 'Êyn Chaddâh (1),
fountain of sharpness

EN-HAKKORE
5875 'Êyn haq-Qôwrê'
(1), *fountain of One
calling*

EN-HAZOR
5877 'Êyn Châtsôwr (1),
fountain of a village

EN-MISHPAT
5880 'Êyn Mishpâṭ (1),
fountain of judgment

EN-RIMMON
5884 'Êyn Rimmôwn (1),
*fountain of a
pomegranate*

EN-ROGEL
5883 'Êyn Rôgêl (4),
fountain of a traveller

EN-SHEMESH
5885 'Êyn Shemesh (2),
fountain of (the) sun

EN-TAPPUAH
5887 'Êyn Tappûwach
(1), *fountain of an
apple tree*

ENABLED
1743 ĕndunamŏŏ (1), *to
empower, strengthen*

ENAM
5879 'Êynayim (1),
double fountain

ENAN
5881 'Êynân (5), *having
eyes*

ENCAMP
2583 chânâh (11), *to
encamp for abode or
siege*

ENCAMPED
2583 chânâh (33), *to
encamp*

ENCAMPETH
2583 chânâh (2), *to
encamp*

ENCAMPING
2583 chânâh (1), *to
encamp*

ENCHANTER
5172 nâchash (1), *to
prognosticate*

ENCHANTERS
6049 'ânan (1), *to cover,
becloud; to act covertly*

ENCHANTMENT
3908 lachash (1),
incantation; amulet
5172 nâchash (2), *to
prognosticate*

ENCHANTMENTS
2267 cheber (2), *society,
group; magic spell*
3858 lahaṭ (1), *blaze;
magic*
3909 lâṭ (3), *incantation;
secrecy; covertly*
5172 nâchash (4), *to
prognosticate*

ENCOUNTERED
4820 sumballō (1), *to
consider; to aid; to join*

ENCOURAGE
2388 châzaq (4), *to be
strong; courageousd,
restrain, conquer*

ENCOURAGED
2388 châzaq (5), *to be
strong; courageous*

END
319 'achărîyth (21),
future; posterity
657 'epheç (1), *end; no
further*
1104 bâla' (1), *to
swallow; to destroy*
1584 gâmar (1), *to end;
to complete; to fail*
1700 dibrâh (1), *reason,
suit or style; because*
2583 chânâh (1), *to
encamp*
2856 châtham (1), *to
close up; to affix a seal*
3318 yâtsâ' (1), *to go,
bring out*
3615 kâlâh (56), *to
complete, prepare*
4390 mâlê' (1), *to fill; be
full*
4616 ma'an (8), *in order
that*
5239 nâlâh (1), *to
complete, attain*
5331 netsach (2),
splendor; lasting
5486 çûwph (1), *to
terminate*
5490 çôwph (3),
termination; end
5491 çôwph (Ch.) (5), *end*
5704+5769+5703 'ad (1),
during; while; until
6118 'êqeb (2), *on
account of*
6285 pê'âh (1), *direction;
region; extremity*
6310 peh (3), *mouth;
opening*
7078 qenets (1),
perversion
7093 qêts (51), *extremity;
after*
7097 qâtseh (48),
extremity
7098 qâtsâh (4),
termination; fringe
7117 qᵉtsâth (3),
termination; portion
7118 qᵉtsâth (Ch.) (2),
termination; portion

7999 shâlam (2), *to be
safe; complete*
8503 taklîyth (2),
extremity
8537 tôm (1),
completeness
8552 tâmam (2), *to
complete, finish*
8622 tᵉqûwphâh (2),
revolution, course
165+3588+165 aiōn (1),
perpetuity, ever; world
206 akrŏn (1), *extremity:
end, top*
1519 ĕis (4), *to or into*
1545 ĕkbasis (1), *exit,
way out*
2078 ĕschatŏs (1),
farthest, final
3796 ŏpsĕ (1), *late in the
day*
4009 pĕras (1), *extremity,
end, limit*
4930 suntĕlĕia (6), *entire
completion*
5049 tĕlĕiŏs (1),
completely
5055 tĕlĕŏ (1), *to end, i.e.
complete, conclude*
5056 tĕlŏs (34),
conclusion

ENDAMAGE
5142 nᵉzaq (Ch.) (1), *to
suffer, inflict loss*

ENDANGER
2325 chûwb (1), *to tie, to
owe, to forfeit*

ENDANGERED
5533 çâkan (1), *to
damage; to grow*

ENDEAVOUR
4704 spŏudazō (1), *to
make effort*

ENDEAVOURED
2212 zētĕō (1), *to seek*
4704 spŏudazō (1), *to
make effort*

ENDEAVOURING
4704 spŏudazō (1), *to
make effort*

ENDEAVOURS
4611 ma'ălâl (1), *act,
deed*

ENDED
3615 kâlâh (7), *to cease,
be finished, perish*
7999 shâlam (2), *to be
safe; be complete*
8552 tâmam (5), *to
complete, finish*
1096 ginŏmai (1), *to be,
become*
4137 plērŏŏ (2), *to fill,
make complete*
4931 suntĕlĕō (4), *to
complete entirely*

ENDETH
2308 châdal (1), *to desist,
stop; be fat*

ENDING
5056 tĕlŏs (1), *conclusion
of an act or state*

ENDLESS
179 akatalutŏs (1),
permanent

562 apĕrantŏs (1),
without a finish

ENDOW
4117 mâhar (1), *to wed a
wife by bargaining*

ENDS
657 'epheç (13), *end; no
further*
1383 gablûth (2), *twisted
chain or lace*
3671 kânâph (2), *edge or
extremity; wing*
4020 migbâlâh (1),
border on garb
7097 qâtseh (7), *extremity*
7098 qâtsâh (17),
termination; fringe
7099 qetsev (4), *limit,
borders*
7218 rô'sh (2), *head*
2078 ĕschatŏs (1),
farthest, final
4009 pĕras (1), *extremity,
end, limit*
5056 tĕlŏs (1), *conclusion
of an act or state*

ENDUED
2064 zâbad (1), *to confer,
bestow a gift*
3045 yâda' (2), *to know*
1746 ĕnduō (1), *to dress*
1990 ĕpistēmōn (1),
intelligent, learned

ENDURE
1961 hâyâh (3), *to exist,
i.e. be or become*
3201 yâkôl (2), *to be able*
3427 yâshab (2), *to dwell,
to remain; to settle*
3885 lûwn (1), *to be
obstinate*
5975 'âmad (3), *to stand*
6440 pânîym (1), *face;
front*
6965 qûwm (1), *to rise*
7272 regel (1), *foot; step*
430 anĕchŏmai (2), *put
up with, endure*
2076 ĕsti (1), *he (she or
it) is; they are*
2553 kakŏpathĕō (2), *to
undergo hardship*
5278 hupŏmĕnō (5), *to
undergo (trials)*
5297 hupŏphĕrō (1), *to
undergo hardship*
5342 phĕrō (1), *to bear or
carry*

ENDURED
1961 hâyâh (1), *to exist,
i.e. be or become*
2594 kartĕrĕō (1), *to be
steadfast or patient*
3114 makrŏthumĕō (1),
to be forbearing, patient
5278 hupŏmĕnō (3), *to
undergo (trials)*
5297 hupŏphĕrō (1), *to
undergo hardship*
5342 phĕrō (1), *to bear or
carry*

ENDURETH
1097 bᵉlîy (1), *without,
not yet; lacking;*
5975 'âmad (4), *to stand*
3306 mĕnō (2), *to stay,
remain*

5278 hupŏmĕnō (3), to undergo (trials)

ENDURING
5975 'âmad (1), to stand
3306 mĕnō (1), to stay, remain
5281 hupŏmŏnē (1), endurance, constancy

ENEMIES
341 'ôyêb (199), adversary, enemy
6145 'âr (1), foe
6146 'âr (Ch.) (1), foe
6862 tsar (26), trouble; opponent
6887 tsârar (9), to cramp
6965 qûwm (1), to rise
7790 shûwr (1), foe as lying in wait
8130 sânê' (3), to hate
8324 shârar (5), opponent
2190 ĕchthrŏs (19), adversary

ENEMIES'
341 'ôyêb (3), adversary, enemy

ENEMY
340 'âyab (1), to be hostile, be an enemy
341 'ôyêb (78), adversary, enemy
6145 'âr (1), foe
6862 tsar (9), trouble; opponent
6887 tsârar (5), to cramp
8130 sânê' (2), to hate
2190 ĕchthrŏs (11), adversary

ENEMY'S
341 'ôyêb (1), adversary, enemy
6862 tsar (2), trouble; opponent

ENFLAMING
2552 châmam (1), to be hot; to be in a rage

ENGAGED
6148 'ârab (1), to intermix

ENGINES
2810 chishshâbôwn (1), machination, scheme
4239 mᵉchîy (1), stroke of a battering-ram

ENGRAFTED
1721 ĕmphutŏs (1), implanted

ENGRAVE
6605 pâthach (2), to open wide; to plow, carve

ENGRAVEN
1795 ĕntupŏō (1), to engrave, carve

ENGRAVER
2796 chârâsh (3), skilled fabricator or worker

ENGRAVINGS
6603 pittûwach (5), sculpture; engraving

ENJOIN
2004 ĕpitassō (1), to order, command

ENJOINED
6485 pâqad (1), to visit, care for, count

6965 qûwm (1), to rise
1781 ĕntĕllŏmai (1), to enjoin, give orders

ENJOY
1086 bâlâh (1), to wear out; consume, spend
1961 hâyâh (1), to exist, i.e. be or become
3423 yârash (2), to inherit; to impoverish
7200 râ'âh (4), to see
7521 râtsâh (3), to be pleased with; to satisfy
619 apŏlausis (1), full enjoyment, pleasure
2192+619 ĕchō (1), to have; hold; keep
5177 tugchanō (1), to take part in; to obtain

ENJOYED
7521 râtsâh (1), to be pleased with; to satisfy

ENLARGE
6601 pâthâh (1), to be, make simple; to delude
7235 râbâh (1), to increase
7337 râchab (7), to broaden
3170 mĕgalunō (1), to increase or extol

ENLARGED
7337 râchab (8), to broaden
3170 mĕgalunō (1), to increase or extol
4115 platunō (2), to widen

ENLARGEMENT
7305 revach (1), room; deliverance

ENLARGETH
7337 râchab (2), to broaden
7849 shâtach (1), to expand

ENLARGING
7337 râchab (1), to broaden

ENLIGHTEN
5050 nâgahh (1), to illuminate

ENLIGHTENED
215 'ôwr (4), to be luminous
5461 phōtizō (2), to shine or to brighten up

ENLIGHTENING
215 'ôwr (1), to be luminous

ENMITY
342 'êybâh (2), hostility
2189 ĕchthra (5), hostility; opposition

ENOCH
2585 Chănôwk (9), initiated
1802 Ĕnōch (3), initiated

ENOS
583 'Ĕnôwsh (6), man; person, human
1800 Ĕnōs (1), man

ENOSH
583 'Ĕnôwsh (1), man; person, human

ENOUGH
1767 day (6), enough, sufficient
1952 hôwn (2), wealth
3027 yâd (1), hand; power
3605 kôl (1), all, any or every
4672 mâtsâ' (1), to find or acquire; to occur
7227 rab (7), great
7654 sob'âh (2), satiety
566 apĕchĕi (1), it is sufficient
713 arkĕtŏs (1), satisfactory, enough
714 arkĕō (1), to avail; be satisfactory
2425 hikanŏs (1), ample; fit
2880 kŏrĕnnumi (1), to cram, i.e. glut or sate
4052 pĕrissĕuō (1), to superabound

ENQUIRE
1158 bâ'âh (2), to ask; be bulging, swelling
1239 bâqar (2), to inspect, admire, care for, consider
1240 bᵉqar (Ch.) (1), to inspect, admire, care for, consider
1875 dârash (32), to pursue or search; to seek or ask; to worship
7592 shâ'al (7), to ask
1231 diaginōskō (1), ascertain exactly
1833 ĕxĕtazō (1), to ascertain or interrogate
1934 ĕpizĕtĕō (1), to search (inquire) for
2212 zētĕō (2), to seek
4441 punthanŏmai (1), to ask for information
4802 suzētĕō (1), to discuss, controvert

ENQUIRED
1245 bâqash (2), to search; to strive after
1875 dârash (10), to pursue or search
7592 shâ'al (15), to ask
7836 shâchar (1), to search for
198 akribŏō (2), to ascertain, find out
1567 ĕkzĕtĕō (1), to seek
4441 punthanŏmai (1), to ask for information

ENQUIREST
1245 bâqash (1), to search; to strive after

ENQUIRY
1239 bâqar (1), to inspect, admire, care
1331 diĕrōtaō (1), to question throughout

ENRICH
6238 'âshar (2), to grow, make rich

ENRICHED
4148 plŏutizō (2), to make wealthy

ENRICHEST
6238 'âshar (1), to grow, make rich

ENSAMPLE
5179 tupŏs (1), shape or resemblance; "type"
5262 hupŏdĕigma (1), exhibit, specimen

ENSAMPLES
5179 tupŏs (3), shape or resemblance; "type"

ENSIGN
226 'ôwth (1), signal, sign
5251 nêç (6), flag; signal
5264 nâçaç (1), to gleam; to flutter a flag

ENSIGNS
226 'ôwth (1), signal, sign

ENSNARED
4170 môwqêsh (1), noose for catching animals

ENSUE
1377 diōkō (1), to pursue; to persecute

ENTANGLE
3802 pagidĕuō (1), to ensnare, entrap

ENTANGLED
943 bûwk (1), to be confused
1707 ĕmplĕkō (1), to involve with
1758 ĕnĕchō (1), to keep a grudge

ENTANGLETH
1707 ĕmplĕkō (1), to involve with

ENTER
935 bôw' (81), to go or come
1980 hâlak (1), to walk; live a certain way
5674 'âbar (1), to cross over; to transition
1525 ĕisĕrchŏmai (63), to enter
1529 ĕisŏdŏs (1), entrance
1531 ĕispŏrĕuŏmai (1), to enter

ENTERED
935 bôw' (38), to go or come
305 anabainō (2), to go up, rise
1524 ĕisĕimi (1), to enter
1525 ĕisĕrchŏmai (53), to enter
1531 ĕispŏrĕuŏmai (3), to enter
1684 ĕmbainō (7), to embark; to reach
2064 ĕrchŏmai (2), to go or come
3922 parĕisĕrchŏmai (1), to supervene

ENTERETH
935 bôw' (9), to go or come
5181 nâchath (1), to sink, descend; to press down
1531 ĕispŏrĕuŏmai (5), to enter
1535 ĕitĕ (4), if too

ENTERING
935 bôw' (15), to go, come
3996 mâbôw' (3),
entrance; sunset; west
6607 pethach (17),
opening; entrance way
1525 ĕisĕrchŏmai (4), to
enter
1529 ĕisŏdŏs (1),
entrance
1531 ĕispŏrĕuŏmai (4), to
enter
1684 ĕmbainō (1), to
embark; to reach
1910 ĕpibainō (1), to
mount, arrive

ENTERPRISE
8454 tûwshîyâh (1),
ability, undertaking

ENTERTAIN
5381 philŏnĕxia (1),
hospitableness

ENTERTAINED
3579 xĕnizō (1), to be a
host; to be a guest

ENTICE
5496 çûwth (1), to
stimulate; to seduce
6601 pâthâh (7), to be,
make simple; to delude

ENTICED
6601 pâthâh (2), to be,
make simple; to delude
1185 dĕlĕazō (1), to
delude, seduce

ENTICETH
6601 pâthâh (1), to be,
make simple; to delude

ENTICING
3981 pĕithŏs (1),
persuasive
4086 pithanŏlŏgia (1),
persuasive language

ENTIRE
3648 hŏlŏklĕrŏs (1),
entirely sound in body

ENTRANCE
935 bôw' (2), to go or
come
2978 yᵉ'îthôwn (1), entry
3996 mâbôw' (3),
entrance; sunset; west
6607 pethach (2),
opening; entrance way
6608 pêthach (1), opening
1529 ĕisŏdŏs (2),
entrance

ENTRANCES
6607 pethach (1),
opening; entrance way

ENTREAT
6293 pâga' (1), to impinge
2559 kakŏŏ (1), to injure;
to oppress; to embitter

ENTREATED
818 atimazō (1), to
maltreat, dishonor
2559 kakŏŏ (1), to injure;
to oppress; to embitter
5195 hubrizō (3), to
exercise violence
5530 chraŏmai (1), to
employ or to act toward

ENTRIES
6607 pethach (1),
opening; entrance way

ENTRY
872 bᵉ'âh (1), entrance
3996 mâbôw' (6),
entrance; sunset; west
6310 peh (1), mouth;
opening
6607 pethach (7),
opening; entrance way

ENVIED
7065 qânâ' (5), to be,
make jealous, envious
7068 qin'âh (1), jealousy
or envy

ENVIES
5355 phthŏnŏs (1),
spiteful jealousy, envy

ENVIEST
7065 qânâ' (1), to be,
make jealous, envious

ENVIETH
2206 zĕlŏŏ (1), to have
warmth of feeling for

ENVIOUS
7065 qânâ' (4), to be,
make jealous, envious

ENVIRON
5437 çâbab (1), to
surround

ENVY
7065 qânâ' (3), to be,
make zealous, jealous
or envious
7068 qin'âh (7), jealousy
or envy
2205 zĕlŏs (1), zeal,
ardor; jealousy, malice
2206 zĕlŏŏ (2), to have
warmth of feeling for
5355 phthŏnŏs (7),
spiteful jealousy, envy

ENVYING
2205 zĕlŏs (4), zeal,
ardor; jealousy, malice
5354 phthŏnĕŏ (1), to be
jealous of

ENVYINGS
2205 zĕlŏs (1), zeal,
ardor; jealousy, malice
5355 phthŏnŏs (1),
spiteful jealousy, envy

EPAENETUS
1866 Ĕpainĕtŏs (1),
praised

EPAPHRAS
1889 Ĕpaphras (3),
devoted to Venus

EPAPHRODITUS
1891 Ĕpaphrŏditŏs (3),
devoted to Venus

EPHAH
374 'êyphâh (34), dry
grain measure
5891 'Êyphâh (5),
obscurity

EPHAI
5778 'Ôwphay (1),
birdlike

EPHER
6081 'Êpher (4), gazelle

EPHES-DAMMIM
658 'Epheç Dammîym
(1), boundary of blood

EPHESIAN
2180 Ĕphĕsiŏs (1),
Ephesian

EPHESIANS
2180 Ĕphĕsiŏs (5),
Ephesian

EPHESUS
2181 Ĕphĕsŏs (17),
Ephesus

EPHLAL
654 'Ephlâl (2), judge

EPHOD
641 'Êphôd (1), Ephod
642 'ephuddâh (2),
plating
646 'êphôwd (49), ephod

EPHPHATHA
2188 ĕphphatha (1), be
opened!

EPHRAIM
669 'Ephrayim (171),
double fruit
2187 Ĕphraïm (1), double
fruit

EPHRAIM'S
669 'Ephrayim (4),
double fruit

EPHRAIMITE
673 'Ephrâthîy (1),
Ephrathite or
Ephraimite

EPHRAIMITES
669 'Ephrayim (5),
double fruit

EPHRAIN
6085 'Ephrôwn (1),
fawn-like

EPHRATAH
672 'Ephrâth (5),
fruitfulness

EPHRATH
672 'Ephrâth (5),
fruitfulness

EPHRATHITE
673 'Ephrâthîy (3),
Ephrathite or
Ephraimite

EPHRATHITES
673 'Ephrâthîy (1),
Ephrathite or
Ephraimite

EPHRON
6085 'Ephrôwn (13),
fawn-like

EPICUREANS
1946 Ĕpikŏurĕiŏs (1),
servant

EPISTLE
1992 ĕpistŏlĕ (13),
written message

EPISTLES
1992 ĕpistŏlĕ (2), written
message

EQUAL
1809 dâlal (1), to
slacken, dangle
4339 mêyshâr (1),
straightness; rectitude

ERRED 87

ERRED
7683 shâgag (5), to stray;
to sin
7686 shâgâh (2), to stray,
wander; to transgress
8582 tâ'âh (2), to
vacillate, i.e. stray

6186 'ârak (2), to set in a
row, i.e. arrange,
6187 'êrek (1), pile,
equipment, estimate
7737 shâvâh (3), to level,
i.e. equalize
8505 tâkan (7), to
balance, i.e. measure
2465 isaggĕlŏs (1),
angelic, like an angel
2470 isŏs (4), similar
2471 isŏtēs (1), likeness;
fairness

EQUALITY
2471 isŏtēs (2), likeness;
fairness

EQUALLY
7947 shâlab (1), to make
equidistant

EQUALS
4915 sunēlikiōtēs (1),
alike, contemporary

EQUITY
3476 yôsher (1), right
3477 yâshâr (1), straight
3788 kishrôwn (1),
success; advantage
4334 mîyshôwr (2), plain;
justice
4339 mêyshâr (4),
straightness; rectitude
5229 nᵉkôchâh (1),
integrity; truth

ER
6147 'Êr (10), watchful
2262 Ēr (1), watchful

ERAN
6197 'Êrân (1), watchful

ERANITES
6198 'Êrânîy (1), Eranite

ERASTUS
2037 Ĕrastŏs (3), beloved

ERE
2962 ţerem (4), not yet or
before
3808 lô' (4), no, not
4250 prin (1), prior,
sooner, before

ERECH
751 'Erek (1), length

ERECTED
5324 nâtsab (1), to station

ERI
6179 'Êrîy (2), watchful

ERITES
6180 'Êrîy (1), Erite

ERR
7686 shâgâh (4), to stray,
wander; to transgress
8582 tâ'âh (14), to
vacillate, i.e. stray
4105 planaō (6), to roam,
wander; to deceive

ERRAND
1697 dâbâr (3), word;
matter; thing

ERRED
7683 shâgag (5), to stray;
to sin
7686 shâgâh (2), to stray,
wander; to transgress
8582 tâ'âh (2), to
vacillate, i.e. stray

E

635 apŏplanaō (1), to
lead astray; to wander
795 astŏchĕō (2), deviate
or wander from truth

ERRETH
7686 shâgâh (1), to stray,
wander; to transgress
8582 tâ'âh (1), to
vacillate, i.e. stray

ERROR
4879 mᵉshûwgâh (1),
mistake
7684 shᵉgâgâh (2),
mistake
7944 shal (1), fault
7960 shâlûw (Ch.) (1),
fault, error
8432 tâvek (1), center,
middle
4106 planē (7),
fraudulence; straying

ERRORS
7691 shᵉgîy'âh (1), moral
mistake
8595 ta'tûa' (2), fraud
51 agnŏēma (1), sin
committed in ignorance

ESAIAS
2268 Hēsaïas (21),
Jehovah has saved

ESAR-HADDON
634 'Êçar-Chaddôwn (3),
Esar-chaddon

ESAU
6215 'Êsâv (84), rough
2269 Êsau (3), rough

ESAU'S
6215 'Êsâv (12), rough

ESCAPE
3318 yâtsâ' (1), to go,
bring out
4422 mâlaṭ (22), to
escape; be delivered
4498+6 mânôwç (1),
fleeing; place of refuge
4655 miphlâṭ (1), escape,
shelter
5337 nâtsal (1), to
deliver; to be snatched
5674 'âbar (1), to cross
over; to transition
6403 pâlaṭ (2), to slip out,
i.e. escape; to deliver
6405 pallêṭ (1), escape
6412 pâlîyṭ (12), refugee
6413 pᵉlêyṭâh (9),
escaped portion
1309 diaphĕugō (1), to
escape, flee
1545 ĕkbasis (1), exit,
way out
1628 ĕkphĕugō (4), to
flee out, escape
5343 phĕugō (1), to run
away; to vanish
5343+575 phĕugō (1), to
run away; to vanish

ESCAPED
3318 yâtsâ' (1), to go,
bring out
4422 mâlaṭ (25), to
escape; be delivered
5337 nâtsal (1), to
deliver; to be snatched
6412 pâlîyṭ (8), refugee

6413 pᵉlêyṭâh (11),
escaped portion
7611 shᵉ'êrîyth (1),
remainder or residual
668 apŏphĕugō (3), to
escape from
1295 diasōzō (3), to cure,
preserve, rescue
1628 ĕkphĕugō (1), to
flee out, escape
1831 ĕxĕrchŏmai (1), to
issue; to leave
5343 phĕugō (2), to run
away; to vanish

ESCAPETH
4422 mâlaṭ (3), to escape;
be delivered; be smooth
6412 pâlîyṭ (2), refugee
6413 pᵉlêyṭâh (1),
escaped portion

ESCAPING
6413 pᵉlêyṭâh (1),
escaped portion

ESCHEW
1578 ĕkklinō (1), to shun;
to decline

ESCHEWED
5493 çûwr (1), to turn off

ESCHEWETH
5493 çûwr (2), to turn off

ESEK
6230 'Êseq (1), strife

ESH-BAAL
792 'Eshba'al (2), man of
Baal

ESHBAN
790 'Eshbân (2), vigorous

ESHCOL
812 'Eshkôl (6), bunch of
grapes

ESHEAN
824 'Esh'ân (1), support

ESHEK
6232 'Êsheq (1),
oppression

ESHKALONITES
832 'Eshqᵉlôwnîy (1),
Ashkelonite

ESHTAOL
847 'Eshtâ'ôl (7), entreaty

ESHTAULITES
848 'Eshtâ'ûlîy (1),
Eshtaolite

ESHTEMOA
851 'Eshtᵉmôa' (5),
Eshtemoa or Eshtemoh

ESHTEMOH
851 'Eshtᵉmôa' (1),
Eshtemoa or Eshtemoh

ESHTON
850 'Eshtôwn (2), restful

ESLI
2069 Ĕsli (1), Esli

ESPECIALLY
3966 mᵉ'ôd (1), very,
utterly
3122 malista (4), in the
greatest degree

ESPIED
7200 râ'âh (1), to see
8446 tûwr (1), to wander,
meander

ESPOUSALS
2861 chăthunnâh (1),
wedding
3623 kᵉlûwlâh (1),
bridehood

ESPOUSED
781 'âras (1), to engage
for matrimony, betroth
718 harmŏzō (1), to
betroth for marriage
3423 mnēstĕuō (3), to
betroth, be engaged

ESPY
6822 tsâphâh (1), to peer;
to observe, await
7270 râgal (1), to
reconnoiter; to slander

ESROM
2074 Ĕsrōm (3),
court-yard

ESTABLISH
3322 yâtsag (1), to place
permanently
3427 yâshab (1), to dwell,
to remain; to settle
3559 kûwn (14), to set up:
establish, fix, prepare
5324 nâtsab (1), to station
5582 çâ'ad (1), to support
5975 'âmad (3), to stand
6965 qûwm (17), to rise
6966 qûwm (Ch.) (2), to
rise
2476 histēmi (3), to
stand, establish
4741 stērizō (1), to turn
resolutely; to confirm

ESTABLISHED
539 'âman (7), to be firm,
faithful, true; to trust
553 'âmats (1), to be
strong; be courageous
2388 châzaq (1), to
fasten upon; to seize
3245 yâçad (2), settle,
establish a foundation
3559 kûwn (44), to set up:
establish, fix, prepare
5564 çâmak (1), to lean
upon; take hold of
5975 'âmad (1), to stand
6965 qûwm (9), to rise
8627 tᵉqan (Ch.) (1), to
straighten up, confirm
950 bĕbaiŏō (1), to
stabilitate, keep strong
2476 histēmi (2), to
stand, establish
3549 nŏmŏthĕtĕō (1), to
be founded, enacted
4732 stĕrĕŏō (1), to be,
become strong
4741 stērizō (2), to turn
resolutely; to confirm

ESTABLISHETH
5975 'âmad (1), to stand
6965 qûwm (1), to rise
6966 qûwm (Ch.) (1), to
rise

ESTABLISHMENT
571 'emeth (1), certainty,
truth, trustworthiness

ESTATE
1700 dibrâh (1), reason,
suit or style; because

3653 kên (5), pedestal or
station of a basin
8448 tôwr (1), manner
3588+4012 hŏ (1), "the,"
i.e. the definite article

ESTEEM
2803 châshab (1), to plot;
to think, regard
6186 'ârak (1), to set in a
row, i.e. arrange,
2233 hēgĕŏmai (2), to
deem, i.e. consider

ESTEEMED
2803 châshab (3), to plot;
to think, regard
5034 nâbêl (1), to wilt; to
fall away; to be foolish
6845 tsâphan (1), to
deny; to protect; to lurk
7043 qâlal (2), to be,
make light
1848 ĕxŏuthĕnĕō (1), to
treat with contempt

ESTEEMETH
2803 châshab (1), to plot;
to think, regard
2919 krinō (2), to decide;
to try, condemn, punish
3049 lŏgizŏmai (1), to
credit; to think, regard

ESTEEMING
2233 hēgĕŏmai (1), to
lead; to deem, consider

ESTHER
635 'Eçtêr (52), Esther

ESTHER'S
635 'Eçtêr (3), Esther

ESTIMATE
6186 'ârak (2), to set in a
row, i.e. arrange,

ESTIMATION
6187 'êrek (23), pile,
equipment, estimate

ESTIMATIONS
6187 'êrek (1), pile,
equipment, estimate

ESTRANGED
2114 zûwr (4), to be
foreign, strange
5234 nâkar (1), to treat
as a foreigner

ETAM
5862 'Êyṭâm (5),
hawk-ground

ETERNAL
5769 'ôwlâm (1), eternity;
ancient; always
6924 qedem (1), eastern;
antiquity; before
126 aïdiŏs (1),
everduring, eternal
165 aiōn (2), perpetuity;
ever; world
166 aiōniŏs (42),
perpetual, long ago

ETERNITY
5703 'ad (1), perpetuity;
ancient

ETHAM
864 'Êthâm (4), Etham

ETHAN
387 'Êythân (8),
permanent

ETHANIM
388 Êythânîym (1), *permanent* brooks

ETHBAAL
856 'Ethba'al (1), *with Baal*

ETHER
6281 'Ether (2), *abundance*

ETHIOPIA
3568 Kûwsh (19), *Cush*
128 Aithiŏps (1), *inhabitant of Æthiop*

ETHIOPIAN
3569 Kûwshîy (8), *Cushite*

ETHIOPIANS
3569 Kûwshîy (12), *Cushite*
128 Aithiŏps (1), *inhabitant of Æthiop*

ETHNAN
869 'Ethnan (1), *gift price of harlotry*

ETHNI
867 'Ethnîy (1), *munificence, lavishness*

EUBULUS
2103 Êubŏulŏs (1), *good-willer*

EUNICE
2131 Êunikē (1), *victorious*

EUNUCH
5631 çârîyç (2), *eunuch; official* of state
2135 ĕunŏuchŏs (5), *castrated; impotent*

EUNUCHS
5631 çârîyç (15), *eunuch; official* of state
2134 ĕunŏuchizō (3), to *castrate*
2135 ĕunŏuchŏs (2), *castrated; impotent*

EUODIAS
2136 Êuŏdia (1), *fine travelling*

EUPHRATES
6578 Pᵉrâth (19), *rushing*
2166 Êuphratēs (2), *Euphrates*

EUROCLYDON
2148 Êurŏkludōn (1), *wind* from the east

EUTYCHUS
2161 Êutuchŏs (1), *fortunate*

EVANGELIST
2099 ĕuaggĕlistēs (2), *preacher* of the gospel

EVANGELISTS
2099 ĕuaggĕlistēs (1), *preacher* of the gospel

EVE
2332 Chavvâh (2), *life-giver*
2096 Êua (2), *life-giver*

EVEN
227 'âz (1), *at that time* or *place; therefore*
389 'ak (2), *surely; only, however*

518 'îm (1), *whether?; if, although; Oh that!*
637 'aph (7), *also* or *yea; though*
853 'êth (25), *not translated*
1571 gam (50), *also; even; yea; though*
1887 hê' (1), *Lo!, Look!*
3588 kîy (7), *for, that because*
3602 kâkâh (5), *just so*
3651 kên (3), *just; right, correct*
4334 mîyshôwr (1), *plain; justice*
5704 'ad (3), *as far (long) as; during; while; until*
5705 'ad (Ch.) (2), *as far (long) as; during*
6153 'ereb (71), *dusk*
6664 tsedeq (1), *right*
7535 raq (1), *merely; although*
737 arti (1), *just now; at once*
891 achri (1), *until* or *up to*
1063 gar (1), *for, indeed, but, because*
1161 dĕ (3), *but, yet; and then*
2089 ĕti (1), *yet, still*
2193 hĕŏs (2), *until*
2504 kagō (7), *and also, even*
2509 kathapĕr (2), *exactly as*
2531 kathōs (24), *just* or *inasmuch as, that*
2532 kai (108), *and; or; even; also*
2548 kakĕinŏs (2), *likewise that* or *those*
3303 mĕn (1), *not translated*
3483 nai (4), *yes*
3676 hŏmōs (1), *at the same time, yet still*
3761 ŏudĕ (3), *neither, nor, not even*
3779 hŏutō (3), *in this way; likewise*
3796 ŏpsĕ (2), *late* in the day
3798 ŏpsiŏs (8), *late; early eve; later eve*
5037 tĕ (1), *both* or *also*
5613 hōs (5), *which, how,* i.e. *in that manner*
5615 hōsautōs (1), *in the same way*
5618 hōspĕr (2), *exactly like*

EVENING
6150 'ârab (2), to *grow dusky* at sundown
6153 'ereb (49), *dusk*
2073 hĕspĕra (2), *evening*
3798 ŏpsiŏs (5), *late; early eve; later eve*

EVENINGS
6160 'ărâbâh (1), *desert, wasteland*

EVENINGTIDE
6256+6153 'êth (2), *time*

EVENT
4745 miqreh (3), *accident* or *fortune*

EVENTIDE
6153 'ereb (1), *dusk*
6256+6153 'êth (2), *time*
2073 hĕspĕra (1), *evening*

EVER
753+3117 'ôrek (2), *length*
3605+3117 kôl (18), *all, any* or *every*
3808 lô' (1), *no, not*
3809 lâ' (Ch.) (1), *as nothing*
5331 netsach (23), *splendor; lasting*
5703 'ad (40), *perpetuity; ancient*
5704+5769 'ad (1), *as far (long) as; during; while*
5750 'ôwd (1), *again; repeatedly; still; more*
5757 'Avvîy (1), *Avvite*
5769 'ôwlâm (266), *ancient; always*
5769+5703 'ôwlâm (1), *ancient; always*
5865 'êylôwm (1), *forever*
5957 'âlam (Ch.) (11), *forever*
6783 tsᵉmîythûth (2), *perpetually*
6924 qedem (1), *eastern; antiquity; before*
8548 tâmîyd (3), *constantly, regularly*
104 aĕi (1), *ever, always*
165 aiōn (49), *perpetuity, ever; world*
166 aiōniŏs (1), *perpetual, long ago*
1336 diēnĕkĕs (2), *perpetually, endless*
2250+165 hēmĕra (1), *day; period of time*
3364 ŏu mē (1), *not* at all, *absolutely not*
3745 hŏsŏs (1), *as much as*
3842 pantŏtĕ (6), *at all times*
3956+165 pas (1), *all, any, every, whole*
4218 pŏtĕ (1), *at some time, ever*
4253 prŏ (1), *before in time* or *space*

EVERLASTING
5703 'ad (2), *perpetuity; ancient*
5769 'ôwlâm (60), *ancient; always*
5957 'âlam (Ch.) (4), *forever*
6924 qedem (1), *eastern; antiquity; before*
126 aïdiŏs (1), *everduring, eternal*
166 aiōniŏs (25), *perpetual, long ago*

EVERMORE
1755 dôwr (1), *dwelling*
3605+3117 kôl (2), *all, any* or *every*
5331 netsach (1), *splendor; lasting*
5703 'ad (1), *perpetuity; ancient*

5769 'ôwlâm (15), *ancient; always*
8548 tâmîyd (1), *constantly, regularly*
3588+165 hŏ (3), *"the,"* i.e. the definite article
3842 pantŏtĕ (2), *at all times*

EVERY
259 'echâd (5), *first*
376 'îysh (125), *man; male; someone*
802 'ishshâh (4), *woman, wife; women, wives*
1397 geber (1), *person, man*
3605 kôl (451), *all, any* or *every*
3606 kôl (Ch.) (4), *all, any* or *every*
3632 kâlîyl (1), *whole, entire; complete; whole*
5437 çâbab (26), to *surround*
7218 rô'sh (1), *head*
303 ana (2), *each; in turn; among*
376 anapĕrŏs (1), *maimed; crippled*
537 hapas (2), *all, every one, whole*
1330 diĕrchŏmai (1), to *traverse, travel through*
1538 hĕkastŏs (73), *each* or *every*
2596 kata (15), *down; according to*
3596 hŏdŏipŏrĕŏ (2), to *travel*
3650 hŏlŏs (2), *whole* or *all,* i.e. *complete*
3836 pantachŏthĕn (1), *from all directions*
3837 pantachŏu (6), *universally, everywhere*
3840 pantŏthĕn (1), *from, on all sides*
3956 pas (162), *all, any, every, whole*
5100 tis (3), *some* or *any person* or *object*
5101 tis (1), *who?, which?* or *what?*

EVI
189 'Êvîy (2), *desirous*

EVIDENCE
5612 çêpher (6), *writing*
1650 ĕlĕgchŏs (1), *proof, conviction*

EVIDENCES
5612 çêpher (2), *writing*

EVIDENT
5921+6440 'al (1), *above, over, upon,* or *against*
1212 dēlŏs (1), *clear, plain, evident*
1732 ĕndĕixis (1), *demonstration*
2612 katadēlŏs (1), *manifest, clear*
4271 prŏdēlŏs (1), *obvious, evident*

EVIDENTLY
4270 prŏgraphō (1), to *announce, prescribe*
5320 phanĕrŏs (1), *plainly,* i.e. *clearly*

EVIL
205 'âven (1), *trouble,
vanity, wickedness*
1100 bᵉlîya'al (1),
wickedness, trouble
1681 dibbâh (1), *slander,
bad report*
7451 ra' (434), *bad; evil*
7455 rôa' (11), *badness,
evil*
7462 râ'âh (1), *to
associate* with
7489 râ'a' (24), *to be
good for nothing*
92 adikēma (1), *wrong
done*
987 blasphēmēō (9), *to
speak impiously*
988 blasphēmia (1),
impious speech
1426 dusphēmia (1),
defamation, slander
2549 kakia (1),
depravity; malignity
2551 kakŏlŏgĕō (1), *to
revile, curse*
2554 kakŏpŏiĕō (4), *to
injure; to sin, do wrong*
2556 kakŏs (44), *bad,
evil, wrong*
2557 kakŏurgŏs (1),
criminal, evildoer
2559 kakŏō (3), *to injure;
to oppress; to embitter*
2560 kakŏs (2), *badly;
wrongly; ill*
2635 katalalĕō (4), *to
speak slander*
2636 katalalia (1),
defamation, slander
4190 pŏnērŏs (49),
malice, wicked, bad
4190+4487 pŏnērŏs (1),
malice, wicked, bad
5337 phaulŏs (4), *foul or
flawed,* i.e. *wicked*

EVIL-MERODACH
192 'Ĕvîyl Mᵉrôdak (2),
Evil-Merodak

EVILDOER
7489 râ'a' (1), *to be good
for nothing*
2555 kakŏpŏiŏs (1),
bad-doer; criminal

EVILDOERS
7489 râ'a' (9), *to be good
for nothing*
2555 kakŏpŏiŏs (3),
bad-doer; criminal

EVILFAVOUREDNESS
1697+7451 dâbâr (1),
word; matter; thing

EVILS
7451 ra' (8), *bad; evil*
4190 pŏnērŏs (1), *malice,
wicked, bad; crime*

EWE
3535 kibsâh (6), *ewe
sheep*
7716 seh (1), *sheep or
goat*

EWES
5763 'ûwl (1), *to suckle,*
i.e. *give milk*
7353 râchêl (2), *ewe*

EXACT
5065 nâgas (3), *to
exploit; to tax, harass*
5378 nâshâ' (2), *to lend
on interest*
5383 nâshâh (2), *to lend
or borrow*
4238 prassō (1), *to
execute, accomplish*

EXACTED
3318 yâtsâ' (1), *to go,
bring out*
5065 nâgas (1), *to
exploit; to tax, harass*

EXACTETH
5382 nâshâh (1), *to forget*

EXACTION
4855 mashshâ' (1), *loan;
interest on a debt*

EXACTIONS
1646 gᵉrûshâh (1),
dispossession

EXACTORS
5065 nâgas (1), *to
exploit; to tax, harass*

EXALT
1361 gâbahh (3), *to be
lofty; to be haughty*
5375 nâsâ' (2), *to lift up*
5549 çâlal (1), *to mound
up; to exalt; to oppose*
7311 rûwm (17), *to be
high; to rise or raise*
1869 ĕpairō (1), *to raise
up, look up*
5312 hupsŏō (2), *to
elevate; to exalt*

EXALTED
1361 gâbahh (5), *to be
lofty; to be haughty*
5375 nâsâ' (8), *to lift up*
5927 'âlâh (2), *to ascend,
be high, mount*
7311 rûwm (28), *to be
high; to rise or raise*
7426 râmam (2), *to rise*
7682 sâgab (5), *to be,
make lofty; be safe*
5229 hupĕrairŏmai (2),
to raise oneself over
5251 hupĕrupsŏō (1), *to
raise to the highest*
5311 hupsŏs (1), *altitude;
sky; dignity*
5312 hupsŏō (10), *to
elevate; to exalt*

EXALTEST
5549 çâlal (1), *to mound
up; to exalt; to oppose*

EXALTETH
1361 gâbahh (1), *to be
lofty; to be haughty*
7311 rûwm (3), *to be
high; to rise or raise*
7682 sâgab (1), *to be,
make lofty; be safe*
1869 ĕpairō (1), *to raise
up, look up*
5229 hupĕrairŏmai (1),
to raise oneself over
5312 hupsŏō (1), *to
elevate; to exalt*

EXAMINATION
351 anakrisis (1),
judicial investigation

EXAMINE
974 bâchan (1), *to test; to
investigate*
1875 dârash (1), *to seek
or ask; to worship*
350 anakrinō (1), *to
interrogate, determine*
1381 dŏkimazō (1), *to
test; to approve*
3985 pĕirazō (1), *to
endeavor, scrutinize*

EXAMINED
350 anakrinō (4), *to
interrogate, determine*
426 anĕtazō (2), *to
investigate; to question*

EXAMINING
350 anakrinō (1), *to
interrogate, determine*

EXAMPLE
1164 dĕigma (1),
specimen, example
3856 paradĕigmatizō (1),
to expose to infamy
5179 tupŏs (1), *shape,
resemblance; "type"*
5261 hupŏgrammŏs (1),
copy, example, model
5262 hupŏdĕigma (4),
exhibit; specimen

EXAMPLES
5179 tupŏs (1), *shape,
resemblance; "type"*

EXCEED
3254 yâçaph (2), *to add
or augment*
4052 pĕrissĕuō (2), *to
superabound*

EXCEEDED
1396 gâbar (1), *to be
strong; to prevail*
1431 gâdal (2), *to be
great, make great*

EXCEEDEST
3254 yâçaph (1), *to add
or augment*

EXCEEDETH
3254 yâçaph (1), *to add
or augment*

EXCEEDING
430 'ĕlôhîym (1), *the true
God; gods; great ones*
1419 gâdôwl (1), *great*
2302 châdâh (1), *to
rejoice, be glad*
2493 chêlem (Ch.) (1),
dream
3493 yattîyr (Ch.) (1),
preeminent; very
3499 yether (1),
remainder; small rope
3966 mᵉ'ôd (18), *very,
utterly*
4605 ma'al (2), *upward,
above, overhead*
5628 çârach (1), *to
extend even to excess*
7235 râbâh (1), *to
increase*
7235+3966 râbâh (1), *to
increase*
7689 saggîy' (1), *mighty*
8057 simchâh (1),
blithesomeness or *glee*
1519+5236 ĕis (1), *to or
into*

EXAMINE (col 4 continues)
2596+5236 kata (1),
down; according to
3029 lian (5), *very much*
3588+2316 hŏ (1), *"the,"*
i.e. the definite article
4036 pĕrilupŏs (3),
intensely sad
4970 sphŏdra (4),
vehemently, much
5228 hupĕr (1), *over;
above; beyond*
5235 hupĕrballō (3), *to
surpass*
5248 hupĕrpĕrissĕuō (1),
to superabound
5250 hupĕrplĕŏnazō (1),
to superabound

EXCEEDINGLY
413+1524 'êl (1), *to,
toward*
1419 gâdôwl (5), *great*
1419+3966 gâdôwl (1),
great
3493 yattîyr (Ch.) (1),
preeminent; very
3966 mᵉ'ôd (9), *very,
utterly*
4605 ma'al (4), *upward,
above, overhead*
7227 rab (2), *great*
7235 râbâh (1), *to
increase*
7235+3966 râbâh (1), *to
increase*
8057 simchâh (1),
blithesomeness or *glee*
1613 ĕktarassō (1), *to
disturb wholly*
1630 ĕkphŏbŏs (1),
frightened out of one's
wits
4056 pĕrissŏtĕrŏs (3),
more superabundantly
4057 pĕrissŏs (1),
superabundantly
4970 sphŏdra (1),
vehemently, much
4971 sphŏdrŏs (1), *very
much*
5228+1537+4053 hupĕr
(1), *over; above; beyond*
5401+3173 phŏbŏs (1),
alarm, or *fright*

EXCEL
1368 gibbôwr (1),
powerful; great warrior
3498 yâthar (1), *to
remain or be left*
5329 nâtsach (1), i.e. *to
be eminent*
4052 pĕrissĕuō (1), *to
superabound*

EXCELLED
7227 rab (1), *great*

EXCELLENCY
1346 ga'ăvâh (3),
arrogance; majesty
1347 gâ'ôwn (10),
ascending; majesty
1363 gôbahh (1), *height;
grandeur; arrogance*
1926 hâdâr (2),
magnificence
3499 yether (2),
remainder; small rope
3504 yithrôwn (1),
preeminence, gain

E

7613 se'êth (2), *elevation; swelling* scab
7863 sîy' (1), *elevation*
5236 hupĕrbŏlē (1), *super-eminence*
5242 hupĕrĕchō (1), to *excel; be superior*
5247 hupĕrŏchē (1), *superiority*

EXCELLENT
117 'addîyr (4), *powerful; majestic*
977 bâchar (1), *select, chose, prefer*
1347 gâ'ôwn (1), *ascending; majesty*
1348 gê'ûwth (1), *ascending; majesty*
1420 gᵉdûwlâh (1), *greatness, grandeur*
1431 gâdal (1), to *be great, make great*
3368 yâqâr (1), *valuable*
3493 yattîyr (Ch.) (5), *preeminent; very*
3499 yether (1), *remainder;* small *rope*
5057 nâgîyd (1), *commander, official*
5716 'ădîy (1), *finery; outfit; headstall*
7119 qar (1), *cool; quiet; cool-headed*
7218 rô'sh (1), *head*
7230 rôb (1), *abundance*
7682 sâgab (1), to *be, make lofty; be safe*
7689 saggîy' (1), *mighty*
7991 shâlîysh (1), *officer; of the third rank*
8446 tûwr (1), to *wander, meander*
1308 diaphĕrō (2), to *differ; to surpass*
1313 diaphŏrŏs (2), *varying; surpassing*
2596+5236 kata (1), *down; according to*
2903 kratistŏs (2), *very honorable*
3169 mĕgalŏprĕpēs (1), *befitting greatness*
4119 plĕiŏn (1), *more*

EXCELLEST
5927 'âlâh (1), to *ascend, be high, mount*

EXCELLETH
3504 yithrôwn (2), *preeminence, gain*
5235 hupĕrballō (1), to *surpass*

EXCEPT
369 'ayin (1), *there is no, i.e., not exist, none*
905 bad (1), *chief; apart, only, besides*
1115 biltîy (3), *not, except, without, unless*
3588 kîy (2), *for, that because*
3861 lâhên (Ch.) (3), *therefore; except*
3884 lûwlê' (3), *if not*
7535 raq (1), *merely; although*
1508 ei mē (7), *if not*
1509 ei mē ti (3), *if not somewhat*

2228 ē (1), *or; than*
3362 ĕan mē (33), *if not, i.e. unless*
3923 parĕisphĕrō (1), to *bear in alongside*
4133 plēn (1), *albeit, save that, rather, yet*

EXCEPTED
1622 ĕktŏs (1), *aside from, besides; except*

EXCESS
192 akrasia (1), *lack of control of self*
401 anachusis (1), *excessively pour out*
810 asōtia (1), *profligacy, debauchery*
3632 ŏinŏphlugia (1), *drunkenness*

EXCHANGE
4171 mûwr (1), to *alter; to barter, to dispose of*
8545 tᵉmûwrâh (2), *barter, compensation*
465 antallagma (2), *equivalent exchange*

EXCHANGERS
5133 trapĕzitēs (1), *money-broker*

EXCLUDE
1576 ĕkklĕiō (1), to *shut out, exclude*

EXCLUDED
1576 ĕkklĕiō (1), to *shut out, exclude*

EXCUSE
379 anapŏlŏgētŏs (1), *without excuse*
626 apŏlŏgĕŏmai (1), to *give an account*
3868 paraitĕŏmai (1), to *deprecate, decline*

EXCUSED
3868 paraitĕŏmai (2), to *deprecate, decline*

EXCUSING
626 apŏlŏgĕŏmai (1), to *give an account*

EXECRATION
423 'âlâh (2), *curse, oath, public agreement*

EXECUTE
1777 dîyn (1), to *judge; to strive or contend for*
5647 'âbad (1), to *do, work, serve*
6213 'âsâh (25), to *do or make*
8199 shâphaṭ (2), to *judge*
4160 pŏiĕō (2), to *do*

EXECUTED
5648 'ăbad (Ch.) (1), to *do, work, serve*
6213 'âsâh (15), to *do or make*
2407 hiĕratĕuō (1), to *be a priest*

EXECUTEDST
6213 'âsâh (1), to *do*

EXECUTEST
6213 'âsâh (1), to *do*

EXECUTETH
6213 'âsâh (5), to *do*

EXECUTING
6213 'âsâh (1), to *do*

EXECUTION
6213 'âsâh (1), to *do*

EXECUTIONER
4688 spĕkŏulatōr (1), *life-guardsman*

EXEMPTED
5355 nâqîy (1), *innocent*

EXERCISE
1980 hâlak (1), to *walk; live a certain way*
6213 'âsâh (1), to *do or make*
778 askĕō (1), to *strive for one's best*
1128 gumnazō (1), to *train by exercise*
1129 gumnasia (1), *training of the body*
1850 ĕxŏusiazō (1), to *control, master another*
2634 katakuriĕuō (2), to *control, subjugate*
2715 katĕxŏusiazō (2), to *wield full privilege over*
2961 kuriĕuō (1), to *rule, be master of*

EXERCISED
6031 'ânâh (2), to *afflict, be afflicted*
1128 gumnazō (3), to *train by exercise*

EXERCISETH
4160 pŏiĕō (1), to *do*

EXHORT
3867 parainĕō (1), to *recommend or advise*
3870 parakalĕō (14), to *call, invite*

EXHORTATION
3870 parakalĕō (2), to *call, invite*
3874 paraklēsis (8), *imploring, exhortation*

EXHORTED
3870 parakalĕō (3), to *call, invite*

EXHORTETH
3870 parakalĕō (1), to *call, invite*

EXHORTING
3870 parakalĕō (3), to *call, invite*
4389 prŏtrĕpŏmai (1), to *encourage*

EXILE
1540 gâlâh (1), to *denude; uncover*
6808 tsâ'âh (1), to *tip over; to depopulate*

EXORCISTS
1845 ĕxŏrkistēs (1), *exorcist, i.e. conjurer*

EXPECTATION
4007 mabbâṭ (3), *expectation, hope*
8615 tiqvâh (7), *cord; expectancy*
603 apŏkaradŏkia (2), *intense anticipation*
4328 prŏsdŏkaō (1), to *anticipate; to await*

4329 prŏsdŏkia (1), *apprehension of evil*

EXPECTED
8615 tiqvâh (1), *cord; expectancy*

EXPECTING
1551 ĕkdĕchŏmai (1), to *await, expect*
4328 prŏsdŏkaō (1), to *anticipate; to await*

EXPEDIENT
4851 sumphĕrō (7), to *collect; to conduce*

EXPEL
1644 gârash (1), to *drive out; to expatriate*
1920 hâdaph (1), to *push away or down; drive out*

EXPELLED
3423 yârash (2), to *inherit; to impoverish*
5080 nâdach (1), to *push off, scattered*
1544 ĕkballō (1), to *throw out*

EXPENCES
5313 niphqâ' (Ch.) (2), *outgo, i.e. expense*

EXPERIENCE
5172 nâchash (1), to *prognosticate*
7200 râ'âh (1), to *see*
1382 dŏkimē (2), *test, i.e. trustiness*

EXPERIMENT
1382 dŏkimē (1), *test, i.e. trustiness*

EXPERT
3925 lâmad (1), to *teach, train*
6186 'ârak (3), to *set in a row, i.e. arrange,*
7919 sâkal (1), to *be or act circumspect*
1109 gnōstēs (1), *knower, expert*

EXPIRED
3615 kâlâh (1), to *cease, be finished, perish*
4390 mâlê' (3), to *fill; be full*
8666 tᵉshûwbâh (3), *recurrence; reply*
4137 plērŏō (1), to *fill, make complete*
5055 tĕlĕō (1), to *end, i.e. complete, execute*

EXPOUND
5046 nâgad (1), to *announce*

EXPOUNDED
5046 nâgad (1), to *announce*
1329 diĕrmēnĕuō (1), to *explain thoroughly*
1620 ĕktithēmi (3), to *expose; to declare*
1956 ĕpiluō (1), to *explain; to decide*

EXPRESS
5481 charaktēr (1), *exact copy or representation*

EXPRESSED
5344 nâqab (5), to
specify, designate, libel

EXPRESSLY
559 'âmar (1), to say
4490 rhētōs (1),
out-spoken, distinctly

EXTEND
4900 mâshak (1), to draw
out; to be tall
5186 nâṭâh (1), to stretch
or spread out

EXTENDED
5186 nâṭâh (2), to stretch
or spread out

EXTINCT
1846 dâ'ak (1), to be
extinguished; to expire
2193 zâ'ak (1), to
extinguish

EXTOL
5549 çâlal (1), to mound
up; to exalt; to oppose
7311 rûwm (2), to be
high; to rise or raise
7313 rûwm (Ch.) (1),
elation, arrogance

EXTOLLED
5375 nâsâ' (1), to lift up
7318 rôwmâm (1),
exaltation, praise

EXTORTION
6233 'ôsheq (1), fraud;
distress; unjust gain
724 harpagē (1), pillage;
greediness; robbery

EXTORTIONER
4160 mûwts (1), to
oppress
5383 nâshâh (1), to lend
or borrow
727 harpax (1),
rapacious; robbing

EXTORTIONERS
727 harpax (3),
rapacious; robbing

EXTREME
2746 charchûr (1), hot
fever

EXTREMITY
6580 pash (1), stupidity
as a result of grossness

EYE
5869 'ayin (73), eye;
sight; fountain
5870 'ayin (Ch.) (1), eye;
sight
3442 mŏnŏphthalmŏs
(2), one-eyed
3788 ŏphthalmŏs (29),
eye
5168 trumalia (2),
needle's eye
5169 trupēma (1),
needle's eye

EYE'S
5869 'ayin (1), eye; sight;
fountain

EYEBROWS
1354+5869 gab (1),
rounded: top or rim;
arch

EYED
5770 'âvan (1), to watch
with jealousy
5869 'ayin (1), eye; sight;
fountain

EYELIDS
6079 'aph'aph (9),
fluttering eyelash

EYES
5869 'ayin (417), eye;
sight; fountain
5870 'ayin (Ch.) (5), eye;
sight
3659 ŏmma (1), eye
3788 ŏphthalmŏs (70),
eye

EYESALVE
2854 kŏllŏuriŏn (1),
poultice

EYESERVICE
3787 ŏphthalmŏdŏulĕia
(2), service that needs
watching

EYESIGHT
5869 'ayin (1), eye; sight;
fountain

EYEWITNESSES
845 autŏptēs (1),
eyewitness
2030 ĕpŏptēs (1),
looker-on

EZAR
687 'Etser (1), treasure

EZBAI
229 'Ezbay (1),
hyssop-like

EZBON
675 'Etsbôwn (2), Etsbon

EZEKIAS
1478 Ĕzĕkias (2),
strengthened of
Jehovah

EZEKIEL
3168 Yᵉchezqê'l (2), God
will strengthen

EZEL
237 'ezel (1), departure

EZEM
6107 'Etsem (1), bone

EZER
687 'Etser (4), treasure
5827 'Ezer (1), help
5829 'Ezer (4), aid

EZION-GABER
6100 'Etsyôwn (short (4),
backbone-like of a man

EZION-GEBER
6100 'Etsyôwn (short (3),
backbone-like of a man

EZNITE
6112 'Etsen (1), spear

EZRA
5830 'Ezrâ' (26), aid

EZRAHITE
250 'Ezrâchîy (3),
Ezrachite

EZRI
5836 'Ezrîy (1), helpful

FABLES
3454 muthŏs (5), tale,
fiction, myth

FACE
600 'ănaph (Ch.) (1), face
639 'aph (19), nose or
nostril; face; person
5869 'ayin (9), eye; sight;
fountain
6440 pânîym (313), face;
front
1799 ĕnôpiŏn (1), in the
face of, before
3799 ŏpsis (1), face;
appearance
4383 prŏsōpŏn (48), face,
presence
4750 stŏma (4), mouth;
edge

FACES
639 'aph (3), nose or
nostril; face; person
6440 pânîym (62), face;
front
4383 prŏsōpŏn (5), face,
presence

FADE
5034 nâbêl (5), to wilt; to
fall away; to be foolish
3133 marainō (1), to pass
away, fade away

FADETH
5034 nâbêl (5), to wilt; to
fall away; to be foolish
262 amarantinŏs (1),
fadeless
263 amarantŏs (1),
perpetual, never fading

FADING
5034 nâbêl (2), to wilt; to
fall away; to be foolish

FAIL
235 'âzal (1), to disappear
656 'âphêç (1), to cease
1238 bâqaq (1), to
depopulate, ruin
1584 gâmar (1), to end;
to complete; to fail
1809 dâlal (1), to
slacken, dangle
2637 châçêr (3), to lack;
to fail, want, make less
2638 châçêr (2), lacking
3543 kâhâh (1), to grow
dull, fade; to be faint
3576 kâzab (1), to lie,
deceive
3584 kâchash (2), to lie,
disown; to disappoint
3615 kâlâh (14), to cease,
be finished, perish
3772 kârath (6), to cut
(off, down or asunder)
3808+539 lô' (1), no, not
5307 nâphal (2), to fall
5405 nâshath (1), to dry
up
5674 'âbar (2), to cross
over; to transition
5737 'âdar (1), to
arrange as a battle
5848 'âṭaph (1), to
shroud, to languish
6461 paçaç (1), to
disappear
6565 pârar (1), to break
up; to violate, frustrate
7503 râphâh (4), to
slacken

7673 shâbath (2), to
repose; to desist
7960 shâlûw (Ch.) (2),
fault, error
8266 shâqar (1), to cheat,
i.e. be untrue in words
1587 ĕklĕipō (3), to die;
to spot
1952 ĕpilĕipō (1), to be
insufficient for
2673 katargĕō (1), to be,
render entirely useless
4098 piptō (1), to fall
5302 hustĕrĕō (1), to be
inferior; to fall short

FAILED
6 'âbad (1), perish;
destroy
2308 châdal (1), to desist,
stop; be fat
3318 yâtsâ' (2), to go,
bring out
3615 kâlâh (1), to cease,
be finished, perish
5307 nâphal (4), to fall
5405 nâshath (1), to dry
up
8552 tâmam (2), to
complete, finish

FAILETH
6 'âbad (1), perish;
destroy
369 'ayin (1), there is no,
i.e., not exist, none
656 'âphêç (1), to cease
1602 gâ'al (1), to detest;
to reject; to fail
2638 châçêr (1), lacking
3584 kâchash (1), to lie,
disown; to disappoint
3615 kâlâh (4), to cease,
be finished, perish
3782 kâshal (1), to totter,
waver; to falter
5405 nâshath (1), to dry
up
5737 'âdar (3), to
arrange as a battle
5800 'âzab (2), to loosen;
relinquish; permit
413 anĕklĕiptŏs (1), not
failing
1601 ĕkpiptō (1), to drop
away

FAILING
3631 killâyôwn (1),
pining, destruction
674 apŏpsuchō (1), to
faint

FAIN
1272 bârach (1), to flee
suddenly
1937 ĕpithumĕō (1), to
long for

FAINT
1738 dâvâh (1), to be in
menstruation cycle
1739 dâveh (1),
menstrual; fainting
1742 davvây (3), sick;
troubled, afflicted
3286 yâ'aph (3), to tire
3287 yâ'êph (2),
exhausted
3543 kâhâh (1), to grow
dull, fade; to be faint

4127 mûwg (3), *to soften, flow down, disappear*
4549 mâçaç (1), *to waste; to faint*
5774 'ûwph (3), *to cover, to fly; to faint*
5848 'âṭaph (1), *to shroud, to languish*
5889 'âyêph (6), *languid*
5968 'âlaph (1), *to be languid, faint*
6296 pâgar (2), *to become exhausted*
7401 râkak (2), *to soften*
7503 râphâh (2), *to slacken*
1573 ĕkkakĕŏ (4), *to be weak, fail*
1590 ĕkluō (5), *to lose heart*

FAINTED
1961 hâyâh (1), *to exist, i.e. be or become*
3021 yâga' (1), *to be exhausted, to tire,*
3856 lâhahh (1), *to languish*
5848 'âṭaph (2), *to shroud, to languish*
5968 'âlaph (2), *to be languid, faint*
5969 'ulpeh (1), *mourning*
6313 pûwg (1), *to be sluggish; be numb*
1590 ĕkluō (1), *to lose heart*
2577 kamnō (1), *to tire; to faint, sicken*

FAINTEST
3811 lâ'âh (1), *to tire; to be, make disgusted*

FAINTETH
3286 yâ'aph (1), *to tire*
3615 kâlâh (2), *to cease, be finished, perish*
4549 mâçaç (1), *to waste; to faint*

FAINTHEARTED
3824+7401 lêbâb (1), *heart*
4127 mûwg (1), *to soften; to fear, faint*
7390+3824 rak (1), *tender; weak*

FAINTNESS
4816 môrek (1), *despondent fear*

FAIR
2091 zâhâb (1), *gold, golden colored*
2603 chânan (1), *to implore*
2889 ṭâhôwr (2), *pure, clean, flawless*
2896 ṭôwb (6), *good; well*
2896+4758 ṭôwb (1), *good; well*
2897+4758 Ṭôwb (1), *good*
2898 ṭûwb (1), *good; goodness; beauty*
3302 yâphâh (12), *to be beautiful*
3303 yâpheh (14), *beautiful; handsome*
3303+8389 yâpheh (1), *beautiful; handsome*

3304 yᵉphêh-phîyâh (1), *very beautiful*
3948 leqach (1), *instruction*
6320 pûwk (1), *stibium*
8209 sappîyr (Ch.) (2), *beautiful*
8597 tiph'ârâh (3), *ornament*
791 astĕiŏs (1), *handsome*
2105 ĕudia (1), *clear sky, i.e. fine weather*
2129 ĕulŏgia (1), *benediction*
2146 ĕuprŏsōpĕō (1), *to make a good display*
2568 Kalŏi Limĕnĕs (1), *Good Harbors*

FAIRER
2896 ṭôwb (2), *good; well*
3302 yâphâh (1), *to be beautiful*

FAIREST
3303 yâpheh (3), *beautiful; handsome*

FAIRS
5801 'izzâbôwn (6), *trade, merchandise*

FAITH
529 'êmûwn (1), *trustworthiness; faithful*
530 'êmûwnâh (1), *fidelity; steadiness*
1680 ĕlpis (1), *expectation; hope*
3640 ŏligŏpistŏs (5), *lacking full confidence*
4102 pistis (238), *faithfulness; faith, belief*

FAITHFUL
529 'êmûwn (3), *trustworthiness; faithful*
530 'êmûwnâh (3), *fidelity; steadiness*
539 'âman (20), *to be firm, faithful, true*
540 'âman (Ch.) (1), *to be firm, faithful, true*
571 'emeth (1), *certainty, truth, trustworthiness*
4103 pistŏs (53), *trustworthy; reliable*

FAITHFULLY
530 'êmûwnâh (5), *fidelity; steadiness*
571 'emeth (2), *certainty, truth, trustworthiness*
4103 pistŏs (1), *trustworthy; reliable*

FAITHFULNESS
530 'êmûwnâh (18), *fidelity; steadiness*
3559 kûwn (1), *to render sure, proper*

FAITHLESS
571 apistŏs (4), *without faith; untrustworthy*

FALL
2342 chûwl (2), *to dance, whirl; to writhe in pain*
3318 yâtsâ' (1), *to go, bring out*
3381 yârad (1), *to descend*

3782 kâshal (22), *to totter, waver; to falter*
3783 kishshâlôwn (1), *ruin*
3832 lâbaṭ (3), *to overthrow; to fall*
3872 Lûwchîyth (1), *floored*
4131 môwṭ (1), *to slip, shake, fall*
4383 mikshôwl (1), *stumbling-block*
4658 mappeleth (7), *down-fall; ruin; carcase*
5034 nâbêl (1), *to wilt; to fall away; be foolish*
5064 nâgar (1), *to pour out; to deliver over*
5203 nâṭash (1), *to disperse; to thrust off*
5307 nâphal (149), *to fall*
5308 nᵉphal (Ch.) (3), *to fall*
5456 çâgad (2), *to prostrate oneself*
6293 pâga' (8), *to impinge*
7264 râgaz (1), *to quiver*
7812 shâchâh (2), *to prostrate in homage*
7997 shâlal (1), *to drop or strip; to plunder*
868 aphistēmi (1), *to desist, desert*
1601 ĕkpiptō (4), *to drop away*
1706 ĕmpiptō (3), *to be entrapped by*
3895 parapiptō (1), *to apostatize, fall away*
3900 paraptōma (2), *error; transgression*
4045 pĕripiptō (1), *to fall into the hands of*
4098 piptō (22), *to fall*
4417 ptaiō (1), *to trip up, stumble morally*
4431 ptōsis (2), *downfall, crash*
4625 skandalŏn (1), *snare*

FALLEN
935 bôw' (1), *to go or come*
3782 kâshal (2), *to totter, waver; to falter*
4131+3027 môwṭ (1), *to slip, shake, fall*
4803 mâraṭ (2), *to polish; to make bald*
5307 nâphal (55), *to fall*
1601 ĕkpiptō (3), *to drop away*
1706 ĕmpiptō (1), *to be entrapped by*
1968 ĕpipiptō (1), *to embrace; to seize*
2064 ĕrchŏmai (1), *to go or come*
2667 katapiptō (2), *to fall down*
2702 kataphĕrō (1), *to bear down*
2837 kŏimaō (2), *to slumber; to decease*
4098 piptō (4), *to fall*

FALLEST
5307 nâphal (1), *to fall*

FALLETH
3918 layish (1), *lion*
5034 nâbêl (1), *to wilt; to fall away; be foolish*
5307 nâphal (15), *to fall*
5308 nᵉphal (Ch.) (2), *to fall*
5456 çâgad (2), *to prostrate oneself*
7122 qârâ' (1), *to encounter, to happen*
1601 ĕkpiptō (2), *to drop away*
1911 ĕpiballō (1), *to throw upon*
4098 piptō (3), *to fall*

FALLING
1762 dᵉchîy (2), *stumbling fall*
3782 kâshal (1), *to totter, waver; to falter*
4131 môwṭ (1), *to slip, shake, fall*
5034 nâbêl (1), *to wilt; to fall away; be foolish*
5307 nâphal (3), *to fall*
646 apŏstasia (1), *defection, rebellion*
679 aptaistŏs (1), *not stumbling, without sin*
2597 katabainō (1), *to descend*
4045 pĕripiptō (1), *to fall into the hands of*
4098 piptō (1), *to fall*
4248+1096 prĕnēs (1), *headlong*
4363 prŏspiptō (1), *to prostrate oneself*

FALLOW
3180 yachmûwr (1), *kind of deer*
5215 nîyr (2), *freshly plowed land*

FALLOWDEER
3180 yachmûwr (1), *kind of deer*

FALSE
205 'âven (1), *trouble, vanity, wickedness*
2555 châmâç (2), *violence; malice*
3577 kâzâb (1), *falsehood; idol*
4820 mirmâh (2), *fraud*
7423 rᵉmîyâh (1), *remissness; treachery*
7723 shâw' (5), *ruin; guile; idolatry*
8267 sheqer (20), *untruth; sham*
1228 diabŏlŏs (2), *traducer, i.e. Satan*
4811 sukŏphantĕō (1), *to defraud, extort*
5569 psĕudadĕlphŏs (2), *pretended associate*
5570 psĕudapŏstŏlŏs (1), *pretended preacher*
5571 psĕudēs (1), *erroneous, deceitful*
5572 psĕudŏdidaskalŏs (1), *propagator of erroneous doctrine*
5573 psĕudŏlŏgŏs (4), *promulgating erroneous doctrine*

5575 psĕudŏmartur (3), bearer of untrue testimony
5576 psĕudŏmarturĕō (6), to offer falsehood
5577 psĕudŏmarturia (1), untrue testimony
5578 psĕudŏprŏphētēs (6), pretended foreteller
5580 psĕudŏchristŏs (2), spurious Messiah

FALSEHOOD
4604 ma'al (1), sinful treachery
8267 sheqer (13), untruth; sham

FALSELY
3584 kâchash (1), to lie, disown; to disappoint
5921+8267 'al (1), above, over, upon, or against
7723 shâv' (1), ruin; guile; idolatry
8266 shâqar (2), to cheat, i.e. be untrue in words
8267 sheqer (12), untruth; sham
5574 psĕudŏmai (1), to utter an untruth
5581 psĕudŏnumŏs (1), untruly named

FALSIFYING
5791 'âvath (1), to wrest, twist

FAME
6963 qôwl (1), voice or sound
8034 shêm (4), appellation, i.e. name
8052 shᵉmûw'âh (2), announcement
8088 shêma' (5), something heard
8089 shôma' (4), report; reputation
189 akŏĕ (3), hearing; thing heard
1310 diaphēmizō (1), to spread news
2279 ēchŏs (1), roar; rumor
3056 lŏgŏs (1), word, matter, thing; Word
5345 phēmē (2), news, report

FAMILIAR
3045 yâda' (1), to know
7965 shâlôwm (1), safe; well; health, prosperity

FAMILIARS
7965 shâlôwm (1), safe; well; health, prosperity

FAMILIES
1004 bayith (2), house; temple; family, tribe
1004+1 bayith (2), house; temple; family, tribe
2945 ṭaph (1), family of children and women
4940 mishpâchâh (169), family, clan, people

FAMILY
504 'eleph (1), ox; cow or cattle
1004 bayith (1), house; temple; family, tribe

4940 mishpâchâh (120), family, clan, people
3965 patria (1), family, race, nation

FAMINE
3720 kâphân (2), hunger
7458 râ'âb (86), hunger
7459 reᵉ'âbôwn (3), famine
3042 limŏs (4), scarcity of food, famine

FAMINES
3042 limŏs (3), scarcity of food, famine

FAMISH
7329 râzâh (1), to make, become thin
7456 râ'êb (1), to hunger

FAMISHED
7456 râ'êb (1), to hunger
7458 râ'âb (1), hunger

FAMOUS
117 'addîyr (2), powerful; majestic
3045 yâda' (1), to know
7121 qârâ' (2), to call out
7148 qârîy' (1), called, i.e. select
8034 shêm (4), appellation, i.e. name

FAN
2219 zârâh (4), to toss about; to winnow
4214 mizreh (1), winnowing shovel
4425 ptuŏn (2), winnowing-fork

FANNERS
2114 zûwr (1), to be foreign, strange

FAR
1419 gâdôwl (1), great
2008 hênnâh (2), from here; from there
2186 zânach (1), to reject, forsake, fail
2486 châlîylâh (9), far be it!, forbid!
3966 meᵉ'ôd (3), very, utterly
4801 merchâq (15), distant place; from afar
5048 neged (3), over against or before
5079 niddâh (1), time of menstrual impurity
7350 râchôwq (59), remote, far
7352 rachîyq (Ch.) (1), far away; aloof
7368 râchaq (39), to recede; remove
7369 râchêq (2), remote, far
891 achri (2), until or up to
1519 ĕis (1), to or into
2193 hĕōs (4), until
2436 hilĕōs (1), God be gracious!, far be it!
3112 makran (6), at a distance, far away
3113 makrŏthĕn (1), from a distance or afar
3117 makrŏs (2), long, in place or time

4054 pĕrissŏtĕrŏn (1), in a superabundant way
4183 pŏlus (3), much, many
4206 pŏrrhō (2), forwards, at a distance
5231 hupĕranō (2), above, upward

FARE
7939 sâkâr (1), payment, salary; compensation
7965 shâlôwm (1), safe; well; health, prosperity
4517 rhŏnnumi (1), to strengthen

FARED
2165 ĕuphrainō (1), to rejoice, be glad

FAREWELL
657 apŏtassŏmai (2), to say adieu; to renounce
4517 rhŏnnumi (1), to strengthen
5463 chairō (1), to be cheerful

FARM
68 agrŏs (1), farmland, countryside

FARTHER
4008 pĕran (1), across, beyond
4260 prŏbainō (1), to advance
4281 prŏĕrchŏmai (1), to go onward, precede

FARTHING
787 assariŏn (1), assarius
2835 kŏdrantēs (2), quadrans

FARTHINGS
787 assariŏn (1), assarius

FASHION
1823 deᵉmûwth (1), resemblance, likeness
3559 kûwn (1), to set up: establish, fix, prepare
4941 mishpâṭ (2), verdict; formal decree; justice
8498 teᵉkûwnâh (1), structure; equipage
1491 ĕidŏs (1), form, appearance, sight
3778 hŏutŏs (1), this or that
4383 prŏsōpŏn (1), face, presence
4976 schēma (2), form or appearance
5179 tupŏs (1), shape, resemblance; "type"

FASHIONED
3335 yâtsar (3), to form; potter; to determine
3559 kûwn (2), to set up: establish, fix, prepare
6213 'âsâh (1), to do or make
4832 summŏrphŏs (1), similar, conformed to

FASHIONETH
3335 yâtsar (1), to form; potter; to determine

FASHIONING
4964 suschēmatizō (1), to conform to the same

FASHIONS
4941 mishpâṭ (1), verdict; formal decree; justice

FAST
629 'oçparnâ' (Ch.) (1), diligently
3966 meᵉ'ôd (1), very, utterly
6684 tsûwm (8), to fast from food
6685 tsôwm (16), fast from food
472 antĕchŏmai (1), to adhere to; to care for
805 asphalizō (1), to render secure
2722 katĕchō (3), to hold down fast
3521 nēstĕia (1), abstinence
3522 nēstĕuō (16), to abstain from food

FASTED
6684 tsûwm (12), to fast from food
3522 nēstĕuō (3), to abstain from food

FASTEN
2388 châzaq (1), to fasten upon; to seize
5414 nâthan (3), to give
8628 tâqa' (1), to clatter, slap, drive, clasp

FASTENED
270 'âchaz (3), to seize, grasp; possess
2388 châzaq (1), to fasten upon; to seize
2883 ṭâba' (1), to sink; to be drowned
3559 kûwn (1), to set up: establish, fix, prepare
5193 nâṭa' (1), to plant
5414 nâthan (2), to give
6775 tsâmad (1), to link, i.e. gird
6795 tsânach (1), to descend, i.e. drive down
8628 tâqa' (4), to clatter, slap, drive, clasp
816 atĕnizō (2), to gaze intently
2510 kathaptō (1), to seize upon

FASTENING
816 atĕnizō (1), to gaze intently

FASTEST
2522 kathēmĕrinŏs (1), quotidian, i.e. daily

FASTING
2908 ṭeᵉvâth (Ch.) (1), hunger
6685 tsôwm (8), fast
777 asitŏs (1), without taking food
3521 nēstĕia (4), abstinence
3522 nēstĕuō (1), to abstain from food
3523 nēstis (2), abstinent from food

FASTINGS
6685 tsôwm (1), fast
3521 nēstĕia (3), abstinence

F

6342 pâchad (1), *to be startled; to fear*
5399 phŏbĕŏ (4), *to fear, be in awe of, revere*

FEARFUL
3372 yârê' (2), *to fear; to revere*
3373 yârê' (2), *fearing; reverent*
4116 mâhar (1), *to hurry; promptly*
1169 dĕilŏs (3), *timid, i.e. faithless*
5398 phŏbĕrŏs (2), *frightful, i.e. formidable*
5400 phŏbĕtrŏn (1), *frightening thing*

FEARFULLY
3372 yârê' (1), *to fear; to revere*

FEARFULNESS
3374 yir'âh (1), *fear; reverence*
6427 pallâtsûwth (1), *affright, trembling fear*
7461 ra'ad (1), *shudder*

FEARING
3372 yârê' (1), *to fear; to revere*
2125 ĕulabĕŏmai (1), *to have reverence*
5399 phŏbĕŏ (6), *to fear, be in awe of, revere*

FEARS
2849 chathchath (1), *terror, horror*
4035 mᵉgûwrâh (2), *fright; granary*
5401 phŏbŏs (1), *alarm, or fright; reverence*

FEAST
2282 chag (53), *solemn festival*
2287 châgag (4), *to observe a festival*
3899 lechem (1), *food, bread*
3900 lᵉchem (Ch.) (1), *food, bread*
4150 môw'êd (3), *assembly, congregation*
4960 mishteh (21), *drink; banquet or feast*
755 architriklinŏs (3), *director of the entertainment*
1408 drŏmŏs (2), *career, course of life*
1456 ĕgkainia (1), *Feast of Dedication*
1858 hĕŏrtazō (1), *to observe a festival*
1859 hĕŏrtē (26), *festival*
4910 sunĕuŏchĕō (2), *to feast together*

FEASTED
6213+4960 'âsâh (1), *to do or make*

FEASTING
4960 mishteh (7), *drink; banquet or feast*

FEASTS
2282 chag (5), *solemn festival*
4150 môw'êd (19), *assembly, congregation*

4580 mâ'ôwg (1), *cake of bread, provision*
4960 mishteh (2), *drink; banquet or feast*
1173 dĕipnŏn (3), *principal meal*

FEATHERED
3671 kânâph (2), *edge or extremity; wing*

FEATHERS
84 'ebrâh (2), *pinion*
2624 chăçîydâh (1), *stork*
5133 nôwtsâh (3), *plumage*

FED
398 'âkal (5), *to eat*
1277 bârîy' (1), *fatted or plump; healthy*
2109 zûwn (1), *to nourish; feed*
2110 zûwn (Ch.) (1), *to nourish; feed*
2939 ţᵉ'am (Ch.) (1), *to feed*
3557 kûwl (3), *to keep in; to measure*
4806 mᵉrîy' (1), *stall-fed animal*
5095 nâhal (1), *to flow; to protect, sustain*
7462 râ'âh (10), *to tend a flock, i.e. pasture it*
1006 bŏskō (2), *to pasture a flock*
4222 pŏtizō (1), *to furnish drink, irrigate*
5142 trĕphō (1), *to nurse, feed, care for*
5526 chŏrtazō (1), *to supply food*

FEEBLE
535 'âmal (1), *to be weak; to be sick*
537 'ămêlâl (1), *languid, feeble*
2826 châshal (1), *make unsteady*
3766 kâra' (1), *to make miserable*
3782 kâshal (4), *to totter, waver; to falter*
3808+3524 lô' (1), *no, not*
3808+6099 lô' (1), *no, not*
5848 'âţaph (1), *to shroud; to languish*
6313 pûwg (1), *to be sluggish; be numb*
7503 râphâh (6), *to slacken*
772 asthĕnēs (1), *strengthless, weak*
3886 paraluō (1), *to be paralyzed or enfeebled*

FEEBLEMINDED
3642 ŏligŏpsuchŏs (1), *timid, faint-hearted*

FEEBLENESS
7510 riphyôwn (1), *slackness*

FEEBLER
5848 'âţaph (1), *to shroud, to languish*

FEED
398 'âkal (8), *to eat*
1197 bâ'ar (1), *to be brutish, be senseless*

2963 ţâraph (1), *to supply, provide food*
3557 kûwl (3), *to keep in; to measure*
3938 lâ'aţ (1), *to swallow greedily, gulp*
7462 râ'âh (55), *to tend a flock, i.e. pasture it*
1006 bŏskō (3), *to pasture a flock*
4165 pŏimainō (4), *to tend as a shepherd*
5142 trĕphō (1), *to nurse, feed, care for*
5595 psōmizō (2), *to nourish, feed*

FEEDEST
398 'âkal (1), *to eat*
7462 râ'âh (1), *to tend a flock, i.e. pasture it*

FEEDETH
7462 râ'âh (5), *to tend a flock, i.e. pasture it*
4165 pŏimainō (1), *to tend as a shepherd*
5142 trĕphō (2), *to nurse, feed, care for*

FEEDING
7462 râ'âh (4), *to tend a flock, i.e. pasture it*
1006 bŏskō (3), *to pasture a flock*
4165 pŏimainō (2), *to tend as a shepherd*

FEEL
995 bîyn (1), *to understand; discern*
3045 yâda' (2), *to know*
4184 mûwsh (2), *to touch, feel*
4959 mâshash (1), *to feel of; to grope*
5584 psēlaphaō (1), *to verify by contac*

FEELING
524 apalgĕō (1), *become apathetic, callous*
4834 sumpathĕō (1), *to commiserate*

FEET
4772 margᵉlâh (5), *at the foot*
6471 pa'am (6), *time; step; occurence*
7166 qarçôl (2), *ankles*
7271 rᵉgal (Ch.) (7), *pair of feet*
7272 regel (151), *foot; step*
939 basis (1), *foot*
4228 pŏus (76), *foot*

FEIGN
5234 nâkar (1), *to treat as a foreigner*
5271 hupŏkrinŏmai (1), *to pretend*

FEIGNED
4820 mirmâh (1), *fraud*
4112 plastŏs (1), *artificial, fabricated*

FEIGNEDLY
8267 sheqer (1), *untruth; sham*

FEIGNEST
908 bâdâ' (1), *to invent; to choose*

FELIX
5344 Phēlix (8), *happy*

FELIX'
5344 Phēlix (1), *happy*

FELL
1961 hâyâh (7), *to exist, i.e. be or become*
3318 yâtsâ' (2), *to go, bring out*
3381 yârad (2), *to descend*
3766 kâra' (2), *to prostrate*
3782 kâshal (2), *to totter, waver; to falter*
5307 nâphal (122), *to fall*
5308 nᵉphal (Ch.) (5), *to fall*
5927 'âlâh (2), *to ascend, be high, mount*
6293 pâga' (4), *to impinge*
6298 pâgash (1), *to come in contact with*
6584 pâshaţ (2), *to strip, i.e. unclothe, plunder*
7257 râbats (1), *to recline, repose, brood*
7812 shâchâh (2), *to prostrate*
634 apŏpiptō (1), *to fall off, drop off*
1096 ginŏmai (1), *to be, become*
1356 diŏpĕtēs (1), *sky-fallen*
1601 ĕkpiptō (1), *to drop away*
1706 ĕmpiptō (1), *to be entrapped by*
1968 ĕpipiptō (10), *to embrace; to seize*
2597 katabainō (1), *to descend*
4045 pĕripiptō (1), *to fall into the hands of*
4098 piptō (56), *to fall*
4363 prŏspiptō (6), *to prostrate oneself*

FELLED
5307 nâphal (1), *to fall*

FELLER
3772 kârath (1), *to cut (off, down or asunder)*

FELLEST
5307 nâphal (1), *to fall*

FELLING
5307 nâphal (1), *to fall*

FELLOES
2839 chishshûq (1), *wheel-spoke*

FELLOW
376 'îysh (1), *man; male; someone*
2270 châbêr (1), *associate, friend*
5997 'âmîyth (1), *comrade or kindred*
7453 rêa' (9), *associate; one close*

FELLOW'S
7453 rêa' (1), *associate; one close*

FELLOWCITIZENS
4847 sumpŏlitēs (1), *fellow citizen*

FELLOWDISCIPLES
4827 summathētēs (1), co-learner

FELLOWHEIRS
4789 sugklērŏnŏmŏs (1), participant in common

FELLOWHELPER
4904 sunĕrgŏs (1), fellow-worker

FELLOWHELPERS
4904 sunĕrgŏs (1), fellow-worker

FELLOWLABOURER
4904 sunĕrgŏs (2), fellow-worker

FELLOWLABOURERS
4904 sunĕrgŏs (2), fellow-worker

FELLOWPRISONER
4869 sunaichmalōtŏs (2), co-captive

FELLOWPRISONERS
4869 sunaichmalōtŏs (1), co-captive

FELLOWS
582 'ĕnôwsh (1), *man; person, human*
2269 chăbar (Ch.) (2), *associate, friend*
2270 châbêr (3), *associate, friend*
2273 chabrâh (Ch.) (1), *similar, associated*
7453 rêa' (1), *associate; one close*
7464 rê'âh (1), *female associate*
435 anēr (1), *man; male*
2083 hĕtairŏs (1), *comrade, friend*
3353 mĕtŏchŏs (1), *sharer, associate*

FELLOWSERVANT
4889 sundŏulŏs (6), *servitor of the same master*

FELLOWSERVANTS
4889 sundŏulŏs (4), *servitor of the same master*

FELLOWSHIP
2266 châbar (1), to *fascinate by spells*
8667+3027 tᵉsûwmeth (1), *deposit, i.e. pledging*
2842 kŏinōnia (12), *benefaction; sharing*
2844 kŏinōnŏs (1), *associate, partner*
3352 mĕtŏchē (1), *something in common*
4790 sugkŏinōnĕō (1), to *co-participate*

FELLOWSOLDIER
4961 sustratiōtēs (1), *soldier together with*

FELT
3045 yâda' (1), to *know*
4959 mâshash (2), to *feel of;* to *grope*
1097 ginōskō (1), to *know*
3958 paschō (1), to *experience* pain

FEMALE
802 'ishshâh (2), *woman, wife; women, wives*
5347 nᵉqêbâh (19), *female, woman*
2338 thēlus (3), *female*

FENCE
1447 gâdêr (1), *enclosure, wall or fence*

FENCED
1211 betsel (1), *onion*
1219 bâtsar (15), to *be inaccessible*
1443 gâdar (1), to *build a stone wall*
4013 mibtsâr (12), *fortification; defender*
4390 mâlê' (1), to *fill; be full*
4692 mâtsôwr (1), *siege-mound; distress*
4694 mᵉtsûwrâh (5), *rampart, fortification*
5823 'âzaq (1), to *grub over, dig*
7753 sûwk (1), to *shut in with hedges*

FENS
1207 bitstsâh (1), *swamp, marsh*

FERRET
604 'ănâqâh (1), *gecko*

FERRY
5679 'âbârâh (1), *crossing-place*

FERVENT
1618 ĕktĕnēs (1), *intent, earnest*
2204 zĕō (2), to *be fervid or earnest*
2205 zēlŏs (1), *zeal, ardor; jealousy, malice*

FERVENTLY
1619 ĕktĕnōs (1), *intently, earnestly*

FESTUS
5347 Phēstŏs (12), *festal*

FESTUS'
5347 Phēstŏs (1), *festal*

FETCH
935 bôw' (1), to *go or come*
3318 yâtsâ' (1), to *go, bring out*
3947 lâqach (20), to *take*
5375 nâsâ' (1), to *lift up*
5437 çâbab (1), to *surround*
5670 'âbaṭ (1), to *pawn; to lend; to entangle*
5927 'âlâh (1), to *ascend, be high, mount*
7725 shûwb (1), to *turn back; to return*
1806 ĕxagō (1), to *lead forth, escort*

FETCHED
622 'âçaph (1), to *gather, collect*
3318 yâtsâ' (1), to *go, bring out*
3947 lâqach (10), to *take*
5375 nâsâ' (1), to *lift up*
5927 'âlâh (1), to *ascend, be high, mount*

FETCHETH
5080 nâdach (1), to *push off, scattered*

FETCHT
3947 lâqach (1), to *take*

FETTERS
2131 zîyqâh (1), *arrow; bond, fetter*
3525 kebel (2), *fetter, shackles*
5178 nᵉchôsheth (5), *copper; bronze*
3976 pĕdē (3), *shackle for the feet*

FEVER
6920 qaddachath (1), *inflammation*
4445 purĕssō (2), to *burn with a fever*
4446 purĕtŏs (6), *fever*

FEW
259 'echâd (3), *first*
4213 miz'âr (1), *fewness, smallness*
4557 miçpâr (5), *number*
4591 mâ'aṭ (4), to *be, make small or few*
4592 mᵉ'aṭ (24), *little or few*
4962 math (4), *men*
7116 qâtsêr (1), *short*
1024 brachus (1), *little, short*
3641 ŏligŏs (20), *puny, small*
4935 suntŏmōs (1), *briefly*

FEWER
4592 mᵉ'aṭ (1), *little or few*

FEWEST
4592 mᵉ'aṭ (1), *little or few*

FEWNESS
4591 mâ'aṭ (1), to *be, make small or few*

FIDELITY
4102 pistis (1), *faithfulness; faith, belief*

FIELD
776 'erets (1), *earth, land, soil; country*
1251 bar (Ch.) (8), *field*
2513 chelqâh (2), *flattery; allotment*
7704 sâdeh (246), *field*
68 agrŏs (22), *farmland, countryside*
5564 chōriŏn (3), *spot or plot of ground*

FIELDS
2351 chûwts (2), *outside, outdoors; countryside*
3010 yâgêb (1), *plowed field*
7704 sâdeh (46), *field*
7709 shᵉdêmâh (4), *cultivated field*
8309 shᵉrêmâh (1), *common*
68 agrŏs (1), *farmland, countryside*
5561 chōra (2), *space of territory*

FIERCE
393 'akzâr (1), *violent, deadly; brave*
2300 châdad (1), to *be, make sharp; fierce*
2740 chârôwn (23), *burning of anger*
2750 chŏrîy (3), *burning anger*
3267 yâ'az (1), to *be obstinate, be arrogant*
5794 'az (4), *strong, vehement, harsh*
7826 shachal (3), *lion*
434 anĕmĕrŏs (1), *brutal, savage*
2001 ĕpischuŏ (1), to *insist stoutly*
4642 sklērŏs (1), *hard or tough; harsh, severe*
5467 chalĕpŏs (1), *difficult, furious*

FIERCENESS
2740 chârôwn (9), *burning of anger*
7494 ra'ash (1), *bounding, uproar*
2372 thumŏs (2), *passion, anger*

FIERCER
7185 qâshâh (1), to *be tough or severe*

FIERY
784 'êsh (1), *fire*
799 'eshdâth (1), *fire-law*
5135 nûwr (Ch.) (10), *fire*
8314 sârâph (5), *poisonous serpent*
4442 pur (1), *fire*
4448 purŏō (1), to *be ignited, glow*
4451 purōsis (1), *ignition, conflagration, calamity*

FIFTEEN
2568+6240 châmêsh (16), *five*
6235+2568 'eser (1), *ten*
7657+2568 shib'îym (3), *seventy*
1178 dĕkapĕntĕ (3), *fifteen*
1440+4002 hĕbdŏmĕkŏnta (1), *seventy*

FIFTEENTH
2568+6240 châmêsh (17), *five*
4003 pĕntĕkaidĕkatŏs (1), *five and tenth*

FIFTH
2549 chămîyshîy (44), *fifth; fifth part*
2567 châmash (1), to *tax a fifth*
2568 châmêsh (6), *five*
2569 chômesh (1), *fifth tax*
2570 chômesh (4), *abdomen, belly*
3991 pĕmptŏs (4), *fifth*

FIFTIES
2572 chămishshîym (5), *fifty*
4004 pĕntĕkŏnta (2), *fifty*

FIFTIETH
2572 chămishshîym (4), *fifty*

FIFTY
2572 chămishshîym (148), *fifty*
4002+3461 pĕntĕ (1), *five*
4004 pĕntēkŏnta (5), *fifty*

FIG
8384 tᵉ'ên (24), *fig tree or fruit*
4808 sukē (16), *fig-tree*

FIGHT
3898 lâcham (85), to *fight a battle*, i.e. *consume*
4421 milchâmâh (5), *battle; war; fighting*
4634 ma'ărâkâh (1), *row; pile*; military *array*
6633 tsâbâ' (4), to *mass an army or servants*
73 agōn (1), *contest, struggle*
75 agōnizŏmai (2), to *struggle*; to *contend*
119 athlēsis (1), *struggle, contest*
2313 thĕŏmachĕō (1), to *resist deity*
2314 thĕŏmachŏs (1), *opponent of deity*
3164 machŏmai (1), to *war*, i.e. to *quarrel*
4170 pŏlĕmĕō (1), to *battle, make war*
4171 pŏlĕmŏs (1), *warfare; battle; fight*
4438 puktĕō (1), to *box as a sporting event*

FIGHTETH
3898 lâcham (3), to *fight a battle*, i.e. *consume*

FIGHTING
3898 lâcham (2), to *fight a battle*, i.e. *consume*
6213+4421 'âsâh (1), to *do or make*

FIGHTINGS
3163 machē (2), *controversy, conflict*

FIGS
6291 pag (1), *unripe fig*
8384 tᵉ'ên (15), *fig tree or fruit*
3653 ŏlunthŏs (1), *unripe fig*
4810 sukŏn (4), *fig*

FIGURE
5566 çemel (1), *likeness*
8403 tabnîyth (1), *model, resemblance*
499 antitupŏn (1), *representative*
3345 mĕtaschēmatizō (1), to *transfigure*
3850 parabŏlē (2), *fictitious narrative*
5179 tupŏs (1), *shape, resemblance; "type"*

FIGURES
4734 miqla'ath (1), *bas-relief sculpture*
499 antitupŏn (1), *representative*
5179 tupŏs (1), *shape, resemblance; "type"*

FILE
6477+6310 pᵉtsîyrâh (1), *bluntness*

FILL
4390 mâlê' (33), to *fill; be full*
4393 mᵉlô' (2), *fulness*
5433 çâbâ' (1), to *quaff to satiety*
7301 râvâh (1), to *slake thirst or appetites*
7646 sâba' (1), *fill to satiety*
7648 sôba' (2), *satisfaction*
466 antanaplērŏō (1), to *fill up*
878 aphrōn (1), *ignorant; egotistic; unbelieving*
1072 gĕmizō (1), to *fill entirely*
2767 kĕrannumi (1), to *mingle*, i.e. to *pour*
4137 plērŏō (3), to *fill, make complete*
4138 plērōma (1), *what fills; what is filled*
5526 chŏrtazō (1), to *supply food*

FILLED
4390 mâlê' (74), to *fill; be full*
4391 mᵉlâ' (Ch.) (1), to *fill; be full*
7059 qâmaṭ (1), to *pluck*, i.e. *destroy*
7301 râvâh (1), to *slake thirst or appetites*
7646 sâba' (22), *fill to satiety*
1072 gĕmizō (7), to *fill entirely*
1705 ĕmpiplēmi (3), to *satisfy*
2767 kĕrannumi (1), to *mingle*, i.e. to *pour*
4130 plēthō (17), to *fulfill, complete*
4137 plērŏō (17), to *fill, make complete*
4138 plērōma (1), *what fills; what is filled*
4845 sumplērŏō (1), to *be complete, fulfill*
5055 tĕlĕō (1), to *end*, i.e. *complete, execute*
5526 chŏrtazō (11), to *supply food*

FILLEDST
4390 mâlê' (1), to *fill; be full*
7646 sâba' (1), *fill to satiety*

FILLEST
4390 mâlê' (1), to *fill; be full*

FILLET
2339 chûwṭ (1), *string; measuring tape; line*

FILLETED
2836 châshaq (3), to *join; to love, delight*

FILLETH
4390 mâlê' (2), to *fill; be full*
5844 'âṭah (1), to *wrap*, i.e. *cover, veil, clothe*
7646 sâba' (2), *fill to satiety*

FILLETS
2838 châshûq (8), *fence-rail or rod*

FILLING
1705 ĕmpiplēmi (1), to *satisfy*

FILTH
6675 tsôw'âh (1), *pollution*
4027 pĕrikatharma (1), *refuse, scum*
4509 rhupŏs (1), *dirt*, i.e. moral *depravity*

FILTHINESS
2932 ṭum'âh (7), *ceremonial impurity*
5079 niddâh (2), *time of menstrual impurity*
5178 nᵉchôsheth (1), *copper; bronze*
6675 tsôw'âh (2), *pollution*
151 aischrŏtēs (1), *obscenity*
168 akathartēs (1), *state of impurity*
3436 mŏlusmŏs (1), *contamination*
4507 rhuparia (1), *moral dirtiness*

FILTHY
444 'âlach (3), to *be or turn morally corrupt*
4754 mârâ' (1), to *rebel; to lash with whip; flap*
5708 'êd (1), *periodical menstrual flux*
6674 tsôw' (2), *excrementitious, soiled*
147 aischrŏkĕrdŏs (1), *sordidly, greedily*
148 aischrŏlŏgia (1), *filthy speech*
150 aischrŏs (2), *shameful thing, base*
766 asĕlgĕia (1), *debauchery, lewdness*
4510 rhupŏŏ (2), to *become morally dirty*

FINALLY
3063 lŏipŏn (5), *finally*
5056 tĕlŏs (1), *conclusion*

FIND
2803 châshab (1), to *think, regard; to value*
4672 mâtsâ' (100), to *find or acquire; to occur*
7912 shᵉkach (Ch.) (6), to *discover, find out*
2147 hĕuriskō (46), to *find*

FINDEST
4672 mâtsâ' (2), to *find or acquire; to occur*

FINDETH
4672 mâtsâ' (11), to *find or acquire; to occur*
2147 hĕuriskō (12), to *find*

FINDING
2714 chêqer (1), *examination*
4672 mâtsâ' (2), to *find or acquire; to occur*

FINISHED
4131 plēktēs (1), *pugnacious*

FILLETS
2838 châshûq (8), *fence-rail or rod*

(see above)

421 anĕxichniastŏs (1), *unsearchable*
429 anĕuriskŏ (1), to *find out*
2147 hĕuriskŏ (4), to *find*

FINE
2212 zâqaq (1), to *strain, refine; extract, clarify*
2869 ṭâb (Ch.) (1), *good*
2896 ṭôwb (2), *good; well*
6668 tsâhab (1), to *be golden in color*
8305 sᵉrîyqâh (1), *linen cloth*
4585 sĕmidalis (1), *fine wheat flour*

FINER
6884 tsâraph (1), to *fuse metal; to refine*

FINEST
2459 cheleb (2), *fat; choice part*

FINGER
676 'etsba' (19), *finger; toe*
1147 daktulŏs (5), *finger*

FINGERS
676 'etsba' (11), *finger; toe*
677 'etsba' (Ch.) (1), *finger; toe*
1147 daktulŏs (3), *finger*

FINING
4715 mitsrêph (2), *crucible*

FINISH
1214 bâtsa' (1), to *plunder; to finish*
3607 kâlâ' (1), to *hold back or in; to prohibit*
3615 kâlâh (1), to *cease, be finished, perish*
535 apartismŏs (1), *completion*
1615 ĕktĕlĕō (2), to *complete fully, finish*
2005 ĕpitĕlĕō (1), to *terminate; to undergo*
4931 suntĕlĕō (1), to *complete entirely*
5048 tĕlĕiŏō (3), to *perfect, complete*

FINISHED
3319 yᵉtsâ' (Ch.) (1), to *complete*
3615 kâlâh (19), to *cease, be finished, perish*
3635 kᵉlal (Ch.) (1), to *complete*
7999 shâlam (3), to *be safe; be complete*
8000 shᵉlam (Ch.) (2), to *complete, to restore*
8552 tâmam (4), to *complete, finish*
658 apŏtĕlĕō (1), to *bring to completion*
1096 ginŏmai (1), to *be, become*
1274 dianuō (1), to *accomplish thoroughly*
5048 tĕlĕiŏō (1), to *perfect, complete*
5055 tĕlĕō (8), to *end, complete, conclude*

FINISHER
5047 tĕlĕiŏtēs (1),
completeness; maturity

FINS
5579 çᵉnappîyr (5), fin

FIR
1265 bᵉrôwsh (20), (poss.)
cypress
1266 bᵉrôwth (1), (poss.)
cypress

FIRE
215 'ôwr (1), to be
luminous
217 'ûwr (4), flame; East
784 'êsh (375), fire
1200 bᵉ'êrâh (1), burning
3857 lâhaṭ (4), to blaze
5135 nûwr (Ch.) (8), fire
4442 pur (73), fire
4443 pura (2), fire
4447 purinŏs (1), fiery,
i.e. flaming
4448 purŏŏ (1), to be
ignited, glow
5394 phlŏgizŏ (2), to
cause a blaze
5457 phŏs (2),
luminousness, light

FIREBRAND
181 'ûwd (1), poker stick
for a fire
3940 lappîyd (1), flaming
torch, lamp or flame

FIREBRANDS
181 'ûwd (1), poker stick
for a fire
2131 zîyqâh (1), flash of
fire
3940 lappîyd (1), flaming
torch, lamp or flame

FIREPANS
4289 machtâh (4), pan
for live coals

FIRES
217 'ûwr (1), flame; East

FIRKINS
3355 mĕtrētēs (1), liquid
measure: 8-10 gallons

FIRM
1277 bârîy' (1), fatted or
plump; healthy
3332 yâtsaq (2), to pour
out
3559 kûwn (2), to set up:
establish, fix, prepare
8631 tᵉqêph (Ch.) (1), to
become, make mighty
949 bĕbaiŏs (1), stable,
certain, binding

FIRMAMENT
7549 râqîya' (17), expanse

FIRST
259 'echâd (34), first
1061 bikkûwr (1),
first-fruits of the crop
1069 bâkar (1), bear the
first born
1073 bakkûrâh (1),
first-ripe fruit of a fig
1121 bên (51), son,
descendant
1323 bath (3), daughter,
descendant, woman
2298 chad (Ch.) (4), one;
single; first; at once

2490 châlal (1), to
profane, defile
3138 yôwreh (1), autumn
rain showers
4395 mᵉlê'âh (1),
fulfilled; abundance
6440 pânîym (1), face;
front
6933 qadmay (Ch.) (3),
first
7218 rô'sh (6), head
7223 rî'shôwn (130), first,
in place, time or rank
7224 rî'shônîy (1), first
7225 rê'shîyth (11), first
8462 tᵉchillâh (7),
original; originally
509 anŏthĕn (1), from
above; from the first
746 archē (4), first in
rank; first in time
1207 dĕutĕrŏprŏtŏs (1),
second-first
1722+4413 ĕn (1), in;
during; because of
3391 mia (7), one or first
3891 paranŏmĕŏ (1), to
transgress, violate law
4272 prŏdidōmi (1), to
give before
4276 prŏĕlpizō (1), to
hope in advance of
4295 prŏkĕimai (1), to be
present to the mind
4386 prŏtĕrŏn (3),
previously
4412 prŏtŏn (58), firstly
4413 prŏtŏs (84), foremost
4416 prŏtŏtŏkŏs (1),
first-born

FIRSTBEGOTTEN
4416 prŏtŏtŏkŏs (1),
first-born

FIRSTBORN
1060 bᵉkôwr (101),
firstborn
1062 bᵉkôwrâh (1), state
of, rights of first born
1067 bᵉkîyrâh (6), first
born, eldest daughter
1069 bâkar (1), bear the
first born
4416 prŏtŏtŏkŏs (7),
first-born

FIRSTFRUIT
7225 rê'shîyth (1), first
536 aparchē (1), first-fruit

FIRSTFRUITS
1061 bikkûwr (13),
first-fruits of the crop
7225 rê'shîyth (11), first
536 aparchē (7), first-fruit

FIRSTLING
1060 bᵉkôwr (8),
firstborn, i.e. oldest son
1069 bâkar (1), bear the
first born
6363 peṭer (4), firstling,
first born

FIRSTLINGS
1060 bᵉkôwr (1),
firstborn, i.e. oldest son
1062 bᵉkôwrâh (5), state
of, rights of first born

FIRSTRIPE
1061 bikkûwr (1),
first-fruits of the crop

1063 bikkûwrâh (3),
early fig

FISH
1709 dâg (11), fish; fishes
1710 dâgâh (14), fish;
fishes
1770 dîyg (1), to catch
fish
5315 nephesh (1), life;
breath; soul; wind
2486 ichthus (5), fish
3795 ŏpsariŏn (3), small
fish

FISH'S
1710 dâgâh (1), fish;
fishes

FISHER'S
1903 ĕpĕndutēs (1), outer
garment, coat

FISHERMEN
231 haliĕus (1), one who
fishes for a living

FISHERS
1728 davvâg (2),
fisherman
1771 dayâg (1), fisherman
231 haliĕus (4), one who
fishes for a living

FISHES
1709 dâg (8), fish; fishes
2485 ichthudiŏn (2), little
fish
2486 ichthus (15), fish
3795 ŏpsariŏn (2), small
fish

FISHHOOKS
5518+1729 çîyr (1), thorn;
hook

FISHING
232 haliĕuō (1), to catch
fish

FISHPOOLS
1295 bᵉrêkâh (1),
reservoir, pool

FIST
106 'egrôph (2), clenched
hand

FISTS
2651 chôphen (1), pair of
fists

FIT
6257 'âthad (1), to
prepare
6261 'ittîy (1), timely
433 anĕkŏ (1), be proper,
fitting
2111 ĕuthĕtŏs (2),
appropriate, suitable
2520 kathēkŏ (1),
becoming, proper

FITCHES
3698 kuççemeth (1), spelt
7100 qetsach (3),
fennel-flower

FITLY
5921+655 'al (1), above,
over, upon, or against
5921+4402 'al (1), above,
over, upon, or against
4883 sunarmŏlŏgĕŏ (2),
to render close-jointed

FITTED
3474 yâshar (1), to be
straight; to make right

3559 kûwn (1), to render
sure, proper
2675 katartizŏ (1), to
repair; to prepare

FITTETH
6213 'âsâh (1), to do or
make

FIVE
2568 châmêsh (271), five
3999 pĕntakis (1), five
times
4000 pĕntakischiliŏi (16),
five times a thousand
4001 pĕntakŏsiŏi (2), five
hundred
4002 pĕntĕ (25), five

FIXED
3559 kûwn (4), to render
sure, proper
4741 stērizŏ (1), to turn
resolutely; to confirm

FLAG
260 'âchûw (1), bulrush
or any marshy grass

FLAGON
809 'ăshîyshâh (2), cake
of raisins

FLAGONS
809 'ăshîyshâh (2), cake
of raisins
5035 nebel (1), skin-bag
for liquids; vase; lyre

FLAGS
5488 çûwph (3), papyrus
reed; reed

FLAKES
4651 mappâl (1), chaff;
flap or fold of skin

FLAME
785 'êsh (Ch.) (1), fire
3632 kâlîyl (1), whole,
entire; complete; whole
3827 labbâh (1), flame
3851 lahab (6), flame of
fire; flash of a blade
3852 lehâbâh (12), flame;
flash
4864 mas'êth (2), raising;
beacon; present
7631 sᵉbîyb (Ch.) (2),
flame tongue
7957 shalhebeth (3),
flare, flame of fire
5395 phlŏx (6), flame;
blaze

FLAMES
3851 lahab (2), flame of
fire; flash of a blade
3852 lehâbâh (1), flame;
flash

FLAMING
784 'êsh (1), fire
3852 lehâbâh (5), flame;
flash
3857 lâhaṭ (1), to blaze
3858 lahaṭ (1), blaze;
magic
5395 phlŏx (1), flame;
blaze

FLANKS
3689 keçel (6), loin;
back; viscera

FLASH
965 bâzâq (1), flash of
lightning

FLAT
2763 charam (1), to *devote* to destruction
8478 tachath (2), *bottom; underneath;* in *lieu of*

FLATTER
2505 châlaq (1), to *be smooth; be slippery*
6601 pâthâh (1), to *be, make simple;* to *delude*

FLATTERETH
2505 châlaq (5), to *be smooth; be slippery*
6601 pâthâh (1), to *be, make simple;* to *delude*

FLATTERIES
2514 chălaqqâh (1), *smoothness; flattery*
2519 chălaqlaqqâh (2), *smooth; treacherous*

FLATTERING
2506 chêleq (1), *smoothness* of tongue
2509 châlâq (2), *smooth, slippery* of tongue
2513 chelqâh (2), *smoothness; flattery*
3665 kâna' (2), to *humiliate, vanquish*
2850 *kŏlakĕia* (1), *flattery*

FLATTERY
2506 chêleq (1), *smoothness* of tongue
2513 chelqâh (1), *smoothness; flattery*

FLAX
6593 pishteh (7), linen, made of *carded* thread
6594 pishtâh (3), *flax; flax wick*
3043 *linŏn* (1), flax *linen*

FLAY
6584 pâshaṭ (3), to *strip,* i.e. *unclothe, flay*

FLAYED
6584 pâshaṭ (1), to *strip,* i.e. *unclothe, flay*

FLEA
6550 par'ôsh (2), *flea*

FLED
1272 bârach (40), to *flee* suddenly
5074 nâdad (8), to *rove, flee;* to *drive* away
5127 nûwç (83), to *vanish* away, *flee*
5132 nûwts (1), to *fly* away, *leave*
1628 *ĕkphĕugō* (2), to *flee out, escape*
2703 *kataphĕugō* (2), to *flee down*
5343 *phĕugō* (11), to *run away;* to *shun*

FLEDDEST
1272 bârach (1), to *flee* suddenly
5127 nûwç (1), to *vanish* away, *flee*

FLEE
1227 Baqbûwq (1), gurgling *bottle*
1272 bârach (14), to *flee* suddenly
3680 kâçâh (1), to *cover*
4498 mânôwç (1), *fleeing;* place of *refuge*
5074 nâdad (4), to *rove, flee;* to *drive* away
5110 nûwd (1), to *waver;* to *wander, flee*
5127 nûwç (62), to *vanish* away, *flee*
5323 nâtsâ' (1), to *go away*
5756 'ûwz (1), to *save* by fleeing
7368 râchaq (1), to *recede; remove*
5343 *phĕugō* (15), to *run away;* to *shun*

FLEECE
1488 gêz (2), shorn *fleece;* mown *grass*
1492 gazzâh (7), wool *fleece*

FLEEING
4499 m^{e}nuwçâh (1), *retreat, fleeing*
5127 nûwç (1), to *vanish* away, *flee*
6207 'âraq (1), to *gnaw;* a *pain*

FLEETH
1272 bârach (1), to *flee* suddenly
5127 nûwç (4), to *vanish* away, *flee*
5211 nîyç (1), *fugitive*
5775 'ôwph (1), *bird*
5343 *phĕugō* (2), to *run away;* to *shun*

FLESH
829 'eshpâr (2), measured *portion*
1320 bâsâr (253), *flesh; body; person*
1321 b^{e}sar (Ch.) (3), *flesh; body; person*
2878 ṭibehâh (1), *butchery*
3894 lâchûwm (1), *flesh*
7607 sh^{e}'êr (7), *flesh, meat; kindred* by blood
2907 *krĕas* (2), butcher's *meat*
4561 *sarx* (143), *flesh*

FLESHHOOK
4207 mazlêg (2), three-tined meat *fork*

FLESHHOOKS
4207 mazlêg (5), three-tined meat *fork*

FLESHLY
4559 *sarkikŏs* (2), *pertaining to flesh*

FLESHY
4560 *sarkinŏs* (1), *similar to flesh*

FLEW
5774 'ûwph (1), to *cover,* to *fly;* to *faint*
6213 'âsâh (1), to *do* or *make*

FLIES
2070 z^{e}bûwb (1), stinging *fly*
6157 'ârôb (2), swarming *mosquitoes*

FLIETH
1675 dâ'âh (1), to *fly* rapidly, *soar*
5774 'ûwph (2), to *cover,* to *fly;* to *faint*
5775 'ôwph (1), *bird*

FLIGHT
1272 bârach (1), to *flee* suddenly
4498 mânôwç (1), *fleeing;* place of *refuge*
4499 m^{e}nuwçâh (1), *retreat, fleeing*
5127 nûwç (1), to *vanish* away, *flee*
7291 râdaph (1), to *run after* with hostility
5437 *phugē* (2), *escape, flight, fleeing*

FLINT
2496 challâmîysh (3), *flint, flinty rock*
6864 tsôr (2), flint-*stone knife*

FLINTY
2496 challâmîysh (1), *flint, flinty rock*

FLOATS
1702 dôb^{e}râh (1), *raft, collection of logs*

FLOCK
5739 'êder (16), *muster, flock*
6629 tsô'n (83), *flock*
4167 *pŏimnē* (4), *flock*
4168 *pŏimniŏn* (5), *flock*

FLOCKS
2835 châsîph (1), small *company, flock*
4735 miqneh (3), *stock*
4830 mir'îyth (1), *pasturage; flock*
5739 'êder (16), *muster, flock*
6251 'asht^{e}râh (4), *flock of ewes*
6629 tsô'n (54), *flock*

FLOOD
2229 zâram (1), to *gush* water, *pour forth*
2230 zerem (1), *gush* of water, *flood*
2975 y^{e}'ôr (6), Nile *River;* Tigris *River*
3999 mabbûwl (13), *deluge*
5104 nâhâr (8), *stream;* Nile; Euphrates; Tigris
5158 nachal (3), *valley, ravine;* mine *shaft*
7858 sheṭeph (3), *deluge, torrent*
2627 *kataklusmŏs* (4), *inundation, flood*
4182 *pŏlupŏikilŏs* (1), *many-sided*
4215 *pŏtamŏs* (2), *current, brook*
4216 *pŏtamŏphŏrētŏs* (1), *overwhelmed by a stream*

FLOODS
5104 nâhâr (10), *stream;* Nile; Euphrates; Tigris
5140 nâzal (3), to *drip,* or *shed* by trickling
5158 nachal (2), *valley, ravine;* mine *shaft*
7641 shibbôl (1), *stream;* ear of grain
7858 sheṭeph (1), *deluge, torrent*
4215 *pŏtamŏs* (2), *current, brook*

FLOOR
1637 gôren (10), open *area*
7136 qârâh (1), to *bring about;* to *impose*
7172 qarqa' (6), *floor* of a building or the sea
257 *halōn* (2), threshing-*floor*

FLOORS
1637 gôren (1), open *area*

FLOTES
7513 raphçôdâh (1), log *raft*

FLOUR
1217 bâtsêq (1), fermenting *dough*
5560 çôleth (52), *fine* flour
7058 qemach (4), *flour*
4585 *sĕmidalis* (1), fine wheat *flour*

FLOURISH
5006 nâ'ats (1), to *scorn*
6524 pârach (9), to *break* forth; to *bloom, flourish*
6692 tsûwts (3), to *blossom, flourish*

FLOURISHED
6524 pârach (1), to *break* forth; to *bloom, flourish*
330 *anathallō* (1), to *flourish;* to *revive*

FLOURISHETH
6692 tsûwts (2), to *blossom, flourish*

FLOURISHING
7487 ra'ănan (Ch.) (1), *prosperous*
7488 ra'ănân (1), *verdant; prosperous*

FLOW
2151 zâlal (1), to *be loose* morally, *worthless*
3212 yâlak (2), to *walk;* to *live;* to *carry*
5064 nâgar (1), to *pour* out; to *deliver* over
5102 nâhar (5), to *sparkle;* to *flow*
5140 nâzal (3), to *drip,* or *shed* by trickling
4482 *rhĕō* (1), to *flow* water

FLOWED
2151 zâlal (1), to *be loose* morally, *worthless*
3212 yâlak (1), to *walk;* to *live;* to *carry*
6687 tsûwph (1), to *overflow*

FLOWER
582 'ĕnôwsh (1), *man; person, human*
5328 nitstsâh (2), *blossom*
6525 perach (5), *calyx flower; bloom*

6731 tsîyts (6), burnished
plate; bright *flower*
6733 tsîytsâh (1), *flower*
438 anthŏs (4), flower
blossom
5230 hupĕrakmŏs (1),
past the *bloom* of youth

FLOWERS
4026 migdâl (1), *tower;
rostrum*
5079 niddâh (2), time of
menstrual *impurity;*
idolatry
5339 nitstsân (1), *blossom*
6525 perach (9), *calyx
flower; bloom*
6731 tsîyts (4), burnished
plate; bright *flower*

FLOWETH
2100 zûwb (12), to *flow*
freely, *gush*

FLOWING
2100 zûwb (9), to *flow*
freely, *gush*
5042 nâba' (1), to *gush*
forth; to *utter*
5140 nâzal (1), to *drip*, or
shed by trickling
7857 shâtaph (1), to
gush; to *inundate*

FLUTE
4953 mashrôwqîy (Ch.)
(4), musical *pipe*

FLUTTERETH
7363 râchaph (1), to
brood; to *be relaxed*

FLUX
1420 dusĕntĕria (1),
dysentery

FLY
82 'âbar (1), to *soar*
1675 dâ'âh (3), to *fly*
rapidly, *soar*
2070 zᵉbûwb (1), *fly*
3286 yâ'aph (1), to *tire*
5774 'ûwph (13), to *cover,*
to *fly;* to *faint*
5860 'îyt (1), to *swoop*
down upon; to *insult*
6524 pârach (2), to *break*
forth; to *bloom;* to *fly*
4072 pĕtŏmai (3), to *fly*

FLYING
3671 kânâph (1), *edge* or
extremity; wing
5774 'ûwph (6), to *cover,*
to *fly;* to *faint*
5775 'ôwph (2), *bird*
4072 pĕtŏmai (2), to *fly*

FOAL
1121 bên (1), *son,
descendant*
5895 'ayîr (1), young
donkey or *ass*
5207 huiŏs (1), *son*

FOALS
5895 'ayîr (1), young
donkey or *ass*

FOAM
7110 qetseph (1), *rage* or
strife

FOAMETH
875 aphrizŏ (1), to *froth*
at the mouth

876 aphrŏs (1), *froth,
foam*

FOAMING
875 aphrizŏ (1), to *froth*
at the mouth
1890 ĕpaphrizŏ (1), to
foam upon

FODDER
1098 bᵉlîyl (1), *feed,
fodder*

FOES
341 'ôyêb (2), *adversary,
enemy*
6862 tsar (2), *trouble;
opponent*
8130 sânê' (1), to *hate*
2190 ĕchthrŏs (2),
adversary

FOLD
1699 dôber (1), grazing
pasture
4356 miklâ'âh (1), sheep
or goat *pen*
5116 nâveh (3), *at home;
lovely; home*
7257 râbats (1), to
recline, repose, brood
833 aulê (1), *palace;
house; sheepfold*
1667 hĕlissŏ (1), to *coil,
roll up, or wrap*
4167 pŏimnē (1), *flock*

FOLDEN
5440 çâbak (1), to
entwine

FOLDETH
2263 châbaq (1), to *clasp*
the hands, *embrace*

FOLDING
1550 gâlîyl (2), *valve* of a
folding door
2264 chibbûq (2), *folding*

FOLDS
1448 gᵉdêrâh (3),
enclosure for flocks
4356 miklâ'âh (1), sheep
or goat *pen*
5116 nâveh (1), *at home;
lovely; home*

FOLK
3816 lᵉ'ôm (1),
community, nation
5971 'am (2), *people;
tribe; flock*

FOLLOW
310 'achar (5), *after*
935+310 bôw' (1), to *go or
come*
1692 dâbaq (1), to *cling
or adhere;* to *catch*
1961 hâyâh (3), to *exist,*
i.e. *be or become*
1961+310 hâyâh (1), to
exist, i.e. *be or become*
1980+310 hâlak (1), to
walk; live a certain way
1980+7272 hâlak (1), to
walk; live a certain way
3212+310 yâlak (8), to
walk; to *live;* to *carry*
7272 regel (3), *foot; step*
7291 râdaph (1), to *run*
after with hostility
190 akŏlŏuthĕŏ (30), to
accompany, follow

1205+3694 dĕutĕ (1),
come hither!
1377 diōkō (8), to *pursue;*
to *persecute*
1811 ĕxakŏlŏuthĕŏ (1), to
imitate, obey
1872 ĕpakŏlŏuthĕŏ (2), to
accompany, follow
2071 ĕsŏmai (1), *will be*
2517 kathĕxēs (1), *in a
sequence*
3326+5023 mĕta (1), *with,
among; after, later*
3401 mimĕŏmai (4), to
imitate, i.e. *model*
3877 parakŏlŏuthĕŏ (1),
to *attend; trace out*
4870 sunakŏlŏuthĕŏ (1),
to *follow, accompany*

FOLLOWED
310 'achar (16), *after*
1692 dâbaq (4), to *cling
or adhere;* to *catch*
1961+310 hâyâh (2), to
exist, i.e. *be or become*
1980+310 hâlak (7), to
walk; live a certain way
3112+310 Yôwyâkîyn (1),
Jehovah will establish
3212+310 yâlak (9), to
walk; to *live;* to *carry*
3318+310 yâtsâ' (1), to
go, bring out
6213 'âsâh (1), to *do or
make*
7272 regel (1), *foot; step*
7291 râdaph (2), to *run*
after with hostility
190 akŏlŏuthĕŏ (53), to
accompany, follow
1096 ginŏmai (1), to *be,
become*
1377 diōkō (2), to *pursue;*
to *persecute*
1811 ĕxakŏlŏuthĕŏ (1), to
imitate, obey
1872 ĕpakŏlŏuthĕŏ (1), to
accompany, follow
2076+3326 ĕsti (1), he
(she or it) *is*
2614 katadiōkō (1), to
search for, look for
2628 katakŏlŏuthĕŏ (2),
to *accompany closely*
4870 sunakŏlŏuthĕŏ (1),
to *follow, accompany*

FOLLOWEDST
3212+310 yâlak (1), to
walk; to *live;* to *carry*

FOLLOWERS
3402 mimētēs (7),
imitator, example
4831 summimētēs (1),
co-imitator

FOLLOWETH
310 'achar (1), *after*
935+310 bôw' (2), to *go or
come*
1692 dâbaq (1), to *cling
or adhere;* to *catch*
7291 râdaph (6), to *run*
after with hostility
190 akŏlŏuthĕŏ (5), to
accompany, follow

FOLLOWING
310 'achar (26), *after*
310+3651 'achar (1), *after*

312 'achêr (1), *other,
another, different; next*
314 'achărôwn (1), *late*
or *last; behind; western*
3212+310 yâlak (2), to
walk; to *live;* to *carry*
190 akŏlŏuthĕŏ (3), to
accompany, follow
1811 ĕxakŏlŏuthĕŏ (1), to
imitate, obey
1836 hĕxēs (1),
successive, next
1872 ĕpakŏlŏuthĕŏ (1), to
accompany, follow
1887 ĕpauriŏn (2),
to-morrow
1966 ĕpiŏusa (1), *ensuing*
2192 ĕchō (1), to *have;
hold; keep*

FOLLY
200 'ivveleth (13),
silliness, foolishness
3689 keçel (2), *loin;
back; viscera; silliness*
3690 kiçlâh (1), *trust;
silliness*
5039 nᵉbâlâh (10), moral
wickedness; crime
5529 çekel (1), *silliness;
dolts*
5531 çiklûwth (5),
silliness
8417 tohŏlâh (1), *bluster,
braggadocio,* i.e. *fatuity*
8604 tiphlâh (2), *frivolity,
foolishness*
454 anŏia (1), *stupidity;
rage*
877 aphrŏsunē (1),
senselessness

FOOD
398 'âkal (1), to *eat*
400 'ôkel (16), *food*
402 'oklâh (1), *food*
944 bûwl (1), *produce*
3899 lechem (21), *food,
bread*
3978 ma'ăkâl (5), *food,*
something to *eat*
4361 makkôleth (1),
nourishment
6718 tsayid (1), hunting
game; lunch, food
7607 shᵉ'êr (1), *flesh,
meat; kindred* by blood
1035 brōsis (1), *food;
rusting corrosion*
1304 diatribō (1), to
remain, stay
5160 trŏphē (2),
nourishment; rations

FOOL
191 ĕvîyl (11), *silly; fool*
3684 kᵉçîyl (34), *stupid*
or *silly*
5030 nâbîy' (1), *prophet;
inspired* man
5036 nâbâl (3), *stupid;
impious*
5528 çâkal (1), to *be silly*
5530 çâkâl (3), *silly*
5536 çal (1), *basket*
876 aphrŏs (6), *froth,
foam*
3474 mōrŏs (2), *heedless,*
moral *blockhead*
3912 paraphrŏnĕō (1), to
be insane

F

FOOL'S
191 'ĕvîyl (2), *silly; fool*
3684 kᵉçîyl (5), *stupid or silly*

FOOLISH
191 'ĕvîyl (6), *silly; fool*
196 'ĕvîlîy (1), *silly, foolish*
200 'ivveleth (1), *silliness, foolishness*
1198 ba'ar (1), *brutishness; stupidity*
1984 hâlal (2), *to boast*
2973 yâ'al (1), *to be or act foolish*
3684 kᵉçîyl (9), *stupid or silly*
3687 kᵉçîylûwth (1), *silliness, stupidity*
3688 kâçal (1), *silly, stupid*
5036 nâbâl (6), *stupid; impious*
5039 nᵉbâlâh (1), *moral wickedness; crime*
5528 çâkal (1), *to be silly*
5530 çâkâl (2), *silly*
6612 pᵉthîy (1), *silly, i.e. seducible*
8602 tâphêl (1), *to plaster; frivolity*
453 anŏētŏs (4), *unintelligent, senseless*
801 asunētŏs (2), *senseless, dull; wicked*
878 aphrōn (2), *ignorant; egotistic; unbelieving*
3471 mōrainō (1), *to become insipid*
3473 mōrŏlŏgia (1), *buffoonery, foolish talk*
3474 mōrŏs (7), *heedless, moral blockhead*

FOOLISHLY
200 'ivveleth (1), *silliness, foolishness*
1984 hâlal (1), *to boast*
2973 yâ'al (1), *to be or act foolish*
5034 nâbêl (1), *to wilt; to fall away; to be foolish or wicked*
5528 çâkal (5), *to be silly*
8604 tiphlâh (1), *frivolity, foolishness*
1722+877 ĕn (2), *in; during; because of*

FOOLISHNESS
200 'ivveleth (10), *silliness, foolishness*
5528 çâkal (1), *to be silly*
5531 çiklûwth (2), *silliness*
877 aphrŏsunē (1), *senselessness*
3472 mōria (5), *absurdity, foolishness*
3474 mōrŏs (1), *heedless, moral blockhead*

FOOLS
191 'ĕvîyl (7), *silly; fool*
1984 hâlal (2), *to boast*
2973 yâ'al (1), *to be or act foolish*
3684 kᵉçîyl (22), *stupid or silly*
5036 nâbâl (2), *stupid; impious*

453 anŏētŏs (1), *unintelligent, senseless*
781 asŏphŏs (1), *unwise, foolish*
878 aphrōn (2), *ignorant; egotistic; unbelieving*
3471 mōrainō (1), *to become insipid*
3474 mōrŏs (3), *heedless, moral blockhead*

FOOT
947 bûwç (2), *to trample down; oppress*
3653 kên (8), *pedestal or station of a basin*
4001 mᵉbûwçâh (1), *trampling, oppression*
4823 mirmâç (1), *abasement*
5541 çâlâh (1), *to contemn, reject*
7272 regel (61), *foot; step*
7273 raglîy (1), *footman soldier*
2662 katapatĕō (2), *to trample down; to reject*
3979 pĕzĕᵢ (1), *on foot*
4158 pŏdērēs (1), *robe reaching the ankles*
4228 pŏus (9), *foot*

FOOTBREADTH
3709+4096+7272 kaph (1), *sole of foot*

FOOTMEN
376+7273 'îysh (4), *man; male; someone*
7273 raglîy (7), *footman soldier*
7328 râz (Ch.) (1), *mystery*

FOOTSTEPS
6119 'âqêb (3), *track, footprint; rear position*
6471 pa'am (1), *time; step; occurence*

FOOTSTOOL
1916+7272 hădôm (6), *foot-stool*
3534 kebesh (1), *footstool*
5286 hupŏpŏdiŏn (1), *under the feet*
5286+3588+4228 hupŏpŏdiŏn (8), *under the feet, i.e. a foot-rest*

FORASMUCH
310 'achar (1), *after*
310+834 'achar (2), *after*
854+834 'êth (1), *with; by; at; among*
3282 ya'an (1), *because, for this reason*
3282+365 ya'an (2), *because, for this reason*
3282+834 ya'an (5), *because, for this reason*
3588 kîy (1), *for, that because*
3588+5921+3651 kîy (1), *for, that because*
3606+6903+1768 kôl (Ch.) (8), *all, any or every*
5704 'ad (1), *as far (long) as; during; while; until*
1487 ĕi (1), *if, whether, that*
1893 ĕpĕi (2), *since*

1894 ĕpĕidē (1), *when, whereas*
1895 ĕpĕidēpĕr (1), *since indeed*
5607 ōn (1), *being, existence*

FORBAD
6680 tsâvâh (1), *to constitute, enjoin*
1254 diakōluō (1), *utterly prohibit or prevent*
2967 kōluō (3), *to stop*

FORBARE
2308 châdal (3), *to desist, stop; be fat*

FORBEAR
1826 dâmam (1), *to stop, cease; to perish*
2308 châdal (15), *to desist, stop; be fat*
2820 châsak (1), *to restrain or refrain*
4900 mâshak (1), *to draw out; to be tall*
3361 mē (1), *not; lest*
4722 stĕgō (2), *to endure patiently*
5339 phĕidŏmai (1), *to abstain; treat leniently*

FORBEARANCE
463 anŏchē (2), *tolerance, clemency*

FORBEARETH
2308 châdal (1), *to desist, stop; be fat*
2310 châdêl (1), *ceasing or destitute*

FORBEARING
639 'aph (1), *nose or nostril; face; person*
3557 kûwl (1), *to maintain*
430 anĕchŏmai (2), *put up with, endure*
447 aniēmi (1), *to slacken, loosen*

FORBID
2486 châlîylâh (12), *far be it!, forbid!*
3607 kâlâ' (1), *to hold back or in; to prohibit*
2967 kōluō (9), *to stop*
3361+1096 mē (14), *not; lest*

FORBIDDEN
3808 lô' (1), *no, not*
6680 tsâvâh (1), *to constitute, enjoin*
2967 kōluō (1), *to stop*

FORBIDDETH
2967 kōluō (1), *to stop*

FORBIDDING
209 akōlutōs (1), *in an unhindered manner*
2967 kōluō (3), *to stop*

FORBORN
2308 châdal (1), *to desist, stop; be fat*

FORCE
153 'edra' (Ch.) (1), *power*
202 'ôwn (1), *ability, power; wealth*
1369 gᵉbûwrâh (1), *force; valor; victory*
1497 gâzal (1), *to rob*

2388 châzaq (1), *to fasten upon; to seize*
2394 chozqâh (2), *vehemence, harshness*
3027 yâd (2), *hand; power*
3533 kâbash (1), *to conquer, subjugate*
3581 kôach (3), *force, might; strength*
3893 lêach (1), *fresh strength, vigor*
6031 'ânâh (1), *to afflict, be afflicted*
726 harpazō (3), *to seize*
949 bᵉbaiŏs (1), *stable, certain, binding*

FORCED
662 'âphaq (1), *to abstain*
3905 lâchats (1), *to press; to distress*
5080 nâdach (1), *to push off, scattered*
6031 'ânâh (4), *to afflict, be afflicted*

FORCES
2428 chayil (14), *army; wealth; virtue; valor*
3981 ma'ămâts (1), *strength; resources*
4581 mâ'ôwz (1), *fortified place; defense*

FORCIBLE
4834 mârats (1), *to be pungent or vehement*

FORCING
4330 mîyts (1), *pressure*
5080 nâdach (1), *to push off, scattered*

FORD
4569 ma'ăbâr (1), *crossing-place*

FORDS
4569 ma'ăbâr (3), *crossing-place*

FORECAST
2803 châshab (2), *to plot; to think, regard*

FOREFATHERS
4269 prŏgŏnŏs (1), *ancestor*

FOREFRONT
4136+6440 mûwl (1), *in front of, opposite*
4136+6440 mûwl (3), *in front of, opposite*
6440 pânîym (4), *face; front*
7218 rô'sh (1), *head*
8127 shên (1), *tooth; ivory; cliff*

FOREHEAD
639 'aph (1), *nose or nostril; face; person*
1371 gibbêach (1), *bald forehead*
1372 gabbachath (3), *baldness on forehead*
4696 mêtsach (9), *forehead*
3359 mĕtōpŏn (2), *forehead*

FOREHEADS
4696 mêtsach (2), *forehead*

3359 mĕtôpŏn (6), forehead

FOREIGNER
5237 nokrîy (1), foreign; non-relative; different
8453 tôwshâb (1), temporary dweller

FOREIGNERS
5237 nokrîy (1), foreign; non-relative; different
3941 parŏikŏs (1), strange; stranger

FOREKNEW
4267 prŏginōskō (1), to know beforehand

FOREKNOW
4267 prŏginōskō (1), to know beforehand

FOREKNOWLEDGE
4268 prŏgnōsis (2), forethought

FOREMOST
7223 rî'shôwn (3), first

FOREORDAINED
4267 prŏginōskō (1), to know beforehand

FOREPART
6440 pânîym (4), face; front
4408 prōra (1), prow, i.e. forward part of a vessel

FORERUNNER
4274 prŏdrŏmŏs (1), runner ahead

FORESAW
4308 prŏŏraō (1), to notice previously

FORESEEING
4375 prŏsphilēs (1), acceptable, pleasing

FORESEETH
7200 râ'âh (2), to see

FORESHIP
4408 prōra (1), prow, i.e. forward part of a vessel

FORESKIN
6188 'ârêl (1), to refrain from using
6190 'orlâh (8), prepuce or penile foreskin

FORESKINS
6190 'orlâh (5), prepuce or penile foreskin

FOREST
3293 ya'ar (37), honey in the comb
6508 pardêç (1), park, cultivated garden area

FORESTS
2793 chôresh (1), wooded forest
3293 ya'ar (1), honey in the comb
3295 ya'ărâh (1), honey in the comb

FORETELL
4302 prŏlĕgō (1), to predict, forewarn

FORETOLD
4280 prŏĕrĕō (1), to say already, predict
4293 prŏkataggĕllō (1), to predict, foretell

FOREWARN
5263 hupŏdĕiknumi (1), to exemplify, instruct

FOREWARNED
4277 prŏĕpō (1), to say already, to predict

FORFEITED
2763 charam (1), to devote to destruction

FORGAT
5382 nâshâh (1), to forget
7911 shâkach (7), to be oblivious of, forget

FORGAVE
3722 kâphar (1), to cover; to expiate
863 aphiēmi (2), to leave; to pardon, forgive
5483 charizŏmai (4), to grant as a favor, pardon

FORGAVEST
5375 nâsâ' (2), to lift up

FORGED
2950 ţâphal (1), to impute falsely

FORGERS
2950 ţâphal (1), to impute falsely

FORGET
5382 nâshâh (2), to forget
7911 shâkach (48), to be oblivious of, forget
7913 shâkêach (2), oblivious, forgetting
1950 ĕpilanthanŏmai (2), to lose out of mind

FORGETFUL
1950 ĕpilanthanŏmai (1), to lose out of mind
1953 ĕpilēsmŏnē (1), negligence

FORGETFULNESS
5388 neshîyâh (1), oblivion

FORGETTEST
7911 shâkach (2), to be oblivious of, forget

FORGETTETH
7911 shâkach (2), to be oblivious of, forget
7913 shâkêach (1), oblivious, forgetting
1950 ĕpilanthanŏmai (1), to lose out of mind

FORGETTING
1950 ĕpilanthanŏmai (1), to lose out of mind

FORGIVE
3722 kâphar (1), to cover; to expiate
5375 nâsâ' (8), to lift up
5545 çâlach (18), to forgive
5546 çallâch (1), placable, tolerant
630 apŏluō (1), to relieve, release; to pardon
863 aphiēmi (22), to leave; to pardon, forgive
5483 charizŏmai (3), to grant as a favor, pardon

FORGIVEN
3722 kâphar (1), to cover; to expiate

5375 nâsâ' (4), to lift up
5545 çâlach (13), to forgive
630 apŏluō (1), to relieve, release; to pardon
863 aphiēmi (21), to leave; to pardon, forgive
5483 charizŏmai (2), to grant as a favor, pardon

FORGIVENESS
5547 çelîychâh (1), pardon
859 aphĕsis (6), pardon, freedom

FORGIVENESSES
5547 çelîychâh (1), pardon

FORGIVETH
5545 çâlach (1), to forgive
863 aphiēmi (1), to leave; to pardon, forgive

FORGIVING
5375 nâsâ' (2), to lift up
5483 charizŏmai (2), to grant as a favor, pardon

FORGOT
7911 shâkach (1), to be oblivious of, forget

FORGOTTEN
5382 nâshâh (1), to forget
7911 shâkach (39), to be oblivious of, forget
7913 shâkêach (1), oblivious, forgetting
1585 ĕklanthanŏmai (1), to forget
1950 ĕpilanthanŏmai (3), to lose out of mind
3024+2983 lēthē (1), forgetfulness

FORKS
7969+7053 shâlôwsh (1), three; third; thrice

FORM
3335 yâtsar (1), to form; potter; to determine
4758 mar'eh (1), appearance; vision
4941 mishpâţ (1), verdict; formal decree; justice
6440 pânîym (1), face; front
6699 tsûwrâh (2), rock; form as if pressed out
6755 tselem (Ch.) (1), idolatrous figure
7299 rêv (Ch.) (2), aspect, appearance
8389 tô'ar (1), outline, i.e. figure, appearance
8403 tabnîyth (3), model, resemblance
8414 tôhûw (2), waste, desolation, formless
3444 mŏrphē (3), shape, form; nature, character
3446 mŏrphōsis (2), appearance; semblance
5179 tupŏs (1), shape resemblance; "type"
5296 hupŏtupōsis (1), example, pattern

FORMED
2342 chûwl (5), to dance, whirl; to writhe in pain

3335 yâtsar (23), to form; potter; to determine
7169 qârats (1), to bite the lips, blink the eyes
3445 mŏrphŏō (1), to fashion, take on a form
4110 plasma (2), molded, what is formed
4111 plassō (1), to mold, i.e. shape or fabricate

FORMER
570 'emesh (1), last night
3138 yôwreh (2), autumn rain showers
3335 yâtsar (2), to form; potter; to determine
4175 môwreh (2), archer; teaching; early rain
6440 pânîym (1), face; front
6927 qadmâh (3), priority in time; before; past
6931 qadmôwnîy (2), anterior time; eastern
7223 rî'shôwn (32), first
4386 prŏtĕrŏn (2), previously
4387 prŏtĕrŏs (1), prior or previous
4413 prōtŏs (2), foremost

FORMETH
3335 yâtsar (2), to form; potter; to determine

FORMS
6699 tsûwrâh (2), rock; form as if pressed out

FORNICATION
2181 zânâh (3), to commit adultery
8457 taznûwth (1), harlotry
1608 ĕkpŏrnĕuō (1), to fornicate
4202 pŏrnĕia (24), sexual immorality
4203 pŏrnĕuō (7), to indulge unlawful lust

FORNICATIONS
8457 taznûwth (1), harlotry
4202 pŏrnĕia (2), sexual immorality

FORNICATOR
4205 pŏrnŏs (2), sexually immoral person

FORNICATORS
4205 pŏrnŏs (3), sexually immoral person

FORSAKE
2308 châdal (1), to desist, stop; be fat
5203 nâţash (7), to disperse; to abandon
5800 'âzab (45), to loosen; relinquish
7503 râphâh (2), to slacken
646+575 apŏstasia (1), defection, rebellion
1459 ĕgkatalĕipō (1), to desert, abandon

FORSAKEN
488 'almân (1), discarded, forsaken
5203 nâţash (6), to disperse; to abandon

F

5428 nâthash (1), to *tear away, be uprooted*
5800 'âzab (60), to *loosen; relinquish*
7971 shâlach (1), to *send away*
863 aphíēmi (2), to *leave; to pardon, forgive*
1459 ĕgkataléipō (4), to *desert, abandon*
2641 kataléipō (1), to *abandon*

FORSAKETH
5800 'âzab (5), to *loosen; relinquish; permit*
657 apŏtassŏmai (1), to *say adieu; to renounce*

FORSAKING
5805 'âzûwbâh (1), *desertion, forsaking*
1459 ĕgkataléipō (1), to *desert, abandon*

FORSOMUCH
2530 kathŏti (1), *as far or inasmuch as*

FORSOOK
5203 nâṭash (2), to *disperse; to abandon*
5800 'âzab (16), to *loosen; relinquish*
863 aphíēmi (4), to *leave; to pardon, forgive*
1459 ĕgkataléipō (1), to *desert, abandon*
2641 kataléipō (1), to *abandon*

FORSOOKEST
5800 'âzab (2), to *loosen; relinquish; permit*

FORSWEAR
1964 ĕpiŏrkĕō (1), to *commit perjury*

FORT
1785 dâyêq (3), *battering-tower*
4581 mâ'ôwz (1), *fortified place; defense*
4686 mâtsûwd (1), *net or capture; fastness*
4869 misgâb (1), *high refuge*

FORTH
935 bôw' (1), to *go or come*
1310 bâshal (1), to *boil up, cook; to ripen*
1319 bâsar (1), to *announce* (good news)
1518 gîyach (4), to *issue forth; to burst forth*
1645 geresh (1), *produce, yield*
1876 dâshâ' (1), to *sprout new plants*
1921 hâdar (1), to *favor or honor; to be high*
2254 châbal (2), to *writhe in labor pain*
2315 cheder (1), *apartment, chamber*
2330 chûwd (4), to *propound a riddle*
2342 chûwl (4), to *dance, whirl; to writhe* in pain
2590 chânaṭ (1), to *embalm; to ripen*

2904 ṭûwl (3), to *cast down or out, hurl*
2986 yâbal (1), to *bring*
3205 yâlad (26), to *bear young; to father a child*
3209 yillôwd (1), *born*
3318 yâtsâ' (403), to *go, bring out*
3329 yâtsîy' (1), *issue forth, i.e. offspring*
4161 môwtsâ' (11), *going forth*
4163 môwtsâ'âh (3), *family descent*
4866 mishbêr (1), *vaginal opening*
5066 nâgash (2), to *be, come, bring near*
5107 nûwb (2), to *(make) flourish; to utter*
5132 nûwts (1), to *fly away, leave*
5221 nâkâh (1), to *strike, kill*
5265 nâça' (5), *start on a journey*
5312 nᵉphaq (Ch.) (7), to *issue forth; to bring out*
5375 nâsâ' (2), to *lift up*
5414 nâthan (1), to *give*
5608 çâphar (1), to *inscribe; to enumerate*
5674 'âbar (2), to *cross over; to transition*
5975 'âmad (1), to *stand*
6213 'âsâh (10), to *do or make*
6398 pâlach (1), to *slice; to break* open; to *pierce*
6440 pânîym (1), *face; front*
6509 pârâh (1), to *bear fruit*
6556 perets (1), *break, gap*
6566 pâras (1), to *break apart, disperse, scatter*
6605 pâthach (1), to *open wide; to loosen, begin*
6631 tse'ĕtsâ' (1), *produce, children*
6779 tsâmach (4), to *sprout*
7126 qârab (1), to *approach, bring near*
7737 shâvâh (1), to *level, i.e. equalize*
7971 shâlach (27), to *send away*
8317 shârats (5), to *swarm, or abound*
8444 tôwtsâ'âh (2), *exit, boundary; deliverance*
321 anagō (3), to *lead up; to bring out; to sail*
392 anatassŏmai (1), to *arrange*
584 apŏdĕiknumi (1), to *demonstrate*
616 apŏkuĕō (1), to *bring into being*
649 apŏstĕllō (11), to *send out* on a mission
669 apŏphthĕggŏmai (1), *declare, address*
985 blastanō (1), to *yield fruit*
1032 bruō (1), to *gush, pour forth*

1080 gĕnnaō (1), to *procreate, regenerate*
1544 ĕkballō (7), to *throw out*
1554 ĕkdidōmi (2), to *lease, rent*
1584 ĕklampō (1), to *be resplendent, shine*
1599 ĕkpĕmpō (1), to *despatch, send out*
1600 ĕkpĕtannumi (1), to *extend, spread out*
1607 ĕkpŏrĕuŏmai (4), to *depart, be discharged*
1614 ĕktĕinō (17), to *stretch*
1627 ĕkphĕrō (3), to *bear out; to produce*
1631 ĕkphuō (2), to *sprout up, put forth*
1632 ĕkchĕō (1), to *pour forth; to bestow*
1731 ĕndĕiknumi (1), to *show, display*
1754 ĕnĕrgĕō (2), to *be active, efficient, work*
1804 ĕxaggĕllō (1), to *declare, proclaim*
1806 ĕxagō (1), to *lead forth, escort*
1821 ĕxapŏstĕllō (4), to *despatch, or to dismiss*
1831 ĕxĕrchŏmai (32), to *issue; to leave*
1854 ĕxō (8), *out, outside*
1901 ĕpĕktĕinŏmai (1), to *stretch oneself forward*
1907 ĕpĕchō (1), to *retain; to detain*
1911 ĕpiballō (1), to *throw upon*
2164 ĕuphŏrĕō (1), to *be fertile, produce a crop*
2564 kalĕō (1), to *call*
2592 karpŏphŏrĕō (2), to *be fertile*
2604 kataggĕlĕus (1), *proclaimer*
2609 katagō (1), to *lead down; to moor a vessel*
3004 lĕgō (1), to *say*
3318 Mĕsŏpŏtamia (2), *between the Rivers*
3855 paragō (1), to *go along or away*
3860 paradidōmi (1), to *hand over*
3908 paratithēmi (2), to *present something*
3928 parĕrchŏmai (1), to *go by; to perish*
4160 pŏiĕō (14), to *do*
4198 pŏrĕuŏmai (1), to *go, come; to travel*
4254 prŏagō (2), to *lead forward; to precede*
4261 prŏballō (1), to *push to the front, germinate*
4270 prŏgraphō (1), to *announce, prescribe*
4295 prŏkĕimai (1), to *stand forth*
4311 prŏpĕmpō (1), to *send forward*
4388 prŏtithēmai (1), to *place before, exhibit*
4393 prŏphĕrō (2), to *bear forward*

4486 rhēgnumi (1), to *break, burst forth*
5087 tithēmi (1), to *place*
5088 tiktō (9), to *produce from seed*
5319 phanĕrŏō (1), to *render apparent*
5348 phthanō (1), to *be beforehand, precede*

FORTHWITH
629 'oçparnâ' (Ch.) (1), *with diligence*
2112 ĕuthĕōs (7), *at once or soon*
2117 ĕuthus (1), *at once, immediately*
3916 parachrēma (1), *instantly, immediately*

FORTIETH
705 'arbâ'îym (4), *forty*

FORTIFIED
2388 châzaq (2), to *fasten upon; be strong*
4692 mâtsôwr (1), *siege-mound; distress*
5800 'âzab (1), to *loosen; relinquish; permit*

FORTIFY
553 'âmats (1), to *be strong; be courageous*
1219 bâtsar (2), to *be inaccessible*
2388 châzaq (1), to *fasten upon; be strong*
5800 'âzab (1), to *loosen; relinquish; permit*
6696 tsûwr (1), to *cramp, i.e. confine; to harass*

FORTRESS
4013 mibtsâr (4), *fortification; defender*
4581 mâ'ôwz (3), *fortified place; defense*
4686 mâtsûwd (6), *net or capture; fastness*
4693 mâtsôwr (2), *limit, border*

FORTRESSES
4013 mibtsâr (2), *fortification; defender*

FORTS
1785 dâyêq (3), *battering-tower*
4679 mᵉtsad (1), *stronghold*
4694 mᵉtsûwrâh (1), *rampart, fortification*
6076 'ôphel (1), *tumor; fortress*

FORTUNATUS
5415 Phŏrtŏunatŏs (2), *fortunate*

FORTY
702+7239 'arba' (2), *four*
705 'arbâ'îym (126), *forty*
5062 tĕssarakŏnta (22), *forty*
5063 tĕssarakŏntaĕtēs (2), *of forty years* of age

FORTY'S
705 'arbâ'îym (1), *forty*

FORUM
675 'Appiŏs (1), *Appius*

FORWARD
1973 hâl‍ᵉâh (5), *far away; thus far*
1980 hâlak (1), to *walk; live a certain way*
3276 yâ'al (1), to *be valuable*
4605 ma'al (2), *upward, above, overhead*
5265 nâça' (18), *start on a journey*
5921 'al (3), *above, over, upon, or against*
6440 pânîym (4), *face; front*
6584 pâshaṭ (1), to *strip, i.e. unclothe, plunder*
6924 qedem (1), *eastern; antiquity; before*
2309 thĕlō (1), to *will; to desire; to choose*
4261 prŏballō (1), to *push to the front, germinate*
4281 prŏĕrchŏmai (1), to *go onward, precede*
4311 prŏpĕmpō (1), to *send forward*
4704 spŏudazō (1), to *make effort*
4707 spŏudaiŏtĕrŏs (1), *more earnest*

FORWARDNESS
4288 prŏthumia (1), *alacrity, eagerness*
4710 spŏudē (1), *despatch; eagerness*

FOUGHT
3898 lâcham (58), to *fight a battle, i.e. consume*
6633 tsâbâ' (1), to *mass an army or servants*
75 agōnizŏmai (1), to *struggle; to contend*
2341 thēriŏmachĕō (1), to *be a beast fighter*
4170 pŏlĕmĕō (2), to *battle, make war*

FOUL
2560 châmar (1), to *ferment, foam; to glow*
7515 râphas (1), to *trample, i.e. roil water*
169 akathartŏs (2), *impure; evil*
5494 chĕimōn (1), *winter season; stormy weather*

FOULED
4833 mirpâs (1), *muddied water*

FOULEDST
7515 râphas (1), to *trample, i.e. roil water*

FOUND
2713 châqar (2), to *examine, search*
4672 mâtsâ' (267), to *find or acquire; to occur*
7912 shᵉkach (Ch.) (11), to *discover, find out*
429 anĕuriskō (1), to *find out*
1096 ginŏmai (1), to *be, become*
2147 hĕuriskō (111), to *find*
2638 katalambanō (1), to *seize; to possess*

FOUNDATION
787 'ôsh (Ch.) (1), *foundation*
3245 yâçad (15), *settle, establish a foundation*
3247 yᵉçôwd (7), *foundation*
3248 yᵉçûwdâh (5), *foundation*
4143 mûwçâd (2), *foundation*
4527 maççad (1), *foundation*
2310 thĕmĕliŏs (12), *substruction*
2311 thĕmĕliŏō (1), to *erect; to consolidate*
2602 katabŏlē (10), *conception, beginning*

FOUNDATIONS
134 'eden (1), *base, footing*
787 'ôsh (Ch.) (2), *foundation*
803 'âshûwyâh (1), *foundation*
808 'âshîysh (1), (ruined) *foundation*
3245 yâçad (4), *settle, establish a foundation*
3247 yᵉçôwd (3), *foundation*
4146 môwçâdâh (13), *foundation*
4328 mᵉyuççâdâh (1), *foundation*
4349 mâkôwn (1), *basis; place*
8356 shâthâh (1), *basis*
2310 thĕmĕliŏs (4), *substruction*

FOUNDED
3245 yâçad (8), *settle, establish a foundation*
2311 thĕmĕliŏō (2), to *erect; to consolidate*

FOUNDER
6884 tsâraph (5), to *fuse metal; to refine*

FOUNDEST
4672 mâtsâ' (1), to *find or acquire; to occur*

FOUNTAIN
953 bôwr (1), *pit hole, cistern, well*
4002 mabbûwa' (1), *fountain, water spring*
4599 ma'yân (9), *fountain; source*
4726 mâqôwr (11), *flow*
5869 'ayin (7), *eye; sight; fountain*
4077 pēgē (4), *source or supply*

FOUNTAINS
4599 ma'yân (7), *fountain; source*
5869 'ayin (4), *eye; sight; fountain*
4077 pēgē (4), *source or supply*

FOUR
702 'arba' (258), *four*
703 'arba' (Ch.) (8), *four*
5064 tĕssarĕs (43), *four*
5066 tĕtartaiŏs (1), *of the fourth day*

5067 tĕtartŏs (1), *fourth*
5070 tĕtrakischiliŏi (5), *four times a thousand*
5071 tĕtrakŏsiŏi (2), *four hundred*
5072 tĕtramēnŏn (1), *four months' time*

FOURFOLD
706 'arba'tayim (1), *fourfold*
5073 tĕtraplŏŏs (1), *quadruple, i.e. four-fold*

FOURFOOTED
5074 tĕtrapŏus (3), *quadruped*

FOURSCORE
8084 shᵉmônîym (34), *eighty; eightieth*
3589 ŏgdŏēkŏnta (2), *ten times eight*

FOURSQUARE
7243 rᵉbîy'îy (1), *fourth; fourth*
7251 râba' (8), to *be four sided, to be quadrate*
5068 tĕtragōnŏs (1), *four-cornered*

FOURTEEN
702+6240 'arba' (2), *four*
702+6246 'arba' (4), *four*
702+7657 'arba' (3), *four*
1180 dĕkatĕssarĕs (5), *fourteen*

FOURTEENTH
702+6240 'arba' (23), *four*
5065 tĕssarĕskaidĕkatŏs (2), *fourteenth*

FOURTH
702 'arba' (5), *four*
7243 rᵉbîy'îy (55), *fourth; fourth*
7244 rᵉbîy'ay (Ch.) (5), *fourth; fourth*
7253 reba' (2), *fourth part or side*
7255 rôba' (2), *quarter*
7256 ribbêa' (4), *fourth; fourth generation*
5067 tĕtartŏs (9), *fourth*

FOWL
1257 barbûr (1), *fowl*
5775 'ôwph (23), *bird*
5776 'ôwph (Ch.) (1), *bird*
5861 'ayiṭ (1), *bird of prey (poss.) hawk*
6833 tsippôwr (5), *little hopping bird*

FOWLER
3353 yâqûwsh (3), *snarer, trapper of fowl*

FOWLERS
3369 yâqôsh (1), to *ensnare, trap*

FOWLS
5775 'ôwph (36), *winged bird*
5776 'ôwph (Ch.) (1), *winged bird*
5861 'ayiṭ (3), *bird of prey (poss.) hawk*
6833 tsippôwr (1), *little hopping bird*
6853 tsᵉphar (Ch.) (3), *bird*
3732 ŏrnĕŏn (2), *bird*

4071 pĕtĕinŏn (9), *bird which flies*

FOX
7776 shûw'âl (1), *jackal*
258 alōpĕx (1), *fox*

FOXES
7776 shûw'âl (6), *jackal*
258 alōpĕx (2), *fox*

FRAGMENTS
2801 klasma (7), *piece, bit*

FRAIL
2310 châdêl (1), *ceasing or destitute*

FRAME
3335 yâtsar (1), to *form; potter; to determine*
3336 yêtser (1), *form*
3559 kûwn (1), to *set up: establish, fix, prepare*
4011 mibneh (1), *building*
5414 nâthan (1), to *give*

FRAMED
3335 yâtsar (1), to *form; potter; to determine*
3336 yêtser (1), *form*
2675 katartizō (1), to *repair; to prepare*
4883 sunarmŏlŏgĕō (1), to *render close-jointed*

FRAMETH
3335 yâtsar (1), to *form; potter; to determine*
6775 tsâmad (1), to *link, i.e. gird*

FRANKINCENSE
3828 lᵉbôwnâh (15), *frankincense*
3030 libanŏs (2), *fragrant incense resin or gum*

FRANKLY
5435 Phrugia (1), *Phrygia*

FRAUD
8496 tôk (1), *oppression*
650 apŏstĕrĕō (1), to *deprive; to despoil*

FRAY
2729 chârad (3), to *shudder; to hasten*

FRECKLED
933 bôhaq (1), *white scurf, rash*

FREE
2600 chinnâm (1), *gratis, free*
2666 châphash (1), to *loose; free from slavery*
2670 chophshîy (16), *exempt, free*
5071 nᵉdâbâh (2), *abundant gift*
5081 nâdîyb (1), *magnanimous*
5082 nᵉdîybâh (1), *nobility, i.e. reputation*
5352 nâqâh (2), to *be, make clean; to be bare*
5355 nâqîy (1), *innocent*
6362 pâṭar (1), to *burst through; to emit*
6605 pâthach (1), to *open wide; to loosen, begin*
1658 ĕlĕuthĕrŏs (20), *not a slave*

F

1659 ĕlĕuthĕrŏō (6), to *exempt, liberate*
5486 charisma (2), spiritual *endowment*

FREED
3772 kârath (1), to *cut* (off, down or asunder)
1344 dikaiŏō (1), *show* or *regard* as *innocent*

FREEDOM
2668 chuphshâh (1), *liberty* from slavery
4174 pŏlitĕia (1), *citizenship*

FREELY
2600 chinnâm (1), *gratis, free*
5071 nᵉdâbâh (2), *abundant* gift
1432 dōrĕan (6), *gratuitously, freely*
3326+3954 mĕta (1), *with, among; after, later*
3955 parrhēsiazŏmai (1), to *be confident*

FREEMAN
558 apĕlĕuthĕrŏs (1), *freedman*

FREEWILL
5069 nᵉdab (Ch.) (2), *be, give without coercion*
5071 nᵉdâbâh (15), *abundant* gift

FREEWOMAN
1658 ĕlĕuthĕrŏs (2), *not a slave*

FREQUENT
4056 pĕrissŏtĕrŏs (1), *more superabundantly*

FRESH
2319 châdâsh (1), *new, recent*
3955 lᵉshad (1), *juice; vigor;* sweet or fat *cake*
7488 ra'ănân (1), *new; prosperous*
1099 glukus (1), *sweet, fresh*

FRESHER
7375 rûwṭăphash (1), to *be rejuvenated*

FRET
2734 chârâh (4), to *blaze* up
6356 pᵉchetheth (1), mildewed garment *hole*
7107 qâtsaph (1), to *burst* out in rage
7481 râ'am (1), to *crash* thunder; to *irritate*

FRETTED
7264 râgaz (1), to *quiver*

FRETTETH
2196 zâ'aph (1), to *be angry*

FRETTING
3992 mâ'ar (3), to *be painful; destructive*

FRIED
7246 râbak (1), to *soak* bread in oil

FRIEND
157 'âhab (4), to *have affection, love*

7451 ra' (1), *bad; evil*
7453 rêa' (27), *associate;* one *close*
7462 râ'âh (1), to *associate* as a friend
7463 rê'eh (3), male *advisor*
2083 hĕtairŏs (3), *comrade, friend*
3982 pĕithō (1), to *pacify* or *conciliate*
5384 philŏs (12), *friend; friendly*

FRIENDLY
3820 lêb (2), *heart*
7489 râ'a' (1), to *make, be good for nothing*

FRIENDS
157 'âhab (8), to *have affection, love*
441 'allûwph (2), *friend,* one *familiar; chieftain*
605+7965 'ânash (1), to *be frail, feeble*
4828 mêrêa' (3), close *friend*
4962 math (1), *men*
7453 rêa' (14), *associate;* one *close*
3588+3844 hŏ (1), "the," i.e. the definite article
4674 sŏs (1), things that are *yours*
5384 philŏs (17), *friend; friendly*

FRIENDSHIP
7462 râ'âh (1), to *associate* as a friend
5373 philia (1), *fondness*

FRINGE
6734 tsîytsîth (2), *fore-lock* of hair; *tassel*

FRINGES
1434 gᵉdîl (1), *tassel; festoon*
6734 tsîytsîth (1), *fore-lock* of hair; *tassel*

FRO
235 'âzal (1), to *disappear*
7725 shûwb (1), to *turn* back; to *return*
7751 shûwṭ (8), to *travel, roam*
8264 shâqaq (1), to *seek* greedily
2831 kludōnizŏmai (1), to *fluctuate back and forth on the waves*

FROGS
6854 tsᵉphardêa' (13), *frog, leaper*
944 batrachŏs (1), *frog*

FRONT
6440 pânîym (2), *face; front*

FRONTIERS
7097 qâtseh (1), *extremity*

FRONTLETS
2903 ṭôwphâphâh (3), *sign* or *symbolic box*

FROST
2602 chănâmâl (1), *aphis* or *plant-louse*
3713 kᵉphôwr (3), *bowl;* white *frost*

7140 qerach (3), *ice; hail;* rock *crystal*

FROWARD
2019 hăphakpak (1), *very perverse, crooked*
3868 lûwz (2), to *depart;* to *be perverse*
6141 'iqqêsh (6), *distorted, warped, false*
6143 'iqqᵉshûwth (2), *perversity*
6617 pâthal (3), to *struggle;* to be *tortuous*
8419 tahpûkâh (6), *perversity* or *fraud*
4646 skŏliŏs (1), *crooked; perverse*

FROWARDLY
7726 shôwbâb (1), *apostate,* i.e. *idolatrous*

FROWARDNESS
8419 tahpûkâh (3), *perversity* or *fraud*

FROZEN
3920 lâkad (1), to *catch;* to *capture*

FRUIT
4 'êb (Ch.) (3), *green* plant
1061 bikkûwr (2), *first-fruits* of the crop
2981 yᵉbûwl (3), *produce, crop; harvest*
3206 yeled (1), *young* male
3899 lechem (1), *food, bread*
3978 ma'ăkâl (1), *food,* something to *eat*
4395 mᵉlê'âh (1), *fulfilled; abundance*
5107 nûwb (1), to *(make) flourish;* to *utter*
5108 nôwb (2), agricultural *produce*
6509 pârâh (1), to *bear* fruit
6529 pᵉrîy (106), *fruit*
7920 sᵉkal (Ch.) (1), to *be* or *act circumspect*
8270 shôr (1), umbilical cord; *strength*
8393 tᵉbûw'âh (7), *income,* i.e. *produce*
8570 tᵉnûwbâh (1), *crop, produce*
175 akarpŏs (1), *barren, unfruitful*
1081 gĕnnĕma (3), *offspring; produce*
2590 karpŏs (54), *fruit; crop*
2592 karpŏphŏrĕō (7), to *be fertile*
5052 tĕlĕsphŏrĕō (1), to *ripen* fruit
5352 phthinŏpōrinŏs (1), *autumnal*

FRUITFUL
1121+8081 bên (1), *people* of a class or kind
2233 zera' (1), *seed; fruit, plant, sowing-time*
3759 karmel (7), *planted field; garden produce*
6500 pârâ' (1), to *bear* fruit

6509 pârâh (21), to *bear* fruit
6529 pᵉrîy (2), *fruit*
2592 karpŏphŏrĕō (1), to *be fertile*
2593 karpŏphŏrŏs (1), *fruitbearing*

FRUITS
3 'êb (1), *green* plant
1061 bikkûwr (1), *first-fruits* of the crop
2173 zimrâh (1), *choice* fruit
3581 kôach (1), *force, might; strength*
4395 mᵉlê'âh (1), *fulfilled; abundance*
6529 pᵉrîy (7), *fruit*
8393 tᵉbûw'âh (6), *income,* i.e. *produce*
8570 tᵉnûwbâh (1), *crop, produce*
1081 gĕnnĕma (2), *offspring; produce*
2590 karpŏs (12), *fruit; crop*
3703 ŏpōra (1), *ripe* fruit

FRUSTRATE
656 'âphêç (1), to *cease*
114 athĕtĕō (1), to *disesteem, neutralize*

FRUSTRATETH
6565 pârar (1), to *break* up; to *violate, frustrate*

FRYING
4802 marchesheth (1), *stew-pan*

FRYINGPAN
4802 marchesheth (1), *stew*-pan

FUEL
402 'oklâh (3), *food*
3980 ma'ăkôleth (2), *fuel* for *fire*

FUGITIVE
5128 nûwa' (2), to *waver*

FUGITIVES
1280 bᵉrîyach (1), *bolt; cross-bar* of a door
4015 mibrâch (1), *refugee*
5307 nâphal (1), to *fall*
6412 pâlîyṭ (1), *refugee*

FULFIL
3615 kâlâh (1), to *complete, consume*
4390 mâlê' (7), to *fill; be* full
6213 'âsâh (2), to *do* or *make*
378 anaplĕrŏō (1), to *complete;* to *occupy*
4137 plĕrŏō (6), to *fill, make complete*
4160 pŏiĕō (2), to *make* or *do*
5055 tĕlĕō (3), to *end,* i.e. *complete, execute*

FULFILLED
1214 bâtsa' (1), to *finish;* to *stop*
3615 kâlâh (2), to *complete, consume*
4390 mâlê' (20), to *fill; be* full
5487 çûwph (Ch.) (1), to *come to an end*

6213 'âsâh (1), to do
378 anaplērŏō (1), to complete; accomplish
1096 ginŏmai (3), to be, become
1603 ĕkplērŏō (1), to accomplish, fulfill
4137 plērŏō (45), to fill, make complete
4931 suntĕlĕō (1), to complete entirely
5048 tĕlĕiŏō (2), to perfect, complete
5055 tĕlĕō (4), to end, i.e. complete, execute

FULFILLING
6213 'âsâh (1), to do or make
4138 plērōma (1), what fills; what is filled
4160 pŏiĕō (1), to do

FULL
3117 yôwm (10), day; time period
3624 kelach (1), maturity
3759 karmel (1), planted field; garden produce
4390 mâlê' (50), to fill; be full
4391 mᵉlâ' (Ch.) (1), to fill; be full
4392 mâlê' (52), full; filling; fulness; fully
4393 mᵉlô' (11), fulness
7227 rab (1), great
7235 râbâh (1), to increase
7646 sâba' (20), fill to satiety
7648 sôba' (3), satisfaction
7649 sâbêa' (2), satiated
7654 sob'âh (3), satiety
7999 shâlam (1), to be safe; be, make complete
8003 shâlêm (2), complete; friendly; safe
8537 tôm (1), completeness
8549 tâmîym (1), entire, complete; integrity
8552 tâmam (1), to complete, finish
1072 gĕmizō (1), to fill entirely
1073 gĕmō (11), to swell out, i.e. be full
1705 ĕmpiplēmi (1), to satisfy
2880 kŏrĕnnumi (1), to cram, i.e. glut or sate
3324 mĕstŏs (8), replete, full
3325 mĕstŏō (1), to intoxicate
4130 plēthō (1), to fulfill, complete
4134 plērĕs (17), replete, full, complete
4135 plērŏphŏrĕō (1), fill completely
4136 plērŏphŏria (3), full assurance
4137 plērŏō (9), to fill, make complete
4138 plērōma (1), what fills; what is filled
5046 tĕlĕiŏs (1), complete; mature

5460 phōtĕinŏs (4), well-illuminated
5526 chŏrtazō (1), to supply food until full

FULLER
1102 gnaphĕus (1), cloth-dresser

FULLER'S
3526 kâbaç (3), to wash

FULLERS'
3526 kâbaç (1), to wash

FULLY
3615 kâlâh (1), to complete, consume
4390 mâlê' (3), to fill; be full
4392 mâlê' (1), full; filling; fulness; fully
5046 nâgad (1), to announce
3877 parakŏlŏuthĕō (1), to attend; trace out
4135 plērŏphŏrĕō (3), to fill completely
4137 plērŏō (1), to fill, make complete
4845 sumplērŏō (1), to be complete, fulfill

FULNESS
4390 mâlê' (1), to fill; be full
4393 mᵉlô' (8), fulness
4395 mᵉlê'âh (1), fulfilled; abundance
7648 sôba' (1), satisfaction
7653 sib'âh (1), satiety
4138 plērōma (13), what fills; what is filled

FURBISH
4838 mâraq (1), to polish; to sharpen; to rinse

FURBISHED
4803 mâraṭ (5), to polish; to sharpen

FURIOUS
1167+2534 ba'al (1), master; owner; citizen
2534 chêmâh (4), heat; anger; poison
7108 qᵉtsaph (Ch.) (1), to become enraged

FURIOUSLY
2534 chêmâh (1), heat; anger; poison
7697 shiggâ'ôwn (1), craziness

FURLONGS
4712 stadiōn (5), length of about 200 yards

FURNACE
861 'attûwn (Ch.) (10), fire furnace
3536 kibshân (4), smelting furnace
3564 kûwr (9), smelting furnace
5948 'ăliyl (1), (poss.) crucible
8574 tannûwr (2), fire-pot
2575 kaminŏs (4), furnace

FURNACES
8574 tannûwr (2), fire-pot

FURNISH
4390 mâlê' (1), to fill; be full
6059 'ânaq (1), to collar; to fit out
6186 'ârak (1), to set in a row, i.e. arrange,
6213+3627 'âsâh (1), to do or make

FURNISHED
5375 nâsâ' (1), to lift up
6186 'ârak (1), to set in a row, i.e. arrange,
1822 ĕxartizō (1), to finish out; to equip fully
4130 plēthō (1), to fulfill, complete
4766 strōnnumi (2), strew, spread a carpet

FURNITURE
3627 kᵉlîy (7), implement, thing
3733 kar (1), saddle bag

FURROW
8525 telem (1), bank or terrace

FURROWS
1417 gᵉdûwd (1), furrow ridge
4618 ma'ănâh (1), furrow, plow path
5869 'ayin (1), eye; sight; fountain
6170 'ărûwgâh (2), parterre, kind of garden
8525 telem (3), bank or terrace

FURTHER
3148 yôwthêr (1), moreover; rest; gain
3254 yâçaph (4), to add or augment
5750 'ôwd (2), again; repeatedly; still; more
6329 pûwq (1), to issue; to furnish; to secure
1339 diïstēmi (1), to remove, intervene
2089 ĕti (6), yet, still
4206 pŏrrhō (1), forwards, at a distance

FURTHERANCE
4297 prŏkŏpē (2), progress, advancement

FURTHERED
5375 nâsâ' (1), to lift up

FURTHERMORE
637 'aph (1), also or yea; though
5750 'ôwd (1), again; repeatedly; still; more
1161 dĕ (1), but, yet; and then
1534 ĕita (1), succession, then, moreover
3063 lŏipŏn (1), remaining; finally

FURY
2528 chĕmâ' (Ch.) (2), anger
2534 chêmâh (67), heat; anger; poison
2740 chârôwn (1), burning of anger

GAAL
1603 Ga'al (9), loathing

GAASH
1608 Ga'ash (4), quaking

GABA
1387 Geba' (3), Geba

GABBAI
1373 Gabbay (1), collective

GABBATHA
1042 gabbatha (1), knoll

GABRIEL
1403 Gabrîy'êl (2), man of God
1043 Gabriēl (2), man of God

GAD
1410 Gâd (71), Gad
1045 Gad (1), Gad

GADARENES
1046 Gadarēnŏs (3), inhabitant of Gadara

GADDEST
235 'âzal (1), to disappear

GADDI
1426 Gaddîy (1), Gaddi

GADDIEL
1427 Gaddîy'êl (1), fortune of God

GADI
1424 Gâdîy (2), fortunate

GADITE
1425 Gâdîy (1), Gadite

GADITES
1425 Gâdîy (14), Gadite

GAHAM
1514 Gacham (1), flame

GAHAR
1515 Gachar (2), lurker

GAIN
1214 bâtsa' (9), to plunder; to finish; to stop
2084 zᵉban (Ch.) (1), to acquire by purchase
4242 mᵉchîyr (1), price, payment, wages
8393 tᵉbûw'âh (1), income, i.e. produce
8636 tarbîyth (1), percentage or bonus
2039 ĕrgasia (1), occupation; profit
2770 kĕrdainō (9), to gain; to spare
2771 kĕrdŏs (2), gain, profit
4122 plĕŏnĕktĕō (2), to be covetous
4200 pŏrismŏs (2), money-getting

GAINED
1214 bâtsa' (2), to plunder; to finish
1281 diapragmatĕuŏmai (1), to earn, make gain
2770 kĕrdainō (5), to gain; to spare
4160 pŏiĕō (1), to make or do
4333 prŏsĕrgazŏmai (1), to acquire besides

GAINS
2039 ĕrgasia (1), occupation; profit

G

GAINSAY
471 antěpō (1), to *refute*
or *deny*

GAINSAYERS
483 antilěgō (1), to
dispute, refuse

GAINSAYING
369 anantirrhětōs (1),
*without raising
objection*
483 antilěgō (1), to
dispute, refuse
485 antilŏgia (1),
dispute, disobedience

GAIUS
1050 Gaïŏs (5), *Gaïus*

GALAL
1559 Gâlâl (3), *great*

GALATIA
1053 Galatia (4), *Galatia*
1054 Galatikŏs (2),
relating to Galatia

GALATIANS
1052 Galatēs (2),
inhabitant of Galatia

GALBANUM
2464 chelbᵉnâh (1),
fragrant resin gum

GALEED
1567 Gal'êd (2), *heap of
testimony*

GALILAEAN
1057 Galilaiŏs (3),
belonging to Galilæa

GALILAEANS
1057 Galilaiŏs (5),
belonging to Galilæa

GALILEE
1551 Gâlîyl (6), *circle* as
a special *circuit*
1056 Galilaia (66),
heathen *circle*

GALL
4845 mᵉrêrâh (1), bitter
bile of the gall bladder
4846 mᵉrôrâh (2), bitter
bile; venom of a serpent
7219 rô'sh (9), *poisonous
plant; poison*
5521 chŏlē (2), *gall* or
bile; bitterness

GALLANT
117 'addîyr (1), *powerful;
majestic*

GALLERIES
862 'attûwq (3), *ledge* or
offset
7298 rahaṭ (1), *ringlet* of
hair

GALLERY
862 'attûwq (1), *ledge* or
offset

GALLEY
590 'ŏnîy (1), *ship; fleet* of
ships

GALLIM
1554 Gallîym (2), *springs*

GALLIO
1058 Galliōn (3), *Gallion,*
i.e. *Gallio*

GALLOWS
6086 'êts (8), *wood,*
things made of *wood*

GAMALIEL
1583 Gamliy'êl (5),
reward of God
1059 Gamaliēl (2),
reward of God

GAMMADIMS
1575 Gammâd (1),
warrior

GAMUL
1577 Gâmûwl (1),
rewarded

GAP
6556 perets (1), *break,
gap*

GAPED
6473 pâ'ar (1), to *open*
wide
6475 pâtsâh (1), to *rend,*
i.e. *open*

GAPS
6556 perets (1), *break,
gap*

GARDEN
1588 gan (39), *garden*
1593 gannâh (3), *garden,
grove*
1594 ginnâh (4), *garden,
grove*
2779 kĕpŏs (5), *garden,
grove*

GARDENER
2780 kĕpŏurŏs (1),
gardener

GARDENS
1588 gan (3), *garden*
1593 gannâh (9), *garden,
grove*

GAREB
1619 Gârêb (3), *scabby*

GARLANDS
4725 stĕmma (1), *wreath*

GARLICK
7762 shûwm (1), *garlic*

GARMENT
155 'addereth (4), *large;
splendid*
899 beged (36), *clothing;
treachery* or *pillage*
3801 kᵉthôneth (2),
garment that *covers*
3830 lᵉbûwsh (7),
garment; wife
3831 lᵉbûwsh (Ch.) (1),
garment
4055 mad (3), *vesture,
garment; carpet*
4594 ma'ăṭeh (1),
vestment, garment
7897 shîyth (1), *garment*
8008 salmâh (4), *clothing*
8071 simlâh (4), *dress,
mantle*
8162 sha'aṭnêz (1), *linen
and woolen*
8509 takrîyk (1), *wrapper*
or *robe*
1742 ĕnduma (2),
apparel, outer *robe*
2440 himatiōn (15), to
put on clothes
4158 pŏdērēs (1), *robe
reaching the ankles*
4749 stŏlē (1),
long-fitting *gown* as a
mark of dignity

GARMENTS
899 beged (69), *clothing;
treachery* or *pillage*
3801 kᵉthôneth (3),
garment that *covers*
3830 lᵉbûwsh (2),
garment; wife
3831 lᵉbûwsh (Ch.) (1),
garment
4055 mad (1), *vesture,
garment; carpet*
4060 middâh (1), *portion;
vestment; tribute*
4063 medev (2), *dress,
garment*
8008 salmâh (4), *clothing*
8071 simlâh (2), *dress,
mantle*
2067 ĕsthēsis (1), *clothing*
2440 himatiōn (15), to
put on clothes

GARMITE
1636 Garmîy (1), *strong*

GARNER
596 apŏthēkē (2),
granary, grain barn

GARNERS
214 'ôwtsâr (1),
depository
4200 mezev (1), *granary*

GARNISH
2885 kŏsmĕō (1), to
decorate; to *snuff*

GARNISHED
6823 tsâphâh (1), to
sheet over with metal
8235 shiphrâh (1),
brightness of skies
2885 kŏsmĕō (3), to
decorate; to *snuff*

GARRISON
4673 matstsâb (7), *spot;
office;* military *post*
4675 matstsâbâh (1),
military *guard*
5333 nᵉtsîyb (4), military
post; statue
5432 phrŏurĕō (1), to
post spies at gates

GARRISONS
4676 matstsêbâh (1),
column or *stone*
5333 nᵉtsîyb (5), military
post; statue

GASHMU
1654 Geshem (1), *rain
downpour*

GAT
622 'âçaph (1), to *gather,
collect*
935 bôw' (2), to *go* or
come
3212 yâlak (4), to *walk;*
to *live;* to *carry*
5927 'âlâh (7), to *ascend,
be high, mount*
6213 'âsâh (2), to *do* or
make
7392 râkab (1), to *ride*

GATAM
1609 Ga'tâm (3), *Gatam*

GATE
6607 pethach (4),
opening; door; entrance
8179 sha'ar (240),
opening, door or *gate*
8651 tᵉra' (Ch.) (1), *door*
2374 thura (1), *entrance,*
i.e. *door, gate*
4439 pulē (8), *gate*
4440 pulōn (5), *gate-way,
door-way*

GATES
1817 deleth (14), *door;
gate*
5592 çaph (2), *dish*
6607 pethach (3),
opening; door, entrance
8179 sha'ar (112),
opening, door or *gate*
4439 pulē (2), *gate*
4440 pulōn (11),
gate-way, door-way

GATH
1661 Gath (33),
wine-press or *vat*

GATH-HEPHER
1662 Gath-ha-Chêpher
(1), *wine-press of* (the)
well

GATH-RIMMON
1667 Gath-Rimmôwn (4),
wine-press of (the)
pomegranate

GATHER
103 'âgar (1), to *harvest*
622 'âçaph (36), to
gather, collect
1219 bâtsar (2), to *gather*
grapes
1413 gâdad (2), to *gash,*
slash oneself
1481 gûwr (3), to *sojourn,*
live as an alien
1716 dâgar (1), to *brood*
over; to *care for* young
2490 châlal (1), to
profane, defile
3259 yâ'ad (1), to *meet;*
to *summon;* to *direct*
3664 kânaç (5), to
collect; to *enfold*
3673 kânash (Ch.) (1), to
assemble
3950 lâqaṭ (13), to *pick*
up, *gather;* to *glean*
3953 lâqash (1), to *gather*
the *after* crop
4390 mâlê' (2), to *fill; be
full*
5619 çâqal (1), to *throw
large stones*
5756 'ûwz (3), to
strengthen
6908 qâbats (56), to
collect, assemble
6910 qᵉbûtsâh (1), *hoard,
gathering*
6950 qâhal (8), to
convoke, gather
7197 qâshash (4), to
assemble
346 anakĕphalaiŏmai
(1), to *sum up*
1996 ĕpisunagō (2), to
collect upon
4816 sullĕgō (6), to
collect, gather

4863 sunagō (11), to *gather together*
5166 trugaō (2), to *collect* the vintage

GATHERED
622 'âçaph (97), to *gather, collect*
626 'âçêphâh (1), (collect) *together*
717 'ârâh (1), to *pluck, pick fruit*
1219 bâtsar (1), to *gather* grapes
1481 gûwr (2), to *sojourn, live as an alien*
2199 zâ'aq (4), to *call out, announce*
3254 yâçaph (1), to *add or augment*
3259 yâ'ad (3), to *meet; to summon; to direct*
3664 kânaç (2), to *collect; to enfold*
3673 kânash (Ch.) (2), to *assemble*
3950 lâqaṭ (11), to *pick up, gather; to glean*
4390 mâlê' (1), to *fill; be full*
5413 nâthak (2), to *flow forth, pour out*
5596 çâphach (1), to *associate; be united*
6192 'âram (1), to *pile up*
6213 'âsâh (1), to *do or make*
6651 tsâbar (2), to *aggregate, gather*
6817 tsâ'aq (5), to *shriek; to proclaim*
6908 qâbats (57), to *collect, assemble*
6950 qâhal (19), to *convoke, gather*
6960 qâvâh (2), to *collect; to expect*
7035 qâlahh (1), to *assemble*
7197 qâshash (1), to *assemble*
7408 râkash (1), to *lay up,* i.e. *collect*
8085 shâma' (1), to *hear intelligently*
1865 ĕpathrŏizō (1), to *accumulate, increase*
1996 ĕpisunagō (4), to *collect upon*
3792 ŏchlŏpŏiĕō (1), to *raise a disturbance*
4816 sullĕgō (2), to *collect, gather*
4863 sunagō (29), to *gather together*
4867 sunathrŏizō (1), to *convene*
4896 sunĕimi (1), to *assemble, gather*
4962 sustrĕphō (1), to *collect a bundle, crowd*
5166 trugaō (1), to *collect* the vintage

GATHERER
1103 bâlaç (1), to *pinch sycamore figs*

GATHEREST
1219 bâtsar (1), to *gather* grapes

GATHERETH
103 'âgar (2), to *harvest*
622 'âçaph (4), to *gather, collect*
3664 kânaç (2), to *collect; to enfold*
3950 lâqaṭ (1), to *pick up, gather; to glean*
6908 qâbats (4), to *collect, assemble*
1996 ĕpisunagō (1), to *collect upon*
4863 sunagō (3), to *gather together*

GATHERING
625 'ôçeph (2), fruit *harvest collection*
962 bâzaz (1), to *plunder, take booty*
3349 yiqqâhâh (1), *obedience*
4723 miqveh (1), *confidence; collection*
7197 qâshash (3), to *assemble*
1997 ĕpisunagōgĕ (1), *meeting, gathering*
4822 sumbibazō (1), to *drive together*
4863 sunagō (1), to *gather together*

GATHERINGS
3048 lŏgia (1), *contribution, collection*

GAVE
935 bôw' (1), to *go, come*
1696 dâbar (3), to *speak, say; to subdue*
3052 yᵉhab (Ch.) (4), to *give*
3254 yâçaph (1), to *add or augment*
3289 yâ'ats (2), to *advise*
5414 nâthan (252), to *give*
5462 çâgar (3), to *shut up; to surrender*
7121 qârâ' (3), to *call out*
7311 rûwm (4), to *be high; to rise or raise*
7725 shûwb (1), to *turn back; to return*
7760 sûwm (4), to *put, place*
7971 shâlach (1), to *send away*
437 anthŏmŏlŏgĕŏmai (1), to *give thanks*
591 apŏdidōmi (2), to *give away*
1291 diastĕllŏmai (1), to *distinguish*
1325 didōmi (77), to *give*
1433 dōrĕŏmai (1), to *bestow gratuitously*
1502 ĕikō (1), to *be weak,* i.e. *yield*
1781 ĕntĕllŏmai (1), to *enjoin, give orders*
1788 ĕntrĕpō (1), to *respect; to confound*
1907 ĕpĕchō (1), to *retain; to detain*
1929 ĕpididōmi (2), to *give over*
2010 ĕpitrĕpō (3), *allow, permit*
2702 kataphĕrō (1), to *bear down*

2753 kĕlĕuō (1), to *order, direct*
3140 marturĕō (3), to *testify; to commend*
3860 paradidōmi (7), to *hand over*
4160 pŏiĕō (2), to *make or do*
4222 pŏtizō (5), to *furnish drink, irrigate*
4337 prŏsĕchō (3), to *pay attention to*
4823 sumbŏulĕuō (1), to *recommend, deliberate*
5483 charizŏmai (2), to *grant as a favor, pardon*

GAVEST
5414 nâthan (21), to *give*
7760 sûwm (1), to *put, place*
1325 didōmi (11), to *give*

GAY
2986 lamprŏs (1), *clear; magnificent*

GAZA
5804 'Azzâh (18), *strong*
1048 Gaza (1), *strong*

GAZATHITES
5841 'Azzâthîy (1), *Azzathite*

GAZE
7200 râ'âh (1), to *see*

GAZER
1507 Gezer (2), *portion, piece*

GAZEZ
1495 Gâzêz (2), *shearer*

GAZING
1689 ĕmblĕpō (1), to *observe; to discern*

GAZINGSTOCK
7210 rŏ'îy (1), *sight; spectacle*
2301 thĕatrizō (1), to *expose as a spectacle*

GAZITES
5841 'Azzâthîy (1), *Azzathite*

GAZZAM
1502 Gazzâm (2), *devourer*

GEBA
1387 Geba' (12), *Geba*

GEBAL
1381 Gᵉbâl (2), *mountain*

GEBER
1398 Geber (2), *(valiant) man*

GEBIM
1374 Gêbîym (1), *cisterns*

GEDALIAH
1436 Gᵉdalyâh (32), *Jehovah has become great*

GEDEON
1066 Gĕdĕōn (1), *warrior*

GEDER
1445 Geder (1), *wall or fence*

GEDERAH
1449 Gᵉdêrâh (1), *enclosure for flocks*

GEDERATHITE
1452 Gᵉdêrâthîy (1), *Gederathite*

GEDERITE
1451 Gᵉdêrîy (1), *Gederite*

GEDEROTH
1450 Gᵉdêrôwth (2), *walls*

GEDEROTHAIM
1453 Gᵉdêrôthayim (1), *double wall*

GEDOR
1446 Gᵉdôr (7), *enclosure*

GEHAZI
1522 Gêychăzîy (12), *valley of a visionary*

GELILOTH
1553 Gᵉlîylôwth (1), *circles*

GEMALLI
1582 Gᵉmalliy (1), *camel-driver*

GEMARIAH
1587 Gᵉmaryâh (5), *Jehovah has perfected*

GENDER
7250 râba' (1), to *lay down; have sex*
1080 gĕnnaō (1), to *procreate, regenerate*

GENDERED
3205 yâlad (1), to *bear young; to father a child*

GENDERETH
5674 'âbar (1), to *cross over; to transition*
1080 gĕnnaō (1), to *procreate, regenerate*

GENEALOGIES
3187 yâchas (6), to *enroll by family list*
1076 gĕnĕalŏgia (2), *genealogy, lineage*

GENEALOGY
3188 yachas (15), *family list*

GENERAL
8269 sar (1), *head person, ruler*
3831 panĕguris (1), *mass-meeting*

GENERALLY
3605 kôl (1), *all, any or every*

GENERATION
1755 dôwr (50), *dwelling*
1859 dâr (Ch.) (2), *age; generation*
1074 gĕnĕa (30), *generation; age*
1078 genesis (1), *nativity, nature*
1081 gĕnnĕma (4), *offspring; produce*
1085 gĕnŏs (1), *kin, offspring in kind*

GENERATIONS
1755 dôwr (73), *dwelling*
8435 tôwlᵉdâh (39), *family descent, family record*

G

1074 gĕnĕa (6),
generation; age

GENNESARET
1082 Gĕnnēsarĕt (3),
(poss.) *harp*-shaped

GENTILE
1672 Hĕllēn (2), *Greek
(-speaking)*

GENTILES
1471 gôwy (30), *foreign
nation; Gentiles*
1483 ĕthnikŏs (1), *as a
Gentile*
1484 ĕthnŏs (93), *race;
tribe; pagan*
1672 Hĕllēn (5), *Greek
(-speaking)*

GENTLE
1933 ĕpiĕikēs (3), *mild,
gentle*
2261 ēpiŏs (2), *affable,*
i.e. *mild or kind*

GENTLENESS
6031 'ânâh (1), to *afflict,
be afflicted*
6038 'ănâvâh (1),
modesty, clemency
1932 ĕpiĕikĕia (1),
mildness, gentleness
5544 chrēstŏtēs (1),
moral excellence

GENTLY
3814 lâ'ţ (1), *silently*

GENUBATH
1592 Gᵉnûbath (2), *theft*

GERA
1617 Gêrâ' (9), *cereal
grain*

GERAHS
1626 gêrâh (5), *measure*

GERAR
1642 Gᵉrâr (10), *rolling*
country

GERGESENES
1086 Gĕrgĕsēnŏs (1),
Gergesene

GERIZIM
1630 Gᵉrîzîym (4), *rocky*

GERSHOM
1648 Gêrᵉshôwn (14),
refugee

GERSHON
1647 Gêrᵉshôm (17),
refugee

GERSHONITE
1649 Gerᵉshunnîy (3),
Gereshonite

GERSHONITES
1649 Gerᵉshunnîy (9),
Gereshonite

GESHAM
1529 Gêyshân (1),
lumpish

GESHEM
1654 Geshem (3), *rain
downpour*

GESHUR
1650 Gᵉshûwr (8), *bridge*

GESHURI
1651 Gᵉshûwrîy (2),
Geshurite

GESHURITES
1651 Gᵉshûwrîy (5),
Geshurite

GET
776 'erets (1), *earth,
land, soil; country*
935 bôw' (8), to *go or
come*
1214 bâtsa' (1), to
plunder; to finish
1245 bâqash (1), to
search; to strive after
1980 hâlak (1), to *walk;
live a certain way*
3212 yâlak (17), to *walk;
to live; to carry*
3318 yâtsâ' (7), to *go,
bring out*
3381 yârad (9), to
descend
3513 kâbad (1), to *be
heavy, severe, dull*
3947 lâqach (5), to *take*
4422 mâlaţ (1), to *escape
as if by slipperiness*
4672 mâtsâ' (2), to *find
or acquire; to occur*
5110 nûwd (1), to *waver;
to wander, flee*
5111 nûwd (Ch.) (1), to
flee
5265 nâça' (1), *start* on a
journey
5381 nâsag (6), to *reach*
5674 'âbar (1), to *cross
over; to transition*
5927 'âlâh (18), to
ascend, be high, mount
6213 'âsâh (2), to *do or
make*
6965 qûwm (1), to *rise*
7069 qânâh (8), to *create;
to procure*
7426 râmam (1), to *rise*
7725 shûwb (1), to *turn
back; to return*
1684 ĕmbainŏ (2), to
embark; to reach
1826 ĕxĕimi (1), *leave;
escape*
1831 ĕxĕrchŏmai (3), to
issue; to leave
2147 hĕuriskō (1), to *find*
2597 katabainō (1), to
descend
4122 plĕŏnĕktĕō (1), to
be covetous
5217 hupagō (4), to
withdraw or retire

GETHER
1666 Gether (2), *Gether*

GETHSEMANE
1068 Gĕthsēmanē (2),
oil-press

GETTETH
3947 lâqach (1), to *take*
5060 nâga' (1), to *strike*
5927 'âlâh (1), to *ascend,
be high, mount*
6213 'âsâh (1), to *do or
make*
6329 pûwq (1), to *issue;
to furnish; to secure*
7069 qânâh (3), to *create;
to procure*

GETTING
6467 pô'al (1), *act or
work, deed*
7069 qânâh (1), to *create;
to procure*
7075 qinyân (1),
acquisition, purchase

GEUEL
1345 Gᵉ'ûw'êl (1),
majesty of God

GEZER
1507 Gezer (13), *portion,
piece*

GEZRITES
1511 Gizrîy (1), *Gezerite;
Girzite*

GHOST
1478 gâva' (9), to *expire,
die*
5315 nephesh (2), *life;
breath; soul; wind*
1606 ĕkpnĕŏ (3), to *expire*
1634 ĕkpsuchō (3), to
expire, die
4151 pnĕuma (92), *spirit*

GIAH
1520 Gîyach (1), *fountain*

GIANT
1368 gibbôwr (1),
powerful; great warrior
7497 râphâ' (7), *giant*

GIANTS
1368 gibbôwr (1),
powerful; great warrior
5303 nᵉphîyl (2), *bully or
tyrant*
7497 râphâ' (10), *giant*

GIBBAR
1402 Gibbâr (1), *Gibbar*

GIBBETHON
1405 Gibbᵉthôwn (6),
hilly spot

GIBEA
1388 Gib'â' (1), *hill*

GIBEAH
1390 Gib'âh (48), *hillock*

GIBEATH
1394 Gib'ath (1), *hilliness*

GIBEATHITE
1395 Gib'âthîy (1),
Gibathite

GIBEON
1391 Gib'ôwn (35), *hilly*

GIBEONITE
1393 Gib'ônîy (2),
Gibonite

GIBEONITES
1393 Gib'ônîy (6),
Gibonite

GIBLITES
1382 Giblîy (1), *Gebalite*

GIDDALTI
1437 Giddaltîy (2), *I have
made great*

GIDDEL
1435 Giddêl (4), *stout*

GIDEON
1439 Gîd'ôwn (39),
warrior

GIDEONI
1441 Gid'ônîy (5), *warlike*

GIDOM
1440 Gid'ôm (1),
desolation

GIER
7360 râchâm (2), *kind of
vulture*

GIFT
4503 minchâh (1),
tribute; offering
4976 mattân (4), *present,
gift*
4979 mâttânâh (5),
present; offering; bribe
4991 mattâth (3), *present*
5379 nissê'th (1), *present*
7810 shachad (6), to
bribe; gift
1390 dŏma (1), *present,
gift*
1394 dŏsis (1), *gift*
1431 dŏrĕa (11), *gratuity,
gift*
1434 dŏrēma (1),
bestowment, gift
1435 dŏrŏn (10),
sacrificial present
5485 charis (1),
gratitude; benefit given
5486 charisma (10),
spiritual endowment

GIFTS
814 'eshkâr (1), *gratuity,
gift; payment*
4503 minchâh (6),
tribute; offering
4864 mas'êth (1), *tribute;
reproach*
4976 mattân (1), *present,
gift*
4978 mattᵉnâ' (Ch.) (3),
present, gift
4979 mâttânâh (11),
present; offering; bribe
5078 nêdeh (1), *bounty,
reward for prostitution*
5083 nâdân (1), *present
for prostitution*
7810 shachad (4), to
bribe; gift
8641 tᵉrûwmâh (1),
tribute, present
334 anathēma (1), *votive
offering to God*
1390 dŏma (2), *present,
gift*
1435 dŏrŏn (9),
sacrificial present
3311 mĕrismŏs (1),
distribution
5486 charisma (7),
spiritual endowment

GIHON
1521 Gîychôwn (6),
stream

GILALAI
1562 Gîlălay (1), *dungy*

GILBOA
1533 Gilbôa' (8),
bubbling fountain

GILEAD
1568 Gil'âd (100), *Gilad*

GILEAD'S
1568 Gil'âd (1), *Gilad*

GILEADITE
1569 Gil'âdîy (9), *Giladite*

G

GILEADITES
1569 Gil'âdîy (4), *Giladite*

GILGAL
1537 Gilgâl (39), *wheel*

GILOH
1542 Gîlôh (2), *open*

GILONITE
1526 Gîylônîy (2), *Gilonite*

GIMZO
1579 Gimzôw (1), Gimzo

GIN
4170 môwqêsh (1), *noose*
6341 pach (2), thin metallic *sheet; net*

GINATH
1527 Gîynath (2), *Ginath*

GINNETHO
1599 Ginn^ethôwn (1), *gardener*

GINNETHON
1599 Ginn^ethôwn (2), *gardener*

GINS
4170 môwqêsh (2), *noose*

GIRD
247 'âzar (4), to *belt*
640 'âphad (1), to *fasten, gird*
2290 chăgôwr (1), *belt for the waist*
2296 châgar (16), to *gird on a belt; put on* armor
328 anazônnumi (1), to *gird, bind afresh*
2224 zônnumi (2), to *bind about*
4024 pĕrizônnumi (2), to *fasten on one's belt*

GIRDED
247 'âzar (7), to *belt*
631 'âçar (1), to *fasten;* to *join* battle
2280 châbash (1), to *wrap* firmly, *bind*
2289 chăgôwr (1), *belted around waist*
2296 châgar (18), to *gird on a belt; put on* armor
8151 shânaç (1), to *compress*
1241 diazônnumi (2), to *gird tightly, wrap*
4024 pĕrizônnumi (2), to *fasten on one's belt*

GIRDEDST
2224 zônnumi (1), to *bind about*

GIRDETH
247 'âzar (1), to *belt*
631 'âçar (1), to *fasten;* to *join* battle
2296 châgar (2), to *gird on a belt; put on* armor

GIRDING
2296 châgar (1), to *gird on a belt; put on* armor
4228 machăgôreth (1), *girdle* of sackcloth

GIRDLE
73 'abnêṭ (6), *belt*
232 'êzôwr (13), *belt; band around waist*

GIRDLE (cont.)
2290 chăgôwr (5), *belt for the waist*
2805 chêsheb (8), *belt, waistband*
4206 mâzîyach (1), leather *belt*
2223 zônĕ (5), *belt, sash*

GIRDLES
73 'abnêṭ (3), *belt*
232 'êzôwr (1), *belt; band around waist*
2289 chăgôwr (1), *belted around waist*
2223 zônĕ (1), *belt, sash*

GIRGASHITE
1622 Girgâshîy (1), *Girgashite*

GIRGASHITES
1622 Girgâshîy (5), *Girgashite*

GIRGASITE
1622 Girgâshîy (1), *Girgashite*

GIRL
3207 yaldâh (1), *young female*

GIRLS
3207 yaldâh (1), *young female*

GIRT
247 'âzar (1), to *belt*
1241 diazônnumi (1), to *gird tightly, wrap*
4024 pĕrizônnumi (2), to *fasten on one's belt*

GISPA
1658 Gishpâ' (1), *Gishpa*

GITTAH-HEPHER
1662 Gath-ha-Chêpher (1), *wine-press of* (the) *well*

GITTAIM
1664 Gittayim (2), *double wine-press*

GITTITE
1663 Gittîy (8), *Gittite*

GITTITES
1663 Gittîy (2), *Gittite*

GITTITH
1665 Gittîyth (3), *harp*

GIVE
1262 bârâh (1), to *feed*
1478 gâva' (3), to *expire, die*
1696 dâbar (1), to *speak, say;* to *subdue*
1961+413 hâyâh (1), to *exist, i.e. be or become*
3051 yâhab (24), to *give*
3052 y^ehab (Ch.) (2), to *give*
3190 yâṭab (1), to *be, make well*
4900 mâshak (1), to *draw out;* to *be tall*
4991 mattâth (2), *present*
5066 nâgash (1), to *be, come, bring near*
5414 nâthan (482), to *give*
5415 n^ethan (Ch.) (2), to *give*
5441 çôbek (1), *copse* or *thicket*

GLAD (column 3)
5534 çâkar (1), to *shut up;* to *surrender*
6213 'âsâh (1), to *do or make*
7311 rûwm (1), to *be high;* to *rise or raise*
7725 shûwb (3), to *turn back;* to *return or restore*
7760 sûwm (5), to *put, place*
7761 sûwm (Ch.) (1), to *put, place*
7999 shâlam (1), to *be safe; be, make complete*
402 anachôrĕō (1), to *retire, withdraw*
591 apŏdidōmi (8), to *give away*
1096 ginŏmai (1), to *be, become*
1239 diadidōmi (1), to *divide up, distribute*
1325 didōmi (139), to *give*
1929 ĕpididōmi (5), to *give over*
2014 ĕpiphainō (1), to *become known*
2468 isthi (1), *be thou*
3330 mĕtadidōmi (1), to *share, distribute*
3844 para (1), *from; with; besides; on account of*
3860 paradidōmi (1), to *hand over*
3930 parĕchō (1), to *hold near, i.e. to present*
3936 paristēmi (1), to *stand beside, present*
4222 pŏtizō (3), to *furnish drink, irrigate*
4342 prŏskartĕrĕō (1), to *attend;* to *adhere*
4980 schŏlazō (1), to *devote oneself wholly to*
5461 phōtizō (1), to *shine or to brighten up*
5483 charizŏmai (1), to *grant as a favor*

GIVEN
1167 ba'al (2), *master; husband; owner; citizen*
1478 gâva' (1), to *expire, die*
1576 g^emûwl (1), *act; reward, recompense*
2505 châlaq (1), to *be smooth; be slippery*
2603 chânan (1), to *implore*
3052 y^ehab (Ch.) (16), to *give*
3254 yâçaph (1), to *add or augment*
3289 yâ'ats (2), to *advise*
5221 nâkâh (3), to *strike, kill*
5301 nâphach (1), to *inflate, blow, scatter*
5375 nâsâ' (1), to *lift up*
5414 nâthan (253), to *give*
5462 çâgar (1), to *shut up;* to *surrender*
6213 'âsâh (1), to *do or make*
7760 sûwm (1), to *put, place*
7761 sûwm (Ch.) (1), to *put, place*

GLAD (column 4)
1325 didōmi (123), to *give*
1377 diōkō (1), to *pursue; to persecute*
1402 dŏulŏō (1), to *enslave*
1433 dōrĕŏmai (2), to *bestow gratuitously*
1547 ĕkgamizō (1), to *marry off* a daughter
2227 zōŏpŏiĕō (1), to *(re-) vitalize, give life*
3860 paradidōmi (2), to *hand over*
3930 parĕchō (1), to *present, afford, exhibit*
3943 parŏinŏs (2), *tippling*
4272 prŏdidōmi (1), to *give before*
4337 prŏsĕchō (1), to *pay attention to*
4369 prŏstithēmi (1), to *lay beside, repeat*
5483 charizŏmai (5), to *grant as a favor*

GIVER
1395 dŏtĕs (1), *giver*

GIVEST
5414 nâthan (7), to *give*
7971 shâlach (1), to *send away*

GIVETH
1478 gâva' (1), to *expire, die*
3052 y^ehab (Ch.) (1), to *give*
5414 nâthan (77), to *give*
5415 n^ethan (Ch.) (3), to *give*
1325 didōmi (13), to *give*
3330 mĕtadidōmi (1), to *share, distribute*
3930 parĕchō (1), to *present, afford, exhibit*
5087 tithēmi (1), to *place*
5524 chŏrēgĕō (1), to *furnish, supply, provide*

GIVING
4646 mappâch (1), *expiring, dying*
5414 nâthan (5), to *give*
632 apŏnĕmō (1), *bestow, treat with respect*
1325 didōmi (3), to *give*
1394 dŏsis (1), *gift*
3004 lĕgō (1), to *say*
3548 nŏmŏthĕsia (1), *legislation, law*
3923 parĕisphĕrō (1), to *bear in alongside*

GIZONITE
1493 Gizownîy (1), *Gizonite*

GLAD
1523 gîyl (6), *rejoice*
1528 gîyr (Ch.) (4), *lime for plaster*
2302 châdâh (1), to *rejoice, be glad*
2868 ṭ^e'êb (Ch.) (1), to *rejoice, be pleased*
2896 ṭôwb (2), *good; well*
7796 Sôwrêq (2), *vine*
7797 sûws (1), to *be bright, i.e. cheerful*
7996 Shalleketh (1), *felling* of trees

8056 sâmêach (49), *blithe* or *gleeful*
8190 Sha'ashgaz (1), *Shaashgaz*
21 agalliaō (2), to *exult*
2097 ĕuaggĕlizō (4), to *announce good news*
2165 ĕuphrainō (1), to *rejoice, be glad*
5463 chairō (14), to be *cheerful*

GLADLY
780 asmĕnōs (2), *with pleasure, gladly*
2234 hēdĕōs (3), *with pleasure, with delight*
2236 hēdista (2), *with great pleasure*

GLADNESS
1524 gîyl (1), *age, stage in life*
2304 chedvâh (1), *rejoicing, joy*
2898 ṭûwb (1), *good; goodness; gladness*
7440 rinnâh (1), *shout*
8057 simchâh (34), *blithesomeness* or *glee*
8342 sâsôwn (2), *cheerfulness; welcome*
20 agalliasis (3), *exultation, delight*
2167 ĕuphrŏsunē (1), *joyfulness, cheerfulness*
5479 chara (3), *calm delight, joy*

GLASS
7209 rᵉ'îy (1), *mirror*
2072 ĕsŏptrŏn (2), *mirror for looking into*
2734 katŏptrizŏmai (1), to *see reflected*
5193 hualinŏs (3), *pertaining to glass*
5194 hualŏs (2), *glass, crystal*

GLASSES
1549 gîllâyôwn (1), *tablet for writing; mirror*

GLEAN
3950 lâqaṭ (7), to *pick up, gather; to glean*
5953 'âlal (3), to *glean; to overdo*

GLEANED
3950 lâqaṭ (5), to *pick up, gather; to glean*
5953 'âlal (1), to *glean; to overdo*

GLEANING
3951 leqeṭ (1), *gleaning after a harvest*
5955 'ôlêlâh (4), *gleaning; gleaning-time*

GLEANINGS
3951 leqeṭ (1), *gleaning*

GLEDE
7201 râ'âh (1), bird of prey (poss. *vulture*)

GLISTERING
6320 pûwk (1), *stibium*
1823 ĕxastraptō (1), to be *radiant*

GLITTER
1300 bârâq (1), *lightning; flash of lightning*

GLITTERING
1300 bârâq (5), *lightning; flash of lightning*
3851 lahab (1), *flame of fire; flash of a blade*

GLOOMINESS
653 'ăphêlâh (2), *duskiness, darkness*

GLORIEST
1984 hâlal (1), to *shine, flash, radiate*

GLORIETH
1984 hâlal (1), to *shine, flash, radiate*
2744 kauchaŏmai (2), to *glory in, rejoice in*

GLORIFIED
1922 hădar (Ch.) (1), to *magnify, glorify*
3513 kâbad (6), to be *heavy, severe, dull; to be rich, glorious*
6286 pâ'ar (6), to *shake a tree*
1392 dŏxazō (34), to *render, esteem glorious*
1740 ĕndŏxazō (2), to *glorify*
4888 sundŏxazō (1), to *share glory with*

GLORIFIETH
3513 kâbad (1), to be *rich, glorious*

GLORIFY
3513 kâbad (7), to be *rich, glorious*
6286 pâ'ar (1), to *shake a tree*
1392 dŏxazō (17), to *render, esteem glorious*

GLORIFYING
1392 dŏxazō (3), to *render, esteem glorious*

GLORIOUS
117 'addîyr (1), *powerful; majestic*
142 'âdar (2), *magnificent; glorious*
215 'ôwr (1), to be *luminous*
1921 hâdar (1), to *favor or honor; to be high or proud*
1926 hâdâr (1), *magnificence*
1935 hôwd (1), *grandeur, majesty*
3513 kâbad (5), to be *rich, glorious*
3519 kâbôwd (11), *splendor, wealth*
3520 kᵉbûwddâh (1), *magnificence, wealth*
6643 tsᵉbîy (5), *conspicuous splendor*
8597 tiph'ârâh (3), *ornament*
1223+1391 dia (1), *through, by means of*
1391 dŏxa (6), *glory; brilliance*
1392 dŏxazō (1), to *render, esteem glorious*

1722+1391 ĕn (3), *in; during; because of*
1741 ĕndŏxŏs (2), *splendid; noble*

GLORIOUSLY
3519 kâbôwd (1), *splendor, copiousness*

GLORY
155 'addereth (1), *large; splendid*
1925 heder (1), *honor*
1926 hâdâr (7), *magnificence*
1935 hôwd (9), *grandeur, majesty*
1984 hâlal (12), to *shine, flash, radiate*
2892 ṭôhar (1), *brightness; purification*
3367 yᵉqâr (Ch.) (5), *glory, honor*
3513 kâbad (1), to be *rich, glorious*
3519 kâbôwd (155), *splendor, wealth*
6286 pâ'ar (1), to *shake a tree*
6643 tsᵉbîy (7), *conspicuous splendor*
7623 shâbach (1), to *address; to pacify*
8597 tiph'ârâh (22), *ornament*
1391 dŏxa (146), *glory; brilliance*
1392 dŏxazō (3), to *render, esteem glorious*
2620 katakauchaŏmai (1), to *exult against*
2744 kauchaŏmai (18), to *glory in, rejoice in*
2745 kauchēma (3), *boast; brag*
2746 kauchēsis (1), *boasting; bragging*
2755 kĕnŏdŏxŏs (1), *self-conceited*
2811 klĕŏs (1), *renown, credited honor*

GLORYING
2744 kauchaŏmai (1), to *glory in, rejoice in*
2745 kauchēma (2), *boast; brag*
2746 kauchēsis (1), *boasting; bragging*

GLUTTON
2151 zâlal (2), to be loose morally, *worthless*

GLUTTONOUS
5314 phagŏs (2), *glutton*

GNASH
2786 châraq (2), to *grate, grind the teeth*

GNASHED
2786 châraq (1), to *grate, grind the teeth*
1031 bruchō (1), to *grate, grind teeth*

GNASHETH
2786 châraq (2), to *grate, grind the teeth*
5149 trizō (1), to *grate the teeth in frenzy*

GNASHING
1030 brugmŏs (7), *grinding of teeth*

GNAT
2971 kōnōps (1), *stinging mosquito*

GNAW
1633 gâram (1), to *crunch the bones*

GNAWED
3145 massaŏmai (1), to *chew, gnaw*

GO
236 'ăzal (Ch.) (1), to *depart*
258 'âchad (1), to *unify, i.e. collect*
833 'âshar (2), to *go forward; guide*
935 bôw' (154), to *go, come*
1718 dâdâh (1), to *walk gently; lead*
1869 dârak (2), to *tread, trample; to walk, lead*
1946 hûwk (Ch.) (1), to *go, come*
1961 hâyâh (2), to *exist, i.e. be or become*
1980 hâlak (83), to *walk; live a certain way*
1982 hêlek (1), *wayfarer, visitor; flowing*
2498 châlaph (1), to *hasten away; to pass on*
2559 châmaq (1), to *depart, i.e. turn about*
3051 yâhab (4), to *give*
3212 yâlak (351), to *walk; to live; to carry*
3312 Yᵉphunneh (1), *he will be prepared*
3318 yâtsâ' (185), to *go, bring out*
3381 yârad (73), to *descend*
3518 kâbâh (1), to *extinguish*
4161 môwtsâ' (1), *going forth*
4609 ma'ălâh (1), *thought arising*
4994 nâ' (2), *I pray!, please!, I beg you!*
5066 nâgash (2), to be, *come, bring near*
5181 nâchath (1), to *sink, descend; to press down*
5186 nâṭâh (1), to *stretch or spread out*
5265 nâça' (7), *start on a journey*
5362 nâqaph (2), to *strike; to surround*
5437 çâbab (7), to *surround*
5472 çûwg (1), to *go back, to retreat*
5493 çûwr (4), to *turn off*
5503 çâchar (1), to *travel round; to palpitate*
5674 'âbar (51), to *cross over; to transition*
5927 'âlâh (129), to *ascend, be high, mount*
5930 'ôlâh (1), *sacrifice wholly consumed in fire*
6213 'âsâh (1), to *do*

6310 peh (1), *mouth; opening*
6485 pâqad (1), *to visit, care for, count*
6544 pâra' (1), *to absolve, begin*
6585 pâsa' (1), *to stride*
6805 tsâ'ad (1), *to pace, step regularly*
6806 tsa'ad (1), *pace or regular step*
6923 qâdam (1), *to hasten, meet*
7126 qârab (3), *to approach, bring near*
7368 râchaq (3), *to recede; remove*
7503 râphâh (4), *to slacken*
7686 shâgâh (2), *to stray, wander; to transgress*
7725 shûwb (15), *to turn back; to return*
7751 shûwṭ (1), *to travel, roam*
7847 sâṭâh (1), *to deviate from duty, go astray*
7971 shâlach (76), *to send away*
8582 tâ'âh (4), *to vacillate, reel or stray*
8637 tirgal (1), *to cause to walk*
33 agĕ (2), *to come on*
71 agō (6), *to lead; to bring, drive; to weigh*
305 anabainō (9), *to go up, rise*
565 apĕrchŏmai (25), *to go off, i.e. depart, withdraw*
630 apŏluō (13), *to relieve, release*
863 aphiēmi (1), *to leave; to pardon, forgive*
1330 diĕrchŏmai (4), *to traverse, travel through*
1524 ĕisĕimi (1), *to enter*
1525 ĕisĕrchŏmai (11), *to enter*
1607 ĕkpŏrĕuŏmai (1), *to depart, proceed, project*
1830 ĕxĕrĕunaō (1), *to explore*
1831 ĕxĕrchŏmai (14), *to issue; to leave*
1881 ĕpanistamai (2), *to stand up on, to attack*
1931 ĕpiduō (1), *to set*
1994 ĕpistrĕphō (1), *to revert, turn back to*
2064 ĕrchŏmai (2), *to go or come*
2212 zētĕō (1), *to seek*
2597 katabainō (2), *to descend*
3327 mĕtabainō (1), *to depart, move from*
3928 parĕrchŏmai (1), *to go by; to perish*
4043 pĕripatĕō (1), *to walk; to live a life*
4198 pŏrĕuŏmai (74), *to go, come; to travel*
4254 prŏagō (5), *to lead forward; to precede*
4281 prŏĕrchŏmai (2), *to go onward, precede*

4313 prŏpŏrĕuŏmai (2), *to precede*
4320 prŏsanabainō (1), *to be promoted*
4334 prŏsĕrchŏmai (1), *to come near, visit*
4782 sugkatabainō (1), *to descend with*
4905 sunĕrchŏmai (1), *to go with*
5217 hupagō (54), *to withdraw or retire*
5233 hupĕrbainō (1), *to transcend, to overreach*
5342 phĕrō (1), *to bear or carry*

GOAD
4451 malmâd (1), *ox-goad*

GOADS
1861 dorbôwn (2), *iron goad stick*

GOAT
689 'aqqôw (1), *ibex*
5795 'êz (9), *she-goat; goat's hair*
6842 tsâphîyr (3), *male goat*
8163 sâ'îyr (21), *shaggy; he-goat; goat idol*
8495 tayish (1), *buck or he-goat*

GOATH
1601 Gô'âh (1), *lowing, bellowing*

GOATS
3277 yâ'êl (3), *ibex animal*
5795 'êz (45), *she-goat; goat's hair*
6260 'attûwd (26), *he-goats; leaders*
6842 tsâphîyr (1), *he-goat*
8163 sâ'îyr (3), *shaggy; he-goat; goat idol*
8495 tayish (3), *he-goat*
2055 ĕriphiŏn (1), *goat*
2056 ĕriphŏs (3), *kid or goat*
5131 tragŏs (4), *he-goat*

GOATS'
5795 'êz (10), *she-goat; goat's hair*

GOATSKINS
122+1192 aigĕiŏs (1), *belonging to a goat*

GOB
1359 Gôb (2), *pit*

GOBLET
101 'aggân (1), *bowl*

GOD
136 'Ădônây (1), *the Lord*
401 'Ûkâl (1), *devoured*
410 'êl (217), *mighty; the Almighty*
426 'ĕlâhh (Ch.) (79), *God*
430 'ĕlôhîym (2340), *God; gods; great ones*
433 'ĕlôwahh (55), *the true God; god*
1008 Bêyth-'Êl (5), *house of God*
3068 Yᵉhôwâh (4), *Jehovah, the self-Existent or Eternal*

3069 Yᵉhôvîh (301), *Jehovah, (the) self-Existent or Eternal*
3609 Kil'âb (1), *restraint of (his) father*
4010 mablîygîyth (1), *desolation*
6697 tsûwr (2), *rock*
112 athĕŏs (1), *godless*
2312 thĕŏdidaktŏs (1), *divinely instructed*
2313 thĕŏmachĕō (1), *to resist deity*
2314 thĕŏmachŏs (1), *opponent of deity*
2315 thĕŏpnĕustŏs (1), *divinely breathed in*
2316 thĕŏs (1292), *deity; the Supreme Deity*
2318 thĕŏsĕbēs (1), *pious, devout, God-fearing*
2319 thĕŏstugēs (1), *impious, God-hating*
2962 kuriŏs (1), *supreme, controller, Mr.*
3361+1096 mē (15), *not; lest*
5377 philŏthĕŏs (1), *pious, i.e. loving God*
5537 chrēmatizō (1), *to utter an oracle*

GOD'S
410 'êl (2), *mighty; the Almighty*
430 'ĕlôhîym (7), *the true God; gods; great ones*
433 'ĕlôwahh (1), *the true God; god*
2316 thĕŏs (15), *deity; the Supreme Deity*

GOD-WARD
4136+430 mûwl (1), *in front of, opposite*
4314+2316 prŏs (2), *for; on, at; to, toward*

GODDESS
430 'ĕlôhîym (2), *god; gods; great ones*
2299 thĕa (3), *female deity, goddess*

GODHEAD
2304 thĕiŏs (1), *divinity*
2305 thĕiŏtēs (1), *divinity*
2320 thĕŏtēs (1), *divinity*

GODLINESS
2150 ĕusĕbĕia (14), *piety, religious*
2317 thĕŏsĕbĕia (1), *piety, worship of deity*

GODLY
430 'ĕlôhîym (1), *the true God; gods; great ones*
2623 châçiyd (3), *religiously pious, godly*
516+2316 axiŏs (1), *appropriately, suitable*
2152 ĕusĕbēs (1), *pious*
2153 ĕusĕbōs (2), *piously*
2316 thĕŏs (3), *deity; the Supreme Deity*
2596+2316 kata (3), *down; according to*

GODS
410 'êl (2), *mighty; the Almighty*
426 'ĕlâhh (Ch.) (14), *God*

430 'ĕlôhîym (214), *God; gods; judges, great ones*
1140 daimŏniŏn (1), *demonic being; god*
2316 thĕŏs (8), *deity; the Supreme Deity*

GOEST
935 bôw' (13), *to go or come*
1980 hâlak (5), *to walk; live a certain way*
3212 yâlak (13), *to walk; to live; to carry*
3318 yâtsâ' (7), *to go, bring out*
5927 'âlâh (1), *to ascend, be high, mount*
565 apĕrchŏmai (1), *to go off, i.e. depart*
5217 hupagō (5), *to withdraw or retire*

GOETH
732 'ârach (1), *to travel, wander*
925 bâhîyr (1), *shining, bright*
935 bôw' (14), *to go or come*
1869 dârak (1), *to tread, trample; to walk, lead*
1980 hâlak (19), *to walk; live a certain way*
3212 yâlak (2), *to walk; to live; to carry*
3318 yâtsâ' (31), *to go, bring out*
3381 yârad (5), *to descend*
3518 kâbâh (2), *to extinguish*
3996 mâbôw' (1), *entrance; sunset; west*
4609 ma'ălâh (1), *thought arising*
5186 nâṭâh (1), *to stretch or spread out*
5493 çûwr (1), *to turn off*
5648 'ăbad (Ch.) (1), *to do, work, serve*
5674 'âbar (6), *to cross over; to transition*
5927 'âlâh (1), *to ascend, be high, mount*
6437 pânâh (1), *to turn, to face*
7126 qârab (1), *to approach, bring near*
7847 sâṭâh (1), *to deviate from duty, go astray*
305 anabainō (1), *to go up, rise*
565 apĕrchŏmai (1), *to go off, i.e. depart*
1525 ĕisĕrchŏmai (1), *to enter*
1607 ĕkpŏrĕuŏmai (3), *to depart, be discharged*
2212 zētĕō (1), *to seek*
3597 hŏdŏipŏria (1), *traveling*
4198 pŏrĕuŏmai (7), *to go/come; to travel*
4254 prŏagō (2), *to lead forward; to precede*
4334 prŏsĕrchŏmai (1), *to come near, visit*
5217 hupagō (9), *to withdraw or retire*

5562 chôrĕō (1), *to pass, enter; to hold, admit*

GOG
1463 Gôwg (10), *Gog*
1136 Gōg (1), *Gog*

GOING
235 'âzal (1), *to disappear*
838 'âshshûwr (1), *step; track*
935 bôw' (7), *to go or come*
1980 hâlak (8), *to walk; live a certain way*
3212 yâlak (5), *to walk; to live; to carry*
3318 yâtsâ' (13), *to go, bring out*
3381 yârad (3), *to descend*
3996 mâbôw' (5), *entrance; sunset; west*
4161 môwtsâ' (5), *going forth*
4174 môwrâd (3), *descent, slope*
4606 mê'al (Ch.) (1), *setting of the sun*
4608 ma'âleh (9), *elevation; platform*
5362 nâqaph (1), *to strike; to surround*
5674 'âbar (2), *to cross over; to transition*
5927 'âlâh (4), *to ascend, be high, mount*
5944 'ălîyâh (2), *upper things; second-story*
6807 tse'âdâh (2), *stepping march*
7751 shûwṭ (2), *to travel, roam*
8444 tôwtsâ'âh (1), *exit, boundary; deliverance*
8582 tâ'âh (1), *to vacillate, reel or stray*
71 agō (1), *to lead; to bring, drive; to weigh*
305 anabainō (2), *to go up, rise*
565 aperchŏmai (1), *to go off, i.e. depart*
1330 dierchŏmai (1), *to traverse, travel through*
1607 ĕkpŏrĕuŏmai (1), *depart, be discharged*
2212 zētĕō (1), *to seek*
2597 katabainō (1), *to descend*
4105 planaō (1), *to roam, wander; to deceive*
4108 planŏs (1), *roving, impostor or misleader*
4198 pŏrĕuŏmai (1), *go/come; to travel*
4254 prŏagō (2), *to lead forward; to precede*
4260 prŏbainō (1), *to advance*
4281 prŏĕrchŏmai (1), *to go onward, precede*
5217 hupagō (1), *to withdraw or retire*

GOINGS
838 'âshshûwr (2), *step; track*
1979 hălîykâh (2), *walking; procession*

4161 môwtsâ' (4), *going forth*
4163 môwtsâ'âh (1), *family descent*
4570 ma'gâl (2), *circular track or camp rampart*
4703 mits'âd (1), *step; companionship*
6471 pa'am (1), *time; step; occurrence*
6806 tsa'ad (1), *pace or regular step*
8444 tôwtsâ'âh (12), *exit, boundary; deliverance*

GOLAN
1474 Gôwlân (4), *captive*

GOLD
1220 betser (2), *gold*
1222 bᵉtsar (1), *gold*
1722 dᵉhab (Ch.) (14), *gold*
2091 zâhâb (340), *gold, golden colored*
2742 chârûwts (6), *mined gold; trench*
3800 kethem (7), *pure gold*
5458 çᵉgôwr (1), *breast; gold*
6337 pâz (9), *pure gold*
5552 chrusĕŏs (3), *made of gold*
5553 chrusiŏn (9), *golden thing*
5554 chrusŏdaktuliŏs (1), *gold-ringed*
5557 chrusŏs (13), *gold; golden article*

GOLDEN
1722 dᵉhab (Ch.) (9), *gold*
2091 zâhâb (38), *gold, golden colored*
3800 kethem (1), *pure gold*
4062 madhêbâh (1), *gold making*
5552 chrusĕŏs (15), *made of gold*

GOLDSMITH
6884 tsâraph (3), *to fuse metal; to refine*

GOLDSMITH'S
6885 Tsôrᵉphîy (1), *refiner*

GOLDSMITHS
6884 tsâraph (2), *to fuse metal; to refine*

GOLGOTHA
1115 Golgŏtha (3), *skull knoll*

GOLIATH
1555 Golyath (6), *exile*

GOMER
1586 Gômer (6), *completion*

GOMORRAH
6017 'Ămôrâh (19), *(ruined) heap*
1116 Gŏmŏrrha (1), *ruined heap*

GOMORRHA
1116 Gŏmŏrrha (4), *ruined heap*

GONE
230 'âzad (Ch.) (2), *firm, assured*

235 'âzal (2), *to disappear*
369 'ayin (4), *there is no, i.e., not exist, none*
656 'âpheç (1), *to cease*
935 bôw' (10), *to go or come*
1540 gâlâh (1), *to denude; uncover*
1961 hâyâh (1), *to exist, i.e. be or become*
1980 hâlak (22), *to walk; live a certain way*
2114 zûwr (1), *to be foreign, strange*
3212 yâlak (17), *to walk; to live; to carry*
3318 yâtsâ' (31), *to go, bring out*
3381 yârad (14), *to descend*
4059 middad (1), *flight*
4161 môwtsâ' (2), *going forth*
4185 mûwsh (1), *to withdraw*
5128 nûwa' (1), *to waver*
5186 nâṭâh (1), *to stretch or spread out*
5312 nᵉphaq (Ch.) (1), *to issue forth; to bring out*
5362 nâqaph (2), *to surround or circulate*
5437 çâbab (1), *to surround*
5472 çûwg (1), *to go back, to retreat*
5493 çûwr (2), *to turn off*
5674 'âbar (16), *to cross over; to transition*
5927 'âlâh (22), *to ascend, be high, mount*
6805 tsa'ad (1), *to pace, step regularly*
7725 shûwb (2), *to turn back; to return*
7751 shûwṭ (1), *to travel, roam*
7847 sâṭâh (2), *to deviate from duty, go astray*
8582 tâ'âh (2), *to vacillate, reel or stray*
305 anabainō (2), *to go up, rise*
402 anachôrĕō (1), *to retire, withdraw*
565 aperchŏmai (4), *to go off, i.e. depart*
576 apŏbainō (1), *to disembark*
1276 diaperaō (1), *to cross over*
1330 dierchŏmai (4), *to traverse, travel through*
1339 diïstēmi (1), *to remove, intervene*
1525 ĕisĕrchŏmai (1), *to enter*
1578 ĕkklinō (1), *to shun; to decline*
1607 ĕkpŏrĕuŏmai (1), *depart, proceed, project*
1826 ĕxĕimi (1), *leave; escape*
1831 ĕxĕrchŏmai (11), *to issue; to leave*
3985 pĕirazō (1), *to endeavor, scrutinize*
4105 planaō (2), *to roam, wander*

4198 pŏrĕuŏmai (3), *to go, come; to travel*
4260 prŏbainō (1), *to advance*
4570 sbĕnnumi (1), *to extinguish, snuff out*
5055 tĕlĕō (1), *to end, i.e. complete, execute*

GOOD
1319 bâsar (7), *to announce (good news)*
1390 Gib'âh (1), *hillock*
1580 gâmal (1), *to benefit or requite; to wean*
2492 châlam (1), *to be, make plump; to dream*
2617 cheçed (1), *kindness, favor*
2623 châçîyd (1), *religiously pious, godly*
2869 ṭâb (Ch.) (1), *good*
2895 ṭowb (6), *to be good*
2896 ṭôwb (363), *good; well*
2898 ṭûwb (11), *good; goodness; beauty; gladness, welfare*
3190 yâṭab (20), *to be, make well*
3191 yᵉṭab (Ch.) (1), *to be, make well*
3276 yâ'al (1), *to be valuable*
3474 yâshar (1), *to be straight; to make right*
3788 kishrôwn (1), *success; advantage*
3966 mᵉ'ôd (3), *very, utterly*
5750 'ôwd (1), *again; repeatedly; still; more*
6743 tsâlach (1), *to push forward*
7368 râchaq (2), *to recede; remove*
7522 râtsôwn (2), *delight*
7965 shâlôwm (1), *safe; well; health, prosperity*
7999 shâlam (6), *to be safe; be, make complete*
8232 shᵉphar (Ch.) (1), *to be beautiful*
14 agathŏĕrgĕō (1), *to do good work*
15 agathŏpŏiĕō (6), *to be a well-doer*
18 agathŏs (98), *good*
515 axiŏō (1), *to deem entitled or fit, worthy*
865 aphilagathŏs (1), *hostile to virtue*
979 biŏs (1), *livelihood; property*
2095 ĕu (1), *well*
2097 ĕuaggĕlizō (2), *to announce good news*
2106 ĕudŏkĕō (1), *to think well, i.e. approve*
2107 ĕudŏkia (3), *delight, kindness, wish*
2108 ĕuĕrgĕsia (1), *beneficence*
2109 ĕuĕrgĕtĕō (1), *to be philanthropic*
2133 ĕunŏia (1), *eagerly, with a whole heart*
2140 ĕupŏiïa (1), *beneficence, doing good*

2162 *ĕuphēmia* (1), good *repute*
2163 *ĕuphēmŏs* (1), *reputable*
2425 *hikanŏs* (1), *ample; fit*
2480 *ischuō* (1), to *have* or *exercise force*
2565 *kalliĕlaiŏs* (1), *cultivated olive*
2567 *kalŏdidaskalŏs* (1), *teacher of* the *right*
2570 *kalŏs* (78), good; *beautiful; valuable*
2573 *kalōs* (3), *well*, i.e. *rightly*
2750 *kĕiria* (2), *swathe of cloth*
3112 *makran* (1), *at a distance, far away*
4851 *sumphĕrō* (1), to *collect;* to *conduce*
5358 *philagathŏs* (1), *promoter of virtue*
5542 *chrēstŏlŏgia* (1), *fair speech, plausibility*
5543 *chrēstŏs* (1), *employed*, i.e. *useful*
5544 *chrēstŏtēs* (1), moral *excellence*

GOODLIER
2896 ṭôwb (1), *good; well*

GOODLIEST
2896 ṭôwb (2), good; *well*

GOODLINESS
2617 cheçed (1), *kindness, favor*

GOODLY
117 'addîyr (1), *powerful; majestic*
145 'eder (1), *mantle; splendor*
155 'addereth (1), *large; splendid*
410 'êl (1), *mighty;* the *Almighty*
1926 hâdâr (1), *magnificence*
1935 hôwd (1), *grandeur, majesty*
2530 châmad (1), to *delight* in; *lust for*
2532 chemdâh (1), *delight*
2896 ṭôwb (11), *good; well*
4261 machmâd (1), *delightful*
4758 mar'eh (1), *appearance; vision*
6287 p^{e}'êr (1), fancy *head-dress*
6643 ts^{e}bîy (1), *conspicuous* splendor
7443 renen (1), female *ostrich*
8231 shâphar (1), to *be, make fair*
8233 shepher (1), *beauty*
2573 *kalōs* (2), *well*, i.e. *rightly*
2986 *lamprŏs* (2), *radiant; magnificent*

GOODMAN
376 'îysh (1), *man; male; someone*
3611 *ŏikĕō* (5), to *reside, inhabit, remain*

GOODNESS
2617 cheçed (12), *kindness, favor*
2896 ṭôwb (16), *good; well*
2898 ṭûwb (13), *good; goodness; beauty*
19 *agathōsunē* (4), *virtue* or *beneficence*
5543 *chrēstŏs* (1), *employed*, i.e. *useful*
5544 *chrēstŏtēs* (4), moral *excellence*

GOODNESS'
2898 ṭûwb (1), *good; goodness; beauty*

GOODS
202 'ôwn (1), *ability, power; wealth*
2428 chayil (2), *army; wealth; virtue; valor*
2896 ṭôwb (2), *good; well*
2898 ṭûwb (3), *good; goodness; beauty*
4399 m^{e}lâ'kâh (2), *work; property*
5232 n^{e}kaç (Ch.) (2), *treasure, riches*
7075 qinyân (2), *purchase, wealth*
7399 r^{e}kûwsh (12), *property*
18 *agathŏs* (2), good
3776 *ŏusia* (1), *wealth, property, possessions*
4147 *plŏutĕō* (1), to *be, become wealthy*
4632 *skĕuŏs* (2), *vessel, implement, equipment*
4674 *sŏs* (1), things that are *yours*
5223 *huparxis* (1), *property, wealth*
5224 *huparchŏnta* (7), *property* or *possessions*

GOPHER
1613 gôpher (1), (poss.) *cypress*

GORE
5055 nâgach (1), to *butt* with bull's horns

GORED
5055 nâgach (2), to *butt* with bull's horns

GORGEOUS
2986 *lamprŏs* (1), *radiant; magnificent*

GORGEOUSLY
4358 miklôwl (1), *perfection; splendidly*
1741 *ĕndŏxŏs* (1), *splendid; noble*

GOSHEN
1657 Gôshen (15), *Goshen*

GOSPEL
2097 *ĕuaggĕlizō* (24), to *announce good news*
2098 *ĕuaggĕliŏn* (73), *good message*
4283 *prŏĕuaggĕlizŏmai* (1), to *announce* glad news *in advance*

GOSPEL'S
2098 *ĕuaggĕliŏn* (3), *good message*

GOT
3318 yâtsâ' (2), to *go, bring out*
3423 yârash (1), to *inherit;* to *impoverish*
7069 qânâh (3), to *create;* to *procure*
7408 râkash (1), to *lay up*, i.e. *collect*

GOTTEN
622 'âçaph (1), to *gather, collect*
3254 yâçaph (1), to *add* or *augment*
4069 maddûwa' (1), *why?, what?*
4672 mâtsâ' (2), to *find* or *acquire;* to *occur*
5414 nâthan (1), to *give*
6213 'âsâh (8), to *do* or *make*
7069 qânâh (1), to *create;* to *procure*
7408 râkash (3), to *lay up*, i.e. *collect*
645 *apŏspaō* (1), *unsheathe; withdraw*

GOURD
7021 qîyqâyôwn (5), *gourd* plant

GOURDS
6498 paqqû'âh (1), *wild cucumber*

GOVERN
2280 châbash (1), to *wrap* firmly, *bind*
5148 nâchâh (1), to *guide*
6213 'âsâh (1), to *do*

GOVERNMENT
4475 memshâlâh (1), *rule; realm* or a *ruler*
4951 misrâh (2), *empire*
2963 *kuriŏtēs* (1), *rulers, masters*

GOVERNMENTS
2941 *kubĕrnēsis* (1), *directorship*

GOVERNOR
441 'allûwph (1), *friend,* one *familiar; chieftain*
4910 mâshal (3), to *rule*
5057 nâgîyd (3), *commander, official*
5387 nâsîy' (1), *leader;* rising *mist, fog*
5921 'al (1), *above, over, upon,* or *against*
6346 pechâh (10), *prefect, officer*
6347 pechâh (Ch.) (6), *prefect, officer*
6485 pâqad (5), to *visit, care for, count*
7989 shallîyṭ (1), *prince* or *warrior*
8269 sar (4), *head* person, *ruler*
755 *architriklinŏs* (2), *director of* the *entertainment*
1481 *ĕthnarchēs* (1), *governor of a district*
2116 *ĕuthunō* (1), to *straighten* or *level*
2230 *hēgĕmŏnĕuō* (3), to *act as ruler*
2232 *hēgĕmōn* (15), *chief* person
2233 *hēgĕŏmai* (2), to *lead*, i.e. *command*

GOVERNOR'S
2232 *hēgĕmōn* (1), *chief* person

GOVERNORS
441 'allûwph (2), *friend,* one *familiar; chieftain*
2710 châqaq (2), to *engrave;* to *enact* laws
4910 mâshal (1), to *rule*
5461 çâgân (5), *prfect* of a province
6346 pechâh (7), *prefect, officer*
8269 sar (2), *head* person, *ruler*
2232 *hēgĕmōn* (2), *chief* person
3623 *ŏikŏnŏmŏs* (1), *overseer, manager*

GOZAN
1470 Gôwzân (5), *quarry*

GRACE
2580 chên (37), *graciousness; beauty*
8467 t^{e}chinnâh (1), *gracious entreaty, supplication*
2143 *ĕuprĕpĕia* (1), *gracefulness*
5485 *charis* (127), *gratitude; benefit given*

GRACIOUS
2580 chên (2), *graciousness; beauty*
2587 channûwn (14), *gracious*
2589 channôwth (1), *supplication*
2603 chânan (11), to *implore*
5485 *charis* (1), *gratitude; benefit given*
5543 *chrēstŏs* (1), *employed*, i.e. *useful*

GRACIOUSLY
2603 chânan (3), to *implore*
2896 ṭôwb (1), *good; well*

GRAFF
1461 *ĕgkĕntrizō* (1), to *engraft*

GRAFFED
1461 *ĕgkĕntrizō* (5), to *engraft*

GRAIN
6872 ts^{e}rôwr (1), *parcel; kernel* or *particle*
2848 *kŏkkŏs* (6), *kernel*

GRANDMOTHER
3125 *mammē* (1), *grandmother*

GRANT
5414 nâthan (12), to *give*
7558 rîshyôwn (1), *permit*
1325 *didōmi* (7), to *give*
2036 *ĕpō* (1), to *speak* or *say*

GRANTED
935 bôw' (1), to *go* or *come*
5414 nâthan (9), to *give*

G

6213 'âsâh (1), to *do* or
make
1325 didōmi (3), to *give*
5483 charizŏmai (1), to
grant as a *favor*

GRAPE
1154 beçer (1),
immature, sour grapes
1155 bôçer (3),
immature, sour grapes
5563 çᵉmâdar (2), vine
blossom
6025 'ênâb (1), *grape*
cluster
6528 pereṭ (1), *stray* or
single berry

GRAPEGATHERER
1219 bâtsar (1), to *gather*
grapes

GRAPEGATHERERS
1219 bâtsar (2), to *gather*
grapes

GRAPEGLEANINGS
5955 'ôlêlâh (1),
gleaning; gleaning-time

GRAPES
891 bᵉ'ûshîym (2), *rotten
fruit*
1154 beçer (1),
immature, sour grapes
5563 çᵉmâdar (1), vine
blossom
6025 'ênâb (15), *grape*
cluster
4718 staphulē (3), *cluster
of grapes*

GRASS
1758 dûwsh (1), to
trample or *thresh*
1877 deshe' (7), *sprout;
green grass*
1883 dethe' (Ch.) (2),
sprout; green *grass*
2682 châtsîyr (17), *grass;
leek plant*
3418 yereq (1), *green*
grass or vegetation
6211 'âsh (5), *moth*
6212 'eseb (16), *grass,* or
any green, tender shoot
5528 chŏrtŏs (12),
pasture, herbage

GRASSHOPPER
697 'arbeh (1), *locust*
2284 châgâb (2), *locust*

GRASSHOPPERS
697 'arbeh (3), *locust*
1462 gôwb (2), *locust*
2284 châgâb (2), *locust*

GRATE
4345 makbêr (6), *grate,
lattice*

GRAVE
1164 bᵉ'îy (1), *prayer*
6603 pittûwach (1),
sculpture; engraving
6605 pâthach (3), to *open
wide;* to *loosen, begin*
6900 qᵉbûwrâh (4),
sepulchre
6913 qeber (19),
sepulchre
7585 shᵉ'ôwl (30), abode
of the *dead*
7845 shachath (1), *pit;
destruction*

86 ha₁dēs (1), *Hades,* i.e.
place of the dead
3419 mnēmĕiŏn (4),
place of interment
4586 sĕmnŏs (3),
honorable, noble

GRAVE'S
7585 shᵉ'ôwl (1), abode
of the *dead*

GRAVECLOTHES
2750 kĕiria (1), *swathe of
cloth*

GRAVED
6605 pâthach (2), to
loosen, plow, carve

GRAVEL
2687 châtsâts (2), *gravel,
grit*
4579 mê'âh (1), *belly*

GRAVEN
2672 châtsab (1), to *cut*
stone or *carve* wood
2710 châqaq (1), to
engrave; to *enact* laws
2790 chârash (1), to
engrave; to *plow*
2801 chârath (1), to
engrave
6456 pᵉçîyl (18), *idol*
6458 pâçal (1), to *carve,*
to *chisel*
6459 peçel (29), *idol*
6605 pâthach (2), to
loosen, plow, carve
5480 charagma (1),
mark, sculptured figure

GRAVES
6913 qeber (16),
sepulchre
3418 mnēma (1),
sepulchral monument
3419 mnēmĕiŏn (4),
place of interment

GRAVETH
2710 châqaq (1), to
engrave; to *enact* laws

GRAVING
2747 chereṭ (1), *chisel;
style* for writing
6603 pittûwach (2),
sculpture; engraving

GRAVINGS
4734 miqla'ath (1),
bas-relief sculpture

GRAVITY
4587 sĕmnŏtēs (2),
venerableness

GRAY
7872 sêybâh (5), old *age*

GRAYHEADED
7867 sîyb (2), to *become
aged,* i.e. to *grow gray*

GREASE
2459 cheleb (1), *fat;
choice* part

GREAT
410 'êl (1), *mighty;* the
Almighty
417 'elgâbîysh (3), *hail*
430 'ĕlôhîym (2), the true
God; gods; great ones
679 'atstsîyl (1), *joint of*
the hand

1004 bayith (1), *house;
temple; family, tribe*
1167 ba'al (1), *master;
husband; owner; citizen*
1241 bâqâr (1), *plowing*
ox; *herd*
1396 gâbar (2), to be
strong; to *prevail;* to
act insolently
1419 gâdôwl (413), *great*
1420 gᵉdûwlâh (3),
greatness, grandeur
1431 gâdal (33), to be
great, make great
1432 gâdêl (2), *large,
powerful*
1462 gôwb (1), *locust*
1560 gᵉlâl (Ch.) (2), *large*
stones
2030 hâreh (1), *pregnant*
2342 chûwl (1), to *dance,
whirl;* to *writhe* in pain
2750 chŏrîy (2), *burning
anger*
3244 yanshûwph (2), *bird*
3514 kôbed (1), *weight,
multitude, vehemence*
3515 kâbêd (8),
numerous; severe
3699 kâçaç (1), to
estimate, determine
3833 lâbîy' (3), *lion,
lioness*
3966 mᵉ'ôd (11), *very,
utterly*
4306 mâṭâr (1), *rain,
shower of rain*
4459 maltâ'âh (1),
grinder, molar tooth
4766 marbeh (1),
increasing; greatness
5006 nâ'ats (1), to *scorn*
6099 'âtsûwm (1),
powerful; numerous
6105 'âtsam (1), to *be,
make powerful*
6343 pachad (1), *sudden
alarm, fear*
7091 qippôwz (1),
arrow-snake
7227 rab (125), *great*
7229 rab (Ch.) (7), *great*
7230 rôb (7), *abundance*
7235 râbâh (9), to
increase
7236 rᵉbâh (Ch.) (1), to
increase
7239 ribbôw (1), *myriad,
indefinite large number*
7260 rabrab (Ch.) (8),
huge; domineering
7350 râchôwq (2),
remote, far
7451 ra' (1), *bad; evil*
7689 saggîy' (1), *mighty*
7690 saggîy' (Ch.) (3),
large
7991 shâlîysh (2), *officer;*
of the *third* rank
8514 tal'ûwbâh (1),
desiccation
1974 ĕpipŏthia (1),
intense longing
2245 hēlikŏs (2), *how
much, how great*
2425 hikanŏs (2), *ample;
fit*
3029 lian (1), very *much*

3112 makran (1), *at a
distance, far away*
3123 mallŏn (1), *in a
greater degree*
3166 mĕgalauchĕŏ (1), to
be arrogant, egotistic
3167 mĕgalĕiŏs (1), *great
things, wonderful works*
3170 mĕgalunŏ (1), to
increase or *extol*
3171 mĕgalōs (1), *much,
greatly*
3173 mĕgas (149), *great,
many*
3175 mĕgistanĕs (2),
great person
3176 mĕgistŏs (1),
greatest or *very great*
3745 hŏsŏs (6), *as much
as*
3819 palai (1), *formerly;
sometime since*
3827 pampŏlus (1), *full
many,* i.e. *immense*
4080 pēlikŏs (1), *how
much, how great*
4118 plĕistŏs (1), *largest
number* or *very large*
4183 pŏlus (60), *much,
many*
4185 pŏlutĕlēs (2),
extremely expensive
4186 pŏlutimŏs (1),
extremely valuable
4214 pŏsŏs (1), *how
much?; how much!*
5082 tēlikŏutŏs (3), *so
vast*
5118 tŏsŏutŏs (5), *such
great*
5246 hupĕrŏgkŏs (2),
insolent, boastful

GREATER
1419 gâdôwl (20), *great*
1431 gâdal (3), to be
great, make great
1980 hâlak (1), to *walk;
live a certain way*
7227 rab (4), *great*
7235 râbâh (2), to
increase
3186 mĕizŏtĕrŏs (1), *still
larger, greater*
3187 mĕizŏn (34), *larger,
greater*
4055 pĕrissŏtĕrŏs (3),
more superabundant
4119 plĕiŏn (6), *more*

GREATEST
1419 gâdôwl (9), *great*
4768 marbîyth (1),
multitude; offspring
3173 mĕgas (2), *great,
many*
3187 mĕizŏn (9), *larger,
greater*

GREATLY
3966 mᵉ'ôd (49), *very,
utterly*
7227 rab (3), *great*
7230 rôb (1), *abundance*
7690 saggîy' (Ch.) (1),
large
1568 ĕkthambĕŏ (1), to
astonish utterly
1569 ĕkthambŏs (1),
utterly astounded

GREATNESS

1971 ĕpipŏthĕō (3), *intensely crave*
3029 lian (4), *very much*
3171 mĕgalōs (1), *much, greatly*
4183 pŏlus (4), *much, many*
4970 sphŏdra (2), *high degree, much*
5479 chara (1), *calm delight, joy*

GREATNESS

1419 gâdôwl (1), *great*
1420 gᵉdûwlâh (7), *greatness, grandeur*
1433 gôdel (11), *magnitude, majesty*
4768 marbîyth (1), *multitude; offspring*
7230 rôb (9), *abundance*
7238 rᵉbûw (Ch.) (2), *increase*
3174 mĕgĕthŏs (1), *greatness*

GREAVES

4697 mitschâh (1), *shin-piece* of armor

GRECIA

3120 Yâvân (3), *effervescent*

GRECIANS

3125 Yᵉvânîy (1), *Jevanite*
1675 Hĕllēnistēs (3), *Hellenist or Greek-speaking Jew*

GREECE

3120 Yâvân (1), *effervescent*
1671 Hĕllas (1), *Hellas*

GREEDILY

8378 ta'ăvâh (1), *longing; delight*
1632 ĕkchĕō (1), *to pour forth; to bestow*

GREEDINESS

4124 plĕŏnĕxia (1), *extortion, avarice*

GREEDY

1214 bâtsa' (2), *to plunder; to finish*
3700 kâçaph (1), *to pine after; to fear*
5794+5315 'az (1), *strong, vehement, harsh*
146 aischrŏkĕrdēs (1), *sordid, greedy*
866 aphilargurŏs (1), *unavaricious*

GREEK

1672 Hĕllēn (7), *Greek (-speaking)*
1673 Hĕllēnikŏs (2), *Grecian language*
1674 Hĕllēnis (1), *Grecian woman*
1676 Hĕllēnisti (2), *Hellenistically, i.e. in the Grecian language*

GREEKS

1672 Hĕllēn (13), *Greek (-speaking)*
1674 Hĕllēnis (1), *Grecian woman*

GREEN

1877 deshe' (1), *sprout; green grass*
3387 yârôwq (1), *green plant*
3410 yarkâ' (Ch.) (1), *thigh*
3418 yereq (5), *green grass or vegetation*
3419 yârâq (1), *vegetable greens*
3768 karpaç (1), *byssus linen*
3892 lach (5), *fresh cut*
6291 pag (1), *unripe fig*
7373 râţôb (1), *moist with sap*
7488 ra'ănân (18), *verdant; new*
5200 hugrŏs (1), *fresh and moist*
5515 chlōrŏs (3), *greenish, i.e. verdant*

GREENISH

3422 yᵉraqraq (2), *yellowishness*

GREENNESS

3 'ēb (1), *green plant*

GREET

7592+7965 shâ'al (1), *to ask*
782 aspazŏmai (14), *to salute, welcome*

GREETETH

782 aspazŏmai (1), *to salute, welcome*

GREETING

5463 chairō (3), *salutation, "be well"*

GREETINGS

783 aspasmŏs (3), *greeting*

GREW

1431 gâdal (9), *to be great, make great*
1432 gâdêl (2), *large, powerful*
6509 pârâh (1), *to bear fruit*
6555 pârats (1), *to break out*
6779 tsâmach (2), *to sprout*
6780 tsemach (2), *sprout, branch*
7236 rᵉbâh (Ch.) (2), *to increase*
305 anabainō (1), *to go up, rise*
837 auxanō (6), *to grow, i.e. enlarge*
2064 ĕrchŏmai (1), *to go or come*

GREY

7872 sêybâh (1), *old age*

GREYHEADED

7872 sêybâh (1), *old age*

GREYHOUND

2223+4975 zarzîyr (1), *fleet animal* (*slender*)

GRIEF

2470 châlâh (2), *to be weak, sick, afflicted*
2483 chŏlîy (3), *malady; anxiety; calamity*

GRIEF (cont.)

3013 yâgâh (1), *to grieve; to torment*
3015 yâgôwn (2), *affliction, sorrow*
3511 kᵉ'êb (2), *suffering; adversity*
3708 ka'aç (7), *vexation, grief*
4341 mak'ôb (2), *anguish; affliction*
4786 môrâh (1), *bitterness; trouble*
6330 pûwqâh (1), *stumbling-block*
7451 ra' (1), *bad; evil*
3076 lupĕō (1), *to distress; to be sad*
3077 lupē (1), *sadness, grief*
4727 stĕnazō (1), *to sigh, murmur, pray* inaudibly

GRIEFS

2483 chŏlîy (1), *malady; anxiety; calamity*

GRIEVANCE

5999 'âmâl (1), *wearing effort; worry*

GRIEVE

109 'âdab (1), *to languish, grieve*
3013 yâgâh (1), *to grieve; to torment*
6087 'âtsab (2), *to worry, have pain or anger*
3076 lupĕō (1), *to distress; to be sad*

GRIEVED

2342 chûwl (2), *to dance, whirl; to writhe in pain*
2470 châlâh (2), *to be weak, sick, afflicted*
2556 châmêts (1), *to be fermented; be soured*
2734 chârâh (1), *to blaze up*
3512 kâ'âh (1), *to despond; to deject*
3707 kâ'aç (1), *to grieve, rage, be indignant*
3735 kârâ' (Ch.) (1), *to grieve, be anxious*
3811 lâ'âh (1), *to tire; to be, make disgusted*
4784 mârâh (1), *to rebel or resist; to provoke*
4843 mârar (1), *to be, make bitter*
5701 'âgam (1), *to be sad*
6087 'âtsab (2), *to worry, have pain or anger*
6962 qûwţ (3), *to detest*
6973 qûwts (1), *to be, make disgusted*
7114 qâtsar (1), *to curtail, cut short*
7489 râ'a' (4), *to break; to be good for nothing*
1278 diapŏnĕō (2), *to be worried*
3076 lupĕō (5), *to distress; to be sad*
4360 prŏsŏchthizō (2), *to be vexed with*
4818 sullupĕō (1), *afflict jointly, sorrow at*

GRIEVETH

3811 lâ'âh (1), *to tire; to be, make disgusted*
4843 mârar (1), *to be, make bitter*

GRIEVING

3510 kâ'ab (1), *to feel pain; to grieve; to spoil*

GRIEVOUS

2342 chûwl (2), *to dance, whirl; to writhe in pain*
2470 châlâh (4), *to be weak, sick, afflicted*
3415 yâra' (1), *to fear*
3513 kâbad (1), *to be heavy, severe, dull*
3515 kâbêd (8), *severe, difficult, stupid*
4834 mârats (1), *to be vehement; to irritate*
5493 çûwr (1), *to turn off*
6089 'etseb (1), *earthen vessel; painful toil*
6277 'âthâq (1), *impudent*
7185 qâshâh (2), *to be tough or severe*
7186 qâsheh (3), *severe*
7451 ra' (2), *bad; evil*
7489 râ'a' (2), *to break; to be good for nothing*
8463 tachălûw' (1), *malady, disease*
926 barus (3), *weighty*
1418 dus- (2), *hard, i.e. with difficulty*
3077 lupē (1), *sadness, grief*
3636 ŏknĕrŏs (1), *irksome; lazy*
4190 pŏnĕrŏs (1), *malice, wicked, bad; crime*

GRIEVOUSLY

2342 chûwl (1), *to dance, whirl; to writhe in pain*
2399 chêţ' (1), *crime or its penalty*
3513 kâbad (1), *to be heavy, severe, dull*
4604 ma'al (1), *sinful treachery*
4784 mârâh (1), *to rebel or resist; to provoke*
1171 dĕinōs (1), *terribly, i.e. excessively, fiercely*
2560 kakōs (1), *badly; wrongly; ill*

GRIEVOUSNESS

3514 kôbed (1), *weight, multitude, vehemence*
5999 'âmâl (1), *wearing effort; worry*

GRIND

2911 ţᵉchôwn (1), hand mill; millstone
2912 ţâchan (4), *to grind* flour meal
3039 likmaō (2), *to grind to powder*

GRINDERS

2912 ţâchan (1), *to grind* flour meal

GRINDING

2913 ţachănâh (1), *chewing, grinding*
229 alēthō (2), *to grind* grain

GRISLED
1261 bârôd (4), *spotted, dappled*

GROAN
584 'ânach (1), to *sigh, moan*
602 'ânaq (1), to *shriek, cry out in groaning*
5008 nâ'aq (2), to *groan*
4727 stěnazō (3), to *sigh, murmur, pray* inaudibly

GROANED
1690 ěmbrimaŏmai (1), to *blame*, to *sigh*

GROANETH
4959 sustěnazō (1), to *moan jointly*

GROANING
585 'ănâchâh (4), *sighing, moaning*
603 'ănâqâh (1), *shrieking, groaning*
5009 nᵉ'âqâh (2), *groaning*
1690 ěmbrimaŏmai (1), to *blame*, to *sigh*
4726 stěnagmŏs (1), *sigh, groan*

GROANINGS
5009 nᵉ'âqâh (2), *groaning*
4726 stěnagmŏs (1), *sigh, groan*

GROPE
1659 gâshash (2), to *feel about, grope* around
4959 mâshash (3), to *feel of*; to *grope*

GROPETH
4959 mâshash (1), to *feel of*; to *grope*

GROSS
6205 'ărâphel (2), *gloom, darkness*
3975 pachunō (2), to *fatten*; to *render callous*

GROUND
127 'ădâmâh (44), *soil; land*
776 'erets (97), *earth, land, soil; country*
2513 chelqâh (1), *smoothness; allotment*
2758 chârîysh (1), *plowing (season)*
2912 ţâchan (3), to *grind* flour meal
6083 'âphâr (1), *dust, earth, mud; clay*,
7383 rîyphâh (1), *grits* cereal
7704 sâdeh (4), *field*
68 agrŏs (1), *farmland, countryside*
1093 gě (18), *soil, region, whole earth*
1474 ědaphizō (1), to *raze, dash to the ground*
1475 ědaphŏs (1), *soil, ground*
1477 hědraiōma (1), *basis, foundation*
5476 chamai (2), *toward the ground*
5561 chōra (1), space of territory

GROUNDED
4145 mûwçâdâh (1), *foundation*
2311 thěměliŏō (2), to *erect*; to *consolidate*

GROVE
815 'êshel (1), *tamarisk* tree
842 'ăshêrâh (16), *happy; Astarte (goddess)*

GROVES
842 'ăshêrâh (24), *happy; Astarte (goddess)*

GROW
1342 gâ'âh (1), to *rise*; to *grow tall; be majestic*
1431 gâdal (2), to *be great, make great*
1711 dâgâh (1), to *become numerous*
3212 yâlak (1), to *walk*; to *live*; to *carry*
3318 yâtsâ' (1), to *go, bring out*
5599 çâphîyach (2), *self-sown crop; freshet*
5927 'âlâh (2), to *ascend, be high, mount*
6335 pûwsh (1), to *spread*; to *act proudly*
6509 pârâh (1), to *bear fruit*
6524 pârach (2), to *break forth*; to *bloom; flourish*
6779 tsâmach (9), to *sprout*
7235 râbâh (1), to *increase*
7680 sᵉgâ' (Ch.) (1), to *increase*
7685 sâgâh (1), to *enlarge, be prosperous*
7735 sûwg (1), to *hedge in, make grow*
7971 shâlach (1), to *send away*
837 auxanō (5), to *grow*, i.e. *enlarge*
1096 ginŏmai (2), to *be, become*
3373 měkunō (1), to *enlarge, grow long*
4886 sunděsmŏs (1), *ligament; control*

GROWETH
2498 châlaph (2), to *spring up*; to *change*
2583 chânâh (1), to *encamp*
3332 yâtsaq (1), to *pour out*
5599 çâphîyach (3), *self-sown crop; freshet*
5927 'âlâh (1), to *ascend, be high, mount*
6524 pârach (1), to *break forth*; to *bloom; flourish*
6779 tsâmach (1), to *sprout*
8025 shâlaph (1), to *pull out, up or off*
305 anabainō (1), to *go up, rise*
837 auxanō (1), to *grow*, i.e. *enlarge*

GROWN
648 'âphîyl (1), *unripe*
1431 gâdal (9), to *be great, make great*
5927 'âlâh (1), to *ascend, be high, mount*
6335 pûwsh (1), to *spread*; to *act proudly*
6779 tsâmach (4), to *sprout*
6965 qûwm (2), to *rise*
7236 rᵉbâh (Ch.) (3), to *increase*
837 auxanō (1), to *grow*, i.e. *enlarge*

GROWTH
3954 leqesh (2), *after crop, second crop*

GRUDGE
3885 lûwn (1), to *be obstinate*
5201 nâţar (1), to *guard*; to *cherish anger*
4727 stěnazō (1), to *sigh, murmur, pray* inaudibly

GRUDGING
1112 gŏggusmŏs (1), *grumbling*

GRUDGINGLY
1537+3077 ěk (1), *out, out of*

GUARD
2876 ţabbâch (29), *king's guard, executioner*
2877 ţabbâch (Ch.) (1), *king's guard, executioner*
4928 mishma'ath (2), *royal court; subject*
4929 mishmâr (3), *guard; deposit; usage; example*
7323 rûwts (14), to *run*
4759 stratŏpědarchěs (1), *military commander*

GUARD'S
2876 ţabbâch (1), *king's guard, executioner*

GUDGODAH
1412 Gudgôdâh (2), *cleft*

GUEST
2647 kataluō (1), to *halt for the night*

GUESTCHAMBER
2646 kataluma (2), *lodging-place*

GUESTS
7121 qârâ' (4), to *call out*
345 anakěimai (2), to *recline at a meal*

GUIDE
441 'allûwph (4), *friend, one familiar; leader*
833 'âshar (1), to *go forward; guide*
1869 dârak (1), to *tread, trample*; to *walk, lead*
3289 yâ'ats (1), to *advise*
3557 kûwl (1), to *keep in*; to *measure*
5090 nâhag (1), to *drive forth*; to *lead*
5095 nâhal (3), to *flow*; to *conduct*; to *protect*

GUIDED
5090 nâhag (1), to *drive forth*; to *lead*
5095 nâhal (2), to *flow*; to *conduct*; to *protect*
5148 nâchâh (2), to *guide*

GUIDES
3595 hŏdēgŏs (2), *conductor, guide*

GUILE
4820 mirmâh (2), *fraud*
6195 'ormâh (1), *trickery; discretion*
7423 rᵉmîyâh (1), *remissness; treachery*
1388 dŏlŏs (7), *wile, deceit, trickery*

GUILTINESS
817 'âshâm (1), *guilt; fault; sin-offering*

GUILTLESS
5352 nâqâh (5), to *be, make clean*; to *be bare*
5355 nâqîy (4), *innocent*
338 anaitiŏs (1), *innocent*

GUILTY
816 'âsham (16), to *be guilty*; to *be punished*
7563 râshâ' (1), *morally wrong; bad person*
1777 ěnŏchŏs (4), *liable*
3784 ŏphěilō (1), to *owe*; to *be under obligation*
5267 hupŏdikŏs (1), *under sentence*

GULF
5490 chasma (1), *chasm or vacancy*

GUNI
1476 Gûwnîy (4), *protected*

GUNITES
1477 Gûwnîy (1), *Gunite*

GUR
1483 Gûwr (1), *cub*

GUR-BAAL
1485 Gûwr-Ba'al (1), *dwelling of Baal*

GUSH
5140 nâzal (1), to *drip, or shed* by trickling

GUSHED
2100 zûwb (3), to *flow freely, gush*
8210 shâphak (1), to *spill forth*; to *expend*
1632 ěkchěō (1), to *pour forth*; to *bestow*

GUTTER
6794 tsinnûwr (1), *culvert, water-shaft*

5148 nâchâh (4), to *guide*
7101 qâtsîyn (1), *magistrate, leader*
2720 katěuthunō (1), to *direct, lead, direct*
3594 hŏdēgěō (2), to *show the way, guide*
3595 hŏdēgŏs (2), *conductor, guide*
3616 ŏikŏděspŏtěō (1), to *be the head of a family*

GUIDED
5090 nâhag (1), to *drive forth*; to *lead*
5095 nâhal (2), to *flow*; to *conduct*; to *protect*
5148 nâchâh (2), to *guide*

GUTTERS
7298 rahaṭ (2), *ringlet of hair*

HA
1889 he'âch (1), *aha!*

HAAHASHTARI
326 'ăchashtărîy (1), *courier*

HABAIAH
2252 Chăbayâh (2), *Jehovah has hidden*

HABAKKUK
2265 Chăbaqqûwq (2), *embrace*

HABAZINIAH
2262 Chăbatstsanyâh (1), *Chabatstsanjah*

HABERGEON
8302 shiryôwn (1), *corslet, coat of mail*
8473 tachărâ' (2), *linen corslet*

HABERGEONS
8302 shiryôwn (2), *corslet, coat of mail*

HABITABLE
8398 têbêl (1), *earth; world; inhabitants*

HABITATION
1628 gêrûwth (1), *(temporary) residence*
2073 zᵉbûwl (3), *residence, dwelling*
2918 ṭîyrâh (1), *fortress; hamlet*
3427 yâshab (3), *to dwell, to remain; to settle*
4186 môwshâb (4), *seat; site; abode*
4349 mâkôwn (2), *basis; place*
4351 mᵉkûwrâh (1), *origin*
4583 mâ'ôwn (9), *retreat or asylum dwelling*
4907 mishkan (Ch.) (1), *residence*
4908 mishkân (3), *residence*
5115 nâvâh (1), *to rest as at home*
5116 nâveh (21), *at home; lovely; home*
7931 shâkan (1), *to reside*
7932 shᵉkan (Ch.) (1), *to reside*
7933 sheken (1), *residence*
1886 ĕpaulis (1), *dwelling, residence*
2732 katŏikētēriŏn (2), *dwelling-place, home*
2733 katŏikia (1), *residence, dwelling*
3613 ŏikētēriŏn (1), *residence, home*

HABITATIONS
4186 môwshâb (8), *seat; site; abode*
4380 mᵉkêrâh (1), *stabbing-sword*
4583 mâ'ôwn (1), *retreat or asylum dwelling*
4585 mᵉ'ôwnâh (1), *abode*
4908 mishkân (2), *residence*

HA
4999 nâ'âh (5), *home, dwelling; pasture*
5116 nâveh (1), *at home; lovely; home*
4638 skēnôma (1), *dwelling: the Temple*

HABOR
2249 Châbôwr (3), *united*

HACHALIAH
2446 Chăkalyâh (2), *darkness (of) Jehovah*

HACHILAH
2444 Chakîylâh (3), *dark*

HACHMONI
2453 Chakmôwnîy (1), *skillful*

HACHMONITE
2453 Chakmôwnîy (1), *skillful*

HAD
935 bôw' (1), *to go, come*
1961 hâyâh (104), *to exist, i.e. be or become*
2370 chăzâ' (Ch.) (1), *to gaze upon; to dream*
3426 yêsh (5), *there is*
3884 lûwlê' (1), *if not*
7760 sûwm (1), *to put*
1096 ginŏmai (1), *to be, become*
1510 ĕimi (8), *I exist, I am*
1746 ĕnduō (1), *to dress*
2192 ĕchō (106), *to have*
2722 katĕchō (1), *to hold down fast*
2983 lambanō (2), *to take, receive*
3844 para (1), *from; with; besides; on account of*
5607 ōn (1), *being, existence*

HADAD
1908 Hădad (13), *Hadad*
2301 Chădad (1), *fierce*

HADADEZER
1909 Hădad'ezer (9), *Hadad (is his) help*

HADADRIMMON
1910 Hădadrimmôwn (1), *Hadad-Rimmon*

HADAR
1924 Hădar (2), *magnificence*

HADAREZER
1928 Hădar'ezer (12), *Hadad is his help*

HADASHAH
2322 Chădâshâh (1), *new*

HADASSAH
1919 Hădaççâh (1), *Esther*

HADATTAH
2675 Châtsôwr Chădattâh (1), *new village*

HADID
2307 Châdîyd (3), *peak*

HADLAI
2311 Chadlay (1), *idle*

HADORAM
1913 Hădôwrâm (4), *Hadoram*

HADRACH
2317 Chadrâk (1), *Syrian deity*

HAFT
5325 nitstsâb (1), *handle of a sword or dagger*

HAGAB
2285 Châgâb (1), *locust*

HAGABA
2286 Chăgâbâ' (1), *locust*

HAGABAH
2286 Chăgâbâ' (1), *locust*

HAGAR
1904 Hâgâr (12), *Hagar*

HAGARENES
1905 Hagrîy (1), *Hagrite*

HAGARITES
1905 Hagrîy (3), *Hagrite*

HAGERITE
1905 Hagrîy (1), *Hagrite*

HAGGAI
2292 Chaggay (11), *festive*

HAGGERI
1905 Hagrîy (1), *Hagrite*

HAGGI
2291 Chaggîy (2), *festive*

HAGGIAH
2293 Chaggîyâh (1), *festival of Jehovah*

HAGGITES
2291 Chaggîy (1), *festive*

HAGGITH
2294 Chaggiyîth (5), *festive*

HAI
5857 'Ay (2), *ruin*

HAIL
1258 bârad (1), *to rain hail*
1259 bârâd (26), *hail, hailstones*
5463 chairō (6), *salutation, "be well"*
5464 chalaza (4), *frozen ice crystals, i.e. hail*

HAILSTONES
68+417 'eben (3), *stone*
68+1259 'eben (2), *stone*

HAIR
1803 dallâh (1), *loose thread; loose hair*
4748 miqsheh (1), *curl of beautiful tresses*
4803 mâraṭ (2), *to polish; to make bald*
5145 nezer (1), *set apart; royal chaplet*
8177 sᵉ'ar (Ch.) (2), *hair*
8181 sê'âr (23), *tossed hair*
8185 sa'ărâh (5), *hairiness*
2359 thrix (9), *hair; single hair*
2863 kŏmaō (2), *to wear long hair*
2864 kŏmē (1), *long hair*
4117 plĕgma (1), *plait or braid of hair*
5155 trichinŏs (1), *made of hair*

HAIRS
8177 sᵉ'ar (Ch.) (1), *hair*
8181 sê'âr (1), *tossed hair*
8185 sa'ărâh (2), *hairiness*
2359 thrix (5), *hair*

HAIRY
1167+8181 ba'al (1), *master; owner; citizen*
8163 sâ'îyr (2), *shaggy; he-goat; goat idol*
8181 sê'âr (2), *tossed hair*

HAKKATAN
6997 Qâṭân (1), *small*

HAKKOZ
6976 Qôwts (1), *thorns*

HAKUPHA
2709 Chăqûwphâ' (2), *to bend, crooked*

HALAH
2477 Chălach (3), *Chalach*

HALAK
2510 Châlâq (2), *bare*

HALE
2694 katasurō (1), *to arrest judicially*

HALF
1235 beqa' (1), *half shekel*
2673 châtsâh (1), *to cut or split in two; to halve*
2677 chêtsîy (106), *half or middle, midst*
4275 mechĕtsâh (2), *halving, half*
4276 machătsîyth (14), *halving or the middle*
8432 tâvek (1), *center, middle*
2253 hēmithanēs (1), *entirely exhausted*
2255 hēmisu (5), *half*
2256 hēmiōriŏn (1), *half-hour*

HALHUL
2478 Chalchûwl (1), *contorted*

HALI
2482 Chălîy (1), *polished trinket, ornament*

HALING
4951 surō (1), *to trail, drag, sweep*

HALL
833 aulē (2), *palace; house; courtyard*
4232 praitōriŏn (6), *governor's court-room*

HALLOHESH
3873 Lôwchêsh (1), *enchanter*

HALLOW
6942 qâdâsh (15), *to be, make clean*

HALLOWED
4720 miqdâsh (1), *sanctuary of deity*
6942 qâdâsh (10), *to be, make clean*
6944 qôdesh (9), *sacred place or thing*
37 hagiazō (2), *to purify or consecrate*

HALOHESH
3873 Lôwchêsh (1), *enchanter*

HALT
6452 pâçach (1), to *hop, skip* over; to *hesitate*
6761 tsela' (1), *limping*
5560 chôlŏs (4), *limping, crippled*

HALTED
6761 tsela' (2), *limping*

HALTETH
6761 tsela' (2), *limping*

HALTING
6761 tsela' (1), *limping*

HAM
1990 Hâm (1), *Ham*
2526 Châm (16), *hot*

HAMAN
2001 Hâmân (50), *Haman*

HAMAN'S
2001 Hâmân (3), *Haman*

HAMATH
2574 Chămâth (33), *walled*
2579 Chămath Rabbâh (1), *walled of Rabbah*

HAMATH-ZOBAH
2578 Chămath Tsôwbâh (1), *walled of Tsobah*

HAMATHITE
2577 Chămâthîy (2), *Chamathite*

HAMMATH
2575 Chammath (1), *hot springs*

HAMMEDATHA
4099 Mᵉdâthâ (5), *Medatha*

HAMMELECH
4429 Melek (2), *king*

HAMMER
1989 halmûwth (1), *hammer* or *mallet*
4717 maqqâbâh (1), *hammer*
4718 maqqebeth (1), *hammer*
6360 paṭṭîysh (3), *hammer* which *pounds*

HAMMERS
3597 kêylaph (1), *club* or *sledge-hammer*
4717 maqqâbâh (2), *hammer*

HAMMOLEKETH
4447 Môleketh (1), *queen*

HAMMON
2540 Chammôwn (2), *warm* spring

HAMMOTH-DOR
2576 Chammôth Dô'r (1), *hot* springs *of Dor*

HAMON-GOG
1996 Hămôwn Gôwg (2), *multitude of Gog*

HAMONAH
1997 Hămôwnâh (1), *multitude*

HAMOR
2544 Chămôwr (12), male donkey or *ass*

HAMOR'S
2544 Chămôwr (1), male donkey or *ass*

HAMUEL
2536 Chammûw'êl (1), *anger of God*

HAMUL
2538 Châmûwl (3), *pitied*

HAMULITES
2539 Châmûwlîy (1), *Chamulite*

HAMUTAL
2537 Chămûwṭal (3), *father-in-law of dew*

HANAMEEL
2601 Chănam'êl (4), *God has favored*

HANAN
2605 Chânân (12), *favor*

HANANEEL
2606 Chănan'êl (4), *God has favored*

HANANI
2607 Chănânîy (11), *gracious*

HANANIAH
2608 Chănanyâh (29), *Jehovah has favored*

HAND
405 'ekeph (1), *stroke, blow*
854 'êth (1), *with; by; at; among*
2026 hârag (1), to *kill, slaughter*
2651 chôphen (1), *pair of fists*
2947 ṭêphach (1), *palm-breadth*
2948 ṭôphach (4), *palm-breadth*
3027 yâd (1086), *hand; power*
3028 yad (Ch.) (12), *hand; power*
3079 Yᵉhôwyâqîym (2), *Jehovah will raise*
3221 yâm (Ch.) (1), *sea; basin; west*
3225 yâmîyn (87), *right; south*
3227 yᵉmîynîy (1), *right*
3235 yâmar (1), to *exchange*
3325 Yitshârîy (1), *Jitsharite*
3709 kaph (52), *hollow of hand; paw; sole of foot*
4672 mâtsâ' (1), to *find* or *acquire;* to *occur*
7126 qârab (4), to *approach, bring near*
7138 qârôwb (5), *near, close*
8040 sᵉmô'wl (14), *north; left* hand
8041 sâma'l (1), to *use the left* hand or go *left*
8042 sᵉmâ'lîy (2), on the *left* side; *northern*
1448 ĕggizō (9), to *approach*
1451 ĕggus (6), *near, close*
1764 ĕnistēmi (1), to *be present*

HAMOR
2544 Chămôwr (12), male donkey or *ass*

2021 ĕpichĕirĕō (1), to *undertake, try*
2186 ĕphistēmi (1), to *be present; to approach*
5495 chĕir (87), *hand*
5496 chĕiragōgĕō (2), to *guide* a blind person by the hand
5497 chĕiragōgŏs (1), *conductor* of a blind person by the hand

HANDBREADTH
2947 ṭêphach (2), *palm-breadth*
2948 ṭôphach (1), *palm-breadth*

HANDED
3027 yâd (1), *hand; power*

HANDFUL
4390+3709 mâlê' (3), to *fill; be full*
4393+7062 mᵉlô' (2), *fulness*
5995 'âmîyr (1), *bunch of cereal new-cut grain*
6451 piççâh (1), *abundance*
7061 qâmats (1), to *grasp a handful*
7062 qômets (1), *handful; abundance*

HANDFULS
4393+2651 mᵉlô' (1), *fulness*
6653 tsebeth (1), *lock of stalks, bundle of grain*
7062 qômets (1), *handful; abundance*
8168 shô'al (2), *palm of hand; handful*

HANDKERCHIEFS
4676 sŏudariŏn (1), *towel*

HANDLE
270 'âchaz (1), to *seize, grasp; possess*
4184 mûwsh (1), to *touch, feel*
4900 mâshak (1), to *draw out; to be tall*
6186 'ârak (1), to set in a row, i.e. *arrange,*
8610 tâphas (5), to *manipulate, i.e. seize*
2345 thigganō (1), to *touch*
5584 psēlaphaō (1), to *manipulate*

HANDLED
8610+3709 tâphas (1), to *manipulate, i.e. seize*
821 atimŏō (1), to *maltreat, disgrace*
5584 psēlaphaō (1), to *manipulate*

HANDLES
3709 kaph (1), *hollow of hand; paw; sole of foot*

HANDLETH
5921 'al (1), *above, over, upon,* or *against*
8610 tâphas (2), to *manipulate, i.e. seize*

HANDLING
8610 tâphas (1), to *manipulate, i.e. seize*

1389 dŏlŏō (1), to *adulterate, falsify*

HANDMAID
519 'âmâh (22), *female servant* or *slave*
8198 shiphchâh (22), household *female slave*
1399 dŏulē (1), *female slave*

HANDMAIDEN
1399 dŏulē (1), *female slave*

HANDMAIDENS
8198 shiphchâh (2), household *female slave*
1399 dŏulē (1), *female slave*

HANDMAIDS
519 'âmâh (1), *female servant* or *slave*
8198 shiphchâh (7), household *female slave*

HANDS
2651 chôphen (3), *pair of fists*
3027 yâd (274), *hand; power*
3028 yad (Ch.) (4), *hand; power*
3709 kaph (67), *hollow of hand; paw; sole of foot*
849 autŏchĕir (1), *self-handed, personally*
886 achĕirŏpŏiētŏs (3), *unmanufactured*
2902 kratĕō (2), to *seize*
4084 piazō (1), to *seize, arrest,* or *capture*
4475 rhapisma (1), *slap, strike*
5495 chĕir (90), *hand*
5499 chĕirŏpŏiētŏs (6), of *human construction*

HANDSTAVES
4731+3027 maqqêl (1), *shoot; stick; staff*

HANDWRITING
5498 chĕirŏgraphŏn (1), *document or bond*

HANDYWORK
4639+3027 ma'ăseh (1), *action; labor*

HANES
2609 Chânêç (1), *Chanes*

HANG
3363 yâqa' (2), to *be dislocated; to impale*
3381 yârad (1), to *descend*
5414 nâthan (3), to *give*
5628 çârach (2), to *extend* even to *excess*
8511 tâlâ' (1), to *suspend; to be uncertain*
8518 tâlâh (7), to *suspend, hang*
2910 krĕmannumi (2), to *hang*
3935 pariēmi (1), to *neglect; to be weakened*

HANGED
2614 chânaq (1), to *choke* oneself
3363 yâqa' (2), to *be dislocated; to impale*

4223 mᵉchâ' (Ch.) (1), to
strike; to impale
8511 tâlâ' (1), to suspend;
to be uncertain
8518 tâlâh (18), to
suspend, hang
519 apagchŏmai (1), to
strangle oneself
2910 krĕmannumi (4), to
hang
4029 pĕrikĕimai (2), to
enclose, encircle

HANGETH
8518 tâlâh (1), to
suspend, hang
2910 krĕmannumi (1), to
hang

HANGING
4539 mâçâk (17), veil;
shield
8518 tâlâh (1), to
suspend, hang

HANGINGS
1004 bayith (1), house;
temple; family, tribe
7050 qela' (15), slinging
weapon; door screen

HANIEL
2592 Chănnîy'êl (1),
favor of God

HANNAH
2584 Channâh (13),
favored

HANNATHON
2615 Channâthôn (1),
favored

HANNIEL
2592 Chănnîy'êl (1),
favor of God

HANOCH
2585 Chănôwk (5),
initiated

HANOCHITES
2599 Chănôkîy (1),
Chanokite

HANUN
2586 Chânûwn (11),
favored

HAP
4745 miqreh (1),
accident or fortune

HAPHRAIM
2663 Chăphârayîm (1),
double pit

HAPLY
3863 lûw' (1), if; would
that!
686 ara (2), then, so,
therefore
3379 mēpŏtĕ (2), not
ever; if, or lest ever
3381 mēpōs (1), lest
somehow

HAPPEN
579 'ânâh (1), to meet, to
happen
7136 qârâh (2), to bring
about; to impose
4819 sumbainō (1), to
concur, happen

HAPPENED
1961 hâyâh (1), to exist,
i.e. be or become

7122 qârâ' (2), to
encountĕr, to happen
7136 qârâh (2), to bring
about; to impose
1096 ginŏmai (1), to be,
become
4819 sumbainō (5), to
concur, happen

HAPPENETH
4745 miqreh (1),
accident or fortune
5060 nâga' (2), to strike
7136 qârâh (3), to bring
about; to impose

HAPPIER
3107 makariŏs (1),
fortunate, well off

HAPPY
833 'âshar (2), to be
honest, prosper
835 'esher (16), how
happy!
837 'ôsher (1),
happiness, blessedness
7951 shâlâh (1), to be
tranquil, i.e. secure
3106 makarizŏ (1), to
esteem fortunate
3107 makariŏs (5),
fortunate, well off

HARA
2024 Hârâ' (1),
mountainousness

HARADAH
2732 Chărâdâh (2), fear,
anxiety

HARAN
2039 Hârân (1),
mountaineer
2309 chedel (6), state of
the dead, deceased
2771 Chârân (12),
parched

HARARITE
2043 Hărârîy (5),
mountaineer

HARBONA
2726 Charbôwnâ' (1),
Charbona, Charbonah

HARBONAH
2726 Charbôwnâ' (1),
Charbona, Charbonah

HARD
280 'ăchîydâh (Ch.) (1),
enigma
386 'êythân (1),
never-failing; eternal
681 'êtsel (1), side; near
1692 dâbaq (4), to cling
or adhere; to catch
2420 chîydâh (2), puzzle;
conundrum; maxim
3332 yâtsaq (1), to pour
out
3515 kâbêd (2), severe,
difficult, stupid
5066 nâgash (1), to be,
come, bring near
5221 nâkâh (1), to strike,
kill
5564 çâmak (1), to lean
upon; take hold of
5980 'ummâh (1), near,
beside, along with
6277 'âthâq (1), impudent

6381 pâlâ' (5), to be,
make great, difficult
7185 qâshâh (5), to be
tough or severe
7186 qâsheh (6), severe
1421 dusĕrmēnĕutŏs (1),
difficult to explain
1422 duskŏlŏs (1),
impracticable, difficult
1425 dusnŏētŏs (1),
difficult of perception
4642 sklērŏs (5), hard or
tough; harsh, severe
4927 sunŏmŏrĕŏ (1), to
border together

HARDEN
533 'ammîyts (1), strong;
mighty; brave
2388 châzaq (4), to be
obstinate; to bind
5513 Çîynîy (1), Sinite
5539 çâlad (1), to leap
with joy
7185 qâshâh (2), to be
tough or severe
4645 sklērunŏ (3), to
indurate, be stubborn

HARDENED
553 'âmats (1), to be
strong; be courageous
2388 châzaq (9), to be
obstinate; to bind
3513 kâbad (4), to be
heavy, severe, dull
3515 kâbêd (3), severe,
difficult, stupid
7185 qâshâh (8), to be
tough or severe
7188 qâshach (2), to be,
make unfeeling
8631 tᵉqêph (Ch.) (1), to
be obstinate
4456 pōrŏŏ (3), to render
stupid or callous
4645 sklērunŏ (2), to
indurate, be stubborn

HARDENETH
5810 'âzaz (1), to be
stout; be bold
7185 qâshâh (2), to be
tough or severe
4645 sklērunŏ (1), to
indurate, be stubborn

HARDER
2388 châzaq (1), to be
obstinate; to bind
2389 châzâq (1), strong;
severe, hard, violent

HARDHEARTED
7186+3820 qâsheh (1),
severe

HARDLY
6031 'ânâh (1), to afflict,
be afflicted
7185 qâshâh (2), to be
tough or severe
1423 duskŏlōs (3),
impracticably, with
difficulty
3425 mŏgis (1), with
difficulty
3433 mŏlis (1), with
difficulty

HARDNESS
4165 mûwtsâq (1),
casting of metal

2553 kakŏpathĕŏ (1), to
undergo hardship
4457 pōrōsis (1),
stupidity or callousness
4641 sklērŏkardia (3),
hard-heartedness
4643 sklērŏtēs (1),
stubbornness

HARE
768 'arnebeth (2), hare,
rabbit

HAREPH
2780 Chârêph (1),
reproachful

HARETH
2802 Chereth (1), forest

HARHAIAH
2736 Charhăyâh (1),
fearing Jehovah

HARHAS
2745 Charchaç (1), sun

HARHUR
2744 Charchûwr (2),
inflammation

HARIM
2766 Chârîm (11),
snub-nosed

HARIPH
2756 Chârîyph (2),
autumnal

HARLOT
2181 zânâh (33), to
commit adultery
6948 qᵉdêshâh (3),
sacred female
prostitute
4204 pŏrnē (4), strumpet,
i.e. prostitute; idolater

HARLOT'S
2181 zânâh (2), to
commit adultery

HARLOTS
2181 zânâh (2), to
commit adultery
6948 qᵉdêshâh (1),
sacred female
prostitute
4204 pŏrnē (4), strumpet,
i.e. prostitute; idolater

HARLOTS'
2181 zânâh (1), to
commit adultery

HARM
1697+7451 dâbâr (1),
word; matter; thing
2398 châțâ' (1), to sin
3415 yâra' (1), to fear
7451 ra' (4), bad; evil
7489 râ'a' (3), to make,
be good for nothing
824 atŏpŏs (1), improper;
injurious; wicked
2556 kakŏs (2), bad, evil,
wrong
2559 kakŏŏ (1), to injure;
to oppress; to embitter
4190 pŏnērŏs (1), malice,
wicked, bad; crime
5196 hubris (1), insult;
injury

HARMLESS
172 akakŏs (1), innocent,
blameless

185 akĕraiŏs (2), *innocent*

HARNEPHER
2774 Charnepher (1), *Charnepher*

HARNESS
631 'âçar (1), to *fasten*; to *join* battle
5402 nesheq (1), military *arms, arsenal*
8302 shiryôwn (2), *corslet, coat of mail*

HARNESSED
2571 châmûsh (1), able-bodied *soldiers*

HAROD
5878 'Êyn Chărôd (1), *fountain of trembling*

HARODITE
2733 Chărôdîy (1), *Charodite*

HAROEH
7204 Rô'êh (1), *seer*

HARORITE
2033 Hărôwrîy (1), *mountaineer*

HAROSHETH
2800 Chărôsheth (3), skilled *worker*

HARP
3658 kinnôwr (25), *harp*
7030 qîythârôç (Ch.) (4), *lyre*
2788 kithara (1), *lyre*

HARPED
2789 kitharizō (1), to *play a lyre*

HARPERS
2790 kitharō̧dŏs (2), one who *plays a lyre*

HARPING
2789 kitharizō (1), to *play a lyre*

HARPS
3658 kinnôwr (17), *harp*
2788 kithara (3), *lyre*

HARROW
7702 sâdad (1), to *harrow* a field

HARROWS
2757 chârîyts (2), *threshing-sledge; slice*

HARSHA
2797 Charshâ' (2), *magician*

HART
354 'ayâl (9), *stag* deer

HARTS
354 'ayâl (2), *stag* deer

HARUM
2037 Hârûm (1), *high, exalted*

HARUMAPH
2739 Chărûwmaph (1), *snub-nosed*

HARUPHITE
2741 Chărûwphîy (1), *Charuphite*

HARUZ
2743 Chârûwts (1), *earnest*

HARVEST
7105 qâtsîyr (47), *harvest; limb* of a tree
2326 thĕrismŏs (13), *harvest, crop*

HARVESTMAN
7105 qâtsîyr (1), *harvest; limb* of a tree
7114 qâtsar (1), to *curtail, cut short*

HASADIAH
2619 Chăçadyâh (1), *Jehovah has favored*

HASENUAH
5574 Çᵉnûw'âh (1), *pointed*

HASHABIAH
2811 Chăshabyâh (15), *Jehovah has regarded*

HASHABNAH
2812 Chăshabnâh (1), *inventiveness*

HASHABNIAH
2813 Chăshabnᵉyâh (2), *thought of Jehovah*

HASHBADANA
2806 Chashbaddânâh (1), *considerate judge*

HASHEM
2044 Hâshêm (1), *wealthy*

HASHMONAH
2832 Chashmônâh (2), *fertile*

HASHUB
2815 Chashshûwb (4), *intelligent*

HASHUBAH
2807 Chăshûbâh (1), *estimation*

HASHUM
2828 Châshûm (5), *enriched*

HASHUPHA
2817 Chăsûwphâ' (1), *nakedness*

HASRAH
2641 Chaçrâh (1), *want*

HASSENAAH
5570 Çᵉnâ'âh (1), *thorny*

HASSHUB
2815 Chashshûwb (1), *intelligent*

HAST
1961 hâyâh (2), to *exist*, i.e. *be* or *become*
3426 yêsh (3), there *is* or *are*
2076 ĕsti (1), he (she or it) *is*; they *are*
2192 ĕchō (28), to *have; hold; keep*
5224 huparchŏnta (1), *property* or *possessions*

HASTE
213 'ûwts (1), to *be close, hurry, withdraw*
924 bᵉhîylûw (Ch.) (1), *hastily, at once*
926 bâhal (1), to *hasten, hurry anxiously*
927 bᵉhal (Ch.) (3), to *terrify; hasten*

1272 bârach (1), to *flee* suddenly
2363 chûwsh (11), to *hurry; to be eager*
2439 chîysh (1), to *hurry, hasten*
2648 châphaz (5), to *hasten* away, to *fear*
2649 chîppâzôwn (3), *hasty flight*
4116 mâhar (20), to *hurry; promptly*
5169 nâchats (1), to *be urgent*
4692 spĕudō (4), to *urge* on diligently
4710 spŏudē (2), *despatch; eagerness*

HASTED
213 'ûwts (2), to *be close, hurry, withdraw*
926 bâhal (1), to *hasten, hurry anxiously*
1765 dâchaph (2), to *urge; to hasten*
2363 chûwsh (2), to *hurry; to be eager*
2648 châphaz (2), to *hasten* away, to *fear*
4116 mâhar (14), to *hurry; promptly*
4692 spĕudō (1), to *urge* on diligently

HASTEN
2363 chûwsh (4), to *hurry; to be eager*
4116 mâhar (3), to *hurry; promptly*
8245 shâqad (1), to *be alert,* i.e. *sleepless*

HASTENED
213 'ûwts (2), to *be close, hurry, withdraw*
926 bâhal (1), to *hasten, hurry anxiously*
1765 dâchaph (1), to *urge; to hasten*
4116 mâhar (2), to *hurry; promptly*

HASTENETH
4116 mâhar (1), to *hurry; promptly*

HASTETH
213 'ûwts (1), to *be close, hurry, withdraw*
926 bâhal (1), to *hasten, hurry anxiously*
2363 chûwsh (1), to *hurry; to be eager*
2648 châphaz (1), to *hasten* away, to *fear*
2907 tûws (1), to *pounce* or *swoop upon*
4116 mâhar (3), to *hurry; promptly*
7602 shâ'aph (1), to *be angry; to hasten*

HASTILY
926 bâhal (1), to *hasten, hurry anxiously*
4116 mâhar (2), to *hurry; promptly*
4118 mahêr (2), *in a hurry*
4120 mᵉhêrâh (1), *hurry; promptly*
7323 rûwts (1), to *run*

5030 tachĕôs (1), *speedily, rapidly*

HASTING
4106 mâhîyr (1), *skillful*
4692 spĕudō (1), to *urge* on diligently

HASTY
213 'ûwts (2), to *be close, hurry, withdraw*
926 bâhal (2), to *hasten, hurry anxiously*
1061 bikkûwr (1), *first-fruits* of the crop
2685 chătsaph (Ch.) (1), to *be severe*
4116 mâhar (2), to *hurry; promptly*
7116 qâtsêr (1), *short*

HASUPHA
2817 Chăsûwphâ' (1), *nakedness*

HATACH
2047 Hăthâk (4), *Hathak*

HATCH
1234 bâqa' (2), to *cleave, break, tear open*

HATCHETH
3205 yâlad (1), to *bear* young; to *father a child*

HATE
7852 sâṭam (2), to *persecute*
8130 sânê' (67), to *hate*
8131 sᵉnê' (Ch.) (1), *enemy*
3404 misĕō (16), to *detest,* to *love less*

HATED
7852 sâṭam (2), to *persecute*
8130 sânê' (42), to *hate*
8135 sin'âh (2), *hate, malice*
8146 sânîy' (1), *hated*
3404 misĕō (12), to *detest; to love less*

HATEFUL
8130 sânê' (1), to *hate*
3404 misĕō (1), to *detest, persecute; to love less*
4767 stugnētŏs (1), *hated,* i.e. *odious*

HATEFULLY
8135 sin'âh (1), *hate, malice*

HATERS
8130 sânê' (1), to *hate*
2319 thĕŏstugēs (1), *impious, God-hating*

HATEST
8130 sânê' (5), to *hate*
3404 misĕō (1), to *detest, persecute; to love less*

HATETH
7852 sâṭam (1), to *persecute*
8130 sânê' (20), to *hate*
3404 misĕō (9), to *detest, persecute; to love less*

HATH
413 'êl (1), *to, toward*
1167 ba'al (3), *master; husband; owner; citizen*

1172 ba'ălâh (2),
mistress; female owner
1933 hâvâ' (1), to be, to
exist
1961 hâyâh (6), to exist,
i.e. be or become
3426 yêsh (3), there is or
are
4672 mâtsâ' (1), to find
or acquire; to occur,
meet or be present
2192 ĕchō (128), to have;
hold; keep
5220 hupandrŏs (1),
married woman
5224 huparchŏnta (2),
property or possessions

HATHATH
2867 Chăthath (1),
dismay

HATING
8130 sânê' (1), to hate
3404 misĕō (2), to detest,
persecute; to love less

HATIPHA
2412 Chătîyphâ' (2),
robber

HATITA
2410 Chătîyţa' (2),
explorer

HATRED
342 'êybâh (2), hostility
4895 masţêmâh (2),
enmity
8135 sin'âh (13), hate,
malice
2189 ĕchthra (1),
hostility; opposition

HATS
3737 karbẽlâ' (Ch.) (1),
mantle

HATTIL
2411 Chaţţîyl (2),
fluctuating

HATTUSH
2407 Chaţţûwsh (5),
Chattush

HAUGHTILY
7317 rôwmâh (1), proudly

HAUGHTINESS
1346 ga'ăvâh (2),
arrogance; majesty
7312 rûwm (3), elevation;
elation

HAUGHTY
1361 gâbahh (5), to be
lofty; to be haughty
1363 gôbahh (1), height;
grandeur; arrogance
1364 gâbôahh (1), high;
powerful; arrogant
3093 yâhîyr (1), arrogant
4791 mârôwm (1),
elevation; haughtiness
7311 rûwm (1), to be
high; to rise or raise

HAUNT
1980 hâlak (1), to walk;
live a certain way
3427 yâshab (1), to dwell,
to remain; to settle
7272 regel (1), foot; step

HAURAN
2362 Chavrân (2),
cavernous

HAVE
270 'âchaz (1), to seize,
grasp; possess
383 'îythay (Ch.) (3),
there is
935 bôw' (1), to go, come
1167 ba'al (1), master;
husband; owner; citizen
1934 hăvâ' (Ch.) (2), to
be, to exist
1961 hâyâh (87), to exist,
i.e. be or become
3045 yâda' (2), to know
3318 yâtsâ' (3), to go,
bring out
3426 yêsh (12), there is
3947 lâqach (1), to take
4672 mâtsâ' (1), to find
or acquire; to occur
5307 nâphal (1), to fall
5375 nâsâ' (1), to lift up
5674 'âbar (1), to cross
over; to transition
5921 'al (1), above, over,
upon, or against
474 antiballō (1), to
exchange words
568 apĕchō (4), to be
distant
1096 ginŏmai (1), to be,
become
1099 glukus (1), sweet,
fresh
1526 ĕisi (1), they are
1699 ĕmŏs (1), my
1751 ĕnĕimi (1), to be
within
2070 ĕsmĕn (1), we are
2071 ĕsŏmai (6), will be
2076 ĕsti (11), he (she or
it) is; they are
2192 ĕchō (266), to have;
hold; keep
2701 katatrĕchō (1), to
hasten, run
2983 lambanō (1), to
take, receive
3335 mĕtalambanō (1),
to accept and use
3918 parĕimi (1), to be
present; to have come
5224 huparchŏnta (1),
property or possessions
5225 huparchō (1), to
come into existence

HAVEN
2348 chôwph (2), cove,
sheltered bay
4231 mâchôwz (1),
harbor
3040 limēn (2), harbor

HAVENS
2568 Kalŏi Limĕnĕs (1),
Good Harbors

HAVILAH
2341 Chăvîylâh (7),
circular

HAVING
1167 ba'al (2), master;
husband; owner; citizen
5414 nâthan (1), to give
1746 ĕnduō (1), to dress
2192 ĕchō (85), to have;
hold; keep

HAVOCK
3075 lumainŏmai (1), to
insult, maltreat

HAVOTH-JAIR
2334 Chavvôwth Yâ'îyr
(2), hamlets of Jair

HAWK
5322 nêts (3), flower;
hawk
8464 tachmâç (2),
unclean bird (poss.) owl

HAY
2682 châtsîyr (2), grass;
leek plant
5528 chŏrtŏs (1), pasture,
herbage or vegetation

HAZAEL
2371 Chăzâ'êl (23), God
has seen

HAZAIAH
2382 Chăzâyâh (1),
Jehovah has seen

HAZAR-ADDAR
2692 Chătsar 'Addâr (1),
village of Addar

HAZAR-ENAN
2703 Chătsar 'Êynôwn
(1), village of springs
2704 Chătsar 'Êynân (3),
village of springs

HAZAR-GADDAH
2693 Chătsar Gaddâh
(1), village of Fortune

HAZAR-HATTICON
2694 Chătsar
hat-Tîykôwn (1), village
of the middle

HAZAR-SHUAL
2705 Chătsar Shûw'âl
(4), village of (the) fox

HAZAR-SUSAH
2701 Chătsar Çûwçâh
(1), village of cavalry

HAZAR-SUSIM
2702 Chătsar Çûwçîym
(1), village of horses

HAZARDED
3860 paradidōmi (1), to
hand over

HAZARMAVETH
2700 Chătsarmâveth (2),
village of death

HAZAZON-TAMAR
2688 Chatsẽtsôwn
Tâmâr (1), row of (the)
palm-tree

HAZEL
3869 lûwz (1), nut-tree,
(poss.) almond

HAZELELPONI
6753 Tsẽlelpôwnîy (1),
shade-facing

HAZERIM
2699 Chătsêrîym (1),
yards

HAZEROTH
2698 Chătsêrowth (6),
yards

HAZEZON-TAMAR
2688 Chatsẽtsôwn
Tâmâr (1), row of (the)
palm-tree

HAZIEL
2381 Chăzîy'êl (1), seen
of God

HAZO
2375 Chăzow (1), seer

HAZOR
2674 Châtsôwr (18),
village
2675 Châtsôwr
Chădattâh (1), new
village

HEAD
1270 barzel (2), iron; iron
implement
1538 gulgôleth (1), skull
3852 lehâbâh (1), flame;
flash
4763 mẽra'ăshâh (1),
headpiece; head-rest
6936 qodqôd (8), crown
of the head
7217 rẽ'sh (Ch.) (11),
head
7218 rô'sh (262), head
2775 kĕphalaiŏō (1), to
strike on the head
2776 kĕphalē (55), head

HEADBANDS
7196 qishshŭr (1), girdle
or sash for women

HEADLONG
2630 katakrĕmnizō (1),
to precipitate down
4248 prēnēs (1), head
foremost, headlong

HEADS
7217 rẽ'sh (Ch.) (1), head
7218 rô'sh (83), head
2776 kĕphalē (19), head

HEADSTONE
68+7222 'eben (1), stone

HEADY
4312 prŏpĕtēs (1), falling
forward headlong

HEAL
7495 râphâ' (21), to cure,
heal
1295 diasōzō (1), to cure,
preserve, rescue
2323 thĕrapĕuō (10), to
relieve disease
2390 iaŏmai (6), to cure,
heal
2392 iasis (2), curing

HEALED
5414+7499 nâthan (1), to
give
7495 râphâ' (31), to cure,
heal
2323 thĕrapĕuō (25), to
relieve disease
2390 iaŏmai (18), to cure,
heal
4982 sōzō (3), to deliver;
to protect

HEALER
2280 châbash (1), to
wrap firmly, bind

HEALETH
7495 râphâ' (4), to cure,
heal

HEALING
3545 kêhâh (1),
alleviation, i.e. a cure
4832 marpê' (3), cure;
deliverance; placidity
8585 tẽ'âlâh (1), bandage
or plaster

HEALINGS column 1

2322 thĕrapĕia (2), *cure, healing; domestics*
2323 thĕrapĕuō (3), *to relieve disease*
2386 iama (2), *cure*
2390 iaŏmai (1), *to cure, heal*
2392 iasis (1), *curing*

HEALINGS
2386 iama (1), *cure*

HEALTH
724 'ărûwkâh (4), *wholeness, health*
3444 yᵉshûw'âh (2), *aid; victory; prosperity*
4832 marpê' (5), *cure; deliverance; placidity*
7500 riph'ûwth (1), *cure, healing*
7965 shâlôwm (2), *safe; well; health, prosperity*
4491 rhiza (1), *root*
5198 hugiainō (1), *to have sound health*

HEAP
1530 gal (12), *heap; ruins*
2266 châbar (1), *to fascinate* by spells
2563 chômer (1), *clay; dry measure*
2846 châthâh (1), *to lay hold of; to pick* up fire
3664 kânaç (1), *to collect; to enfold*
4596 mᵉ'îy (1), *pile* of rubbish, *ruin*
5067 nêd (6), *mound, heap, dam*
5595 çâphâh (1), *to scrape; to accumulate*
5856 'îy (1), *ruin; rubble*
6194 'ârêm (3), *heap, mound; sheaf*
6651 tsâbar (2), *to aggregate, gather*
7235 râbâh (1), *to increase*
7760 sûwm (1), *to put, place*
8510 têl (4), *mound*
2002 ĕpisōrĕuō (1), *to accumulate further*
4987 sōrĕuō (1), *to pile up, load up*

HEAPED
6651 tsâbar (1), *to aggregate, gather*
2343 thēsaurizō (1), *to amass or reserve, store*

HEAPETH
6651 tsâbar (1), *to aggregate, gather*
6908 qâbats (1), *to collect, assemble*

HEAPS
1530 gal (6), *heap; ruins*
2563 chômer (1), *clay; dry measure*
2565 chămôrâh (1), *heap*
5856 'îy (3), *ruin; rubble*
6194 'ârêm (6), *heap, mound; sheaf*
6632 tsâb (1), *lizard; covered cart*
8564 tamrûwr (1), *erection, i.e. pillar*

HEAR column 2
238 'âzan (2), *to listen*
2045 hâshmâ'ûwth (1), *communication*
6030 'ânâh (28), *to respond, answer*
7181 qâshab (1), *to prick up* the ears
8085 shâma' (364), *to hear*
8086 shᵉma' (Ch.) (4), *to hear*
191 akŏuō (131), *to hear; obey*
1251 diakŏuŏmai (1), *to patiently listen*
1522 ĕisakŏuō (1), *to listen to*
3878 parakŏuō (2), *to disobey*

HEARD
6030 'ânâh (11), *to respond, answer*
7181 qâshab (1), *to prick up* the ears
8085 shâma' (376), *to hear*
8086 shᵉma' (Ch.) (4), *to hear*
189 akŏē (1), *hearing; thing heard*
191 akŏuō (239), *to hear; obey*
1522 ĕisakŏuō (4), *to listen to*
1873 ĕpakŏuō (1), *to hearken* favorably *to*
1874 ĕpakrŏaŏmai (1), *to listen intently to*
4257 prŏakŏuō (1), *to hear beforehand*

HEARDEST
6030 'ânâh (1), *to respond, answer*
8085 shâma' (11), *to hear*

HEARER
202 akrŏatēs (2), *hearer*

HEARERS
191 akŏuō (2), *to hear; obey*
202 akrŏatēs (2), *hearer*

HEAREST
6030 'ânâh (1), *to respond, answer*
8085 shâma' (6), *to hear*
191 akŏuō (4), *to hear; obey*

HEARETH
8085 shâma' (29), *to hear*
191 akŏuō (22), *to hear; obey*

HEARING
241 'ôzen (5), *ear*
4926 mishmâ' (1), *report*
7182 qesheb (1), *hearkening*
8085 shâma' (6), *to hear*
8088 shêma' (1), *something heard*
189 akŏē (10), *hearing; thing heard*
191 akŏuō (13), *to hear; obey*
201 akrŏatēriŏn (1), *audience-room*

HEAR column 3
1233 diagnōsis (1), *magisterial examination*

HEARKEN
238 'âzan (5), *to listen*
7181 qâshab (21), *to prick up* the ears
8085 shâma' (119), *to hear*
191 akŏuō (6), *to hear; obey*
1801 ĕnōtizŏmai (1), *to take in one's ear*
5219 hupakŏuō (1), *to listen attentively*

HEARKENED
238 'âzan (1), *to listen*
7181 qâshab (5), *to prick up* the ears
8085 shâma' (74), *to hear*
3980 pĕitharchĕō (1), *to submit to authority*

HEARKENEDST
8085 shâma' (1), *to hear*

HEARKENETH
8085 shâma' (2), *to hear*

HEARKENING
8085 shâma' (1), *to hear*

HEART
1079 bâl (Ch.) (1), *heart, mind*
3820 lêb (479), *heart*
3821 lêb (Ch.) (1), *heart*
3823 lâbab (2), *to transport* with love
3824 lêbâb (207), *heart*
3825 lᵉbab (Ch.) (7), *heart*
3826 libbâh (2), *heart*
4578 mê'âh (1), *viscera; anguish, tenderness*
5315 nephesh (12), *life; breath; soul; wind*
7130 qereb (1), *nearest part, i.e. the center*
7907 sekvîy (1), *mind*
2588 kardia (101), *heart, i.e. thoughts or feelings*
4641 sklērŏkardia (2), *hard-heartedness*
5590 psuchē (1), *soul, vitality; heart, mind*

HEART'S
3820 lêb (1), *heart*
5315 nephesh (1), *life; breath; soul; wind*
2588 kardia (1), *heart, i.e. thoughts or feelings*

HEARTED
3820 lêb (8), *heart*

HEARTH
254 'âch (3), *fire-pot*
3344 yâqad (1), *to burn*
3595 kîyôwr (1), *dish; caldron; washbowl*
4168 môwqêd (1), *conflagration, burning*

HEARTILY
1537+5590 ĕk (1), *out, out of*

HEARTS
3820 lêb (21), *heart*
3824 lêbâb (22), *heart*
3826 libbâh (6), *heart*
5315 nephesh (2), *life; breath; soul; wind*

HEART column 4
674 apŏpsuchō (1), *to faint*
2588 kardia (57), *heart, i.e. thoughts or feelings*
2589 kardiŏgnōstēs (2), *heart-knower*
4641 sklērŏkardia (1), *hard-heartedness*

HEARTS'
3820 lêb (1), *heart*

HEARTY
5315 nephesh (1), *life; breath; soul; wind*

HEAT
228 'ăzâ' (Ch.) (1), *to heat*
2527 chôm (9), *heat*
2534 chêmâh (1), *heat; anger; poison*
2535 chammâh (1), *heat of sun*
2552 châmam (2), *to be hot; to be in a rage*
2721 chôreb (6), *parched; ruined*
2750 chŏrîy (1), *burning anger*
3179 yâcham (1), *to conceive*
7565 resheph (1), *flame*
8273 shârâb (2), *glow of the hot air; mirage*
2329 thĕrmē (1), *warmth, heat*
2738 kauma (2), *scorching heat*
2741 kausŏō (2), *to set on fire*
2742 kausōn (3), *burning heat, hot day*

HEATED
228 'ăzâ' (Ch.) (1), *to heat*
1197 bâ'ar (1), *to be brutish, be senseless*

HEATH
6176 'ărôw'êr (2), *juniper bush*

HEATHEN
1471 gôwy (143), *foreign nation; Gentiles*
1482 ĕthnikŏs (2), *Gentile*
1484 ĕthnŏs (5), *race; tribe; pagan*

HEAVE
7311 rûwm (1), *to be high; to rise or raise*
8641 tᵉrûwmâh (28), *sacrifice, tribute*

HEAVED
7311 rûwm (3), *to be high; to rise or raise*

HEAVEN
1534 galgal (1), *wheel; something round*
7834 shachaq (2), *firmament, clouds*
8064 shâmayim (285), *sky; unseen celestial places*
8065 shâmayin (Ch.) (35), *sky; unseen celestial places*
2032 ĕpŏuraniŏs (1), *above the sky, celestial*
3321 mĕsŏuranēma (3), *mid-sky, mid-heaven*

3771 ŏuranŏthĕn (2),
from the *sky* or *heaven*
3772 ŏuranŏs (248), *sky;
air; heaven*

HEAVEN'S
3772 ŏuranŏs (1), *sky;
air; heaven*

HEAVENLY
1537+3772 ĕk (1), *out, out
of*
2032 ĕpŏuraniŏs (16),
above the *sky, celestial*
3770 ŏuraniŏs (6),
belonging to or coming
from the *sky* or *heaven*

HEAVENS
6160 'ărâbâh (1), *desert,
wasteland*
6183 'ărîyph (1), *sky*
8064 shâmayim (107),
*sky; unseen celestial
places*
8065 shâmayin (Ch.) (3),
*sky; unseen celestial
places*
3772 ŏuranŏs (19), *sky;
air; heaven*

HEAVIER
3513 kâbad (3), to *be
heavy, severe, dull*

HEAVILY
3513 kâbad (1), to *be
heavy, severe, dull*
3517 kᵉbêdûth (1),
difficulty
6957 qav (1), *rule* for
measuring; *rim*

HEAVINESS
1674 dᵉ'âgâh (1), *anxiety*
3544 kêheh (1), *feeble;
obscure*
5136 nûwsh (1), to *be sick*
6440 pânîym (1), *face;
front*
8386 ta'ănîyâh (1),
lamentation
8424 tûwgâh (3),
depression; grief
8589 ta'ănîyth (1),
affliction of self, *fasting*
85 adēmŏnĕŏ (1), to *be in*
mental *distress*
2726 katĕphĕia (1),
sadness, dejection
3076 lupĕŏ (1), to
distress; to be sad
3077 lupē (2), *sadness,
grief*

HEAVY
3513 kâbad (16), to *be
heavy, severe, dull*
3514 kôbed (2), *weight,
multitude, vehemence*
3515 kâbêd (8), *severe,
difficult, stupid*
4133 môwṭâh (1), *pole;
ox-bow; yoke*
4751 mar (1), *bitter;
bitterness; bitterly*
5620 çar (2), *peevish,
sullen*
7186 qâsheh (1), *severe*
7451 ra' (1), *bad; evil*
85 adēmŏnĕŏ (2), to *be in*
mental *distress*
916 barĕŏ (3), to *weigh*
down, *cause pressure*

926 barus (1), *weighty*

HEBER
2268 Cheber (10),
community
5677 'Êber (2), regions
beyond
1443 Ēbĕr (1), regions
beyond

HEBER'S
2268 Cheber (1),
community

HEBERITES
2277 Chebrîy (1),
Chebrite

HEBREW
5680 'Ibrîy (14), *Eberite*
(i.e. Hebrew)
1444 Hĕbraïkŏs (1),
Hebraïc or the *Jewish*
language
1446 Hĕbraïs (4), *Hebrew*
or *Jewish* language
1447 Hĕbraïsti (6),
Hebraistically or in the
Jewish language

HEBREWESS
5680 'Ibrîy (1), *Eberite*
(i.e. Hebrew)

HEBREWS
5680 'Ibrîy (17), *Eberite*
(i.e. Hebrew)
1445 Hĕbraiŏs (3),
Hebrew or *Jew*

HEBREWS'
5680 'Ibrîy (1), *Eberite*
(i.e. Hebrew)

HEBRON
2275 Chebrôwn (72),
seat of *association*

HEBRONITES
2276 Chebrôwnîy (6),
Chebronite

HEDGE
1447 gâdêr (3),
enclosure, wall or *fence*
4534 mᵉçûwkâh (1),
thorn-hedge
4881 mᵉsûwkâh (2),
thorn hedge
7753 sûwk (2), to *shut* in
with hedges
5418 phragmŏs (1), *fence*
or enclosing *barrier*

HEDGED
1443 gâdar (1), to *build a*
stone *wall*
5526 çâkak (1), to
entwine; to *fence in*
5418+4060 phragmŏs (1),
fence or *barrier*

HEDGES
1447 gâdêr (1),
enclosure, wall or *fence*
1448 gᵉdêrâh (4),
enclosure for flocks
5418 phragmŏs (1), *fence*
or enclosing *barrier*

HEED
238 'âzan (1), to *listen*
2095 zᵉhar (Ch.) (1), *be
admonished, be careful*
5414+3820 nâthan (1), to
give
5535 çâkath (1), to *be
silent*

7181 qâshab (3), to *prick
up* the ears
7182 qesheb (1),
hearkening
7200 râ'âh (2), to *see*
8104 shâmar (35), to
watch
433 anēkŏ (1), *be proper,
fitting*
991 blĕpŏ (14), to *look at*
1907 ĕpĕchŏ (2), to
detain; to *pay attention*
3708 hŏraŏ (5), to *stare,
see clearly;* to *discern*
4337 prŏsĕchŏ (11), to
pay attention to
4648 skŏpĕŏ (1), to *watch
out for,* i.e. to *regard*

HEEL
6117 'âqab (1), to *seize* by
the *heel;* to *circumvent*
6119 'âqêb (4), *track,
footprint; rear* position
4418 ptĕrna (1), *heel*

HEELS
6119 'âqêb (2), *track,
footprint; rear* position
6120 'âqêb (1), *one who
lies in wait*
8328 sheresh (1), *root*

HEGAI
1896 Hêgê' (3), *Hege* or
Hegai

HEGE
1896 Hêgê' (1), *Hege* or
Hegai

HEIFER
5697 'eglâh (11), *cow calf*
6510 pârâh (6), *heifer*
1151 damalis (1), *heifer*

HEIFER'S
5697 'eglâh (1), *cow calf*

HEIGHT
1361 gâbahh (2), to *be
lofty;* to *be haughty*
1363 gôbahh (8), *height;
grandeur; arrogance*
1364 gâbôahh (2), *high;
powerful; arrogant*
4791 mârôwm (9),
elevation; elation
6967 qôwmâh (30), *height*
7218 rô'sh (1), *head*
7312 rûwm (2), *elevation;
elation*
7314 rûwm (Ch.) (4),
altitude, tallness
7419 râmûwth (1), *heap*
of carcases
5311 hupsŏs (2), *altitude;
sky; dignity*
5313 hupsōma (1),
altitude; barrier

HEIGHTS
1116 bâmâh (1),
elevation, high place
4791 mârôwm (1),
elevation; elation

HEINOUS
2154 zimmâh (1), *bad
plan*

HEIR
3423 yârash (9), to
inherit; to *impoverish*
2816 klērŏnŏmĕŏ (1), to
be an heir to, inherit

2818 klērŏnŏmŏs (8),
*possessor by
inheritance*

HEIRS
3423 yârash (1), to
inherit; to *impoverish*
2816 klērŏnŏmĕŏ (1), to
be an heir to, inherit
2818 klērŏnŏmŏs (7),
*possessor by
inheritance*
4789 sugklērŏnŏmŏs (2),
participant in common

HELAH
2458 Chel'âh (2), *rust*

HELAM
2431 Chêylâm (2),
fortress

HELBAH
2462 Chelbâh (1), *fertility*

HELBON
2463 Chelbôwn (1),
fruitful

HELD
270 'âchaz (3), to *seize,
grasp; possess*
631 'âçar (1), to *fasten;* to
join battle
1102 bâlam (1), to
muzzle, control
1826 dâmam (1), to *be
silent;* to *be astonished*
2244 châbâ' (1), to *secrete*
2388 châzaq (6), to
fasten upon; to *seize*
2790 chârash (10), to
engrave; to *plow*
2814 châshâh (2), to
hush or *keep quiet*
2820 châsak (1), to
restrain or *refrain*
3447 yâshaṭ (2), to *extend*
3557 kûwl (1), to *keep in;*
to *measure*
5582 çâ'ad (1), to *support*
6213 'âsâh (1), to *do*
6901 qâbal (1), to *admit;*
to *take*
7311 rûwm (2), to *be
high;* to *rise* or *raise*
8557 temeç (1), *melting
disappearance*
2192 ĕchŏ (1), to *have;
hold; keep*
2258 ēn (1), I *was*
2270 hēsuchazŏ (2), to
refrain
2722 katĕchŏ (1), to *hold
down fast*
2902 kratĕŏ (2), to *seize*
2983 lambanŏ (1), to
take, receive
4160 pŏiĕŏ (1), to *make*
4601 sigaŏ (2), to *keep
silent*
4623 siōpaŏ (4), to *be
quiet*
4912 sunĕchŏ (1), to *hold
together*

HELDAI
2469 Chelday (2),
worldliness

HELEB
2460 Chêleb (1), *fatness*

HEREOF
5921+2063 'al (1), above, over, upon, or against
1722+5129 ĕn (7), in; during; because of

HEREOF
3778 hŏutŏs (1), this or that
5026 tautē₁ (1), (toward or of) this

HERES
2776 Chereç (1), shining

HERESH
2792 Cheresh (1), magical craft; silence

HERESIES
139 hairĕsis (3), party, sect; disunion or heresy

HERESY
139 hairĕsis (1), party, sect; disunion or heresy

HERETICK
141 hairĕtikŏs (1), schismatic, division

HERETOFORE
865 'ethmôwl (1), heretofore, formerly
8543 tᵉmôwl (6), yesterday
4258 prŏamartanō (1), to sin previously

HEREUNTO
1519+5124 ĕis (1), to or into

HEREWITH
2063 zô'th (2), this

HERITAGE
3425 yᵉrushâh (1), conquest
4181 môwrâshâh (1), possession
5157 nâchal (1), to inherit
5159 nachălâh (26), occupancy
2819 klĕrŏs (1), lot, portion

HERITAGES
5159 nachălâh (1), occupancy

HERMAS
2057 Hĕrmas (1), born of god Hermes

HERMES
2060 Hĕrmēs (1), born of god Hermes

HERMOGENES
2061 Hĕrmŏgĕnēs (1), born of god Hermes

HERMON
2768 Chermôwn (13), abrupt

HERMONITES
2769 Chermôwnîym (1), peaks of Hermon

HEROD
2264 Hĕrōdēs (40), heroic

HEROD'S
2264 Hĕrōdēs (4), heroic

HERODIANS
2265 Hĕrōdianŏi (3), Herodians

HERODIAS
2266 Hĕrōdias (4), heroic

HERODIAS'
2266 Hĕrōdias (2), heroic

HERODION
2267 Hĕrōdiōn (1), heroic

HERON
601 'ănâphâh (2), (poss.) parrot

HESED
2618 Cheçed (1), favor

HESHBON
2809 Cheshbôwn (38), contrivance; plan

HESHMON
2829 Cheshmôwn (1), opulent

HETH
2845 Chêth (14), terror

HETHLON
2855 Chethlôn (2), enswathed

HEW
1414 gᵉdad (Ch.) (2), to cut down
1438 gâda' (1), to fell a tree; to destroy
2404 châṭab (1), to chop or carve wood
2672 châtsab (2), to cut stone or carve wood
3772 kârath (3), to cut (off, down or asunder)
6458 pâçal (3), to carve, to chisel

HEWED
1496 gâzîyth (5), dressed stone
2672 châtsab (3), to cut stone or carve wood
4274 machtsêb (1), quarry stone
5408 nâthach (1), to dismember, cut up
6458 pâçal (2), to carve, to chisel
8158 shâçaph (1), to hack in pieces, i.e. kill

HEWER
2404 châṭab (1), to chop or carve wood

HEWERS
2404 châṭab (5), to chop or carve wood
2672 châtsab (4), to cut stone or carve wood

HEWETH
2672 châtsab (2), to cut stone or carve wood
3772 kârath (1), to cut (off, down or asunder)

HEWN
1438 gâda' (1), to fell a tree; to destroy
1496 gâzîyth (5), dressed stone
2672 châtsab (2), to cut stone or carve wood
4274 machtsêb (2), quarry stone
7060 qâmal (1), to wither
1581 ĕkkŏptō (3), to cut off; to frustrate
2991 laxĕutŏs (1), rock-quarried
2998 latŏmĕŏ (2), to quarry

HEZEKI
2395 Chizqîy (1), strong

HEZEKIAH
2396 Chizqîyâh (128), strengthened of Jehovah

HEZION
2383 Chezyôwn (1), vision

HEZIR
2387 Chêzîyr (2), protected

HEZRAI
2695 Chetsrôw (1), enclosure

HEZRO
2695 Chetsrôw (1), enclosure

HEZRON
2696 Chetsrôwn (17), court-yard

HEZRON'S
2696 Chetsrôwn (1), court-yard

HEZRONITES
2697 Chetsrôwnîy (2), Chetsronite

HID
2244 châbâ' (25), to secrete
2934 ṭâman (16), to hide
3582 kâchad (6), to destroy; to hide
3680 kâçâh (2), to cover
4301 maṭmôwn (2), secret storehouse
5641 çâthar (30), to hide by covering
5956 'âlam (11), to veil from sight, i.e. conceal
6845 tsâphan (5), to hide; to hoard or reserve
8587 ta'ălummâh (1), secret
613 apŏkruptō (5), to keep secret, conceal
614 apŏkruphŏs (2), secret; hidden things
1470 ĕgkruptō (2), incorporate with, mix in
2572 kaluptō (1), to cover up
2927 kruptŏs (3), private, unseen
2928 kruptō (10), to conceal
2990 lanthanō (2), to lie hid; unwittingly
3871 parakaluptō (1), to veil, be hidden
4032 pĕrikruptō (1), to conceal all around

HIDDAI
1914 Hidday (1), Hiddai

HIDDEKEL
2313 Chiddeqel (2), Tigris river

HIDDEN
2664 châphas (1), to seek; to mask
2934 ṭâman (1), to hide
4301 maṭmôwn (1), secret storehouse
4710 mitspûn (1), secret

HIDE
5341 nâtsar (1), to guard; to conceal, hide
5640 çâtham (1), to stop up; to keep secret
5956 'âlam (1), to veil from sight, i.e. conceal
6381 pâlâ' (1), to be, make great, difficult
6845 tsâphan (3), to hide; to hoard or reserve
613 apŏkruptō (1), to keep secret, conceal
2927 kruptŏs (3), private, unseen
2928 kruptō (1), to conceal
2990 lanthanō (1), to lie hid; unwittingly

HIDE
2244 châbâ' (6), to secrete
2247 châbah (5), to hide
2934 ṭâman (5), to hide
3582 kâchad (10), to destroy; to hide
3680 kâçâh (3), to cover
5127 nûwç (1), to vanish away, flee
5641 çâthar (33), to hide by covering
5785 'ôwr (2), skin, leather
5956 'âlam (8), to veil from sight, i.e. conceal
6004 'âmam (2), to overshadow by huddling together
6845 tsâphan (5), to hide; to hoard or reserve
2572 kaluptō (1), to cover
2928 kruptō (2), to conceal

HIDEST
5641 çâthar (5), to hide by covering
5956 'âlam (1), to veil from sight, i.e. conceal

HIDETH
2244 châbâ' (1), to secrete
2821 châshak (1), to be dark; to darken
2934 ṭâman (2), to hide
3680 kâçâh (1), to cover
5641 çâthar (5), to hide by covering
5848 'âṭaph (1), to shroud, i.e. clothe
5956 'âlam (2), to veil from sight, i.e. conceal
6845 tsâphan (1), to hide; to hoard or reserve
2928 kruptō (1), to conceal

HIDING
2253 chebyôwn (1), concealment, hiding
2934 ṭâman (1), to hide
4224 machăbê' (1), refuge, shelter
5643 çêther (3), cover, shelter

HIEL
2419 Chîy'êl (1), living of God

HIERAPOLIS
2404 Hiĕrapŏlis (1), holy city

HIGGAION
1902 higgâyôwn (1), *musical notation*

HIGH
376 'îysh (2), *man; male; someone*
753 'ôrek (1), *length*
1111 Bâlâq (1), *waster*
1116 bâmâh (99), *elevation, high place*
1361 gâbahh (4), *to be lofty; to be haughty*
1362 gâbâhh (3), *high; lofty*
1363 gôbahh (2), *height; grandeur; arrogance*
1364 gâbôahh (25), *high; powerful; arrogant*
1386 gabnôn (2), *peak of hills*
1419 gâdôwl (22), *great*
1870 derek (1), *road; course of life*
4546 mᵉçillâh (1), *main thoroughfare; viaduct*
4605 ma'al (7), *upward, above, overhead*
4608 ma'âleh (1), *elevation; platform*
4791 mârôwm (33), *elevation; elation*
4796 Mârôwth (1), *bitter springs*
4869 misgâb (4), high *refuge*
5375 nâsâ' (1), *to lift up*
5920 'al (3), the *Highest God*
5943 'illay (Ch.) (9), the *supreme God*
5945 'elyôwn (37), *loftier, higher; Supreme God*
5946 'elyôwn (Ch.) (4), the *Supreme God*
6381 pâlâ' (1), *to be, make great, difficult*
6877 tsᵉrîyach (1), *citadel*
6967 qôwmâh (5), *height*
7218 rô'sh (3), *head*
7311 rûwm (25), *to be high; to rise or raise*
7312 rûwm (3), *elevation; elation*
7315 rôwm (1), *aloft, on high*
7319 rôwmᵉmâh (1), *exaltation*, i.e. *praise*
7413 râmâh (4), *height; high seat of idolatry*
7682 sâgab (6), *to be, make lofty; be safe*
8192 shâphâh (1), *to bare*
8203 Shᵉphatyâh (2), *Jehovah has judged*
8205 shᵉphîy (7), *bare hill or plain*
8564 tamrûwr (1), *erection*, i.e. *pillar*
8643 tᵉrûw'âh (1), *battle-cry; clangor*
507 anō (1), *upward or on the top, heavenward*
749 archiĕrĕus (59), *high-priest, chief priest*
2032 ĕpŏuraniŏs (1), *above the sky, celestial*
2409 hiĕrĕus (1), *priest*
3173 mĕgas (2), *great, many*

5308 hupsēlŏs (9), *lofty* in place or character
5310 hupsistŏs (5), the *Supreme God*
5311 hupsŏs (3), *altitude; sky; dignity*
5313 hupsōma (1), *altitude; barrier*

HIGHER
1354 gab (1), *mounded or rounded: top or rim*
1361 gâbahh (4), *to be lofty; to be haughty*
1364 gâbôahh (5), *high; powerful; arrogant*
3201 yâkôl (1), *to be able*
5945 'elyôwn (4), *loftier, higher; Supreme God*
6706 tsᵉchîyach (1), *glaring*
7311 rûwm (2), *to be high; to rise or raise*
511 anōtĕrŏs (1), *upper part; former part*
5242 hupĕrĕchŏ (1), *to excel; superior*
5308 hupsēlŏs (1), *lofty*

HIGHEST
1364 gâbôahh (1), *high; powerful; arrogant*
4791 mârôwm (1), *elevation; elation*
5945 'elyôwn (3), *loftier, higher; Supreme God*
6788 tsammereth (2), *foliage*
7218 rô'sh (1), *head*
4410 prōtŏkathĕdria (1), *pre-eminence in council*
4411 prōtŏklisia (1), *pre-eminence at meals*
5310 hupsistŏs (8), the *Supreme God*

HIGHLY
1537+4053 ĕk (1), *out of*
2371 thumŏmachĕŏ (1), *to be exasperated*
5251 hupĕrupsŏō (1), *to raise to the highest*
5252 hupĕrphrŏnĕŏ (1), *to esteem oneself overmuch*
5308 hupsēlŏs (1), *lofty* in place or character

HIGHMINDED
5187 tuphŏō (1), *to inflate with self-conceit*
5309 hupsēlŏphrŏnĕŏ (2), *to be lofty in mind*

HIGHNESS
1346 ga'ăvâh (1), *arrogance; majesty*
7613 sᵉ'êth (1), *elevation; swelling leprous scab*

HIGHWAY
4546 mᵉçillâh (13), main *thoroughfare; viaduct*
4547 maçlûwl (1), main *thoroughfare*
3598 hŏdŏs (1), *road*

HIGHWAYS
734 'ôrach (1), *well-traveled road; manner of life*
2351 chûwts (1), *outside, outdoors; open market*

4546 mᵉçillâh (6), main *thoroughfare; viaduct*
1327+3598 diĕxŏdŏs (1), open *square*
3598 hŏdŏs (2), *road*

HILEN
2432 Chîylên (1), *fortress*

HILKIAH
2518 Chilqîyâh (33), *portion* (of) *Jehovah*

HILKIAH'S
2518 Chilqîyâh (1), *portion* (of) *Jehovah*

HILL
1389 gib'âh (30), *hillock*
2022 har (34), *mountain or range of hills*
4608 ma'âleh (1), *elevation; platform*
7161 qeren (1), *horn*
697 Arĕiŏs Pagŏs (1), *rock of Ares*
1015 bŏunŏs (1), *small hill*
3714 ŏrĕinŏs (2), *Highlands of Judæa*
3735 ŏrŏs (3), *hill, mountain*

HILL'S
2022 har (1), *mountain or range of hills*

HILLEL
1985 Hillêl (2), *praising* (God)

HILLS
1389 gib'âh (39), *hillock*
2022 har (23), *mountain or range of hills*
2042 hârâr (2), *mountain*
1015 bŏunŏs (1), *small hill*

HIN
1969 hîyn (22), *liquid measure*

HIND
355 'ayâlâh (1), *doe deer*
365 'ayeleth (1), *doe deer*

HINDER
268 'âchôwr (3), *behind, backward; west*
309 'âchar (1), *to remain; to delay*
310 'achar (1), *after*
314 'achărôwn (1), *late or last; behind; western*
4513 mâna' (1), *to deny, refuse*
5490 çôwph (1), *termination; end*
6213+8442 'âsâh (1), *to do or make*
7725 shûwb (2), *to turn back; to return*
348 anakŏptō (1), *to beat back*, i.e. *check*
2967 kōluō (2), *to stop*
4403 prumna (2), *stern of a ship*
5100+1464+1325 tis (1), *some* or *any person*

HINDERED
989 bᵉtêl (Ch.) (1), *to stop*
1465 ĕgkŏptō (2), *to impede, detain*

4546 mᵉçillâh (6), main *thoroughfare; viaduct*
1581 ĕkkŏptō (1), *to cut off; to frustrate*
2967 kōluō (1), *to stop*

HINDERETH
2820 châsak (1), *to restrain or refrain*

HINDERMOST
314 'achărôwn (1), *late or last; behind; western*
319 'achărîyth (1), *future; posterity*

HINDMOST
314 'achărôwn (1), *late or last; behind; western*
2179 zânab (2), *militarily attack the rear position*

HINDS
355 'ayâlâh (4), *doe deer*

HINDS'
355 'ayâlâh (3), *doe deer*

HINGES
6596 pôth (1), *hole; hinge; female genitals*
6735 tsîyr (1), *hinge*

HINNOM
2011 Hinnôm (13), *Hinnom*

HIP
7785 shôwq (1), lower *leg*

HIRAH
2437 Chîyrâh (2), *splendor*

HIRAM
2438 Chîyrâm (22), *noble*

HIRAM'S
2438 Chîyrâm (1), *noble*

HIRE
868 'ethnan (7), *gift price of harlotry*
4242 mᵉchîyr (1), *price, payment, wages*
7936 sâkar (2), *to hire*
7939 sâkâr (8), *payment, salary; compensation*
3408 misthŏs (3), *pay for services*
3409 misthŏō (1), *to hire*

HIRED
7916 sâkîyr (11), *man at wages, hired hand*
7917 sᵉkîyrâh (1), *hiring*
7936 sâkar (14), *to hire*
8566 tânâh (2), *to bargain with a harlot*
3407 misthiŏs (2), *hired-worker*
3409 misthŏō (1), *to hire*
3410 misthōma (1), *rented building*
3411 misthōtŏs (1), *wage-worker*

HIRELING
7916 sâkîyr (6), *man at wages, hired hand*
3411 misthōtŏs (2), *wage-worker*

HIRES
868 'ethnan (1), *gift price of harlotry*

HIREST
7806 shâzar (1), *to twist a thread of straw*

HISS
8319 shâraq (12), to whistle or *hiss*

HISSING
8292 sh^erûwqâh (1), *whistling; scorn*
8322 sh^erêqâh (7), *derision*

HIT
4672 mâtsâ' (2), to *find* or *acquire; to occur*

HITHER
1988 hălôm (6), *hither, to here*
2008 hênnâh (2), *from here; from there*
5066 nâgash (7), to *be, come, bring near*
6311 pôh (1), *here* or *hence*
1204 děurŏ (2), *hither!; hitherto*
1759 ĕnthadĕ (4), *here, hither*
3333 mĕtakalĕō (1), to *summon for, call for*
5602 hōdĕ (14), *here* or *hither*

HITHERTO
227 'âz (1), *at that time* or *place; therefore*
1973 hâl^eâh (2), *far away; thus far*
1988 hălôm (2), *hither, to here*
5704+2008 'ad (6), *as far (long) as; during*
5704+3541 'ad (2), *as far (long) as; during*
5704+6311 'ad (1), *as far (long) as; during*
5705+3542 'ad (Ch.) (1), *as far (long) as; during*
891+1204 achri (1), *until* or *up to*
2193+737 hĕōs (2), *until*
3768 ŏupō (1), *not yet*

HITTITE
2850 Chittîy (26), *Chittite*

HITTITES
2850 Chittîy (22), *Chittite*

HIVITE
2340 Chivvîy (9), *villager*

HIVITES
2340 Chivvîy (16), *villager*

HIZKIAH
2396 Chizqîyâh (1), *strengthened of Jehovah*

HIZKIJAH
2396 Chizqîyâh (1), *strengthened of Jehovah*

HO
1945 hôwy (3), *oh!, woe!*

HOAR
3713 k^ephôwr (2), *bowl; white frost*
7872 sêybâh (3), *old age*

HOARY
3713 k^ephôwr (1), *bowl; white frost*
7872 sêybâh (3), *old age*

HOBAB
2246 Chôbâb (2), *cherished*

HOBAH
2327 chôwbâh (1), *hiding place*

HOD
1963 hêyk (1), *how?*

HODAIAH
1939 Howday^evâhûw (1), *majesty of Jehovah*

HODAVIAH
1938 Hôwdavyâh (3), *majesty of Jehovah*

HODESH
2321 Chôdesh (1), *new moon*

HODEVAH
1937 Hôwd^evâh (1), *majesty of Jehovah*

HODIAH
1940 Hôwdîyâh (1), *Jewess*

HODIJAH
1940 Hôwdîyâh (5), *Jewess*

HOGLAH
2295 Choglâh (4), *partridge*

HOHAM
1944 Hôwhâm (1), *Hoham*

HOISED
1869 ĕpairō (1), to *raise up, look up*

HOLD
270 'âchaz (26), to *seize, grasp; possess*
816 'âsham (1), to *be guilty; to be punished*
1225 bitstsârôwn (1), *fortress*
2013 hâçâh (2), to *hush, be quiet*
2388 châzaq (35), to *fasten upon; to seize*
2790 chârash (16), to *engrave; to plow*
2814 châshâh (6), to *hush* or *keep quiet*
3447 yâshaţ (1), to *extend*
3557 kûwl (1), to *keep in; to maintain*
3905 lâchats (1), to *press; to distress*
3943 lâphath (1), to *clasp; to turn around*
4013 mibtsâr (1), *fortification; defender*
4581 mâ'ôwz (1), *fortified place; defense*
4672 mâtsâ' (2), to *find* or *acquire; to occur*
4679 m^etsad (2), *stronghold*
4686 mâtsûwd (7), *net* or *capture; fastness*
4692 mâtsôwr (1), *distress; fastness*
5253 nâçag (1), to *retreat*
5375 nâsâ' (1), to *lift up*
5381 nâsag (5), to *reach*
5553 çela' (1), *craggy rock; fortress*
5582 çâ'ad (1), to *support*

6076 'ôphel (1), *tumor; fortress*
6877 ts^erîyach (3), *citadel*
6901 qâbal (1), to *admit; to take*
6965 qûwm (1), to *rise*
8551 tâmak (4), to *obtain, keep fast*
8610 tâphas (7), to *manipulate, i.e. seize*
472 antĕchŏmai (2), to *adhere to; to care for*
1949 ĕpilambanŏmai (5), to *seize*
2192 ĕchō (3), to *have; hold; keep*
2722 katĕchō (5), to *hold down fast*
2902 kratĕō (19), to *seize*
4601 sigaō (2), to *keep silent*
4623 siōpaō (5), to *be quiet*
5083 tērĕō (1), to *keep, guard, obey*
5084 tērēsis (1), *observance; prison*
5392 phimŏō (2), to *restrain to silence*
5438 phulakē (1), *guarding* or *guard*

HOLDEN
270 'âchaz (1), to *seize, grasp; possess*
2388 châzaq (1), to *fasten upon; to seize*
2814 châshâh (1), to *hush* or *keep quiet*
3920 lâkad (1), to *catch; to capture*
5564 çâmak (1), to *lean upon; take hold* of
5582 çâ'ad (1), to *support*
6213 'âsâh (2), to *do* or *make*
8551 tâmak (1), to *obtain, keep fast*
2902 kratĕō (2), to *seize*

HOLDEST
270 'âchaz (1), to *seize, grasp; possess*
2790 chârash (2), to *engrave; to plow*
2803 châshab (1), to *weave, fabricate*
8610 tâphas (1), to *manipulate, i.e. seize*
2902 kratĕō (1), to *seize*

HOLDETH
270 'âchaz (1), to *seize, grasp; possess*
2388 châzaq (2), to *fasten upon; to seize*
2790 chârash (2), to *engrave; to plow*
7760 sûwm (1), to *put, place*
8551 tâmak (2), to *obtain, keep fast*
2902 kratĕō (2), to *seize*

HOLDING
3557 kûwl (1), to *keep in; to measure*
8551 tâmak (1), to *obtain, keep fast*
472 antĕchŏmai (1), to *adhere to; to care for*

HOLDS
4013 mibtsâr (11), *fortification; defender*
4581 mâ'ôwz (1), *fortified place; defense*
4679 m^etsad (6), *stronghold*
4686 mâtsûwd (1), *net* or *capture; fastness*
4694 m^etsûwrâh (1), *rampart, fortification*

HOLE
2356 chôwr (4), *cavity, socket, den*
4718 maqqebeth (1), *hammer*
5357 nâqîyq (1), *cleft, crevice*
6310 peh (6), *mouth; opening*

HOLE'S
6354 pachath (1), *pit*

HOLES
2356 chôwr (4), *cavity, socket, den*
4526 miçgereth (1), *margin; stronghold*
4631 m^e'ârâh (1), *dark cavern*
5344 nâqab (1), to *puncture, perforate*
5357 nâqîyq (2), *cleft, crevice*
5454 phōlĕŏs (2), *burrow, den hole*

HOLIER
6942 qâdâsh (1), to *be, make clean*

HOLIEST
39 hagiŏn (3), *sacred thing, place or person*

HOLILY
3743 hŏsiōs (1), *piously*

HOLINESS
6944 qôdesh (30), *sacred place or thing*
38 hagiasmŏs (5), *state of purity*
41 hagiŏtēs (1), *state of holiness*
42 hagiōsunē (3), *quality of holiness*
2150 ĕusĕbĕia (1), *piety, religious*
2412 hiĕrŏprĕpēs (1), *reverent*
3742 hŏsiŏtēs (2), *piety*

HOLLOW
3709 kaph (4), *hollow of hand; paw; sole* of foot
4388 maktêsh (1), *mortar; socket*
5014 nâbab (3), to *be hollow; be foolish*
8168 shô'al (1), *palm of hand; handful*
8258 sh^eqa'rûwrâh (1), *depression*

HOLON
2473 Chôlôwn (3), *sandy*

HOLPEN
2220 zᵉrôwa' (1), *arm; foreleg; force, power*
5826 'âzar (3), *to protect or aid*
482 antilambanŏmai (1), *to come to the aid*

HOLY
2623 châçîyd (5), *religiously pious, godly*
4720 miqdâsh (3), *sanctuary of deity*
6918 qâdôwsh (100), *sacred*
6922 qaddîysh (Ch.) (7), *sacred*
6942 qâdâsh (7), *to be, make clean*
6944 qôdesh (297), *sacred place or thing*
37 hagiazō (1), *to purify or consecrate*
39 hagiŏn (3), *sacred thing, place or person*
40 hagiŏs (162), *sacred, holy*
2413 hiĕrŏs (2), *sacred, set apart for God*
3741 hŏsiŏs (6), *hallowed, pious, sacred*

HOLYDAY
2287 châgag (1), *to observe a festival*
1859 hĕŏrtē (1), *festival*

HOMAM
1950 Hôwmâm (1), *raging*

HOME
168 'ôhel (1), *tent*
1004 bayith (26), *house; temple; family; tribe*
4725 mâqôwm (3), *general locality, place*
5115 nâvâh (1), *to rest as at home*
7725 shûwb (5), *to turn back; to return*
8432 tâvek (1), *center, middle*
1438 hĕautŏu (1), *himself, herself, itself*
1736 ĕndēmĕŏ (1), *to be at home*
2398 idiŏs (2), *private or separate*
3614 ŏikia (1), *abode; family*
3624 ŏikŏs (4), *dwelling; family*
3626 ŏikŏurŏs (1), *domestically inclined*

HOMEBORN
249 'ezrâch (1), *native born*
1004 bayith (1), *house; temple; family, tribe*

HOMER
2563 chômer (10), *clay; dry measure*

HOMERS
2563 chômer (1), *clay; dry measure*

HONEST
2570 kalŏs (5), *good; valuable; virtuous*
4586 sĕmnŏs (1), *honorable, noble*

HONESTLY
2156 ĕuschēmŏnōs (2), *fittingly, properly*
2573 kalŏs (1), *well, i.e. rightly*

HONESTY
4587 sĕmnŏtēs (1), *venerableness*

HONEY
1706 dᵉbash (52), *honey*
3192 mĕli (4), *honey*

HONEYCOMB
3293 ya'ar (1), *honey in the comb*
3295+1706 ya'ărâh (1), *honey in the comb*
5317 nôpheth (4), *honey from the comb*
5317+6688 nôpheth (1), *honey from the comb*
6688+1706 tsûwph (1), *comb of dripping honey*
3193+2781 mĕlissiŏs (1), *honeybee comb*

HONOUR
1921 hâdar (2), *to favor or honor; to be high*
1922 hâdar (Ch.) (1), *to magnify, glorify*
1923 hădar (Ch.) (2), *magnificence, glory*
1926 hâdâr (5), *magnificence*
1927 hădârâh (1), *ornament; splendor*
1935 hôwd (6), *grandeur, majesty*
3366 yᵉqâr (12), *wealth; costliness; dignity*
3367 yᵉqâr (Ch.) (2), *glory, honor*
3513 kâbad (22), *to be rich, glorious*
3515 kâbêd (1), *severe, difficult, stupid*
3519 kâbôwd (32), *splendor, wealth*
8597 tiph'ârâh (4), *ornament*
820 atimŏs (2), *dishonoured*
1391 dŏxa (6), *glory; brilliance*
5091 timaō (14), *to revere, honor*
5092 timē (31), *esteem; nobility; money*

HONOURABLE
142 'âdar (1), *magnificent; glorious*
1935 hôwd (2), *grandeur, majesty*
3368 yâqâr (1), *valuable*
3513 kâbad (13), *to be rich, glorious*
3519 kâbôwd (2), *splendor, wealth*
5375+6440 nâsâ' (4), *to lift up*
820 atimŏs (1), *dishonoured*
1741 ĕndŏxŏs (1), *noble; honored*
1784 ĕntimŏs (1), *valued, considered precious*
2158 ĕuschēmŏn (3), *decorous, proper; noble*

5093 timiŏs (1), *costly; honored, esteemed*

HONOURED
1921 hâdar (1), *to favor or honor; to be high*
1922 hădar (Ch.) (1), *to magnify, glorify*
3513 kâbad (5), *to be rich, glorious*
1392 dŏxazō (1), *to render, esteem glorious*
5092 timē (1), *esteem; nobility; money*

HONOUREST
3513 kâbad (1), *to be rich, glorious*

HONOURETH
3513 kâbad (4), *to be rich, glorious*
1392 dŏxazō (1), *to render, esteem glorious*
5091 timaō (3), *to revere, honor, show respect*

HONOURS
5091 timaō (1), *to revere, honor, show respect*

HOODS
6797 tsânîyph (1), *head-dress, turban*

HOOF
6541 parçâh (12), *split hoof*

HOOFS
6536 pâraç (1), *to break in pieces; to split*
6541 parçâh (5), *split hoof*

HOOK
100 'agmôwn (1), *rush; rope of rushes*
2397 châch (2), *ring for the nose or lips*
2443 chakkâh (1), *fish hook*
44 agkistrŏn (1), *fish hook*

HOOKS
2053 vâv (13), *hook*
2397 châch (2), *ring for the nose or lips*
6793 tsinnâh (1), *large shield; piercing cold*
8240 shâphâth (1), *two-pronged hook*

HOPE
982 bâṭach (1), *to trust, be confident or sure*
983 beṭach (1), *safety, security, trust*
986 biṭṭâchôwn (1), *trust*
2342 chûwl (1), *to dance, whirl; to wait; to pervert*
2620 châçâh (1), *to flee to; to confide in*
2976 yâ'ash (3), *to despond, despair*
3176 yâchal (19), *to wait; to be patient, hope*
3689 keçel (1), *loin; back; viscera; trust*
4009 mibṭâch (1), *security; assurance*
4268 machâçeh (2), *shelter; refuge*
4723 miqveh (4), *confidence; collection*

7663 sâbar (1), *to expect with hope*
7664 sêber (2), *expectation*
8431 tôwcheleth (6), *hope, expectation*
8615 tiqvâh (23), *cord; expectancy*
1679 ĕlpizō (7), *to expect or confide, hope for*
1680 ĕlpis (51), *hope; confidence*

HOPE'S
1679 ĕlpizō (1), *to expect or confide, hope for*

HOPED
982 bâṭach (1), *to trust, be confident or sure*
3176 yâchal (1), *to wait; to be patient, hope*
7663 sâbar (2), *to expect with hope*
1679 ĕlpizō (4), *to expect or confide, hope for*

HOPETH
1679 ĕlpizō (1), *to expect or confide, hope for*

HOPHNI
2652 Chophnîy (5), *pair of fists*

HOPING
560 apĕlpizō (1), *to fully expect in return*
1679 ĕlpizō (1), *to expect or confide, hope for*

HOR
2023 Hôr (12), *mountain*

HOR-HAGIDGAD
2735 Chôr hag-Gidgâd (2), *hole of the cleft*

HORAM
2036 Hôrâm (1), *high, exalted*

HOREB
2722 Chôrêb (17), *desolate*

HOREM
2765 Chŏrêm (1), *devoted*

HORI
2753 Chôrîy (4), *cave-dweller*

HORIMS
2752 Chôrîy (2), *cave-dweller*

HORITE
2752 Chôrîy (1), *cave-dweller*

HORITES
2752 Chôrîy (3), *cave-dweller*

HORMAH
2767 Chormâh (9), *devoted*

HORN
7161 qeren (28), *horn*
7162 qeren (Ch.) (5), *horn*
2768 kĕras (1), *horn*

HORNET
6880 tsir'âh (2), *wasp*

HORNETS
6880 tsir'âh (1), *wasp*

HORNS
3104 yôwbêl (3), *blast of a ram's horn*
7160 qâran (1), *to protrude out horns*
7161 qeren (46), *horn*
7162 qeren (Ch.) (5), *horn*
2768 kĕras (10), *horn*

HORONAIM
2773 Chôrŏnayim (4), *double cave-town*

HORONITE
2772 Chôrŏnîy (3), *Choronite*

HORRIBLE
2152 zal'âphâh (1), *glow; famine*
7588 shâ'ôwn (1), *uproar; destruction*
8186 sha'ărûwrâh (4), *something fearful*

HORRIBLY
8175 sâ'ar (1), *to storm; to shiver, i.e. fear*
8178 sa'ar (1), *tempest; terror*

HORROR
367 'êymâh (1), *fright*
2152 zal'âphâh (1), *glow; famine*
6427 pallâtsûwth (2), *affright, trembling fear*

HORSE
5483 çûwç (35), *horse*
2462 hippŏs (8), *horse*

HORSEBACK
5483 çûwç (1), *horse*
7392 râkab (2), *to ride*
7392+5483 râkab (2), *to ride*

HORSEHOOFS
6119+5483 'âqêb (1), *track, footprint*

HORSELEACH
5936 'ălûwqâh (1), *leech*

HORSEMAN
6571 pârâsh (1), *horse; chariot driver*
7395 rakkâb (1), *charioteer*

HORSEMEN
6571 pârâsh (56), *horse; chariot driver*
2460 hippĕus (2), *member of a cavalry*
2461 hippikŏn (1), *cavalry force*

HORSES
5483 çûwç (96), *horse*
5484 çûwçâh (1), *mare*
2462 hippŏs (7), *horse*

HORSES'
5483 çûwç (1), *horse*
2462 hippŏs (1), *horse*

HOSAH
2621 Chôçâh (5), *hopeful*

HOSANNA
5614 hōsanna (6), *"oh save!"*

HOSEA
1954 Hôwshêä' (3), *deliverer*

HOSEN
6361 paṭṭîysh (Ch.) (1), *garment*

HOSHAIAH
1955 Hôwshi'yâh (3), *Jehovah has saved*

HOSHAMA
1953 Hôwshâmâ' (1), *Jehovah has heard*

HOSHEA
1954 Hôwshêä' (11), *deliverer*

HOSPITALITY
5381 philŏnĕxia (1), *hospitableness*
5382 philŏxĕnŏs (3), *hospitable*

HOST
2426 chêyl (2), *rampart, battlement*
2428 chayil (28), *army; wealth; virtue; valor*
4264 machăneh (54), *encampment*
6635 tsâbâ' (100), *army, military host*
3581 xĕnŏs (1), *alien; guest or host*
3830 pandŏchĕus (1), *innkeeper*
4756 stratia (2), *army; celestial luminaries*

HOSTAGES
1121+8594 bên (2), *son, descendant; people*

HOSTS
2428 chayil (1), *army; wealth; virtue; valor*
4264 machăneh (4), *encampment*
6635 tsâbâ' (293), *army, military host*

HOT
228 'ăzâ' (Ch.) (1), *to heat*
784 'êsh (1), *fire*
2525 châm (1), *hot, sweltering*
2527 chôm (4), *heat*
2534 chêmâh (3), *heat; anger; poison*
2552 châmam (3), *to be hot; to be in a rage*
2734 chârâh (10), *to blaze up*
3179 yâcham (2), *to conceive*
7565 resheph (1), *flame*
2200 zĕstŏs (3), *hot, i.e. fervent*
2743 kautēriazō (1), *to brand or cauterize*

HOTHAM
2369 Chôwthâm (1), *seal*

HOTHAN
2369 Chôwthâm (1), *seal*

HOTHIR
1956 Hôwthîyr (2), *he has caused to remain*

HOTLY
1814 dâlaq (1), *to flame; to pursue*

HOTTEST
2389 châzâq (1), *strong; severe, hard, violent*

HOUGH
6131 'âqar (1), *to pluck up roots; to hamstring*

HOUGHED
6131 'âqar (3), *to pluck up roots; to hamstring*

HOUR
8160 shâ'âh (Ch.) (5), *immediately*
734 Artĕmas (1), *gift of Artemis*
2256 hēmiōriŏn (1), *half-hour*
5610 hōra (85), *hour, i.e. a unit of time*

HOURS
5610 hōra (3), *hour, i.e. a unit of time*

HOUSE
1004 bayith (1745), *house; temple; family*
1005 bayith (Ch.) (41), *house; temple; family*
1008 Bêyth-'Êl (5), *house of God*
1035 Bêyth Lechem (1), *house of bread*
5854 'Aṭrôwth Bêyth Yôw'âb (1), *crowns of (the) house of Joäb*
3609 ŏikĕiŏs (1), *of the household*
3613 ŏikētēriŏn (1), *residence, home*
3614 ŏikia (84), *abode; family*
3616 ŏikŏdĕspŏtĕō (1), *to be the head of a family*
3617 ŏikŏdĕspŏtēs (7), *head of a family*
3624 ŏikŏs (96), *dwelling; family*
3832 panŏiki (1), *with the whole family*

HOUSEHOLD
1004 bayith (47), *house; temple; family, tribe*
5657 'ăbuddâh (1), *service*
2322 thĕrapĕia (2), *cure, healing; domestics*
3609 ŏikĕiŏs (2), *of the household*
3610 ŏikĕtēs (1), *menial domestic servant*
3614 ŏikia (1), *abode; family*
3615 ŏikiakŏs (2), *relatives*
3624 ŏikŏs (3), *dwelling; family*

HOUSEHOLDER
3617 ŏikŏdĕspŏtēs (4), *head of a family*

HOUSEHOLDS
1004 bayith (7), *house; temple; family, tribe*

HOUSES
490 'almânâh (1), *widow*
1004 bayith (116), *house; temple; family, tribe*
1005 bayith (Ch.) (2), *house; temple; family*
4999 nâ'âh (1), *home, dwelling; pasture*

3614 ŏikia (8), *abode; family*
3624 ŏikŏs (5), *dwelling; family*

HOUSETOP
1406 gâg (2), *roof; top*
1430 dōma (5), *roof, housetop*

HOUSETOPS
1406 gâg (5), *roof; top*
1430 dōma (2), *roof, housetop*

HOW
335 'ay (1), *where?*
346 'ayêh (2), *where?*
349 'êyk (75), *how? or how!; where?*
434 'ĕlûwl (1), *good for nothing*
637 'aph (18), *also or yea; though*
834 'ăsher (26), *how, because, in order that*
1963 hêyk (2), *how?*
3588 kîy (11), *for, that because*
4069 maddûwa' (1), *why?, what?*
4100 mâh (59), *how?, how!; what, whatever*
4101 mâh (Ch.) (3), *how?, how!; what, whatever*
5704 'ad (47), *as far (long) as; during*
2193 hĕŏs (6), *until*
2245 hēlikŏs (1), *how much, how great*
2531 kathōs (11), *just or inasmuch as, that*
3386 mētigĕ (1), *not to say (the rather still)*
3704 hŏpōs (4), *in the manner that*
3745 hŏsŏs (7), *as much as*
3754 hŏti (14), *that; because; since*
4012 pĕri (1), *about; around*
4080 pēlikŏs (2), *how much, how great*
4212 pŏsakis (2), *how many times*
4214 pŏsŏs (26), *how much?; how much!*
4219 pŏtĕ (1), *at what time?*
4459 pōs (96), *in what way?; how?; how much!*
4559 sarkikŏs (2), *pertaining to flesh*
5101 tis (11), *who?, which? or what?*
5613 hōs (19), *which, how, i.e. in that manner*

HOWBEIT
199 'ûwlâm (1), *however or on the contrary*
389 'ak (1), *surely; only, however*
657 'ephĕç (1), *end; no further*
3651 kên (1), *just; right, correct*
7535 raq (1), *merely; although*
235 alla (8), *but, yet, except, instead*

1161 dĕ (1), *but, yet*
3305 mĕntōi (1), *however*

HOWL
3213 yâlal (27), to *howl,
wail, yell*
3649 ŏlŏluzō (1), to *howl,*
i.e. *shriek or wail*

HOWLED
3213 yâlal (1), to *howl,
wail, yell*

HOWLING
3213 yâlal (5), to *howl,
wail, yell*
3214 yᵉlêl (1), *howl, wail*

HOWLINGS
3213 yâlal (1), to *howl,
wail, yell*

HOWSOEVER
1961+4101 hâyâh (1), to
exist, i.e. *be or become*
3605+834 kôl (1), *all, any
or every*
7535 raq (1), *merely;
although*

HUGE
7230 rôb (1), *abundance*

HUKKOK
2712 Chuqqôq (1),
appointed

HUKOK
2712 Chuqqôq (1),
appointed

HUL
2343 Chûwl (2), *circle*

HULDAH
2468 Chuldâh (2), *weasel*

HUMBLE
3665 kâna' (2), to
*humiliate, vanquish,
subdue*
6031 'ânâh (4), to *afflict,
be afflicted*
6041 'ânîy (5), *depressed*
7511 râphaç (1), to
trample; to prostrate
7807+5869 shach (1),
sunk, i.e. *downcast*
8213 shâphêl (2), to
humiliate
8217 shâphâl (3),
depressed, low
5011 tapĕinŏs (2),
humiliated, lowly
5013 tapĕinŏō (5), to
depress; to humiliate

HUMBLED
1792 dâkâ' (1), to be
contrite, be humbled
3665 kâna' (13), to
humiliate, vanquish
6031 'ânâh (7), to *afflict,
be afflicted*
7743 shûwach (1), to *sink*
8213 shâphêl (4), to
humiliate
8214 shᵉphal (Ch.) (1), to
humiliate
5013 tapĕinŏō (1), to
depress; to humiliate

HUMBLEDST
3665 kâna' (1), to
humiliate, vanquish

HUMBLENESS
5012 tapĕinŏphrŏsunē
(1), *modesty, humility*

HUMBLETH
3665 kâna' (2), to
humiliate, vanquish
7817 shâchach (1), to
sink or depress
8213 shâphêl (2), to
humiliate
5013 tapĕinŏō (2), to
depress; to humiliate

HUMBLY
6800 tsâna' (1), to
humiliate
7812 shâchâh (1), to
prostrate in homage

HUMILIATION
5014 tapĕinōsis (1),
humbleness, lowliness

HUMILITY
6038 'ănâvâh (3),
condescension
5012 tapĕinŏphrŏsunē
(4), *modesty, humility*

HUMTAH
2457 chel'âh (1), *rust*

HUNDRED
520 'ammâh (1), *cubit*
3967 mê'âh (545),
hundred
3969 mᵉ'âh (Ch.) (7),
hundred
1250 diakŏsiŏi (8), *two
hundred*
1540 hĕkatŏn (14),
hundred
1541 hĕkatŏntaĕtēs (1),
centenarian
3461 murias (1),
ten-thousand
4001 pĕntakŏsiŏi (2), *five
hundred*
5071 tĕtrakŏsiŏi (4), *four
hundred*
5145 triakŏsiŏi (2), *three
hundred*
5516 chi xi stigma (2), 666

HUNDREDFOLD
3967+8180 mê'âh (1),
hundred
1540 hĕkatŏn (2),
hundred
1542 hĕkatŏntaplasiŏn
(3), *hundred times*

HUNDREDS
3967 mê'âh (27), *hundred*
1540 hĕkatŏn (1),
hundred

HUNDREDTH
3967 mê'âh (3), *hundred*

HUNGER
7456 râ'êb (5), to *hunger*
7457 râ'êb (8), *hungry*
3042 limŏs (3), *scarcity,
famine*
3983 pĕinaō (8), to
famish; to crave

HUNGERBITTEN
7457 râ'êb (1), *hungry*

HUNGERED
3983 pĕinaō (2), to
famish; to crave

HUNGRED
3983 pĕinaō (9), to
famish; to crave

HUNGRY
7456 râ'êb (25), to *hunger*
3983 pĕinaō (4), to
famish; to crave
4361 prŏspĕinŏs (1),
intensely hungry

HUNT
6679 tsûwd (11), to *lie in
wait; to catch*
7291 râdaph (1), to *run
after with hostility*

HUNTED
4686 mâtsûwd (1), *net or
capture; fastness*

HUNTER
6718 tsayid (4), *hunting
game; lunch, food*

HUNTERS
6719 tsayâd (1),
huntsman

HUNTEST
6658 tsâdâh (1), to
desolate
6679 tsûwd (1), to *lie in
wait; to catch*

HUNTETH
6679 tsûwd (1), to *lie in
wait; to catch*

HUNTING
6718 tsayid (2), *hunting
game; lunch, food*

HUPHAM
2349 Chûwphâm (1),
protection

HUPHAMITES
2350 Chûwphâmîy (1),
Chuphamite

HUPPAH
2647 Chuppâh (1),
canopy

HUPPIM
2650 Chuppîym (3),
canopies

HUR
2354 Chûwr (16), *cell of a
prison or white linen*

HURAI
2360 Chûwray (1),
linen-worker

HURAM
2361 Chûwrâm (6), *noble*
2438 Chîyrâm (6), *noble*

HURI
2359 Chûwrîy (1),
linen-worker

HURL
7993 shâlak (1), to *throw
out, down or away*

HURLETH
8175 sâ'ar (1), to *storm;
to shiver,* i.e. *fear*

HURT
1697 dâbâr (1), *word;
matter; thing*
2248 chăbûwlâh (Ch.)
(1), *crime, wrong*
2250 chabbûwrâh (1),
weal, bruise
2255 chăbal (Ch.) (1), to
ruin, destroy

HUSBANDS
2257 chăbal (Ch.) (2),
harm, wound
3637 kâlam (2), to *taunt
or insult*
5062 nâgaph (2), to
inflict a disease
5142 nᵉzaq (Ch.) (1), to
suffer, inflict loss
6031 'ânâh (1), to *afflict,
be afflicted*
6087 'âtsab (1), to *worry,
have pain or anger*
6485 pâqad (1), to *visit,
care for, count*
7451 ra' (20), *bad; evil*
7489 râ'a' (7), to *break to
pieces*
7665 shâbar (3), to *burst*
7667 sheber (4), *fracture;
ruin*
91 adikĕŏ (10), to *do
wrong*
984 blaptŏ (2), to *hinder,*
i.e. *to injure*
2559 kakŏō (1), to *injure;
to oppress; to embitter*
5196 hubris (1), *insult;
injury*

HURTFUL
5142 nᵉzaq (Ch.) (1), to
suffer, inflict loss
7451 ra' (1), *bad; evil*
983 blabĕrŏs (1),
injurious, harmful

HURTING
7489 râ'a' (1), to *break to
pieces*

HUSBAND
376 'îysh (66), *man;
male; someone*
1167 ba'al (13), *master;
husband; owner; citizen*
2860 châthân (2),
bridegroom
435 anēr (38), *man; male*
5220 hupandrŏs (1),
married woman

HUSBAND'S
376 'îysh (2), *man; male;
someone*
2992 yâbam (2), to *marry
a dead brother's widow*
2993 yâbâm (2),
husband's brother

HUSBANDMAN
376+127 'îysh (1), *man;
male; someone*
406 'ikkâr (2), *farmer*
5647 'âbad (1), to *do,
work, serve*
1092 gĕŏrgŏs (3), *farmer;
tenant farmer*

HUSBANDMEN
406 'ikkâr (3), *farmer*
1461 gûwb (1), to *dig*
3009 yâgab (1), to *dig or
plow*
1092 gĕŏrgŏs (16),
farmer; tenant farmer

HUSBANDRY
127 'ădâmâh (1), *soil;
land*
1091 gĕŏrgiŏn (1),
cultivable, i.e. *farm*

HUSBANDS
376 'îysh (1), *man; male*

582 'ĕnôwsh (3), *man; person, human*
1167 ba'al (2), *master; husband; owner; citizen*
435 *anēr* (12), *man; male*
5362 *philandrŏs* (1), *affectionate as a wife to her husband*

HUSHAH
2364 Chûwshâh (1), *haste*

HUSHAI
2365 Chûwshay (14), *hasty*

HUSHAM
2367 Chûwshâm (4), *hastily*

HUSHATHITE
2843 Chûshâthîy (5), *Chushathite*

HUSHIM
2366 Chûwshîym (4), those who *hasten*

HUSK
2085 zâg (1), grape *skin*
6861 tsiqlôn (1), tied up *sack*

HUSKS
2769 *kĕratiŏn* (1), *pod*

HUZ
5780 'Ûwts (1), *consultation*

HUZZAB
5324 nâtsab (1), to *station*

HYMENAEUS
5211 Humĕnaiŏs (2), *one dedicated to the god of weddings*

HYMN
5214 humnĕŏ (1), to *celebrate God in song*

HYMNS
5215 humnŏs (2), *hymn or religious ode*

HYPOCRISIES
5272 hupŏkrisis (1), *deceit, hypocrisy*

HYPOCRISY
2612 chôneph (1), moral *filth,* i.e. *wickedness*
505 anupŏkritŏs (1), *sincere, genuine*
5272 hupŏkrisis (4), *deceit, hypocrisy*

HYPOCRITE
120+2611 'âdâm (1), *human being; mankind*
2611 chânêph (6), *soiled* (i.e. with sin), *impious*
5273 hupŏkritēs (3), *dissembler, hypocrite*

HYPOCRITE'S
2611 chânêph (1), *soiled* (i.e. with sin), *impious*

HYPOCRITES
120+2611 'âdâm (1), *human being; mankind*
2611 chânêph (2), *soiled* (i.e. with sin), *impious*
5273 hupŏkritēs (17), *dissembler, hypocrite*

HYPOCRITICAL
2611 chânêph (2), *soiled* (i.e. with sin), *impious*

HYSSOP
231 'êzôwb (10), *hyssop*
5301 hussōpŏs (2), *hyssop plant*

I-CHABOD
350 Îy-kâbôwd (1), *inglorious*

I-CHABOD'S
350 Îy-kâbôwd (1), *inglorious*

IBHAR
2984 Yibchar (3), *choice*

IBLEAM
2991 Yibleʻâm (3), *devouring people*

IBNEIAH
2997 Yibneyâh (1), *built of Jehovah*

IBNIJAH
2998 Yibnîyâh (1), *building of Jehovah*

IBRI
5681 'Ibrîy (1), *Eberite* (i.e. Hebrew)

IBZAN
78 'Ibtsân (2), *splendid*

ICE
7140 qerach (3), *ice; hail; rock crystal*

ICONIUM
2430 Ikŏniŏn (6), *image-like*

IDALAH
3030 Yidʻălâh (1), *Jidalah*

IDBASH
3031 Yidbâsh (1), *honeyed*

IDDO
112 'Iddôw (2), *Iddo*
3035 Yiddôw (1), *praised*
3260 Yeʻdîy (1), *appointed*
5714 'Iddôw (10), *timely*

IDLE
7423 remîyâh (1), *remissness; treachery*
7504 râpheh (2), *slack*
692 argŏs (6), *lazy; useless*
3026 lêrŏs (1), *twaddle,* i.e. an *incredible story*

IDLENESS
6104 'atslûwth (1), *indolence*
8220 shiphlûwth (1), *remissness, idleness*
8252 shâqaṭ (1), to *repose*

IDOL
205 'âven (1), *trouble, vanity, wickedness*
457 'ĕlîyl (1), *vain idol*
4656 miphletseth (4), *terror idol*
5566 çemel (2), *likeness*
6089 'etseb (1), *earthen vessel; painful toil*
6090 'ôtseb (1), *fashioned idol; pain*
1494 ĕidōlŏthutŏn (1), *idolatrous offering*
1497 ĕidōlŏn (4), *idol,* or the *worship of such*

IDOL'S
1493 ĕidōlĕiŏn (1), *idol temple*

IDOLATER
1496 ĕidōlŏlatrēs (2), *image-worshipper*

IDOLATERS
1496 ĕidōlŏlatrēs (5), *image-worshipper*

IDOLATRIES
1495 ĕidōlŏlatrĕia (1), *image-worship*

IDOLATROUS
3649 kâmâr (1), *pagan priest*

IDOLATRY
8655 terâphîym (1), *healer*
1495 ĕidōlŏlatrĕia (3), *image-worship*
2712 katĕidōlŏs (1), *utterly idolatrous*

IDOLS
367 'êymâh (1), *fright*
410 'êl (1), *mighty;* the *Almighty*
457 'ĕlîyl (16), *vain idol*
1544 gillûwl (47), *idol*
2553 chammân (1), *sun-pillar*
6091 'âtsâb (16), *image, idol*
6736 tsîyr (1), *carved idolatrous image*
8251 shiqqûwts (1), *disgusting; idol*
8655 terâphîym (1), *healer*
1494 ĕidōlŏthutŏn (9), *idolatrous offering*
1497 ĕidōlŏn (7), *idol,* or the *worship of such*

IDUMAEA
2401 Idŏumaia (1), *Idumæa,* i.e. *Edom*

IDUMEA
123 'Ědôm (4), *red*

IF
176 'ôw (3), *or, whether*
194 'ûwlay (9), *if not*
432 'illûw (1), *if*
518 'îm (557), *whether?; if*
834 'âsher (19), *who, which, what, that*
2005 hên (3), *lo!; if!*
2006 hên (Ch.) (11), *lo; whether, but, if*
3588 kîy (159), *for, that because*
3808 lô' (1), *no, not*
3863 lûw' (7), *if; would that!*
3883 lûwl (1), *spiral step*
3884 lûwlê' (2), *if not*
6112 'Êtsen (1), *spear*
148 aischrŏlŏgia (3), *vile conversation*
1437 ĕan (216), *in case that, although*
1477 hĕdraiōma (5), *basis, foundation*
1487 ĕi (305), *if, whether*
1489 ĕigĕ (5), *if indeed*
1490 ĕi dĕ mē(gĕ) (4), *but if not*
1499 ĕi kai (6), *if also*

1512 ĕi pĕr (4), *if perhaps*
1513 ĕi pōs (4), *if somehow*
1535 ĕitĕ (1), *if too*
2579 kan (5), *and if*
3379 mēpŏtĕ (1), *not ever; if,* or *lest ever*

IGAL
3008 Yig'âl (2), *avenger*

IGDALIAH
3012 Yigdalyâhûw (1), *magnified of Jehovah*

IGEAL
3008 Yig'âl (1), *avenger*

IGNOMINY
7036 qâlôwn (1), *disgrace*

IGNORANCE
7684 shegâgâh (12), *mistake, transgression*
7686 shâgâh (1), to *transgress by mistake*
52 agnŏia (4), *ignorance*
56 agnōsia (1), state of *ignorance*

IGNORANT
3808+3045 lô' (3), no, *not know; not understand*
50 agnŏĕō (10), to *not know; not understand*
2399 idiōtēs (1), *not initiated; untrained*
2990 lanthanō (2), to *lie hid; unwittingly*

IGNORANTLY
1097+1847 beliy (1), *not yet; lacking;*
7683 shâgag (1), to *sin through oversight*
50 agnŏĕō (2), to *not know; not understand*

IIM
5864 'Iyîym (2), *ruins*

IJE-ABARIM
5863 'Iyêy hâ-'Ăbârîym (2), *ruins of the passers*

IJON
5859 'Iyôwn (3), *ruin*

IKKESH
6142 'Iqqêsh (3), *perverse*

ILAI
5866 'Îylay (1), *elevated*

ILL
3415 yâra' (2), to *fear*
6709 tsachănâh (1), *stench*
7451 ra' (8), *bad; evil*
7489 râ'a' (3), to *be good for nothing*
2556 kakŏs (1), *bad, evil, wrong*

ILLUMINATED
5461 phōtizō (1), to *shine* or to *brighten up*

ILLYRICUM
2437 Illurikŏn (1), *Illyricum*

IMAGE
4676 matstsêbâh (3), *column* or *stone*
4906 maskîyth (1), *carved figure*
5566 çemel (2), *likeness*
6459 peçel (2), *idol*
6676 tsavva'r (Ch.) (1), *back of the neck*

6754 tselem (6),
phantom; idol
6755 tselem (Ch.) (16),
idolatrous *figure*
6816 tsa'tsûa' (1),
sculpture work
8544 tᵉmûwnâh (1),
something *fashioned*
8655 tᵉrâphîym (2),
healer
1504 ĕikŏn (22), *likeness*
5481 charaktēr (1), exact
copy or *representation*

IMAGE'S
6755 tselem (Ch.) (1),
idolatrous *figure*

IMAGERY
4906 maskîyth (1),
carved *figure*

IMAGES
457 'ĕlîyl (1), *vain idol*
1544 gillûwl (1), *idol*
2553 chammân (6),
sun-pillar
4676 matstsêbâh (14),
column or *stone*
6091 'âtsâb (1), *image,
idol*
6456 pᵉçîyl (2), *idol*
6754 tselem (9),
phantom; idol
8655 tᵉrâphîym (5),
healer

IMAGINATION
3336 yêtser (4), *form*
8307 shᵉrîyrûwth (9),
obstinacy
1271 dianŏia (1), *mind*
or *thought*

IMAGINATIONS
3336 yêtser (1), *form*
4284 machăshâbâh (3),
contrivance; plan
1261 dialŏgismŏs (1),
consideration; debate
3053 lŏgismŏs (1),
reasoning; conscience

IMAGINE
1897 hâgâh (2), to
murmur, ponder
2050 hâthath (1), to
assail, verbally attack
2554 châmaç (1), to be
violent; to maltreat
2790 chârash (1), to be
silent; to be deaf
2803 châshab (5), to *plot;*
to *think, regard*
3191 mĕlĕtaŏ (1), to *plot,
think about*

IMAGINED
2161 zâmam (1), to *plan*
2803 châshab (2), to *plot;*
to *think, regard*

IMAGINETH
2803 châshab (1), to *plot;*
to *think, regard*

IMLA
3229 Yimlâ' (2), *full*

IMLAH
3229 Yimlâ' (2), *full*

IMMANUEL
6005 'Immânûw'êl (2),
with us (is) *God*

IMMEDIATELY
1824 ĕxautēs (3),
instantly, at once
2112 ĕuthĕōs (35), *at
once or soon*
2117 ĕuthus (3), *at once,
immediately*
3916 parachrēma (13),
instantly, immediately

IMMER
564 'Immêr (10),
talkative

IMMORTAL
862 aphthartŏs (1),
undecaying, immortal

IMMORTALITY
110 athanasia (3),
deathlessness
861 aphtharsia (2),
unending existence

IMMUTABILITY
276 amĕtathĕtŏs (1),
unchangeable

IMMUTABLE
276 amĕtathĕtŏs (1),
unchangeable

IMNA
3234 Yimnâ' (1), *he will
restrain*

IMNAH
3232 Yimnâh (2),
prosperity

IMPART
3330 mĕtadidōmi (2), to
share, distribute

IMPARTED
2505 châlaq (1), to be
smooth; be slippery
3330 mĕtadidōmi (1), to
share, distribute

IMPEDIMENT
3424 mŏgilalŏs (1),
hardly talking

IMPENITENT
279 amĕtanŏētŏs (1),
unrepentant

IMPERIOUS
7986 shalleṭeth (1),
dominant woman

IMPLACABLE
786 aspŏndŏs (1), *not
reconcilable*

IMPLEAD
1458 ĕgkalĕō (1), to
charge, criminate

IMPORTUNITY
335 anaidĕia (1),
importunity, boldness

IMPOSE
7412 rᵉmâh (Ch.) (1), to
throw; to set; to assess

IMPOSED
1942 ĕpikaluma (1),
pretext, covering

IMPOSSIBLE
101 adunatĕō (2), to be
impossible
102 adunatŏs (6), *weak;
impossible*
418 anĕndĕktŏs (1),
impossible

IMPOTENT
102 adunatŏs (1), *weak;
impossible*
770 asthĕnĕō (2), to be
feeble
772 asthĕnēs (1),
strengthless, weak

IMPOVERISH
7567 râshash (1), to
demolish

IMPOVERISHED
1809 dâlal (1), to be
feeble; to be oppressed
5533 çâkan (1), to *grow,
make poor*
7567 râshash (1), to
demolish

IMPRISONED
5439 phulakizō (1), to
incarcerate, imprison

IMPRISONMENT
613 'ĕçûwr (Ch.) (1),
manacles, chains
5438 phulakē (1), *watch;
prison; haunt*

IMPRISONMENTS
5438 phulakē (1), *watch;
prison; haunt*

IMPUDENT
2389+4696 châzâq (1),
severe, hard, violent
5810 'âzaz (1), to be
stout; be bold
7186+6440 qâsheh (1),
severe

IMPUTE
2803 châshab (1), to
regard; to *compute*
7760 sûwm (1), to *put,
place*
3049 lŏgizŏmai (1), to
credit; to *think, regard*

IMPUTED
2803 châshab (2), to
think, regard; compute
1677 ĕllŏgĕō (1), to
charge to one's account
3049 lŏgizŏmai (5), to
credit; to *think, regard*

IMPUTETH
2803 châshab (1), to
think, regard; compute
3049 lŏgizŏmai (1), to
credit; to *think, regard*

IMPUTING
3049 lŏgizŏmai (1), to
credit; to *think, regard*

IMRAH
3236 Yimrâh (1),
interchange

IMRI
556 'amtsâh (2),
strength, force

INASMUCH
1115 biltîy (1), *except,
without, unless, besides*
3588 kîy (1), *for, that
because*
2526 kathŏ (1), *precisely
as, in proportion as*

INCENSE
3828 lᵉbôwnâh (6),
frankincense

6999 qâṭar (58), to *turn
into fragrance* by fire
7002 qiṭṭêr (1), *perfume*
7004 qᵉṭôreth (57),
fumigation
2368 thumiama (4),
incense offering
2370 thumiaŏ (1), to
offer aromatic *fumes*

INCENSED
2734 chârâh (2), to *blaze*

INCLINE
5186 nâṭâh (15), to
stretch or spread out
7181 qâshab (1), to *prick
up* the ears

INCLINED
5186 nâṭâh (13), to
stretch or spread out

INCLINETH
7743 shûwach (1), to *sink*

INCLOSE
6696 tsûwr (1), to *cramp,*
i.e. *confine;* to *harass*

INCLOSED
1443 gâdar (1), to *build a
stone wall*
3803 kâthar (1), to
enclose, besiege; to *wait*
4142 mûwçabbâh (2),
backside; fold
5274 nâ'al (1), to *fasten
up, lock*
5362 nâqaph (1), to
surround or *circulate*
5462 çâgar (1), to *shut
up;* to *surrender*
4788 sugklĕiō (1), to *net
fish;* to *lock up* persons

INCLOSINGS
4396 millû'âh (2), *setting*

INCONTINENCY
192 akrasia (1), *lack of
control of self*

INCONTINENT
193 akratēs (1), *without
self-control*

INCORRUPTIBLE
862 aphthartŏs (4),
undecaying, immortal

INCORRUPTION
861 aphtharsia (4),
unending existence

INCREASE
2981 yᵉbûwl (10),
produce, crop; harvest
3254 yâçaph (6), to *add
or augment*
4768 marbîyth (3),
interest on money
5107 nûwb (1), to (*make*)
flourish; to *utter*
6555 pârats (1), to *break
out*
7235 râbâh (18), to
increase
7239 ribbôw (1), *myriad,
indefinite large number*
7685 sâgâh (2), to
enlarge, be prosperous
7698 sheger (4), *what
comes forth*
8393 tᵉbûw'âh (23),
income, i.e. *produce*

INCREASED
8570 tᵉnûwbâh (2), *crop, produce*
8635 tarbûwth (6), *progeny, brood*
837 auxanō (4), *to grow, i.e. enlarge*
838 auxēsis (2), *growth, increase*
4052 pĕrissĕuō (1), *to superabound*
4121 plĕŏnazō (1), *to increase; superabound*
4298 prŏkŏptō (1), *to go ahead, advance*
4369 prŏstithēmi (1), *to lay beside, annex*

INCREASED
1431 gâdal (1), *to be great, make great*
3254 yâçaph (5), *to add or augment*
5927 'âlâh (3), *to ascend, be high, mount*
6105 'âtsam (4), *to be, make numerous*
6509 pârâh (3), *to bear fruit*
6555 pârats (4), *to break out*
7227 rab (2), *great*
7230 rôb (1), *abundance*
7231 râbab (3), *to increase; to multiply*
7235 râbâh (15), *to increase*
8317 shârats (1), *to swarm, or abound*
837 auxanō (3), *to grow, i.e. enlarge*
1743 ĕndunamŏō (1), *to empower, strengthen*
4052 pĕrissĕuō (1), *to superabound*
4147 plŏutĕō (1), *to be, become wealthy*
4298 prŏkŏptō (1), *to go ahead, advance*

INCREASEST
7235 râbâh (1), *to increase*

INCREASETH
553 'âmats (1), *to be strong; be courageous*
1342 gâ'âh (1), *to rise; to grow tall; be majestic*
3254 yâçaph (4), *to add or augment*
5927 'âlâh (1), *to ascend, be high, mount*
7235 râbâh (5), *to increase*
7679 sâgâ' (1), *to laud, extol*
837 auxanō (1), *to grow, i.e. enlarge*

INCREASING
837 auxanō (1), *to grow, i.e. enlarge*

INCREDIBLE
571 apistŏs (1), *without faith; incredible*

INCURABLE
369+4832 'ayin (1), *there is no, i.e., not exist*
605 'ânash (5), *to be frail, feeble*

INDEBTED
3784 ŏphĕilō (1), *to owe; to be under obligation*

INDEED
61 'ăbâl (2), *truly, surely; yet, but*
389 'ak (1), *surely; only, however*
546 'omnâh (2), *surely*
551 'omnâm (2), *verily, indeed, truly*
552 'umnâm (3), *verily, indeed, truly*
1571 gam (1), *also; even; yea; though*
230 alēthōs (6), *truly, surely*
235 alla (1), *but, yet, except, instead*
1063 gar (2), *for, indeed, but, because*
2532 kai (2), *and; or; even; also*
3303 měn (22), *indeed*
3689 ŏntōs (6), *really, certainly*

INDIA
1912 Hôdûw (2), *India*

INDIGNATION
2194 zâ'am (4), *to be enraged*
2195 za'am (20), *fury, anger*
2197 za'aph (2), *anger, rage*
2534 chêmâh (1), *heat; anger; poison*
3707 kâ'aç (1), *to grieve, rage, be indignant*
3708 ka'aç (1), *vexation, grief*
7110 qetseph (3), *rage or strife*
23 aganaktĕō (4), *to be indignant*
24 aganaktēsis (1), *indignation*
2205 zēlŏs (2), *zeal, ardor; jealousy, malice*
2372 thumŏs (1), *passion, anger*
3709 ŏrgē (1), *ire; punishment*

INDITING
7370 râchash (1), *to gush*

INDUSTRIOUS
6213+4399 'âsâh (1), *to do or make*

INEXCUSABLE
379 anapŏlŏgētŏs (1), *without excuse*

INFAMOUS
2931+8034 ţâmê' (1), *foul; ceremonially impure*

INFAMY
1681 dibbâh (2), *slander, bad report*

INFANT
5764 'ûwl (1), *nursing babe*
5768 'ôwlêl (1), *suckling child*

INFANTS
5768 'ôwlêl (2), *suckling child*
1025 brĕphŏs (1), *infant*

INFERIOR
772 'ăra' (Ch.) (1), *earth, ground, land; inferior*
5307 nâphal (2), *to fall*
2274 hēttaō (1), *to rate lower, be inferior*

INFIDEL
571 apistŏs (2), *without faith; untrustworthy*

INFINITE
369+4557 'ayin (1), *there is no, i.e., not exist*
369+7093 'ayin (2), *there is no, i.e., not exist*

INFIRMITIES
769 asthĕnĕia (10), *feebleness; malady*
771 asthĕnēma (1), *failing, weakness*
3554 nŏsŏs (1), *malady, disease*

INFIRMITY
1738 dâvâh (1), *to be in menstruation cycle*
2470 châlâh (1), *to be weak, sick, afflicted*
4245 machăleh (1), *sickness*
769 asthĕnĕia (7), *feebleness; malady*

INFLAME
1814 dâlaq (1), *to flame; to pursue*

INFLAMMATION
1816 dalleqeth (1), *burning fever*
6867 tsârebeth (1), *conflagration*

INFLUENCES
4575 ma'ădannâh (1), *bond, i.e. group*

INFOLDING
3947 lâqach (1), *to take*

INFORM
3384 yârâh (1), *to point; to teach*

INFORMED
995 bîyn (1), *to understand; discern*
1718 ĕmphanizō (3), *to show forth*
2727 katēchĕō (2), *to indoctrinate*

INGATHERING
614 'âçîyph (2), *harvest, gathering in of crops*

INHABIT
3427 yâshab (8), *to dwell, to remain; to settle*
7931 shâkan (2), *to reside*

INHABITANT
1481 gûwr (1), *to sojourn, live as an alien*
3427 yâshab (31), *to dwell, to remain*
7934 shâkên (1), *resident; fellow-citizen*

INHABITANTS
1753 dûwr (Ch.) (2), *to reside, live in*
3427 yâshab (190), *to dwell, to remain*
7934 shâkên (2), *resident; fellow-citizen*

INHABITED
8453 tôwshâb (1), *temporary dweller*
2730 katŏikĕō (1), *to reside, live in*

INHABITED
1509 gᵉzêrâh (1), *desert, unfertile place*
3427 yâshab (29), *to dwell, to remain*
4186 môwshâb (1), *seat; site; abode*
7931 shâkan (1), *to reside*

INHABITERS
2730 katŏikĕō (2), *to reside, live in*

INHABITEST
3427 yâshab (1), *to dwell, to remain; to settle*

INHABITETH
3427 yâshab (1), *to dwell, to remain; to settle*
7931 shâkan (1), *to reside*

INHABITING
6728 tsîyîy (1), *desert-dweller; wild beast*

INHERIT
3423 yârash (21), *to inherit; to impoverish*
5157 nâchal (25), *to inherit*
5159 nachălâh (2), *occupancy*
2816 klĕrŏnŏmĕō (14), *to be an heir to, inherit*

INHERITANCE
2490 châlal (1), *to profane, defile*
2506 chêleq (1), *allotment*
3423 yârash (1), *to inherit; to impoverish*
3425 yᵉrushâh (1), *conquest*
4181 môwrâshâh (2), *possession*
5157 nâchal (18), *to inherit*
5159 nachălâh (189), *occupancy*
2817 klĕrŏnŏmia (14), *inherited possession*
2819 klĕrŏs (2), *lot, portion*
2820 klĕrŏō (2), *to allot*

INHERITANCES
5159 nachălâh (1), *occupancy*

INHERITED
3423 yârash (2), *to inherit; to impoverish*
5157 nâchal (3), *to inherit*
2816 klĕrŏnŏmĕō (1), *to be an heir to, inherit*

INHERITETH
5157 nâchal (1), *to inherit*

INHERITOR
3423 yârash (1), *to inherit; to impoverish*

INIQUITIES
1647+5771 Gêrᵉshôm (1), *refugee*
5758 'ivyâ' (Ch.) (1), *perverseness*
5766 'evel (1), *moral evil*
5771 'âvôn (47), *evil*

92 adikēma (1), *wrong done*

458 anŏmia (3), *violation of law, wickedness*

4189 pŏnēria (1), *malice, evil, wickedness*

INIQUITY
205 'âven (47), *trouble, vanity, wickedness*
1942 havvâh (1), *desire; craving*
5753 'âvâh (4), *to be crooked*
5766 'evel (35), moral *evil*
5771 'âvôn (170), moral *evil*
5932 'alvâh (1), *moral perverseness*
5999 'âmâl (1), *wearing effort; worry*
7562 resha' (1), moral *wrong*
93 adikia (6), *wrongfulness*
458 anŏmia (8), *violation of law, wickedness*
3892 paranŏmia (1), *transgression*

INJURED
91 adikĕŏ (1), *to do wrong*

INJURIOUS
5197 hubristēs (1), *maltreater, violent*

INJUSTICE
2555 châmâç (1), *violence; malice*

INK
1773 dᵉyôw (1), *ink*
3188 mĕlan (3), *black ink*

INKHORN
7083 qeçeth (3), *ink-stand*

INN
4411 mâlôwn (3), *lodgment for night*
2646 kataluma (1), *lodging-place*
3829 pandŏchĕiŏn (1), public *lodging-place*

INNER
2315 cheder (4), *apartment, chamber*
6441 pᵉnîymâh (1), *indoors, inside*
6442 pᵉnîymîy (30), *interior, inner*
2080 ĕsō (1), *inside, inner, in*
2082 ĕsōtĕrŏs (1), *interior, inner*

INNERMOST
2315 cheder (2), *apartment, chamber*

INNOCENCY
2136 zâkûw (Ch.) (1), *purity; justice*
5356 niqqâyôwn (4), *clearness; cleanness*

INNOCENT
2600 chinnâm (1), *gratis, free*
2643 chaph (1), *pure, clean*

5352 nâqâh (5), *to be, make clean; to be bare*
5355 nâqîy (29), *innocent*
121 athŏŏs (2), *not guilty*

INNOCENTS
5355 nâqîy (2), *innocent*

INNUMERABLE
369+4557 'ayin (4), *there is no, i.e., not exist*
382 anarithmētŏs (1), *without number*
3461 murias (2), *ten-thousand*

INORDINATE
5691 'ăgâbâh (1), *love, amorousness*
3806 pathŏs (1), *passion, concupiscence*

INQUISITION
1245 bâqash (1), *to search; to strive after*
1875 dârash (2), to *pursue or search*

INSCRIPTION
1924 ĕpigraphō (1), *to inscribe, write upon*

INSIDE
1004 bayith (1), *house; temple; family, tribe*

INSOMUCH
1519 ĕis (1), *to or into*
5620 hŏstĕ (17), *thus, therefore*

INSPIRATION
5397 nᵉshâmâh (1), *breath, life*
2315 thĕŏpnĕustŏs (1), *divinely breathed in*

INSTANT
6621 petha' (2), *wink, i.e. moment; quickly*
7281 rega' (2), *very short space of time*
1945 ĕpikĕimai (1), to *rest upon; press upon*
2186 ĕphistĕmi (1), *to be present; to approach*
4342 prŏskartĕrĕŏ (1), *to attend; to adhere*
5610 hōra (1), *hour, i.e. a unit of time*

INSTANTLY
1722+1616 ĕn (1), *in; during; because of*
4705 spŏudaiŏs (1), *prompt, energetic*

INSTEAD
8478 tachath (35), *underneath; in lieu of*

INSTRUCT
995 bîyn (1), *to understand; discern*
3250 yiççôwr (1), *reprover, corrector*
3256 yâçar (3), *to chastise; to instruct*
3925 lâmad (1), *to teach, train*
7919 sâkal (2), *to be or act circumspect*
4822 sumbibazŏ (1), *to unite; to show, teach*

INSTRUCTED
995 bîyn (2), *to understand; discern*

3045 yâda' (1), *to know*
3245 yâçad (1), *settle, consult, establish*
3256 yâçar (5), to *chastise; to instruct*
3384 yârâh (1), *to point; to teach*
3925 lâmad (2), *to teach, train*
7919 sâkal (1), to *be or act circumspect*
2727 katĕchĕŏ (3), *to indoctrinate*
3100 mathētĕuō (1), *to become a student*
3453 muĕŏ (1), *to initiate*
4264 prŏbibazŏ (1), *to bring to the front*

INSTRUCTER
3913 lâţash (1), *to sharpen; to pierce*

INSTRUCTERS
3807 paidagōgŏs (1), *tutor, cf. pedagogue*

INSTRUCTING
3811 paidĕuō (1), *to educate or discipline*

INSTRUCTION
4148 mûwçâr (30), *reproof, warning*
4561 môçâr (1), *admonition*
3809 paidĕia (1), *disciplinary correction*

INSTRUCTOR
3810 paidĕutēs (1), *teacher or discipliner*

INSTRUMENT
3627 kᵉlîy (2), *implement, thing*

INSTRUMENTS
1761 dachăvâh (Ch.) (1), *musical instrument*
3627 kᵉlîy (37), *implement, thing*
4482 mên (1), *part; musical chord*
7991 shâlîysh (1), *triangle instrument*
3696 hŏplŏn (2), *implement, or utensil*

INSURRECTION
5376 nᵉsâ' (Ch.) (1), *to lift up*
7285 regesh (1), *tumultuous crowd*
2721 katĕphistĕmi (1), *rush upon in an assault*
4714 stasis (1), one *leading an uprising*
4955 sustasiastēs (1), *fellow-insurgent*

INTEGRITY
8537 tôm (11), *prosperity; innocence*
8538 tummâh (5), *innocence*

INTELLIGENCE
995 bîyn (1), *to understand; discern*

INTEND
559 'âmar (2), *to say*
1014 bŏulŏmai (1), *to be willing, desire; choose*

3195 mĕllō (1), *to intend, i.e. be about to*

INTENDED
5186 nâţâh (1), *to stretch or spread out*

INTENDEST
559 'âmar (1), *to say*

INTENDING
1011 bŏulĕuō (1), *to deliberate; to resolve*
2309 thĕlō (1), *to will; to desire; to choose*
3195 mĕllō (1), *to intend, i.e. be about to*

INTENT
1701 dibrâh (Ch.) (1), *because, on account of*
4616 ma'an (2), *on account of; in order*
5668 'âbûwr (1), *on account of; in order*
2443 hina (2), *in order that*
3056 lŏgŏs (1), *word, matter, thing*

INTENTS
4209 mᵉzimmâh (1), *plan; sagacity*
1771 ĕnnŏia (1), *moral understanding*

INTERCESSION
6293 pâga' (4), *to impinge*
1793 ĕntugchanō (4), *to entreat, petition*
5241 hupĕrĕntugchanō (1), *to intercede*

INTERCESSIONS
1783 ĕntĕuxis (1), *intercession*

INTERCESSOR
6293 pâga' (1), *to impinge*

INTERMEDDLE
6148 'ârab (1), *to intermix*

INTERMEDDLETH
1566 gâla' (1), *to be obstinate; to burst forth*

INTERMISSION
2014 hăphûgâh (1), *relaxation*

INTERPRET
6622 pâthar (4), *to interpret a dream*
1329 diĕrmĕnĕuō (4), *to explain thoroughly*

INTERPRETATION
4426 mᵉlîytsâh (1), *aphorism, saying*
6591 pᵉshar (Ch.) (30), *interpretation*
6592 pêsher (1), *interpretation*
6623 pithrôwn (5), *interpretation*
7667 sheber (1), *solution of a dream*
1329 diĕrmĕnĕuō (1), *to explain thoroughly*
1955 ĕpilusis (1), *interpretation*
2058 hĕrmēnĕia (2), *translation*
2059 hĕrmēnĕuō (3), *to translate*
3177 mĕthĕrmēnĕuō (1), *to translate*

INTERPRETATIONS
6591 pᵉshar (Ch.) (1), *interpretation*
6623 pithrôwn (1), *interpretation*

INTERPRETED
6622 pâthar (3), to *interpret a dream*
8638 tirgam (1), to *translate, interpret*
2059 hĕrmēnĕuō (1), to translate
3177 mĕthĕrmēnĕuō (6), to translate

INTERPRETER
3887 lûwts (2), to *scoff; to interpret; to intercede*
6622 pâthar (1), to *interpret a dream*
1328 diĕrmēnĕutēs (1), explainer, translator

INTERPRETING
6591 pᵉshar (Ch.) (1), *interpretation*

INTREAT
2470 châlâh (3), to *be weak, sick, afflicted*
6279 'âthar (6), *intercede*
6293 pâga' (2), to *impinge*
6419 pâlal (1), to *intercede, pray*
2065 ĕrōtaō (1), to interrogate; to request
3870 *parakalĕō (2), to call, invite*

INTREATED
2470 châlâh (1), to *be weak, sick, afflicted*
2589 channôwth (1), *supplication*
2603 chânan (1), to *implore*
6279 'âthar (12), *intercede in prayer*
2138 ĕupĕithēs (1), compliant, submissive
3862 paradŏsis (1), precept; tradition
3870 *parakalĕō (1), to call, invite*

INTREATIES
8469 tachănûwn (1), *earnest prayer, plea*

INTREATY
3874 paraklēsis (1), imploring, exhortation

INTRUDING
1687 ĕmbatĕuō (1), to intrude on

INVADE
935 bôw' (1), to *go or come*
1464 gûwd (1), to *attack*

INVADED
935 bôw' (1), to *go or come*
6584 pâshaṭ (4), to *strip, i.e. unclothe, plunder*

INVASION
6584 pâshaṭ (1), to *strip, i.e. unclothe, plunder, flay*

INVENT
2803 châshab (1), to *weave, fabricate*

INVENTED
2803 châshab (1), to *weave, fabricate*

INVENTIONS
2810 chishshâbôwn (1), *machination, scheme*
4209 mᵉzimmâh (1), *plan; sagacity*
4611 ma'ălâl (2), *act, deed*
5949 'ălîylâh (1), *opportunity, action*

INVENTORS
2182 ĕphĕurētēs (1), contriver, inventor

INVISIBLE
517 aŏratŏs (5), invisible, not seen

INVITED
7121 qârâ' (3), to *call out*

INWARD
1004 bayith (7), *house; temple; family, tribe*
2315 cheder (2), *apartment, chamber*
2910 tûwchâh (2), *inmost thought*
5475 çôwd (1), *intimacy; consultation; secret*
6441 pᵉnîymâh (2), *indoors, inside*
6442 pᵉnîymîy (1), *interior, inner*
7130 qereb (5), *nearest part, i.e. the center*
2080 ĕsō (1), *inside, inner, in*
2081 ĕsōthĕn (2), *from inside; inside*
4698 splagchnŏn (1), intestine; affection, pity or sympathy

INWARDLY
7130 qereb (1), *nearest part, i.e. the center*
1722+2927 ĕn (1), in; during; because of
2081 ĕsōthĕn (1), *from inside; inside*

INWARDS
7130 qereb (19), *nearest part, i.e. the center*

IPHEDEIAH
3301 Yiphdᵉyâh (1), *Jehovah will liberate*

IR
5893 'Îyr (1), *city, town, unwalled-village*

IR-NAHASH
5904 'Îyr Nâchâsh (1), *city of a serpent*

IR-SHEMESH
5905 'Îyr Shemesh (1), *city of* (the) *sun*

IRA
5896 'Îyrâ' (6), *wakefulness*

IRAD
5897 'Îyrâd (2), *fugitive*

IRAM
5902 'Îyrâm (2), *city-wise*

IRI
5901 'Îyrîy (1), *urbane*

IRIJAH
3376 Yir'îyâyh (2), *fearful of Jehovah*

IRON
1270 barzel (72), *iron; iron implement*
3375 Yir'ôwn (1), *fearfulness*
6523 parzel (Ch.) (19), *iron*
4603 sidĕrĕŏs (5), made of iron
4604 sidĕrŏs (1), iron

IRONS
7905 sukkâh (1), *dart, harpoon*

IRPEEL
3416 Yirpᵉ'êl (1), *God will heal*

IRU
5902 'Îyrâm (1), *city-wise*

ISAAC
3327 Yitschâq (104), *laughter*
3446 Yischâq (4), *he will laugh*
2464 Isaak (20), he will laugh

ISAAC'S
3327 Yitschâq (4), *laughter*

ISAIAH
3470 Yᵉsha'yâh (32), *Jehovah has saved*

ISCAH
3252 Yiçkâh (1), *observant*

ISCARIOT
2469 Iskariōtēs (11), inhabitant of Kerioth

ISH-BOSHETH
378 'Îysh-Bôsheth (11), *man of shame*

ISH-TOB
382 'Îysh-Ṭôwb (2), *man of Tob*

ISHBAH
3431 Yishbach (1), *he will praise*

ISHBAK
3435 Yishbâq (2), *he will leave*

ISHBI-BENOB
3430 Yishbôw bᵉ-Nôb (1), *his dwelling* (is) *in Nob*

ISHI
376 'îysh (1), *man; male; someone*
3469 Yish'îy (5), *saving*

ISHIAH
3449 Yishshîyâh (1), *Jehovah will lend*

ISHIJAH
3449 Yishshîyâh (1), *Jehovah will lend*

ISHMA
3457 Yishmâ' (1), *desolate*

ISHMAEL
3458 Yishmâ'ê'l (47), *God will hear*

ISHMAEL'S
3458 Yishmâ'ê'l (1), *God will hear*

ISHMAELITE
3458 Yishmâ'ê'l (1), *God will hear*

ISHMAELITES
3459 Yishmâ'ê'lîy (2), *Jishmaëlite*

ISHMAIAH
3460 Yishma'yâh (1), *Jehovah will hear*

ISHMEELITE
3459 Yishmâ'ê'lîy (1), *Jishmaëlite*

ISHMEELITES
3459 Yishmâ'ê'lîy (4), *Jishmaëlite*

ISHMERAI
3461 Yishmᵉray (1), *preservative*

ISHOD
379 'Îyshhôwd (1), *man of renown*

ISHPAN
3473 Yishpân (1), *he will hide*

ISHUAH
3438 Yishvâh (1), *he will level*

ISHUAI
3440 Yishvîy (1), *level*

ISHUI
3440 Yishvîy (1), *level*

ISLAND
336 'îy (1), *not*
338 'îy (1), *solitary wild creature that howls*
3519 nēsiŏn (1), *small island*
3520 nēsŏs (6), *island*

ISLANDS
338 'îy (1), *solitary wild creature that howls*
339 'îy (6), *dry land; coast; island*

ISLE
339 'îy (3), *coast; island*
3520 nēsŏs (3), *island*

ISLES
339 'îy (27), *dry land; coast; island*

ISMACHIAH
3253 Yiçmakyâhûw (1), *Jehovah will sustain*

ISMAIAH
3460 Yishma'yâh (1), *Jehovah will hear*

ISPAH
3472 Yishpâh (1), *he will scratch*

ISRAEL
3478 Yisrâ'êl (2477), *he will rule* (as) *God*
3479 Yisrâ'êl (Ch.) (8), *he will rule* (as) *God*
3481 Yisrᵉ'êlîy (1), *Jisreëlite*
2474 Israēl (70), he will rule (as) *God*
2475 Israēlitēs (5), descendants of Israel

ISRAEL'S
3478 Yisrâ'êl (10), *he will rule (as) God*

ISRAELITE
1121+3478 bên (1), *son, descendant; people*
3481 Yisrᵉ'êlîy (1), *Jisreëlite*
2475 Isrâēlîtēs (2), descendants *of Israel*

ISRAELITES
3478 Yisrâ'êl (16), *he will rule (as) God*
2475 Isrâēlîtēs (2), descendants *of Israel*

ISRAELITISH
3482 Yisrᵉ'êlîyth (3), *Jisreëlitess*

ISSACHAR
3485 Yissâˢkâr (43), *he will bring a reward*
2466 Isachar (1), *he will bring a reward*

ISSHIAH
3449 Yishshîyâh (2), *Jehovah will lend*

ISSUE
2100 zûwb (16), to *flow freely, gush*
2101 zôwb (11), *flux or discharge*
2231 zirmâh (1), *emission* of semen
3318 yâtsâ' (3), to *go, bring out*
4138 môwledeth (1), *offspring, family*
4726 mâqôwr (1), *flow*
6849 tsᵉphî'âh (1), *outcast thing, offshoots*
131 haimŏrrhĕŏ (1), to *have a hemorrhage*
4511 rhusis (3), *flux*
4690 spĕrma (1), *seed, offspring*

ISSUED
3318 yâtsâ' (4), to *go, bring out*
5047 nᵉgad (Ch.) (1), to *flow*
1607 ĕkpŏrĕuŏmai (2), to *depart, be discharged*

ISSUES
8444 tôwtsâ'âh (2), *exit, boundary; source*

ISUAH
3440 Yishvîy (1), *level*

ISUI
3440 Yishvîy (1), *level*

ITALIAN
2483 Italikŏs (1), *belonging to Italia*

ITALY
2482 Italia (4), *Italia*

ITCH
2775 chereç (1), *itch; sun*

ITCHING
2833 knēthō (1), to *tickle, feel an itch*

ITHAI
863 'Ittay (1), *near*

ITHAMAR
385 'Îythâmâr (21), *coast* of the *palm-tree*

ITHIEL
384 'Îythîy'êl (3), *God has arrived*

ITHMAH
3495 Yithmâh (1), *orphanage*

ITHNAN
3497 Yithnân (1), *extensive*

ITHRA
3501 Yithrâ' (1), *wealth*

ITHRAN
3506 Yithrân (3), *excellent*

ITHREAM
3507 Yithrᵉ'âm (2), *excellence of people*

ITHRITE
3505 Yithrîy (4), *Jithrite*

ITHRITES
3505 Yithrîy (1), *Jithrite*

ITTAH-KAZIN
6278 'Êth Qâtsîyn (1), *time of a judge*

ITTAI
863 'Ittay (8), *near*

ITURAEA
2434 hilasmŏs (1), *atonement, expiator*

IVAH
5755 'Ivvâh (3), *overthrow, ruin*

IVORY
8127 shên (10), *tooth; ivory; cliff*
8143 shenhabbîym (2), *elephant's ivory tusk*
1661 ĕlĕphantinŏs (1), of *ivory*

IZEHAR
3324 Yitshâr (1), *olive oil; anointing*

IZEHARITES
3325 Yitshârîy (1), *Jitsharite*

IZHAR
3324 Yitshâr (8), *olive oil; anointing*

IZHARITES
3325 Yitshârîy (3), *Jitsharite*

IZRAHIAH
3156 Yizrachyâh (2), *Jehovah will shine*

IZRAHITE
3155 Yizrâch (1), *Ezrachite or Zarchite*

IZRI
3342 yeqeb (1), *wine-vat; wine-press*

JAAKAN
3292 Ya'ăqân (1), *Jaakan*

JAAKOBAH
3291 Ya'ăqôbâh (1), *heel-catcher*

JAALA
3279 Ya'ălâ' (1), to *be valuable*

JAALAH
3279 Ya'ălâ' (1), to *be valuable*

JAALAM
3281 Ya'lâm (4), *occult*

JAANAI
3285 Ya'ănay (1), *responsive*

JAARE-OREGIM
3296 Ya'ărêy 'Orᵉgîym (1), *woods of weavers*

JAASAU
3299 Ya'ăsûw (1), *they will do*

JAASIEL
3300 Ya'ăsîy'êl (1), *made of God*

JAAZANIAH
2970 Ya'ăzanyâh (4), *heard of Jehovah*

JAAZER
3270 Ya'ăzêyr (2), *helpful*

JAAZIAH
3269 Ya'ăzîyâhûw (2), *emboldened of Jehovah*

JAAZIEL
3268 Ya'ăzîy'êl (1), *emboldened of God*

JABAL
2989 Yâbâl (1), *stream*

JABBOK
2999 Yabbôq (7), *pouring forth*

JABESH
3003 Yâbêsh (12), *dry*

JABESH-GILEAD
3003+1568 Yâbêsh (12), *dry*

JABEZ
3258 Ya'bêts (4), *sorrowful*

JABIN
2985 Yâbîyn (7), *intelligent*

JABIN'S
2985 Yâbîyn (1), *intelligent*

JABNEEL
2995 Yabnᵉ'êl (2), *built of God*

JABNEH
2996 Yabneh (1), *building*

JACHAN
3275 Ya'kân (1), *troublesome*

JACHIN
3199 Yâkîyn (8), *he* (or *it*) *will establish*

JACHINITES
3200 Yâkîynîy (1), *Jakinite*

JACINTH
5191 huakinthinŏs (1), *deep blue color*
5192 huakinthŏs (1), *blue gem*, (poss.) *zircon*

JACOB
3290 Ya'ăqôb (331), *heel-catcher*
2384 Iakōb (26), *heel-catcher*

JACOB'S
3290 Ya'ăqôb (17), *heel-catcher*

JAKOB
2384 Iakōb (1), *heel-catcher*

JADA
3047 Yâdâ' (2), *knowing*

JADAU
3035 Yiddôw (1), *praised*

JADDUA
3037 Yaddûwa' (3), *knowing*

JADON
3036 Yâdôwn (1), *thankful*

JAEL
3278 Yâ'êl (6), *ibex animal*

JAGUR
3017 Yâgûwr (1), *lodging*

JAH
3050 Yâhh (1), *Jehovah*, (the) self-*Existent or Eternal One*

JAHATH
3189 Yachath (8), *unity*

JAHAZ
3096 Yahats (5), *threshing-floor*

JAHAZA
3096 Yahats (1), *threshing-floor*

JAHAZAH
3096 Yahats (2), *threshing-floor*

JAHAZIAH
3167 Yachzᵉyâh (1), *Jehovah will behold*

JAHAZIEL
3166 Yachăzîy'êl (6), *beheld of God*

JAHDAI
3056 Yehday (1), *Judaistic*

JAHDIEL
3164 Yachdîy'êl (1), *unity of God*

JAHDO
3163 Yachdôw (1), *his unity*

JAHLEEL
3177 Yachlᵉ'êl (2), *expectant of God*

JAHLEELITES
3178 Yachlᵉ'êlîy (1), *Jachleëlite*

JAHMAI
3181 Yachmay (1), *hot*

JAHZAH
3096 Yahats (1), *threshing-floor*

JAHZEEL
3183 Yachtsᵉ'êl (2), *God will allot*

JAHZEELITES
3184 Yachtsᵉ'êlîy (1), *Jachtseëlite*

JAHZERAH
3170 Yachzêrâh (1), *protection*

JAHZIEL
3185 Yachtsîy'êl (1), *allotted of God*

JAILER
1200 dĕsmŏphulax (1), jailer

JAIR
2971 Yâ'îyr (10), enlightener

JAIRITE
2972 Yâ'îrîy (1), Jaïrite

JAIRUS
2383 Iaĕirŏs (2), enlightener

JAKAN
3292 Ya'ăqân (1), Jaakan

JAKEH
3348 Yâqeh (1), obedient

JAKIM
3356 Yâqîym (2), he will raise

JALON
3210 Yâlôwn (1), lodging

JAMBRES
2387 Iambrēs (1), Jambres

JAMES
2385 Iakōbŏs (41), heel-catcher

JAMIN
3226 Yâmîyn (6), right; south

JAMINITES
3228 Yᵉmîynîy (1), Jeminite

JAMLECH
3230 Yamlêk (1), he will make king

JANGLING
3150 mataiŏlŏgia (1), babble, meaningless talk

JANNA
2388 Ianna (1), Janna

JANNES
2389 Iannēs (1), Jannes

JANOAH
3239 Yânôwach (1), quiet

JANOHAH
3239 Yânôwach (2), quiet

JANUM
3241 Yânîym (1), asleep

JAPHETH
3315 Yepheth (11), expansion

JAPHIA
3309 Yâphîya' (5), bright

JAPHLET
3310 Yaphlêṭ (3), he will deliver

JAPHLETI
3311 Yaphlêṭîy (1), Japhletite

JAPHO
3305 Yâphôw (1), beautiful

JARAH
3294 Ya'râh (2), honey in the comb

JAREB
3377 Yârêb (2), he will contend

JARED
3382 Yered (5), descent
2391 Iarĕd (1), descent

JARESIAH
3298 Ya'ăreshyâh (1), Jaareshjah

JARHA
3398 Yarchâ' (2), Jarcha

JARIB
3402 Yârîyb (3), contentious; adversary

JARMUTH
3412 Yarmûwth (7), elevation

JAROAH
3386 Yârôwach (1), (born at the) new moon

JASHEN
3464 Yâshên (1), sleepy

JASHER
3477 yâshâr (2), straight

JASHOBEAM
3434 Yâshob'âm (3), people will return

JASHUB
3437 Yâshûwb (3), he will return

JASHUBI-LEHEM
3433 Yâshûbîy Lechem (1), returner of bread

JASHUBITES
3432 Yâshûbîy (1), Jashubite

JASIEL
3300 Ya'ăsîy'êl (1), made of God

JASON
2394 Iasōn (5), about to cure

JASPER
3471 yâshᵉphêh (3), jasper stone
2393 iaspis (4), jasper

JATHNIEL
3496 Yathnîy'êl (1), continued of God

JATTIR
3492 Yattîyr (4), redundant

JAVAN
3120 Yâvân (7), effervescent

JAVELIN
2595 chănîyth (6), lance, spear
7420 rômach (1), iron pointed spear

JAW
3895 lᵉchîy (3), jaw; jaw-bone
4973 mᵉthallᵉ'âh (1), tooth

JAWBONE
3895 lᵉchîy (3), jaw; jaw-bone

JAWS
3895 lᵉchîy (4), jaw; jaw-bone
4455 malqôwach (1), spoil, plunder
4973 mᵉthallᵉ'âh (1), tooth

JAZER
3270 Ya'ăzêyr (11), helpful

JAZIZ
3151 Yâzîyz (1), he will make prominent

JEALOUS
7065 qânâ' (11), to be, make zealous, jealous
7067 qannâ' (4), jealous
7072 qannôw' (2), jealous
2206 zēlŏō (1), to have warmth of feeling for

JEALOUSIES
7068 qin'âh (1), jealousy or envy

JEALOUSY
7065 qânâ' (5), to be, make zealous, jealous
7068 qin'âh (23), jealousy
7069 qânâh (1), to create; to procure
2205 zēlŏs (1), zeal, ardor; jealousy, malice

JEARIM
3297 Yᵉ'ârîym (1), forests

JEATERAI
2979 Yᵉ'âthᵉray (1), stepping

JEBERECHIAH
3000 Yᵉberekyâhûw (1), blessed of Jehovah

JEBUS
2982 Yᵉbûwç (4), trodden

JEBUSI
2983 Yᵉbûwçîy (2), Jebusite

JEBUSITE
2983 Yᵉbûwçîy (14), Jebusite

JEBUSITES
2983 Yᵉbûwçîy (25), Jebusite

JECAMIAH
3359 Yᵉqamyâh (1), Jehovah will rise

JECHOLIAH
3203 Yᵉkolyâh (1), Jehovah will enable

JECHONIAS
2423 Iĕchŏnias (2), Jehovah will establish

JECOLIAH
3203 Yᵉkolyâh (1), Jehovah will enable

JECONIAH
3204 Yᵉkonyâh (7), Jehovah will establish

JEDAIAH
3042 Yᵉdâyâh (2), praised of Jehovah
3048 Yᵉda'yâh (11), Jehovah has known

JEDIAEL
3043 Yᵉdîy'ă'êl (6), knowing God

JEDIDAH
3040 Yᵉdîydâh (1), beloved

JEDIDIAH
3041 Yᵉdîydᵉyâh (1), beloved of Jehovah

JEDUTHUN
3038 Yᵉdûwthûwn (16), laudatory

JEEZER
372 'Iy'ezer (1), helpless

JEEZERITES
373 'Iy'ezrîy (1), Iezrite

JEGAR-SAHADUTHA
3026 Yᵉgar Sahădûwthâ' (Ch.) (1), heap of the testimony

JEHALELEEL
3094 Yᵉhallel'êl (1), praising God

JEHALELEL
3094 Yᵉhallel'êl (1), praising God

JEHDEIAH
3165 Yechdîyâhûw (2), unity of Jehovah

JEHEZEKEL
3168 Yᵉchezqê'l (1), God will strengthen

JEHIAH
3174 Yᵉchîyâh (1), Jehovah will live

JEHIEL
3171 Yᵉchîy'êl (14), God will live
3273 Yᵉ'îy'êl (2), carried away of God

JEHIELI
3172 Yᵉchîy'êlîy (2), Jechiëlite

JEHIZKIAH
3169 Yᵉchizqîyâh (1), strengthened of Jehovah

JEHOADAH
3085 Yᵉhôw'addâh (2), Jehovah-adorned

JEHOADDAN
3086 Yᵉhôw'addîyn (2), Jehovah-pleased

JEHOAHAZ
3059 Yᵉhôw'âchâz (21), Jehovah-seized
3099 Yôw'âchâz (1), Jehovah-seized

JEHOASH
3060 Yᵉhôw'âsh (17), Jehovah-fired

JEHOHANAN
3076 Yᵉhôwchânân (6), Jehovah-favored

JEHOIACHIN
3078 Yᵉhôwyâkîyn (10), Jehovah will establish

JEHOIACHIN'S
3112 Yôwyâkîyn (1), Jehovah will establish

JEHOIADA
3111 Yôwyâdâ' (52), Jehovah-known

JEHOIAKIM
3079 Yᵉhôwyâqîym (37), Jehovah will raise

JEHOIARIB
3080 Yᵉhôwyârîyb (2), Jehovah will contend

J

JEHONADAB
3082 Yᵉhôwnâdâb (3), *Jehovah-largessed*

JEHONATHAN
3083 Yᵉhôwnâthân (3), *Jehovah-given*

JEHORAM
3088 Yᵉhôwrâm (23), *Jehovah-raised*

JEHOSHABEATH
3090 Yᵉhôwshab'ath (2), *Jehovah-sworn*

JEHOSHAPHAT
3046 yᵉda' (Ch.) (1), to *know*
3092 Yᵉhôwshâphâṭ (84), *Jehovah-judged*

JEHOSHEBA
3089 Yᵉhôwsheba' (1), *Jehovah-sworn*

JEHOSHUA
3091 Yᵉhôwshûw'a (1), *Jehovah-saved*

JEHOSHUAH
3091 Yᵉhôwshûw'a (1), *Jehovah-saved*

JEHOVAH
3068 Yᵉhôvâh (4), (the) self-*Existent* or Eternal

JEHOVAH-JIREH
3070 Yᵉhôvâh Yir'eh (1), *Jehovah will see* (to it)

JEHOVAH-NISSI
3071 Yᵉhôvâh Niççîy (1), *Jehovah* (is) *my banner*

JEHOVAH-SHALOM
3073 Yᵉhôvâh Shâlôwm (1), *Jehovah* (is) *peace*

JEHOZABAD
3075 Yᵉhôwzâbâd (4), *Jehovah-endowed*

JEHOZADAK
3087 Yᵉhôwtsâdâq (2), *Jehovah-righted*

JEHU
3058 Yêhûw' (57), *Jehovah* (is) *He*

JEHUBBAH
3160 Yᵉchubbâh (1), *hidden*

JEHUCAL
3081 Yᵉhûwkal (1), *potent*

JEHUD
3055 Yᵉhûd (1), *celebrated*

JEHUDI
3065 Yᵉhûwdîy (4), *Jehudite*

JEHUDIJAH
3057 Yᵉhûdîyâh (1), *celebrated*

JEHUSH
3266 Yᵉ'ûwsh (1), *hasty*

JEIEL
3273 Yᵉ'îy'êl (11), *carried away of God*

JEKABZEEL
3343 Yᵉqabtsᵉ'êl (1), *God will gather*

JEKAMEAM
3360 Yᵉqam'âm (2), *people will rise*

JEKAMIAH
3359 Yᵉqamyâh (2), *Jehovah will rise*

JEKUTHIEL
3354 Yᵉqûwthîy'êl (1), *obedience of God*

JEMIMA
3224 Yᵉmîymâh (1), *dove*

JEMUEL
3223 Yᵉmûw'êl (2), *day of God*

JEOPARDED
2778 châraph (1), to spend the *winter*

JEOPARDY
2793 kindunĕuō (2), to undergo peril

JEPHTHAE
2422 Iĕphthaĕ (1), *he will open*

JEPHTHAH
3316 Yiphtâch (29), *he will open*

JEPHUNNEH
3312 Yᵉphunneh (16), *he will be prepared*

JERAH
3392 Yerach (2), *lunar month*

JERAHMEEL
3396 Yᵉrachmᵉ'êl (8), *God will be compassionate*

JERAHMEELITES
3397 Yᵉrachmᵉ'êlîy (2), *Jerachmeëlite*

JERED
3382 Yered (2), *descent*

JEREMAI
3413 Yᵉrêmay (1), *elevated*

JEREMIAH
3414 Yirmᵉyâh (146), *Jehovah will rise*

JEREMIAH'S
3414 Yirmᵉyâh (1), *Jehovah will rise*

JEREMIAS
2408 Hiĕrĕmias (1), *Jehovah will rise*

JEREMOTH
3406 Yᵉrîymôwth (5), *elevations*

JEREMY
2408 Hiĕrĕmias (2), *Jehovah will rise*

JERIAH
3404 Yᵉrîyâh (2), *Jehovah will throw*

JERIBAI
3403 Yᵉrîybay (1), *contentious*

JERICHO
3405 Yᵉrîychôw (57), *its month*, or *fragrant*
2410 Hiĕrichô (7), *its month* or *fragrant*

JERIEL
3400 Yᵉrîy'êl (1), *thrown of God*

JERIJAH
3404 Yᵉrîyâh (1), *Jehovah will throw*

JERIMOTH
3406 Yᵉrîymôwth (8), *elevations*

JERIOTH
3408 Yᵉrîy'ôwth (1), *curtains*

JEROBOAM
3379 Yârob'âm (102), *people will contend*

JEROBOAM'S
3379 Yârob'âm (2), *people will contend*

JEROHAM
3395 Yᵉrôchâm (10), *compassionate*

JERUBBAAL
3378 Yᵉrubba'al (14), *Baal will contend*

JERUBBESHETH
3380 Yᵉrubbesheth (1), *the idol will contend*

JERUEL
3385 Yᵉrûw'êl (1), *founded of God*

JERUSALEM
3389 Yᵉrûwshâlaim (640), *founded peaceful*
3390 Yᵉrûwshâlêm (Ch.) (26), *founded peaceful*
2414 Hiĕrŏsŏluma (61), *founded peaceful*
2419 Hiĕrŏusalēm (81), *founded peaceful*

JERUSALEM'S
3389 Yᵉrûwshâlaim (3), *founded peaceful*

JERUSHA
3388 Yᵉrûwshâ' (1), *possessed*

JERUSHAH
3388 Yᵉrûwshâ' (1), *possessed*

JESAIAH
3470 Yᵉsha'yâh (2), *Jehovah has saved*

JESHAIAH
3740 kêrâh (5), *purchase*

JESHANAH
3466 Yᵉshânâh (1), *old*

JESHARELAH
3480 Yᵉsar'êlâh (1), *right towards God*

JESHEBEAB
3434 Yâshob'âm (1), *people will return*

JESHER
3475 Yêsher (1), *right*

JESHIMON
3452 yᵉshîymôwn (5), *desolation*

JESHISHAI
3454 Yᵉshîyshay (1), *aged*

JESHOHAIAH
3439 Yᵉshôwchâyâh (1), *Jehovah will empty*

JESHUA
3442 Yêshûwa' (28), *he will save*
3443 Yêshûwa' (Ch.) (2), *he will save*

JESHURUN
3484 Yᵉshûrûwn (3), *upright*

JESIAH
3449 Yishshîyâh (2), *Jehovah will lend*

JESIMIEL
3450 Yᵉsîymâ'êl (1), *God will place*

JESSE
3448 Yîshay (41), *extant*
2421 Iĕssai (5), *extant*

JESTING
2160 ĕutrapĕlia (1), *ribaldry*

JESUI
3440 Yishvîy (1), *level*

JESUITES
3441 Yishvîy (1), *Jishvite*

JESURUN
3484 Yᵉshûrûwn (1), *upright*

JESUS
846 autŏs (1), *he, she, it*
2424 Iēsŏus (967), *Jehovah-saved*

JESUS'
2424 Iēsŏus (10), *Jehovah-saved*

JETHER
3500 Yether (8), *remainder*

JETHETH
3509 Yᵉthêyth (2), *Jetheth*

JETHLAH
3494 Yithlâh (1), *be high*

JETHRO
3503 Yithrôw (10), *his excellence*

JETUR
3195 Yᵉṭûwr (3), *enclosed*

JEUEL
3262 Yᵉ'ûw'êl (1), *carried away of God*

JEUSH
3266 Yᵉ'ûwsh (8), *hasty*

JEUZ
3263 Yᵉ'ûwts (1), *counselor*

JEW
3064 Yᵉhûwdîy (10), *Jehudite*
2453 Iŏudaiŏs (22), *belonging to Jehudah*

JEWEL
3627 kᵉlîy (1), *implement, thing*
5141 nezem (2), *nose-ring*

JEWELS
2484 chelyâh (2), *trinket, ornament*
3627 kᵉlîy (18), *implement, thing*
5141 nezem (1), *nose-ring*
5459 çᵉgullâh (1), *wealth*

JEWESS
2453 Iŏudaiŏs (2), belonging to *Jehudah*

JEWISH
2451 Iŏudaïkŏs (1), resembling a *Judæan*

JEWRY
3061 Y^{e}hûwd (Ch.) (1), *celebrated*
2449 Iŏudaia (2), *Judæan* land

JEWS
3054 yâhad (1), to *become Jewish*
3062 Y^{e}hûwdâ'îy (Ch.) (8), *Jew*
3064 Y^{e}hûwdîy (65), *Jehudite*
2450 Iŏudaïzō (1), to *Judaize, live as a Jew*
2452 Iŏudaïkōs (1), *in a Judæan manner*
2453 Iŏudaiŏs (167), belonging to *Jehudah*

JEWS'
3064 Y^{e}hûwdîy (4), *Jehudite*
3066 Y^{e}hûwdîyth (4), *in* the *Jewish language*
2453 Iŏudaiŏs (4), belonging to *Jehudah*
2454 Iŏudaismŏs (2), *Jewish faith*

JEZANIAH
3153 Y^{e}zanyâh (2), *heard of Jehovah*

JEZEBEL
348 'Îyzebel (21), *chaste*
2403 Iĕzabēl (1), *chaste*

JEZEBEL'S
348 'Îyzebel (1), *chaste*

JEZER
3337 Yêtser (3), *form*

JEZERITES
3339 Yitsrîy (1), *formative*

JEZIAH
3150 Yizzîyâh (1), *sprinkled of Jehovah*

JEZIEL
3149 Y^{e}zav'êl (1), *sprinkled of God*

JEZLIAH
3152 Yizlîy'ah (1), *he will draw out*

JEZOAR
3328 Yitschar (1), *he will shine*

JEZRAHIAH
3156 Yizrachyâh (1), *Jehovah will shine*

JEZREEL
3157 Yizr^{e}'ê'l (36), *God will sow*

JEZREELITE
3158 Yizr^{e}'ê'lîy (8), *Jizreëlite*

JEZREELITESS
3159 Yizr^{e}'ê'lîyth (5), *Jezreëlitess*

JIBSAM
3005 Yibsâm (1), *fragrant*

JIDLAPH
3044 Yidlâph (1), *tearful*

JIMNA
3232 Yimnâh (1), *prosperity*

JIMNAH
3232 Yimnâh (1), *prosperity*

JIMNITES
3232 Yimnâh (1), *prosperity*

JIPHTAH
3316 Yiphtâch (1), *he will open*

JIPHTHAH-EL
3317 Yiphtach-'êl (2), *God will open*

JOAB
3097 Yôw'âb (137), *Jehovah-fathered*
5854 'Aṭrôwth Bêyth Yôw'âb (1), *crowns of* (the) *house of Joäb*

JOAB'S
3097 Yôw'âb (8), *Jehovah-fathered*

JOAH
3098 Yôw'âch (11), *Jehovah-brothered*

JOAHAZ
3098 Yôw'âch (1), *Jehovah-brothered*

JOANNA
2489 Iōanna (3), *Jehovah-favored*

JOASH
3101 Yôw'âsh (47), *Jehovah-fired*
3135 Yôw'âsh (2), *Jehovah-hastened*

JOATHAM
2488 Iōatham (2), *Jehovah* (is) *perfect*

JOB
347 'Îyôwb (57), *persecuted*
3102 Yôwb (1), *Job*
2492 Iōb (1), *persecuted*

JOB'S
347 'Îyôwb (1), *persecuted*

JOBAB
3103 Yôwbâb (9), *howler*

JOCHEBED
3115 Yôwkebed (2), *Jehovah-gloried*

JOED
3133 Yôw'êd (1), *appointer*

JOEL
3100 Yôw'êl (19), *Jehovah* (is his) *God*
2493 Iōēl (1), *Jehovah* (is his) *God*

JOELAH
3132 Yôw'ê'lâh (1), *furthermore*

JOEZER
3134 Yôw'ezer (1), *Jehovah* (is his) *help*

JOGBEHAH
3011 Yogb^{e}hâh (2), *hillock*

JOGLI
3020 Yoglîy (1), *exiled*

JOHA
3109 Yôwchâ' (2), *Jehovah-revived*

JOHANAN
3076 Y^{e}hôwchânân (3), *Jehovah-favored*
3110 Yôwchânân (24), *Jehovah-favored*

JOHN
2491 Iōannēs (131), *Jehovah-favored*

JOHN'S
2491 Iōannēs (2), *Jehovah-favored*

JOIADA
3111 Yôwyâdâ' (4), *Jehovah-known*

JOIAKIM
3113 Yôwyâqîym (4), *Jehovah will raise*

JOIARIB
3114 Yôwyârîyb (5), *Jehovah will contend*

JOIN
2266 châbar (2), to *fascinate* by spells
2859 châthan (1), to *become related*
3254 yâçaph (1), to *add* or *augment*
3867 lâvâh (2), to *unite;* to *remain;* to *borrow*
5060 nâga' (1), to *strike*
5526 çâkak (1), to *entwine;* to *fence* in
7126 qârab (1), to *approach, bring near*
2853 kŏllaō (3), to *glue together*

JOINED
977 bâchar (1), *select, chose, prefer*
1692 dâbaq (2), to *cling* or *adhere;* to *catch*
2266 châbar (8), to *fascinate* by spells
2302 châdâh (1), to *rejoice, be glad*
2338 chûwṭ (Ch.) (1), to *repair; lay a foundation*
2859 châthan (1), to *become related*
3161 yâchad (1), to *be, become one*
3867 lâvâh (8), to *unite;* to *remain;* to *borrow*
5208 nîychôwach (Ch.) (1), *pleasure*
5595 çâphâh (1), to *scrape;* to *accumulate*
6186 'ârak (1), to set in a row, i.e. *arrange,*
6775 tsâmad (3), to *link,* i.e. *gird*
7000 qâṭar (1), to *enclose*
7126 qârab (1), to *approach, bring near*
7194 qâshar (1), to *tie, bind*
2675 katartizō (1), to *repair;* to *prepare*
2853 kŏllaō (3), to *glue together*
4347 prŏskŏllaō (2), to *glue to,* i.e. to *adhere*
4801 suzĕugnumi (2), to *conjoin* in marriage
4883 sunarmŏlŏgĕō (1), to *render close-jointed*
4927 sunŏmŏrĕō (1), to *border together*

JOINING
1692 dâbaq (1), to *cling* or *adhere;* to *catch*

JOININGS
4226 m^{e}chabb^{e}râh (1), *joiner,* brace or cramp

JOINT
3363 yâqa' (1), to *be dislocated*
4154 mûw'edeth (1), *dislocated*
6504 pârad (1), to *spread* or *separate*
860 haphē (1), fastening *ligament, joint*

JOINT-HEIRS
4789 sugklērŏnŏmŏs (1), *participant in common*

JOINTS
1694 debeq (2), *joint*
2542 chammûwq (1), *wrapping,* i.e. *drawers*
7001 q^{e}ṭar (Ch.) (1), *riddle; vertebra*
719 harmŏs (1), *articulation,* body-joint
860 haphē (1), fastening *ligament, joint*

JOKDEAM
3347 Yoqd^{e}'âm (1), *burning of* (the) *people*

JOKIM
3137 Yôwqîym (1), *Jehovah will raise*

JOKMEAM
3361 Yoqm^{e}'âm (1), *people will be raised*

JOKNEAM
3362 Yoqn^{e}'âm (4), *people will be lamented*

JOKSHAN
3370 Yoqshân (4), *insidious*

JOKTAN
3355 Yoqṭân (6), *he will be made little*

JOKTHEEL
3371 Yoqth^{e}'êl (2), *veneration of God*

JONA
2495 Iōnas (1), *dove*

JONADAB
3082 Y^{e}hôwnâdâb (4), *Jehovah-largessed*
3122 Yôwnâdâb (8), *Jehovah-largessed*

JONAH
3124 Yôwnâh (19), *dove*

JONAN
2494 Iōnan (1), *Jehovah-favored* or a *dove*

JONAS
2495 Iōnas (12), *dove*

J

JONATH-ELEM-RECHOKIM
3128 Yôwnath 'êlem
rᵉchôqîym (1), dove of
(the) silence

JONATHAN
3083 Yᵉhôwnâthân (81),
Jehovah-given
3129 Yôwnâthân (37),
Jehovah-given

JONATHAN'S
3129 Yôwnâthân (3),
Jehovah-given

JOPPA
3305 Yâphôw (3),
beautiful
2445 Iŏppē (10), beautiful

JORAH
3139 Yôwrâh (1), rainy

JORAI
3140 Yôwray (1), rainy

JORAM
3141 Yôwrâm (19),
Jehovah-raised
3088 Yᵉhôwrâm (7),
Jehovah-raised
2496 Iŏram (2),
Jehovah-raised

JORDAN
3383 Yardên (182),
descender
2446 Iŏrdanēs (15),
descender

JORIM
2497 Iŏrĕim (1), (poss.)
Jehovah-raised

JORKOAM
3421 Yorqᵉ'âm (1),
people will be poured
forth

JOSABAD
3107 Yôwzâbâd (1),
Jehovah-endowed

JOSAPHAT
2498 Iŏsaphat (2),
Jehovah-judged

JOSE
2499 Iŏsē (1), (poss.) let
him add

JOSEDECH
3087 Yᵉhôwtsâdâq (6),
Jehovah-righted

JOSEPH
3084 Yᵉhôwçêph (1), let
him add or adding
3130 Yôwçêph (193), let
him add or adding
2501 Iŏsēph (33), let him
add or adding

JOSEPH'S
3130 Yôwçêph (20), let
him add or adding
2501 Iŏsēph (2), let him
add or adding

JOSES
2500 Iŏsēs (6), (poss.) let
him add

JOSHAH
3144 Yôwshâh (1), Joshah

JOSHAPHAT
3146 Yôwshâphât (1),
Jehovah-judged

JOSHAVIAH
3145 Yôwshavyâh (1),
Jehovah-set

JOSHBEKASHAH
3436 Yoshbᵉqâshâh (2),
hard seat

JOSHUA
3091 Yᵉhôwshûw'a (215),
Jehovah-saved

JOSIAH
2977 Yô'shîyâh (53),
founded of Jehovah

JOSIAS
2502 Iŏsias (2), founded
of Jehovah

JOSIBIAH
3143 Yôwshîbyâh (1),
Jehovah will cause to
dwell

JOSIPHIAH
3131 Yôwçiphyâh (1),
Jehovah (is) adding

JOT
2503 iŏta (1), iota

JOTBAH
3192 Yoṭbâh (1),
pleasantness

JOTBATH
3193 Yoṭbâthâh (1),
pleasantness

JOTBATHAH
3193 Yoṭbâthâh (2),
pleasantness

JOTHAM
3147 Yôwthâm (24),
Jehovah (is) perfect

JOURNEY
1870 derek (23), road;
course of life; mode of
action
4109 mahălâk (3),
passage or a distance
4550 maçça' (1),
departure
5265 nâça' (12), start on
a journey
5575+7272 çanvêr (1),
blindness
589 apŏdēmĕŏ (2), visit a
foreign land
590 apŏdēmŏs (1),
foreign traveller
1279 diapŏrĕuŏmai (1),
to travel through
2137 ĕuŏdŏō (1), to
succeeᴄ' in business
3596 hŏdŏipŏrĕŏ (1), to
travel
3597 hŏdŏipŏria (1),
traveling
3598 hŏdŏs (6), road
4198 pŏrĕuŏmai (2), to
go, come; to travel

JOURNEYED
5265 nâça' (28), start on
a journey
6213+1870 'âsâh (1), to
do or make
3593 hŏdĕuŏ (1), to travel
4198 pŏrĕuŏmai (2), to
go/come; to travel
4922 sunŏdĕuŏ (1), to
travel in company with

JOURNEYING
4550 maçça' (1),
departure
5265 nâça' (1), start on a
journey
4197+4160 pŏrĕia (1),
journey; life's conduct

JOURNEYINGS
4550 maçça' (1),
departure
3597 hŏdŏipŏria (1),
traveling

JOURNEYS
4550 maçça' (9),
departure

JOY
1523 gîyl (2), rejoice
1524 gîyl (3), age, stage
in life
1525 gîylâh (1), joy,
delight
2304 chedvâh (1),
rejoicing, joy
2305 chedvâh (Ch.) (1),
rejoicing, joy
2898 ṭûwb (1), good;
beauty, gladness
4885 mâsôws (12), delight
7440 rinnâh (3), shout
7442 rânan (3), to shout
for joy
7796 Sôwrêq (1), vine
8055 sâmach (4), to be,
make gleesome
8056 sâmêach (2), blithe
or gleeful
8057 simchâh (43),
blithesomeness or glee
8342 sâsôwn (14),
cheerfulness; welcome
8643 tᵉrûw'âh (2),
battle-cry; clangor
20 agalliasis (2),
exultation, delight
21 agalliaō (1), to exult
2167 ĕuphrŏsunē (1),
joyfulness, cheerfulness
2744 kauchaŏmai (1), to
glory in, rejoice in; to
boast
3685 ŏninēmi (1), to
gratify, derive pleasure
5468 chalinagōgĕō (3), to
curb, hold in check
5479 chara (51), calm
delight, joy
5485 charis (1),
gratitude; benefit given

JOYED
5463 chairō (1), to be
cheerful

JOYFUL
1523 gîyl (4), rejoice
2896 ṭôwb (1), good; well
5937 'âlaz (2), to jump for
joy
5970 'âlats (1), to jump
for joy
7442 rânan (1), to shout
for joy
7445 rᵉnânâh (2), shout
for joy
8055 sâmach (2), to be,
make gleesome
8056 sâmêach (3), blithe
or gleeful

8643 tᵉrûw'âh (1),
battle-cry; clangor of
trumpets
5479 chara (1), calm
delight, joy

JOYFULLY
2416 chay (1), alive; raw;
fresh; life
3326+5479 mĕta (1), with,
among; after, later
5463 chairō (1), to be
cheerful

JOYFULNESS
8057 simchâh (1),
blithesomeness or glee
5479 chara (1), calm
delight, joy

JOYING
5463 chairō (1), to be
cheerful

JOYOUS
5947 'allîyz (3), exultant;
reveling
5479 chara (1), calm
delight, joy

JOZABAD
3107 Yôwzâbâd (9),
Jehovah-endowed

JOZACHAR
3108 Yôwzâkâr (1),
Jehovah-remembered

JOZADAK
3136 Yôwtsâdâq (5),
Jehovah-righted

JUBAL
3106 Yûwbâl (1), stream

JUBILE
3104 yôwbêl (21), blast of
a ram's horn
8643 tᵉrûw'âh (1),
battle-cry; clangor

JUCAL
3116 Yûwkal (1), potent

JUDA
2448 Iŏuda (1),
celebrated
2455 Iŏudas (7),
celebrated

JUDAEA
2449 Iŏudaia (41),
Judæan land
2453 Iŏudaiŏs (1),
belonging to Jehudah
2499 Iŏsē (1), (poss.) let
him add

JUDAH
3061 Yᵉhûwd (Ch.) (5),
celebrated
3063 Yᵉhûwdâh (806),
celebrated
3064 Yᵉhûwdîy (1),
Jehudite
2455 Iŏudas (1),
celebrated

JUDAH'S
3063 Yᵉhûwdâh (4),
celebrated

JUDAS
2455 Iŏudas (33),
celebrated

JUDE
2455 Iŏudas (1),
celebrated

JUDEA
3061 Yᵉhûwd (Ch.) (1), *celebrated*

JUDGE
430 'ĕlôhîym (1), *God; magistrates, judges*
1777 dîyn (14), to *judge;* to *strive* or *contend for*
1781 dayân (1), *judge; advocate*
1784 Dîynay (Ch.) (1), *Dinaite*
3198 yâkach (1), to *decide, justify, convict*
6416 pᵉlîylîy (1), *judicial*
8199 shâphaṭ (102), to *judge*
350 anakrinō (1), to *interrogate, determine*
1252 diakrinō (3), to *decide; to hesitate*
1348 dikastēs (3), one who *judges*
2919 krinō (45), to *decide; to try*
2922 kritēriŏn (1), *rule; tribunal; lawsuit*
2923 kritēs (13), *judge*

JUDGED
1777 dîyn (2), to *judge;* to *strive* or *contend for*
4941 mishpâṭ (1), *verdict; formal decree; justice*
5307 nâphal (1), to *fall*
6419 pâlal (1), to *intercede, pray*
8199 shâphaṭ (28), to *judge*
350 anakrinō (3), to *interrogate, determine*
2233 hēgĕŏmai (1), to *deem, i.e. consider*
2919 krinō (26), to *decide; to try, condemn, punish*

JUDGES
148 'ădargâzêr (Ch.) (2), *chief diviner*
430 'ĕlôhîym (4), *God; magistrates, judges*
1782 dayân (Ch.) (1), *judge*
6414 pâlîyl (3), *magistrate*
8199 shâphaṭ (38), to *judge*
2923 kritēs (4), *judge*

JUDGEST
8199 shâphaṭ (2), to *judge*
2919 krinō (6), to *decide;* to *try, condemn, punish*

JUDGETH
1777 dîyn (1), to *judge;* to *strive* or *contend for*
8199 shâphaṭ (5), to *judge*
350 anakrinō (1), to *interrogate, determine*
2919 krinō (10), to *try, condemn, punish*

JUDGING
8199 shâphaṭ (4), to *judge*
2919 krinō (2), to *decide;* to *try, condemn, punish*

JUDGMENT
1777 dîyn (1), to *judge;* to *strive* or *contend for*

1779 dîyn (9), *judge; judgment; law suit*
1780 dîyn (Ch.) (5), *judge; judgment*
2940 ṭa'am (1), *perception; mandate*
4055 mad (1), *vesture, garment; carpet*
4941 mishpâṭ (187), *verdict; decree; justice*
6415 pᵉlîylâh (1), *justice*
6417 pᵉlîylîyâh (1), *judgment*
6419 pâlal (1), to *intercede, pray*
6485 pâqad (2), to *visit, care for, count*
8196 shᵉphôwṭ (2), *sentence, punishment*
8199 shâphaṭ (2), to *judge*
8201 shepheṭ (2), *criminal sentence*
144 aisthēsis (1), *discernment*
968 bēma (10), *tribunal platform; judging place*
1106 gnōmē (3), *cognition, opinion*
1341 dikaiŏkrisia (1), *just sentence*
1345 dikaiōma (1), *statute or decision*
1349 dikē (1), *justice*
2250 hēmĕra (1), *day; period of time*
2917 krima (12), *decision*
2920 krisis (39), *decision; tribunal; justice*
2922 kritēriŏn (1), *rule; tribunal; lawsuit*
4232 praitōriŏn (5), *governor's court-room*

JUDGMENTS
4941 mishpâṭ (108), *verdict; decree; justice*
8201 shepheṭ (14), *criminal sentence*
1345 dikaiōma (1), *deed; statute or decision*
2917 krima (1), *decision*
2920 krisis (2), *decision; tribunal; justice*
2922 kritēriŏn (1), *rule; tribunal; lawsuit*

JUDITH
3067 Yᵉhûwdîyth (1), *Jewess*

JUICE
6071 'âçîyç (1), *expressed fresh grape-juice*

JULIA
2456 Iŏulia (1), *Julia*

JULIUS
2457 Iŏuliŏs (2), *Julius*

JUMPING
7540 râqad (1), to *spring about wildly or for joy*

JUNIA
2458 Iŏunias (1), *Junias*

JUNIPER
7574 rethem (4), *broom tree*

JUPITER
1356 diŏpĕtēs (1), *sky-fallen*

2203 Zĕus (2), *Jupiter or Jove*

JURISDICTION
1849 ĕxŏusia (1), *authority, dominion*

JUSHAB-HESED
3142 Yûwshab Cheçed (1), *kindness will be returned*

JUST
3477 yâshâr (1), *straight*
4941 mishpâṭ (1), *verdict; formal decree; justice*
6662 tsaddîyq (42), *just*
6663 tsâdaq (3), to *be, make right*
6664 tsedeq (8), *right*
8003 shâlêm (1), *complete; friendly; safe*
1342 dikaiŏs (33), *equitable, holy*
1738 ĕndikŏs (2), *equitable, deserved, just*

JUSTICE
4941 mishpâṭ (1), *verdict; formal decree; justice*
6663 tsâdaq (2), to *be, make right*
6664 tsedeq (10), *right*
6666 tsᵉdâqâh (15), *rightness*

JUSTIFICATION
1345 dikaiōma (1), *deed; statute or decision*
1347 dikaiōsis (2), *acquittal, vindication*

JUSTIFIED
6663 tsâdaq (12), to *be, make right*
1344 dikaiŏō (31), *show or regard as just*

JUSTIFIER
1344 dikaiŏō (1), *show or regard as just*

JUSTIFIETH
6663 tsâdaq (2), to *be, make right*
1344 dikaiŏō (2), *show or regard as just*

JUSTIFY
6663 tsâdaq (7), to *be, make right*
1344 dikaiŏō (4), *show or regard as just*

JUSTIFYING
6663 tsâdaq (2), to *be, make right*

JUSTLE
8264 shâqaq (1), to *seek greedily*

JUSTLY
4941 mishpâṭ (1), *verdict; formal decree; justice*
1346 dikaiŏs (2), *equitably*

JUSTUS
2459 Iŏustŏs (3), *just*

JUTTAH
3194 Yuṭṭâh (2), *extended*

KABZEEL
6909 Qabtsᵉ'êl (3), *God has gathered*

KADESH
6946 Qâdêsh (17), *sanctuary*

KADESH-BARNEA
6947 Qâdêsh Barnêa' (10), Kadesh of (the) *Wilderness of Wandering*

KADMIEL
6934 Qadmîy'êl (8), *presence of God*

KADMONITES
6935 Qadmônîy (1), *ancient*

KALLAI
7040 Qallay (1), *frivolous*

KANAH
7071 Qânâh (3), *reediness*

KAREAH
7143 Qârêach (13), *bald*

KARKAA
7173 Qarqa' (1), *ground-floor*

KARKOR
7174 Qarqôr (1), *foundation*

KARTAH
7177 Qartâh (1), *city*

KARTAN
7178 Qartân (1), *city-plot*

KATTATH
7005 Qaṭṭâth (1), *littleness*

KEDAR
6938 Qêdâr (12), *dusky*

KEDEMAH
6929 Qêdᵉmâh (2), *precedence*

KEDEMOTH
6932 Qᵉdêmôwth (4), *beginnings*

KEDESH
6943 Qedesh (11), *sanctum*

KEDESH-NAPHTALI
6943+5321 Qedesh (1), *sanctum*

KEEP
1692 dâbaq (3), to *cling or adhere; to catch*
1961 hâyâh (1), to *exist, i.e. be or become*
2287 châgag (12), to *observe a festival*
2820 châsak (1), to *refuse, spare, preserve*
3533 kâbash (1), to *conquer, subjugate*
3607 kâlâ' (1), to *hold back or in; to prohibit*
4513 mâna' (2), to *deny, refuse*
4931 mishmereth (1), *watch, sentry, post*
5201 nâṭar (3), to *guard; to cherish anger*
5341 nâtsar (26), to *guard, protect*
5647 'âbad (1), to *do, work, serve*
5737 'âdar (2), to *arrange as a battle*

6113 'âtsar (1), to *hold back; to maintain, rule*
6213 'âsâh (30), to *do or make*
6485 pâqad (1), to *visit, care for, count*
6942 qâdâsh (1), to *be, make clean*
7069 qânâh (1), to *create; to procure*
7368 râchaq (1), to *recede; remove*
8104 shâmar (186), to *watch*
1301 diatērĕō (1), to *observe* strictly
1314 diaphulassō (1), to *protect, guard carefully*
1858 hĕŏrtazō (1), to *observe a festival*
2722 katĕchō (3), to *hold down fast*
2853 kŏllaō (1), to *glue together*
3557 nŏsphizōmai (1), to *sequestrate, embezzle*
4160 pŏiĕō (2), to *do*
4238 prassō (1), to *execute, accomplish*
4601 sigaō (2), to *keep silent*
4874 sunanamignumi (1), to *associate with*
4912 sunĕchō (1), to *hold together*
5083 tērĕō (32), to *keep, guard, obey*
5299 hupōpiazō (1), to *beat up; to wear out*
5432 phrŏurĕō (1), to *hem in, protect*
5442 phulassō (13), to *watch, i.e. be on guard*

KEEPER
5201 nâțar (1), to *guard; to cherish* anger
5341 nâtsar (1), to *guard, protect, maintain*
7462 râ'âh (1), to *tend a flock, i.e. pasture it*
8104 shâmar (13), to *watch*
8269 sar (3), *head person, ruler*
1200 dĕsmŏphulax (2), *jailer*

KEEPERS
5201 nâțar (1), to *guard; to cherish* anger
8104 shâmar (15), to *watch*
3626 ŏikŏurŏs (1), *domestically inclined*
5083 tērĕō (1), to *keep, guard, obey*
5441 phulax (3), *watcher or sentry*

KEEPEST
8104 shâmar (3), to *watch*
5442 phulassō (1), to *watch, i.e. be on guard*

KEEPETH
2820 châsak (1), to *refuse, spare, preserve*
4513 mâna' (1), to *deny, refuse*
5307 nâphal (1), to *fall*

5341 nâtsar (7), to *guard, protect, maintain*
7462 râ'âh (1), to *tend a flock, i.e. pasture it*
7623 shâbach (1), to *address; to pacify*
8104 shâmar (18), to *watch*
4160 pŏiĕō (1), to *do*
5083 tērĕō (10), to *keep, guard, obey*
5442 phulassō (1), to *watch, i.e. be on guard*

KEEPING
5341 nâtsar (1), to *guard, protect, maintain*
7462 râ'âh (1), to *tend a flock, i.e. pasture it*
8104 shâmar (7), to *watch*
5084 tērĕsis (1), *observance; prison*
5442 phulassō (1), to *watch, i.e. be on guard*

KEHELATHAH
6954 Qᵉhêlâthâh (2), *convocation*

KEILAH
7084 Qᵉ'îylâh (18), *citadel*

KELAIAH
7041 Qêlâyâh (1), *insignificance*

KELITA
7042 Qᵉlîyţâ' (3), *maiming*

KEMUEL
7055 Qᵉmûw'êl (3), *raised of God*

KENAN
7018 Qêynân (1), *fixed*

KENATH
7079 Qᵉnâth (2), *possession*

KENAZ
7073 Qᵉnaz (11), *hunter*

KENEZITE
7074 Qᵉnizzîy (3), *Kenizzite*

KENITE
7014 Qayin (2), *lance*
7017 Qêynîy (4), *Kenite*

KENITES
7017 Qêynîy (8), *Kenite*

KENIZZITES
7074 Qᵉnizzîy (1), *Kenizzite*

KEPT
631 'âçar (1), to *fasten; to join* battle
680 'âtsal (1), to *select; refuse; narrow*
1639 gâra' (1), to *shave, remove, or withhold*
1692 dâbaq (1), to *cling or adhere; to catch*
2287 châgag (1), to *observe a festival*
2790 chârash (2), to *engrave; to plow*
2820 châsak (2), to *refuse, spare, preserve*
3607 kâlâ' (1), to *hold back or in; to prohibit*

4513 mâna' (2), to *deny, refuse*
4931 mishmereth (6), *watch, sentry, post*
5201 nâțar (1), to *guard; to cherish* anger
5202 nᵉțar (Ch.) (1), to *retain*
5341 nâtsar (4), to *guard, protect, maintain*
5641 châthar (2), to *hide by covering*
5648 'ăbad (Ch.) (1), to *do, work, serve*
6113 'âtsar (2), to *hold back; to maintain, rule*
6213 'âsâh (18), to *do or make*
6942 qâdâsh (1), to *be, make clean*
7462 râ'âh (3), to *tend a flock, i.e. pasture it*
7673 shâbath (1), to *repose; to desist*
8104 shâmar (70), to *watch*
71 agō (1), to *lead; to bring, drive; to weigh*
650 apŏstĕrĕō (1), to *deprive; to despoil*
1006 bŏskō (1), to *pasture a flock*
1096 ginŏmai (1), to *be, become*
1301 diatērĕō (1), to *observe* strictly
2192 ĕchō (1), to *have; hold; keep*
2343 thēsaurizō (1), to *amass or reserve, store*
2377 thurōrŏs (2), *doorkeeper*
2621 katakĕimai (1), to *lie down in bed*
2902 kratĕō (1), to *seize*
2967 kōluō (1), to *stop*
3557 nŏsphizōmai (1), to *sequestrate, embezzle*
3930 parĕchō (1), to *hold near, i.e. to present*
4160 pŏiĕō (1), to *do*
4601 sigaō (2), to *keep silent*
4933 suntĕrĕō (1), to *protect*
5083 tērĕō (15), to *keep, guard, obey*
5288 hupŏstĕllō (1), to *conceal (reserve)*
5432 phrŏurĕō (3), to *hem in, protect*
5442 phulassō (8), to *watch, i.e. be on guard*

KERCHIEFS
4556 miçpachath (2), *scurf, rash*

KEREN-HAPPUCH
7163 Qeren Hap-pûwk (1), *horn of cosmetic*

KERIOTH
7152 Qᵉrîyôwth (3), *buildings*

KERNELS
2785 chartsan (1), *sour, tart grape*

KEROS
7026 Qêyrôç (2), *ankled*

KETTLE
1731 dûwd (1), *pot, kettle; basket*

KETURAH
6989 Qᵉțûwrâh (4), *perfumed*

KEY
4668 maphtêach (2), *opening; key*
2807 klĕis (4), *key*

KEYS
2807 klĕis (2), *key*

KEZIA
7103 Qᵉtsîy'âh (1), *cassia*

KEZIZ
7104 Qᵉtsîyts (1), *abrupt*

KIBROTH-HATTAAVAH
6914 Qibrôwth hat-Ta'ăvâh (5), *graves of the longing*

KIBZAIM
6911 Qibtsayim (1), *double heap*

KICK
1163 bâ'aț (1), *kick*
2979 laktizō (2), to *recalcitrate, kick back*

KICKED
1163 bâ'aț (1), *kick*

KID
1423 gᵉdîy (8), *young male goat*
1423+5795 gᵉdîy (5), *young male goat*
5795 'êz (1), *she-goat; goat's hair*
8163 sâ'îyr (26), *shaggy; he-goat; goat idol*
8166 sᵉ'îyrâh (2), *she-goat*
2056 ĕriphŏs (1), *kid or goat*

KIDNEYS
3629 kilyâh (18), *kidney; mind, heart, spirit*

KIDRON
6939 Qidrôwn (11), *dusky place*

KIDS
1423 gᵉdîy (4), *young male goat*
5795 'êz (1), *she-goat; goat's hair*
8163 sâ'îyr (2), *shaggy; he-goat; goat idol*

KILL
2026 hârag (17), to *kill, slaughter*
2076 zâbach (3), to *(sacrificially) slaughter*
2491 châlâl (2), *pierced to death, one slain*
2873 țâbach (1), to *kill, butcher*
4191 mûwth (24), to *die; to kill*
5221 nâkâh (4), to *strike, kill*
5362 nâqaph (1), to *strike; to surround*
7523 râtsach (4), to *murder*
7819 shâchaț (22), to *slaughter; butcher*

337 anairĕō (6), *to abolish, murder*
615 apŏktĕinō (28), *to kill outright; to destroy*
1315 diachĕirizŏmai (1), *to lay hands upon*
2380 thuō (3), *to kill; to butcher; to sacrifice*
4969 sphazō (1), *to slaughter or to maim*
5407 phŏnĕuō (8), *to commit murder*

KILLED
2026 hârag (3), *to kill, slaughter*
2076 zâbach (1), *to (sacrificially) slaughter*
2873 tâbach (3), *to kill, butcher*
3076 Yᵉhôwchânân (1), *Jehovah-favored*
4191 mûwth (6), *to die; to kill*
5221 nâkâh (3), *to strike, kill*
7523 râtsach (1), *to murder*
7819 shâchaṭ (15), *to slaughter; butcher*
337 anairĕō (3), *to take away, murder*
615 apŏktĕinō (22), *to kill outright; to destroy*
2289 thanatŏō (2), *to kill*
2380 thuō (3), *to kill; to butcher; to sacrifice*
5407 phŏnĕuō (2), *to commit murder*

KILLEDST
2026 hârag (2), *to kill, slaughter*

KILLEST
615 apŏktĕinō (2), *to kill outright; to destroy*

KILLETH
2026 hârag (1), *to kill, slaughter*
4191 mûwth (2), *to die; to kill*
5221 nâkâh (13), *to strike, kill*
6991 qâṭal (1), *to put to death*
7819 shâchaṭ (3), *to slaughter; butcher*
615 apŏktĕinō (3), *to kill outright; to destroy*

KILLING
2026 hârag (1), *to kill, slaughter*
7523 râtsach (1), *to murder*
7819 shâchaṭ (1), *to slaughter; butcher*
7821 shᵉchîyṭâh (1), *slaughter*
615 apŏktĕinō (1), *to kill outright; to destroy*

KIN
1320 bâsâr (2), *flesh; body; person*
7138 qârôwb (1), *near, close*
7607 shᵉ'êr (2), *flesh, meat; kindred by blood*
4773 suggĕnēs (1), *blood relative; countryman*

KINAH
7016 Qîynâh (1), *dirge*

KIND
2896 ṭôwb (1), *good; well*
4327 mîyn (29), *sort, i.e. species*
1085 gĕnŏs (3), *kin, offspring in kind*
5100 tis (1), *some or any person or object*
5449 phusis (1), *genus or sort*
5541 chrēstĕuŏmai (1), *to show oneself useful*
5543 chrēstŏs (2), *employed, i.e. useful*

KINDLE
215 'ôwr (1), *to be luminous*
1197 bâ'ar (4), *to be brutish, be senseless*
1814 dâlaq (2), *to flame; to pursue*
2787 chârar (1), *to melt, burn, dry up*
3341 yâtsath (8), *to burn or set on fire*
3344 yâqad (1), *to burn*
6919 qâdach (1), *to inflame*
6999 qâṭar (1), *to turn into fragrance by fire*

KINDLED
1197 bâ'ar (9), *to be brutish, be senseless*
2734 chârâh (43), *to blaze up*
3341 yâtsath (4), *to burn or set on fire*
3648 kâmar (1), *to shrivel with heat*
5400 nâsaq (1), *to catch fire*
6919 qâdach (3), *to inflame*
8313 sâraph (1), *to be, set on fire*
381 anaptō (2), *to kindle, set on fire*
681 haptō (1), *to set on fire*

KINDLETH
3857 lâhaṭ (1), *to blaze*
5400 nâsaq (1), *to catch fire*
381 anaptō (1), *to kindle, set on fire*

KINDLY
2617 cheçed (5), *kindness, favor*
2896 ṭôwb (2), *good; well*
5921+3820 'al (2), *above, over, upon, or against*
5387 philŏstŏrgŏs (1), *fraternal, devoted*

KINDNESS
2617 cheçed (40), *kindness, favor*
2896 ṭôwb (1), *good; well*
5360 philadĕlphia (2), *fraternal affection*
5363 philanthrōpia (1), *benevolence*
5544 chrēstŏtēs (4), *moral excellence*

KINDRED
250 'Ezrâchîy (1), *Ezrachite*
1353 gᵉullâh (1), *blood relationship*
4130 môwda'ath (1), *distant relative*
4138 môwledeth (11), *lineage, family*
4940 mishpâchâh (6), *family, clan, people*
1085 gĕnŏs (3), *kin*
4772 suggĕnĕia (3), *relatives; one's people*
5443 phulē (2), *race or clan*

KINDREDS
4940 mishpâchâh (3), *family, clan, people*
3965 patria (1), *family, group, race, i.e. nation*
5443 phulē (4), *race or clan*

KINDS
2177 zan (5), *form or sort*
4327 mîyn (1), *sort, i.e. species*
4940 mishpâchâh (2), *family, clan, people*
1085 gĕnŏs (2), *kin, offspring in kind*

KINE
504 'eleph (4), *ox; cow or cattle*
1241 bâqâr (2), *plowing ox; herd*
6510 pârâh (18), *heifer*

KING
4427 mâlak (43), *to reign as king*
4428 melek (1957), *king*
4430 melek (Ch.) (140), *king*
935 basilĕus (86), *sovereign*

KING'S
4410 mᵉlûwkâh (2), *realm, rulership*
4428 melek (259), *king*
4430 melek (Ch.) (18), *king*
4467 mamlâkâh (1), *royal dominion*
935 basilĕus (2), *sovereign*
937 basilikŏs (1), *befitting the sovereign*

KINGDOM
4410 mᵉlûwkâh (18), *realm, rulership*
4437 malkûw (Ch.) (45), *dominion*
4438 malkûwth (47), *rule; dominion*
4467 mamlâkâh (61), *royal dominion*
4468 mamlâkûwth (8), *royal dominion*
932 basilĕia (155), *rule; realm*

KINGDOMS
4437 malkûw (Ch.) (2), *dominion*
4438 malkûwth (1), *rule; dominion*
4467 mamlâkâh (49), *royal dominion*

932 basilĕia (5), *rule; realm*

KINGLY
4437 malkûw (Ch.) (1), *dominion*

KINGS
4428 melek (283), *king*
4430 melek (Ch.) (13), *king*
935 basilĕus (29), *sovereign*
936 basilĕuō (1), *to rule*

KINGS'
4428 melek (3), *king*
933 basilĕiŏn (1), *royal palace*
935 basilĕus (1), *sovereign*

KINSFOLK
7138 qârôwb (1), *near, close*
4773 suggĕnēs (1), *blood relative; countryman*

KINSFOLKS
1350 gâ'al (1), *to redeem; to be the next of kin*
3045 yâda' (1), *to know*
4773 suggĕnēs (1), *blood relative; countryman*

KINSMAN
1350 gâ'al (12), *to be the next of kin*
3045 yâda' (1), *to know*
7607 shᵉ'êr (1), *flesh, meat; kindred by blood*
4773 suggĕnēs (2), *blood relative; countryman*

KINSMAN'S
1350 gâ'al (1), *to redeem; to be the next of kin*

KINSMEN
1350 gâ'al (1), *to redeem; to be the next of kin*
7138 qârôwb (1), *near, close*
4773 suggĕnēs (5), *blood relative; countryman*

KINSWOMAN
4129 môwda' (1), *distant relative*
7607 shᵉ'êr (2), *flesh, meat; kindred by blood*

KINSWOMEN
7608 sha'ărâh (1), *female kindred by blood*

KIR
7024 Qîyr (5), *fortress*

KIR-HARASETH
7025 Qîyr Cheres (1), *fortress of earthenware*

KIR-HARESETH
7025 Qîyr Cheres (1), *fortress of earthenware*

KIR-HARESH
7025 Qîyr Cheres (1), *fortress of earthenware*

KIR-HERES
7025 Qîyr Cheres (2), *fortress of earthenware*

KIRIATHAIM
7156 Qiryâthayim (3), *double city*

K

7741 Shâvêh
Qiryâthayim (1), *plain
of a double city*

KIRIOTH
7152 Qᵉrîyôwth (1),
buildings

KIRJATH
7157 Qiryath Yᵉ'ârîym
(1), *city of forests*

KIRJATH-ARBA
7153 Qiryath 'Arba' (6),
*city of Arba or of the
four* (giants)

KIRJATH-ARIM
7157 Qiryath Yᵉ'ârîym
(1), *city of forests or of
towns*

KIRJATH-BAAL
7154 Qiryath Ba'al (2),
city of Baal

KIRJATH-HUZOTH
7155 Qiryath Chûtsôwth
(1), *city of streets*

KIRJATH-JEARIM
7157 Qiryath Yᵉ'ârîym
(18), *city of forests*

KIRJATH-SANNAH
7158 Qiryath Çannâh
(1), *city of branches or
of a book*

KIRJATH-SEPHER
7158 Qiryath Çannâh
(4), *city of branches or
of a book*

KIRJATHAIM
7156 Qiryâthayim (3),
double city

KISH
7027 Qîysh (20), *bow*

KISHI
7029 Qîyshîy (1), *bowed*

KISHION
7191 Qishyôwn (1), *hard
ground*

KISHON
7028 Qîyshôwn (5),
winding
7191 Qishyôwn (1), *hard
ground*

KISON
7028 Qîyshôwn (1),
winding

KISS
5401 nâshaq (9), *to kiss*
2705 kataphilĕō (1), *to
kiss earnestly*
5368 philĕō (3), *to be a
friend, to kiss*
5370 philēma (7), *kiss*

KISSED
5401 nâshaq (21), *to kiss*
2705 kataphilĕō (5), *to
kiss earnestly*

KISSES
5390 nᵉshîyqâh (2), *kiss*

KITE
344 'ayâh (2), *hawk*

KITHLISH
3798 Kithlîysh (1), *wall of
a man*

KITRON
7003 Qiṭrôwn (1),
fumigative

KITTIM
3794 Kittîy (2), *islander*

KNEAD
3888 lûwsh (2), *to knead*

KNEADED
3888 lûwsh (3), *to knead*

KNEADINGTROUGHS
4863 mish'ereth (2),
kneading-trough

KNEE
1290 berek (1), *knee*
1119 gŏnu (3), *knee*

KNEEL
1288 bârak (2), *to bless*

KNEELED
1288 bârak (1), *to bless*
1289 bᵉrak (Ch.) (1), *to
bless*
1120 gŏnupĕtĕō (1), *to
fall on the knee, kneel*
5087+1119 tithēmi (5), *to
place, put*

KNEELING
3766 kâra' (1), *to
prostrate*
1120 gŏnupĕtĕō (2), *to
fall on the knee, kneel*

KNEES
755 'arkûbâh (Ch.) (1),
knees
1290 berek (24), *knee*
1291 berek (Ch.) (1), *knee*
1119 gŏnu (4), *knee joint*

KNEW
1847 da'ath (1),
knowledge
3045 yâda' (83), *to know*
3046 yᵉda' (Ch.) (2), *to
know*
5234 nâkar (9), *to
acknowledge*
50 agnŏĕō (1), *to not
know; understand*
1097 ginōskō (30), *to
know*
1492 ĕidō (27), *to know*
1912 ĕpibarĕō (1), *to be
severe toward*
1921 ĕpiginōskō (13), *to
acknowledge*
4267 prŏginōskō (1), *to
know beforehand*

KNEWEST
3045 yâda' (5), *to know*
3046 yᵉda' (Ch.) (1), *to
know*
1097 ginōskō (1), *to know*
1492 ĕidō (3), *to know*

KNIFE
2719 chereb (2), *knife,
sword*
3979 ma'ăkeleth (3),
knife
7915 sakkîyn (1), *knife*

KNIT
2270 châbêr (1),
associate, friend
3162 yachad (1), *unitedly*
7194 qâshar (1), *to tie,
bind*
1210 dĕō (1), *to bind*

4822 sumbibazō (2), *to
drive together*

KNIVES
2719 chereb (3), *knife,
sword*
3979 ma'ăkeleth (1),
knife
4252 machălâph (1),
butcher knife

KNOCK
2925 krŏuō (4), *to rap,
knock*

KNOCKED
2925 krŏuō (1), *to rap,
knock*

KNOCKETH
1849 dâphaq (1), *to
knock; to press severely*
2925 krŏuō (3), *to rap,
knock*

KNOCKING
2925 krŏuō (1), *to rap,
knock*

KNOP
3730 kaphtôr (10),
capital; button or disk

KNOPS
3730 kaphtôr (6), *capital;
button or disk*
6497 peqa' (3),
ornamental semi-globe

KNOW
995 bîyn (1), *to
understand; discern*
1847 da'ath (4),
knowledge
3045 yâda' (429), *to know*
3046 yᵉda' (Ch.) (15), *to
know*
5234 nâkar (9), *to
acknowledge*
50 agnŏĕō (2), *to not
know; not understand*
1097 ginōskō (92), *to
know*
1110 gnōstŏs (1),
well-known
1231 diaginōskō (1),
ascertain exactly
1492 ĕidō (176), *to know*
1921 ĕpiginōskō (8), *to
acknowledge*
1987 ĕpistamai (9), *to be
acquainted with*
2467 isĕmi (2), *to know*
4267 prŏginōskō (1), *to
know beforehand*
4892 sunĕdriŏn (1), *head
Jewish tribunal*

KNOWEST
1847 da'ath (1),
knowledge
3045 yâda' (66), *to know*
1097 ginōskō (5), *to know*
1492 ĕidō (15), *to know*
1921 ĕpiginōskō (1), *to
acknowledge*
2589 kardiŏgnōstēs (1),
heart-knower

KNOWETH
854 'êth (1), *with; by; at;
among*
3045 yâda' (59), *to know*
3046 yᵉda' (Ch.) (1), *to
know*

5234 nâkar (1), *to
acknowledge*
1097 ginōskō (16), *to
know*
1492 ĕidō (22), *to know*
1921 ĕpiginōskō (2), *to
acknowledge*
1987 ĕpistamai (1), *to
comprehend*
2589 kardiŏgnōstēs (1),
heart-knower

KNOWING
3045 yâda' (2), *to know*
50 agnŏĕō (1), *to not
know; not understand*
1097 ginōskō (5), *to know*
1492 ĕidō (38), *to know*
1921 ĕpiginōskō (2), *to
acknowledge*
1987 ĕpistamai (3), *to
comprehend*

KNOWLEDGE
998 bîynâh (3),
understanding
1843 dêa' (2), *knowledge*
1844 dê'âh (6),
knowledge
1847 da'ath (82),
knowledge
3045 yâda' (19), *to know*
4093 maddâ' (4),
intelligence
5234 nâkar (2), *to treat
as a foreigner*
5869 'ayin (1), *eye; sight;
fountain*
7922 sekel (1),
intelligence; success
56 agnōsia (1), *state of
ignorance*
1097 ginōskō (1), *to know*
1108 gnōsis (28),
knowledge
1492 ĕidō (1), *to know*
1921 ĕpiginōskō (3), *to
acknowledge*
1922 ĕpignōsis (16), *full
discernment*
1990 ĕpistēmōn (1),
intelligent, learned
4907 sunĕsis (1),
intelligence, intellect

KNOWN
3045 yâda' (105), *to know*
3046 yᵉda' (Ch.) (24), *to
know*
5234 nâkar (2), *to
acknowledge*
319 anagnōrizŏmai (1),
to make oneself known
1097 ginōskō (46), *to
know*
1107 gnōrizō (16), *to
make known, reveal*
1110 gnōstŏs (11),
well-known
1232 diagnōrizō (1), *to
tell abroad*
1492 ĕidō (6), *to know*
1921 ĕpiginōskō (4), *to
acknowledge*
3877 parakŏlŏuthĕō (1),
to attend; trace out
4135 plērŏphŏrĕō (1), *to
assure or convince*
5318 phanĕrŏs (3),
apparent, visible, clear

KOA
6970 Qôwa' (1),
curtailment

KOHATH
6955 Qᵉhâth (32), *allied*

KOHATHITES
6956 Qŏhâthîy (15),
Kohathite

KOLAIAH
6964 Qôwlâyâh (2), *voice
of Jehovah*

KORAH
7141 Qôrach (37), *ice*

KORAHITE
7145 Qorchîy (1),
Korchite

KORAHITES
7145 Qorchîy (1),
Korchite

KORATHITES
7145 Qorchîy (1),
Korchite

KORE
6981 Qôwrê' (3), *crier*
7145 Qorchîy (1),
Korchite

KORHITES
7145 Qorchîy (4),
Korchite

KOZ
6976 Qôwts (4), *thorns*

KUSHAIAH
6984 Qûwshâyâhûw (1),
entrapped of Jehovah

LAADAH
3935 La'dâh (1), *Ladah*

LAADAN
3936 La'dân (7), *Ladan*

LABAN
3837 Lâbân (51), *white*

LABAN'S
3837 Lâbân (4), *white*

LABOUR
213 'ûwts (1), to *be close,
hurry, withdraw*
1518 gîyach (1), to *issue
forth; to burst forth*
3018 yᵉgîya (12), *toil,
work; produce, property*
3021 yâga' (8), to *be
exhausted, to tire,*
3023 yâgêa (1), *tiresome*
3027 yâd (1), *hand; power*
3205 yâlad (2), to *bear
young; to father a child*
4399 mᵉlâ'kâh (1), *work;
property*
4639 ma'ăseh (1), *action;
labor*
5445 çâbal (1), to *carry*
5647 'âbad (2), to *do,
work, serve*
5656 'ăbôdâh (1), *work of
any kind*
5998 'âmal (2), to *work
severely, put forth effort*
5999 'âmâl (25), *wearing
effort; worry*
6001 'âmêl (1), *toiling;
laborer; sorrowful*
6089 'etseb (1), *earthen
vessel; painful toil*
6213 'âsâh (2), to *do*

LABOURED
3021 yâga' (4), to *be
exhausted, to tire,*
3022 yâgâ' (1), *earnings,
i.e. the product of toil*
5998 'âmal (5), to *work
severely, put forth effort*
6001 'âmêl (1), *toiling;
laborer; sorrowful*
6213 'âsâh (1), to *do or
make*
7712 shᵉdar (Ch.) (1), to
endeavor, strive
2872 kŏpiaō (5), to *feel
fatigue; to work hard*
4866 sunathlĕō (1), to
wrestle with

LABOURER
2040 ĕrgatēs (2), *toiler,
worker*

LABOURERS
2040 ĕrgatēs (8), *toiler,
worker*
4904 sunĕrgŏs (1),
fellow-worker

LABOURETH
5998 'âmal (1), to *work
severely, put forth effort*
6001 'âmêl (2), *toiling;
laborer; sorrowful*
2872 kŏpiaō (2), to *feel
fatigue; to work hard*

LABOURING
5647 'âbad (1), to *do,
work, serve*
75 agōnizŏmai (1), to
struggle; to contend
2872 kŏpiaō (1), to *feel
fatigue; to work hard*
2873 kŏpŏs (1), *toil; pains*

LABOURS
3018 yᵉgîya (3), *toil,
work; produce, property*
4639 ma'ăseh (3), *action;
labor*
6089 'etseb (1), *earthen
vessel; painful toil;
mental pang*
6092 'âtsêb (1), *hired
workman*
2873 kŏpŏs (5), *toil; pains*

LACE
6616 pâthîyl (4), *twine,
cord*

LACHISH
3923 Lâchîysh (24),
Lakish

LACK
1097 bᵉlîy (3), *without,
not yet; lacking;*
2637 châçêr (4), to *lack;
to fail, want, make less*

LABOURED (second column continued)
6468 pᵉ'ullâh (2), *work,
deed*
2038 ĕrgazŏmai (1), to
toil
2041 ĕrgŏn (1), *work*
2872 kŏpiaō (11), to *feel
fatigue; to work hard*
2873 kŏpŏs (8), *toil; pains*
4704 spŏudazō (1), to
make effort
4904 sunĕrgŏs (1),
fellow-worker
5389 philŏtimĕŏmai (1),
to be *eager or earnest*

4270 machçôwr (1),
impoverishment
7326 rûwsh (1), to *be
destitute*
1641 ĕlattŏnĕō (1), to *fall
short, have too little*
3007 lĕipō (1), to *fail or
be absent*
5302 hustĕrĕō (1), to *be
inferior; to fall short*
5303 hustĕrēma (1),
deficit; poverty; lacking
5332 pharmakĕus (1),
magician, sorcerer

LACKED
2637 châçêr (2), to *lack;
to fail, want, make less*
2638 châçêr (1), *lacking*
5737 'âdar (2), to
arrange as a battle
6485 pâqad (1), to *visit,
care for, count*
170 akairĕŏmai (1), to
fail of a proper occasion
1729 ĕndĕēs (1), *lacking;
deficient in; needy*
3361+2192 mē (1), *not;
lest*
5302 hustĕrĕō (2), to *be
inferior; to fall short*

LACKEST
3007 lĕipō (1), to *fail or
be absent*
5302 hustĕrĕō (1), to *be
inferior; to fall short*

LACKETH
2638 châçêr (3), *lacking*
6485 pâqad (1), to *visit,
care for, count*
3361+3918 mē (1), *not;
lest*

LACKING
5737 'âdar (1), to
arrange as a battle
6485 pâqad (2), to *visit,
care for, count*
7038 qâlaṭ (1), to *be
maim*
7673 shâbath (1), to
repose; to desist
5303 hustĕrēma (3),
deficit; poverty; lacking

LAD
5288 na'ar (32), *male
child; servant*
3808 paidariŏn (1), *little
boy*

LAD'S
5288 na'ar (1), *male
child; servant*

LADDER
5551 çullâm (1),
stair-case

LADE
2943 ṭâ'an (1), to *load a
beast*
6006 'âmaç (1), to *impose
a burden*
5412 phŏrtizō (1), to
overburden

LADED
5375 nâsâ' (1), to *lift up*
6006 'âmaç (2), to *impose
a burden*
2007 ĕpitithēmi (1), to
impose

LADEN
3515 kâbêd (1), *severe,
difficult, stupid*
5375 nâsâ' (2), to *lift up*
4987 sōrĕuō (1), to *pile
up, load up*
5412 phŏrtizō (1), to
overburden

LADETH
3515 kâbêd (1), *severe,
difficult, stupid*

LADIES
8282 sârâh (2), *female
noble*

LADING
6006 'âmaç (1), to *impose
a burden*
5414 phŏrtŏs (1), *cargo of
a ship*

LADS
5288 na'ar (1), *male
child; servant*

LADY
1404 gᵉbereth (2),
mistress, noblewoman
2959 Kuria (2), *Lady*

LAEL
3815 Lâ'êl (1), *belonging
to God*

LAHAD
3854 lahag (1), *mental
application*

LAHAI-ROI
883 Bᵉ'êr la-Chay Rô'îy
(2), *well of a living
(One) my seer*

LAHMAM
3903 Lachmâç (1),
food-like

LAHMI
3902 Lachmîy (1), *foodful*

LAID
935 bôw' (1), to *go or
come*
2470 châlâh (1), to *be
weak, sick, afflicted*
2630 châçan (1), to
hoard, store up
2934 ṭâman (2), to *hide*
3052 yᵉhab (Ch.) (1), to
give
3240 yânach (1), to *allow
to stay*
3241 Yânîym (8), *asleep*
3318 yâtsâ' (2), to *go,
bring out*
3332 yâtsaq (1), to *pour
out*
3369 yâqôsh (1), to
ensnare, trap
3384 yârâh (1), to *point;
to teach*
3515 kâbêd (1),
numerous; severe
3647 kâmaç (1), to *store
away*
5060 nâga' (1), to *strike*
5182 nᵉchath (Ch.) (1), to
descend; to depose
5186 nâṭâh (1), to *stretch
or spread out*
5324 nâtsab (1), to *station*
5375 nâsâ' (4), to *lift up*
5414 nâthan (13), to *give*

5446 çᵉbal (Ch.) (1), to *raise*

5493 çûwr (1), to *turn* off

5564 çâmak (6), to *lean* upon; *take hold of*

5674 'âbar (1), to *cross over; to transition*

5927 'âlâh (1), to *ascend, be high, mount*

6293 pâga' (1), to *impinge*

6485 pâqad (2), to *visit, care for, count*

6486 pᵉquddâh (1), *visitation; punishment*

6845 tsâphan (3), to *hide; to hoard or reserve; to deny; to protect; to lurk*

7737 shâvâh (3), to *level,* i.e. *equalize*

7760 sûwm (38), to *put, place*

7896 shîyth (8), to *place, put*

7901 shâkab (17), to *lie down*

7971 shâlach (6), to *send away*.

8371 shâthath (1), to *place,* i.e. *array; to lie*

8610 tâphas (1), to *manipulate,* i.e. *seize*

347 anaklinō (1), to *lean back, recline*

606 apŏkĕimai (3), to *be reserved; to await*

659 apŏtithēmi (1), to *put away; get rid of*

906 ballō (3), to *throw*

1096 ginŏmai (1), to *be, become*

1462 ĕgklēma (2), *accusation*

1911 ĕpiballō (7), to *throw upon*

1945 ĕpikĕimai (2), to *rest upon; press upon*

2007 ĕpitithēmi (13), to *impose*

2071 ĕsŏmai (1), *will be*

2698 katatithēmi (1), to *place down*

2749 kĕimai (6), to *lie outstretched*

3049 lŏgizŏmai (1), to *credit; to think, regard*

4369 prŏstithēmi (1), to *lay beside, annex*

5087 tithēmi (29), to *place, put*

5294 hupŏtithēmi (1), to *hazard; to suggest*

5342 phĕrō (1), to *bear*

LAIDST
7760 sûwm (1), to *put*

LAIN
3045+4904 yâda' (1), to *know*

5414+7903 nâthan (1), to *give*

7901 shâkab (2), to *lie down*

2749 kĕimai (1), to *lie outstretched*

LAISH
3919 Layish (7), *lion*

LAKE
3041 limnē (10), *pond; lake*

LAKUM
3946 Laqqûwm (1), (poss.) *fortification*

LAMA
2982 lama (2), *why?*

LAMB
2924 ṭâleh (2), *lamb*

3532 kebes (44), *young ram*

3535 kibsâh (5), *ewe sheep*

3733 kar (1), *ram sheep; battering ram*

3775 keseb (3), *young ram sheep*

3776 kisbâh (1), *young ewe sheep*

6629 tsô'n (1), *flock of sheep or goats*

7716 seh (17), *sheep or goat*

286 amnŏs (4), *lamb*

721 arniŏn (27), *lamb, sheep*

LAMB'S
721 arniŏn (2), *lamb, sheep*

LAMBS
563 'immar (Ch.) (3), *lamb*

1121+6629 bên (2), *son, descendant; people*

2922 ṭᵉlâ' (1), *lamb*

3532 kebes (60), *young ram*

3535 kibsâh (3), *ewe sheep*

3733 kar (9), *ram sheep; battering ram*

3775 keseb (1), *young ram sheep*

704 arēn (1), male *lamb*

721 arniŏn (1), *lamb, sheep*

LAME
5223 nâkeh (2), *maimed; dejected*

6452 pâçach (1), to *hop, skip* over; *to hesitate*

6455 piççêach (14), *lame*

5560 chōlŏs (10), *limping, crippled*

LAMECH
3929 Lemek (11), *Lemek*

2984 Lamĕch (1), *Lemek*

LAMENT
56 'âbal (2), to *bewail*

421 'âlâh (1), to *bewail, mourn*

578 'ânâh (1), to *groan, lament*

5091 nâhâh (1), to *bewail; to assemble*

5594 çâphad (9), to *tear the hair, wail*

6969 qûwn (4), to *chant or wail* at a funeral

8567 tânâh (1), to *ascribe* praise, i.e. *celebrate*

2354 thrēnĕŏ (1), to *bewail, lament*

2875 kŏptō (1), to *beat the breast*

LAMENTABLE
6088 'ătsab (Ch.) (1), to *afflict; be afflicted*

LAMENTATION
592 'ănîyâh (1), *groaning*

1058 bâkâh (1), to *weep, moan*

4553 miçpêd (3), *lamentation, howling*

5092 nᵉhîy (3), *elegy*

7015 qîynâh (14), *dirge*

2355 thrēnŏs (1), *wailing, funeral song*

2870 kŏpĕtŏs (1), *mourning*

LAMENTATIONS
7015 qîynâh (3), *dirge*

LAMENTED
56 'âbal (1), to *bewail*

5091 nâhâh (1), to *bewail; to assemble*

5594 çâphad (4), to *tear the hair, wail*

6969 qûwn (3), to *chant or wail* at a funeral

2354 thrēnĕŏ (1), to *bewail, lament*

2875 kŏptō (1), to *beat the breast*

LAMP
3940 lappîyd (3), *flaming torch, lamp or flame*

5216 nîyr (9), *lamp; lamplight*

2985 lampas (1), *lamp, lantern, torch*

LAMPS
3940 lappîyd (5), *flaming torch, lamp or flame*

5216 nîyr (26), *lamp; lamplight*

2985 lampas (6), *lamp, lantern, torch*

LANCE
3591 kîydôwn (1), *dart, javelin*

LANCETS
7420 rômach (1), iron *pointed spear*

LAND
127 'ădâmâh (123), *soil; land*

249 'ezrâch (2), *native born*

776 'erets (1505), *earth, land, soil; country*

3004 yabbâshâh (1), *dry ground*

7704 sâdeh (7), *field*

68 agrŏs (1), *farmland, countryside*

1093 gē (42), *soil, region, whole earth*

3584 xērŏs (1), *scorched; arid; withered*

5561 chōra (3), *space of territory*

5564 chōriŏn (2), *spot or plot of ground*

LANDED
2609 katagō (1), to *lead down; to moor a vessel*

2718 katĕrchŏmai (1), to *go/come down*

LANDING
2609 katagō (1), to *lead down; to moor a vessel*

LANDMARK
1366 gᵉbûwl (4), *boundary, border*

LANDMARKS
1367 gᵉbûwlâh (1), *boundary marker*

LANDS
127 'ădâmâh (3), *soil; land*

776 'erets (34), *earth, land, soil; country, nation*

7704 sâdeh (4), *field*

68 agrŏs (3), *farmland, countryside*

5564 chōriŏn (1), *spot or plot of ground*

LANES
4505 rhumē (1), *alley or crowded avenue*

LANGUAGE
1697 dâbâr (1), *word; matter; thing*

3937 lâ'az (1), to *speak in a foreign tongue*

3956 lâshôwn (9), *tongue; tongue-shaped*

3961 lishshân (Ch.) (1), *nation*

8193 sâphâh (7), *lip, language, speech*

1258 dialĕktŏs (1), known *language*

LANGUAGES
3956 lâshôwn (1), *tongue; tongue-shaped*

3961 lishshân (Ch.) (6), *nation*

LANGUISH
535 'âmal (5), to *be weak; to be sick*

LANGUISHED
535 'âmal (1), to *be weak; to be sick*

LANGUISHETH
535 'âmal (8), to *be weak; to be sick*

LANGUISHING
1741 dᵉvay (1), *sickness*

LANTERNS
5322 phanŏs (1), *light; lantern,* i.e. *torch*

LAODICEA
2993 Laŏdikĕia (5), *Laodicea*

LAODICEANS
2994 Laŏdikĕus (2), *inhabitant of Laodicea*

LAP
899 beged (1), *clothing; treachery or pillage*

2436 chêyq (1), *bosom, heart*

2684 chôtsen (1), *bosom*

LAPIDOTH
3941 Lappîydôwth (1), *flaming torch, lamp*

LAPPED
3952 lâqaq (2), to *lick or lap*

LAPPETH
3952 lâqaq (2), to *lick or lap*

LAPWING
1744 dûwkîyphath (2), hoopoe; (poss.) grouse

LARGE
4800 merchâb (5), open space; liberty
7304 râvach (1), to revive; to have ample room
7337 râchab (2), to broaden
7342 râchâb (5), roomy, spacious
2425 hikanŏs (1), ample; fit
3173 mĕgas (2), great, many
4080 pēlikŏs (1), how much, how great
5118 tŏsŏutŏs (1), such great

LARGENESS
7341 rôchab (1), width

LASCIVIOUSNESS
766 asĕlgĕia (6), licentiousness

LASEA
2996 Lasaia (1), Lasæa

LASHA
3962 Lesha' (1), boiling spring

LASHARON
8289 Shârôwn (1), plain

LAST
314 'achărôwn (20), late or last; behind; western
318 'ochŏrêyn (Ch.) (1), at last, finally
319 'achărîyth (10), future; posterity
6119 'âqêb (1), track, footprint; rear position
2078 ĕschatŏs (48), farthest, final
4218 pŏtĕ (1), at some time, ever
5305 hustĕrŏn (4), more lately, i.e. eventually

LASTED
1961 hâyâh (1), to exist, i.e. be or become

LASTING
5769 'ôwlâm (1), eternity; ancient; always

LATCHET
8288 sᵉrôwk (1), sandal thong
2438 himas (3), strap; lash

LATE
309 'âchar (1), to delay; to procrastinate
865 'ethmôwl (1), formerly; yesterday
3568 nun (1), now; the present or immediate

LATELY
4373 prŏsphatŏs (1), recently

LATIN
4513 Rhōmaïkŏs (2), Latin

LATTER
314 'achărôwn (8), late or last; behind; western
319 'achărîyth (20), future; posterity
320 'achărîyth (Ch.) (1), later, end
3954 leqesh (2), after crop, second crop
4456 malqôwsh (8), spring rain
2078 ĕschatŏs (1), farthest, final
3797 ŏpsimŏs (1), later, i.e. vernal showering
5305 hustĕrŏn (1), more lately, i.e. eventually

LATTICE
822 'eshnâb (1), latticed window
2762 cherek (1), window lattice
7639 sᵉbâkâh (1), net-work balustrade

LAUD
1867 ĕpainĕō (1), to applaud, commend

LAUGH
3932 lâ'ag (4), to deride; to speak unintelligibly
6711 tsâchaq (3), to laugh; to scorn
6712 tsᵉchôq (1), laughter; scorn
7832 sâchaq (8), to laugh; to scorn; to play
1070 gĕlaō (2), to laugh

LAUGHED
3932 lâ'ag (3), to deride; to speak unintelligibly
6711 tsâchaq (3), to laugh; to scorn
6712 tsᵉchôq (1), laughter; scorn
7832 sâchaq (3), to laugh; to scorn; to play
2606 katagĕlaō (3), to laugh down, i.e. deride

LAUGHETH
7832 sâchaq (1), to laugh; to scorn; to play

LAUGHING
7814 sᵉchôwq (1), laughter; scorn

LAUGHTER
7814 sᵉchôwq (6), laughter; scorn
1071 gĕlōs (1), laughter

LAUNCH
1877 ĕpanagō (1), to put out to sea; to return

LAUNCHED
321 anagō (4), to bring out; to sail away

LAVER
3595 kîyôwr (15), caldron; washbowl

LAVERS
3595 kîyôwr (5), caldron; washbowl

LAVISH
2107 zûwl (1), to treat lightly

LAW
1881 dâth (6), royal edict or statute
1882 dâth (Ch.) (9), Law; royal edict or statute
2524 châm (4), father-in-law
2545 châmôwth (11), mother-in-law
2706 chôq (4), appointment; allotment
2710 châqaq (1), to engrave; to enact laws; to prescribe
2859 châthan (32), to become related
2860 châthân (5), relative by marriage
2994 yᵉbêmeth (2), sister-in-law
3618 kallâh (17), bride; son's wife
4687 mitsvâh (1), command
4941 mishpât (2), verdict; formal decree; justice
8451 tôwrâh (206), precept or statute
60 agŏraiŏs (1), people of the market place
458 anŏmia (1), violation of law, wickedness
459 anŏmŏs (3), without Jewish law
460 anŏmŏs (1), lawlessly
1772 ĕnnŏmŏs (1), legal, or subject to law
2917 krima (1), decision
2919 krinō (2), to decide; to try, condemn, punish
3544 nŏmikŏs (1), expert in the (Mosaic) law
3547 nŏmŏdidaskalŏs (3), a Rabbi
3548 nŏmŏthĕsia (1), legislation, law
3549 nŏmŏthĕtĕō (1), to be given law
3551 nŏmŏs (192), law
3565 numphē (3), young married woman
3891 paranŏmĕō (1), to transgress, violate law
3994 pĕnthĕra (3), wife's mother, mother-in-law
3995 pĕnthĕrŏs (1), wife's father
4160+458 pŏiĕō (1), to make or do

LAWFUL
4941 mishpât (7), verdict; formal decree; justice
6662 tsaddîyq (1), just
7990 shallîyt (Ch.) (1), premier, sovereign
1772 ĕnnŏmŏs (1), legal, or subject to law
1832 ĕxĕsti (12), it is right, it is proper
1833 ĕxĕtazō (17), to ascertain or interrogate

LAWFULLY
3545 nŏmimŏs (2), agreeably to the rules

LAWGIVER
2710 châqaq (6), to engrave; to enact laws

LAW
3550 nŏmŏthĕtēs (1), legislator, lawgiver

LAWLESS
459 anŏmŏs (1), without Jewish law

LAWS
1881 dâth (3), royal edict or statute
1882 dâth (Ch.) (2), Law; royal edict or statute
8451 tôwrâh (12), precept or codified statute
8541 timmâhôwn (1), consternation, panic
3551 nŏmŏs (2), law

LAWYER
3544 nŏmikŏs (3), expert in the (Mosaic) law

LAWYERS
3544 nŏmikŏs (5), expert in the (Mosaic) law

LAY
3241 Yânîym (10), asleep
3331 yâtsa' (1), to strew as a surface
3885 lûwn (1), to be obstinate
4422 mâlat (1), to be delivered; be smooth
5117 nûwach (1), to rest; to settle down
5186 nâtâh (1), to stretch or spread out
5307 nâphal (4), to fall
5414 nâthan (20), to give
5493 çûwr (1), to turn off
5564 çâmak (12), to lean upon; take hold of
6651 tsâbar (1), to aggregate, gather
6845 tsâphan (2), to hide; to hoard or reserve
7126 qârab (1), to approach, bring near
7257 râbats (3), to recline, repose, brood
7258 rebets (1), place of repose
7760 sûwm (26), to put, place
7871 shîybâh (1), residence
7896 shîyth (5), to place, put
7901 shâkab (45), to lie down
7902 shᵉkâbâh (2), lying down
7931 shâkan (1), to reside
7971 shâlach (8), to send away
659 apŏtithēmi (2), to put away; get rid of
1458 ĕgkalĕō (1), to charge, criminate
1474 ĕdaphizō (1), to dash to the ground
1911 ĕpiballō (2), to throw upon
1945 ĕpikĕimai (2), to rest upon; press upon
1949 ĕpilambanŏmai (2), to seize
2007 ĕpitithēmi (7), to impose
2343 thēsaurizō (1), to amass or reserve, store

2476 histēmi (1), to
stand, establish
2621 katakĕimai (5), to
lie down; to recline
2749 kĕimai (1), to lie
outstretched
2827 klinō (2), to slant or
slope
5087 tithēmi (13), to place

LAYEDST
5087 tithēmi (1), to place

LAYEST
7760 sûwm (1), to put

LAYETH
5381 nâsag (1), to reach
5414 nâthan (1), to give
6845 tsâphan (2), to hide;
to hoard or reserve
7760 sûwm (1), to place
7896 shîyth (1), to place
7971 shâlach (1), to send
away
2007 ĕpitithēmi (1), to
impose

LAYING
2934 ţâman (1), to hide
597 apŏthēsaurizō (1), to
store treasure away
659 apŏtithēmi (1), to put
away; get rid of
863 aphiēmi (1), to leave;
to pardon, forgive
1748 ĕnĕdrĕuō (1), to lurk
1917 ĕpibŏulĕ (1), plot,
plan
1936 ĕpithĕsis (3),
imposition
2598 kataballō (1), to
throw down
4160 pŏiĕō (1), to make
or do

LAZARUS
2976 Lazarŏs (15), God
(is) helper

LEAD
833 'âshar (1), to go
forward; guide
1869 dârak (2), to tread,
trample; to walk, lead
1980 hâlak (1), to walk;
live a certain way
2986 yâbal (1), to bring
3212 yâlak (2), to walk;
to live; to carry
3318 yâtsâ' (1), to go,
bring out
5090 nâhag (9), to drive
forth; to lead, carry
5095 nâhal (2), to flow; to
conduct; to protect
5148 nâchâh (16), to
guide
5777 'ôwphereth (9),
mineral lead
7218 rô'sh (1), head
71 agō (1), to lead; to
bring, drive; to weigh
162 aichmalōtĕuō (1), to
capture
520 apagō (2), to take
away
1236 diagō (1), to pass
time, conduct one's life
1533 ĕisphĕrō (2), to
carry inward
1806 ĕxagō (1), to lead
forth, escort

3594 hŏdēgĕō (3), to
show the way, i.e. lead
4013 pĕriagō (1), to take
around as a companion
5497 chĕiragōgŏs (1),
conductor of the blind

LEADER
5057 nâgîyd (3),
commander, official

LEADERS
833 'âshar (1), to go
forward; guide
5057 nâgîyd (1),
commander, official
3595 hŏdēgŏs (1),
conductor, guide

LEADEST
5090 nâhag (1), to drive
forth; to lead away

LEADETH
1869 dârak (1), to tread,
trample; to walk, lead
3212 yâlak (3), to walk;
to live; to carry
5090 nâhag (1), to drive
forth; to lead away
5095 nâhal (1), to flow; to
conduct; to protect
71 agō (1), to lead; to
bring, drive; to weigh
399 anaphĕrō (1), to take
up; to lead up
520 apagō (2), to take
away
1806 ĕxagō (1), to lead
forth, escort
4863 sunagō (1), to
gather together
5342 phĕrō (1), to bear or
carry

LEAF
5929 'âleh (11), leaf;
foliage

LEAGUE
1285 bᵉrîyth (17),
compact, agreement
2266 châbar (1), to
fascinate by spells
3772 kârath (1), to cut
(off, down or asunder)

LEAH
3812 Lê'âh (29), weary

LEAH'S
3812 Lê'âh (5), weary

LEAN
1800 dal (1), weak, thin;
humble, needy
5564 çâmak (2), to lean
upon; take hold of
7329 râzâh (1), to make,
become thin
7330 râzeh (2), thin, lean
7534 raq (1), emaciated,
lank
8172 shâ'an (4), to
support, rely on

LEANED
5564 çâmak (1), to lean
upon; take hold of
8172 shâ'an (4), to
support, rely on
377 anapiptō (1), lie
down, lean back

LEANETH
2388 châzaq (1), to
fasten upon; to seize
8127 shên (1), tooth;
ivory; cliff

LEANFLESHED
1851+1320 daq (2),
crushed; small or thin
7534 raq (1), emaciated,
lank

LEANING
7514 râphaq (1), to
recline
345 anakĕimai (1), to
recline at a meal

LEANNESS
3585 kachash (1),
emaciation; hypocrisy
7332 râzôwn (2), thinness
7334 râzîy (1), thinness

LEANNOTH
6030 'ânâh (1), to sing,
shout

LEAP
1801 dâlag (2), to spring
up, ascend
2178 zan (Ch.) (1), sort,
kind
4422 mâlaţ (1), to escape
as if by slipperiness
5425 nâthar (1), to jump;
to be agitated
5927 'âlâh (1), to ascend,
be high, mount
7520 râtsad (1), to look
askant; to be jealous
7540 râqad (1), to spring
about wildly or for joy
4640 skirtaō (1), to jump

LEAPED
1801 dâlag (2), to spring
up, ascend
5927 'âlâh (1), to ascend,
be high, mount
6452 pâçach (1), to hop,
skip over; to limp
242 hallŏmai (1), to jump
up; to gush up
2177 ĕphallŏmai (1), to
spring upon, leap upon
4640 skirtaō (2), to jump

LEAPING
1801 dâlag (1), to spring
up, ascend
6339 pâzaz (1), to solidify
by refining; to spring
242 hallŏmai (1), to jump
up; to gush up
1814 ĕxallŏmai (1), to
spring forth

LEARN
502 'âlaph (1), to learn;
to teach
3925 lâmad (17), to
teach, train
3129 manthanō (13), to
learn
3811 paidĕuō (1), to
educate or discipline

LEARNED
3045+5612 yâda' (3), to
know
3925 lâmad (5), to teach,
train
3928 limmûwd (2),
instructed one

5172 nâchash (1), to
prognosticate
3129 manthanō (10), to
learn
3811 paidĕuō (1), to
educate or discipline

LEARNING
3948 leqach (4),
instruction
5612 çêpher (2), writing
1121 gramma (1),
writing; education
1319 didaskalia (1),
instruction
3129 manthanō (1), to
learn

LEASING
3577 kâzâb (2),
falsehood; idol

LEAST
176 'ôw (1), or, whether;
desire
389 'ak (1), surely; only,
however
4591 mâ'aţ (1), to be,
make small or few
6810 tsâ'îyr (4), little in
number; few in age
6994 qâţôn (1), to be,
make diminutive
6996 qâţân (10), small,
least, youngest
7535 raq (1), merely;
although
1646 ĕlachistŏs (9), least
1647 ĕlachistŏtĕrŏs (1),
far less
1848 ĕxŏuthĕnĕō (1), to
treat with contempt
2534 kaigĕ (1), and at
least (or even, indeed)
2579 kan (1), and if
3398 mikrŏs (6), small,
little

LEATHER
5785 'ôwr (1), skin,
leather

LEATHERN
1193 dĕrmatinŏs (1),
made of leather hide

LEAVE
2308 châdal (3), to desist,
stop; be fat
3241 Yânîym (14), asleep
3322 yâtsag (1), to place
3498 yâthar (7), to
remain or be left
3499 yether (1),
remainder; small rope
5157 nâchal (1), to inherit
5203 nâţash (6), to
disperse; to thrust off
5414 nâthan (2), to give
5800 'âzab (30), to
loosen; relinquish
6168 'ârâh (1), to be,
make bare; to empty
7503 râphâh (1), to
slacken
7592 shâ'al (1), to ask
7604 shâ'ar (13), to leave,
remain
7662 shᵉbaq (Ch.) (3), to
allow to remain
8338 shâwshâw (1),
(poss.) to annihilate

LEAVED

447 aniēmi (1), to *desert*, *desist* from
657 apŏtassŏmai (2), to *say adieu*; to *renounce*
782 aspazŏmai (1), to *give salutation*
863 aphiēmi (11), to *leave*; to *pardon, forgive*
1459 ĕgkataleipō (1), to *desert, abandon*
1544 ĕkballō (1), to *throw out*
2010 ĕpitrĕpō (2), *allow, permit*
2641 kataleipō (6), to *abandon*

LEAVED
1817 deleth (1), *door; gate*

LEAVEN
2557 châmêts (5), *ferment, yeasted*
4682 matstsâh (1), *unfermented cake*
7603 se'ôr (4), yeast-cake for *fermentation*
2219 zumē (13), *ferment*

LEAVENED
2557 châmêts (11), *ferment, yeasted*
7603 se'ôr (1), yeast-cake for *fermentation*
2220 zumŏō (2), to *cause to ferment*

LEAVENETH
2220 zumŏō (2), to *cause to ferment*

LEAVES
1817 deleth (3), *door; gate*
2529 chem'âh (1), *curds, milk* or *cheese*
2964 țereph (1), *fresh torn prey*
6074 'ŏphîy (Ch.) (3), *foliage*
6763 tsêlâ' (1), *side*
7050 qela' (1), *slinging weapon; door screen*
5444 phullŏn (6), *leaf*

LEAVETH
5800 'âzab (2), to *loosen; relinquish; permit*
863 aphiēmi (2), to *leave*; to *pardon, forgive*

LEAVING
863 aphiēmi (3), to *leave*; to *pardon, forgive*
2641 kataleipō (1), to *abandon*
5277 hupŏlimpanō (1), to *leave behind*

LEBANA
3848 lebash (Ch.) (1), to *clothe*

LEBANAH
3848 lebash (Ch.) (1), to *clothe*

LEBANON
3844 Lebânôwn (71), *white snow mountain*

LEBAOTH
3822 Lebâ'ôwth (1), *lionesses*

LEBBAEUS
3002 Lĕbbaiŏs (1), *Lebbæus*

LEBONAH
3829 Lebôwnâh (1), *frankincense*

LECAH
3922 Lêkâh (1), *journey*

LED
833 'âshar (1), to *go forward; guide*
935 bôw' (2), to *go*
1869 dârak (2), to *tread, trample; to walk, lead*
2986 yâbal (1), to *bring*
3212 yâlak (13), to *walk; to live; to carry*
5090 nâhag (4), to *drive forth; to lead away*
5148 nâchâh (6), to *guide*
5437 çâbab (3), to *surround*
71 agō (11), to *lead; to bring, drive; to weigh*
162 aichmalōtĕuō (1), to *capture*
163 aichmalōtizō (1), to *make captive*
321 anagō (2), to *lead up; to bring out*
520 apagō (8), to *take away*
1521 ĕisagō (1), to *lead into*
1806 ĕxagō (3), to *lead forth, escort*
4879 sunapagō (1), to *take off together*
5496 chĕiragōgĕō (2), to *guide* a blind person

LEDDEST
3318 yâtsâ' (2), to *go, bring out*
5148 nâchâh (2), to *guide*
1806 ĕxagō (1), to *lead forth, escort*

LEDGES
3027 yâd (2), *hand; power*
7948 shâlâb (3), *interval*

LEEKS
2682 châtsîyr (1), *grass; leek plant*

LEES
8105 shemer (4), *settlings* of wine, *dregs*

LEFT
2308 châdal (7), to *desist, stop; be fat*
2790 chârash (1), to *be silent; to be deaf*
3240 yânach (8), to *allow to stay*
3241 Yânîym (3), *asleep*
3498 yâthar (47), to *remain* or *be left*
3499 yether (3), *remainder; small rope*
3615 kâlâh (3), to *cease, be finished, perish*
3885 lûwn (1), to *be obstinate with*
4672 mâtsâ' (2), to *find* or *acquire; to occur*
5203 nâțash (7), to *disperse; to thrust off*
5414 nâthan (1), to *give*

LEBBAEUS
5493 çûwr (1), to *turn* off
5800 'âzab (43), to *loosen; relinquish*
5975 'âmad (2), to *stand*
6275 'âthaq (1), to *remove; to grow old*
7604 shâ'ar (65), to *leave, remain*
7611 she'êrîyth (1), *remainder* or *residual*
7662 shebaq (Ch.) (1), to *allow to remain*
7673 shâbath (1), to *repose; to desist*
7971 shâlach (1), to *send away*
8040 semô'wl (55), *north; left* hand
8041 sâma'l (4), to *use the left* hand or go *left*
8042 semâ'lîy (9), on the *left* side; *northern*
8300 sârîyd (3), *survivor; remainder*
620 apŏleipō (3), to *leave behind; to forsake*
710 aristĕrŏs (3), *left* hand
863 aphiēmi (36), to *leave*; to *pardon, forgive*
1439 ĕaō (1), to *let be*, i.e. *permit* or *leave* alone
1459 ĕgkataleipō (1), to *desert, abandon*
2176 ĕuōnumŏs (10), *left; at the left* hand; *south*
2641 kataleipō (15), to *abandon*
3973 pauō (2), to *stop*, i.e. *restrain, quit*
4051 pĕrissĕuma (1), *superabundance*
4052 pĕrissĕuō (1), to *superabound*
5275 hupŏleipō (1), to *remain, survive*

LEFTEST
5800 'âzab (1), to *loosen; relinquish; permit*

LEFTHANDED
334+3027+3225 'iṭṭêr (2), *impeded* (as to the right hand), *left-handed*

LEG
7640 shôbel (1), lady's garment *train*

LEGION
3003 lĕgĕōn (3), *legion*

LEGIONS
3003 lĕgĕōn (1), *legion*

LEGS
3767 kârâ' (9), *leg*
6807 tse'âdâh (1), *march; ankle-chain*
7272 regel (1), *foot; step*
7785 shôwq (1), *lower leg*
8243 shâq (Ch.) (1), *shank, or whole leg*
4628 skĕlŏs (3), *leg*

LEHABIM
3853 Lehâbîym (2), *flames*

LEHI
3896 Lechîy (3), *jaw-bone*

LEISURE
2119 ĕukairĕō (1), to *have leisure*

LEMUEL
3927 Lemûw'êl (2), *(belonging)* to *God*

LEND
3867 lâvâh (4), to *unite; to remain; to lend*
5383 nâshâh (2), to *lend* or *borrow*
5391 nâshak (3), to *strike; to oppress*
5414 nâthan (1), to *give*
5670 'âbaț (2), to *pawn; to lend; to entangle*
1155 danĕizō (3), to *loan on interest; to borrow*
5531 chraō (1), to *loan, lend*

LENDER
3867 lâvâh (2), to *unite; to borrow; to lend*

LENDETH
3867 lâvâh (3), to *unite; to borrow; to lend*
5383 nâshâh (1), to *lend* or *borrow*

LENGTH
319 'achărîyth (1), *future; posterity*
753 'ôrek (70), *length*
3372 mĕkŏs (3), *length*
4218 pŏtĕ (1), at *some time, ever*

LENGTHEN
748 'ârak (2), to *be, make long*

LENGTHENED
748 'ârak (1), to *be, make long*

LENGTHENING
754 'arkâ' (Ch.) (1), *length*

LENT
5383 nâshâh (2), to *lend* or *borrow*
5391 nâshak (1), to *strike; to oppress*
7592 shâ'al (4), to *ask*

LENTILES
5742 'âdâsh (4), *lentil bean*

LEOPARD
5245 nemar (Ch.) (1), *leopard*
5246 nâmêr (4), *leopard*
3917 pardalis (1), *leopard, panther*

LEOPARDS
5246 nâmêr (2), *leopard*

LEPER
6879 tsâra' (13), to *be stricken with leprosy*
3015 lĕprŏs (4), *leper*

LEPERS
6879 tsâra' (1), to *be stricken with leprosy*
3015 lĕprŏs (5), *leper*

LEPROSY
6883 tsâra'ath (35), *leprosy*
3014 lĕpra (4), *leprosy*

LEPROUS
6879 tsâra' (6), to *be stricken with leprosy*

LESHEM
3959 Leshem (2), *jacinth stone*

LESS
657 'epheç (1), *end; no further*
4295 maṭṭâh (1), *below or beneath*
4591 mâ'aṭ (4), *to be, make small or few*
6996 qâṭân (3), *small, least, youngest*
253 alupŏtĕrŏs (1), *more without grief*
820 atimŏs (1), *without honor*
1640 ĕlassŏn (1), *smaller*
1647 ĕlachistŏtĕrŏs (1), *far less*
2276 hēttŏn (1), *worse; less*
3398 mikrŏs (2), *small, little*

LESSER
6996 qâṭân (2), *small, least, youngest*
7716 seh (1), *sheep or goat*

LEST
1077 bal (1), *nothing; not at all; lest*
1115 biltîy (3), *not, except, without, unless*
3808 lô' (12), *no, not*
6435 pên (120), *lest, not*
3361 mē (13), *not; lest*
3379 mĕpŏtĕ (20), *not ever; if, or lest ever*
3381 mĕpōs (12), *lest somehow*

LET
3212 yâlak (1), *to walk; to live; to carry*
3240 yânach (3), *to allow to stay*
3381 yârad (7), *to descend*
5117 nûwach (1), *to rest; to settle down*
5186 nâṭâh (1), *to stretch or spread out*
5414 nâthan (3), *to give*
6544 pâra' (1), *to loosen*
7503 râphâh (2), *to slacken*
7725 shûwb (1), *to turn back; to return*
7971 shâlach (2), *to send away*
630 apŏluō (10), *to relieve, release*
863 aphiēmi (16), *to leave; to pardon, forgive*
1439 ĕaō (4), *to let be, i.e. permit or leave alone*
1554 ĕkdidōmi (4), *to lease, rent*
1832 ĕxĕsti (1), *it is right, it is proper*
1929 ĕpididōmi (1), *to give over*
2010 ĕpitrĕpō (1), *allow, permit*
2524 kathiĕmi (1), *to lower, let down*
2722 katĕchō (1), *to hold down fast*
2967 kōluō (1), *to stop*

5465 chalaō (5), *to lower as into a void*

LETTER
104 'iggᵉrâ' (Ch.) (3), *epistle, letter*
107 'iggereth (4), *epistle, letter*
5406 nishtᵉvân (2), *written epistle*
5407 nishtᵉvân (Ch.) (3), *written epistle*
5612 çêpher (13), *writing*
6600 pithgâm (Ch.) (1), *decree; report*
1121 gramma (6), *writing; education*
1989 ĕpistĕllō (1), *to communicate by letter*
1992 ĕpistŏlē (3), *written message*

LETTERS
107 'iggereth (6), *epistle, letter*
5612 çêpher (16), *writing*
1121 gramma (3), *writing; education*
1992 ĕpistŏlē (6), *written message*

LETTEST
8257 shâqa' (1), *to be overflowed; to cease*
630 apŏluō (1), *to relieve, release*

LETTETH
6362 pâṭar (1), *to burst through; to emit*
2722 katĕchō (1), *to hold down fast*

LETUSHIM
3912 Lᵉṭûwshîm (1), *oppressed ones*

LEUMMIM
3817 Lᵉ'ummîym (1), *communities*

LEVI
3878 Lêvîy (64), *attached*
3017 Lĕuï (5), *attached*
3018 Lĕuïs (3), *attached*

LEVIATHAN
3882 livyâthân (5), *serpent (crocodile)*

LEVITE
3881 Lêvîyîy (26), *Levite*
3019 Lĕuïtēs (2), *descendants of Levi*

LEVITES
3878 Lêvîy (1), *attached*
3879 Lêvîy (Ch.) (4), *attached*
3881 Lêvîyîy (259), *Levite*
3019 Lĕuïtēs (1), *descendants of Levi*

LEVITICAL
3020 Lĕuïtikŏs (1), *relating to the Levites*

LEVY
4522 maç (4), *forced labor*
5927 'âlâh (1), *to ascend, be high, mount*
7311 rûwm (1), *to be high; to rise or raise*

LEWD
2154 zimmâh (2), *bad plan*

4190 pŏnērŏs (1), *malice, wicked, bad; crime*

LEWDLY
2154 zimmâh (1), *bad plan*

LEWDNESS
2154 zimmâh (14), *bad plan*
4209 mᵉzimmâh (1), *plan; sagacity*
5040 nablûwth (1), *female genitals*
4467 rhaᵢdiŏurgēma (1), *crime, legal fraction*

LIAR
376+3576 'îysh (1), *man; male; someone*
391 'akzâb (1), *deceit; treachery*
3576 kâzab (2), *to lie, deceive*
8267 sheqer (1), *untruth; sham*
5583 psĕustēs (8), *falsifier*

LIARS
907 bad (2), *brag or lie; liar, boaster*
3576 kâzab (1), *to lie, deceive*
3584 kâchash (1), *to lie, disown; to disappoint*
5571 psĕudēs (2), *erroneous, deceitful*
5583 psĕustēs (2), *falsifier*

LIBERAL
1293 bᵉrâkâh (1), *benediction, blessing*
5081 nâdîyb (3), *generous*
572 haplŏtēs (1), *sincerity; generosity*

LIBERALITY
572 haplŏtēs (1), *sincerity; generosity*
5485 charis (1), *graciousness*

LIBERALLY
6059 'ânaq (1), *to collar; to fit out*
574 haplōs (1), *bountifully, generously*

LIBERTINES
3032 Libĕrtinŏs (1), *Freedman*

LIBERTY
1865 dᵉrôwr (7), *freedom; clear, pure*
2670 chophshîy (1), *exempt from bondage*
7342 râchâb (1), *roomy, spacious*
425 anĕsis (1), *relaxation; relief*
630 apŏluō (2), *to relieve, release; to pardon*
859 aphĕsis (1), *pardon, freedom*
1657 ĕlĕuthĕria (11), *freedom*
1658 ĕlĕuthĕrŏs (1), *unrestrained*
1849 ĕxŏusia (1), *authority, power, right*
2010 ĕpitrĕpō (1), *to allow*

LIBNAH
3841 Libnâh (18), *storax-tree*

LIBNI
3845 Libnîy (5), *white*

LIBNITES
3864 Lûwbîy (2), *dry region*

LIBYA
6316 Pûwṭ (2), *Put, person*
3033 Libuē (1), *south region*

LIBYANS
3864 Lûwbîy (1), *dry region*
6316 Pûwṭ (1), *Put, person*

LICE
3654 kên (6), *stinging bug*

LICENCE
2010 ĕpitrĕpō (1), *allow, permit*
5117 tŏpŏs (1), *place*

LICK
3897 lâchak (4), *to lick*
3952 lâqaq (1), *to lick*

LICKED
3897 lâchak (1), *to lick*
3952 lâqaq (2), *to lick*
621 apŏlĕichō (1), *to lick off clean*

LICKETH
3897 lâchak (1), *to lick*

LID
1817 deleth (1), *door; gate*

LIE
391 'akzâb (1), *deceit; treachery*
693 'ârab (2), *to ambush, lie in wait*
2583 chânâh (2), *to encamp*
3576 kâzab (12), *to lie, deceive*
3584 kâchash (1), *to lie, disown; to disappoint*
3885 lûwn (2), *to be obstinate*
4769 marbêts (1), *reclining or resting place*
5203 nâṭash (1), *to disperse; to abandon*
5307 nâphal (1), *to fall*
5414+7903 nâthan (3), *to give*
6658 tsâdâh (1), *to desolate*
7250 râba' (2), *to lay down; have sex*
7257 râbats (15), *to recline, repose, brood*
7258 rebets (1), *place of repose*
7693 shâgal (1), *to copulate*
7901 shâkab (59), *to lie down*
8266 shâqar (5), *to cheat, i.e. be untrue in words*
8267 sheqer (8), *untruth; sham*
893 apsĕudēs (1), *veracious, free of deceit*
2621 katakĕimai (1), *to lie down; to recline*

LIED

2749 kĕimai (1), to *lie* outstretched
3180 mĕthŏdĕia (1), trickery, scheming
3582 xĕstēs (1), vessel
5574 pseŭdŏmai (11), to utter an untruth
5579 pseŭdŏs (7), falsehood

LIED

3576 kâzab (2), to *lie*, deceive
3584 kâchash (1), to *lie*, disown; to disappoint
5574 pseŭdŏmai (1), to utter an untruth

LIEN

7693 shâgal (1), to copulate with
7901 shâkab (1), to *lie* down

LIES

907 bad (3), brag or *lie*; liar, boaster
1697+3576 dâbâr (1), word; matter; thing
1697+8267 dâbâr (1), word; matter; thing
3576 kâzab (22), to *lie*, deceive
3585 kachash (4), emaciation; hypocrisy
7723 shâv' (1), ruin; guile; idolatry
8267 sheqer (17), untruth; sham
8383 te'ûn (1), toil
5573 pseŭdŏlŏgŏs (1), promulgating erroneous doctrine

LIEST

5307 nâphal (1), to *fall*
7901 shâkab (4), to *lie* down

LIETH

3318 yâtsâ' (3), to *go*, bring out
3584 kâchash (1), to *lie*, disown; to disappoint
4904 mishkâb (1), bed; sleep; intercourse
5564 çâmak (1), to *lean* upon; take hold of
6437 pânâh (1), to *turn*, to face
7257 râbats (2), to recline, repose, brood
7901 shâkab (20), to *lie* down
8172 shâ'an (1), to support, rely on
906 ballō (1), to *throw*
991 blĕpō (1), to *look* at
2192 ĕchō (1), to *have*; hold; keep
2749 kĕimai (2), to *lie* outstretched

LIEUTENANTS

323 'ăchashdarpan (4), satrap

LIFE

2416 chay (143), *alive*; raw; fresh; life
2417 chay (Ch.) (1), *alive*; life
2421 châyâh (10), to *live*; to revive

2425 châyay (1), to *live*; to revive
3117 yôwm (3), day; time period
3117+5921 yôwm (1), day; time period
5315 nephesh (90), life; breath; soul; wind
6106 'etsem (1), bone; body; substance
72 agōgē (1), mode of living, way of life
895 apsuchŏs (1), lifeless, i.e. inanimate
979 biŏs (5), present state of existence
981 biōsis (1), mode of living
982 biōtikŏs (3), relating to the present existence
2198 zaō (1), to *live*
2222 zōē (132), life
2227 zōŏpŏiĕō (2), to (re-) vitalize, give life
4151 pnĕuma (1), spirit
5590 psuchē (36), soul, vitality; heart, mind

LIFETIME

2416 chay (1), alive; raw; fresh; life
2198 zaō (1), to *live*
2222 zōē (1), life

LIFT

5127 nûwç (1), to *vanish* away, flee
5130 nûwph (3), to quiver, vibrate, rock
5375 nâsâ' (66), to *lift* up
5414 nâthan (1), to *give*
6030 'ânâh (1), to respond, answer
6670 tsâhal (1), to be cheerful; to sound
6965 qûwm (3), to *rise*
7311 rûwm (18), to be high; to rise or raise
352 anakuptō (1), to straighten up
461 anŏrthŏō (1), to straighten up
1458 ĕgkalĕō (1), to charge, criminate
1869 ĕpairō (4), to raise up, look up
5312 hupsŏō (1), to elevate; to exalt

LIFTED

935 bôw' (1), to *go* or come
1361 gâbahh (7), to be lofty; to be haughty
1431 gâdal (1), to be great, make great
1802 dâlâh (1), to *draw* out water); to deliver
5130 nûwph (1), to quiver, vibrate, rock
5191 ne'tal (Ch.) (2), to raise; to repent
5264 nâçaç (1), to *gleam*; to flutter a flag
5375 nâsâ' (92), to *lift* up
5423 nâthaq (1), to tear off
5782 'ûwr (3), to *awake*
5927 'âlâh (1), to *ascend*, be high, mount

6075 'âphal (1), to *swell*; be elated
7213 râ'am (1), to *rise*
7311 rûwm (15), to be high; to rise or raise
7313 rûwm (Ch.) (2), elation, arrogance
7426 râmam (2), to *rise*
142 airō (4), to *lift*, to take up
352 anakuptō (2), to straighten up
450 anistēmi (1), to stand up; to come back to life
1453 ĕgĕirō (3), to waken, i.e. rouse
1869 ĕpairō (10), to raise up, look up
5188 tuphō (1), to make a smoke
5312 hupsŏō (5), to elevate; to exalt

LIFTER

7311 rûwm (1), to be high; to rise or raise

LIFTEST

5375 nâsâ' (1), to *lift* up
5414 nâthan (1), to *give*
7311 rûwm (2), to be high; to rise or raise

LIFTETH

4754 mârâ' (1), to *rebel*; to lash with whip; flap
5375 nâsâ' (2), to *lift* up
5749 'ûwd (1), to duplicate or repeat
5927 'âlâh (2), to *ascend*, be high, mount
7311 rûwm (4), to be high; to rise or raise

LIFTING

1348 gē'ûwth (1), ascending; majesty
1466 gēvâh (1), exaltation; arrogance
4607 mô'al (1), raising of the hands
4864 mas'êth (1), raising; beacon; present
5375 nâsâ' (1), to *lift* up
5782 'ûwr (1), to *awake*
7311 rûwm (1), to be high; to rise or raise
7427 rômêmûth (1), exaltation
1869 ĕpairō (1), to raise up, look up

LIGHT

215 'ôwr (1), to be luminous
216 'ôwr (126), luminary; lightning; happiness
217 'ûwr (1), flame; East
219 'ôwrâh (2), luminousness, light
3313 yâpha' (1), to *shine*
3974 mâ'ôwr (15), luminary, light source
4237 mechĕzâh (2), window
5051 nôgahh (1), brilliancy
5094 ne'hîyr (Ch.) (3), illumination
5105 ne'hârâh (1), daylight

5117 nûwach (1), to *rest*; to settle down
5216 nîyr (4), lamp; lamplight
5927 'âlâh (2), to *ascend*, be high, mount
6348 pâchaz (2), to be unimportant
7031 qal (1), rapid, swift
7034 qâlâh (1), to be *light*
7043 qâlal (7), to be, make light
7052 qe'lôqêl (1), insubstantial food
7136 qârâh (1), to *bring* about; to impose
7837 shachar (1), dawn
272 amĕlĕō (1), to be careless of, neglect
681 haptō (1), to set on fire
1645 ĕlaphrŏs (2), light, i.e. easy
2014 ĕpiphainō (1), to become visible
2017 ĕpiphauō (1), to illuminate, shine on
2545 kaiō (1), to set on fire
2989 lampō (1), to radiate brilliancy
3088 luchnŏs (5), lamp or other illuminator
4098 piptō (1), to *fall*
5338 phĕggŏs (2), brilliancy, radiance
5457 phōs (65), luminousness, light
5458 phōstēr (1), celestial luminary
5460 phōtĕinŏs (4), well-illuminated
5461 phōtizō (4), to *shine* or to brighten up
5462 phōtismŏs (2), light; illumination

LIGHTED

3381 yârad (2), to descend
4672 mâtsâ' (1), to *find* or acquire; to occur
5307 nâphal (1), to *fall*
5927 'âlâh (2), to *ascend*, be high, mount
6293 pâga' (1), to impinge
6795 tsânach (2), to descend, i.e. drive down
681 haptō (2), to set on fire

LIGHTEN

215 'ôwr (2), to be luminous
5050 nâgahh (1), to illuminate
7043 qâlal (2), to be, make light
602 apŏkalupsis (1), disclosure, revelation
5461 phōtizō (1), to *shine* or to brighten up

LIGHTENED

215 'ôwr (1), to be luminous
5102 nâhar (1), to sparkle; to be cheerful
1546+4160 ĕkbŏlē (1), jettison of cargo

2893 kŏuphizŏ (1), to
unload, make lighter
5461 phōtizō (1), to shine
or to brighten up

LIGHTENETH
215 'ôwr (1), to be
luminous
797 astraptō (1), to flash
as lightning

LIGHTER
7043 qâlal (4), to be,
make light

LIGHTEST
5927 'âlâh (1), to ascend,
be high, mount

LIGHTETH
4672 mâtsâ' (1), to find
or acquire; to occur
5927 'âlâh (1), to ascend,
be high, mount
5461 phōtizō (1), to shine
or to brighten up

LIGHTING
5183 nachath (1),
descent; quiet
2064 ĕrchŏmai (1), to go
or come

LIGHTLY
4592 mᵉ'aṭ (1), little or
few
5034 nâbêl (1), to wilt; to
fall away; to be foolish
7034 qâlâh (1), to be light
7043 qâlal (3), to be,
make light
5035 tachu (1), without
delay, soon, suddenly

LIGHTNESS
6350 pachăzûwth (1),
frivolity
6963 qôwl (1), voice or
sound
1644 ĕlaphria (1),
fickleness

LIGHTNING
216 'ôwr (1), luminary;
lightning; happiness
965 bâzâq (1), flash of
lightning
1300 bârâq (5), lightning;
flash of lightning
2385 chăzîyz (2), flash of
lightning
796 astrapē (4),
lightning; light's glare

LIGHTNINGS
1300 bârâq (9), lightning;
flash of lightning
3940 lappîyd (1), flaming
torch, lamp or flame
796 astrapē (4),
lightning; light's glare

LIGHTS
216 'ôwr (1), luminary;
lightning; happiness
3974 mâ'ôwr (4),
luminary, light source
8261 shâqûph (1),
opening
2985 lampas (1), lamp,
lantern, torch
3088 luchnŏs (1), lamp
or other illuminator
5457 phōs (1),
luminousness, light

5458 phōstēr (1),
celestial luminary

LIGURE
3958 leshem (2), (poss.)
jacinth

LIKE
251 'âch (1), brother;
relative; member
1571 gam (2), also; even
1819 dâmâh (16), to
resemble, liken
1821 dᵉmâh (Ch.) (2), to
resemble; be like
1823 dᵉmûwth (2),
resemblance, likeness
1825 dimyôwn (1),
resemblance, likeness
1922 hădar (Ch.) (1), to
magnify, glorify
2088 zeh (1), this or that
2421 châyâh (1), to live;
to revive
2654 châphêts (2), to be
pleased with, desire
2803 châshab (1), to
think, regard; to value
3541 kôh (1), thus
3644 kᵉmôw (61), like,
as; for; with
3651 kên (7), just; right,
correct
4711 mâtsats (1), to suck
4911 mâshal (5), to use
figurative language
4915 môshel (1), empire;
parallel
5973 'îm (2), with
5974 'îm (Ch.) (1), with
7737 shâvâh (2), to
resemble; to adjust
407 andrizŏmai (1), to
act manly
499 antitupŏn (1),
representative
871 aphŏmŏiŏō (1), to be
like
1381 dŏkimazŏ (1), to
test; to approve
1503 ĕikō (1), to
resemble, be like
2470 isŏs (1), similar
2472 isŏtimŏs (1), of
equal value or honor
2504 kagō (1), and also
2532 kai (1), and; or
3663 hŏmŏiŏpathēs (2),
similarly affected
3664 hŏmŏiŏs (47),
similar
3665 hŏmŏiŏtēs (1),
resemblance, similarity
3666 hŏmŏiŏō (4), to
become like
3667 hŏmŏiōma (1),
form; resemblance
3779 hŏutō (2), in this
way; likewise
3945 parŏmŏiazō (2), to
resemble, be like
3946 parŏmŏiŏs (2),
similar, like
4832 summŏrphŏs (1),
similar, conformed to
5024 tauta (2), in the
same way
5108 tŏiŏutŏs (1), truly
this, i.e. of this sort
5613 hōs (10), which,
how, i.e. in that manner

5615 hōsautōs (2), in the
same way
5616 hōsĕi (6), as if
5618 hōspĕr (1), exactly
like

LIKED
7521 râtsâh (1), to be
pleased with; to satisfy

LIKEMINDED
2473 isŏpsuchŏs (1), of
similar spirit
3588+846+5426 hŏ (2),
"the," definite article

LIKEN
1819 dâmâh (4), to
resemble, liken
3666 hŏmŏiŏō (5), to
become like

LIKENED
1819 dâmâh (2), to
resemble, liken
3666 hŏmŏiŏō (4), to
become like

LIKENESS
1823 dᵉmûwth (19),
resemblance, likeness
8403 tabnîyth (5),
resemblance
8544 tᵉmûwnâh (5),
something fashioned
3666 hŏmŏiŏō (1), to
become like
3667 hŏmŏiōma (3),
form; resemblance

LIKETH
157 'âhab (1), to have
affection, love
2896 tôwb (2), good; well

LIKEWISE
1571 gam (15), also;
even; yea; though
2063 zō'th (2), this
3162 yachad (1), unitedly
3651 kên (14), just; right
36 agĕnēs (2), ignoble,
lowly
437 anthŏmŏlŏgĕŏmai
(1), respond in praise
2532 kai (11), and; or
3668 hŏmŏiŏs (29), in the
same way
3779 hŏutō (5), in this
way; likewise
3898 paraplēsiŏs (1), in a
manner near by
5615 hōsautōs (13), in
the same way

LIKHI
3949 Liqchîy (1), learned

LIKING
2492 châlam (1), to be,
make plump; to dream

LILIES
7799 shûwshan (8), white
lily; straight trumpet
2918 krinŏn (2), lily

LILY
7799 shûwshan (5), white
lily; straight trumpet

LIME
7875 sîyd (2), lime

LIMIT
1366 gᵉbûwl (1),
boundary, border

LIMITED
8428 tâvâh (1), to grieve,
bring pain

LIMITETH
3724 hŏrizō (1), to
appoint, decree, specify

LINE
2256 chebel (5),
company, band
2339 chûwṭ (1), string;
line
6616 pâthîyl (1), twine,
cord
6957 qav (14), rule;
musical string
8279 sered (1),
scribing-awl
8515 Tᵉla'ssar (1),
Telassar
8615 tiqvâh (1), cord;
expectancy
2583 kanŏn (1), rule,
standard

LINEAGE
3965 patria (1), family,
group, race, i.e. nation

LINEN
906 bad (23), linen
garment
948 bûwts (9), Byssus,
(poss.) cotton
4723 miqveh (4),
confidence; collection
5466 çâdîyn (2), shirt
6593 pishteh (9), linen,
from carded thread
8162 sha'aṭnêz (1), linen
and woolen
8336 shêsh (37), white
linen; white marble
1039 bussinŏs (4), linen
1040 bussŏs (2), white
linen
3043 linŏn (1), flax linen
3608 ŏthŏniŏn (5), strips
of linen bandage
4616 sindōn (6), byssos,
i.e. bleached linen

LINES
2256 chebel (2),
company, band

LINGERED
4102 mâhahh (2), to be
reluctant

LINGERETH
691 argĕŏ (1), to delay,
grow weary

LINTEL
352 'ayil (1), chief; ram;
oak tree
3730 kaphtôr (1), capital;
wreath-like button
4947 mashqôwph (2),
lintel

LINTELS
3730 kaphtôr (1), capital;
wreath-like button

LINUS
3044 Linŏs (1), (poss.)
flax linen

LION
738 'ărîy (56), lion
739 'ărîy'êl (2), Lion of
God

LION'S
3715 k^ephîyr (16), *walled village; young lion*
3833 lâbîy' (9), *lion, lioness*
3918 layish (3), *lion*
7826 shachal (6), *lion*
3023 lĕôn (6), lion

LION'S
738 'ărîy (4), *lion*
3833 lâbîy' (1), *lion, lioness*
7830 shachats (1), *haughtiness; dignity*

LIONESS
3833 lâbîy' (1), *lion, lioness*

LIONESSES
3833 lâbîy' (1), *lion, lioness*

LIONLIKE
739 'ărîy'êl (2), *Lion of God*

LIONS
738 'ărîy (17), *lion*
744 'aryêh (Ch.) (8), *lion*
3715 k^ephîyr (14), *walled village; young lion*
3833 lâbîy' (1), *lion, lioness*
3023 lĕôn (3), lion

LIONS'
738 'ărîy (2), *lion*
744 'aryêh (Ch.) (1), *lion*

LIP
822 'eshnâb (1), *latticed window*
8193 sâphâh (2), *lip, language, speech*

LIPS
2193 zâ'ak (1), to *extinguish*
8193 sâphâh (109), *lip, language, speech*
8222 sâphâm (3), *beard*
5491 chêilŏs (6), lip

LIQUOR
4197 mezeg (1), *tempered wine*
4952 mishrâh (1), *steeped juice*

LIQUORS
1831 dema' (1), *juice*

LISTED
2309 thĕlō (2), to will; to desire; to choose

LISTEN
8085 shâma' (1), to *hear intelligently*

LISTETH
2309 thĕlō (1), to will; to desire; to choose
3730+1014 hŏrmē (1), impulse, i.e. onset

LITTERS
6632 tsâb (1), *lizard; covered cart*

LITTLE
1851 daq (1), *crushed; small or thin*
2191 z^e'êyr (3), *small, little*
2192 z^e'êyr (Ch.) (1), *small, little*

LO
718 'ărûw (Ch.) (1), *lo!, behold!*
1883 dethe' (Ch.) (1), *sprout; green grass*
1888 hê' (Ch.) (1), *Lo!, Look!*
2005 hên (13), *lo!; if!*
2009 hinnêh (103), *lo!; Look!*
2114 zûwr (1), to *be foreign, strange*
7200 râ'âh (3), to *see*
2395 iatrŏs (1), physician
2396 idĕ (2), surprise!, lo!, look!
2400 idŏu (29), lo!, note!, see!

LO-AMMI
3818 Lô' 'Ammîy (1), *not my people*

LO-DEBAR
3810 Lô' D^ebar (3), *pastureless*

LO-RUHAMAH
3819 Lô' Rûchâmâh (2), *not pitied*

LOADEN
6006 'âmaç (1), to *impose a burden*

LOADETH
6006 'âmaç (1), to *impose a burden*

LOAF
3603 kikkâr (2), *round loaf; talent*
740 artos (1), loaf of bread

LOAN
7596 sh^e'êlâh (1), *petition*

LOATHE
3988 mâ'aç (1), to *spurn; to disappear*

LOATHETH
947 bûwç (1), to *trample down; oppress*
6973 qûwts (1), to *be, make disgusted*

LOATHSOME
887 bâ'ash (1), to *be a moral stench*
2214 zârâ' (1), *disgusting, loathing*
3988 mâ'aç (1), to *spurn; to disappear*
7033 qâlâh (1), to *toast, scorch*

LOAVES
3603 kikkâr (2), *round loaf; talent*
3899 lechem (5), *food, bread*
740 artos (22), loaf of bread

LOCK
4514 man'ûwl (1), *bolt on door*
6734 tsîytsîth (1), *fore-lock of hair; tassel*

LOCKED
5274 nâ'al (2), to *fasten up, lock*

2835 châsîph (1), *small company, flock*
2945 ṭaph (32), *family of children and women*
3530 kibrâh (3), *measure of length*
3563 kôwç (2), *cup; (poss.) owl*
4591 mâ'aṭ (3), to *be, make small or few*
4592 m^e'aṭ (52), *little or few*
4704 mitsts^e'îyrâh (1), *diminutive*
4705 mits'âr (3), *little; short time*
5759 'ăvîyl (1), *infant, young child*
5768 'ôwlêl (1), *suckling child*
6810 tsâ'îyr (4), *little in number; few in age*
6819 tsâ'ar (1), to *be small; be trivial*
6966 qûwm (Ch.) (1), to *rise*
6995 qôṭen (2), *little finger*
6996 qâṭân (20), *small, least, youngest*
8102 shemets (2), *inkling*
8241 shetseph (1), *outburst of anger*
8585 t^e'âlâh (1), *channel; bandage or plaster*
974 bibliaridiŏn (4), little scroll
1024 brachus (6), little, short
1646 ĕlachistŏs (1), least
2365 thugatriŏn (1), little daughter
2485 ichthudiŏn (1), little fish
3357 mĕtriŏs (1), moderately, i.e. slightly
3397 mikrŏn (14), small space of time or degree
3398 mikrŏs (16), small, little
3640 ŏligŏpistŏs (5), little confidence
3641 ŏligŏs (9), puny, small
3813 paidiŏn (12), child: immature
4142 plŏiariŏn (2), small boat
5040 tĕkniŏn (9), infant, i.e. a darling Christian
5177 tugchanō (1), to take part in; to obtain

LIVE
2414 châṭaph (3), to *seize as a prisoner*
2416 chay (44), *alive; raw; fresh; life*
2418 chăyâ' (Ch.) (2), to *live*
2421 châyâh (110), to *live; to revive*
2425 châyay (15), to *live; to revive*
3117 yôwm (2), *day; time period*
7531 ritspâh (1), *hot stone; pavement*
390 anastrĕphō (2), to remain, to live

---

980 biŏō (1), to live life
1514 ĕirēnĕuō (2), to be, act peaceful
2068 ĕsthiō (1), to eat
2071+3118 ĕsŏmai (1), will be
2198 zaō (53), to live
2225 zōŏgŏnĕō (1), to rescue; be saved
4800 suzaō (3), to live in common with
5225 huparchō (1), to come into existence

LIVED
2416 chay (5), *alive; raw; fresh; life*
2421 châyâh (39), to *live; to revive*
2425 châyay (5), to *live; to revive*
326 anazaō (1), to recover life, live again
2198 zaō (4), to live
4176 pŏlitĕuŏmai (1), to behave as a citizen
5171 truphaō (1), to live indulgently

LIVELY
2416 chay (1), *alive; raw; fresh; life*
2422 châyeh (1), *vigorous*
2198 zaō (3), to live

LIVER
3516 kâbêd (14), *liver*

LIVES
2416 chay (2), *alive; raw; fresh; life*
2417 chay (Ch.) (1), *alive; life*
2421 châyâh (2), to *live; to revive*
5315 nephesh (18), *life; breath; soul; wind*
5590 psuchē (5), soul, vitality; heart, mind

LIVEST
2416 chay (1), *alive; raw; fresh; life*
3117 yôwm (1), *day; time period*
2198 zaō (2), to live

LIVETH
2416 chay (61), *alive; raw; fresh; life*
2421 châyâh (1), to *live; to revive*
2425 châyay (2), to *live; to revive*
3117 yôwm (1), *day; time period*
2198 zaō (24), to live

LIVING
2416 chay (98), *alive; raw; fresh; life*
2417 chay (Ch.) (4), *alive; life*
2424 chayûwth (1), *life, lifetime*
979 biŏs (5), present state of existence
1236 diagō (1), to pass time or life
2198 zaō (34), to live

LIZARD
3911 l^eṭâ'âh (1), *kind of lizard*

LOCKS
4253 machlâphâh (2), *ringlet* or *braid*, of hair
4514 man'ûwl (5), *bolt* on door
6545 pera' (2), *hair* as *dishevelled*
6777 tsammâh (4), *veil*
6977 qᵉvutstsâh (2), *forelock* of hair

LOCUST
697 'arbeh (9), *locust*
5556 çol'âm (1), destructive *locust* kind
6767 tsᵉlâtsal (1), *cricket*

LOCUSTS
697 'arbeh (11), *locust*
1357 gêb (1), *locust* swarm
2284 châgâb (1), *locust*
200 akris (4), *locust*

LOD
3850 Lôd (4), *Lod*

LODGE
3885 lûwn (22), to *be obstinate*
4412 mᵉlûwnâh (1), *hut*
2647 kataluō (1), to *halt* for the night
2681 kataskēnŏō (2), to *remain, live*
3579 xĕnizō (1), to be a *host*; to be a *guest*

LODGED
3885 lûwn (12), to *be obstinate*
4411 mâlôwn (1), *lodging* for night
7901 shâkab (1), to *lie down*
835 aulizŏmai (1), to *pass the night*
2681 kataskēnŏō (1), to *remain, live*
3579 xĕnizō (4), to be a *host*; to be a *guest*
3580 xĕnŏdŏchĕō (1), to *be hospitable*

LODGEST
3885 lûwn (1), to *be obstinate*

LODGETH
3579 xĕnizō (1), to be a *host*; to be a *guest*

LODGING
3885 lûwn (1), to *be obstinate*
4411 mâlôwn (3), *lodgment* for night
3578 xĕnia (2), *place of entertainment*

LODGINGS
4411 mâlôwn (1), *lodgment* for night

LOFT
5944 'ălîyâh (1), *upper things; second-story*

LOFTILY
4791 mârôwm (1), *elevation; elation*

LOFTINESS
1363 gôbahh (1), *height; grandeur; arrogance*
1365 gabhûwth (1), *pride, arrogance*

LOFTY
1364 gâbôahh (2), *high; powerful; arrogant*
1365 gabhûwth (1), *pride, arrogance*
5375 nâsâ' (1), to *lift up*
7311 rûwm (3), to be *high; to rise* or *raise*
7682 sâgab (1), to *be, make lofty; be safe*

LOG
3849 lôg (5), liquid *measure*

LOINS
2504 châlâts (9), *loins, areas of the waist*
2788 chârêr (1), *arid, parched*
3409 yârêk (2), leg or *shank, flank; side*
3689 keçel (1), *loin; back; viscera*
4975 môthen (42), *loins*
3751 ŏsphus (8), *loin; belt*

LOIS
3090 Lŏïs (1), *Lois*

LONG
748 'ârak (4), to *be, make long*
752 'ârôk (2), *long*
753 'ôrek (23), *length*
954 bûwsh (1), to *be delayed*
1419 gâdôwl (1), *great*
2442 châkâh (1), to *await; hope for*
3117 yôwm (16), *day; time period*
4101 mâh (Ch.) (1), *what?, how?, why?*
4900 mâshak (2), to *draw out; to be tall*
4970 mâthay (1), *when; when?, how long?*
5704 'ad (51), *as far (long) as; during*
5750 'ôwd (1), *again; repeatedly; still; more*
5769 'ôwlâm (3), *eternity; ancient; always*
5973 'îm (1), *with*
6256 'êth (1), *time*
6440 pânîym (1), *face; front*
7221 rî'shâh (1), *beginning*
7227 rab (11), *great*
7230 rôb (2), *abundance*
7235 râbâh (3), to *increase*
7350 râchôwq (3), *remote, far*
8615 tiqvâh (1), *cord; expectancy*
1909 ĕpi (1), *on, upon*
1909+4119 ĕpi (1), *on, upon*
1971 ĕpipŏthĕō (3), *intensely crave*
2118 ĕuthutēs (1), *rectitude, uprightness*
2193 hĕŏs (7), *until*
2425 hikanŏs (6), *ample; fit*
2863 kŏmaō (2), to *wear long hair*
3114 makrŏthumĕō (3), to *be forbearing, patient*

3117 makrŏs (3), *long*, in place or time
3752 hŏtan (1), *inasmuch as, at once*
3756+3641 ŏu (1), *no* or *not*
3819 palai (1), *formerly; sometime since*
4183 pŏlus (4), *much, many*
4214 pŏsŏs (1), *how much?; how much!*
5118 tŏsŏutŏs (2), *such great*
5550 chrŏnŏs (4), *space of time, period*

LONGED
183 'âvâh (2), to *wish* for, *desire*
2968 yâ'ab (1), to *desire, long for*
3615 kâlâh (1), to *cease, be finished, perish*
8373 tâ'ab (2), to *desire*
1971 ĕpipŏthĕō (1), *intensely crave*
1973 ĕpipŏthĕtŏs (1), *yearned upon*

LONGEDST
3700 kâçaph (1), to *pine after; to fear*

LONGER
752 'ârôk (1), *long*
3254 yâçaph (1), to *add* or *augment*
5750 'ôwd (4), *again; repeatedly; still; more*
2089 ĕti (4), *yet, still*
3370 Mēdŏs (5), *inhabitant of Media*
4119 plĕiŏn (1), *more*

LONGETH
183 'âvâh (1), to *wish* for, *desire*
2836 châshaq (1), to *join; to love, delight*
3642 kâmahh (1), to *pine after, long for*
3700 kâçaph (1), to *pine after; to fear*

LONGING
8264 shâqaq (1), to *seek greedily*
8375 ta'ăbâh (1), *desire*

LONGSUFFERING
750+639 'ârêk (4), *patient*
3114 makrŏthumĕō (1), to *be forbearing, patient*
3115 makrŏthumia (12), *forbearance; fortitude*

LONGWINGED
750+83 'ârêk (1), *patient*

LOOK
2342 chûwl (1), to *wait; to pervert*
2372 châzâh (3), to *gaze at; to perceive*
2376 chêzev (Ch.) (1), *sight, revelation*
4758 mar'eh (6), *appearance; vision*
5027 nâbaṭ (24), to *scan; to regard* with favor
5869 'ayin (3), *eye; sight*
6437 pânâh (13), to *turn, to face*

6440 pânîym (1), *face; front*
6485 pâqad (1), to *visit, care for, count*
6822 tsâphâh (2), to *peer into the distance*
6960 qâvâh (4), to *collect; to expect*
7200 râ'âh (53), to *see*
7210 rŏ'îy (1), *sight; spectacle*
7688 shâgach (1), to *glance sharply at*
7760 sûwm (2), to *put, place*
7789 shûwr (1), to *spy out, survey*
7896 shîyth (1), to *place, put*
8159 shâ'âh (4), to *inspect, consider*
8259 shâqaph (3), to *peep or gaze*
308 anablĕpō (1), to *look up; to recover sight*
352 anakuptō (1), to *straighten up*
553 apĕkdĕchŏmai (2), to *expect fully*
816 atĕnizō (2), to *gaze intently*
991 blĕpō (5), to *look at*
1492 ĕidō (1), to *know*
1551 ĕkdĕchŏmai (1), to *await, expect*
1914 ĕpiblĕpō (1), to *gaze at*
1980 ĕpiskĕptŏmai (1), to *inspect; to go to see*
2300 thĕaŏmai (1), to *look closely at*
3700 ŏptanŏmai (2), to *appear*
3706 hŏrasis (1), *vision*
3879 parakuptō (1), to *lean over to peer within*
4328 prŏsdŏkaō (5), to *anticipate; to await*
4648 skŏpĕō (2), to *watch out for*, i.e. to *regard*

LOOKED
5027 nâbaṭ (12), to *scan; to regard* with favor
6437 pânâh (18), to *turn, to face*
6440 pânîym (1), *face; front*
6960 qâvâh (8), to *collect; to expect*
6970 Qôwa' (1), *curtailment*
7200 râ'âh (55), to *see*
7805 shâzaph (1), to *scan*
8159 shâ'âh (1), to *inspect, consider*
8259 shâqaph (12), to *peep or gaze*
8559 Tâmâr (1), *palm tree*
308 anablĕpō (6), to *look up; to recover sight*
816 atĕnizō (4), to *gaze intently*
991 blĕpō (1), to *look at*
1492 ĕidō (7), to *know*
1551 ĕkdĕchŏmai (1), to *await, expect*
1689 ĕmblĕpō (2), to *observe; to discern*

1869 ĕpairō (1), to *raise
up, look up*
2300 thĕaŏmai (1), to
look closely at
4017 pĕriblĕpō (6), to
look all around
4327 prŏsdĕchŏmai (1),
to *receive; to await for*
4328 prŏsdŏkaō (2), to
anticipate; to await

LOOKEST
5027 nâbaṭ (1), to *scan;
to regard with favor*
8104 shâmar (1), to
watch

LOOKETH
995 bîyn (1), to
understand; discern
4758+5869 mar'eh (1),
appearance; vision
5027 nâbaṭ (3), to *scan;
to regard with favor*
6437 pânâh (8), to *turn,
to face*
6440 pânîym (2), *face;
front*
6822 tsâphâh (2), to *peer
into the distance*
6960 qâvâh (1), to *collect;
to expect*
7200 râ'âh (4), to *see*
7688 shâgach (2), to
glance sharply at
7789 shûwr (1), to *spy
out, survey*
8259 shâqaph (4), to *peep
or gaze*
991 blĕpō (1), to *look at*
3879 parakuptō (1), to
lean over to peer within
4328 prŏsdŏkaō (2), to
anticipate; to await

LOOKING
6437 pânâh (9), to *turn,
to face*
7209 rᵉ'îy (1), *mirror*
8259 shâqaph (1), to *peep
or gaze*
308 anablĕpō (3), to *look
up; to recover sight*
816 atĕnizō (1), to *gaze
intently*
872 aphŏraō (1), to
consider attentively
991 blĕpō (1), to *look at*
1561 ĕkdŏchĕ (1),
expectation
1689 ĕmblĕpō (2), to
observe; to discern
1983 ĕpiskŏpĕō (1), to
oversee; to beware
2334 thĕōrĕō (2), to *see;
to discern*
4017 pĕriblĕpō (1), to
look all around
4327 prŏsdĕchŏmai (3),
to *receive; to await for*
4328 prŏsdŏkaō (2), to
anticipate; to await
4329 prŏsdŏkia (1),
apprehension of evil

LOOKINGGLASSES
4759 mar'âh (1), *vision;
mirror*

LOOKS
5869 'ayin (3), *eye; sight;
fountain*

6400 pelach (2), *slice*

LOOPS
3924 lûlâ'âh (13), curtain
loop

LOOSE
2502 châlats (1), to *pull
off; to strip; to depart*
5394 nâshal (1), to *divest,
eject, or drop*
5425 nâthar (1), to
terrify; shake off; untie
6605 pâthach (7), to *open
wide; to loosen, begin*
7971 shâlach (3), to *send
away*
8271 shᵉrê' (Ch.) (1), to
free, separate; unravel
3089 luō (15), to *loosen*

LOOSED
2118 zâchach (2), to
shove or displace
2502 châlats (1), to *pull
off; to strip; to depart*
4549 mâçaç (1), to *waste
with disease; to faint*
5203 nâṭash (1), to
disperse; to thrust off
5425 nâthar (1), to
terrify; shake off; untie
6605 pâthach (5), to *open
wide; to loosen, begin*
7368 râchaq (1), to
recede; remove
8271 shᵉrê' (Ch.) (1), to
free, separate; unravel
321 anagō (2), to *lead
up; to bring out; to sail*
447 aniēmi (2), to
slacken, loosen
630 apŏluō (2), to *relieve,
release; to pardon*
2673 katargĕō (1), to be,
render entirely useless
3080 lusis (1), *divorce*
3089 luō (10), to *loosen*

LOOSETH
5425 nâthar (1), to
terrify; shake off; untie
6605 pâthach (1), to *open
wide; to loosen, begin*

LOOSING
142 airō (1), to *lift, to
take up*
321 anagō (1), to *lead
up; to bring out; to sail*
3089 luō (2), to *loosen*

LOP
5586 çâ'aph (1), to
dis-branch a tree

LORD
113 'âdôwn (201),
sovereign, i.e. controller
136 'Ădônây (430), the
Lord
1376 gᵉbîyr (2), *master*
3050 Yâhh (50), *Jehovah,
self-Existent or Eternal*
3068 Yᵉhôvâh (6394),
Jehovah, self-Existent
4756 mârê' (Ch.) (4),
master
7229 rab (Ch.) (1), *great*
7991 shâlîysh (3), *officer;
of the third rank*
1203 dĕspŏtēs (4),
absolute *ruler*

2961 kuriĕuō (1), to *rule,
be master of*
2962 kuriŏs (694),
supreme, controller, Mr.
4462 rhabbŏni (1), *my
master*

LORD'S
113 'âdôwn (8),
sovereign, i.e. controller
136 'Ădônây (1), the *Lord*
3068 Yᵉhôvâh (108),
Jehovah, self-Existent
2960 kuriakŏs (2),
belonging to the Lord
2962 kuriŏs (15),
supreme, controller, Mr.

LORDLY
117 'addîyr (1), *powerful;
majestic*

LORDS
113 'âdôwn (4),
sovereign, i.e. controller
1167 ba'al (2), *master;
husband; owner; citizen*
5633 çeren (21), *axle;
peer*
7261 rabrᵉbân (Ch.) (6),
magnate, noble
7300 rûwd (1), to *ramble
free or disconsolate*
7991 shâlîysh (1), *officer;
of the third rank*
8269 sar (1), *head
person, ruler*
2634 katakuriĕuō (1), to
control, subjugate, lord
2961 kuriĕuō (1), to *rule,
be master of*
2962 kuriŏs (3), *supreme,
controller, Mr.*
3175 mĕgistanĕs (1),
great person

LORDSHIP
2634 katakuriĕuō (1), to
subjugate, lord over
2961 kuriĕuō (1), to *rule,
be master of*

LOSE
6 'âbad (1), *perish;
destroy*
622 'âçaph (1), to *gather,
collect*
3772 kârath (1), to *cut
(off, down or asunder)*
5307 nâphal (1), to *fall*
7843 shâchath (1), to
decay; to ruin
622 apŏllumi (17), to
perish or lose
2210 zēmiŏō (2), to *suffer
loss*

LOSETH
622 apŏllumi (1), to
perish or lose

LOSS
2398 châṭâ' (1), to *sin*
7674 shebeth (1), *rest,
interruption, cessation*
7921 shâkôl (2), to
miscarry
580 apŏbŏlĕ (1),
rejection, loss
2209 zēmia (3),
detriment; loss
2210 zēmiŏō (2), to *suffer
loss*

LOST
6 'âbad (9), to *perish*
9 'ăbêdâh (4), *destruction*
5307 nâphal (2), to *fall*
7908 shᵉkôwl (1),
bereavement
7923 shikkûlîym (1),
childlessness
358+1096 analŏs (1),
saltless, i.e. insipid
622 apŏllumi (13), to
perish or lose
3471 môrainō (2), to
become insipid

LOT
1486 gôwrâl (60), *lot,
allotment*
2256 chebel (3),
company, band
3876 Lôwṭ (32), *veil*
2624 kataklĕrŏdŏtĕō (1),
to *apportion an estate*
2819 klĕrŏs (2), *lot,
portion*
2975 lagchanō (1), to
determine by lot
3091 Lōt (3), *veil*

LOT'S
3876 Lôwṭ (1), *veil*

LOTAN
3877 Lôwṭân (5), *covering*

LOTAN'S
3877 Lôwṭân (2), *covering*

LOTHE
3811 lâ'âh (1), to *tire; to
be, make disgusted*
6962 qûwṭ (3), to *detest*

LOTHED
1602 gâ'al (2), to *detest;
to reject; to fail*
7114 qâtsar (1), to
curtail, cut short

LOTHETH
1602 gâ'al (1), to *detest;
to reject; to fail*

LOTHING
1604 gô'al (1), *abhorrence*

LOTS
1486 gôwrâl (16), *lot,
allotment*
2819 klĕrŏs (6), *lot,
portion*
2975 lagchanō (1), to
determine by lot

LOUD
1419 gâdôwl (19), *great*
1993 hâmâh (1), to *be in
great commotion*
2389 châzâq (1), *strong;
severe, hard, violent*
5797 'ôz (1), *strength*
7311 rûwm (1), to *be
high; to rise or raise*
8085 shâma' (2), to *hear*
3173 mĕgas (33), *great,
many*

LOUDER
3966 mᵉ'ôd (1), *very,
utterly*

LOVE
157 'âhab (73), to *have
affection, love*
160 'ahăbâh (34),
affection, love

L

1730 dôwd (7), *beloved, friend; uncle, relative*
2836 châshaq (3), *to join; to love, delight*
5690 'egeb (1), *amative words, words of love*
5691 'ăgâbâh (1), *love, amorousness*
7355 râcham (1), *to be compassionate*
7474 ra'yâh (9), *female associate*
25 agapaō (70), *to love*
26 agapē (85), *love; love-feast*
2309 thělō (1), *to will; to desire; to choose*
5360 philadělphia (4), *fraternal affection*
5361 philadělphŏs (1), *fraternal*
5362 philandrŏs (1), *affectionate as a wife to her husband*
5363 philanthrōpia (1), *benevolence*
5365 philarguria (1), *avarice, greedy love of possessions*
5368 philěō (10), *to be a friend, have affection*
5388 philŏtěknŏs (1), *loving one's child(ren)*

LOVE'S
26 agapē (1), *love*

LOVED
157 'âhab (48), *to have affection, love*
160 'ăhăbâh (7), *affection, love*
2245 châbab (1), *to cherish*
25 agapaō (37), *to love*
26 agapē (1), *love*
5368 philěō (3), *to be a friend, have affection*

LOVEDST
157 'âhab (1), *to have affection, love*
25 agapaō (1), *to love*

LOVELY
157 'âhab (1), *to have affection, love*
4261 machmâd (1), *object of affection*
5690 'egeb (1), *amative words, words of love*
4375 prŏsphilěs (1), *acceptable, pleasing*

LOVER
157 'âhab (2), *to have affection, love*
5358 philagathŏs (1), *promoter of virtue*
5382 philŏxěnŏs (1), *hospitable*

LOVERS
157 'âhab (17), *to have affection, love*
158 'ahab (1), *affection, love*
5689 'âgab (1), *to lust sensually*
7453 rêa' (1), *associate; one close*
5367 philautŏs (1), *selfish*

5369 philēdŏnŏs (1), *loving pleasure*
5377 philŏthěŏs (1), *pious,* i.e. *loving God*

LOVES
159 'ôhab (1), *affection, love*
1730 dôwd (1), *beloved, friend; uncle, relative*
3039 yᵉdîyd (1), *loved*

LOVEST
157 'âhab (7), *to have affection, love*
25 agapaō (2), *to love*
5368 philěō (3), *to be a friend, have affection*

LOVETH
157 'âhab (37), *to have affection, love*
25 agapaō (19), *to love*
5368 philěō (6), *to be a friend, have affection*
5383 philŏprōtěuō (1), *loving to be first*

LOVING
157 'âhab (1), *to have affection, love*
158 'ahab (1), *affection, love*
2896 ṭôwb (1), *good; well*

LOVINGKINDNESS
2617 cheçed (26), *kindness, favor*

LOVINGKINDNESSES
2617 cheçed (4), *kindness, favor*

LOW
120 'âdâm (1), *human being; mankind*
1809 dâlal (3), *to slacken, dangle*
3665 kâna' (2), *to humiliate, subdue*
3766 kâra' (1), *to prostrate*
4295 maṭṭâh (1), *below or beneath*
4355 mâkak (2), *to tumble in ruins*
6030 'ânâh (1), *to respond, answer*
6819 tsâ'ar (1), *to be small; be trivial*
7817 shâchach (3), *to sink or depress*
8213 shâphêl (11), *to humiliate*
8216 shephel (1), *humble state or rank*
8217 shâphâl (5), *depressed, low*
8219 shᵉphêlâh (5), *lowland,*
8482 tachtîy (2), *lowermost; depths*
5011 tapěinŏs (3), *humiliated, lowly*
5013 tapěinŏō (1), *to depress; to humiliate*
5014 tapěinōsis (2), *humbleness, lowliness*

LOWER
2637 châçêr (1), *to lack; to fail, want, make less*
8213 shâphêl (1), *to humiliate*

8217 shâphâl (4), *depressed, low*
8481 tachtôwn (5), *bottommost*
8482 tachtîy (4), *lowermost; depths*
1642 ĕlattŏō (2), *to lessen*
2737 katōtěrŏs (1), *inferior, lower*

LOWEST
7098 qâtsâh (3), *termination; fringe*
8481 tachtôwn (2), *bottommost*
8482 tachtîy (4), *lowermost; depths*
2078 ĕschatŏs (2), *farthest, final*

LOWETH
1600 gâ'âh (1), *to bellow,* i.e. *low of a cow*

LOWING
1600 gâ'âh (1), *to bellow,* i.e. *low of a cow*
6963 qôwl (1), *voice or sound*

LOWLINESS
5012 tapěinŏphrŏsunē (2), *modesty, humility*

LOWLY
6041 'ânîy (3), *depressed*
6800 tsâna' (1), *to humiliate*
8217 shâphâl (1), *depressed, low*
5011 tapěinŏs (1), *humiliated, lowly*

LOWRING
4768 stugnazō (1), *to be overcast, somber*

LUBIM
3864 Lûwbîy (2), *dry region*

LUBIMS
3864 Lûwbîy (1), *dry region*

LUCAS
3065 Lŏukas (2), *Lucanus*

LUCIFER
1966 hêylêl (1), *Venus* (i.e. *morning star*)

LUCIUS
3066 Lŏukiŏs (2), *illuminative*

LUCRE
1215 betsa' (1), *plunder; unjust gain*
146 aischrŏkěrdēs (2), *shamefully greedy*
147 aischrŏkěrdŏs (1), *sordidly, greedily*
866 aphilargurŏs (1), *unavaricious*

LUCRE'S
2771 kěrdŏs (1), *gain, profit*

LUD
3865 Lûwd (4), *Lud*

LUDIM
3866 Lûwdîy (2), *Ludite*

LUHITH
3872 Lûwchîyth (2), *floored*

LUKE
3065 Lŏukas (2), *Lucanus*

LUKEWARM
5513 chliarŏs (1), *tepid*

LUMP
1690 dᵉbêlâh (2), *cake of pressed figs*
5445 phurama (5), *lump of clay; mass of dough*

LUNATICK
4583 sělěniazŏmai (2), *to be moon-struck*

LURK
6845 tsâphan (2), *to hide; to hoard; to lurk*

LURKING
3427 yâshab (1), *to dwell, to remain; to settle*
3993 ma'ărâb (1), *ambuscade, ambush*
4224 machăbě' (1), *refuge, shelter*

LUST
2530 châmad (1), *to delight in; lust for*
5315 nephesh (2), *life; breath; soul; wind*
8307 shᵉrîyrûwth (1), *obstinacy*
8378 ta'ăvâh (1), *longing; delight*
1511+1938 ĕinai (1), *to exist*
1937 ĕpithuměō (2), *to long for*
1939 ĕpithumia (9), *longing*
3715 ŏrěxis (1), *longing after, lust, desire*
3806 pathŏs (1), *passion, especially concupiscence*

LUSTED
183 'âvâh (2), *to wish for, desire*
1937 ĕpithuměō (2), *to long for*

LUSTETH
183 'âvâh (4), *to wish for, desire*
1937 ĕpithuměō (1), *to long for*
1971 ĕpipŏthěō (1), *intensely crave*

LUSTING
8378 ta'ăvâh (1), *longing; delight*

LUSTS
1939 ĕpithumia (22), *longing*
2237 hēdŏnē (2), *delight; desire*

LUSTY
8082 shâmên (1), *rich; fertile*

LUZ
3870 Lûwz (7), *Luz*

LYCAONIA
3071 Lukaŏnia (2), *Lycaonia*

LYCIA
3073 Lukia (1), *Lycia*

LYDDA
3069 Ludda (3), *Lod*

3421 mnēmŏnĕuŏ (1), to exercise memory
3447 mŏschŏpŏiĕŏ (1), to fabricate a bull image
3471 mŏrainŏ (1), to become insipid
3489 nauagĕŏ (1), to be shipwrecked
3666 hŏmŏiŏŏ (2), to become like
3670 hŏmŏlŏgĕŏ (1), to acknowledge, agree
3822 palaiŏŏ (1), to make, become worn out
3903 paraskĕuazŏ (1), to get ready, prepare
3982 pĕithŏ (1), to pacify or conciliate
4087 pikrainŏ (1), to embitter, turn sour
4147 plŏutĕŏ (2), to be, become wealthy
4160 pŏiĕŏ (51), to make
4161 pŏiĕma (1), what is made, product
4198 pŏrĕuŏmai (1), to go, come; to travel
4222 pŏtizŏ (2), to furnish drink, irrigate
4364 prŏspŏiĕŏmai (1), to pretend as if about to
4483 rhĕŏ (1), to utter, i.e. speak or say
4692 spĕudŏ (1), to urge; to await eagerly
4732 stĕrĕŏŏ (1), to be, become strong
4776 sugkathizŏ (1), to give, take a seat in company with
4832 summŏrphŏs (1), similar, conformed to
4955 sustasiastēs (1), fellow-insurgent
4982 sōzŏ (9), to deliver; to protect
5014 tapeinōsis (1), humbleness, lowliness
5048 tĕlĕiŏŏ (9), to perfect, complete
5055 tĕlĕŏ (1), to end, i.e. complete, execute
5087 tithēmi (3), to place
5293 hupŏtassŏ (2), to subordinate; to obey
5319 phanĕrŏŏ (13), to render apparent
5487 charitŏŏ (1), to give special honor
5499 chĕirŏpŏiētŏs (6), of human construction

MADEST
3045 yâda' (1), to know
3772 kârath (1), to cut (off, down or asunder)
6213 'âsâh (1), to make
387 anastatŏŏ (1), to disturb, cause trouble
1642 ĕlattŏŏ (1), to lessen

MADIAN
3099 Madian (1), contest or quarrel

MADMANNAH
4089 Madmannâh (2), dunghill

MADMEN
4086 Madmên (1), dunghill

MADMENAH
4088 Madmênâh (1), dunghill

MADNESS
1947 hôwlêlâh (4), folly, delusion
1948 hôwlêlûwth (1), folly, delusion
7697 shiggâ'ôwn (2), craziness
454 anŏia (1), stupidity; rage
3913 paraphrŏnia (1), foolhardiness, insanity

MADON
4068 Mâdôwn (2), height

MAGBISH
4019 Magbîysh (1), stiffening

MAGDALA
3093 Magdala (1), tower

MAGDALENE
3094 Magdalēnē (12), of Magdala

MAGDIEL
4025 Magdîy'êl (2), preciousness of God

MAGICIAN
2749 charṭôm (Ch.) (1), horoscopist, magician

MAGICIANS
2748 charṭôm (11), horoscopist, magician
2749 charṭôm (Ch.) (4), horoscopist, magician

MAGISTRATE
3423+6114 yârash (1), to inherit; to impoverish
758 archŏn (1), first

MAGISTRATES
8200 sh⁰phaṭ (Ch.) (1), to judge
746 archē (1), first in rank; first in time
3980 pĕitharchĕŏ (1), to submit to authority
4755 stratēgŏs (5), military governor

MAGNIFICAL
1431 gâdal (1), to be great, make great

MAGNIFICENCE
3168 mĕgalĕiŏtēs (1), grandeur or splendor

MAGNIFIED
1431 gâdal (17), to be great, make great
5375 nâsâ' (1), to lift up
3170 mĕgalunŏ (3), to increase or extol

MAGNIFY
1431 gâdal (15), to be great, make great
7679 sâgâ' (1), to laud, extol
1392 dŏxazŏ (1), to render, esteem glorious
3170 mĕgalunŏ (2), to increase or extol

MAGOG
4031 Mâgôwg (4), Magog
3098 Magŏg (1), Magog

MAGOR-MISSABIB
4036 Mâgôwr miç-Çâbîyb (1), affright from around

MAGPIASH
4047 Magpîy'âsh (1), exterminator of (the) moth

MAHALAH
4244 Machlâh (1), sickness

MAHALALEEL
4111 Mahălal'êl (7), praise of God

MAHALATH
4257 Machălath (2), sickness
4258 Machălath (2), sickness

MAHALI
4249 Machlîy (1), sick

MAHANAIM
4266 Machănayim (13), double camp

MAHANEH-DAN
4265 Machănêh-Dân (1), camp of Dan

MAHARAI
4121 Mahăray (3), hasty

MAHATH
4287 Machath (3), erasure

MAHAVITE
4233 Machăvîym (1), Machavite

MAHAZIOTH
4238 Machăzîy'ôwth (2), visions

MAHER-SHALAL-HASH-BAZ
4122 Mahêr Shâlâl Châsh Baz (2), hasting is he to the booty, swift to the prey

MAHLAH
4244 Machlâh (4), sickness

MAHLI
4249 Machlîy (10), sick

MAHLITES
4250 Machlîy (2), Machlite

MAHLON
4248 Machlôwn (3), sick

MAHLON'S
4248 Machlôwn (1), sick

MAHOL
4235 Mâchôwl (1), (round) dance

MAID
519 'âmâh (5), female servant or slave
1330 b⁰thûwlâh (4), virgin maiden
1331 b⁰thûwlîym (2), virginity
5291 na'ărâh (4), female child; servant
5347 n⁰qêbâh (1), female, woman
5959 'almâh (2), lass, young woman

8198 shiphchâh (12), household female slave
2877 kŏrasiŏn (2), little girl
3814 paidiskĕ (2), female slave or servant
3816 pais (1), child; slave or servant

MAID'S
5291 na'ărâh (1), female child; servant

MAIDEN
1330 b⁰thûwlâh (2), virgin maiden
5291 na'ărâh (3), female child; servant
8198 shiphchâh (2), household female slave
3816 pais (1), child; slave or servant

MAIDENS
1330 b⁰thûwlâh (3), virgin maiden
5291 na'ărâh (13), female child; servant
8198 shiphchâh (1), household female slave
3814 paidiskĕ (1), female slave or servant

MAIDS
519 'âmâh (3), female servant or slave
1330 b⁰thûwlâh (3), virgin maiden
5291 na'ărâh (2), female child; servant
3814 paidiskĕ (1), female slave or servant

MAIDSERVANT
519 'âmâh (13), female servant or slave
8198 shiphchâh (3), household female slave

MAIDSERVANT'S
519 'âmâh (1), female servant or slave

MAIDSERVANTS
519 'âmâh (4), female servant or slave
8198 shiphchâh (5), household female slave

MAIDSERVANTS'
519 'âmâh (1), female servant or slave

MAIL
7193 qasqeseth (2), fish scales; coat of mail

MAIMED
2782 chârats (1), to be alert, to decide
376 anapĕrŏs (2), maimed; crippled
2948 kullŏs (4), crippled, i.e. maimed

MAINSAIL
736 artĕmŏn (1), foresail or jib

MAINTAIN
2388 châzaq (1), to bind, restrain, conquer
3198 yâkach (1), to be correct; to argue
6213 'âsâh (6), to do or make

4291 *prŏistēmi* (2), to preside; to practice

MAINTAINED
6213 *'âsâh* (1), to *do* or *make*

MAINTAINEST
8551 *tâmak* (1), to *obtain, keep fast*

MAINTENANCE
2416 *chay* (1), *alive; raw; fresh; life*
4415 m^e*lach* (Ch.) (1), to *eat salt*

MAJESTY
1347 *gâ'ôwn* (7), *ascending; majesty*
1348 *gê'ûwth* (2), *ascending; majesty*
1420 g^e*dûwlâh* (1), *greatness, grandeur*
1923 *hădar* (Ch.) (1), *magnificence, glory*
1926 *hâdâr* (7), *magnificence*
1935 *hôwd* (4), *grandeur, majesty*
7238 r^e*bûw* (Ch.) (3), *increase*
3168 *mĕgalĕiŏtēs* (1), *grandeur or splendor*
3172 *mĕgalōsunē* (3), *divinity, majesty*

MAKAZ
4739 *Mâqats* (1), *end*

MAKE
1124 b^e*nâ'* (Ch.) (1), to *build*
1254 *bârâ'* (1), to *create; fashion*
1443 *gâdar* (2), to *build a* stone *wall*
2015 *hâphak* (1), to *change, overturn*
3331 *yâtsa'* (1), to *strew* as a surface
3335 *yâtsar* (1), to *form; potter; to determine*
3635 k^e*lal* (Ch.) (2), to *complete*
3772 *kârath* (31), to *cut* (off, down or asunder)
3823 *lâbab* (1), *transport* with love; to *stultify*
5414 *nâthan* (64), to *give*
5674 *'âbar* (2), to *cross* over; to *transition*
6014 *'âmar* (1), to *gather* grain into sheaves
6213 *'âsâh* (238), to *make*
6381 *pâlâ'* (1), to *be, make great, wonderful*
7760 *sûwm* (65), to *put, place*
7761 *sûwm* (Ch.) (5), to *put, place*
7896 *shîyth* (9), to *place*
8074 *shâmêm* (1), to *devastate; to stupefy*
142 *airō* (1), to *lift, to take up*
347 *anaklinō* (2), to *lean back, recline*
805 *asphalizō* (1), to *render secure*
1107 *gnōrizō* (6), to *make known, reveal*

1303 *diatithēmai* (2), to *put apart, i.e. dispose*
1325 *didōmi* (2), to *give*
1510 *ĕimi* (1), I *exist, I am*
1519 *ĕis* (1), *to or into*
1659 *ĕlĕuthĕrŏō* (2), to *exempt, liberate*
1710 *ĕmpŏrĕuŏmai* (1), to *trade, do business*
1793 *ĕntugchanō* (1), to *entreat, petition*
2005 *ĕpitĕlĕō* (1), to *terminate; to undergo*
2090 *hĕtŏimazō* (6), to *prepare*
2116 *ĕuthunō* (1), to *straighten or level*
2146 *ĕuprŏsōpĕō* (1), to *make a good display*
2165 *ĕuphrainō* (3), to *rejoice, be glad*
2350 *thŏrubĕō* (1), to *disturb; clamor*
2433 *hilaskŏmai* (1), to *conciliate, to atone* for
2476 *histēmi* (1), to *stand, establish*
2511 *katharizō* (5), to *cleanse*
2525 *kathistēmi* (6), to *designate, constitute*
2625 *kataklinō* (1), to *recline, take a place*
2673 *katargĕō* (3), to *be, render entirely useless*
2675 *katartizō* (2), to *repair; to prepare*
2758 *kĕnŏō* (1), to *make empty*
2936 *ktizō* (1), to *fabricate, create*
3076 *lupĕō* (1), to *distress; to be sad*
3753 *hŏtĕ* (1), *when; as*
3856 *paradĕigmatizō* (1), to *expose to infamy*
3868 *paraitĕŏmai* (1), to *deprecate, decline*
4052 *pĕrissĕuō* (1), to *superabound*
4062 *pĕritrĕpō* (1), to *drive crazy*
4087 *pikrainō* (1), to *embitter, turn sour*
4115 *platunō* (1), to *widen*
4121 *plĕŏnazō* (1), to *increase; superabound*
4122 *plĕŏnĕktĕō* (2), to *be covetous*
4135 *plērŏphŏrĕō* (1), to *fill completely; assure*
4137 *plērŏō* (1), to *fill, make complete*
4160 *pŏiĕō* (48), to *make*
4170 *pŏlĕmĕō* (3), to *battle, make war*
4294 *prŏkatartizō* (1), to *prepare in advance*
4336 *prŏsĕuchŏmai* (3), to *supplicate, pray*
4400 *prŏchĕirizŏmai* (1), to *purpose*
4624 *skandalizō* (2), to *entrap, i.e. trip up*
4679 *sŏphizō* (1), to *be cleverly invented*
4692 *spĕudō* (2), to *urge on*

4766 *strōnnumi* (1), *strew, i.e. spread*
4820 *sumballō* (1), to *aid; to join, attack*
4921 *sunistaō* (1), to *set together, to introduce*
4931 *suntĕlĕō* (1), to *complete entirely*
5055 *tĕlĕō* (3), to *end, i.e. complete, execute*
5087 *tithēmi* (6), to *place*
5319 *phanĕrŏō* (2), to *render apparent*
5461 *phōtizō* (1), to *shine* or to *brighten* up

MAKER
3335 *yâtsar* (4), to *form; potter; to determine*
6213 *'âsâh* (13), to *make*
6466 *pâ'al* (1), to *make*
6467 *pô'al* (1), *act or work, deed*
1217 *dēmiŏurgŏs* (1), *worker, mechanic*

MAKERS
2796 *chârâsh* (1), skilled *fabricator* or worker

MAKEST
6213 *'âsâh* (6), to *make*
7760 *sûwm* (1), to *place*
7896 *shîyth* (1), to *place*
2744 *kauchaŏmai* (2), to *glory in, rejoice in*
4160 *pŏiĕō* (4), to *make*

MAKETH
3772 *kârath* (1), to *cut* (off, down or asunder)
5414 *nâthan* (2), to *give*
6213 *'âsâh* (23), to *make*
6466 *pâ'al* (1), to *make*
7706 *Shadday* (1), the *Almighty God*
7737 *shâvâh* (1), to *level, i.e. equalize*
7760 *sûwm* (6), to *place*
393 *anatĕllō* (1), to *cause* to *arise*
1252 *diakrinō* (1), to *decide; to hesitate*
1308 *diaphĕrō* (1), to *bear, carry; to differ*
1793 *ĕntugchanō* (3), to *entreat, petition*
2165 *ĕuphrainō* (1), to *rejoice, be glad*
2390 *iaŏmai* (1), to *cure, heal*
2525 *kathistēmi* (1), to *designate, constitute*
2617 *kataischunō* (1), to *disgrace or shame*
4160 *pŏiĕō* (6), to *make*
4977 *schizō* (1), to *split* or *sever*
5241 *hupĕrĕntugchanō* (1), to *intercede in behalf of*
5319 *phanĕrŏō* (1), to *render apparent*

MAKHELOTH
4721 *maqhêl* (2), *assembly*

MAKING
3772 *kârath* (1), to *cut* (off, down or asunder)
4639 *ma'ăseh* (2), *action; labor*

6213 *'âsâh* (1), to *make*
208 *akurŏō* (1), to *invalidate, nullify*
1189 *dĕŏmai* (1), to *beg, petition, ask*
1252 *diakrinō* (1), to *decide; to hesitate*
2350 *thŏrubĕō* (1), to *disturb; clamor*
4148 *plŏutizō* (1), to *make wealthy*
4160 *pŏiĕō* (7), to *make*
5567 *psallō* (1), to *play* a stringed instrument

MAKKEDAH
4719 *Maqqêdâh* (9), *herding-fold*

MAKTESH
4389 *Maktêsh* (1), *dell*

MALACHI
4401 *Mal'âkîy* (1), *ministrative*

MALCHAM
4445 *Malkâm* (2), *Malcam or Milcom*

MALCHI-SHUA
4444 *Malkîyshûwa'* (3), *king of wealth*

MALCHIAH
4441 *Malkîyâh* (9), *appointed by Jehovah*

MALCHIEL
4439 *Malkîy'êl* (3), *appointed by God*

MALCHIELITES
4440 *Malkîy'êlîy* (1), *Malkiëlite*

MALCHIJAH
4441 *Malkîyâh* (6), *appointed by Jehovah*

MALCHIRAM
4443 *Malkîyrâm* (1), *king of a high one*

MALCHUS
3124 *Malchŏs* (1), *king*

MALE
376 *'îysh* (2), *man; male*
2138 *zâkûwr* (1), *male*
2142 *zâkar* (1), to *be male*
2145 *zâkâr* (47), *male*
730 *arrhēn* (1), *male*

MALEFACTOR
2555 *kakŏpŏiŏs* (1), *bad-doer; criminal*

MALEFACTORS
2557 *kakŏurgŏs* (3), *criminal, evildoer*

MALELEEL
3121 *Malĕlĕēl* (1), *praise of God*

MALES
2138 *zâkûwr* (2), *male*
2145 *zâkâr* (30), *male*

MALICE
2549 *kakia* (6), *depravity; malignity*

MALICIOUS
4190 *pŏnĕrŏs* (1), *malice, wicked, bad; crime*

MALICIOUSNESS
2549 *kakia* (2), *depravity; malignity*

MALIGNITY
2550 kakŏĕthĕia (1),
mischievousness

MALLOTHI
4413 Mallôwthîy (2),
loquacious

MALLOWS
4408 mallûwach (1),
salt-purslain

MALLUCH
4409 Mallûwk (6),
regnant

MAMMON
3126 mammōnas (4),
wealth, riches

MAMRE
4471 Mamrê' (10), *lusty*

MAN
120 'âdâm (388), *human
being; mankind*
375 'êyphôh (1), *where?;
when?; how?*
376 'îysh (967), *man;
male; someone*
376+2145 'îysh (1), *man;
male; someone*
582 'ĕnôwsh (32), *man;
person, human*
606 'ĕnâsh (Ch.) (8), *man*
935 bôw' (1), *to go, come*
1121 bên (3), *son,
descendant; people*
1121+120 bên (1), *son,
descendant; people*
1167 ba'al (5), *master;
husband; owner; citizen*
1201 Ba'shâ' (1),
offensiveness
1396 gâbar (1), *to be
strong; to prevail*
1397 geber (54), *person,
man*
1400 gᵉbar (Ch.) (2),
person; someone
1538 gulgôleth (2), *skull*
2145 zâkâr (11), *male*
5315 nephesh (3), *life;
breath; soul; wind*
5958 'elem (1), *lad,
young man*
435 anēr (75), *man; male*
442 anthrōpinŏs (2),
human
444 anthrōpŏs (347),
human being; mankind
730 arrhēn (2), *male*
1520 hĕis (3), *one*
1538 hĕkastŏs (3), *each
or every*
2478 ischurŏs (1),
forcible, powerful
3367 mēdĕis (33), *not
even one*
3494 nĕanias (4), *youth*
3495 nĕaniskŏs (5), *youth*
3762 ŏudĕis (96), *none,
nobody, nothing*
3956 pas (3), *all, any,
every, whole*
5100 tis (40), *some or any*

MAN'S
120 'âdâm (17), *human
being; mankind*
312 'achēr (1), *other,
another, different*
376 'îysh (42), *man;
male; someone*

582 'ĕnôwsh (3), *man;
person, human*
606 'ĕnâsh (Ch.) (3), *man*
1167 ba'al (1), *master;
husband; owner; citizen*
1397 geber (2), *person,
man*
245 allŏtriŏs (4), *not
one's own*
435 anēr (1), *man; male*
442 anthrōpinŏs (3),
human
444 anthrōpŏs (10),
human being; mankind
3494 nĕanias (1), *youth*
3762 ŏudĕis (1), *none,
nobody, nothing*
5100 tis (3), *some or any*

MANAEN
3127 Manaĕn (1),
Manaĕn

MANAHATH
4506 Mânachath (3), *rest*

MANAHETHITES
2679 Chătsîy
ham-Mᵉnûchôwth (1),
*midst of the
resting-places*
2680 Chătsîy
ham-Mᵉnachtîy (1),
Chatsi-ham-Menachtite

MANASSEH
4519 Mᵉnashsheh (141),
causing to forget
4520 Mᵉnashshîy (2),
Menashshite

MANASSEH'S
4519 Mᵉnashsheh (4),
causing to forget

MANASSES
3128 Manassēs (3),
causing to forget

MANASSITES
4519 Mᵉnashsheh (1),
causing to forget
4520 Mᵉnashshîy (2),
Menashshite

MANDRAKES
1736 dûwday (6),
mandrake

MANEH
4488 mâneh (1), *weight*

MANGER
5336 phatnē (3), *crib;
stall*

MANIFEST
1305 bârar (1), *to
examine; select*
852 apribĕia (1),
non-apparent, invisible
1212 dēlŏs (1), *clear,
plain, evident*
1552 ĕkdēlŏs (1), *wholly
evident, clear*
1717 ĕmphanēs (1),
apparent, seen, visible
1718 ĕmphanizō (2), *to
show forth*
4271 prŏdēlŏs (1),
obvious, evident
5318 phanĕrŏs (7),
apparent, visible, clear
5319 phanĕrŏō (23), *to
render apparent*

MANIFESTATION
602 apŏkalupsis (1),
disclosure, revelation
5321 phanĕrōsis (2),
manifestation

MANIFESTED
5319 phanĕrŏō (10), *to
render apparent*

MANIFESTLY
5319 phanĕrŏō (1), *to
render apparent*

MANIFOLD
7227 rab (3), *great*
7231 râbab (1), *to
increase*
4164 pŏikilŏs (2), *various*
4179 pŏllaplasiōn (1),
very much more
4182 pŏlupŏikilŏs (1),
multifarious

MANKIND
1320+376 bâsâr (1), *flesh;
body; person*
2145 zâkâr (2), *male*
733 arsĕnŏkŏitēs (2),
sodomite
5449+442 phusis (1),
genus or sort

MANNA
4478 mân (14), *manna,
i.e. a "whatness?"*
3131 manna (5), *edible
gum-like food*

MANNER
734 'ôrach (1), *road;
manner of life*
1571 gam (1), *also; even;
yea; though*
1697 dâbâr (15), *word;
matter; thing*
1699 dôber (1), *grazing
pasture*
1823 dᵉmûwth (1),
resemblance, likeness
1870 derek (8), *road;
course of life*
1881 dâth (1), *royal edict
or statute*
2177 zan (1), *form or sort*
3541 kôh (6), *thus*
3605 kôl (1), *all, any or
every*
3651 kên (3), *just; right;
correct*
3654 kên (1), *stinging bug*
4941 mishpâṭ (36),
verdict; decree; justice
8452 tôwrâh (1), *custom*
72 agōgē (1), *mode of
living, way of life*
195 apribĕia (1),
thoroughness
442 anthrōpinŏs (1),
human
686 ara (3), *then, so,
therefore*
981 biōsis (1), *mode of
living*
1483 ĕthnikōs (1), *as a
Gentile*
1485 ĕthŏs (5), *usage
prescribed*
1486 ĕthō (1), *to be used
by habit or convention*
3592 hŏdĕ (1), *this or
that; these or those*

3634 hŏiŏs (2), *such or
what sort of*
3697 hŏpŏiŏs (2), *what
kind of, what sort of*
3779 hŏutō (5), *in this
way; likewise*
4012 pĕri (1), *about;
around*
4169 pŏiŏs (1), *what sort
of?; which one?*
4217 pŏtapŏs (6), *of what
possible sort?*
4458 -pōs (1), *particle
used in composition*
5158 trŏpŏs (2),
deportment, character
5179 tupŏs (1), *shape,
resemblance; "type"*
5615 hōsautōs (2), *in the
same way*

MANNERS
2708 chuqqâh (1), *to
delineate*
4941 mishpâṭ (2), *verdict;
formal decree; justice*
2239 ēthŏs (1), *usage, i.e.
moral habits*
4187 pŏlutrŏpōs (1), *in
many ways*
5159 trŏpŏphŏrĕō (1), *to
endure one's habits*

MANOAH
4495 Mânôwach (18), *rest*

MANSERVANT
5650 'ebed (12), *servant*

MANSERVANT'S
5650 'ebed (1), *servant*

MANSERVANTS
5650 'ebed (1), *servant*

MANSIONS
3438 mŏnē (1), *residence,
dwelling place*

MANSLAYER
7523 râtsach (2), *to
murder*

MANSLAYERS
409 andrŏphŏnŏs (1),
murderer

MANTLE
155 'addereth (5), *large;
splendid*
4598 mᵉ'îyl (7), *outer
garment or robe*
8063 sᵉmîykâh (1), *rug*

MANTLES
4595 ma'ăṭâphâh (1),
cloak

MANY
1995 hâmôwn (3), *noise,
tumult; many; crowd*
3513 kâbad (2), *to be
heavy, severe, dull*
3605 kôl (1), *all, any or
every*
7227 rab (196), *great*
7230 rôb (4), *abundance*
7231 râbab (6), *to
increase; to multiply*
7233 rᵉbâbâh (1), *myriad*
7235 râbâh (27), *to
increase*
7690 saggîy' (Ch.) (2),
large
2425 hikanŏs (11),
ample; fit

3745 hŏsŏs (31), *as much as*

4119 plĕiŏn (14), *more*

4183 pŏlus (207), *much, many*

4214 pŏsŏs (11), *how much?; how much!*

5118 tŏsŏutŏs (6), *such great*

MAOCH
4582 Mâ'ôwk (1), *oppressed*

MAON
4584 Mâ'ôwn (7), *residence*

MAONITES
4584 Mâ'ôwn (1), *residence*

MAR
3510 kâ'ab (1), to feel pain; to grieve; to spoil
5420 nâthaç (1), to tear up
7843 shâchath (4), to decay; to ruin

MARA
4755 Mârâ' (1), *bitter*

MARAH
4785 Mârâh (5), *bitter*

MARALAH
4831 Mar'ălâh (1), (poss.) *earthquake*

MARANATHA
3134 maran atha (1), *Come, Lord!*

MARBLE
7898 shayith (1), wild *growth* of weeds
8336 shêsh (2), *white* linen; *white* marble
8338 shâwshâw (1), (poss.) to *annihilate*
3139 marmarŏs (1), sparkling *white marble*

MARCH
1980 hâlak (1), to *walk; live a certain way*
3212 yâlak (2), to *walk; to live; to carry*
6805 tsâ'ad (2), to *pace, step* regularly

MARCHED
5265 nâça' (1), *start on a journey*

MARCHEDST
6805 tsâ'ad (1), to *pace, step* regularly

MARCUS
3138 Markŏs (3), *Marcus*

MARESHAH
4762 Mar'êshâh (8), *summit*

MARINERS
4419 mallâch (4), *salt-water sailor*
7751 shûwt (1), to *travel, roam*

MARISHES
1360 gebe' (1), *reservoir; marsh*

MARK
226 'ôwth (1), *signal, sign*

995 bîyn (1), to *understand; discern*
3045 yâda' (3), to *know*
4307 maṭṭârâ' (3), *jail (guard*-house); *aim*
4645 miphgâ' (1), *object of attack, target*
6437 pânâh (1), to *turn, to face*
7181 qâshab (1), to *prick up* the ears
7200 râ'âh (1), to *see*
7760 sûwm (2), to *place*
7896 shîyth (1), to *place*
8104 shâmar (4), to *watch*
8420 tâv (2), *mark; signature*
3138 Markŏs (5), *Marcus*
4648 skŏpĕŏ (2), to *watch out for, i.e. to regard*
4649 skŏpŏs (1), *goal*
5480 charagma (8), *mark, stamp*

MARKED
2856 châtham (1), to *close up; to affix a seal*
3799 kâtham (1), to *inscribe* indelibly
7181 qâshab (1), to *prick up* the ears
8104 shâmar (2), to *watch*
1907 ĕpĕchō (1), to *pay attention to*

MARKEST
8104 shâmar (1), to *watch*

MARKET
4627 ma'ărâb (4), mercantile *goods*
58 agŏra (2), *town-square, market*

MARKETH
8104 shâmar (1), to *watch*
8388 tâ'ar (2), to *delineate; to extend*

MARKETPLACE
58 agŏra (3), *town-square, market*

MARKETPLACES
58 agŏra (1), *town-square, market*

MARKETS
58 agŏra (4), *town-square, market*

MARKS
7085 qa'ăqa' (1), *incision* or gash
4742 stigma (1), *mark, scar* of service

MAROTH
4796 Mârôwth (1), *bitter springs*

MARRED
4893 mishchâth (1), *disfigurement*
7843 shâchath (3), to *decay; to ruin*
622 apŏllumi (1), to *destroy* fully

MARRIAGE
1984 hâlal (1), to *shine, flash, radiate*

5772 'ôwnâh (1), marital cohabitation
1061 gamiskō (1), to *espouse*
1062 gamŏs (9), *nuptials*
1547 ĕkgamizō (3), to *marry off* a daughter
1548 ĕkgamiskō (4), to *marry off* a daughter

MARRIAGES
2859 châthan (3), to *be related* by marriage

MARRIED
802 'ishshâh (3), *woman, wife; women, wives*
1166 bâ'al (7), to *be master; to marry*
1166+802 bâ'al (1), to *be master; to marry*
3427 yâshab (1), to *dwell, to remain; to settle*
3947 lâqach (4), to *take*
5375 nâsâ' (1), to *lift up*
1060 gamĕō (9), to *wed*
1096 ginŏmai (3), to *be, become*

MARRIETH
1166 bâ'al (1), to *be master; to marry*
1060 gamĕō (3), to *wed*

MARROW
2459 cheleb (1), *fat; choice* part
4221 môach (1), bone *marrow*
4229 mâchâh (1), to *erase; to grease*
8250 shiqqûwy (1), *beverage; refreshment*
3452 muĕlŏs (1), *marrow*

MARRY
802 'ishshâh (2), *woman, wife; women, wives*
1166 bâ'al (1), to *be master; to marry*
1961+376 hâyâh (1), to *exist, i.e. be or become*
2992 yâbam (1), to *marry* a dead brother's widow
1060 gamĕō (16), to *wed*
1918 ĕpigambrĕuō (1), to *form an affinity with*

MARRYING
3427 yâshab (1), to *dwell, to remain; to settle*
1060 gamĕō (1), to *wed*

MARS'
697 Arĕiŏs Pagŏs (1), *rock of Ares*

MARSENA
4826 Marçᵉnâ' (1), *Marsena*

MART
5505 çâchar (1), *profit from trade*

MARTHA
3136 Martha (12), *mistress, i.e. lady lord*

MARTYR
3144 martus (2), *witness*

MARTYRS
3144 martus (1), *witness*

MARVEL
8539 tâmahh (1), to *be astounded*

2296 thaumazō (9), to *wonder; to admire*
2298 thaumastŏs (1), *wonderful, marvelous*

MARVELLED
8539 tâmahh (2), to *be astounded*
2296 thaumazō (21), to *wonder; to admire*

MARVELLOUS
6381 pâlâ' (16), to *be, make great, wonderful*
6382 pele' (1), *miracle*
6395 pâlâh (1), to *distinguish*
2298 thaumastŏs (6), *wonderful, marvelous*

MARVELLOUSLY
6381 pâlâ' (2), to *be, make great, wonderful*
8539 tâmahh (1), to *be astounded*

MARVELS
6381 pâlâ' (1), to *be, make great, wonderful*

MARY
3137 Maria (54), *rebelliously*

MASCHIL
4905 maskîyl (13), *instructional* poem

MASH
4851 Mash (1), *Mash*

MASHAL
4913 Mâshâl (1), *request*

MASONS
1443 gâdar (2), to *build a* stone *wall*
2672 châtsab (3), to *cut* stone *or carve* wood

MASREKAH
4957 Masrêqâh (2), *vineyard*

MASSA
4854 Massâ' (2), *burden*

MASSAH
4532 Maççâh (4), *testing*

MAST
2260 chibbêl (1), ship's *mast*
8650 tôren (1), mast ship pole; flag-staff pole

MASTER
113 'âdôwn (75), *sovereign, i.e. controller*
729 'âraz (2), of *cedar*
1167 ba'al (3), *master; husband; owner; citizen*
5782 'ûwr (1), to *awake*
7227 rab (1), *great*
8269 sar (1), *head person, ruler*
1320 didaskalŏs (47), *instructor*
1988 ĕpistatēs (6), *commander*
2519 kathēgĕtēs (2), *teacher*
2942 kubĕrnētēs (1), *helmsman, captain*
2962 kuriŏs (1), *supreme, controller, Mr.*
3617 ŏikŏdĕspŏtēs (2), *head of a family*

M

4461 rhabbi (8), *my master*

MASTER'S
113 'âdôwn (22), *sovereign*, i.e. *controller*
1167 ba'al (1), *master; husband; owner; citizen*
1203 *děspŏtēs* (1), *absolute ruler*

MASTERBUILDER
753 *architĕktōn* (1), *architect, expert builder*

MASTERS
113 'âdôwn (5), *sovereign*, i.e. *controller*
1167 ba'al (1), *master; husband; owner; citizen*
1203 *děspŏtēs* (4), *absolute ruler*
1320 didaskalŏs (1), *instructor*
2519 kathēgētēs (1), *teacher*
2962 kuriŏs (8), *supreme, controller, Mr.*

MASTERS'
113 'âdôwn (1), *sovereign*, i.e. *controller*
2962 kuriŏs (1), *supreme, controller, Mr.*

MASTERY
1369 gᵉbûwrâh (1), *force; valor; victory*
6981 Qôwrê' (1), *crier*

MASTS
8650 tôren (1), mast ship *pole*; flag-staff *pole*

MATE
7468 rᵉ'ûwth (2), *female associate*

MATHUSALA
3103 Mathŏusala (1), *man of a dart*

MATRED
4308 Maṭrêd (2), *propulsive*

MATRI
4309 Maṭrîy (1), *rainy*

MATRIX
7358 rechem (5), *womb*

MATTAN
4977 Mattân (3), *present, gift*

MATTANAH
4980 Mattânâh (2), *present;* sacrificial *offering; bribe*

MATTANIAH
4983 Mattanyâh (16), *gift of Jehovah*

MATTATHA
3160 Mattatha (1), *gift of Jehovah*

MATTATHAH
4992 Mattattâh (1), *gift of Jehovah*

MATTATHIAS
3161 Mattathias (2), *gift of Jehovah*

MATTENAI
4982 Mattᵉnay (3), *liberal*

MATTER
1697 dâbâr (48), *word; matter; thing*
1836 dên (Ch.) (1), *this*
2659 châphêr (1), *to shame, reproach*
2941 ṭa'am (Ch.) (1), *sentence, command*
3602 kâkâh (1), *just so*
4405 millâh (1), *word; discourse; speech*
4406 millâh (Ch.) (4), *command, discourse*
6600 pithgâm (Ch.) (2), *decree; report*
1308 diaphěrō (1), *to bear, carry; to differ*
2596 kata (1), *down; according to*
3056 lŏgŏs (4), *word, matter, thing*
4229 pragma (3), *matter, deed, affair*
5208 hulē (1), *forest*, i.e. *wood fuel*

MATTERS
1419 gâdôwl (1), *great*
1697 dâbâr (15), *word; matter; thing*
4406 millâh (Ch.) (1), *word, command*

MATTHAN
3157 Matthan (2), *present, gift*

MATTHAT
3158 Matthat (2), *gift of Jehovah*

MATTHEW
3156 Matthaiŏs (5), *gift of Jehovah*

MATTHIAS
3159 Matthias (2), *gift of Jehovah*

MATTITHIAH
4993 Mattithyâh (8), *gift of Jehovah*

MATTOCK
4281 machărêshâh (1), *(poss.) pick-axe*
4576 ma'dêr (1), *hoe*

MATTOCKS
2719 chereb (1), *knife, sword*
4281 machărêshâh (1), *(poss.) pick-axe*

MAUL
4650 mêphîyts (1), *mallet-club*

MAW
6896 qêbâh (1), *paunch cavity; stomach*

MAY
194 'ûwlay (4), *if not; perhaps*
3201 yâkôl (11), *to be able*
1410 dunamai (9), *to be able or possible*
1832 ĕxěsti (1), *it is right, it is proper*
2481 isŏs (1), *perhaps*

MAYEST
3201 yâkôl (5), *to be able*
1410 dunamai (2), *to be able or possible*

1832 ĕxěsti (1), *it is right, it is proper*

MAZZAROTH
4216 Mazzârâh (1), *constellation*

ME-JARKON
4313 Mêy hay-Yarqôwn (1), *water of the yellowness*

MEADOW
260 'âchûw (2), *bulrush or any marshy grass*

MEADOWS
4629 ma'ăreh (1), *nude place*, i.e. a *common*

MEAH
3968 Mê'âh (2), *hundred*

MEAL
7058 qemach (9), *flour*
7058+5560 qemach (1), *flour*
224 alĕurŏn (2), *flour*

MEALTIME
6256+400 'êth (1), *time*

MEAN
120 'âdâm (3), *human being; mankind*
2823 châshôk (1), *obscure*
5704+3541 'ad (1), *as far (long) as; during*
767 asēmŏs (1), *ignoble*, i.e. *ordinary*
1498 ĕiēn (1), *might could, would*
2076 ĕsti (1), *he (she or it) is; they are*
2309+1511 thĕlō (1), *will; to desire; to choose*
3342 mĕtaxu (2), *betwixt; meanwhile*
4160 pŏiĕō (1), *to make*

MEANETH
1819 dâmâh (1), *to resemble, liken*
2076 ĕsti (2), *he (she or it) is; they are*
2309+1511 thĕlō (1), *will; to desire; to choose*

MEANING
998 bîynâh (1), *understanding*
1411 dunamis (1), *force, power, miracle*
3195 mĕllō (1), *to intend*, i.e. *be about to*

MEANS
1157 bᵉ'ad (1), *at, beside, among, behind, for*
3027 yâd (1), *hand; power*
4284 machăshâbâh (1), *contrivance; plan*
6903 qᵉbêl (Ch.) (1), *on account of, so as, since*
1096 ginŏmai (1), *to be, become*
3361 mē (1), *not; lest*
3364 ŏu mē (1), *not at all, absolutely not*
3843 pantŏs (2), *entirely; at all events*
4458 -pōs (9), *particle used in composition*
4459 pōs (2), *in what way?; how?; how much!*

5158 trŏpŏs (2), *deportment, character*

MEANT
2803 châshab (1), *to think, regard; to value*
1498 ĕiēn (2), *might could, would be*

MEARAH
4632 Mᵉ'ârâh (1), *cave*

MEASURE
374 'êyphâh (2), *dry grain measure*
520 'ammâh (1), *cubit*
2706 chôq (1), *appointment; allotment*
4055 mad (1), *vesture, garment; carpet*
4058 mâdad (7), *to measure*
4060 middâh (15), *measure; portion*
4884 mᵉsûwrâh (4), *liquid measure*
4941 mishpâṭ (2), *verdict; formal decree; justice*
4971 mathkôneth (1), *proportion*
5429 çᵉ'âh (3), *volume measure for grain*
5432 ça.çᵉ'âh (1), *moderation*
7991 shâlîysh (2), *three-fold measure*
8506 tôken (1), *fixed quantity*
280 amĕtrŏs (2), *immoderate*
3354 mĕtrĕō (3), *to admeasure*
3358 mĕtrŏn (13), *what is apportioned*
4053 pĕrissŏs (1), *superabundant*
4057 pĕrissŏs (1), *superabundantly*
5234 hupĕrballŏntōs (1), *to a greater degree*
5236 hupĕrbŏlē (2), *super-eminence*
5249 hupĕrpĕrissōs (1), *beyond all measure*
5518 chŏinix (1), *about a dry quart measure*

MEASURED
4058 mâdad (40), *to measure*
4128 mûwd (1), *to shake*
488 antimĕtrĕō (2), *to measure in return*
3354 mĕtrĕō (3), *to admeasure*

MEASURES
374 'êyphâh (2), *dry grain measure*
3734 kôr (8), *dry measure*
4055 mad (1), *vesture, garment; carpet*
4060 middâh (12), *measure; portion*
4461 mêmad (1), *measurement*
5429 çᵉ'âh (6), *volume measure for grain*
943 batŏs (1), *measure for liquids*
2884 kŏrŏs (1), *dry bushel measure*

4568 satŏn (2), *measure of about 12 dry quarts*
5518 chŏinix (1), *about a dry quart measure*

MEASURING
4060 middâh (10), *measure; portion*
3354 mĕtrĕŏ (1), to *admeasure*

MEAT
396 'ăkîylâh (1), *food*
398 'âkal (5), to *eat*
400 'ôkel (18), *food*
402 'oklâh (1), *food*
1262 bârâh (1), to *feed*
1267 bârûwth (1), *food*
1279 biryâh (3), *food*
2964 ţereph (3), *fresh torn prey*
3899 lechem (18), *food, bread*
3978 ma'ăkâl (22), *food, something to eat*
4202 mâzôwn (1), *food, provisions*
4203 mâzôwn (Ch.) (2), *food, provisions*
6595 path (1), *bit, morsel*
6598 pathbag (6), *dainty food*
6720 tsêydâh (1), *food, supplies*
1033 brōma (10), *food*
1034 brōsimŏs (1), *eatable*
1035 brōsis (7), *food; rusting corrosion*
4371 prŏsphagiŏn (1), *little fish*
4620 sitŏmĕtrŏn (1), *allowance or ration*
5132 trapĕza (1), *four-legged table*
5160 trŏphē (13), *nourishment; rations*
5315 phagō (3), *outer garment, i.e. a mantle*

MEATS
1033 brōma (6), *food*

MEBUNNAI
4012 Mᵉbunnay (1), *built up*

MECHERATHITE
4382 Mᵉkêrâthîy (1), *Mekerathite*

MEDAD
4312 Mêydâd (2), *affectionate*

MEDAN
4091 Mᵉdân (2), *contest or quarrel*

MEDDLE
1624 gârâh (4), to *provoke to anger*
6148 'ârab (2), to *intermix*

MEDDLED
1566 gâla' (1), to *be obstinate; to burst forth*

MEDDLETH
5674 'âbar (1), to *cross over; to transition*

MEDDLING
1566 gâla' (1), to *be obstinate; to burst forth*

MEDE
4075 Mâday (1), *Madian*

MEDEBA
4311 Mêydᵉbâ' (5), *water of quiet*

MEDES
4074 Mâday (9), *Madai*
4076 Mâday (Ch.) (4), *Madai*
3370 Mēdŏs (1), *inhabitant of Media*

MEDIA
4074 Mâday (6), *Madai*

MEDIAN
4077 Mâday (Ch.) (1), *Madian*

MEDIATOR
3316 mĕsitēs (6), *reconciler, intercessor*

MEDICINE
1456 gêhâh (1), *medicinal cure*
8644 tᵉrûwphâh (1), *remedy, healing*

MEDICINES
7499 rᵉphû'âh (2), *medicament, healing*

MEDITATE
1897 hâgâh (6), to *murmur, ponder*
7742 sûwach (1), to *muse pensively*
7878 sîyach (5), to *ponder, muse aloud*
3191 mĕlĕtaō (1), to *plot, think about*
4304 prŏmĕlĕtaō (1), to *premeditate*

MEDITATION
1900 hâgûwth (1), *musing, meditation*
1901 hâgîyg (1), *complaint, sighing*
1902 higgâyôwn (1), *musical notation*
7879 sîyach (1), uttered *contemplation*
7881 sîychâh (2), *reflection; devotion*

MEEK
6035 'ânâv (13), *needy; oppressed*
4235 pra¡ŏs (1), *gentle, i.e. humble*
4239 praüs (3), *mild, humble, gentle*

MEEKNESS
6037 'anvâh (1), *mildness; oppressed*
6038 'ănâvâh (1), *modesty, clemency*
4236 pra¡ŏtēs (9), *gentleness, humility*
4240 praütēs (3), *humility, meekness*

MEET
749 'ărak (Ch.) (1), to *suit*
1121 bên (1), *son, descendant; people*
3259 yâ'ad (8), to *meet; to summon; to direct*
3474 yâshar (1), to *be straight; to make right*
3476 yôsher (1), *right*
3477 yâshâr (1), *straight*

3559 kûwn (1), to *set up: establish, fix, prepare*
4672 mâtsâ' (2), to *find or acquire; to occur*
5828 'êzer (2), *aid*
6213 'âsâh (2), to *make*
6293 pâga' (5), to *impinge*
6298 pâgash (6), to *come in contact with*
6440 pânîym (3), *face; front*
6743 tsâlach (1), to *push forward*
7125 qîr'âh (70), to *encounter, to happen*
7136 qârâh (1), to *bring about; to impose*
7200 râ'âh (1), to *see*
514 axiŏs (4), *deserving, comparable or suitable*
528 apantaō (2), *encounter, meet*
529 apantēsis (4), *friendly encounter*
1163 dĕi (2), *it is (was) necessary*
1342 dikaiŏs (2), *equitable, holy*
2111 ĕuthĕtŏs (1), *appropriate, suitable*
2173 ĕuchrēstŏs (1), *useful, serviceable*
2425 hikanŏs (1), *ample; fit*
2427 hikanŏō (1), to *make competent*
2570 kalŏs (2), *good; beautiful; valuable*
4876 sunantaō (1), to *meet with; to occur*
4877 sunantēsis (1), *meeting with*
5222 hupantēsis (1), *encounter; concurrence*

MEETEST
3477 yâshâr (1), *straight*
6293 pâga' (1), to *impinge*

MEETETH
6293 pâga' (2), to *impinge*
6298 pâgash (1), to *come in contact with*

MEETING
6116 'ătsârâh (1), *assembly*
7125 qîr'âh (1), to *encounter, to happen*

MEGIDDO
4023 Mᵉgiddôwn (11), *rendezvous*

MEGIDDON
4023 Mᵉgiddôwn (1), *rendezvous*

MEHETABEEL
4105 Mᵉhêyţab'êl (1), *bettered of God*

MEHETABEL
4105 Mᵉhêyţab'êl (2), *bettered of God*

MEHIDA
4240 Mᵉchîydâ' (2), *junction*

MEHIR
4243 Mᵉchîyr (1), *price*

MEHOLATHITE
4259 Mᵉchôlâthîy (2), *Mecholathite*

MEHUJAEL
4232 Mᵉchûwyâ'êl (2), *smitten of God*

MEHUMAN
4104 Mᵉhûwmân (1), *Mehuman*

MEHUNIM
4586 Mᵉ'ûwnîy (1), *Menite*

MEHUNIMS
4586 Mᵉ'ûwnîy (1), *Menite*

MEKONAH
4368 Mᵉkônâh (1), *base*

MELATIAH
4424 Mᵉlaţyâh (1), *Jehovah has delivered*

MELCHI
3197 Mĕlchi (2), *king*

MELCHI-SHUA
4444 Malkîyshûwa' (2), *king of wealth*

MELCHIAH
4441 Malkîyâh (1), *appointed by Jehovah*

MELCHISEDEC
3198 Mĕlchisĕdĕk (9), *king of right*

MELCHIZEDEK
4442 Malkîy-Tsedeq (2), *king of right*

MELEA
3190 Mĕlĕas (1), *Meleas*

MELECH
4429 Melek (2), *king*

MELICU
4409 Mallûwk (1), *regnant*

MELITA
3194 Mĕlitē (1), *Melita*

MELODY
2172 zimrâh (2), *song*
5059 nâgan (1), to *play; to make music*
5567 psallō (1), to *play a stringed instrument*

MELONS
20 'ăbaţţîyach (1), *melon*

MELT
3988 mâ'aç (1), to *spurn; to disappear*
4127 mûwg (4), to *soften, flow down, disappear*
4529 mâçâh (1), to *dissolve, melt*
4549 mâçaç (6), to *waste; to faint*
5413 nâthak (2), to *pour out; to liquefy, melt*
6884 tsâraph (1), to *fuse metal; to refine*
3089 luŏ (1), to *loosen*
5080 tēkō (1), to *liquefy, melt*

MELTED
2046 hittûwk (1), *melting*
4127 mûwg (3), to *soften, flow down, disappear*
4549 mâçaç (6), to *waste; to faint fear or grief*
5140 nâzal (1), to *drip, or shed by trickling*
5413 nâthak (2), to *pour out; to liquefy, melt*

M

MELTETH
1811 dâlaph (1), to *drip*
4549 mâçaç (3), to *waste*; to *faint*
5258 nâçak (1), to *pour a libation*
6884 tsâraph (1), to *fuse metal*; to *refine*
8557 temeç (1), *melting disappearance*

MELTING
2003 hâmâç (1), dry *twig* or *brushwood*

MELZAR
4453 Meltsâr (2), court *officer* (poss.) *butler*

MEMBER
3196 mĕlŏs (5), *limb* or part of the body

MEMBERS
3338 yâtsûr (1), *structure, human frame*
3196 mĕlŏs (29), *limb* or part of the body

MEMORIAL
234 'azkârâh (7), *remembrance-offering*
2143 zêker (5), *recollection; commemoration*
2146 zikrôwn (17), *commemoration*
3422 mnēmŏsunŏn (3), *memorandum*

MEMORY
2143 zêker (5), *commemoration*

MEMPHIS
4644 Môph (1), *Moph*

MEMUCAN
4462 Mᵉmûwkân (3), *Memucan* or *Momucan*

MEN
120 'âdâm (107), *human being; mankind*
376 'îysh (211), *man; male; someone*
582 'ĕnôwsh (491), *man; person, human*
606 'ĕnâsh (Ch.) (12), *man*
1121 bên (16), *son, descendant; people*
1167 ba'al (20), *master; husband; owner; citizen*
1368 gibbôwr (1), *powerful; great warrior*
1397 geber (6), *person, man*
1400 gᵉbar (Ch.) (18), *person; someone*
2145 zâkâr (1), *male*
2388 châzaq (1), to *be strong; courageous*
4962 math (14), *men*
4974 mᵉthôm (1), *completely*
407 andrizŏmai (1), to *act manly*
435 anēr (79), *man; male*
442 anthrŏpinŏs (1), *human*
444 anthrŏpŏs (192), *human being; mankind*
730 arrhēn (3), *male*
3495 nĕaniskŏs (5), *youth*

MERAIAH
4811 Mᵉrâyâh (1), *rebellion*

MERAIOTH
4812 Mᵉrâyôwth (7), *rebellious*

MERARI
4847 Mᵉrârîy (39), *bitter*

MERARITES
4848 Mᵉrârîy (1), *Merarite*

MERATHAIM
4850 Mᵉrâthayim (1), *double bitterness*

MERCHANDISE
4267 machănaq (1), *choking, strangling*
4627 ma'ărâb (4), *mercantile goods*
4819 markôleth (1), *mart, market*
5504 çachar (4), *profit from trade*
5505 çâchar (2), *profit from trade*
5506 çᵉchôrâh (1), *traffic*
6014 'âmar (2), to *gather grain into sheaves*
7404 rᵉkullâh (2), *peddled trade*
1117 gŏmŏs (2), *cargo, wares* or *freight*
1711 ĕmpŏria (1), *traffic, business trade*
1712 ĕmpŏriŏn (1), *emporium* marketplace

MERCHANT
3667 Kᵉna'an (3), *humiliated*
5503 çâchar (4), to *travel round*; to *palpitate*
7402 râkal (3), to *travel for trading*
1713 ĕmpŏrŏs (1), *tradesman, merchant*

MERCHANTMEN
5503 çâchar (1), to *travel round*; to *palpitate*
8446 tûwr (1), to *wander, meander* for trade

MERCHANTS
3669 Kᵉna'ănîy (1), *Kenaanite; merchant*
5503 çâchar (9), to *travel round*; to *palpitate*
7402 râkal (14), to *travel for trading*
1713 ĕmpŏrŏs (4), *tradesman, merchant*

MERCHANTS'
5503 çâchar (1), to *travel round*; to *palpitate*

MERCIES
2617 cheçed (9), *kindness, favor*
7356 racham (25), *compassion; womb*
7359 rᵉchêm (Ch.) (1), *pity*
3628 ŏiktirmŏs (4), *pity, compassion*
3741 hŏsiŏs (1), *hallowed, pious, sacred*

MERCIES'
2617 cheçed (3), *kindness, favor*
7356 racham (1), *compassion; womb*

MERCIFUL
2551 chemlâh (1), *commiseration, pity*
2603 chânan (11), to *implore*
2616 châçad (2), to *reprove, shame*
2617 cheçed (5), *kindness, favor*
2623 châçîyd (3), *religiously pious, godly*
3722 kâphar (2), to *cover*; to *expiate*
7349 rachûwm (8), *compassionate*
7355 râcham (1), to *be compassionate*
1655 ĕlĕĕmŏn (2), *compassion*
2433 hilaskŏmai (1), to *conciliate*, to *atone for*
2436 hilĕŏs (1), God be *gracious!, far* be it!
3629 ŏiktirmŏn (2), *compassionate*

MERCURIUS
2060 Hērmēs (1), *born of god Hermes*

MERCY
2603 chânan (16), to *implore*
2604 chânan (Ch.) (1), to *favor*
2617 cheçed (137), *kindness, favor*
3727 kappôreth (27), *lid, cover*
7355 râcham (31), to *be compassionate*
7356 racham (4), *compassion; womb*
448 anilĕŏs (1), *inexorable, merciless*
1653 ĕlĕĕŏ (27), to *give out compassion*
1656 ĕlĕŏs (28), *compassion*
3628 ŏiktirmŏs (1), *pity, compassion*
3629 ŏiktirmŏn (1), *compassionate*

MERCYSEAT
2435 hilastēriŏn (1), *expiatory place*

MERED
4778 Mered (2), *rebellion*

MEREMOTH
4822 Mᵉrêmôwth (6), *heights*

MERES
4825 Mereç (1), *Meres*

MERIB-BAAL
4807 Mᵉrîyb Ba'al (3), *quarreller of Baal*
4810 Mᵉrîy Ba'al (1), *rebellion against Baal*

MERIBAH
4809 Mᵉrîybâh (6), *quarrel*

4753 stratĕuma (1), body of *troops*
5046 tĕlĕiŏs (1), *complete; mature*

MEN'S
120 'âdâm (10), *human being; mankind*
582 'ĕnôwsh (2), *man; person, human*
444 anthrŏpŏs (4), *human being; mankind*
4283 prŏĕuaggĕlizŏmai (1), to *announce glad news in advance*

MENAHEM
4505 Mᵉnachêm (8), *comforter*

MENAN
3104 Maïnan (1), *Maïnan*

MEND
2388 châzaq (1), to *fasten upon*; to *bind*

MENDING
2675 katartizŏ (2), to *repair*; to *prepare*

MENE
4484 menê' (Ch.) (2), *numbered*

MENPLEASERS
441 anthrŏparĕskŏs (2), *man-courting, fawning*

MENSERVANTS
5650 'ebed (9), *servant*
3816 pais (1), *child; slave* or *servant*

MENSTEALERS
405 andrapŏdistēs (1), *enslaver, kidnapper*

MENSTRUOUS
1739 dâveh (1), *menstrual; fainting*
5079 niddâh (2), time of menstrual *impurity*

MENTION
2142 zâkar (18), to *remember*; to *mention*
3417 mnĕia (4), *recollection; recital*
3421 mnēmŏnĕuŏ (1), to *exercise memory*

MENTIONED
935 bôw' (1), to *go, come*
2142 zâkar (3), to *remember*; to *mention*
5927 'âlâh (1), to *ascend, be high, mount*
7121 qârâ' (1), to *call out*
8052 shᵉmûw'âh (1), *announcement*

MEONENIM
6049 'ânan (1), to *cover, becloud*; to *act covertly*

MEONOTHAI
4587 Mᵉ'ôwnôthay (1), *habitative*

MEPHAATH
4158 Môwpha'ath (4), *illuminative*

MEPHIBOSHETH
4648 Mᵉphîybôsheth (15), *dispeller of Shame*

MERAB
4764 Mêrâb (3), *increase*

MERIBAH-KADESH
4809+6946 Mᵉrîybâh (1), quarrel

MERODACH
4781 Mᵉrôdâk (1), Merodak

MERODACH-BALADAN
4757 Mᵉrô'dak Bal'ădân (1), Merodak-Baladan

MEROM
4792 Mêrôwm (2), height

MERONOTHITE
4824 Mêrônôthîy (2), Meronothite

MEROZ
4789 Mêrôwz (1), Meroz

MERRILY
8056 sâmêach (1), blithe or gleeful

MERRY
1974 hillûwl (1), harvest celebration
2896 ṭôwb (7), good; well
3190 yâṭab (5), to be, make well
7832 sâchaq (2), to laugh; to scorn; to play
7937 shâkar (1), to become tipsy, to satiate
8055 sâmach (2), to be, make gleesome
8056 sâmêach (3), blithe or gleeful
2114 ĕuthumĕō (1), to be cheerful; keep courage
2165 ĕuphrainō (6), to rejoice, be glad

MERRYHEARTED
8056+3820 sâmêach (1), blithe or gleeful

MESECH
4902 Meshek (1), Meshek

MESHA
4331 Mêyshâ' (1), departure
4337 Mêyshâ' (1), safety
4338 Mêysha' (1), safety
4852 Mêshâ' (1), Mesha

MESHACH
4335 Mêyshak (1), Meshak
4336 Mêyshak (Ch.) (14), Meshak

MESHECH
4902 Meshek (8), Meshek

MESHELEMIAH
4920 Mᵉshelemyâh (4), ally of Jehovah

MESHEZABEEL
4898 Mᵉshêyzab'êl (3), delivered of God

MESHILLEMITH
4921 Mᵉshillêmîyth (1), reconciliation

MESHILLEMOTH
4919 Mᵉshillêmôwth (2), reconciliations

MESHOBAB
4877 Mᵉshôwbâb (1), returned

MESHULLAM
4918 Mᵉshullâm (25), allied

MESHULLEMETH
4922 Mᵉshullemeth (1), Meshullemeth

MESOBAITE
4677 Mᵉtsôbâyâh (1), found of Jehovah

MESOPOTAMIA
763 'Ăram Nahărayim (5), Aram of (the) two rivers
3318 Mĕsŏpŏtamia (2), between the Rivers

MESS
4864 mas'êth (2), raising; beacon; present

MESSAGE
1697 dâbâr (3), word; matter; thing
4400 mal'ăkûwth (1), message
31 aggĕlia (1), message
1860 ĕpaggĕlia (1), divine assurance
4242 prĕsbĕia (1), delegates

MESSENGER
1319 bâsar (1), to announce (good news)
4397 mal'âk (24), messenger
5046 nâgad (2), to announce
6680 tsâvâh (1), to constitute, enjoin
6735 tsîyr (1), hinge; herald or errand-doer
32 aggĕlŏs (4), messenger; angel
652 apŏstŏlŏs (1), commissioner of Christ

MESSENGERS
4397 mal'âk (74), messenger
6735 tsîyr (1), hinge; herald or errand-doer
32 aggĕlŏs (3), messenger; angel
652 apŏstŏlŏs (1), commissioner of Christ

MESSES
4864 mas'êth (1), raising; beacon; present

MESSIAH
4899 mâshîyach (2), consecrated; Messiah

MESSIAS
3323 Mĕssias (2), consecrated

MET
3259 yâ'ad (1), to meet; to summon; to direct
4672 mâtsâ' (3), to occur, meet or be present
6293 pâga' (4), to impinge
6298 pâgash (7), to come in contact with
6923 qâdam (2), to anticipate, meet
7122 qârâ' (2), to encounter, to happen
7125 qir'âh (3), to encounter, to happen
7135 qârâh (1), coolness, cold
7136 qârâh (4), to bring about; to impose

MESHULLEMETH
296 amphŏdŏn (1), fork in the road
528 apantaō (5), encounter, meet
3909 paratugchanō (1), to chance near
4820 sumballō (1), to aid; to join, attack
4876 sunantaō (4), to meet with; to occur
5221 hupantaō (5), to meet, encounter

METE
4058 mâdad (3), to measure
3354 mĕtrĕō (3), to admeasure

METED
6978 qav-qav (2), stalwart
8505 tâkan (1), to balance, i.e. measure

METEYARD
4060 middâh (1), measure; portion

METHEG-AMMAH
4965 Metheg hâ-'Ammâh (1), bit of the metropolis

METHUSAEL
4967 Mᵉthûwshâ'êl (2), man who (is) of God

METHUSELAH
4968 Mᵉthûwshelach (6), man of a dart

MEUNIM
4586 Mᵉ'ûwnîy (1), Menite

MEZAHAB
4314 Mêy Zâhâb (2), water of gold

MIAMIN
4326 Mîyâmîn (2), from (the) right hand

MIBHAR
4006 Mibchâr (1), select, i.e. best

MIBSAM
4017 Mibsâm (3), fragrant

MIBZAR
4014 Mibtsâr (2), fortification; defender

MICAH
4316 Mîykâ' (1), who (is) like Jehovah?
4318 Mîykâh (22), who (is) like Jehovah?
4319 Mîykâhûw (4), who (is) like Jehovah?
4320 Mîykâyâh (1), who (is) like Jehovah?

MICAH'S
4318 Mîykâh (3), who (is) like Jehovah?

MICAIAH
4318 Mîykâh (1), who (is) like Jehovah?
4319 Mîykâhûw (1), who (is) like Jehovah?
4321 Mîykâyᵉhûw (16), who (is) like Jehovah?

MICE
5909 'akbâr (4), mouse

MICHA
4316 Mîykâ' (4), who (is) like Jehovah?

MICHAEL
4317 Mîykâ'êl (13), who (is) like God?
3413 Michaêl (2), who (is) like God?

MICHAH
4318 Mîykâh (3), who (is) like Jehovah?

MICHAIAH
4320 Mîykâyâh (3), who (is) like Jehovah?
4321 Mîykâyᵉhûw (2), who (is) like Jehovah?
4322 Mîykâyâhûw (2), who (is) like Jehovah?

MICHAL
4324 Mîykâl (18), rivulet

MICHMAS
4363 Mikmâç (2), hidden

MICHMASH
4363 Mikmâç (9), hidden

MICHMETHAH
4366 Mikmᵉthâth (2), concealment

MICHRI
4381 Mikrîy (1), salesman

MICHTAM
4387 Miktâm (6), poem

MIDDAY
4276+3117 machătsîyth (1), halving or middle
6672 tsôhar (1), window; noon time
2250+3319 hēmĕra (1), day; period of time

MIDDIN
4081 Middîyn (1), contest or quarrel

MIDDLE
2677 chêtsîy (1), half or middle, midst
2872 ṭabbûwr (1), summit
8432 tâvek (6), center, middle
8484 tîykôwn (9), central, middle
3320 mᵉsŏtŏichŏn (1), partition wall

MIDDLEMOST
8484 tîykôwn (2), central, middle

MIDIAN
4080 Midyân (39), contest or quarrel

MIDIANITE
4084 Midyânîy (1), Midjanite

MIDIANITES
4080 Midyân (20), contest or quarrel
4084 Midyânîy (3), Midjanite
4092 Mᵉdânîy (1), Midjanite

MIDIANITISH
4084 Midyânîy (3), Midjanite

MIDNIGHT
2676+3915 châtsôwth (3),
middle of the night
2677+3915 chêtsîy (3),
half or *middle, midst*
8432+3915 tâvek (1),
center, middle
3317 mĕsŏnuktiŏn (4),
midnight watch
3319+3571 mĕsŏs (2),
middle

MIDST
1459 gav (Ch.) (10),
middle
2436 chêyq (1), *bosom,
heart*
2673 châtsâh (1), *to cut*
or *split* in two; *to halve*
2677 chêtsîy (8), *half* or
middle, midst
2686 châtsats (1), *to
curtail; to distribute*
2872 ṭabbûwr (1), *summit*
3820 lêb (12), *heart*
3824 lêbâb (1), *heart*
7130 qereb (73), *nearest
part*, i.e. *the center*
8432 tâvek (209), *center,
middle*
8484 tîykôwn (1), *central,
middle*
3319 mĕsŏs (41), *middle*
3321 mĕsŏuranĕma (3),
mid-sky, mid-heaven
3322 mĕsŏŏ (1), *to be at
midpoint*

MIDWIFE
3205 yâlad (3), *to bear
young; to father a child*

MIDWIVES
3205 yâlad (7), *to bear
young; to father a child*

MIGDAL-EL
4027 Migdal-'Êl (1),
tower of God

MIGDAL-GAD
4028 Migdal-Gâd (1),
tower of Fortune

MIGDOL
4024 Migdôwl (4), *tower*

MIGHT
202 'ôwn (2), *ability,
power; wealth*
410 'êl (1), *mighty*; the
Almighty
1369 gᵉbûwrâh (27),
force; valor; victory
1370 gᵉbûwrâh (Ch.) (2),
power, strength
2428 chayil (6), *army;
wealth; virtue; strength*
3201 yâkôl (2), *to be able*
3581 kôach (7), *force,
might; strength*
3966 mᵉ'ôd (2), *very,
utterly*
5797 'ôz (2), *strength*
5807 'ĕzûwz (1),
forcibleness
6108 'ôtsem (1), *power;
framework of the body*
8632 tᵉqôph (Ch.) (1),
power
1410 dunamai (6), *to be
able* or *possible*
1411 dunamis (4), *force,
power, miracle*

2479 ischus (2),
forcefulness, power
2480 ischuŏ (1), *to have*
or *exercise force*

MIGHTIER
117 'addîyr (1), *powerful;
majestic*
6099 'âtsûwm (7),
powerful; numerous
6105 'âtsam (1), *to be,
make powerful*
8623 taqqîyph (1),
powerful
2478 ischurŏs (3),
forcible, powerful

MIGHTIES
1368 gibbôwr (2),
powerful; great warrior

MIGHTIEST
1368 gibbôwr (1),
powerful; great warrior

MIGHTILY
2393 chezqâh (2),
prevailing power
3966 mᵉ'ôd (2), *very,
utterly*
1722+1411 ĕn (1), *in;
during; because of*
1722+2479 ĕn (1), *in;
during; because of*
2159 ĕutŏnŏs (1),
intensely, cogently
2596+2904 kata (1),
down; according to

MIGHTY
46 'âbîyr (6), *mighty*
47 'abbîyr (4), *mighty*
117 'addîyr (5), *powerful;
majestic*
193 'ûwl (1), *powerful;
mighty*
352 'ayil (2), *chief; ram;
oak* tree
376 'îysh (2), *man; male;
someone*
386 'êythân (4),
never-failing; eternal
410 'êl (5), *mighty*; the
Almighty
430 'ĕlôhîym (2), the true
God; great ones
533 'ammîyts (1), *strong;
mighty; brave*
650 'âphîyq (1), *valley;
stream; mighty, strong*
1121+410 bên (1), *son,
descendant; people*
1219 bâtsar (1), *to be
inaccessible*
1368 gibbôwr (135),
powerful; great warrior
1369 gᵉbûwrâh (7), *force;
valor; victory*
1396 gâbar (1), *to be
strong; to prevail*
1397 geber (2), *person,
man*
1401 gibbâr (Ch.) (1),
valiant man, or *warrior*
1419 gâdôwl (7), *great*
2220 zᵉrôwa' (1), *arm;
foreleg; force, power*
2388 châzaq (2), *to be
strong; courageous*
2389 châzâq (20), *strong;
severe, hard, violent*

2428 chayil (1), *army;
wealth; virtue; strength*
3524 kabbîyr (5), *mighty;
aged; mighty*
3966 mᵉ'ôd (1), *very,
utterly*
5794 'az (3), *strong,
vehement, harsh*
5797 'ôz (1), *strength*
5868 'ăyâm (1), (poss.)
strength
6099 'âtsûwm (8),
powerful; numerous
6105 'âtsam (4), *to be,
make powerful*
6184 'ârîyts (1), *powerful*
or *tyrannical*
6697 tsûwr (2), *rock*
7227 rab (5), *great*
7989 shallîyṭ (1), *prince*
or *warrior*
8624 taqqîyph (Ch.) (2),
powerful
972 biaiŏs (1), *violent*
1411 dunamis (14), *force,
power, miracle*
1413 dunastēs (1), *ruler*
or *officer*
1414 dunatĕŏ (1), *to be
efficient, able, strong*
1415 dunatŏs (7),
powerful or *capable*
1754 ĕnĕrgĕŏ (1), *to be
active, efficient, work*
2478 ischurŏs (7),
forcible, powerful
2479 ischus (1),
forcefulness, power
2900 krataiŏs (1),
powerful, mighty
3168 mĕgalĕiŏtēs (1),
grandeur or *splendor*
3173 mĕgas (1), *great,
many*
5082 tēlikŏutŏs (1), *so
vast*

MIGRON
4051 Migrôwn (2),
precipice

MIJAMIN
4326 Mîyâmîn (2), *from
(the) right hand*

MIKLOTH
4732 Miqlôwth (4), *rods*

MIKNEIAH
4737 Miqnêyâhûw (2),
possession of Jehovah

MILALAI
4450 Mîlălay (1),
talkative

MILCAH
4435 Milkâh (11), *queen*

MILCH
3243 yânaq (1), *to suck;
to give milk*
5763 'ûwl (2), *to suckle*,
i.e. *give milk*

MILCOM
4445 Malkâm (3),
Malcam or *Milcom*

MILDEW
3420 yêrâqôwn (5),
paleness; mildew

MILE
3400 miliŏn (1), *about
4,850 feet, Roman mile*

MILETUM
3399 Milētŏs (1), *Miletus*

MILETUS
3399 Milētŏs (2), *Miletus*

MILK
2461 châlâb (42), *milk*
4711 mâtsats (1), *to suck*
1051 gala (5), *milk*

MILL
7347 rêcheh (1),
mill-stone
3459 mulôn (1),
mill-house

MILLET
1764 dôchan (1), *millet
cereal grain*

MILLIONS
7233 rᵉbâbâh (1), *myriad
number*

MILLO
4407 millôw' (10), *citadel*

MILLS
7347 rêcheh (1),
mill-stone

MILLSTONE
7347 rêcheh (1),
mill-stone
7393 rekeb (2), *upper
millstone*
3037+3457 lithŏs (1),
stone
3458 mulŏs (2), *grinder
millstone*
3458+3684 mulŏs (2),
grinder millstone

MILLSTONES
7347 rêcheh (2),
mill-stone

MINCING
2952 ṭâphaph (1), *to trip*
or *step*

MIND
3336 yêtser (1), *form*
3820 lêb (12), *heart*
3824 lêbâb (4), *heart*
5315 nephesh (11), *life;
breath; soul; wind*
5973 'îm (1), *with*
6310 peh (1), *mouth;
opening*
7307 rûwach (6), *breath;
wind; life-spirit*
363 anamimnēskŏ (1), *to
remind; to recollect*
1106 gnŏmē (2),
cognition, opinion
1271 dianŏia (7), *mind*
or *thought*
1771 ĕnnŏia (1), *moral
understanding*
1878 ĕpanamimnēskŏ
(1), *to remind again of*
3563 nŏus (15), *intellect,
mind; understanding*
3661 hŏmŏthumadŏn (1),
unanimously
3675 hŏmŏphrŏn (1),
like-minded
4288 prŏthumia (4),
alacrity, eagerness
4290 prŏthumŏs (1), *with
alacrity, with eagerness*
4993 sŏphrŏnĕŏ (2), *to be
in a right state of mind*

4995 sōphrŏnismŏs (1), self-discipline
5012 tapĕinŏphrŏsunē (1), modesty, humility
5279 hupŏmimnĕskō (1), to suggest to memory
5426 phrŏnĕō (9), to be mentally disposed
5427 phrŏnēma (2), inclination or purpose
5590 psuchē (1), soul, vitality; heart, mind

MINDED
5973+3820 'îm (1), with
1011 bŏulĕuō (1), to deliberate; to resolve
1014 bŏulŏmai (3), to be willing, desire
1374 dipsuchŏs (2), vacillating
4993 sōphrŏnĕō (1), to be in a right state of mind
5426 phrŏnĕō (3), to be mentally disposed
5427 phrŏnēma (2), mental inclination

MINDFUL
2142 zâkar (6), to remember; to mention
3403 mimnĕskō (3), to remind or to recall
3421 mnēmŏnĕuō (1), to exercise memory

MINDING
3195 mĕllō (1), to intend, i.e. be about to

MINDS
5315 nephesh (4), life; breath; soul; wind
1271 dianŏia (2), mind or thought
3540 nŏēma (4), perception, i.e. purpose
3563 nŏus (2), intellect, mind; understanding
5590 psuchē (2), soul, vitality; heart, mind

MINGLE
4537 mâçak (1), to mix
6151 'ărab (Ch.) (1), to co-mingle, mix

MINGLED
1101 bâlal (37), to mix; confuse; to feed
3610 kil'ayim (2), two different kinds of thing
3947 lâqach (1), to take
4537 mâçak (4), to mix
6148 'ârab (2), to intermix
6154 'êreb (4), mixed or woven things
3396 mignumi (4), to mix, mingle

MINIAMIN
4509 Minyâmîyn (3), from (the) right hand

MINISH
1639 gâra' (1), to shave, remove, lessen

MINISHED
4591 mâ'aṭ (1), to be, make small or few

MINISTER
1777 dîyn (1), to judge; to strive or contend for

8334 shârath (50), to attend as a menial
8335 shârêth (1), service
1247 diakŏnĕō (8), to act as a deacon
1248 diakŏnia (1), attendance, aid, service
1249 diakŏnŏs (14), waiter; deacon (-ess)
1325 didōmi (1), to give
2038 ĕrgazŏmai (1), to toil
3008 lĕitŏurgĕō (1), to perform religious or charitable functions
3011 lĕitŏurgŏs (2), functionary in the Temple or Gospel
3930 parĕchō (1), to hold near, i.e. to present
5256 hupĕrĕtĕō (1), to be a subordinate
5257 hupĕrĕtēs (3), servant, attendant
5524 chŏrēgĕō (1), to furnish, supply, provide

MINISTERED
8120 shᵉmash (Ch.) (1), to serve
8334 shârath (15), to attend as a menial
1247 diakŏnĕō (14), to wait upon, serve
2023 ĕpichŏrēgĕō (2), to fully supply; to aid
3008 lĕitŏurgĕō (1), to perform religious or charitable functions
3011 lĕitŏurgŏs (1), functionary in the Temple or Gospel
5256 hupĕrĕtĕō (1), to be a subordinate

MINISTERETH
2023 ĕpichŏrēgĕō (2), to fully supply; to aid

MINISTERING
5656 'ăbôdâh (1), work of any kind
8334 shârath (1), to attend as a menial
1247 diakŏnĕō (1), to wait upon, serve
1248 diakŏnia (3), attendance, aid, service
2418 hiĕrŏurgĕō (1), officiate as a priest
3008 lĕitŏurgĕō (1), to perform religious or charitable functions
3010 lĕitŏurgikŏs (1), engaged in holy service

MINISTERS
6399 pᵉlach (Ch.) (1), to serve or worship
8334 shârath (15), to attend as a menial
1249 diakŏnŏs (6), attendant, deacon
3011 lĕitŏurgŏs (2), functionary in the Temple or Gospel
5257 hupĕrĕtēs (2), servant, attendant

MINISTRATION
1248 diakŏnia (6), attendance, aid, service

3009 lĕitŏurgia (1), service, ministry

MINISTRY
3027 yâd (2), hand; power
5656 'ăbôdâh (1), work
8335 shârêth (1), service in the Temple
1248 diakŏnia (16), attendance, aid, service
3009 lĕitŏurgia (2), service, ministry

MINNI
4508 Minnîy (1), Minni

MINNITH
4511 Minnîyth (2), enumeration

MINSTREL
5059 nâgan (2), to play; to make music

MINSTRELS
834 aulētēs (1), flute-player

MINT
2238 hĕduŏsmŏn (2), sweet-scented, mint

MIPHKAD
4663 Miphqâd (1), assignment

MIRACLE
4159 môwphêth (1), miracle; token or omen
1411 dunamis (1), force, power, miracle
4592 sēmĕiŏn (7), indication, sign, signal

MIRACLES
226 'ôwth (2), signal, sign
4159 môwphêth (1), miracle; token or omen
6381 pâlâ' (1), to be, make great, wonderful
1411 dunamis (8), force, power, miracle
4592 sēmĕiŏn (15), indication, sign, signal

MIRE
1206 bôts (1), mud
1207 bitstsâh (1), swamp, marsh
2563 chômer (2), clay; dry measure
2916 ṭîyṭ (8), mud or clay
3121 yâvên (1), mud, sediment
7516 rephesh (1), mud of the sea
1004 bŏrbŏrŏs (1), mud

MIRIAM
4813 Miryâm (15), rebelliously

MIRMA
4821 Mirmâh (1), fraud

MIRTH
4885 mâsôws (3), delight
7797 sûws (1), to be bright, i.e. cheerful
8057 simchâh (8), blithesomeness or glee
8342 sâsôwn (3), cheerfulness; welcome

MIRY
1207 bitstsâh (1), swamp, marsh

2917 ṭîyn (Ch.) (2), wet clay
3121 yâvên (1), mud, sediment

MISCARRYING
7921 shâkôl (1), to miscarry

MISCHIEF
205 'âven (4), trouble, vanity, wickedness
611 'âçôwn (5), hurt, injury
1943 hôvâh (2), ruin, disaster
2154 zimmâh (3), bad plan
4827 mêra' (1), wickedness
5771 'âvôn (1), moral evil
5999 'âmâl (9), wearing effort; worry
7451 ra' (19), bad; evil
7489 râ'a' (1), to be good for nothing
4468 rhaₑdiŏurgia (1), malignity, trickery

MISCHIEFS
1942 havvâh (1), desire; craving
7451 ra' (2), bad; evil

MISCHIEVOUS
1942 havvâh (2), desire; craving
4209 mᵉzimmâh (2), plan; sagacity
7451 ra' (1), bad; evil

MISERABLE
5999 'âmâl (1), wearing effort; worry
1652 ĕlĕĕinŏs (2), worthy of mercy

MISERABLY
2560 kakŏs (1), badly; wrongly; ill

MISERIES
4788 mârûwd (1), outcast; destitution
5004 talaipōria (1), calamity, distress

MISERY
4788 mârûwd (1), outcast; destitution
5999 'âmâl (3), wearing effort; worry
6001 'âmêl (1), toiling; laborer; sorrowful
7451 ra' (1), bad; evil
5004 talaipōria (1), calamity, distress

MISGAB
4869 misgâb (1), high refuge

MISHAEL
4332 Mîyshâ'êl (8), who (is) what God (is)?

MISHAL
4861 Mish'âl (1), request

MISHAM
4936 Mish'âm (1), inspection

MISHEAL
4861 Mish'âl (1), request

MISHMA
4927 Mishmâ' (4), report

M

MISHMANNAH
4925 Mishmannâh (1), *fatness*

MISHRAITES
4954 Mishrâ'îy (1), *extension*

MISPERETH
4559 Miçpereth (1), *enumeration*

MISREPHOTH-MAIM
4956 Misr^{e}phôwth Mayim (2), *burnings of water*

MISS
2398 châṭâ' (1), to *sin*
6485 pâqad (1), to *visit, care for, count*

MISSED
6485 pâqad (3), to *visit, care for, count*

MISSING
6485 pâqad (2), to *visit, care for, count*

MIST
108 'êd (1), *fog*
887 *achlus* (1), *dimness* of sight, i.e. *cataract*
2217 *zŏphŏs* (1), *gloom*

MISTRESS
1172 ba'ălâh (2), *mistress; female owner*
1404 g^{e}bereth (7), *mistress, noblewoman*

MISUSED
8591 tâ'a' (1), to *cheat;* to *maltreat*

MITE
3016 *lĕptŏn* (1), small *coin*

MITES
3016 *lĕptŏn* (2), small *coin*

MITHCAH
4989 Mithqâh (2), *sweetness*

MITHNITE
4981 Mithnîy (1), *slenderness*

MITHREDATH
4990 Mithr^{e}dâth (2), *Mithredath*

MITRE
4701 mitsnepheth (11), royal/priestly *turban*
6797 tsânîyph (2), *head-dress, turban*

MITYLENE
3412 *Mitulēnē* (1), *abounding in shell-fish*

MIXED
1101 bâlal (1), to *mix; confuse;* to *feed*
4107 mâhal (1), to *dilute* a mixture
4469 mamçâk (1), *mixed*-wine
6151 'ărab (Ch.) (3), to *co-mingle, mix*
6154 'êreb (2), *mixed* or *woven* things
4786 *sugkĕrannumi* (1), to *combine; assimilate*

MIXTURE
4538 meçek (1), wine *mixture* with spices
194 *akratŏs* (1), *undiluted*
3395 *migma* (1), *compound, mixture*

MIZAR
4706 Mits'âr (1), *little*

MIZPAH
4708 Mitspeh (5), *observatory*
4709 Mitspah (18), *observatory*

MIZPAR
4558 Miçpâr (1), *number*

MIZPEH
4708 Mitspeh (9), *observatory*
4709 Mitspah (14), *observatory*

MIZRAIM
4714 Mitsrayim (4), double *border*

MIZZAH
4199 Mizzâh (3), *terror*

MNASON
3416 *Mnasōn* (1), *Mnason*

MOAB
4124 Môw'âb (165), *from* mother's *father*
4125 Môw'âbîy (2), *Moäbite* or *Moäbitess*

MOABITE
4125 Môw'âbîy (3), *Moäbite* or *Moäbitess*

MOABITES
4124 Môw'âb (16), *from* mother's *father*
4125 Môw'âbîy (3), *Moäbite* or *Moäbitess*

MOABITESS
4125 Môw'âbîy (6), *Moäbite* or *Moäbitess*

MOABITISH
4125 Môw'âbîy (1), *Moäbite* or *Moäbitess*

MOADIAH
4153 Môw'adyâh (1), *assembly of Jehovah*

MOCK
2048 hâthal (1), to *deride, mock*
3887 lûwts (1), to *scoff;* to *interpret;* to *intercede*
3932 lâ'ag (2), to *deride;* to *speak unintelligibly*
5953 'âlal (1), to *glean;* to *overdo*
6711 tsâchaq (2), to *scorn;* to make *sport* of
7046 qâlaç (1), to *disparage*, i.e. *ridicule*
7832 sâchaq (1), to *laugh;* to *scorn;* to *play*
1702 *ĕmpaizō* (3), *deride, ridicule*

MOCKED
2048 hâthal (4), to *deride, mock*
3931 lâ'ab (1), to *deride, mock*
3932 lâ'ag (2), to *deride;* to *speak unintelligibly*
5953 'âlal (1), to *glean;* to *overdo*
6711 tsâchaq (1), to *scorn;* to make *sport* of
7046 qâlaç (1), to *disparage*, i.e. *ridicule*
7832 sâchaq (1), to *laugh;* to *scorn;* to *play*
1702 *ĕmpaizō* (8), *deride, ridicule*
3456 *muktērizō* (1), to *ridicule*
5512 *chlĕuazō* (1), *jeer* at, *sneer* at

MOCKER
3887 lûwts (1), to *scoff;* to *interpret;* to *intercede*

MOCKERS
2049 hâthôl (1), *derision, mockery*
3887 lûwts (1), to *scoff;* to *interpret;* to *intercede*
3934 lâ'êg (1), *buffoon; foreigner*
7832 sâchaq (1), to *laugh;* to *scorn;* to *play*
1703 *ĕmpaiktēs* (1), *derider; false teacher*

MOCKEST
3932 lâ'ag (1), to *deride;* to *speak unintelligibly*

MOCKETH
2048 hâthal (1), to *deride, mock*
3932 lâ'ag (3), to *deride;* to *speak unintelligibly*
7832 sâchaq (1), to *laugh;* to *scorn;* to *play*

MOCKING
6711 tsâchaq (1), to *scorn;* to make *sport* of
7048 qallâçâh (1), *ridicule*
1702 *ĕmpaizō* (2), to *deride, ridicule*
5512 *chlĕuazō* (1), *jeer* at, *sneer* at

MOCKINGS
1701 *ĕmpaigmŏs* (1), *derision, jeering*

MODERATELY
6666 ts^{e}dâqâh (1), *rightness*

MODERATION
1933 *ĕpiĕikēs* (1), *mild, gentle*

MODEST
2887 *kŏsmiŏs* (1), *orderly*

MOIST
3892 lach (1), *fresh* cut, i.e. unused or undried

MOISTENED
8248 shâqâh (1), to *quaff*, i.e. to *irrigate*

MOISTURE
3955 l^{e}shad (1), *juice; vigor;* sweet or fat *cake*
2429 *hikmas* (1), *dampness, dampness*

MOLADAH
4137 Môwlâdâh (4), *birth*

MOLE
8580 tanshemeth (1), (poss.) *tree-toad*

MOLECH
4432 Môlek (8), *king*

MOLES
2661 chăphôr (1), *hole*, i.e. a *burrowing rat*

MOLID
4140 Môwlîyd (1), *genitor*

MOLLIFIED
7401 râkak (1), to *soften*

MOLOCH
4432 Môlek (1), *king*
3434 *Mŏlŏch* (1), *king*

MOLTEN
3332 yâtsaq (6), to *pour* out
4541 maççêkâh (25), *cast* image); *libation*
4549 mâçaç (1), to *waste;* to *faint*
5258 nâçak (1), to *pour* a libation
5262 neçek (4), *libation; cast idol*
5413 nâthak (1), to *flow* forth, *pour* out
6694 tsûwq (1), to *pour* out; *melt*

MOMENT
7281 rega' (19), very *short space* of time
823 *atŏmŏs* (1), *indivisible* unit of time
3901 *pararrhuĕō* (1), to *flow by*
4743 *stigmē* (1), *point* of time, i.e. an *instant*

MONEY
3701 keçeph (112), *silver money*
3702 k^{e}çaph (Ch.) (1), *silver money*
7192 q^{e}sîyṭah (2), *coin* of unknown weight
694 *arguriŏn* (11), *silver; silver money*
2772 *kĕrma* (1), *coin*
2773 *kĕrmatistēs* (1), *money-broker*
3546 *nŏmisma* (1), *coin*
4715 *statēr* (1), *coin worth four day's wage*
5365 *philarguria* (1), *avarice*
5475 *chalkŏs* (2), *copper*
5536 *chrēma* (4), *wealth, price*

MONEYCHANGERS
2855 *kŏllubistēs* (2), *coin-dealer*

MONSTERS
8577 tannîyn (1), *sea-serpent; jackal*

MONTH
2320 chôdesh (215), *new moon; month*
3391 yerach (6), *lunar* month
3393 y^{e}rach (Ch.) (1), *lunar* month
3376 *mēn* (4), *month; month's* time

MONTHLY
2320 chôdesh (1), *new moon; month*

MONTHS
2320 chôdesh (37), *new moon; month*
3391 yerach (5), *lunar month*
3393 yᵉrach (Ch.) (1), *lunar* month
3376 mên (14), *month; month's time*
5072 tĕtramĕnŏn (1), *four months' time*
5150 trimĕnŏn (1), *three months' space*

MONUMENTS
5341 nâtsar (1), to *guard, protect, maintain*

MOON
2320 chôdesh (9), *new moon; month*
3391 yerach (2), *lunar month*
3394 yârêach (26), *moon*
3842 lᵉbânâh (3), *white moon*
3561 nŏumĕnia (1), *festival of new moon*
4582 sĕlēnē (9), *moon*

MOONS
2320 chôdesh (11), *new moon; month*

MORASTHITE
4183 Mowrashtîy (2), *Morashtite*

MORDECAI
4782 Mordᵉkay (58), *Mordecai*

MORDECAI'S
4782 Mordᵉkay (2), *Mordecai*

MORE
637 'aph (1), *also or yea; though*
1058 bâkâh (1), to *weep, moan*
1490 gizbâr (Ch.) (3), *treasurer*
1980 hâlak (1), to *walk; live a certain way*
2351 chûwts (1), *outside, outdoors; open market; countryside*
3148 yôwthêr (3), *moreover; rest; gain*
3254 yâçaph (59), to *add or augment*
3499 yether (1), *remainder; small rope*
3513 kâbad (1), to *be heavy, severe, dull*
3651 kên (2), *just; right, correct*
4480 min (4), *from, out of*
4481 min (Ch.) (1), *from or out of*
5674 'âbar (1), to *cross over; to transition*
5720 'Âdîyn (1), *voluptuous*
5736 'âdaph (1), to *be redundant, have surplus*
5750 'ôwd (196), *again; repeatedly; still; more*
5922 'al (Ch.) (1), *above, over, upon, or against*
5973 'îm (1), *with*

6105 'âtsam (2), to *be, make numerous*
6440 pânîym (1), *face; front*
7138 qârôwb (1), *near, close*
7227 rab (14), *great*
7230 rôb (1), *abundance*
7231 râbab (2), to *increase*
7235 râbâh (11), to *increase*
7608 sha'ărâh (1), *female kindred by blood*
7725 shûwb (1), to *turn back; to return*
8145 shênîy (3), *second; again*
197 akribĕstĕrŏn (4), *more exactly*
243 allŏs (1), *different, other*
316 anagkaiŏs (1), *necessary*
414 anĕktŏtĕrŏs (6), *more bearable*
1065 gĕ (1), *particle of emphasis*
1308 diaphĕrō (2), to *differ; to surpass*
1508 ĕi mē (1), *if not*
1617 ĕktĕnĕstĕrŏn (1), *more intently*
1833 ĕxĕtazō (1), to *ascertain or interrogate*
2001 ĕpischuō (7), to *insist stoutly*
2089 ĕti (39), *yet, still*
2115 ĕuthumŏs (1), *cheerful, encouraged*
3122 malista (1), *in the greatest degree*
3123 mallŏn (47), *in a greater degree*
3185 mĕizŏn (1), *in greater degree*
3187 mĕizōn (1), *larger, greater*
3370 Mēdŏs (3), *inhabitant of Media*
3745 hŏsŏs (1), *as much as*
3761 ŏudĕ (1), *neither, nor, not even*
3765 ŏukĕti (17), *not yet, no longer*
3844 para (2), *from; with; besides; on account of*
4053 pĕrissŏs (2), *superabundant*
4054 pĕrissŏtĕrŏn (1), *more superabundant*
4055 pĕrissŏtĕrŏs (10), *more superabundant*
4056 pĕrissŏtĕrŏs (10), *more superabundantly*
4057 pĕrissŏs (1), *superabundantly*
4065 pĕriphrŏnĕō (1), to *depreciate, contemn*
4119 plĕiōn (25), *more*
4179 pŏllaplasiōn (1), *very much more*
4325 prŏsdapanaō (1), to *expend additionally*
4369 prŏstithēmi (1), to *lay beside, repeat*
4707 spŏudaiŏtĕrŏs (2), *more prompt*

5112 tŏlmĕrŏtĕrŏn (1), *more daringly*
5228 hupĕr (4), *over; above; beyond*
5245 hupĕrnikaō (1), to *gain* a decisive *victory*

MOREH
4176 Môwreh (3), *archer; teaching; early rain*

MOREOVER
518 'îm (1), *whether?; if, although; Oh that!*
637 'aph (2), *also or yea; though*
1571 gam (25), *also; even; yea; though*
3148 yôwthêr (1), *moreover; rest; gain*
3254 yâçaph (1), to *add or augment*
5750 'ôwd (6), *again; repeatedly; still; more*
1161 dĕ (12), *but, yet; and then*
2089 ĕti (1), *yet, still*
2532 kai (1), *and; or; even; also*

MORESHETH-GATH
4182 Môwresheth Gath (1), *possession of Gath*

MORIAH
4179 Môwrîyâh (2), *seen of Jehovah*

MORNING
216 'ôwr (1), *luminary; lightning; happiness*
1242 bôqer (187), *morning*
4891 mishchâr (1), *dawn*
5053 nôgahh (Ch.) (1), *dawn*
6843 tsᵉphîyrâh (2), *mishap*
7836 shâchar (1), to *search for*
7837 shachar (12), *dawn*
7904 shâkâh (1), to *roam because of lust*
7925 shâkam (1), to *start early in the morning*
3720 ŏrthrinŏs (1), *matutinal, i.e. early*
4404 prŏï (6), *at dawn; day-break* watch
4405 prŏïa (3), *day-dawn, early morn*
4407 prŏïnŏs (1), *matutinal, i.e. early*

MORROW
1242 bôqer (7), *morning*
4279 mâchar (45), *tomorrow; hereafter*
4283 mochŏrâth (28), *tomorrow, next day*
839 auriŏn (14), *to-morrow*
1836 hĕxēs (1), *successive, next*
1887 ĕpauriŏn (8), *to-morrow*

MORSEL
3603 kikkâr (1), *round loaf; talent*
6595 path (8), *bit, morsel*
1035 brōsis (1), *food; rusting corrosion*

MORSELS
6595 path (1), *bit, morsel*

MORTAL
582 'ĕnôwsh (1), *man; person, human*
2349 thnētŏs (5), *liable to die, i.e. mortal*

MORTALITY
2349 thnētŏs (1), *liable to die, i.e. mortal*

MORTALLY
5315 nephesh (1), *life; breath; soul; wind*

MORTAR
4085 mᵉdôkâh (1), *mortar for bricks*
4388 maktêsh (1), *mortar; socket*

MORTER
2563 chômer (4), *clay; dry measure*
6083 'âphâr (2), *dust, earth, mud; clay,*

MORTGAGED
6148 'ârab (1), to *intermix; to give or be security*

MORTIFY
2289 thanatŏō (1), to *kill*
3499 nĕkrŏō (1), to *deaden, i.e. to subdue*

MOSERA
4149 Môwçêrâh (1), *corrections*

MOSEROTH
4149 Môwçêrâh (2), *corrections*

MOSES
4872 Môsheh (749), *drawing out of the water*
4873 Môsheh (Ch.) (1), *drawing out of the water*
3475 Mōsĕus (77), *drawing out of the water*

MOSES'
4872 Môsheh (16), *drawing out of the water*
3475 Mōsĕus (3), *drawing out of the water*

MOST
2429 chayil (Ch.) (1), *army; strength*
2896 ţôwb (1), *good; well*
3524 kabbîyr (1), *mighty; aged; mighty*
3800 kethem (1), *pure gold*
4581 mâ'ôwz (1), *fortified place; defense*
4971 mathkôneth (1), *proportion*
5920 'al (2), *the Highest God*
5943 'illay (Ch.) (9), *the supreme God*
5945 'elyôwn (25), *loftier, higher; Supreme God*
5946 'elyôwn (Ch.) (3), *the Supreme God*

M

6579 partam (1), *grandee, noble*
6944 qôdesh (48), *sacred place or thing*
7230 rôb (1), *abundance*
8077 sheʹmâmâh (1), *devastation*
8563 tamrûwr (1), *bitterness*
40 hagiŏs (1), *sacred, holy*
2236 hēdista (1), *with great pleasure*
2903 kratistŏs (4), *very honorable*
3122 malista (1), *in the greatest degree*
4118 plěistŏs (1), *very large, i.e. the most*
4119 plěiŏn (3), *more*
5310 hupsistŏs (5), *highest; the Supreme God*

MOTE
2595 karphŏs (6), *dry twig or straw*

MOTH
6211 'âsh (7), *moth*
4597 sēs (3), *moth* insect

MOTHEATEN
4598 sētŏbrōtŏs (1), *moth-eaten*

MOTHER
517 'êm (143), *mother*
2545 chămôwth (11), *mother-in-law*
2859 châthan (1), *to become related by marriage,*
282 amētōr (1), *of unknown maternity*
3384 mētēr (76), *mother*
3994 pěnthěra (6), *wife's mother*

MOTHER'S
517 'êm (67), *mother*
3384 mētēr (7), *mother*

MOTHERS
517 'êm (3), *mother*
3384 mētēr (2), *mother*
3389 mētralō₁as (1), *matricide*

MOTHERS'
517 'êm (1), *mother*

MOTIONS
3804 pathēma (1), *passion; suffering*

MOULDY
5350 niqqud (2), *crumb, morsel; biscuit*

MOUNT
55 'âbak (1), *to coil upward*
1361 gâbahh (1), *to be lofty; to be haughty*
2022 har (222), *mountain or range of hills*
2042 hârâr (1), *mountain*
4674 mutstsâb (1), *station, military post*
5550 çôlʹlâh (5), *military siege mound, rampart*
5927 'âlah (4), *to ascend, be high, mount*
7311 rûwm (1), *to be high; to rise or raise*

3735 ŏrŏs (21), *hill, mountain*

MOUNTAIN
2022 har (104), *mountain or range of hills*
2042 hârâr (2), *mountain*
2906 ṭûwr (Ch.) (2), *rock or hill*
3735 ŏrŏs (28), *hill, mountain*

MOUNTAINS
2022 har (155), *mountain or range of hills*
2042 hârâr (8), *mountain*
3735 ŏrŏs (13), *hill, mountain*

MOUNTED
7426 râmam (1), *to rise*

MOUNTING
4608 ma'ăleh (1), *elevation; platform*

MOUNTS
5550 çôlʹlâh (3), *military siege mound, rampart*

MOURN
56 'âbal (15), *to bewail*
57 'âbêl (3), *lamenting*
578 'ânâh (1), *to groan, lament*
584 'ânach (1), *to sigh, moan*
1897 hâgâh (4), *to murmur, utter a sound*
5098 nâham (2), *to growl, groan*
5110 nûwd (1), *to deplore; to taunt*
5594 çâphad (9), *to tear the hair, wail*
6937 qâdar (2), *to mourn in dark garments*
7300 rûwd (1), *to ramble*
2875 kŏptō (1), *to beat the breast*
3996 pěnthěō (5), *to grieve*

MOURNED
56 'âbal (10), *to bewail*
1058 bâkâh (2), *to weep, moan*
5594 çâphad (6), *to tear the hair, wail*
2354 thrēněō (2), *to bewail, lament*
3996 pěnthěō (2), *to grieve*

MOURNER
56 'âbal (1), *to bewail*

MOURNERS
57 'âbêl (2), *lamenting*
205 'âven (1), *trouble, vanity, wickedness*
5594 çâphad (1), *to tear the hair, wail*

MOURNETH
56 'âbal (8), *to bewail*
57 'âbêl (1), *lamenting*
1669 dâ'ab (1), *to pine, feel sorrow*
5594 çâphad (1), *to tear the hair, wail*

MOURNFULLY
6941 qeʹdôrannîyth (1), *in sackcloth*

MOURNING
56 'âbal (2), *to bewail*
57 'âbêl (2), *lamenting*
60 'êbel (24), *lamentation*
205 'âven (1), *trouble, vanity, wickedness*
585 'ănâchâh (1), *sighing, moaning*
1086 bâlâh (1), *to wear out, decay; consume*
1899 hegeh (1), *muttering; mourning*
1993 hâmâh (1), *to be in great commotion*
3382 Yered (1), *descent*
4553 miçpêd (6), *lamentation, howling*
4798 marzêach (1), *cry of lamentation*
6937 qâdar (4), *to mourn in dark garments*
6969 qûwn (1), *to chant or wail at a funeral*
8386 ta'ănîyâh (1), *lamentation*
3602 ŏdurmŏs (2), *lamentation*
3997 pěnthŏs (2), *grief, mourning, sadness*

MOUSE
5909 'akbâr (2), *mouse*

MOUTH
1627 gârôwn (1), *throat*
2441 chêk (14), *area of mouth*
5716 'ădîy (2), *finery; outfit; headstall*
6310 peh (326), *mouth; opening*
6433 pûm (Ch.) (5), *mouth*
8651 teʹra' (Ch.) (1), *door; palace*
3056 lŏgŏs (1), *word, matter, thing*
4750 stŏma (69), *mouth; edge*

MOUTHS
6310 peh (12), *mouth; opening*
6433 pûm (Ch.) (1), *mouth*
1993 ěpistŏmizō (1), *to silence*
4750 stŏma (4), *mouth; edge*

MOVE
2782 chârats (1), *to be alert, to decide*
5110 nûwd (1), *to waver; to wander, flee*
5128 nûwa' (1), *to waver*
5130 nûwph (1), *to quiver, vibrate, rock*
6328 pûwq (1), *to waver*
6470 pâ'am (1), *to tap; to impel or agitate*
7264 râgaz (2), *to quiver*
8318 sherets (1), *swarm, teeming mass*
2795 kiněō (2), *to stir, move, remove*
3056+4160 lŏgŏs (1), *word, matter, thing*

MOVEABLE
5128 nûwa' (1), *to waver*

MOVED
1607 gâ'ash (3), *to agitate violently, shake*
1949 hûwm (1), *to make an uproar; agitate*
1993 hâmâh (1), *to be in great commotion*
2111 zûwâ' (1), *to shake with fear, tremble*
2782 chârats (1), *to be alert, to decide*
4131 môwṭ (19), *to slip, shake, fall*
4132 môwṭ (3), *pole; yoke*
5074 nâdad (1), *to rove, flee; to drive away*
5120 nûwṭ (1), *to quake*
5128 nûwa' (5), *to waver*
5425 nâthar (1), *to jump; to be agitated*
5496 çûwth (4), *to stimulate; to seduce*
5648 'âbad (Ch.) (1), *to do, work, serve*
7043 qâlal (1), *to be, make light, swift*
7264 râgaz (5), *to quiver*
7363 râchaph (1), *to brood; to be relaxed*
7430 râmas (1), *to glide swiftly, move, swarm*
7493 râ'ash (2), *to undulate, quake*
23 aganaktěō (1), *to be indignant*
383 anaseiō (1), *to excite, stir up*
761 asaleutŏs (1), *immovable, fixed*
2125 ěulaběŏmai (1), *to have reverence*
2206 zēlŏō (2), *to have warmth of feeling for*
2795 kiněō (2), *to stir, move, remove*
3334 mětakiněō (1), *to be removed, shifted from*
4525 sainō (1), *to shake; to disturb*
4531 saleuō (1), *to waver, i.e. agitate, rock, topple*
4579 sěiō (1), *to vibrate; to agitate*
4697 splagchnizŏmai (5), *to feel sympathy, to pity*
5342 phěrō (1), *to bear or carry*

MOVEDST
5496 çûwth (1), *to stimulate; to seduce*

MOVER
2795 kiněō (1), *to stir, move, remove*

MOVETH
1980 hâlak (1), *to walk; live a certain way*
2654 châphêts (1), *to be pleased with, desire*
7430 râmas (5), *to glide swiftly, i.e. crawl, move, swarm*
8317 shârats (1), *to wriggle, swarm*

MOVING
5205 nîyd (1), *motion of the lips in speech*
7169 qârats (1), *to bite the lips, blink the eyes*

7430 râmas (1), to *glide swiftly*, *crawl, move*
8318 sherets (1), *swarm, teeming* mass
2796 kinêsis (1), *stirring, motion*

MOWER
7114 qâtsar (1), to *curtail, cut short*

MOWINGS
1488 gêz (1), shorn *fleece;* mown *grass*

MOWN
1488 gêz (1), shorn *fleece;* mown *grass*

MOZA
4162 Môwtsâ' (5), *going forth*

MOZAH
4681 Môtsâh (1), *drained*

MUCH
634 'Êçar-Chaddôwn (1), *Esar-chaddon*
637 'aph (15), *also or yea; though*
834 'âsher (2), *how, because, in order that*
1431 gâdal (2), to *be great, make great*
1571 gam (2), *also; even; yea; though*
1767 day (2), *enough, sufficient*
1931 hûw' (1), *he, she, it; this or that*
2479 chalchâlâh (1), *writhing* in childbirth
3254 yâçaph (1), to *add or augment*
3498 yâthar (1), to *remain or be left*
3515 kâbêd (2), *numerous; severe*
3524 kabbîyr (2), *mighty; aged; mighty*
3605 kôl (1), *all, any*
3966 m⁰ʻôd (9), *very, utterly*
4276 machătsîyth (1), *halving* or the *middle*
4767 mirbâh (1), *great quantity*
5704 'ad (2), *as far (long) as; during; while; until*
6079 'aph'aph (1), *fluttering eyelash*
6581 pâsâh (4), to *spread*
7114 qâtsar (1), to *curtail, cut short*
7225 rê'shîyth (1), *first*
7227 rab (38), *great*
7230 rôb (7), *abundance*
7235 râbâh (31), to *increase*
7335 râzam (1), to *twinkle* the eye
7690 saggîy' (Ch.) (4), *large*
23 aganaktĕō (2), to *be indignant*
1280 diapŏrĕō (1), to *be thoroughly puzzled*
2425 hikanŏs (6), *ample*
2470 isŏs (1), *similar*
2579 kan (1), *and (or even) if*

3123 mallŏn (3), *in a greater degree*
3366 mĕdĕ (1), *but not, not even; nor*
3383 mĕtĕ (1), *neither or nor; not even*
3386 mĕtigĕ (1), *not to say (the rather still)*
3433 mŏlis (1), *with difficulty*
3588 hŏ (2), *"the,"* i.e. the definite article
3745 hŏsŏs (4), *as much as*
3761 ŏudĕ (4), *neither, nor, not even*
4055 pĕrissŏtĕrŏs (1), *more superabundant*
4056 pĕrissŏtĕrŏs (1), *more superabundantly*
4124 plĕŏnĕxia (2), *extortion, avarice*
4180 pŏlulŏgia (1), *prolixity, wordiness*
4183 pŏlus (73), *much, many*
4214 pŏsŏs (11), *how much?; how much!*
5118 tŏsŏutŏs (7), *such great*
5248 hupĕrpĕrissĕuō (2), to *super-abound*

MUFFLERS
7479 ra'ălâh (1), long *veil*

MULBERRY
1057 bâkâ' (4), (poss.) *balsam* tree

MULE
6505 pered (6), *mule*
6506 pirdâh (3), *she-mule*

MULES
3222 yêm (1), *warm spring*
6505 pered (8), *mule*
7409 rekesh (2), *relay of animals on a post-route*

MULES'
6505 pered (1), *mule*

MULTIPLIED
1995 hâmôwn (1), *noise, tumult; many, crowd*
6280 'âthar (1), to *be, make abundant*
7231 râbab (3), to *increase*
7235 râbâh (29), to *increase*
7680 sᵉgâ' (Ch.) (2), to *increase*
4129 plĕthunō (8), to *increase*

MULTIPLIEDST
7235 râbâh (1), to *increase*

MULTIPLIETH
3527 kâbar (1), to *augment; accumulate*
7235 râbâh (2), to *increase*

MULTIPLY
7227 rab (1), *great*
7231 râbab (1), to *increase*
7233 rᵉbâbâh (1), *myriad number*

7235 râbâh (41), to *increase*
4129 plĕthunō (2), to *increase*

MULTIPLYING
7235 râbâh (1), to *increase*
4129 plĕthunō (1), to *increase*

MULTITUDE
527 'âmôwn (4), *throng of people, crowd*
582 'ěnôwsh (1), *man; person, human*
628 'açpᵉçûph (1), *assemblage*
1995 hâmôwn (55), *noise, tumult; many, crowd*
2416 chay (1), *alive; raw; fresh; life*
4392 mâlê' (1), *full; filling; fulness; fully*
4393 mᵉlô' (2), *fulness*
4768 marbîyth (1), *multitude; offspring*
5519 çâk (1), *crowd*
5712 'êdâh (1), *assemblage; crowd*
6154 'êreb (1), *mixed or woven things*
6951 qâhâl (3), *assemblage*
7227 rab (7), *great*
7230 rôb (68), *abundance*
7379 rîyb (1), *contest*
7393 rekeb (1), *upper millstone*
8229 shiph'âh (1), *copiousness*
3461 murias (1), *ten-thousand*
3793 ŏchlŏs (59), *throng*
4128 plĕthŏs (29), *large number, throng*

MULTITUDES
1995 hâmôwn (2), *noise, tumult; many, crowd*
3793 ŏchlŏs (20), *throng*
4128 plĕthŏs (1), *large number, throng*

MUNITION
4685 mâtsôwd (1), *net or snare; besieging tower*
4694 mᵉtsûwrâh (1), *rampart; fortification*

MUNITIONS
4679 mᵉtsad (1), *stronghold*

MUPPIM
4649 Muppîym (1), *wavings*

MURDER
2026 hârag (1), to *kill, slaughter*
7523 râtsach (3), to *murder*
5407 phŏnĕuō (1), to *commit murder*
5408 phŏnŏs (4), *slaying; murder*

MURDERER
2026 hârag (1), to *kill, slaughter*
7523 râtsach (13), to *murder*

443 anthrŏpŏktŏnŏs (3), *killer of humans*
5406 phŏnĕus (3), *murderer*

MURDERERS
2026 hârag (1), to *kill, slaughter*
5221 nâkâh (1), to *strike, kill*
7523 râtsach (1), to *murder*
3389 mĕtralō₁as (1), *matricide*
3964 patralō₁as (1), *parricide*
4607 sikariŏs (1), *dagger-man*
5406 phŏnĕus (4), *murderer*

MURDERS
5408 phŏnŏs (4), *slaying; murder*

MURMUR
3885 lûwn (7), to *be obstinate with* words
1111 gŏgguzō (2), to *grumble, mutter*

MURMURED
3885 lûwn (7), to *be obstinate with* words
7279 râgan (3), to *grumbling rebel*
1111 gŏgguzō (6), to *grumble, mutter*
1234 diagŏgguzō (2), to *complain throughout*
1690 ĕmbrimaŏmai (1), to *blame, warn sternly*

MURMURERS
1113 gŏggustĕs (1), *grumbler*

MURMURING
1112 gŏggusmŏs (2), *grumbling*

MURMURINGS
8519 tᵉlûwnâh (8), *grumbling*
1112 gŏggusmŏs (1), *grumbling*

MURRAIN
1698 deber (1), *pestilence, plague*

MUSE
7878 sîyach (1), to *ponder, muse aloud*

MUSED
1260 dialŏgizŏmai (1), to *deliberate*

MUSHI
4187 Mûwshîy (8), *sensitive*

MUSHITES
4188 Mûwshîy (2), *Mushite*

MUSICAL
7705 shiddâh (1), *wife* (as *mistress* of the house)
7892 shîyr (2), *song; singing*

MUSICIAN
5329 nâtsach (55), i.e. to *be eminent*

MUSICIANS
3451 mŏusikŏs (1),
minstrel, musician

MUSICK
2170 z°mâr (Ch.) (4),
instrumental *music*
4485 mangîynâh (1),
satire, mocking
5058 n°gîynâh (1),
stringed instrument
7892 shîyr (7), *song;
singing*
4858 sumphōnia (1),
concert of instruments

MUSING
1901 hâgîyg (1),
complaint, sighing

MUST
318 anagkē (1),
constraint; distress
1163 děi (63), *it is (was)
necessary*
2192 ěchō (1), to *have;
hold; keep*
2443 hina (1), in order
that
3784 ŏphěilō (1), to *owe;*
to *be under obligation*

MUSTARD
4615 sinapi (5), *mustard*

MUSTERED
6633 tsâbâ' (2), to *mass*
an army or servants

MUSTERETH
6485 pâqad (1), to *visit,
care for, count*

MUTH-LABBEN
4192 Mûwth (1), "*To die
for the son*"

MUTTER
1897 hâgâh (1), to
murmur, utter a sound

MUTTERED
1897 hâgâh (1), to
murmur, utter a sound

MUTUAL
1722+240 ěn (1), *in;
during; because of*

MUZZLE
2629 châçam (1), to
muzzle; block
5392 phimŏō (2), to
muzzle; silence

MYRA
3460 Mura (1), *Myra*

MYRRH
3910 lôṭ (2), *sticky gum
resin (poss.) ladanum*
4753 môr (12), *myrrh*
4666 smurna (2), *myrrh*
4669 smurnizō (1), to
mix with myrrh

MYRTLE
1918 hădaç (6), *myrtle*

MYSIA
3463 muriŏi (2), *ten
thousand*

MYSTERIES
3466 mustēriŏn (5), *secret*

MYSTERY
3466 mustēriŏn (22),
secret

NAAM
5277 Na'am (1), *pleasure*

NAAMAH
5279 Na'ămâh (5),
pleasantness

NAAMAN
5283 Na'ămân (15),
pleasantness
3497 Něěman (1),
pleasantness

NAAMAN'S
5283 Na'ămân (1),
pleasantness

NAAMATHITE
5284 Na'ămâthîy (4),
Naamathite

NAAMITES
5280 Na'âmîy (1),
Naamanite

NAARAH
5292 Na'ărâh (3), female
child; servant

NAARAI
5293 Na'ăray (1), *youthful*

NAARAN
5295 Na'ărân (1), *juvenile*

NAARATH
5292 Na'ărâh (1), female
child; servant

NAASHON
5177 Nachshôwn (1),
enchanter

NAASSON
3476 Naassōn (3),
enchanter

NABAL
5037 Nâbâl (18), *dolt*

NABAL'S
5037 Nâbâl (4), *dolt*

NABOTH
5022 Nâbôwth (22), *fruits*

NACHON'S
5225 Nâkôwn (1),
prepared

NACHOR
5152 Nâchôwr (1), *snorer*
3493 Nachōr (1), *snorer*

NADAB
5070 Nâdâb (20), *liberal*

NAGGE
3477 Naggai (1), (poss.)
brilliancy

NAHALAL
5096 Nahălâl (1), *pasture*

NAHALIEL
5160 Nachălîy'êl (2),
valley of God

NAHALLAL
5096 Nahălâl (1), *pasture*

NAHALOL
5096 Nahălâl (1), *pasture*

NAHAM
5163 Nacham (1),
consolation

NAHAMANI
5167 Nachămânîy (1),
consolatory

NAHARAI
5171 Nachăray (1), *snorer*

NAHARI
5171 Nachăray (1), *snorer*

NAHASH
5176 Nâchâsh (9), *snake*

NAHATH
5184 Nachath (5), *quiet*

NAHBI
5147 Nachbîy (1), *occult*

NAHOR
5152 Nâchôwr (15),
snorer

NAHOR'S
5152 Nâchôwr (2), *snorer*

NAHSHON
5177 Nachshôwn (9),
enchanter

NAHUM
5151 Nachûwm (1),
comfortable

NAIL
3489 yâthêd (8), tent *peg*

NAILING
4338 prŏsēlŏō (1), to *nail*
to something

NAILS
2953 ṭ°phar (Ch.) (2),
finger-*nail; claw*
4548 maçmêr (4), *peg*
4930 masm°râh (1), *pin*
on the end of a goad
6856 tsippôren (1), *nail;
point of a pen*
2247 hēlŏs (2), *stud,* i.e.
spike or *nail*

NAIN
3484 Naïn (1), cf. a *home,
dwelling; pasture*

NAIOTH
5121 Nâvîyth (6),
residence

NAKED
4636 ma'ărôm (1), *bare,
stripped*
5783 'ûwr (1), to (be) bare
5903 'êyrôm (9), *naked;
nudity*
6168 'ârâh (1), to *be,
make bare;* to *empty*
6174 'ârôwm (16), *nude;*
partially *stripped*
6181 'eryâh (1), *nudity*
6544 pâra' (3), to *loosen;*
to *expose, dismiss*
1130 gumnētěuō (1), go
poorly clad, be in rags
1131 gumnŏs (14), *nude*
or poorly clothed

NAKEDNESS
4589 mâ'ôwr (1),
nakedness; exposed
4626 ma'ar (1), *bare
place; nakedness*
5903 'êyrôm (1), *naked;
nudity*
6172 'ervâh (50), *nudity;
disgrace; blemish*
1132 gumnŏtēs (3),
nudity or poorly clothed

NAME
559 'âmar (2), to *say*
8034 shêm (735),
appellation
8036 shum (Ch.) (8),
name

NARHARI
2564 kalěō (1), to *call*
3686 ŏnŏma (170), *name*

NAME'S
8034 shêm (19),
appellation, i.e. name
3686 ŏnŏma (11), *name*

NAMED
559 'âmar (1), to *say*
1696 dâbar (1), to *speak,
say;* to *subdue*
5344 nâqab (1), to
specify, designate, libel
7121 qârâ' (5), to *call* out
7121+8034 qârâ' (1), to
call out
8034 shêm (4),
appellation, i.e. name
8034+7121 shêm (1),
appellation, i.e. name
8036 shum (Ch.) (1),
name
2564 kalěō (2), to *call*
3004 lěgō (2), to *say*
3686 ŏnŏma (28), *name*
3687 ŏnŏmazō (7), to
give a name

NAMELY
1722 ěn (1), *in; during;
because of*

NAMES
8034 shêm (82),
appellation, i.e. name
8036 shum (Ch.) (3),
name
3686 ŏnŏma (11), *name*

NAMETH
3687 ŏnŏmazō (1), to
give a name

NAOMI
5281 No'ŏmîy (20),
pleasant

NAOMI'S
5281 No'ŏmîy (1),
pleasant

NAPHISH
5305 Nâphîysh (2),
refreshed

NAPHTALI
5321 Naphtâlîy (49), *my
wrestling*

NAPHTUHIM
5320 Naphtûchîym (1),
Naphtuchim

NAPKIN
4676 sŏudariŏn (3), *towel*

NAPHTHUHIM
5320 Naphtûchîym (1),
Naphtuchim

NARCISSUS
3488 Narkissŏs (1),
stupefaction

NARROW
213 'ûwts (1), to *be close,
hurry, withdraw*
331 'âṭam (4), to *close*
3334 yâtsar (1), to *be in
distress*
6862 tsar (2), *trouble;
opponent*
2346 thlibō (1), to *crowd,
press, trouble*

NARROWED
4052 migrâ'âh (1), *ledge*
or offset

NARROWER
6887 tsârar (1), to *cramp*

NARROWLY
8104 shâmar (1), to *watch*

NATHAN
5416 Nâthân (42), *given*
3481 Nathan (1), *given*

NATHAN-MELECH
5419 Nᵉthan-Melek (1), *given of* (the) *king*

NATHANAEL
3482 Nathanaël (6), *given of God*

NATION
249 'ezrâch (1), *native born*
524 'ummâh (Ch.) (1), *community, clan, tribe*
1471 gôwy (105), *foreign nation; Gentiles*
3816 lᵉ'ôm (1), *community, nation*
5971 'am (2), *people; tribe; troops*
246 allŏphulŏs (1), *Gentile, foreigner*
1074 gĕnĕa (1), *generation; age*
1085 gĕnŏs (2), *kin, offspring in kind*
1484 ĕthnŏs (24), *race; tribe; pagan*

NATIONS
523 'ummâh (1), *community, clan, tribe*
524 'ummâh (Ch.) (7), *community, clan, tribe*
776 'erets (1), *earth, land, soil; nation*
1471 gôwy (266), *foreign nation; Gentiles*
3816 lᵉ'ôm (9), *community, nation*
5971 'am (14), *people; tribe; troops*
1484 ĕthnŏs (37), *race; tribe; pagan*

NATIVE
4138 môwledeth (1), *lineage, native country*

NATIVITY
4138 môwledeth (6), *lineage, native country*
4351 mᵉkûwrâh (1), *origin*

NATURAL
3893 lêach (1), *fresh strength, vigor*
1083 gĕnnĕsis (1), *nativity*
2596+6449 kata (2), *down; according to*
5446 phusikŏs (3), *instinctive, natural*
5591 psuchikŏs (3), *physical* and *brutish*

NATURALLY
1103 gnēsiŏs (1), *genuine, true*
5447 phusikŏs (1), *instinctively, naturally*

NATURE
1078 genesis (1), *nativity, nature*

5449 phusis (10), *genus or sort; disposition*

NAUGHT
7451 ra' (2), *bad; evil*

NAUGHTINESS
1942 havvâh (1), *desire; craving*
7455 rôa' (1), *badness, evil*
2549 kakia (1), *depravity; malignity; trouble*

NAUGHTY
1100 bᵉlîya'al (1), *wickedness, trouble*
1942 havvâh (1), *desire; craving*
7451 ra' (1), *bad; evil*

NAUM
3486 Naŏum (1), *comfortable*

NAVEL
8270 shôr (2), *umbilical cord; strength*
8306 shârîyr (1), *sinew*
8326 shôrer (1), *umbilical cord*

NAVES
1354 gab (1), *mounded: top, rim; arch, bulwarks*

NAVY
590 'ŏnîy (6), *ship; fleet of ships*

NAY
408 'al (8), *not; nothing*
1571 gam (2), *also; even*
3808 lô' (17), *no, not*
6440 pânîym (1), *face; front*
235 alla (4), *but, yet*
3304 mĕnŏungĕ (1), *so then at least*
3756 ŏu (8), *no or not*
3780 ŏuchi (5), *not indeed*

NAZARENE
3480 Nazŏraiŏs (1), *inhabitant of Nazareth*

NAZARENES
3480 Nazŏraiŏs (1), *inhabitant of Nazareth*

NAZARETH
3478 Nazarĕth (29), *Nazareth or Nazaret*

NAZARITE
5139 nâzîyr (9), *prince; separated Nazirite*

NAZARITES
5139 nâzîyr (3), *prince; separated Nazirite*

NEAH
5269 Nê'âh (1), *motion*

NEAPOLIS
3496 Nĕapŏlis (1), *new town*

NEAR
413 'êl (1), *to, toward*
681 'êtsel (3), *side; near*
3027 yâd (2), *hand; power*
5060 nâga' (4), *to strike*
5066 nâgash (58), *to be, come, bring near*
5921 'al (1), *above, over, upon, or against*
5973 'îm (1), *with*

7126 qârab (54), *to approach, bring near*
7127 qᵉrêb (Ch.) (5), *to approach, bring near*
7131 qârêb (2), *near*
7132 qᵉrâbâh (1), *approach*
7138 qârôwb (42), *near, close*
7200 râ'âh (1), *to see*
7607 shᵉ'êr (4), *flesh, meat; kindred* by blood
7608 sha'ărâh (1), *female kindred* by blood
316 anagkaiŏs (1), *necessary*
1448 ĕggizō (10), *to approach*
1451 ĕggus (4), *near, close*
4139 plēsiŏn (1), *neighbor, fellow*
4317 prŏsagō (1), *to bring near*
4334 prŏsĕrchŏmai (3), *to come near, visit*

NEARER
7138 qârôwb (1), *near, close*
1452 ĕggutĕrŏn (1), *nearer, closer*

NEARIAH
5294 Nᵉ'aryâh (3), *servant of Jehovah*

NEBAI
5109 Nôwbay (1), *fruitful*

NEBAIOTH
5032 Nᵉbâyôwth (2), *fruitfulnesses*

NEBAJOTH
5032 Nᵉbâyôwth (3), *fruitfulnesses*

NEBALLAT
5041 Nᵉballâṭ (1), *foolish secrecy*

NEBAT
5028 Nᵉbâṭ (25), *regard*

NEBO
5015 Nᵉbôw (13), *Nebo*

NEBUCHADNEZZAR
5019 Nᵉbûwkadne'tstsar (29), *Nebukadnetstsar*
5020 Nᵉbûwkadnetstsar (Ch.) (31), *Nebukadnetstsar*

NEBUCHADREZZAR
5019 Nᵉbûwkadne'tstsar (31), *Nebukadnetstsar*

NEBUSHASBAN
5021 Nᵉbûwshazbân (1), *Nebushazban*

NEBUZAR-ADAN
5018 Nᵉbûwzar'ădân (15), *Nebuzaradan*

NECESSARY
2706 chôq (1), *appointment; allotment*
316 anagkaiŏs (5), *necessary*
318 anagkē (1), *constraint; distress*
1876 ĕpanagkĕs (1), *necessarily*
4314+3588+5532 prŏs (1), *for; on, at; to, toward*

NECESSITIES
318 anagkē (2), *constraint; distress*
5532 chrĕia (1), *demand, requirement*

NECESSITY
316 anagkaiŏs (1), *necessary*
318 anagkē (6), *constraint; distress*
2192+318 ĕchō (1), *to have; hold; keep*
5532 chrĕia (2), *demand, requirement*

NECHO
5224 Nᵉkôw (3), *Neko*

NECK
1621 gargᵉrôwth (4), *throat*
1627 gârôwn (1), *throat*
4665 miphreketh (1), *vertebra of the neck*
6202 'âraph (3), *to break the neck, to destroy*
6203 'ôreph (12), *nape or back of the neck*
6676 tsavva'r (Ch.) (5), *back of the neck*
6677 tsavvâ'r (30), *back of the neck*
5137 trachēlŏs (6), *throat or neck; life*

NECKS
1627 gârôwn (1), *throat*
6203 'ôreph (6), *nape or back of the neck*
6677 tsavvâ'r (10), *back of the neck*
5137 trachēlŏs (1), *throat or neck; life*

NECROMANCER
1875+4191 dârash (1), *to seek or ask; to worship*

NEDABIAH
5072 Nᵉdabyâh (1), *largess of Jehovah*

NEED
2637 châcêr (1), *to lack; to fail, want, make less*
2638 châcêr (1), *lacking*
2818 chăshach (Ch.) (1), *to need*
4270 machçôwr (1), *impoverishment*
6878 tsôrek (1), *need*
1163 dĕi (1), *it is (was) necessary*
2121 ĕukairŏs (1), *opportune, suitable*
2192+5532 ĕchō (8), *to have; hold; keep*
3784 ŏphĕilō (1), *to owe; to be under obligation*
5532 chrĕia (26), *demand, requirement*
5535 chrĕịzō (1), *to have necessity, be in want of*

NEEDED
2192+5532 ĕchō (1), *to have; hold; keep*
4326 prŏsdĕŏmai (1), *to require additionally*

NEEDEST
2192+5532 ĕchō (1), *to have; hold; keep*

NEEDETH
422 anĕpaischuntŏs (1), unashamed
2192+318 ĕchō (1), to have; hold; keep
2192+5532 ĕchō (1), to have; hold; keep
5532 chrĕia (1), demand, requirement
5535 chrȩ̄zō (1), to have necessity, be in want of

NEEDFUL
2819 chashchûwth (1), necessity
316 anagkaiŏs (1), necessary
318 anagkē (1), constraint; distress
1163 dĕi (1), it is (was) necessary
2006 ĕpitĕdĕiŏs (1), requisite, needful
5532 chrĕia (1), demand, requirement

NEEDLE
4476 rhaphis (2), sewing needle

NEEDLE'S
4476 rhaphis (1), sewing needle

NEEDLEWORK
4639+7551 ma'ăseh (1), action; labor
7551 râqam (5), variegation; embroider
7553 riqmâh (3), variegation of color; embroidery

NEEDS
318 anagkē (3), constraint; distress
3843 pantŏs (1), entirely; at all events

NEEDY
34 'ebyôwn (35), destitute; poor
1800 dal (2), weak, thin; humble, needy
7326 rûwsh (1), to be destitute

NEESINGS
5846 'ăṭîyshâh (1), sneezing

NEGINAH
5058 nᵉgîynâh (1), stringed instrument

NEGINOTH
5058 nᵉgîynâh (6), stringed instrument

NEGLECT
272 amĕlĕō (2), to be careless of, neglect
3878 parakŏuō (2), to disobey

NEGLECTED
3865 parathĕōrĕō (1), to overlook or disregard

NEGLECTING
857 aphĕidia (1), austerity, asceticism

NEGLIGENT
7952 shâlâh (1), to mislead
272 amĕlĕō (1), to be careless of, neglect

NEHELAMITE
5161 Nechĕlâmîy (3), dreamed

NEHEMIAH
5166 Nᵉchemyâh (8), consolation of Jehovah

NEHILOTH
5155 Nᵉchîylâh (1), flute

NEHUM
5149 Nᵉchûwm (1), comforted

NEHUSHTA
5179 Nᵉchushtâ' (1), copper

NEHUSHTAN
5180 Nᵉchushtân (1), copper serpent

NEIEL
5272 Nᵉ'îy'êl (1), moved of God

NEIGHBOUR
5997 'âmîyth (7), comrade or kindred
7138 qârôwb (2), near, close
7453 rêa' (74), associate; one close
7468 rᵉ'ûwth (2), female associate
7934 shâkên (6), resident; fellow-citizen
4139 plĕsiŏn (16), neighbor, fellow

NEIGHBOUR'S
5997 'âmîyth (2), comrade or kindred
7453 rêa' (26), associate; one close

NEIGHBOURS
7138 qârôwb (3), near, close
7453 rêa' (2), associate; one close
7934 shâkên (11), resident; fellow-citizen
1069 gĕitōn (4), neighbour
4040 pĕriŏikŏs (1), neighbor

NEIGHBOURS'
7453 rêa' (1), associate; one close

NEIGHED
6670 tsâhal (1), to be cheerful; to sound

NEIGHING
4684 matshâlâh (1), whinnying

NEIGHINGS
4684 matshâlâh (1), whinnying

NEITHER
369 'ayin (40), there is no, i.e., not exist, none
408 'al (66), not; nothing
518 'îm (5), whether?; if, although; Oh that!
1077 bal (3), nothing; not at all; lest
1115 biltîy (4), not, except, without, unless
1571 gam (5), also; even
3608 kele' (2), prison

3804 kether (1), royal headdress
3808 lô' (475), no, not
3809 lâ' (Ch.) (3), as nothing
4480 min (2), from, out of
2228 ē (4), or; than
3361 mē (5), not; lest
3366 mĕdĕ (34), but not, not even; nor
3383 mĕtĕ (19), neither or nor; not even
3756 ŏu (12), no or not
3761 ŏudĕ (67), neither, nor, not even
3763 ŏudĕpŏtĕ (1), never at all
3777 ŏutĕ (39), not even

NEKEB
5346 Neqeb (1), dell

NEKODA
5353 Nᵉqôwdâ' (4), distinction

NEMUEL
5241 Nᵉmûw'êl (3), day of God

NEMUELITES
5242 Nᵉmûw'êlîy (1), Nemuelite

NEPHEG
5298 Nepheg (4), sprout

NEPHEW
5220 neked (2), offspring

NEPHEWS
1121 bên (1), son, descendant; people
1549 ĕkgŏnŏn (1), grandchild

NEPHISH
5305 Nâphîysh (1), refreshed

NEPHISHESIM
5300 Nᵉphûwshᵉçîym (1), expansions

NEPHTHALIM
3508 Nĕphthalĕim (2), my wrestling

NEPHTOAH
5318 Nephtôwach (2), spring

NEPHUSIM
5304 Nᵉphîyçîym (1), expansions

NEPTHALIM
3508 Nĕphthalĕim (1), my wrestling

NER
5369 Nêr (16), lamp

NEREUS
3517 Nĕrĕus (1), wet

NERGAL
5370 Nêrgal (1), Nergal

NERGAL-SHAREZER
5371 Nêrgal Shar'etser (3), Nergal-Sharetser

NERI
3518 Nĕri (1), light of Jehovah

NERIAH
5374 Nêrîyâh (10), light of Jehovah

NERO
3505 Nĕrōn (1), Nero

NEST
7064 qên (12), nest; nestlings; chamber
7077 qânan (3), to nestle

NESTS
7077 qânan (2), to nestle
2682 kataskēnōsis (2), perch or nest

NET
2764 chêrem (5), doomed object
4364 makmâr (1), hunter's snare-net
4685 mâtsôwd (2), net or snare; besieging tower
4686 mâtsûwd (2), net or capture; fastness
7568 resheth (20), hunting net; network
293 amphiblēstrŏn (2), fishing net which is cast
1350 diktuŏn (6), drag net
4522 sagēnē (1), seine

NETHANEEL
5417 Nᵉthan'êl (14), given of God

NETHANIAH
5418 Nᵉthanyâh (20), given of Jehovah

NETHER
7347 rêcheh (1), mill-stone
8481 tachtôwn (5), bottommost
8482 tachtîy (9), lowermost; depths

NETHERMOST
8481 tachtôwn (1), bottommost

NETHINIMS
5411 Nâthîyn (17), ones given to duty
5412 Nᵉthîyn (Ch.) (1), ones given to duty

NETOPHAH
5199 Nᵉṭôphâh (2), distillation

NETOPHATHI
5200 Nᵉṭôphâthîy (1), Netophathite

NETOPHATHITE
5200 Nᵉṭôphâthîy (8), Netophathite

NETOPHATHITES
5200 Nᵉṭôphâthîy (2), Netophathite

NETS
2764 chêrem (4), doomed object
4364 makmâr (1), hunter's snare-net
4365 mikmereth (1), fishing-net
7638 sâbâk (1), netting
1350 diktuŏn (6), drag net

NETTLES
2738 chârûwl (3), bramble, thorny weed
7057 qimmôwsh (2), prickly plant

NETWORK
4640+7568 Ma'say (2),
operative
7639 sᵉbâkâh (5),
net-work balustrade

NETWORKS
2355 chôwr (1), *white
linen*
7639 sᵉbâkâh (2),
net-work balustrade

NEVER
369 'ayin (2), *there is no,
i.e., not exist, none*
408 'al (1), *not; nothing*
1253 bôr (1), *vegetable
lye as soap; flux*
1755 dôwr (1), *dwelling*
3808 lô' (17), *no, not*
165 aiōn (1), *perpetuity,
ever; world*
3361 mē (1), *not; lest*
3364 ŏu mē (1), *not at all,
absolutely not*
3368 mēdĕpŏtĕ (1), *not
even ever*
3756 ŏu (5), *no or not*
3762 ŏudĕis (1), *none,
nobody, nothing*
3763 ŏudĕpŏtĕ (14),
never at all
3764 ŏudĕpō (2), *not
even yet*

NEVERTHELESS
61 'ăbâl (2), *truly, surely;
yet, but*
389 'ak (11), *surely; only,
however*
403 'âkên (1), *surely!,
truly!; but*
657 'ephĕç (1), *end; no
further*
1297 bᵉram (Ch.) (1),
however, but
1571 gam (3), *also; even*
3588 kîy (4), *for, that
because*
7535 raq (5), *merely;
although*
235 alla (10), *but, yet,
except, instead*
1161 dĕ (11), *but, yet;
and then*
2544 kaitŏigĕ (1),
although really
3305 mĕntŏi (1), *however*
4133 plēn (8), *albeit, save
that, rather, yet*

NEW
1069 bâkar (1), *bear the
first born*
1278 bᵉrîy'âh (1), *creation*
2319 châdâsh (50), *new,
recent*
2320 chôdesh (20), *new
moon; month*
2323 chădath (Ch.) (1),
new
2961 ţârîy (1), *fresh*
8492 tîyrôwsh (11), fresh
squeezed grape-juice
46 agnaphŏs (2), *new,
unshrunk cloth*
1098 glĕukŏs (1), *sweet
wine*
2537 kainŏs (44),
freshness, i.e. new
3501 nĕŏs (11), *new*

NEW MOON
3561 nŏumēnia (1),
festival of new moon
4372 prŏsphatŏs (1),
lately made, i.e. new

NEWBORN
738 artigĕnnētŏs (1), *new
born; young convert*

NEWLY
6965 qûwm (1), *to rise*
7138 qârôwb (1), *near,
close*

NEWNESS
2538 kainŏtēs (2),
renewal, newness

NEWS
8052 shᵉmûw'âh (1),
announcement

NEXT
312 'acher (2), *other,
another, different; next*
4283 mochŏrâth (3),
tomorrow, next day
4932 mishneh (7),
duplicate copy; double
7138 qârôwb (5), *near,
close*
839 auriŏn (1), *to-morrow*
1206 dĕutĕraiŏs (1), *on
the second day*
1836 hĕxēs (2),
successive, next
1887 ĕpauriŏn (7),
to-morrow
1966 ĕpiŏusa (3), *ensuing*
2064 ĕrchŏmai (1), *to go
or come*
2087 hĕtĕrŏs (2), *other or
different*
2192 ĕchō (3), *to have;
hold; keep*
3342 mĕtaxu (1), *betwixt;
meanwhile*

NEZIAH
5335 Nᵉtsîyach (2),
conspicuous

NEZIB
5334 Nᵉtsîyb (1), *station*

NIBHAZ
5026 Nibchaz (1),
Nibchaz

NIBSHAN
5044 Nibshân (1),
Nibshan

NICANOR
3527 Nikanŏr (1),
victorious

NICODEMUS
3530 Nikŏdēmŏs (5),
*victorious among his
people*

NICOLAITANES
3531 Nikŏlaïtēs (2),
adherent of Nicolaüs

NICOLAS
3532 Nikŏlaŏs (1),
*victorious over the
people*

NICOPOLIS
3533 Nikŏpŏlis (2),
victorious city

NIGER
3526 Nigĕr (1), *black*

NIGH
4952 mishrâh (1),
steeped juice
5060 nâga' (3), *to strike*
5066 nâgash (12), *to be,
come, bring near*
7126 qârab (32), *to
approach, bring near*
7138 qârôwb (4), *near,
close*
7607 shᵉ'êr (1), *flesh,
meat; kindred by blood*
7934 shâkên (1),
resident; fellow-citizen
1448 ĕggizō (21), *to
approach*
1451 ĕggus (18), *near,
close*
3844 para (2), *from; with;
besides; on account of*
3897 paraplēsiŏn (1),
almost
4314 prŏs (1), *for; on, at;
to, toward; against*

NIGHT
956 bûwth (Ch.) (1), *to
lodge over night*
2822 chôshek (1),
darkness; misery
3915 layil (208), *night;
adversity*
3916 leylᵉyâ' (Ch.) (4),
night
5399 nesheph (3), *dusk,
dawn*
6153 'ereb (4), *dusk*
6916 qiddâh (1), *cassia
bark*
8464 tachmâç (2),
unclean bird (poss.) owl
1273 dianuktĕrĕuō (1), *to
pass, spend the night*
3571 nux (60), *night*
3574 nuchthēmĕrŏn (1),
full day

NIGHTS
3915 layil (15), *night;
adversity*
3571 nux (3), *night*

NIMRAH
5247 Nimrâh (1), *clear
water*

NIMRIM
5249 Nimrîym (2), *clear
waters*

NIMROD
5248 Nimrôwd (4),
Nimrod

NIMSHI
5250 Nimshîy (5),
extricated

NINE
8672 têsha' (44), *nine;
ninth*
1767 ĕnnĕa (1), *nine*
1768 ĕnnĕnĕkŏntaĕnnĕa
(4), *ninety-nine*

NINETEEN
8672+6240 têsha' (3),
nine; ninth

NINETEENTH
8672+6240 têsha' (4),
nine; ninth

NINETY
8673 tish'îym (20), *ninety*

1768 ĕnnĕnĕkŏntaĕnnĕa
(4), *ninety-nine*

NINEVE
3535 Ninĕuï (1), *Nineveh*

NINEVEH
5210 Nîynᵉvêh (17),
Nineveh
3536 Ninĕuïtēs (1),
inhabitant of Nineveh

NINEVITES
3536 Ninĕuïtēs (1),
inhabitant of Nineveh

NINTH
8671 tᵉshîy'îy (18), *ninth*
8672 têsha' (6), *nine;
ninth*
1766 ĕnnatŏs (10), *ninth*

NISAN
5212 Nîyçân (2), *Nisan*

NISROCH
5268 Niçrôk (2), *Nisrok*

NITRE
5427 nether (2), *mineral
potash for washing*

NOADIAH
5129 Nôw'adyâh (2),
convened of Jehovah

NOAH
5146 Nôach (44), *rest*
5270 Nô'âh (4),
movement
3575 Nŏē (3), *rest*

NOAH'S
5146 Nôach (2), *rest*

NOB
5011 Nôb (6), *fruit*

NOBAH
5025 Nôbach (3), *bark*

NOBLE
3358 yaqqîyr (Ch.) (1),
precious
6579 partam (1),
grandee, noble
2104 ĕugĕnēs (2), *high in
rank; generous*
2908 krĕissŏn (2), *better,
i.e. greater advantage*

NOBLEMAN
937 basilikŏs (2),
befitting the sovereign
2104+444 ĕugĕnēs (1),
high in rank; generous

NOBLES
117 'addîyr (7), *powerful;
majestic*
678 'âtsîyl (1), *extremity;
noble*
1281 bârîyach (1),
fleeing, gliding serpent
1419 gâdôwl (1), *great*
2715 chôr (13), *noble, i.e.
in high rank*
3513 kâbad (1), *to be
rich, glorious*
5057 nâgîyd (1),
commander, official
5081 nâdîyb (4),
magnanimous
6579 partam (1),
grandee, noble

NOD
5113 Nôwd (1), *vagrancy*

NODAB
5114 Nôwdâb (1), *noble*

NOE
3575 Nôĕ (5), *rest*

NOGAH
5052 Nôgahh (2), *brilliancy*

NOHAH
5119 Nôwchâh (1), *quietude*

NOISE
1949 hûwm (2), *to make an uproar; agitate*
1993 hâmâh (4), *to be in great commotion*
1995 hâmôwn (4), *noise, tumult; many, crowd*
1998 hemyâh (1), *sound, tone*
6476 pâtsach (1), *to break out in sound*
6963 qôwl (48), *voice or sound*
7267 rôgez (1), *disquiet; anger*
7452 rêa' (1), *crash; noise; shout*
7588 shâ'ôwn (8), *uproar; destruction*
8085 shâma' (2), *to hear intelligently*
8643 tᵉrûw'âh (1), *battle-cry; clangor*
8663 tᵉshú'âh (1), *crashing or clamor*
2350 thŏrubĕŏ (1), *to disturb; clamor*
4500 rhŏizĕdŏn (1), *with a crash, with a roar*
5456 phŏnē (1), *voice, sound*

NOISED
191 akŏuŏ (1), *to hear; obey*
1096+5408 ginŏmai (1), *to be, become*
1255 dialalĕŏ (1), *to converse, discuss*

NOISOME
1942 havvâh (1), *desire; craving*
7451 ra' (2), *bad; evil*
2556 kakŏs (1), *bad, evil, wrong*

NON
5126 Nûwn (1), *perpetuity*

NOON
6672 tsôhar (11), *window; noon time*
3314 mĕsĕmbria (1), *midday; south*

NOONDAY
6672 tsôhar (10), *window; noon time*

NOONTIDE
6256+6672 'êth (1), *time*

NOPH
5297 Nôph (7), *Noph*

NOPHAH
5302 Nôphach (1), *gust*

NORTH
4215 mᵉzâreh (1), *north wind*
6828 tsâphôwn (128), *north, northern*

1005 borrhas (2), *north*
5566 chŏrŏs (1), *north-west wind*

NORTHERN
6828 tsâphôwn (1), *north, northern*
6830 tsᵉphôwnîy (1), *northern*

NORTHWARD
6828 tsâphôwn (24), *north, northern*

NOSE
639 'aph (11), *nose or nostril; face; person*
2763 charam (1), *to devote to destruction*

NOSES
639 'aph (1), *nose or nostril; face; person*

NOSTRILS
639 'aph (13), *nose or nostril; face; person*
5156 nᵉchîyr (1), *pair of nostrils*
5170 nachar (1), *snorting*

NOTABLE
2380 châzûwth (2), *striking appearance*
1110 gnŏstŏs (1), *well-known*
1978 ĕpisēmŏs (1), *eminent, prominent*
2016 ĕpiphanēs (1), *conspicuous*

NOTE
2710 châqaq (1), *to engrave; to enact laws*
1978 ĕpisēmŏs (1), *eminent, prominent*
4593 sēmĕiŏŏ (1), *to mark for avoidance*

NOTED
7559 râsham (1), *to record*

NOTHING
369 'ayin (23), *there is no, i.e., not exist, none*
408 'al (3), *not; nothing*
657 'epheç (2), *end; no further*
1099 bᵉlîymâh (1), *nothing whatever*
1115 biltîy (3), *not, except, without, unless*
1697 dâbâr (2), *word; matter; thing*
2600 chinnâm (2), *gratis, free*
3605 kôl (1), *all, any or every*
3808 lô' (25), *no, not*
3809 lâ' (Ch.) (1), *as nothing*
4591 mâ'aṭ (1), *to be, make small or few*
7535 raq (1), *merely; although*
8414 tôhûw (1), *waste, desolation, formless*
114 athĕtĕŏ (1), *to disesteem, neutralize*
3361 mē (1), *not; lest*
3367 mēdĕis (27), *not even one*
3385 mēti (2), *whether at all*

3756 ŏu (4), *no or not*
3762 ŏudĕis (66), *none, nobody, nothing*
3777 ŏutĕ (1), *not even*

NOTICE
5234 nâkar (1), *to acknowledge*
4293 prŏkataggĕllŏ (1), *to predict, promise*

NOTWITHSTANDING
389 'ak (6), *surely; only, however*
657 'epheç (1), *end; no further*
7535 raq (2), *merely; although*
235 alla (1), *but, yet, except, instead*
4133 plēn (4), *albeit, save that, rather, yet*

NOUGHT
205 'âven (1), *trouble, vanity, wickedness*
369 'ayin (1), *there is no, i.e., not exist, none*
408+3972 'al (1), *not; nothing*
434 'ĕlûwl (1), *good for nothing*
656 'âphêç (1), *to cease*
657 'epheç (1), *end; no further*
659 'êpha' (1), *nothing*
2600 chinnâm (6), *gratis, free*
3808 lô' (1), *no, not*
3808+1697 lô' (1), *no, not*
3808+1952 lô' (1), *no, not*
5034 nâbêl (1), *to wilt; to fall away; to be foolish*
6331 pûwr (1), *to crush*
6544 pâra' (1), *to loosen; to expose, dismiss*
6565 pârar (2), *to break up; to violate, frustrate*
8045 shâmad (1), *to desolate*
8414 tôhûw (2), *waste, desolation, formless*
557 apĕlĕgmŏs (1), *refutation, discrediting*
1432 dōrĕan (1), *gratuitously, freely*
1847 ĕxŏudĕnŏŏ (1), *to be treated with contempt*
1848 ĕxŏuthĕnĕŏ (3), *to treat with contempt*
2049 ĕrēmŏŏ (1), *to lay waste*
2647 kataluŏ (1), *to demolish*
2673 katargĕŏ (2), *to be, render entirely useless*
3762 ŏudĕis (1), *none, nobody, nothing*

NOURISH
1431 gâdal (2), *to be great, make great*
2421 châyâh (1), *to live; to revive*
3557 kûwl (2), *to keep in; to maintain*

NOURISHED
1431 gâdal (1), *to be great, make great*

2421 châyâh (1), *to live; to revive*
3557 kûwl (1), *to keep in; to measure*
7235 râbâh (1), *to increase*
397 anatrĕphŏ (2), *to rear, care for*
1789 ĕntrĕphŏ (1), *to educate; to be trained*
5142 trĕphŏ (3), *to nurse, feed, care for*

NOURISHER
3557 kûwl (1), *to keep in; to measure*

NOURISHETH
1625 ĕktrĕphŏ (1), *to cherish or train*

NOURISHING
1431 gâdal (1), *to be great, make great*

NOURISHMENT
2023 ĕpichŏrēgĕŏ (1), *to fully supply; to aid*

NOVICE
3504 nĕŏphutŏs (1), *young convert*

NOW
116 'ĕdayin (Ch.) (2), *then*
227 'âz (1), *at that time or place; therefore*
645 'êphôw (10), *then*
1768 dîy (Ch.) (1), *that; of*
2008 hênnâh (1), *from here; from there*
2088 zeh (3), *this or that*
3117 yôwm (4), *day; time period*
3528 kᵉbâr (4), *long ago, formerly, hitherto*
3588 kîy (2), *for, that because*
3705 kᵉ'an (Ch.) (14), *now*
4994 nâ' (172), *I pray!, please!, I beg you!*
6254 'Ashtᵉrâthîy (1), *Ashterathite*
6258 'attâh (401), *at this time, now*
6288 pᵉ'ôrâh (3), *foliage, branches*
6471 pa'am (5), *time; step; occurence*
737 arti (25), *just now; at once*
1160 dapanē (2), *expense, cost*
1161 dĕ (160), *but, yet; and then*
1211 dē (1), *now, then; indeed, therefore*
2235 ēdē (3), *even now*
2236 hēdista (38), *with great pleasure*
2532 kai (5), *and; or; even; also*
3063 lŏipŏn (2), *remaining; finally*
3568 nun (127), *now; the present or immediate*
3570 nuni (20), *just now, indeed, in fact*
3765 ŏukĕti (5), *not yet, no longer*
3767 ŏun (12), *certainly; accordingly*

NUMBER

2714 chêqer (1), *examination*
3187 yâchas (1), to *enroll by family list*
4373 mikçâh (1), *valuation* of a thing
4487 mânâh (7), to *allot; to enumerate* or enroll
4507 Mᵉnîy (1), *Apportioner*, i.e. Fate
4510 minyân (Ch.) (1), *enumeration, number*
4557 miçpâr (108), *number*
4557+3187 miçpâr (1), *number*
4662 miphqâd (2), *designated spot; census*
5608 çâphar (10), to *inscribe; to enumerate*
5736 'âdaph (1), to *be redundant*
6485 pâqad (14), to *visit, care for, count*
705 arithmĕō (1), to *enumerate or count*
706 arithmŏs (18), *reckoned number*
1469 ĕgkrinō (1), to *count among*
2639 katalĕgō (1), to *enroll, put on a list*
3793 ŏchlŏs (2), *throng*

NUMBERED

4483 mᵉnâ' (Ch.) (1), to *count, appoint*
4487 mânâh (7), to *allot; to enumerate* or enroll
4557 miçpâr (1), *number*
5608 çâphar (11), to *inscribe; to enumerate*
6485 pâqad (102), to *visit, care for, count*
705 arithmĕō (2), to *enumerate or count*
2674 katarithmĕō (1), to *be numbered among*
3049 lŏgizŏmai (1), to *credit; to think, regard*
4785 sugkatapsēphizō (1), to *number with*

NUMBEREST

5608 çâphar (1), to *inscribe; to enumerate*
6485 pâqad (2), to *visit, care for, count*

NUMBERING

5608 çâphar (1), to *inscribe; to enumerate*
5610 çᵉphâr (1), *census*

NUMBERS

4557 miçpâr (1), *number*
5615 çᵉphôrâh (1), *numeration*
6486 pᵉquddâh (1), *visitation; punishment*

NUN

5126 Nûwn (29), *perpetuity*

NURSE

539 'âman (2), to *be firm, faithful, true; to trust*
3243 yânaq (7), to *suck; to give milk*
5162 trŏphŏs (1), *nurse-mother*

NURSED

539 'âman (1), to *be firm, faithful, true; to trust*
5134 nûwq (1), to *suckle*

NURSING

539 'âman (2), to *be firm, faithful, true; to trust*
3243 yânaq (1), to *suck; to give milk*

NURTURE

3809 paidĕia (1), *disciplinary correction*

NUTS

93 'ĕgôwz (1), *nut*
992 bôṭen (1), *pistachio*

NYMPHAS

3564 Numphas (1), *nymph-born*

OAK

424 'êlâh (11), *oak*
427 'allâh (1), *oak*
437 'allôwn (3), *oak*

OAKS

352 'ayîl (1), *chief; ram; oak tree*
437 'allôwn (5), *oak*

OAR

4880 mâshôwṭ (1), *oar*

OARS

4880 mâshôwṭ (1), *oar*
7885 shayiṭ (1), *oar*

OATH

423 'âlâh (14), *curse, oath*
7621 shᵉbûw'âh (26), *sworn oath*
7650 shâba' (7), to *swear*
332 anathĕmatizō (1), to *declare* or vow an *oath*
3727 hŏrkŏs (7), *sacred restraint*, i.e. an *oath*
3728 hŏrkōmŏsia (4), *asseveration on oath*

OATH'S

3727 hŏrkŏs (2), *sacred restraint*, i.e. an *oath*

OATHS

7621 shᵉbûw'âh (2), *sworn oath*
3727 hŏrkŏs (1), *sacred restraint*, i.e. an *oath*

OBADIAH

5662 'Ôbadyâh (20), *serving Jehovah*

OBAL

5745 'Ôwbâl (1), *Obal*

OBED

5744 'Ôwbêd (9), *serving*
5601 Obēd (3), *serving*

OBED-EDOM

5654 'Ôbêd 'Ĕdôwm (20), *worker of Edom*

OBEDIENCE

5218 hupakŏē (11), *compliance, submission*
5293 hupŏtassō (1), to *subordinate; to obey*

OBEDIENT

8085 shâma' (8), to *hear intelligently*
5218 hupakŏē (2), *compliance, submission*
5219 hupakŏuō (2), to *heed* or conform

OBEISANCE

7812 shâchâh (9), to *prostrate in homage*

OBEY

3349 yiqqâhâh (1), *obedience*
4928 mishma'ath (1), *obedience; royal subject*
8085 shâma' (40), to *hear intelligently*
8086 shᵉma' (Ch.) (1), to *hear intelligently*
544 apĕithĕō (3), to *disbelieve*
3980 pĕitharchĕō (3), to *submit to authority*
3982 pĕithō (5), to *pacify or conciliate; to assent*
5218 hupakŏē (1), *compliance, submission*
5219 hupakŏuō (13), to *heed or conform*
5255+1036 hupēkŏŏs (1), to *listen attentively*

OBEYED

8085 shâma' (34), to *hear*
3982 pĕithō (2), to *pacify or conciliate; to assent*
5219 hupakŏuō (5), to *heed or conform*

OBEYEDST

8085 shâma' (2), to *hear*

OBEYETH

8085 shâma' (3), to *hear*

OBEYING

8085 shâma' (2), to *hear*
5218 hupakŏē (1), *compliance, submission*

OBIL

179 'Ôwbîyl (1), *mournful*

OBJECT

2723 katēgŏrĕō (1), to *bring a charge*

OBLATION

4503 minchâh (5), *tribute; offering*
4541 maççêkâh (1), *libation; woven coverlet*
7133 qorbân (11), *sacrificial present*
8641 tᵉrûwmâh (17), *sacrifice, tribute*
8642 tᵉrûwmîyâh (1), *sacrificial offering*

OBLATIONS

4503 minchâh (1), *sacrificial offering*
4864 mas'êth (1), *raising; beacon; present*
7133 qorbân (1), *sacrificial present*
8641 tᵉrûwmâh (2), *sacrifice, tribute*

OBOTH

88 'Ôbôth (4), *water-skins*

OBSCURE

380 'îyshôwn (1), *pupil, eyeball; middle*

OBSCURITY

652 'ôphel (1), *dusk, darkness*
2822 chôshek (2), *darkness; misery*

OBSERVATION

3907 paratērēsis (1), *careful observation*

OBSERVE

5172 nâchash (1), to *prognosticate*
5341 nâtsar (1), to *guard, protect, maintain*
6049 'ânan (1), to *cover, becloud; to act covertly*
6213 'âsâh (3), to *do or make*
7789 shûwr (1), to *spy out, survey*
8104 shâmar (41), to *watch*
3906 paratērĕō (1), to *note insidiously*
4160 pŏiĕō (1), to *make*
5083 tērĕō (3), to *keep, guard, obey*
5442 phulassō (1), to *watch*, i.e. *be on guard*

OBSERVED

6049 'ânan (2), to *cover, becloud; to act covertly*
6213 'âsâh (1), to *do or make*
7789 shûwr (1), to *spy out, survey*
8104 shâmar (3), to *watch*
8107 shimmûr (2), *observance*
4933 suntērĕō (1), to *preserve in memory*
5442 phulassō (1), to *watch*, i.e. *be on guard*

OBSERVER

6049 'ânan (1), to *cover, becloud; to act covertly*

OBSERVERS

6049 'ânan (1), to *cover, becloud; to act covertly*

OBSERVEST

8104 shâmar (1), to *watch*

OBSERVETH

8104 shâmar (1), to *watch*

OBSTINATE

553 'âmats (1), to *be strong; be courageous*
7186 qâsheh (1), *severe*

OBTAIN

1129 bânâh (1), to *build; to establish*
2388 châzaq (1), to *fasten upon; to seize*
5381 nâsag (2), to *reach*
6329 pûwq (1), to *issue; to furnish; to secure*
1653 ĕlĕĕō (2), to *give out compassion*
2013 ĕpitugchanō (1), to *attain, obtain*
2638 katalambanō (1), to *seize; to possess*
2983 lambanō (2), to *take, receive*

OFFERINGS

5927 'âlâh (9), to *ascend, be high, mount*
5930 'ôlâh (1), *sacrifice wholly consumed in fire*
6213 'âsâh (2), to *make*
7126 qârab (1), to *approach, bring near*
7133 qorbân (66), *sacrificial present*
8573 tᵉnûwphâh (6), *undulation of offerings*
8641 tᵉrûwmâh (40), *sacrifice, tribute*
4374 prŏsphĕrŏ (2), to *present to; to treat as*
4376 prŏsphŏra (8), *presentation; oblation*

OFFERINGS

1890 habhâb (1), *gift given as a sacrifice*
2077 zebach (5), *animal flesh; sacrifice*
4503 minchâh (16), *tribute; offering*
5262 neçek (1), *libation; cast idol*
7133 qorbân (1), *sacrificial present*
8641 tᵉrûwmâh (10), *sacrifice, tribute*
1435 dōrŏn (1), *sacrificial present*
3646 hŏlŏkautōma (3), *wholly-consumed sacrifice*
4376 prŏsphŏra (1), *presentation; oblation*

OFFICE

3653 kên (1), *pedestal or station of a basin*
4612 ma'ămâd (1), *position; attendant*
5656 'ăbôdâh (1), *work*
6486 pᵉquddâh (8), *visitation; punishment*
1247 diakŏnĕŏ (2), to *wait upon, serve*
1248 diakŏnia (1), *attendance, aid, service*
1984 ĕpiskŏpĕ (1), *episcopate*
2405 hiĕratĕia (2), *priestly office*
2407 hiĕratĕuŏ (1), to be *a priest*
4234 praxis (1), *act; function*

OFFICER

5324 nâtsab (1), to *station*
5333 nᵉtsîyb (1), *military post; statue*
5631 çârîyç (5), *eunuch; official of state*
6496 pâqîyd (2), *superintendent, officer*
4233 praktōr (2), *official collector*
5257 hupērĕtēs (1), *servant, attendant*

OFFICERS

5324 nâtsab (6), to *station*
5631 çârîyç (7), *eunuch; official of state*
6213 'âsâh (1), to *do*
6485 pâqad (3), to *visit, care for, count*
6486 pᵉquddâh (3), *visitation; punishment*

6496 pâqîyd (3), *superintendent, officer*
7227 rab (1), *great*
7860 shôṭêr (23), to *write; official who is a scribe*
5257 hupērĕtēs (10), *servant, attendant*

OFFICES

4929 mishmâr (1), *guard; deposit; usage; example*
4931 mishmereth (1), *watch, sentry, post*
6486 pᵉquddâh (2), *visitation; punishment*

OFFSCOURING

5501 çᵉchîy (1), *refuse*
4067 pĕripsōma (1), *scum, garbage*

OFFSPRING

6631 tse'ĕtsâ' (9), *produce, children*
1085 gĕnŏs (3), *kin*

OFT

1767 day (1), *enough, sufficient*
3740 hŏsakis (1), *as often as, when*
4178 pŏllakis (5), *many times, i.e. frequently*
4183 pŏlus (1), *much, many*
4212 pŏsakis (1), *how many times*
4435 pugmē (1), *with the fist*

OFTEN

3740 hŏsakis (6), *as often as, when*
4178 pŏllakis (3), *many times, i.e. frequently*
4212 pŏsakis (2), *how many times*
4437 puknŏs (2), *frequent; frequently*

OFTENER

4437 puknŏs (1), *frequent; frequently*

OFTENTIMES

6471+7227 pa'am (1), *time; step; occurence*
6471+7969 pa'am (1), *time; step; occurence*
4178 pŏllakis (3), *many times, i.e. frequently*
4183+5550 pŏlus (1), *much, many*

OFTTIMES

4178 pŏllakis (3), *many times, i.e. frequently*

OG

5747 'Ôwg (22), *round*

OH

518 'îm (1), *whether?; if, although; Oh that!*
577 'ânnâ' (1), *oh now!, I ask you!*
994 bîy (7), *Oh that!*
3863 lûw' (2), *if; would that!*
4994 nâ' (6), *I pray!, please!, I beg you!*

OHAD

161 'Ôhad (2), *unity*

OHEL

169 'Ôhel (1), *Ohel*

OIL

3323 yitshâr (21), *olive oil; anointing*
4887 mᵉshach (Ch.) (2), *olive oil*
6671 tsâhar (1), to *press out olive oil*
8081 shemen (163), *olive oil, wood, lotions*
1637 ĕlaiŏn (11), *olive oil*

OILED

8081 shemen (2), *olive oil, wood, lotions*

OINTMENT

4841 merqâchâh (1), *unguent-kettle*
4842 mirqachath (1), *aromatic unguent*
4888 mishchâh (1), *unction; gift*
7545 rôqach (1), *aromatic, fragrance*
8081 shemen (11), *olive oil, wood, lotions*
3464 murŏn (12), *perfumed oil*

OINTMENTS

8081 shemen (3), *olive oil, wood, lotions*
3464 murŏn (2), *perfumed oil*

OLD

227 'âz (2), *at that time or place; therefore*
865 'ethmôwl (1), *heretofore, formerly*
1086 bâlâh (11), to *wear out, decay; consume*
1087 bâleh (5), *worn out*
1094 bᵉlôw' (3), *rags, worn out fabric*
1121 bên (132), *son, descendant; people*
1247 bar (Ch.) (1), *son, child; descendant*
1323 bath (1), *daughter, descendant, woman*
2204 zâqên (26), to be *old, venerated*
2205 zâqên (41), *old, venerated*
2208 zâqûn (4), *old age*
2209 ziqnâh (6), *old age*
2416 chay (1), *alive; raw; fresh; life*
3117 yôwm (1), *day; time period*
3117+8140+3117 yôwm (1), *day; time period*
3453 yâshîysh (1), *old man*
3462 yâshên (2), to *sleep; to grow old, stale*
3465 yâshân (7), *old*
3833 lâbîy' (1), *lion, lioness*
3918 layish (1), *lion*
5288 na'ar (1), *male child; servant*
5669 'âbûwr (2), *kept over; stored grain*
5703 'ad (1), *perpetuity; ancient*
5769 'ôwlâm (26), *eternity; ancient*
5957 'âlam (Ch.) (2), *forever*

6275 'âthaq (2), to *remove; to grow old*
6440 pânîym (3), *face; front*
6924 qedem (17), *East, eastern; antiquity*
6927 qadmâh (1), *priority in time; before; past*
6931 qadmôwnîy (2), *anterior time; oriental*
7223 rî'shôwn (2), *first*
7350 râchôwq (2), *remote, far*
7872 sêybâh (6), *old age*
7992 shᵉlîyshîy (2), *third*
8027 shâlash (3), to *be, triplicate*
744 archaiŏs (11), *original or primeval*
1088 gĕrōn (1), *aged, old person*
1094 gĕras (1), *senility, old age*
1095 gĕraskō (2), to be *senescent, grow old*
1126 graŏdēs (1), *old lady-like, i.e. silly*
1332 diĕtēs (1), *of two years in age*
1541 hĕkatŏntaĕtēs (1), *centenarian*
1597 ĕkpalai (1), *long ago, for a long while*
3819 palai (2), *formerly; sometime since*
3820 palaiŏs (19), *not recent, worn out, old*
3822 palaiŏō (3), to *become worn out*
4218 pŏtĕ (2), *at some time, ever*
4245 prĕsbutĕrŏs (1), *elderly; older; presbyter*
4246 prĕsbutēs (1), *old man*
5550 chrŏnŏs (1), *space of time, period*

OLDNESS

3821 palaiŏtēs (1), *antiquatedness*

OLIVE

2132 zayith (27), *olive*
8081 shemen (4), *olive oil, wood, lotions*
65 agriĕlaiŏs (2), *wild olive tree*
1636 ĕlaia (4), *olive*
2565 kalliĕlaiŏs (1), *cultivated olive*

OLIVES

2132 zayith (4), *olive*
1636 ĕlaia (11), *olive*

OLIVET

2132 zayith (1), *olive*
1638 ĕlaiŏn (1), *Mt. of Olives*

OLIVEYARD

2132 zayith (1), *olive*

OLIVEYARDS

2132 zayith (5), *olive*

OLYMPAS

3632 ŏinŏphlugia (1), *drunkenness*

OMAR

201 'Ôwmâr (3), *talkative*

OMEGA
5598 Ō (4), last letter of the Greek alphabet

OMER
6016 'ômer (5), sheaf of grain; dry measure

OMERS
6016 'ômer (1), sheaf of grain; dry measure

OMITTED
863 aphiēmi (1), to leave; to pardon, forgive

OMNIPOTENT
3841 pantŏkratōr (1), Absolute sovereign

OMRI
6018 'Omrîy (18), heaping

ONAM
208 'Ôwnâm (4), strong

ONAN
209 'Ôwnân (8), strong

ONCE
227 'âz (1), at that time or place; therefore
259 'echâd (15), first
996 bêyn (1), between; "either...or"
3162 yachad (1), unitedly
4118 mahêr (1), in a hurry
5750 'ôwd (1), again; repeatedly; still; more
6471 pa'am (10), time; step; occurence
6471+259 pa'am (1), time; step; occurence
530 hapax (15), once for all
2178 ĕphapax (5), upon one occasion
3366 mēdĕ (1), but not, not even; nor
3826 pamplēthĕi (1), in full multitude
4218 pŏtĕ (2), at some time, ever

ONE
259 'echâd (658), first
376 'îysh (173), man; male; someone
428 'êl-leh (2), these or those
492 'almônîy (1), certain so and so; whoever
802 'ishshâh (8), woman, wife; women, wives
1397 geber (1), person, man
1571 gam (1), also; even
1668 dâ' (Ch.) (2), this
1836 dên (Ch.) (1), this
2063 zô'th (1), this
2088 zeh (10), this or that
2297 chad (1), one
2298 chad (Ch.) (5), one; single; first; at once
3605 kôl (1), all, any
3627 kᵉlîy (1), implement, thing
3671 kânâph (1), edge or extremity; wing
5315 nephesh (1), life; breath; soul; wind
6918 qâdôwsh (2), sacred
240 allēlōn (77), one another

243 allŏs (4), different, other
1438 hĕautŏu (6), himself, herself, itself
1515 ĕirēnē (1), peace; health; prosperity
1520 hĕis (231), one
2087 hĕtĕrŏs (1), other or different
3303 mĕn (2), not translated
3391 mia (56), one or first
3442 mŏnŏphthalmŏs (2), one-eyed
3661 hŏmŏthumadŏn (12), unanimously
3675 hŏmŏphrōn (1), like-minded
3739 hŏs (1), who, which, what, that
3956 pas (2), all, any, every, whole
4861 sumpsuchŏs (1), similar in sentiment
5100 tis (35), some or any person or object
5129 tŏutō₁ (1), in this person or thing

ONES
1121 bên (1), son, descendant; people

ONESIMUS
3682 Ŏnēsimŏs (4), profitable

ONESIPHORUS
3683 Ŏnēsiphŏrŏs (2), profit-bearer

ONIONS
1211 betsel (1), onion

ONLY
259 'echâd (2), first
389 'ak (33), surely; only, however
905 bad (35), apart, only, besides
910 bâdâd (1), separate, alone
2108 zûwlâh (1), except; apart from; besides
3162 yachad (2), unitedly
3173 yâchîyd (7), only son; alone; beloved
3535 kibsâh (1), ewe sheep
3697 kâçam (1), to shear, clip
7535 raq (52), merely; although
1520 hĕis (1), one
3439 mŏnŏgĕnēs (9), sole, one and only
3440 mŏnŏn (62), merely; just
3441 mŏnŏs (24), single, only; by oneself

ONO
207 'Ôwnôw (5), strong

ONYCHA
7827 shᵉchêleth (1), scale or shell, mussel

ONYX
7718 shôham (11), (poss.) pale green beryl stone

OPEN
1540 gâlâh (6), to denude; uncover

3605 kôl (1), all, any or every
4725 mâqôwm (1), general locality, place
5869 'ayin (1), eye; sight; fountain
6358 pâṭûwr (4), opened; bud
6363 peṭer (1), firstling, first born
6440 pânîym (13), face; front
6475 pâtsâh (3), to rend, i.e. open
6491 pâqach (10), to open the eyes
6555 pârats (1), to break out
6566 pâras (1), to break apart, disperse, scatter
6605 pâthach (49), to open wide; to loosen
6606 pᵉthach (Ch.) (1), to open
6610 pithchôwn (1), act of opening the mouth
8365 shâtham (2), to unveil, i.e. open
71 agō (1), to lead; to bring, drive; to weigh
343 anakaluptō (1), to unveil
455 anŏigō (21), to open up
1722+457 ĕn (1), in; during; because of
3856 paradĕigmatizō (1), to expose to infamy
4271 prŏdēlŏs (1), obvious, evident

OPENED
1540 gâlâh (3), to denude; uncover
3738 kârâh (1), to dig; to plot; to bore, hew
6473 pâ'ar (3), to open wide
6475 pâtsâh (7), to rend, i.e. open
6491 pâqach (7), to open the eyes
6589 pâsaq (1), to dispart, i.e., spread
6605 pâthach (51), to open wide; to loosen
6606 pᵉthach (Ch.) (1), to open
380 anaptussō (1), to unroll a scroll
455 anŏigō (53), to open up
1272 dianŏigō (6), to open thoroughly
4977 schizō (1), to split or sever
5136 trachēlizō (1), to lay bare

OPENEST
6605 pâthach (2), to open wide; to loosen, begin

OPENETH
1540 gâlâh (3), to denude; uncover
6363 peṭer (7), firstling, first born
6491 pâqach (2), to open the eyes

6589 pâsaq (1), to dispart, i.e., spread
6605 pâthach (4), to open wide; to loosen, begin
455 anŏigō (3), to open up
1272 dianŏigō (1), to open thoroughly

OPENING
4668 maphtêach (1), opening; key
4669 miphtâch (1), utterance of lips
6491 pâqach (1), to open the eyes
6495 pᵉqach-qôwach (1), jail-delivery; salvation
6605 pâthach (1), to open wide; to loosen, begin
6610 pithchôwn (1), act of opening the mouth
1272 dianŏigō (1), to open thoroughly

OPENINGS
6607 pethach (1), opening; door, entrance

OPENLY
5879 'Êynayim (1), double fountain
1219 dēmŏsiŏs (1), public; in public
1717 ĕmphanēs (1), apparent in self, seen
1722+3588+5318 ĕn (3), in; during; because of
1722+3954 ĕn (2), in; during; because of
3954 parrhēsia (4), frankness, boldness
5320 phanĕrōs (2), plainly, i.e. clearly

OPERATION
4639 ma'ăseh (2), action; labor
1753 ĕnĕrgĕia (1), efficiency, energy

OPERATIONS
1755 ĕnĕrgēma (1), effect, activity

OPHEL
6077 'Ôphel (5), fortress

OPHIR
211 'Ôwphîyr (13), Ophir

OPHNI
6078 'Ophnîy (1), Ophnite

OPHRAH
6084 'Ophrâh (8), female fawn

OPINION
1843 dêa' (3), knowledge

OPINIONS
5587 çâ'îph (1), divided in mind; sentiment

OPPORTUNITY
170 akairĕŏmai (1), to fail of a proper occasion
2120 ĕukairia (2), favorable occasion
2540 kairŏs (2), occasion, set time

OPPOSE
475 antidiatithĕmai (1), be disputatious

OPPOSED
498 antitassŏmai (1), *oppose, resist*

OPPOSEST
7852 sâṭam (1), to *persecute*

OPPOSETH
480 antikĕimai (1), to be an *opponent*

OPPOSITIONS
477 antithĕsis (1), *opposition*

OPPRESS
1792 dâkâ' (1), to *pulverize; be contrite*
3238 yânâh (5), to *suppress; to maltreat*
3905 lâchats (5), to *press; to distress*
6206 'ârats (1), to *awe; to dread; to harass*
6231 'âshaq (9), to *oppress; to defraud*
7703 shâdad (1), to *ravage*
2616 katadunastĕuō (1), to *oppress, exploit*

OPPRESSED
1790 dak (3), *injured, oppressed*
2541 châmôwts (1), *violent*
3238 yânâh (3), to *suppress; to maltreat*
3905 lâchats (7), to *press; to distress*
5065 nâgas (2), to *exploit; tax, harass*
6217 'âshûwq (1), used *tyranny*
6231 'âshaq (11), to *oppress; to defraud*
6234 'oshqâh (1), *anguish, trouble*
7533 râtsats (6), to *crack in pieces, smash*
2616 katadunastĕuō (1), to *oppress, exploit*
2669 katapŏnĕŏ (1), to *harass, oppress*

OPPRESSETH
3905 lâchats (1), to *press; to distress*
6231 'âshaq (3), to *oppress; to defraud*
6887 tsârar (1), to *cramp*

OPPRESSING
3238 yânâh (3), to *suppress; to maltreat*

OPPRESSION
3238 yânâh (1), to *suppress; to maltreat*
3906 lachats (7), *distress*
4939 mispâch (1), *slaughter*
6115 'ôtser (1), *closure; constraint*
6125 'âqâh (1), *constraint*
6233 'ôsheq (12), *injury; fraud; distress*
7701 shôd (1), *violence, ravage, destruction*

OPPRESSIONS
4642 ma'ăshaqqâh (1), *oppression*

6217 'âshûwq (2), used *tyranny*

OPPRESSOR
376+2555 'îysh (1), *man; male; someone*
3238 yânâh (1), to *suppress; to maltreat*
4642 ma'ăshaqqâh (1), *oppression*
5065 nâgas (5), to *exploit; to tax, harass*
6184 'ârîyts (1), *powerful or tyrannical*
6216 'âshôwq (1), *tyrant*
6231 'âshaq (2), to *oppress; to defraud*
6693 tsûwq (2), to *oppress, distress*

OPPRESSORS
3905 lâchats (1), to *press; to distress*
5065 nâgas (2), to *exploit; to tax, harass*
6184 'ârîyts (2), *powerful or tyrannical*
6231 'âshaq (2), to *oppress; to defraud*
7429 râmaç (1), to *tread upon*

ORACLE
1687 dᵉbîyr (16), *inmost part of the sanctuary*
1697 dâbâr (1), *word; matter; thing*

ORACLES
3051 lŏgiŏn (4), *utterance of God*

ORATION
1215 dēmēgŏrĕŏ (1), to *address an assembly*

ORATOR
3908 lachash (1), *incantation; amulet*
4489 rhētōr (1), legal *advocate*

ORCHARD
6508 pardêç (1), *park, cultivated garden area*

ORCHARDS
6508 pardêç (1), *park, cultivated garden area*

ORDAIN
3245 yâçad (1), *settle, establish a foundation*
7760 sûwm (1), to *put, place*
8239 shâphath (1), to *place or put*
1299 diatassō (1), to *institute, prescribe*
2525 kathistēmi (1), to *designate, constitute*

ORDAINED
3245 yâçad (1), *settle, establish a foundation*
3559 kûwn (1), to *set up: establish, fix, prepare*
4483 mᵉnâ' (Ch.) (1), to *count, appoint*
5414 nâthan (2), to *give*
5975 'âmad (1), to *stand*
6186 'ârak (2), to *set in a row, i.e. arrange,*
6213 'âsâh (3), to *do or make*
6965 qûwm (1), to *rise*

7760 sûwm (2), to *put, place*
1096 ginŏmai (1), to *be, become*
1299 diatassō (2), to *institute, prescribe*
2525 kathistēmi (2), to *designate, constitute*
2680 kataskĕuazō (1), to *prepare thoroughly*
2919 krinō (1), to *decide; to try, condemn, punish*
3724 hŏrizō (2), to *appoint, decree, specify*
4160 pŏiĕŏ (1), to *make or do*
4270 prŏgraphō (1), to *announce, prescribe*
4282 prŏĕtŏimazō (1), to *fit up in advance*
4304 prŏmĕlĕtaō (1), to *premeditate*
5021 tassō (2), to *arrange, assign*
5087 tithēmi (2), to *place*
5500 chĕirŏtŏnĕō (3), to *select or appoint*

ORDAINETH
6466 pâ'al (1), to *do, make or practice*

ORDER
631 'âçar (1), to *fasten; to join battle*
1700 dibrâh (1), *reason, suit or style; because*
3027 yâd (2), *hand; power*
3559 kûwn (3), to *set up: establish, fix, prepare*
4634 ma'ărâkâh (1), *arrangement, row; pile*
4941 mishpâṭ (5), *verdict; formal decree; justice*
5468 çeder (1), to *arrange, order*
6186 'ârak (19), to *set in a row, i.e. arrange,*
6187 'êrek (1), *pile, equipment, estimate*
6471 pa'am (1), *time; step; occurence*
6680 tsâvâh (3), to *constitute, enjoin*
7947 shâlab (1), to *make equidistant*
8626 tâqan (1), to *straighten; to compose*
1299 diatassō (3), to *institute, prescribe*
1930 ĕpidiŏrthŏō (1), to *arrange additionally*
2517 kathĕxēs (3), *in a sequence, subsequent*
5001 tagma (1), *series or succession*
5010 taxis (10), *succession; kind*

ORDERED
3559 kûwn (1), to *set up: establish, fix, prepare*
4634 ma'ărâkâh (1), *arrangement, row; pile*
6186 'ârak (2), to *set in a row, i.e. arrange,*

ORDERETH
7760 sûwm (1), to *put, place*

ORDERINGS
6486 pᵉquddâh (1), *visitation; punishment*

ORDERLY
4748 stŏichĕō (1), to *follow, walk; to conform*

ORDINANCE
2706 chôq (6), *appointment; allotment*
2708 chuqqâh (12), to *delineate*
3027 yâd (1), *hand; power*
4931 mishmereth (3), *watch, sentry, post*
4941 mishpâṭ (5), *verdict; formal decree; justice*
1296 diatagē (1), *institution*
2937 ktisis (1), *formation*

ORDINANCES
2706 chôq (3), *appointment; allotment*
2708 chuqqâh (10), to *delineate*
4687 mitsvâh (1), *command*
4941 mishpâṭ (6), *verdict; formal decree; justice*
1345 dikaiōma (3), *statute or decision*
1378 dŏgma (2), *law*
1379 dŏgmatizō (1), to *submit to a certain rule*
3862 paradŏsis (1), *precept; tradition*

ORDINARY
2706 chôq (1), *appointment; allotment*

OREB
6157 'ârôb (6), *swarming mosquitoes*

OREN
767 'Ôren (1), *ash tree*

ORGAN
5748 'ûwgâb (3), *reed-instrument*

ORGANS
5748 'ûwgâb (1), *reed-instrument*

ORION
3685 Kᵉçîyl (3), *constellation Orion*

ORNAMENT
642 'êphuddâh (1), *plating*
2481 châlîy (1), *polished trinket, ornament*
3880 livyâh (2), *wreath*
5716 'ădîy (2), *finery; outfit; headstall*

ORNAMENTS
5716 'ădîy (9), *finery; outfit; headstall*
5914 'ekeç (1), *anklet, bangle*
6287 pᵉ'êr (1), *fancy head-dress*
6807 tsᵉ'âdâh (1), *march; ankle-chain*
7720 sahărôn (2), *round pendant or crescent*

ORNAN
771 'Ornân (11), *strong*

ORPAH
6204 'Orpâh (2), *mane*

ORPHANS
3490 yâthôwm (1), child alone, fatherless child

OSEE
5617 Hōsēē (1), deliverer

OSHEA
1954 Hôwshêä' (2), deliverer

OSPRAY
5822 'oznîyâh (2), (poss.) sea-eagle

OSSIFRAGE
6538 pereç (2), kind of eagle

OSTRICH
5133 nôwtsâh (1), plumage

OSTRICHES
3283 yâ'ên (1), ostrich

OTHER
251 'âch (1), brother; relative; member
259 'echâd (32), first
269 'achôwth (1), sister
312 'achêr (99), other, another, different; next, more
317 'ochŏrîy (Ch.) (1), other, another
321 'ochŏrân (Ch.) (3), other, another
428 'êl-leh (3), these or those
2063 zô'th (2), this
2088 zeh (16), this or that
3541 kôh (1), thus
3671 kânâph (1), edge or extremity; wing
5048 neged (2), over against or before
5676 'êber (25), opposite side; east
6311 pôh (5), here or hence
7453 rêa' (2), associate; one close
7605 she'âr (1), remainder
8145 shênîy (36), second; again
237 allachŏthĕn (1), from elsewhere
240 allēlōn (5), one another
243 allŏs (51), different, other
244 allotriĕpiskŏpŏs (1), meddler, busybody
245 allŏtriŏs (2), not one's own
492 antiparĕrchŏmai (2), to go along opposite
846 autŏs (1), he, she, it
1520 hĕis (7), one
1565 ĕkĕinŏs (2), that one
1622 ĕktŏs (1), aside from, besides; except
2084 hĕtĕrŏglŏssŏs (1), foreigner
2085 hĕtĕrŏdidaskalĕō (1), to instruct differently
2087 hĕtĕrŏs (34), other or different
2548 kakĕinŏs (2), likewise that or those

3062 lŏipŏi (16), remaining ones
3739 hŏs (2), who, which, what, that
4008 pĕran (12), across, beyond

OTHERS
312 'achêr (9), other, another, different; next
428 'êl-leh (1), these
243 allŏs (29), different, other
245 allŏtriŏs (1), not one's own
2087 hĕtĕrŏs (11), other or different
3062 lŏipŏi (9), remaining ones
3588 hŏ (2), "the," i.e. the definite article
3739 hŏs (1), who, which

OTHERWISE
176 'ôw (1), or, whether
3808 lô' (1), no, not
243 allŏs (1), different, other
247 allōs (1), differently
1490 ĕi dĕ mĕ(gĕ) (3), but if not
1893 ĕpĕi (4), since
2085 hĕtĕrŏdidaskalĕō (1), to instruct differently
2088 hĕtĕrōs (1), differently, otherly

OTHNI
6273 'Otnîy (1), forcible

OTHNIEL
6274 'Othnîy'êl (7), force of God

OUCHES
4865 mishbeᵉtsâh (8), reticulated setting

OUGHT
1697 dâbâr (2), word; matter; thing
3972 mᵉ'ûwmâh (6), something; anything
4465 mimkâr (1), merchandise
1163 dĕi (29), it is (was) necessary
3762 ŏudĕis (1), none, nobody, nothing
3784 ŏphĕilō (15), to owe; to be under obligation
5100 tis (8), some or any
5534 chrē (1), it needs (must or should) be

OUGHTEST
1163 dĕi (3), it is (was) necessary

OUTCAST
5080 nâdach (1), to push off, scattered

OUTCASTS
1760 dâchâh (3), to push down; to totter
5080 nâdach (4), to push off, scattered

OUTER
2435 chîytsôwn (1), outer wall side; exterior; secular
1857 ĕxōtĕrŏs (3), exterior, outer

OUTGOINGS
4161 môwtsâ' (1), going forth
8444 tôwtsâ'âh (7), exit, boundary; deliverance

OUTLANDISH
5237 nokrîy (1), foreign; non-relative

OUTLIVED
748+3117+310 'ârak (1), to be, make long

OUTMOST
7020 qîytsôwn (1), terminal, end
7097 qâtseh (2), extremity

OUTRAGEOUS
7858 sheţeph (1), deluge, torrent

OUTRUN
4370+5032 prŏstrĕchō (1), to hasten by running

OUTSIDE
2351 chûwts (2), outside, outdoors; open market
7097 qâtseh (3), extremity
1623 hĕktŏs (1), sixth
1855 ĕxōthĕn (2), outside, external (-ly)

OUTSTRETCHED
5186 nâţâh (3), to stretch or spread out

OUTWARD
2435 chîytsôwn (8), outer wall side; exterior
5869 'ayin (1), eye; sight; fountain
1722+3588+5318 ĕn (1), in; during; because of
1854 ĕxō (1), out, outside
1855 ĕxōthĕn (2), outside, external (-ly)
4383 prŏsōpŏn (1), face, presence

OUTWARDLY
1722+5318 ĕn (1), in; during; because of
1855 ĕxōthĕn (1), outside, external (-ly)

OUTWENT
4281 prŏĕrchŏmai (1), to go onward, precede

OVEN
8574 tannûwr (10), fire-pot
2823 klibanŏs (2), earthen pot

OVENS
8574 tannûwr (1), fire-pot

OVER
413 'êl (19), to, toward
1157 bᵉ'ad (1), up to or over against
1541 gᵉlâh (Ch.) (1), to reveal mysteries
1591 gᵉnêbâh (1), something stolen
1869 dârak (1), to tread, trample; to walk, lead
2498 châlaph (1), to hasten away; to pass on
3148 yôwthêr (1), moreover; rest; gain
4136 mûwl (14), in front of, opposite
4480 min (1), from, out of

4605 ma'al (3), upward, above, overhead
5048 neged (27), over against or before
5226 nêkach (1), opposite
5227 nôkach (9), opposite, in front of
5414 nâthan (1), to give
5462 çâgar (2), to shut up; to surrender
5534 çâkar (1), to shut up; to surrender
5674 'âbar (171), to cross over; to transition
5736 'âdaph (3), to have surplus
5764 'ûwl (2), nursing babe
5848 'âţaph (1), to shroud, i.e. clothe
5921 'al (406), above, over, upon, or against
5922 'al (Ch.) (12), above, over, upon, or against
5924 'êllâ' (Ch.) (1), above
5927 'âlâh (1), to ascend, be high, mount
5975 'âmad (1), to stand
5980 'ummâh (23), near, beside, along with
6440 pânîym (2), face; front
6743 tsâlach (1), to push forward
6903 qᵉbêl (Ch.) (1), in front of, before
7235 râbâh (2), to increase
481 antikru (1), opposite of
495 antipĕran (1), on the opposite side
561 apĕnanti (2), opposite, before
1224 diabainō (1), to pass by, over, across
1276 diapĕraō (5), to cross over
1277 diaplĕō (1), to sail through, across
1330 diĕrchŏmai (4), to traverse, travel through
1537 ĕk (3), out, out of
1608 ĕkpŏrnĕuō (1), to be utterly unchaste
1722 ĕn (1), in; during; because of
1883 ĕpanō (6), over or on
1909 ĕpi (49), on, upon
1924 ĕpigraphō (1), to inscribe, write upon
2596 kata (2), down; according to
2634 katakuriĕuō (1), to control, lord over
2713 katĕnanti (4), directly opposite
3346 mĕtatithĕmi (1), to transport; to exchange
3860 paradidōmi (2), to hand over
3928 parĕrchŏmai (1), to go by; to perish
4008 pĕran (3), across, beyond
4012 pĕri (2), about; around
4052 pĕrissĕuō (1), to superabound

4121 plĕŏnazŏ (1), to
superabound
4291 prŏïstēmi (1), to
preside; to practice
5055 tĕlĕŏ (1), to end, i.e.
complete, execute
5228 hupĕr (1), over;
above; beyond
5231 hupĕranŏ (1),
above, upward
5240 hupĕrĕkchunŏ (1),
to overflow

OVERCAME
2634 katakuriĕuŏ (1), to
control, lord over
3528 nikaŏ (2), to
subdue, conquer

OVERCHARGE
1912 ĕpibarĕŏ (1), to be
severe toward

OVERCHARGED
925 barunŏ (1), to
burden; to grieve

OVERCOME
1464 gûwd (2), to attack
1986 hâlam (1), to strike,
beat, stamp, conquer
2476 châlûwshâh (1),
defeat
3201 yâkôl (1), to be able
3898 lâcham (2), to fight
a battle
5674 'âbar (1), to cross
over; to transition
7292 râhab (1), to urge
severely, i.e. importune
2274 hĕttaŏ (2), to rate
lower, be inferior
3528 nikaŏ (10), to
subdue, conquer

OVERCOMETH
3528 nikaŏ (11), to
subdue, conquer

OVERDRIVE
1849 dâphaq (1), to
knock; to press severely

OVERFLOW
6687 tsûwph (1), to
overflow
7783 shûwq (2), to
overflow
7857 shâtaph (10), to
gush; to inundate

OVERFLOWED
7857 shâtaph (1), to
gush; to inundate
2626 katakluzŏ (1), to
deluge, flood

OVERFLOWETH
4390 mâlê' (1), to fill; be
full

OVERFLOWING
1065 bᵉkîy (1), weeping
2230 zerem (1), gush of
water, flood
7857 shâtaph (8), to
gush; to inundate
7858 sheteph (1), deluge,
torrent

OVERFLOWN
3332 yâtsaq (1), to pour
out
4390 mâlê' (1), to fill; be
full

7857 shâtaph (1), to
gush; to inundate

OVERLAID
2645 châphâh (4), to
cover; to veil, to encase
5968 'âlaph (1), to be
languid, faint
6823 tsâphâh (28), to
sheet over with metal
7901 shâkab (1), to lie
down
4028 pĕrikaluptŏ (1), to
cover eyes; to plait

OVERLAY
2902 tûwach (1), to
whitewash
6823 tsâphâh (12), to
sheet over with metal

OVERLAYING
6826 tsippûwy (2),
encasement with metal

OVERLIVED
748+3117+310 'ârak (1),
to be, make long

OVERMUCH
4055 pĕrissŏtĕrŏs (1),
more superabundant

OVERPASS
5674 'âbar (1), to cross
over; to transition

OVERPAST
5674 'âbar (2), to cross
over; to transition

OVERPLUS
5736 'âdaph (1), to have
surplus

OVERRAN
5674 'âbar (1), to cross
over; to transition

OVERRUNNING
5674 'âbar (1), to cross
over; to transition

OVERSEE
5329 nâtsach (1), i.e. to
be eminent

OVERSEER
6485 pâqad (2), to visit,
care for, count
6496 pâqîyd (4),
superintendent, officer
7860 shôtēr (1), to write;
official who is a scribe

OVERSEERS
5329 nâtsach (2), i.e. to
be eminent
6485 pâqad (2), to visit,
care for, count
6496 pâqîyd (1),
superintendent, officer
1985 ĕpiskŏpŏs (1),
overseer, supervisor

OVERSHADOW
1982 ĕpiskiazŏ (2), to
cast a shade upon

OVERSHADOWED
1982 ĕpiskiazŏ (3), to
cast a shade upon

OVERSIGHT
4870 mishgeh (1), error
5414 nâthan (1), to give
5921 'al (2), above, over,
upon, or against
6485 pâqad (4), to visit,
care for, count

6486 pᵉquddâh (2),
visitation; punishment
1983 ĕpiskŏpĕŏ (1), to
oversee; to beware

OVERSPREAD
5310 nâphats (1), to dash
to pieces; to scatter

OVERSPREADING
3671 kânâph (1), edge or
extremity; wing

OVERTAKE
5066 nâgash (2), to be,
come, bring near
5381 nâsag (14), to reach
2638 katalambanŏ (1), to
seize; to possess

OVERTAKEN
5381 nâsag (1), to reach
4301 prŏlambanŏ (1), to
take before

OVERTAKETH
5381 nâsag (1), to reach

OVERTHREW
2015 hâphak (4), to
change, overturn
4114 mahpêkâh (3),
destruction
5286 nâ'ar (1), to growl
5287 nâ'ar (1), to tumble
about
390 anastrĕphŏ (1), to
remain, to live
2690 katastrĕphŏ (2), to
upset, overturn

OVERTHROW
1760 dâchâh (1), to push
down; to totter
2015 hâphak (5), to
change, overturn
2018 hăphêkâh (1),
destruction, demolition
2040 hâraç (2), to pull
down; break, destroy
4073 mᵉdachphâh (1),
ruin
4114 mahpêkâh (2),
destruction
5186 nâtâh (1), to stretch
or spread out
5307 nâphal (2), to fall
5422 nâthats (1), to tear
down
396 anatrĕpŏ (1), to
overturn, destroy
2647 kataluŏ (1), to
demolish
2692 katastrŏphê (1),
catastrophical ruin

OVERTHROWETH
2040 hâraç (1), to pull
down; break, destroy
5557 çâlaph (4), to
wrench; to subvert

OVERTHROWN
2015 hâphak (4), to
change, overturn
2040 hâraç (2), to pull
down; break, destroy
3782 kâshal (2), to totter,
waver; to falter
4114 mahpêkâh (1),
destruction
5307 nâphal (3), to fall
5791 'âvath (1), to wrest,
twist

8045 shâmad (1), to
desolate
8058 shâmat (1), to
jostle; to let alone
2693 katastrŏnnumi (1),
to prostrate, i.e. slay

OVERTOOK
1692 dâbaq (3), to cling
or adhere; to catch
5381 nâsag (7), to reach

OVERTURN
2015 hâphak (1), to
change, overturn
5754 'avvâh (1),
overthrow, ruin

OVERTURNED
2015 hâphak (1), to
change, overturn

OVERTURNETH
2015 hâphak (3), to
change, overturn

OVERWHELM
5307 nâphal (1), to fall

OVERWHELMED
3680 kâçâh (2), to cover
5848 'âtaph (5), to
shroud, i.e. clothe
7857 shâtaph (1), to
gush; to inundate

OWE
3784 ŏphĕilŏ (1), to owe;
to be under obligation

OWED
3781 ŏphĕilĕtēs (1),
person indebted
3784 ŏphĕilŏ (2), to owe;
to be under obligation

OWEST
3784 ŏphĕilŏ (3), to owe;
to be under obligation
4359 prŏsŏphĕilŏ (1), to
be indebted

OWETH
3784 ŏphĕilŏ (1), to owe;
to be under obligation

OWL
1323+3284 bath (2),
daughter, descendant
3244 yanshûwph (3), bird
3563 kôwç (3), cup;
(poss.) owl
3917 lîylîyth (1), night
spectre (spirit)
7091 qippôwz (1),
arrow-snake

OWLS
1323+3284 bath (6),
daughter, descendant

OWN
249 'ezrâch (15), native
born
3548 kôhên (2), one
officiating as a priest
5315 nephesh (1), life;
breath; soul; wind
7522 râtsôwn (1), delight
830 authairĕtŏs (1),
self-chosen
846 autŏs (1), he, she, it
848 hautou (15), self
849 autŏchĕïr (1),
self-handed, personally
1103 gnēsiŏs (2),
genuine, true

1438 hĕautŏu (24),
himself, herself, itself
1683 ĕmautŏu (2), *myself*
1699 ĕmŏs (2), *my*
2398 idiŏs (76), *private or
separate*
2596 kata (1), *down;
according to*
4572 sĕautŏu (2), *of
yourself*

OWNER
113 'âdôwn (1),
sovereign, i.e. *controller*
1167 ba'al (10), *master;
husband; owner; citizen*
7069 qânâh (1), *to create;
to procure*
3490 nauklērŏs (1), *ship
captain*

OWNERS
1167 ba'al (4), *master;
husband; owner; citizen*
2962 kuriŏs (1), *supreme,
controller, Mr.*

OWNETH
2076 ĕsti (1), *he* (she or
it) *is; they are*

OX
441 'allûwph (1), *friend,*
one *familiar; chieftain,
leader*
1241 bâqâr (3), *plowing*
ox; *herd*
7794 shôwr (53), *bullock*
8377 t°'ôw (1), *antelope*
1016 bŏus (4), *ox, cattle*

OXEN
441 'allûwph (1), *friend,*
one *familiar; chieftain*
504 'eleph (2), *ox; cow or
cattle*
1241 bâqâr (74), *plowing*
ox; *herd*
5091 nâhâh (1), *to
bewail; to* assemble
6499 par (2), *bullock*
7794 shôwr (8), *bullock*
8450 tôwr (Ch.) (4), *bull*
1016 bŏus (4), *ox, cattle*
5022 taurŏs (2), *bullock,
ox*

OZEM
684 'Ôtsem (2), *strong*

OZIAS
3604 Ŏzias (2), *strength
of Jehovah*

OZNI
244 'Oznîy (1), *having*
(quick) *ears*

OZNITES
244 'Oznîy (1), *having*
(quick) *ears*

PAARAI
6474 Pa'ăray (1), *yawning*

PACATIANA
3818 Pakatianē (1),
Pacatianian

PACES
6806 tsa'ad (1), *pace* or
regular *step*

PACIFIED
3722 kâphar (1), *to
placate* or *cancel*
7918 shâkak (1), *to lay* a
trap; *to allay*

PACIFIETH
3240 yânach (1), *to allow
to stay*
3711 kâphâh (1), *to tame*
or *subdue*

PACIFY
3722 kâphar (1), *to
cover; to placate*

PADAN
6307 Paddân (1),
table-land of Aram

PADAN-ARAM
6307 Paddân (10),
table-land of Aram

PADDLE
3489 yâthêd (1), *tent peg*

PADON
6303 Pâdôwn (2), *ransom*

PAGIEL
6295 Pag'îy'êl (5),
accident of God

PAHATH-MOAB
6355 Pachath Môw'âb
(6), *pit of Moáb*

PAI
6464 Pâ'ûw (1),
screaming

PAID
3052 y°hab (Ch.) (1), *to
give*
5414 nâthan (1), *to give*
591 apŏdidōmi (2), *to
give away*

PAIN
2256 chebel (1),
company, band
2342 chûwl (6), *to dance,
whirl; to writhe in pain*
2427 chîyl (3), *throe* of
painful childbirth
2470 châlâh (1), *to be
weak, sick, afflicted*
2479 chalchâlâh (4),
writhing in childbirth
3510 kâ'ab (1), *to feel
pain; to grieve; to spoil*
3511 k°'êb (1), *suffering;
adversity*
4341 mak'ôb (2),
anguish; affliction
5999 'âmâl (1), *wearing
effort; worry*
4192 pŏnŏs (2), *toil,* i.e.
anguish

PAINED
2342 chûwl (3), *to dance,
whirl; to writhe* in pain
3176 yâchal (1), *to wait;
to be patient, hope*
928 basanizŏ (1), *to
torture, torment*

PAINFUL
5999 'âmâl (1), *wearing
effort; worry*

PAINFULNESS
3449 mŏchthŏs (1),
sadness

PAINS
4712 mêtsar (1), *trouble*
6735 tsîyr (1), *hinge;
trouble*
4192 pŏnŏs (1), *toil,* i.e.
anguish

5604 ŏdin (1), *pang* of
childbirth; *agony*

PAINTED
4886 mâshach (1), *to rub
or smear* with oil
7760+6320 sûwm (1), *to
put, place*

PAINTEDST
3583 kâchal (1), *to paint
the eyes with stibnite*

PAINTING
6320 pûwk (1), *stibium*

PAIR
2201 zĕugŏs (1), *team,
pair*
2218 zugŏs (1), *coupling,
yoke*

PALACE
643 'appeden (1),
pavilion or palace-tent
759 'armôwn (4), *citadel,
high fortress*
1002 bîyrâh (17), *palace,
citadel*
1004 bayith (1), *house;
temple; family, tribe*
1055 bîythân (3), *large
house*
1964 hêykâl (8), *palace;
temple; hall*
1965 hêykal (Ch.) (4),
palace; temple
2038 harmôwn (1), *high
castle or fortress*
2918 ṭîyrâh (1), *fortress;
hamlet*
833 aulē (7), *palace;
house; courtyard*
4232 praitōriŏn (1),
court-room or *palace*

PALACES
759 'armôwn (27),
citadel, high fortress
1964 hêykâl (3), *palace;
temple; hall*
2918 ṭîyrâh (1), *fortress;
hamlet*

PALAL
6420 Pâlâl (1), *judge*

PALE
2357 châvar (1), *to
blanch* with shame
5515 chlōrŏs (1),
greenish, verdant

PALENESS
3420 yêrâqôwn (1),
paleness; mildew

PALESTINA
6429 P°lesheth (3),
migratory

PALESTINE
6429 P°lesheth (1),
migratory

PALLU
6396 Pallûw' (4),
distinguished

PALLUITES
6384 Pallû'îy (1), *Palluïte*

PALM
3709 kaph (2), *hollow of
hand; paw; sole* of foot
8558 tâmâr (12), *palm
tree*

8560 tômer (2), *palm
trunk*
8561 timmôr (17),
palm-like pilaster
4475 rhapisma (1), *slap,
strike*
5404 phŏinix (1),
palm-tree

PALMERWORM
1501 gâzâm (3), *kind of
locust*

PALMS
3709 kaph (4), *hollow of
hand; paw; sole* of foot
4474 rhapizō (1), *to slap,
rap, strike*
4475 rhapisma (1), *slap,
strike*
5404 phŏinix (1),
palm-tree

PALSIES
3886 paraluō (1), *to be
paralyzed or enfeebled*

PALSY
3885 paralutikŏs (10),
lame person
3886 paraluō (3), *to be
paralyzed or enfeebled*

PALTI
6406 Palṭîy (1), *delivered*

PALTIEL
6409 Palṭîy'êl (1),
deliverance of God

PALTITE
6407 Palṭîy (1), *Paltite*

PAMPHYLIA
3828 Pamphulia (5),
every-tribal, i.e.
heterogeneous

PAN
3595 kîyôwr (1), *caldron;
washbowl*
4227 machăbath (6),
metal *pan* for baking in
4958 masrêth (1), *pan*

PANGS
2256 chebel (2),
company, band
2427 chîyl (2), *throe* of
painful childbirth
6735 tsîyr (3), *hinge;
herald, trouble*
6887 tsârar (2), *to cramp*

PANNAG
6436 Pannag (1), *food,*
(poss.) *pastry*

PANS
2281 châbêth (1),
griddle-cake
5518 çîyr (1), *thorn; hook*
6517 pârûwr (1), *skillet*
6745 tsêlâchâh (1),
flattened out *platter*

PANT
7602 shâ'aph (1), *to be
angry; to hasten*

PANTED
7602 shâ'aph (1), *to be
angry; to hasten*
8582 tâ'âh (1), *to
vacillate,* i.e. *reel*

PANTETH
5503 çâchar (1), *to travel
round; to palpitate*

6165 'ârag (2), to *long* for, *pant for*

PAPER
6169 'ârâh (1), *bulrushes, reeds*
5489 chartēs (1), *sheet of* papyrus *paper*

PAPHOS
3974 Paphŏs (2), *Paphus*

PAPS
7699 shad (1), *female breast*
3149 mastŏs (3), *female breast; chest* area

PARABLE
4912 mâshâl (17), *pithy maxim; taunt*
3850 parabŏlē (31), *fictitious narrative*
3942 parŏimia (1), *illustration; adage*

PARABLES
4912 mâshâl (1), *pithy maxim; taunt*
3850 parabŏlē (15), *fictitious narrative*

PARADISE
3857 paradĕisŏs (3), *park*

PARAH
6511 Pârâh (1), *heifer*

PARAMOURS
6370 pîylegesh (1), *concubine; paramour*

PARAN
6290 Pâ'rân (11), *ornamental*

PARBAR
6503 Parbâr (2), *Parbar* or *Parvar*

PARCEL
2513 chelqâh (5), *allotment*
5564 chŏriŏn (1), *spot or plot of ground*

PARCHED
2788 chârêr (1), *arid, parched*
7039 qâlîy (6), *roasted ears of cereal grain*
8273 shârâb (1), *glow of the hot air; mirage*

PARCHMENTS
3200 mĕmbrana (1), sheep-*skin for writing*

PARDON
3722 kâphar (1), *to cover; to expiate*
5375 nâsâ' (3), *to lift up*
5545 çâlach (11), *to forgive*
5547 çᵉlîychâh (1), *pardon*

PARDONED
5545 çâlach (2), *to forgive*
7521 râtsâh (1), *to be pleased with; to satisfy*

PARDONETH
5375 nâsâ' (1), *to lift up*

PARE
6213 'âsâh (1), *to do or make*

PARENTS
1118 gŏnĕus (19), *parents*

3962 patēr (1), *father*
4269 prŏgŏnŏs (1), *ancestor*

PARLOUR
3957 lishkâh (1), *room*
5944 'ălîyâh (4), *upper things; second-story*

PARLOURS
2315 cheder (1), *apartment, chamber*

PARMASHTA
6534 Parmashtâ' (1), *Parmashta*

PARMENAS
3937 Parmĕnas (1), *constant*

PARNACH
6535 Parnak (1), *Parnak*

PAROSH
6551 Par'ôsh (5), *flea*

PARSHANDATHA
6577 Parshandâthâ' (1), *Parshandatha*

PART
2505 châlaq (3), *to be smooth; be slippery*
2506 chêleq (19), *allotment*
2513 chelqâh (1), *flattery; allotment*
2673 châtsâh (1), *to cut or split in two; to halve*
2677 chêtsîy (3), *half or middle, midst*
4481 min (Ch.) (5), *from or out of*
4490 mânâh (1), *ration; lot or portion*
4940 mishpâchâh (2), *family, clan, people*
5337 nâtsal (1), *to deliver; snatched away*
6418 pelek (7), *spindle-whorl; crutch*
6447 paç (Ch.) (2), *palm of the hand*
6504 pârad (1), *to spread or separate*
6626 pâthath (1), *to break, crumble*
7117 qᵉtsâth (1), *termination; portion*
2819 klērŏs (2), *lot, portion*
3307 mĕrizō (1), *to apportion, share*
3310 mĕris (5), *portion, share, participation*
3313 mĕrŏs (17), *division or share*
3348 mĕtĕchō (1), *to share or participate*
4119 plĕiŏn (1), *more*
4403 prumna (1), *stern of a ship*

PARTAKER
2506 chêleq (1), *smoothness; allotment*
2841 kŏinōnĕō (2), *to share or participate*
2844 kŏinōnŏs (1), *associate, partner*
3335 mĕtalambanō (1), *to participate*
3348 mĕtĕchō (2), *to share or participate*

4777 sugkakŏpathĕō (1), to *suffer hardship with*
4791 sugkŏinōnŏs (1), *co-participant*

PARTAKERS
482 antilambanŏmai (1), *to succor; aid*
2841 kŏinōnĕō (3), to *share or participate*
2844 kŏinōnŏs (4), *associate, partner*
3310 mĕris (1), *portion, share, participation*
3335 mĕtalambanō (1), *to participate*
3348 mĕtĕchō (3), *to share or participate*
3353 mĕtŏchŏs (4), *sharer, associate*
4790 sugkŏinōnĕō (1), *to co-participate in*
4791 sugkŏinōnŏs (1), *co-participant*
4829 summĕrizŏmai (1), *to share jointly*
4830 summĕtŏchŏs (2), *co-participant*

PARTAKEST
1096+4791 Bêlṭᵉsha'tstsar (Ch.) (1), *Belteshatstsar*

PARTED
2505 châlaq (2), *to be smooth; be slippery*
2673 châtsâh (1), *to cut or split in two; to halve*
6504 pârad (2), *to spread or separate*
1266 diamĕrizō (6), *to have dissension*
1339 diïstēmi (1), *to remove, intervene*

PARTETH
6504 pârad (1), *to spread or separate*
6536 pâraç (2), *to break in pieces; to split*

PARTHIANS
3934 Parthŏs (1), *inhabitant of Parthia*

PARTIAL
5375+6440 nâsâ' (1), *to lift up*
1252 diakrinō (1), *to decide; to hesitate*

PARTIALITY
87 adiakritŏs (1), *impartial*
4346 prŏsklisis (1), *favoritism*

PARTICULAR
3313 mĕrŏs (1), *division or share*
3588+1520 hŏ (1), *"the," i.e. the definite article*

PARTICULARLY
1520+1538+2596 hĕis (1), *one*
2596+3313 kata (1), *down; according to*

PARTING
517 'êm (1), *mother*

PARTITION
5674 'âbar (1), *to cross over; to transition*

5418 phragmŏs (1), *fence or enclosing barrier*

PARTLY
7118 qᵉtsâth (Ch.) (1), *termination; portion*
1161 dĕ (1), *but, yet*
3313+5100 mĕrŏs (1), *division or share*
5124+3303 tŏutŏ (1), *that thing*

PARTNER
2505 châlaq (1), *to be smooth; be slippery*
2844 kŏinōnŏs (2), *associate, partner*

PARTNERS
2844 kŏinōnŏs (1), *associate, partner*
3353 mĕtŏchŏs (1), *sharer, associate*

PARTRIDGE
7124 qôrê' (2), *calling partridge*

PARTS
905 bad (1), *limb, member; bar*
1335 bether (2), *section, piece*
1506 gezer (1), *portion, piece*
1697 dâbâr (1), *word; matter; thing*
2506 chêleq (6), *smoothness; allotment*
2677 chêtsîy (1), *half or middle, midst*
3027 yâd (3), *hand; power*
3411 yᵉrêkâh (2), *recesses, far places*
5409 nêthach (1), *fragment*
6310 peh (1), *mouth; opening*
7098 qâtsâh (1), *termination; fringe*
2825 klinē (1), *couch*
3313 mĕrŏs (6), *division or share*

PARUAH
6515 Pârûwach (1), *blossomed*

PARVAIM
6516 Parvayim (1), *Parvajim*

PAS-DAMMIM
6450 Paç Dammîym (1), *dell of bloodshed*

PASACH
6457 Pâçak (1), *divider*

PASEAH
6454 Pâçêach (3), *limping*

PASHUR
6583 Pashchûwr (14), *liberation*

PASS
935 bôw' (3), *to go or come*
1980 hâlak (1), *to walk; live a certain way*
2498 châlaph (2), *to hasten away; to pass on*
2499 chălaph (Ch.) (4), *to have time pass by*
3615 kâlâh (1), *to cease, be finished, perish*

4569 ma'ăbâr (1),
crossing-place
5674 'âbar (153), to *cross*
over; to *transition*
5709 'ădâ' (Ch.) (1), to
pass on or *continue*
6213 'âsâh (5), to *do* or
make
6452 pâçach (2), to *hop,
skip* over; to *hesitate*
390 anastrĕphō (1), to
remain, to live
1224 diabainō (1), to
pass by, over, across
1276 diapĕraō (1), to
cross over
1279 diapŏrĕuŏmai (1),
to *travel through*
1330 diĕrchŏmai (7), to
traverse, travel through
3928 parĕrchŏmai (19),
to *go by*; to *perish*
5230 hupĕrakmŏs (1),
past the bloom of youth

PASSAGE
1552 gᵉlîylâh (1), *circuit*
or *region*
4569 ma'ăbâr (2),
crossing-place
5674 'âbar (1), to *cross*
over; to *transition*

PASSAGES
4569 ma'ăbâr (4),
crossing-place
5676 'êber (1), *opposite*
side; *east*

PASSED
1431 gâdal (1), to *be
great, make great*
2498 châlaph (2), to
hasten away; to *pass on*
5674 'âbar (117), to *cross*
over; to *transition*
5709 'ădâ' (Ch.) (1), to
pass on or *continue*
5710 'ădâh (1), to *pass on*
or *continue; to remove*
6437 pânâh (1), to *turn,*
to *face*
6452 pâçach (1), to *hop,
skip* over; to *hesitate*
492 antiparĕrchŏmai (2),
to *go along opposite*
565 apĕrchŏmai (1), to
go off, i.e. depart
1224 diabainō (1), to
pass by, over, across
1276 diapĕraō (3), to
cross over
1330 diĕrchŏmai (11), to
traverse, travel through
1353 diŏdĕuō (1), to
travel through
3327 mĕtabainō (2), to
depart, move from
3855 paragō (6), to *go
along* or *away*
3899 parapŏrĕuŏmai (4),
to *travel near*
3928 parĕrchŏmai (3), to
go by; to *perish, neglect*
4281 prŏĕrchŏmai (1), to
go onward, precede

PASSEDST
5674 'âbar (1), to *cross*
over; to *transition*

PASSENGERS
5674 'âbar (4), to *cross*
over; to *transition*
5674+1870 'âbar (1), to
cross over; to *transition*

PASSEST
5674 'âbar (5), to *cross*
over; to *transition*

PASSETH
1980 hâlak (4), to *walk;
live a certain way*
2498 châlaph (1), to
hasten away; to *pass on*
5674 'âbar (28), to *cross*
over; to *transition*
3855 paragō (2), to *go
along* or *away*
3928 parĕrchŏmai (1), to
go by; to *perish*
5235 hupĕrballō (1), to
surpass
5242 hupĕrĕchō (1), to
excel; superior

PASSING
5674 'âbar (7), to *cross*
over; to *transition*
1330 diĕrchŏmai (2), to
traverse, travel through
2064 ĕrchŏmai (1), to *go,
come*
3881 paralĕgŏmai (1), to
sail past
3928 parĕrchŏmai (1), to
go by; to *perish*

PASSION
3958 paschō (1), to
experience pain

PASSIONS
3663 hŏmŏiŏpathēs (2),
similarly affected

PASSOVER
6453 Peçach (48),
Passover
3957 pascha (28),
Passover events

PASSOVERS
6453 Peçach (1), *Passover*

PAST
369 'ayin (1), *there is no,
i.e., not exist, none*
5493 çûwr (2), to *turn* off
5674 'âbar (8), to *cross*
over; to *transition*
6924 qedem (1), *eastern;
antiquity; before*
7223 rî'shôwn (1), *first*
7291 râdaph (1), to *run
after* with hostility
7725 shûwb (1), to *turn*
back; to *return*
8032 shilshôwm (9), *day
before yesterday*
421 anĕxichniastŏs (1),
untraceable
524 apalgĕō (1), *become
apathetic*
565 apĕrchŏmai (2), to
go off, i.e. depart
1096 ginŏmai (2), to *be,
become*
1230 diaginŏmai (1), to
have time elapse
1330 diĕrchŏmai (1), to
traverse, travel through
3819 palai (1), *formerly;
sometime since*

3844 para (1), *from; with;
besides; on account of*
3855 paragō (1), to *go
along* or *away*
3928 parĕrchŏmai (3), to
go by; to *perish*
3944 parŏichŏmai (1), to
escape along
4266 prŏginŏmai (1), to
*have previously
transpired*
4302 prŏlĕgō (1), to
predict, forewarn

PASTOR
7462 râ'âh (1), to *tend* a
flock, i.e. *pasture* it

PASTORS
7462 râ'âh (7), to *tend* a
flock, i.e. *pasture* it
4166 pŏimēn (1),
shepherd

PASTURE
4829 mir'eh (11),
pasture; haunt
4830 mir'îyth (8),
pasturage; flock
3542 nŏmē (1), *pasture,
i.e. the act of feeding*

PASTURES
3733 kar (2), *ram sheep*
4829 mir'eh (1), *pasture;
haunt*
4830 mir'îyth (1),
pasturage; flock
4945 mashqeh (1), *butler;
drink; well-watered*
4999 nâ'âh (5), *home,
dwelling; pasture*
7471 rᵉ'îy (1), *pasture*

PATARA
3959 Patara (1), *Patara*

PATE
6936 qodqôd (1), *crown*
of the head

PATH
734 'ôrach (9), *road;
manner of life*
4546 mᵉçillâh (1), *main
thoroughfare; viaduct*
4570 ma'gâl (3), *circular
track* or *camp rampart*
4934 mish'ôwl (1),
narrow passage
5410 nâthîyb (8),
(beaten) *track, path*
7635 shâbîyl (1), *track* or
passage-way

PATHROS
6624 Pathrôwç (5),
Pathros

PATHRUSIM
6625 Pathrûçîy (2),
Pathrusite

PATHS
734 'ôrach (16), *road;
manner of life*
4546 mᵉçillâh (1), *main
thoroughfare; viaduct*
4570 ma'gâl (6), *circular
track* or *camp rampart*
5410 nâthîyb (14),
(beaten) *track, path*
7635 shâbîyl (1), *track* or
passage-way
5147 tribŏs (3), *rut,* or
worn track

5163 trŏchia (1), *course*
of conduct, *path* of life

PATHWAY
1870+5410 derek (1),
road; course of life

PATIENCE
3114 makrŏthumĕō (3),
to *be forbearing, patient*
3115 makrŏthumia (2),
forbearance; fortitude
5281 hupŏmŏnē (29),
endurance, constancy

PATIENT
750 'ârêk (1), *patient*
420 anĕxikakŏs (1),
forbearing
1933 ĕpiĕikēs (1), *mild,
gentle*
3114 makrŏthumĕō (3),
to *be forbearing, patient*
5278 hupŏmĕnō (1), to
undergo, bear (trials)
5281 hupŏmŏnē (2),
perseverence

PATIENTLY
2342 chûwl (1), to *dance,
whirl*; to *wait*; to *pervert*
6960 qâvâh (1), to *collect;
to expect*
3114 makrŏthumĕō (1),
to *be forbearing, patient*
3116 makrŏthumōs (1),
*with long, enduring
temper, i.e. leniently*
5278 hupŏmĕnō (2), to
undergo, bear (trials)

PATMOS
3963 Patmŏs (1), *Patmus*

PATRIARCH
3966 patriarchēs (2),
progenitor or patriarch

PATRIARCHS
3966 patriarchēs (2),
progenitor or patriarch

PATRIMONY
1+5921 'âb (1), *father*

PATROBAS
3969 Patrŏbas (1),
father's life

PATTERN
4758 mar'eh (1),
appearance; vision
8403 tabnîyth (9),
structure; model
8508 toknîyth (1),
admeasurement
5179 tupŏs (2), *shape,
resemblance; "type"*
5296 hupŏtupōsis (1),
example, pattern

PATTERNS
5262 hupŏdĕigma (1),
exhibit; specimen

PAU
6464 Pâ'ûw (1),
screaming

PAUL
3972 Paulŏs (157), *little*

PAUL'S
3972 Paulŏs (6), *little*

PAULUS
3972 Paulŏs (1), *little*

PAVED
3840 libnâh (1), transparency
7528 râtsaph (1), to tessellate, embroider

PAVEMENT
4837 martsepheth (1), pavement, stone base
7531 ritspâh (7), hot stone; pavement
3037 lithŏs (1), stone

PAVILION
5520 çôk (1), hut of entwined boughs
5521 çukkâh (2), tabernacle; shelter
8237 shaphrûwr (1), tapestry or canopy

PAVILIONS
5521 çukkâh (3), tabernacle; shelter

PAW
3027 yâd (2), hand; power

PAWETH
2658 châphar (1), to delve, to explore

PAWS
3709 kaph (1), hollow of hand; paw; sole of foot

PAY
5414 nâthan (2), to give
5414+4377 nâthan (1), to give
5415 nᵉthan (Ch.) (1), to give
5927 'âlâh (1), to ascend, be high, mount
7725 shûwb (1), to turn back; to return
7999 shâlam (19), to be safe; be, make complete
8254 shâqal (4), to suspend in trade
586 apŏdĕkatŏŏ (1), to tithe, give a tenth
591 apŏdidōmi (7), to give away
5055 tĕlĕŏ (2), to end, discharge (a debt)

PAYED
7999 shâlam (1), to be safe; be, make complete
1183 dĕkatŏŏ (1), to give or take a tenth

PAYETH
7999 shâlam (1), to be safe; be, make complete

PAYMENT
591 apŏdidōmi (1), to give away

PEACE
1826 dâmam (1), to be silent; to be astonished
2013 hâçâh (2), to hush, be quiet
2790 chârash (26), to be silent; to be deaf
2814 châshâh (9), to hush or keep quiet
6963 qôwl (1), voice or sound
7962 shalvâh (1), security, ease
7965 shâlôwm (169), safe; well; health, peace

7999 shâlam (11), to be safe; be, make complete
8001 shᵉlâm (Ch.) (4), prosperity
8002 shelem (87), thank offering
1515 ĕirēnē (87), peace; health; prosperity
1517 ĕirēnŏpŏiĕŏ (1), to harmonize, make peace
1518 ĕirēnŏpŏiŏs (3), peaceable
2270 hēsuchazŏ (2), to refrain
4263 prŏbatŏn (1), sheep
4601 sigaŏ (4), to keep silent
4623 siōpaŏ (9), to be quiet
5392 phimŏŏ (2), to muzzle; restrain to silence

PEACEABLE
7961 shâlêv (1), careless, carefree; security
7965 shâlôwm (2), safe; well; health, peace
7999 shâlam (1), to be safe; be, make complete
8003 shâlêm (1), complete; friendly; safe
1516 ĕirēnikŏs (2), pacific, peaceful
2272 hēsuchiŏs (1), still, undisturbed

PEACEABLY
7962 shalvâh (2), security, ease
7965 shâlôwm (9), safe; well; health, peace
1518 ĕirēnŏpŏiŏs (1), peaceable

PEACEMAKERS
1518 ĕirēnŏpŏiŏs (1), peaceable

PEACOCKS
7443 renen (1), female ostrich
8500 tukkîy (2), (poss.) peacock

PEARL
3135 margaritēs (2), pearl

PEARLS
1378 gâbîysh (1), crystal
3135 margaritēs (7), pearl

PECULIAR
5459 çᵉgullâh (5), wealth
1519+4047 ĕis (1), to or into
4041 pĕriŏusiŏs (1), special, one's very own

PEDAHEL
6300 Pᵉdah'êl (1), God has ransomed

PEDAHZUR
6301 Pᵉdâhtsûwr (5), Rock has ransomed

PEDAIAH
6305 Pᵉdâyâh (8), Jehovah has ransomed

PEDIGREES
3205 yâlad (1), to bear young; to father a child

PEELED
4178 môwrâṭ (2), obstinate, independent
4803 mâraṭ (1), to polish; to make bald

PEEP
6850 tsâphaph (1), to coo or chirp as a bird

PEEPED
6850 tsâphaph (1), to coo or chirp as a bird

PEKAH
6492 Peqach (11), watch

PEKAHIAH
6494 Pᵉqachyâh (3), Jehovah has observed

PEKOD
6489 Pᵉqôwd (2), punishment

PELAIAH
6411 Pᵉlâyâh (3), Jehovah has distinguished

PELALIAH
6421 Pᵉlalyâh (1), Jehovah has judged

PELATIAH
6410 Pᵉlaṭyâh (5), Jehovah has delivered

PELEG
6389 Peleg (7), earthquake

PELET
6404 Peleṭ (2), escape

PELETH
6431 Peleth (2), swiftness

PELETHITES
6432 Pᵉlêthîy (7), courier or official messenger

PELICAN
6893 qâ'ath (3), pelican

PELONITE
6397 Pᵉlôwnîy (3), separate

PEN
2747 chereṭ (1), chisel; style for writing
5842 'êṭ (4), stylus; reed pen
7626 shêbeṭ (1), stick; clan, family
2563 kalamŏs (1), reed; pen

PENCE
1220 dēnariŏn (5), denarius

PENIEL
6439 Pᵉnûw'êl (1), face of God

PENINNAH
6444 Pᵉninnâh (3), round pearl

PENKNIFE
8593 ta'ar (1), knife; razor; scabbard

PENNY
1220 dēnariŏn (9), denarius

PENNYWORTH
1220 dēnariŏn (2), denarius

PENTECOST
4005 pĕntēkŏstē (3), the festival of Pentecost

PENUEL
6439 Pᵉnûw'êl (7), face of God

PENURY
4270 machçôwr (1), impoverishment
5303 hustĕrēma (1), deficit; poverty; lacking

PEOPLE
376 'îysh (1), man; male; someone
523 'ummâh (1), community, clan, tribe
528 'Âmôwn (1), Amon
582 'ĕnôwsh (1), man; person, human
1121 bên (1), son, descendant; people
1471 gôwy (11), foreign nation; Gentiles
3816 lᵉ'ôm (24), community, nation
5712 'êdâh (1), assemblage; family
5971 'am (1827), people; tribe; troops
5972 'am (Ch.) (15), people, nation
1218 dēmŏs (4), public, crowd
1484 ĕthnŏs (2), race; tribe; pagan
2992 laŏs (138), people; public
3793 ŏchlŏs (83), throng

PEOPLE'S
5971 'am (2), people; tribe; troops
2992 laŏs (2), people; public

PEOPLES
2992 laŏs (2), people; public

PEOR
6465 Pᵉ'ôwr (4), gap

PEOR'S
6465 Pᵉ'ôwr (1), gap

PERADVENTURE
194 'ûwlay (23), if not; perhaps
3863 lûw' (1), if; would that!
6435 pên (1), lest, not
3379 mēpŏtĕ (1), not ever; if, or lest ever
5029 tacha (1), shortly, i.e. possibly

PERAZIM
6559 Pᵉrâtsîym (1), breaks

PERCEIVE
995 bîyn (1), to understand; discern
3045 yâda' (7), to know
7200 râ'âh (1), to see
8085 shâma' (1), to hear intelligently
991 blĕpŏ (1), to look at
1097 ginōskŏ (2), to know
1492 ĕidŏ (3), to know
2334 thĕōrĕŏ (4), to see; to discern

2638 katalambanō (1), to seize; to possess
3539 nŏiĕŏ (2), to exercise the mind
3708 hŏraō (1), to stare, see clearly; to discern

PERCEIVED
238 'âzan (1), to listen
995 bîyn (3), to understand; discern
3045 yâda' (11), to know
5234 nâkar (1), to acknowledge
7200 râ'âh (4), to see
8085 shâma' (1), to hear intelligently
143 aisthanŏmai (1), to apprehend
1097 ginōskō (7), to know
1921 ĕpiginōskō (3), to become fully acquainted with
2147 hĕuriskō (1), to find
2638 katalambanō (1), to possess; to understand
2657 katanŏĕō (1), to observe fully

PERCEIVEST
3045 yâda' (1), to know
2657 katanŏĕō (1), to observe fully

PERCEIVETH
995 bîyn (1), to understand; discern
2938 ţâ'am (1), to taste; to perceive, experience
7789 shûwr (1), to spy out, survey

PERCEIVING
1492 ĕidō (3), to know

PERDITION
684 apōlĕia (8), ruin or loss

PERES
6537 pᵉraç (Ch.) (1), to split up

PERESH
6570 Peresh (1), excrement

PEREZ
6557 Perets (3), breech

PEREZ-UZZA
6560 Perets 'Uzza' (1), break of Uzza

PEREZ-UZZAH
6560 Perets 'Uzzâ' (1), break of Uzza

PERFECT
1584 gâmar (1), to end; to complete; to fail
1585 gᵉmar (Ch.) (1), to complete
3559 kûwn (1), to render sure, proper
3632 kâlîyl (3), whole, entire; complete; whole
3634 kâlal (1), to complete
4357 miklâh (1), wholly, solidly
7999 shâlam (1), to be safe; be, make complete
8003 shâlêm (15), complete; friendly; safe

8503 taklîyth (1), extremity
8535 tâm (9), morally pious; gentle, dear
8537 tôm (1), prosperity
8549 tâmîym (18), entire, complete; integrity
8552 tâmam (2), to complete, finish
195 akribĕia (1), exactness
197 akribĕstĕrŏn (1), more exactly
199 akribōs (1), exactly, carefully
739 artiŏs (1), complete, thorough, capable
2005 ĕpitĕlĕō (1), to terminate; to undergo
2675 katartizō (5), to repair; to prepare
3647 hŏlŏklēria (1), wholeness
4137 plērŏō (1), to fill, make complete
5046 tĕlĕiŏs (17), complete; mature
5048 tĕlĕiŏō (13), to perfect, complete

PERFECTED
3634 kâlal (1), to complete
5927+724 'âlâh (1), to ascend, be high, mount
8003 shâlêm (1), complete; friendly; safe
2675 katartizō (1), to repair; to prepare
5048 tĕlĕiŏō (4), to perfect, complete

PERFECTING
2005 ĕpitĕlĕō (1), to terminate; to undergo
2677 katartismŏs (1), complete furnishing

PERFECTION
3632 kâlîyl (1), whole, entire; complete; whole
4359 miklâl (1), perfection of beauty
4512 minleh (1), wealth
8502 tiklâh (1), completeness
8503 taklîyth (2), extremity
8537 tôm (1), completeness
2676 katartisis (1), thorough equipment
5050 tĕlĕiōsis (1), completion; verification
5051 tĕlĕiŏtēs (1), consummator, perfecter
5052 tĕlĕsphŏrĕō (1), to ripen fruit

PERFECTLY
998 bîynâh (1), discernment
197 akribĕstĕrŏn (3), more exactly
199 akribōs (1), exactly, carefully
1295 diasōzō (1), to cure, preserve, rescue
2675 katartizō (1), to repair; to prepare

PERFECTNESS
5047 tĕlĕiŏtēs (1), completeness; maturity

PERFORM
5414 nâthan (1), to give
6213 'âsâh (12), to do or make
6633 tsâbâ' (1), to mass an army or servants
6965 qûwm (13), to rise
7999 shâlam (4), to be safe; be, make complete
591 apŏdidōmi (1), to give away
2005 ĕpitĕlĕō (2), to terminate; to undergo
2716 katĕrgazŏmai (1), to finish; to accomplish
4160 pŏiĕō (2), to do

PERFORMANCE
2005 ĕpitĕlĕō (1), to terminate; to undergo
5050 tĕlĕiōsis (1), completion; verification

PERFORMED
1214 bâtsa' (1), to plunder; to finish
6213 'âsâh (5), to do or make
6965 qûwm (11), to rise
7999 shâlam (1), to be safe; be, make complete
1096 ginŏmai (1), to be, become
2005 ĕpitĕlĕō (1), to terminate; to undergo
5055 tĕlĕō (1), to end, i.e. complete, execute

PERFORMETH
1584 gâmar (1), to end; to complete; to fail
6965 qûwm (1), to rise
7999 shâlam (2), to be safe; be, make complete

PERFORMING
6381 pâlâ' (2), to be, make great, wonderful

PERFUME
7004 qᵉţôreth (3), fumigation

PERFUMED
5130 nûwph (1), to quiver, vibrate, rock
6999 qâţar (1), to turn into fragrance by fire

PERFUMES
7547 raqqûach (1), scented ointment

PERGA
4011 Pĕrgē (3), tower

PERGAMOS
4010 Pĕrgamŏs (2), fortified

PERHAPS
686 ara (1), then, so, therefore
3381 mēpōs (1), lest somehow
5029 tacha (1), shortly, i.e. possibly

PERIDA
6514 Pᵉrûwdâ' (1), dispersion

PERIL
2794 kindunŏs (1), danger, risk

PERILOUS
5467 chalĕpŏs (1), difficult, i.e. dangerous

PERILS
2794 kindunŏs (8), danger, risk

PERISH
6 'âbad (73), perish; destroy
7 'âbad (Ch.) (2), perish; destroy
8 'ôbêd (2), wretched; destruction
1478 gâva' (1), to expire, die
1820 dâmâh (2), to be silent; to fail, cease
3772 kârath (1), to cut (off, down or asunder)
5307 nâphal (1), to fall
5486 çûwph (1), to terminate
5595 çâphâh (2), to scrape; to remove
5674 'âbar (1), to cross over; to transition
6544 pâra' (1), to loosen; to expose, dismiss
7843 shâchath (1), to decay; to ruin
622 apŏllumi (25), to destroy fully; to perish
853 aphanizō (1), to disappear, be destroyed
1311 diaphthĕirō (1), to ruin, to decay
1510+1519+604 ĕimi (1), I exist, I am
2704 kataphthĕirō (1), to spoil entirely
5356 phthŏra (1), ruin; depravity, corruption

PERISHED
6 'âbad (17), perish; destroy
1478 gâva' (1), to expire, die
8045 shâmad (1), to desolate
599 apŏthnēskō (1), to die off
622 apŏllumi (5), to destroy fully; to perish
4881 sunapŏllumi (1), to destroy, be slain with

PERISHETH
6 'âbad (6), perish; destroy
622 apŏllumi (3), to destroy fully; to perish

PERISHING
5674 'âbar (1), to cross over; to transition

PERIZZITE
6522 Pᵉrîzziy (5), of the open country

PERIZZITES
6522 Pᵉrîzziy (18), of the open country

PERJURED
1965 ĕpiŏrkŏs (1), forswearer, perjurer

PERMISSION
4774 suggnṓmē (1), concession

PERMIT
2010 ĕpitrĕpō (2), allow, permit

PERMITTED
2010 ĕpitrĕpō (2), allow, permit

PERNICIOUS
684 apṓlĕia (1), ruin or loss

PERPETUAL
5331 netsach (4), splendor; lasting
5769 'ôwlâm (22), eternity; always
8548 tâmîyd (2), constantly, regularly

PERPETUALLY
3605+3711 kôl (2), all, any or every
5703 'ad (1), perpetuity

PERPLEXED
943 bûwk (2), to be confused
639 apŏrĕō (1), be at a mental loss, be puzzled
1280 diapŏrĕō (2), to be thoroughly puzzled

PERPLEXITY
3998 mᵉbûwkâh (2), perplexity, confusion
640 apŏria (1), state of quandary, perplexity

PERSECUTE
1814 dâlaq (1), to flame; to pursue
7291 râdaph (14), to run after with hostility
7921+310 shâkôl (1), to miscarry
1377 diōkō (8), to pursue; to persecute
1559 ĕkdiōkō (1), to expel or persecute

PERSECUTED
4783 murdâph (1), persecuted
7291 râdaph (5), to run after with hostility
1377 diōkō (13), to pursue; to persecute
1559 ĕkdiōkō (1), to expel or persecute

PERSECUTEST
1377 diōkō (6), to pursue; to persecute

PERSECUTING
1377 diōkō (1), to pursue; to persecute

PERSECUTION
7291 râdaph (1), to run after with hostility
1375 diōgmŏs (5), persecution
1377 diōkō (3), to pursue; to persecute
2347 thlipsis (1), pressure, trouble

PERSECUTIONS
1375 diōgmŏs (5), persecution

PERSECUTOR
1376 diōktēs (1), persecutor

PERSECUTORS
1814 dâlaq (1), to flame; to pursue
7291 râdaph (7), to run after with hostility

PERSEVERANCE
4343 prŏskartĕrēsis (1), perseverance

PERSIA
6539 Pâraç (27), Paras
6540 Pâraç (Ch.) (2), Paras

PERSIAN
6523 parzel (Ch.) (1), iron
6542 Parçîy (1), Parsite

PERSIANS
6539 Pâraç (1), Paras
6540 Pâraç (Ch.) (4), Paras

PERSIS
4069 Pĕrsis (1), Persis

PERSON
120 'âdâm (2), human being; mankind
376 'îysh (3), man; male; someone
376+120 'îysh (1), man; male; someone
1167 ba'al (1), master; husband; owner; citizen
5315 nephesh (14), life; breath; soul; wind
6440 pânîym (10), face; front
4383 prŏsōpŏn (5), face, presence
5287 hupŏstasis (1), essence; assurance

PERSONS
120 'âdâm (3), human being; mankind
376 'îysh (8), man; male; someone
582 'ĕnôwsh (2), man; person, human
4962 math (1), men
5315 nephesh (12), life; breath; soul; wind
5315+120 nephesh (4), life; breath; soul; wind
6440 pânîym (11), face; front
678 aprŏsōpŏlēptōs (2), without prejudice
4380 prŏsōpŏlēptĕō (1), to show partiality
4381 prŏsōpŏlēptēs (1), exhibiting partiality
4382 prŏsōpŏlēpsia (4), favoritism
4383 prŏsōpŏn (2), face, presence

PERSUADE
5496 çûwth (3), to stimulate; to seduce
6601 pâthâh (3), to be, make simple; to delude
3982 pĕithō (3), to assent to evidence

PERSUADED
5496 çûwth (1), to stimulate; to seduce

PERSUADEST
3982 pĕithō (1), to assent to evidence

PERSUADETH
5496 çûwth (1), to stimulate; to seduce
374 anapĕithō (1), to incite, persuade

PERSUADING
3982 pĕithō (2), to assent to evidence

PERSUASION
3988 pĕismŏnē (1), persuadableness

PERTAINED
1961 hâyâh (1), to exist

PERTAINETH
1961 hâyâh (1), to exist
3627 kᵉlîy (1), implement, thing
3348 mĕtĕchō (1), to share or participate

PERTAINING
4012 pĕri (1), about

PERUDA
6514 Pᵉrûwdâ' (1), dispersion

PERVERSE
1942 havvâh (1), desire; craving
2015 hâphak (1), to change, pervert
3399 yârat (1), to be rash
3868 lûwz (1), to depart; to be perverse
3891 lᵉzûwth (1), perverseness
5753 'âvâh (2), to be crooked
5773 'av'eh (1), perversity
6140 'âqash (2), to knot or distort; to pervert
6141 'iqqêsh (4), distorted, warped, false
8419 tahpûkâh (1), perversity or fraud
1294 diastrĕphō (4), to be morally corrupt
3859 paradiatribē (1), meddlesomeness

PERVERSELY
5753 'âvâh (2), to be crooked
5791 'âvath (1), to wrest, twist

PERVERSENESS
3868 lûwz (1), to depart; to be perverse
4297 mutteh (1), distortion; iniquity
5558 çeleph (2), distortion; viciousness
5766 'evel (1), moral evil
5999 'âmâl (1), wearing effort; worry

PERVERT
5186 nâtâh (2), to stretch or spread out

PEULTHAI
6469 Pᵉ'ull'thay (1), laborious

(Column 3)

6601 pâthâh (1), to be, make simple; to delude
3982 pĕithō (16), to assent to evidence
4135 plērŏphŏrĕō (2), to assure or convince

PERSUADEST
3982 pĕithō (1), to assent to evidence

PERSUADETH
5496 çûwth (1), to stimulate; to seduce
374 anapĕithō (1), to incite, persuade

PERSUADING
3982 pĕithō (2), to assent to evidence

PERSUASION
3988 pĕismŏnē (1), persuadableness

PERTAINED
1961 hâyâh (1), to exist

PERTAINETH
1961 hâyâh (1), to exist
3627 kᵉlîy (1), implement, thing
3348 mĕtĕchō (1), to share or participate

PERTAINING
4012 pĕri (1), about

PERUDA
6514 Pᵉrûwdâ' (1), dispersion

PERVERSE
1942 havvâh (1), desire; craving
2015 hâphak (1), to change, pervert
3399 yârat (1), to be rash
3868 lûwz (1), to depart; to be perverse
3891 lᵉzûwth (1), perverseness
5753 'âvâh (2), to be crooked
5773 'av'eh (1), perversity
6140 'âqash (2), to knot or distort; to pervert
6141 'iqqêsh (4), distorted, warped, false
8419 tahpûkâh (1), perversity or fraud
1294 diastrĕphō (4), to be morally corrupt
3859 paradiatribē (1), meddlesomeness

PERVERSELY
5753 'âvâh (2), to be crooked
5791 'âvath (1), to wrest, twist

PERVERSENESS
3868 lûwz (1), to depart; to be perverse
4297 mutteh (1), distortion; iniquity
5558 çeleph (2), distortion; viciousness
5766 'evel (1), moral evil
5999 'âmâl (1), wearing effort; worry

PERVERT
5186 nâtâh (2), to stretch or spread out

(Column 4)

PERVERTED
2015 hâphak (1), to change, pervert
5186 nâtâh (1), to stretch or spread out
5753 'âvâh (2), to be crooked
7725 shûwb (1), to turn back; to return

PERVERTETH
5186 nâtâh (1), to stretch or spread out
5557 çâlaph (2), to wrench; to subvert
6140 'âqash (1), to knot or distort; to pervert
654 apŏstrĕphō (1), to turn away or back

PERVERTING
1294 diastrĕphō (1), to be morally corrupt

PESTILENCE
1698 deber (47), pestilence, plague

PESTILENCES
3061 lŏimŏs (2), plague; disease; pest

PESTILENT
3061 lŏimŏs (1), plague; disease; pest

PESTLE
5940 'ĕlîy (1), mortar pestle

PETER
4074 Pĕtrŏs (157), piece of rock

PETER'S
4074 Pĕtrŏs (4), piece of rock

PETHAHIAH
6611 Pᵉthachyâh (4), Jehovah has opened

PETHOR
6604 Pᵉthôwr (2), Pethor

PETHUEL
6602 Pᵉthûw'êl (1), enlarged of God

PETITION
1159 bâ'ûw (Ch.) (2), request; prayer
7596 shᵉ'êlâh (10), petition

PETITIONS
4862 mish'âlâh (1), request

PEULTHAI
6469 Pᵉ'ull'thay (1), laborious

(Column 5)

PERVERTED
5557 çâlaph (1), to wrench; to subvert
5791 'âvath (3), to wrest, twist
6140 'âqash (1), to knot or distort; to pervert
8138 shânâh (1), to fold, to transmute
1294 diastrĕphō (1), to be morally corrupt
3344 mĕtastrĕphō (1), to transmute; corrupt

PHALEC
5317 Phalĕk (1),
earthquake

PHALLU
6396 Pallûw' (1),
distinguished

PHALTI
6406 Palţîy (1), delivered

PHALTIEL
6409 Palţîy'êl (1),
deliverance of God

PHANUEL
5323 Phanŏuēl (1), face
of God

PHARAOH
6547 Par'ôh (221), Paroh
5328 Pharaō (3), Pharaoh

PHARAOH'S
6547 Par'ôh (46), Paroh
5328 Pharaō (2), Pharaoh

PHARAOH-HOPHRA
6548 Par'ôh Chophra'
(1), Paroh-Chophra

PHARAOH-NECHO
6549 Par'ôh Nᵉkôh (1),
Paroh-Nekoh (or -Neko)

PHARAOH-NECHOH
6549 Par'ôh Nᵉkôh (4),
Paroh-Nekoh (or -Neko)

PHARES
5329 Pharĕs (3), breech

PHAREZ
6557 Perets (12), breech

PHARISEE
5330 Pharisaiŏs (10),
separatist

PHARISEE'S
5330 Pharisaiŏs (2),
separatist

PHARISEES
5330 Pharisaiŏs (86),
separatist

PHARISEES'
5330 Pharisaiŏs (1),
separatist

PHAROSH
6551 Par'ôsh (1), flea

PHARPAR
6554 Parpar (1), rapid

PHARZITES
6558 Partsîy (1), Partsite

PHASEAH
6454 Pâçêach (1), limping

PHEBE
5402 Phŏibē (2), bright

PHENICE
5403 Phŏinikē (2),
palm-country
5405 Phŏinix (1),
palm-tree

PHENICIA
5403 Phŏinikē (1),
palm-country

PHICHOL
6369 Pîykôl (3), mouth of
all

PHILADELPHIA
5359 Philadĕlphĕia (2),
fraternal

PHILEMON
5371 Philēmōn (2),
friendly

PHILETUS
5372 Philētŏs (1), amiable

PHILIP
5376 Philippŏs (33), fond
of horses

PHILIP'S
5376 Philippŏs (3), fond
of horses

PHILIPPI
5375 Philippŏi (8),
Philippi

PHILIPPIANS
5374 Philippēsiŏs (1),
native of Philippi

PHILISTIA
6429 Pᵉlesheth (3),
migratory

PHILISTIM
6430 Pᵉlishtîy (1),
Pelishtite

PHILISTINE
6430 Pᵉlishtîy (33),
Pelishtite

PHILISTINES
6430 Pᵉlishtîy (250),
Pelishtite

PHILISTINES'
6430 Pᵉlishtîy (4),
Pelishtite

PHILOLOGUS
5378 Philŏlŏgŏs (1),
argumentative, learned

PHILOSOPHERS
5386 philŏsŏphŏs (1), one
fond of wise things, i.e.
philosopher

PHILOSOPHY
5385 philŏsŏphia (1),
wise things

PHINEHAS
6372 Pîynᵉchâç (24),
mouth of a serpent

PHINEHAS'
6372 Pîynᵉchâç (1),
mouth of a serpent

PHLEGON
5393 Phlĕgōn (1), blazing

PHRYGIA
5435 Phrugia (4), Phrygia

PHURAH
6513 Pûrâh (2), foliage

PHUT
6316 Pûwţ (2), Put

PHUVAH
6312 Pûw'âh (1), blast

PHYGELLUS
5436 Phugĕllŏs (1),
fugitive

PHYLACTERIES
5440 phulaktēriŏn (1),
guard-case

PHYSICIAN
7495 râphâ' (1), to cure,
heal
2395 iatrŏs (5), physician

PHYSICIANS
7495 râphâ' (4), to cure,
heal

2395 iatrŏs (2), physician

PI-BESETH
6364 Pîy-Beçeth (1),
Pi-Beseth

PI-HAHIROTH
6367 Pîy ha-Chîrôth (4),
mouth of the gorges

PICK
5365 nâqar (1), to bore;
to gouge

PICTURES
4906 maskîyth (2),
carved figure
7914 sᵉkîyâh (1),
conspicuous object

PIECE
95 'ăgôwrâh (1), coin
829 'eshpâr (2), portion
915 bâdâl (1), part
1335 bether (1), piece
2513 chelqâh (3),
flattery; allotment
3603 kikkâr (2), round
loaf; talent
4060 middâh (7),
measure; portion
4749 miqshâh (1), work
molded by hammering
5409 nêthach (2),
fragment
6400 peiach (6), slice
6595 path (2), bit, morsel
1406 drachmē (2), coin
1915 ĕpiblēma (4), patch
3313 merŏs (1), division
or share
4138 plērōma (1), what
fills; what is filled

PIECES
1506 gezer (1), portion,
piece
1917 haddâm (Ch.) (2),
bit, piece
5409 nêthach (9),
fragment
6595 path (3), bit, morsel
7168 qera' (3), rag, torn
pieces
7518 rats (1), fragment
1288 diaspaō (1), to sever
or dismember
1406 drachmē (1), coin

PIERCE
4272 mâchats (1), to
crush; to subdue
5344 nâqab (2), to
puncture, perforate
1330 dierchŏmai (1), to
traverse, travel through

PIERCED
738 'ărîy (1), lion
1856 dâqar (1), to stab,
pierce
4272 mâchats (1), to
crush; to subdue
5365 nâqar (1), to bore;
to gouge
1574 ĕkkĕntĕō (2), to
pierce or impale
3572 nussō (1), to pierce,
stab
4044 pĕripĕirō (1), to
penetrate entirely

PIERCETH
5344 nâqab (1), to
puncture, perforate

PIERCING
1281 bârîyach (1),
fleeing, gliding serpent
1338 diïknĕŏmai (1),
penetrate, pierce

PIERCINGS
4094 madqârâh (1),
wound

PIETY
2151 ĕusĕbĕō (1), to put
show piety toward

PIGEON
1469 gôwzâl (1), young of
a bird
3123 yôwnâh (1), dove

PIGEONS
3123 yôwnâh (9), dove
4058 pĕristĕra (1),
pigeon, dove

PILATE
4091 Pilatŏs (55), firm

PILDASH
6394 Pildâsh (1), Pildash

PILE
4071 mᵉdûwrâh (2), pile

PILEHA
6401 Pilchâ' (1), slicing

PILGRIMAGE
4033 mâgûwr (4), abode

PILGRIMS
3927 parepidēmŏs (2),
resident foreigner

PILLAR
4676 matstsêbâh (10),
column or stone
4678 matstsebeth (4),
stock of a tree
5324 nâtsab (1), to station
5333 nᵉtsîyb (1), military
post; statue
5982 'ammûwd (29),
column, pillar
4769 stulŏs (2),
supporting pillar; leader

PILLARS
547 'ômᵉnâh (1), column
4552 miç'âd (1),
balustrade for stairs
4676 matstsêbâh (2),
column or stone
4690 mâtsûwq (1),
column; hilltop
5982 'ammûwd (79),
column, pillar
8490 tîymârâh (2),
column, i.e. cloud
4769 stulŏs (2),
supporting pillar; leader

PILLED
6478 pâtsal (2), to peel

PILLOW
3523 kᵉbîyr (2), matrass,
quilt of animal hair
4344 prŏskĕphalaiŏn (1),
cushion pillow

PILLOWS
3704 keçeth (2), cushion
or pillow
4763 mᵉra'ăshâh (2),
headpiece; head-rest

PILOTS
2259 chôbêl (4), sailor

PILTAI
6408 Pilṭay (1), *Piltai*

PIN
3489 yâthêd (3), tent *peg*

PINE
2100 zûwb (1), to *waste away*
4743 mâqaq (4), to *melt; to flow, dwindle, vanish*
6086+8081 'êts (1), *wood*
8410 tidhâr (2), *lasting tree (poss.) oak*

PINETH
3583 xĕrainŏ (1), to *shrivel, to mature*

PINING
1803 dallâh (1), loose *hair; indigent, needy*

PINNACLE
4419 pṭĕrugiŏn (2), *winglet, i.e. extremity*

PINON
6373 Pîynôn (2), *Pinon*

PINS
3489 yâthêd (10), tent *peg*

PIPE
2485 châlîyl (3), *flute*
836 aulŏs (1), *flute*

PIPED
2490 châlal (1), to *play the flute*
832 aulĕŏ (3), to play the *flute*

PIPERS
834 aulētēs (1), *flute-player*

PIPES
2485 châlîyl (3), *flute instrument*
4166 mûwtsâqâh (1), *tube*
5345 neqeb (1), *bezel, gem mounting*
6804 tsantârâh (1), *tube, pipe*

PIRAM
6502 Pir'âm (1), *wildly*

PIRATHON
6552 Pir'âthôwn (1), *chieftaincy*

PIRATHONITE
6553 Pir'âthôwnîy (5), *Pirathonite*

PISGAH
6449 Piçgâh (5), *cleft*

PISIDIA
4099 Pisidia (2), *Pisidia*

PISON
6376 Pîyshôwn (1), *dispersive*

PISPAH
6462 Piçpâh (1), *dispersion*

PISS
7890 shayin (2), *urine*

PISSETH
8366 shâthan (6), to *urinate as a male*

PIT
875 bᵉ'êr (3), *well, cistern*
953 bôwr (41), *pit hole, cistern, well; prison*
1360 gebe' (1), *reservoir*

1475 gûwmmâts (1), *pit*
6354 pachath (8), *pit for catching animals*
7585 shᵉ'ôwl (3), *abode of the dead*
7743+7882 shûwach (1), to *sink*
7745 shûwchâh (2), *chasm*
7816 shᵉchûwth (1), *pit*
7845 shachath (14), *pit; destruction*
7882 shîychâh (1), *pit-fall*
999 bŏthunŏs (1), *cistern, pit-hole*
5421 phrĕar (5), *cistern or water well; abyss*

PITCH
167 'âhal (1), to pitch a tent
2203 zepheth (3), *asphalt*
2583 chânâh (11), to *encamp*
3724 kôpher (1), *village; bitumen; henna*
6965 qûwm (1), to *rise*
8628 tâqa' (1), to *clatter, slap, drive, clasp*

PITCHED
167 'âhal (1), to pitch a tent
2583 chânâh (70), to *encamp*
5186 nâṭâh (8), to *stretch or spread out*
8628 tâqa' (2), to *clatter, slap, drive, clasp*
4078 pĕgnumi (1), to *set up a tent*

PITCHER
3537 kad (10), *jar, pitcher*
2765 kĕramiŏn (2), *earthenware vessel*

PITCHERS
3537 kad (4), *jar, pitcher*
5035 nebel (1), *skin-bag for liquids; vase; lyre*

PITHOM
6619 Pîthôm (1), *Pithom*

PITHON
6377 Pîythôwn (2), *expansive*

PITIED
2347 chûwç (1), to be *compassionate*
2550 châmal (4), to *spare, have pity on*
7356 racham (1), *compassion; womb*

PITIETH
4263 machmâl (1), *delight*
7355 râcham (2), to be *compassionate*

PITIFUL
7362 rachmânîy (1), *compassionate*
2155 ĕusplagchnŏs (1), *compassionate*
4184 pŏlusplagchnŏs (1), *extremely compassionate*

PITS
953 bôwr (1), *pit hole, cistern, well; prison*

1356 gêb (1), *well, cistern; pit*
7745 shûwchâh (1), *chasm*
7825 shᵉchîyth (1), *pit-fall*
7882 shîychâh (1), *pit-fall*

PITY
2347 chûwç (6), to be *compassionate*
2550 châmal (14), to *spare, have pity on*
2551 chemlah (1), *commiseration, pity*
2603 chânan (3), to *implore*
2617 cheçed (1), *kindness, favor*
5110 nûwd (1), to *console, deplore; to taunt*
7355 râcham (1), to be *compassionate*
7356 racham (1), *compassion; womb*
1653 ĕlĕĕŏ (1), to give out *compassion*

PLACE
870 'âthar (Ch.) (5), *after*
1004 bayith (7), *house; temple; family, tribe*
1367 gᵉbûwlâh (1), *region*
3027 yâd (7), *hand; power*
3241 Yânîym (1), *asleep*
3427 yâshab (2), to *dwell, to remain; to settle*
3653 kên (1), *pedestal or station of a basin*
4349 mâkôwn (11), *basis; place*
4612 ma'ămâd (1), *position; attendant*
4634 ma'ărâkâh (1), *arrangement, row; pile*
4724 miqvâh (1), *water reservoir*
4725 mâqôwm (373), *general locality, place*
4800 merchâb (1), *open space; liberty*
5182 nᵉchath (Ch.) (1), to *descend; to depose*
5414 nâthan (3), to *give*
5977 ômed (6), *fixed spot*
6607 pethach (1), *opening; door*
7675 shebeth (1), *abode or locality*
7760 sûwm (1), to *place*
7931 shâkan (5), to *reside*
8414 tôhûw (1), *waste, desolation, formless*
8478 tachath (17), *bottom; underneath*
201 akrŏatēriŏn (1), *audience-room*
402 anachôrĕŏ (1), to *retire, withdraw*
1502 ĕikŏ (1), to be weak, i.e. *yield*
1564 ĕkĕithĕn (1), *from there*
1786 ĕntŏpiŏs (1), *local resident*
3692 ŏpē (1), *hole, i.e. cavern; spring of water*
3699 hŏpŏu (1), *at whichever spot*
4042 pĕriŏchē (1), *passage of Scripture*

5117 tŏpŏs (74), *place*
5562 chôrĕŏ (1), to *pass, enter; to hold, admit*
5564 chôriŏn (2), *spot or plot of ground*
5602 hŏdĕ (2), *here*

PLACED
776 'erets (1), *earth, land, soil; country*
3240 yânach (2), to *allow to stay*
3427 yâshab (5), to *dwell, to remain; to settle*
3947 lâqach (1), to *take*
5414 nâthan (1), to *give*
5975 'âmad (1), to *stand*
7760 sûwm (1), to *place*
7931 shâkan (2), to *reside*

PLACES
168 'ôhel (1), *tent*
1004 bayith (9), *house; temple; family, tribe*
2723 chorbâh (1), *desolation, dry desert*
3027 yâd (1), *hand; power*
4585 mᵉ'ôwnâh (1), *abode*
4725 mâqôwm (20), *general locality, place*
5439 çâbîyb (1), *circle; environs; around*
8478 tachath (1), *bottom; underneath; in lieu of*
3837 pantachŏu (1), *universally, everywhere*
5117 tŏpŏs (7), *place*

PLAGUE
4046 maggêphâh (20), *pestilence; defeat*
4347 makkâh (2), *blow; wound; pestilence*
5061 nega' (64), *infliction, affliction; leprous spot*
5063 negeph (7), *infliction of disease*
3148 mastix (2), *flogging device*
4127 plēgē (2), *stroke; wound; calamity*

PLAGUED
4046 maggêphâh (1), *pestilence; defeat*
5060 nâga' (3), to *strike*
5062 nâgaph (2), to *inflict a disease*

PLAGUES
1698 deber (1), *pestilence, plague*
4046 maggêphâh (1), *pestilence; defeat*
4347 makkâh (8), *blow; wound; pestilence*
5061 nega' (1), *infliction, affliction; leprous spot*
3148 mastix (2), *flogging device*
4127 plēgē (10), *stroke; wound; calamity*

PLAIN
58 'âbêl (1), *meadow*
436 'êlôwn (7), *oak*
874 bâ'ar (1), to *explain*
1236 biq'â (Ch.) (1), *wide level valley*
1237 biq'âh (7), *wide level valley*

3603 kikkâr (13), *tract or region; round loaf*
4334 mîyshôwr (14), *plain; justice*
5228 nâkôach (1), *equitable, correct*
5549 çâlal (1), to *mound up; to exalt; to oppose*
6160 'ărâbâh (22), *desert, wasteland*
7737 shâvâh (1), to *level, i.e. equalize*
8219 sh°phêlâh (3), *lowland,*
8535 tâm (1), *morally pious; gentle, dear*
3723 ŏrthŏs (1), *correctly, rightly*
5117+3977 tŏpŏs (1), *place*

PLAINLY
559 'âmar (1), to *say*
874 bâ'ar (1), to *explain*
1540 gâlâh (1), to *denude; uncover*
5046 nâgad (1), to *announce*
6568 p°rash (Ch.) (1), to *specify, translate*
6703 tsach (1), *dazzling, i.e. sunny, bright*
1718 ĕmphanizŏ (1), to *show forth*
3954 parrhēsia (4), *frankness, boldness*

PLAINNESS
3954 parrhēsia (1), *frankness, boldness*

PLAINS
436 'êlôwn (2), *oak*
4334 mîyshôwr (1), *plain; justice*
6160 'ărâbâh (20), *desert, wasteland*
8219 sh°phêlâh (2), *lowland,*

PLAISTER
1528 gîyr (Ch.) (1), *lime for plaster*
2902 tûwach (1), to *whitewash*
4799 mârach (1), to *apply by rubbing*
7874 sîyd (2), to *plaster, whitewash with lime*

PLAISTERED
2902 tûwach (2), to *whitewash*

PLAITING
1708 ĕmplŏkē (1), *braiding of the hair*

PLANES
4741 maqtsû'âh (1), *wood-carving chisel*

PLANETS
4208 mazzâlâh (1), *constellations*

PLANKS
5646 'âb (1), *architrave*
6086 'êts (1), *wood, things made of wood*
6763 tsêlâ' (1), *side*

PLANT
4302 maṭṭâ' (1), *something planted*
5193 nâṭa' (31), to *plant*

5194 neṭa' (3), *plant; plantation; planting*
5414 nâthan (1), to *give*
7880 sîyach (1), *shrubbery*
8362 shâthal (2), to *transplant*
5451 phutĕia (1), *shrub or vegetable*

PLANTATION
4302 maṭṭâ' (1), *something planted*

PLANTED
5193 nâṭa' (21), to *plant*
8362 shâthal (8), to *transplant*
4854 sumphutŏs (1), *closely united to*
5452 phutĕuŏ (8), to *implant, i.e. to instill doctrine*

PLANTEDST
5193 nâṭa' (2), to *plant*

PLANTERS
5193 nâṭa' (1), to *plant*

PLANTETH
5192 nêṭel (2), *burden*
5452 phutĕuŏ (3), to *implant, i.e. to instill*

PLANTING
4302 maṭṭâ' (2), *something planted*

PLANTINGS
4302 maṭṭâ' (1), *something planted*

PLANTS
4302 maṭṭâ' (1), *something planted*
5189 n°ṭîyshâh (1), *tendril plant shoot*
5194 neṭa' (2), *plant; plantation; planting*
5195 nâṭîya' (1), *plant*
7973 shelach (1), *spear; shoot of growth*
8291 sarûwq (1), *choice grapevine*
8363 sh°thîyl (1), *sucker plant*

PLAT
2513 chelqâh (2), *smoothness; flattery*

PLATE
6731 tsîyts (3), *burnished plate; bright flower*

PLATES
3871 lûwach (1), *tablet*
5633 çeren (1), *axle; peer*
6341 pach (2), *thin metallic sheet; net*

PLATTED
4120 plĕkŏ (3), to *twine or braid*

PLATTER
3953 parŏpsis (2), *side-dish receptacle*
4094 pinax (1), *plate, platter, dish*

PLAY
5059 nâgan (4), to *play; to make music*
6711 tsâchaq (1), to *laugh; to make sport of*

7832 sâchaq (5), to *laugh; to scorn; to play*
8173 shâ'a' (1), to *fondle, please or amuse (self)*
3815 paizŏ (1), to *indulge in (sexual) revelry*

PLAYED
5059 nâgan (4), to *play; to make music*
7832 sâchaq (3), to *laugh; to scorn; to play*

PLAYER
5059 nâgan (1), to *play; to make music*

PLAYERS
2490 châlal (1), to *play the flute*
5059 nâgan (1), to *play; to make music*

PLAYING
5059 nâgan (1), to *play; to make music*
7832 sâchaq (2), to *laugh; to scorn; to play*

PLEA
1779 dîyn (1), *judge; judgment; law suit*

PLEAD
1777 dîyn (2), to *judge; to strive or contend for*
3198 yâkach (3), to *correct; to argue*
7378 rîyb (23), to *hold a controversy; to defend*
8199 shâphaṭ (9), to *judge*

PLEADED
7378 rîyb (2), to *hold a controversy; to defend*
8199 shâphaṭ (1), to *judge*

PLEADETH
7378 rîyb (1), to *hold a controversy; to defend*
8199 shâphaṭ (1), to *judge*

PLEADINGS
7379 rîyb (1), *contest, personal or legal*

PLEASANT
2530 châmad (3), to *delight in; lust for*
2531 chemed (2), *delight*
2532 chemdâh (11), *delight*
2580 chên (1), *graciousness; beauty*
2656 chêphets (1), *pleasure; desire*
2896 ṭôwb (2), *good; well*
3303 yâpheh (1), *beautiful; handsome*
4022 meged (3), *valuable*
4261 machmâd (5), *delightful*
4262 machmûd (3), *desired; valuable*
4999 nâ'âh (1), *home, dwelling; pasture*
5116 nâveh (1), *at home; lovely; home*
5273 nâ'îym (8), *delightful; sweet*
5276 nâ'êm (5), to *be agreeable*
5278 no'am (2), *agreeableness, delight*
6027 'ôneg (1), *luxury*
6148 'ârab (1), to *intermix*

7832 sâchaq (5), to *laugh; to scorn; to play*
8173 shâ'a' (1), to *fondle, please or amuse (self)*
3815 paizŏ (1), to *indulge in (sexual) revelry*

6643 ts°bîy (1), *conspicuous splendor*
8191 sha'shûa' (2), *enjoyment*
8378 ta'ăvâh (1), *longing; delight*
8588 ta'ănûwg (1), *luxury; delight*

PLEASANTNESS
5278 no'am (1), *agreeableness*

PLEASE
2654 châphêts (5), to *be pleased with, desire*
2655 châphêts (1), *pleased with*
2894 ṭûw' (3), to *sweep away*
2895 ṭowb (6), to *be good*
2896 ṭôwb (2), *good; well*
3190 yâṭab (2), to *be, make well*
3477+5869 yâshâr (1), *straight*
5606 çâphaq (1), to *be enough; to vomit*
7451+5869 ra' (1), *bad; evil*
7521 râtsâh (3), to *be pleased with; to satisfy*
700 arĕskŏ (11), to *seek to please*
701 arĕstŏs (1), *agreeable; desirable; fit*
2001+1511 ĕpischuŏ (1), to *insist stoutly*
2100 ĕuarĕstĕŏ (1), to *gratify entirely, please*

PLEASED
2654 châphêts (8), to *be pleased with, desire*
2895 ṭowb (1), to *be good*
2896+5869 ṭôwb (1), *good; well*
2974 yâ'al (1), to *assent; to undertake, begin*
3190 yâṭab (2), to *be, make well*
3190+5869 yâṭab (10), to *be, make well*
3477+5869 yâshâr (7), *straight*
7451+5869 ra' (1), *bad; evil*
7521 râtsâh (4), to *be pleased with; to satisfy*
8232 sh°phar (Ch.) (1), to *be beautiful*
700 arĕskŏ (5), to *seek to please*
701 arĕstŏs (1), *agreeable; desirable; fit*
1380 dŏkĕŏ (2), to *think, regard, seem good*
2100 ĕuarĕstĕŏ (2), to *gratify entirely, please*
2106 ĕudŏkĕŏ (12), to *think well, i.e. approve*
2309 thĕlŏ (1), to *will; to desire; to choose*
4909 sunĕudŏkĕŏ (2), to *assent to, feel gratified*

PLEASETH
2654 châphêts (1), to *be pleased with, desire*
2896+5869 ṭôwb (2), *good; well*

2896+6440 tôwb (1),
good; well
3190+5869 yâṭab (1), to
be, make well
3477+5869 yâshâr (1),
straight

PLEASING
2896 tôwb (1), *good; well*
6148 'ârab (1), to *give or
be security*
699 arĕskĕia (1),
complaisance, amiable
700 arĕskō (2), to *seek to
please*
701 arĕstŏs (1),
agreeable; desirable; fit

PLEASURE
185+5315 'avvâh (1),
longing
2654 châphêts (3), to *be
pleased with, desire*
2655 châphêts (2),
pleased with
2656 chêphets (16),
pleasure; desire
2837 chêsheq (1),
delight, desired thing
2896 tôwb (2), *good; well*
5315 nephesh (3), *life;
breath; soul; wind*
5730 'êden (1), *pleasure*
6148 'ârab (1), to *give or
be security*
7470 rᵉ'ûwth (Ch.) (1),
desire
7521 râtsâh (6), to *be
pleased with; to satisfy
a debt*
7522 râtsôwn (5), *delight*
8057 simchâh (1),
blithesomeness or glee
2106 ĕudŏkĕō (6), to
think well, i.e. *approve*
2107 ĕudŏkia (4),
delight, kindness, wish
2237 hēdŏnē (1), *delight;
desire*
2307 thĕlēma (1), *decree;
inclination*
3588+1380 hŏ (1), "*the,*"
i.e. *the definite article*
4684 spatalaō (1), to *live
in luxury*
4909 sunĕudŏkĕō (1), to
assent to, feel gratified
5171 truphaō (1), to
indulge in luxury
5485 charis (2),
gratitude; benefit given

PLEASURES
5273 nâ'îym (2),
delightful; sweet
5719 'âdîyn (1),
voluptuous
5730 'êden (1), *pleasure*
2237 hēdŏnē (2), *delight;
desire*
5569 psĕudadĕlphŏs (1),
pretended associate

PLEDGE
2254 châbal (10), to *bind
by a pledge; to pervert*
2258 châbôl (4), *pawn,
pledge as security*
5667 'âbôwṭ (4), *pledged
item*
6161 'ărubbâh (1), as
security; bondsman

6162 'ărâbôwn (3), *pawn,
security pledge*

PLEDGES
6148 'ârab (2), to *give or
be security*

PLEIADES
3598 Kîymâh (2), *cluster
of stars, Pleiades*

PLENTEOUS
1277 bârîy' (1), *fatted or
plump; healthy*
3498 yâthar (2), to
remain or be left
7227 rab (3), *great*
7235 râbâh (1), to
increase
7647 sâbâ' (2),
copiousness
8082 shâmên (1), *rich;
fertile*
4180 pŏlulŏgia (1),
prolixity, wordiness

PLENTEOUSNESS
4195 môwthar (1), *gain;
superiority*
7647 sâbâ' (1),
copiousness

PLENTIFUL
3759 karmel (3), *planted
field; garden produce*
5071 nᵉdâbâh (1),
abundant gift

PLENTIFULLY
3499 yether (1),
remainder; small rope
7230 rôb (1), *abundance*
2164 ĕuphŏrĕō (1), to *be
fertile, produce a crop*

PLENTY
398 'âkal (1), to *eat*
4723 miqveh (1),
confidence; collection
7230 rôb (3), *abundance*
7235 râbâh (1), to
increase
7646 sâba' (2), *fill to
satiety*
7647 sâbâ' (4),
copiousness
8443 tôw'âphâh (1),
treasure; speed

PLOTTETH
2161 zâmam (1), to *plan*

PLOUGH
723 arŏtrŏn (1), *plow*

PLOW
2790 chârash (6), to
engrave; to plow
722 arŏtriŏō (1), to
plough, make furrows

PLOWED
2790 chârash (5), to
engrave; to plow

PLOWERS
2790 chârash (1), to
engrave; to plow

PLOWETH
722 arŏtriŏō (1), to
plough, make furrows

PLOWING
2790 chârash (2), to
engrave; to plow
5215 nîyr (1), *freshly
plowed land*

722 arŏtriŏō (1), to
plough, make furrows

PLOWMAN
2790 chârash (2), to
engrave; to plow

PLOWMEN
406 'ikkâr (2), *farmer*

PLOWSHARES
855 'êth (3), *digging
implement*

PLUCK
717 'ârâh (1), to *pluck,
pick fruit*
1497 gâzal (2), to *rob*
3318 yâtsâ' (1), to *go,
bring out*
3615 kâlâh (1), to *cease,
be finished, perish*
5255 nâçach (1), to *tear
away*
5375 nâsâ' (1), to *lift up*
5423 nâthaq (2), to *tear
off*
5428 nâthash (10), to
tear away, be uprooted
5493 çûwr (1), to *turn off*
6131 'âqar (1), to *pluck
up roots; to hamstring*
6998 qâṭaph (1), to *strip
off, pick off*
8045 shâmad (1), to
desolate
726 harpazō (2), to *seize*
1544 ĕkballō (1), to
throw out
1807 ĕxairĕō (1), to *tear
out; to select; to release*
1808 ĕxairō (1), to
remove, drive away
5089 tillō (2), to *pull off
grain heads*

PLUCKED
1497 gâzal (2), to *rob*
3318 yâtsâ' (1), to *go,
bring out*
4803 mâraṭ (3), to *polish;
to make bald*
4804 mᵉraṭ (Ch.) (1), to
pull off, tear off
5255 nâçach (1), to *tear
away*
5337 nâtsal (2), to *be
snatched away*
5423 nâthaq (1), to *tear
off*
5428 nâthash (4), to *tear
away, be uprooted*
6132 'âqar (Ch.) (1), to
pluck up roots
7993 shâlak (1), to *throw
out, down or away*
8025 shâlaph (1), to *pull
out, up or off*
1288 diaspaō (1), to *sever
or dismember*
1610 ĕkrizŏō (2), to
uproot
1846 ĕxŏrussō (1), to *dig
out*
5089 tillō (1), to *pull off
grain heads*

PLUCKETH
2040 hâraç (1), to *pull
down; break, destroy*

PLUCKT
2965 ṭârâph (1), *freshly
picked vegetation*

722 arŏtriŏō (1), to
plough, make furrows

PLOWMAN
2790 chârash (2), to
engrave; to plow

PLOWMEN
406 'ikkâr (2), *farmer*

PLUMBLINE
594 'ănâk (4),
plumb-line, plummet

PLUMMET
68+913 'eben (1), *stone*
4949 mishqeleth (2),
plummet weight

PLUNGE
2881 ṭâbal (1), to *dip*

POCHERETH
6380 Pôkereth
Tsᵉbâyîym (2), *trap of
gazelles*

POETS
4163 pŏiētēs (1),
performer; poet

POINT
19 'ibchâh (1),
brandishing of a sword
184 'âvâh (1), to *extend
or mark out*
1980 hâlak (1), to *walk;
live a certain way*
6856 tsippôren (1), *nail;
point of a style or pen*
8376 tâ'âh (2), to *mark
off,* i.e. *designate*
2079 ĕschatŏs (1), *finally,*
i.e. *at the extremity*
3195 mĕllō (1), to *intend,*
i.e. *be about to*

POINTED
2742 chârûwts (1),
threshing-sledge

POINTS
5980 'ummâh (1), *near,
beside, along with*

POISON
2534 chêmâh (5), *heat;
anger; poison*
7219 rô'sh (1), *poisonous
plant; poison*
2447 iŏs (2), *corrosion;
venom*

POLE
5251 nêç (2), *flag; signal;
token*

POLICY
7922 sekel (1),
intelligence; success

POLISHED
1305 bârar (1), to
brighten; purify
2404 châṭab (1), to *chop
or carve wood*
7044 qâlâl (1),
brightened, polished

POLISHING
1508 gizrâh (1), *figure,
appearance; enclosure*

POLL
1494 gâzaz (1), to *shear;
shave; destroy*
1538 gulgôleth (1), *skull*
3697 kâçam (1), to *shear,
clip*

POLLED
1548 gâlach (3), to *shave;
to lay waste*

POLLS
1538 gulgôleth (6), *skull*

POLLUTE
2490 châlal (8), to
profane, defile

P

2610 chânêph (1), to *soil,*
be defiled
2930 ṭâmê' (2), to *be*
morally contaminated

POLLUTED
947 bûwç (2), to *trample*
down; oppress
1351 gâ'al (7), to *soil,*
stain; desecrate
2490 châlal (13), to
profane, defile
2610 chânêph (3), to *soil,*
be defiled
2930 ṭâmê' (12), to *be*
morally contaminated
2931 ṭâmê' (1), *foul;*
ceremonially impure
6121 'âqôb (1),
fraudulent; tracked
2840 kŏinŏō (1), to *make*
profane

POLLUTING
2490 châlal (2), to
profane, defile

POLLUTION
2931 ṭâmê' (1), *foul;*
ceremonially impure

POLLUTIONS
234 alisgĕma (1),
ceremonially polluted
3393 miasma (1),
foulness, corruption

POLLUX
1359 Diŏskŏurŏi (1),
twins of Zeus

POMEGRANATE
7416 rimmôwn (10),
pomegranate

POMEGRANATES
7416 rimmôwn (22),
pomegranate

POMMELS
1543 gullâh (3), *fountain;*
bowl or globe

POMP
1347 gâ'ôwn (5),
ascending; majesty
7588 shâ'ôwn (1), *uproar;*
destruction
5325 phantasia (1), *vain*
show, i.e. *pomp*

PONDER
6424 pâlaç (2), to *weigh*
mentally

PONDERED
4820 sumballō (1), to
consider; to aid; to join,
attack

PONDERETH
6424 pâlaç (1), to *weigh*
mentally
8505 tâkan (2), to
balance, i.e. *measure*

PONDS
98 'ăgam (2), *marsh;*
pond; pool
99 'âgêm (1), *sad*

PONTIUS
4194 Pŏntiŏs (4), *bridged*

PONTUS
4195 Pŏntŏs (3), *sea*

POOL
98 'ăgam (2), *marsh;*
pond; pool

1295 bᵉrêkâh (15),
reservoir, pool
2861 kŏlumbēthra (5),
pond

POOLS
98 'ăgam (2), *marsh;*
pond; pool
1293 bᵉrâkâh (1),
benediction, blessing
1295 bᵉrêkâh (1),
reservoir, pool
4723 miqveh (1),
confidence; collection

POOR
34 'ebyôwn (25),
destitute; poor
1800 dal (44), *weak, thin;*
humble, needy
1803 dallâh (4), *indigent,*
needy
2489 chêlᵉkâ' (3),
unhappy wretch
3423 yârash (2), to
impoverish; to ruin
4134 mûwk (4), to *be*
impoverished
4270 machçôwr (1),
impoverishment
4542 miçkên (4),
indigent, needy
6033 'ănâh (Ch.) (1), to
afflict, be afflicted
6035 'ânâv (1), *needy;*
oppressed
6035+6041 'ânâv (3),
needy; oppressed
6041 'ânîy (56), *depressed*
7326 rûwsh (21), to *be*
destitute
3993 pĕnēs (1), *poor*
3998 pĕnichrŏs (1),
needy, impoverished
4433 ptōchĕuō (1), to
become indigent, poor
4434 ptōchŏs (31),
pauper, beggar

POORER
4134 mûwk (1), to *be*
impoverished

POOREST
1803 dallâh (1), *indigent,*
needy

POPLAR
3839 libneh (1), *whitish*
tree, (poss.) *storax*

POPLARS
3839 libneh (1), *whitish*
tree, (poss.) *storax*

POPULOUS
527 'âmôwn (1), *crowd*
7227 rab (1), *great*

PORATHA
6334 Pôwrâthâ' (1),
Poratha

PORCH
197 'ûwlâm (33),
vestibule, portico
4528 miçdᵉrôwn (1),
colonnade or portico
4259 prŏauliŏn (1),
vestibule, i.e. *alley-way*
4440 pulōn (1), *gate-way,*
door-way
4745 stŏa (3), *colonnade*
or interior piazza

PORCHES
197 'ûwlâm (1), *vestibule,*
portico
4745 stŏa (1), *colonnade*
or interior piazza

PORCIUS
4201 Pŏrkiŏs (1), *swinish*

PORT
8179 sha'ar (1), *opening,*
i.e. *door or gate*

PORTER
7778 shôw'êr (4), *janitor,*
door-keeper
2377 thurŏrŏs (2), *gate-*
warden, doorkeeper

PORTERS
7778 shôw'êr (31),
janitor, door-keeper
8179 sha'ar (1), *opening,*
i.e. *door or gate*
8652 târâ' (Ch.) (1),
doorkeeper

PORTION
270 'âchaz (2), to *seize,*
grasp; possess
1697 dâbâr (4), *word;*
matter; thing
2256 chebel (2),
company, band
2505 châlaq (1), to *be*
smooth; be slippery
2506 chêleq (36),
allotment
2508 chălâq (Ch.) (3),
part, portion
2513 chelqâh (6),
allotment
2706 chôq (3),
appointment; allotment
4490 mânâh (4), *ration;*
lot or portion
4521 mᵉnâth (4),
allotment
6310 peh (2), *mouth;*
opening
6598 pathbag (5), *dainty*
food
7926 shᵉkem (1), *neck;*
spur of a hill
3313 mĕrŏs (3), *division*
or share
4620 sitŏmĕtrŏn (1),
allowance or ration

PORTIONS
2256 chebel (2),
company, band
2506 chêleq (4),
allotment
4256 machălôqeth (1),
section or division
4490 mânâh (6), *ration;*
lot or portion
4521 mᵉnâth (3),
allotment

POSSESS
423 'âlâh (2), *public*
agreement
2631 chăçan (Ch.) (1), to
take possession
3423 yârash (93), to
inherit; to impoverish
5157 nâchal (5), to *inherit*
2932 ktaŏmai (3), to *get*

POSSESSED
270 'âchaz (1), to *seize,*
grasp; possess

2631 chăçan (Ch.) (1), to
take possession
3423 yârash (19), to
inherit; to impoverish
7069 qânâh (3), to *create;*
to procure
1139 daimŏnizŏmai (11),
to be demon-possessed
2192 echō (2), to *have;*
hold; keep
2722 katĕchō (1), to *hold*
down fast
5224 huparchŏnta (1),
property or possessions

POSSESSEST
3423 yârash (1), to
inherit; to impoverish

POSSESSETH
3423 yârash (1), to
inherit; to impoverish
5224 huparchŏnta (1),
property or possessions

POSSESSING
2722 katĕchō (1), to *hold*
down fast

POSSESSION
270 'âchaz (1), to *seize,*
grasp; possess
272 'ăchuzzâh (64),
possession
3423 yârash (6), to
inherit; to impoverish
3424 yᵉrêshâh (2),
occupancy
3425 yᵉrushâh (11),
conquest
4180 môwrâsh (1),
possession
4181 môwrâshâh (6),
possession
4735 miqneh (3),
live-stock
4736 miqnâh (1),
acquisition
5157 nâchal (1), to *inherit*
5159 nachălâh (1),
occupancy
7272 regel (1), *foot; step*
2697 kataschĕsis (2),
occupancy, possession
2933 ktēma (1), *estate;*
wealth, possessions
4047 pĕripŏiēsis (1),
acquisition

POSSESSIONS
270 'âchaz (3), to *seize,*
grasp; possess
272 'ăchuzzâh (2),
possession
4180 môwrâsh (1),
possession
4639 ma'ăseh (1), *action;*
labor
4735 miqneh (2),
live-stock
2933 ktēma (3), *estate;*
wealth, possessions
5564 chōriŏn (1), *spot or*
plot of ground

POSSESSOR
7069 qânâh (2), to *create;*
to procure

POSSESSORS
7069 qânâh (1), to *create;*
to procure
2935 ktētōr (1), *land*
owner

POSSIBLE
102 adunatŏs (1), *weak; impossible*
1410 dunamai (1), *to be able or possible*
1415 dunatŏs (13), *capable; possible*

POST
352 'ayîl (4), *chief; ram; oak tree*
4201 mᵉzûwzâh (4), *door-post*
4947 mashqôwph (1), *lintel*
7323 rûwts (2), to *run*

POSTERITY
310 'achar (4), *after*
319 'achărîyth (3), *future; posterity*
1755 dôwr (1), *dwelling*
7611 shᵉ'êrîyth (1), *remainder or residual*

POSTS
352 'ayîl (17), *chief; ram; oak tree*
520 'ammâh (1), *cubit*
4201 mᵉzûwzâh (15), *door-post*
5592 çaph (3), *dish*
7323 rûwts (6), to *run*

POT
610 'âçûwk (1), oil-*flask*
1731 dûwd (1), *pot, kettle; basket*
3627 kᵉlîy (1), *implement, thing*
4715 mitsrêph (2), *crucible*
5518 çîyr (12), *thorn; hook*
6517 pârûwr (2), *skillet*
6803 tsintseneth (1), *vase, receptacle*
4713 stamnŏs (1), *jar or earthen tank*

POTENTATE
1413 dunastēs (1), *ruler or officer*

POTI-PHERAH
6319 Pôwṭîy Phera' (3), *Poti-Phera*

POTIPHAR
6318 Pôwṭîyphar (2), *Potiphar*

POTS
1375 gᵉbîya' (1), *goblet; bowl*
1731 dûwd (1), *pot, kettle; basket*
5518 çîyr (9), *thorn; hook*
8240 shâphâth (1), *hook; hearth*
3582 xēstēs (2), *vessel; measure*

POTSHERD
2789 cheres (4), *piece of earthenware pottery*

POTSHERDS
2789 cheres (1), *piece of earthenware pottery*

POTTAGE
5138 nâzîyd (6), *boiled soup or stew*

POTTER
3335 yâtsar (8), to *form; potter; to determine*
2763 kĕramĕus (1), *potter*
2764 kĕramikŏs (1), *made of clay*

POTTER'S
3335 yâtsar (7), to *form; potter; to determine*
2763 kĕramĕus (2), *potter*

POTTERS
3335 yâtsar (1), to *form; potter; to determine*

POTTERS'
3335 yâtsar (1), to *form; potter; to determine*
6353 pechâr (Ch.) (1), *potter*

POUND
4488 mâneh (2), *fixed weight*
3046 litra (2), 12 oz. measure, i.e. a *pound*
3414 mna (4), *certain weight*

POUNDS
4488 mâneh (2), *fixed weight*
3414 mna (5), *certain weight*

POUR
2212 zâqaq (1), to *strain, refine; extract, clarify*
3332 yâtsaq (13), to *pour out*
5042 nâba' (1), to *gush forth; to utter*
5064 nâgar (2), to *pour out; to deliver over*
5140 nâzal (2), to *drip, or shed by trickling*
5258 nâçak (6), to *pour a libation; to anoint*
5414 nâthan (1), to *give*
7324 rûwq (1), to *pour out, i.e. empty*
8210 shâphak (33), to *spill forth; to expend*
1632 ĕkchĕŏ (3), to *pour forth; to bestow*

POURED
2229 zâram (1), to *gush water, pour forth*
3251 yâçak (1), to *pour*
3332 yâtsaq (3), to *pour*
5064 nâgar (1), to *pour out; to deliver over*
5258 nâçak (10), to *pour a libation; to anoint*
5413 nâthak (13), to *flow forth, pour out*
6168 'ârâh (1), to *empty, pour out; demolish*
6694 tsûwq (2), to *melt*
7324 rûwq (1), to *pour out, i.e. empty*
8210 shâphak (25), to *spill forth*
8211 shephek (2), ash-*heap, dump*
906 ballō (1), to *throw*
1632 ĕkchĕŏ (9), to *pour forth; to bestow*
2708 katachĕŏ (2), to *pour down or out*

POUREDST
8210 shâphak (1), to *spill forth; to expend*

POURETH
1811 dâlaph (1), to *drip*
5042 nâba' (2), to *gush forth; to utter*
5064 nâgar (1), to *pour out; to deliver over*
8210 shâphak (6), to *spill forth; to expend*
906 ballō (1), to *throw*

POURING
8210 shâphak (1), to *spill forth; to expend*

POURTRAY
2710 châqaq (1), to *engrave; to enact laws*

POURTRAYED
2707 châqah (2), to *carve; to delineate*
2710 châqaq (1), to *engrave; to enact laws*

POVERTY
2639 cheçer (1), *lack; destitution*
3423 yârash (3), to *impoverish; to ruin*
4270 machçôwr (1), *impoverishment*
7389 rêysh (7), *poverty*
4432 ptōchĕia (3), *indigence, poverty*

POWDER
80 'âbâq (1), *fine dust; cosmetic powder*
1854 dâqaq (2), to *crush; crumble*
6083 'âphâr (3), *dust, earth, mud; clay*
3039 likmaō (2), to *grind to powder*

POWDERS
81 'âbâqâh (1), *cosmetic powder*

POWER
410 'êl (3), *mighty; the Almighty*
1369 gᵉbûwrâh (9), *force; valor; victory*
2220 zᵉrôwa' (3), *arm; foreleg; force, power*
2428 chayil (9), *army; wealth; virtue; strength*
2429 chayil (Ch.) (1), *army; strength; loud sound*
2632 chêçen (Ch.) (2), *strength, powerful rule*
3027 yâd (13), *hand; power*
3028 yad (Ch.) (1), *hand; power*
3201 yâkôl (1), to *be able*
3581 kôach (47), *force, might; strength*
3709 kaph (1), *hollow of hand; paw; sole of foot*
4475 memshâlâh (1), *rule; realm or a ruler*
4910 mâshal (2), to *rule*
5794 'az (1), *strong, vehement, harsh*
5797 'ôz (11), *strength*

POWEREST
5808 'izzûwz (1), *forcible; army*
6184 'ârîyts (1), *powerful or tyrannical*
7786 sûwr (1), to *rule, crown*
7980 shâlaṭ (3), to *dominate, i.e. govern*
7981 shᵉlêṭ (Ch.) (1), to *dominate, i.e. govern*
7983 shilṭôwn (2), *potentate*
7989 shallîyṭ (1), *prince or warrior*
8280 sârâh (2), to *prevail, contend*
8592 ta'ătsûmâh (1), *might*
8617 tᵉqûwmâh (1), *resistfulness*
8633 tôqeph (1), *might*
746 archē (1), *first in rank; first in time*
1325 didōmi (1), to *give*
1410 dunamai (1), to *be able or possible*
1411 dunamis (71), *force, power, miracle*
1415 dunatŏs (1), *powerful or capable; possible*
1849 ĕxŏusia (61), *authority, power, right*
1850 ĕxŏusiazō (3), to *control, master another*
2479 ischus (1), *forcefulness, power*
2904 kratŏs (6), *vigor, strength*
3168 mĕgalĕiŏtēs (1), *grandeur or splendor*

POWERFUL
3581 kôach (1), *force, might; strength*
1756 ĕnĕrgēs (1), *active, operative*
2478 ischurŏs (1), *forcible, powerful*

POWERS
1411 dunamis (6), *force, power, miracle*
1849 ĕxŏusia (8), *authority, power, right*

PRACTISE
5953 'âlal (1), to *glean; to overdo*
6213 'âsâh (3), to *do or make*

PRACTISED
2790 chârash (1), to *engrave; to plow*
6213 'âsâh (1), to *do*

PRAETORIUM
4232 praitōriŏn (1), *governor's court-room*

PRAISE
1288 bârak (1), to *bless*
1974 hillûwl (1), *harvest celebration*
1984 hâlal (92), to *praise; thank; boast*
2167 zâmar (4), to *play music*
3034 yâdâh (52), to *revere or worship*
4110 mahălâl (1), *fame, good reputation*

7623 shâbach (4), to
address; to pacify
7624 sh°bach (Ch.) (2), to
adulate, i.e. adore
8416 t°hillâh (52),
laudation; hymn
8426 tôwdâh (5),
expressions of thanks
133 ainĕsis (1),
thank-offering. praise
134 ainĕō (3), to praise
136 ainŏs (2), praise
1391 dŏxa (4), glory;
brilliance
1867 ĕpainĕō (3), to
applaud, commend
1868 ĕpainŏs (12),
laudation
5214 humnĕō (1), to
celebrate in song

PRAISED
1288 bârak (1), to bless
1984 hâlal (19), to praise;
thank; boast
3034 yâdâh (1), to throw;
to revere or worship
7623 shâbach (1), to
address
7624 sh°bach (Ch.) (3), to
adulate, i.e. adore
2127 ĕulŏgĕō (1), to
invoke a benediction

PRAISES
1984 hâlal (1), to praise;
thank; boast
8416 t°hillâh (5),
laudation; hymn
8426 tôwdâh (1),
expressions of thanks
703 arĕtē (1), excellence,
virtue

PRAISETH
1984 hâlal (1), to praise;
thank; boast

PRAISING
1984 hâlal (4), to praise;
thank; boast
134 ainĕō (6), to praise

PRANSING
1725 dâhar (1), to prance

PRANSINGS
1726 dahăhar (2), gallop

PRATING
8193 sâphâh (2), lip,
language, speech
5396 phluarĕō (1), to
berate

PRAY
577 'ânnâ' (2), oh now!, I
ask you!
2470 châlâh (3), to be
weak, sick, afflicted
2603 chânan (1), to
implore
3863 lûw' (1), if; would
that!
4994 nâ' (195), I pray!,
please!, I beg you!
6279 'âthar (1), intercede
6293 pâga' (1), to impinge
6419 pâlal (34), to
intercede, pray
6739 ts°lâ' (Ch.) (1), pray
7592 shâ'al (2), to ask
7878 sîyach (1), to
ponder, muse aloud

1189 dĕŏmai (7), to beg,
petition, ask
2065 ĕrōtaō (10), to
interrogate; to request
2172 ĕuchŏmai (2), to
wish for; to pray
3870 parakalĕō (4), to
call, invite
4336 prŏsĕuchŏmai (42),
to supplicate, pray

PRAYED
6419 pâlal (30), to
intercede, pray
6739 ts°lâ' (Ch.) (1), pray
1189 dĕŏmai (3), to beg,
petition, ask
2065 ĕrōtaō (4), to
interrogate; to request
3870 parakalĕō (2), to
call, invite
4336 prŏsĕuchŏmai (25),
to supplicate, pray

PRAYER
2470 châlâh (1), to be
weak, sick, afflicted
3908 lachash (1),
incantation; amulet
6279 'âthar (1), intercede
in prayer
6419 pâlal (2), to
intercede, pray
7878 sîyach (1), to
ponder, muse aloud
7879 sîyach (1), uttered
contemplation
8605 t°phillâh (75),
intercession
1162 dĕēsis (7), petition,
request
1783 ĕntĕuxis (1),
intercession
2171 ĕuchē (1), wish,
petition
4335 prŏsĕuchē (21),
prayer; prayer chapel
4336 prŏsĕuchŏmai (1),
to supplicate, pray

PRAYERS
8605 t°phillâh (2),
intercession
1162 dĕēsis (5), petition,
request
4335 prŏsĕuchē (15),
prayer; prayer chapel
4336 prŏsĕuchŏmai (2),
to supplicate, pray

PRAYEST
4336 prŏsĕuchŏmai (2),
to supplicate, pray

PRAYETH
6419 pâlal (4), to
intercede, pray
4336 prŏsĕuchŏmai (3),
to supplicate, pray

PRAYING
1156 b°'â' (Ch.) (1), to
seek or ask
6419 pâlal (5), to
intercede, pray
1189 dĕŏmai (2), to beg,
petition, ask
4336 prŏsĕuchŏmai (12),
to supplicate, pray

PREACH
1319 bâsar (1), to
announce (good news)
7121 qârâ' (2), to call out

1229 diaggĕllō (1), to
herald thoroughly
2097 ĕuaggĕlizō (18), to
announce good news
2605 kataggĕllō (4), to
proclaim, promulgate
2784 kĕrussō (22), to
herald
2980 lalĕō (1), to talk

PREACHED
1319 bâsar (1), to
announce (good news)
189 akŏē (1), hearing;
thing heard
1256 dialĕgŏmai (1), to
discuss
2097 ĕuaggĕlizō (22), to
announce good news
2605 kataggĕllō (6), to
proclaim, promulgate
2784 kĕrussō (20), to
herald
2907 krĕas (1), meat
2980 lalĕō (4), to talk
3954 parrhĕsia (1),
frankness, boldness
4137 plĕrŏō (1), to fill,
make complete
4283 prŏĕuaggĕlizŏmai
(1), to announce glad
news in advance
4296 prŏkĕrussō (2), to
proclaim in advance

PREACHER
6953 qôheleth (7),
assembler i.e. lecturer
2783 kĕrux (3), herald
2784 kĕrussō (1), to
herald

PREACHEST
2784 kĕrussō (1), to
herald

PREACHETH
2097 ĕuaggĕlizō (1), to
announce good news
2784 kĕrussō (2), to
herald

PREACHING
7150 q°rîy'âh (1),
proclamation
1256 dialĕgŏmai (1), to
discuss
2097 ĕuaggĕlizō (6), to
announce good news
2782 kĕrugma (8),
proclamation
2784 kĕrussō (8), to
herald
2980 lalĕō (1), to talk
3056 lŏgŏs (1), word,
matter, thing; Word

PRECEPT
4687 mitsvâh (1),
command
6673 tsav (4), injunction
1785 ĕntŏlē (2),
prescription, regulation

PRECEPTS
4687 mitsvâh (3),
command
6490 piqqûwd (21),
mandate of God, Law

PRECIOUS
2530 châmad (3), to
delight in; lust for

2532 chemdâh (1),
delight
2580 chên (1),
graciousness; beauty
2667 chôphesh (1), carpet
2896 tôwb (4), good; well
3365 yâqar (8), to be
valuable; to make rare
3366 y°qâr (4), wealth;
costliness; dignity
3368 yâqâr (25), valuable
4022 meged (5), valuable
4030 migdânâh (3),
preciousness, i.e. a gem
4901 meshek (1), sowing;
possession
5238 n°kôth (2),
valuables
927 barutimŏs (1), highly
valuable
1784 ĕntimŏs (2), valued,
considered precious
2472 isŏtimŏs (1), of
equal value or honor
4185 pŏlutĕlēs (1),
extremely expensive
5092 timē (1), esteem;
nobility; money
5093 timiŏs (11), costly;
honored, esteemed

PREDESTINATE
4309 prŏŏrizō (2), to
predetermine

PREDESTINATED
4309 prŏŏrizō (2), to
predetermine

PREEMINENCE
4195 môwthar (1), gain;
superiority
4409 prōtĕuō (1), to be
first
5383 philŏprōtĕuō (1),
loving to be first

PREFER
5927 'âlâh (1), to ascend,
be high, mount

PREFERRED
5330 n°tsach (Ch.) (1), to
become chief
8138 shânâh (1), to fold,
to transmute
1096 ginŏmai (3), to be,
become

PREFERRING
4285 prŏĕgĕŏmai (1), to
show deference
4299 prŏkrima (1),
prejudgment, partiality

PREMEDITATE
3191 mĕlĕtaō (1), to plot,
think about

PREPARATION
3559 kûwn (2), to set up;
establish, fix, prepare
2091 hĕtŏimasia (1),
preparation
3904 paraskĕuē (6),
readiness

PREPARATIONS
4633 ma'ărâk (1), mental
disposition, plan

PREPARE
631 'âçar (1), to fasten; to
join battle
3559 kûwn (41), to set up;
establish, fix, prepare

4487 mânâh (1), to *allot*; to *enumerate* or enroll
6186 'ârak (2), to set in a row, i.e. *arrange*,
6213 'âsâh (9), to *do* or *make*
6437 pânâh (4), to *turn*, to *face*
6942 qâdâsh (7), to *be, make clean*
2090 hĕtŏimazō (11), to *prepare*
2680 kataskĕuazō (3), to *prepare thoroughly*
3903 paraskĕuazō (1), to *get ready, prepare*

PREPARED
2164 zᵉman (Ch.) (1), to *agree, conspire*
2502 châlats (2), to *deliver, equip*
3559 kûwn (53), to *set up: establish, fix, prepare*
3739 kârâh (1), to *purchase by bargaining*
4487 mânâh (4), to *allot*; to *enumerate* or enroll
6186 'ârak (2), to set in a row, i.e. *arrange*,
6213 'âsâh (13), to *do* or *make*
6437 pânâh (1), to *turn*, to *face*
7543 râqach (1), to *perfume, blend spice*
2090 hĕtŏimazō (18), to *prepare*
2092 hĕtŏimŏs (1), *ready, prepared*
2675 katartizō (1), to *repair*; to *prepare*
2680 kataskĕuazō (2), to *prepare thoroughly*
4282 prŏĕtŏimazō (1), to *fit up in advance*

PREPAREDST
6437 pânâh (1), to *turn*, to *face*

PREPAREST
3559 kûwn (1), to *set up: establish, fix, prepare*
6186 'ârak (1), to set in a row, i.e. *arrange*,
6213 'âsâh (1), to *do* or *make*

PREPARETH
3559 kûwn (3), to *set up: establish, fix, prepare*

PREPARING
6213 'âsâh (1), to *do* or *make*
2680 kataskĕuazō (1), to *prepare thoroughly*

PRESBYTERY
4244 prĕsbutĕriŏn (1), *order of elders*

PRESCRIBED
3789 kâthab (1), to *write*

PRESCRIBING
3792 kᵉthâb (Ch.) (1), *writing, record or book*

PRESENCE
5048 neged (8), *over against* or *before*
5869 'ayin (9), *eye; sight; fountain*

5921 'al (1), *above, over, upon,* or *against*
6440 pânîym (76), *face; front*
6925 qŏdâm (Ch.) (1), *before*
561 apĕnanti (1), *before* or *against*
1715 ĕmprŏsthĕn (1), *in front of*
1799 ĕnōpiŏn (9), *in the face of, before*
2714 katĕnōpiŏn (1), *directly in front of*
3952 parŏusia (2), *coming; presence*
4383 prŏsōpŏn (7), *face, presence*

PRESENT
814 'eshkâr (1), *gratuity, gift; payment*
1293 bᵉrâkâh (3), *benediction, blessing*
3320 yâtsab (5), to *station, offer, continue*
3557 kûwl (1), to *keep in; to measure*
4503 minchâh (22), *tribute; offering*
4672 mâtsâ' (17), to *find* or *acquire; to occur*
5307 nâphal (3), to *fall*
5324 nâtsab (1), to *station*
5975 'âmad (6), to *stand*
7810 shachad (2), to *bribe; gift*
7862 shay (1), *gift*
7964 shillûwach (1), *daughter's dower*
8670 tᵉshûwrâh (1), *gift*
737 arti (2), *just now; at once*
1736 ĕndēmĕō (2), to *be at home*
1764 ĕnistēmi (5), to *be present*
2186 ĕphistēmi (1), to *be present; to approach*
2476 histēmi (1), to *stand, establish*
3306 mĕnō (1), to *stay, remain*
3568 nun (4), *now; the present or immediate*
3854 paraginŏmai (1), to *arrive; to appear*
3873 parakĕimai (2), to *be at hand*
3918 parĕimi (14), to *be present; to have come*
3936 paristēmi (7), to *stand beside, present*
4840 sumparĕimi (1), to *be now present*

PRESENTED
3320 yâtsab (4), to *station, offer, continue*
3322 yâtsag (1), to *place*
4672 mâtsâ' (3), to *find meet or be present*
5066 nâgash (1), to *be, come, bring near*
5307 nâphal (1), to *fall*
5414 nâthan (1), to *give*
5975 'âmad (1), to *stand*
7126 qârab (2), to *approach, bring near*
7200 râ'âh (1), to *see*

3936 paristēmi (2), to *stand beside, present*
4374 prŏsphĕrō (1), to *present to; to treat as*

PRESENTING
5307 nâphal (1), to *fall*

PRESENTLY
3117 yōwm (2), *day; time period*
1824 ĕxautēs (1), *instantly, at once*
3916 parachrēma (1), *instantly, immediately*
3936 paristēmi (1), to *stand beside, present*

PRESENTS
4030 migdânâh (1), *preciousness, i.e. a gem*
4503 minchâh (6), *tribute; offering*
7862 shay (2), *gift*
7964 shillûwach (1), *daughter's dower*

PRESERVE
2421 châyâh (4), to *live; to revive*
3498 yâthar (1), to *remain or be left*
4241 michyâh (1), *preservation of life*
4422 mâlaṭ (1), to *escape as if by slipperiness*
5341 nâtsar (11), to *guard, protect*
7760 sûwm (1), to *put*
8104 shâmar (9), to *watch*
2225 zōŏgŏnĕō (1), to *rescue; be saved*
4982 sōzō (1), to *deliver; to protect*

PRESERVED
3467 yâsha' (4), to make *safe, free*
5336 nâtsîyr (1), *delivered*
5337 nâtsal (1), to *deliver; to be snatched*
8104 shâmar (6), to *watch*
4933 suntērĕō (2), to *preserve in memory*
5083 tērĕō (2), to *keep, guard, obey*

PRESERVER
5314 nâphash (1), to *be refreshed*

PRESERVEST
2421 châyâh (1), to *live; to revive*
3467 yâsha' (1), to make *safe, free*

PRESERVETH
2421 châyâh (1), to *live; to revive*
5341 nâtsar (1), to *guard, protect, maintain*
8104 shâmar (6), to *watch*

PRESIDENTS
5632 çârêk (Ch.) (5), *emir, high official*

PRESS
1660 gath (1), *wine-press or vat*
6333 pûwrâh (1), *wine-press trough*

598 apŏthlibō (1), to *crowd, press up* against
1377 diōkō (1), to *pursue; to persecute*
3793 ŏchlŏs (5), *throng, i.e. crowd or mob*

PRESSED
1765 dâchaph (1), to *urge; to hasten*
4600 mâ'ak (1), to *press*
5781 'ûwq (2), to *pack, be pressed*
6484 pâtsar (2), to *stun or dull*
6555 pârats (2), to *break out*
6693 tsûwq (1), to *oppress, distress*
7818 sâchaṭ (1), to *tread out, i.e. squeeze grapes*
916 barĕō (1), to *weigh down, cause pressure*
1945 ĕpikĕimai (1), to *rest upon; press upon*
1968 ĕpipiptō (1), to *embrace; to seize*
4085 piĕzō (1), to *pack down firm*
4912 sunĕchō (1), to *hold together, compress*

PRESSES
3342 yeqeb (2), *wine-vat, wine-press*

PRESSETH
5181 nâchath (1), to *sink, descend; to press down*
971 biazō (1), to *crowd oneself into*

PRESSFAT
3342 yeqeb (1), *wine-vat, wine-press*

PRESUME
2102 zûwd (1), to *be insolent*
4390 mâlê' (1), to *fill; be full*

PRESUMED
6075 'âphal (1), to *swell; be elated*

PRESUMPTUOUS
2086 zêd (1), *arrogant, proud*
5113 tŏlmētēs (1), *daring (audacious) man*

PRESUMPTUOUSLY
2087 zâdôwn (2), *arrogance, pride*
2102 zûwd (3), to *be insolent*
3027 yâd (1), *hand; power*

PRETENCE
4392 prŏphasis (3), *pretext, excuse*

PREVAIL
1396 gâbar (5), to *act insolently*
2388 châzaq (2), to *bind, restrain, conquer*
3201 yâkôl (13), to *be able*
3898 lâcham (1), to *fight a battle*
5810 'âzaz (1), to *be stout; be bold*
6113 'âtsar (1), to *hold back; to maintain, rule*

P

6206 'ârats (1), to *awe*; to
dread; to *harass*
8630 tâqaph (2), to
overpower
2729 *katischuō* (1), to
overpower, prevail
5623 ŏphĕlĕō (2), to
benefit, be of use

PREVAILED
553 'âmats (1), to *be
strong; be courageous*
1396 gâbar (9), to *be
strong; to prevail*
2388 châzaq (8), to *bind,
restrain, conquer*
3201 yâkôl (9), to *be able*
3202 yᵉkêl (Ch.) (1), to *be
able*
3513 kâbad (1), to *be
heavy, severe, dull*
5810 'âzaz (2), to *be
stout; be bold*
7186 qâsheh (1), *severe*
2480 ischuō (3), to *have
or exercise force*
2729 *katischuō* (1), to
overpower, prevail
3528 nikaō (1), to
subdue, conquer

PREVAILEST
8630 tâqaph (1), to
overpower

PREVAILETH
7287 râdâh (1), to
subjugate; to crumble

PREVENT
6923 qâdam (6), to
anticipate, hasten
5348 phthanō (1), to
anticipate or precede

PREVENTED
6923 qâdam (8), to
anticipate, hasten
4399 prŏphthanō (1), to
anticipate

PREVENTEST
6923 qâdam (1), to
anticipate, hasten

PREY
400 'ôkel (2), *food*
957 baz (17), *plunder, loot*
961 bizzâh (4), *booty,
plunder*
962 bâzaz (9), to *plunder,
take booty*
2863 chetheph (1),
robber or robbery
2963 ţâraph (1), to *pluck
off or pull to pieces*
2964 ţereph (18), *fresh
torn prey*
4455 malqôwach (6),
spoil, plunder
5706 'ad (3), *booty*
7997 shâlal (1), to *drop
or strip; to plunder*
7998 shâlâl (11), *booty*

PRICE
3365 yâqar (1), to *be
valuable; to make rare*
3701 keçeph (3), *silver
money*
4242 mᵉchîyr (11), *price,
payment, wages*
4377 meker (1),
merchandise; value

4736 miqnâh (2),
acquisition
4901 meshek (1), *sowing;
possession*
6187 'êrek (1), *pile,
equipment, estimate*
7939 sâkâr (2), *payment,
salary; compensation*
4185 pŏlutĕlēs (1),
extremely expensive
4186 pŏlutimŏs (1),
extremely valuable
5092 timē (7), *esteem;
nobility; money*

PRICES
5092 timē (1), *esteem;
nobility; money*

PRICKED
8150 shânan (1), to
pierce; to inculcate
2669 katapŏnĕō (1), to
harass, oppress

PRICKING
3992 mâ'ar (1), to *be
painful; destructive*

PRICKS
7899 sêk (1), *brier of a
hedge*
2759 kĕntrŏn (2), *sting;
goad*

PRIDE
1344 gê'âh (1),
arrogance, pride
1346 ga'ăvâh (9),
arrogance; majesty
1347 gâ'ôwn (20),
ascending; majesty
1348 gê'ûwth (2),
ascending; majesty
1363 gôbahh (2), *height;
grandeur; arrogance*
1466 gêvâh (3),
arrogance, pride
2087 zâdôwn (6),
arrogance, pride
2103 zûwd (Ch.) (1), to *be
proud*
7407 rôkeç (1), *snare as
of tied meshes*
7830 shachats (1),
haughtiness; dignity
212 alazŏnĕia (1),
boasting
5187 tuphŏō (1), to
inflate with self-conceit
5243 hupĕrēphania (1),
haughtiness, arrogance

PRIEST
3547 kâhan (2), to
officiate as a priest
3548 kôhên (423), one
officiating as a priest
3549 kâhên (Ch.) (1), one
officiating as a priest
748 archiĕratikŏs (1),
high-priestly
749 archiĕrĕus (53),
high-priest, chief priest
2409 hiĕrĕus (16), *priest*

PRIEST'S
3547 kâhan (20), to
officiate as a priest
3548 kôhên (17), one
officiating as a priest
3550 kᵉhunnâh (4),
priesthood

749 archiĕrĕus (4),
high-priest, chief priest
2405 hiĕratĕia (1),
priestly office
2407 hiĕratĕuō (1), to *be
a priest*

PRIESTHOOD
3550 kᵉhunnâh (9),
priesthood
2405 hiĕratĕia (1),
priestly office
2406 hiĕratĕuma (2),
priestly order
2420 hiĕrōsunē (4),
priestly office

PRIESTS
3548 kôhên (300), one
officiating as a priest
3549 kâhên (Ch.) (6), one
officiating as a priest
3649 kâmâr (1), *pagan
priest*
749 archiĕrĕus (67),
high-priest, chief priest
2409 hiĕrĕus (15), *priest*

PRIESTS'
3548 kôhên (8), one
officiating as a priest

PRINCE
5057 nâgîyd (8),
commander, official
5081 nâdîyb (4), *grandee
or tyrant*
5387 nâsîy' (56), *leader;
rising mist, fog*
7101 qâtsîyn (2),
magistrate; leader
7333 râzôwn (1),
dignitary
8269 sar (19), *head
person, ruler*
8323 sârar (1), to *have,
exercise, get dominion*
747 archĕgŏs (2), *chief
leader; founder*
758 archōn (8), *first*

PRINCE'S
5081 nâdîyb (1), *grandee
or tyrant*
5387 nâsîy' (2), *leader;
rising mist, fog*

PRINCES
324 ăchashdarpan (Ch.)
(9), *satrap*
2831 chashmân (1),
(poss.) *wealthy*
3548 kôhên (1), one
officiating as a priest
5057 nâgîyd (1),
commander, official
5081 nâdîyb (10),
grandee or tyrant
5257 nᵉçîyk (3), *libation;
molten image; prince*
5387 nâsîy' (40), *leader;
rising mist, fog*
5461 çâgân (1), *prfect of
a province*
6579 partam (1),
grandee, noble
7101 qâtsîyn (2),
magistrate; leader
7227 rab (2), *great*
7261 rabrᵉbân (Ch.) (2),
magnate, noble
7336 râzan (5), *honorable*

7991 shâlîysh (1), *officer;
of the third rank*
8269 sar (190), *head
person, ruler*
758 archōn (3), *first*
2232 hĕgĕmōn (1), *chief*

PRINCESS
8282 sârâh (1), *female
noble*

PRINCESSES
8282 sârâh (1), *female
noble*

PRINCIPAL
1 'âb (1), *father*
117 'addîyr (3), *powerful;
majestic*
3548 kôhên (1), one
officiating as a priest
5257 nᵉçîyk (1), *libation;
molten image; prince*
7218 rô'sh (5), *head*
7225 rê'shîyth (1), *first*
7795 sôwrâh (1), *row*
8269 sar (2), *head
person, ruler*
8291 sarûwq (1), *choice
grapevine*

PRINCIPALITIES
4761 mar'âshâh (1),
headship, dominion
746 archē (6), *first in
rank; first in time*

PRINCIPALITY
746 archē (2), *first in
rank; first in time*

PRINCIPLES
746 archē (1), *first in
rank; first in time*
4747 stŏichĕiŏn (1), *basic
principles*

PRINT
2707 châqah (1), to
carve; to delineate
5414 nâthan (1), to *give*
5179 tupŏs (2), *shape,
resemblance; "type"*

PRINTED
2710 châqaq (1), to
engrave; to enact laws

PRISCA
4251 Priska (1), *ancient*

PRISCILLA
4252 Priskilla (5), *little
Prisca*

PRISED
3365 yâqar (1), to *be
valuable; to make rare*

PRISON
631 'âçar (2), to *fasten; to
join battle*
1004+612 bayith (3),
house; temple; family
1004+3608 bayith (7),
house; temple; family
1004+5470 bayith (8),
house; temple; family
1004+6486 bayith (1),
house; temple; family
3608 kele' (4), *prison*
4115 mahpeketh (2),
stocks for punishment
4307 maţţârâ' (13), *jail
(guard-house); aim*
4525 maçgêr (3), *prison;
craftsman*

4929 mishmâr (1), *guard; deposit; usage; example*

6115 'ôtser (1), *closure; constraint*

6495 p^eqach-qôwach (1), *jail-delivery; salvation*

1200 dĕsmŏphulax (2), *jailer*

1201 dĕsmōtēriŏn (4), *dungeon, jail*

3612 ŏikēma (1), *jail cell*

3860 paradidōmi (2), *to hand over*

5084 tērēsis (1), *observance; prison*

5438 phulakē (33), *night watch; prison; haunt*

PRISONER

615 'âçîyr (1), *captive, prisoner*

616 'açčîyr (1), *captive, prisoner*

1198 dĕsmiŏs (11), *bound captive; one arrested*

PRISONERS

615 'âçîyr (8), *captive, prisoner*

616 'açčîyr (3), *captive, prisoner*

631 'âçar (2), *to fasten; to join battle*

7628 sh^ebîy (2), *exile; booty*

1198 dĕsmiŏs (3), *bound captive; one arrested*

1202 dĕsmōtēs (2), *captive*

PRISONS

5438 phulakē (3), *night watch; prison; haunt*

PRIVATE

2398 idiŏs (1), *private or separate*

PRIVATELY

2596+2398 kata (8), *down; according to*

PRIVILY

652 'ôphel (1), *dusk, darkness*

2934 ţaman (3), *to hide*

3909 lâţ (1), *incantation; secrecy; covertly*

5643 çêther (1), *cover, shelter*

6845 tsâphan (1), *to hide; to protect; to lurk*

8649 tormâh (1), *fraud*

2977 lathra (3), *privately, secretly*

3918 parĕimi (1), *to be present; to have come*

3922 parĕisĕrchŏmai (1), *to supervene stealthily*

PRIVY

2314 châdar (1), *to enclose; to beset*

3045 yâda' (1), *to know*

8212 shophkâh (1), *penis*

4894 sunĕidŏ (1), *to understand*

PRIZE

1017 brabĕiŏn (2), *prize in the public games*

PROCEED

3254 yâçaph (2), *to add or augment*

3318 yâtsâ' (8), *to go, bring out*

1607 ĕkpŏrĕuŏmai (3), *to proceed, project*

1831 ĕxĕrchŏmai (1), *to issue; to leave*

4298 prŏkŏptō (1), *to go ahead, advance*

PROCEEDED

3254 yâçaph (1), *to add or augment*

3318 yâtsâ' (2), *to go, bring out*

4161 môwtsâ' (1), *going forth*

1607 ĕkpŏrĕuŏmai (3), *to proceed, project*

1831 ĕxĕrchŏmai (1), *to issue; to leave*

4369 prŏstithēmi (1), *to annex, repeat*

PROCEEDETH

3318 yâtsâ' (6), *to go, bring out*

4161 môwtsâ' (1), *going forth*

1607 ĕkpŏrĕuŏmai (3), *to proceed, project*

1831 ĕxĕrchŏmai (1), *to issue; to leave*

PROCEEDING

1607 ĕkpŏrĕuŏmai (1), *to proceed, project*

PROCESS

7093 qêts (1), *extremity; after*

7227 rab (1), *great*

7235 râbâh (1), *to increase*

PROCHORUS

4402 Prŏchŏrŏs (1), *before the dance*

PROCLAIM

5674 'âbar (1), *to cross over; to transition*

6942 qâdâsh (1), *to be, make clean*

7121 qârâ' (21), *to call out*

PROCLAIMED

2199 zâ'aq (1), *to call out, announce*

5674 'âbar (1), *to cross over; to transition*

7121 qârâ' (11), *to call out*

8085 shâma' (1), *to hear*

2784 kērussō (1), *to herald*

PROCLAIMETH

7121 qârâ' (1), *to call out*

PROCLAIMING

7121 qârâ' (2), *to call out*

2784 kērussō (1), *to herald*

PROCLAMATION

3745 k^eraz (Ch.) (1), *to proclaim*

5674+6963 'âbar (4), *cross over; to transition*

6963 qôwl (1), *voice or sound*

7121 qârâ' (1), *to call out*

7440 rinnâh (1), *shout*

8085 shâma' (1), *to hear*

PROCURE

6213 'âsâh (2), *to make*

PROCURED

6213 'âsâh (2), *to make*

PROCURETH

1245 bâqash (1), *to search out*

PRODUCE

7126 qârab (1), *to approach, bring near*

PROFANE

2455 chôl (4), *profane, common, not holy*

2490 châlal (18), *to profane, defile*

2491 châlâl (3), *pierced to death, one slain*

2610 chânêph (1), *to soil, be defiled*

952 bĕbēlŏs (5), *irreligious, profane*

953 bĕbēlŏō (2), *to desecrate, profane*

PROFANED

2490 châlal (15), *to profane, defile*

PROFANENESS

2613 chănûphâh (1), *impiety, ungodliness*

PROFANETH

2490 châlal (1), *to profane, defile*

PROFANING

2490 châlal (2), *to profane, defile*

PROFESS

5046 nâgad (1), *to announce*

3670 hŏmŏlŏgĕō (2), *to acknowledge, declare*

PROFESSED

3670 hŏmŏlŏgĕō (1), *to acknowledge, declare*

3671 hŏmŏlŏgia (1), *acknowledgment*

PROFESSING

1861 ĕpaggĕllō (2), *to assert*

5335 phaskō (1), *to assert a claim*

PROFESSION

3671 hŏmŏlŏgia (4), *acknowledgment*

PROFIT

1215 betsa (3), *plunder; unjust gain*

3148 yôwthêr (1), *moreover; rest; gain*

3276 yâ'al (18), *to be valuable*

3504 yithrôwn (5), *preeminence, gain*

4195 môwthar (1), *gain; superiority*

7737 shâvâh (1), *to resemble; to adjust*

3786 ŏphĕlŏs (2), *accumulate or benefit*

4851 sumphĕrō (4), *to collect; advantage*

5539 chrēsimŏs (1), *useful, valued*

5622 ŏphĕlĕia (1), *value, advantage*

5623 ŏphĕlĕō (4), *to benefit, be of use*

PROFITABLE

3276 yâ'al (1), *to be valuable*

3504 yithrôwn (1), *preeminence, gain*

5532 çâkan (2), *to be serviceable to*

6743 tsâlach (1), *to push forward*

2173 ĕuchrēstŏs (2), *useful, serviceable*

4851 sumphĕrō (3), *to conduce; advantage*

5624 ŏphĕlimŏs (3), *advantageous, useful*

PROFITED

7737 shâvâh (1), *to resemble; to adjust*

4298 prŏkŏptō (1), *to go ahead, advance*

5623 ŏphĕlĕō (4), *to benefit, be of use*

PROFITETH

3276 yâ'al (1), *to be valuable*

5532 çâkan (1), *to be serviceable to*

5623 ŏphĕlĕō (3), *to benefit, be of use*

5624+2076 ŏphĕlimŏs (1), *useful, valuable*

PROFITING

4297 prŏkŏpē (1), *progress, advancement*

PROFOUND

6009 'âmaq (1), *to be, make deep*

PROGENITORS

2029 hârâh (1), *to conceive, be pregnant*

PROGNOSTICATORS

3045 yâda' (1), *to know*

PROLONG

748 'ârak (12), *to be, make long*

3254 yâçaph (1), *to add or augment*

5186 nâţâh (1), *to stretch or spread out*

PROLONGED

748 'ârak (5), *to be, make long*

754+3052 'arkâ' (Ch.) (1), *length*

4900 mâshak (3), *to draw out; to be tall*

PROLONGETH

748 'ârak (1), *to be, make long*

3254 yâçaph (1), *to add or augment*

PROMISE

562 'ômer (1), *something said*

1697 dâbâr (6), *word; matter; thing*

1860 ĕpaggĕlia (40), *divine assurance*

1861 ĕpaggĕllō (3), *to assert*

1862 ĕpaggĕlma (1), *self-committal*

PROMISED
559 'âmar (5), to say
1696 dâbar (29), to
speak, say; to subdue
1843 ĕxŏmŏlŏgĕō (1), to
acknowledge or agree
1861 ĕpaggĕllō (10), to
assert
3670 hŏmŏlŏgĕō (1), to
acknowledge, agree
4279 prŏĕpaggĕllŏmai
(1), to promise before

PROMISEDST
559 'âmar (1), to say
1696 dâbar (2), to speak

PROMISES
1860 ĕpaggĕlia (12),
divine assurance
1862 ĕpaggĕlma (1),
self-committal

PROMISING
2421 châyâh (1), to live;
to revive

PROMOTE
1431 gâdal (1), to make
great, enlarge
3513 kâbad (3), to be
rich, glorious
7311 rûwm (1), to be
high; to rise or raise

PROMOTED
1431 gâdal (1), to make
great, enlarge
5128 nûwa' (3), to waver
6744 tsᵉlach (Ch.) (1), to
advance; promote

PROMOTION
7311 rûwm (2), to be
high; to rise or raise

PRONOUNCE
981 bâṭâ' (1), to babble,
speak rashly
1696 dâbar (1), to speak

PRONOUNCED
1691 Diblayim (2), two
cakes
1696 dâbar (11), to speak
7126 qârab (1), to
approach, bring near

PRONOUNCING
981 bâṭâ' (1), to babble,
speak rashly

PROOF
1382 dŏkimē (3), test, i.e.
trustiness
1732 ĕndĕixis (1),
demonstration
4135 plērŏphŏrĕō (1), to
assure or convince

PROOFS
5039 tĕkmēriŏn (1),
criterion of certainty

PROPER
5459 çᵉgullâh (1), wealth
791 astĕiŏs (1),
handsome
2398 idiŏs (2), private or
separate

PROPHECIES
4394 prŏphētĕia (2),
prediction

PROPHECY
4853 massâ' (2), burden,
utterance

5016 nᵉbûw'âh (3),
prediction
5030 nâbîy' (1), prophet;
inspired man
4394 prŏphētĕia (14),
prediction
4397 prŏphētikŏs (1),
prophetic

PROPHESIED
5012 nâbâ' (40), to speak
as a prophet
5013 nᵉbâ' (Ch.) (1), to
speak as a prophet
4395 prŏphētĕuō (9), to
foretell events, divine

PROPHESIETH
5012 nâbâ' (3), to speak
as a prophet
4395 prŏphētĕuō (4), to
foretell events, divine

PROPHESY
2372 châzâh (2), to gaze
at; have a vision
5012 nâbâ' (66), to speak
as a prophet
5197 nâṭaph (5), to speak
by inspiration
4395 prŏphētĕuō (14), to
foretell events, divine

PROPHESYING
5012 nâbâ' (2), to speak
as a prophet
5017 nᵉbûw'âh (Ch.) (1),
inspired teaching
4394 prŏphētĕia (2),
prediction
4395 prŏphētĕuō (1), to
foretell events, divine

PROPHESYINGS
4394 prŏphētĕia (1),
prediction

PROPHET
5012 nâbâ' (2), to speak
as a prophet
5029 nᵉbîy' (Ch.) (2),
prophet
5030 nâbîy' (164),
prophet; inspired man
5197 nâṭaph (1), to speak
by inspiration
4396 prŏphētēs (67),
foreteller
5578 psĕudŏprŏphētēs
(4), pretended foreteller

PROPHET'S
5030 nâbîy' (1), prophet;
inspired man
4396 prŏphētēs (1),
foreteller

PROPHETESS
5031 nᵉbîy'âh (6),
prophetess
4398 prŏphētis (2),
female foreteller

PROPHETS
2374 chôzeh (1),
beholder in vision
5029 nᵉbîy' (Ch.) (2),
prophet
5030 nâbîy' (147),
prophet; inspired man
4396 prŏphētēs (80),
foreteller
4397 prŏphētikŏs (1),
prophetic

5578 psĕudŏprŏphētēs
(7), pretended foreteller

PROPITIATION
2434 hilasmŏs (2),
atonement
2435 hilastēriŏn (1),
expiatory place

PROPORTION
4626 ma'ar (1), vacant
space
6187 'êrek (1), pile,
equipment, estimate
356 analŏgia (1),
proportion

PROSELYTE
4339 prŏsēlutŏs (2),
convert, i.e. proselyte

PROSELYTES
4339 prŏsēlutŏs (2),
convert, i.e. proselyte

PROSPECT
6440 pânîym (6), face;
front

PROSPER
3787 kâshêr (1), to be
straight or right
6743 tsâlach (37), to push
forward
7919 sâkal (7), to be or
act circumspect
7951 shâlâh (3), to be
secure or successful
2137 ĕuŏdŏō (1), to
succeed in business

PROSPERED
1980 hâlak (1), to walk;
live a certain way
6743 tsâlach (6), to push
forward
6744 tsᵉlach (Ch.) (2), to
advance; promote
7919 sâkal (1), to be or
act circumspect
7965 shâlôwm (1), safe;
well; health, prosperity
7999 shâlam (1), to be
safe; be, make complete
2137 ĕuŏdŏō (1), to
succeed in business

PROSPERETH
6743 tsâlach (1), to push
forward
6744 tsᵉlach (Ch.) (1), to
advance; promote
7919 sâkal (1), to be or
act circumspect
2137 ĕuŏdŏō (1), to
succeed in business

PROSPERITY
2896 ṭôwb (6), good; well
6743 tsâlach (1), to push
forward
7961 shâlêv (2), careless,
carefree; security
7962 shalvâh (3),
security, ease
7965 shâlôwm (4), safe;
well; health, prosperity

PROSPEROUS
6743 tsâlach (5), to push
forward
7965 shâlôwm (1), safe;
well; health, prosperity
7999 shâlam (1), to be
safe; be, make complete

2137 ĕuŏdŏō (1), to
succeed in business

PROSPEROUSLY
6743 tsâlach (2), to push
forward

PROSTITUTE
2490 châlal (1), to
profane, defile

PROTECTION
5643 çêther (1), cover,
shelter

PROTEST
5749 'ûwd (2), to protest
3513 nê (1), as sure as

PROTESTED
5749 'ûwd (3), to protest

PROTESTING
5749 'ûwd (1), to protest

PROUD
1341 gê' (2), haughty,
proud
1343 gê'eh (8), arrogant,
haughty
1346 ga'ăvâh (1),
arrogance; majesty
1347 gâ'ôwn (1),
ascending; majesty
1349 ga'ăyôwn (1),
haughty, arrogant
1362 gâbâhh (2), high;
lofty
1364 gâbôahh (1), high;
powerful; arrogant
1419 gâdôwl (1), great
2086 zêd (12), arrogant,
proud
2087 zâdôwn (3),
arrogance, pride
2102 zûwd (1), to seethe,
to be insolent
2121 zêydôwn (1),
boiling, raging wave
3093 yâhîyr (1), arrogant
7293 rahab (2), bluster
7295 râhâb (1), insolent
7311 rûwm (1), to be
high; to rise or raise
7342 râchâb (3), roomy,
spacious
5187 tuphŏō (1), to
inflate with self-conceit
5244 hupĕrēphanŏs (5),
haughty, arrogant

PROUDLY
1346 ga'ăvâh (1),
arrogance; majesty
1348 gê'ûwth (1),
ascending; majesty
1364 gâbôahh (1), high;
powerful; arrogant
1431 gâdal (1), to be
great, make great
2102 zûwd (4), to seethe;
to be insolent
7292 râhab (1), to urge,
embolden

PROVE
974 bâchan (1), to test; to
investigate
5254 nâçâh (14), to test,
attempt
584 apŏdĕiknumi (1), to
demonstrate
1381 dŏkimazō (6), to
test; to approve

3936 paristēmi (1), to
stand beside, present
3985 pĕirazō (1), to
endeavor, scrutinize

PROVED
974 bâchan (6), to *test*; to
investigate
5254 nâçâh (5), to *test*,
attempt
1381 dŏkimazō (3), to
test; to *approve*
4256 prŏaitiaŏmai (1), to
previously charge

PROVENDER
1098 bᵉlîyl (1), *feed*,
fodder
1101 bâlal (1), to *mix*;
confuse; to *feed*
4554 miçpôw' (5), *fodder*,
animal feed

PROVERB
2420 chîydâh (1), *puzzle*;
conundrum; *maxim*
4911 mâshal (4), to *use*
figurative language
4912 mâshâl (12), *pithy*
maxim; *taunt*
3850 parabŏlē (1),
fictitious narrative
3942 parŏimia (2),
illustration; *adage*

PROVERBS
4911 mâshal (2), to *use*
figurative language
4912 mâshâl (5), *pithy*
maxim; *taunt*
3942 parŏimia (2),
illustration; *adage*

PROVETH
5254 nâçâh (1), to *test*,
attempt

PROVIDE
2372 châzâh (1), to *gaze*
at; to *perceive*
3559 kûwn (2), to *set up*:
establish, fix, prepare
6213 'âsâh (1), to *do*
7200 râ'âh (2), to *see*
2532 kai (1), *and*; *or*
3936 paristēmi (1), to
stand beside, present
4160 pŏiĕō (1), to *do*
4306 prŏnŏĕō (2), to *look*
out for *beforehand*

PROVIDED
3559 kûwn (1), to *set up*:
establish, fix, prepare
6213 'âsâh (1), to *do*
7200 râ'âh (2), to *see*
2090 hĕtŏimazō (1), to
prepare
4265 prŏblĕpō (1), to
furnish in advance

PROVIDENCE
4307 prŏnŏia (1),
provident *care, supply*

PROVIDETH
3559 kûwn (2), to *set up*:
establish, fix, prepare

PROVIDING
4306 prŏnŏĕō (1), to *look*
out for *beforehand*

PROVINCE
4082 mᵉdîynâh (20),
governmental *region*

4083 mᵉdîynâh (Ch.) (5),
governmental *region*
1885 ĕparchia (2),
Roman *præfecture*

PROVINCES
4082 mᵉdîynâh (29),
governmental *region*
4083 mᵉdîynâh (Ch.) (1),
governmental *region*

PROVING
1381 dŏkimazō (1), to
test; to *approve*
4822 sumbibazō (1), to
infer, show, teach

PROVISION
1697 dâbâr (1), *word*;
matter; *thing*
3557 kûwl (1), to
measure; to *maintain*
3559 kûwn (1), to *set up*:
establish, fix, prepare
3740 kêrâh (1), *purchase*
3899 lechem (1), *food*,
bread
6679 tsûwd (1), to *lie in*
wait; to *catch*
6718 tsayid (2), *hunting*
game; *lunch, food*
6720 tsêydâh (2), *food*,
supplies
4307 prŏnŏia (1),
provident *care, supply*

PROVOCATION
3708 ka'aç (4), *vexation*,
grief
4784 mârâh (1), to *rebel*
or *resist*; to *provoke*
4808 mᵉrîybâh (1),
quarrel
3894 parapikrasmŏs (2),
irritation

PROVOCATIONS
3708 ka'aç (1), *vexation*,
grief
5007 nᵉ'âtsâh (2), *scorn*;
to *bloom*

PROVOKE
4784 mârâh (2), to *rebel*
or *resist*; to *provoke*
4843 mârar (1), to *be*,
make bitter
5006 nâ'ats (2), to *scorn*
7264 râgaz (1), to *quiver*
653 apŏstŏmatizō (1), to
question carefully
2042 ĕrĕthizō (1), to
stimulate, provoke
3863 parazēlŏō (4), to
excite to rivalry
3893 parapikrainō (1), to
embitter alongside
3948 parŏxusmŏs (1),
incitement to good
3949 parŏrgizō (1), to
enrage, exasperate

PROVOKED
3707 kâ'aç (4), to *grieve*,
rage, be indignant
4784 mârâh (4), to *rebel*
or *resist*; to *provoke*
5006 nâ'ats (3), to *scorn*
5496 çûwth (1), to
stimulate; to *seduce*
7265 rᵉgaz (Ch.) (1), to
quiver
2042 ĕrĕthizō (1), to
stimulate, provoke

3947 parŏxunō (1), to
exasperate

PROVOKETH
5674 'âbar (1), to *cross*
over; to *transition*

PROVOKING
3707 kâ'aç (1), to *grieve*,
rage, be indignant
4784 mârâh (1), to *rebel*
or *resist*; to *provoke*
4292 prŏkalĕŏmai (1), to
irritate

PRUDENCE
6195 'ormâh (1), *trickery*;
discretion
7922 sekel (1),
intelligence; *success*
5428 phrŏnēsis (1), moral
insight, understanding

PRUDENT
995 bîyn (8), to
understand; *discern*
6175 'ârûwm (8),
cunning; *clever*
6191 'âram (1), to *be*
cunning; *be prudent*
7080 qâçam (1), to *divine*
magic
7919 sâkal (2), to *be* or
act circumspect
4908 sunĕtŏs (4),
sagacious, learned

PRUDENTLY
7919 sâkal (1), to *be* or
act circumspect

PRUNE
2168 zâmar (2), to *trim*
or a *vine*

PRUNED
2167 zâmar (1), to *play*
music

PRUNINGHOOKS
4211 mazmêrâh (4),
pruning-knife

PSALM
2172 zimrâh (2), *song*
4210 mizmôwr (58),
poem set to *music*
5568 psalmŏs (2), *psalm*;
book of the *Psalms*

PSALMIST
2158 zâmîyr (1), *song*

PSALMS
2158 zâmîyr (1), *song*
2167 zâmar (2), to *play*
music
5567 psallō (1), to *play* a
stringed instrument
5568 psalmŏs (5), *psalm*;
book of the *Psalms*

PSALTERIES
3627 kᵉlîy (1),
implement, thing
5035 nebel (13), skin-*bag*
for liquids; *vase*; *lyre*

PSALTERY
3627 kᵉlîy (1),
implement, thing
5035 nebel (8), skin-*bag*
for liquids; *vase*; *lyre*
6460 pᵉçanţêrîyn (Ch.)
(4), *lyre instrument*

PTOLEMAIS
4424 Ptŏlĕmaïs (1), of
Ptolemy

PUA
6312 Pûw'âh (1), *blast*

PUAH
6312 Pûw'âh (2), *blast*
6326 Pûw'âh (1),
brilliancy

PUBLICAN
5057 tĕlōnēs (6),
collector of revenue

PUBLICANS
754 architĕlōnēs (1),
chief tax-gatherer
5057 tĕlōnēs (16),
collector of revenue

PUBLICK
3856 paradĕigmatizō (1),
to *expose to infamy*

PUBLICKLY
1219 dēmŏsiŏs (2),
public; *in public*

PUBLISH
1319 bâsar (2), to
announce (good news)
7121 qârâ' (1), to *call* out
8085 shâma' (11), to *hear*
2784 kērussō (2), to
herald

PUBLISHED
559 'âmar (1), to *say*
1319 bâsar (1), to
announce (good news)
1540 gâlâh (2), to *reveal*
1696 dâbar (1), to *speak*
8085 shâma' (1), to *hear*
1096 ginŏmai (1), to *be*,
become
1308 diaphĕrō (1), to
bear, carry; to *differ*
2784 kērussō (3), to
herald

PUBLISHETH
8085 shâma' (4), to *hear*

PUBLIUS
4196 Pŏpliŏs (2), *popular*

PUDENS
4227 Pŏudēs (1), *modest*

PUFFED
5448 phusiŏō (6), to
inflate, i.e. make proud

PUFFETH
6315 pûwach (2), to *blow*,
to *fan, kindle*; to *utter*
5448 phusiŏō (1), to
inflate, i.e. make proud

PUHITES
6336 Pûwthîy (1), *hinge*

PUL
6322 Pûwl (4), *Pul, i.e.* a
person or tribe

PULL
2040 hâraç (3), to *pull*
down; *break, destroy*
3318 yâtsâ' (1), to *go*,
bring out
5422 nâthats (2), to *tear*
down
5423 nâthaq (3), to *tear*
off
6584 pâshaṭ (1), to *strip*,
i.e. *unclothe, plunder*

7725 shûwb (1), to *turn back*; to *return*
385 anaspaō (1), to *take up or extricate*
1544 ĕkballō (3), to *throw out*
2507 kathairĕō (1), to *lower, or demolish*

PULLED
935 bôw' (1), to *go, come*
4026 migdâl (1), *tower; rostrum*
5256 nᵉçach (Ch.) (1), to *tear away*
5414 nâthan (1), to *give*
5428 nâthash (1), to *tear away, be uprooted*
6582 pâshach (1), to *tear in pieces*
1288 diaspaō (1), to *sever or dismember*

PULLING
726 harpazō (1), to *seize*
2506 kathairĕsis (1), *demolition*

PULPIT
4026 migdâl (1), *tower; rostrum*

PULSE
2235 zêrôa' (2), *vegetable*

PUNISH
3256 yâçar (1), to *chastise; to instruct*
5221 nâkâh (1), to *strike, kill*
6064 'ânash (1), to *inflict a penalty, to fine*
6485 pâqad (27), to *visit, care for, count*
7489 râ'a' (1), to *break to pieces*
2849 kŏlazō (1), to *chastise, punish*

PUNISHED
2820 châsak (1), to *restrain or refrain*
5358 nâqam (2), to *avenge or punish*
6064 'ânash (4), to *inflict a penalty, to fine*
6485 pâqad (4), to *visit, care for, count*
1349+5099 dikē (1), *justice*
2849 kŏlazō (1), to *chastise, punish*
5097 timōrĕō (2), to *avenge*

PUNISHMENT
2399 chêṭ' (1), *crime or its penalty*
2403 chaṭṭâ'âh (3), *offence; sin offering*
5771 'âvôn (9), moral *evil*
6066 'ônesh (1), *fine*
1557 ĕkdikēsis (1), *retaliation, punishment*
2009 ĕpitimia (1), *penalty*
2851 kŏlasis (1), *infliction, punishment*
5098 timōria (1), *penalty, punishment*

PUNISHMENTS
5771 'âvôn (2), moral *evil*

PUNITES
6324 Pûwnîy (1), *turn*

PUNON
6325 Pûwnôn (2), *perplexity*

PUR
6332 Pûwr (3), *lot cast*

PURCHASE
1350 gâ'al (1), to *redeem; to be the next of kin*
4736 miqnâh (6), *acquisition*
4046 pĕripŏiĕŏmai (1), to *acquire; to gain*

PURCHASED
7069 qânâh (5), to *create; to procure*
2932 ktaŏmai (2), to *get, i.e. acquire*
4046 pĕripŏiĕŏmai (1), to *acquire; to gain*
4047 pĕripŏiēsis (1), *acquisition*

PURE
1249 bar (2), *beloved; pure; empty*
1305 bârar (3), to *brighten; purify*
1865 dᵉrôwr (1), *freedom; clear, pure*
2134 zak (9), *pure; clear*
2135 zâkâh (1), to *be innocent*
2141 zâkak (1), to *be transparent; clean, pure*
2561 chemer (1), *fermenting wine*
2888 Ṭabbath (2), *Tabbath*
2889 ṭâhôwr (40), *pure, clean, flawless*
2891 ṭâhêr (2), to *be pure, unadulterated*
3795 kâthîyth (1), *pure oil from beaten olives*
5343 nᵉqê' (Ch.) (1), *clean, pure*
5462 çâgar (8), to *shut up; to surrender*
6337 pâz (1), *pure gold*
6884 tsâraph (2), to *fuse metal; to refine*
53 hagnŏs (4), *innocent, modest, perfect, pure*
1506 ĕilikrinēs (1), *tested as genuine, i.e. pure*
2513 katharŏs (16), *clean, pure*

PURELY
1252 bôr (1), *purity, cleanness*

PURENESS
1252 bôr (1), *purity, cleanness*
2890 ṭᵉhôwr (1), *purity*
54 hagnŏtēs (1), *blamelessness, purity*

PURER
2141 zâkak (1), to *be transparent; clean, pure*
2889 ṭâhôwr (1), *pure, clean, flawless*

PURGE
1305 bârar (2), to *brighten; purify*
2212 zâqaq (1), to *strain, refine; extract, clarify*
2398 châṭâ' (1), to *sin*

2891 ṭâhêr (1), to *be pure, unadulterated*
3722 kâphar (4), to *cover; to expiate*
6884 tsâraph (1), to *fuse metal; to refine*
1245 diakatharizō (2), to *cleanse perfectly*
1571 ĕkkathairō (2), to *cleanse thoroughly*
2511 katharizō (1), to *cleanse*

PURGED
1740 dûwach (1), to *rinse clean, wash*
2891 ṭâhêr (4), to *be pure, unadulterated*
3722 kâphar (5), to *cover; to expiate*
2508 kathairō (1), to *prune dead wood*
2511 katharizō (1), to *cleanse*
2512 katharismŏs (1), *ablution; expiation*
4160+2512 pŏiĕō (1), to *make or do*

PURGETH
2508 kathairō (1), to *prune dead wood*

PURGING
2511 katharizō (1), to *cleanse*

PURIFICATION
2403 chaṭṭâ'âh (2), *offence; sin offering*
2893 ṭohŏrâh (2), *ceremonial purification*
8562 tamrûwq (2), *scouring, perfumery*
49 hagnismŏs (1), *purification*
2512 katharismŏs (1), *ablution; expiation*

PURIFICATIONS
4795 mârûwq (1), *rubbing*

PURIFIED
1305 bârar (1), to *brighten; purify*
2212 zâqaq (1), to *strain, refine; extract, clarify*
2398 châṭâ' (3), to *sin*
2891 ṭâhêr (3), to *be pure, unadulterated*
6942 qâdâsh (1), to *be, make clean*
48 hagnizō (2), *sanctify; to cleanse in ritual*
2511 katharizō (1), to *cleanse*

PURIFIER
2891 ṭâhêr (1), to *be pure, unadulterated*

PURIFIETH
2398 châṭâ' (1), to *sin*
48 hagnizō (1), *sanctify; to cleanse in ritual*

PURIFY
2398 châṭâ' (7), to *sin*
2891 ṭâhêr (3), to *be pure, unadulterated*
48 hagnizō (3), *sanctify; to cleanse in ritual*
2511 katharizō (1), to *cleanse*

PURIFYING
2403 chaṭṭâ'âh (1), *offence; sin offering*
2892 ṭôhar (2), *ceremonial purification*
2893 ṭohŏrâh (3), *ceremonial purification*
8562 tamrûwq (1), *scouring, perfumery*
48 hagnizō (1), *sanctify; to cleanse in ritual*
2511 katharizō (1), to *cleanse*
2512 katharismŏs (2), *ablution; expiation*
2514 katharŏtēs (1), *cleanness*

PURIM
6332 Pûwr (5), *lot cast*

PURITY
47 hagnĕia (2), moral *chastity, purity*

PURLOINING
3557 nŏsphizŏmai (1), to *embezzle*

PURPLE
710 'argᵉvân (1), *purple*
713 'argâmân (38), *purple*
4209 pŏrphura (5), *red-blue color*
4210 pŏrphurŏus (3), *bluish-red*
4211 pŏrphurŏpōlis (1), *trader in bluish-red cloth*

PURPOSE
559 'âmar (2), to *say*
1697 dâbâr (1), *word; matter; thing*
2656 chêphets (3), *pleasure; desire*
2803 châshab (2), to *plot; to think, regard*
4284 machăshâbâh (3), *contrivance; plan*
4639 ma'ăseh (1), *action; labor*
6098 'êtsâh (2), *advice; plan; prudence*
6640 tsᵉbûw (Ch.) (1), *determination*
7385 rîyq (1), *emptiness; worthless thing; in vain*
7997 shâlal (1), to *drop or strip; to plunder*
1011 bŏulĕuō (2), to *deliberate; to resolve*
1013 bŏulēma (1), *resolve, willful choice*
4286 prŏthĕsis (8), *setting forth*

PURPOSED
2161 zâmam (2), to *plan*
2803 châshab (4), to *plot; to think, regard*
3289 yâ'ats (5), to *advise*
3335 yâtsar (1), to *form; potter; to determine*
6440 pânîym (1), *face; front*
7760 sûwm (1), to *put, place*
1096+1106 ginŏmai (1), to *be, become*
4160 pŏiĕō (1), to *do*
4388 prŏtithĕmai (2), to *propose, determine*

5087 tithēmi (1), to *place*

PURPOSES
2154 zimmâh (1), *plan*
4284 machăshâbâh (3), *contrivance; plan*
8356 shâthâh (1), *basis*

PURPOSETH
4255 prŏairĕŏmai (1), to *propose, intend, decide*

PURSE
3599 kîyç (1), *cup;* utility *bag*
905 balantiŏn (3), *money pouch*
2223 zōnē (1), *belt, sash*

PURSES
2223 zōnē (1), *belt, sash*

PURSUE
3212 yâlak (1), to *walk;* to *live;* to *carry*
7291 râdaph (28), to *run after* with hostility

PURSUED
1692 dâbaq (1), to *cling* or *adhere;* to *catch*
1814 dâlaq (2), to *flame;* to *pursue*
7291 râdaph (35), to *run after* with hostility

PURSUER
7291 râdaph (1), to *run after* with hostility

PURSUERS
7291 râdaph (5), to *run after* with hostility

PURSUETH
7291 râdaph (7), to *run after* with hostility

PURSUING
310 'achar (2), *after*
7291 râdaph (4), to *run after* with hostility
7873 sîyg (1), *withdrawal* into a private place

PURTENANCE
7130 qereb (1), *nearest* part, i.e. the *center*

PUSH
5055 nâgach (6), to *butt*
5056 naggâch (2), act of *butting*
7971 shâlach (1), to *send away*

PUSHED
5055 nâgach (1), to *butt*

PUSHING
5055 nâgach (1), to *butt*

PUT
622 'âçaph (2), to *gather, collect*
935 bôw' (10), to *go, come*
1197 bâ'ar (13), to *be brutish, be senseless*
1396 gábar (1), to *be strong; to prevail*
1644 gârash (2), to *drive* out; to *divorce*
1645 geresh (1), *produce, yield*
1846 dâ'ak (6), to *be extinguished; to expire*
1911 hâdâh (1), to *stretch forth* the hand

1921 hâdar (1), to *favor* or *honor;* to *be high*
2026 hârag (1), to *kill, slaughter*
2280 châbash (2), to *wrap* firmly, *bind*
2296 châgar (1), to *gird* on a belt; *put on armor*
2330 chûwd (4), to *propound* a riddle
2502 châlats (1), to *pull* off; to *strip;* to *depart*
3240 yânach (5), to *allow to stay*
3254 yâçaph (5), to *add* or *augment*
3318 yâtsâ' (2), to *go, bring out*
3322 yâtsag (2), to *place*
3381 yârad (2), to *descend*
3455 yâsam (1), to *put*
3518 kâbâh (3), to *extinguish*
3637 kâlam (1), to *taunt* or *insult*
3722 kâphar (1), to *cover; to expiate*
3847 lâbash (41), to *clothe*
3947 lâqach (1), to *take*
4191 mûwth (3), to *die;* to *kill*
4229 mâchâh (3), to *touch,* i.e. reach to
4916 mishlôwach (1), *sending* out
5056 naggâch (1), act of *butting*
5079 niddâh (2), time of menstrual *impurity*
5114 Nôwdâb (3), *noble*
5148 nâchâh (1), to *guide*
5186 nâṭâh (1), to *stretch* or spread out
5365 nâqar (2), to *bore;* to *gouge*
5381 nâsag (1), to *reach*
5394 nâshal (2), to *divest, eject,* or *drop*
5411 Nâthîyn (1), ones *given* to duty
5414 nâthan (187), to *give*
5493 çûwr (19), to *turn* off
5564 çâmak (5), to *lean* upon; *take hold* of
5595 çâphâh (1), to *scrape;* to *remove*
5596 çâphach (1), to *associate;* be *united*
5674 'âbar (4), to *cross* over; to *transition*
5786 'âvar (3), to *blind*
5927 'âlâh (3), to *ascend,* be high, mount
6006 'âmaç (1), to *impose* a burden
6186 'ârak (1), to *set in a row,* i.e. *arrange,*
6213 'âsâh (1), to *do*
6316 Pûwṭ (2), *Put*
6319 Pôwṭîy Phera' (2), *Poti-Phera*
6584 pâshaṭ (6), to *strip,* i.e. *unclothe, plunder*
6605 pâthach (1), to *open* wide; to *loosen, begin*
6695 tsôwq (1), *distress*

7368 râchaq (4), to *recede; remove*
7392 râkab (2), to *ride*
7673 shâbath (2), to *repose; to desist*
7725 shûwb (7), to *turn* back; to *return*
7760 sûwm (150), to *put*
7896 shîyth (11), to *put*
7971 shâlach (45), to *send away*
7972 sheʰlach (Ch.) (1), to *send away*
7973 shelach (1), *spear; shoot* of growth
8214 sheʰphal (Ch.) (1), to *humiliate*
115 athĕtēsis (1), *cancellation*
142 airō (1), to *lift,* to *take up*
337 anairĕō (2), to *take away,* i.e. *abolish*
363 anamimnēskō (1), to *remind; to recollect*
506 anupŏtaktŏs (1), *independent*
520 apagō (1), to *take away*
554 apĕkduŏmai (1), to *divest wholly* oneself
595 apŏthĕsis (1), *laying aside*
615 apŏktĕinō (6), to *kill* outright; to *destroy*
630 apŏluō (13), to *relieve, release*
654 apŏstrĕphō (1), to *turn away* or *back*
659 apŏtithēmi (2), to *put away; get rid of*
683 apōthĕŏmai (2), to *push off;* to *reject*
863 aphiēmi (2), to *leave;* to *pardon, forgive*
906 ballō (14), to *throw*
1096 ginŏmai (1), to *be, become*
1252 diakrinō (1), to *decide; to hesitate*
1325 didōmi (5), to *give*
1544 ĕkballō (4), to *throw out*
1614 ĕktĕinō (3), to *stretch*
1677 ĕllŏgĕō (1), *attribute*
1688 ĕmbibazō (1), to *transfer*
1746 ĕnduō (16), to *dress*
1749 ĕnĕdrŏn (1), *ambush*
1808 ĕxairō (1), to *remove, drive away*
1911 ĕpiballō (1), to *throw upon*
2007 ĕpitithēmi (9), to *impose*
2289 thanatŏō (7), to *kill*
2507 kathairĕō (1), to *lower, or demolish*
2673 katargĕō (2), to *be, render entirely useless*
3004 lĕgō (1), to *say*
3089 luō (1), to *loosen*
3179 mĕthistēmi (1), to *move*
3856 paradĕigmatizō (1), to *expose to infamy*

3860 paradidōmi (1), to *hand over*
3908 paratithēmi (2), to *present*
3982 pĕithō (1), to *pacify* or *conciliate*
4016 pĕriballō (1), to *wrap around, clothe*
4060 pĕritithēmi (5), to *present*
4160 pŏiĕō (3), to *do*
4374 prŏsphĕrō (1), to *present to;* to *treat as*
5087 tithēmi (15), to *place, put*
5279 hupŏmimnēskō (4), to *suggest to memory*
5293 hupŏtassō (9), to *subordinate;* to *obey*
5294 hupŏtithēmi (1), to *hazard; to suggest*
5392 phimŏō (1), to *restrain to silence*
5562 chōrĕō (2), to *pass, enter;* to *hold, admit*

PUTEOLI
4223 Pŏtiŏlŏi (1), *little wells*

PUTIEL
6317 Pûwṭîy'êl (1), *contempt of God*

PUTRIFYING
2961 ṭârîy (1), *fresh*

PUTTEST
4916 mishlôwach (2), *presentation; seizure*
5414 nâthan (1), to *give*
5596 çâphach (1), to *associate; be united*
7673 shâbath (1), to *repose; to desist*
7760 sûwm (2), to *put, place*

PUTTETH
2590 chânaṭ (1), to *embalm; to ripen*
5414 nâthan (4), to *give*
5844 'âṭâh (1), to *wrap,* i.e. *cover, veil, clothe*
6605 pâthach (1), to *open* wide; to *loosen, begin*
7760 sûwm (5), to *put*
7971 shâlach (2), to *send away*
8213 shâphêl (1), to *humiliate*
630 apŏluō (1), to *relieve, release; divorce*
649 apŏstĕllō (1), to *send out* on a mission
906 ballō (2), to *throw*
1544 ĕkballō (1), to *throw out*
1631 ĕkphuō (2), to *sprout up, put forth*
1911 ĕpiballō (2), to *throw upon*
5087 tithēmi (2), to *place, put*

PUTTING
5414 nâthan (1), to *give*
7760 sûwm (1), to *put, place*
7971 shâlach (2), to *send away*
555 apĕkdusis (1), *divestment, removal*

P

595 apŏthĕsis (1), *laying aside*
659 apŏtithēmi (1), *to put away; get rid of*
1745 ĕndusis (1), *investment*
1746 ĕnduō (1), *to dress*
1878 ĕpanamimnĕskō (1), *to remind again of*
1936 ĕpithĕsis (1), *imposition*
2007 ĕpitithēmi (2), *to impose*
4261 prŏballō (1), *to push to the front, germinate*
5087 tithēmi (1), *to place, put*
5279 hupŏmimnĕskō (1), *to suggest to memory*

PYGARG
1787 Dîyshôwn, (1), *antelope*

QUAILS
7958 sᵉlâv (4), *quail bird*

QUAKE
7264 râgaz (1), *to quiver*
7493 râ'ash (1), *to undulate, quake*
1790 ĕntrŏmŏs (1), *terrified*
4579 sĕiŏ (1), *to vibrate; to agitate*

QUAKED
2729 chârad (1), *to shudder*
7264 râgaz (1), *to quiver*

QUAKING
2731 chărâdâh (1), *fear, anxiety*
7494 ra'ash (1), *vibration, uproar*

QUARREL
579 'ânâh (1), *to meet, to happen*
5359 nâqâm (1), *revenge*
1758 ĕnĕchō (1), *to keep a grudge*
3437 mŏmphē (1), *blame*

QUARRIES
6456 pᵉçîyl (2), *idol*

QUARTER
5676 'êber (1), *opposite side; east*
6285 pê'âh (4), *region; extremity*
7098 qâtsâh (2), *termination; fringe*
3836 pantachŏthĕn (1), *from all directions*

QUARTERS
1366 gᵉbûwl (1), *boundary, border*
3411 yᵉrêkâh (1), *far away places*
3671 kânâph (1), *edge or extremity; wing*
7098 qâtsâh (1), *termination; fringe*
7307 rûwach (1), *breath; wind; life-spirit*
1137 gōnia (1), *angle; cornerstone*
5117 tŏpŏs (2), *place*

QUARTUS
2890 Kŏuartŏs (1), *fourth*

QUATERNIONS
5069 tĕtradiŏn (1), *squad of four Roman soldiers*

QUEEN
1377 gᵉbîyrâh (6), *mistress*
4427 mâlak (2), *to reign as king*
4433 malkâ' (Ch.) (2), *queen*
4436 malkâh (33), *queen*
4446 mᵉleketh (5), *queen*
7694 shêgâl (2), *queen*
938 basilissa (4), *queen*

QUEENS
4436 malkâh (2), *queen*
8282 sârâh (1), *female noble*

QUENCH
3518 kâbâh (8), *to extinguish*
7665 shâbar (1), *to burst*
4570 sbĕnnumi (3), *to extinguish, snuff out*

QUENCHED
1846 dâ'ak (1), *to be extinguished; to expire*
3518 kâbâh (9), *to extinguish*
8257 shâqa' (1), *to be overflowed; to cease*
762 asbĕstŏs (2), *not extinguished*
4570 sbĕnnumi (4), *to extinguish, snuff out*

QUESTION
1458 ĕgkalĕō (1), *to bring crimination*
2213 zētēma (2), *debate, dispute*
2214 zētēsis (1), *dispute or its theme*
2919 krinō (2), *to decide; to try, condemn, punish*
3056 lŏgŏs (1), *word, matter, thing; Word*
4802 suzētĕō (2), *to discuss, controvert*

QUESTIONED
1875 dârash (1), *to seek or ask; to worship*
1905 ĕpĕrōtaō (1), *to inquire, seek*
4802 suzētĕō (1), *to discuss, controvert*

QUESTIONING
4802 suzētĕō (2), *to discuss, controvert*

QUESTIONS
1697 dâbâr (2), *word; matter; thing*
2420 chîydâh (2), *puzzle; conundrum; maxim*
1905 ĕpĕrōtaō (1), *to inquire, seek*
2213 zētēma (3), *debate, dispute*
2214 zētēsis (5), *dispute*

QUICK
2416 chay (3), *alive; raw; fresh; life*
4241 michyâh (2), *preservation of life*
2198 zaō (4), *to live*

QUICKEN
2421 châyâh (12), *to live*

2227 zōŏpŏiĕō (1), *to (re-)vitalize, give life*

QUICKENED
2421 châyâh (2), *to live*
2227 zōŏpŏiĕō (2), *to (re-)vitalize, give life*
4806 suzōŏpŏiĕō (2), *to reanimate conjointly*

QUICKENETH
2227 zōŏpŏiĕō (5), *to (re-)vitalize, give life*

QUICKENING
2227 zōŏpŏiĕō (1), *to (re-)vitalize, give life*

QUICKLY
3966 mᵉ'ôd (1), *very*
4116 mâhar (3), *to hurry*
4118 mahêr (8), *in a hurry*
4120 mᵉhêrâh (10), *hurry; promptly*
1722+5034 ĕn (2), *in; during; because of*
5030 tachĕŏs (2), *speedily, rapidly*
5032 tachiŏn (1), *more rapidly, more speedily*
5035 tachu (12), *without delay, soon, suddenly*

QUICKSANDS
4950 surtis (1), *sand drawn by the waves*

QUIET
2790 chârash (1), *to be silent; to be deaf*
4496 mᵉnûwchâh (1), *peacefully; consolation*
5117 nûwach (1), *to rest; to settle down*
5183 nachath (1), *descent; quiet*
7282 râgêa' (1), *restful, i.e. peaceable*
7599 shâ'an (2), *to loll, i.e. be peaceful*
7600 sha'ănân (2), *secure; haughty*
7961 shâlêv (1), *carefree; security, at ease*
8003 shâlêm (1), *complete; friendly; safe*
8252 shâqaṭ (15), *to repose*
8367 shâthaq (1), *to subside*
2263 ērĕmŏs (1), *tranquil, peaceful*
2270 hēsuchazō (1), *to refrain*
2272 hēsuchiŏs (1), *still, undisturbed*
2687 katastĕllō (1), *to quell, quiet*

QUIETED
1826 dâmam (1), *to be silent; to stop, cease*
5117 nûwach (1), *to rest; to settle down*

QUIETETH
8252 shâqaṭ (1), *to repose*

QUIETLY
7987 shᵉlîy (1), *privacy*

QUIETNESS
5183 nachath (1), *quiet*
7961 shâlêv (1), *carefree; security, at ease*

7962 shalvâh (1), *security, ease*
8252 shâqaṭ (4), *to repose*
8253 sheqeṭ (1), *tranquillity*
1515 ĕirēnē (1), *peace; health; prosperity*
2271 hēsuchia (1), *stillness*

QUIT
1961 hâyâh (1), *to exist, i.e. be or become*
5352 nâqâh (1), *to be bare, i.e. extirpated*
5355 nâqîy (2), *innocent*
407 andrizŏmai (1), *to act manly*

QUITE
3615 kâlâh (1), *to cease, be finished, perish*
5080 nâdach (1), *to push off, scattered*
6181 'eryâh (1), *nudity*

QUIVER
827 'ashpâh (6), *quiver*
8522 tᵉlîy (1), *quiver*

QUIVERED
6750 tsâlal (1), *to tinkle, to rattle together*

RAAMAH
7484 Ra'mâh (5), *horse's mane*

RAAMIAH
7485 Ra'amyâh (1), *Jehovah has shaken*

RAAMSES
7486 Ra'mᵉçêç (1), *Rameses or Raamses*

RAB-MAG
7248 Rab-Mâg (2), *chief Magian*

RAB-SARIS
7249 Rab-Çârîyç (3), *chief chamberlain*

RAB-SHAKEH
7262 Rabshâqêh (8), *chief butler*

RABBAH
7237 Rabbâh (13), *great*

RABBATH
7237 Rabbâh (2), *great*

RABBI
4461 rhabbi (7), *my master*

RABBITH
7245 Rabbîyth (1), *multitude*

RABBONI
4462 rhabbŏni (1), *my master*

RABSHAKEH
7262 Rabshâqêh (8), *chief butler*

RACA
4469 rhaka (1), *O empty one, i.e. worthless*

RACE
734 'ôrach (1), *road; manner of life*
4793 mêrôwts (1), *running foot-race*
73 agōn (1), *contest, struggle*

RACHAB
4712 stadiŏn (1), *length of about 200 yards*

RACHAB
4477 Rhachab (1), *proud*

RACHAL
7403 Râkâl (1), *merchant*

RACHEL
7354 Râchêl (41), *ewe*
4478 Rhachêl (1), *ewe*

RACHEL'S
7354 Râchêl (5), *ewe*

RADDAI
7288 Radday (1), *domineering*

RAFTERS
7351 reçhîyt (1), *panel*

RAGAU
4466 Rhagau (1), *friend*

RAGE
1984 hâlal (2), *to boast*
2195 za'am (1), *fury*
2197 za'aph (2), *anger*
2534 chêmâh (2), *heat; anger; poison*
5678 'ebrâh (2), *outburst*
7264 râgaz (5), *to quiver*
7266 regaz (Ch.) (1), *violent anger*
7267 rôgez (1), *disquiet; anger*
7283 râgash (1), *to be tumultuous*
5433 phruassŏ (1), *to make a tumult*

RAGED
1993 hâmâh (1), *to be in great commotion*

RAGETH
5674 'âbar (1), *to cross over; to transition*

RAGING
1348 gê'ûwth (1), *ascending; majesty*
1993 hâmâh (1), *to be in great commotion*
2197 za'aph (1), *anger, rage*
66 agriŏs (1), *wild (country)*
2830 kludŏn (1), *surge, raging*

RAGS
899 beged (1), *clothing; treachery or pillage*
4418 mâlâch (2), *rag or old garment*
7168 qera' (1), *rag, torn pieces*

RAGUEL
7467 Re'ûw'êl (1), *friend of God*

RAHAB
7294 Rahab (3), *boaster*
7343 Râchâb (5), *proud*
4460 Rhaab (2), *proud*

RAHAM
7357 Racham (1), *pity*

RAHEL
7354 Râchêl (1), *ewe*

RAIL
2778 châraph (1), *to spend the winter*

RAILED
5860 'îyt (1), *to swoop down upon; to insult*
987 blasphēmĕŏ (2), *to speak impiously*

RAILER
3060 lŏidŏrŏs (1), *verbal abuser*

RAILING
988 blasphēmia (1), *impious speech*
989 blasphēmŏs (1), *slanderous*
3059 lŏidŏria (1), *slander*

RAILINGS
988 blasphēmia (1), *impious speech*

RAIMENT
899 beged (12), *clothing; treachery or pillage*
3682 keçûwth (1), *cover; veiling*
3830 lebûwsh (1), *garment; wife*
4055 mad (1), *vesture, garment; carpet*
4254 machălâtsâh (1), *mantle, garment*
4403 malbûwsh (3), *garment, clothing*
7553 riqmâh (1), *variegation of color*
8008 salmâh (5), *clothing*
8071 simlâh (11), *dress*
1742 ĕnduma (5), *apparel, outer robe*
2066 ĕsthēs (1), *to clothe*
2440 himatiŏn (12), *to put on clothes*
2441 himatismŏs (2), *clothing*
4629 skĕpasma (1), *clothing; covering*

RAIN
1653 geshem (30), *rain*
3138 yôwreh (1), *autumn rain showers*
3384 yârâh (2), *to throw, shoot an arrow*
4175 môwreh (3), *archer; teaching; early rain*
4305 mâtar (11), *to rain*
4306 mâtâr (37), *rain, shower of rain*
4456 malqôwsh (6), *spring rain*
8164 sâ'îyr (1), *shower*
1026 brĕchŏ (2), *to make wet; to rain*
1026+5205 brĕchŏ (1), *to make wet; to rain*
1028 brŏchē (2), *rain*
5205 huĕtŏs (5), *rain; rain shower*

RAINBOW
2463 iris (2), *rainbow*

RAINED
1656 gôshem (1), *rain downpour*
4305 mâtar (6), *to rain*
1026 brĕchŏ (2), *to make wet; to rain*

RAINY
5464 çagrîyd (1), *pouring rain*

RAISE
5375 nâsâ' (2), *to lift up*
5549 çâlal (2), *to mound up; to exalt*
5782 'ûwr (6), *to awake*
6965 qûwm (30), *to rise*
450 anistēmi (8), *to rise; to come to life*
1453 ĕgĕirō (8), *to waken, i.e. rouse*
1817 ĕxanistēmi (2), *to beget, raise up*
1825 ĕxĕgĕirō (1), *to resuscitate; release*

RAISED
1361 gâbahh (1), *to be lofty; to be haughty*
5782 'ûwr (12), *to awake*
5927 'âlâh (3), *to ascend, be high, mount*
5975 'âmad (1), *to stand*
6209 'ârar (1), *to bare; to demolish*
6965 qûwm (10), *to rise*
6966 qûwm (Ch.) (1), *to rise*
386 anastasis (1), *resurrection from death*
450 anistēmi (6), *to rise; to come to life*
1326 diĕgĕirō (1), *to arouse, stimulate*
1453 ĕgĕirō (45), *to waken, i.e. rouse*
1825 ĕxĕgĕirō (1), *to resuscitate; release*
1892 ĕpĕgĕirō (1), *to excite against, stir up*
4891 sunĕgĕirō (1), *to raise up with*

RAISER
5674 'âbar (1), *to cross over; to transition*

RAISETH
2210 zâqaph (2), *to lift up, comfort*
5975 'âmad (1), *to stand*
6965 qûwm (2), *to rise*
7613 se'êth (1), *elevation; swelling leprous scab*
1453 ĕgĕirō (2), *to waken, i.e. rouse*

RAISING
5872 'Êyn Gedîy (1), *fountain of a kid*
4160+1999 pŏiĕŏ (1), *to do*

RAISINS
6778 tsammûwq (4), *lump of dried grapes*

RAKEM
7552 Reqem (1), *versi-color*

RAKKATH
7557 Raqqath (1), *beach (as expanded shingle)*

RAKKON
7542 Raqqôwn (1), *thinness*

RAM
352 'ayîl (89), *chief; ram*
7410 Râm (7), *high*

RAM'S
3104 yôwbêl (1), *blast of a ram's horn*

RAMA
4471 Rhama (1), *height*

RAMAH
7414 Râmâh (36), *height*

RAMATH
7418 Râmôwth-Negeb (1), *heights of* (the) *South*

RAMATH-LEHI
7437 Râmath Lechîy (1), *height of* (a) *jaw-bone*

RAMATH-MIZPEH
7434 Râmath ham-Mitspeh (1), *height of the watch-tower*

RAMATHAIM-ZOPHIM
7436 Râmâthayim Tsôwphîym (1), *double height of watchers*

RAMATHITE
7435 Râmâthîy (1), *Ramathite*

RAMESES
7486 Ra'meçêç (4), *Rameses or Raamses*

RAMIAH
7422 Ramyâh (1), *Jehovah has raised*

RAMOTH
3406 Yerîymôwth (1), *elevations*
7216 Râ'môwth (6), *heights*
7418 Râmôwth-Negeb (1), *heights of* (the) *South*

RAMOTH-GILEAD
7433 Râmôth Gil'âd (19), *heights of Gilad*

RAMPART
2426 chêyl (2), *rampart, battlement*

RAMS
352 'ayîl (61), *chief; ram*
1798 dekar (Ch.) (3), *male sheep*
3733 kar (2), *ram sheep; battering ram*
6260 'attûwd (2), *he-goats; leaders*

RAMS'
352 'ayîl (5), *chief; ram*
3104 yôwbêl (4), *blast of a ram's horn*

RAN
1272 bârach (1), *to flee suddenly*
1980 hâlak (2), *to walk; live a certain way*
3331 yâtsa' (1), *to strew as a surface*
3332 yâtsaq (1), *to pour out*
5064 nâgar (1), *to pour out; to deliver over*
6379 pâkâh (1), *to pour, trickle*
6584 pâshat (1), *to strip, i.e. unclothe, plunder*
7323 rûwts (30), *to run*
7519 râtsâ' (1), *to run; to delight in*
7857 shâtaph (1), *to gush; to inundate*

R

1530 ĕispēdaō (1), to
rush in
1532 ĕistrĕchō (1), to
hasten inward
1632 ĕkchēō (1), to pour
forth; to bestow
2027 ĕpŏkĕllō (1), to
beach a ship vessel
2701 katatrĕchō (1), to
hasten, run
3729 hŏrmaō (4), to dash
or plunge, stampede
4063 pĕritrĕchō (1), to
traverse, run about
4370 prŏstrĕchō (1), to
hasten by running
4390 prŏtrĕchō (1), to run
ahead, i.e. to precede
4890 sundrŏmē (1),
(riotous) concourse
4936 suntrĕchō (2), to
rush together
5143 trĕchō (6), to run or
walk hastily; to strive

RANG
1949 hûwm (2), to make
an uproar; agitate

RANGE
3491 yâthûwr (1),
gleaning

RANGES
3600 kîyr (1), portable
cooking range
7713 sᵉdêrâh (3), row, i.e.
rank of soldiers; story

RANGING
8264 shâqaq (1), to seek

RANK
1277 bârîy' (2), fatted or
plump; healthy
4634 ma'ărâkâh (1), row;
pile; military array
5737 'âdar (1), to
arrange; hoe a vineyard

RANKS
734 'ôrach (1), road;
manner of life
6471 pa'am (2), time;
step; occurence
4237 prasia (1),
arranged group

RANSOM
3724 kôpher (8), village;
redemption-price
6299 pâdâh (1), to
ransom; to release
6306 pidyôwm (1),
ransom; payment
487 antilutrŏn (1),
redemption-price
3083 lutrŏn (2),
redemption-price

RANSOMED
1350 gâ'al (2), to redeem;
to be the next of kin
6299 pâdâh (1), to
ransom; to release

RAPHA
7498 Râphâ' (2), giant

RAPHU
7505 Râphûw' (1), cured

RARE
3358 yaqqîyr (Ch.) (1),
precious

RASE
6168 'ârâh (1), to be,
make bare; demolish

RASH
926 bâhal (1), to tremble;
hasten, hurry anxiously
4116 mâhar (1), to hurry;
promptly

RASHLY
4312 prŏpĕtēs (1), falling
forward headlong

RASOR
8593 ta'ar (1), knife;
razor; scabbard

RATE
1697 dâbâr (5), word;
matter; thing

RATHER
408 'al (2), not; nothing
977 bâchar (1), select,
chose, prefer
2228 ē (3), or; than
2309 thĕlō (1), to will; to
desire; to choose
3123 mallŏn (34), in a
greater degree
3304 mĕnŏungĕ (1), so
then at least
4056 pĕrissŏtĕrōs (1),
more superabundantly
4133 plēn (2), rather, yet

RATTLETH
7439 rânâh (1), to whiz,
rattle

RATTLING
7494 ra'ash (1),
vibration, bounding

RAVEN
6158 'ôrêb (6),
dusky-hue raven

RAVENING
2963 țâraph (3), to pluck
off or pull to pieces
724 harpagē (1), pillage;
greediness; robbery
727 harpax (1),
rapacious; robbing

RAVENOUS
5861 'ayiț (2), bird of
prey (poss.) hawk
6530 pᵉrîyts (1), violent

RAVENS
6158 'ôrêb (4),
dusky-hue raven
2876 kŏrax (1), crow or
raven

RAVIN
2963 țâraph (1), to pluck
off or pull to pieces
2966 țᵉrêphâh (1), torn
prey

RAVISHED
3823 lâbab (2), transport
with love; to stultify
6031 'ânâh (1), to afflict,
be afflicted
7686 shâgâh (2), to stray,
wander; to transgress
7693 shâgal (2), to
copulate with

RAW
2416 chay (6), alive; raw;
fresh; life
4995 nâ' (1), uncooked

RAZOR
4177 môwrâh (3), razor
8593 ta'ar (2), knife;
razor; scabbard

REACH
1272 bârach (1), to flee
suddenly
1961 hâyâh (1), to exist,
i.e. be or become
4229 mâchâh (1), to
touch, i.e. reach to
5060 nâga' (5), to strike
5381 nâsag (2), to reach
2185 ĕphiknĕŏmai (1), to
extend to, reach to
5342 phĕrō (2), to bear or
carry

REACHED
4291 mᵉțâ' (Ch.) (2), to
arrive, to extend
5060 nâga' (1), to strike
6293 pâga' (1), to impinge
6642 tsâbaț (1), to hand
out food
190 akŏlŏuthĕō (1), to
accompany, follow
2185 ĕphiknĕŏmai (1), to
extend to, reach to

REACHETH
4291 mᵉțâ' (Ch.) (1), to
arrive, to extend
5060 nâga' (4), to strike
6293 pâga' (5), to impinge
7971 shâlach (1), to send
away

REACHING
5060 nâga' (3), to strike
1901 ĕpĕktĕinŏmai (1), to
stretch oneself forward

READ
7121 qârâ' (35), to call
out
7123 qᵉrâ' (Ch.) (7), to
call out
314 anaginōskō (28), to
read aloud in public

READEST
314 anaginōskō (2), to
read aloud in public

READETH
7121 qârâ' (1), to call out
314 anaginōskō (3), to
read aloud in public

READINESS
2092 hĕtŏimŏs (1), ready,
prepared
4288 prŏthumia (2),
alacrity, eagerness

READING
4744 miqrâ' (1), public
meeting
7121 qârâ' (2), to call out
320 anagnōsis (3), act of
public reading

READY
631 'âçar (4), to fasten; to
join battle
1951 hûwn (1), to be, act
light
2363 chûwsh (1), to
hurry; to be eager
2896 țôwb (1), good; well
3559 kûwn (17), to set up;
establish, fix, prepare
4106 mâhîyr (2), skillful

4116 mâhar (2), to hurry;
promptly
4131 môwț (1), to slip,
shake, fall
4672 mâtsâ' (1), to find
or acquire; to occur
5750 'ôwd (1), again;
repeatedly; still; more
6257 'âthad (1), to
prepare
6263 'ăthîyd (Ch.) (1),
prepared
6264 'âthîyd (4),
prepared; treasure
7126 qârab (1), to
approach, bring near
7138 qârôwb (1), near,
close
8003 shâlêm (1),
complete; friendly; safe
1451 ĕggus (1), near,
close
2090 hĕtŏimazō (10), to
prepare
2092 hĕtŏimŏs (15),
ready, prepared
2093 hĕtŏimŏs (3), in
readiness
2130 ĕumĕtadŏtŏs (1),
liberal, generous
3195 mĕllō (4), to intend,
i.e. be about to
3903 paraskĕuazō (3), to
get ready, prepare
4288 prŏthumia (1),
alacrity, eagerness
4289 prŏthumŏs (3),
alacrity, eagerness
4689 spĕndō (1), to pour
out as a libation

REAIA
7211 Rᵉ'âyâh (1),
Jehovah has seen

REAIAH
7211 Rᵉ'âyâh (3),
Jehovah has seen

REALM
4437 malkûw (Ch.) (3),
dominion
4438 malkûwth (4), rule;
dominion

REAP
7114 qâtsar (18), to
curtail, cut short
2325 thĕrizō (13), to
harvest, reap a crop

REAPED
7114 qâtsar (1), to
curtail, cut short
270 amaō (1), reap, mow
down grain
2325 thĕrizō (2), to
harvest, reap a crop

REAPER
7114 qâtsar (1), to
curtail, cut short

REAPERS
7114 qâtsar (7), to
curtail, cut short
2327 thĕristēs (2),
harvester, reaper

REAPEST
7114 qâtsar (1), to
curtail, cut short
2325 thĕrizō (1), to
harvest, reap a crop

REAPETH
7114 qâtsar (1), to
curtail, cut short
2325 *thĕrizō* (3), to
harvest, reap a crop

REAPING
7114 qâtsar (1), to
curtail, cut short
2325 *thĕrizō* (2), to
harvest, reap a crop

REAR
6965 qûwm (3), to *rise*
1453 *ĕgĕirō* (1), to
waken, i.e. *rouse*

REARED
5324 nâtsab (1), to *station*
6965 qûwm (9), to *rise*

REASON
413 'êl (1), *to, toward*
1697 dâbâr (1), *word;
matter; thing*
2808 cheshbôwn (1),
intelligent plan
2940 ṭa'am (1), *taste;
intelligence; mandate*
3198 yâkach (3), to *be
correct*; to *argue*
4480 min (5), *from, out of*
4486 manda' (Ch.) (1),
wisdom or intelligence
5921 'al (1), *above, over,
upon*, or *against*
5973 'îm (1), *with*
6440 pânîym (9), *face;
front*
6903 qᵉbêl (Ch.) (1), *on
account of, so as, since*
8199 shâphaṭ (1), to *judge*
701 *arĕstŏs* (1),
agreeable; desirable; fit
1223 *dia* (5), *through, by
means of; because of*
1260 *dialŏgizŏmai* (5), to
deliberate
1537 *ĕk* (3), *out, out of*
1752 *hĕnĕka* (1), *on
account of*
3056 *lŏgŏs* (2), *word,
matter, thing; Word*

REASONABLE
3050 *lŏgikŏs* (1),
rational, logical

REASONED
1256 *dialĕgŏmai* (4), to
discuss
1260 *dialŏgizŏmai* (5), to
deliberate
3049 *lŏgizŏmai* (1), to
credit; to *think, regard*
4802 *suzĕtĕō* (1), to
discuss, controvert
4817 *sullŏgizŏmai* (1), to
reckon together

REASONING
8433 tôwkêchâh (1),
correction, refutation
1260 *dialŏgizŏmai* (1), to
deliberate
1261 *dialŏgismŏs* (1),
consideration; debate
4802 *suzĕtĕō* (1), to
discuss, controvert
4803 *suzĕtĕsis* (1),
discussion, dispute

REASONS
8394 tâbûwn (1),
intelligence; argument

REBA
7254 Reba' (2), *fourth*

REBECCA
4479 *Rhĕbĕkka* (1),
fettering (by beauty)

REBEKAH
7259 Ribqâh (28),
fettering (by beauty)

REBEKAH'S
7259 Ribqâh (2), *fettering*
(by beauty)

REBEL
4775 mârad (9), to *rebel*
4784 mârâh (4), to *rebel
or resist*; to *provoke*
5493 çûwr (1), to *turn off*

REBELLED
4775 mârad (12), to *rebel*
4784 mârâh (16), to *rebel
or resist*; to *provoke*
6586 pâsha' (5), to *break
away from authority*
6856 tsippôren (1), *nail;
point* of a style or pen

REBELLEST
4775 mârad (2), to *rebel*

REBELLION
4776 mᵉrad (Ch.) (1),
rebellion
4779 mârâd (Ch.) (1),
rebellious
4805 mᵉrîy (4), *rebellion,
rebellious*
5627 çârâh (2), *apostasy;
crime; remission*
6588 pesha' (1), *revolt*

REBELLIOUS
4775 mârad (1), to *rebel*
4779 mârâd (Ch.) (2),
rebellious
4780 mardûwth (1),
rebelliousness
4784 mârâh (9), to *rebel
or resist*; to *provoke*
4805 mᵉrîy (17),
rebellion, rebellious
5637 çârar (6), to *be
refractory, stubborn*

REBELS
4775 mârad (1), to *rebel*
4784 mârâh (1), to *rebel
or resist*; to *provoke*
4805 mᵉrîy (1), *rebellion,
rebellious*

REBUKE
1605 gâ'ar (7), to *chide,
reprimand*
1606 gᵉ'ârâh (12),
chiding, rebuke
2781 cherpâh (2),
contumely, disgrace
3198 yâkach (8), to *be
correct*; to *argue*
4045 mig'ereth (1),
reproof (i.e. a curse)
8433 tôwkêchâh (4),
refutation, proof
298 *amōmĕtŏs* (1),
unblemished
1651 *ĕlĕgchō* (4), to
admonish, rebuke

REBUKED
1605 gâ'ar (4), to *chide,
reprimand*
3198 yâkach (1), to *be
correct*; to *argue*
7378 rîyb (1), to *hold a
controversy*; to *defend*
1651 *ĕlĕgchō* (1), to
admonish, rebuke
2008 *ĕpitimaō* (17), to
rebuke, warn, forbid
2192+1649 *ĕchō* (1), to
have; hold; keep

REBUKER
4148 mûwçâr (1),
reproof, warning

REBUKES
8433 tôwkêchâh (3),
correction, refutation

REBUKETH
1605 gâ'ar (1), to *chide,
reprimand*
3198 yâkach (3), to *be
correct*; to *argue*

REBUKING
1606 gᵉ'ârâh (1), *chiding,
rebuke*
2008 *ĕpitimaō* (1), to
rebuke, warn, forbid

RECALL
7725 shûwb (1), to *turn
back*; to *return*

RECEIPT
5058 *tĕlōniŏn* (3),
tax-gatherer's booth

RECEIVE
1878 dâshên (1), to
fatten; to *satisfy*
3557 kûwl (2), to *keep in;
to measure*
3947 lâqach (35), to *take*
5162 nâcham (1), to *be
sorry*; to *pity, console*
5375 nâsâ' (3), to *lift up*
6901 qâbal (3), to *admit;
to take*
6902 qᵉbal (Ch.) (1), to
acquire
8254 shâqal (1), to
suspend in trade
308 *anablĕpō* (7), to *look
up*; to *recover sight*
568 *apĕchō* (1), to *be
distant*
588 *apŏdĕchŏmai* (1), to
welcome; approve
618 *apŏlambanō* (8), to
receive; *be repaid*
1209 *dĕchŏmai* (24), to
receive, welcome
1325 *didōmi* (1), to *give*
1523 *ĕisdĕchŏmai* (1), to
take into one's favor
1926 *ĕpidĕchŏmai* (1), to
admit, welcome
2210 *zēmiŏō* (1), to
experience detriment
2865 *kŏmizō* (6), to
provide for
2983 *lambanō* (61), to
take, receive

REASONS *1969 ĕpiplēssō* (1), to
upbraid, rebuke
2008 *ĕpitimaō* (6), to
rebuke, warn, forbid

3858 paradĕchŏmai (4),
to *accept, receive*
3880 *paralambanō* (1), to
assume an office
4327 *prŏsdĕchŏmai* (2),
to *receive*; to *await for*
4355 *prŏslambanō* (4), to
welcome, receive
5562 *chōrĕō* (5), to *pass,
enter*; to *hold, admit*

RECEIVED
622 'âçaph (1), to *gather,
collect*
1961 hâyâh (2), to *exist*,
i.e. *be* or *become*
2388 châzaq (1), to
fasten upon; to *seize*
2505 châlaq (1), to *be
smooth, be slippery*
3947 lâqach (22), to *take*
4672 mâtsâ' (1), to *find
or acquire*; to *occur*
6901 qâbal (3), to *admit;
to take*
308 *anablĕpō* (8), to *look
up*; to *recover sight*
324 *anadĕchŏmai* (2), to
entertain as a guest
353 *analambanō* (3), to
take up, bring up
354 *analĕpsis* (1),
ascension
568 *apĕchō* (1), to *be
distant*
588 *apŏdĕchŏmai* (4),
welcome; approve
618 *apŏlambanō* (1), to
receive; *be repaid*
1183 *dĕkatŏō* (1), to *give
or take* a tenth
1209 *dĕchŏmai* (16), to
receive, welcome
1653 *ĕlĕĕō* (1), to *give out
compassion*
2865 *kŏmizō* (3), to
provide for, to *carry* off
2983 *lambanō* (56), to
take, receive
3336 *mĕtalĕmpsis* (1),
participation, sharing
3549 *nŏmŏthĕtĕō* (1), to
be given law
3880 *paralambanō* (13),
to *assume* an office
4355 *prŏslambanō* (3), to
welcome, receive
4687 *spĕirō* (4), to
scatter, i.e. *sow* seed
4732 *stĕrĕŏō* (1), to *be,
become strong*
5264 *hupŏdĕchŏmai* (4),
to *entertain hospitably*
5274 *hupŏlambanō* (1),
to *take up*, i.e. *continue*

RECEIVEDST
618 *apŏlambanō* (1), to
receive; *be repaid*

RECEIVER
8254 shâqal (1), to
suspend in trade

RECEIVETH
622 'âçaph (1), to *gather,
collect*
3947 lâqach (4), to *take*
1209 *dĕchŏmai* (8), to
receive, welcome
1926 *ĕpidĕchŏmai* (1), to
admit, welcome

R

2983 *lambanō* (14), to take, receive
3335 *mĕtalambanō* (1), to participate
3858 *paradĕchŏmai* (1), to accept, receive
4327 *prŏsdĕchŏmai* (1), to receive; to await for

RECEIVING
3947 lâqach (1), to take
618 apŏlambanō (1), to receive; be repaid
2865 kŏmizō (1), to provide for, to carry off
2983 lambanō (1), to take, receive
3028 lēmpsis (1), act of receipt
3880 paralambanō (1), to assume an office
4356 prŏslēpsis (1), admission, acceptance

RECHAB
7394 Rêkâb (13), rider

RECHABITES
7397 Rêkâh (4), softness

RECHAH
7397 Rêkâh (1), softness

RECKON
2803 châshab (3), to think, regard; to value
5608 çâphar (1), to inscribe; to enumerate
6485 pâqad (1), to visit, care for, count
3049 lŏgizŏmai (2), to credit; to think, regard
4868 sunairō (1), to compute an account

RECKONED
2803 châshab (4), to think, regard; to value
3187 yâchas (12), to enroll by family list
7737 shâvâh (1), to resemble; to adjust
3049 lŏgizŏmai (4), to credit; to think, regard

RECKONETH
4868+3056 sunairō (1), to compute an account

RECKONING
2803 châshab (1), to think, regard; to value
6486 pᵉquddâh (1), visitation; punishment

RECOMMENDED
3860 paradidōmi (2), to hand over

RECOMPENCE
1576 gᵉmûwl (9), act; reward, recompense
7966 shillûwm (1), requital; retribution; fee
8005 shillêm (1), requital
8545 tᵉmûwrâh (1), barter, compensation
468 antapŏdŏma (2), requital, recompense
489 antimisthia (2), correspondence
3405 misthapŏdŏsia (3), requital, good or bad

RECOMPENCES
1578 gᵉmûwlâh (1), act; reward, recompense
7966 shillûwm (1), requital; retribution; fee

RECOMPENSE
1580 gâmal (2), to benefit or requite; to wean
5414 nâthan (9), to give
7725 shûwb (3), to return or restore
7999 shâlam (7), to be safe; to reciprocate
467 antapŏdidōmi (3), to requite good or evil
591 apŏdidōmi (1), to give away

RECOMPENSED
5414 nâthan (1), to give
7725 shûwb (5), to return or restore
7999 shâlam (2), to be safe; to reciprocate
467 antapŏdidōmi (2), to requite good or evil

RECOMPENSEST
7999 shâlam (1), to be safe; to reciprocate

RECOMPENSING
5414 nâthan (1), to give

RECONCILE
3722 kâphar (2), to placate or cancel
7521 râtsâh (1), to be pleased with; to satisfy
604 apŏkatallassō (2), to reconcile fully, reunite

RECONCILED
604 apŏkatallassō (1), to reconcile fully, reunite
1259 diallassō (1), to be reconciled
2644 katallassō (5), to change mutually

RECONCILIATION
2398 châṭâ' (1), to sin
3722 kâphar (4), to placate or cancel
2433 hilaskŏmai (1), to conciliate, to atone for
2643 katallagē (2), restoration

RECONCILING
3722 kâphar (1), to cover; to expiate
2643 katallagē (1), restoration
2644 katallassō (1), to change mutually

RECORD
1799 dikrôwn (Ch.) (1), official register
2142 zâkar (2), to remember; to mention
5749 'ûwd (3), to duplicate or repeat
7717 sâhêd (1), witness
3140 marturĕō (13), to testify; to commend
3141 marturia (7), evidence given
3143 marturŏmai (1), to witness
3144 martus (2), witness

RECORDED
3789 kâthab (1), to write

RECORDER
2142 zâkar (9), to remember; to mention

RECORDS
1799 dikrôwn (Ch.) (2), official register
2146 zikrôwn (1), commemoration

RECOUNT
2142 zâkar (1), to remember; to mention

RECOVER
622 'âçaph (4), to gather, collect
1082 bâlag (1), to be comforted
2421 châyâh (6), to live; to revive
2492 châlam (1), to be, make plump; to dream
4241 michyâh (1), preservation of life; sustenance
5337 nâtsal (3), to deliver; to be snatched
6113 'âtsar (1), to hold back; to maintain, rule
7069 qânâh (1), to create; to procure
7725 shûwb (1), to turn back; to return
366 ananēphō (1), to regain one's senses
2192+2573 ĕchō (1), to have; hold; keep

RECOVERED
2388 châzaq (1), to fasten upon; to seize
2421 châyâh (2), to live; to revive
5337 nâtsal (2), to deliver; to be snatched
5927 'âlâh (1), to ascend, be high, mount
7725 shûwb (1), to turn back; to return

RECOVERING
309 anablĕpsis (1), restoration of sight

RED
119 'âdam (9), to be red in the face
122 'âdôm (7), rosy, red
132 'admônîy (1), reddish, ruddy
923 bahaṭ (1), white marble
2447 chaklîyl (1), darkly flashing eyes; brilliant
2560 châmar (1), to ferment, foam; to glow
2561 chemer (1), fermenting wine
5488 çûwph (24), papyrus reed; reed
5489 Çûwph (1), reed
5492 çûwphâh (1), hurricane wind
2281 thalassa (2), sea or lake
4449 purrhazō (2), to redden
4450 purrhŏs (2), fire-like, flame-colored

REDDISH
125 'ădamdâm (6), reddish

REDEEM
1350 gâ'al (23), to redeem; be next of kin
1353 gᵉullâh (5), redemption
6299 pâdâh (24), to ransom; to release
6304 pᵉdûwth (1), distinction; deliverance
1805 ĕxagŏrazō (1), to buy up, ransom
3084 lutrŏō (1), to free by paying a ransom

REDEEMED
1350 gâ'al (24), to redeem; be next of kin
1353 gᵉullâh (2), redemption
6299 pâdâh (23), to ransom; to release
6302 pâdûwy (2), ransom
6306 pidyôwm (2), ransom payment
6561 pâraq (1), to break off or crunch; to deliver
7069 qânâh (1), to create; to procure
59 agŏrazō (3), to purchase; to redeem
1805 ĕxagŏrazō (1), to buy up, ransom
3084 lutrŏō (2), to free by paying a ransom
4160+3085 pŏiĕō (1), to make or do

REDEEMEDST
6299 pâdâh (1), to ransom; to release

REDEEMER
1350 gâ'al (18), to redeem; be next of kin

REDEEMETH
1350 gâ'al (1), to redeem; to be the next of kin
6299 pâdâh (1), to ransom; to release

REDEEMING
1353 gᵉullâh (1), redemption
1805 ĕxagŏrazō (2), to buy up, ransom

REDEMPTION
1353 gᵉullâh (5), redemption
6304 pᵉdûwth (2), distinction; deliverance
6306 pidyôwm (2), ransom payment
629 apŏlutrōsis (9), ransom in full
3085 lutrōsis (2), ransoming

REDNESS
2498 châlaph (1), to hasten away; to pass on

REDOUND
4052 pĕrissĕuō (1), to superabound

REED
7070 qâneh (21), reed
2563 kalamŏs (11), reed

REEDS
98 'âgam (1), marsh; pond; pool
7070 qâneh (6), reed

REEL
2287 châgag (1), to
observe a festival
5128 nûwa' (1), to waver

REELAIAH
7480 Re'êlâyâh (1),
fearful of Jehovah

REFINE
6884 tsâraph (1), to fuse
metal; to refine

REFINED
2212 zâqaq (3), to strain,
refine; extract, clarify
6884 tsâraph (2), to fuse
metal; to refine

REFINER
6884 tsâraph (1), to fuse
metal; to refine

REFINER'S
6884 tsâraph (1), to fuse
metal; to refine

REFORMATION
1357 diŏrthōsis (1),
Messianic restoration

REFORMED
3256 yâçar (1), to
chastise; to instruct

REFRAIN
662 'âphaq (2), to abstain
2413 châtam (1), to stop,
restrain
2820 châsak (1), to
restrain or refrain
4513 mâna' (2), to deny
7368 râchaq (1), to
recede; remove
868 aphistēmi (1), to
desist, desert
3973 pauō (1), to stop

REFRAINED
662 'âphaq (3), to abstain
2820 châsak (1), to
restrain or refrain
3601 kîyshôwr (1),
spindle
3607 kâlâ' (1), to hold
back; to prohibit, stop
6113 'âtsar (1), to hold
back; to maintain, rule

REFRAINETH
2820 châsak (1), to
restrain or refrain

REFRESH
5582 çâ'ad (1), to support
373 anapauō (1), to
repose; to refresh
1958+5177 ĕpimĕlĕia (1),
carefulness

REFRESHED
5314 nâphash (3), to be
refreshed
7304 râvach (2), to
revive; to have room
373 anapauō (3), to
repose; to refresh
404 anapsuchō (1), to
relieve
4875 sunanapauŏmai
(1), to recruit oneself

REFRESHETH
7725 shûwb (1), to return
or restore

REFRESHING
4774 margê'âh (1), place
of rest
403 anapsuxis (1),
revival, relief

REFUGE
2620 châçâh (1), to flee
to; to confide in
4268 machăçeh (15),
shelter; refuge
4498 mânôwç (4), fleeing;
place of refuge
4585 me'ôwnâh (1), abode
4733 miqlât (20), asylum,
place of protection
4869 misgâb (5), high
refuge
2703 kataphĕugō (1), to
flee down

REFUSE
3973 mâ'ôwç (1), refuse
3985 mâ'ên (10), to
refuse, reject
3986 mâ'ên (4),
unwilling, refusing
3987 mê'ên (1),
refractory, stubborn
3988 mâ'aç (3), to spurn;
to disappear
4549 mâçaç (1), to waste;
to faint
4651 mappâl (1), chaff;
flap or fold of skin
6544 pâra' (1), to loosen;
to expose, dismiss
3868 paraitĕŏmai (4), to
deprecate, decline

REFUSED
3985 mâ'ên (24), to
refuse, reject
3988 mâ'aç (5), to spurn;
to disappear
579 apŏblētŏs (1),
rejected
720 arnĕŏmai (2), to
disavow, reject
3868 paraitĕŏmai (1), to
deprecate, decline

REFUSEDST
3985 mâ'ên (1), to refuse,
reject

REFUSETH
3985 mâ'ên (5), to refuse,
reject
3988 mâ'aç (1), to spurn;
to disappear
5800 'âzab (1), to loosen;
relinquish; permit
6544 pâra' (2), to loosen;
to expose, dismiss

REGARD
995 bîyn (4), to
understand; discern
1875 dârash (1), to
pursue or search
2803 châshab (1), to
think, regard; to value
3820 lêb (3), heart
5027 nâbat (4), to scan;
to regard with favor
5375 nâsâ' (3), to lift up
5375+6440 nâsâ' (1), to
lift up
5869+2437+5921 'ayin (1),
eye; sight; fountain
5921+1700 'al (1), above,
over, upon, or against

6437 pânâh (3), to turn,
to face
7200 râ'âh (1), to see
7789 shûwr (1), to spy
out, survey
8104 shâmar (2), to
watch
8159 shâ'âh (1), to
inspect, consider
1788 ĕntrĕpō (1), to
respect; to confound
4337 prŏsĕchō (1), to pay
attention to
5426 phrŏnĕŏ (1), to be
mentally disposed

REGARDED
3820 lêb (1), heart
7181 qâshab (1), to prick
up the ears
7182 qesheb (1),
hearkening
7200 râ'âh (2), to see
7761+2942 sûwm (Ch.)
(1), to put, place
272 amĕlĕŏ (1), to be
careless of, neglect
1788 ĕntrĕpō (1), to
respect; to confound
1914 ĕpiblĕpō (1), to gaze
at

REGARDEST
995 bîyn (1), to
understand; discern
991 blĕpō (2), to look at

REGARDETH
995 bîyn (1), to
understand; discern
2803 châshab (1), to
think, regard; to value
3045 yâda' (1), to know
5234 nâkar (1), to
respect, revere
5375 nâsâ' (1), to lift up
6437 pânâh (1), to turn,
to face
7200 râ'âh (1), to see
7761+2942 sûwm (Ch.)
(1), to put, place
8085 shâma' (1), to hear
8104 shâmar (3), to
watch
5426 phrŏnĕŏ (2), to be
mentally disposed

REGARDING
7760 sûwm (1), to put,
place
3851 parabŏulĕuŏmai
(1), to misconsult, i.e.
disregard

REGEM
7276 Regem (1),
stone-heap

REGEM-MELECH
7278 Regem Melek (1),
king's heap

REGENERATION
3824 paliggĕnĕsia (2),
renovation; restoration

REGION
2256 chebel (3),
company, band
5299 nâphâh (1), height;
sieve
4066 pĕrichōrŏs (6),
surrounding country
5561 chōra (4), territory

REGIONS
2825 klinē (2), couch
5561 chōra (1), territory

REGISTER
3791 kâthâb (2), writing,
record or book
5612 çêpher (1), writing

REHABIAH
7345 Rechabyâh (5),
Jehovah has enlarged

REHEARSE
7760 sûwm (1), to put,
place
8567 tânâh (1), to
commemorate

REHEARSED
1696 dâbar (1), to speak,
say; to subdue
5046 nâgad (1), to
announce
312 anaggĕllō (1), to
announce in detail
756 archŏmai (1), to
begin

REHOB
7340 Rechôb (10), myriad

REHOBOAM
7346 Rechab'âm (50),
people has enlarged

REHOBOTH
7344 Rechôbôwth (4),
streets

REHUM
7348 Rechûwm (8),
compassionate

REI
7472 Rê'îy (1), social

REIGN
4427 mâlak (117), to
reign as king
4437 malkûw (Ch.) (4),
dominion
4438 malkûwth (21),
rule; dominion
4467 mamlâkâh (2),
royal dominion
4468 mamlâkûwth (1),
royal dominion
4910 mâshal (3), to rule
6113 'âtsar (1), to hold
back; to rule, assemble
7287 râdâh (1), to
subjugate
757 archō (1), to rule, be
first in rank
936 basilĕuō (13), to rule
2231 hēgĕmŏnia (1),
rulership, leadership
4821 sumbasilĕuō (2), to
be co-regent

REIGNED
4427 mâlak (159), to
reign as king
4910 mâshal (3), to rule
7786 sûwr (1), to rule,
crown
936 basilĕuō (6), to rule

REIGNEST
4910 mâshal (1), to rule

REIGNETH
4427 mâlak (11), to reign
as king
936 basilĕuō (1), to rule
2192+932 ĕchō (1), to
have; hold; keep

R

REIGNING
4427 mâlak (1), to *reign as king*

REINS
2504 châlâts (1), *loins, areas of the waist*
3629 kilyâh (13), *kidney; mind, heart, spirit*
3510 nĕphrŏs (1), *inmost mind*

REJECT
3988 mâ'aç (1), to *spurn; to disappear*
114 athĕtĕō (2), to *disesteem, neutralize*
3868 paraitĕŏmai (1), to *deprecate, decline*

REJECTED
2310 châdêl (1), *ceasing or destitute*
3988 mâ'aç (17), to *spurn; to disappear*
96 adŏkimŏs (1), *failing the test, worthless*
114 athĕtĕō (1), to *disesteem, neutralize*
593 apŏdŏkimazō (7), to *repudiate, reject*
1609 ĕkptuō (1), to *spurn, scorn*

REJECTETH
14 agathŏĕrgĕō (1), to do *good work*

REJOICE
1523 gîyl (23), *rejoice*
1524 gîyl (2), *age, stage in life*
4885 mâsôws (1), *delight*
5937 'âlaz (8), to *jump for joy*
5947 'allîyz (3), *exultant; reveling*
5965 'âlaç (1), to *leap for joy, i.e. exult, wave*
5970 'âlats (4), to *jump for joy*
7442 rânan (11), to *shout for joy*
7797 sûws (14), to *be bright, i.e. cheerful*
7832 sâchaq (1), to *laugh; to scorn; to play*
8055 sâmach (70), to *be, make gleesome*
8056 sâmêach (5), *blithe or gleeful*
8057 simchâh (4), *blithesomeness or glee*
21 agalliaō (4), to *exult*
2165 ĕuphrainō (5), to *rejoice, be glad*
2744 kauchaŏmai (4), to *glory in, rejoice in*
2745 kauchēma (1), *boast; brag*
4796 sugchairō (5), to *sympathize in gladness*
5463 chairō (24), to be *cheerful*

REJOICED
1523 gîyl (2), *rejoice*
2302 châdâh (1), to *rejoice, be glad*
5937 'âlaz (2), to *jump for joy*
6670 tsâhal (1), to *be cheerful*

REJOICEST
5937 'âlaz (1), to *jump for joy*

REJOICETH
1523 gîyl (1), *rejoice*
4885 mâsôws (1), *delight*
5937 'âlaz (1), to *jump for joy*
5938 'âlêz (1), *exultant*
5970 'âlats (2), to *jump for joy*
7797 sûws (3), to *be bright, i.e. cheerful*
8055 sâmach (4), to *be, make gleesome*
2620 katakauchaŏmai (1), to *exult over*
4796 sugchairō (1), to *sympathize in gladness*
5463 chairō (3), to *be cheerful*

REJOICING
1524 gîyl (1), *age, stage in life*
1525 gîylâh (1), *joy, delight*
5947 'allîyz (1), *exultant; reveling*
5951 'ălîytsûwth (1), *exultation*
7440 rinnâh (3), *shout*
7832 sâchaq (2), to *laugh; to scorn; to play*
8055 sâmach (1), to *be, make gleesome*
8056 sâmêach (1), *blithe or gleeful*
8057 simchâh (2), *blithesomeness or glee*
8342 sâsôwn (1), *cheerfulness; welcome*
8643 tᵉrûw'âh (1), *battle-cry; clangor*
2745 kauchēma (4), *boast; brag*
2746 kauchēsis (4), *boasting; bragging*
5463 chairō (5), to be *cheerful*

REKEM
7552 Reqem (5), *versi-color*

RELEASE
2010 hănâchâh (1), *quiet*
8058 shâmaṭ (2), to *let alone, desist, remit*
8059 shᵉmiṭṭâh (5), *remission of debt*
630 apŏluō (13), to *relieve, release*

RELEASED
630 apŏluō (4), to *relieve, release; to divorce*

RELIED
8172 shâ'an (3), to *support, rely on*

RELIEF
1248 diakŏnia (1), *attendance, aid, service*

RELIEVE
833 'âshar (1), to *go forward; guide; prosper*
2388 châzaq (1), to *bind, restrain, conquer*
7725 shûwb (3), to *turn back; to return*
1884 ĕparkĕō (2), to *help*

RELIEVED
1884 ĕparkĕō (1), to *help*

RELIEVETH
5749 'ûwd (1), to *protest, testify; to restore*

RELIGION
2356 thrēskĕia (3), *observance, religion*
2454 Iŏudaismŏs (2), *Jewish faith*

RELIGIOUS
2357 thrēskŏs (1), *ceremonious, pious*
4576 sĕbŏmai (1), to *revere, i.e. adore*

RELY
8172 shâ'an (1), to *support, rely on*

REMAIN
1481 gûwr (1), to *sojourn, live as an alien*
1961 hâyâh (1), to *exist, i.e. be or become*
3241 Yânîym (1), *asleep*
3427 yâshab (11), to *dwell, to remain*
3498 yâthar (13), to *remain or be left*
3885 lûwn (5), to *be obstinate with*
5117 nûwach (1), to *rest; to settle down*
5975 'âmad (3), to *stand*
6965 qûwm (1), to *rise*
7604 shâ'ar (15), to *leave, remain*
7611 shᵉ'êrîyth (1), *remainder or residual*
7931 shâkan (3), to *reside*
8245 shâqad (1), to *be alert, i.e. sleepless*
8300 sârîyd (8), *survivor; remainder*
3062 Iôipŏi (1), *remaining ones*
3306 mĕnō (8), to *remain*
4035 pĕrilĕipō (2), to *survive, be left, remain*
4052 pĕrissĕuō (1), to *superabound*

REMAINDER
3498 yâthar (4), to *remain or be left*
7611 shᵉ'êrîyth (2), *remainder or residual*

REMAINED
1961 hâyâh (1), to *exist, i.e. be or become*

RELEASE
3427 yâshab (10), to *dwell, to remain*
3462 yâshên (1), to *sleep; to grow old, stale*
3498 yâthar (5), to *remain or be left*
5975 'âmad (4), to *stand*
7604 shâ'ar (23), to *leave, remain*
8277 sârad (1), to *escape or survive*
8300 sârîyd (1), *survivor; remainder*
1265 diamĕnō (1), to *stay constantly*
3306 mĕnō (3), to *remain*
4052 pĕrissĕuō (3), to *superabound*

REMAINEST
3427 yâshab (1), to *dwell, to remain; to settle*
1265 diamĕnō (1), to *stay constantly*

REMAINETH
3117 yôwm (1), *day; time period*
3427 yâshab (1), to *dwell, to remain; to settle*
3498 yâthar (4), to *remain or be left*
3885 lûwn (2), to *be obstinate with*
5736 'âdaph (4), to *be redundant*
5975 'âmad (1), to *stand*
7604 shâ'ar (8), to *leave, remain*
7931 shâkan (1), to *reside*
8300 sârîyd (3), *survivor; remainder*
620 apŏlĕipō (3), to *leave behind; to forsake*
3306 mĕnō (5), to *stay, remain*
3588+3063 hŏ (1), "the," i.e. the definite article

REMAINING
3320 yâtsab (1), to *station, offer, continue*
3498 yâthar (1), to *remain or be left*
7931 shâkan (1), to *reside*
8300 sârîyd (9), *survivor; remainder*
3306 mĕnō (1), to *remain*

REMALIAH
7425 Rᵉmalyâhûw (11), *Jehovah has bedecked*

REMALIAH'S
7425 Rᵉmalyâhûw (2), *Jehovah has bedecked*

REMEDY
4832 marpê' (3), *cure; deliverance; placidity*

REMEMBER
2142 zâkar (120), to *remember; to mention*
6485 pâqad (1), to *visit, care for, count*
3403 mimnēskō (1), to *remind or to recall*
3415 mnaŏmai (9), to *bear in mind*
3421 mnēmŏnĕuō (16), to *exercise memory*
5279 hupŏmimnēskō (1), to *suggest to memory*

REMEMBERED
2142 zâkar (48), to
remember; to mention
2143 zêker (1),
commemoration
3415 mnaŏmai (6), to
recollect
3421 mnĕmŏnĕuō (1), to
recall
5279 hupŏmimnĕskō (1),
to remind oneself

REMEMBEREST
2142 zâkar (1), to
remember; to mention
3415 mnaŏmai (1), to
recollect

REMEMBERETH
2142 zâkar (3), to
remember; to mention
363 anamimnĕskō (1), to
remind; to recollect
3421 mnĕmŏnĕuō (1), to
recall

REMEMBERING
2142 zâkar (1), to
remember; to mention
3421 mnĕmŏnĕuō (1), to
recall

REMEMBRANCE
2142 zâkar (13), to
remember; to mention
2143 zêker (11),
recollection
2146 zikrôwn (5),
commemoration
6485 pâqad (1), to visit,
care for, count
363 anamimnĕskō (3), to
remind; to recollect
364 anamnēsis (5),
recollection
3415 mnaŏmai (3), to
recollect
3417 mnĕia (3),
recollection; recital
3418 mnēma (1),
sepulchral monument
5179 tupŏs (2), shape,
resemblance; "type"
5279 hupŏmimnĕskō (2),
to remind oneself
5280 hupŏmnēsis (3),
reminding
5294 hupŏtithēmi (1), to
hazard; to suggest

REMEMBRANCES
2146 zikrôwn (1),
commemoration

REMETH
7432 Remeth (1), height

REMISSION
859 aphĕsis (9), pardon,
freedom
3929 parĕsis (1),
toleration, passing over

REMIT
863 aphiĕmi (1), to leave;
to pardon, forgive

REMITTED
863 aphiĕmi (1), to leave;
to pardon, forgive

REMMON
7417 Rimmôwn (1),
pomegranate

REMMON-METHOAR
7417 Rimmôwn (1),
pomegranate

REMNANT
310 'achar (1), after
319 'achărîyth (1), future;
posterity
3498 yâthar (4), to
remain or be left
3499 yether (14),
remainder; small rope
5629 çerach (1),
redundancy
6413 pᵉlêyţâh (1),
escaped portion
7604 shâ'ar (4), to leave,
remain
7605 shᵉ'âr (11),
remainder
7611 shᵉ'êrîyth (44),
remainder or residual
8293 shêrûwth (1),
freedom
8300 sârîyd (2), survivor;
remainder
2640 katalĕimma (1),
few, remnant
3005 lĕimma (1),
remainder, remnant
3062 lŏipŏi (4),
remaining ones

REMOVE
1540 gâlâh (2), to
denude; uncover
1556 gâlal (1), to roll; to
commit
4185 mûwsh (4), to
withdraw
5110 nûwd (4), to waver;
to wander, flee
5253 nâçag (4), to retreat
5265 nâça' (1), start
5437 çâbab (2), to
surround
5472 çûwg (1), to go
back, to retreat
5493 çûwr (15), to turn off
7368 râchaq (5), to
recede; remove
7493 râ'ash (1), to
undulate, quake
2795 kinĕō (1), to stir,
move, remove
3179 mĕthistēmi (1), to
move
3327 mĕtabainō (2), to
depart, move from
3911 paraphĕrō (1), to
carry off; to avert

REMOVED
167 'âhal (1), to pitch a
tent
1540 gâlâh (3), to
denude; uncover
1556 gâlal (1), to roll; to
commit
2186 zânach (1), to
reject, forsake, fail
2189 za'ăvâh (6),
agitation,
maltreatment
3014 yâgâh (1), to push
away, be removed
3670 kânaph (1), to
withdraw
4131 môwţ (5), to slip,
shake, fall

4171 mûwr (1), to alter;
to barter, to dispose of
4185 mûwsh (2), to
withdraw
5074 nâdad (1), to rove,
flee; to drive away
5079 niddâh (2), time of
menstrual impurity
5110 nûwd (1), to waver;
to wander, flee
5128 nûwa' (1), to waver
5206 nîydâh (1), removal
5265 nâça' (26), start
5437 çâbab (1), to
surround
5493 çûwr (21), to turn off
5674 'âbar (1), to cross
over; to transition
6275 'âthaq (4), to remove
7368 râchaq (4), to recede
142 airō (2), to lift, to
take up
3179 mĕthistēmi (1), to
move
3346 mĕtatithēmi (1), to
transport; to exchange
3351 mĕtŏikizō (1), to
transfer as a settler

REMOVETH
5253 nâçag (1), to retreat
5265 nâça' (1), start
5493 çûwr (1), to turn off
5709 'ădâ' (Ch.) (1), to
pass on or continue
6275 'âthaq (1), to remove

REMOVING
1473 gôwlâh (2), exile;
captive
5493 çûwr (2), to turn off
3331 mĕtathĕsis (1),
transferral to heaven

REMPHAN
4481 Rhĕmphan (1),
Kijun (a pagan god)

REND
1234 bâqa' (3), to cleave,
break, tear open
6533 pâram (2), to tear,
be torn
7167 qâra' (11), to rend
4486 rhēgnumi (1), to
tear to pieces
4977 schizō (1), to split
or sever

RENDER
5415 nᵉthan (Ch.) (1), to
give
7725 shûwb (16), to turn
back; to return
7999 shâlam (7), to be
safe; be, make complete
467 antapŏdidōmi (1), to
requite good or evil
591 apŏdidōmi (8), to
give away

RENDERED
7725 shûwb (4), to turn
back; to return

RENDEREST
7999 shâlam (1), to be
safe; be, make complete

RENDERETH
7999 shâlam (1), to be
safe; be, make complete

RENDERING
591 apŏdidōmi (1), to
give away

RENDING
6561 pâraq (1), to break
off or crunch; to deliver

RENEW
2318 châdash (3), to be
new, renew; to rebuild
2498 châlaph (2), to
spring up; to change
340 anakainizō (1), to
restore, bring back

RENEWED
2318 châdash (2), to be
new, renew; to rebuild
2498 châlaph (1), to
spring up; to change
341 anakainŏō (1), to
renovate, renew
365 ananĕŏō (1), to
renovate, i.e. reform

RENEWEST
2318 châdash (2), to be
new, renew; to rebuild

RENEWING
342 anakainōsis (2),
renovation, renewal

RENOUNCED
550 apĕipŏmĕn (1), to
disown

RENOWN
8034 shêm (7), name,
appellation

RENOWNED
1984 hâlal (1), to boast
7121 qârâ' (3), to call out

RENT
1234 bâqa' (5), to cleave,
break, tear open
2963 ţâraph (1), to pluck
off or pull to pieces
5364 niqpâh (1), rope
6533 pâram (1), to tear,
be torn
6561 pâraq (1), to break
off or crunch; to deliver
7167 qâra' (43), to rend
8156 shâça' (2), to split
or tear; to upbraid
1284 diarrhēssō (3), to
tear asunder
4048 pĕrirrhēgnumi (1),
to tear all around
4682 sparassō (1), to
convulse with epilepsy
4977 schizō (5), to split
or sever
4978 schisma (2),
divisive dissension

RENTEST
7167 qâra' (1), to rend

REPAID
7999 shâlam (1), to be
safe; to reciprocate

REPAIR
918 bâdaq (1), to mend a
breach
2318 châdash (3), to be
new, renew; to rebuild
2388 châzaq (8), to
fasten upon; to seize
2393 chezqâh (1),
prevailing power
5975 'âmad (1), to stand

REPAIRED
1129 bânâh (2), to *build;*
to *establish*
2388 châzaq (39), to
fasten upon; to *seize*
2421 châyâh (1), to *live;*
to *revive*
5462 çâgar (1), to *shut*
up; to *surrender*
7495 râphâ' (1), to *cure,*
heal

REPAIRER
1443 gâdar (1), to *build a*
stone wall

REPAIRING
3247 yᵉçôwd (1),
foundation

REPAY
7999 shâlam (5), to *be*
complete; to *reciprocate*
457 anŏixis (1), act of
opening
591 apŏdidōmi (1), to
give away
661 apŏtinō (1), to *pay* in
full, *make restitution*

REPAYETH
7999 shâlam (1), to *be*
complete; to *reciprocate*

REPEATETH
8138 shânâh (1), to *fold,*
i.e. *duplicate*

REPENT
5162 nâcham (19), to *be*
sorry; to *pity, rue*
7725 shûwb (3), to *turn*
back; to *return*
3338 mĕtamĕllŏmai (2),
to *regret*
3340 mĕtanŏĕō (21), to
reconsider

REPENTANCE
5164 nôcham (1),
ruefulness
278 amĕtamĕlētŏs (1),
irrevocable
3341 mĕtanŏia (24),
reversal

REPENTED
5162 nâcham (17), to *be*
sorry; to *pity, rue*
278 amĕtamĕlētŏs (1),
irrevocable
3338 mĕtamĕllŏmai (3),
to *regret*
3340 mĕtanŏĕō (11), to
reconsider

REPENTEST
5162 nâcham (1), to *be*
sorry; to *pity, rue*

REPENTETH
5162 nâcham (3), to *be*
sorry; to *pity, rue*
3340 mĕtanŏĕō (2), to
reconsider

REPENTING
5162 nâcham (1), to *be*
sorry; to *pity, rue*

REPENTINGS
5150 nichûwm (1),
consoled; solace

REPETITIONS
945 battŏlŏgĕō (1), to
prate tediously, *babble*

REPHAEL
7501 Rᵉphâ'êl (1), *God*
has cured

REPHAH
7506 Rephach (1),
support

REPHAIAH
7509 Rᵉphâyâh (5),
Jehovah has cured

REPHAIM
7497 râphâ' (6), *giant*

REPHAIMS
7497 râphâ' (2), *giant*

REPHIDIM
7508 Rᵉphîydîym (5),
balusters

REPLENISH
4390 mâlê' (2), to *fill; be*
full

REPLENISHED
4390 mâlê' (5), to *fill; be*
full

REPLIEST
470 antapŏkrinŏmai (1),
to *contradict* or *dispute*

REPORT
1681 dibbâh (3), *slander,*
bad report
1697 dâbâr (2), *word;*
matter; thing
5046 nâgad (1), to
announce
8034 shêm (1), *name,*
appellation
8052 shᵉmûw'âh (4),
announcement
8088 shêma' (5),
something heard
189 akŏē (2), *hearing;*
thing heard
518 apaggĕllō (1), to
announce, proclaim
1426 dusphēmia (1),
defamation, slander
2162 ĕuphēmia (1), good
repute
2163 ĕuphēmŏs (1),
reputable
3140 marturĕō (6), to
testify; to *commend*
3141 marturia (1),
evidence given

REPORTED
559 'âmar (2), to *say*
7725 shûwb (1), to *turn*
back; to *return*
8085 shâma' (2), to *hear*
191 akŏuō (1), to *hear*
312 anaggĕllō (1), to
announce, report
518 apaggĕllō (1), to
announce, proclaim
987 blasphēmĕō (1), to
speak impiously
1310 diaphēmizō (1), to
spread news
3140 marturĕō (2), to
testify; to *commend*

REPROACH
2617 cheçed (1),
kindness, favor
2659 châphêr (1), to
shame, reproach
2778 châraph (10), to
spend the *winter*

2781 cherpâh (65),
contumely, disgrace
3637 kâlam (1), to *taunt*
or *insult*
3639 kᵉlimmâh (1),
disgrace, scorn
7036 qâlôwn (1), *disgrace*
819 atimia (1), *disgrace*
3679 ŏnĕidizō (2), to *rail*
at, chide, taunt
3680 ŏnĕidismŏs (3),
with insult
3681 ŏnĕidŏs (1),
notoriety, i.e. a *taunt*

REPROACHED
2778 châraph (12), to
spend the *winter*
3637 kâlam (1), to *taunt*
or *insult*
3679 ŏnĕidizō (2), to *rail*
at, chide, taunt

REPROACHES
1421 giddûwph (1),
vilification, scorn
2781 cherpâh (1),
contumely, disgrace
3679 ŏnĕidizō (1), to *rail*
at, chide, taunt
3680 ŏnĕidismŏs (1),
with insult
5196 hubris (1), *insult*

REPROACHEST
5195 hubrizō (1), to
exercise violence, abuse

REPROACHETH
1442 gâdaph (1), to
revile, blaspheme
2778 châraph (5), to
spend the *winter*
2781 cherpâh (1),
contumely, disgrace

REPROACHFULLY
2781 cherpâh (1),
contumely, disgrace
5484+3059 charin (1), *on*
account of, *because* of

REPROBATE
3988 mâ'aç (1), to *spurn;*
to *disappear*
96 adŏkimŏs (3), *failing*
the test, worthless

REPROBATES
96 adŏkimŏs (3), *failing*
the test, worthless

REPROOF
1606 gᵉ'ârâh (2), *chiding,*
rebuke
8433 tôwkêchâh (12),
correction, refutation
1650 ĕlĕgchŏs (1), *proof,*
conviction

REPROOFS
8433 tôwkêchâh (2),
correction, refutation

REPROVE
3198 yâkach (16), to *be*
correct; to *argue*
1651 ĕlĕgchō (3), to
confute, admonish

REPROVED
1605 gâ'ar (1), to *chide,*
reprimand
3198 yâkach (4), to *be*
correct; to *argue*

8433 tôwkêchâh (2),
correction, refutation
1651 ĕlĕgchō (3), to
confute, admonish

REPROVER
3198 yâkach (2), to *be*
correct; to *argue*

REPROVETH
3198 yâkach (3), to *be*
correct; to *argue*
3256 yâçar (1), to
chastise; to *instruct*

REPUTATION
3368 yâqâr (1), *valuable*
1380 dŏkĕō (1), to *think,*
regard, seem good
1784 ĕntimŏs (1), *valued,*
considered precious
2758 kĕnŏō (1), to *make*
empty
5093 timiŏs (1), *costly;*
honored, esteemed

REPUTED
2804 chăshab (Ch.) (2), to
regard

REQUEST
782 'ăresheth (1),
longing for
1245 bâqash (3), to
search; to *strive after*
1246 baqqâshâh (8),
petition, request
1697 dâbâr (2), *word;*
matter; thing
7596 shᵉ'êlâh (3), *petition*
1162 dĕēsis (1), *petition,*
request
1189 dĕŏmai (1), to *beg,*
petition, ask

REQUESTED
1156 bᵉ'â' (Ch.) (1), to
seek or *ask*
1245 bâqash (1), to
search; to *strive after*
7592 shâ'al (3), to *ask*

REQUESTS
155 aitēma (1), *thing*
asked, request

REQUIRE
977 bâchar (1), *select,*
chose, prefer
1245 bâqash (10), to
search; to *strive after*
1875 dârash (11), to
pursue or *search*
3117 yôwm (1), *day; time*
period
7592 shâ'al (3), to *ask*
7593 shᵉ'êl (Ch.) (1), to
ask
154 aitĕō (1), to *ask* for
1096 ginŏmai (1), to *be,*
become

REQUIRED
1245 bâqash (3), to
search; to *strive after*
1875 dârash (2), to
pursue or *search*
1961 hâyâh (1), to *exist,*
i.e. *be* or *become*
3117 yôwm (3), *day; time*
period
7592 shâ'al (4), to *ask*
155 aitēma (1), *thing*
asked, request

373 anapauō (1), to
  repose; to refresh

RESTING
4496 m°nûwchâh (2),
  peacefully; consolation
5118 nûwach (1), *quiet*
7258 rebets (1), place of
  repose

RESTINGPLACE
7258 rebets (1), place of
  repose

RESTITUTION
7999 shâlam (4), to *make
  complete; to reciprocate*
8545 t°mûwrâh (1),
  barter, compensation
605 apŏkatastasis (1),
  reconstitution

RESTORE
5927 'âlâh (1), to *ascend,
  be high, mount*
7725 shûwb (27), to
  return or restore
7999 shâlam (8), to *make
  complete; to reciprocate*
591 apŏdidōmi (1), to
  give away
600 apŏkathistēmi (2), to
  reconstitute
2675 katartizō (1), to
  repair; to prepare

RESTORED
2421 châyâh (4), to *live;
  to revive*
5414 nâthan (1), to *give*
7725 shûwb (16), to
  return or restore
8421 tûwb (Ch.) (1), to
  come back with answer
600 apŏkathistēmi (5), to
  reconstitute

RESTORER
7725 shûwb (2), to *return
  or restore*

RESTORETH
7725 shûwb (1), to *return
  or restore*
600 apŏkathistēmi (1), to
  reconstitute

RESTRAIN
1639 gâra' (1), to *shave,
  remove, lessen*
2296 châgar (1), to *gird
  on a belt; put on armor*

RESTRAINED
662 'âphaq (1), to *abstain*
1219 bâtsar (1), to be
  inaccessible
3543 kâhâh (1), to *grow
  dull, fade; to be faint*
3607 kâlâ' (1), to *hold
  back or in; to prohibit*
4513 mâna' (1), to *deny,
  refuse*
6113 'âtsar (1), to *hold
  back; to maintain, rule*
2664 katapauō (1), to
  cause to desist

RESTRAINEST
1639 gâra' (1), to *remove,
  lessen, or withhold*

RESTRAINT
4622 ma'tsôwr (1),
  hindrance

RESURRECTION
386 anastasis (39),
  resurrection from death
1454 ĕgĕrsis (1),
  resurgence from death
1815 ĕxanastasis (1),
  rising from death

RETAIN
2388 châzaq (1), to
  fasten upon; to seize;
3607 kâlâ' (1), to *hold
  back or in; to prohibit*
6113 'âtsar (1), to *hold
  back; to maintain, rule*
8551 tâmak (2), to
  obtain, keep fast
2192 ĕchō (1), to *have;
  hold; keep*
2902 kratĕō (1), to *seize*

RETAINED
2388 châzaq (2), to
  fasten upon; to seize
6113 'âtsar (2), to *hold
  back; to maintain, rule*
2722 katĕchō (1), to *hold
  down fast*
2902 kratĕō (1), to *seize*

RETAINETH
2388 châzaq (1), to
  fasten upon; to seize
8551 tâmak (2), to
  obtain, keep fast

RETIRE
5756 'ûwz (1), to
  strengthen; to save
7725 shûwb (1), to *return
  or restore*

RETIRED
2015 hâphak (1), to
  return, pervert
6327 pûwts (1), to *dash
  in pieces; to disperse*

RETURN
3427 yâshab (1), to *dwell,
  to remain; to settle*
6437 pânâh (1), to *turn,
  to face*
7725 shûwb (242), to *turn
  back; to return*
8666 t°shûwbâh (3),
  recurrence; reply
344 anakamptō (1), to
  turn back, come back
360 analuō (1), to *depart*
390 anastrĕphō (1), to
  remain; to return
844 autŏmatŏs (1),
  spontaneous, by itself
1994 ĕpistrĕphō (4), to
  revert, turn back to
5290 hupŏstrĕphō (5), to
  turn under, to return

RETURNED
5437 çâbab (2), to
  surround
7725 shûwb (151), to *turn
  back; to return*
8421 tûwb (Ch.) (2), to
  reply
344 anakamptō (1), to
  turn back, come back
390 anastrĕphō (1), to
  remain, to return
1877 ĕpanagō (1), to *put
  out to sea; to return*
1880 ĕpanĕrchŏmai (1),
  return home

1994 ĕpistrĕphō (2), to
  revert, turn back to
5290 hupŏstrĕphō (24), to
  turn under, to return

RETURNETH
7725 shûwb (6), to *turn
  back; to return*
8138 shânâh (1), to *fold,
  to transmute*

RETURNING
7729 shûwbâh (1),
  return, i.e. repentance
5290 hupŏstrĕphō (3), to
  turn under, to return

REU
7466 R°'ûw (5), *friend*

REUBEN
7205 R°'ûwbên (72), *see
  ye a son*
7206 R°'ûwbênîy (1),
  Rebenite
4502 Rhŏubēn (1), *see ye
  a son*

REUBENITE
7206 R°'ûwbênîy (1),
  Rebenite

REUBENITES
7206 R°'ûwbênîy (16),
  Rebenite

REUEL
7467 R°'ûw'êl (10), *friend
  of God*

REUMAH
7208 R°'ûwmâh (1),
  raised

REVEAL
1540 gâlâh (2), to
  denude; to reveal
1541 g°lâh (Ch.) (1), to
  reveal mysteries
601 apŏkaluptō (4),
  disclose, reveal

REVEALED
1540 gâlâh (11), to
  denude; to reveal
1541 g°lâh (Ch.) (2), to
  reveal mysteries
601 apŏkaluptō (22),
  disclose, reveal
602 apŏkalupsis (2),
  disclosure, revelation
5537 chrēmatizō (1), to
  utter an oracle

REVEALER
1541 g°lâh (Ch.) (1), to
  reveal mysteries

REVEALETH
1540 gâlâh (3), to
  denude; to reveal
1541 g°lâh (Ch.) (3), to
  reveal mysteries

REVELATION
602 apŏkalupsis (10),
  disclosure, revelation

REVELATIONS
602 apŏkalupsis (2),
  disclosure, revelation

REVELLINGS
2970 kōmŏs (2),
  carousal, reveling, orgy

REVENGE
5358 nâqam (1), to
  avenge or punish

5360 n°qâmâh (2),
  avengement
1556 ĕkdikĕō (1), to
  vindicate; retaliate
1557 ĕkdikēsis (1),
  vindication; retaliation

REVENGED
5358 nâqam (1), to
  avenge or punish

REVENGER
1350 gâ'al (6), to *redeem;
  to be the next of kin*
1558 ĕkdikŏs (1),
  punisher, avenger

REVENGERS
1350 gâ'al (1), to *redeem;
  to be the next of kin*

REVENGES
6546 par'âh (1),
  leadership

REVENGETH
5358 nâqam (2), to
  avenge or punish

REVENGING
5360 n°qâmâh (1),
  avengement

REVENUE
674 'app°thôm (Ch.) (1),
  revenue
8393 t°bûw'âh (2),
  income, i.e. produce

REVENUES
8393 t°bûw'âh (3),
  income, i.e. produce

REVERENCE
3372 yârê' (2), to *fear; to
  revere*
7812 shâchâh (5), to
  prostrate in homage
127 aidōs (1), *modesty;
  awe*
1788 ĕntrĕpō (4), to
  respect; to confound
5399 phŏbĕō (1), to be in
  awe of, i.e. revere

REVERENCED
7812 shâchâh (1), to
  prostrate in homage

REVEREND
3372 yârê' (1), to *fear; to
  revere*

REVERSE
7725 shûwb (3), to *turn
  back; to return*

REVILE
7043 qâlal (1), to be *easy,
  trifling, vile*
3679 ŏnĕidizō (1), to *rail
  at, chide, taunt*

REVILED
486 antilŏidŏrĕō (1), to
  rail in reply, retaliate
937 basilikŏs (1),
  befitting the sovereign
3058 lŏidŏrĕō (2), *vilify,
  insult*
3679 ŏnĕidizō (1), to *rail
  at, chide, taunt*

REVILERS
3060 lŏidŏrŏs (1), verbal
  abuser

REVILEST
3058 lŏidŏrĕō (1), *vilify,
  insult*

REVILINGS
1421 giddûwph (2), *vilification, scorn*

REVIVE
2421 châyâh (8), *to live; to revive*

REVIVED
2421 châyâh (4), *to live; to revive*
326 anazaō (2), *to recover life, live again*

REVIVING
4241 michyâh (2), *preservation of life*

REVOLT
5627 çârâh (2), *apostasy; crime; remission*
6586 pâsha' (1), *to break away from authority*

REVOLTED
5498 çâchab (1), *to trail along*
5627 çârâh (1), *apostasy; crime; remission*
6586 pâsha' (5), *to break away from authority*

REVOLTERS
5637 çârar (2), *to be refractory, stubborn*
7846 sêṭ (1), *departure*

REVOLTING
5637 çârar (1), *to be refractory, stubborn*

REWARD
319 'achărîyth (2), *future; posterity*
868 'ethnan (3), *gift price of harlotry*
1309 bᵉsôwrâh (1), *glad tidings, good news*
1576 gᵉmûwl (3), *reward, recompense*
1578 gᵉmûwlâh (1), *reward, recompense*
1580 gâmal (1), *to benefit or requite; to wean*
4864 mas'êth (1), *tribute; reproach*
4909 maskôreth (1), *wages; reward*
4991 mattâth (1), *present*
6118 'êqeb (3), *unto the end; for ever*
6468 pᵉ'ullâh (1), *work, deed*
6529 pᵉrîy (1), *fruit*
7725 shûwb (2), *to turn back; to return*
7809 shâchad (1), *to bribe; gift*
7810 shachad (7), *to bribe; gift*
7938 seker (1), *wages, reward*
7939 sâkâr (5), *payment, salary; compensation*
7966 shillûwm (1), *requital; retribution; fee*
7999 shâlam (6), *to make complete; to reciprocate*
8011 shillumâh (1), *retribution*
469 antapŏdŏsis (1), *requital, reward*
514 axiōs (1), *deserving, comparable or suitable*

591 apŏdidōmi (6), *to give away*
2603 katabrabĕuō (1), *to award the price*
3405 misthapŏdŏsia (3), *requital, good or bad*
3408 misthŏs (24), *pay*

REWARDED
1580 gâmal (7), *to benefit or requite; to wean*
7760 sûwm (1), *to place*
7939 sâkâr (2), *payment, salary; compensation*
7999 shâlam (3), *to make complete; to reciprocate*
591 apŏdidōmi (1), *to give away*

REWARDER
3406 misthapŏdŏtēs (1), *rewarder*

REWARDETH
7725 shûwb (1), *to turn back; to return*
7936 sâkar (2), *to hire*
7999 shâlam (3), *to make complete; to reciprocate*

REWARDS
866 'êthnâh (1), *gift price of harlotry*
5023 nᵉbizbâh (Ch.) (2), *largess, gift*
8021 shalmôn (1), *bribe, gift*

REZEPH
7530 Retseph (2), *hot stone for baking*

REZIA
7525 Ritsyâ' (1), *delight*

REZIN
7526 Rᵉtsîyn (10), *delight*

REZON
7331 Rᵉzôwn (1), *prince*

RHEGIUM
4484 Rhēgiŏn (1), *Rhegium*

RHESA
4488 Rhēsa (1), (poss.) *Jehovah has cured*

RHODA
4498 Rhŏdē (1), *rose*

RHODES
4499 Rhŏdŏs (1), *rose*

RIB
6763 tsêlâ' (1), *side*

RIBAI
7380 Rîybay (2), *contentious*

RIBBAND
6616 pâthîyl (1), *twine, cord*

RIBLAH
7247 Riblâh (11), *fertile*

RIBS
6763 tsêlâ' (2), *side*

RICH
1952 hôwn (1), *wealth*
3513 kâbad (1), *to be rich, glorious*
5381 nâsag (1), *to reach*
6223 'âshîyr (23), *rich; rich person*
6238 'âshar (13), *to grow, make rich*

7771 shôwa' (1), *noble, i.e. liberal; opulent*
4145 plŏusiŏs (28), *wealthy; abounding*
4147 plŏutĕō (11), *to be, become wealthy*
4148 plŏutizō (1), *to make wealthy*

RICHER
6238 'âshar (1), *to grow, make rich*

RICHES
1952 hôwn (9), *wealth*
1995 hâmôwn (1), *noise, tumult; many, crowd*
2428 chayil (11), *army; wealth; virtue; valor*
2633 chôçen (1), *wealth, stored riches*
3502 yithrâh (1), *wealth, abundance*
4301 maṭmôwn (1), *secret storehouse*
5233 nekeç (1), *treasure*
6239 'ôsher (37), *wealth*
7075 qinyân (1), *purchase, wealth*
7399 rᵉkûwsh (5), *property*
7769 shûwa' (1), *call*
4149 plŏutŏs (22), *abundant riches*
5536 chrēma (3), *wealth*

RICHLY
4146 plŏusiŏs (2), *copiously, abundantly*

RID
5337 nâtsal (3), *to deliver; to be snatched*
6475 pâtsâh (2), *to rend*
7673 shâbath (1), *to repose; to desist*

RIDDANCE
3615 kâlâh (1), *to cease, be finished, perish*
3617 kâlâh (1), *complete destruction*

RIDDEN
7392 râkab (1), *to ride*

RIDDLE
2420 chîydâh (9), *puzzle; conundrum; maxim*

RIDE
7392 râkab (20), *to ride*

RIDER
7392 râkab (7), *to ride*

RIDERS
7392 râkab (5), *to ride*

RIDETH
7392 râkab (7), *to ride*

RIDGES
8525 telem (1), *bank or terrace*

RIDING
7392 râkab (10), *to ride*

RIE
3698 kuççemeth (2), *spelt*

RIFLED
8155 shâçaç (1), *to plunder, ransack*

RIGHT
541 'âman (1), *to take the right hand road*

571 'emeth (3), *certainty, truth, trustworthiness*
1353 gᵉullâh (1), *blood relationship*
3225 yâmîyn (136), *right; south*
3227 yᵉmîynîy (1), *right*
3231 yâman (4), *to be right-handed*
3233 yᵉmânîy (31), *right*
3474 yâshar (2), *to be straight; to make right*
3476 yôsher (2), *right*
3477 yâshâr (52), *straight*
3559 kûwn (4), *to render sure, proper*
3651 kên (3), *just; right*
3787 kâshêr (1), *to be straight or right*
3788 kishrôwn (1), *success; advantage*
4334 mîyshôwr (1), *plain; justice*
4339 mêyshâr (3), *straightness; rectitude*
4941 mishpâṭ (19), *verdict; decree; justice*
5227 nôkach (2), *forward, in behalf of*
5228 nâkôach (2), *equitable, correct*
5229 nᵉkôchâh (2), *integrity; truth*
6227 'âshân (1), *smoke*
6437 pânâh (1), *to turn, to face*
6440 pânîym (1), *face; front*
6664 tsedeq (3), *right*
6666 tsᵉdâqâh (9), *rightness*
1188 dĕxiŏs (53), *right*
1342 dikaiŏs (5), *equitable, holy*
1849 ĕxŏusia (2), *authority, power, right*
2117 ĕuthus (3), *at once, immediately*
3723 ŏrthŏs (1), *rightly*
4993 sōphrŏnĕō (2), *to be in a right state of mind*

RIGHTEOUS
3477 yâshâr (8), *straight*
6662 tsaddîyq (166), *just*
6663 tsâdaq (8), *to be, make right*
6664 tsedeq (9), *right*
6666 tsᵉdâqâh (3), *rightness*
1341 dikaiŏkrisia (1), *proper judgment*
1342 dikaiŏs (39), *equitable, holy*
1343 dikaiŏsunē (1), *equity, justification*

RIGHTEOUSLY
4334 mîyshôwr (1), *plain; justice*
4339 mêyshâr (1), *straightness; rectitude*
6664 tsedeq (3), *right*
6666 tsᵉdâqâh (1), *rightness*
1346 dikaiŏs (2), *equitably*

RIGHTEOUSNESS
6663 tsâdaq (1), *to be, make right*

R

6664 tsedeq (78), *right*
6665 tsidqâh (Ch.) (1), *beneficence*
6666 tsᵉdâqâh (124), *rightness*
1343 dikaiŏsunē (91), *equity, justification*
1345 dikaiōma (4), *equitable deed; statute*
1346 dikaiŏs (1), *equitably*
2118 ĕuthutēs (1), *rectitude, uprightness*

RIGHTEOUSNESS'
6664 tsedeq (1), *right*
6666 tsᵉdâqâh (1), *rightness*
1343 dikaiŏsunē (2), *equity, justification*

RIGHTEOUSNESSES
6666 tsᵉdâqâh (3), *rightness*

RIGHTLY
3588 kîy (1), *for, that because*
3723 ŏrthōs (3), *rightly*

RIGOUR
6531 perek (5), *severity*

RIMMON
7417 Rimmôwn (14), *pomegranate*

RIMMON-PAREZ
7428 Rimmôn Perets (2), *pomegranate of* (the) *breach*

RING
2885 ṭabba'ath (9), *ring; signet ring for sealing*
1146 daktuliŏs (1), *finger-ring*
5554 chrusŏdaktuliŏs (1), *gold-ringed*

RINGLEADER
4414 prōtŏstatēs (1), *leader, ring leader*

RINGS
1354 gab (2), *mounded or rounded: top or rim*
1550 gâlîyl (2), *curtain ring*
2885 ṭabba'ath (39), *ring; signet ring for sealing*

RINGSTRAKED
6124 'âqôd (7), *striped, streaked* animals

RINNAH
7441 Rinnâh (1), *shout*

RINSED
7857 shâṭaph (3), *to inundate, cleanse*

RIOT
810 asōtia (2), *profligacy, debauchery*
5172 truphē (1), *luxury or debauchery*

RIOTING
2970 kōmŏs (1), *carousal, reveling, orgy*

RIOTOUS
2151 zâlal (2), *to be loose morally, worthless*
811 asōtōs (1), *with debauchery*

RIP
1234 bâqa' (1), *to cleave, break, tear open*

RIPE
1310 bâshal (2), *to boil up, cook; to ripen*
187 akmazō (1), *to be mature, be ripe*
3583 xērainō (1), *to shrivel, to mature*

RIPENING
1580 gâmal (1), *to benefit or require; to wean*

RIPHATH
7384 Rîyphath (2), *Riphath*

RIPPED
1234 bâqa' (3), *to cleave, break, tear open*

RISE
2224 zârach (1), *to rise; to be bright*
5927 'âlâh (6), *to ascend, be high, mount*
6965 qûwm (76), *to rise*
6966 qûwm (Ch.) (1), *to rise*
7925 shâkam (5), *to load up, i.e. to start early*
8618 tᵉqôwmêm (1), *opponent*
305 anabainō (1), *to go up, rise*
386 anastasis (1), *resurrection from death*
393 anatĕllō (2), *to cause to arise*
450 anistēmi (23), *to rise; to come back to life*
1453 ĕgĕirō (23), *to waken, i.e. rouse*
1881 ĕpanistamai (2), *to stand up on*

RISEN
1342 gâ'âh (1), *to rise; to grow tall; be majestic*
2224 zârach (2), *to rise; to be bright*
3318 yâtsâ' (1), *to go, bring out*
6965 qûwm (16), *to rise*
393 anatĕllō (1), *to cause to arise*
450 anistēmi (6), *to rise; to come back to life*
1453 ĕgĕirō (22), *to waken, i.e. rouse*
4891 sunĕgĕirō (2), *to raise up with*

RISEST
6965 qûwm (2), *to rise*

RISETH
2224 zârach (2), *to rise; to be bright*
5927 'âlâh (1), *to ascend, be high, mount*
6965 qûwm (9), *to rise*
7837 shachar (1), *dawn*
1453 ĕgĕirō (1), *to waken, i.e. rouse*

RISING
510 'alqûwm (1), *resistlessness*
2225 zerach (1), *rising* of light, *dawning*

4217 mizrâch (8), *place of sunrise; east*
5927 'âlâh (1), *to ascend, be high, mount*
6965 qûwm (1), *to rise*
7012 qîymâh (1), *arising*
7613 sᵉ'êth (7), *elevation; swelling*
7836 shâchar (1), *to search for*
7925 shâkam (14), *to load up, to start early*
305 anabainō (1), *to rise*
386 anastasis (1), *resurrection from death*
393 anatĕllō (1), *to cause to arise*
450 anistēmi (1), *to rise; to come back to life*

RISSAH
7446 Riççâh (2), *ruin*

RITES
2708 chuqqâh (1), *to delineate*

RITHMAH
7575 Rithmâh (2), *broom tree*

RIVER
180 'ûwbâl (3), *stream*
2975 yᵉ'ôr (35), Nile *River*; Tigris *River*
3105 yûwbal (1), *stream*
5103 nᵉhar (Ch.) (14), *river*; Euphrates *River*
5104 nâhâr (66), *stream*; Nile; Euphrates; Tigris
5158 nachal (46), *valley*
4215 pŏtamŏs (6), *current, brook*

RIVER'S
2975 yᵉ'ôr (3), Nile *River*; Tigris *River*
5104 nâhâr (1), *stream*; Nile; Euphrates; Tigris

RIVERS
650 'âphîyq (10), *valley; stream; mighty, strong*
2975 yᵉ'ôr (15), Nile *River*; Tigris *River*
5103 nᵉhar (Ch.) (9), *river*; Euphrates *River*
5104 nâhâr (22), *stream*; Nile; Euphrates; Tigris
5158 nachal (8), *valley*
6388 peleg (8), *small irrigation channel*
6390 pᵉlaggâh (1), *gully*
8585 tᵉ'âlâh (1), *irrigation channel*
4215 pŏtamŏs (3), *current, brook*

RIZPAH
7532 Ritspâh (4), *hot stone; pavement*

ROAD
6584 pâshaṭ (1), *to strip, i.e. unclothe, plunder*

ROAR
1993 hâmâh (6), *to be in great commotion*
5098 nâham (2), *to growl, groan*
6873 tsârach (1), *to whoop*
7481 râ'am (2), *to crash thunder; to irritate*

7580 shâ'ag (12), *to rumble or moan*

ROARED
1993 hâmâh (1), *to be in great commotion*
7580 shâ'ag (4), *to rumble or moan*

ROARETH
1993 hâmâh (1), *to be in great commotion*
7580 shâ'ag (1), *to rumble or moan*
3455 mukaŏmai (1), *to roar*

ROARING
1897 hâgâh (1), *to murmur, utter a sound*
5098 nâham (1), *to growl, groan*
5099 naham (2), *snarl, growl*
5100 nᵉhâmâh (1), *snarling, growling*
7580 shâ'ag (2), *to rumble or moan*
7581 shᵉ'âgâh (6), *rumbling or moan*
2278 ĕchĕŏ (1), *to reverberate, ring out*
5612 ŏruŏmai (1), *to roar*

ROARINGS
7581 shᵉ'âgâh (1), *rumbling or moan*

ROAST
1310 bâshal (1), *to boil up, cook; to ripen*
6740 tsâlâh (1), *to roast*
6748 tsâlîy (3), *roasted*

ROASTED
1310 bâshal (1), *to boil up, cook; to ripen*
6740 tsâlâh (1), *to roast*
7033 qâlâh (1), *to toast*

ROASTETH
740 'Ărî'êl (1), *Lion of God*
2760 chârak (1), *to catch*

ROB
962 bâzaz (3), *to plunder, take booty*
1497 gâzal (2), *to rob*
6906 qâba' (1), *to defraud, rob*
7921 shâkôl (1), *to miscarry*
8154 shâçâh (1), *to plunder*

ROBBED
962 bâzaz (4), *to plunder, take booty*
1497 gâzal (1), *to rob*
5100 nᵉhâmâh (1), *snarling, growling*
5749 'ûwd (1), *to encompass, restore*
6906 qâba' (2), *to defraud, rob*
7909 shakkuwl (2), *bereaved*
8154 shâçâh (1), *to plunder*
4813 sulaŏ (1), *to despoil, rob*

ROBBER
6530 pᵉrîyts (1), *violent*

6782 tsammîym (2), *noose, snare*
3027 lêⱼstēs (2), *brigand*

ROBBERS
962 bâzaz (1), *to plunder, take booty*
6530 pᵉrîyts (3), *violent*
7703 shâdad (2), *to ravage*
2417 hiĕrŏsulŏs (1), *temple-despoiler*
3027 lêⱼstēs (2), *brigand*

ROBBERY
1498 gâzêl (3), *robbery, stealing*
6503 Parbâr (1), *Parbar or Parvar*
7701 shôd (2), *violence, ravage, destruction*
725 harpagmŏs (1), *plunder*

ROBBETH
1497 gâzal (1), *to rob*

ROBE
145 'eder (1), *mantle; splendor*
155 'addereth (1), *large; splendid*
3301 Yiphdᵉyâh (1), *Jehovah will liberate*
4598 mᵉʻîyl (17), *outer garment or robe*
2066 ĕsthēs (1), *to clothe*
2440 himatiŏn (2), *to put on clothes*
4749 stŏlē (1), *long-fitting gown*
5511 chlamus (2), *military cloak*

ROBES
899 beged (4), *clothing; treachery or pillage*
4598 mᵉʻîyl (2), *outer garment or robe*
4749 stŏlē (5), *long-fitting gown*

ROBOAM
4497 Rhŏbŏam (2), *people has enlarged*

ROCK
2496 challâmîysh (1), *flint, flinty rock*
4581 mâʻôwz (1), *fortified place; defense*
5553 çela' (44), *craggy rock; fortress*
5558 çeleph (2), *distortion; viciousness*
6697 tsûwr (56), *rock*
4073 pĕtra (13), *mass of rock*

ROCKS
3710 kêph (2), *hollow rock*
5553 çela' (10), *craggy rock; fortress*
6697 tsûwr (7), *rock*
4073 pĕtra (3), *mass of rock*
5138+5117 trachus (1), *uneven, jagged, rocky*

ROD
2415 chôter (2), *twig; shoot of a plant*
4294 maṭṭeh (42), *tribe; rod, scepter; club*

4731 maqqêl (2), *shoot; stick; staff*
7626 shêbeṭ (34), *stick; clan, family*
4464 rhabdŏs (6), *stick, rod*

RODE
7392 râkab (15), *to ride*

RODS
4294 maṭṭeh (8), *tribe; rod, scepter; club*
4731 maqqêl (6), *shoot; stick; staff*
4463 rhabdizō (1), *to strike with a stick*

ROE
3280 ya'ălâh (1), *ibex*
6643 tsᵉbîy (6), *gazelle*

ROEBUCK
6643 tsᵉbîy (4), *gazelle*

ROEBUCKS
6643 tsᵉbîy (1), *gazelle*

ROES
6643 tsᵉbîy (1), *gazelle*
6646 tsᵉbîyâh (2), *gazelle*

ROGELIM
7274 Rôgᵉlîym (2), *fullers as tramping the cloth*

ROHGAH
7303 Rôwhăgâh (1), *outcry*

ROLL
1549 gîllâyôwn (1), *tablet for writing; mirror*
1556 gâlal (4), *to roll; to commit*
4039 mᵉgillâh (14), *roll, scroll*
4040 mᵉgillâh (Ch.) (7), *roll, scroll*
6428 pâlash (1), *to roll in dust*
617 apŏkuliō (1), *to roll away, roll back*

ROLLED
1556 gâlal (6), *to roll; to commit*
617 apŏkuliō (3), *to roll away, roll back*
1507 hĕilissō (1), *to roll, coil or wrap*
4351 prŏskuliō (2), *to roll towards*

ROLLER
2848 chittûwl (1), *bandage for a wound*

ROLLETH
1556 gâlal (1), *to roll*

ROLLING
1534 galgal (1), *wheel; something round*

ROLLS
5609 çᵉphar (Ch.) (1), *book*

ROMAMTI-EZER
7320 Rôwmamtîy 'Ezer (2), *I have raised up a help*

ROMAN
4514 Rhŏmaiŏs (5), *Roman; of Rome*

ROMANS
4514 Rhŏmaiŏs (7), *Roman; of Rome*

ROME
4516 Rhŏmē (15), *strength*

ROOF
1406 gâg (11), *roof; top*
2441 chêk (5), *area of mouth*
6982 qôwrâh (1), *rafter; roof*
4721 stĕgē (1), *roof*

ROOFS
1406 gâg (2), *roof; top*

ROOM
4725 mâqôwm (3), *general locality, place*
4800 merchâb (1), *open space; liberty*
7337 râchab (2), *to broaden*
8478 tachath (11), *bottom; underneath*
473 anti (1), *instead of, because of*
508 anŏgĕŏn (1), *dome or a balcony*
1240 diadŏchŏs (1), *successor in office*
4411 prŏtŏklisia (1), *pre-eminence at meals*
5117 tŏpŏs (5), *place*
5253 hupĕrŏⱼŏn (1), *upper room*
5362 philandrŏs (1), *affectionate as a wife to her husband*

ROOMS
7064 qên (1), *nest; nestlings; chamber*
8478 tachath (2), *bottom; underneath; in lieu of*
4411 prŏtŏklisia (4), *pre-eminence at meals*

ROOT
5428 nâthash (2), *to tear away, be uprooted*
8327 shârash (7), *to root, insert; to uproot*
8328 sheresh (17), *root*
1610 ĕkrizŏō (2), *to uproot*
4491 rhiza (15), *root*

ROOTED
5255 nâçach (1), *to tear away*
5423 nâthaq (1), *to tear off*
5428 nâthash (1), *to tear away, be uprooted*
6131 'âqar (1), *to pluck up roots; to hamstring*
8327 shârash (1), *to root, insert; to uproot*
1610 ĕkrizŏō (1), *to uproot*
4492 rhizŏō (2), *to root; to become stable*

ROOTS
5428 nâthash (1), *to tear away, be uprooted*
6132 'âqar (Ch.) (1), *to pluck up roots*
8328 sheresh (13), *root*

8330 shôresh (Ch.) (3), *root*
1610 ĕkrizŏō (1), *to uproot*
4491 rhiza (1), *root*

ROPE
5688 'ăbôth (1), *entwined things: a string, wreath*

ROPES
2256 chebel (3), *band*
5688 'ăbôth (2), *entwined things: a string, wreath*
4979 schŏiniŏn (1), *withe or tie or rope*

ROSE
2224 zârach (3), *to rise; to be bright*
2261 chăbatstseleth (2), *meadow-saffron*
5927 'âlâh (2), *to ascend, be high, mount*
6965 qûwm (71), *to rise*
7925 shâkam (29), *to load up, to start early*
305 anabainō (1), *to go up, rise*
450 anistēmi (18), *to rise; to come back to life*
1453 ĕgĕirō (3), *to waken, i.e. rouse*
1817 ĕxanistēmi (1), *to beget, raise up*
4911 sunĕphistēmi (1), *to resist or assault jointly*

ROSH
7220 Rô'sh (1), *head*

ROT
5307 nâphal (3), *to fall*
7537 râqab (2), *to decay by worm-eating*

ROTTEN
4418 mâlach (2), *rag or old garment*
5685 'âbash (1), *to dry up*
7538 râqâb (1), *decay by caries*
7539 riqqâbôwn (1), *decay by caries*

ROTTENNESS
4716 maq (1), *putridity, stench*
7538 râqâb (4), *decay by caries*

ROUGH
386 'êythân (1), *never-failing; eternal*
5569 çâmâr (1), *shaggy*
7186 qâsheh (1), *severe*
7406 rekeç (1), *ridgy*
8163 sâ'îyr (1), *shaggy; he-goat; goat idol*
8181 sê'âr (1), *tossed hair*
5138 trachus (1), *uneven, jagged, rocky, reefy*

ROUGHLY
5794 'az (1), *strong, vehement, harsh*
7186 qâsheh (5), *severe*

ROUND
1754 dûwr (1), *circle; ball; pile*
2636 chaçpaç (1), *to peel; to be scale-like*
3803 kâthar (2), *to enclose, besiege; to wait*

4524 mêçab (3), *divan couch; around*
5362 nâqaph (4), to *strike; to surround*
5437 çâbab (7), to *surround*
5439 çâbîyb (254), *circle; environs; around*
5469 çahar (1), *roundness*
5696 'âgôl (6), *circular*
5921 'al (2), *above, over*
7720 sahârôn (1), round *pendant or crescent*
2943 kuklôthĕn (10), *from the circle*
2944 kuklŏō (2), to *surround, encircle*
3840 pantôthĕn (1), *from, on all sides*
4015 pĕriastraptō (2), to *shine around*
4017 pĕriblĕpō (5), to *look all around*
4026 pĕriistēmi (1), to *stand around; to avoid*
4033 pĕrikuklŏō (1), to *blockade completely*
4034 pĕrilampō (2), to *shine all around*
4038 pĕrix (1), all *around*
4039 pĕriŏikĕō (1), to *be a neighbor*
4066 pĕrichōrŏs (9), *surrounding country*

ROUSE
6965 qûwm (1), to *rise*

ROW
2905 ṭûwr (14), *row, course* built into a *wall*
4635 ma'ăreketh (2), *pile* of loaves, *arrangement*
5073 nidbâk (Ch.) (1), *layer, row*

ROWED
2864 châthar (1), to *row*
1643 ĕlaunō (1), to *push*

ROWERS
7751 shûwṭ (1), to *travel, roam*

ROWING
1643 ĕlaunō (1), to *push*

ROWS
2905 ṭûwr (12), *row, course* built into a *wall*
2918 ṭîyrâh (1), *fortress; hamlet*
4634 ma'ărâkâh (1), *arrangement, row; pile*
5073 nidbâk (Ch.) (1), *layer, row*
8447 tôwr (1), *succession*

ROYAL
4410 mᵉlûwkâh (4), *realm, rulership*
4428 melek (2), *king*
4430 melek (Ch.) (1), *king*
4438 malkûwth (13), *rule; dominion*
4467 mamlâkâh (4), royal *dominion*
8237 shaphrûwr (1), *tapestry or canopy*
934 basilĕiŏs (1), *royal, kingly* in nature
937 basilikŏs (2), *befitting the sovereign*

RUBBING
5597 psōchō (1), to *rub out grain kernels*

RUBBISH
6083 'âphâr (2), *dust, earth, mud; clay,*

RUBIES
6443 pânîyn (6), (poss.) *round pearl*

RUDDER
4079 pēdaliŏn (1), *blade*

RUDDY
119 'âdam (1), to *red in the face*
132 'admônîy (3), *reddish, ruddy*

RUDE
2399 idiōtēs (1), not *initiated; untrained*

RUDIMENTS
4747 stŏichĕiŏn (2), *elementary* truths

RUE
4076 pēganŏn (1), *rue*

RUFUS
4504 Rhŏuphŏs (2), red

RUHAMAH
7355 râcham (1), to *be compassionate*

RUIN
4072 midcheh (1), *overthrow, downfall*
4288 mᵉchittâh (1), *ruin; consternation*
4383 mikshôwl (1), *obstacle; enticement*
4384 makshêlâh (1), *enticement*
4654 mappâlâh (2), *ruin*
4658 mappeleth (2), *down-fall; ruin; carcase*
6365 pîyd (1), *misfortune*
4485 rhēgma (1), *ruin*

RUINED
2040 hâraç (2), to *pull down; break, destroy*
3782 kâshal (1), to *totter, waver; to falter*

RUINOUS
4654 mappâlâh (1), *ruin*
5327 nâtsâh (2), to *be desolate, to lay waste*

RUINS
2034 hărîyçâh (1), *demolished, ruins*
4383 mikshôwl (1), *obstacle; enticement*
2679 kataskaptō (1), to *destroy, be ruined*

RULE
4427 mâlak (1), to *reign as king*
4475 memshâlâh (4), *rule; realm* or a *ruler*
4623 ma'tsâr (1), *self-control*
4910 mâshal (25), to *rule*
7287 râdâh (10), to *subjugate; to crumble*
7980 shâlaṭ (3), to *dominate, i.e. govern*
7981 shᵉlêṭ (Ch.) (1), to *dominate, i.e. govern*

7990 shallîyṭ (Ch.) (1), *premier, sovereign*
8323 sârar (3), to *have, exercise, get dominion*
746 archē (1), *first*
757 archō (1), to *rule, be first in rank*
1018 brabĕuō (1), to *govern; to prevail*
2233 hēgĕŏmai (3), to *lead, i.e. command*
2583 kanōn (4), *rule, standard*
4165 pŏimainō (4), to *tend as a shepherd*
4291 prŏistēmi (2), to *preside; to practice*

RULED
4474 mimshâl (1), *ruler; dominion, rule*
4910 mâshal (5), to *rule*
5401 nâshaq (1), to *kiss; to equip with weapons*
7287 râdâh (3), to *subjugate; to crumble*
7990 shallîyṭ (Ch.) (2), *premier, sovereign*
8199 shâphaṭ (1), to *judge*

RULER
834+5921 'âsher (1), *who, which, what, that*
4910 mâshal (13), to *rule*
5057 nâgîyd (19), *commander, official*
5387 nâsiy' (3), *leader; rising mist, fog*
6485 pâqad (2), to *visit, care for, count*
7101 qâtsîyn (2), *magistrate; leader*
7287 râdâh (1), to *subjugate; to crumble*
7860 shôṭêr (1), to *write; official who is a scribe*
7981 shᵉlêṭ (Ch.) (4), to *dominate, i.e. govern*
7989 shallîyṭ (1), *prince or warrior*
7990 shallîyṭ (Ch.) (2), *premier, sovereign*
8269 sar (10), *head person, ruler*
752 archisunagōgŏs (6), *director of the synagogue services*
755 architriklinŏs (1), *director of the entertainment*
758 archōn (9), *first*
2525 kathistēmi (6), to *designate, constitute*

RULER'S
4910 mâshal (1), to *rule*
758 archōn (1), *first*

RULERS
4043 mâgên (1), small *shield (buckler)*
4910 mâshal (4), to *rule*
5057 nâgîyd (1), *commander, official*
5387 nâsiy' (3), *leader; rising mist, fog*
5461 çâgân (16), *prefect*
6485 pâqad (1), to *visit, care for, count*
7101 qâtsîyn (2), *magistrate; leader*
7218 rô'sh (2), *head*

7336 râzan (1), *honorable*
7984 shiltôwn (Ch.) (2), *official*
8269 sar (21), *ruler*
752 archisunagōgŏs (2), *director of the synagogue services*
758 archōn (14), *first*
2232 hēgĕmōn (2), *chief*
2888 kŏsmŏkratōr (1), *world-ruler*
4178 pŏllakis (2), *many times, i.e. frequently*

RULEST
4910 mâshal (2), to *rule*

RULETH
4910 mâshal (7), to *rule*
7300 rûwd (1), to *ramble*
7980 shâlaṭ (4), to *dominate, i.e. govern*
4291 prŏistēmi (2), to *preside; to practice*

RULING
4910 mâshal (2), to *rule*
4291 prŏistēmi (1), to *preside; to practice*

RUMAH
7316 Rûwmâh (1), *height*

RUMBLING
1995 hâmôwn (1), *noise, tumult; many, crowd*

RUMOUR
8052 shᵉmûw'âh (8), *announcement*
3056 lŏgŏs (1), *word, matter, thing*

RUMOURS
189 akŏē (2), *hearing; thing heard*

RUMP
451 'alyâh (5), fat *tail*

RUN
935 bôw' (1), to *go, come*
1556 gâlal (1), to *roll; to commit*
1980 hâlak (3), to *walk; live a certain way*
2100 zûwb (1), to *flow freely, gush*
3212 yâlak (1), to *walk; to live; to carry*
3381 yârad (6), to *descend*
6293 pâga' (1), to *impinge*
6805 tsâ'ad (1), to *pace*
7323 rûwts (36), to *run*
7325 rûwr (1), to *emit a fluid*
7751 shûwṭ (6), to *travel, roam*
8264 shâqaq (2), to *seek*
4936 suntrĕchō (1), to *rush together*
5143 trĕchō (8), to *run or walk hastily; to strive*

RUNNEST
7323 rûwts (1), to *run*

RUNNETH
935 bôw' (1), to *go, come*
3381 yârad (2), to *descend*
7310 rᵉvâyâh (1), *satisfaction*
7323 rûwts (4), to *run*

1632 ĕkchĕŏ (1), to *pour forth; to bestow*
5143 trĕchō (2), to *run*

RUNNING
1980 hâlak (1), to *walk*
2100 zûwb (2), to *discharge; waste away*
2416 chay (7), *alive; raw*
4794 mᵉrûwtsâh (2), *race*
4944 mashshâq (1), rapid *traversing motion*
5140 nâzal (1), to *drip*
7323 rûwts (6), to *run*
1998 ĕpisuntrĕchō (1), to *hasten together upon*
4370 próstrĕchō (2), to *hasten by running*
5143 trĕchō (1), to *run*
5240 hupĕrĕkchunō (1), to *overflow*
5295 hupŏtrĕchō (1), to *run under*

RUSH
100 'agmôwn (2), *rush*
1573 gôme' (1), *papyrus*
7582 shâ'âh (1), to *moan*

RUSHED
6584 pâshaṭ (2), to *strip*
3729 hŏrmaō (1), to *dash*

RUSHES
1573 gôme' (1), *papyrus*

RUSHETH
7857 shâṭaph (1), to *gush*

RUSHING
7494 ra'ash (3), *uproar*
7582 shâ'âh (1), to *moan*
7588 shâ'ôwn (1), *uproar*
5342 phĕrō (1), to *bear*

RUST
1035 brōsis (2), *food; rust*
2447 iŏs (1), *corrosion*

RUTH
7327 Rûwth (12), *friend*
4503 Rhŏuth (1), *friend*

SABACHTHANI
4518 sabachthani (2), *thou hast left me*

SABAOTH
4519 sabaōth (2), *armies*

SABBATH
7673 shâbath (1), to *repose; to desist*
7676 shabbâth (73), day *of rest*
7677 shabbâthôwn (3), *special holiday*
4315 prŏsabbatŏn (1), *Sabbath-eve*
4521 sabbatŏn (59), day *of repose*

SABBATHS
4868 mishbâth (1), *cessation; destruction*
7676 shabbâth (34), day *of rest*

SABEANS
5433 çâbâ' (1), to *quaff*
5436 Çᵉbâ'îy (1), *Sebaite*
7614 Shᵉbâ' (1), *Sheba*
7615 Shᵉbâ'îy (1), *Shebaïte*

SABTA
5454 Çabtâ' (1), *Sabta or Sabtah*

SABTAH
5454 Çabtâ' (1), *Sabta or Sabtah*

SABTECHA
5455 Çabtᵉkâ' (1), *Sabteca*

SABTECHAH
5455 Çabtᵉkâ' (1), *Sabteca*

SACAR
7940 Sâkar (2), *recompense*

SACK
572 'amtêchath (5), *sack*
8242 saq (4), *bag*

SACK'S
572 'amtêchath (3), *sack*

SACKBUT
5443 çabbᵉkâ' (Ch.) (4), *lyre musical instrument*

SACKCLOTH
8242 saq (41), *coarse cloth or sacking; bag*
4526 sakkŏs (4), *sack-cloth*

SACKCLOTHES
8242 saq (1), *coarse cloth or sacking; bag*

SACKS
572 'amtêchath (6), *sack*
3672 Kinnᵉrôwth (1), (poss.) *harp*-shaped
8242 saq (2), *bag*

SACKS'
572 'amtêchath (1), *sack*

SACRIFICE
2076 zâbach (48), to *(sacrificially) slaughter*
2077 zebach (102), *animal flesh; sacrifice*
2282 chag (2), *solemn festival*
4503 minchâh (5), *tribute; offering*
6213 'âsâh (1), to *make*
7133 qorbân (1), *sacrificial present*
1494 ĕidōlŏthutŏn (3), *idolatrous offering*
2378 thusia (17), *sacrifice*
2380 thuō (4), to *sacrifice*

SACRIFICED
2076 zâbach (29), to *(sacrificially) slaughter*
6213 'âsâh (1), to *make*
1494 ĕidōlŏthutŏn (2), *idolatrous offering*
2380 thuō (1), to *kill; to butcher; to sacrifice*

SACRIFICEDST
2076 zâbach (1), to *(sacrificially) slaughter*

SACRIFICES
1685 dᵉbach (Ch.) (1), *animal sacrifice*
2077 zebach (53), *animal flesh; sacrifice*
2282 chag (1), *solemn festival*
2378 thusia (12), *sacrifice, offering*

SACRIFICETH
2076 zâbach (6), to *(sacrificially) slaughter*

SACRIFICING
2076 zâbach (2), to *(sacrificially) slaughter*

SACRILEGE
2416 hiĕrŏsulĕō (1), to *be a temple-robber*

SAD
2196 zâ'aph (1), to *be angry*
3510 kâ'ab (1), to *feel pain; to grieve; to spoil*
3512 kâ'âh (1), to *despond; to deject*
5620 çar (1), *sullen*
7451 ra' (2), *bad; evil*
7489 râ'a' (1), to *be good for nothing*
4659 skuthrōpŏs (2), *gloomy, mournful*
4768 stugnazō (1), to *be overcast; somber*

SADDLE
2280 châbash (3), to *wrap firmly, bind*
4817 merkâb (1), *chariot; seat in chariot*

SADDLED
2280 châbash (10), to *wrap firmly, bind*

SADDUCEES
4523 Saddŏukaiŏs (14), *of Tsadok*

SADLY
7451 ra' (1), *bad; evil*

SADNESS
7455 rôa' (1), *badness*

SADOC
4524 Sadōk (1), *just*

SAFE
983 beṭach (2), *safety*
3467 yâsha' (1), to *make safe, free*
6403 pâlaṭ (1), to *slip out, i.e. escape; to deliver*
7682 sâgab (2), to *be safe*
7965 shâlôwm (3), *safe*
809 aschēmōn (1), *inelegant, indecent*
1295 diasōzō (2), to *cure, preserve, rescue*
5198 hugiainō (1), to *have sound health*

SAFEGUARD
4931 mishmereth (1), *watch, sentry, post*

SAFELY
983 beṭach (17), *safety*
7965 shâlôwm (1), *safe*
806 asphalōs (2), *securely*

SAFETY
983 beṭach (9), *safety*
3468 yesha' (3), *liberty, deliverance, prosperity*
7951 shâlâh (1), to *be secure or successful*
8668 tᵉshûw'âh (4), *rescue, deliverance*
803 asphalĕia (2), *security; certainty*

SAFFRON
3750 karkôm (1), *crocus*

SAID
559 'âmar (2772), to *say*

SAINTS

560 'âmar (Ch.) (41), to *say*
1696 dâbar (85), to *say*
1697 dâbâr (8), *word; matter; thing*
4448 mâlal (1), to *speak*
4449 mᵉlal (Ch.) (1), to *speak, say*
5002 nᵉ'ûm (9), *oracle*
6030 'ânâh (1), to *respond*
7121 qârâ' (1), to *call out*
669 apŏphthĕggŏmai (1), *declare, address*
2036 ĕpō (756), to *speak*
2046 ĕrĕō (21), to *utter*
2063 ĕruthrŏs (3), *red*
2980 lalĕō (7), to *talk*
3004 lĕgō (200), to *say*
4280 prŏĕrĕō (4), to *say already, predict*
4483 rhĕō (15), to *utter*
5346 phēmi (48), to *make known one's thoughts*

SAIDST
559 'âmar (20), to *say*
1696 dâbar (1), to *speak*
2046 ĕrĕō (1), to *utter*

SAIL
5251 nêç (2), *flag; signal*
321 anagō (1), to *sail*
636 apŏplĕō (1), to *set sail, sail away*
3896 paraplĕō (1), to *sail near*
4126 plĕō (2), to *travel in a ship*
4632 skĕuŏs (1), *vessel, implement, equipment*

SAILED
321 anagō (2), to *lead up; to sail away*
636 apŏplĕō (3), to *set sail, sail away*
1020 braduplŏĕō (1), to *sail slowly*
1277 diaplĕō (1), to *sail through, across*
1602 ĕkplĕō (3), to *depart by ship*
3881 paralĕgŏmai (1), to *sail past*
4126 plĕō (2), to *travel in a ship*
5284 hupŏplĕō (2), to *sail under the lee of*

SAILING
1276 diapĕraō (1), to *cross over*
4126 plĕō (1), to *travel in a ship*
4144 plŏŏs (1), *navigation, voyage*

SAILORS
3492 nautēs (1), *sailor*

SAINT
6918 qâdôwsh (3), *sacred*
40 hagiŏs (1), *holy*

SAINTS
2623 châçîyd (19), *religiously pious, godly*
6918 qâdôwsh (9), *sacred*
6922 qaddîysh (Ch.) (6), *sacred*
6944 qôdesh (1), *sacred*
40 hagiŏs (60), *holy*

SAINTS'
40 hagiŏs (1), holy

SAITH
559 'âmar (581), to say
1696 dâbar (7), to speak
5001 nâ'am (10), to utter
as an oracle
5002 nᵉ'ûm (353), oracle
6310 peh (1), mouth
2036 ĕpō (1), to speak
2980 laleō (2), to talk
3004 lĕgō (297), to say
5346 phēmi (5), to make
known one's thoughts

SAKE
182 'ôwdôwth (1), on
account of; because
1558 gâlâl (3), on
account of, because of
1697 dâbâr (2), word;
matter; thing
4616 ma'an (45), on
account of
5668 'âbûwr (15), on
account of
7068 qin'âh (1), jealousy
7945 shel (1), on account
of; whatsoever
8478 tachath (2), bottom;
underneath; in lieu of
1722 ĕn (1), because of
1752 hĕnĕka (14), on
account of

SAKES
1558 gâlâl (1), on
account of, because of
1697 dâbâr (1), matter
1701 dibrâh (Ch.) (1),
because, on account of
5668 'âbûwr (1), on
account of
5921 'al (3), above, over
6616 pâthîyl (6), twine

SALA
4527 Sala (1), spear

SALAH
7974 Shelach (6), spear

SALAMIS
4529 Salamis (1), surge

SALATHIEL
7597 Shᵉ'altîy'êl (1), I
have asked God
4528 Salathiĕl (3), I have
asked God

SALCAH
5548 Çalkâh (2), walking

SALCHAH
5548 Çalkâh (2), walking

SALE
4465 mimkâr (3),
merchandise

SALEM
8004 Shâlêm (2), peaceful
4532 Salēm (2), peaceful

SALIM
4530 Salĕim (1), (poss.)
waver

SALLAI
5543 Çallûw (2), weighed

SALLU
5543 Çallûw (3), weighed

SALMA
8007 Salmâ' (4), clothing

SALMON
6756 Tsalmôwn (1),
shady
8009 Salmâh (1), clothing
8012 Salmôwn (1),
investiture
4533 Salmōn (3),
investiture

SALMONE
4534 Salmōnē (1), (poss.)
surge on the shore

SALOME
4539 Salōmē (2), peace

SALT
4416 mᵉlach (Ch.) (2), salt
4417 melach (27), salt
4420 mᵉlêchâh (1),
salted land, i.e. a desert
5898 'Îyr ham-Melach
(1), city of (the) salt
217 halas (8), salt
251 hals (1), salt
252 halukŏs (1), salty

SALTED
4414 mâlach (1), to salt
233 halizō (3), to salt

SALTNESS
1096+358 ginōmai (1), to
be, become

SALTPITS
4417 melach (1), salt

SALU
5543 Çallûw (1), weighed

SALUTATION
783 aspasmŏs (6),
greeting

SALUTATIONS
783 aspasmŏs (1),
greeting

SALUTE
1288 bârak (4), to bless
7592+7965 shâ'al (1), to
ask
7965 shâlôwm (2), safe;
well; health, prosperity
782 aspazŏmai (32), to
give salutation

SALUTED
1288 bârak (1), to bless
7592+7965 shâ'al (3), to
ask
782 aspazŏmai (5), to
give salutation

SALUTETH
782 aspazŏmai (5), to
give salutation

SALVATION
3444 yᵉshûw'âh (65),
deliverance; aid
3467 yâsha' (3), to make
safe, free
3468 yesha' (32), liberty,
deliverance, prosperity
4190 môwshâ'âh (1),
deliverance
8668 tᵉshûw'âh (17),
rescue, deliverance
4991 sōtēria (40), rescue
4992 sōtēriŏn (5),
defender or defence

SAMARIA
8111 Shômᵉrown (109),
watch-station

8115 Shomrayin (Ch.)
(2), watch-station
4540 Samarĕia (13),
watch-station

SAMARITAN
4541 Samarĕitēs (3),
inhabitant of Samaria

SAMARITANS
8118 Shômᵉrônîy (1),
Shomeronite
4541 Samarĕitēs (6),
inhabitant of Samaria

SAME
428 'êl-leh (1), these
1459 gav (Ch.) (1), middle
1791 dêk (Ch.) (1), this
1797 dikkên (Ch.) (1), this
1931 hûw' (73), this
1933 hâvâ' (1), to be
1992 hêm (4), they
2063 zô'th (1), this
2088 zeh (9), this or that
6106 'etsem (6), selfsame
8478 tachath (1), bottom
846 autŏs (87), he, she, it
1565 ĕkĕinŏs (24), that
2532 kai (1), even; also
3673 hŏmŏtĕchnŏs (1), of
the same trade
3748 hŏstis (1), whoever
3761 ŏudĕ (1), neither
3778 hŏutŏs (37), this
4954 sussōmŏs (1),
fellow-member
5023 tauta (2), these
5026 tautē̦ (5), (toward
or of) this
5126 tŏutŏn (2), to this
5129 tŏutō̦ (1), in this
5615 hōsautōs (1), in the
same way

SAMGAR-NEBO
5562 Çamgar Nᵉbôw (1),
Samgar-Nebo

SAMLAH
8072 Samlâh (4), mantle

SAMOS
4544 Samŏs (1), Samus

SAMOTHRACIA
4543 Samŏthra̦kē (1),
Samos of Thrace

SAMSON
8123 Shimshôwn (35),
sunlight
4546 Sampsōn (1),
sunlight

SAMSON'S
8123 Shimshôwn (3),
sunlight

SAMUEL
8050 Shᵉmûw'êl (135),
heard of God
4545 Samŏuêl (3), heard
of God

SANBALLAT
5571 Çanballaṭ (10),
Sanballat

SANCTIFICATION
38 hagiasmŏs (5), state
of purity

SANCTIFIED
6942 qâdâsh (46), to be,
make clean
37 hagiazō (16), to purify

SANCTIFIETH
37 hagiazō (4), to purify

SANCTIFY
6942 qâdâsh (63), to be,
make clean
37 hagiazō (6), to purify

SANCTUARIES
4720 miqdâsh (5),
sanctuary of deity

SANCTUARY
4720 miqdâsh (64),
sanctuary of deity
6944 qôdesh (68), sacred
39 hagiŏn (4), sacred

SAND
2344 chôwl (23), sand
285 ammŏs (5), sand

SANDALS
4547 sandaliŏn (2),
sandal

SANG
6030 'ânâh (2), to sing
7442 rânan (1), to shout
for joy
7891 shîyr (7), to sing
5214 humnĕō (1), to
celebrate God in song

SANK
3381 yârad (1), to
descend
6749 tsâlal (1), to settle

SANSANNAH
5578 Çançannâh (1),
bough

SAPH
5593 Çaph (1), dish

SAPHIR
8208 Shâphîyr (1),
beautiful

SAPPHIRA
4551 Sapphĕirē (1),
sapphire or lapis-lazuli

SAPPHIRE
5601 çappîyr (8),
sapphire
4552 sapphĕirŏs (1),
sapphire or lapis-lazuli

SAPPHIRES
5601 çappîyr (3),
sapphire

SARA
4564 Sarrha (1), princess

SARAH
8283 Sârâh (36), princess
8294 Serach (1),
superfluity
4564 Sarrha (2), princess

SARAH'S
8283 Sârâh (2), princess
4564 Sarrha (1), princess

SARAI
8297 Sâray (16),
dominative

SARAI'S
8297 Sâray (1),
dominative

SARAPH
8315 Sâraph (1), burning
one, serpent

SARDINE
4555 sardinŏs (1), sard

SARDIS
4554 *Sardĕis* (3), *Sardis*

SARDITES
5625 *Çardîy* (1), *Seredite*

SARDIUS
124 'ôdem (3), *ruby*
4556 *sardiŏs* (1), *sardian*

SARDONYX
4557 *sardŏnux* (1),
sard-onyx

SAREPTA
4558 *Sarĕpta* (1),
refinement

SARGON
5623 *Çargŏwn* (1),
Sargon

SARID
8301 *Sârîyd* (2), *survivor*

SARON
4565 *Sarŏn* (1), *plain*

SARSECHIM
8310 *Sarçᵉkîym* (1),
Sarsekim

SARUCH
4562 *Sarŏuch* (1), *tendril*

SAT
3427 *yâshab* (94), to *dwell*
8497 *tâkâh* (1), to *camp*
339 *anakathizō* (2), to *sit up*
345 *anakĕimai* (6), to
recline at a meal
347 *anaklinō* (1), to *lean back, recline*
377 *anapiptō* (4), *lie down, lean back*
2516 *kathĕzŏmai* (4), to
sit down, be seated
2521 *kathēmai* (43), to
sit down; to remain
2523 *kathizō* (21), to *seat down, dwell*
2621 *katakĕimai* (3), to
lie down; recline
2625 *kataklinō* (1), to
recline, take a place
3869 *parakathizō* (1), to
sit down near, beside
4775 *sugkathēmai* (2), to
seat oneself with
4873 *sunanakĕimai* (8),
to *recline with*

SATAN
7854 *sâṭân* (18), *opponent*
4567 *Satanas* (34),
accuser, i.e. the *Devil*

SATAN'S
4567 *Satanas* (1),
accuser, i.e. the *Devil*

SATEST
3427 *yâshab* (2), to *settle*

SATIATE
7301 *râvâh* (1), to *slake*
7646 *sâba'* (1), to *fill*

SATIATED
7301 *râvâh* (1), to *slake*

SATISFACTION
3724 *kôpher* (2),
redemption-price

SATISFIED
4390 *mâlê'* (1), to *fill*
7301 *râvâh* (1), to *slake*
7646 *sâba'* (36), *fill*

SATISFIEST
7646 *sâba'* (1), to *fill*

SATISFIETH
7646 *sâba'* (2), to *fill*
7654 *sob'âh* (1), *satiety*

SATISFY
4390 *mâlê'* (1), to *fill*
7301 *râvâh* (1), to *slake*
7646 *sâba'* (7), to *fill*
5526 *chŏrtazō* (1), to
supply food

SATISFYING
7648 *sôba'* (1),
satisfaction
4140 *plēsmŏnē* (1),
gratification

SATISIFED
7649 *sâbêa'* (1), *satiated*

SATYR
8163 *sâ'îyr* (1), *shaggy; he-goat; goat idol*

SATYRS
8163 *sâ'îyr* (1), *shaggy; he-goat; goat idol*

SAUL
7586 *Shâ'ûwl* (367), *asked*
4569 *Saulŏs* (23), *asked*

SAUL'S
7586 *Shâ'ûwl* (31), *asked*

SAVE
389 'ak (1), *surely; only*
518 'îm (1), *Oh that!*
657 'epheç (1), *end; no further*
1107 *bil'ădêy* (4), *except*
1115 *biltîy* (2), *except*
1115+518 *biltîy* (1), *not, except, without, unless*
2108 *zûwlâh* (6), *except*
2421 *châyâh* (21), to *live; to revive*
2425 *châyay* (1), to *live; to revive*
3444 *yᵉshûw'âh* (1),
deliverance; aid
3467 *yâsha'* (106), to
make safe, free
3588+518 *kîy* (12), *for, that because*
3861 *lâhên* (Ch.) (2),
therefore; except
4422 *mâlaṭ* (4), to *escape*
7535 *raq* (3), *although*
8104 *shâmar* (1), to *watch*
235 *alla* (2), *except*
1295 *diasōzō* (1), to *cure, preserve, rescue*
1508 *ĕi mē* (18), *if not*
2228 *ē* (1), *or; than*
3844 *para* (1), *besides*
4133 *plēn* (1), *save that*
4982 *sōzō* (41), to *deliver*

SAVED
2421 *châyâh* (8), to *live; to revive*
3467 *yâsha'* (35), to *make safe, free*
4422 *mâlaṭ* (1), to *escape*
5337 *nâtsal* (1), to *deliver*
8104 *shâmar* (1), to *watch*
1295 *diasōzō* (1), to *cure, preserve, rescue*

SAVEST
4982 *sōzō* (53), to *deliver*
4991 *sōtēria* (2), *rescue*
5442 *phulassō* (1), to *watch*, i.e. *be on guard*

SAVEST
3467 *yâsha'* (3), to *make safe, free*

SAVETH
3467 *yâsha'* (7), to *make safe, free*

SAVING
518 'îm (1), *Oh that!*
657 'epheç (1), *end; no further*
2421 *châyâh* (1), to *live; to revive*
3444 *yᵉshûw'âh* (2),
deliverance; aid
3468 *yesha'* (1), *liberty, deliverance, prosperity*
1508 *ĕi mē* (2), *if not*
3924 *parĕktŏs* (1), *besides*
4047 *pĕripŏiēsis* (1),
preservation
4991 *sōtēria* (1), *rescue*

SAVIOUR
3467 *yâsha'* (13), to *make safe, free*
4990 *sōtēr* (24), *Deliverer*

SAVIOURS
3467 *yâsha'* (2), to *make safe, free*

SAVOUR
6709 *tsachănâh* (1),
stench
7381 *rêyach* (46), *odor*
2175 *ĕuŏdia* (1), *aroma*
3471 *mōrainō* (2), to
become insipid
3744 *ŏsmē* (4), *fragrance*

SAVOUREST
5426 *phrŏnĕō* (2), to be
mentally disposed

SAVOURS
5208 *nîychôwach* (Ch.)
(1), *pleasure*

SAVOURY
4303 *maṭ'am* (6), *delicacy*

SAW
2370 *chăzâ'* (Ch.) (9), to
gaze upon; to dream
2372 *châzâh* (8), to *gaze at; to perceive*
4883 *massôwr* (1), *saw*
7200 *râ'âh* (306), to *see*
7805 *shâzaph* (1), to *scan*
991 *blĕpō* (9), to *look at*
1492 *ĕidō* (188), to *know*
1689 *ĕmblĕpō* (1), to
observe; to discern
2147 *hĕuriskō* (1), to *find*
2300 *thĕaŏmai* (8), to
look closely at
2334 *thĕōrĕō* (9), to *see*
3708 *hŏraō* (4), to *stare, see clearly; to discern*

SAWED
1641 *gârar* (1), to *saw*

SAWEST
2370 *chăzâ'* (Ch.) (7), to
gaze upon; to dream
2372 *châzâh* (8), to *gaze at; to perceive*
7200 *râ'âh* (6), to *see*
1492 *ĕidō* (7), to *know*

SAWN
4249 *prizō* (1), to *saw in two*

SAWS
4050 *mᵉgêrâh* (3), *saw*

SAY
559 'âmar (573), to *say*
560 'ămar (Ch.) (2), to *say*
1696 *dâbar* (28), to *speak*
1697 *dâbâr* (1), *word*
4405 *millâh* (2), *word*
471 *antĕpō* (1), to *refute*
2036 *ĕpō* (66), to *speak*
2046 *ĕrĕō* (39), to *utter*
2980 *lalĕō* (6), to *talk*
3004 *lĕgō* (293), to *say*
3056 *lŏgŏs* (1), *word*
5335 *phaskō* (1), to
assert a claim
5346 *phēmi* (6), to *make known one's thoughts*

SAYEST
559 'âmar (18), to *say*
2036 *ĕpō* (1), to *speak*
3004 *lĕgō* (20), to *say*

SAYING
559 'âmar (916), to *say*
560 'ămar (Ch.) (2), to *say*
1697 *dâbâr* (20), *word*
2420 *chîydâh* (1), *puzzle; conundrum; maxim*
2036 *ĕpō* (18), to *speak*
2981 *lalia* (1), *talk*
3004 *lĕgō* (380), to *say*
3007 *lĕipō* (5), to *fail*
3056 *lŏgŏs* (33), *word*
3058 *lŏidŏrĕō* (1), to
vilify, insult
4487 *rhēma* (6),
utterance; matter
5335 *phaskō* (1), to *assert*

SAYINGS
561 'êmer (2), *saying*
1697 *dâbâr* (5), *word*
2420 *chîydâh* (2), *puzzle; conundrum; maxim*
6310 *peh* (1), *mouth*
3004 *lĕgō* (1), to *say*
3056 *lŏgŏs* (16), *word*
4487 *rhēma* (3),
utterance; matter

SCAB
1618 *gârâb* (1), *itching*
4556 *miçpachath* (3),
scurf, rash
5597 *çappachath* (3),
skin mange

SCABBARD
8593 *ta'ar* (1), *scabbard*

SCABBED
3217 *yallepheth* (2), *scurf*

SCAFFOLD
3595 *kîyôwr* (1), *caldron*

SCALES
650+4043 'âphîyq (1),
valley; stream; mighty
6425 *peleç* (1), *balance*
7193 *qasqeseth* (7), *fish scales; coat of mail*
3013 *lĕpis* (1), *flake, scale*

SCALETH
5927 'âlâh (1), to *ascend, be high, mount*

SCALL
5424 *netheq* (14), *scurf*

S

SCALP
6936 qodqôd (1), *crown of the head*

SCANT
7332 râzôwn (1), *thinness*

SCAPEGOAT
5799 'ăzâ'zêl (4), *goat of departure; scapegoat*

SCARCE
3433 mŏlis (2), *with difficulty*

SCARCELY
3433 mŏlis (2), *with difficulty*

SCARCENESS
4544 miçkênûth (1), *indigence, poverty*

SCAREST
2865 châthath (1), *to break down*

SCARLET
711 'argᵉvân (Ch.) (3), *purple*
8144 shânîy (9), *crimson*
8144+8438 shânîy (33), *crimson dyed stuffs*
8529 tâla' (1), *to dye crimson*
2847 kŏkkinŏs (6), *crimson*

SCATTER
921 bᵉdar (Ch.) (1), *to scatter*
967 bâzar (2), *to scatter*
2210 zâqaph (1), *to lift up*
2219 zârâh (11), *to diffuse*
2236 zâraq (2), *to sprinkle, scatter*
5128 nûwa' (1), *to waver*
5310 nâphats (1), *to dash*
6284 pâ'âh (1), *to blow away*
6327 pûwts (18), *to dash*

SCATTERED
2219 zârâh (6), *to diffuse*
4900 mâshak (2), *to draw out; to be tall*
5310 nâphats (2), *to dash*
6327 pûwts (34), *to dash*
6340 pâzar (7), *to scatter*
6504 pârad (2), *to spread*
6555 pârats (1), *to break out*
6566 pâras (3), *to scatter*
1262 dialuō (1), *to break up*
1287 diaskŏrpizō (4), *scatter; to squander*
1289 diaspĕirō (3), *to scatter like seed*
1290 diaspŏra (2), *dispersion*
4496 rhiptō (1), *to fling*
4650 skŏrpizō (1), *to dissipate*

SCATTERETH
2219 zârâh (2), *to diffuse*
6327 pûwts (3), *to dash in pieces; to disperse*
6340 pâzar (2), *to scatter*
4650 skŏrpizō (3), *to dissipate*

SCATTERING
5311 nephets (1), *storm which disperses*

SCENT
2143 zêker (1), *commemoration*
7381 rêyach (2), *odor*

SCEPTRE
7626 shêbeț (9), *stick*
8275 sharbîyț (4), *ruler's rod*
4464 rhabdŏs (2), *stick*

SCEPTRES
7626 shêbeț (1), *stick*

SCEVA
4630 Skĕuas (1), *left-handed*

SCHISM
4978 schisma (1), *divisive dissension*

SCHOLAR
6030 'ânâh (1), *to respond*
8527 talmîyd (1), *pupil*

SCHOOL
4981 schŏlē (1), *lecture hall, i.e. school*

SCHOOLMASTER
3807 paidagōgŏs (2), *tutor, cf. pedagogue*

SCIENCE
4093 maddâ' (1), *intelligence*
1108 gnōsis (1), *knowledge*

SCOFF
7046 qâlaç (1), *to disparage, i.e. ridicule*

SCOFFERS
1703 ĕmpaiktēs (1), *derider; false teacher*

SCORCH
2739 kaumatizō (1), *to burn, scorch, sear*

SCORCHED
2739 kaumatizō (3), *burn, scorch, sear*

SCORN
959 bâzâh (1), *to scorn*
3887 lûwts (1), *to scoff*
3933 la'ag (1), *scoffing*
4890 mischâq (1), *laughing-stock*
2606 katagĕlaō (3), *laugh down, i.e. deride*

SCORNER
3887 lûwts (11), *to scoff*

SCORNERS
3887 lûwts (3), *to scoff*
3945 lâtsats (1), *to scoff*

SCORNEST
3887 lûwts (1), *to scoff*
7046 qâlaç (1), *to disparage, i.e. ridicule*

SCORNETH
3887 lûwts (2), *to scoff; to interpret; to intercede*
7832 sâchaq (2), *to scorn*

SCORNFUL
3887 lûwts (1), *to scoff*
3944 lâtsôwn (2), *scoffing*

SCORNING
3933 la'ag (2), *scoffing*
3944 lâtsôwn (1), *scoffing*

SCORPION
4651 skŏrpiŏs (2), *scorpion*

SCORPIONS
6137 'aqrâb (6), *scorpion*
4651 skŏrpiŏs (3), *scorpion*

SCOURED
4838 mâraq (1), *to polish*

SCOURGE
7752 shôwṭ (4), *lash*
7885 shayiṭ (1), *oar*
3147 mastizō (1), *to whip*
3164 machŏmai (5), *to war, i.e. to quarrel*
5416 phragĕlliŏn (1), *lash*

SCOURGED
1244 biqqôreth (1), *due punishment*
3146 mastigŏō (1), *to punish by flogging*
5417 phragĕllŏō (2), *to whip, i.e. to lash*

SCOURGES
7850 shôṭêṭ (1), *goad, flogging device*

SCOURGETH
3146 mastigŏō (1), *to punish by flogging*

SCOURGING
3148 mastix (1), *flogging device*

SCOURGINGS
3148 mastix (1), *flogging device*

SCRABBLED
8427 tâvâh (1), *to mark*

SCRAPE
1623 gârad (1), *to rub off*
5500 çâchâh (1), *to sweep away*
7096 qâtsâh (1), *to cut off*

SCRAPED
7096 qâtsâh (1), *to cut off*
7106 qâtsa' (1), *to scrape*

SCREECH
3917 lîylîyth (1), *night spectre (spirit)*

SCRIBE
5608 çâphar (42), *to inscribe; to enumerate*
5613 çâphêr (Ch.) (6), *scribe, recorder*
1122 grammatĕus (4), *secretary, scholar*

SCRIBE'S
5608 çâphar (2), *to inscribe; to enumerate*

SCRIBES
5608 çâphar (6), *to inscribe; to enumerate*
1122 grammatĕus (62), *secretary, scholar*

SCRIP
3219 yalqûwṭ (1), *pouch*
4082 pēra (6), *wallet*

SCRIPTURE
3791 kâthâb (1), *writing*
1124 graphē (31), *document, i.e. holy Writ*

SCRIPTURES
1121 gramma (1), *writing*

SCROLL
1124 graphē (20), *document, i.e. holy Writ*

SCROLL
5612 çêpher (1), *writing*
975 bibliŏn (1), *scroll*

SCUM
2457 chel'âh (5), *rust*

SCURVY
1618 gârâb (2), *itching*

SCYTHIAN
4658 Skuthēs (1), *Scythene*

SEA
3220 yâm (291), *sea*
3221 yâm (Ch.) (2), *sea*
1724 ĕnaliŏs (1), *marine*
2281 thalassa (93), *sea*
3864 parathalassiŏs (1), *by the lake*
3882 paraliŏs (1), *maritime; seacoast*
3989 pĕlagŏs (1), *open sea*

SEAFARING
3220 yâm (1), *sea; basin*

SEAL
2368 chôwthâm (5), *seal*
2856 châtham (6), *to close up; to affix a seal*
4972 sphragizō (4), *to stamp with a signet*
4973 sphragis (11), *stamp impressed*

SEALED
2856 châtham (14), *to close up; to affix a seal*
2857 châtham (Ch.) (1), *to affix a seal*
2696 katasphragizō (1), *to seal closely*
4972 sphragizō (20), *to stamp with a signet*

SEALEST
2856 châtham (1), *to close up; to affix a seal*

SEALETH
2856 châtham (3), *to close up; to affix a seal*

SEALING
4972 sphragizō (1), *to stamp with a signet*

SEALS
4973 sphragis (5), *stamp*

SEAM
729 arrhaphŏs (1), *without seam*

SEARCH
1239 bâqar (1), *to inspect, admire*
1240 bᵉqar (Ch.) (4), *to inspect, admire*
1875 dârash (4), *to pursue or search*
2658 châphar (3), *delve, to explore*
2664 châphas (8), *to seek; to let be sought*
2665 chêphes (1), *secret trick, plot*
2713 châqar (11), *to examine, search*
2714 chêqer (3), *examination*

4290 machtereth (1), *burglary*
8446 tûwr (9), to *meander*
1833 ĕxĕtazō (1), to *ascertain* or *interrogate*
2045 ĕrĕunaō (2), to *seek*, i.e. to *investigate*

SEARCHED
2664 châphas (3), to *seek*
2713 châqar (7), to *examine* intimately
2714 chĕqer (1), *examination*
4959 mâshash (2), to *feel*
7270 râgal (1), to *reconnoiter; to slander*
8446 tûwr (4), to *meander*
350 anakrinō (1), to *interrogate, determine*
1830 ĕxĕrĕunaō (1), to *explore*

SEARCHEST
1875 dârash (1), to *search*
2664 châphas (1), to *seek*

SEARCHETH
1875 dârash (2), to *search*
2713 châqar (3), to *search*
2045 ĕrĕunaō (3), to *seek*

SEARCHING
2664 châphas (1), to *seek*
2714 chĕqer (2), *examination*
8446 tûwr (1), to *meander*
2045 ĕrĕunaō (1), to *seek*

SEARCHINGS
2714 chĕqer (1), *examination*

SEARED
2743 kautĕriazō (1), to *brand* or *cauterize*

SEAS
3220 yâm (24), *sea*
1337 dithalassŏs (1), *having two seas*

SEASON
2165 zᵉmân (1), *time*
2166 zᵉmân (Ch.) (1), *time, appointed*
3117 yôwm (3), *day; time*
4150 môw'êd (10), *place of meeting*
4414 mâlach (1), to *disappear* as dust
6256 'êth (14), *time*
171 akairōs (1), *inopportunely*
741 artuō (1), to *spice*
2121 ĕukairōs (1), *opportune, suitable*
2540 kairŏs (11), *set* or *proper* time
3641 ŏligŏs (1), *puny*
4340 prŏskairŏs (1), *temporary*
5550 chrŏnŏs (3), *time*
5610 hōra (3), *hour*

SEASONED
741 artuō (2), to *spice*

SEASONS
2166 zᵉmân (Ch.) (1), *time, appointed*
4150 môw'êd (3), *place of meeting; assembly*
6256 'êth (2), *time*
2540 kairŏs (4), *set* or *proper* time

5550 chrŏnŏs (1), *time*

SEAT
3678 kiççê' (7), *throne*
4186 môwshâb (7), *seat*
7674 shebeth (1), *rest*
7675 shebeth (2), *abode*
8499 tᵉkûwnâh (1), something *arranged*
968 bēma (10), *tribunal platform; judging place*
2362 thrŏnŏs (3), *throne*
2515 kathĕdra (1), *bench*

SEATED
5603 çâphan (1), to *roof*

SEATS
2362 thrŏnŏs (4), *throne*
2515 kathĕdra (2), *bench*
4410 prŏtŏkathĕdria (4), *pre-eminence* in council

SEBA
5434 Çᵉbâ' (4), *Seba*

SEBAT
7627 Shᵉbâṭ (1), *Shebat*

SECACAH
5527 Çᵉkâkâh (1), *enclosure*

SECHU
7906 Sĕkûw (1), *Seku*

SECOND
4932 mishneh (12), *double; second*
8138 shânâh (3), to *fold*, i.e. *duplicate*
8145 shênîy (99), *second*
8147 shᵉnayim (10), *two-fold*
8578 tinyân (Ch.) (1), *second*
8648 tᵉrêyn (Ch.) (1), *two*
1207 dĕutĕrŏprŏtŏs (1), *second-first*
1208 dĕutĕrŏs (42), *second; secondly*

SECONDARILY
1208 dĕutĕrŏs (1), *second; secondly*

SECRET
328 'aṭ (1), *gently, softly*
2934 ṭâman (1), to *hide*
4565 miçtâr (8), *covert hiding place*
5475 çôwd (8), *secret*
5640 çâtham (1), to *repair; to keep secret*
5641 çâthar (4), to *hide*
5642 çᵉthar (Ch.) (1), to *demolish*
5643 çêther (15), *cover*
5956 'âlam (2), to *conceal*
6383 pil'îy (1), *remarkable*
6596 pôth (1), *hole; hinge*
6845 tsâphan (2), to *hide*
7328 râz (Ch.) (6), *mystery*
8368 sâthar (1), to *break out* as an *eruption*
614 apŏkruphŏs (1), *secret, hidden things*
2926 kruptē (1), *hidden*
2927 kruptŏs (10), *private*
2928 kruptō (1), to *conceal*
2931 kruphē (1), *in secret*
4601 sigaō (1), to *keep silent*

5009 tamĕiŏn (1), *room*

SECRETLY
1589 gânab (1), to *deceive*
2244 châbâ' (1), to *secrete*
2644 châphâ' (1), to *act covertly*
2790 chârash (1), to *engrave; to plow*
2791 cheresh (1), *magical craft; silence*
3909 lâṭ (1), *secrecy*
4565 miçtâr (2), *covert hiding place*
5643 çêther (9), *cover*
6845 tsâphan (1), to *hide*
2928 kruptō (1), to *conceal*
2977 lathra (1), *secretly*

SECRETS
4016 mâbûsh (1), *male genitals*
5475 çôwd (2), *secret*
7328 râz (Ch.) (3), *mystery*
8587 ta'ălummâh (2), *secret*
2927 kruptŏs (2), *private*

SECRET
139 hairĕsis (5), *sect*

SECUNDUS
4580 Sĕkŏundŏs (1), *second*

SECURE
982 bâṭach (4), to *trust*
983 beṭach (1), *security*
987 baṭṭûchôwth (1), *security*
4160+275 mûwts (1), to *oppress*

SECURELY
983 beṭach (2), *safety, security, trust*

SECURITY
2425 hikanŏs (1), *ample*

SEDITION
849 'eshtaddûwr (Ch.) (2), *rebellion*
4714 stasis (3), one leading an *uprising*

SEDITIONS
1370 dichŏstasia (1), *dissension*

SEDUCE
635 apŏplanaō (1), to *lead astray; to wander*
4105 planaō (2), to *deceive*

SEDUCED
2937 ṭâ'âh (1), to *lead astray*
8582 tâ'âh (2), to *stray*

SEDUCERS
1114 gŏēs (1), *imposter*

SEDUCETH
8582 tâ'âh (1), to *stray*

SEDUCING
4108 planŏs (1), *roving*

SEE
2009 hinnêh (2), *Look!*
2370 châzâ' (Ch.) (4), to *gaze* upon; to *dream*
2372 châzâh (15), to *gaze at; to perceive*

2374 chôzeh (2), *beholder* in vision
4758 mar'eh (1), *appearance; vision*
5027 nâbaṭ (4), to *scan; to regard* with favor
7200 râ'âh (346), to *see*
7789 shûwr (4), to *spy out, survey*
308 anablĕpō (1), to *look up; to recover sight*
542 apĕidō (1), to *see fully*
991 blĕpō (46), to *look at*
1227 diablĕpō (2), to *see clearly, recover vision*
1492 ĕidō (79), to *know*
1689 ĕmblĕpō (1), to *observe; to discern*
2300 thĕaŏmai (4), to *look closely at*
2334 thĕŏrĕō (17), to *see*
2396 idĕ (1), *lo!, look!*
2400 idŏu (3), *lo!, see!*
2477 histŏrĕō (1), to *visit*
3467 muŏpazō (1), to *see indistinctly, be myopic*
3700 ŏptanŏmai (29), to *appear*
3708 hŏraō (11), to *stare, see clearly; to discern*
5461 phŏtizō (1), to *shine* or to *brighten up*

SEED
2233 zera' (218), *seed*
2234 zᵉra' (Ch.) (1), *posterity, progeny*
6507 pᵉrûdâh (1), *kernel*
4687 spĕirō (4), to *scatter*, i.e. *sow* seed
4690 spĕrma (41), *seed*
4701 spŏra (1), *sowing*
4703 spŏrŏs (5), *seed*

SEED'S
2233 zera' (1), *seed; fruit*

SEEDS
4690 spĕrma (3), *seed*

SEEDTIME
2233 zera' (1), *seed; fruit*

SEEING
310 achar (1), *after*
518 'im (1), *whether?; if*
1768 dîy (Ch.) (1), *that; of*
3282 ya'an (1), *because*
3588 kîy (9), *for, that*
6493 piqqêach (1), *clear-sighted*
7200 râ'âh (16), to *see*
990 blemma (1), *vision*
991 blĕpō (1), to *look at*
1063 gar (1), *for, indeed, but, because*
1492 ĕidō (8), to *know*
1512 ĕi pĕr (1), *if perhaps*
1893 ĕpĕi (4), *since*
1894 ĕpĕidē (2), *whereas*
1897 ĕpĕipĕr (1), *since*
2334 thĕŏrĕō (1), to *see*
3708 hŏraō (1), to *stare, see clearly; to discern*
3754 hŏti (1), *that; since*
4275 prŏĕidō (1), to *foresee*

SEEK
1239 bâqar (3), to *inspect, admire*

1245 bâqash (112), to *search* out; to *strive*
1556 gâlal (1), to *roll*
1875 dârash (56), to *seek*
2713 châqar (1), to *search*
7125 qîr'âh (1), to *encounter; to happen*
7836 shâchar (8), to *search* for
8446 tûwr (1), to *wander*
327 anazētĕō (1), to *search out*
1567 ĕkzētĕō (2), to *seek out*
1934 ĕpizētĕō (6), to *search (inquire) for*
2212 zētĕō (48), to *seek*

SEEKEST
1245 bâqash (7), to *search* out; to *strive*
2212 zētĕō (2), to *seek*

SEEKETH
579 'ânâh (1), to *meet*
1243 baqqârâh (1), *looking after*
1245 bâqash (19), to *search* out; to *strive*
1875 dârash (6), to *seek*
2658 châphar (1), to *delve*
7836 shâchar (1), to *search* for
1567 ĕkzētĕō (1), to *seek out*
1934 ĕpizētĕō (3), to *search (inquire) for*
2212 zētĕō (9), to *seek*

SEEKING
1875 dârash (2), to *seek*
2212 zētĕō (12), to *seek*

SEEM
3191 yᵉ'ṭab (Ch.) (1), to *be, make well*
4591 mâ'aṭ (1), to *be, make small or few*
4758 mar'eh (1), *appearance; vision*
5869 'ayin (2), *eye; sight*
7034 qâlâh (1), to *be light*
7185 qâshâh (1), to *be tough or severe*
1380 dŏkĕō (5), to *seem*

SEEMED
5869 'ayin (4), *eye; sight*
1380 dŏkĕō (6), to *think, regard, seem* good
5316 phainō (1), to *lighten; to appear*

SEEMETH
5869 'ayin (18), *eye; sight*
6440 pânîym (2), *face*
7200 râ'âh (1), to *see*
1380 dŏkĕō (5), to *seem*

SEEMLY
5000 nâ'veh (2), *suitable*

SEEN
2370 chăzâ' (Ch.) (3), to *gaze upon; to dream*
2372 châzâh (9), to *gaze at; to perceive*
7200 râ'âh (162), to *see*
7210 rô'îy (2), *sight*
7805 shâzaph (1), to *scan*
991 blĕpō (9), to *look at*
1492 ĕidō (33), to *know*
2300 thĕaŏmai (8), to *look closely at*

2334 thĕōrĕō (2), to *see*
2529 kathŏraō (1), to *see clearly*
3700 ŏptanŏmai (8), to *appear*
3708 hŏraō (32), to *stare, see clearly; to discern*
3780 ŏuchi (1), *not indeed*
4308 prŏŏraō (1), to *notice previously*
5316 phainō (2), to *lighten; be visible*

SEER
2374 chôzeh (11), *beholder* in vision
7200 râ'âh (10), to *see*

SEER'S
7200 râ'âh (1), to *see*

SEERS
2374 chôzeh (5), *beholder* in vision
7200 râ'âh (1), to *see*

SEEST
2372 châzâh (2), to *gaze at; to perceive*
7200 râ'âh (27), to *see*
7210 rô'îy (1), *sight; spectacle*
991 blĕpō (5), to *look at*
2334 thĕōrĕō (1), to *see*

SEETH
2372 châzâh (3), to *gaze at; to perceive*
7200 râ'âh (27), to *see*
7210 rô'îy (1), *sight; spectacle*
991 blĕpō (11), to *look at*
2334 thĕōrĕō (9), to *see*
3708 hŏraō (1), to *stare*

SEETHE
1310 bâshal (8), to *boil*

SEETHING
1310 bâshal (1), to *boil*
5301 nâphach (2), to *inflate, blow, kindle*

SEGUB
7687 Sᵉgûwb (3), *aloft*

SEIR
8165 Sê'îyr (39), *rough*

SEIRATH
8167 Sᵉ'îyrâh (1), *roughness*

SEIZE
3423 yârash (1), to *inherit; to impoverish*
3451 yᵉshîymâh (1), *desolation*
3947 lâqach (1), to *take*
2722 katĕchō (1), to *hold down fast*

SEIZED
2388 châzaq (1), to *seize*

SELA
5554 Çela' (1), *craggy rock; fortress*

SELA-HAMMAHLEKOTH
5555 Çela' ham-machlᵉqôwth (1), *rock of the divisions*

SELAH
5542 Çelâh (74), *suspension* of music
5554 Çela' (1), *craggy rock; fortress*

SELED
5540 Çeled (1), *exultation*

SELEUCIA
4581 Sĕlĕukĕia (1), of *Seleucus*

SELFWILL
7522 râtsôwn (1), *delight*

SELFWILLED
829 authadēs (2), *self-pleasing, arrogant*

SELL
4376 mâkar (24), to *sell*
7666 shâbar (3), to *deal*
1710 ĕmpŏrĕuŏmai (1), to *trade, do business*
4453 pōlĕō (7), to *barter*

SELLER
4376 mâkar (3), to *sell*
4211 pŏrphurŏpōlis (1), *female trader in bluish-red cloth*

SELLERS
4376 mâkar (1), to *sell*

SELLEST
4376 mâkar (1), to *sell*

SELLETH
4376 mâkar (5), to *sell*
7666 shâbar (1), to *deal*
4453 pōlĕō (1), to *barter*

SELVEDGE
7098 qâtsâh (2), *termination; fringe*

SEM
4590 Sĕm (1), *name*

SEMACHIAH
5565 Çᵉmakyâhûw (1), *supported of Jehovah*

SEMEI
4584 Sĕmĕï (1), *famous*

SENAAH
5570 Çᵉnâ'âh (2), *thorny*

SENATE
1087 gĕrŏusia (1), Jewish *Sanhedrin*

SENATORS
2205 zâqēn (1), *old, venerated*

SEND
935 bôw' (1), to *go, come*
5042 nâba' (1), to *gush*
5130 nûwph (1), to *rock*
5414 nâthan (6), to *give*
7136 qârâh (1), to *bring about; to impose*
7971 shâlach (157), to *send away*
7972 shᵉlach (Ch.) (1), to *send away*
630 apŏluō (6), to *relieve, release; divorce*
649 apŏstĕllō (23), to *send out on a mission*
906 ballō (3), to *throw*
1032 bruō (1), to *gush*
1544 ĕkballō (3), to *throw out*
1821 ĕxapŏstĕllō (1), to *despatch, or to dismiss*
3343 mĕtapĕmpō (2), to *summon or invite*
3992 pĕmpō (25), to *send*

SENDEST
7971 shâlach (6), to *send away*

SENDETH
5414 nâthan (2), to *give*
7971 shâlach (8), to *send away*
649 apŏstĕllō (4), to *send out on a mission*
1026 brĕchō (1), to *make wet; to rain*

SENDING
4916 mishlôwach (3), *sending out*
4917 mishlachath (1), *mission; release; army*
7971 shâlach (9), to *send away*
3992 pĕmpō (1), to *send*

SENEH
5573 Çeneh (1), *thorn*

SENIR
8149 Shᵉnîyr (2), *peak*

SENNACHERIB
5576 Çanchêrîyb (13), *Sancherib*

SENSE
7922 sekel (1), *intelligence; success*

SENSES
145 aisthētēriŏn (1), *judgment, sense*

SENSUAL
5591 psuchikŏs (2), *physical and brutish*

SENT
1980 hâlak (1), to *walk*
2904 ṭûwl (1), to *cast down or out, hurl*
3947 lâqach (1), to *take*
5414 nâthan (5), to *give*
5674 'âbar (2), to *cross over; to transition*
6680 tsâvâh (1), to *constitute, enjoin*
7725 shûwb (1), to *return*
7964 shillûwach (1), *divorce; dower*
7971 shâlach (459), to *send away*
7972 shᵉlach (Ch.) (12), to *send away*
375 anapĕmpō (4), to *send up or back*
628 apŏlŏuō (2), to *wash fully*
630 apŏluō (6), to *release; divorce*
640 apŏria (1), state of *quandarý, perplexity*
649 apŏstĕllō (104), to *send out on a mission*
652 apŏstŏlŏs (2), *commissioner of Christ*
657 apŏtassŏmai (1), to *say adieu; to renounce*
863 aphiēmi (2), to *leave*
1524 ĕisĕimi (1), to *enter*
1544 ĕkballō (1), to *throw out*
1599 ĕkpĕmpō (2), to *despatch, send out*
1821 ĕxapŏstĕllō (10), to *despatch, or to dismiss*
3343 mĕtapĕmpō (4), to *summon or invite*

SENTENCE

3992 pĕmpō (49), to send
4842 sumpĕmpō (2), to
dispatch with
4882 sunapŏstĕllō (1), to
despatch with

SENTENCE

1697 dâbâr (3), word
4941 mishpâṭ (2), verdict;
formal decree; justice
6310 peh (1), mouth
6599 pithgâm (1),
judicial sentence; edict
7081 qeçem (1),
divination
610 apŏkrima (1),
decision or sentence
1948 ĕpikrinō (1), to
adjudge, decide
2919 krinō (1), to decide

SENTENCES

280 'ăchîydâh (Ch.) (1),
enigma
2420 chîydâh (1), puzzle

SENTEST

7971 shâlach (4), to send
away

SENUAH

5574 Çᵉnûw'âh (1),
pointed

SEORIM

8188 Sᵉ'ôrîym (1), barley

SEPARATE

914 bâdal (7), to divide
1508 gizrâh (7), figure,
appearance; enclosure
2505 châlaq (1), to be
smooth; be slippery
3995 mibdâlâh (1),
separation; separate
5139 nâzîyr (1), prince;
separated Nazirite
5144 nâzar (4), to set
apart, devote
6381 pâlâ' (1), to be,
make great, difficult
6504 pârad (2), to spread
873 aphŏrizō (5), to limit,
exclude, appoint
5562 chŏrĕō (3), to pass,
enter; to hold, admit

SEPARATED

914 bâdal (17), to divide
5139 nâzîyr (1), prince;
separated Nazirite
5144 nâzar (1), to set
apart, devote
6395 pâlâh (2), to
distinguish
6504 pârad (8), to spread
873 aphŏrizō (4), to limit,
exclude, appoint

SEPARATETH

5144 nâzar (3), to set
apart, devote
6504 pârad (2), to spread

SEPARATING

5144 nâzar (1), to set
apart, devote

SEPARATION

914 bâdal (1), to divide
5079 niddâh (14), time of
menstrual impurity
5145 nezer (11), set
apart; dedication

SEPHAR

5611 Çᵉphâr (1), census

SEPHARAD

5614 Çᵉphârâd (1),
Sepharad

SEPHARVAIM

5617 Çᵉpharvayim (6),
Sepharvajim

SEPHARVITES

5616 Çᵉpharvîy (1),
Sepharvite

SEPULCHRE

6900 qᵉbûwrâh (5),
sepulchre
6913 qeber (14),
sepulchre
3418 mnēma (4),
sepulchral monument
3419 mnēmĕiŏn (26),
place of interment
5028 taphŏs (5), grave

SEPULCHRES

6913 qeber (12),
sepulchre
3419 mnēmĕiŏn (3),
place of interment
5028 taphŏs (1), grave

SERAH

8294 Serach (2),
superfluity

SERAIAH

8304 Sᵉrâyâh (20),
Jehovah has prevailed

SERAPHIMS

8314 sârâph (2), saraph

SERED

5624 Çered (2), trembling

SERGIUS

4588 Sĕrgiŏs (1), Sergius

SERJEANTS

4465 rhabdŏuchŏs (2),
constable

SERPENT

5175 nâchâsh (25), snake
8314 sârâph (3),
poisonous serpent
8577 tannîyn (2),
sea-serpent; jackal
3789 ŏphis (8), snake

SERPENT'S

5175 nâchâsh (2), snake

SERPENTS

2119 zâchal (1), to crawl
5175 nâchâsh (4), snake
8577 tannîyn (1),
sea-serpent; jackal
2062 hĕrpĕtŏn (1), reptile
3789 ŏphis (6), snake

SERUG

8286 Sᵉrûwg (5), tendril

SERVANT

5288 na'ar (30), servant
5647 'âbad (1), to serve
5649 'âbad (Ch.) (1),
servant
5650 'ebed (363), servant
7916 sâkîyr (8), man at
wages, hired hand
8334 shârath (4), to
attend
1248 diakŏnia (2),
attendance, aid, service
1249 diakŏnŏs (3),
attendant, deacon

SERVANT'S

1401 dŏulŏs (66), servant
1402 dŏulŏō (1), to
enslave
2324 thĕrapōn (1),
menial attendant
3610 ŏikĕtēs (3), menial
domestic servant
3816 pais (8), servant

SERVANT'S

5650 'ebed (8), servant
1401 dŏulŏs (1), servant

SERVANTS

582 'ĕnôwsh (1), man
5288 na'ar (21), servant
5647 'âbad (4), to serve
5649 'âbad (Ch.) (6),
servant
5650 'ebed (367), servant
5657 'ăbuddâh (1),
service
8334 shârath (1), to
attend as a menial
341 anakainŏō (1), to
renovate, renew
1249 diakŏnŏs (2),
attendant, deacon
1401 dŏulŏs (55), servant
1402 dŏulŏō (1), to
enslave
3407 misthiŏs (2),
hired-worker
3610 ŏikĕtēs (1), menial
domestic servant
3816 pais (1), servant
5257 hupĕrĕtēs (4),
servant, attendant

SERVANTS'

5650 'ebed (4), servant

SERVE

5647 'âbad (162), to serve
5656 'ăbôdâh (1), work
5975+6440 'âmad (1), to
stand
6399 pᵉlach (Ch.) (7), to
serve or worship
8334 shârath (4), to
attend as a menial
1247 diakŏnĕō (7), to
wait upon, serve
1398 dŏulĕuō (13), to
serve as a slave
3000 latrĕuō (13), to
minister to God

SERVED

1580 gâmal (1), to benefit
or requite; to wean
5647 'âbad (61), to serve
5975+6440 'âmad (1), to
stand
6213 'âsâh (1), to do
8334 shârath (4), to
attend as a menial
1247 diakŏnĕō (1), to
wait upon, serve
1398 dŏulĕuō (1), to
serve as a slave
3000 latrĕuō (2), to
minister to God
5256 hupĕrĕtĕō (1), to be
a subordinate

SERVEDST

5647 'âbad (1), to serve

SERVEST

6399 pᵉlach (Ch.) (2), to
serve or worship

SERVETH

5647 'âbad (2), to serve
5656 'ăbôdâh (1), work
1247 diakŏnĕō (2), to
wait upon, serve
1398 dŏulĕuō (1), to
serve as a slave

SERVICE

3027 yâd (2), hand; power
5647 'âbad (4), to serve
5656 'ăbôdâh (98), work
5673 'ăbîydâh (Ch.) (1),
labor or business
6402 polchân (Ch.) (1),
worship
6635 tsâbâ' (4), army,
military host
8278 sᵉrâd (4), stitching
8334 shârath (3), to
attend as a menial
1248 diakŏnia (1),
attendance, aid, service
1398 dŏulĕuō (3), to
serve as a slave
2999 latrĕia (5), worship,
ministry service
3000 latrĕuō (1), to
minister to God
3009 lĕitŏurgia (3),
service, ministry

SERVILE

5656 'ăbôdâh (12), work

SERVING

5647 'âbad (2), to serve
1248 diakŏnia (1),
attendance, aid, service
1398 dŏulĕuō (3), to
serve as a slave
3000 latrĕuō (1), to
minister to God

SERVITOR

8334 shârath (1), to
attend as a menial

SERVITUDE

5656 'ăbôdâh (2), work

SET

530 'ĕmûwnâh (5),
fidelity; steadiness
631 'âçar (1), to fasten
935 bôw' (1), to go, come
1129 bânâh (2), to build
1197 bâ'ar (1), to be
brutish, be senseless
1379 gâbal (1), to set a
boundary line, limit
1431 gâdal (1), to be
great, make great
2211 zᵉqaph (Ch.) (1), to
impale by hanging
2232 zâra' (1), to sow
seed; to disseminate
2706 chôq (1),
appointment; allotment
2710 châqaq (1), to
engrave; to enact laws
3051 yâhab (1), to give
3240 yânach (8), to allow
to stay
3245 yâçad (1), settle,
consult, establish
3259 yâ'ad (1), to meet;
to summon; to direct
3320 yâtsab (5), to
station, offer, continue
3322 yâtsag (8), to place
3332 yâtsaq (1), to pour
out

3335 yâtsar (1), to *form*
3341 yâtsath (1), to *burn*
3427 yâshab (13), to *settle*
3488 yᵉthîb (Ch.) (2), to *sit*
3559 kûwn (6), to *set up*
3635 kᵉlal (Ch.) (4), to *complete*
3966 mᵉʼôd (2), *very*
4142 mûwçabbâh (1), *backside; fold*
4150 môwʻêd (10), *place of meeting*
4390 mâlêʼ (5), to *fill*
4394 millûʼ (4), *fulfilling; setting; consecration*
4427 mâlak (1), to *reign as king*
4483 mᵉnâʼ (Ch.) (3), to *count, appoint*
4487 mânâh (1), to *allot*
4853 massâʼ (1), *burden*
5079 niddâh (1), *time of menstrual impurity*
5117 nûwach (2), to *rest; to settle* down
5128 nûwaʻ (1), to *waver*
5183 nachath (1), *descent; quiet*
5258 nâçak (2), to *pour*
5265 nâçaʼ (16), *start*
5324 nâtsab (18), to *station*
5329 nâtsach (4), to *be eminent*
5375 nâsâʼ (9), to *lift up*
5414 nâthan (103), to *give*
5473 çûwg (1), to *hem in*
5496 çûwth (1), to *stimulate; to seduce*
5526 çâkak (1), to *entwine; to fence in*
5564 çâmak (1), to *lean* upon; *take hold* of
5774 ʻûwph (1), to *cover, to fly; to faint*
5927 ʻâlâh (2), to *ascend, be high, mount*
5975 ʻâmad (44), to *stand*
6186 ʼârak (1), to set in a row, i.e. *arrange,*
6187 ʼêrek (1), *pile, equipment, estimate*
6213 ʼâsâh (3), to *do*
6395 pâlâh (1), to *distinguish*
6485 pâqad (7), to *care*
6496 pâqîyd (1), *superintendent, officer*
6584 pâshaṭ (1), to *strip*
6605 pâthach (1), to *open*
6845 tsâphan (1), to *hide*
6965 qûwm (28), to *rise*
6966 qûwm (Ch.) (11), to *rise*
7311 rûwm (7), to *rise*
7313 rûwm (Ch.) (1), *elation, arrogance*
7392 râkab (2), to *ride*
7660 shâbats (1), to *interweave*
7682 sâgab (1), to *be, make lofty; be safe*
7725 shûwb (1), to *return*
7737 shâvâh (1), to *level*
7760 sûwm (129), to *put*
7761 sûwm (Ch.) (2), to *put, place*
7896 shîyth (22), to *place*
7931 shâkan (3), to *reside*

7947 shâlab (1), to *make equidistant*
7971 shâlach (5), to *send away*
8239 shâphath (2), to *put*
8371 shâthath (1), to *place,* i.e. *array; to lie*
8427 tâvâh (1), to *mark* out; *imprint*
321 anagō (1), to *lead up; to bring out*
345 anakĕimai (1), to *recline at a meal*
377 anapiptō (1), *lie down, lean back*
392 anatassŏmai (1), to *arrange*
461 anŏrthŏō (1), to *strengthen, build*
584 apŏdĕiknumi (1), to *demonstrate*
630 apŏluō (2), to *relieve, release; divorce*
649 apŏstĕllō (1), to *send out* on a mission
816 atĕnizō (1), to *gaze*
968 bēma (1), *tribunal platform; judging place*
1299 diatassō (1), to *institute, prescribe*
1325 didōmi (1), to *give*
1369 dichazō (1), to *sunder,* i.e. *alienate*
1416 dunō (1), to *have the sun set*
1847 ĕxŏudĕnŏō (1), to *be treated with contempt*
1848 ĕxŏuthĕnĕō (3), to *treat with contempt*
1913 ĕpibibazō (3), to *cause to mount*
1930 ĕpidiŏrthŏō (1), to *set in order*
1940 ĕpikathizō (1), to *seat upon*
2007 ĕpitithēmi (3), to *impose*
2064 ĕrchŏmai (1), to *go*
2350 thŏrubĕō (1), to *clamor; start a riot*
2476 histēmi (11), to *stand, establish*
2521 kathēmai (1), to *sit down; to remain, reside*
2523 kathizō (6), to *seat down, dwell*
2525 kathistēmi (1), to *designate, constitute*
2749 kĕimai (6), to *lie outstretched*
3908 paratithēmi (9), to *present something*
4060 pĕritithēmi (1), to *present*
4270 prŏgraphō (1), to *announce, prescribe*
4295 prŏkĕimai (4), to be *present to the mind*
4388 prŏtithēmai (1), to *place before*
4741 stērizō (1), to *turn resolutely; to confirm*
4776 sugkathizō (1), to *give, take a seat with*
4900 sunĕlaunō (1), to *drive together*
4972 sphragizō (2), to *stamp* with a signet

5002 taktŏs (1), *appointed or stated*
5021 tassō (1), to *arrange, assign*
5087 tithēmi (5), to *place*
5394 phlŏgizō (1), to *cause a blaze, ignite*
5426 phrŏnĕō (1), to be *mentally disposed*

SETH
8352 Shêth (7), *put*
4589 Sēth (1), *put*

SETHUR
5639 Çᵉthûwr (1), *hidden*

SETTER
2604 kataggĕlĕus (1), *proclaimer*

SETTEST
4916 mishlôwach (3), *sending* out
5324 nâtsab (1), to *station*
7760 sûwm (1), to *put*
7896 shîyth (1), to *place*

SETTETH
3320 yâtsab (1), to *station, offer, continue*
3427 yâshab (1), to *dwell, to remain; to settle*
3559 kûwn (1), to *set up: establish, fix, prepare*
3857 lâhaṭ (1), to *blaze*
5265 nâçaʼ (2), *start*
5375 nâsâʼ (1), to *lift up*
5496 çûwth (1), to *stimulate; to seduce*
5927 ʼâlâh (2), to *ascend, be high, mount*
5975 ʼâmad (2), to *stand*
6966 qûwm (Ch.) (2), to *rise*
7034 qâlâh (1), to be *light*
7311 rûwm (1), to *raise*
7760 sûwm (1), to *put*
7918 shâkak (1), to *lay a* trap; to *allay*
2007 ĕpitithēmi (1), to *impose*
2476 histēmi (1), to *stand*
5394 phlŏgizō (1), to *cause a blaze,* i.e. *ignite*

SETTING
5414 nâthan (1), to *give*
1416 dunō (1), to *have the sun set*
3326 mĕta (1), *with*

SETTINGS
4396 millûʼâh (1), *setting*

SETTLE
3427 yâshab (1), to *settle*
5835 ʼăzârâh (6), *enclosure; border*
5975 ʼâmad (1), to *stand*
2311 thĕmĕliŏō (1), to *erect; to consolidate*
5087 tithēmi (1), to *place*

SETTLED
2883 ṭâbaʼ (1), to *sink*
4349 mâkôwn (1), *place*
5324 nâtsab (1), to *station*
5975 ʼâmad (1), to *stand*
7087 qâphâʼ (1), to *thicken, congeal*
8252 shâqaṭ (1), to *repose*
1476 hĕdraiŏs (1), *immovable; steadfast*

SETTLEST
5181 nâchath (1), to *sink*

SEVEN
3598 Kîymâh (1), *cluster* of stars, the *Pleiades*
7651 sheba' (346), *seven*
7655 shibʻâh (Ch.) (6), *satiety*
7658 shibʻânâh (1), *seven*
7659 shibʻâthayim (1), *seven-fold*
2033 hĕpta (80), *seven*
2034 hĕptakis (4), *seven times*
2035 hĕptakischiliŏi (1), *seven times a thousand*

SEVENFOLD
7659 shibʻâthayim (6), *seven-fold*

SEVENS
7651 sheba' (2), *seven*

SEVENTEEN
7651+6240 sheba' (9), *seven*
7657+7651 shibʻîym (1), *seventy*

SEVENTEENTH
7651+6240 sheba' (6), *seven*

SEVENTH
7637 shᵉbîyʻîy (96), *seventh*
7651 sheba' (13), *seven*
1442 hĕbdŏmŏs (9), *seventh*
2035 hĕptakischiliŏi (1), *seven times a thousand*

SEVENTY
7657 shibʻîym (58), *seventy*
1440 hĕbdŏmĕkŏnta (2), *seventy*
1441 hĕbdŏmĕkŏntakis (1), *seventy times*

SEVER
914 bâdal (1), to *divide, separate, distinguish*
6395 pâlâh (2), to *distinguish*
873 aphŏrizō (1), to *limit, exclude, appoint*

SEVERAL
2669 chôphshûwth (2), *prostration by sickness*
2398 idiŏs (1), *private*

SEVERALLY
2398 idiŏs (1), *private*

SEVERED
914 bâdal (2), to *divide*
6504 pârad (1), to *spread*

SEVERITY
663 apŏtŏmia (2), *rigor, severity*

SEW
8609 tâphar (2), to *sew*

SEWED
8609 tâphar (2), to *sew*

SEWEST
2950 ṭâphal (1), to *impute* falsely

SEWETH
1976 ĕpirrhaptō (1), to *stitch upon*

SHAALABBIN
8169 Sha'albîym (1),
fox-holes

SHAALBIM
8169 Sha'albîym (2),
fox-holes

SHAALBONITE
8170 Sha'albônîy (2),
Shaalbonite

SHAAPH
8174 Sha'aph (2),
fluctuation

SHAARAIM
8189 Sha'ărayim (2),
double gates

SHAASHGAZ
8190 Sha'ashgaz (1),
Shaashgaz

SHABBETHAI
7678 Shabbᵉthay (3),
restful

SHACHIA
7634 Shobyâh (1),
captivation

SHADE
6783 tseᵐîythûth (1),
perpetually

SHADOW
2927 ṭᵉlal (Ch.) (1), to
cover with shade
6738 tsêl (47), *shade*
6752 tsêlel (1), *shade*
6757 tsalmâveth (16),
shade of death
644 apŏskiasma (1),
shading off
4639 skia (7), *shade*

SHADOWING
6751 tsâlal (1), to *shade*;
to *grow dark*
6767 tseᵉlâtsal (1),
whirring of wings
2683 kataskiazō (1), to
cover, overshadow

SHADOWS
6752 tsêlel (3), *shade*

SHADRACH
7714 Shadrak (1),
Shadrak
7715 Shadrak (Ch.) (14),
Shadrak

SHADY
6628 tse'el (2), *lotus* tree

SHAFT
2671 chêts (1), *shaft*
3409 yârêk (3), *shank*

SHAGE
7681 Shâgê' (1), *erring*

SHAHAR
7837 shachar (1), *dawn*

SHAHARAIM
7842 Shachărayim (1),
double dawn

SHAHAZIMAH
7831 Shachatsôwm (1),
proudly

SHAKE
2554 châmaç (1), to *be
violent*; to *maltreat*
4571 mâ'ad (1), to *waver*
5128 nûwa' (2), to *waver*
5130 nûwph (5), to
quiver, vibrate, rock

5287 nâ'ar (4), to *tumble*
5426 neᵉthar (Ch.) (1), to
tear off; to *shake off*
6206 'ârats (2), to *dread*
6342 pâchad (1), to *fear*
7264 râgaz (1), to *quiver*
7363 râchaph (1), to
brood; to be relaxed
7493 râ'ash (14), to *quake*
660 apŏtinassō (1), to
brush off, shake off
1621 ĕktinassō (2), to
shake violently
4531 salĕuō (1), to *waver*
4579 sĕiō (2), to *agitate*

SHAKED
5128 nûwa' (1), to *waver*

SHAKEN
1607 gâ'ash (1), to *agitate*
5086 nâdaph (1), to
disperse, be windblown
5110 nûwd (1), to *waver*
5128 nûwa' (3), to *waver*
5287 nâ'ar (2), to *tumble*
6327 pûwts (1), to *dash*
7477 râ'al (1), to *reel*
4531 salĕuō (11), to *waver*
4579 sĕiō (1), to *agitate*

SHAKETH
2342 chûwl (2), to *writhe*
4131 môwṭ (1), to *shake*
5130 nûwph (2), to *rock*
5287 nâ'ar (1), to *tumble*
7264 râgaz (1), to *quiver*

SHAKING
4493 mânôwd (1), *nod*
5363 nôqeph (2),
threshing of olives
7494 ra'ash (3),
vibration, bounding
8573 teᵉnûwphâh (2),
undulation of offerings

SHALEM
8003 shâlêm (1),
complete; friendly; safe

SHALIM
8171 Sha'ălîym (1), *foxes*

SHALISHA
8031 Shâlîshâh (1),
trebled land

SHALLECHETH
7996 Shalleketh (1),
felling of trees

SHALLUM
7967 Shallûwm (27),
retribution

SHALLUN
7968 Shallûwn (1),
retribution

SHALMAI
8014 Salmay (1), *clothed*
8073 Shamlay (1), *clothed*

SHALMAN
8020 Shalman (1),
Shalman

SHALMANESER
8022 Shalman'eçer (2),
Shalmaneser

SHAMA
8091 Shâmâ' (1), *obedient*

SHAMBLES
3111 makĕllŏn (1),
butcher's stall

SHAME
954 bûwsh (9), be
ashamed
955 bûwshâh (4), *shame*
1317 boshnâh (1),
shamefulness
1322 bôsheth (20), *shame*
2616 châçad (1), to
reprove, shame
2659 châphêr (4), to *be
ashamed*
2781 cherpâh (3),
contumely, disgrace
3637 kâlam (6), to *taunt*
3639 keᵉlimmâh (20),
disgrace, scorn
3640 keᵉlimmûwth (1),
disgrace, scorn
6172 'ervâh (1), *disgrace*
7036 qâlôwn (13),
disgrace
8103 shimtsâh (1),
scornful whispering
149 aischrŏn (3),
shameful thing
152 aischunē (5), *shame*
808 aschēmŏsunē (1),
indecency; shame
818 atimazō (1), to
maltreat, dishonor
819 atimia (1), *disgrace*
1788 ĕntrĕpō (1), to
respect; to confound
1791 ĕntrŏpē (2), *shame*
2617 kataischunō (1), to
disgrace or shame
3856 paradĕigmatizō (1),
to *expose to infamy*

SHAMED
937 bûwz (1), *disrespect*
954 bûwsh (1), to *be
ashamed*
3001 yâbêsh (1), to *dry
up; to wither*
8106 Shemer (1),
settlings of wine, *dregs*

SHAMEFACEDNESS
127 aidōs (1), *modesty*

SHAMEFUL
1322 bôsheth (1), *shame*
7022 qîyqâlôwn (1),
disgrace

SHAMEFULLY
3001 yâbêsh (1), to *dry
up; to wither*
818 atimazō (1), to
maltreat, dishonor
821 atimŏō (1), to
maltreat, disgrace
5195 hubrizō (1), to
exercise violence, abuse

SHAMELESSLY
1540 gâlâh (1), to *denude*

SHAMER
8106 Shemer (2),
settlings of wine, *dregs*

SHAMETH
3637 kâlam (1), to *taunt*

SHAMGAR
8044 Shamgar (2),
Shamgar

SHAMHUTH
8049 Shamhûwth (1),
desolation

SHAMIR
8053 Shâmûwr (1),
observed
8069 Shâmîyr (3), *thorn*
or (poss.) *diamond*

SHAMMA
8037 Shammâ' (1),
desolation

SHAMMAH
8048 Shammâh (8),
desolation

SHAMMAI
8060 Shammay (6),
destructive

SHAMMOTH
8054 Shammôwth (1),
ruins

SHAMMUA
8051 Shammûwa' (4),
renowned

SHAMMUAH
8051 Shammûwa' (1),
renowned

SHAMSHERAI
8125 Shamsheᵉray (1),
sun-like

SHAPE
1491 ĕidŏs (2), *form,
appearance, sight*

SHAPEN
2342 chûwl (1), to *dance,
whirl*; to *writhe* in pain

SHAPES
3667 hŏmŏiōma (1), *form*

SHAPHAM
8223 Shâphâm (1), *baldly*

SHAPHAN
8227 shâphân (30), *hyrax*

SHAPHAT
8202 Shâphâṭ (8), *judge*

SHAPHER
8234 Shepher (2), *beauty*

SHARAI
8298 Shâray (1), *hostile*

SHARAIM
8189 Sha'ărayim (1),
double gates

SHARAR
8325 Shârâr (1), *hostile*

SHARE
4282 machăresheth (1),
(poss.) *hoe*

SHAREZER
8272 Shar'etser (2),
Sharetser

SHARON
8289 Shârôwn (6), *plain*

SHARONITE
8290 Shârôwnîy (1),
Sharonite

SHARP
2299 chad (4), *sharp
sword*
2303 chaddûwd (1),
pointed, jagged
2742 chârûwts (2),
threshing-sledge
3913 lâṭash (1), to
sharpen; to pierce
6697 tsûwr (2), *rock*
6864 tsôr (1), flint-*stone
knife*

S

8127 shên (2), *tooth*
8150 shânan (4), to *pierce*
3691 ŏxus (7), *sharp*

SHARPEN
3913 lâṭash (1), to
  sharpen; to *pierce*
5324 nâtsab (1), to *station*

SHARPENED
2300 châdad (3), to *be,
  make sharp; severe*
8150 shânan (1), to
  pierce; to *inculcate*

SHARPENETH
2300 châdad (2), to *be,
  make sharp; severe*
3913 lâṭash (1), to
  sharpen; to *pierce*

SHARPER
5114 tŏmŏtĕrŏs (1), *more
  keen*

SHARPLY
2394 chozqâh (1),
  vehemence, harshness
664 apŏtŏmōs (1),
  abruptly, peremptorily

SHARPNESS
664 apŏtŏmōs (1),
  abruptly, peremptorily

SHARUHEN
8287 Shârûwchen (1),
  abode of pleasure

SHASHAI
8343 Shâshay (1), *whitish*

SHASHAK
8349 Shâshaq (2),
  pedestrian

SHAUL
7586 Shâ'ûwl (7), *asked*

SHAULITES
7587 Shâ'ûwlîy (1),
  Shalite

SHAVE
1548 gâlach (12), to *shave*
5674+8593 'âbar (1), to
  cross over; to *transition*
3587 xuraŏ (1), to *shave*

SHAVED
1494 gâzaz (1), to *shave*
1548 gâlach (3), to *shave*

SHAVEH
7740 Shâvêh (1), *plain*
7741 Shâvêh
  Qiryâthayim (1), *plain
  of a double city*

SHAVEN
1548 gâlach (5), to *shave*
3587 xuraŏ (2), to *shave*

SHAVSHA
7798 Shavshâ' (1), *joyful*

SHEAF
485 'ălummâh (2), *sheaf*
5995 'âmîyr (1), *bunch*
6016 'ômer (6), *measure*

SHEAL
7594 Shë'âl (1), *request*

SHEALTIEL
7597 Shë'altîy'êl (9), *I
  have asked God*

SHEAR
1494 gâzaz (4), to *shear*

SHEAR-JASHUB
7610 Shë'âr Yâshûwb (1),
  remnant will return

SHEARER
2751 kĕirŏ (1), to *shear*

SHEARERS
1494 gâzaz (3), to *shear*

SHEARIAH
8187 Shë'aryâh (2),
  Jehovah has stormed

SHEARING
1044 Bêyth 'Êqed (1),
  house of (the) *binding*
1044+7462 Bêyth 'Êqed
  (1), *house of* (the)
  binding
1494 gâzaz (1), to *shear*

SHEATH
5084 nâdân (1), *sheath*
8593 ta'ar (6), *scabbard*
2336 thĕkĕ (1), *scabbard*

SHEAVES
485 'ălummâh (3), *sheaf*
5995 'âmîyr (2), *bunch*
6016 'ômer (2), *measure*
6194 'ârêm (1), *sheaf*

SHEBA
7614 Shëbâ' (22), *Sheba*
7652 Sheba' (10), *seven*

SHEBAH
7656 Shib'âh (1), *seventh*

SHEBAM
7643 Sᵉbâm (1), *spice*

SHEBANIAH
7645 Shᵉbanyâh (7),
  Jehovah has prospered

SHEBARIM
7671 Shᵉbârîym (1), *ruins*

SHEBER
7669 Sheber (1), *crushing*

SHEBNA
7644 Shebnâ' (9), *growth*

SHEBUEL
7619 Shᵉbûw'êl (3),
  captive (or *returned) of
  God*

SHECANIAH
7935 Shᵉkanyâh (2),
  Jehovah has dwelt

SHECHANIAH
7935 Shᵉkanyâh (8),
  Jehovah has dwelt

SHECHEM
7927 Shᵉkem (45), *ridge*
7928 Shekem (17),
  shoulder

SHECHEM'S
7927 Shᵉkem (2), *ridge*

SHECHEMITES
7930 Shikmîy (1),
  Shikmite

SHED
5064 nâgar (1), to *pour*
7760 sûwm (1), to *put*
8210 shâphak (35), to
  spill forth; to *expend;*
1632 ĕkchĕŏ (11), to *pour*

SHEDDER
8210 shâphak (1), to *spill
  forth;* to *expend*

SHEDDETH
8210 shâphak (2), to *spill*

SHEDDING
130 haimatĕkchusia (1),
  pouring of blood

SHEDEUR
7707 Shᵉdêy'ûwr (5),
  spreader of light

SHEEP
3532 kebes (2), *young
  ram*
3775 keseb (9), *young
  ram sheep*
6629 tsô'n (111), *flock of
  sheep or goats*
6792 tsônê' (2), *flock*
7353 râchêl (2), *ewe*
7716 seh (16), *sheep*
4262 prŏbatikŏs (1),
  Sheep Gate
4263 prŏbatŏn (39), *sheep*

SHEEP'S
4263 prŏbatŏn (1), *sheep*

SHEEPCOTE
5116 nâveh (2), *at home;
  lovely; home*

SHEEPCOTES
1448+6629 gᵉdêrâh (1),
  enclosure for flocks

SHEEPFOLD
833+4263 aulē (1), *house;
  courtyard; sheepfold*

SHEEPFOLDS
1488+6629 gêz (1), *shorn
  fleece;* mown *grass*
4356+6629 miklâ'âh (1),
  sheep or goat pen
4942 mishpâth (1), *pair
  of stalls for cattle*

SHEEPMASTER
5349 nôqêd (1), *owner or
  tender of sheep*

SHEEPSHEARERS
1494 gâzaz (2), to *shear;
  shave; destroy*
1494+6629 gâzaz (1), to
  shear; shave; destroy

SHEEPSKINS
3374 mēlōtē (1),
  sheep-skin

SHEET
3607 ŏthŏnē (2), *linen
  sail cloth*

SHEETS
5466 çâdîyn (2), *shirt*

SHEHARIAH
7841 Shᵉcharyâh (1),
  Jehovah has sought

SHEKEL
1235 beqa' (1), *half
  shekel*
8255 sheqel (41),
  standard weight

SHEKELS
8255 sheqel (45),
  standard weight

SHELAH
7956 Shêlâh (10), *request*
7974 Shelach (1), *spear*

SHELANITES
8024 Shêlânîy (1),
  Shelanite

SHELEMIAH
8018 Shelemyâh (10),
  *thank-offering of
  Jehovah*

SHELEPH
8026 Sheleph (2), *extract*

SHELESH
8028 Shelesh (1), *triplet*

SHELOMI
8015 Shᵉlômîy (1),
  peaceable

SHELOMITH
8013 Shᵉlômôwth (4),
  pacifications
8019 Shᵉlômîyth (5),
  peaceableness

SHELOMOTH
8013 Shᵉlômôwth (1),
  pacifications

SHELTER
4268 machăçeh (2),
  shelter; refuge

SHELUMIEL
8017 Shᵉlûmîy'êl (5),
  peace of God

SHEM
8035 Shêm (17), *name*

SHEMA
8087 Shema' (6), *heard*

SHEMAAH
8094 Shᵉmâ'âh (1),
  annunciation

SHEMAIAH
8098 Shᵉma'yâh (40),
  Jehovah has heard

SHEMARIAH
8114 Shᵉmaryâh (4),
  Jehovah has guarded

SHEMEBER
8038 Shem'êber (1),
  illustrious

SHEMER
8106 Shemer (2),
  settlings of wine, dregs

SHEMIDA
8061 Shᵉmîydâ' (2),
  name of knowing

SHEMIDAH
8061 Shᵉmîydâ' (1),
  name of knowing

SHEMIDAITES
8062 Shᵉmîydâ'îy (1),
  Shemidaite

SHEMININH
8067 shᵉmîynîyth (3),
  (poss.) *eight*-stringed
  lyre

SHEMIRAMOTH
8070 Shᵉmîyrâmôwth
  (4), *name of heights*

SHEMUEL
8050 Shᵉmûw'êl (3),
  heard of God

SHEN
8129 Shên (1), *crag*

SHENAZAR
8137 Shen'atstsar (1),
  Shenatstsar

SHENIR
8149 Shᵉnîyr (2), *peak*

SHEPHAM
8221 Sheᵖhâm (2), *bare*

SHEPHATIAH
8203 Sheᵖhaṭyâh (13), *Jehovah has judged*

SHEPHERD
7462 râ'âh (27), to *tend a flock, i.e. pasture it*
7462+6629 râ'âh (1), to *tend a flock*
7473 rô'îy (1), *shepherd*
750 archipŏimēn (1), *head shepherd*
4166 pŏimēn (13), *shepherd*

SHEPHERD'S
7462 râ'âh (1), to *tend a flock, i.e. pasture it*
7473 rô'îy (1), *shepherd*

SHEPHERDS
7462 râ'âh (31), to *tend a flock, i.e. pasture it*
7462+6629 râ'âh (2), to *tend a flock*
4166 pŏimēn (4), *shepherd*

SHEPHERDS'
7462 râ'âh (1), to *tend a flock, i.e. pasture it*

SHEPHI
8195 Sheᵖhôw (1), *baldness*

SHEPHO
8195 Sheᵖhôw (1), *baldness*

SHEPHUPHAN
8197 Sheᵖhûwphâm (1), *serpent-like*

SHERAH
7609 She'ĕrâh (1), *kindred by blood*

SHERD
2789 cheres (1), *pottery*

SHERDS
2789 cheres (1), *pottery*

SHEREBIAH
8274 Shêrêbyâh (8), *Jehovah has brought heat*

SHERESH
8329 Sheresh (1), *root*

SHEREZER
8272 Shar'etser (1), *Sharetser*

SHERIFFS
8614 tiphtay (Ch.) (2), *lawyer, officer*

SHESHACH
8347 Shêshak (2), *Sheshak*

SHESHAI
8344 Shêshay (3), *whitish*

SHESHAN
8348 Shêshân (4), *lily*

SHESHBAZZAR
8339 Shêshbatstsar (4), *Sheshbatstsar*

SHETH
8352 Shêth (2), *put, i.e. substituted*

SHETHAR
8369 Shêthâr (1), *Shethar*

SHETHAR-BOZNAI
8370 Sheᵗhar Bôwzeᵉnay (4), *Shethar-Bozenai*

SHEVA
7724 Sheᵛâ' (2), *false*

SHEW
1319 bâsar (3), to *announce* (good news)
1540 gâlâh (5), to *reveal*
1971 hakkârâh (1), *respect, i.e. partiality*
2324 chăvâ' (Ch.) (13), to *show*
2331 châvâh (5), to *show*
3045 yâda' (12), to *know*
3313 yâpha' (1), to *shine*
5046 nâgad (37), to *announce*
5414 nâthan (5), to *give*
5608 çâphar (5), to *inscribe; to enumerate*
6213 'âsâh (21), to *do*
6754 tselem (1), *phantom; idol*
7200 râ'âh (27), to *see*
7760 sûwm (1), to *put*
7896 shîyth (1), to *place*
8085 shâma' (3), to *hear*
312 anaggĕllō (4), to *announce in detail*
322 anadĕiknumi (1), to *indicate, appoint*
518 apaggĕllō (5), to *announce, proclaim*
1165 dĕigmatizō (1), to *exhibit, expose*
1166 dĕiknuō (20), to *show, make known*
1325 didōmi (3), to *give*
1334 diēgĕŏmai (1), to *relate fully, describe*
1731 ĕndĕiknumi (7), to *show, display*
1754 ĕnĕrgĕō (2), to be *active, efficient, work*
1804 ĕxaggĕllō (1), to *declare, proclaim*
1925 ĕpidĕiknumi (6), to *exhibit, call attention to*
2097 ĕuaggĕlizō (1), to *announce good news*
2146 ĕuprŏsōpĕō (1), to *make a good display*
2151 ĕusĕbĕō (1), to *put religion into practice*
2605 kataggĕllō (3), to *proclaim, promulgate*
2698 katatithēmi (1), to *place down, to deposit*
3004 lĕgō (1), to *say*
3056 lŏgŏs (1), *word, matter, thing; Word*
3377 mēnuō (1), to *report, declare*
3936 paristēmi (1), to *stand beside, present*
4392 prŏphasis (1), *pretext, excuse*
5263 hupŏdĕiknumi (2), to *exemplify*
5319 phanĕrŏō (1), to *render apparent*

SHEWBREAD
3899+4635 lechem (4), *food, bread*
3899+6440 lechem (6), *food, bread*

4635 ma'ăreketh (3), *pile of loaves, arrangement*
6440 pânîym (1), *face*
740+4286 artos (3), *loaf of bread*
4286+740 prŏthĕsis (1), *setting forth*

SHEWED
1540 gâlâh (2), to *reveal*
3045 yâda' (5), to *know*
3190 yâṭab (1), to be, *make well*
3384 yârâh (1), to *throw*
5046 nâgad (18), to *announce*
5186 nâṭâh (1), to *stretch*
5414 nâthan (1), to *give*
6213 'âsâh (17), to *do*
6567 pârash (1), to *separate; to disperse*
7200 râ'âh (37), to *see*
7760 sûwm (1), to *put*
8085 shâma' (4), to *hear*
312 anaggĕllō (2), to *announce in detail*
518 apaggĕllō (6), to *announce, proclaim*
1096 ginŏmai (1), to be *show, make known*
1166 dĕiknuō (8), to *show, make known*
1213 dēlŏō (1), to *make plain by words*
1325+1717+1096 didōmi (1), to *give*
1718 ĕmphanizō (1), to *show forth*
1731 ĕndĕiknumi (1), to *show, display*
1925 ĕpidĕiknumi (1), to *exhibit, call attention to*
3170 mĕgalunō (1), to *increase or extol*
3377 mēnuō (2), to *report, declare*
3700 ŏptanŏmai (1), to *appear*
3930 parĕchō (1), to *hold near, i.e. to present*
3936 paristēmi (1), to *stand beside, present*
4160 pŏiĕō (4), to *make*
4293 prŏkataggĕllō (2), to *predict, promise*
5268 hupŏzugiŏn (1), *donkey*
5319 phanĕrŏō (4), to *render apparent*

SHEWEDST
5414 nâthan (1), to *give*
7200 râ'âh (1), to *see*

SHEWEST
6213 'âsâh (1), to *do*
1166 dĕiknuō (1), to *show*
4160 pŏiĕō (1), to *make*

SHEWETH
1540+241 gâlâh (2), to *denude; uncover*
2331 châvâh (2), to *show*
5046 nâgad (6), to *announce*
6213 'âsâh (2), to *do*
7200 râ'âh (3), to *see*
1166 dĕiknuō (2), to *show*
1658 ĕlĕuthĕrŏs (2), *unrestrained*

SHEWING
263 'achăvâh (Ch.) (1), *solution*
5608 çâphar (1), to *inscribe; to enumerate*
6213 'âsâh (2), to *do*
6692 tsûwts (1), to *twinkle, i.e. glance*
323 anadĕixis (1), act of *public exhibition*
584 apŏdĕiknumi (1), to *demonstrate*
1731 ĕndĕiknumi (2), to *show, display*
1925 ĕpidĕiknumi (2), to *exhibit, call attention to*
3930 parĕchō (1), to *hold near, i.e. to present*

SHIBBOLETH
7641 shibbôl (1), *stream; ear of grain*

SHIBMAH
7643 Seᵇbâm (1), *spice*

SHICRON
7942 Shikkeᵉrôwn (1), *drunkenness*

SHIELD
3591 kîydôwn (2), *dart*
4043 mâgên (33), small *shield (buckler)*
6793 tsinnâh (9), large *shield; piercing cold*
2375 thurĕŏs (1), large *door-shaped shield*

SHIELDS
4043 mâgên (15), small *shield (buckler)*
6793 tsinnâh (1), large *shield; piercing cold*
7982 sheleṭ (7), *shield*

SHIGGAION
7692 Shiggâyôwn (1), *dithyramb or poem*

SHIGIONOTH
7692 Shiggâyôwn (1), *dithyramb or poem*

SHIHON
7866 Shî'yôwn (1), *ruin*

SHIHOR
7883 Shîychôwr (1), *dark, i.e. turbid*

SHIHOR-LIBNATH
7884 Shîychôwr Libnâth (1), *darkish whiteness*

SHILHI
7977 Shilchîy (2), *armed*

SHILHIM
7978 Shilchîym (1), *javelins or sprouts*

SHILLEM
8006 Shillêm (2), *requital*

SHILLEMITES
8016 Shillêmîy (1), *Shilemite*

SHILOAH
7975 Shilôach (1), *small stream*

SHILOH
7886 Shîylôh (1), *tranquil*
7887 Shîylôh (32), *tranquil*

SHILONI
8023 Shîlônîy (1), *Shiloni*

S

SHILONITE
7888 Shiylôwnîy (5),
Shilonite

SHILONITES
7888 Shiylôwnîy (1),
Shilonite

SHILSHAH
8030 Shilshâh (1),
triplication

SHIMEA
8092 Shim'â' (4),
annunciation

SHIMEAH
8039 Shim'âh (1),
obedient
8092 Shim'â' (1),
annunciation
8093 Shim'âh (2),
annunciation

SHIMEAM
8043 Shim'âm (1),
obedient

SHIMEATH
8100 Shim'âth (2),
annunciation

SHIMEATHITES
8101 Shim'âthiy (1),
Shimathite

SHIMEI
8096 Shim'iy (41), famous
8097 Shim'iy (1), Shimite

SHIMEON
8095 Shim'ôwn (1),
hearing

SHIMHI
8096 Shim'iy (1), famous

SHIMI
8096 Shim'iy (1), famous

SHIMITES
8097 Shim'iy (1), Shimite

SHIMMA
8092 Shim'â' (1),
annunciation

SHIMON
7889 Shîymôwn (1),
desert

SHIMRATH
8119 Shimrâth (1),
guardship

SHIMRI
8113 Shimriy (3),
watchful

SHIMRITH
8116 Shimrîyth (1),
female guard

SHIMROM
8110 Shimrôwn (1),
guardianship

SHIMRON
8110 Shimrôwn (4),
guardianship

SHIMRON-MERON
8112 Shimrôwn Mᵉr'ôwn
(1), guard of lashing

SHIMRONITES
8117 Shimrônîy (1),
Shimronite

SHIMSHAI
8124 Shimshay (Ch.) (4),
sunny

SHINAB
8134 Shin'âb (1), father
has turned

SHINAR
8152 Shin'âr (7), Shinar

SHINE
215 'ôwr (11), to be
luminous
1984 hâlal (1), to shine
2094 zâhar (1), to
enlighten
3313 yâpha' (4), to shine
5050 nâgahh (3), to
illuminate
5774 'ûwph (1), to cover
6245 'âshath (1), to be
sleek; to excogitate
6670 tsâhal (1), to be
cheerful; to sound
826 augazō (1), to beam
forth
1584 ĕklampō (1), to be
resplendent, shine
2989 lampō (3), to
radiate brilliancy
5316 phainō (3), to shine

SHINED
215 'ôwr (1), to be
luminous
1984 hâlal (2), to shine
3313 yâpha' (2), to shine
5050 nâgahh (1), to
illuminate
2989 lampō (2), to
radiate brilliancy
4015 pĕriastraptō (1), to
envelop in light, shine

SHINETH
166 'âhal (1), to be bright
215 'ôwr (2), to be
luminous
2989 lampō (1), to radiate
5316 phainō (5), to shine

SHINING
5051 nôgahh (6),
brilliancy
796 astrapē (1),
lightning; light's glare
797 astraptō (1), to flash
4034 pĕrilampō (1), to
shine all around
4744 stilbō (1), to gleam
5316 phainō (1), to shine

SHIP
591 'ŏnîyâh (4), ship
5600 çᵉphîynâh (1),
sea-going vessel
6716 tsîy (1), ship
3490 nauklērŏs (1), ship
captain
3491 naus (1), boat
4142 plŏiariŏn (2), small
boat
4143 plŏiŏn (58), ship

SHIPHI
8230 Shiph'îy (1), copious

SHIPHMITE
8225 Shiphmîy (1),
Shiphmite

SHIPHRAH
8236 Shiphrâh (1),
brightness of skies

SHIPHTAN
8204 Shiphṭân (1),
judge-like

SHIPMASTER
7227+2259 rab (1), great
2942 kubĕrnētēs (1),
helmsman, captain

SHIPMEN
582+591 'ĕnôwsh (1),
man; person, human
3492 nautēs (2), sailor

SHIPPING
4143 plŏiŏn (1), ship

SHIPS
591 'ŏnîyâh (26), ship
6716 tsîy (3), ship
4142 plŏiariŏn (1), small
boat
4143 plŏiŏn (8), boat

SHIPWRECK
3489 nauagĕō (2), to be
shipwrecked

SHISHA
7894 Shîyshâ' (1),
whiteness

SHISHAK
7895 Shîyshaq (7),
Shishak

SHITRAI
7861 Shiṭray (1),
magisterial

SHITTAH
7848 shiṭṭâh (1), acacia

SHITTIM
7848 shiṭṭâh (27), acacia
7851 Shiṭṭîym (5), acacia

SHIVERS
4937 suntribō (1), to
crush completely

SHIZA
7877 Shîyzâ' (1), Shiza

SHOA
7772 Shôwa' (1), rich

SHOBAB
7727 Shôwbâb (4),
rebellious

SHOBACH
7731 Shôwbâk (2), (poss.)
thicket

SHOBAI
7630 Shôbay (2), captor

SHOBAL
7732 Shôwbâl (9),
overflowing

SHOBEK
7733 Shôwbêq (1),
forsaking

SHOBI
7629 Shôbîy (1), captor

SHOCHO
7755 Sôwkôh (1), hedged

SHOCHOH
7755 Sôwkôh (2), hedged

SHOCK
1430 gâdîysh (1), stack of
sheaves, shock of grain

SHOCKS
1430 gâdîysh (1), stack of
sheaves, shock of grain

SHOCO
7755 Sôwkôh (1), hedged

SHOD
5274 nâ'al (2), to fasten
up, to put on sandals

SHOES
4515 man'âl (1), bolt on
gate
5275 na'al (11), sandal
5266 hupŏdēma (9),
sandal

SHOHAM
7719 Shôham (1), beryl

SHOMER
7763 Shôwmêr (2),
keeper

SHONE
2224 zârach (1), to rise;
to be bright
7160 qâran (3), to shine
4015 pĕriastraptō (1), to
envelop in light, shine
4034 pĕrilampō (1), to
shine all around
5316 phainō (1), to shine

SHOOK
1607 gâ'ash (3), to
agitate violently, shake
5287 nâ'ar (1), to tumble
7264 râgaz (1), to quiver
7493 râ'ash (2), to quake
8058 shâmaṭ (1), to jostle
660 apŏtinassō (1), to
brush off, shake off
1621 ĕktinassō (2), to
shake violently
4531 salĕuō (1), to waver

SHOOT
1272 bârach (1), to flee
1869 dârak (1), to tread;
to string a bow
3034 yâdâh (1), to throw
3384 yârâh (10), to
throw, shoot an arrow
5414 nâthan (2), to give
6362 pâṭar (1), to burst
through; to emit
7971 shâlach (1), to send
away
4261 prŏballō (1), to push
to the front, germinate

SHOOTERS
3384 yârâh (1), to throw,
shoot an arrow

SHOOTETH
3318 yâtsâ' (1), to go,
bring out
7971 shâlach (1), to send
away
4160 pŏiĕō (1), to do

SHOOTING
5927 'âlâh (1), to ascend,
be high, mount

SHOPHACH
7780 Shôwphâk (2),
poured

SHOE
5275 na'al (9), sandal

SHOE'S
5266 hupŏdēma (1),
sandal

SHOELATCHET
8288+5275 sᵉrôwk (1),
sandal thong

SHIPMASTER column (right):
5265 hupŏdĕō (2), to put
on shoes or sandals

SHOPHAN
5855 'Aṭrôwth Shôwphân (1), crowns of Shophan

SHORE
2348 chôwph (2), cove
7097 qâtseh (1), extremity
8193 sâphâh (6), edge
123 aigialŏs (6), beach
4358 prŏsŏrmizō (1), to moor to, i.e. land at
5491 chĕilŏs (1), lip

SHORN
7094 qâtsab (1), to clip
2751 kĕirō (3), to shear

SHORT
2465 cheled (1), fleeting
7114 qâtsar (1), to curtail
7138 qârôwb (2), near
3641 ŏligŏs (2), small
4932 suntĕmnō (2), to cut short, i.e. do speedily
4958 sustĕllō (1), to draw together, i.e. enwrap
5302 hustĕrĕō (2), to be inferior; to fall short
5610 hōra (1), hour

SHORTENED
7114 qâtsar (5), to curtail
2856 kŏlŏbŏō (4), shorten

SHORTER
7114 qâtsar (2), to curtail

SHORTLY
4116 mâhar (1), to hurry
4120 m^{e}hêrâh (1), hurry
7138 qârôwb (1), near
1722+5034 ĕn (4), in; during; because of
2112 ĕuthĕōs (1), at once
5030 tachĕōs (4), speedily
5031 tachinŏs (1), soon
5032 tachiŏn (2), more rapidly, more speedily

SHOSHANNIM
7799 shûwshan (2), white lily; straight trumpet

SHOSHANNIM-EDUTH
7802 Shûwshan 'Êdûwth (1), lily (or trumpet) of assemblage

SHOT
3384 yârâh (7), to shoot
5927 'âlâh (1), to ascend, be high, mount
7232 râbab (2), to shoot
7819 shâchaṭ (1), to slaughter; butcher
7971 shâlach (5), to send away

SHOULD
1163 dĕi (3), it is (was) necessary
3195 mĕllō (25), to intend, i.e. be about to
3784 ŏphĕilō (1), to owe

SHOULDER
2220 z^{e}rôwa' (2), arm
3802 kâthêph (9), shoulder-piece; wall
7785 shôwq (13), lower leg
7926 sh^{e}kem (12), neck
7929 shikmâh (1), shoulder-bone

SHOULDERPIECES
3802 kâthêph (4), shoulder-piece; wall

SHOULDERS
3802 kâthêph (13), shoulder-piece; wall
7926 sh^{e}kem (5), neck
5606 ōmŏs (2), shoulder

SHOUT
1959 hêydâd (1), acclamation, shout
6030 'ânâh (1), to shout
6670 tsâhal (1), to be cheerful; to sound
6681 tsâvach (1), to screech exultingly
7321 rûwa' (12), to shout
7442 rânan (6), to shout
7768 shâva' (1), to halloo, call for help
8643 t^{e}rûw'âh (9), battle-cry; clangor
2019 ĕpiphōnĕō (1), to exclaim, shout
2752 kĕlĕuma (1), cry of incitement

SHOUTED
7321 rûwa' (11), to shout
7442 rânan (1), to shout
7452 rêa' (1), shout
8643 t^{e}rûw'âh (1), battle-cry; clangor

SHOUTETH
7442 rânan (1), to shout

SHOUTING
1959 hêydâd (4), shout of joy
7321 rûwa' (1), to shout
7440 rinnâh (1), shout
8643 t^{e}rûw'âh (8), battle-cry; clangor

SHOUTINGS
8663 t^{e}shû'âh (1), crashing or clamor

SHOVEL
7371 rachath (1), winnowing-fork

SHOVELS
3257 yâ' (9), shove

SHOWER
1653 geshem (3), rain
3655 ŏmbrŏs (1), storm

SHOWERS
1653 geshem (2), rain
2230 zerem (1), flood
7241 râbîyb (6), rain

SHRANK
5384 nâsheh (2), rheumatic or crippled

SHRED
6398 pâlach (1), to slice

SHRINES
3485 naŏs (1), shrine

SHROUD
2793 chôresh (1), forest

SHRUBS
7880 sîyach (1), shrubbery

SHUA
7770 Shûwa' (1), halloo
7774 Shûw'â' (1), wealth

SHUAH
7744 Shûwach (2), dell
7746 Shûwchâh (1), chasm
7770 Shûwa' (2), halloo

SHUAL
7777 Shûw'âl (2), jackal

SHUBAEL
2619 Chăçadyâh (3), Jehovah has favored

SHUHAM
7748 Shûwchâm (1), humbly

SHUHAMITES
7749 Shûwchâmîy (2), Shuchamite

SHUHITE
7747 Shuchîy (5), Shuchite

SHULAMITE
7759 Shûwlammîyth (2), peaceful

SHUMATHITES
8126 Shûmâthîy (1), Shumathite

SHUN
4026 pĕriistēmi (1), to avoid, shun

SHUNAMMITE
7767 Shûwnammîyth (8), Shunammitess

SHUNEM
7766 Shûwnêm (3), quietly

SHUNI
7764 Shûwnîy (2), quiet

SHUNITES
7765 Shûwnîy (1), Shunite

SHUNNED
5288 hupŏstĕllō (1), to cower or shrink

SHUPHAM
8197 Sh^{e}phûwphâm (1), serpent-like

SHUPHAMITES
7781 Shûwphâmîy (1), Shuphamite

SHUPPIM
8206 Shuppîym (3), serpents

SHUR
7793 Shûwr (6), wall

SHUSHAN
7800 Shûwshan (21), lily

SHUSHAN-EDUTH
7802 Shûwshan 'Êdûwth (1), lily (or trumpet) of assemblage

SHUT
332 'âṭar (1), to close up
1479 gûwph (1), to shut
2902 ṭûwach (1), to whitewash
3607 kâlâ' (4), to stop
5274 nâ'al (1), to lock
5462 çâgar (55), to shut
5463 ç^{e}gar (Ch.) (1), to close up
5526 çâkak (1), to entwine; to fence in
5640 çâtham (2), to stop
6113 'âtsar (16), to hold
6887 tsârar (1), to cramp
7092 qâphats (3), to draw together, to leap; to die
8173 shâ'a' (1), to fondle, please or amuse (self)
608 apŏklĕiō (1), to close
2623 kataklĕiō (2), to incarcerate, lock up
2808 klĕiō (13), to close
4788 sugklĕiō (1), to net fish; to lock up persons

SHUTHALHITES
8364 Shûthalchîy (1), Shuthalchite

SHUTHELAH
7803 Shûwthelach (4), crash of breakage

SHUTTETH
331 'âṭam (1), to close
5462 çâgar (1), to shut
5640 çâtham (1), to stop
6095 'âtsâh (1), to close
6105 'âtsam (1), to be, make powerful
2808 klĕiō (3), to shut

SHUTTING
5462 çâgar (1), to shut

SHUTTLE
708 'ereg (1), shuttle

SIA
5517 Çîy'â' (1), congregation

SIAHA
5517 Çîy'â' (1), congregation

SIBBECAI
5444 Çibb^{e}kay (2), thicket-like

SIBBECHAI
5444 Çibb^{e}kay (2), thicket-like

SIBBOLETH
5451 Çibbôleth (1), ear of grain

SIBMAH
7643 S^{e}bâm (4), spice

SIBRAIM
5453 Çibrayim (1), double hope

SICHEM
7927 Sh^{e}kem (1), ridge

SICK
605 'ânash (1), to be frail
1739 dâveh (1), menstrual; fainting
2470 châlâh (34), to be weak, sick, afflicted
2483 chŏlîy (1), malady
8463 tachălûw' (1), malady, disease
732 arrhōstŏs (4), infirmed, ill
770 asthĕnĕō (17), to be feeble
772 asthĕnēs (6), weak
2192+2560 ĕchō (8), to have; hold; keep
2577 kamnō (1), to sicken
3885 paralutikŏs (11), lame person
4445 purĕssō (2), to burn with a fever

SICKLE
2770 chermêsh (2), sickle
4038 maggâl (2), sickle

1407 drĕpanŏn (8), gathering *hook*

SICKLY
732 arrhōstŏs (1), *infirmed, ill*

SICKNESS
1739 dâveh (1), *menstrual; fainting*
2483 chŏlîy (11), *malady*
4245 machăleh (3), *sickness*
769 asthĕnĕia (1), *feebleness* of body
3554 nŏsŏs (3), *malady*

SICKNESSES
2483 chŏlîy (1), *malady*
8463 tachălûw' (1), *malady, disease*
3554 nŏsŏs (2), *malady*

SIDDIM
7708 Siddîym (3), *flats*

SIDE
2296 châgar (1), to *gird*
2348 chôwph (1), *cove*
3027 yâd (5), *hand; power*
3225 yâmîyn (4), *right*
3409 yârêk (7), *side*
3411 yᵉrêkâh (2), *far away places*
3541 kôh (2), *thus*
3802 kâthêph (29), *side-piece*
4217 mizrâch (2), *east*
4975 môthen (4), *loins*
5048 neged (2), *beside*
5437 çâbab (1), to *surround*
5439 çâbîyb (26), *circle*
5675 'ăbar (Ch.) (7), *region across*
5676 'êber (56), *opposite*
6285 pê'âh (50), *direction*
6311 pôh (2), *here*
6654 tsad (20), *side*
6753 Tsᵉlelpôwnîy (2), *shade-facing*
6763 tsêlâ' (22), *side*
6921 qâdîym (1), *East; eastward; east wind*
6924 qedem (2), *East, eastern; antiquity*
6954 Qᵉhêlâthâh (1), *convocation*
7023 qîyr (2), *side-wall*
7097 qâtseh (1), *extremity*
7307 rûwach (5), *breath; wind; life-spirit*
7859 sᵉṭar (Ch.) (1), *side*
8040 sᵉmô'wl (1), *left*
8193 sâphâh (3), *edge*
492 antiparĕrchŏmai (2), to *go along opposite*
1188 dĕxiŏs (2), *right*
1782 ĕntĕuthĕn (2), on *both sides*
3313 mĕrŏs (1), *division*
3840 pantŏthĕn (1), *from, on all sides*
3844 para (15), *besides*
4008 pĕran (13), *across*
4125 plĕura (5), *side*

SIDES
3411 yᵉrêkâh (19), *far away places*
3802 kâthêph (4), *shoulder-piece; wall*
5676 'êber (4), *opposite*

6285 pê'âh (1), *direction*
6654 tsad (9), *side*
6763 tsêlâ' (4), *side*
7023 qîyr (2), *side-wall*
7253 reba' (3), *fourth*
7307 rûwach (1), *breath; wind; life-spirit*

SIDON
6721 Tsîydôwn (2), *fishery*
4605 Sidōn (12), *fishery*

SIDONIANS
6722 Tsîydônîy (5), *Tsidonian*

SIEGE
4692 mâtsôwr (13), *siege-mound; distress*
6696 tsûwr (3), to *cramp*

SIEVE
3531 kᵉbârâh (1), *sieve*
5299 nâphâh (1), *sieve*

SIFT
5128 nûwa' (1), to *waver*
5130 nûwph (1), to *quiver, vibrate, rock*
4617 siniazō (1), to *shake in a sieve*

SIFTED
5128 nûwa' (1), to *waver*

SIGH
584 'ânach (7), to *sigh*

SIGHED
584 'ânach (1), to *sigh*
389 anastĕnazō (1), to *sigh deeply*
4727 stĕnazō (1), to *sigh*

SIGHEST
584 'ânach (1), to *sigh*

SIGHETH
584 'ânach (1), to *sigh*

SIGHING
585 'ănâchâh (5), *sighing*
603 'ănâqâh (2), *shrieking, groaning*

SIGHS
585 'ănâchâh (1), *sighing*

SIGHT
2379 chăzôwth (Ch.) (2), *view, visible sight*
4758 mar'eh (18), *appearance; vision*
5048 neged (2), *before*
5869 'ayin (218), *sight*
6440 pânîym (39), *face*
7200 râ'âh (1), to *see*
308 anablĕpō (15), to *look up; to recover sight*
309 anablĕpsis (1), *restoration of sight*
991 blĕpō (2), to *look at*
1491 ĕidŏs (1), *sight*
1715 ĕmprŏsthĕn (3), in *front of*
1726 ĕnantiŏn (1), in the *presence of*
1799 ĕnôpiŏn (21), *before*
2335 thĕōria (1), *sight*
2714 katĕnōpiŏn (2), *directly in front of*
3705 hŏrama (1), *supernatural spectacle*
3706 hŏrasis (1), *appearance, vision*
3788 ŏphthalmŏs (1), *eye*
3844 para (1), *from; with; besides; on account of*

5324 phantazō (1), to *appear; spectacle, sight*

SIGHTS
5400 phŏbētrŏn (1), *frightening thing*

SIGN
226 'ôwth (33), *sign*
4159 môwphêth (8), *miracle; token or omen*
4864 mas'êth (1), *beacon*
5251 nêç (1), *flag; signal*
6725 tsîyûwn (1), *guiding pillar, monument*
7560 rᵉsham (Ch.) (1), to *record*
3902 parasēmŏs (1), *labeled, marked*
4592 sēmĕiŏn (29), *sign*

SIGNED
7560 rᵉsham (Ch.) (4), to *record*

SIGNET
2368 chôwthâm (8), *signature-ring, seal*
2858 chôthemeth (1), *signet ring seal*
5824 'izqâ' (Ch.) (2), *signet or signet-ring*

SIGNETS
2368 chôwthâm (1), *signature-ring, seal*

SIGNIFICATION
880 aphŏnŏs (1), *mute, silent; unmeaning*

SIGNIFIED
4591 sēmainō (2), to *indicate, make known*

SIGNIFIETH
1213 dēlŏō (1), to *make plain by words*

SIGNIFY
1213 dēlŏō (1), to *make plain by words*
1229 diaggĕllō (1), to *herald thoroughly*
1718 ĕmphanizō (1), to *show forth*
4591 sēmainō (1), to *indicate, make known*

SIGNIFYING
1213 dēlŏō (1), to *make plain by words*
4591 sēmainō (3), to *indicate, make known*

SIGNS
226 'ôwth (27), *sign*
852 'âth (Ch.) (3), *sign*
1770 ĕnnĕuŏ (1), to *signal*
4591 sēmainō (17), to *indicate, make known*
4592 sēmĕiŏn (5), *sign*

SIHON
5511 Çîychôwn (37), *tempestuous*

SIHOR
7883 Shîychôwr (3), *dark, i.e. turbid*

SILAS
4609 Silas (13), *sylvan*

SILENCE
481 'âlam (1), to *be silent*
1745 dûwmâh (2), *silence*
1747 dûwmîyâh (1), *silently; quiet, trust*

1820 dâmâh (1), to *be silent; to fail, cease*
1824 dᵉmîy (2), *quiet*
1826 dâmam (6), to *be silent; to be astonished*
1827 dᵉmâmâh (1), *quiet*
2013 hâçâh (3), to *hush*
2790 chârash (5), to *be silent; to be deaf*
2814 châshâh (2), to *hush*
2271 hēsuchia (3), *stillness*
4601 sigaō (3), to *keep silent*
4602 sigē (2), *silence*
5392 phimŏō (2), to *restrain to silence*

SILENT
1748 dûwmâm (1), *silently*
1826 dâmam (4), to *be silent; to be astonished*
1947 hôwlêlâh (1), *folly*
2013 hâçâh (1), to *hush*
2790 chârash (2), to *be silent; to be deaf*

SILK
4897 meshîy (2), *silk*
8336 shêsh (1), *white linen; white* marble
2596 kata (1), *down; according to*

SILLA
5538 Çillâ' (1), *embankment*

SILLY
6601 pâthâh (2), to *be, make simple; to delude*
1133 gunaikariŏn (1), *little, i.e. foolish woman*

SILOAH
7975 Shilôach (1), *rill*

SILOAM
4611 Silōam (3), *rill*

SILVANUS
4610 Silŏuanŏs (4), *sylvan*

SILVER
3701 keçeph (280), *silver*
3702 kᵉçaph (Ch.) (12), *silver money*
7192 qᵉsîytah (1), *coin*
693 argurĕŏs (3), *made of silver*
694 arguriŏn (9), *silver*
696 argurŏs (5), *silver*
1406 drachmē (1), *silver coin*

SILVERLINGS
3701 keçeph (1), *silver*

SILVERSMITH
695 argurŏkŏpŏs (1), *worker of silver*

SIMEON
8095 Shim'ôwn (43), *hearing*
8099 Shim'ôniy (1), *Shimonite*
4826 Sumĕōn (6), *hearing*

SIMEONITES
8099 Shim'ôniy (1), *Shimonite*

SIMILITUDE
1823 dᵉmûwth (2), *resemblance, likeness*

8403 tabnîyth (2), *model, resemblance*
8544 t°mûwnâh (4), *something fashioned*
3665 hŏmŏiŏtēs (1), *resemblance, similarity*
3667 hŏmŏiōma (1), *form; resemblance*
3669 hŏmŏiōsis (1), *resemblance, likeness*

SIMILITUDES
1819 dâmâh (1), *to liken*

SIMON
4613 Simōn (67), *hearing*

SIMON'S
4613 Simōn (7), *hearing*

SIMPLE
6612 p°thîy (17), *silly*
6615 p°thayûwth (1), *silliness,* i.e. *seducible*
172 akakŏs (1), *innocent*
185 akĕraiŏs (1), *innocent*

SIMPLICITY
6612 p°thîy (1), *silly*
8537 tôm (1), *innocence*
572 haplŏtēs (3), *sincerity*

SIMRI
8113 Shimriy (1), *watchful*

SIN
817 'âshâm (3), *guilt*
819 'ashmâh (2), *guiltiness*
2398 châṭâ' (68), *to sin*
2399 chêṭ' (22), *crime*
2401 chăṭâ'âh (8), *offence*
2402 chaṭṭâ'âh (Ch.) (2), *offence,* and *penalty*
2403 chaṭṭâ'âh (215), *offence; sin* offering
2409 chaṭṭâyâ' (Ch.) (1), *expiation, sin* offering
5512 Çîyn (6), *Sin*
5771 'âvôn (1), *moral evil*
6588 pesha' (1), *revolt*
7686 shâgâh (1), *to stray*
264 hamartanō (15), *to miss* the mark, *to err*
265 hamartēma (1), *sin*
266 hamartia (91), *sin*
361 anamartētŏs (1), *sinless*

SINA
4614 Sina (2), *Sinai*

SINAI
5514 Çîynay (35), *Sinai*
4614 Sina (2), *Sinai*

SINCE
227 'âz (3), *therefore*
310 'achar (2), *after*
518 'îm (1), *whether?; if, although; Oh that!*
1767 day (3), *enough, sufficient*
2008 hênnâh (1), *from here; from there*
3588 kîy (1), *for, that*
4480 min (12), *from*
4480+227 min (1), *from*
4481 min (Ch.) (1), *from*
5750 'ôwd (2), *more*
575 apŏ (9), *from, away*
575+3739 apŏ (3), *from*
1537 ĕk (1), *out, out of*
1893 ĕpĕi (1), *since*

1894 ĕpĕidē (1), *when*
3326 mĕta (1), *after, later*
5613 hōs (1), *which, how*

SINCERE
97 adŏlŏs (1), *pure*
1506 ĕilikrinēs (1), *pure*

SINCERELY
8549 tâmîym (2), *entire*
55 hagnōs (1), *purely*

SINCERITY
8549 tâmîym (1), *integrity*
861 aphtharsia (2), *genuineness*
1103 gnēsiŏs (1), *genuine*
1505 ĕilikrinĕia (3), *purity, sincerity*

SINEW
1517 gîyd (3), *tendon*

SINEWS
1517 gîyd (4), *tendon*
6207 'âraq (1), *to gnaw*

SINFUL
2398 châṭâ' (1), *to sin*
2400 chaṭṭâ' (1), *guilty*
2401 chăṭâ'âh (1), *offence or sacrifice*
266 hamartia (1), *sin*
268 hamartōlŏs (4), *sinner; sinful*

SING
1984 hâlal (2), *to speak praise; thank*
2167 zâmar (33), *to play music*
5414+6963 nâthan (1), *to give*
6030 'ânâh (4), *to sing*
6031 'ânâh (2), *to afflict*
7440 rinnâh (1), *shout*
7442 rânan (25), *to shout*
7788 shûwr (1), *to travel*
7891 shîyr (32), *to sing*
7892 shîyr (1), *singing*
103 a₁dō (1), *to sing*
5214 humnĕō (1), *to celebrate God in song*
5567 psallō (4), *to play a stringed instrument*

SINGED
2761 chărak (Ch.) (1), *to scorch, singe*

SINGER
5329 nâtsach (1), i.e. *to be eminent*
7891 shîyr (1), *to sing*

SINGERS
2171 zammâr (Ch.) (1), *musician*
7891 shîyr (35), *to sing*
7892 shîyr (1), *singing*

SINGETH
7891 shîyr (1), *to sing*

SINGING
2158 zâmîyr (1), *song*
7440 rinnâh (9), *shout*
7442 rânan (2), *to shout for joy*
7445 r°nânâh (1), *shout for joy*
7891 shîyr (5), *to sing*
7892 shîyr (4), *singing*
103 a₁dō (2), *to sing*

SINGLE
573 haplŏus (2), *single*

SINGLENESS
572 haplŏtēs (2), *sincerity*
858 aphĕlŏtēs (1), *simplicity; sincerity*

SINGULAR
6381 pâlâ' (1), *to be, make great, difficult*

SINIM
5515 Çîynîym (1), *Sinim*

SINITE
5513 Çîynîy (2), *Sinite*

SINK
2883 ṭâba' (2), *to sink*
8257 shâqa' (1), *to be overflowed; to abate*
1036 buthizō (1), *to sink*
2670 katapŏntizō (1), *to submerge, be drowned*
5087 tithēmi (1), *to place*

SINNED
2398 châṭâ' (102), *to sin*
264 hamartanō (15), *to miss* the mark, *to sin*
4258 prŏamartanō (2), *to sin previously*

SINNER
2398 châṭâ' (8), *to sin*
2403 chaṭṭâ'âh (1), *offence; sin* offering
268 hamartōlŏs (12), *sinner; sinful*

SINNERS
2400 chaṭṭâ' (16), *guilty*
268 hamartōlŏs (30), *sinner; sinful*
3781 ŏphĕilĕtēs (1), *person indebted*

SINNEST
2398 châṭâ' (1), *to sin*

SINNETH
2398 châṭâ' (13), *to sin*
6213 'âsâh (1), *to do*
7683 shâgag (1), *to sin*
264 hamartanō (7), *to sin*

SINNING
2398 châṭâ' (2), *to sin*

SINS
819 'ashmâh (2), *guiltiness*
2399 chêṭ' (8), *crime*
2403 chaṭṭâ'âh (71), *offence; sin* offering
2408 chăṭîy (Ch.) (1), *sin*
6588 pesha' (1), *revolt*
265 hamartēma (3), *sin*
266 hamartia (78), *sin*
3900 paraptōma (3), *error; transgression*

SION
6726 Tsîyôwn (1), *capital*
7865 Sîy'ôn (1), *peak*
4622 Siōn (7), *capital*

SIPHMOTH
8224 Siphmôwth (1), *Siphmoth*

SIPPAI
5598 Çippay (1), *bason-like*

SIR
113 'âdôwn (1), *sovereign,* i.e. *controller*
2962 kuriŏs (11), *supreme, controller, Mr.*

SIRAH
5626 Çîrâh (1), *departure*

SIRION
8304 S°râyâh (2), *Jehovah has prevailed*

SIRS
435 anēr (6), *man; male*
2962 kuriŏs (1), *supreme, controller, Mr.*

SISAMAI
5581 Çiçmay (2), *Sismai*

SISERA
5516 Çîyç°râ' (21), *Sisera*

SISTER
269 'achôwth (91), *sister*
1733 dôwdâh (1), *aunt*
2994 y°bêmeth (2), *sister-in-law*
79 adĕlphē (15), *sister*

SISTER'S
269 'achôwth (5), *sister*
79 adĕlphē (1), *sister*
431 anĕpsiŏs (1), *cousin*

SISTERS
269 'achôwth (11), *sister*
79 adĕlphē (8), *sister*

SIT
3427 yâshab (65), *to dwell, to settle*
3488 y°thîb (Ch.) (2), *to sit*
5414 nâthan (1), *to give*
5437 çâbab (1), *to surround*
7674 shebeth (1), *rest*
347 anaklinō (6), *to recline*
377 anapiptō (5), *lie down, lean back*
2521 kathēmai (12), *to sit down; to remain*
2523 kathizō (15), *to seat down, dwell*
2621 katakĕimai (1), *to lie down*
2625 kataklinō (2), *to recline, take a place*
4776 sugkathizō (1), *to give, take a seat with*
4873 sunanakĕimai (1), *to recline with at meal*

SITH
518 'îm (1), *whether?; if, although; Oh that!*

SITNAH
7856 Siṭnâh (1), *opposition*

SITTEST
3427 yâshab (6), *to settle*
2521 kathēmai (1), *to sit*

SITTETH
1716 dâgar (1), *to brood over; to care for* young
3427 yâshab (25), *to settle*
345 anakĕimai (2), *to recline at a meal*
2521 kathēmai (10), *to sit down; or reside*
2523 kathizō (3), *to seat down, dwell*

SITTING
3427 yâshab (15), *to settle*
4186 môwshâb (2), *seat*
7257 râbats (1), *to recline*
1910 ĕpibainō (1), *to mount, ascend*

2516 kathĕzŏmai (2), to *sit down, be seated*
2521 kathēmai (21), to *sit down; to reside*
2523 kathizō (1), to *seat down, dwell*

SITUATE
3427 yâshab (2), to *settle*
4690 mâtsûwq (1), *column; hilltop*

SITUATION
4186 môwshâb (1), *site*
5131 nôwph (1), *elevation*

SIVAN
5510 Çîyvân (1), *Sivan*

SIX
8337 shêsh (185), *six; sixth*
8353 shêth (Ch.) (1), *six; sixth*
1803 hĕx (11), *six*
1812 hĕxakŏsiŏi (1), *six hundred*
5516 chi xi stigma (1), 666

SIXSCORE
3967+6242 mê'âh (1), *hundred*
8147+6240+7239 sh°nayim (1), *two-fold*

SIXTEEN
8337+6240 shêsh (22), *six; sixth*
1440+1803 hĕbdŏmĕkŏnta (1), *seventy*

SIXTEENTH
8337+6240 shêsh (3), *six; sixth*

SIXTH
8337 shêsh (2), *six; sixth*
8338 shâwshâw (1), (poss.) to *annihilate*
8341 shâshâh (1), to *divide into sixths*
8345 shishshîy (26), *sixth*
8353 shêth (Ch.) (1), *six; sixth*
1623 hĕktŏs (14), *sixth*

SIXTY
8346 shishshîym (11), *sixty*
1835 hĕxēkŏnta (3), *sixty*

SIXTYFOLD
1835 hĕxēkŏnta (1), *sixty*

SIZE
4060 middâh (3), *measure; portion*
7095 qetseb (2), *shape*

SKIES
7834 shachaq (5), *clouds*

SKILFUL
995 bîyn (1), to *discern*
2451 chokmâh (1), *wisdom*
2796 chârâsh (1), skilled *fabricator or worker*
3045 yâda' (2), to *know*
3925 lâmad (1), to *teach*
7919 sâkal (1), to *be or act circumspect*

SKILFULLY
3190 yâṭab (1), to *be, make well*

SKILFULNESS
8394 tâbûwn (1), *intelligence; argument*

SKILL
995 bîyn (1), to *discern*
3045 yâda' (4), to *know*
7919 sâkal (2), to *be or act circumspect*

SKIN
1320 bâsâr (1), *flesh*
1539 geled (1), *skin*
5785 'ôwr (71), *skin*
1193 dĕrmatinŏs (1), made of leather *hide*

SKINS
5785 'ôwr (20), *skin*

SKIP
7540 râqad (1), to *spring*

SKIPPED
7540 râqad (2), to *spring*

SKIPPEDST
5110 nûwd (1), to *waver*

SKIPPING
7092 qâphats (1), to *leap*

SKIRT
3671 kânâph (12), *wing*

SKIRTS
3671 kânâph (2), *wing*
6310 peh (1), *mouth*
7757 shûwl (4), *skirt*

SKULL
1538 gulgôleth (2), *skull*
2898 kraniŏn (3), *skull*

SKY
7834 shachaq (2), *clouds*
3772 ŏuranŏs (5), *sky*

SLACK
309 'âchar (2), to *delay*
6113 'âtsar (1), to *hold back; to maintain, rule*
7423 r°mîyâh (1), *remissness; treachery*
7503 râphâh (3), to *slacken*
1019 bradunō (1), to *delay, hesitate*

SLACKED
6313 pûwg (1), to *be sluggish; be numb*

SLACKNESS
1022 bradutēs (1), *tardiness, slowness*

SLAIN
2026 hârag (31), to *kill*
2027 hereg (1), *kill*
2076 zâbach (2), to (sacrificially) *slaughter*
2490 châlal (1), to *profane, defile*
2491 châlâl (75), *slain*
2717 chârab (1), to *desolate, destroy*
2873 ṭâbach (1), to *kill*
4191 mûwth (18), to *kill*
5062 nâgaph (2), to *strike*
5221 nâkâh (20), to *kill*
6992 q°ṭal (Ch.) (4), to *kill*
7523 râtsach (3), to *murder*
7819 shâchaṭ (5), to *slaughter; butcher*
337 anairĕō (3), to *take away, murder*
615 apŏktĕinō (7), to *kill*

1722+5408+599 ĕn (1), *in; during; because of*
4968 sphagiŏn (1), *offering for slaughter*
4969 sphazō (6), to *slaughter or to maim*

SLANDER
1681 dibbâh (3), *slander*

SLANDERED
7270 râgal (1), to *slander*

SLANDERERS
1228 diabŏlŏs (1), *traducer, i.e. Satan*

SLANDEREST
5414+1848 nâthan (1), to *give*

SLANDERETH
3960 lâshan (1), to *calumniate, malign*

SLANDEROUSLY
987 blasphēmĕō (1), to *speak impiously*

SLANDERS
7400 râkîyl (2), *scandal-monger*

SLANG
7049 qâla' (1), to *sling*

SLAUGHTER
2027 hereg (4), *kill*
2028 hărêgâh (5), *kill*
2873 ṭâbach (5), to *kill*
2875 Ṭebach (9), *massacre*
2878 ṭibehâh (1), *butchery*
4046 maggêphâh (3), *pestilence; defeat*
4293 maṭbêach (1), *slaughter place*
4347 makkâh (14), *blow; wound; pestilence*
4660 mappâts (1), *striking to pieces*
5221 nâkâh (5), to *kill*
6993 qeṭel (1), *death*
7524 retsach (1), *crushing; murder-cry*
7819 shâchaṭ (1), to *slaughter; butcher*
2871 kŏpē (1), *carnage*
4967 sphagē (3), *butchery*
5408 phŏnŏs (1), *slaying*

SLAVES
4983 sōma (1), *body*

SLAY
1194 Be'ôn (1), *Beon*
2026 hârag (38), to *kill*
2717 chârab (1), to *desolate, destroy*
2763 charam (1), to *devote to destruction*
2873 ṭâbach (1), to *kill, butcher*
2875 Ṭebach (1), *massacre*
4191 mûwth (43), to *kill*
5221 nâkâh (11), to *kill*
5221+5315 nâkâh (1), to *strike, kill*
6991 qâṭal (2), to *put to death*
6992 q°ṭal (Ch.) (1), to *kill*
7819 shâchaṭ (9), to *slaughter; butcher*

337 anairĕō (2), to *take away, murder*
615 apŏktĕinō (3), to *kill*
2380 thuō (1), to *kill*
2695 katasphattō (1), to *slaughter, strike down*

SLAYER
2026 hârag (1), to *kill*
5221 nâkâh (1), to *kill*
7523 râtsach (17), to *murder*

SLAYETH
2026 hârag (2), to *kill*
2490 châlal (1), to *profane, defile*
4191 mûwth (1), to *kill*
7523+5315 râtsach (1), to *murder*

SLAYING
2026 hârag (3), to *kill*
4191 mûwth (1), to *kill*
5221 nâkâh (2), to *kill*
7819 shâchaṭ (1), to *slaughter; butcher*

SLEEP
3462 yâshên (11), to *sleep; to grow old*
3463 yâshên (4), *sleepy*
7290 râdam (3), to *stupefy*
7901 shâkab (11), to *lie*
8139 sh°nâh (Ch.) (1), *sleep*
8142 shênâh (24), *sleep*
8639 tardêmâh (4), *trance, deep sleep*
1852 ĕxupnizō (1), *waken, rouse*
1853 ĕxupnŏs (1), *awake*
2518 kathĕudō (7), to *fall asleep*
2837 kŏimaō (5), to *slumber; to decease*
5258 hupnŏs (6), *sleep*

SLEEPER
7290 râdam (1), to *stupefy*

SLEEPEST
3462 yâshên (1), to *sleep*
7901 shâkab (1), to *lie*
2518 kathĕudō (2), to *fall asleep*

SLEEPETH
3463 yâshên (2), *sleepy*
7290 râdam (1), to *stupefy*
2518 kathĕudō (3), to *fall asleep*
2837 kŏimaō (1), to *slumber; to decease*

SLEEPING
1957 hâzâh (1), to *dream*
3463 yâshên (1), *sleepy*
2518 kathĕudō (2), to *fall asleep*
2837 kŏimaō (2), to *slumber; to decease*

SLEIGHT
2940 kubĕia (1), *artifice or fraud, deceit*

SLEPT
3462 yâshên (5), to *sleep*
3463 yâshên (1), *sleepy*
5123 nûwm (1), to *slumber*
7901 shâkab (37), to *lie*

2518 kathĕudō (2), to *fall asleep*
2837 kŏimaō (3), to *slumber; to decease*

SLEW
2026 hârag (55), to *kill*
2076 zâbach (3), to (sacrificially) *slaughter*
2126 Zîynâ' (1), well-*fed*
2490 châlal (1), to *profane, defile*
2491 châlâl (3), *slain*
4191 mûwth (40), to *kill*
5221 nâkâh (57), to *kill*
5307 nâphal (1), to *fall*
6992 qᵉṭal (Ch.) (2), to *kill*
7819 shâchaṭ (21), to *slaughter; butcher*
337 anairĕō (3), to *take away, murder*
615 apŏktĕinō (4), to *kill*
1315 diachĕirizŏmai (1), to *lay hands* upon
4969 sphazō (2), to *slaughter* or to *maim*
5407 phŏnĕuō (1), to *commit murder*

SLEWEST
5221 nâkâh (1), to *kill*

SLIDDEN
7725 shûwb (1), to *return*

SLIDE
4131 môwṭ (1), to *slip*
4571 mâ'ad (2), to *waver*

SLIDETH
5637 çârar (1), to *be refractory, stubborn*

SLIGHTLY
7043 qâlal (2), to *be, make light*

SLIME
2564 chêmâr (2), *bitumen*

SLIMEPITS
2564 chêmâr (2), *bitumen*

SLING
4773 margêmâh (1), sling for *stones*
7049 qâla' (3), to *sling*
7050 qela' (4), *sling*

SLINGERS
7051 qallâ' (1), *slinger*

SLINGS
7050 qela' (1), *sling*

SLINGSTONES
68+7050 'eben (1), *stone*

SLIP
4131 môwṭ (1), to *slip*
4571 mâ'ad (3), to *waver*
3901 pararrhuĕō (1), to *flow by*, to pass (*miss*)

SLIPPED
6362 pâṭar (1), to *burst through; to emit*
8210 shâphak (1), to *spill forth; to expend*

SLIPPERY
2513 chelqâh (1), *smoothness; flattery*
2519 chălaqlaqqâh (2), *smooth; treacherous*

SLIPPETH
4131 môwṭ (2), to *slip*
5394 nâshal (1), to *drop*

SLIPS
2156 zᵉmôwrâh (1), *twig, vine branch*

SLOTHFUL
6101 'âtsal (1), to *be slack*
6102 'âtsêl (8), *indolent*
7423 rᵉmîyâh (2), *remissness; treachery*
7503 râphâh (1), to *slacken*
3576 nôthrŏs (1), *lazy*
3636 ŏknêrŏs (2), *lazy*

SLOTHFULNESS
6103 'atslâh (2), *indolence*

SLOW
750 'ârêk (10), *patient*
3515 kâbêd (1), *stupid*
692 argŏs (1), *lazy*
1021 bradus (2), *slow*

SLOWLY
1020 braduplŏĕō (1), to *sail slowly*

SLUGGARD
6102 'âtsêl (6), *indolent*

SLUICES
7938 seker (1), *wages*

SLUMBER
5123 nûwm (5), to *slumber*
8572 tᵉnûwmâh (4), *drowsiness, i.e. sleep*
2659 katanuxis (1), *stupor, bewilderment*

SLUMBERED
3573 nustazō (1), to *fall asleep; to delay*

SLUMBERETH
3573 nustazō (1), to *fall asleep; to delay*

SLUMBERINGS
8572 tᵉnûwmâh (1), *drowsiness, i.e. sleep*

SMALL
1571 gam (1), *also; even*
1639 gâra' (1), to *lessen*
1851 daq (5), *small*
1854 dâqaq (5), to *crush*
3190 yâṭab (1), to *be, make well*
4213 miz'âr (1), *fewness*
4592 mᵉ'aṭ (9), *little*
4705 mits'âr (2), *little; short time*
4962 math (1), *men*
6694 tsûwq (1), to *pour out; melt*
6810 tsâ'îyr (2), *small*
6819 tsâ'ar (1), to *be small; be trivial*
6862 tsar (1), *trouble; opponent*
6994 qâṭôn (2), to *be, make diminutive*
6996 qâṭân (34), *small*
7116 qâtsêr (1), *short*
1646 ĕlachistŏs (2), *least*
2485 ichthudiŏn (1), *little fish*
3398 mikrŏs (6), *small*
3641 ŏligŏs (5), *small*
3795 ŏpsariŏn (1), *small fish*
4142 plŏiariŏn (1), small boat

SMALLEST
6996 qâṭân (1), *small*
1646 ĕlachistŏs (1), *least*

SMART
7321+7451 rûwa' (1), to *shout* for alarm or joy

SMELL
1314 besem (1), *spice*
7306 rûwach (5), to *smell*
7381 rêyach (10), *odor*
7382 rêyach (Ch.) (1), *odor*
2175 ĕuŏdia (1), *fragrance, aroma*

SMELLED
7306 rûwach (2), to *smell*

SMELLETH
7306 rûwach (1), to *smell*

SMELLING
5674 'âbar (2), to *cross over; to transition*
3750 ŏsphrēsis (1), *smell*

SMITE
1986 hâlam (1), to *strike*
3807 kâthath (1), to *strike*
4272 mâchats (2), to *crush; to subdue*
5062 nâgaph (9), to *strike*
5221 nâkâh (94), to *strike*
5307 nâphal (1), to *fall*
5596 çâphach (1), to *associate; be united*
5606 çâphaq (1), to *clap*
6221 'Ăsîy'êl (2), *made of God*
6375 pîyq (1), *tottering*
1194 dĕrō (1), to *flay*
3960 patassō (5), to *strike*
4474 rhapizō (1), to *slap*
5180 tuptō (3), to *strike*

SMITERS
5221 nâkâh (1), to *strike*

SMITEST
5221 nâkâh (1), to *strike*
1194 dĕrō (1), to *flay*

SMITETH
4272 mâchats (1), to *crush; to subdue*
5221 nâkâh (11), to *strike*
5180 tuptō (1), to *strike*

SMITH
2796 chârâsh (2), skilled *fabricator* or worker
2796+1270 chârâsh (1), skilled *fabricator*

SMITHS
4525 maçgêr (4), *prison; craftsman*

SMITING
5221 nâkâh (5), to *strike*

SMITTEN
1792 dâkâ' (1), to *pulverize; be contrite*
3807 kâthath (1), to *strike*
5060 nâga' (1), to *strike*
5062 nâgaph (15), to *inflict; to strike*
5221 nâkâh (43), to *strike*
4141 plēssō (1), to *pound*
5180 tuptō (1), to *strike*

SMOKE
6225 'âshan (5), to *envelope in smoke*

4979 schŏiniŏn (1), *rope*

SMALLEST
6996 qâṭân (1), *small*
1646 ĕlachistŏs (1), *least*

6227 'âshân (24), *smoke*
7008 qîyṭôwr (3), *fume*
2586 kapnŏs (13), *smoke*

SMOKING
3544 kêheh (1), *feeble; obscure*
6226 'âshên (2), *smoky*
6227 'âshân (1), *smoke*
5187 tuphŏō (1), to *inflate* with self-conceit

SMOOTH
2509 châlâq (1), *smooth*
2511 challâq (1), *smooth*
2512 challûq (1), *smooth*
2513 chelqâh (2), *smoothness; flattery*
3006 lĕiŏs (1), *smooth*

SMOOTHER
2505 châlaq (1), to *be smooth; be slippery*
2513 chelqâh (1), *smoothness; flattery*

SMOOTHETH
2505 châlaq (1), to *be smooth; be slippery*

SMOTE
1986 hâlam (2), to *strike*
3766 kâra' (1), to *prostrate*
4223 mᵉchâ' (Ch.) (2), to *strike; to impale*
4277 mâchaq (1), to *crush*
4347 makkâh (1), *blow*
5060 nâga' (2), to *strike*
5062 nâgaph (6), to *strike*
5221 nâkâh (194), to *strike*
5368 nᵉqash (Ch.) (1), to *knock; to be frightened*
5606 çâphaq (2), to *clap*
8628 tâqa' (1), to *slap*
851 aphairĕō (1), to *remove, cut off*
1194 dĕrō (1), to *flay, i.e. to scourge* or *thrash*
1325+4475 didōmi (1), to *give*
3817 paiō (4), to *hit*
3960 patassō (4), to *strike*
4474 rhapizō (1), to *strike*
5180 tuptō (4), to *strike*

SMOTEST
5221 nâkâh (1), to *strike*

SMYRNA
4667 Smurna (1), *myrrh*
4668 Smurnaiŏs (1), *inhabitant of Smyrna*

SNAIL
2546 chômeṭ (1), *lizard*
7642 shablûwl (1), *snail*

SNARE
2256 chebel (1), *band*
3369 yâqôsh (1), to *trap*
4170 môwqêsh (14), *noose*
4686 mâtsûwd (2), *net*
5367 nâqash (1), to *entrap with a noose*
6315 pûwach (1), to *blow, to fan, kindle; to utter*
6341 pach (17), *net*
6354 pachath (1), *pit for catching animals*
6983 qôwsh (1), to *set a trap*
7639 sᵉbâkâh (1), *snare*

SONGS
5058 nᵉgîynâh (4), *instrument, poem*
7892 shîyr (62), *song*
5603 õ₁dĕ (5), *religious chant or ode*

SONGS
2158 zâmîyr (3), *song*
5058 nᵉgîynâh (1), *instrument; poem*
7438 rôn (1), *shout of deliverance*
7440 rinnâh (1), *shout*
7892 shîyr (12), *song*
5603 õ₁dĕ (3), *religious chant or ode*

SONS
1121 bên (1024), *son*
1123 bên (Ch.) (3), *son*
2860 châthân (2), *relative; bridegroom*
3206 yeled (3), *young male*
3211 yâlîyd (2), *born; descendants*
5043 tĕknŏn (6), *child*
5206 huiŏthĕsia (1), *placing as a son*
5207 huiŏs (24), *son*

SONS'
1121 bên (26), *son*

SOON
834 'ăsher (6), *because, in order that*
1571 gam (1), *also; even*
2440 chîysh (1), *hurry*
4116 mâhar (3), *to hurry*
4120 mᵉhêrâh (1), *hurry*
4592 mᵉ'aṭ (2), *little*
4758 mar'eh (1), *appearance; vision*
7116 qâtsêr (1), *short*
7323 rûwts (1), *to run*
1096 ginŏmai (1), *to be*
2112 ĕuthĕŏs (2), *soon*
3711 ŏrgilŏs (1), *irascible, hot-tempered*
3752 hŏtan (2), *inasmuch as, at once*
3753 hŏtĕ (2), *when; as*
3916 parachrĕma (1), *instantly, immediately*
5030 tachĕŏs (2), *speedily, rapidly*

SOONER
5032 tachiŏn (1), *more rapidly, more speedily*

SOOTHSAYER
7080 qâçam (1), *to divine magic*

SOOTHSAYERS
1505 gᵉzar (Ch.) (4), *to determine by divination*
6049 'ânan (2), *to cover, becloud; to act covertly*

SOOTHSAYING
3132 mantĕuŏmai (1), *to utter spells, fortune-tell*

SOP
5596 psŏmiŏn (4), *morsel*

SOPATER
4986 Sŏpatrŏs (1), *of a safe father*

SOPE
1287 bôrîyth (2), *alkali soap*

SOPHERETH
5618 Çôphereth (2), *female scribe*

SORCERER
3097 magŏs (2), *Oriental scientist, i.e. magician*

SORCERERS
3784 kâshaph (3), *to enchant*
3786 kashshâph (1), *magician, sorcerer*
5332 pharmakĕus (1), *magician, sorcerer*
5333 pharmakŏs (1), *magician, sorcerer*

SORCERESS
6049 'ânan (1), *to cover, becloud; to act covertly*

SORCERIES
3785 kesheph (2), *sorcery*
3095 magĕia (1), *sorcery*
5331 pharmakĕia (2), *magic, witchcraft*

SORCERY
3096 magĕuō (1), *to practice magic, sorcery*

SORE
1419 gâdôwl (3), *great*
2388 châzaq (4), *to fasten upon; to seize*
2389 châzâq (3), *severe*
2470 châlâh (2), *to be weak, sick, afflicted*
3027 yâd (1), *hand; power*
3510 kâ'ab (2), *to feel pain; to grieve; to spoil*
3513 kâbad (3), *to be heavy, severe, dull*
3515 kâbêd (4), *severe*
3708 ka'aç (4), *vexation*
3966 mᵉ'ôd (22), *very*
4834 mârats (1), *to be pungent or vehement*
5061 nega' (5), *infliction, affliction; leprous spot*
5704+3966 'ad (1), *as far (long) as; during*
7185 qâshâh (1), *to be tough or severe*
7186 qâsheh (1), *severe*
7188 qâshach (1), *to be, make unfeeling*
7235 râbâh (1), *to increase*
7451 ra' (9), *bad; evil*
7690 saggîy' (Ch.) (1), *large*
8178 sa'ar (1), *tempest; terror*
23 aganaktĕŏ (1), *to be indignant*
1568 ĕkthambĕŏ (1), *to astonish utterly*
1630 ĕkphŏbŏs (1), *frightened out*
1668 hĕlkŏs (1), *sore*
2425 hikanŏs (1), *ample*
2560 kakŏs (1), *badly; wrongly; ill*
3029 lian (1), *very much*
3173 mĕgas (1), *great*
4183 pŏlus (1), *much*
4970 sphŏdra (1), *much*

SOREK
7796 Sôwrêq (1), *vine*

SORELY
4843 mârar (1), *to embitter*

SORER
5501 chĕirōn (1), *more evil or aggravated*

SORES
4347 makkâh (1), *wound*
1668 hĕlkŏs (2), *sore*
1669 hĕlkŏō (1), *to be ulcerous*

SORROW
17 'âbŏwy (1), *want*
205 'âven (1), *trouble, vanity, wickedness*
592 'ănîyâh (1), *groaning*
1669 dâ'ab (1), *to pine*
1670 dᵉ'âbâh (1), *pining*
1671 dᵉ'âbôwn (1), *pining*
1674 dᵉ'âgâh (1), *anxiety*
1727 dûwb (1), *to pine*
2342 chûwl (1), *to dance, whirl; to writhe in pain*
2427 chîyl (2), *throe*
2490 châlal (1), *to profane, defile*
3015 yâgôwn (12), *sorrow*
3511 kᵉ'êb (3), *suffering*
3708 ka'aç (4), *vexation*
4044 mᵉginnâh (1), *covering, veil*
4341 mak'ôb (6), *anguish*
4620 ma'ătsêbâh (1), *anguish place*
5999 'âmâl (2), *worry*
6089 'etseb (2), *painful toil; mental pang*
6090 'ôtseb (2), *pain*
6093 'itstsâbôwn (2), *labor or pain*
6094 'atstsebeth (2), *pain or wound, sorrow*
6862 tsar (1), *trouble; opponent*
7451 ra' (1), *bad; evil*
7455 rôa' (1), *badness*
8424 tûwgâh (1), *grief*
3076 lupĕō (1), *to be sad*
3077 lupĕ (10), *sadness*
3601 ŏdunē (1), *grief*
3997 pĕnthŏs (3), *grief*

SORROWED
3076 lupĕō (2), *to be sad*

SORROWETH
1672 dâ'ag (1), *be anxious, be afraid*

SORROWFUL
1669 dâ'ab (1), *to pine*
1741 dᵉvay (1), *sickness*
2342 chûwl (1), *to dance, whirl; to writhe in pain*
3013 yâgâh (1), *to grieve*
3510 kâ'ab (2), *to feel pain; to grieve; to spoil*
7186 qâsheh (1), *severe*
253 alupŏtĕrŏs (1), *more without grief*
3076 lupĕō (6), *to be sad*
4036 pĕrilupŏs (4), *intensely sad*

SORROWING
3600 ŏdunaō (2), *to grieve*

SORROWS
2256 chebel (10), *company, band*
4341 mak'ôb (5), *anguish*

SORRY
1672 dâ'ag (1), *be anxious, be afraid*
2470 châlâh (1), *to be weak, sick, afflicted*
5110 nûwd (1), *to console*
6087 'âtsab (1), *to worry*
3076 lupĕō (9), *to be sad*
4036 pĕrilupŏs (1), *intensely sad*

SORT
1524 gîyl (1), *age, stage*
1697 dâbâr (1), *thing*
3660 kᵉnêmâ' (Ch.) (1), *so or thus*
3671 kânâph (2), *edge*
516 axiŏs (1), *suitable*
3313 mĕrŏs (1), *division*
3697 hŏpŏiŏs (1), *what kind of, what sort of*

SORTS
4358 miklôwl (1), *perfection; splendidly*
4360 miklûl (1), *perfectly splendid garment*

SOSIPATER
4989 Sŏsipatrŏs (1), *of a safe father*

SOSTHENES
4988 Sŏsthĕnēs (2), *of safe strength*

SOTAI
5479 Çôwṭay (2), *roving*

SOTTISH
5530 çâkâl (1), *silly*

SOUGHT
1156 bᵉ'â' (Ch.) (1), *to seek or ask*
1158 bâ'âh (3), *to ask*
1245 bâqash (55), *to search; to strive after*
1875 dârash (25), *to seek or ask; to worship*
2713 châqar (1), *to examine, search*
8446 tûwr (1), *to wander search out*
1567 ĕkzētĕō (1), *to seek*
1934 ĕpizētĕō (1), *to search (inquire) for*
2212 zētĕō (36), *to seek*

SOUL
5082 nᵉdîybâh (1), *nobility, i.e. reputation*
5315 nephesh (416), *soul*
5590 psuchē (39), *soul*

SOUL'S
5315 nephesh (1), *soul*

SOULS
5315 nephesh (58), *soul*
5397 nᵉshâmâh (1), *breath, life*
5590 psuchē (19), *soul*

SOUND
1899 hegeh (1), *muttering; rumbling*
1902 higgâyôwn (1), *musical notation*

1993 hâmâh (3), to *be in great commotion*
4832 marpê' (1), *cure; deliverance; placidity*
5674 'âbar (2), to *cross over; to transition*
6310 peh (1), *mouth*
6963 qôwl (39), *sound*
7032 qâl (Ch.) (4), *sound*
7321 rûwa' (2), to *shout*
8085 shâma' (3), to *hear*
8454 tûwshîyâh (3), *ability, help*
8549 tâmîym (1), *entire, complete; integrity*
8629 têqa' (1), *blast* of a *trumpet*
8643 t^erûw'âh (1), *battle-cry; clangor*
2279 ēchŏs (2), *roar*
4537 salpizō (5), to *sound a trumpet blast*
4995 sōphrŏnismŏs (1), *self-control*
5198 hugiainō (8), to *have sound health*
5199 hugiēs (1), *well*
5353 phthŏggŏs (1), *utterance; musical*
5456 phōnē (8), *sound*

SOUNDED
2690 châtsar (3), to *blow the trumpet*
2713 châqar (1), to *search*
8628 tâqa' (2), to *clatter, slap, drive, clasp*
1001 bŏlizō (2), to *heave a weight*
1096 ginŏmai (1), to *be*
1837 ĕxēchĕŏmai (1), to *echo forth, i.e. resound*
4537 salpizō (7), to *sound a trumpet blast*

SOUNDING
1906 hêd (1), *shout of joy*
1995 hâmôwn (1), *noise*
2690 châtsar (1), to *blow the trumpet*
8085 shâma' (1), to *hear*
8643 t^erûw'âh (2), *battle-cry; clangor*
2278 ēchĕō (1), to *reverberate, ring out*

SOUNDNESS
4974 m^ethôm (3), *wholesomeness*
3647 hŏlŏklēria (1), *wholeness*

SOUNDS
5353 phthŏggŏs (1), *utterance; musical*

SOUR
1155 bôçer (4), *immature, sour grapes*
5493 çûwr (1), to *turn off*

SOUTH
1864 dârôwm (17), *south; south wind*
2315 cheder (1), *apartment, chamber*
3220 yâm (1), *sea; west*
3225 yâmîyn (3), *south*
4057 midbâr (1), *desert*
5045 negeb (97), *South*
8486 têymân (14), *south; southward; south wind*
3047 lips (1), *southwest*

3314 mĕsēmbria (1), *midday; south*
3558 nŏtŏs (7), *south*

SOUTHWARD
5045 negeb (17), *south*
8486 têymân (7), *south*

SOW
2232 zâra' (28), to *sow seed; to disseminate*
4687 spĕirō (8), to *scatter, i.e. sow* seed
5300 hus (1), *swine*

SOWED
2232 zâra' (2), to *sow seed; to disseminate*
4687 spĕirō (8), to *scatter, i.e. sow seed*

SOWEDST
2232 zâra' (1), to *sow seed; to disseminate*

SOWER
2232 zâra' (2), to *sow seed; to disseminate*
4687 spĕirō (6), to *scatter, i.e. sow seed*

SOWEST
4687 spĕirō (3), to *scatter, i.e. sow seed*

SOWETH
2232 zâra' (2), to *sow seed; to disseminate*
4900 mâshak (1), to *draw out; to be tall*
7971 shâlach (3), to *send away*
4687 spĕirō (9), to *scatter, i.e. sow seed*

SOWING
2221 zêrûwa' (1), *plant*
2233 zera' (1), *seed; fruit, plant, sowing-time*

SOWN
2221 zêrûwa' (1), *plant*
2232 zâra' (14), to *sow seed; to disseminate*
4218 mizrâ' (1), *planted field*
4687 spĕirō (15), to *scatter, i.e. sow seed*

SPACE
1366 g^ebûwl (2), *border*
3117 yôwm (3), *day; time*
4390 mâlê' (1), to *fill*
4725 mâqôwm (1), *place*
5750 'ôwd (1), *again*
7281 rega' (1), *very short space* of time
7305 revach (1), *room*
7350 râchôwq (1), *remote*
575 apŏ (1), *from, away*
1024 brachus (1), *short*
1292 diastēma (1), *interval of time*
1339 diïstēmi (1), to *remove, intervene*
1909 ĕpi (3), *on, upon*
4158 pŏdērēs (1), *robe reaching the ankles*
5550 chrŏnŏs (2), *space of time, period*

SPAIN
4681 Spania (2), *Spania*

SPAKE
559 'âmar (109), to *say*
560 'âmar (Ch.) (1), to *say*

981 bâṭâ' (1), to *babble*
1696 dâbar (318), to *say*
4449 m^elal (Ch.) (2), to *speak, say*
5002 n^e'ûm (1), *oracle*
6030 'ânâh (3), to *respond*
6032 'ănâh (Ch.) (14), to *respond, answer*
400 anaphōnĕō (1), to *exclaim*
483 antilĕgō (2), to *dispute, refuse*
626 apŏlŏgĕŏmai (1), to *give an account*
2036 ĕpō (30), to *speak*
2046 ĕrĕō (3), to *utter*
2551 kakŏlŏgĕō (1), to *revile, curse*
2980 lalĕō (72), to *talk*
3004 lĕgō (17), to *say*
4227 Pŏudēs (1), *modest*
4377 prŏsphōnĕō (3), to *address, exclaim*
4814 sullalĕō (1), to *talk together, i.e. converse*
5537 chrēmatizō (1), to *utter an oracle*

SPAKEST
559 'âmar (1), to *say*
1696 dâbar (8), to *speak*
1697 dâbâr (1), *word*

SPAN
2239 zereth (7), *span*
2949 ṭippûch (1), *nursing, caring for*

SPANNED
2946 ṭâphach (1), to *extend, spread out*

SPARE
2347 chûwç (14), to *be compassionate*
2550 châmal (13), to *spare, have pity on*
2820 châsak (3), to *refuse, spare, preserve*
5375 nâsâ' (3), to *lift up*
5545 çâlach (1), to *forgive*
8159 shâ'âh (1), to *inspect, consider*
4052 pĕrissĕuō (1), to *superabound*
5339 phĕidŏmai (4), to *treat leniently*

SPARED
2347 chûwç (2), to *be compassionate*
2550 châmal (4), to *spare, have pity on*
2820 châsak (2), to *refuse, spare, preserve*
5339 phĕidŏmai (4), to *treat leniently*

SPARETH
2550 châmal (1), to *spare, have pity on*
2820 châsak (3), to *refuse, spare, preserve*

SPARING
5339 phĕidŏmai (1), to *treat leniently*

SPARINGLY
5340 phĕidŏmĕnōs (2), *stingily, sparingly*

SPARK
5213 nîytsôwts (1), *spark*
7632 shâbîyb (1), *flame*

SPARKLED
5340 nâtsats (1), to *be bright-colored*

SPARKS
1121+7565 bên (1), *son, descendant; people*
2131 zîyqâh (2), *flash*
3590 kîydôwd (1), *spark*

SPARROW
6833 tsippôwr (1), *little hopping bird*

SPARROWS
4765 strŏuthiŏn (4), *little sparrow*

SPAT
4429 ptuō (1), to *spit*

SPEAK
559 'âmar (47), to *say*
560 'âmar (Ch.) (2), to *say*
1680 dâbab (1), to *move slowly, i.e. glide*
1696 dâbar (276), to *speak*
1897 hâgâh (3), to *murmur, utter a sound*
2790 chârash (1), to *engrave; to plow*
4405 millâh (1), *word; discourse; speech*
4448 mâlal (1), to *speak*
4449 m^elal (Ch.) (1), to *speak, say*
4911 mâshal (2), to *use figurative language*
5608 çâphar (2), to *recount an event*
5790 'ûwth (1), to *succor*
6030 'ânâh (5), to *answer*
6315 pûwach (1), to *utter*
7878 sîyach (4), to *ponder, muse aloud*
653 apŏstŏmatizō (1), to *question carefully*
669 apŏphthĕggŏmai (1), *declare, address*
987 blasphēmĕō (5), to *speak impiously*
1097 ginōskō (1), to *know*
2036 ĕpō (6), to *speak*
2046 ĕrĕō (2), to *utter*
2551 kakŏlŏgĕō (1), to *revile, curse*
2635 katalalĕō (3), to *speak slander*
2980 lalĕō (101), to *talk*
3004 lĕgō (30), to *say*
4354 prŏslalĕō (1), to *converse with*
5350 phthĕggŏmai (2), to *utter a clear sound*

SPEAKER
376+3956 'îysh (1), *man*
3056 lŏgŏs (1), *word*

SPEAKEST
1696 dâbar (11), to *speak*
2980 lalĕō (4), to *talk*
3004 lĕgō (2), to *say*

SPEAKETH
559 'âmar (7), to *say*
981 bâṭâ' (1), to *babble*
1696 dâbar (22), to *say*
1897 hâgâh (1), to *murmur, utter a sound*
4448 mâlal (1), to *speak*
5046 nâgad (1), to *announce*

SPEAKING
6315 pûwach (5), to *utter*
6963 qôwl (1), *voice*
483 antilĕgō (1), to *dispute, refuse*
1256 dialĕgŏmai (1), to *discuss*
2036 ĕpō (2), to *speak*
2635 katalalĕō (2), to *speak slander*
2980 lalĕō (22), to *talk*
3004 lĕgō (4), to *say*

SPEAKING
1696 dâbar (37), to *speak*
2790 chârash (1), to *engrave; to plow*
4405 millâh (2), *word; discourse; speech*
4449 mᵉlal (Ch.) (1), to *speak, say*
226 alēthĕuō (1), to *be true*
987 blasphĕmĕō (1), to *speak impiously*
988 blasphēmia (1), *impious speech*
2980 lalĕō (11), to *talk*
3004 lĕgō (1), to *say*
4180 pŏlulŏgia (1), *prolixity, wordiness*
4354 prŏslalĕō (1), to *converse with*
5350 phthĕggŏmai (1), to *utter* a clear sound
5573 psĕudŏlŏgŏs (1), *promulgating erroneous doctrine*

SPEAKINGS
2636 katalalia (1), *defamation, slander*

SPEAR
2595 chănîyth (34), *lance, spear*
3591 kîydôwn (5), *dart, javelin*
7013 qayin (1), *lance*
7420 rômach (3), iron pointed spear
3057 lŏgchē (1), *lance, spear*

SPEAR'S
2595 chănîyth (1), *lance, spear*

SPEARMEN
7070 qâneh (1), *reed*
1187 dĕxiŏlabŏs (1), *guardsman*

SPEARS
2595 chănîyth (6), *lance, spear*
6767 tsᵉlâtsal (1), *whirring* of wings
7420 rômach (9), iron pointed spear

SPECIAL
5459 çᵉgullâh (1), *wealth*
3756+3858+5177 ŏu (1), *no* or *not*

SPECIALLY
3122 malista (5), *particularly*

SPECKLED
5348 nâqôd (9), *spotted*
6641 tsâbûwa' (1), *hyena*
8320 sâruq (1), *bright red, bay* colored

SPECTACLE
2302 thĕatrŏn (1), *audience-room*

SPED
4672 mâtsâ' (1), to *find* or *acquire; to occur*

SPEECH
562 'ômer (2), something *said*
565 'imrâh (7), something *said*
1697 dâbâr (7), *word*
1999 hămullâh (1), *sound, roar, noise*
3066 Yᵉhûwdîyth (2), *in* the *Jewish language*
3948 leqach (1), *instruction*
4057 midbâr (1), *desert;* also *speech; mouth*
4405 millâh (4), *word; discourse; speech*
6310 peh (1), *mouth; opening*
8088 shêma' (1), something *heard*
8193 sâphâh (6), *lip, language, speech*
2981 lalia (3), *talk, speech*
3056 lŏgŏs (8), *word*
3072 Lukaŏnisti (1), *in* Lycaonian language
3424 mŏgilalŏs (1), *hardly talking*

SPEECHES
561 'êmer (2), something *said*
2420 chîydâh (1), *puzzle; conundrum; maxim*
4405 millâh (2), *word; discourse; speech*
2129 ĕulŏgia (1), *benediction*

SPEECHLESS
1769 ĕnnĕŏs (1), *speechless, silent*
2974 kŏphŏs (1), *silent*
5392 phimŏō (1), *torestrain to silence*

SPEED
553 'âmats (2), to *be strong; be courageous*
629 'oçparnâ' (Ch.) (1), *with diligence*
4116 mâhar (2), to *hurry*
4120 mᵉhêrâh (2), *hurry*
7136 qârâh (1), to *bring about; to impose*
5463 chairō (2), *salutation, "be well"*
5613+5033 hōs (1), *which, how,* i.e. *in that manner*

SPEEDILY
629 'oçparnâ' (Ch.) (4), *with diligence*
926 bâhal (1), to *hasten, hurry anxiously*
1980 hâlak (1), to *walk; live a certain way*
4116 mâhar (1), to *hurry; promptly*
4118 mahêr (4), *in a hurry*
4120 mᵉhêrâh (4), *hurry; promptly*

SPED
4672 mâtsâ' (1), to *find* or *acquire; to occur*

SPEECH

4422 mâlaṭ (1), to *escape* as if by *slipperiness*
5674 'âbar (1), to *cross over; to transition*
1722+5034 ĕn (1), *in; during; because of*

SPEEDY
926 bâhal (1), to *hasten, hurry anxiously*

SPEND
3615 kâlâh (4), to *cease, be finished, perish*
8254 shâqal (1), to *suspend in trade*
1159 dapanaō (1), to *incur cost; to waste*
5551 chrŏnŏtribĕō (1), to *procrastinate, linger*

SPENDEST
4325 prŏsdapanaō (1), to *expend additionally*

SPENDETH
6 'âbad (1), *perish; destroy*
1104 bâla' (1), to *swallow; to destroy*
6213 'âsâh (1), to *do*

SPENT
235 'âzal (1), to *disappear*
3615 kâlâh (4), to *complete, consume*
7286 râdad (1), to *conquer; to overlay*
8552 tâmam (3), to *complete, finish*
1159 dapanaō (2), to *incur cost; to waste*
1230 diaginŏmai (1), to *have time elapse*
1550 ĕkdapanaō (1), to *exhaust, be exhausted*
2119 ĕukairĕō (1), to *have opportunity*
2827 klinō (1), to *slant*
4160 pŏiĕō (1), to *do*
4298 prŏkŏptō (1), to *go ahead, advance*
4321 prŏsanaliskō (1), to *expend further*

SPEWING
7022 qîyqâlôwn (1), *disgrace*

SPICE
1313 bâsâm (1), *balsam*
1314 besem (2), *spice; fragrance; balsam*
7402 râkal (1), to *travel*
7543 râqach (1), to *perfume, blend spice*

SPICED
7544 reqach (1), *spice*

SPICERY
5219 nᵉkô'th (1), *gum,* (poss.) *styrax*

SPICES
1314 besem (22), *spice; fragrance; balsam*
5219 nᵉkô'th (1), *gum,* (poss.) *styrax*
5561 çam (3), *aroma*
759 arōma (4), *scented oils, perfumes, spices*

SPIDER
8079 sᵉmâmîyth (1), *lizard*

SPIDER'S
5908 'akkâbîysh (2), *web-making spider*

SPIED
7200 râ'âh (5), to *see*
7270 râgal (1), to *reconnoiter; to slander*

SPIES
871 'Ăthârîym (1), *places to step*
7270 râgal (10), to *reconnoiter; to slander*
8104 shâmar (1), to *watch*
1455 ĕgkathĕtŏs (1), *spy*
2685 kataskŏpŏs (1), *reconnoiterer,* i.e. a *spy*

SPIKENARD
5373 nêrd (3), *nard*
3487+4101 nardŏs (2), oil from spike-*nard* root

SPILLED
7843 shâchath (1), to *decay; to ruin*
1632 ĕkchĕō (2), to *pour forth; to bestow*

SPILT
5064 nâgar (1), to *pour out; to deliver over*

SPIN
2901 ṭâvâh (1), to *spin yarn*
3514 nēthō (2), to *spin yarn*

SPINDLE
3601 kîyshôwr (1), *spindle* or shank

SPIRIT
178 'ôwb (7), *wineskin; necromancer, medium*
5397 nᵉshâmâh (2), *breath, life*
7307 rûwach (226), *breath; wind; life-spirit*
7308 rûwach (Ch.) (8), *breath; wind; life-spirit*
4151 pnĕuma (255), *spirit*
5326 phantasma (2), *spectre, apparition*

SPIRITS
178 'ôwb (9), *wineskin; necromancer, medium*
7307 rûwach (5), *breath; wind; life-spirit*
4151 pnĕuma (32), *spirit*

SPIRITUAL
7307 rûwach (1), *breath; wind; life-spirit*
4151 pnĕuma (1), *spirit*
4152 pnĕumatikŏs (25), *spiritual*

SPIRITUALLY
3588+4151 hŏ (1), "*the,*" i.e. the definite article
4153 pnĕumatikŏs (2), *non-physical*

SPIT
3417 yâraq (2), to *spit*
7536 rôq (1), *spittle, saliva*
7556 râqaq (1), to *spit*
1716 ĕmptuō (5), to *spit at*
4429 ptuō (2), to *spit*

S

SPITE
3708 ka'aç (1), *vexation*

SPITEFULLY
5195 hubrizō (2), to *exercise violence, abuse*

SPITTED
1716 ĕmptuō (1), to *spit at*

SPITTING
7536 rôq (1), *spittle*

SPITTLE
7388 rîyr (1), *saliva; broth*
7536 rôq (1), *spittle*
4427 ptusma (1), *saliva*

SPOIL
957 baz (4), *plunder, loot*
961 bizzâh (6), *plunder*
962 bâzaz (8), to *plunder*
1500 gᵉzêlâh (1), *robbery, stealing; things stolen*
2254 châbal (1), to *pervert, destroy*
2488 châlîytsâh (1), *spoil, booty* of the dead
2964 țereph (1), *fresh torn prey*
4882 mᵉshûwçâh (1), *spoilation, loot*
4933 mᵉshiççâh (3), *plunder*
5337 nâtsal (1), to *deliver; to be snatched*
6584 pâshaț (1), to *strip*
6906 qâba' (1), to *defraud, rob*
7701 shôd (5), *violence, ravage, destruction*
7703 shâdad (8), to *ravage*
7921 shâkôl (1), to *miscarry*
7997 shâlal (4), to *drop or strip; to plunder*
7998 shâlâl (62), *booty*
8154 shâçâh (3), to *plunder*
8155 shâçaç (1), to *plunder, ransack*
1283 diarpazō (4), *plunder, rob*
4812 sulagōgĕō (1), to *take captive as booty*

SPOILED
957 baz (2), *plunder, loot*
958 bâzâ' (2), to *divide*
962 bâzaz (6), to *plunder*
1497 gâzal (7), to *rob*
5337 nâtsal (1), to *deliver; to be snatched*
6906 qâba' (1), to *defraud*
7701 shôd (3), *violence, ravage, destruction*
7703 shâdad (20), to *ravage*
7758 shôwlâl (2), *stripped; captive*
7997 shâlal (4), to *drop or strip; to plunder*
8154 shâçâh (3), to *plunder*
8155 shâçaç (3), to *plunder, ransack*
554 apĕkduŏmai (1), to *despoil*

SPOILER
7701 shôd (1), *violence, ravage, destruction*

7703 shâdad (8), to *ravage*

SPOILERS
7703 shâdad (3), to *ravage*
7843 shâchath (2), to *decay; to ruin*
8154 shâçâh (2), to *plunder*

SPOILEST
7703 shâdad (1), to *ravage*

SPOILETH
1497 gâzal (1), to *rob*
6584 pâshaț (2), to *strip*
7703 shâdad (1), to *ravage*

SPOILING
7701 shôd (3), *violence, ravage, destruction*
7908 shᵉkôwl (1), *bereavement*
724 harpagē (1), *pillage*

SPOILS
698 'orŏbâh (1), *ambuscades*
7998 shâlâl (2), *booty*
205 akrŏthiniŏn (1), *best of the booty*
4661 skulŏn (1), *plunder*

SPOKEN
559 'âmar (15), to *say*
560 'âmar (Ch.) (1), to *say*
1696 dâbar (174), to *speak, say*
1697 dâbâr (2), *word*
6310 peh (1), *mouth*
312 anaggĕllō (1), to *announce, report*
369 anantirrhĕtōs (1), *without objection*
483 antilĕgō (2), to *dispute, refuse*
987 blasphēmĕō (5), to *speak impiously*
2036 ĕpō (19), to *speak*
2046 ĕrĕō (4), to *utter*
2605 kataggĕllō (1), to *proclaim, promulgate*
2980 lalĕō (33), to *talk*
3004 lĕgō (7), to *say*
4280 prŏĕrĕō (2), to *say already, predict*
4369 prŏstithēmi (1), to *repeat*
4483 rhĕō (15), to *utter*

SPOKES
2840 chishshûr (1), *hub*

SPOKESMAN
1696 dâbar (1), to *speak*

SPOON
3709 kaph (12), *bowl; handle*

SPOONS
3709 kaph (12), *bowl; handle*

SPORT
6026 'ânag (1), to *be soft or pliable*
6711 tsâchaq (1), to *laugh; to make sport* of
7814 sᵉchôwq (1), *laughter; scorn*
7832 sâchaq (3), to *laugh; to scorn; to play*

SPORTING
6711 tsâchaq (1), to *laugh; to make sport* of
1792 ĕntruphaŏ (1), to *revel in, carouse*

SPOT
933 bôhaq (1), *white scurf, rash*
934 bôhereth (9), *whitish, bright* spot
3971 m'ûwm (3), *blemish; fault*
8549 tâmîym (6), *entire, complete; integrity*
299 amōmŏs (1), *unblemished, blameless*
784 aspilŏs (3), *unblemished*
4696 spilŏs (1), *stain or blemish*, i.e. *defect*

SPOTS
934 bôhereth (2), *whitish, bright* spot
2272 chăbarbûrâh (1), *streak, stripe*
4694 spilas (1), *ledge or reef* of rock in the sea
4696 spilŏs (1), *stain or blemish*, i.e. *defect*

SPOTTED
2921 țâlâ' (6), to *be spotted or variegated*
4695 spilŏŏ (1), to *soil*

SPOUSE
3618 kallâh (6), *bride; son's wife*

SPOUSES
3618 kallâh (2), *bride; son's wife*

SPRANG
305 anabainō (1), to *go up, rise*
393 anatĕllō (1), to *cause to arise*
1080 gĕnnaŏ (1), to *procreate, regenerate*
1530 ĕispēdaŏ (1), to *rush in*
1816 ĕxanatĕllō (1), to *germinate, spring forth*
4855 sumphuō (1), to *grow jointly*
5453 phuō (1), to *germinate or grow*

SPREAD
2219 zârâh (2), to *toss about; to diffuse*
3212 yâlak (2), to *walk; to live; to carry*
3318 yâtsâ' (1), to *go, bring out*
3331 yâtsa' (2), to *strew*
4894 mishṭôwach (2), *spreading-place*
5186 nâțâh (5), to *stretch or spread out*
5203 nâțash (4), to *disperse; to thrust off*
5259 nâçak (1), to *interweave*
6327 pûwts (2), to *dash in pieces; to disperse*
6335 pûwsh (1), to *spread; to act proudly*
6555 pârats (1), to *break out*

SPORTING

SPREAD
6566 pâras (49), to *break apart, disperse, scatter*
6581 pâsâh (17), to *spread*
6584 pâshaț (2), to *strip*
6605 pâthach (1), to *open wide; to loosen, begin*
7286 râdad (1), to *conquer; to overlay*
7554 râqa' (4), to *pound*
7849 shâțach (3), to *expand*
1268 dianĕmō (1), to *spread information*
1310 diaphēmizō (1), to *spread news*
1831 ĕxĕrchōmai (2), to *issue; to leave*
4766 strŏnnumi (3), *strew*, i.e. *spread*
5291 hupŏstrŏnnumi (1), to *strew underneath*

SPREADEST
4666 miphrâs (1), *expansion*

SPREADETH
4969 mâthach (1), to *stretch* out
5186 nâțâh (1), to *stretch or spread out*
6566 pâras (6), to *break apart, disperse, scatter*
6576 parshêz (1), to *expand*
6581 pâsâh (1), to *spread*
7502 râphad (1), to *spread a bed; to refresh*
7554 râqa' (2), to *pound*
7971 shâlach (1), to *send away*

SPREADING
4894 mishṭôwach (1), *spreading-place*
5628 çârach (1), to *extend even to excess*
6168 'ârâh (1), to *pour out; demolish*
6524 pârach (1), to *break forth; to bloom; to fly*

SPREADINGS
4666 miphrâs (1), *expansion*

SPRIGS
2150 zalzal (1), *twig, shoot*
6288 pᵉ'ôrâh (1), *foliage, branches*

SPRING
1530 gal (1), *heap; ruins*
1876 dâshâ' (1), to *sprout new plants*
3318 yâtsâ' (1), to *go, bring out*
4161 môwtsâ' (2), *going forth*
4726 mâqôwr (2), *flow of liquids, or ideas*
5927 'âlâh (3), to *ascend, be high, mount*
6524 pârach (1), to *break forth; to bloom; to fly*
6779 tsâmach (10), to *sprout*
6780 tsemach (1), *sprout, branch*
985 blastanō (1), to *yield fruit*

SPRINGETH
3318 yâtsâ' (1), to go, bring out
6524 pârach (1), to break forth; to bloom; to fly
7823 shâchîyç (2), after-growth

SPRINGING
2416 chay (1), alive; raw; fresh; life
6780 tsemach (1), sprout, branch
242 hallŏmai (1), to jump up; to gush up
5453 phuŏ (1), to germinate or grow

SPRINGS
794 'ăshêdâh (3), ravine
1543 gullâh (4), fountain; bowl or globe
4002 mabbûwa' (2), fountain, water spring
4161 môwtsâ' (1), going forth
4599 ma'yân (2), fountain; source
4726 mâqôwr (1), flow
5033 nêbek (1), fountain

SPRINKLE
2236 zâraq (14), to sprinkle, scatter
5137 nâzâh (17), to splash or sprinkle

SPRINKLED
2236 zâraq (16), to sprinkle, scatter
5137 nâzâh (6), to splash or sprinkle
4472 rhantizō (3), to asperse, sprinkle

SPRINKLETH
2236 zâraq (1), to sprinkle, scatter
5137 nâzâh (1), to splash or sprinkle

SPRINKLING
4378 prŏschusis (1), affusion, sprinkling
4472 rhantizō (1), to asperse, sprinkle
4473 rhantismŏs (2), aspersion, sprinkling

SPROUT
2498 châlaph (1), to spring up; to pierce

SPRUNG
6524 pârach (1), to break forth; to bloom; to fly
6779 tsâmach (2), to sprout
305 anabainō (1), to go up, rise
393 anatĕllō (1), to cause to arise
985 blastanō (1), to yield fruit
1816 ĕxanatĕllō (1), to germinate, spring forth
5453 phuŏ (1), to germinate or grow

SPUE
6958 qôw' (2), to vomit
7006 qâyâh (1), to vomit
1692 ĕmĕŏ (1), to vomit

SPUED
6958 qôw' (1), to vomit

SPUN
2901 ţâvâh (1), to spin yarn
4299 maţveh (1), something spun

SPUNGE
4699 spŏggŏs (3), sponge

SPY
7200 râ'âh (2), to see
7270 râgal (7), to reconnoiter; to slander
8446 tûwr (2), to wander, meander
2684 kataskŏpĕŏ (1), to inspect, spy on

SQUARE
7251 râba' (3), to be four sided, to be quadrate

SQUARED
7251 râba' (1), to be four sided, to be quadrate

SQUARES
7253 reba' (2), fourth

STABILITY
530 'ĕmûwnâh (1), fidelity; steadiness

STABLE
3559 kûwn (1), to set up: establish, fix, prepare
5116 nâveh (1), at home; lovely; home

STABLISH
3559 kûwn (2), to set up: establish, fix, prepare
5324 nâtsab (1), to station
6965 qûwm (3), to rise
4741 stērizō (6), to confirm

STABLISHED
3559 kûwn (2), to set up: establish, fix, prepare
5975 'âmad (1), to stand
950 bĕbaiŏō (1), to stabilitate, keep strong

STABLISHETH
3559 kûwn (1), to set up: establish, fix, prepare
950 bĕbaiŏō (1), to stabilitate, keep strong

STACHYS
4720 Stachus (1), head of grain

STACKS
1430 gâdîysh (1), stack of sheaves, shock of grain

STACTE
5198 nâţâph (1), drop; aromatic gum resin

STAFF
2671 chêts (1), arrow; shaft of a spear
4132 môwţ (1), pole; yoke
4294 maţţeh (15), tribe; rod, scepter; club
4731 maqqêl (7), shoot; stick; staff
4938 mish'ênâh (11), walking-stick
6086 'êts (3), wood
6418 pelek (1), spindle-whorl; crutch
7626 shêbeţ (2), stick
4464 rhabdŏs (2), stick, rod

STAGGER
5128 nûwa' (2), to waver
8582 tâ'âh (1), to vacillate, i.e. reel

STAGGERED
1252 diakrinō (1), to decide; to hesitate

STAGGERETH
8582 tâ'âh (1), to vacillate, i.e. reel

STAIN
1350 gâ'al (1), to redeem; to be the next of kin
1351 gâ'al (1), to soil, stain; desecrate
2490 châlal (1), to profane, defile

STAIRS
3883 lûwl (1), spiral step
4095 madrêgâh (1), steep or inaccessible place
4608 ma'ăleh (1), platform; stairs
4609 ma'ălâh (5), thought arising
304 anabathmŏs (2), stairway step

STAKES
3489 yâthêd (2), tent peg

STALK
7054 qâmâh (1), stalk of grain
7070 qâneh (2), reed

STALKS
6086 'êts (1), wood

STALL
4770 marbêq (2), stall
5336 phatnē (1), stall

STALLED
75 'âbaç (1), to feed

STALLS
723 'urvâh (3), herding-place
7517 repheth (1), stall for cattle

STAMMERERS
5926 'illêg (1), stuttering, stammering

STAMMERING
3932 lâ'ag (1), to deride; to speak unintelligibly
3934 lâ'êg (1), buffoon; foreigner

STAMP
1854 dâqaq (1), to crush
7554 râqa' (1), to pound

STAMPED
1854 dâqaq (3), to crush
3807 kâthath (1), to bruise, strike, beat
7429 râmaç (2), to tread
7512 rᵉphaç (Ch.) (2), to trample; to ruin
7554 râqa' (1), to pound

STAMPING
8161 sha'ăţâh (1), clatter of hoofs

STANCHED
2476 histēmi (1), to stand, establish

STAND
539 'âman (1), to be firm, faithful, true; to trust

STANDING
1481 gûwr (1), to sojourn
1826 dâmam (1), to stop, cease; to perish
3318 yâtsâ' (1), to go, bring out
3320 yâtsab (22), to station, offer, continue
5066 nâgash (1), to be, come, bring near
5324 nâtsab (9), to station
5564 çâmak (1), to lean upon; take hold of
5749 'ûwd (1), to protest, testify; to restore
5975 'âmad (144), to stand
5976 'âmad (1), to shake
6965 qûwm (31), to rise
6966 qûwm (Ch.) (2), to rise
7126 qârab (1), to approach, bring near
8617 tᵉqûwmâh (1), resistfulness
450 anistēmi (2), to rise; to come back to life
639 apŏrĕŏ (1), be at a mental loss, be puzzled
1453 ĕgĕirō (1), to waken, i.e. rouse
1510 ĕimi (1), I exist, I am
2476 histēmi (36), to stand, establish
3306 mĕnō (1), to stay
3936 paristēmi (3), to stand beside, present
4026 pĕriistēmi (1), to stand around; to avoid
4739 stēkō (7), to persevere, be steadfast

STANDARD
1714 degel (10), flag, standard, banner
5127 nûwç (1), to vanish
5251 nêç (7), flag; signal

STANDARD-BEARER
5264 nâçaç (1), to gleam; to flutter a flag

STANDARDS
1714 degel (3), flag, standard, banner

STANDEST
5975 'âmad (4), to stand
2476 histēmi (2), to stand

STANDETH
3559 kûwn (1), to set up
5324 nâtsab (4), to station
5975 'âmad (14), to stand
2476 histēmi (8), to stand
4739 stēkō (1), to persevere, be steadfast

STANDING
98 'ăgam (2), marsh; pond; pool
3320 yâtsab (1), to station, offer, continue
4613 mo'ŏmâd (1), foothold
4676 matstsêbâh (2), column or stone
5324 nâtsab (4), to station
5975 'âmad (12), to stand
5979 'emdâh (1), station
7054 qâmâh (5), stalk
2186 ĕphistēmi (1), to be present; to approach

4496 mᵉnûwchâh (1), *peacefully; consolation*
5265 nâça' (1), to *start*
5750 'ôwd (19), *still; more*
5975 'âmad (3), to *stand*
7503 râphâh (1), to *slacken*
7673 shâbath (2), to *repose; to desist*
8252 shâqaṭ (2), to *repose*
2089 ĕti (4), *yet, still*
2476 histēmi (4), to *stand, establish*
4357 prŏsmĕnŏ (1), to *remain* in a place
5392 phimŏŏ (1), to *restrain to silence*

STILLED
2013 hâçâh (1), to *hush*
2814 châshâh (1), to *hush* or *keep quiet*

STILLEST
7623 shâbach (1), to *pacify*

STILLETH
7623 shâbach (1), to *pacify*

STING
2759 kĕntrŏn (2), *sting*

STINGETH
6567 pârash (1), to *wound*

STINGS
2759 kĕntrŏn (1), *sting*

STINK
887 bâ'ash (4), to *smell bad*
889 bᵉ'ôsh (3), *stench*
4716 maq (1), *putridity, stench*

STINKETH
887 bâ'ash (1), to *smell bad*
3605 ŏzŏ (1), to *stink*

STINKING
887 bâ'ash (1), to *smell bad*

STIR
5782 'ûwr (13), to *awake*
5927 'âlâh (1), to *ascend, be high, mount*
6965 qûwm (1), to *rise*
329 anazŏpurĕŏ (1), to *re-enkindle, fan a flame*
1326 diĕgĕirŏ (1), to *arouse, stimulate*
5017 tarachŏs (2), *disturbance, tumult*

STIRRED
1624 gârâh (3), to *provoke to anger*
5375 nâsâ' (3), to *lift up*
5496 çûwth (2), to *stimulate; to seduce*
5782 'ûwr (5), to *awake*
5916 'âkar (1), to *disturb* or *afflict*
6965 qûwm (3), to *rise*
1892 ĕpĕgĕirŏ (1), to *excite* against, *stir up*
3947 parŏxunŏ (1), to *exasperate*
3951 parŏtrunŏ (1), to *stimulate to hostility*

4531 salĕuŏ (1), to *waver*, i.e. *agitate, rock, topple*
4787 sugkinĕŏ (1), to *excite to sedition*
4797 sugchĕŏ (1), to *throw into disorder*

STIRRETH
1624 gârâh (3), to *provoke to anger*
5782 'ûwr (4), to *awake*
383 anasĕiŏ (1), to *excite, stir up*

STIRS
8663 tᵉshu'âh (1), *crashing* or *clamor*

STOCK
944 bûwl (1), *produce*
1503 geza' (2), *stump*
6086 'êts (2), *wood*
6133 'êqer (1), *naturalized* citizen
1085 gĕnŏs (2), *kin*

STOCKS
4115 mahpeketh (2), *stocks* for punishment
5465 çad (2), *stocks*
5914 'ekeç (1), *anklet*
6086 'êts (2), (of) *wood*
6729 tsîynôq (1), *pillory*
3586 xulŏn (1), (of) *timber*

STOICKS
4770 Stŏïkŏs (1), *porch*

STOLE
1589 gânab (4), to *thieve*
2813 klĕptŏ (2), to *steal*

STOLEN
1589 gânab (14), to *thieve*

STOMACH'S
4751 stŏmachŏs (1), *stomach*

STOMACHER
6614 pᵉthîygîyl (1), *fine mantle for holidays*

STONE
68 'eben (104), *stone*
69 'eben (Ch.) (6), *stone*
1496 gâzîyth (3), *dressed stone*
5619 çâqal (7), to *throw large stones*
6697 tsûwr (1), *rock*
6872 tsᵉrôwr (1), *parcel; kernel* or *particle*
7275 râgam (10), to *cast stones*
8068 shâmîyr (1), *thorn;* (poss.) *diamond*
2642 katalithazŏ (1), to *stone to death*
2991 laxĕutŏs (1), *rock-quarried*
3034 lithazŏ (4), to *lapidate, to stone*
3035 lithinŏs (3), *made of stone*
3036 lithŏbŏlĕŏ (1), to *throw stones*
3037 lithŏs (36), *stone*
4074 Pĕtrŏs (1), *piece of rock*
5586 psĕphŏs (2), *pebble stone*

STONE'S
3037 lithŏs (1), *stone*

STONED
5619 çâqal (8), to *throw large stones*
7275 râgam (5), to *cast stones*
3034 lithazŏ (4), to *lapidate, to stone*
3036 lithŏbŏlĕŏ (5), to *throw stones*

STONES
68 'eben (136), *stone*
69 'eben (Ch.) (2), *stone*
810 'eshek (1), *testicle*
1496 gâzîyth (4), *dressed stone*
2106 zâvîyth (1), *angle, corner* (as projecting)
2687 châtsâts (1), *gravel*
2789 cheres (1), *piece of earthenware pottery*
5553 çela' (1), *craggy rock; fortress*
5619 çâqal (1), to *throw large stones*
6344 pachad (1), *male testicle*
6697 tsûwr (1), *rock*
3036 lithŏbŏlĕŏ (1), to *throw stones*
3037 lithŏs (16), *stone*

STONESQUARERS
1382 Giblîy (1), *Gebalite*

STONEST
3036 lithŏbŏlĕŏ (2), to *throw stones*

STONING
5619 çâqal (1), to *throw large stones*

STONY
68 'eben (2), *stone*
5553 çela' (1), *craggy rock; fortress*
4075 pĕtrŏdēs (4), *rocky*

STOOD
1826 dâmam (1), to *stop, cease; to perish*
3320 yâtsab (7), to *station, offer, continue*
3559 kûwn (1), to *set up*
4673 matstsâb (2), *fixed spot; office; post*
5324 nâtsab (19), to *station*
5568 çâmar (1), to *bristle*
5975 'âmad (189), to *stand*
5977 'ômed (1), *fixed spot*
6965 qûwm (15), to *rise*
6966 qûwm (Ch.) (4), to *rise*
450 anistēmi (7), to *rise; to come back to life*
2186 ĕphistēmi (5), to *be present; to approach*
2476 histēmi (60), to *stand, establish*
2944 kuklŏŏ (1), to *surround, encircle*
3936 paristēmi (14), to *stand beside, present*
4026 pĕriistēmi (1), to *stand around; to avoid*
4836 sumparaginŏmai (1), to *convene; to appear in aid*
4921 sunistaŏ (1), to *set together*

STOODEST
5324 nâtsab (1), to *station*
5975 'âmad (2), to *stand*

STOOL
3678 kiççê' (1), *throne*

STOOLS
70 'ôben (1), *potter's wheel;* midwife's *stool*

STOOP
7164 qâraç (1), to *hunch*
7812 shâchâh (1), to *prostrate* in homage
7817 shâchach (1), to *sink* or *depress*
2955 kuptŏ (1), to *bend forward, stoop down*

STOOPED
3486 yâshêsh (1), *gray-haired, aged*
3766 kâra' (1), to *prostrate*
6915 qâdad (2), to *bend*
2955 kuptŏ (2), to *bend forward, stoop down*
3879 parakuptŏ (1), to *lean over to peer within*

STOOPETH
7164 qâraç (1), to *hunch*

STOOPING
3879 parakuptŏ (2), to *lean over to peer within*

STOP
2629 châçam (1), to *muzzle; block*
5462 çâgar (1), to *shut up*
5640 çâtham (2), to *stop up; to repair*
6113 'âtsar (1), to *hold back; to maintain, rule*
7092 qâphats (1), to *draw together, to leap; to die*
5420 phrassŏ (1), to *fence or enclose, to block up*

STOPPED
2856 châtham (1), to *close up; to affix a seal*
3513 kâbad (1), to *be heavy, severe, dull*
5534 çâkar (2), to *shut up*
5640 çâtham (6), to *stop up; to repair*
8610 tâphas (1), to *manipulate,* i.e. *seize*
1998 ĕpisuntrĕchŏ (1), to *hasten together upon*
4912 sunĕchŏ (1), to *hold together*
5420 phrassŏ (2), to *fence or enclose, to block up*

STOPPETH
331 'âṭam (3), to *close*
7092 qâphats (1), to *draw together, to leap; to die*

STORE
214 'ôwtsâr (1), *depository*
686 'âtsar (3), to *store up*
1995 hâmôwn (2), *noise, tumult; many, crowd*
3462 yâshên (1), to *sleep; to grow old, stale*
4543 miçᵉnâh (5), *storage-magazine*
4863 mish'ereth (2), *kneading-trough*

6487 piqqâdôwn (1), *deposit*
7235 râbâh (1), to *increase*
8498 tᵉkûwnâh (1), *structure; equipage*
597 apŏthēsaurizō (1), to *store treasure away*
2343 thēsaurizō (2), to *amass, reserve, store up*

STOREHOUSE
214 'ôwtsâr (1), *depository*
5009 tamēïôn (1), *room*

STOREHOUSES
214 'ôwtsâr (2), *depository*
618 'âçâm (1), *storehouse, barn*
834 'âsher (1), *who, which, what, that*
3965 ma'ăbûwç (1), *granary, barn*
4543 miçkᵉnâh (1), *storage-magazine*

STORIES
4609 ma'ălâh (1), *thought arising*

STORK
2624 chăçîydâh (5), *stork*

STORM
2230 zerem (3), *flood*
5492 çûwphâh (3), *hurricane wind*
5584 çâ'âh (1), to *rush*
5591 ça'ar (1), *hurricane*
7722 shôw' (1), *tempest; devastation*
8178 sa'ar (1), *tempest*
8183 sᵉ'ârâh (1), *hurricane wind*
2978 lailaps (2), *whirlwind; hurricane*

STORMY
5591 ça'ar (4), *hurricane*

STORY
4097 midrâsh (2), *treatise*

STOUT
1433 gôdel (1), *magnitude, majesty*
2388 châzaq (1), to *be strong; courageous*
7229 rab (Ch.) (1), *great*

STOUTHEARTED
47+3820 'abbîyr (2), *mighty*

STOUTNESS
1433 gôdel (1), *magnitude, majesty*

STRAIGHT
3474 yâshar (9), to *be straight; to make right*
4334 mîyshôwr (2), *plain; justice*
5676 'êber (3), *opposite*
8626 tâqan (2), to *straighten; to compose*
461 anŏrthŏō (1), to *straighten up*
2113 ĕuthudrŏmĕō (2), to *sail direct*
2116 ĕuthunō (1), to *straighten or level*
2117 ĕuthus (5), *at once, immediately*

3717 ŏrthŏs (1), *straight*

STRAIGHTWAY
3651 kên (1), *just; right*
4116 mâhar (1), to *hurry*
6258 'attâh (1), *now*
6597 pith'ôwm (1), *instantly, suddenly*
1824 ĕxautēs (1), *instantly, at once*
2112 ĕuthĕōs (32), *at once or soon*
2117 ĕuthus (2), *at once*
3916 parachrēma (3), *instantly, immediately*

STRAIN
1368 diulizō (1), to *strain out*

STRAIT
6862 tsar (3), *trouble*
6887 tsârar (3), to *cramp*
4728 stĕnŏs (3), *narrow*
4912 sunĕchō (1), to *hold together*

STRAITEN
6693 tsûwq (1), to *oppress*

STRAITENED
680 'âtsal (1), to *select; refuse; narrow*
3334 yâtsar (2), to *be in distress*
4164 mûwtsaq (1), *distress*
7114 qâtsar (1), to *curtail, cut short*
4729 stĕnŏchōrĕō (2), to *hem in closely*
4912 sunĕchō (1), to *hold together*

STRAITENETH
5148 nâchâh (1), to *guide*

STRAITEST
196 akribĕstatŏs (1), *most exact, very strict*

STRAITLY
547 apĕilē (1), *menace, threat*
4183 pŏlus (2), *much*

STRAITNESS
4164 mûwtsaq (1), *distress*
4689 mâtsôwq (4), *confinement; disability*

STRAITS
3334 yâtsar (1), to *be in distress*
4712 mêtsar (1), *trouble*

STRAKE
5465 chalaō (1), to *lower as into a void*

STRAKES
6479 pᵉtsâlâh (1), *peeling*
8258 shᵉqa'rûwrâh (1), *depression*

STRANGE
312 'achêr (1), *different*
1970 hâkar (1), (poss.) to *injure*
2114 zûwr (22), to *be foreign, strange*
3937 lâ'az (1), to *speak in a foreign tongue*
5234 nâkar (1), to *treat as a foreigner*
5235 neker (1), *calamity*

5236 nêkâr (16), *foreigner; heathendom*
5237 nokrîy (20), *foreign; non-relative; different*
6012 'âmêq (2), *obscure*
245 allŏtriŏs (2), *not one's own*
1854 ĕxō (1), *out, outside*
2087 hĕtĕrŏs (1), *different*
3579 xĕnizō (3), to *be a guest; to be strange*
3581 xĕnŏs (3), *alien*
3861 paradŏxŏs (1), *extraordinary*

STRANGELY
5234 nâkar (1), to *treat as a foreigner*

STRANGER
376+1616 'îysh (1), *man; male; someone*
376+2114 'îysh (3), *man; male; someone*
376+5237 'îysh (2), *man; male; someone*
1121+5235 bên (3), *son, descendant; people*
1121+5236 bên (2), *son, descendant; people*
1616 gêr (69), *foreigner*
2114 zûwr (18), to *be foreign, strange*
4033 mâgûwr (3), *abode*
5235 neker (1), *calamity*
5236 nêkâr (3), *foreigner*
5237 nokrîy (14), *foreign*
8453 tôwshâb (2), *temporary dweller*
241 allŏgĕnēs (1), *foreign, i.e. not a Jew*
245 allŏtriŏs (1), *not one's own*
3581 xĕnŏs (4), *alien*
3939 parŏikĕō (1), to *reside as a foreigner*
3941 parŏikŏs (1), *strange; stranger*

STRANGER'S
1121+5236 bên (1), *son, descendant; people*
1616 gêr (1), *foreigner*

STRANGERS
582+1616 'ĕnôwsh (1), *man; person, human*
1121+5236 bên (6), *son, descendant; people*
1481 gûwr (6), to *sojourn*
1616 gêr (18), *stranger*
2114 zûwr (26), to *be foreign, strange*
4033 mâgûwr (1), *abode*
5236 nêkâr (3), *foreigner*
5237 nokrîy (2), *foreign*
8453 tôwshâb (1), *temporary dweller*
245 allŏtriŏs (3), *not one's own*
1722+3940 ĕn (1), *in; during; because of*
1927 ĕpidēmĕō (1), to *make oneself at home*
3580 xĕnŏdŏchĕō (1), to *be hospitable*
3581 xĕnŏs (6), *alien*
3927 parepidēmŏs (1), *resident foreigner*
3941 parŏikŏs (1), *strange; stranger*

5381 philŏnĕxia (1), *hospitableness to strangers*

STRANGERS'
2114 zûwr (1), to *be foreign, strange*

STRANGLED
2614 chânaq (1), to *choke*
4156 pniktŏs (3), *animal choked to death*

STRANGLING
4267 machănaq (1), *choking, strangling*

STRAW
4963 mathbên (1), *straw*
8401 teben (15), *threshed stalks of grain*

STRAWED
2219 zârâh (1), to *toss about; to winnow*
1287 diaskŏrpizō (2), to *scatter; to squander*
4766 strōnnumi (2), *strew, i.e. spread*

STREAM
650 'âphîyq (1), *valley; stream; mighty, strong*
793 'eshed (1), *stream*
5103 nᵉhar (Ch.) (1), *river; Euphrates River*
5158 nachal (7), *valley*
4215 pŏtamŏs (2), *current, brook*

STREAMS
650 'âphîyq (1), *valley; stream; mighty, strong*
2975 yᵉ'ôr (1), Nile *River; Tigris River*
2988 yâbâl (1), *stream*
5104 nâhâr (2), *stream*
5140 nâzal (2), to *drip*
5158 nachal (4), *valley*
6388 peleg (1), *small irrigation channel*

STREET
2351 chûwts (8), *outside, outdoors; open market*
2351+6440 chûwts (1), *outside, outdoors*
7339 rᵉchôb (22), *myriad*
7784 shûwq (1), *street*
4113 platĕia (3), *wide, open square*
4505 rhumē (2), *alley or crowded avenue*

STREETS
2351 chûwts (34), *outside, outdoors*
7339 rᵉchôb (19), *myriad*
7784 shûwq (2), *street*
58 agŏra (1), *town-square, market*
4113 platĕia (6), *wide, open square*
4505 rhumē (1), *alley or crowded avenue*

STRENGTH
193 'ûwl (1), *powerful; mighty*
202 'ôwn (7), *ability, power; wealth*
353 'ĕyâl (1), *strength*
360 'ĕyâlûwth (1), *power*
386 'êythân (2), *never-failing; eternal*

STRENGTHEN

556 'amtsâh (1), *strength, force*
905 bad (2), *limb, member; bar; chief*
1082 bâlag (1), *to be strengthened; invade*
1369 gᵉbûwrâh (17), *force; valor; victory*
1679 dôbe' (1), *leisurely*
2220 zᵉrôwa' (1), *arm; foreleg; force, power*
2388 châzaq (1), *to be strong; courageous*
2391 chêzeq (1), *help*
2392 chôzeq (5), *power*
2394 chozqâh (1), *vehemence, harshness*
2428 chayil (11), *army; wealth; virtue; strength*
2633 chôçen (2), *wealth, stored riches*
3027 yâd (1), *hand; power*
3581 kôach (57), *force, might; strength*
4206 mâzîyach (2), *belt*
4581 mâ'ôwz (24), *fortified place; defense*
5326 nitsbâh (Ch.) (1), *firmness, hardness*
5331 netsach (2), *splendor; lasting*
5332 nêtsach (1), *blood (as if red juice)*
5797 'ôz (60), *strength*
5807 'ĕzûwz (2), *forcibleness*
6106 'etsem (1), *bone; body; substance*
6109 'otsmâh (2), *powerfulness*
6697 tsûwr (5), *rock*
7293 rahab (1), *bluster*
7296 rôhab (1), *pride*
8443 tôw'âphâh (3), *treasure; speed*
8510 têl (1), *mound*
8632 tᵉqôph (Ch.) (1), *power*
8633 tôqeph (1), *might*
772 asthĕnĕs (1), *strengthless, weak*
1411 dunamis (7), *force, power, miracle*
1743 ĕndunamŏŏ (1), *empower, strengthen*
1849 ĕxŏusia (1), *authority, power, right*
2479 ischus (4), *forcefulness, power*
2480 ischuŏ (1), *to have or exercise force*
2904 kratŏs (1), *vigor, strength*
4732 stĕrĕŏŏ (1), *to be, become strong*

STRENGTHEN

553 'âmats (3), *to be strong; be courageous*
1396 gâbar (2), *to be strong; to prevail*
2388 châzaq (14), *to be strong; courageous*
4581 mâ'ôwz (1), *fortified place; defense*
5582 çâ'ad (2), *to support*
5810 'âzaz (2), *to be stout; be bold*
6965 qûwm (1), *to rise*

4599 sthĕnŏŏ (1), *to strengthen*
4741 stĕrizŏ (2), *to turn resolutely; to confirm*

STRENGTHENED

553 'âmats (3), *to be strong; be courageous*
2388 châzaq (28), *to be strong; courageous*
2394 chozqâh (1), *vehemence, harshness*
5810 'âzaz (3), *to be stout; be bold*
1412 dunamŏŏ (1), *to enable, strengthen*
1743 ĕndunamŏŏ (1), *empower, strengthen*
1765 ĕnischuŏ (1), *invigorate oneself*
2901 krataiŏŏ (1), *increase in vigor*

STRENGTHENEDST

7292 râhab (1), *to urge, importune, embolden*

STRENGTHENETH

553 'âmats (3), *to be strong; be courageous*
1082 bâlag (1), *to be strengthened*
1396 gâbar (1), *to be strong; to prevail*
5582 çâ'ad (1), *to support*
5810 'âzaz (1), *to be stout; be bold*
1743 ĕndunamŏŏ (1), *empower, strengthen*

STRENGTHENING

1765 ĕnischuŏ (1), *invigorate oneself*
1991 ĕpistĕrizŏ (1), *re-establish, strengthen*

STRETCH

5186 nâṭâh (28), *to stretch or spread out*
5628 çârach (1), *to extend even to excess*
6566 pâras (2), *to break apart, disperse, scatter*
7323 rûwts (1), *to run*
7971 shâlach (10), *to send away*
8311 sâra' (1), *to be deformed*
1614 ĕktĕinŏ (4), *to stretch*
5239 hupĕrĕktĕinŏ (1), *extend inordinately*

STRETCHED

1457 gâhar (2), *to prostrate, bow down*
4058 mâdad (1), *to be extended*
4900 mâshak (1), *to draw out; to be tall*
5186 nâṭâh (47), *to stretch or spread out*
5203 nâṭash (1), *to disperse; to thrust off*
5628 çârach (1), *to extend even to excess*
6504 pârad (1), *to spread or separate*
6566 pâras (2), *to break apart, disperse, scatter*
7554 râqa' (1), *to pound*
7849 shâṭach (1), *to expand*

7971 shâlach (4), *to send away*
1600 ĕkpĕtannumi (1), *to extend, spread out*
1614 ĕktĕinŏ (7), *to stretch*
1911 ĕpiballŏ (1), *to throw upon*

STRETCHEDST

5186 nâṭâh (1), *to stretch*

STRETCHEST

5186 nâṭâh (1), *to stretch*

STRETCHETH

5186 nâṭâh (6), *to stretch*
6566 pâras (1), *to break apart, disperse, scatter*

STRETCHING

4298 muṭṭâh (1), *expansion, extending*
1614 ĕktĕinŏ (1), *to stretch*

STRICKEN

935 bôw' (7), *to go, come*
1856 dâqar (1), *to stab, pierce; to starve*
2498 châlaph (1), *to pierce; to change*
5060 nâga' (1), *to strike*
5061 nega' (1), *infliction, affliction; leprous spot*
5218 nâkê' (1), *smitten*
5221 nâkâh (3), *to strike, kill*
8628 tâqa' (1), *to slap*
4260 prŏbainŏ (2), *to advance*

STRIFE

1777 dîyn (1), *to judge; to strive or contend for*
1779 dîyn (1), *judge; judgment; law suit*
4066 mâdôwn (7), *contest or quarrel*
4683 matstsâh (1), *quarrel*
4808 mᵉrîybâh (5), *quarrel*
7379 rîyb (14), *contest*
485 antilŏgia (1), *dispute, disobedience*
2052 ĕrithĕia (4), *faction, strife, selfish ambition*
2054 ĕris (4), *quarrel, i.e. wrangling*
5379 philŏnĕikia (1), *dispute, strife*

STRIFES

4090 mᵉdân (1), *contest or quarrel*
2052 ĕrithĕia (1), *faction, strife, selfish ambition*
3055 lŏgŏmachia (1), *disputation*
3163 machê (1), *controversy, conflict*

STRIKE

2498 châlaph (1), *too pierce; to change*
4272 mâchats (1), *to crush; to subdue*
5060 nâga' (1), *to strike*
5130 nûwph (1), *to quiver, vibrate, rock*
5221 nâkâh (1), *to strike, kill*

5344 nâqab (1), *to puncture, perforate*
5414 nâthan (1), *to give*
6398 pâlach (1), *to pierce*
8628 tâqa' (2), *to slap*
906 ballŏ (1), *to throw*

STRIKER

4131 plĕktĕs (2), *pugnacious*

STRIKETH

5606 çâphaq (1), *to clap the hands*
8628 tâqa' (1), *to clatter, slap, drive, clasp*
3817 paiŏ (1), *to hit*

STRING

3499 yether (1), *remainder; small rope*
1199 dĕsmŏn (1), *shackle; impediment*

STRINGED

4482 mên (1), *part; musical chord*
5058 nᵉgîynâh (2), *stringed instrument*

STRINGS

4340 mêythâr (1), *tent-cord; bow-string*

STRIP

6584 pâshaṭ (7), *to strip*

STRIPE

2250 chabbûwrâh (1), *weal, bruise*

STRIPES

2250 chabbûwrâh (1), *weal, bruise*
4112 mahălummâh (1), *blow*
4347 makkâh (2), *blow; wound; pestilence*
5061 nega' (2), *infliction, affliction; leprous spot*
5221 nâkâh (2), *to strike, kill*
3468 mŏlŏps (1), *black eye or blow-mark, welt*
4127 plĕgê (7), *stroke; wound; calamity*

STRIPLING

5958 'elem (1), *lad, young man*

STRIPPED

5337 nâtsal (2), *to deliver; to be snatched*
6584 pâshaṭ (6), *to strip*
7758 shôwlâl (1), *bare-foot; stripped*
1562 ĕkduŏ (2), *to divest*

STRIPT

6584 pâshaṭ (1), *to strip*

STRIVE

1777 dîyn (1), *to judge; to strive or contend for*
3401 yârîyb (2), *contentious; adversary*
5327 nâtsâh (2), *to quarrel, fight*
7378 rîyb (9), *to hold a controversy; to defend*
7379 rîyb (1), *contest*
75 agŏnizŏmai (1), *to struggle; to contend*
118 athlĕŏ (2), *to contend in games*

S

2051 ĕrizō (1), to *wrangle, quarrel*
3054 lŏgŏmachĕō (1), to *be disputatious*
3164 machŏmai (1), to *quarrel, dispute*
4865 sunagōnizŏmai (1), to *struggle with*

STRIVED
5389 philŏtimĕŏmai (1), *eager or earnest to do*

STRIVEN
1624 gârâh (1), to *provoke to anger*

STRIVETH
7378 rîyb (1), to *hold a controversy; to defend*
75 agōnizŏmai (1), to *struggle; to contend*

STRIVING
75 agōnizŏmai (1), to *struggle; to contend*
464 antagōnizŏmai (1), to *struggle against*
4866 sunathlĕō (1), to *wrestle with*

STRIVINGS
7379 rîyb (2), *contest*
3163 machē (1), *controversy, conflict*

STROKE
3027 yâd (1), *hand; power*
4046 maggêphâh (1), *pestilence; defeat*
4273 machats (1), *contusion*
4347 makkâh (2), *blow; wound; pestilence*
5061 nega' (3), *infliction, affliction; leprous spot*
5607 cêpheq (1), *satiety*

STROKES
4112 mahălummâh (1), *blow*

STRONG
47 'abbîyr (3), *mighty*
386 'êythân (5), *never-failing; eternal*
410 'êl (1), *mighty*
533 'ammîyts (4), *strong; mighty; brave*
553 'âmats (4), to be *strong; be courageous*
559 'âmar (1), to *say*
650 'âphîyq (1), *valley; stream; mighty, strong*
1219 bâtsar (1), to be *inaccessible*
1225 bitstsârôwn (1), *fortress*
1368 gibbôwr (5), *powerful; great warrior*
1634 gerem (1), *bone; self*
2364 Chûwshâh (1), *haste*
2388 châzaq (47), to be *strong; courageous*
2389 châzâq (26), *strong; severe, hard, violent*
2393 chezqâh (1), *power*
2394 chozqâh (1), *vehemence, harshness*
2428 chayil (5), *army; wealth; virtue; strength*
2626 chăçîyn (1), *mighty*
2634 châçôn (1), *strong*

3524 kabbîyr (1), *mighty; aged; mighty*
4013 mibtsâr (14), *fortification; defender*
4581 mâ'ôwz (5), *fortified place; defense*
4679 mᵉtsad (5), *stronghold*
4686 mâtsûwd (2), *net or capture; fastness*
4692 mâtsôwr (3), *siege-mound; distress*
4694 mᵉtsûwrâh (1), *rampart, fortification*
5553 çela' (1), *craggy rock; fortress*
5794 'az (12), *strong, vehement, harsh*
5797 'ôz (17), *strength*
5808 'izzûwz (1), *forcible; army*
5810 'âzaz (1), to be *stout; be bold*
6076 'ôphel (1), *tumor; fortress*
6099 'âtsûwm (13), *powerful; numerous*
6105 'âtsam (4), to be, *make powerful*
6108 'ôtsem (1), *power; framework of the body*
6110 'atstsûmâh (1), *defensive argument*
6184 'ârîyts (1), *powerful or tyrannical*
6339 pâzaz (1), to *solidify by refining; to spring*
6697 tsûwr (1), *rock*
7682 sâgab (1), to be *safe, strong*
7941 shêkâr (1), *liquor*
8624 taqqîyph (Ch.) (3), *powerful*
8631 tᵉqêph (Ch.) (3), to *become, make mighty*
1415 dunatŏs (3), *powerful or capable*
1743 ĕndunamŏō (4), to *empower, strengthen*
1753 ĕnĕrgĕia (1), *energy, power*
2478 ischurŏs (11), *forcible, powerful*
2901 krataiŏō (3), *increase in vigor*
3173 mĕgas (1), *great*
3794 ŏchurōma (1), *fortress, stronghold*
4608 sikĕra (1), *intoxicant*
4731 stĕrĕŏs (2), *solid*
4732 stĕrĕŏō (1), to be, *become strong*

STRONGER
553 'âmats (2), to be *strong; be courageous*
555 'ômets (1), *strength*
1396 gâbar (1), to be *strong; to prevail*
2388 châzaq (6), to be *strong; courageous*
2389 châzâq (1), *strong*
2390 châzêq (1), *powerful; loud*
5794 'az (1), *strong*
6105 'âtsam (1), to be, *make powerful*
7194 qâshar (2), to *tie, bind*

2478 ischurŏs (3), *forcible, powerful*

STRONGEST
1368 gibbôwr (1), *powerful; great warrior*

STROVE
1519 gîyach (Ch.) (1), to *rush forth*
5327 nâtsâh (6), to *quarrel, fight*
6229 'âsaq (1), to *quarrel*
7378 rîyb (3), to *hold a controversy; to defend*
1264 diamachŏmai (1), to *fight fiercely*
3164 machŏmai (2), to *war, quarrel, dispute*

STROWED
2236 zâraq (1), to *scatter*

STRUCK
5062 nâgaph (2), to *inflict a disease; strike*
5221 nâkâh (1), to *strike*
8138 shânâh (1), to *fold*
1325+4475 didōmi (1), to *give*
3960 patassō (1), to *strike*
5180 tuptō (1), to *strike*

STRUGGLED
7533 râtsats (1), to *crack in pieces, smash*

STUBBLE
7179 qash (16), *dry straw*
8401 teben (1), *threshed stalks of grain*
2562 kalamē (1), *stubble*

STUBBORN
5637 çârar (4), to be *refractory, stubborn*
7186 qâsheh (1), *severe*

STUBBORNNESS
6484 pâtsar (1), to *stun or dull*
7190 qᵉshîy (1), *obstinacy*

STUCK
1692 dâbaq (1), to *cling or adhere; to catch*
4600 mâ'ak (1), to *press*
2043 ĕrĕidō (1), to *make immovable*

STUDIETH
1897 hâgâh (2), to *murmur, ponder*

STUDS
5351 nᵉquddâh (1), *ornamental boss*

STUDY
3854 lahag (1), *mental application*
4704 spŏudazō (1), to *make effort*
5389 philŏtimĕŏmai (1), *eager or earnest to do*

STUFF
3627 kᵉlîy (14), *thing*
4399 mᵉlâ'kâh (1), *work*
4632 skĕuŏs (1), *vessel*

STUMBLE
3782 kâshal (15), to *stumble*
5062 nâgaph (2), to *inflict a disease; strike*
6328 pûwq (1), to *waver*

4350 prŏskŏptō (1), to *trip up; to strike*

STUMBLED
3782 kâshal (3), to *totter*
8058 shâmaṭ (1), to *jostle; to let alone*
4350 prŏskŏptō (1), to *trip up; to strike*
4417 ptaiō (1), to *trip up*

STUMBLETH
3782 kâshal (1), to *totter*
4350 prŏskŏptō (3), to *trip up; to strike*

STUMBLING
5063 negeph (1), *trip*
4625 skandalŏn (1), *snare*

STUMBLINGBLOCK
4383 mikshôwl (7), *stumbling-block*
4348 prŏskŏmma (2), *occasion of apostasy*
4625 skandalŏn (3), *snare*

STUMBLINGBLOCKS
4383 mikshôwl (1), *stumbling-block*
4384 makshêlâh (1), *stumbling-block*

STUMBLINGSTONE
3037+4348 lithŏs (2), *stone*

STUMP
6136 'iqqar (Ch.) (3), *stock*

SUAH
5477 Çûwach (1), *sweeping*

SUBDUE
1696 dâbar (1), to *subdue*
3533 kâbash (3), to *conquer, subjugate*
3665 kâna' (1), to *humiliate, subdue*
7286 râdad (1), to *conquer; to overlay*
8214 shᵉphal (Ch.) (1), to *humiliate*
5293 hupŏtassō (1), to *subordinate; to obey*

SUBDUED
3381 yârad (1), to *descend*
3533 kâbash (5), to *conquer, subjugate*
3665 kâna' (9), to *humiliate, subdue*
3766 kâra' (2), to *prostrate*
2610 katagōnizŏmai (1), to *overcome, defeat*
5293 hupŏtassō (1), to *subordinate; to obey*

SUBDUEDST
3665 kâna' (1), to *humiliate, subdue*

SUBDUETH
1696 dâbar (1), to *subdue*
2827 chăshal (Ch.) (1), to *crush, pulverize*
7286 râdad (1), to *conquer; to overlay*

SUBJECT
1379 dŏgmatizō (1), to *submit to a certain rule*

1777 ĕnŏchŏs (1), *liable*
3663 hŏmŏiŏpathēs (1),
  similarly affected
5293 hupŏtassō (14), to
  subordinate; to obey

SUBJECTED
5293 hupŏtassō (1), to
  subordinate; to obey

SUBJECTION
3533 kâbash (2), to
  conquer, subjugate
3665 kâna' (1), to
  humiliate, subdue
1396 dŏulagōgĕō (1), to
  enslave, subdue
5292 hupŏtagē (4),
  subordination
5293 hupŏtassō (6), to
  subordinate; to obey

SUBMIT
3584 kâchash (3), to *lie,*
  disown; to cringe
6031 'ânâh (1), to *afflict,*
  be afflicted
7511 râphaç (1), to
  trample; to prostrate
5226 hupeïkō (1), to
  surrender, yield
5293 hupŏtassō (6), to
  subordinate; to obey

SUBMITTED
3584 kâchash (1), to *lie,*
  disown; to cringe
5414+3027 nâthan (1), to
  give
5293 hupŏtassō (1), to
  subordinate; to obey

SUBMITTING
5293 hupŏtassō (1), to
  subordinate; to obey

SUBORNED
5260 hupŏballō (1), to
  throw in stealthily

SUBSCRIBE
3789 kâthab (2), to *write*

SUBSCRIBED
3789 kâthab (2), to *write*

SUBSTANCE
202 'ôwn (1), *ability,*
  power; wealth
1564 gôlem (1), *embryo*
1942 havvâh (1), *desire;*
  craving
1952 hôwn (7), *wealth*
2428 chayil (7), *wealth;*
  virtue; valor; strength
3351 yᵉqûwm (3), *living*
  thing
3426 yêsh (1), there *is*
3428 Yesheb'âb (1), *seat*
  of (his) *father*
3581 kôach (1), *force,*
  might; strength
4678 matstsebeth (2),
  stock of a tree
4735 miqneh (2), *stock*
6108 'ôtsem (1), *power;*
  framework of the body
7009 qîym (1), *opponent*
7075 qinyân (4),
  acquisition, purchase
7399 rᵉkûwsh (11),
  property
7738 shâvâh (1), to
  destroy

3776 ŏusia (1), *wealth,*
  property, possessions
5223 huparxis (1),
  property, possessions
5224 huparchŏnta (1),
  property or possessions
5287 hupŏstasis (1),
  essence; assurance

SUBTIL
2450 châkâm (1), *wise,*
  intelligent, skillful
5341 nâtsar (1), to
  conceal, hide
6175 'ârûwm (1),
  cunning; clever

SUBTILLY
5230 nâkal (1), to *act*
  treacherously
6191 'âram (1), to *be*
  cunning; be prudent
2686 katasŏphizŏmai*
  (1), to *be crafty against*

SUBTILTY
4820 mirmâh (1), *fraud*
6122 'oqbâh (1), *trickery*
6195 'ormâh (1), *trickery;*
  discretion
1388 dŏlŏs (2), *wile,*
  deceit, trickery
3834 panŏurgia (1),
  trickery or sophistry

SUBURBS
4054 migrâsh (110), *open*
  country
6503 Parbâr (1), *Parbar*

SUBVERT
5791 'âvath (1), to *wrest,*
  twist
396 anatrĕpō (1), to
  overturn, destroy

SUBVERTED
1612 ĕkstrĕphō (1), to
  pervert, be warped

SUBVERTING
384 anaskĕuazō (1), to
  upset, trouble
2692 katastrŏphē (1),
  catastrophical ruin

SUCCEED
6965 qûwm (1), to *rise*

SUCCEEDED
3423 yârash (3), to
  impoverish; to ruin

SUCCEEDEST
3423 yârash (2), to
  impoverish; to ruin

SUCCESS
7919 sâkal (1), to *be or*
  act circumspect

SUCCOTH
5523 Çukkôwth (18),
  booths

SUCCOTH-BENOTH
5524 Çukkôwth Bᵉnôwth
  (1), *brothels*

SUCCOUR
5826 'âzar (2), to *aid*
997 bŏēthĕō (1), to *aid*

SUCCOURED
5826 'âzar (1), to *aid*
997 bŏēthĕō (1), to *aid*

SUCCOURER
4368 prŏstatis (1),
  assistant, helper

SUCHATHITES
7756 Sûwkâthîy (1),
  Sukathite

SUCK
3243 yânaq (13), to *suck*
4680 mâtsâh (1), to
  drain; to squeeze out
5966 'âla' (1), to *sip up*
2337 thēlazō (4), to *suck*

SUCKED
3243 yânaq (1), to *suck*
2337 thēlazō (1), to *suck*

SUCKING
2461 châlâb (1), *milk*
3243 yânaq (3), to *suck*
5764 'ûwl (1), *babe*

SUCKLING
3243 yânaq (3), to *suck*

SUCKLINGS
3243 yânaq (3), to *suck*
2337 thēlazō (1), to *suck*

SUDDEN
6597 pith'ôwm (2),
  instantly, suddenly
160 aiphnidiŏs (1),
  suddenly

SUDDENLY
4116 mâhar (1), to *hurry*
4118 mahêr (1), *in a*
  hurry
6597 pith'ôwm (22),
  instantly, suddenly
6621 petha' (4), *wink,* i.e.
  moment; quickly
7280 râga' (2), to *settle,*
  i.e. *quiet; to wink*
7281 rega' (1), very *short*
  space of time
869 aphnō (3), *suddenly*
1810 ĕxaiphnēs (5),
  suddenly, unexpectedly
1819 ĕxapina (1),
  unexpectedly
5030 tachĕŏs (1), *rapidly*

SUE
2919 krinō (1), to *decide;*
  to *try, condemn, punish*

SUFFER
3201 yâkôl (1), to *be able*
3240 yânach (3), to *allow*
  to stay
3803 kâthar (1), to
  enclose, besiege; to *wait*
5375 nâsâ' (5), to *lift up*
5414 nâthan (11), to *give*
430 anĕchŏmai (7), *put*
  up with, endure
818 atimazō (1), to
  maltreat, dishonor
863 aphiĕmi (6), to *leave;*
  to pardon, forgive
1325 didŏmi (2), to *give*
1377 diōkō (3), to *pursue;*
  to persecute
1439 ĕaō (2), to *let be,* i.e.
  permit or leave alone
2010 ĕpitrĕpō (6), *allow*
2210 zēmiŏō (1), to
  experience detriment
2553 kakŏpathĕō (1), to
  undergo suffering
2558 kakŏuchĕō (1), to
  maltreat; to torment
3805 pathētŏs (1),
  doomed to pain

3958 paschō (20), to
  experience pain
4722 stĕgō (1), to *endure*
  patiently
4778 sugkakŏuchĕō (1),
  to *endure persecution*
4841 sumpaschō (2), to
  experience pain jointly
5278 hupŏmĕnō (1), to
  undergo, bear (trials)
5302 hustĕrĕō (1), to *be*
  inferior; to fall short

SUFFERED
3240 yânach (2), to *allow*
  to stay
5203 nâṭash (1), to
  disperse; to thrust off
5375 nâsâ' (1), to *lift up*
5414 nâthan (7), to *give*
863 aphiĕmi (6), to *leave;*
  to pardon, forgive
1439 ĕaō (5), to *let be,* i.e.
  permit or leave alone
2010 ĕpitrĕpō (4), *allow*
2210 zēmiŏō (1), to *suffer*
  loss
2967 kōluō (1), to *stop*
3958 paschō (17), to
  experience pain
4310 prŏpaschō (1), to
  undergo hardship
5159 trŏpŏphŏrĕō (1), to
  endure one's habits

SUFFEREST
1439 ĕaō (1), to *let be*

SUFFERETH
5414 nâthan (1), to *give*
971 biazō (1), to *crowd*
  oneself into
1439 ĕaō (1), to *let be*
3114 makrŏthumĕō (1),
  to *be forbearing, patient*

SUFFERING
2552 kakŏpathĕia (1),
  hardship, suffering
3804 pathēma (1),
  passion; suffering
3958 paschō (1), to
  experience pain
4330 prŏsĕaō (1), to
  permit further progress
5254 hupĕchō (1), to
  endure with patience

SUFFERINGS
3804 pathēma (10),
  passion; suffering

SUFFICE
4672 mâtsâ' (2), to *find*
  or acquire; to occur
5606 çâphaq (1), to *be*
  enough; to vomit
7227 rab (3), *great*
713 arkĕtŏs (1), *enough*

SUFFICED
4672 mâtsâ' (1), to *find*
  or acquire; to occur
7646 sâba' (1), *fill* to
  satiety
7648 sôba' (1),
  satisfaction

SUFFICETH
714 arkĕō (1), to *avail; be*
  satisfactory

SUFFICIENCY
5607 çêpheq (1), *satiety*

SUFFICIENT
841 autarkeia (1), contentedness
2426 hikanŏtēs (1), ability, competence

SUFFICIENT
1767 day (5), *enough*
7227 rab (1), *great*
713 arkĕtŏs (1), enough
714 arkĕō (2), to *avail; be satisfactory*
2425 hikanŏs (3), *ample*

SUFFICIENTLY
4078 madday (1), *sufficiently*
7654 sob'âh (1), *satiety*

SUIT
2470 châlâh (1), to *be weak, sick, afflicted*
6187 'êrek (1), *pile, equipment, estimate*
7379 rîyb (1), *contest*

SUKKIIMS
5525 Çukkîy (1), *hut-dwellers*

SUM
3724 kôpher (1), *redemption-price*
4557 miçpâr (2), *number*
6485 pâqad (1), to *visit, care for, count*
6575 pârâshâh (1), *exposition*
7217 rê'sh (Ch.) (1), *head*
7218 rô'sh (9), *head*
8508 toknîyth (1), *consummation*
8552 tâmam (1), to *complete, finish*
2774 kĕphalaiŏn (2), *principal; amount*
5092 timē (1), *esteem; nobility; money*

SUMMER
4747 mᵉqêrâh (2), *cooling, coolness*
6972 qûwts (1), to *spend the harvest season*
7007 qâyiț (Ch.) (1), *harvest season*
7019 qayits (20), *harvest*
2330 thĕrŏs (3), *summer*

SUMPTUOUSLY
2983 lambanō (1), to *take, receive*

SUN
216 'ôwr (1), *luminary*
2535 chammâh (4), *heat of sun*
2775 chereç (3), *itch; sun*
8121 shemesh (120), *sun*
8122 shemesh (Ch.) (1), *sun*
2246 hēliŏs (30), *sun*

SUNDERED
6504 pârad (1), to *spread or separate*

SUNDRY
4181 pŏlumĕrŏs (1), *in many portions*

SUNG
7891 shîyr (1), to *sing*
103 a↓dō (2), to *sing*
5214 humnĕō (2), to *celebrate God in song*

SUNK
2883 țâba' (5), to *sink*
3766 kâra' (1), to *prostrate*
2702 kataphĕrō (1), to *bear down*

SUNRISING
4217 mizrâch (1), *place of sunrise; east*
4217+8121 mizrâch (9), *place of sunrise; east*

SUP
4041 mᵉgammâh (1), *accumulation*
1172 dĕipnĕō (2), to *eat the principal meal*

SUPERFLUITY
4050 pĕrissĕia (1), *superabundance*

SUPERFLUOUS
8311 sâra' (2), to *be deformed*
4053 pĕrissŏs (1), *superabundant*

SUPERSCRIPTION
1923 ĕpigraphē (5), *superscription*

SUPERSTITION
1175 dĕisidaimŏnia (1), *religion*

SUPERSTITIOUS
1174 dĕisidaimŏnĕstĕrŏs (1), *more religious*

SUPPED
1172 dĕipnĕō (1), to *eat the principal meal*

SUPPER
1172 dĕipnĕō (1), to *eat the principal meal*
1173 dĕipnŏn (13), *principal meal*

SUPPLANT
6117 'âqab (1), to *seize by the heel; to circumvent*

SUPPLANTED
6117 'âqab (1), to *seize by the heel; to circumvent*

SUPPLE
4935 mish'îy (1), *inspection*

SUPPLIANTS
6282 'âthâr (1), *incense; worshipper*

SUPPLICATION
2420 chîydâh (1), *puzzle; conundrum; maxim*
2603 chânan (10), to *implore*
2604 chănan (Ch.) (1), to *favor*
6419 pâlal (1), to *intercede, pray*
8467 tᵉchinnâh (22), *supplication*
1162 dĕēsis (4), *petition*

SUPPLICATIONS
8467 tᵉchinnâh (1), *supplication*
8469 tachănûwn (17), *earnest prayer, plea*
1162 dĕēsis (2), *petition*
2428 hikĕtēria (1), *entreaty, supplication*

SUPPLIED
378 anaplērŏō (1), to *complete; to supply*
4322 prŏsanaplērŏō (1), to *furnish fully*

SUPPLIETH
2024 ĕpichŏrēgia (1), *contribution, aid*
4322 prŏsanaplērŏō (1), to *furnish fully*

SUPPLY
378 anaplērŏō (1), to *complete; to supply*
2024 ĕpichŏrēgia (1), *contribution, aid*
4137 plērŏō (1), to *fill, make complete*

SUPPORT
472 antĕchŏmai (1), to *adhere to; to care for*
482 antilambanŏmai (1), to *succor; aid*

SUPPOSE
559 'âmar (1), to *say*
1380 dŏkĕō (3), to *think, regard, seem good*
3049 lŏgizŏmai (2), to *credit; to think, regard*
3543 nŏmizō (1), to *deem*
3633 ŏiŏmai (1), to *imagine, opine*
5274 hupŏlambanō (2), to *assume, presume*

SUPPOSED
1380 dŏkĕō (2), to *think*
2233 hēgĕŏmai (1), to *deem, i.e. consider*
3543 nŏmizō (4), to *deem*
5282 hupŏnŏĕō (1), to *think; to expect*

SUPPOSING
1380 dŏkĕō (2), to *think*
3543 nŏmizō (4), to *deem*
3633 ŏiŏmai (1), to *imagine, opine*

SUPREME
5242 hupĕrĕchō (1), to *excel; be superior*

SUR
5495 Çûwr (1), *deteriorated*

SURE
539 'âman (11), to *be firm, faithful, true*
546 'omnâh (1), *surely*
548 'ămânâh (1), *covenant*
571 'emeth (1), *certainty, truth, trustworthiness*
982 bâțach (1), to *trust, be confident or sure*
2388 châzaq (1), to *bind*
3045 yâda' (4), to *know*
3245 yâçad (1), *settle, consult, establish*
4009 mibțâch (1), *security; assurance*
6965 qûwm (2), to *rise*
7011 qayâm (Ch.) (1), *permanent*
7292 râhab (1), to *urge, embolden, capture*
8104 shâmar (1), to *watch*
804 asphalēs (1), *secure*

805 *asphalizō* (3), to *render secure*
949 bĕbaiŏs (3), *stable, certain, binding*
1097 ginōskō (2), to *know*
1492 ĕidō (3), to *know*
4103 pistŏs (1), *trustworthy; reliable*
4731 stĕrĕŏs (1), *solid*

SURETIES
6148 'ârab (1), to *give or be security*

SURETISHIP
8628 tâqa' (1), to *clatter, slap, drive, clasp*

SURETY
389 'ak (1), *surely*
552 'umnâm (1), *verily*
3045 yâda' (1), to *know*
6148 'ârab (8), to *give or be security*
6161 'ărubbâh (1), *as security; bondsman*
230 alēthōs (1), *surely*
1450 ĕgguŏs (1), *bondsman, guarantor*

SURFEITING
2897 kraipalē (1), *debauch*

SURMISINGS
5283 hupŏnŏia (1), *suspicion*

SURNAME
3655 kânâh (1), to *address, give title*
1941 ĕpikalĕŏmai (6), to *invoke*
2564 kalĕō (1), to *call*

SURNAMED
3655 kânâh (1), to *address, give title*
1941 ĕpikalĕŏmai (5), to *invoke*
2007+3686 ĕpitithēmi (2), to *impose*

SURPRISED
270 'âchaz (1), to *seize*
8610 tâphas (2), to *seize*

SUSANCHITES
7801 Shûwshankîy (Ch.) (1), *Shushankite*

SUSANNA
4677 Sŏusanna (1), *lily*

SUSI
5485 Çûwçîy (1), *horse-like*

SUSTAIN
3557 kûwl (4), to *maintain*

SUSTAINED
5564 çâmak (3), to *lean upon; take hold of*

SUSTENANCE
3557 kûwl (1), to *maintain*
4241 michyâh (1), *sustenance*
5527 chŏrtasma (1), *food*

SWADDLED
2853 châthal (1), to *swathe, wrap in cloth*
2946 țâphach (1), to *nurse*

SWADDLING
4683 sparganŏŏ (2), to *wrap* with cloth

SWADDLINGBAND
2854 chăthullâh (1), *swathing* cloth to wrap

SWALLOW
1104 bâla' (13), to *swallow; to destroy*
1866 d°rôwr (2), *swallow*
3886 lûwa' (1), to *be rash*
5693 'âgûwr (2), *swallow*
7602 shâ'aph (4), to *be angry; to hasten*
2666 katapinŏ (1), to *devour by swallowing*

SWALLOWED
1104 bâla' (19), to *swallow; to destroy*
1105 bela' (1), *gulp*
3886 lûwa' (1), to *be rash*
7602 shâ'aph (1), to *be angry; to hasten*
2666 katapinŏ (4), to *devour by swallowing*

SWALLOWETH
1572 gâmâ' (1), to *swallow*
7602 shâ'aph (1), to *be angry; to hasten*

SWAN
8580 tanshemeth (2), (poss.) *water-hen*

SWARE
5375 nâsâ' (1), to *lift up*
7650 shâba' (70), to *swear*
3660 ŏmnuŏ (7), to *swear, declare on oath*

SWAREST
7650 shâba' (5), to *swear*

SWARM
5712 'êdâh (1), *assemblage; family*
6157 'ârôb (2), swarming *mosquitoes*

SWARMS
6157 'ârôb (5), swarming *mosquitoes*

SWEAR
422 'âlâh (2), *imprecate, utter a curse*
5375 nâsâ' (2), to *lift up*
7650 shâba' (43), to *swear*
3660 ŏmnuŏ (13), to *swear, declare on oath*

SWEARERS
7650 shâba' (1), to *swear*

SWEARETH
7650 shâba' (7), to *swear*
3660 ŏmnuŏ (4), to *swear, declare on oath*

SWEARING
422 'âlâh (2), *imprecate, utter a curse*
423 'âlâh (2), *imprecation: curse*

SWEAT
2188 zê'âh (1), *sweat*
3154 yeza' (1), *sweat*
2402 hidrōs (1), *sweat*

SWEEP
2894 tûw' (1), to *sweep away*

3261 yâ'âh (1), to *brush aside*
4563 sarŏŏ (1), to *sweep clean*

SWEEPING
5502 çâchaph (1), to *scrape off, sweep off*

SWEET
1314 besem (5), *spice; fragrance; balsam*
2896 tôwb (1), *good; well*
3190 yâṭab (1), to *be, make well*
4452 mâlats (1), to *be smooth; to be pleasant*
4477 mamtaq (2), *sweet*
4575 ma'ădannâh (1), *bond, i.e. group*
4840 merqâch (1), *spicy*
4966 mâthôwq (7), *sweet*
4985 mâthaq (5), to *relish; to be sweet*
5207 nîchôwach (43), *pleasant; delight*
5208 nîychôwach (Ch.) (2), *pleasure*
5273 nâ'îym (2), *delightful; sweet*
5276 nâ'êm (1), to *be agreeable*
5561 çam (16), *aroma*
5674 'âbar (2), to *cross over; to transition*
6071 'âçîyç (2), *expressed fresh grape-juice*
6148 'ârab (5), to *intermix*
6149 'ârêb (2), *agreeable*
8492 tîyrôwsh (1), *wine; squeezed grape-juice*
1099 glukus (3), *sweet*
2175 ĕuŏdia (2), *fragrance, aroma*

SWEETER
4966 mâthôwq (2), *sweet*

SWEETLY
4339 mêyshâr (1), *straightness; rectitude*
4988 mâthâq (1), *sweet food*

SWEETNESS
4966 mâthôwq (2), *sweet*
4986 metheq (2), *pleasantness*
4987 môtheq (1), *sweetness*

SWEETSMELLING
2175 ĕuŏdia (1), *fragrance, aroma*

SWELL
1216 bâtsêq (1), to *blister*
6638 tsâbâh (2), to *array an army against*
6639 tsâbeh (1), *swollen*

SWELLED
1216 bâtsêq (1), to *blister*

SWELLING
1158 bâ'âh (1), to *ask; be bulging, swelling*
1346 ga'ăvâh (1), *arrogance; majesty*
1347 gâ'ôwn (3), *ascending; majesty*
5246 hupĕrŏgkŏs (2), *insolent, boastful*

SWELLINGS
5450 phusiōsis (1), *haughtiness, arrogance*

SWEPT
1640 gâraph (1), to *sweep away*
5502 çâchaph (1), to *scrape off, sweep off*
4563 sarŏŏ (2), to *sweep clean*

SWERVED
795 astŏchĕŏ (1), *deviate*

SWIFT
16 'êbeh (1), *papyrus*
3753 karkârâh (1), cow-*camel*
4116 mâhar (3), to *hurry*
7031 qal (9), *rapid, swift*
7043 qâlal (1), to *be, make light (swift)*
7409 rekesh (1), *relay*
3691 ŏxus (1), *rapid, fast*
5031 tachinŏs (1), *soon, immanent*
5036 tachus (1), *prompt*

SWIFTER
7031 qal (1), *rapid, swift*
7043 qâlal (5), to *be, make light (swift)*

SWIFTLY
3288 y°'âph (1), utterly *exhausted*
4120 m°hêrâh (1), *hurry*
7031 qal (2), *rapid, swift*

SWIM
6687 tsûwph (1), to *overflow*
7811 sâchâh (2), to *swim*
7813 sâchûw (1), *pond for swimming*
1579 ĕkkŏlumbaŏ (1), to *escape by swimming*
2860 kŏlumbaŏ (1), to *plunge into water*

SWIMMEST
6824 tsâphâh (1), *inundation*

SWIMMETH
7811 sâchâh (1), to *swim*

SWINE
2386 chăzîyr (2), *hog*
5519 chŏirŏs (14), *pig*

SWINE'S
2386 chăzîyr (4), *hog*

SWOLLEN
4092 pimprēmi (1), to *become inflamed*

SWOON
5848 'âṭaph (1), to *languish*

SWOONED
5848 'âṭaph (1), to *languish*

SWORD
1300 bârâq (1), *lightning; flash of lightning*
2719 chereb (380), *sword*
7524 retsach (1), *crushing; murder-cry*
7973 shelach (3), *spear*
3162 machaira (22), *short sword*
4501 rhŏmphaia (7), *sabre, cutlass*

SWELLINGS (col 3)

SWORDS
2719 chereb (17), *sword*
6609 p°thîchâh (1), *drawn sword*
3162 machaira (6), *short sword*

SWORN
1167+7621 ba'al (1), *master; husband*
3027+5920+3676 yâd (1), *hand; power*
5375 nâsâ' (1), to *lift up*
7650 shâba' (42), to *swear*
3660 ŏmnuŏ (3), to *swear*

SYCAMINE
4807 sukaminŏs (1), *sycamore-fig tree*

SYCHAR
4965 Suchar (1), *liquor*

SYCHEM
4966 Suchĕm (2), *ridge*

SYCOMORE
8256 shâqâm (6), *sycamore tree*
4809 sukŏmōraia (1), *sycamore-fig tree*

SYCOMORES
8256 shâqâm (1), *sycamore tree*

SYENE
5482 Ç°vênêh (2), the local *Seven*

SYNAGOGUE
656 apŏsunagōgŏs (2), *excommunicated*
752 archisunagōgŏs (7), *director of the synagogue services*
4864 sunagōgē (34), *assemblage*

SYNAGOGUE'S
752 archisunagōgŏs (2), *director of the synagogue services*

SYNAGOGUES
4150 môw'êd (1), *place of meeting; congregation*
656 apŏsunagōgŏs (1), *excommunicated*
4864 sunagōgē (22), *assemblage*

SYNTYCHE
4941 Suntuchē (1), *accident*

SYRACUSE
4946 Surakŏusai (1), *Syracuse*

SYRIA
758 'Arâm (66), *highland*
4947 Suria (8), (poss.) *rock*

SYRIA-DAMASCUS
758+1834 'Arâm (1), *highland*

SYRIA-MAACHAH
758 'Arâm (1), *highland*

SYRIACK
762 'Ărâmîyth (1), *in Araman*

SYRIAN
761 'Ărammîy (7), *Aramite*

762 'Ărâmîyth (4), *in Araman*
4948 Surŏs (1), *native of Syria*

SYRIANS
758 'Arâm (57), *highland*
761 'Ărammîy (4), *Aramite*

SYROPHENICIAN
4949 Surŏphŏinissa (1), *native of Phœnicia*

TAANACH
8590 Ta'ănâk (6), *Taanak or Tanak*

TAANATH-SHILOH
8387 Ta'ănath Shîlôh (1), *approach of Shiloh*

TABBAOTH
2884 Ţabbâ'ôwth (2), *rings*

TABBATH
2888 Ţabbath (1), *Tabbath*

TABEAL
2870 Ţâbᵉ'êl (1), *pleasing* (to) *God*

TABEEL
2870 Ţâbᵉ'êl (1), *pleasing* (to) *God*

TABERAH
8404 Tab'êrâh (2), *burning*

TABERING
8608 tâphaph (1), to *drum* on a tambourine

TABERNACLE
168 'ôhel (187), *tent*
4908 mishkân (114), *residence*
5520 çôk (1), *hut of entwined boughs*
5521 çukkâh (3), *tabernacle; shelter*
5522 çikkûwth (1), *idolatrous booth*
7900 sôk (1), *booth*
4633 skēnē (15), *tent*
4636 skēnŏs (2), *tent*
4638 skēnōma (3), *dwelling*: the *Temple*

TABERNACLES
168 'ôhel (11), *tent*
4908 mishkân (5), *residence*
5521 çukkâh (9), *tabernacle; shelter*
4633 skēnē (4), *tent*
4634 skēnŏpēgia (1), *tabernacles, i.e. booths*

TABITHA
5000 Tabitha (2), *gazelle*

TABLE
3871 lûwach (4), *tablet*
4524 mêçab (1), *divan couch; around*
7979 shulchân (56), *table*
345 anakĕimai (1), to *recline at a meal*
4093 pinakidiŏn (1), *wooden writing tablet*
5132 trapēza (9), *four-legged table or stool*

TABLES
3871 lûwach (34), *tablet*

7979 shulchân (14), *table*
2825 klinē (1), *couch*
4109 plax (3), *tablet*
5132 trapēza (4), *four-legged table or stool*

TABLETS
1004+5315 bayith (1), *house; temple; family*
3558 kûwmâz (2), *jewel*

TABOR
8396 Tâbôwr (10), *broken*

TABRET
8596 tôph (3), *tambourine*
8611 tôpheth (1), *smiting*

TABRETS
8596 tôph (5), *tambourine*

TABRIMON
2886 Ţabrimmôwn (1), *pleasing* (to) *Rimmon*

TACHES
7165 qereç (10), *knob*

TACHMONITE
8461 Tachkᵉmônîy (1), *sagacious*

TACKLING
4631 skĕuē (1), *tackle*

TACKLINGS
2256 chebel (1), *company*

TADMOR
8412 Tadmôr (2), *palm*

TAHAN
8465 Tachan (2), *station*

TAHANITES
8470 Tachănîy (1), *Tachanite*

TAHAPANES
8471 Tachpanchêç (1), *Tachpanches*

TAHATH
8480 Tachath (6), *bottom*

TAHPANHES
8471 Tachpanchêç (5), *Tachpanches*

TAHPENES
8472 Tachpᵉnêyç (3), *Tachpenes*

TAHREA
8475 Tachrêa' (1), (poss.) *earth, ground; low*

TAHTIM-HODSHI
8483 Tachtîym Chodshîy (1), *lower* (ones) *monthly*

TAIL
2180 zânâb (8), *tail*
3769 ŏura (1), *tail*

TAILS
2180 zânâb (2), *tail*
3769 ŏura (4), *tail*

TAKE
6 'âbad (1), to *perish*
270 'âchaz (12), to *seize*
622 'âçaph (3), to *gather*
680 'âtsal (1), to *select*
935 bôw' (1), to *go, come*
962 bâzaz (9), to *plunder*
1197 bâ'ar (4), to *be brutish, be senseless*
1497 gâzal (3), to *rob*

1692 dâbaq (1), to *cling* or *adhere;* to *catch*
1898 hâgâh (2), to *remove, expel*
1961 hâyâh (1), to *exist*
2095 zᵉhar (Ch.) (1), *be admonished, be careful*
2254 châbal (7), to *bind* by a *pledge;* to *pervert*
2388 châzaq (9), to *fasten* upon; to *seize*
2502 châlats (1), to *present, strengthen*
2834 châsaph (1), to *drain away or bail* up
2846 châthâh (3), to *lay hold* of; to *take away*
3051 yâhab (1), to *give*
3212 yâlak (1), to *carry*
3318 yâtsâ' (2), to *go, bring out*
3381 yârad (3), to *descend*
3423 yârash (3), to *inherit*
3615 kâlâh (1), to *complete, prepare*
3920 lâkad (19), to *catch*
3947 lâqach (367), to *take*
5253 nâçag (2), to *retreat*
5267 nᵉçaq (Ch.) (1), to *go up*
5312 nᵉphaq (Ch.) (1), to *issue forth;* to *bring out*
5337 nâtsal (1), to *deliver;* to *be snatched*
5375 nâsâ' (60), to *lift up*
5376 nᵉsâ' (Ch.) (1), to *lift up*
5381 nâsag (5), to *reach*
5414 nâthan (1), to *give*
5493 çûwr (45), to *turn off*
5496 çûwth (1), to *stimulate;* to *seduce*
5535 çâkath (1), to *be silent;* to *observe*
5674 'âbar (2), to *cross over;* to *transition*
5709 'ădâ' (Ch.) (1), to *pass on or continue*
5749 'ûwd (2), to *encompass, restore*
5927 'âlâh (4), to *ascend*
5978 'immâd (1), *with*
6213 'âsâh (1), to *do*
6331 pûwr (1), to *crush*
6679 tsûwd (1), to *catch*
6901 qâbal (1), to *admit*
6902 qᵉbal (Ch.) (1), to *acquire*
7061 qâmats (3), to *grasp*
7126 qârab (1), to *approach, bring near*
7200 râ'âh (2), to *see*
7311 rûwm (11), to *be high;* to *rise or raise*
7760 sûwm (2), to *put*
7896 shîyth (1), to *place*
7901 shâkab (2), to *lie*
7997 shâlal (4), to *drop or strip;* to *plunder*
8175 sâ'ar (1), to *storm;* to *shiver, i.e. fear*
8551 tâmak (2), to *obtain*
8610 tâphas (10), to *manipulate, i.e. seize*
142 airō (35), to *lift up*
353 analambanō (3), to *take up, bring up*
726 harpazō (3), to *seize*

851 aphaireō (5), to *remove, cut off*
1209 dĕchŏmai (3), to *receive, accept*
1949 ĕpilambanŏmai (2), to *seize*
2507 kathaireō (1), to *lower, or demolish*
2722 katĕchō (1), to *hold down fast*
2902 kratĕō (4), to *seize*
2983 lambanō (31), to *take, receive*
3335 mĕtalambanō (1), to *accept and use*
3880 paralambanō (5), to *associate with* oneself
3911 paraphĕrō (1), to *carry off;* to *avert*
4014 pĕriaireō (1), to *unveil;* to *cast off*
4084 piazō (4), to *seize*
4355 prŏslambanō (1), to *take along, receive*
4648 skŏpĕō (1), to *watch out for, i.e. to regard*
4815 sullambanō (3), to *seize* (arrest, capture)
4838 sumparalambanō (2), to *take along*
4868 sunairō (1), to *compute an account*

TAKEN
247 'âzar (1), to *belt*
270 'âchaz (7), to *seize*
622 'âçaph (7), to *gather*
935 bôw' (1), to *go, come*
1197 bâ'ar (2), to *be brutish, be senseless*
1497 gâzal (5), to *rob*
1639 gâra' (4), to *remove, lessen, or withhold*
2254 châbal (1), to *bind* by a *pledge;* to *pervert*
2388 châzaq (5), to *fasten* upon; to *seize*
2502 châlats (1), to *pull off;* to *strip;* to *depart*
2974 yâ'al (2), to *assent;* to *undertake, begin*
3289 yâ'ats (2), to *advise*
3381 yârad (1), to *descend*
3427 yâshab (5), to *dwell*
3885 lûwn (1), to *be obstinate with*
3920 lâkad (42), to *catch*
3921 leked (1), *noose*
3947 lâqach (84), to *take*
4672 mâtsâ' (1), to *find*
5267 nᵉçaq (Ch.) (1), to *go up*
5312 nᵉphaq (Ch.) (2), to *issue forth;* to *bring out*
5337 nâtsal (3), to *deliver;* to *be snatched*
5375 nâsâ' (10), to *lift up*
5381 nâsag (1), to *reach*
5414 nâthan (1), to *give*
5493 çûwr (19), to *turn off*
5674 'âbar (1), to *cross over;* to *transition*
5709 'ădâ' (Ch.) (1), to *remove;* to *bedeck*
5927 'âlâh (9), to *ascend*
6001 'âmêl (1), *laborer*
6213 'âsâh (1), to *make*
6679 tsûwd (1), to *catch*
6813 tsâ'an (1), to *load*

7092 qâphats (1), to *draw together, to leap; to die*
7287 râdâh (1), to *subjugate; to crumble*
7311 rûwm (4), to *be high; to rise or raise*
7628 sh°bîy (2), *booty*
7725 shûwb (1), to *turn back; to return*
8610 tâphas (12), to *manipulate, i.e. seize*
142 airō (16), to *lift up*
259 halōsis (1), *capture*
353 analambanō (3), to *take up, bring up*
522 apairō (3), to *remove, take away*
642 apŏrphanizō (1), to *separate*
782 aspazŏmai (1), to give *salutation*
851 aphairĕō (1), to *remove*
1096 ginŏmai (1), to *be*
1723 ĕnagkalizŏmai (1), *take into one's arms*
1808 ĕxairō (1), to *remove, drive away*
1869 ĕpairō (1), to *raise*
2021 ĕpichĕirĕō (1), to *undertake, try*
2221 zōgrĕō (1), to *capture or ensnare*
2638 katalambanō (2), to *seize; to possess*
2639 katalĕgō (1), to *enroll, put on a list*
2983 lambanō (12), to *take, receive*
3880 paralambanō (5), to *associate with oneself*
4014 pĕriairĕō (3), to *unveil; to cast off*
4084 piazō (2), to *seize*
4355 prŏslambanō (1), to *take along; receive*
4815 sullambanō (2), to *seize (arrest, capture)*
4912 sunĕchō (3), to *hold together*

TAKEST
622 'âçaph (1), to *gather*
1980 hâlak (1), to *walk*
3947 lâqach (2), to *take*
5375 nâsâ' (1), to *lift up*
6001 'âmêl (1), *laborer*
8104 shâmar (1), to *watch*
142 airō (1), to *lift up*

TAKETH
270 'âchaz (2), to *seize*
1197 bâ'ar (1), to *be brutish, be senseless*
2254 châbal (1), to *bind by a pledge; to pervert*
2388 châzaq (4), to *fasten upon; to seize*
2862 châthaph (1), to *clutch, snatch*
3920 lâkad (5), to *catch*
3947 lâqach (11), to *take*
5190 nâtal (1), to *lift; to impose*
5337 nâtsal (1), to *deliver; to be snatched*
5375 nâsâ' (3), to *lift up*
5493 çûwr (2), to *turn off*
5710 'âdâh (1), to *pass on or continue; to remove*

5998 'âmal (2), to *work severely, put forth effort*
6908 qâbats (1), to *collect, assemble*
7953 shâlâh (1), to *draw out or off, i.e. remove*
8610 tâphas (1), to *manipulate, i.e. seize*
142 airō (11), to *lift up*
337 anairĕō (1), to *take away, i.e. abolish*
851 aphairĕō (1), to *remove, cut off*
1405 drassŏmai (1), to *grasp, i.e. entrap*
2018 ĕpiphĕrō (1), to *inflict, bring upon*
2638 katalambanō (1), to *seize; to possess*
2983 lambanō (4), to *take, receive*
3880 paralambanō (8), to *associate with* oneself
4301 prŏlambanō (1), to *take before; be caught*

TAKING
3947 lâqach (1), to *take*
4727 miqqâch (1), *reception*
8610 tâphas (1), to *manipulate, i.e. seize*
142 airō (1), to *lift up*
321 anagō (1), to *lead up; to bring out*
353 analambanō (1), to *take up, bring up*
1325 didōmi (1), to *give*
2983 lambanō (4), to *take*

TALE
1899 hegeh (1), *muttering*
4557 miçpâr (1), *number*
4971 mathkôneth (1), *proportion*
8506 tôken (1), *quantity*

TALEBEARER
1980+7400 hâlak (1), to *walk; live a certain way*
5372 nirgân (3), *slanderer*
7400 râkîyl (2), *scandal-monger*

TALENT
3603 kikkâr (10), *talent*
5006 talantiaiŏs (1), *weight* of 57-80 lbs.
5007 talantŏn (3), *weight*

TALENTS
3603 kikkâr (38), *talent*
3604 kikkêr (Ch.) (1), *talent weight*
5007 talantŏn (12), *weight* of 57-80 lbs.

TALES
7400 râkîyl (1), *scandal-monger*
3026 lērŏs (1), *twaddle*

TALITHA
5008 talitha (1), *young girl*

TALK
1696 dâbar (11), to *speak*
1697 dâbâr (2), *word*
1897 hâgâh (1), to *murmur, utter a sound*
5608 çâphar (1), to *recount an event*
6310 peh (1), *mouth*

7878 sîyach (5), to *ponder, muse aloud*
8193 sâphâh (1), *lip, language, speech*
2980 lalĕō (1), to *talk*
3056 lŏgŏs (1), *word, matter, thing*

TALKED
559 'âmar (1), to *say*
1696 dâbar (29), to *speak*
2980 lalĕō (8), to *talk*
3656 hŏmilĕō (2), to *talk*
4814 sullalĕō (1), to *talk*
4926 sunŏmilĕō (1), to *converse* mutually

TALKERS
3956 lâshôwn (1), *tongue*
3151 mataiŏlŏgŏs (1), *senseless talker*

TALKEST
1696 dâbar (2), to *speak*
2980 lalĕō (1), to *talk*

TALKETH
1696 dâbar (1), to *speak*
2980 lalĕō (1), to *talk*

TALKING
1696 dâbar (3), to *speak*
4405 millâh (1), *word; discourse; speech*
7879 sîyach (1), *uttered contemplation*
2980 lalĕō (1), to *talk*
3473 mōrŏlŏgia (1), *buffoonery, foolish talk*
4814 sullalĕō (2), to *talk together, i.e. converse*

TALL
6967 qôwmâh (2), *height*
7311 rûwm (3), to *be high*

TALLER
7311 rûwm (1), to *be high*

TALMAI
8526 Talmay (6), *ridged*

TALMON
2929 Talmôwn (5), *oppressive*

TAMAH
8547 Temach (1), *Temach*

TAMAR
8559 Tâmâr (24), *palm*

TAME
1150 damazō (2), to *tame*

TAMED
1150 damazō (2), to *tame*

TAMMUZ
8542 Tammûwz (1), *Tammuz*

TANACH
8590 Ta'ănâk (1), *Taanak or Tanak*

TANHUMETH
8576 Tanchûmeth (2), *compassion, solace*

TANNER
1033 brŏma (3), *food*

TAPHATH
2955 Țâphath (1), *dropping* (of ointment)

TAPPUAH
8599 Tappûwach (6), *apple*

8646 Terach (2), *Terach*

TARALAH
8634 Tar'ălâh (1), *reeling*

TARE
1234 bâqa' (1), to *cleave, break, tear open*
7167 qâra' (1), to *rend*
4682 sparassō (1), to *convulse with epilepsy*
4952 susparassō (1), to *convulse violently*

TAREA
8390 Ta'ărêa' (1), (poss.) *earth, ground; low*

TARES
2215 zizaniŏn (8), *darnel*

TARGET
3591 kîydôwn (1), *dart*
6793 tsinnâh (2), *large shield; piercing cold*

TARGETS
6793 tsinnâh (3), *large shield; piercing cold*

TARPELITES
2967 Ṭarp°lay (Ch.) (1), *Tarpelite*

TARRIED
748 'ârak (2), to *be long*
2342 chûwl (1), to *wait*
3176 yâchal (1), to *wait*
3186 yâchar (1), to *delay*
3427 yâshab (6), to *dwell, to remain; to settle*
3885 lûwn (3), to *be obstinate with*
4102 mâhahh (2), to *be reluctant*
5116 nâveh (1), *at home*
5975 'âmad (1), to *stand*
1304 diatribō (2), to *stay*
1961 ĕpimĕnō (3), to *remain; to persevere*
3306 mĕnō (3), to *stay*
4160 pŏiĕō (1), to *do*
4328 prŏsdŏkaō (1), to *anticipate; to await*
4357 prŏsmĕnō (1), to *remain* in a place
5278 hupŏmĕnō (1), to *undergo,* (trials)
5549 chrŏnizō (2), to *take time, i.e. linger*

TARRIEST
3195 mĕllō (1), to *intend,* i.e. *be about to*

TARRIETH
3427 yâshab (1), to *dwell, to remain; to settle*
6960 qâvâh (1), to *expect*

TARRY
309 'âchar (4), to *remain; to delay*
1826 dâmam (1), to *stop, cease; to perish*
2442 châkâh (2), to *await; hope for*
3176 yâchal (2), to *wait*
3427 yâshab (13), to *dwell, to remain*
3559 kûwn (1), to *set up: establish, fix, prepare*
3885 lûwn (7), to *be obstinate with*

T

4102 mâhahh (3), to *be reluctant*
5975 'âmad (1), to *stand*
7663 sâbar (1), to *scrutinize; to expect*
1019 bradunō (1), to *delay, hesitate*
1551 ĕkdĕchŏmai (1), to *await, expect*
1961 ĕpimĕnō (4), to *remain; to persevere*
2523 kathizō (1), to *seat down, dwell*
3306 mĕnō (7), to *stay*
5549 chrŏnizō (1), to *take time, i.e. linger*

TARRYING
309 'âchar (2), to *remain*

TARSHISH
8659 Tarshîysh (24), *merchant vessel*

TARSUS
5018 Tarsĕus (2), *native of Tarsus*
5019 Tarsŏs (3), *flat*

TARTAK
8662 Tartâq (1), *Tartak*

TARTAN
8661 Tartân (2), *Tartan*

TASK
1697 dâbâr (1), *word; matter; thing*
2706 chôq (1), *appointment; allotment*

TASKMASTERS
5065 nâgas (5), to *exploit; to tax, harass*

TASKS
1697 dâbâr (1), *word; matter; thing*

TASTE
2441 chêk (4), area of *mouth*
2938 ţâ'am (6), to *taste*
2940 ţa'am (5), *taste*
1089 gĕuŏmai (7), to *taste*

TASTED
2938 ţâ'am (2), to *taste*
2942 ţe'êm (Ch.) (1), *judgment; account*
1089 gĕuŏmai (5), to *taste; to eat*

TASTETH
2938 ţâ'am (1), to *taste*

TATNAI
8674 Tatteⁿnay (4), *Tattenai*

TATTLERS
5397 phluarŏs (1), *pratery*

TAUGHT
995 bîyn (1), to *understand; discern*
1696 dâbar (2), to *speak*
3045 yâda' (3), to *know*
3256 yâçar (2), to *instruct*
3384 yârâh (5), to *teach*
3925 lâmad (17), to *teach*
3928 limmûwd (1), *instructed* one
4000 mâbôwn (1), *instructing*
7919 sâkal (1), to *be or act circumspect*

8637 tirgal (1), to *cause to walk*
1318 didaktŏs (1), *instructed, taught*
1321 didaskō (36), to *teach*
1322 didachē (1), *instruction*
2258+1321 ēn (4), I *was*
2312 thĕŏdidaktŏs (1), *divinely instructed*
2727 katēchĕō (1), to *indoctrinate*
3100 mathētĕuō (1), to *become a student*
3811 paidĕuō (1), to *educate or discipline*

TAUNT
1422 geⁿdûwphâh (1), *revilement, taunt*
8148 sheⁿnîynâh (1), *gibe, verbal taunt*

TAUNTING
4426 meⁿlîytsâh (1), *aphorism, saying*

TAVERNS
4999 Tabĕrnai (1), *huts*

TAXATION
6187 'êrek (1), *estimate*

TAXED
6186 'ârak (1), to *arrange*
582 apŏgraphē (3), *census registration*

TAXES
5065 nâgas (1), to *exploit; to tax, harass*

TAXING
583 apŏgraphō (2), *enroll, take a census*

TEACH
502 'âlaph (1), to *teach*
2094 zâhar (1), to *enlighten*
3045 yâda' (5), to *know*
3046 yeⁿda' (Ch.) (1), to *know*
3384 yârâh (33), to *teach*
3925 lâmad (32), to *teach*
8150 shânan (1), to *pierce; to inculcate*
1317 didaktikŏs (2), *instructive*
1321 didaskō (26), to *teach*
2085 hĕtĕrŏdidaskalĕō** (2), to *instruct differently*
2605 kataggĕllō (1), to *proclaim, promulgate*
2727 katēchĕō (1), to *indoctrinate*
3100 mathētĕuō (1), to *become a student*
4994 sŏphrŏnizō (1), to *train up*

TEACHER
995 bîyn (1), to *understand; discern*
3384 yârâh (1), to *teach*
1320 didaskalŏs (4), *instructor*

TEACHERS
3384 yârâh (3), to *teach*
3887 lûwts (1), to *scoff; to interpret; to intercede*
3925 lâmad (1), to *teach*

1320 didaskalŏs (6), *instructor*
2567 kalŏdidaskalŏs (1), *teacher of the right*
3547 nŏmŏdidaskalŏs** (1), *Rabbi*
5572 psĕudŏdidaskalŏs** (1), *propagator of erroneous doctrine*

TEACHEST
3925 lâmad (1), to *teach*
1321 didaskō (7), to *teach*

TEACHETH
502 'âlaph (1), to *teach*
3384 yârâh (3), to *teach*
3925 lâmad (5), to *teach*
7919 sâkal (1), to *be or act circumspect*
1318 didaktŏs (2), *taught*
1321 didaskō (3), to *teach*
2727 katēchĕō (1), to *indoctrinate*

TEACHING
3384 yârâh (1), to *teach*
3925 lâmad (1), to *teach*
1319 didaskalia (1), *instruction*
1321 didaskō (21), to *teach*
3811 paidĕuō (1), to *educate or discipline*

TEAR
1234 bâqa' (1), to *cleave, break, tear open*
1758 dûwsh (1), to *trample or thresh*
2963 ţâraph (5), to *pluck off or pull to pieces*
5498 çâchab (1), to *trail along*
6536 pâraç (1), to *break in pieces; to split*
6561 pâraq (1), to *break off or crunch; to deliver*
7167 qâra' (3), to *rend*

TEARETH
2963 ţâraph (4), to *pluck off or pull to pieces*
4486 rhēgnumi (1), to *tear to pieces*
4682 sparassō (1), to *convulse with epilepsy*

TEARS
1058 bâkâh (1), to *weep*
1832 dim'âh (23), *tears*
1144 dakru (11), *teardrop*

TEATS
1717 dad (2), female *breast or bosom*
7699 shad (1), *breast*

TEBAH
2875 Ţebach (1), *massacre*

TEBALIAH
2882 Ţeⁿbalyâhûw (1), *Jehovah has dipped*

TEBETH
2887 Ţêbeth (1), a *month*

TEDIOUS
1465 ĕgkŏptō (1), to *impede, detain*

TEETH
4973 meⁿthalleⁿ'âh (3), *tooth*
6374 pîyphîyâh (1), *tooth*

8127 shên (31), *tooth*
8128 shên (Ch.) (3), *tooth*
3599 ŏdŏus (10), *tooth*
3679 ŏnĕidizō (1), to *rail at, chide, taunt*

TEHAPHNEHES
8471 Tachpanchêç (1), *Tachpanches*

TEHINNAH
8468 Teⁿchinnâh (1), *supplication*

TEIL
424 'êlâh (1), *oak*

TEKEL
8625 teⁿqal (Ch.) (2), to *weigh in a scale*

TEKOA
8620 Teⁿqôwa' (6), *trumpet*

TEKOAH
8620 Teⁿqôwa' (1), *trumpet*
8621 Teⁿqôw'îy (2), *Tekoite*

TEKOITE
8621 Teⁿqôw'îy (3), *Tekoite*

TEKOITES
8621 Teⁿqôw'îy (2), *Tekoite*

TEL-ABIB
8512 Têl 'Âbîyb (1), *mound of green growth*

TEL-HARESHA
8521 Têl Charshâ' (1), *mound of workmanship*

TEL-HARSA
8521 Têl Charshâ' (1), *mound of workmanship*

TEL-MELAH
8528 Têl Melach (2), *mound of salt*

TELAH
8520 Telach (1), *breach*

TELAIM
2923 Ţeⁿlâ'îym (1), *lambs*

TELASSAR
8515 Teⁿla'ssar (1), *Telassar*

TELEM
2928 Ţelem (2), *oppression*

TELL
559 'âmar (29), to *say*
560 'ămar (Ch.) (5), to *say*
1696 dâbâr (7), to *speak*
3045 yâda' (7), to *know*
5046 nâgad (69), to *announce*
5608 çâphar (12), to *recount an event*
8085 shâma' (2), to *hear*
226 alēthĕuō (1), to *be true*
312 anaggĕllō (2), to *announce, report*
518 apaggĕllō (6), to *announce, proclaim*
1334 diĕgĕŏmai (2), to *relate fully, describe*
1492 ĕidō (9), to *know*
1583 ĕklalĕō (1), to *tell*
1650 ĕlĕgchŏs (1), *proof*
2036 ĕpō (28), to *speak*
2046 ĕrĕō (3), to *utter*
2980 lalĕō (2), to *talk*
3004 lĕgō (28), to *say*

4302 prŏlĕgō (1), to predict, forewarn

TELLEST
5608 çâphar (1), to recount an event

TELLETH
1696 dâbar (2), to speak
4487 mânâh (2), to allot; to enumerate or enroll
5046 nâgad (2), to announce
3004 lĕgō (1), to say

TELLING
1696 dâbar (1), to speak
4557 miçpâr (1), number
5608 çâphar (1), to recount an event

TEMA
8485 Têymâ' (5), Tema

TEMAN
8487 Têymân (11), south

TEMANI
8489 Têymânîy (1), Temanite

TEMANITE
8489 Têymânîy (6), Temanite

TEMANITES
8489 Têymânîy (1), Temanite

TEMENI
8488 Têymᵉnîy (1), Temeni

TEMPER
7450 râçaç (1), to moisten with drops

TEMPERANCE
1466 ĕgkratĕia (4), self-control

TEMPERATE
1467 ĕgkratĕuŏmai (1), to exercise self-restraint
1468 ĕgkratēs (1), self-controlled
4998 sōphrōn (1), self-controlled

TEMPERED
1101 bâlal (1), to mix
4414 mâlach (1), to salt
4786 sugkĕrannumi (1), to combine, assimilate

TEMPEST
2230 zerem (3), flood
5492 çûwphâh (1), hurricane wind
5590 çâ'ar (1), to rush upon; to toss about
5591 ça'ar (6), hurricane
7307 rûwach (1), breath; wind; life-spirit
8183 sᵉ'ârâh (1), hurricane wind
2366 thuĕlla (1), blowing
2978 lailaps (1), whirlwind; hurricane
4578 sĕismŏs (1), gale storm; earthquake
5492 chĕimazō (1), to be battered in a storm
5494 chĕimōn (1), winter season; stormy weather

TEMPESTUOUS
5490 çôwph (2), termination; end

8175 sâ'ar (1), to storm
5189 tuphōnikŏs (1), stormy

TEMPLE
1004 bayith (11), house; temple; family, tribe
1964 hêykâl (68), temple
1965 hêykal (Ch.) (8), palace; temple
2411 hiĕrŏn (71), sacred place; sanctuary
3485 naŏs (43), temple
3624 ŏikŏs (1), dwelling

TEMPLES
1964 hêykâl (2), temple
7451 ra' (5), bad; evil
3485 naŏs (2), temple

TEMPORAL
4340 prŏskairŏs (1), temporary

TEMPT
974 bâchan (1), to test
5254 nâçâh (4), to test
1598 ĕkpĕirazō (3), to test thoroughly
3985 pĕirazō (6), to endeavor, scrutinize

TEMPTATION
4531 maççâh (1), testing
3986 pĕirasmŏs (15), test

TEMPTATIONS
4531 maççâh (3), testing
3986 pĕirasmŏs (5), test

TEMPTED
5254 nâçâh (8), to test
551 apĕirastŏs (1), not temptable
1598 ĕkpĕirazō (1), to test thoroughly
3985 pĕirazō (14), to endeavor, scrutinize

TEMPTER
3985 pĕirazō (2), to endeavor, scrutinize

TEMPTETH
3985 pĕirazō (1), to endeavor, scrutinize

TEMPTING
3985 pĕirazō (7), to endeavor, scrutinize

TEN
6218 'âsôwr (4), ten
6235 'eser (164), ten
6236 'âsar (Ch.) (4), ten
7231 râbab (1), to multiply by the myriad
7233 rᵉbâbâh (13), myriad
7239 ribbôw (2), myriad
7240 ribbôw (Ch.) (2), myriad
1176 dĕka (24), ten
3461 murias (3), ten thousand
3463 muriŏi (3), ten thousand; innumerably

TEN'S
6235 'eser (1), ten

TENDER
3126 yôwnêq (1), sucker plant; nursing infant
3127 yôwneqeth (1), sprout, new shoot
7390 rak (10), tender
7401 râkak (2), to soften

527 hapalŏs (2), tender
3629 ŏiktirmōn (1), compassionate
4698 splagchnŏn (1), intestine; affection, pity

TENDERHEARTED
7390+3824 rak (1), tender; weak
2155 ĕusplagchnŏs (1), compassionate

TENDERNESS
7391 rôk (1), softness

TENONS
3027 yâd (6), hand; power

TENOR
6310 peh (2), mouth

TENS
6235 'eser (3), ten

TENT
167 'âhal (3), to pitch a tent
168 'ôhel (89), tent
6898 qubbâh (1), pavilion

TENTH
4643 ma'ăsêr (4), tithe, one-tenth
6218 'âsôwr (13), ten
6224 'ăsîyrîy (26), tenth
6237 'âsar (3), to tithe
6241 'issârôwn (28), tenth
1181 dĕkatē (2), tenth
1182 dĕkatŏs (3), tenth

TENTMAKERS
4635 skĕnŏpŏiŏs (1), manufacturer of tents

TENTS
168 'ôhel (50), tent
2583 chânâh (1), to encamp
4264 machăneh (5), encampment
4908 mishkân (1), residence
5521 çukkâh (1), tabernacle; shelter

TERAH
8646 Terach (11), Terach

TERAPHIM
8655 tᵉrâphîym (6), healer

TERESH
8657 Teresh (2), Teresh

TERMED
559 'âmar (2), to say

TERRACES
4546 mᵉçillâh (1), viaduct; staircase

TERRESTRIAL
1919 ĕpigĕiŏs (2), worldly, earthly

TERRIBLE
366 'âyôm (3), frightful
367 'êymâh (2), fright
574 'emtânîy (Ch.) (1), burly or mighty
1763 dᵉchal (Ch.) (1), to fear; be formidable
2152 zal'âphâh (1), glow
3372 yârê' (30), to fear
6184 'ârîyts (13), powerful or tyrannical
5398 phŏbĕrŏs (1), frightful, i.e. formidable

TERRIBLENESS
3372 yârê' (1), to fear
4172 môwrâ' (1), fearful
8606 tiphletseth (1), fearfulness

TERRIBLY
6206 'ârats (2), to dread

TERRIFIED
6206 'ârats (1), to dread
4422 ptŏĕō (2), to be scared
4426 pturō (1), to be frightened

TERRIFIEST
1204 bâ'ath (1), to fear

TERRIFY
1204 bâ'ath (2), to fear
2865 châthath (1), to break down
1629 ĕkphŏbĕō (1), to frighten utterly

TERROR
367 'êymâh (4), fright
928 behâlâh (1), sudden panic, destruction
1091 ballâhâh (3), sudden destruction
2283 châgâ' (1), terror
2847 chittâh (1), terror
2851 chittîyth (8), terror
4032 mâgôwr (1), fright
4172 môwrâ' (2), fearful
4288 mᵉchittâh (2), ruin; consternation
4637 ma'ărâtsâh (1), terrifying violent power
6343 pachad (2), fear
5401 phŏbŏs (3), alarm, or fright; reverence

TERRORS
367 'êymâh (3), fright
928 behâlâh (1), sudden panic, destruction
1091 ballâhâh (6), sudden destruction
1161 bî'ûwthîym (2), alarms, startling things
4032 mâgôwr (1), fright
4048 mâgar (1), to yield up, be thrown
4172 môwrâ' (1), fearful

TERTIUS
5060 Tĕrtiŏs (1), third

TERTULLUS
5061 Tĕrtullŏs (2), Tertullus

TESTAMENT
1242 diathēkē (11), contract; devisory will
1248 diakŏnia (2), attendance, aid, service

TESTATOR
1303 diatithēmai (2), to put apart, i.e. dispose

TESTIFIED
5749 'ûwd (7), to protest, testify; to encompass
6030 'ânâh (3), to respond, answer
1263 diamarturŏmai (6), to attest earnestly
3140 marturĕō (6), to testify; to commend
3142 marturiŏn (1), something evidential

4303 prŏmarturŏmai (1), to predict beforehand

TESTIFIEDST
5749 'ûwd (2), to protest, testify; to encompass

TESTIFIETH
6030 'ânâh (1), to respond, answer
3140 marturĕō (4), to testify; to commend

TESTIFY
5749 'ûwd (6), to protest, testify; to encompass
6030 'ânâh (8), to respond, answer
1263 diamarturŏmai (4), to attest earnestly
3140 marturĕō (8), to testify; to commend
3143 marturŏmai (2), to be witness, i.e. to obtest
4828 summarturĕō (1), to testify jointly

TESTIFYING
1263 diamarturŏmai (1), to attest earnestly
1957 ĕpimarturĕō (1), to corroborate
3140 marturĕō (1), to testify; to commend

TESTIMONIES
5713 'êdâh (21), testimony
5715 'êdûwth (15), testimony

TESTIMONY
5713 'êdâh (1), testimony
5715 'êdûwth (40), testimony
8584 tᵉ'ûwdâh (3), attestation, precept
3140 marturĕō (3), to testify; to commend
3141 marturia (14), evidence given
3142 marturiŏn (15), something evidential

TETRARCH
5075 tĕtrarchĕō (3), to be a tetrarch
5076 tĕtrarchēs (4), ruler of a fourth part

THADDAEUS
2280 Thaddaiŏs (2), Thaddæus

THAHASH
8477 Tachash (1), (poss.) antelope

THAMAH
8547 Temach (1), Temach

THAMAR
2283 Thamar (1), palm

THANK
2192+5485 zᵉ'êyr (Ch.) (3), small, little
3029 yᵉdâ' (Ch.) (1), to praise
3034 yâdâh (4), to throw; to revere or worship
8426 tôwdâh (3), thanks
1843 ĕxŏmŏlŏgĕō (2), to acknowledge
2168 ĕucharistĕō (11), to express gratitude

5485 charis (3), gratitude; benefit given

THANKED
1288 bârak (1), to bless
2168 ĕucharistĕō (1), to express gratitude
5485 charis (1), gratitude; benefit given

THANKFUL
3034 yâdâh (1), to throw; to revere or worship
2168 ĕucharistĕō (1), to express gratitude
2170 ĕucharistŏs (1), grateful, thankful

THANKFULNESS
2169 ĕucharistia (1), gratitude

THANKING
3034 yâdâh (1), to throw; to revere or worship

THANKS
3029 yᵉdâ' (Ch.) (1), to praise
3034 yâdâh (32), to throw; to revere, worship
8426 tôwdâh (3), thanks
437 anthŏmŏlŏgĕŏmai (1), to give thanks
2168 ĕucharistĕō (26), to express gratitude
2169 ĕucharistia (5), gratitude
3670 hŏmŏlŏgĕō (1), to acknowledge, agree
5485 charis (4), gratitude; benefit given

THANKSGIVING
1960 huyᵉdâh (1), choir
3034 yâdâh (2), to throw; to revere or worship
8426 tôwdâh (16), thanks
2169 ĕucharistia (8), gratitude; grateful

THANKSGIVINGS
8426 tôwdâh (1), thanks
2169 ĕucharistia (1), gratitude; grateful

THANKWORTHY
5485 charis (1), gratitude; benefit given

THARA
2291 Thara (1), Thara

THARSHISH
8659 Tarshîysh (4), merchant vessel

THEATRE
2302 thĕatrŏn (2), audience-room; show

THEBEZ
8405 Têbêts (3), whiteness

THEFT
1591 gᵉnêbâh (2), something stolen

THEFTS
2804 Klaudiŏs (1), Claudius
2829 klŏpē (2), theft

THELASAR
8515 Tᵉla'ssar (1), Telassar

THEOPHILUS
2321 Thĕŏphilŏs (2), friend of God

THERE
2008 hênnâh (1), from here; from there
8033 shâm (440), there
8536 tâm (Ch.) (2), there
847 autŏu (3), in this
1563 ĕkĕi (98), there
1564 ĕkĕithĕn (1), from there
1566 ĕkĕisĕ (2), there
1759 ĕnthadĕ (1), here
1927 ĕpidēmĕō (1), to make oneself at home
5602 hôdĕ (1), here

THEREABOUT
4012+5127 pĕri (1), about

THEREAT
1223+846 dia (1), through, by means of

THEREBY
2004 hên (2), they
5921 'al (2), above, over

THEREFORE
1571 gam (5), also; even
2006 hên (Ch.) (2), lo; therefore, unless
2063 zô'th (1), this
3588 kîy (2), for, that
3651 kên (170), just; right, correct
235 alla (3), but, yet
686 ara (6), therefore
1063 gar (1), for, indeed
1160 dapanē (1), expense, cost
1211 dē (1), therefore
1352 diŏ (9), therefore
1360 diŏti (1), inasmuch as
2532 kai (1), and; or
3747 ŏstĕŏn (1), bone
3757 hŏu (1), at which
3767 ŏun (255), certainly
5105 tŏigarŏun (1), then
5106 tŏinun (3), then
5124 tŏutŏ (1), that thing
5620 hōstĕ (9), thus

THEREIN
413 'êl (2), to, toward
1459 gav (Ch.) (1), middle
2004 hên (4), they
2007 hênnâh (1), themselves
4393 mᵉlô' (7), fulness
5921 'al (9), above, over
7130 qereb (2), nearest
8033 shâm (10), there
8432 tâvek (3), center
5125 tŏutŏis (1), in these

THEREINTO
1519+846 ĕis (1), to

THEREOF
8033 shâm (1), there
846 autŏs (26), he, she, it

THEREON
5921 'al (48), above, over
846 autŏs (2), he, she, it
1911 ĕpiballō (1), to throw upon
1913 ĕpibibazō (1), to cause to mount
1924 ĕpigraphō (1), to inscribe, write upon

1945 ĕpikĕimai (1), to rest upon; press upon
2026 ĕpŏikŏdŏmĕō (1), to rear up, build up

THEREOUT
8033 shâm (1), where, there

THERETO
5921 'al (8), above, over
1928 ĕpidiatassŏmai (1), to appoint besides

THEREUNTO
1519+846+5124 ĕis (1), to
1519+5124 ĕis (2), to
4334 prŏsĕrchŏmai (1), to come near, visit

THEREUPON
2026 ĕpŏikŏdŏmĕō (2), to rear up, build up

THEREWITH
854 'êth (1), with; by; at
5921 'al (2), above, over
1722+846 ĕn (2), in
1909+5125 ĕpi (1), on
5125 tŏutŏis (1), in these

THESSALONIANS
2331 Thĕssalŏnikĕus (5), of Thessalonice

THESSALONICA
2331 Thĕssalŏnikĕus (1), of Thessalonice
2332 Thĕssalŏnikē (5), Thessalonice

THEUDAS
2333 Thĕudas (1), Theudas

THICK
653 'âphêlâh (1), duskiness, darkness
3515 kâbêd (1), numerous; severe
5441 çôbek (1), thicket
5645 'âb (2), thick clouds
5666 'âbâh (1), to be dense
5672 'âbîy (2), density
5687 'âbôth (4), dense
5688 'ăbôth (4), entwined
6282 'âthâr (1), incense; worshipper
7341 rôchab (1), width

THICKER
5666 'âbâh (2), to be dense

THICKET
5441 çôbek (1), thicket
5442 çᵉbâk (1), thicket

THICKETS
2337 châvâch (1), dell or crevice of rock
5442 çᵉbâk (2), thicket
5645 'âb (1), thick clouds; thicket

THICKNESS
5672 'âbîy (2), density
7341 rôchab (2), width

THIEF
1590 gannâb (13), stealer
2812 klĕptēs (12), stealer
3027 lē¡stēs (3), brigand

THIEVES
1590 gannâb (4), stealer
2812 klĕptēs (4), stealer
3027 lē¡stēs (8), brigand

THIGH
3409 yârêk (19), leg or
shank, flank; side
7785 shôwq (1), lower leg
3382 mêrŏs (1), thigh

THIGHS
3409 yârêk (2), leg or
shank, flank; side
3410 yarkâ' (Ch.) (1),
thigh

THIMNATHAH
8553 Timnâh (1), portion

THIN
1809 dâlal (1), to
slacken, dangle
1851 daq (5), thin
4174 môwrâd (1),
descent, slope
7534 raq (1), emaciated

THING
562 'ômer (1), something
said
1697 dâbâr (182), thing
3627 kᵉlîy (11), thing
3651 kên (2), just; right
3972 mᵉ'ûwmâh (3),
something; anything
4399 mᵉlâ'kâh (2), work;
property
4406 millâh (Ch.) (9),
word, command
4859 mashshâ'âh (1),
secured loan
5315 nephesh (2), life;
breath; soul; wind
1520 hĕis (1), one
3056 lŏgŏs (2), word,
matter, thing
4110 plasma (1), molded
4229 pragma (2), matter
4487 rhēma (1), matter
5313 hupsōma (1), barrier

THINGS
1697 dâbâr (47), thing
4406 millâh (Ch.) (1),
word or subject
18 agathŏs (1), good
846 autŏs (1), he, she, it
3056 lŏgŏs (3), thing
4229 pragma (4), matter
4487 rhēma (2), thing
5023 tauta (1), these

THINK
559 'âmar (3), to say
995 bîyn (1), to
understand; discern
1819 dâmâh (1), to
consider, think
2142 zâkar (3), to
remember; to mention
2803 châshab (6), to
think, regard; to value
5452 çᵉbar (Ch.) (1), to
bear in mind, i.e. hope
5869 'ayin (2), eye; sight
6245 'âshath (1), to be
sleek; to excogitate
1380 dŏkĕō (22), to think
1760 ĕnthumĕŏmai (1),
ponder, reflect on
2233 hēgĕŏmai (2), to
deem, i.e. consider
3049 lŏgizŏmai (7), to
credit; to think, regard
3539 nŏiĕō (1), to
exercise the mind

3543 nŏmizō (4), to deem
or regard
3633 ŏiŏmai (1), to
imagine, opine
5252 hupĕrphrŏnĕō (1),
to esteem oneself
5282 hupŏnŏĕō (1), to
think; to expect
5316 phainō (1), to
lighten (shine)
5426 phrŏnĕō (4), to be
mentally disposed

THINKEST
2803 châshab (1), to
think, regard; to value
5869 'ayin (2), eye; sight
1380 dŏkĕō (4), to think
3049 lŏgizŏmai (1), to
think, regard
5426 phrŏnĕō (1), to be
mentally disposed

THINKETH
2803 châshab (1), to
think, regard; to value
7200 râ'âh (1), to see
8176 shâ'ar (1), to
estimate
1380 dŏkĕō (2), to think
3049 lŏgizŏmai (1), to
think, regard

THINKING
559 'âmar (1), to say
1931+1961 hûw' (1), this

THIRD
7969 shâlôwsh (9), three;
third; thrice
7992 shᵉlîyshîy (104),
third
8027 shâlash (2), to be
triplicate
8029 shillêsh (5), great
grandchild
8523 tᵉlîythay (Ch.) (2),
third
8531 tᵉlath (Ch.) (3),
tertiary, i.e. third rank
5152 tristĕgŏn (1), third
story place
5154 tritŏs (56), third
part; third time, thirdly

THIRDLY
5154 tritŏs (1), third part

THIRST
6770 tsâmê' (2), to thirst
6771 tsâmê' (1), thirsty
6772 tsâmâ' (16), thirst
6773 tsim'âh (1), thirst
1372 dipsaō (10), to thirst
1373 dipsŏs (1), thirst

THIRSTED
6770 tsâmê' (2), to thirst

THIRSTETH
6770 tsâmê' (2), to thirst
6771 tsâmê' (1), thirsty

THIRSTY
6770 tsâmê' (2), to thirst
6771 tsâmê' (7), thirsty
6772 tsâmâ' (1), thirst
6774 tsimmâ'ôwn (1),
desert
1372 dipsaō (3), to thirst

THIRTEEN
7969 shâlôwsh (2), three
7969+6240 shâlôwsh (13),
three; third; thrice

THIRTEENTH
7969+6240 shâlôwsh (11),
three; third; thrice

THIRTIETH
7970 shᵉlôwshîym (9),
thirty; thirtieth

THIRTY
7970 shᵉlôwshîym (161),
thirty; thirtieth
8533 tᵉlâthîyn (Ch.) (2),
thirty
5144 triakŏnta (9), thirty

THIRTYFOLD
5144 triakŏnta (2), thirty

THISTLE
1863 dardar (1), thorn
2336 chôwach (4), thorn

THISTLES
1863 dardar (1), thorn
2336 chôwach (1), thorn
5146 tribŏlŏs (1), thorny
caltrop plant

THITHER
1988 hălôm (1), hither
2008 hênnâh (3), from
here; from there
5704 'ad (1), until
8033 shâm (63), there
1563 ĕkĕi (8), thither
1904 ĕpĕrchŏmai (1), to
supervene
3854 paraginŏmai (1), to
arrive; to appear
4370 prŏstrĕchō (1), to
hasten by running

THITHERWARD
2008 hênnâh (1), from
here; from there
8033 shâm (1), there
1563 ĕkĕi (1), thither

THOMAS
2381 Thōmas (12), twin

THONGS
2438 himas (1), strap

THORN
2336 chôwach (2), thorn
4534 mᵉçûwkâh (1),
thorn-hedge
5285 na'ătsûwts (1),
brier; thicket
6975 qôwts (2), thorns
4647 skŏlŏps (1), thorn

THORNS
329 'âţâd (1), buckthorn
2312 chêdeq (1), prickly
2336 chôwach (3), thorn
5285 na'ătsûwts (1),
brier; thicket
5518 çîyr (4), thorn; hook
5544 çillôwn (1), prickle
6791 tsên (2), thorn
6975 qôwts (12), thorns
7063 qimmâshôwn (1),
prickly plant
7898 shayith (7), wild
growth of briers
173 akantha (14), thorn
174 akanthinŏs (2),
thorny

THOROUGHLY
3190 yâţab (1), to be,
make well
7495 râphâ' (1), to cure

THOUGHT
559 'âmar (9), to say

1672 dâ'ag (1), be
anxious, be afraid
1696 dâbar (1), to speak
1697 dâbâr (1), word;
matter; thing
1819 dâmâh (4), to think
2154 zimmâh (1), plan
2161 zâmam (5), to plan
2803 châshab (10), to
think, regard; to value
4093 maddâ' (1),
intelligence
4209 mᵉzimmâh (1), plan
4284 machăshâbâh (1),
contrivance; plan
5869 'ayin (3), eye; sight
6246 'ăshîth (Ch.) (1), to
purpose, plan
6248 'ashtûwth (1),
cogitation, thinking
6419 pâlal (1), to
intercede, pray
7454 rêa' (1), thought
7807 shach (1), sunk
8232+6925 shᵉphar (Ch.)
(1), to be beautiful
1260 dialŏgizŏmai (1), to
deliberate
1261 dialŏgismŏs (1),
consideration; debate
1380 dŏkĕō (5), to think
1760 ĕnthumĕŏmai (2),
ponder, reflect on
1911 ĕpiballō (1), to
throw upon
1963 ĕpinŏia (1),
thought, intention
2106 ĕudŏkĕō (1), to
think well, i.e. approve
2233 hēgĕŏmai (2), to
deem, i.e. consider
2919 krinō (1), to decide;
to try, condemn, punish
3049 lŏgizŏmai (1), to
credit; to think, regard
3309 mĕrimnaō (11), to
be anxious about
3540 nŏēma (1),
perception, i.e. purpose
3543 nŏmizō (1), to deem
4305 prŏmĕrimnaō (1), to
care in advance

THOUGHTEST
1819 dâmâh (1), to
consider, think

THOUGHTS
2031 harhôr (Ch.) (1),
mental conception
2711 chêqeq (1),
enactment, resolution
4180 môwrâsh (1),
possession
4209 mᵉzimmâh (2),
plan; sagacity
4284 machăshâbâh (24),
contrivance; plan
5587 çâ'îph (2), divided
in mind; sentiment
5588 çê'êph (1), divided
in mind; skeptic
6250 'eshtônâh (1),
thinking
7454 rêa' (1), thought
7476 ra'yôwn (Ch.) (5),
mental conception
8312 sar'aph (2),
cogitation
1261 dialŏgismŏs (8),
consideration; debate

1270 dianŏēma (1), *sentiment, thought*
1761 ĕnthumēsis (3), *deliberation; idea*
3053 lŏgismŏs (1), *reasoning; conscience*

THOUSAND
505 'eleph (436), *thousand*
506 'ălaph (Ch.) (3), *thousand*
7233 rᵉbâbâh (4), *myriad*
7239 ribbôw (5), *myriad*
7239+505 ribbôw (1), *myriad, large number*
7240 ribbôw (Ch.) (1), *myriad, large number*
1367 dischilïoi (1), *two thousand*
2035 hĕptakischilïoi (1), *seven times a thousand*
3461 murias (3), *ten thousand*
3463 murïoi (3), *ten thousand*
4000 pĕntakischilïoi (6), *five times a thousand*
5070 tĕtrakischilïoi (5), *four times a thousand*
5153 trischilïoi (1), *three times a thousand*
5505 chilias (21), *one thousand*
5507 chilïoi (11), *thousand*

THOUSANDS
503 'ălaph (1), *increase by thousands*
505 'eleph (46), *thousand*
506 'ălaph (Ch.) (1), *thousand*
7232 râbab (1), *to shoot*
7233 rᵉbâbâh (7), *myriad*
7239 ribbôw (1), *myriad*
3461 murias (2), *ten thousand*
5505 chilias (1), *one thousand*

THREAD
2339 chûwṭ (4), *string*
6616 pâthîyl (1), *twine*

THREATEN
546 apĕilĕō (1), *to menace; to forbid*

THREATENED
546 apĕilĕō (1), *to menace; to forbid*
4324 prŏsapĕilĕō (1), *to menace additionally*

THREATENING
547 apĕilē (1), *menace*

THREATENINGS
547 apĕilē (2), *menace*

THREE
7969 shâlôwsh (377), *three; third; thrice*
7991 shâlîysh (1), *triangle, three*
7992 shᵉlîyshîy (4), *third*
8027 shâlash (6), *to be triplicate*
8032 shilshôwm (1), *day before yesterday*
8532 tᵉlâth (Ch.) (10), *three or third*
5140 trĕis (69), *three*

5145 triakŏsiŏi (2), *three hundred*
5148 triĕtia (1), *three years' period*
5150 trimēnŏn (1), *three months' space*
5151 tris (1), *three times*
5153 trischilïoi (1), *three times a thousand*

THREEFOLD
8027 shâlash (1), *to be triplicate*

THREESCORE
7239 ribbôw (1), *myriad*
7657 shib'îym (38), *seventy*
8346 shishshîym (42), *sixty*
8361 shittîyn (Ch.) (4), *sixty*
1440 hĕbdŏmēkŏnta (3), *seventy*
1835 hĕxēkŏnta (4), *sixty*
5516 chi xi stigma (1), 666

THRESH
1758 dûwsh (3), *to thresh*
1869 dârak (1), *to tread*

THRESHED
1758 dûwsh (2), *to thresh*
2251 châbaṭ (1), *to thresh*

THRESHETH
248 alŏaŏ (1), *to tread*

THRESHING
1758 dûwsh (3), *to thresh*
1786 dayîsh (1), *threshing*-time
2742 chârûwts (2), *threshing-sledge*
4098 mᵉdushshâh (1), *down-trodden people*
4173 môwrag (3), *threshing sledge*

THRESHINGFLOOR
1637 gôren (17), *open area*

THRESHINGFLOORS
147 'iddar (Ch.) (1), *threshing-floor*
1637 gôren (1), *open area*

THRESHINGPLACE
1637 gôren (1), *open area*

THRESHOLD
4670 miphtân (8), *sill*
5592 çaph (6), *dish*

THRESHOLDS
624 'âçûph (1), *collection, stores*
5592 çaph (2), *dish*

THREW
5422 nâthats (1), *to tear down*
5619 çâqal (1), *to throw large stones*
8058 shâmaṭ (1), *to jostle*
906 ballō (2), *to throw*
4952 susparassō (1), *to convulse violently*

THREWEST
7993 shâlak (1), *to throw*

THRICE
7969+6471 shâlôwsh (4), *three; third; thrice*
5151 tris (11), *three times*

THROAT
1627 gârôwn (4), *throat*
3930 lôa' (1), *throat*
2995 larugx (1), *throat*
4155 pnigō (1), *to throttle*

THRONE
3678 kiççê' (120), *throne*
3764 korçê' (Ch.) (2), *throne*
968 bēma (1), *tribunal platform; judging place*
2362 thrŏnŏs (50), *throne*

THRONES
3678 kiççê' (4), *throne*
3764 korçê' (Ch.) (1), *throne*
2362 thrŏnŏs (4), *throne*

THRONG
2346 thlibō (1), *to crowd*
4912 sunĕchō (1), *to hold together*

THRONGED
4846 sumpnigō (1), *to drown; to crowd*
4918 sunthlibō (1), *to compress, i.e. to crowd*

THRONGING
4918 sunthlibō (1), *to compress, i.e. to crowd*

THROUGH
413 'êl (2), *to, toward*
1119 bᵉmôw (1), *in, with*
1157 bᵉ'ad (5), *through*
1234 bâqa' (3), *to cleave*
1811 dâlaph (1), *to drip*
1856 dâqar (2), *to pierce*
1870 derek (1), *road*
2864 châthar (1), *to break or dig into*
2944 ṭâ'an (1), *to stab*
3027 yâd (1), *hand; power*
4480 min (2), *from, out of*
5674 'âbar (10), *to cross*
5921 'al (5), *over, upon*
6440 pânîym (1), *face*
7130 qereb (5), *nearest part, i.e. the center*
7751 shûwṭ (1), *to travel*
8432 tâvek (7), *center*
303 ana (1), *through*
1223 dia (93), *through*
1224 diabainō (1), *to pass by, over, across*
1279 diapŏrĕuŏmai (1), *to travel through*
1330 diĕrchŏmai (8), *to traverse, travel through*
1350 diktuŏn (1), *drag net*
1358 diŏrussō (3), *to penetrate burglariously*
1537 ĕk (3), *out, out of*
1653 ĕlĕĕō (1), *to give out compassion*
1722 ĕn (37), *in; during*
1909 ĕpi (2), *on, upon*
2569 kalŏpŏiĕō (1), *to do well*
2596 kata (4), *down; according to*
2700 katatŏxĕuō (1), *to shoot down*
4044 pĕriĕirō (1), *penetrate entirely*
4063 pĕritrĕchō (1), *traverse, run about*

THROUGHLY
7235 râbâh (1), *to increase*
1245 diakatharizō (2), *to cleanse perfectly*
1722+3956 ĕn (1), *in*
1822 ĕxartizō (1), *to finish out; to equip fully*

THROUGHOUT
5921 'al (2), *above, over*
1223 dia (3), *through*
1330 diĕrchŏmai (2), *to traverse, travel through*
1519 ĕis (6), *to or into*
1722 ĕn (5), *in; during*
1909 ĕpi (2), *on, upon*
2596 kata (8), *down; according to*

THROW
2040 hâraç (6), *to pull down; break, destroy*
5307 nâphal (1), *to fall*
5422 nâthats (1), *to tear down*
8058 shâmaṭ (1), *to jostle*

THROWING
3027 yâd (1), *hand; power*

THROWN
2040 hâraç (7), *to pull down; break, destroy*
5422 nâthats (3), *to tear down*
7411 râmâh (1), *to hurl*
7993 shâlak (1), *to throw*
906 ballō (1), *to throw*
2647 kataluō (3), *to demolish; to halt*
4496 rhiptō (1), *to toss*

THRUST
926 bâhal (1), *to be, make agitated; hasten*
1333 bâthaq (1), *to cut in pieces, hack up*
1644 gârash (6), *to drive out; to expatriate*
1760 dâchâh (1), *to push down; to totter*
1766 dâchaq (1), *to oppress*
1856 dâqar (8), *to stab*
1920 hâdaph (4), *to push away or down; drive out*
2115 zûwr (1), *to press*
2944 ṭâ'an (1), *to stab*
3238 yânâh (1), *to suppress; to maltreat*
3905 lâchats (1), *to press*
5074 nâdad (1), *to rove, flee; to drive away*
5080 nâdach (2), *to push off, scattered*
5365 nâqar (1), *to bore*
5414 nâthan (1), *to give*
8628 tâqa' (2), *to clatter, slap, drive, clasp*
683 apōthĕŏmai (2), *to push off; to reject*
906 ballō (5), *to throw*
1544 ĕkballō (3), *to throw out*
1856 ĕxōthĕō (1), *to expel; to propel*
1877 ĕpanagō (1), *to put out to sea; to return*
2601 katabibazō (1), *to cause to bring down*

2700 katatŏxĕuō (1), to *shoot down*
3992 pĕmpō (2), to *send*

THRUSTETH
5086 nâdaph (1), to *disperse, be windblown*

THUMB
931 bôhen (6), *thumb*

THUMBS
931 bôhen (1), *thumb*
931+3027 bôhen (2), *thumb; big toe*

THUMMIM
8550 Tummîym (5), *perfections*

THUNDER
6963 qôwl (7), *sound*
7481 râ'am (2), to *crash* thunder; to *irritate*
7482 ra'am (6), *peal of* thunder
7483 ra'mâh (1), *horse's* mane
1027 brŏntē (3), *thunder*

THUNDERBOLTS
7565 resheph (1), *flame*

THUNDERED
7481 râ'am (3), to *crash* thunder; to *irritate*
1027+1096 brŏntē (1), *thunder*

THUNDERETH
7481 râ'am (3), to *crash* thunder; to *irritate*

THUNDERINGS
6963 qôwl (2), *sound*
1027 brŏntē (4), *thunder*

THUNDERS
6963 qôwl (3), *sound*
1027 brŏntē (4), *thunder*

THYATIRA
2363 Thuatĕira (4), *Thyatira*

THYINE
2367 thuïnŏs (1), of *citron*

TIBERIAS
5085 Tibĕrias (3), *Tiberius*

TIBERIUS
5086 Tibĕriŏs (1), (poss.) *pertaining to the* river *Tiberis or Tiber*

TIBHATH
2880 Ţibchath (1), *slaughter*

TIBNI
8402 Tibnîy (3), *strawy*

TIDAL
8413 Tid'âl (2), *fearfulness*

TIDINGS
1309 bᵉsôwrâh (6), glad *tidings, good news*
1319 bâsar (16), to *announce* (good news)
1697 dâbâr (4), *word*
8052 shᵉmûw'âh (8), *announcement*
8088 shêma' (2), *something heard*
2097 ĕuaggĕlizō (6), to *announce good news*
3056 lŏgŏs (1), *word*
5334 phasis (1), *news*

TIE
631 'âçar (1), to *fasten*
6029 'ânad (1), to *bind*

TIED
631 'âçar (3), to *fasten*
5414 nâthan (1), to *give*
1210 dĕō (4), to *bind*

TIGLATH-PILESER
8407 Tiglath Pil'eçer (3), *Tiglath-Pileser*

TIKVAH
8616 Tiqvâh (2), *hope*

TIKVATH
8616 Tiqvâh (1), *hope*

TILE
3843 lᵉbênâh (1), *brick*

TILGATH-PILNESER
8407 Tiglath Pil'eçer (3), *Tiglath-Pileser*

TILING
2766 kĕramŏs (1), *clay* roof *tile*

TILL
5647 'âbad (4), to *work*
5704 'ad (90), *until*
5705 'ad (Ch.) (1), *until*
6440 pânîym (1), *face; front*
891 achri (5), *until, up to*
1519 êis (1), *to* or *into*
2193 hĕōs (41), *until*
3360 mĕchri (2), *until*

TILLAGE
5215 nîyr (1), *plowed* land
5656 'ăbôdâh (2), *work*

TILLED
5647 'âbad (2), to *work*

TILLER
5647 'âbad (1), to *work*

TILLEST
5647 'âbad (1), to *work*

TILLETH
5647 'âbad (2), to *work*

TILON
8436 Tûwlôn (1), *suspension*

TIMAEUS
5090 Timaiŏs (1), (poss.) *foul; impure*

TIMBER
636 'â' (Ch.) (3), *wood*
6086 'êts (23), *wood*

TIMBREL
8596 tôph (5), *tambourine*

TIMBRELS
8596 tôph (4), *tambourine*
8608 tâphaph (1), to *drum* on a tambourine

TIME
116 'ĕdayin (Ch.) (1), *then*
227 'âz (5), *at that time*
268 'âchôwr (1), *behind, backward; west*
570 'emesh (1), *yesterday evening*
1767 day (1), *enough*
2165 zᵉmân (2), *time*
2166 zᵉmân (Ch.) (6), *time, appointed*
3117 yôwm (55), *day*
3118 yôwm (Ch.) (2), *day*

4150 môw'êd (3), *assembly*
4279 mâchar (7), *tomorrow; hereafter*
5732 'iddân (Ch.) (7), set *time; year*
5769 'ôwlâm (1), *eternity*
6256 'êth (220), *time*
6258 'attâh (3), *now*
6440 pânîym (2), *front*
6471 pa'am (14), *time*
6635 tsâbâ' (2), *army*
7225 rê'shîyth (1), *first*
7227 rab (2), *great*
7674 shebeth (1), *rest*
8032 shilshôwm (1), *day before yesterday*
8462 tᵉchillâh (2), *original; originally*
8543 tᵉmôwl (1), *yesterday*
744 archaiŏs (3), *original*
1074 gĕnĕa (1), *age*
1208 dĕutĕrŏs (1), *second*
1597 ĕkpalai (1), *long ago*
1909 ĕpi (2), *on, upon*
2119 ĕukairĕō (2), to *have opportunity*
2121 ĕukairŏs (1), *opportune, suitable*
2235 ēdē (1), *even now*
2250 hēmĕra (4), *day*
2540 kairŏs (54), *set time*
3195 mĕllō (1), to *intend*
3379 mēpŏtĕ (6), *never*
3568 nun (2), *now*
3598 hŏdŏs (1), *road*
3819 palai (1), *formerly*
4218 pŏtĕ (12), *ever*
4287 prŏthĕsmiŏs (1), *designated* day or time
4340 prŏskairŏs (1), *temporary*
4455 pōpŏtĕ (3), *at no time*
5119 tŏtĕ (4), *at the time*
5550 chrŏnŏs (28), *time*
5551 chrŏnŏtribĕō (1), to *procrastinate, linger*
5610 hōra (12), *hour*

TIMES
2165 zᵉmân (1), *time*
2166 zᵉmân (Ch.) (3), *time, appointed*
3027 yâd (1), *hand; power*
3117 yôwm (5), *day; time*
4150 môw'êd (1), *assembly*
4151 môw'âd (1), *troop*
4489 môneh (2), *instance*
5732 'iddân (Ch.) (6), set *time; year*
6256 'êth (22), *time*
6471 pa'am (42), *time*
8543 tᵉmôwl (1), *yesterday*
1074 gĕnĕa (1), *age*
1441 hĕbdŏmēkŏntakis (1), *seventy times*
2034 hĕptakis (4), *seven times*
2540 kairŏs (8), *set time*
3999 pĕntakis (1), *five times*
4218 pŏtĕ (3), *ever*
5151 tris (1), *three times*
5550 chrŏnŏs (8), *time*

TIMNA
8555 Timnâ' (4), *restraint*

TIMNAH
8553 Timnâh (3), *portion*
8555 Timnâ' (2), *restraint*

TIMNATH
8553 Timnâh (8), *portion*

TIMNATH-HERES
8556 Timnath Chereç (1), *portion of* (the) *sun*

TIMNATH-SERAH
8556 Timnath Chereç (2), *portion of* (the) *sun*

TIMNITE
8554 Timnîy (1), *Timnite*

TIMON
5096 Timōn (1), *valuable*

TIMOTHEOUS
5095 Timŏthĕŏs (1), *dear to God*

TIMOTHEUS
5095 Timŏthĕŏs (18), *dear to God*

TIMOTHY
5095 Timŏthĕŏs (9), *dear to God*

TIN
913 bᵉdîyl (5), *tin*

TINGLE
6750 tsâlal (3), to *tinkle*

TINKLING
5913 'âkaç (1), to *put on anklets*
214 alalazō (1), to *clang*

TIP
8571 tᵉnûwk (8), *pinnacle, i.e. extremity*
206 akrŏn (1), *extremity*

TIPHSAH
8607 Tiphçach (2), *ford*

TIRAS
8493 Tîyrᵉyâ' (2), *fearful*

TIRATHITES
8654 Tir'âthîy (1), *gate*

TIRE
6287 pᵉ'êr (1), *head-dress*

TIRED
3190 yâţab (1), to *be, make well; successful*

TIRES
6287 pᵉ'êr (1), *fancy head-dress*
7720 sahărôn (1), *round pendant* or *crescent*

TIRHAKAH
8640 Tirhâqâh (2), *Tirhakah*

TIRHANAH
8647 Tirchănâh (1), *Tirchanah*

TIRIA
8493 Tîyrᵉyâ' (1), *fearful*

TIRSHATHA
8660 Tirshâthâ' (5), *deputy* or *governor*

TIRZAH
8656 Tirtsâh (18), *delightsomeness*

TISHBITE
8664 Tishbîy (6), *Tishbite*

TITHE
4643 ma'ăsêr (11), *tithe*
6237 'âsar (1), to *tithe*

586 apŏdĕkatŏō (2), to
tithe

TITHES
4643 ma'ăsêr (16), *tithe*
6237 'âsar (2), *to tithe*
586 apŏdĕkatŏō (2), to
tithe, give a tenth
1181 dĕkatē (1), *tithe*
1183 dĕkatŏō (3), *to give
or take a tenth*

TITHING
4643 ma'ăsêr (1), *tithe*
6237 'âsar (1), *to tithe*

TITLE
6725 tsîyûwn (1), guiding
pillar, monument
5102 titlŏs (2), *title*

TITTLE
2762 kĕraia (2), *horn-like*

TITUS
5103 Titŏs (15), *Titus*

TIZITE
8491 Tîytsîy (1), *Titsite*

TOAH
8430 Tôwach (1), *humble*

TOB
2897 Ţôwb (2), *good*

TOB-ADONIJAH
2899 Ţôwb Ădônîyâhûw
(1), *pleasing (to)
Adonijah*

TOBIAH
2900 Ţôwbîyâh (15),
goodness of Jehovah

TOBIJAH
2900 Ţôwbîyâh (3),
goodness of Jehovah

TOCHEN
8507 Tôken (1), *quantity*

TOE
931 bôhen (6), *big toe*

TOES
676 'etsba' (2), *finger; toe*
677 'etsba' (Ch.) (2), *toe*
931 bôhen (1), *big toe*
931+7272 bôhen (2),
thumb; big toe

TOGARMAH
8425 Tôwgarmâh (4),
Togarmah

TOGETHER
259 'echâd (5), *first*
2298 chad (Ch.) (1), *one*
3162 yachad (125),
unitedly
6776 tsemed (1), *yoke*
240 allēlōn (1), *one
another*
260 hama (3), *together*
346 anakĕphalaiŏmai
(1), to *sum up*
1794 ĕntulissō (1), *wind
up in, enwrap*
1865 ĕpathrŏizō (1), to
accumulate, increase
1996 ĕpisunagō (6), to
collect upon
1997 ĕpisunagōgē (2),
meeting, gathering
1998 ĕpisuntrĕchō (1), to
hasten together upon
2086 hĕtĕrŏzugĕō (1), to
associate discordantly

2675 katartizō (1), to
prepare, equip
3674 hŏmŏu (3), *at the
same place or time*
4776 sugkathizō (2), to
give, take a seat with
4779 sugkalĕō (8), to
convoke, call together
4786 sugkĕrannumi (1),
to *combine, assimilate*
4789 sugklĕrŏnŏmŏs (1),
participant in common
4794 sugkuptō (1), to be
completely overcome
4801 suzĕugnumi (2), to
conjoin in marriage
4802 suzĕtĕō (1), to
discuss, controvert
4806 suzōŏpŏiĕō (2), to
reanimate conjointly
4811 sukŏphantĕō (1), to
defraud, i.e. exact
4816 sullĕgō (1), to *gather*
4822 sumbibazō (2), to
drive together, unite
4831 summimētēs (1),
co-imitator
4836 sumparaginŏmai
(1), to *convene*
4837 sumparakalĕō (1),
to *console jointly*
4851 sumphĕrō (1), to
collect; to conduce
4853 sumphulĕtēs (1),
*native of the same
country*
4854 sumphutŏs (1),
closely united to
4856 sumphōnĕō (1), to
be harmonious
4863 sunagō (31), to
gather together
4865 sunagōnizŏmai (1),
to *struggle with*
4866 sunathlĕō (1), to
wrestle with
4867 sunathrŏizō (3), to
convene
4873 sunanakĕimai (1),
to *recline with*
4883 sunarmŏlŏgĕō (2),
to *render close-jointed*
4886 sundĕsmŏs (1),
ligament; uniting
4888 sundŏxazō (1), to
share glory with
4890 sundrŏmē (1),
(riotous) concourse
4891 sunĕgĕirō (1), to
raise up with
4896 sunĕimi (1), to
assemble, gather
4897 sunĕisĕrchŏmai (1),
to *enter with*
4899 sunĕklĕktŏs (1),
chosen together with
4903 sunĕrgĕō (2), to be
a fellow-worker
4904 sunĕrgŏs (1),
fellow-worker
4905 sunĕrchŏmai (16),
to *gather together*
4911 sunĕphistēmi (1), to
resist or assault jointly
4925 sunŏikŏdŏmĕō (1),
to *construct*
4943 sunupŏurgĕō (1),
assist, join to help

4944 sunōdinō (1), to
sympathize

TOHU
8459 Tôchûw (1),
abasement

TOI
8583 Tô'ûw (3), *error*

TOIL
5999 'âmâl (1), *effort*
6093 'itstsâbôwn (1),
labor or pain
2872 kŏpiaŏ (2), to *feel
fatigue; to work hard*

TOILED
2872 kŏpiaŏ (1), to *feel
fatigue; to work hard*

TOILING
928 basanizō (1), to
torture, torment

TOKEN
226 'ôwth (10), *sign*
1730 ĕndĕigma (1), plain
indication
1732 ĕndĕixis (1),
indication
4592 sēmĕiŏn (1), *sign*
4953 sussēmŏn (1), *sign
in common*

TOKENS
226 'ôwth (4), *signal, sign*

TOLA
8439 Tôwlâ' (6), *worm*

TOLAD
8434 Tôwlâd (1), *posterity*

TOLAITES
8440 Tôwlâ'îy (1), *Tolaite*

TOLD
559 'âmar (13), to *say*
560 'ămar (Ch.) (5), to *say*
1540 gâlâh (2), to *reveal*
1696 dâbar (15), to *speak*
4487 mânâh (1), to *allot;
to enumerate or enroll*
5046 nâgad (152), to
announce
5608 çâphar (27), to
recount an event
8085 shâma' (2), to *hear*
8505 tâkan (1), to
balance, i.e. measure
312 anaggĕllō (4), to
announce, report
513 axinē (3), *axe*
518 apaggĕllō (17), to
announce, proclaim
1285 diasaphĕō (1), to
declare, tell
1334 diēgĕŏmai (2), to
relate fully, describe
1834 ĕxēgĕŏmai (1), to
tell, relate again
2036 ĕpō (13), to *speak*
2046 ĕrĕō (1), to *utter*
2980 lalĕō (10), to *talk*
3004 lĕgō (4), to *say*
3377 mēnuō (1), to *report*
4277 prŏĕpō (1), to *say
already, to predict*
4280 prŏĕrĕō (2), to *say
already, predict*
4302 prŏlĕgō (1), to
predict, forewarn

TOLERABLE
414 anĕktŏtĕrŏs (6),
more endurable

TOLL
4061 middâh (Ch.) (3),
tribute, tax money

TOMB
1430 gâdîysh (1), *stack*
3419 mnēmĕiŏn (2),
place of interment

TOMBS
3418 mnēma (2),
monument
3419 mnēmĕiŏn (3),
place of interment
5028 taphŏs (1), *grave*

TONGS
4457 melqâch (5), *tongs*
4621 ma'ătsâd (1), *axe*

TONGUE
762 'Ărâmîyth (2), *in
Aramean*
2013 hâçâh (1), to *hush*
2790 chârash (4), to *be
silent; to be deaf*
3956 lâshôwn (89),
tongue; tongue-shaped
1100 glōssa (24), *tongue*
1258 dialĕktŏs (5),
language
1447 Hĕbraïsti (3), *in the
Jewish language*

TONGUES
3956 lâshôwn (9), *tongue*
1100 glōssa (26), *tongue*
2084 hĕtĕrŏglōssŏs (1),
foreigner

TOOK
270 'âchaz (6), to *seize*
622 'âçaph (2), to *gather*
680 'âtsal (1), to *select*
935 bôw' (1), to *go, come*
1197 bâ'ar (1), to *be
brutish, be senseless*
1491 gâzâh (1), to *cut off*
1497 gâzal (1), to *rob*
1518 gîyach (1), to *issue
forth; to burst forth*
2388 châzaq (4), to
fasten upon; to seize
3318 yâtsâ' (1), to *bring
out*
3381 yârad (4), to
descend
3920 lâkad (43), to *catch*
3947 lâqach (359), to *take*
4185 mûwsh (1), to
withdraw
5265 nâça' (2), to *start*
5267 n°çaq (Ch.) (1), to
go up
5312 n°phaq (Ch.) (2), to
issue forth; to bring out
5375 nâsâ' (45), to *lift up*
5384 nâsheh (1),
rheumatic or crippled
5414 nâthan (1), to *give*
5493 çûwr (11), to *turn off*
5674 'âbar (2), to *cross
over; to transition*
5709 'ădâ' (Ch.) (1), to
remove
5927 'âlâh (3), to *ascend*
6901 qâbal (3), to *take*
6902 q°bal (Ch.) (1), to
acquire
7287 râdâh (1), to
subjugate; to crumble
7311 rûwm (2), to *be
high; to rise or raise*

7673 shâbath (1), to repose; to desist
7760 sûwm (1), to put
8610 tâphas (1), to manipulate, i.e. seize
142 airō (18), to take up
337 anairĕō (1), to take away, i.e. abolish
353 analambanō (3), to take up, bring up
520 apagō (1), to take away
589 apŏdĕmĕō (2), visit a foreign land
618 apŏlambanō (1), to receive; be repaid
643 apŏskĕuazō (1), to pack up baggage
657 apŏtassŏmai (1), to say adieu; to renounce
941 bastazō (1), to lift
1011 bŏulĕuō (1), to deliberate; to resolve
1209 dĕchŏmai (2), to receive, welcome
1453 ĕgĕirō (1), to waken
1544 ĕkballō (1), to throw out
1562 ĕkduō (2), to divest
1723 ĕnagkalizŏmai (1), take into one's arms
1921 ĕpiginōskō (1), to acknowledge
1949 ĕpilambanŏmai (12), to seize
1959 ĕpimĕlĕŏmai (1), to care for
2021 ĕpichĕirĕō (1), to undertake, try
2192 ĕchō (1), to have
2507 kathairĕō (3), to lower, or demolish
2902 kratĕō (11), to seize
2983 lambanō (57), to take, receive
3348 mĕtĕchō (1), to share or participate
3830 pandŏchĕus (1), innkeeper
3880 paralambanō (16), to associate with
4084 piazō (1), to seize
4160 pŏiĕō (1), to make
4327 prŏsdĕchŏmai (1), to receive; to await for
4355 prŏslambanō (5), to take along
4815 sullambanō (3), to seize (arrest, capture)
4823 sumbŏulĕuō (2), to recommend, deliberate
4838 sumparalambanō (2), to take along with
4863 sunagō (3), to gather together

TOOKEST
3947 lâqach (1), to take

TOOL
2719 chereb (1), knife
3627 kĕlîy (1), thing

TOOTH
8127 shên (6), tooth
3599 ŏdŏus (1), tooth

TOOTH'S
8127 shên (1), tooth

TOP
1406 gâg (8), roof; top

1634 gerem (1), bone; self
5585 çâ'îyph (2), bough
6706 tsᵉchîyach (4), exposed to the sun
6788 tsammereth (3), foliage
6936 qodqŏd (2), crown
7218 rô'sh (67), head
206 akrŏn (1), extremity
509 anŏthĕn (3), from above; from the first

TOPAZ
6357 piṭdâh (4), topaz
5116 tŏpaziŏn (1), topaz

TOPHEL
8603 Tôphel (1), quagmire

TOPHET
8612 Tôpheth (8), smiting
8613 Tophteh (1), place of cremation

TOPHETH
8612 Tôpheth (1), smiting

TOPS
1406 gâg (2), roof; top
5585 çâ'îyph (1), bough
7218 rô'sh (8), head

TORCH
3940 lappîyd (1), torch

TORCHES
3940 lappîyd (1), torch
6393 pᵉlâdâh (1), iron armature
2985 lampas (1), torch

TORMENT
928 basanizō (3), to torture, torment
929 basanismŏs (6), torture, agony
931 basanŏs (1), torture
2851 kŏlasis (1), infliction, punishment

TORMENTED
928 basanizō (5), to torture, torment
2558 kakŏuchĕō (1), to maltreat; to torment
3600 ŏdunaō (2), to grieve

TORMENTORS
930 basanistēs (1), torturer

TORMENTS
931 basanŏs (2), torture

TORN
1497 gâzal (1), to rob
2963 ṭâraph (4), to pluck
2966 ṭᵉrêphâh (8), torn prey
5478 çûwchâh (1), filth
7665 shâbar (2), to burst
4682 sparassō (1), to convulse with epilepsy

TORTOISE
6632 tsâb (1), lizard

TORTURED
5178 tumpanizō (1), to beat to death

TOSS
1607 gâ'ash (1), to agitate violently, shake
6802 tsᵉnêphâh (1), ball

TOSSED
5086 nâdaph (1), to disperse, be windblown

5287 nâ'ar (1), to tumble
928 basanizō (1), to torture, torment
2831 kludŏnizŏmai (1), to fluctuate on waves
4494 rhipizō (1), to be tossed about
5492 chĕimazō (1), to be battered in a storm

TOSSINGS
5076 nâdûd (1), tossing and rolling on the bed

TOTTERING
1760 dâchâh (1), to totter

TOU
8583 Tô'ûw (2), error

TOUCH
5060 nâga' (31), to strike
680 haptŏmai (13), to touch
2345 thigganō (2), to touch
4379 prŏspsauō (1), to lay a finger on

TOUCHED
5060 nâga' (24), to strike
5401 nâshaq (1), to touch
680 haptŏmai (21), to touch
2609 katagō (1), to lead down; to moor a vessel
4834 sumpathĕō (1), to commiserate
5584 psēlaphaō (1), to manipulate

TOUCHETH
5060 nâga' (37), to strike
7306 rûwach (1), to smell
680 haptŏmai (2), to touch

TOUCHING
413 'êl (3), to, toward
5921 'al (1), against
1909 ĕpi (2), on, upon
2596 kata (3), down; according to
4012 pĕri (11), about

TOW
5296 nᵉ'ôreth (2), tow
6594 pishtâh (1), flax

TOWEL
3012 lĕntiŏn (2), linen

TOWER
969 bâchôwn (1), assayer
1431 gâdal (1), to be great, make great
4024 Migdôwl (2), tower
4026 migdâl (34), tower
4692 mâtsôwr (1), siege-mound; distress
4869 misgâb (3), refuge
6076 'ôphel (1), fortress
4444 purgŏs (4), tower

TOWERS
971 bachîyn (1), siege-tower
975 bachan (1), watch-tower
4026 migdâl (13), tower
6438 pinnâh (2), pinnacle

TOWN
5892 'îyr (3), city, town
7023 qîyr (2), wall
2968 kōmē (8), town

TOWNCLERK
1122 grammatĕus (1), secretary, scholar

TOWNS
1323 bath (27), outlying village
2333 chavvâh (4), village
2691 châtsêr (1), village
5892 'îyr (3), city, town
6519 pᵉrâzâh (1), rural
2968 kōmē (3), town
2969 kōmŏpŏlis (1), unwalled city

TRACHONITIS
5139 Trachōnitis (1), rough district

TRADE
582 'ĕnôwsh (2), man; person, human
5503 câchar (2), to travel
2038 ĕrgazŏmai (1), to toil

TRADED
5414 nâthan (4), to give
2038 ĕrgazŏmai (1), to toil

TRADING
1281 diapragmatĕuŏmai (1), to earn, make gain

TRADITION
3862 paradŏsis (11), Jewish traditional law

TRADITIONS
3862 paradŏsis (2), Jewish traditional law

TRAFFICK
3667 Kᵉna'an (1), humiliated
4536 miçchâr (1), trade
5503 câchar (1), to travel round; to palpitate
7404 rᵉkullâh (2), peddled trade

TRAFFICKERS
3669 Kᵉna'ăniy (1), Kenaanite; pedlar

TRAIN
2428 chayil (1), army; wealth; virtue; valor
2596 chânak (1), to initiate or discipline
7757 shûwl (1), skirt

TRAINED
2593 chânîyk (1), trained

TRAITOR
4273 prŏdŏtēs (1), betraying

TRAITORS
4273 prŏdŏtēs (1), betraying

TRAMPLE
7429 râmaç (2), to tread
2662 katapatĕō (1), to trample down; to reject

TRANCE
1611 ĕkstasis (3), bewilderment, ecstasy

TRANQUILITY
7963 shᵉlêvâh (Ch.) (1), safety

TRANSFERRED
3345 mĕtaschēmatizō (1), to transfigure

TRANSFIGURED
3339 mĕtamŏrphŏō (2), to *transform*

TRANSFORMED
3339 mĕtamŏrphŏō (1), to *transform*
3345 mĕtaschēmatizō (2), to *transfigure*

TRANSFORMING
3345 mĕtaschēmatizō (1), to *transfigure*

TRANSGRESS
898 bâgad (1), to *act treacherously*
4603 mâ'al (2), to *act treacherously*
5647 'âbad (1), to *do*
5674 'âbar (4), to *cross*
6586 pâsha' (3), to *break away from authority*
3845 *parabainō* (2), to *violate a command*
3848 *parabatēs* (1), *violator, lawbreaker*

TRANSGRESSED
898 bâgad (1), to *act treacherously*
4603 mâ'al (7), to *act treacherously*
5674 'âbar (12), to *cross*
6586 pâsha' (13), to *break from authority*
3928 *parērchŏmai* (1), to *go by; to perish*

TRANSGRESSEST
5674 'âbar (1), to *cross*

TRANSGRESSETH
898 bâgad (1), to *act treacherously*
4603 mâ'al (1), to *act treacherously*
458+4160 *anŏmia* (1), *violation of law*
3845 *parabainō* (1), to *violate a command*

TRANSGRESSING
5674 'âbar (1), to *cross*
6586 pâsha' (1), to *break away from authority*

TRANSGRESSION
4604 ma'al (6), *treachery*
6586 pâsha' (1), to *break away from authority*
6588 pesha' (38), *revolt*
458 *anŏmia* (1), *violation of law, wickedness*
3845 *parabainō* (1), to *violate a command*
3847 *parabasis* (4), *violation, breaking*

TRANSGRESSIONS
6588 pesha' (46), *revolt*
3847 *parabasis* (2), *violation, breaking*

TRANSGRESSOR
898 bâgad (2), to *act treacherously*
6586 pâsha' (1), to *break away from authority*
3848 *parabatēs* (1), *violator, lawbreaker*

TRANSGRESSORS
898 bâgad (8), to *act treacherously*
5674 'âbar (1), to *cross*

6586 pâsha' (8), to *break away from authority*
459 *anŏmŏs* (2), *without Jewish law*
3848 *parabatēs* (1), *violator, lawbreaker*

TRANSLATE
5674 'âbar (1), to *cross*

TRANSLATED
3179 mĕthistēmi (1), to *move*
3346 mĕtatithēmi (2), to *transport; to exchange*

TRANSLATION
3331 mĕtathĕsis (1), *transferral* to heaven

TRANSPARENT
1307 *diaphanēs* (1), *appearing through*

TRAP
4170 môwqêsh (1), *noose*
4434 malkôdeth (1), *snare*
4889 mashchîyth (1), *bird snare; corruption*
2339 *thēra* (1), *hunting*

TRAPS
4170 môwqêsh (1), *noose*

TRAVAIL
2342 chûwl (2), to *dance, whirl; to writhe* in pain
2470 châlâh (1), to *be weak, sick, afflicted*
3205 yâlad (11), to *bear young; to father a child*
5999 'âmâl (3), *worry*
6045 'inyân (6), *labor; affair, care*
8513 t°lâ'âh (1), *distress*
3449 *mŏchthŏs* (2), *sadness*
5088 tiktō (1), to *produce from seed*
5604 ōdin (1), *pang*
5605 ōdinō (1), to *experience labor pains*

TRAVAILED
2342 chûwl (2), to *dance, whirl; to writhe* in pain
3205 yâlad (3), to *bear young; to father a child*

TRAVAILEST
5605 ōdinō (1), to *experience labor pains*

TRAVAILETH
2254 châbal (1), to *writhe* in labor pain
2342 chûwl (1), to *writhe* in pain; to *wait*
3205 yâlad (4), to *bear young; to father a child*
4944 sunōdinō (1), to *sympathize*

TRAVAILING
3205 yâlad (2), to *bear young; to father a child*
5605 ōdinō (1), to *experience labor pains*

TRAVEL
8513 t°lâ'âh (2), *distress*
4898 sunĕkdēmŏs (2), *fellow-traveller*

TRAVELERS
1980+5410 hâlak (1), to *walk*

TRAVELLED
1330 diĕrchŏmai (1), to *traverse, travel through*

TRAVELLER
734 'ôrach (1), *road*
1982 hêlek (1), *wayfarer*

TRAVELLETH
1980 hâlak (2), to *walk*

TRAVELLING
736 'ôr°châh (1), *caravan*
6808 tsâ'âh (1), to *tip over; to depopulate*
589 apŏdēmĕō (1), *visit a foreign land*

TRAVERSING
8308 sârak (1), to *interlace*

TREACHEROUS
898 bâgad (6), to *act treacherously*
900 bôg°dôwth (1), *treachery*
901 bâgôwd (2), *treacherous*

TREACHEROUSLY
898 bâgad (23), to *act treacherously*

TREACHERY
4820 mirmâh (1), *fraud*

TREAD
947 bûwç (6), to *trample*
1758 dûwsh (1), to *trample or thresh*
1759 dûwsh (Ch.) (1), to *trample; destroy*
1869 dârak (14), to *tread*
1915 hâdak (1), to *crush*
6072 'âçaç (1), to *trample*
7429 râmaç (6), to *tread*
7760+4823 sûwm (1), to *put, place*
3961 patĕō (2), to *trample*

TREADER
1869 dârak (1), to *tread*

TREADERS
1869 dârak (1), to *tread*

TREADETH
1758 dûwsh (1), to *trample or thresh*
1869 dârak (4), to *tread*
7429 râmaç (2), to *tread*
248 alŏaō (2), to *tread out grain*
3961 patĕō (1), to *trample*

TREADING
1318 bâshaç (1), to *trample down*
1869 dârak (1), to *tread*
4001 m°bûwçâh (1), *trampling, oppression*
4823 mirmâç (1), *abasement*

TREASON
7195 qesher (5), *unlawful alliance*

TREASURE
214 'ôwtsâr (11), *depository*
1596 g°naz (Ch.) (2), *treasury storeroom*
2633 chôçen (2), *wealth*
4301 matmôwn (1), *secret storehouse*

4543 miçk°nâh (1), *storage-magazine*
1047 gaza (1), *treasure*
2343 thēsaurizō (2), to *amass or reserve*
2344 thēsaurŏs (13), *wealth, what is stored*

TREASURED
686 'âtsar (1), to *store up*

TREASURER
1489 gizbâr (1), *treasurer*
5532 çâkan (1), to *minister to*

TREASURERS
686 'âtsar (1), to *store up*
1411 g°dâbâr (Ch.) (2), *treasurer*
1490 gizbâr (Ch.) (1), *treasurer*

TREASURES
214 'ôwtsâr (50), *depository*
1596 g°naz (Ch.) (1), *treasury storeroom*
4301 matmôwn (3), *secret storehouse*
4362 mikman (1), *hidden-treasure*
6259 'âthûwd (1), *prepared*
8226 sâphan (1), to *conceal*
2344 thēsaurŏs (5), *wealth, what is stored*

TREASUREST
2343 thēsaurizō (1), to *amass or reserve*

TREASURIES
214 'ôwtsâr (7), *depository*
1595 genez (2), *treasury coffer*
1597 ginzak (1), *treasury storeroom*

TREASURY
214 'ôwtsâr (3), *depository*
1049 gazŏphulakiŏn (5), *treasure-house*
2878 kŏrban (1), *votive offering or gift*

TREATISE
3056 lŏgŏs (1), *word*

TREE
363 'îylân (Ch.) (6), *tree*
815 'êshel (2), *tamarisk*
6086 'êts (88), *wood*
65 agriĕlaiŏs (2), *wild olive* tree
1186 dĕndrŏn (17), *tree*
2565 kalliĕlaiŏs (1), *cultivated olive*
3586 xulŏn (10), *timber*
4808 sukē (16), *fig-tree*
4809 sukŏmŏraia (1), *sycamore-fig* tree

TREES
352 'ayîl (2), *oak tree*
6086 'êts (77), *wood*
6097 'êtsâh (1), *timber*
1186 dĕndrŏn (9), *tree*

TREMBLE
2111 zûwâ' (1), to *tremble*
2112 zûwa' (Ch.) (1), to *shake* with fear

2342 chûwl (2), to *writhe*
2648 châphaz (1), to
hasten away, to *fear*
2729 chârad (6), to
shudder with terror
2730 chârêd (2), *fearful*
6426 pâlats (1), to *quiver*
7264 râgaz (9), to *quiver*
7322 rûwph (1), to *quake*
7493 râ'ash (4), to *quake*
5425 *phrissō* (1), to
shudder in *fear*

TREMBLED
2112 zûwa' (Ch.) (1), to
shake with fear
2342 chûwl (2), to *writhe*
2729 chârad (5), to
shudder with terror
2730 chârêd (2), *fearful*
7264 râgaz (2), to *quiver*
7364 râchats (1), to *bathe*
7493 râ'ash (5), to *quake*
1719+1096 ĕmphŏbŏs (1),
alarmed, terrified
1790+1096 ĕntrŏmŏs (1),
terrified
2192+5156 ĕchō (1), to
have; hold; keep

TREMBLETH
2729 chârad (1), to
shudder with terror
2730 chârêd (1), *fearful*
5568 çâmar (1), to *bristle*
7460 râ'ad (1), to *shudder*

TREMBLING
2729 chârad (1), to
shudder with terror
2731 chărâdâh (4), *fear*
6427 pallâtsûwth (1),
trembling fear
7268 raggâz (1), *timid*
7269 rogzâh (1),
trepidation
7460 râ'ad (6), to
shudder violently
7478 ra'al (1), *reeling*
7578 rᵉthêth (1), *terror*
8653 tar'êlâh (2), *reeling*
1096+1790 ginŏmai (1),
to *be, become*
5141 trĕmō (3), to *tremble*
5156 trŏmŏs (4), *quaking*
with *fear*

TRENCH
2426 chêyl (1),
entrenchment
4570 ma'gâl (3), circular
track or camp *rampart*
8565 tan (2), *jackal*
8585 tᵉ'âlâh (1),
irrigation *channel*
5482 *charax* (1), *rampart*

TRESPASS
816 'âsham (2), to *be
guilty;* to *be punished*
817 'âshâm (41), *guilt*
819 'ashmâh (11),
guiltiness
2398 châṭâ' (1), to *sin*
4603 mâ'al (1), to *act
treacherously*
4604 ma'al (18), sinful
treachery
6588 pesha' (5), *revolt*
264 hamartanō (3), to *sin*

TRESPASSED
816 'âsham (2), to *be
guilty;* to *be punished*
819 'ashmâh (1),
guiltiness
4603 mâ'al (8), to *act
treacherously*
4604 ma'al (3), sinful
treachery

TRESPASSES
817 'âshâm (1), *guilt*
819 'ashmâh (1),
guiltiness
4604 ma'al (1), sinful
treachery
3900 paraptōma (9),
error; transgression

TRESPASSING
819 'ashmâh (1),
guiltiness
4603 mâ'al (1), to *act
treacherously*

TRIAL
974 bâchan (1), to *test*
4531 maççâh (1), *testing*
1382 dŏkimē (1), *test*
1383 dŏkimiŏn (1),
testing; trustworthiness
3984 pĕira (1), *attempt*

TRIBE
4294 maṭṭeh (160), *tribe*
7626 shêbeṭ (57), *clan*
5443 *phulē* (19), *clan*

TRIBES
4294 maṭṭeh (20), *tribe*
7625 shᵉbaṭ (Ch.) (1), *clan*
7626 shêbeṭ (84), *clan*
1429 dōdĕkaphulŏn (1),
twelve tribes
5443 *phulē* (6), *clan*

TRIBULATION
6862 tsar (1), *trouble*
6869 tsârâh (2), *trouble*
2346 *thlibō* (1), to *trouble*
2347 *thlipsis* (18), *trouble*

TRIBULATIONS
6869 tsârâh (1), *trouble*
2347 *thlipsis* (3), *trouble*

TRIBUTARIES
4522 maç (4), *labor*

TRIBUTARY
4522 maç (1), *labor*

TRIBUTE
1093 bᵉlôw (Ch.) (3), *tax*
4060 middâh (1), *tribute*
4061 middâh (Ch.) (1),
tribute
4371 mekeç (6),
assessment, census-tax
4522 maç (12), *labor*
4530 miççâh (1), *liberally*
4853 massâ' (1), *burden*
6066 'ônesh (1), *fine*
1323 didrachmŏn (2),
double drachma
2778 *kĕnsŏs* (4),
enrollment
5411 phŏrŏs (4), *tax, toll*

TRICKLETH
5064 nâgar (1), to *pour*
out; to *deliver* over

TRIED
974 bâchan (4), to *test;* to
investigate
976 bôchan (1), *trial*

6884 tsâraph (7), to *refine*
1381 dŏkimazō (1), to
test; to *approve*
1384 dŏkimŏs (1),
acceptable, approved
3985 pĕirazō (3), to
endeavor, scrutinize
4448 purŏō (1), to *be
ignited, glow*

TRIEST
974 bâchan (3), to *test*

TRIETH
974 bâchan (4), to *test;* to
investigate
1381 dŏkimazō (1), to
test; to *approve*

TRIMMED
6213 'âsâh (1), to *do*
2885 kŏsmĕō (1), to *snuff*

TRIMMEST
3190 yâṭab (1), to *be,
make well*

TRIUMPH
5937 'âlaz (2), to *jump for
joy*
5970 'âlats (1), to *jump
for joy*
7321 rûwa' (3), to *shout*
7440 rinnâh (1), *shout*
7442 rânan (1), to *shout
for joy*
7623 shâbach (1), to
address in a loud tone;
to *pacify*
2358 thriambĕuō (1), to
*give victory, lead in
triumphal procession*

TRIUMPHED
1342 gâ'âh (2), to *be
exalted*

TRIUMPHING
7445 rᵉnânâh (1), *shout
for joy*
2358 thriambĕuō (1), to
*give victory, lead in
triumphal procession*

TROAS
5174 Trōas (6), *plain of
Troy*

TRODDEN
947 bûwç (3), to *trample*
1758 dûwsh (2), to
trample or *thresh*
1869 dârak (7), to *tread*
4001 mᵉbûwçâh (2),
trampling, oppression
4823 mirmâç (4),
abasement
5541 çâlâh (2), to
contemn, reject
7429 râmaç (2), to *tread*
2662 katapatĕō (3), to
trample down; to *reject*
3961 patĕō (2), to *trample*

TRODE
1869 dârak (2), to *tread*
7429 râmaç (5), to *tread*
2662 katapatĕō (1), to
trample down; to *reject*

TROGYLLIUM
5175 Trōgulliŏn (1),
Trogyllium

TROOP
92 'ăguddâh (2), *band*
1409 gâd (2), *fortune*

1416 gᵉdûwd (7), *band*
2416 chay (2), *alive; raw*

TROOPS
734 'ôrach (1), *road*
1416 gᵉdûwd (3), *band*

TROPHIMUS
5161 Trŏphimŏs (3),
nutritive

TROUBLE
926 bâhal (2), to *tremble*
927 bᵉhal (Ch.) (2), to
terrify; hasten
928 behâlâh (1), *sudden
panic, destruction*
1091 ballâhâh (1),
sudden *destruction*
1205 bᵉ'âthâh (2), *fear*
1804 dâlach (1), to *roil
water, churn up*
2189 za'ăvâh (1),
agitation
2960 ṭôrach (1), *burden*
4103 mᵉhûwmâh (4),
confusion or uproar
5916 'âkar (4), to *disturb*
5999 'âmâl (3), *worry*
6040 'ŏnîy (3), *misery*
6862 tsar (17), *trouble*
6869 tsârâh (34), *trouble*
6887 tsârar (2), to *cramp*
7186+3117 qâsheh (1),
severe
7267 rôgez (2), *disquiet*
7451 ra' (9), *bad; evil*
7561 râsha' (1), to *be, do,
declare wrong*
8513 tᵉlâ'âh (1), *distress*
387 anastatŏō (1), to
disturb, cause trouble
1613 ĕktarassō (1), to
disturb wholly
1776 ĕnŏchlĕō (1), to
annoy, cause trouble
2346 thlibō (1), to *trouble*
2347 thlipsis (3), *trouble*
2350 thŏrubĕō (1), to
disturb; clamor
2553 kakŏpathĕō (1), to
undergo hardship
2873 kŏpŏs (1), *toil; pains*
2873+3930 kŏpŏs (2), *toil*
3926 parĕnŏchlĕō (1), to
annoy, make trouble
3930 parĕchō (1), to *hold
near,* i.e. to *present*
4660 skullō (2), to *harass*
5015 tarassō (1), to
trouble, disturb

TROUBLED
926 bâhal (12), to *tremble*
927 bᵉhal (Ch.) (6), to
terrify; hasten
1089 bâlahh (1), to *terrify*
1204 bâ'ath (1), to *fear,
be afraid*
1607 gâ'ash (1), to
agitate violently, *shake*
1644 gârash (1), to *drive*
out; to *divorce*
1993 hâmâh (2), to *be in
great commotion*
2000 hâmam (1), to *put
in commotion*
2560 châmar (3), to
ferment, foam
5590 çâ'ar (1), to *rush*
upon; to *toss about*

5753 'âvâh (1), to *be crooked*
5916 'âkar (4), to *disturb*
6031 'ânâh (1), to *afflict*
6470 pâ'am (4), to *impel or agitate*
7114 qâtsar (1), to *curtail, cut short*
7264 râgaz (3), to *quiver*
7481 râ'am (1), to *crash thunder; to irritate*
7515 râphas (1), to *trample*, i.e. *roil* water
1298 diatarassō (1), to *disturb wholly*
2346 thlibō (3), to *crowd, press, trouble*
2360 throĕō (3), to *frighten, be alarmed*
5015 tarassō (14), to *trouble, disturb*
5015+1438 tarassō (1), to *trouble, disturb*
5182 turbazō (1), to *make turbid*

TROUBLEDST
1804 dâlach (1), to *roil* water, *churn up*

TROUBLER
5916 'âkar (1), to *disturb or afflict*

TROUBLES
6869 tsârâh (10), *trouble*
7451 ra' (1), *bad; evil*
5016 tarachē (1), *mob disturbance; roiling*

TROUBLEST
4660 skullō (1), to *harass*

TROUBLETH
598 'ănaç (Ch.) (1), to *distress*
926 bâhal (2), to *tremble*
1204 bâ'ath (1), to *fear, be afraid*
5916 'âkar (4), to *disturb*
3930+2873 parĕchō (1), to *hold near*
5015 tarassō (1), to *trouble, disturb*

TROUBLING
7267 rôgez (1), *disquiet; anger*
5015 tarassō (1), to *trouble, disturb*

TROUBLOUS
5916 'âkar (1), to *disturb or afflict*

TROUGH
8268 shôqeth (1), *watering-trough*

TROUGHS
7298 rahaṭ (1), *ringlet of* hair
8268 shôqeth (1), *watering-trough*

TROW
1380 dŏkĕō (1), to *think, regard, seem good*

TRUCEBREAKERS
786 aspŏndŏs (1), *not reconcilable*

TRUE
551 'omnâm (1), *verily, indeed, truly*

571 'emeth (18), *truth, trustworthiness*
3330 yatstsîyb (Ch.) (2), *fixed, sure*
3651 kên (5), *just; right*
6656 tsᵉdâ' (Ch.) (1), (sinister) *design*
227 alēthēs (22), *true; genuine*
228 alēthinŏs (27), *truthful*
1103 gnēsiŏs (1), *genuine, true*
2227 zōŏpŏiĕō (1), to (re-)*vitalize, give life*
3588+225 hŏ (1), *"the,"* i.e. the definite article
4103 pistŏs (2), *trustworthy; reliable*

TRULY
199 'ûwlâm (4), *however*
389 'ak (3), *surely; only*
403 'âkên (2), *truly!*
530 'ĕmûwnâh (1), *fidelity; steadiness*
551 'omnâm (1), *truly*
571 'emeth (8), *certainty, truth, trustworthiness*
577 'ânnâ' (1), *oh now!*
3588 kîy (1), *for, that*
227 alēthēs (1), *true*
230 alēthŏs (2), *truly*
686 ara (1), *then, so*
1161 dĕ (1), *but, yet*
1909+225 ĕpi (1), *on, upon*
3303 mĕn (12), *truly*

TRUMP
2689 chătsôtsᵉrâh (1), *trumpet*
7782 shôwphâr (1), *curved ram's horn*
4536 salpigx (2), *trumpet*

TRUMPET
3104 yôwbêl (1), *blast of a ram's horn*
7782 shôwphâr (47), *curved ram's horn*
8628 tâqa' (1), to *clatter, slap, drive, clasp*
4536 salpigx (7), *trumpet*
4537 salpizō (1), to *sound a trumpet blast*

TRUMPETERS
2689 chătsôtsᵉrâh (2), *trumpet*
2690 châtsar (1), to *blow* the *trumpet*
4538 salpistēs (1), *trumpeter*

TRUMPETS
2689 chătsôtsᵉrâh (24), *trumpet*
7782 shôwphâr (20), *curved ram's horn*
4536 salpigx (2), *trumpet*

TRUST
539 'âman (4), to *be firm, faithful, true; to trust*
982 bâṭach (61), to *trust, be confident or sure*
2342 chûwl (1), to *wait; to pervert*
2620 châçâh (32), to *confide in*
2622 châçûwth (1), *confidence*

3176 yâchal (2), to *wait; to be patient, hope*
4004 mibchôwr (1), *select,* i.e. *well fortified*
4009 mibṭâch (3), *security; assurance*
4268 machăçeh (1), *shelter; refuge*
1679 ĕlpizō (15), to *confide, hope for*
3892 paranŏmia (1), *wrongdoing*
3982 pĕithō (6), to *rely by inward certainty*
4006 pĕpŏithēsis (1), *reliance, trust*
4100 pistĕuō (3), to *have faith, credit; to entrust*

TRUSTED
539 'âman (1), to *trust,* to *be permanent*
982 bâṭach (18), to *trust, be confident or sure*
1556 gâlal (1), to *roll;* to *commit*
2620 châçâh (1), to *confide in*
7365 rᵉchats (Ch.) (1), to *attend upon, trust*
1679 ĕlpizō (2), to *expect or confide, hope for*
3982 pĕithō (3), to *rely by inward certainty*
4276 prŏĕlpizō (1), to *hope in advance*

TRUSTEDST
982 bâṭach (3), to *trust, be confident or sure*

TRUSTEST
982 bâṭach (6), to *trust, be confident or sure*

TRUSTETH
982 bâṭach (14), to *trust, be confident or sure*
2620 châçâh (2), to *confide in*
1679 ĕlpizō (1), to *expect or confide, hope for*

TRUSTING
982 bâṭach (1), to *trust, be confident or sure*

TRUSTY
539 'âman (1), to *be firm, faithful, true; to trust*

TRUTH
518+3808 'îm (1), *if, although; Oh that!*
529 'êmûwn (1), *trustworthiness; faithful*
530 'ĕmûwnâh (13), *fidelity; steadiness*
544 'ômen (1), *verity, faithfulness*
548 'ămânâh (2), *covenant*
551 'omnâm (3), *verily, indeed, truly*
571 'emeth (90), *certainty, truth*
3321 yᵉtsêb (Ch.) (1), to *speak surely*
3330 yatstsîyb (Ch.) (1), *fixed, sure*
3588+518 kîy (1), *for, that because*
7187 qᵉshôwṭ (Ch.) (2), *fidelity, truth*

7189 qôsheṭ (1), *reality*
225 alētheia (99), *truth, truthfulness*
226 alēthĕuō (8), to *be true*
227 alēthēs (1), *true; genuine*
230 alēthŏs (7), *truly, surely*
3483 nai (1), *yes*
3689 ŏntŏs (1), *really, certainly*

TRUTH'S
571 'emeth (1), *certainty, truth, trustworthiness*
225 alētheia (1), *truth, truthfulness*

TRY
974 bâchan (8), to *test; to investigate*
2713 châqar (1), to *examine, search*
5254 nâçâh (3), to *test, attempt*
6884 tsâraph (3), to *fuse metal; to refine*
1381 dŏkimazō (2), to *test; to approve*
3985 pĕirazō (1), to *endeavor, scrutinize*
4314+3986 prŏs (1), to, *toward; against*

TRYING
1383 dŏkimiŏn (1), *testing; trustworthiness*

TRYPHENA
5170 Truphaina (1), *luxurious*

TRYPHOSA
5173 Truphōsa (1), *luxuriating*

TUBAL
8422 Tûwbal (8), *Tubal*

TUBAL-CAIN
8423 Tûwbal Qayin (2), *offspring of Cain*

TUMBLED
2015 hâphak (1), to *change, overturn*

TUMULT
1993 hâmâh (1), to *be in great commotion*
1995 hâmôwn (4), *noise, tumult; many, crowd*
1999 hămullâh (1), *sound, roar, noise*
4103 mᵉhûwmâh (1), *confusion or uproar*
7588 shâ'ôwn (3), *uproar; destruction*
7600 sha'ănân (2), *secure; haughty*
2351 thŏrubŏs (4), *disturbance*

TUMULTS
4103 mᵉhûwmâh (1), *confusion or uproar*
181 akatastasia (2), *disorder, riot*

TUMULTUOUS
1121+7588 bên (1), *son, descendant; people*
1993 hâmâh (1), to *be in great commotion*

7588 shâ'ôwn (1), *uproar; destruction*

TURN
2015 hâphak (7), *to turn; to change, overturn*
2186 zânach (1), *to reject, forsake, fail*
5186 nâṭâh (17), *to stretch or spread out*
5414 nâthan (1), *to give*
5437 çâbab (14), *to surround*
5493 çûwr (27), *to turn off*
5627 çârâh (1), *apostasy; crime; remission*
5674 'âbar (1), *to cross over; to transition*
6437 pânâh (18), *to turn, to face*
6801 tsânaph (1), *to wrap, i.e. roll or dress*
7725 shûwb (152), *to turn back; to return*
7750 sûwṭ (2), *become derelict*
7760 sûwm (1), *to put, place*
7847 sâṭâh (1), *to deviate from duty, go astray*
8159 shâ'âh (1), *to inspect, consider*
8447 tôwr (2), *string or order*
344 anakamptō (1), *to turn back, come back*
576 apŏbainō (2), *to disembark*
654 apŏstrĕphō (5), *to turn away or back*
665 apŏtrĕpō (1), *to deflect, avoid*
1294 diastrĕphō (1), *to be morally corrupt*
1994 ĕpistrĕphō (10), *to revert, turn back to*
3329 mĕtagō (1), *to turn*
4762 strĕphō (4), *to turn or reverse a course*

TURNED
1750 dûwts (1), *to leap*
2015 hâphak (53), *to turn; to change*
3399 yârâṭ (1), *to be rash*
3943 lâphath (2), *to turn around or aside*
5186 nâṭâh (16), *to stretch or spread out*
5253 nâçag (1), *to retreat*
5414 nâthan (1), *to give*
5437 çâbab (31), *to surround*
5472 çûwg (10), *to go back, to retreat*
5493 çûwr (24), *to turn off*
6437 pânâh (36), *to turn, to face*
7725 shûwb (67), *to turn back; to return*
7734 sûwg (1), *to retreat*
7760 sûwm (1), *to put, place*
387 anastatŏō (1), *to disturb, cause trouble*
402 anachōrĕō (1), *to retire, withdraw*
654 apŏstrĕphō (2), *to turn away or back*
1096 ginŏmai (1), *to be, become*

1624 ĕktrĕpō (1), *to turn away*
1824 ĕxautēs (2), *instantly, at once*
1994 ĕpistrĕphō (11), *to revert, turn back to*
2827 klinō (1), *to slant or slope*
3179 mĕthistēmi (1), *to move*
3329 mĕtagō (1), *to turn*
3344 mĕtastrĕphō (1), *to transmute; corrupt*
4672 Sŏlŏmōn (1), *peaceful*
4762 strĕphō (12), *to turn or reverse a course*
5290 hupŏstrĕphō (2), *to turn under, behind*

TURNEST
6437 pânâh (1), *to turn, to face*
7725 shûwb (2), *to turn back; to return*

TURNETH
2015 hâphak (2), *to turn; to change, overturn*
5186 nâṭâh (2), *to stretch or spread out*
5437 çâbab (2), *to surround*
5493 çûwr (1), *to turn off*
5753 'âvâh (1), *to be crooked*
5791 'âvath (1), *to wrest, twist*
5844 'âṭâh (1), *to wrap, i.e. cover, veil, clothe*
6437 pânâh (4), *to turn, to face*
7725 shûwb (17), *to turn back; to return*
7760 sûwm (2), *to put, place*

TURNING
2015 hâphak (1), *to change, overturn*
2017 hôphek (1), *opposite-ness*
4142 mûwçabbâh (1), *transmutation*
4740 maqtsôwa' (5), *angle; or recess*
4878 mᵉshûwbâh (1), *apostasy*
7257 râbats (1), *to recline, repose, brood*
7725 shûwb (1), *to turn back; to return*
654 apŏstrĕphō (1), *to turn away or back*
1994 ĕpistrĕphō (2), *to revert, turn back to*
3346 mĕtatithēmi (1), *to transport; to exchange*
4762 strĕphō (1), *to turn or reverse a course*
5077 tĕphrŏō (1), *to incinerate*
5157 trŏpē (1), *turn, i.e. revolution (variation)*

TURTLE
8449 tôwr (2), *ring-dove*

TURTLEDOVE
8449 tôwr (3), *ring-dove*

TURTLEDOVES
8449 tôwr (6), *ring-dove*

5167 trugōn (1), *turtle-dove bird*

TURTLES
8449 tôwr (3), *ring-dove*

TUTORS
2012 ĕpitrŏpŏs (1), *manager, guardian*

TWAIN
8147 shᵉnayim (7), *two-fold*
1417 duŏ (10), *two*

TWELFTH
8147+6240 shᵉnayim (20), *two-fold*
1428 dōdĕkatŏs (1), *twelfth*

TWELVE
505 'eleph (1), *thousand*
8147 shᵉnayim (2), *two-fold*
8147+6240 shᵉnayim (107), *two-fold*
8648+6236 tᵉrêyn (Ch.) (2), *two*
1177 dĕkaduŏ (2), *twelve*
1427 dōdĕka (71), *twelve*
1429 dōdĕkaphulŏn (1), *twelve tribes*

TWENTIETH
6242 'esrîym (36), *twenty; twentieth*

TWENTY
6242 'esrîym (275), *twenty; twentieth*
6243 'esrîyn (Ch.) (1), *twenty; twentieth*
7239 ribbôw (3), *myriad, indefinite large number*
1501 êikŏsi (12), *twenty*

TWENTY'S
6242 'esrîym (1), *twenty; twentieth*

TWICE
4932 mishneh (3), *duplicate copy; double*
6471 pa'am (2), *time; step; occurence*
8147 shᵉnayim (5), *two-fold*
1364 dis (4), *twice*

TWIGS
3127 yôwneqeth (1), *sprout, new shoot*
3242 yᵉnîqâh (1), *sucker or sapling*

TWILIGHT
5399 nesheph (6), *dusk, dawn*
5939 'ălâṭâh (3), *dusk*

TWINED
7806 shâzar (21), *to twist a thread of straw*

TWINKLING
4493 rhipē (1), *instant*

TWINS
8380 tâ'ôwm (4), *twin, things doubled*
8382 tâ'am (2), *to be twinned, i.e. duplicate*

TWO
2677 chêtsîy (1), *half or middle, midst*
6471 pa'am (1), *time; step; occurence*

6771 tsâmê' (1), *thirsty*
8147 shᵉnayim (527), *two-fold*
8648 tᵉrêyn (Ch.) (1), *two*
296 amphŏdŏn (1), *fork in the road*
1250 diakŏsiŏi (7), *two hundred*
1332 diĕtēs (1), *of two years in age*
1333 diĕtia (2), *interval of two years*
1337 dithalassŏs (1), *having two seas*
1366 distŏmŏs (1), *double-edged*
1367 dischilïoi (1), *two thousand*
1417 duŏ (122), *two*

TWOEDGED
6310 peh (1), *mouth; opening*
6374 pîyphîyâh (1), *edge or tooth*
1366 distŏmŏs (2), *double-edged*

TWOFOLD
1366 distŏmŏs (1), *double-edged*

TYCHICUS
5190 Tuchikŏs (7), *fortunate*

TYRANNUS
5181 Turannŏs (1), *tyrant*

TYRE
6865 Tsôr (20), *rock*
6876 Tsôrîy (5), *Tsorite*
5184 Turŏs (11), *rock*
5185 tuphlŏs (1), *blindness; blind person*

TYRUS
6865 Tsôr (22), *rock*

UCAL
401 'Ûkâl (1), *devoured*

UEL
177 'Ûw'êl (1), *wish of God*

ULAI
195 'Ûwlay (2), *Ulai or Eulus*

ULAM
198 'Ûwlâm (4), *solitary*

ULLA
5925 'Ullâ (1), *burden*

UMMAH
5981 'Ummâh (1), *association*

UNACCUSTOMED
3808+3925 lô' (1), *no, not*

UNADVISEDLY
981 bâṭâ' (1), *to babble, speak rashly*

UNAWARES
1097+1847 bᵉlîy (1), *without, not yet*
3045 yâda' (1), *to know*
3820+3824 lêb (2), *heart*
7684 shᵉgâgâh (4), *mistake*
160 aiphnidiŏs (1), *suddenly*
2990 lanthanō (1), *to lie hid; unwittingly*

3920 parĕisaktŏs (1), smuggled in, infiltrated
3921 parĕisdunō (1), to slip in secretly

UNBELIEF
543 apĕithĕia (4), disbelief
570 apistia (12), disbelief; disobedience

UNBELIEVERS
571 apistŏs (4), without faith; untrustworthy

UNBELIEVING
544 apĕithĕō (1), to disbelieve
571 apistŏs (5), without faith; untrustworthy

UNBLAMEABLE
299 amŏmŏs (2), unblemished, blameless

UNBLAMEABLY
274 amĕmptŏs (1), faultlessly

UNCERTAIN
82 adēlŏs (1), indistinct, not clear
83 adēlŏtēs (1), uncertainty

UNCERTAINLY
82 adēlŏs (1), indistinct, not clear

UNCHANGEABLE
531 aparabatŏs (1), untransferable

UNCIRCUMCISED
6189 'ârêl (34), to be uncircumcised
6190 'orlâh (2), prepuce or penile foreskin
203+2192 akrŏbustia (1), uncircumcised
564 apĕritmētŏs (1), uncircumcised
1722+3588+203 ĕn (2), in; during; because of
1986 ĕpispaŏmai (1), to efface the mark of circumcision

UNCIRCUMCISION
203 akrŏbustia (16), uncircumcised

UNCLE
1730 dôwd (10), beloved, friend; uncle, cousin

UNCLE'S
1730 dôwd (1), beloved, friend; uncle, cousin
1733 dôwdâh (6), aunt

UNCLEAN
2930 ţâmê' (74), to be morally contaminated
2931 ţâmê' (78), foul; ceremonially impure
2932 ţum'âh (4), ceremonial impurity
5079 niddâh (2), time of menstrual impurity
6172 'ervâh (1), nudity; disgrace; blemish
6945 qâdêsh (1), sacred male prostitute
169 akathartŏs (28), impure; evil
2839 kŏinŏs (3), common, i.e. profane

2840 kŏinŏŏ (1), to make profane

UNCLEANNESS
2930 ţâmê' (1), to be morally contaminated
2932 ţum'âh (25), ceremonial impurity
5079 niddâh (1), time of menstrual impurity
6172 'ervâh (1), nudity; disgrace; blemish
7137 qâreh (1), accidental occurrence
167 akatharsia (10), quality of impurity
3394 miasmŏs (1), act of moral contamination

UNCLEANNESSES
2932 ţum'âh (1), ceremonial impurity

UNCLOTHED
1562 ĕkduō (1), to divest

UNCOMELY
807 aschēmŏnĕō (1), to be, act unbecoming
809 aschēmōn (1), inelegant, indecent

UNCONDEMNED
178 akatakritŏs (2), without legal trial

UNCORRUPTIBLE
862 aphthartŏs (1), undecaying, immortal

UNCORRUPTNESS
90 adiaphthŏria (1), purity of doctrine

UNCOVER
1540 gâlâh (22), to denude; uncover
6168 'ârâh (1), to be, make bare; to empty
6544 pâra' (3), to loosen; to expose, dismiss

UNCOVERED
1540 gâlâh (10), to denude; uncover
2834 châsaph (2), to drain away or bail up
6168 'ârâh (1), to be, make bare; to empty
177 akatakaluptŏs (2), unveiled
648 apŏstĕgazō (1), to unroof, make a hole in a roof

UNCOVERETH
1540 gâlâh (2), to denude; uncover
6168 'ârâh (1), to be, make bare; to empty

UNCTION
5545 chrisma (1), special endowment of the Holy Spirit

UNDEFILED
8535 tâm (2), morally pious; gentle, dear
8549 tâmîym (1), entire, complete; integrity
283 amiantŏs (4), pure

UNDER
413 'êl (2), to, toward
4295 maţţâh (1), below or beneath

5921 'al (9), above, over, upon, or against
8460 tᵉchôwth (Ch.) (4), beneath, under
8478 tachath (231), bottom; underneath
332 anathĕmatizō (2), to declare or vow an oath
506 anupŏtaktŏs (1), independent
1640 ĕlassōn (1), smaller
1722 ĕn (2), in; during; because of
1772 ĕnnŏmŏs (1), legal, or subject to law
1909 ĕpi (3), on, upon
2662 katapatĕō (2), to trample down; to reject
2709 katachthŏniŏs (1), infernal
2736 katō (1), downwards
5259 hupŏ (47), under; by means of; at
5270 hupŏkatō (8), down under, i.e. beneath
5273 hupŏkritēs (1), dissembler, hypocrite
5284 hupŏplĕō (2), to sail under the lee of
5293 hupŏtassō (4), to subordinate; to obey
5295 hupŏtrĕchō (1), to run under
5299 hupŏpiazō (1), to beat up; to wear out

UNDERGIRDING
5269 hupŏzŏnnumi (1), to gird under

UNDERNEATH
4295 maţţâh (2), below or beneath
8478 tachath (1), bottom; underneath; in lieu of

UNDERSETTERS
3802 kâthêph (4), shoulder-piece; wall

UNDERSTAND
995 bîyn (44), to understand; discern
998 bîynâh (1), understanding
3045 yâda' (3), to know
7919 sâkal (9), to be or act circumspect
8085 shâma' (6), to hear intelligently
50 agnŏĕō (1), to not know; not understand
1097 ginōskō (3), to know
1107 gnōrizō (1), to make known, reveal
1492 ĕidō (1), to know
1987 ĕpistamai (1), to comprehend
3539 nŏiĕō (8), to exercise the mind
4920 suniēmi (13), to comprehend

UNDERSTANDEST
995 bîyn (2), to understand; discern
8085 shâma' (1), to hear intelligently
1097 ginōskō (1), to know

UNDERSTANDETH
995 bîyn (5), to understand; discern

7919 sâkal (1), to be or act circumspect
191 akŏuō (1), to hear; obey
1492 ĕidō (1), to know
4920 suniēmi (3), to comprehend

UNDERSTANDING
995 bîyn (33), to understand; discern
998 bîynâh (32), understanding
999 bîynâh (Ch.) (1), understanding
2940 ţa'am (1), taste; intelligence; mandate
3820 lêb (10), heart
3824 lêbâb (3), heart
4486 manda' (Ch.) (1), wisdom or intelligence
7306 rûwach (1), to smell or perceive
7919 sâkal (5), to be or act circumspect
7922 sekel (7), intelligence; success
7924 soklᵉthânûw (Ch.) (3), intelligence
8085 shâma' (1), to hear intelligently
8394 tâbûwn (38), intelligence; argument
801 asunĕtŏs (3), senseless, dull; wicked
1271 dianŏia (3), mind or thought
3563 nŏus (7), intellect, mind; understanding
3877 parakŏlŏuthĕō (1), to attend; trace out
4907 sunĕsis (6), understanding
4920 suniēmi (2), to understand
5424 phrēn (2), mind or cognitive faculties

UNDERSTOOD
995 bîyn (11), to understand; discern
3045 yâda' (4), to know
7919 sâkal (2), to be or act circumspect
8085 shâma' (1), to hear intelligently
50 agnŏĕō (2), to not know; not understand
1097 ginōskō (4), to know
1425 dusnŏētŏs (1), difficult of perception
2154 ĕusēmŏs (1), significant
3129 manthanō (1), to learn
3539 nŏiĕō (1), to exercise the mind
4441 punthanŏmai (1), to ask for information
4920 suniēmi (7), to understand
5426 phrŏnĕō (1), to be mentally disposed

UNDERTAKE
6148 'ârab (1), to intermix; to give or be security

UNDERTOOK
6901 qâbal (1), to admit; to take

UNDO
5425 nâthar (1), to
terrify; shake off; *untie*
6213 'âsâh (1), to *do or
make*

UNDONE
6 'âbad (1), to *perish;
destroy*
1820 dâmâh (1), to *be
silent; to fail, cease*
5493 çûwr (1), to *turn* off

UNDRESSED
5139 nâzîyr (2), *prince;
separated Nazirite*

UNEQUAL
3808+8505 lô' (2), no, *not*

UNEQUALLY
2086 hĕtĕrŏzugĕŏ (1), to
associate discordantly

UNFAITHFUL
898 bâgad (1), to *act
treacherously*

UNFAITHFULLY
898 bâgad (1), to *act
treacherously*

UNFEIGNED
505 anupŏkritŏs (4),
sincere, genuine

UNFRUITFUL
175 akarpŏs (6), *barren,
unfruitful*

UNGIRDED
6605 pâthach (1), to *open
wide; to loosen, begin*

UNGODLINESS
763 asĕbĕia (4),
wickedness, impiety

UNGODLY
1100 bᵉlîya'al (4),
wickedness, trouble
3808+2623 lô' (1), no, *not*
5760 'ăvîyl (1), *morally
perverse*
7563 râshâ' (8), *morally
wrong; bad* person
763 asĕbĕia (3),
wickedness, impiety
764 asĕbĕŏ (2), to *be, act
impious* or *wicked*
765 asĕbēs (8), *impious*
or *wicked*

UNHOLY
2455 chôl (1), *profane,
common, not holy*
462 anŏsiŏs (2), *wicked,
unholy*
2839 kŏinŏs (1),
common, i.e. profane

UNICORN
7214 rᵉ'êm (6), *wild bull*

UNICORNS
7214 rᵉ'êm (3), *wild bull*

UNITE
3161 yâchad (1), to *be,
become one*

UNITED
3161 yâchad (1), to *be,
become one*

UNITY
3162 yachad (1), *unitedly*
1775 hĕnŏtēs (2),
unanimity, unity

UNJUST
205 'âven (1), *trouble,
vanity, wickedness*
5766 'evel (2), moral *evil*
5767 'avvâl (1), *morally
evil*
8636 tarbîyth (1),
percentage or bonus
91 adikĕŏ (1), to *do
wrong*
93 adikia (2),
wrongfulness
94 adikŏs (8), *unjust,
wicked*

UNJUSTLY
5765 'âval (1), to *morally
distort*
5766 'evel (1), moral *evil*

UNKNOWN
50 agnŏĕŏ (2), to *not
know; not understand*
57 agnŏstŏs (1), *unknown*

UNLADE
670 apŏphŏrtizŏmai (1),
to *unload*

UNLAWFUL
111 athĕmitŏs (1),
illegal; detestable
459 anŏmŏs (1), *without
Jewish law*

UNLEARNED
62 agrammatŏs (1),
illiterate, unschooled
261 amathēs (1),
ignorant
521 apaidĕutŏs (1),
stupid, uneducated
2399 idiŏtēs (3), *not
initiated; untrained*

UNLEAVENED
4682 matstsâh (51),
unfermented cake
106 azumŏs (9), made
without yeast; Passover

UNLESS
194 'ûwlay (1), *if not;
perhaps*
3884 lûwlê' (3), *if not*

UNLOOSE
3089 luō (3), to *loosen*

UNMARRIED
22 agamŏs (4),
unmarried

UNMERCIFUL
415 anĕlĕēmōn (1),
merciless, ruthless

UNMINDFUL
7876 shâyâh (1), to *keep
in memory*

UNMOVABLE
277 amĕtakinētŏs (1),
immovable

UNMOVEABLE
761 asalĕutŏs (1),
immovable, fixed

UNNI
6042 'Unnîy (3), *afflicted*

UNOCCUPIED
2308 châdal (1), to *desist,
stop; be fat*

UNPREPARED
532 aparaskĕuastŏs (1),
unready

UNPROFITABLE
5532 çâkan (1), to *be
serviceable* to
255 alusitĕlēs (1),
gainless, pernicious
512 anŏphĕlēs (1), *useless*
888 achrĕiŏs (2), *useless,
i.e. unmeritorious*
889 achrĕiŏŏ (1), *render
useless, i.e. spoil*
890 achrēstŏs (1),
inefficient, detrimental

UNPROFITABLENESS
512 anŏphĕlēs (1), *useless*

UNPUNISHED
5352 nâqâh (11), to *be,
make clean; to be bare*

UNQUENCHABLE
762 asbĕstŏs (2), *not
extinguished*

UNREASONABLE
249 alŏgŏs (1), *irrational,
not reasonable*
824 atŏpŏs (1), *improper;
injurious; wicked*

UNREBUKEABLE
423 anĕpilēptŏs (1), *not
open to blame*

UNREPROVEABLE
410 anĕgklētŏs (1),
irreproachable

UNRIGHTEOUS
205 'âven (2), *trouble,
vanity, wickedness*
2555 châmâç (1),
violence; malice
5765 'âval (1), to *morally
distort*
5767 'avvâl (1), *morally
evil*
94 adikŏs (4), *unjust,
wicked*

UNRIGHTEOUSLY
5766 'evel (1), moral *evil*

UNRIGHTEOUSNESS
3808+6664 lô' (1), no, *not*
5766 'evel (1), moral *evil*
93 adikia (16),
wrongfulness
458 anŏmia (1), *violation
of law, wickedness*

UNRIPE
1154 beçer (1),
immature, sour grapes

UNRULY
183 akataschĕtŏs (1),
unrestrainable
506 anupŏtaktŏs (2),
insubordinate
813 ataktŏs (1),
insubordinate

UNSATIABLE
1115+7654 biltîy (1), *not,
except, without, unless*

UNSAVOURY
6617 pâthal (1), to
struggle; to be tortuous
8602 tâphêl (1), to
plaster; be tasteless

UNSEARCHABLE
369+2714 'ayin (3), *there
is no, i.e., not exist*
419 anĕxĕrĕunētŏs (1),
inscrutable

UNPROFITABLE
421 anĕxichniastŏs (1),
unsearchable

UNSEEMLY
808 aschēmŏsunĕ (1),
indecency; shame

UNSHOD
3182 mĕthuskŏ (1), to
*intoxicate, become
drunk*

UNSKILFUL
552 apĕirŏs (1), *ignorant,
not acquainted with*

UNSPEAKABLE
411 anĕkdiēgētŏs (1),
indescribable
412 anĕklalētŏs (1),
unutterable
731 arrhētŏs (1),
inexpressible

UNSPOTTED
784 aspilŏs (1),
unblemished

UNSTABLE
6349 pachaz (1),
ebullition, turbulence
182 akatastatŏs (1),
inconstant, restless
793 astĕriktŏs (2),
vacillating, unstable

UNSTOPPED
6605 pâthach (1), to *open
wide; to loosen, begin*

UNTAKEN
3361+348 mē (1), *not; lest*

UNTEMPERED
8602 tâphêl (5), to *be
tasteless; frivolity*

UNTHANKFUL
884 acharistŏs (2),
ungrateful

UNTIL
5704 'ad (288), *as far
(long) as; during; until*
891 achri (16), *until* or
up to
1519 ĕis (1), *to or into*
2193 hĕōs (35), *until*
3360 mĕchri (7), *until, to
the point of*

UNTIMELY
5309 nephel (3), *abortive
miscarriage*
3653 ŏlunthŏs (1), *unripe
fig*

UNTOWARD
4646 skŏliŏs (1), *crooked;
perverse*

UNWALLED
6519 pᵉrâzâh (1), *rural,
open country*
6521 pᵉrâzîy (1), *rustic*

UNWASHEN
449 aniptŏs (3), *without
ablution, unwashed*

UNWISE
3808+2450 lô' (2), no, *not*
453 anŏētŏs (1),
unintelligent, senseless
878 aphrōn (1), *ignorant;
egotistic; unbelieving*

UNWITTINGLY
1097+1847 bᵉlîy (2),
without, not yet

7684 shᵉgâgâh (1), *mistake*, inadvertent *transgression*

UNWORTHILY
371 anaxiŏs (2), in a manner *unworthy*

UNWORTHY
370 anaxiŏs (1), *unfit, unworthy*
3756+514 ŏu (1), *no or not*

UPBRAID
2778 châraph (1), to spend the *winter*
3679 ŏnĕidizō (1), to *rail at, chide, taunt*

UPBRAIDED
3679 ŏnĕidizō (1), to *rail at, chide, taunt*

UPBRAIDETH
3679 ŏnĕidizō (1), to *rail at, chide, taunt*

UPHARSIN
6537 pᵉraç (Ch.) (1), to *split* up

UPHAZ
210 'Ûwphâz (2), *Uphaz*

UPHELD
5564 çâmak (1), to *lean* upon; *take hold* of

UPHOLD
5564 çâmak (5), to *lean* upon; *take hold* of
8551 tâmak (3), to *obtain, keep fast*

UPHOLDEN
5582 çâ'ad (1), to *support*
6965 qûwm (1), to *rise*

UPHOLDEST
8551 tâmak (1), to *obtain, keep fast*

UPHOLDETH
5564 çâmak (3), to *lean* upon; *take hold* of
8551 tâmak (1), to *obtain, keep fast*

UPHOLDING
5342 phĕrō (1), to *bear* or *carry*

UPPER
3730 kaphtôr (1), *capital; wreath-like button*
4947 mashqôwph (1), *lintel*
5942 'illîy (2), *higher*
5944 'ălîyâh (4), *upper things; second-story*
5945 'elyôwn (8), *loftier, higher; Supreme* God
7393 rekeb (1), *upper millstone*
8222 sâphâm (1), *beard*
508 anŏgĕŏn (2), *dome* or a *balcony*
510 anŏtĕrikŏs (1), *more remote regions*
5250 hupĕrplĕŏnazō (1), to *superabound*
5253 hupĕrō̧ŏn (3), *room* in the *third story*

UPPERMOST
5945 'elyôwn (1), *loftier, higher; Supreme* God
4410 prōtŏkathĕdria (1), *pre-eminence in council*

4411 prōtŏklisia (2), *pre-eminence at meals*

UPRIGHT
3474 yâshar (1), to *be straight; to make right*
3476 yôsher (1), *right*
3477 yâshâr (43), *straight*
4339 mêyshâr (1), *straightness; rectitude*
4749 miqshâh (1), *work molded by hammering*
5977 'ômed (2), *fixed spot*
6968 qôwmᵉmîyûwth (1), *erectly, with head high*
8535 tâm (1), *morally pious; gentle, dear*
8537 tôm (2), *prosperity; innocence*
8549 tâmîym (8), *entire, complete; integrity*
8549+8552 tâmîym (1), *complete; integrity*
8552 tâmam (2), to *complete, finish*
3717 ŏrthŏs (1), *straight, level*

UPRIGHTLY
3474 yâshar (1), to *be straight; to make right*
3477 yâshâr (1), *straight*
4339 mêyshâr (3), *straightness; rectitude*
8537 tôm (2), *prosperity; innocence*
8549 tâmîym (4), *entire, complete; integrity*
3716 ŏrthŏpŏdĕō (1), to *act rightly*

UPRIGHTNESS
3476 yôsher (9), *right*
3477 yâshâr (1), *straight*
3483 yishrâh (1), *moral integrity*
4334 mîyshôwr (1), *plain; justice*
4339 mêyshâr (3), *straightness; rectitude*
5228 nâkôach (1), *equitable, correct*
5229 nᵉkôchâh (1), *integrity; truth*
8537 tôm (2), *prosperity; innocence*

UPRISING
6965 qûwm (1), to *rise*

UPROAR
1993 hâmâh (1), to *be in great commotion*
387 anastatŏō (1), to *disturb, cause trouble*
2350 thŏrubĕō (1), to *clamor; start a riot*
2351 thŏrubŏs (3), *commotion*
4714 stasis (1), *one leading an uprising*
4797 sugchĕō (1), to *throw into disorder*

UPSIDE
5921+6440 'al (2), *above, over, upon, or against*
389 anastĕnazō (1), to *sigh deeply*

UPWARD
1361 gâbahh (1), to *be lofty; to be haughty*

4605 ma'al (59), *upward, above, overhead*
4791 mârôwm (1), *elevation; elation*

UR
218 'Ûwr (5), *Ur*

URBANE
3779 hŏutō (1), *in this way; likewise*

URGE
1758 ĕnĕchō (1), to *keep a grudge*

URGED
509 'âlats (1), to *press, urge*
6484 pâtsar (4), to *stun* or *dull*
6555 pârats (1), to *break out*

URGENT
2388 châzaq (1), to *fasten upon; to seize*
2685 châtsaph (Ch.) (1), to *be severe*

URI
221 'Ûwrîy (8), *fiery*

URIAH
223 'Ûwrîyâh (27), *flame of Jehovah*

URIAH'S
223 'Ûwrîyâh (1), *flame of Jehovah*

URIAS
3774 Ourias (1), *flame of Jehovah*

URIEL
222 'Ûwrîy'êl (4), *flame of God*

URIJAH
223 'Ûwrîyâh (11), *flame of Jehovah*

URIM
224 'Ûwrîym (7), *lights*

US-WARD
413 'êl (1), *to, toward*
1519+2248 ĕis (2), *to or into*

USE
559 'âmar (1), to *say*
3231 yâman (1), to *be right-handed*
3947 lâqach (1), to *take*
4399 mᵉlâ'kâh (1), *work; property*
4911 mâshal (3), to *use figurative language*
4912 mâshâl (1), *pithy maxim; taunt*
5172 nâchash (1), to *prognosticate*
5656 'ăbôdâh (1), *work*
7080 qâçam (1), to *divine magic*
1838 hĕxis (1), *practice, constant use*
1908 ĕpĕrĕazō (2), to *insult with threats*
5195 hubrizō (1), to *exercise violence, abuse*
5382 philŏxĕnŏs (1), *hospitable*
5530 chraŏmai (7), to *furnish what is needed*

5532 chrĕia (1), *affair; occasion, demand*
5540 chrĕsis (2), *employment*

USED
3928 limmûwd (1), *instructed one*
6213 'âsâh (2), to *do or make*
390 anastrĕphō (1), to *remain, to live*
1247 diakŏnĕō (1), to *wait upon, serve*
1387 dŏliŏō (1), to *practice deceit*
1510 ĕimi (1), I *exist*, I *am*
3096 magĕuō (1), to *practice magic, sorcery*
4238 prassō (1), to *execute, accomplish*
5530 chraŏmai (3), to *furnish* what is needed

USES
5532 chrĕia (1), *affair; occasion, demand*

USEST
4941 mishpâṭ (1), *verdict; formal decree; justice*

USETH
1696 dâbar (1), to *speak, say; to subdue*
3348 mĕtĕchō (1), to *share or participate*

USING
671 apŏchrēsis (1), *consumption, using up*
2192 ĕchō (1), to *have; hold; keep*

USURER
5383 nâshâh (1), to *lend* or *borrow*

USURP
831 authĕntĕō (1), to *dominate*

USURY
5378 nâshâ' (1), to *lend* on interest
5383 nâshâh (5), to *lend* or *borrow*
5391 nâshak (4), to *oppress* through finance
5392 neshek (11), *interest*
5110 tŏkŏs (2), *interest* on money loaned

UTHAI
5793 'Ûwthay (2), *succoring*

UTMOST
314 'achărôwn (2), *late* or *last; behind; western*
7093 qêts (1), *extremity; after*
7097 qâtseh (3), *extremity*
7112 qâtsats (3), to *chop off; to separate*
4009 pĕras (1), *extremity, end, limit*

UTTER
1696 dâbar (5), to *speak, say; to subdue*
1897 hâgâh (1), to *murmur, utter a sound; ponder*

UTTERANCE

2435 chîytsôwn (12), outer *wall side; exterior*
2531 chemed (1), *delight*
3318 yâtsâ' (3), to *go, bring out*
3617 kâlâh (2), *complete destruction*
4448 mâlal (2), to *speak, say*
4911 mâshal (1), to *use figurative language*
5042 nâba' (4), to *gush forth; to utter*
5046 nâgad (3), to *announce*
5414 nâthan (4), to *give*
6030 'ânâh (1), to *respond, answer*
6315 pûwach (1), to *blow, to fan, kindle; to utter*
1325 didōmi (1), to *give*
2044 ĕrĕugŏmai (1), to *speak out*
2980 lalĕō (1), to *talk*

UTTERANCE

669 apŏphthĕggŏmai (1), *declare, address*
3056 lŏgŏs (4), *word, matter, thing*

UTTERED

1696 dâbar (1), to *speak, say; to subdue*
3318 yâtsâ' (1), to *go, bring out*
4008 mibṭâ' (2), *rash utterance*
5046 nâgad (2), to *announce*
5414 nâthan (5), to *give*
6475 pâtsâh (1), to *rend, i.e. open*
215 alalĕtŏs (1), *unspeakable*
2980 lalĕō (3), to *talk*
3004 lĕgō (1), to *say*

UTTERETH

502 'âlaph (1), to *learn; to teach*
559 'âmar (1), to *say*
1696 dâbar (1), to *speak, say; to subdue*
3318 yâtsâ' (2), to *go, bring out*
5042 nâba' (1), to *gush forth; to utter*
5414 nâthan (3), to *give*

UTTERING

1897 hâgâh (1), to *murmur, utter a sound*

UTTERLY

3605 kôl (1), *all, any or every*
3615 kâlâh (1), *complete, prepare*
3632 kâlîyl (1), *whole, entire; complete; whole*
3966 m⁰ôd (2), *very, utterly*
7703 shâdad (1), to *ravage*
2618 katakaiŏ (1), to *consume wholly by burning*
2704 kataphthĕirō (1), to *spoil entirely*
3654 hŏlōs (1), *completely, altogether*

UTTERMOST

314 'achărôwn (1), *late or last; behind; western*
319 'achărîyth (1), *future; posterity*
657 'epheç (1), *end; no further*
3671 kânâph (1), *edge or extremity; wing*
7020 qîytsôwn (3), *terminal, end*
7097 qâtseh (10), *extremity*
7098 qâtsâh (3), *termination; fringe*
206 akrŏn (2), *extremity; end, top*
1231 diaginōskō (1), *ascertain exactly*
2078 ĕschatŏs (2), *farthest, final*
3838 pantĕlĕs (1), *entire; completion*
4009 pĕras (1), *extremity, end, limit*
5056 tĕlŏs (1), *conclusion*

UZ

5780 'Ûwts (7), *consultation*

UZAI

186 'Ûwzay (1), *Uzai*

UZAL

187 'Ûwzâl (2), *Uzal*

UZZA

5798 'Uzzâ' (10), *strength*

UZZAH

5798 'Uzzâ' (4), *strength*

UZZEN-SHERAH

242 'Uzzên She'ĕrâh (1), *land of Sheerah*

UZZI

5813 'Uzzîy (11), *forceful*

UZZIA

5814 'Uzzîyâ' (1), *strength of Jehovah*

UZZIAH

5818 'Uzzîyâh (27), *strength of Jehovah*

UZZIEL

5816 'Uzzîy'êl (16), *strength of God*

UZZIELITES

5817 'Ozzîy'êlîy (2), *Uzziëlite*

VAGABOND

5110 nûwd (2), to *waver; to wander, flee*
4022 pĕriĕrchŏmai (1), to *stroll, vacillate, veer*

VAGABONDS

5128 nûwa' (1), to *waver*

VAIL

4304 miṭpachath (1), *cloak, woman's shawl*
4533 maçveh (3), *veil, cover*
4541 maççêkâh (1), *woven coverlet*
6532 pôreketh (25), *sacred screen, curtain*
6809 tsâ'îyph (3), *veil*
2571 kaluma (4), *veil, covering*

VAILS

7289 râdîyd (1), *veil*

VAIN

205 'âven (1), *trouble, vanity, wickedness*
1891 hâbal (5), to *be vain, be worthless*
1892 hebel (11), *emptiness or vanity*
2600 chinnâm (2), *gratis, free*
3576 kâzab (1), to *lie, deceive*
5014 nâbab (1), to *be hollow; be foolish*
7307 rûwach (2), *breath; wind; life-spirit*
7385 rîyq (8), *emptiness; worthless thing; in vain*
7386 rêyq (7), *empty; worthless*
7387 rêyqâm (1), *emptily; ineffectually*
7723 shâv' (22), *ruin; guile; idolatry*
8193 sâphâh (2), *lip, language, speech*
8267 sheqer (6), *untruth; sham*
8414 tôhûw (4), *waste, formless; in vain*
1432 dōrĕan (1), *gratuitously, freely*
1500 ĕikē (5), *idly, i.e. without reason or effect*
2755 kĕnŏdŏxŏs (1), *self-conceited*
2756 kĕnŏs (14), *empty; vain; useless*
2757 kĕnŏphōnia (2), *fruitless discussion*
2761 kĕnŏs (2), *vainly, i.e. to no purpose*
3150 mataiŏlŏgia (1), *meaningless talk*
3151 mataiŏlŏgŏs (1), *mischievous talker*
3152 mataiŏs (5), *profitless, futile; idol*
3154 mataiŏō (1), *wicked; idolatrous*
3155 matĕn (2), to *no purpose, in vain*

VAINGLORY

2754 kĕnŏdŏxia (1), *self-conceit, vanity*

VAINLY

1500 ĕikē (1), *idly, i.e. without reason or effect*

VAJEZATHA

2055 Vay⁰zâthâ' (1), *Vajezatha*

VALE

6010 'êmeq (4), *broad depression or valley*
8219 sh⁰phêlâh (5), *lowland,*

VALIANT

47 'abbîyr (1), *mighty*
691 'er'êl (1), *hero, brave person*
1121+2428 bên (4), *son, descendant; people*
1368 gibbôwr (6), *powerful; great warrior*
1396 gâbar (1), to *be strong; to prevail*

VANISHED

2428 chayil (16), *army; wealth; virtue; valor*
3524 kabbîyr (1), *mighty; aged; mighty*
2478 ischurŏs (1), *forcible, powerful*

VALIANTEST

1121+2428 bên (1), *son, descendant; people*

VALIANTLY

2388 châzaq (1), to *be strong; courageous*
2428 chayil (5), *army; wealth; virtue; valor*

VALLEY

1237 biq'âh (9), *wide level valley*
1516 gay' (52), *gorge, valley*
5158 nachal (18), *valley, ravine; mine shaft*
6010 'êmeq (54), *broad depression or valley*
8219 sh⁰phêlâh (6), *lowland,*
5327 pharagx (1), *wadi ravine; valley*

VALLEYS

1237 biq'âh (4), *wide level valley*
1516 gay' (8), *gorge, valley*
5158 nachal (5), *valley, ravine; mine shaft*
6010 'êmeq (9), *broad depression or valley*
8219 sh⁰phêlâh (2), *lowland,*

VALOUR

2428 chayil (37), *army; wealth; virtue; valor*

VALUE

457 'ĕlîyl (1), *vain idol*
6186 'ârak (3), to *set in a row, i.e. arrange*
1308 diaphĕrō (2), to *bear, carry; to differ*
5091 timaŏ (1), to *revere, honor, show respect*

VALUED

5541 çâlâh (2), to *contemn, reject*
5091 timaŏ (1), to *revere, honor, show respect*

VALUEST

6187 'êrek (1), *pile, equipment, estimate*

VANIAH

2057 Vanyâh (1), *Vanjah*

VANISH

4414 mâlach (1), to *disappear as dust*
6789 tsâmath (1), to *extirpate, root out*
854 aphanismŏs (1), *disappearance*
2673 katargĕō (1), to *be, render entirely useless*

VANISHED

5628 çârach (1), to *extend even to excess*
1096+855 ginŏmai (1), to *be, become*

VANISHETH

3212 yâlak (1), to *walk*; to *live*; to *carry*
853 aphanizō (1), to *disappear, be destroyed*

VANITIES

1892 hebel (12), *emptiness* or *vanity*
3152 mataiŏs (1), *profitless, futile; idol*

VANITY

205 'âven (6), *trouble, vanity, wickedness*
1892 hebel (49), *emptiness* or *vanity*
7385 rîyq (2), *emptiness; worthless* thing; *in vain*
7723 shâv' (22), *ruin; guile; idolatry*
8414 tôhûw (4), *waste, formless; in vain*
3153 mataiŏtēs (3), *transientness; depravity*

VAPORS

5387 nâsîy' (2), *leader; rising mist, fog*

VAPOUR

108 'êd (1), *fog*
5927 'âlâh (1), to *ascend, be high, mount*
822 atmis (2), *mist, vapor; billows of smoke*

VAPOURS

5387 nâsîy' (1), *leader; rising mist, fog*
7008 qîytôwr (1), *fume,* i.e. *smoke cloud*

VARIABLENESS

3883 parallagē (1), *change or variation*

VARIANCE

1369 dichazō (1), to *sunder,* i.e. *alienate*
2054 ĕris (1), *quarrel,* i.e. *wrangling*

VASHNI

2059 Vashnîy (1), *weak*

VASHTI

2060 Vashtîy (10), *Vashti*

VAUNT

6286 pâ'ar (1), to *shake a* tree

VAUNTETH

4068 pĕrpĕrĕuŏmai (1), to *boast, brag*

VEHEMENT

2759 chărîyshîy (1), *sultry, searing*
3050 Yâhh (1), *Jehovah,* (the) self-*Existent* or Eternal One
1972 ĕpipŏthēsis (1), *longing for*

VEHEMENTLY

1171 dĕinōs (1), *terribly,* i.e. *excessively, fiercely*
1722+4 ĕn (1), *in; during; because of*
2159 ĕutŏnōs (1), *intensely, cogently*
4366 prŏsrēgnumi (2), to *burst upon*

VEIL

7289 râdîyd (1), *veil*

2665 katapĕtasma (6), door *screen*

VEIN

4161 môwtsâ' (1), *going forth*

VENGEANCE

5358 nâqam (4), to *avenge* or *punish*
5359 nâqâm (15), *revenge*
5360 nᵉqâmâh (19), *avengement*
1349 dikē (2), *justice*
1557 ĕkdikēsis (4), *retaliation, punishment*
3709 ŏrgē (1), *ire; punishment*

VENISON

6718 tsayid (7), *hunting game; lunch, food*
6720 tsêydâh (1), *food, supplies*

VENOM

7219 rô'sh (1), *poisonous plant; poison*

VENT

6605 pâthach (1), to *open wide; to loosen, begin*

VENTURE

8537 tôm (2), *prosperity; innocence*

VERIFIED

539 'âman (3), to *be firm, faithful, true; to trust*

VERILY

61 'ăbâl (3), *truly, surely; yet, but*
389 'ak (6), *surely; only, however*
403 'âkên (2), *surely!, truly!; but*
518 'îm (1), *whether?; if, although; Oh that!*
518+3808 'îm (1), *Oh that!*
530 'ĕmûwnâh (1), *fidelity; steadiness*
559 'âmar (1), to *say*
7069 qânâh (1), to *create; to procure*
230 alēthōs (1), *truly, surely*
281 amēn (76), *surely; so be it*
1063 gar (2), *for, indeed, but, because*
1222 dēpou (1), *indeed doubtless*
2532 kai (1), *and; or; even; also*
3303 mĕn (13), *verily*
3303+3767 mĕn (1), *verily*
3304 mĕnŏungĕ (1), *so then at least*
3483 nai (1), *yes*
3689 ŏntōs (1), *really, certainly*

VERITY

571 'emeth (1), *certainty, truth, trustworthiness*
225 alēthĕia (1), *truth, truthfulness*

VERMILION

8350 shâshar (2), *red*

VERY

199 'ûwlâm (2), *however or on the contrary*

430 'ĕlôhîym (1), the true *God; great ones*
552 'umnâm (1), *verily, indeed, truly*
651 'âphêl (1), *dusky, dark*
898 bâgad (1), to *act covertly*
899 beged (2), *clothing; treachery or pillage*
1419 gâdôwl (1), *great*
1767 day (2), *enough, sufficient*
1851 daq (1), *crushed; small or thin*
1854 dâqaq (1), to *crush; crumble*
1942 havvâh (1), *desire; craving*
2088 zeh (2), *this or that*
3190 yâṭab (2), to *be, make well; be successful*
3304 yᵉpheh-phîyâh (1), *very beautiful*
3453 yâshîysh (2), *old man*
3559 kûwn (1), to *render sure, proper*
3966 mᵉ'ôd (136), *very, utterly*
4213 miz'âr (3), *fewness, smallness*
4295 maṭṭâh (1), *below or beneath*
4592 mᵉ'aṭ (1), *little or few*
4605 ma'al (2), *upward, above, overhead*
4801 merchâq (1), *distant place; from afar*
5464 çagrîyd (1), *pouring rain*
5690 'egeb (1), *amative words, words of love*
5704 'ad (2), *as far (long) as; during; while; until*
6106 'etsem (2), *bone; substance; selfsame*
6621 petha' (1), *wink,* i.e. *moment; quickly*
6985 qaṭ (1), *little,* i.e. *merely*
7023 qîyr (1), *wall, side-wall*
7230 rôb (1), *abundance*
7260 rabrab (Ch.) (1), *huge, domineering*
7690 saggîy' (Ch.) (1), *large*
85 adēmŏnĕō (2), to *be in mental distress*
230 alēthōs (1), *truly, surely*
662 apŏtŏlmaō (1), to *venture plainly*
846 autŏs (5), *he, she, it*
927 barutimŏs (1), *highly valuable*
957 bĕltiŏn (1), *better*
1565 ĕkĕinŏs (2), *that one*
1582 ĕkkrĕmamai (1), to *listen closely*
1646 ĕlachistŏs (3), *least*
1888 ĕpautŏphŏrō₁ (1), *in actual crime*
2236 hēdista (1), *with great pleasure*

2532 kai (4), *and; or; even; also*
2566 kalliŏn (1), *better*
2735 katŏrthōma (1), *made fully upright*
3029 lian (2), *very much*
3827 pampŏlus (1), *full many,* i.e. *immense*
4036 pĕrilupŏs (1), *intensely sad*
4118 plĕistŏs (1), *very large,* i.e. *the most*
4119 plĕiŏn (1), *more*
4184 pŏlusplagchnŏs (1), *extremely compassionate*
4185 pŏlutĕlēs (1), *extremely expensive*
4186 pŏlutimŏs (1), *extremely valuable*
4361 prŏspĕinŏs (1), *intensely hungry*
4708 spŏudaiŏtĕrŏs (1), *more speedily*
4970 sphŏdra (4), *high degree, much*
5228 hupĕr (2), *over; above; beyond*

VESSEL

3627 kᵉlîy (33), *implement, thing*
5035 nebel (1), *skin-bag for liquids; vase; lyre*
4632 skĕuŏs (11), *vessel, implement, equipment*

VESSELS

3627 kᵉlîy (129), *implement, thing*
3984 mâ'n (Ch.) (7), *utensil, vessel*
30 aggĕiŏn (2), *receptacle, vessel*
4632 skĕuŏs (8), *vessel, implement, equipment*

VESTMENTS

3830 lᵉbûwsh (1), *garment; wife*
4403 malbûwsh (1), *garment, clothing*

VESTRY

4458 meltâchâh (1), *wardrobe*

VESTURE

3682 kᵉçûwth (1), *cover; veiling*
3830 lᵉbûwsh (2), *garment; wife*
2440 himatiŏn (2), to *put on clothes*
2441 himatismŏs (2), *clothing*
4018 pĕribŏlaiŏn (1), *thrown around*

VESTURES

899 beged (1), *clothing; treachery or pillage*

VEX

926 bâhal (1), to *tremble; be, make agitated*
2000 hâmam (1), to *put in commotion*
2111 zûwâ' (1), to *shake with fear, tremble*
3013 yâgâh (1), to *grieve; to torment*
3238 yânâh (2), to *rage or be violent*

3707 kâ'aç (1), to *grieve, rage, be indignant*
6213+7451 'âsâh (1), to *do or make*
6887 tsârar (5), to *cramp*
6973 qûwts (1), to *be, make anxious*
2559 kakôô (1), to *injure; to oppress; to embitter*

VEXATION
2113 z^e vâ'âh (1), *agitation, fear*
4103 m^e hûwmâh (1), *confusion or uproar*
4164 mûwtsaq (1), *distress*
7469 r^e 'ûwth (7), *grasping* after
7475 ra'yôwn (3), *desire, chasing after*
7667 sheber (1), *fracture; ruin*

VEXATIONS
4103 m^e hûwmâh (1), *confusion or uproar*

VEXED
926 bâhal (3), to *tremble; be, make agitated*
1766 dâchaq (1), to *oppress*
3238 yânâh (2), to *rage or be violent*
3334 yâtsar (1), to *be in distress*
4103 m^e hûwmâh (1), *confusion or uproar*
4843 mârar (2), to *be, make bitter*
6087 'âtsab (1), to *worry, have pain or anger*
6887 tsârar (1), to *cramp*
7114 qâtsar (1), to *curtail, cut short*
7489 râ'a' (1), to *be good for nothing*
7492 râ'ats (1), to *break in pieces; to harass*
7561 râsha' (1), to *be, do, declare wrong*
928 basanizō (1), to *torture, torment*
1139 daimŏnizŏmai (1), to *be exercised by a demon*
2669 katapŏnĕō (1), to *harass, oppress*
3791 ŏchlĕō (2), to *harass, be tormented*
3958 paschō (1), to *experience* pain

VIAL
6378 pak (1), *flask, small jug*
5357 phialē (7), broad shallow *cup*, i.e. a *phial*

VIALS
5357 phialē (5), broad shallow *cup*, i.e. a *phial*

VICTORY
3467 yâsha' (1), to make *safe, free*
5331 netsach (2), *splendor; lasting*
8668 t^e shûw'âh (3), *rescue, deliverance*
3528 nikaō (1), to *subdue, conquer*

3529 nikē (1), *conquest, victory, success*
3534 nikŏs (4), *triumph, victory*

VICTUAL
3557 kûwl (1), to *measure; to maintain*
3978 ma'ăkâl (1), *food, something to eat*
4202 mâzôwn (1), *food, provisions*
6720 tsêydâh (2), *food, supplies*

VICTUALS
400 'ôkel (3), *food*
737 'ărûchâh (1), *ration, portion* of food
3557 kûwl (1), to *measure; to maintain*
3899 lechem (2), *food, bread*
4241 michyâh (1), *sustenance; quick*
6718 tsayid (2), hunting *game; lunch, food*
6720 tsêydâh (4), *food, supplies*
7668 sheber (1), *grain*
1033 brōma (1), *food*
1979 ĕpisitismŏs (1), *food*

VIEW
5048 neged (2), *in front of*
7200 râ'âh (1), to *see*
7270 râgal (1), to *reconnoiter; to slander*

VIEWED
995 bîyn (1), to *understand; discern*
7370 râchash (1), to *gush*
7663 sâbar (2), to *scrutinize; to expect*

VIGILANT
1127 grēgŏrĕuŏ (1), to *watch, guard*
3524 nēphalĕŏs (1), *circumspect, temperate*

VILE
959 bâzâh (2), to *disesteem, ridicule*
2151 zâlal (2), to *be loose morally, worthless*
2933 ţâmâh (1), to *be ceremonially impure*
5034 nâbêl (1), to *wilt; to fall away; to be foolish*
5036 nâbâl (2), *stupid; impious*
5039 n^e bâlâh (1), *moral wickedness; crime*
5240 n^e mibzeh (1), *despised*
7034 qâlâh (1), to *be, hold in contempt*
7043 qâlal (4), to *be easy, trifling, vile*
8182 shô'âr (1), *harsh or horrid*, i.e. *offensive*
819 atimia (1), *disgrace*
4508 rhuparŏs (1), *shabby, dirty; wicked*
5014 tapĕinōsis (1), *humbleness, lowliness*

VILELY
1602 gâ'al (1), to *detest; to reject; to fail*

VILER
5217 nâkâ' (1), to *smite*, i.e. *drive* away

VILEST
2149 zullûwth (1), (poss.) *tempest*

VILLAGE
2968 kōmē (10), *hamlet, town*

VILLAGES
1323 bath (12), *daughter, outlying village*
2691 châtsêr (47), *yard; walled village*
3715 k^e phîyr (1), *walled village; young lion*
3723 kâphâr (2), *walled village*
3724 kôpher (1), *village; bitumen; henna*
6518 pârâz (1), *chieftain*
6519 p^e râzâh (1), *rural, open country*
6520 p^e râzôwn (2), *magistracy, leadership*
6521 p^e râziy (1), *rustic*
2968 kōmē (7), *hamlet, town*

VILLANY
5039 n^e bâlâh (2), *moral wickedness; crime*

VINE
1612 gephen (44), *grape vine*
2156 z^e môwrâh (1), *pruned twig, branch*
3196 yayin (1), *wine; intoxication*
3755 kôrêm (1), *vinedresser*
5139 nâzîyr (2), *prince; unpruned vine*
8321 sôrêq (3), *choice vine stock*
288 ampělŏs (9), *grape vine*

VINEDRESSERS
3755 kôrêm (4), *vinedresser*

VINEGAR
2558 chômets (6), *vinegar*
3690 ŏxŏs (7), *sour wine*

VINES
1612 gephen (9), *grape vine*
3754 kerem (3), *garden or vineyard*

VINEYARD
3657 kannâh (1), *plant*
3754 kerem (44), *garden or vineyard*
289 ampělŏurgŏs (1), *vineyard caretaker*
290 ampělōn (23), *vineyard*

VINEYARDS
3754 kerem (45), *garden or vineyard*

VINTAGE
1208 bâtsôwr (1), *inaccessible*
1210 bâtsîyr (7), *grape crop, harvest*
3754 kerem (1), *garden or vineyard*

VIOL
5035 nebel (2), *skin-bag for liquids; vase; lyre*

VIOLATED
2554 châmaç (1), to *be violent; to maltreat*

VIOLENCE
1497 gâzal (1), to *rob*
1498 gâzêl (1), *robbery, stealing*
1499 gêzel (1), *violence*
1500 g^e zêlâh (3), *robbery, stealing; things stolen*
2554 châmaç (2), to *be violent; to maltreat*
2555 châmâç (39), *violence; malice*
4835 m^e rûtsâh (1), *oppression*
6231 'âshaq (1), to *violate; to overflow*
970 bia (4), *force, pounding violence*
971 biazō (1), to *crowd oneself into*
1286 diasĕiō (1), to *intimidate, extort*
1411 dunamis (1), *force, power, miracle*
3731 hŏrmēma (1), *sudden attack*

VIOLENT
1499 gêzel (1), *violence*
2555 châmâç (7), *violence; malice*
6184 'ârîyts (1), *powerful or tyrannical*
973 biastēs (1), *energetic, forceful one*

VIOLENTLY
1497 gâzal (4), to *rob*
1500 g^e zêlâh (1), *robbery, stealing; things stolen*
2554 châmaç (1), to *be violent; to maltreat*

VIOLS
5035 nebel (2), *skin-bag for liquids; vase; lyre*

VIPER
660 'eph'eh (2), *asp*
2191 ĕchidna (1), *adder*

VIPER'S
660 'eph'eh (1), *asp*

VIPERS
2191 ĕchidna (4), *adder*

VIRGIN
1330 b^e thûwlâh (24), *virgin*
5959 'almâh (2), *lass, young woman*
3933 parthěnŏs (7), *virgin*

VIRGIN'S
3933 parthěnŏs (1), *virgin*

VIRGINITY
1331 b^e thûwlîym (8), *virginity; proof of female virginity*
3932 parthěnia (1), *maidenhood, virginity*

VIRGINS
1330 b^e thûwlâh (14), *virgin*
5959 'almâh (2), *lass, young woman*
3933 parthěnŏs (6), *virgin*

V

VIRTUE
703 arĕtē (4), *excellence, virtue*
1411 dunamis (3), *force, power, miracle*

VIRTUOUS
2428 chayil (3), *army; wealth; virtue; valor*

VIRTUOUSLY
2428 chayil (1), *army; wealth; virtue; valor*

VISAGE
600 'ănaph (Ch.) (1), *face*
4758 mar'eh (1), *appearance; vision*
8389 tô'ar (1), *outline, appearance*

VISIBLE
3707 hŏratŏs (1), *capable of being seen*

VISION
2376 chêzev (Ch.) (2), *sight, revelation*
2377 châzôwn (32), *sight; revelation*
2380 châzûwth (2), *striking appearance*
2384 chizzâyôwn (6), *dream; vision*
4236 machăzeh (4), *vision*
4758 mar'eh (14), *appearance; vision*
4759 mar'âh (3), *vision; mirror*
7203 rô'eh (1), *seer; vision*
3701 ŏptasia (2), *supernatural vision*
3705 hŏrama (12), *supernatural spectacle*
3706 hŏrasis (1), *appearance, vision*

VISIONS
2376 chêzev (Ch.) (9), *sight, revelation*
2377 châzôwn (3), *sight; revelation*
2378 châzôwth (1), *revelation*
2384 chizzâyôwn (3), *dream; vision*
4759 mar'âh (5), *vision; mirror*
7200 râ'âh (1), *to see*
3701 ŏptasia (1), *supernatural vision*
3706 hŏrasis (1), *appearance, vision*

VISIT
6485 pâqad (33), *to visit, care for, count*
1980 ĕpiskĕptŏmai (4), *to inspect, to go to see*

VISITATION
6486 pᵉquddâh (13), *visitation; punishment*
1984 ĕpiskŏpē (2), *episcopate*

VISITED
6485 pâqad (18), *to visit, care for, count*
1980 ĕpiskĕptŏmai (5), *to inspect; to go to see*

VISITEST
6485 pâqad (2), *to visit, care for, count*
1980 ĕpiskĕptŏmai (1), *to inspect; to go to see*

VISITETH
6485 pâqad (1), *to visit, care for, count*

VISITING
6485 pâqad (4), *to visit, care for, count*

VOCATION
2821 klēsis (1), *invitation; station in life*

VOICE
6963 qôwl (379), *voice or sound*
7032 qâl (Ch.) (3), *sound, music*
5456 phônē (116), *voice, sound*
5586 psēphŏs (1), *pebble stone*

VOICES
6963 qôwl (2), *voice or sound*
5456 phônē (15), *voice, sound*

VOID
6 'âbad (1), *perish; destroy*
922 bôhûw (2), *ruin, desolation*
1238 bâqaq (1), *to depopulate, ruin*
1637 gôren (2), *open area*
2638 châçêr (6), *lacking*
4003 mᵉbûwqâh (1), *emptiness, devastation*
5010 nâ'ar (1), *to reject*
6565 pârar (5), *to break up; to violate, frustrate*
7387 rêyqâm (1), *emptily; ineffectually*
677 aprŏskŏpŏs (1), *not led into sin*
2673 katargĕŏ (1), *to be, render entirely useless*
2758 kĕnŏŏ (2), *to make empty*

VOLUME
4039 mᵉgillâh (1), *roll, scroll*
2777 kĕphalis (1), *roll, scroll*

VOLUNTARILY
5071 nᵉdâbâh (1), *abundant gift*

VOLUNTARY
5071 nᵉdâbâh (2), *abundant gift*
7522 râtsôwn (1), *delight*
2309 thĕlŏ (1), *to will; to desire; to choose*

VOMIT
6892 qê' (4), *vomit*
6958 qôw' (3), *to vomit*
1829 ĕxĕrama (1), *vomit*

VOMITED
6958 qôw' (1), *to vomit*

VOMITETH
6958 qôw' (1), *to vomit*

VOPHSI
2058 Vophçîy (1), *additional*

VOW
5087 nâdar (9), *to promise, vow*
5088 neder (30), *promise to God; thing promised*
2171 ĕuchē (2), *wish, petition*

VOWED
5087 nâdar (16), *to promise, vow*
5088 neder (2), *promise to God; thing promised*

VOWEDST
5087 nâdar (1), *to promise, vow*

VOWEST
5087 nâdar (2), *to promise, vow*

VOWETH
5087 nâdar (1), *to promise, vow*

VOWS
5088 neder (30), *promise to God; thing promised*

VOYAGE
4144 plŏŏs (1), *navigation, voyage*

VULTURE
1676 dâ'âh (1), *kite*
1772 dayâh (1), *falcon*

VULTURE'S
344 'ayâh (1), *hawk*

VULTURES
1772 dayâh (1), *falcon*

WAFER
7550 râqîyq (3), *thin cake, wafer*

WAFERS
6838 tsappîychîth (1), *flat thin cake*
7550 râqîyq (4), *thin cake, wafer*

WAG
5110 nûwd (1), *to waver; to wander, flee*
5128 nûwa' (2), *to waver*

WAGES
2600 chinnâm (1), *gratis, free*
4909 maskôreth (3), *wages; reward*
6468 pᵉ'ullâh (1), *work, deed*
7936 sâkar (1), *to hire*
7939 sâkâr (6), *payment, salary; compensation*
3408 misthŏs (2), *pay for services, good or bad*
3800 ŏpsōniŏn (3), *rations, stipend or pay*

WAGGING
2795 kinĕŏ (2), *to stir, move, remove*

WAGON
5699 'ăgâlâh (1), *wheeled vehicle*

WAGONS
5699 'ăgâlâh (8), *wheeled vehicle*
7393 rekeb (1), *vehicle for riding*

WAIL
5091 nâhâh (1), *to bewail; to assemble*
5594 çâphad (1), *to tear the hair, wail*
2875 kŏptō (1), *to beat the breast*

WAILED
214 alalazŏ (1), *to wail; to clang*

WAILING
4553 miçpêd (6), *lamentation, howling*
5089 nôahh (1), *lamentation*
5092 nᵉhîy (4), *elegy*
5204 nîy (1), *lamentation*
2805 klauthmŏs (2), *lamentation, weeping*
3996 pĕnthĕŏ (2), *to grieve*

WAIT
693 'ârab (34), *to ambush, lie in wait*
695 'ereb (1), *hiding place; lair*
696 'ôreb (1), *hiding place; lair*
1748 dûwmâm (1), *silently*
1826 dâmam (1), *to stop, cease; to perish*
2342 chûwl (1), *to wait; to pervert*
2442 châkâh (6), *to await; hope for*
3027 yâd (1), *hand; power*
3176 yâchal (5), *to wait; to be patient, hope*
3993 ma'ărâb (1), *ambuscade, ambush*
6119 'âqêb (1), *track, footprint; rear position*
6633 tsâbâ' (1), *to mass an army or servants*
6658 tsâdâh (1), *to desolate*
6660 tsᵉdîyâh (2), *design, lying in wait*
6960 qâvâh (22), *to collect; to expect*
7663 sâbar (2), *to scrutinize; to expect*
7789 shûwr (1), *to spy out, survey*
8104 shâmar (4), *to watch*
362 anamĕnŏ (1), *to await in expectation*
553 apĕkdĕchŏmai (2), *to expect fully, await*
1096+1917 ginŏmai (1), *to be, become*
1747 ĕnĕdra (1), *ambush*
1748 ĕnĕdrĕuŏ (2), *to lurk*
1917 ĕpibŏulē (2), *plot, plan*
3180 mĕthŏdĕia (1), *trickery, scheming*
4037 pĕrimĕnŏ (1), *to await*
4160+1747 pŏiĕŏ (1), *to make or do*
4327 prŏsdĕchŏmai (1), *to receive; to await for*
4332 prŏsĕdrĕuŏ (1), *to attend as a servant*

4342 prŏskartĕrĕō (1), to
persevere

WAITED
1961+6440 hâyâh (1), to
exist, i.e. *be* or *become*
2342 chûwl (1), to *wait;*
to *pervert*
2442 châkâh (2), to
await; hope for
3176 yâchal (6), to *wait;*
to *be patient, hope*
5975 'âmad (5), to *stand*
6822 tsâphâh (1), to
observe, await
6960 qâvâh (8), to *collect;*
to *expect*
8104 shâmar (1), to
watch
8334 shârath (1), to
attend as a menial
1551 ĕkdĕchŏmai (2), to
await, expect
4327 prŏsdĕchŏmai (2),
to *receive;* to *await for*
4328 prŏsdŏkaō (2), to
anticipate; to *await*
4342 prŏskartĕrĕō (1), to
persevere, be constant

WAITETH
1747 dûwmîyâh (2),
silently; quiet, trust
2442 châkâh (3), to
await; hope for
3176 yâchal (1), to *wait;*
to *be patient, hope*
8104 shâmar (2), to
watch
553 apĕkdĕchŏmai (1),
to *expect fully, await*
1551 ĕkdĕchŏmai (1), to
await, expect

WAITING
6635 tsâbâ' (1), *army,*
military host
8104 shâmar (1), to
watch
553 apĕkdĕchŏmai (2),
to *expect fully, await*
1551 ĕkdĕchŏmai (1), to
await, expect
4327 prŏsdĕchŏmai (1),
to *receive;* to *await for*
4328 prŏsdŏkaō (1), to
anticipate; to *await*

WAKE
5782 'ûwr (1), to *awake*
6974 qûwts (2), to *awake*
1127 grēgŏrĕuō (1), to
watch, guard

WAKED
5782 'ûwr (1), to *awake*

WAKENED
5782 'ûwr (2), to *awake*

WAKENETH
5782 'ûwr (2), to *awake*

WAKETH
5782 'ûwr (1), to *awake*
8245 shâqad (1), to *be*
alert, i.e. *sleepless*

WAKING
8109 shᵉmûrâh (1),
eye-lid

WALK
1869 dârak (2), to *tread,*
trample; to *walk*

1979 hălîykâh (1),
walking; procession
1980 hâlak (61), to *walk;*
live a certain way
1981 hălak (Ch.) (1), to
walk; live a certain way
3212 yâlak (79), to *walk;*
to *live;* to *carry*
4108 mahlêk (1), *access;*
journey
4109 mahălâk (1),
passage or a *distance*
5437 çâbab (1), to
surround
1704 ĕmpĕripatĕō (1), to
be occupied among
4043 pĕripatĕō (55), to
walk; to *live a life*
4198 pŏrĕuŏmai (4), to
go, come; to *travel*
4748 stŏichĕō (4), to
follow, walk; to *conform*

WALKED
1980 hâlak (67), to *walk;*
live a certain way
1981 hălak (Ch.) (1), to
walk; live a certain way
3212 yâlak (32), to *walk;*
to *live;* to *carry*
3716 ŏrthŏpŏdĕō (1), to
act *rightly*
4043 pĕripatĕō (19), to
walk; to *live a life*
4198 pŏrĕuŏmai (1), to
go, come; to *travel*

WALKEDST
4043 pĕripatĕō (1), to
walk; to *live a life*

WALKEST
1980 hâlak (1), to *walk;*
live a certain way
3212 yâlak (3), to *walk;*
to *live;* to *carry*
4043 pĕripatĕō (2), to
walk; to *live a life*
4748 stŏichĕō (1), to
follow, walk; to *conform*

WALKETH
1980 hâlak (31), to *walk;*
live a certain way
3212 yâlak (2), to *walk;*
to *live;* to *carry*
1330 diĕrchŏmai (2), to
traverse, travel through
4043 pĕripatĕō (5), to
walk; to *live a life*

WALKING
1980 hâlak (10), to *walk;*
live a certain way
1981 hălak (Ch.) (1), to
walk; live a certain way
3212 yâlak (3), to *walk;*
to *live;* to *carry*
4043 pĕripatĕō (12), to
walk; to *live a life*
4198 pŏrĕuŏmai (4), to
go, come; to *travel*

WALL
846 'ushsharnâ' (Ch.) (1),
wall
1444 geder (2), *wall* or
fence
1447 gâdêr (5),
enclosure, i.e. *wall*
1448 gᵉdêrâh (1),
enclosure for flocks
2346 chôwmâh (92), *wall*

2426 chêyl (1),
entrenchment
2434 chayits (1), *wall*
2742 chârûwts (1),
mined *gold; trench*
3796 kôthel (1), house
wall
3797 kᵉthal (Ch.) (1),
house *wall*
7023 qîyr (50), *wall,*
side-*wall*
7791 shûwr (3), *wall*
7794 shôwr (1), *bullock*
5038 tĕichŏs (8), house
wall
5109 tŏichŏs (1), *wall*

WALLED
1219 bâtsar (2), to *be*
inaccessible
2346 chôwmâh (2), *wall*

WALLOW
5606 çâphaq (1), to *be*
enough; to *vomit*
6428 pâlash (3), to *roll* in
dust

WALLOWED
1556 gâlal (1), to *roll;* to
commit
2947 kuliŏō (1), to *roll*
about

WALLOWING
2946 kulisma (1),
wallowing in filth

WALLS
846 'ushsharnâ' (Ch.) (1),
wall
1447 gâdêr (1),
enclosure, i.e. *wall*
2346 chôwmâh (39), *wall*
2426 chêyl (1), *rampart,*
battlement
3797 kᵉthal (Ch.) (1),
house *wall*
7023 qîyr (16), *wall,*
side-*wall*
7791 shûwr (4), *wall*
8284 shârâh (1),
fortification
5038 tĕichŏs (1), house
wall

WANDER
5074 nâdad (1), to *rove,*
flee; to *drive away*
5128 nûwa' (4), to *waver*
6808 tsâ'âh (1), to *tip*
over; to *depopulate*
7462 râ'âh (1), to *tend* a
flock, i.e. *pasture* it
7686 shâgâh (2), to *stray,*
wander; to *transgress*
8582 tâ'âh (5), to
vacillate, i.e. *reel, stray*

WANDERED
1980 hâlak (1), to *walk;*
live a certain way
5128 nûwa' (3), to *waver*
7686 shâgâh (1), to *stray,*
wander; to *transgress*
8582 tâ'âh (3), to
vacillate, i.e. *reel, stray*
4022 pĕriĕrchŏmai (1), to
stroll, vacillate, veer
4105 planaō (1), to *roam,*
wander from safety

WANDERERS
5074 nâdad (1), to *rove,*
flee; to *drive away*
6808 tsâ'âh (1), to *tip*
over; to *depopulate*

WANDEREST
6808 tsâ'âh (1), to *tip*
over; to *depopulate;* to
imprison; to *lay down*

WANDERETH
5074 nâdad (5), to *rove,*
flee; to *drive away*
8582 tâ'âh (1), to
vacillate, i.e. *reel, stray*

WANDERING
1981 hălak (Ch.) (1), to
walk; live a certain way
5074 nâdad (1), to *rove,*
flee; to *drive away*
5110 nûwd (1), to *waver;*
to *wander, flee*
8582 tâ'âh (1), to
vacillate, i.e. *reel, stray*
4022 pĕriĕrchŏmai (1), to
stroll, vacillate, veer
4107 planētēs (1), *roving,*
erratic teacher

WANDERINGS
5112 nôwd (1), *exile*

WANT
657 'epheç (1), *end; no*
further
1097 bᵉlîy (2), *without,*
not yet; lacking;
2637 châçêr (4), to *lack;*
to *fail, want, make less*
2638 châçêr (1), *lacking*
2639 cheçer (1), *lack;*
destitution
2640 chôçer (3), *poverty*
3772 kârath (3), to *cut*
(off, down or asunder)
3808 lô' (1), *no, not*
4270 machçôwr (7),
impoverishment
6485 pâqad (1), to *visit,*
care for, count
5302 hustĕrĕō (1), to *be*
inferior; to *fall short* (*be*
deficient)
5303 hustĕrēma (3),
deficit; poverty; lacking
5304 hustĕrēsis (2),
penury, lack, need

WANTED
2637 châçêr (1), to *lack;*
to *fail, want, make less*
5302 hustĕrĕō (2), to *be*
inferior; to *fall short*

WANTETH
2308 châdal (1), to *desist,*
stop; be fat
2637 châçêr (2), to *lack;*
to *fail, want, make less*
2638 châçêr (4), *lacking*

WANTING
2627 chaççîyr (Ch.) (1),
deficient, wanting
2642 cheçrôwn (1),
deficiency
3808 lô' (1), *no, not*
6485 pâqad (2), to *visit,*
care for, count
3007 lĕipō (3), to *fail* or
be absent

WANTON
8265 sâqar (1), to *ogle*,
i.e. *blink coquettishly*
2691 *katastrēniaō* (1), to
be voluptuous against
4684 *spatalaō* (1), to *live
in luxury*

WANTONNESS
766 *asĕlgĕia* (2),
debauchery, lewdness

WANTS
4270 machçôwr (1),
impoverishment
5532 chrĕia (1), *affair;
requirement*

WAR
2428 chayil (1), *army;
wealth; virtue; valor*
2438 Chîyrâm (1), *noble*
3898 lâcham (9), to *fight
a battle*
3901 lâchem (1), *battle,
war*
4421 milchâmâh (151),
battle; war; fighting
4421+7128 milchâmâh
(1), *battle; war; fighting*
6635 tsâbâ' (41), *army,
military host*
6904 qôbel (1),
battering-ram
7128 q^erâb (3), hostile
encounter
7129 q^erâb (Ch.) (1),
hostile *encounter*
4170 *pŏlĕmĕō* (4), to
battle, make war
4171 *pŏlĕmŏs* (6),
warfare; battle; fight
4753 *stratĕuma* (1), body
of *troops*
4754 *stratĕuŏmai* (4), to
serve in military

WARD
4929 mishmâr (11),
guard; deposit; usage
4931 mishmereth (6),
watch, sentry, post
5474 çûwgar (1), *animal
cage*
6488 p^eqîdûth (1),
supervision
5438 *phulakē* (1),
guarding or *guard*

WARDROBE
899 beged (2), *clothing;
treachery* or *pillage*

WARDS
4931 mishmereth (3),
watch, sentry, post

WARE
4377 meker (1),
merchandise; value
4465 mimkâr (1),
merchandise
4728 maqqâchâh (1),
merchandise, wares
1737 *ĕndiduskō* (1), to
clothe
4894 *sunĕidō* (1), to
understand or *be aware*
5442 *phulassō* (1), to
watch, i.e. *be on guard*

WARES
3627 k^elîy (1),
implement, thing

3666 kin'âh (1), *package,
bundle*
4639 ma'ăseh (2), *action;
labor*
5801 'izzâbôwn (1),
trade, merchandise

WARFARE
6635 tsâbâ' (2), *army,
military host*
4752 *stratĕia* (2),
warfare; fight
4754 *stratĕuŏmai* (1), to
serve in military

WARM
2215 zârab (1), to *flow
away, be dry*
2525 châm (1), *hot,
sweltering*
2527 chôm (1), *heat*
2552 châmam (4), to *be
hot; to be in a rage*
3179 yâcham (1), to
conceive

WARMED
2552 châmam (1), to *be
hot; to be in a rage*
2328 *thĕrmainō* (5), to
heat oneself

WARMETH
2552 châmam (2), to *be
hot; to be in a rage*

WARMING
2328 *thĕrmainō* (1), to
heat oneself

WARN
2094 zâhar (8), to
enlighten
3560 *nŏuthĕtĕō* (3), to
caution or *reprove*

WARNED
2094 zâhar (4), to
enlighten
5263 *hupŏdĕiknumi* (2),
to *exemplify*
5537 *chrĕmatizō* (4), to
utter an oracle

WARNING
2094 zâhar (6), to
enlighten
5749 'ûwd (1), to
duplicate or *repeat*
3560 *nŏuthĕtĕō* (1), to
caution or *reprove*

WARP
8359 sh^ethîy (9), *warp* in
weaving

WARRED
3898 lâcham (7), to *fight
a battle*
6633 tsâbâ' (2), to *mass
an army* or *servants*

WARRETH
4754 *stratĕuŏmai* (1), to
serve in military

WARRING
3898 lâcham (2), to *fight
a battle*
497 *antistratĕuŏmai* (1),
destroy, wage war

WARRIOR
5431 çâ'an (1), *soldier
wearing boots*

WARRIORS
6213+4421 'âsâh (2), to
do or *make*

WARS
4421 milchâmâh (9),
battle; war; fighting
4171 *pŏlĕmŏs* (4),
warfare; battle; fight

WASH
3526 kâbaç (39), to *wash*
7364 râchats (36), to
lave, bathe
628 *apŏlŏuō* (1), to *wash
fully*
907 *baptizō* (1), *baptize*
1026 *brĕchō* (1), to *make
wet; to rain*
3538 *niptō* (11), to *wash,
bathe*

WASHED
1740 dûwach (2), to *rinse
clean, wash*
3526 kâbaç (7), to *wash*
7364 râchats (17), to
lave, bathe
7857 shâţaph (2), to
inundate, cleanse
628 *apŏlŏuō* (1), to *wash
fully*
633 *apŏniptō* (1), to *wash
off* hands
907 *baptizō* (1), *baptize*
1026 *brĕchō* (1), to *make
wet; to rain*
3068 *lŏuō* (6), to *bathe; to
wash*
3538 *niptō* (6), to *wash,
bathe*
4150 *plunō* (1), to *wash*
or *launder* clothing

WASHEST
7857 shâţaph (1), to
inundate, cleanse

WASHING
3526 kâbaç (1), to *wash*
4325 mayim (1), *water*
7364 râchats (1), to *lave,
bathe*
7367 rachtsâh (2),
bathing place
637 *apŏplunō* (1), to
rinse off, wash out
909 *baptismŏs* (2),
baptism
3067 *lŏutrŏn* (2),
washing, baptism

WASHINGS
909 *baptismŏs* (1),
baptism

WASHPOT
5518+7366 çîyr (2), *thorn;
hook*

WAST
1961 hâyâh (13), to *exist*,
i.e. *be* or *become*
2258 ēn (5), I *was*
5607 ōn (1), *being,
existence*

WASTE
1086 bâlâh (1), to *wear
out, decay; consume*
1110 bâlaq (2), to
annihilate, devastate
1326 bâthâh (1), *area of
desolation*

2717 chârab (13), to
desolate, destroy
2720 chârêb (6), *ruined;
desolate*
2721 chôreb (2),
parched; ruined
2723 chorbâh (14),
desolation, dry desert
3615 kâlâh (1), to
complete, prepare
3765 kirçêm (1), to *lay
waste, ravage*
4875 m^eshôw'âh (2), *ruin*
5327 nâtsâh (1), to *be
desolate, to lay waste*
7489 râ'a' (1), to *be good
for nothing*
7582 shâ'âh (2), to *moan;
to desolate*
7703 shâdad (5), to
ravage
8047 shammâh (3), *ruin;
consternation*
8074 shâmêm (5), to
devastate; to stupefy
8077 sh^emâmâh (1),
devastation
8414 tôhûw (1), *waste,
desolation, formless*
684 *apŏlĕia* (2), *ruin* or
loss

WASTED
1197 bâ'ar (1), to *be
brutish, be senseless*
2717 chârab (3), to
parch; desolate, destroy
2723 chorbâh (1),
desolation, dry desert
3615 kâlâh (1), to
complete, consume
7582 shâ'âh (1), to *moan;
to desolate*
7703 shâdad (2), to
ravage
7843 shâchath (1), to
decay; to ruin
8437 tôwlâl (1), *oppressor*
8552 tâmam (2), to
complete, finish
1287 *diaskŏrpizō* (2), to
scatter; to squander
4199 *pŏrthĕō* (1), to
ravage, pillage

WASTENESS
7722 shôw' (1), *tempest;
devastation*

WASTER
7843 shâchath (2), to
decay; to ruin

WASTES
2723 chorbâh (7),
desolation, dry desert

WASTETH
2522 châlash (1), to
prostrate, lay low
7703 shâdad (1), to
ravage
7736 shûwd (1), to
devastate

WASTING
7701 shôd (2), *violence,
ravage, destruction*

WATCH
821 'ashmûrâh (4), *night
watch*
4707 mitspeh (1),
military observatory

WATCHED
4929 mishmâr (4), *guard; deposit; usage; example*
4931 mishmereth (5), *watch, sentry, post*
6822 tsâphâh (5), to *observe, await*
8104 shâmar (5), to *watch*
8108 shomrâh (1), *watchfulness*
8245 shâqad (6), to *be on the lookout*
69 agrupnĕŏ (3), to *be sleepless, keep awake*
1127 grēgŏrĕuō (16), to *watch, guard*
2892 kŏustōdia (3), *sentry*
3525 nēphō (2), to *abstain* from wine
5438 phulakē (6), *night watch; prison; haunt*

WATCHED
6822 tsâphâh (1), to *observe, await*
8104 shâmar (2), to *watch*
8245 shâqad (2), to *be on the lookout*
1127 grēgŏrĕuō (2), to *watch, guard*
3906 paratĕrĕŏ (5), to *note insidiously*
5083 tērĕō (1), to *keep, guard, obey*

WATCHER
5894 'îyr (Ch.) (2), *watcher-angel*

WATCHERS
5341 nâtsar (1), to *guard, protect, maintain*
5894 'îyr (Ch.) (1), *watcher-angel*

WATCHES
821 'ashmûrâh (3), night *watch*
4931 mishmereth (2), *watch, sentry, post*

WATCHETH
6822 tsâphâh (1), to *observe, await*
6974 qûwts (1), to *awake*
1127 grēgŏrĕuō (1), to *watch, guard*

WATCHFUL
1127 grēgŏrĕuō (1), to *watch, guard*

WATCHING
6822 tsâphâh (2), to *observe, await*
8245 shâqad (1), to *be on the lookout*
69 agrupnĕō (1), to *be sleepless, keep awake*
1127 grēgŏrĕuō (1), to *watch, guard*
5083 tērĕō (1), to *keep, guard, obey*

WATCHINGS
70 agrupnia (2), *keeping awake*

WATCHMAN
6822 tsâphâh (14), to *peer* into the distance
8104 shâmar (4), to *watch*

WATCHMAN'S
6822 tsâphâh (1), to *peer* into the distance

WATCHMEN
5341 nâtsar (3), to *guard, protect, maintain*
6822 tsâphâh (5), to *peer* into the distance
8104 shâmar (4), to *watch*

WATCHTOWER
4707 mitspeh (1), military *observatory*
6844 tsâphîyth (1), *sentry*

WATER
1119 bᵉmôw (1), *in, with, by*
2222 zarzîyph (1), *pouring rain*
4325 mayim (308), *water*
4529 mâçâh (1), to *dissolve, melt*
7301 râvâh (1), to *slake* thirst or appetites
8248 shâqâh (9), to *quaff, i.e. to irrigate*
504 anudrŏs (2), *dry, arid*
5202 hudrŏpŏtĕō (1), to *drink water exclusively*
5204 hudōr (62), *water*

WATERCOURSE
4161+4325 môwtsâ' (1), *going forth*
8585 tᵉ'âlâh (1), irrigation *channel*

WATERED
3384 yârâh (1), to *point; to teach*
4945 mashqeh (1), *butler; drink; well-watered*
7302 râveh (2), *sated, full* with drink
8248 shâqâh (6), to *quaff, i.e. to irrigate*
4222 pŏtizō (1), to *furnish drink, irrigate*

WATEREDST
8248 shâqâh (1), to *quaff, i.e. to irrigate*

WATEREST
7301 râvâh (1), to *slake* thirst or appetites
7783 shûwq (1), to *overflow*

WATERETH
7301 râvâh (2), to *slake* thirst or appetites
8248 shâqâh (1), to *quaff, i.e. to irrigate*
4222 pŏtizō (2), to *furnish drink, irrigate*

WATERFLOOD
7641+4325 shibbôl (1), *stream; ear of grain*

WATERING
4325 mayim (1), *water*
7377 rîy (1), *irrigation*
4222 pŏtizō (1), to *furnish drink, irrigate*

WATERPOT
5201 hudria (1), *water jar, i.e. receptacle*

WATERPOTS
5201 hudria (2), *water jar, i.e. receptacle*

WATERS
4325 mayim (265), *water*
4215 pŏtamŏs (1), *current, brook, running water*
5204 hudōr (15), *water*

WATERSPOUTS
6794 tsinnûwr (1), *culvert, water-shaft*

WATERSPRINGS
4161+4325 môwtsâ' (2), *going forth*

WAVE
5130 nûwph (11), to *quiver, vibrate, rock*
8573 tᵉnûwphâh (19), official *undulation* of sacrificial offerings
2830 kludōn (1), *surge, raging*

WAVED
5130 nûwph (5), to *quiver, vibrate, rock*
8573 tᵉnûwphâh (1), official *undulation* of sacrificial offerings

WAVERETH
1252 diakrinō (1), to *decide; to hesitate*

WAVERING
186 aklinēs (1), *firm, unswerving*
1252 diakrinō (1), to *decide; to hesitate*

WAVES
1116 bâmâh (1), *elevation, high place*
1530 gal (14), *heap; ruins*
1796 dŏkîy (1), *dashing, pounding* of surf
4867 mishbâr (4), *breaker sea-waves*
2949 kuma (5), *bursting or toppling*
4535 salŏs (1), *billow, i.e. rolling motion of waves*

WAX
1749 dôwnag (4), *bees-wax*
2691 katastrēniaŏ (1), to *be voluptuous against*
3822 palaiŏō (2), to *make, become worn out*
4298 prŏkŏptō (1), to *go ahead, advance*
5594 psuchō (1), to *chill, grow cold*

WAXED
1980 hâlak (5), to *walk; live a certain way*
1096 ginŏmai (2), to *be, become*
2901 krataiŏō (2), *increase in vigor*
3955 parrhēsiazŏmai (1), to *be frank* in utterance
3975 pachunō (2), to *fatten; to render callous*
4147 plŏutĕō (1), to *be, become wealthy*

WAXETH
1095 gēraskō (1), to *be senescent, grow old*

WAXING
3982 pĕithō (1), to *pacify or conciliate; to assent*

WAY
734 'ôrach (18), *road; manner of life*
776 'erets (3), *earth, land, soil; country*
935 bôw' (1), to *go, come*
1870 derek (466), *road; course of life; mode*
2008 hênnâh (1), *from here; from there*
2088 zeh (1), *this or that*
3212 yâlak (6), to *walk; to live; to carry*
3541 kôh (1), *thus*
4498 mânôwç (1), *fleeing; place of refuge*
5265 nâça' (1), *start on a journey*
5410 nâthîyb (2), (beaten) *track, path*
7125 qîr'âh (1), to *encounter, to happen*
7971 shâlach (1), to *send away*
8582 tâ'âh (2), to *vacillate, i.e. reel*
1545 ĕkbasis (1), *exit, way out*
1624 ĕktrĕpō (1), to *turn away*
1722 ĕn (1), *in; during; because of*
3112 makran (2), *at a distance, far away*
3319 mĕsŏs (2), *middle*
3598 hŏdŏs (81), *road*
3938 parŏdŏs (1), *by-road, i.e. a route*
4105 planaŏ (1), to *roam, wander from safety*
4206 pŏrrhō (1), *forwards*
4311 prŏpĕmpō (5), to *send forward*
5158 trŏpŏs (2), *deportment, character*

WAYFARING
732 'ârach (4), to *travel, wander*
1980+1870 hâlak (1), to *walk; live a certain way*
5674+734 'âbar (1), to *cross over; to transition*

WAYMARKS
6725 tsîyûwn (1), *guiding pillar, monument*

WAYS
734 'ôrach (8), *road; manner of life*
735 'ôrach (Ch.) (2), *road*
1870 derek (161), *road; course of life; mode of action*
1979 hălîykâh (2), *walking; procession or march; caravan*
4546 mᵉçillâh (1), *main thoroughfare; viaduct*
4570 ma'gâl (1), *circular track or camp rampart*
7339 rᵉchôb (1), *myriad*
296 amphŏdŏn (1), *fork in the road*
684 apŏlĕia (1), *ruin or loss*
3598 hŏdŏs (11), *road*

4197 pŏrĕia (1), *journey; life's daily conduct*

WAYSIDE
3027+4570 yâd (1), *hand; power*
3197+1870 yak (1), *hand or side*

WEAK
535 'âmal (1), *to be weak; to be sick*
536 'umlal (1), *sick, faint*
2470 châlâh (4), *to be weak, sick, afflicted*
2523 challâsh (1), *frail, weak*
3212 yâlak (2), *to walk; to live; to carry*
3782 kâshal (1), *to totter, waver; to falter*
7390 rak (1), *tender; weak*
7503 râphâh (1), *to slacken*
7504 râpheh (4), *slack*
102 adunatŏs (1), *weak; impossible*
770 asthĕnĕō (19), *to be feeble*
772 asthĕnēs (8), *strengthless, weak*

WEAKEN
2522 châlash (1), *to prostrate, lay low*

WEAKENED
6031 'ânâh (1), *to afflict, be afflicted*
7503 râphâh (2), *to slacken*

WEAKENETH
7503 râphâh (2), *to slacken*

WEAKER
1800 dal (1), *weak, thin; humble, needy*
772 asthĕnēs (1), *strengthless, weak*

WEAKNESS
769 asthĕnĕia (5), *feebleness; frailty*
772 asthĕnēs (2), *strengthless, weak*

WEALTH
1952 hôwn (5), *wealth*
2428 chayil (10), *army; wealth; virtue; valor*
2896 tôwb (3), *good; well*
3581 kôach (1), *force, might; strength*
5233 nekeç (4), *treasure, riches*
2142 ĕupŏria (1), *resources, prosperity*

WEALTHY
7310 rᵉvâyâh (1), *satisfaction*
7961 shâlêv (1), *careless, carefree; security*

WEANED
1580 gâmal (12), *to benefit or requite*

WEAPON
240 'âzēn (1), *spade; paddle*
3627 kᵉlîy (4), *implement, thing*

5402 nesheq (1), *military arms, arsenal*
7973 shelach (2), *spear; shoot of growth*

WEAPONS
3627 kᵉlîy (17), *implement, thing*
5402 nesheq (2), *military arms, arsenal*
3696 hŏplŏn (2), *implement, or utensil*

WEAR
1080 bᵉlâ' (Ch.) (1), *to afflict, torment*
1961 hâyâh (1), *to exist, i.e. be or become*
3847 lâbash (4), *to clothe*
5034 nâbêl (1), *to wilt; to fall away; to be foolish*
5375 nâsâ' (2), *to lift up*
7833 shâchaq (1), *to grind or wear away*
2827 klinō (1), *to slant or slope*
5409 phŏrĕō (1), *to wear*

WEARETH
5409 phŏrĕō (1), *to wear*

WEARIED
3021 yâga' (5), *to be exhausted, to tire,*
3811 lâ'âh (5), *to tire; to be, make disgusted*
5888 'âyêph (1), *to languish*
2577 kamnō (1), *to tire; to faint, sicken*
2872 kŏpiaō (1), *to feel fatigue; to work hard*

WEARIETH
2959 târach (1), *to overburden*
3021 yâga' (1), *to be exhausted, to tire,*

WEARINESS
3024 yᵉgî'âh (1), *fatigue*
4972 mattᵉlâ'âh (1), *what a trouble!*
2873 kŏpŏs (1), *toil; pains*

WEARING
5375 nâsâ' (1), *to lift up*
4025 pĕrithĕsis (1), *putting all around, i.e. decorating oneself with*
5409 phŏrĕō (1), *to wear*

WEARISOME
5999 'âmâl (1), *wearing effort; worry*

WEARY
3019 yâgîya' (1), *tired, exhausted*
3021 yâga' (7), *to be exhausted, to tire,*
3023 yâgêa' (2), *tiresome*
3286 yâ'aph (5), *to tire*
3287 yâ'êph (1), *exhausted*
3811 lâ'âh (10), *to tire; to be, make disgusted*
5354 nâqat (1), *to loathe*
5774 'ûwph (1), *to cover, to fly; to faint*
5889 'âyêph (8), *languid*
6973 qûwts (2), *to be, make disgusted*
7646 sâba' (1), *fill to satiety*

5402 nesheq (1), *military arms, arsenal*

1573 ĕkkakĕō (2), *to be weak, fail*
5299 hupōpiazō (1), *to beat up; to wear out*

WEASEL
2467 chôled (1), *weasel*

WEATHER
2091 zâhâb (1), *gold, piece of gold*
3117 yôwm (1), *day; time period*
2105 ĕudia (1), *clear sky, i.e. fine weather*
5494 chĕimōn (1), *winter season; stormy weather*

WEAVE
707 'ârag (2), *to plait or weave*

WEAVER
707 'ârag (2), *to plait or weave*

WEAVER'S
707 'ârag (4), *to plait or weave*

WEAVEST
707 'ârag (1), *to plait or weave*

WEB
1004 bayith (1), *house; temple; family, tribe*
4545 maççeketh (2), *length-wise threads*
6980 qûwr (1), *spider web*

WEBS
6980 qûwr (1), *spider web*

WEDDING
1062 gamŏs (7), *nuptials*

WEDGE
3956 lâshôwn (2), *tongue; tongue-shaped*

WEDLOCK
5003 nâ'aph (1), *to commit adultery*

WEEDS
5488 çûwph (1), *papyrus reed; reed*

WEEK
7620 shâbûwa' (4), *seven-day week*
4521 sabbatŏn (9), *day of weekly repose*

WEEKS
7620 shâbûwa' (15), *seven-day week*

WEEP
1058 bâkâh (29), *to weep, moan*
1065 bᵉkîy (2), *weeping*
1830 dâma' (1), *to weep*
2799 klaiō (15), *to sob, wail*

WEEPEST
1058 bâkâh (1), *to weep, moan*
2799 klaiō (2), *to sob, wail*

WEEPETH
1058 bâkâh (4), *to weep, moan*

WEEPING
1058 bâkâh (8), *to weep, moan*
1065 bᵉkîy (21), *weeping*

2799 klaiō (9), *to sob, wail*
2805 klauthmŏs (6), *lamentation, weeping*

WEIGH
4948 mishqâl (2), *weight, weighing*
6424 pâlaç (2), *to weigh mentally*
8254 shâqal (2), *to suspend in trade*

WEIGHED
8254 shâqal (12), *to suspend in trade*
8505 tâkan (1), *to balance, i.e. measure*
8625 tᵉqal (Ch.) (1), *to weigh in a balance*

WEIGHETH
8505 tâkan (2), *to balance, i.e. measure*

WEIGHT
68 'eben (4), *stone*
4946 mishqôwl (1), *weight*
4948 mishqâl (44), *weight, weighing*
6425 peleç (1), *balance, scale*
922 barŏs (1), *load, abundance, authority*
3591 ŏgkŏs (1), *burden, hindrance*
5006 talantiaiŏs (1), *weight of 57-80 lbs.*

WEIGHTIER
926 barus (1), *weighty*

WEIGHTS
68 'eben (6), *stone*

WEIGHTY
5192 nêtel (1), *burden*
926 barus (1), *weighty*

WELFARE
2896 tôwb (1), *good; well*
3444 yᵉshûw'âh (1), *victory; prosperity*
7965 shâlôwm (5), *safe; well; health, prosperity*

WELL
71 'Âbânâh (1), *stony*
369 'ayin (1), *there is no, i.e., not exist, none*
375 'êyphôh (2), *where?; when?; how?*
875 bᵉ'êr (21), *well, cistern*
883 Bᵉ'êr la-Chay Rô'îy (1), *well of a living (One) my seer*
953 bôwr (6), *pit hole, cistern, well; prison*
995 bîyn (1), *to understand; discern*
2090 zôh (1), *this or that*
2654 châphêts (1), *to be pleased with, desire*
2895 towb (9), *to be good*
2896 tôwb (20), *good; well*
2898 tûwb (1), *good; goodness; beauty, gladness, welfare*
3190 yâtab (35), *to be, make well*
3303 yâpheh (5), *beautiful; handsome*

W

1535 galgal (Ch.) (1), *wheel*

6471 pa'am (1), *time; step; occurence*

WHELP
1482 gûwr (3), *cub*

WHELPS
1121 bên (2), *son, descendant; people*
1482 gûwr (3), *cub*
1484 gôwr (3), *lion cub*

WHEN
310 'achar (1), *after*
518 'îm (19), *whether?*
834 'ăsher (83), *who, what, that; when*
1767 day (3), *enough, sufficient*
1768 dîy (Ch.) (4), *that; of*
1961 hâyâh (4), *to exist*
3117 yôwm (7), *day; time*
3588 kîy (280), *for, that*
3644 kᵉmôw (1), *like, as*
4970 mâthay (14), *when; when?, how long?*
5704 'ad (3), *as far (long) as; during; while; until*
5750 'ôwd (2), *again; repeatedly; still; more*
5921 'al (1), *above, over, upon, or against*
6256 'êth (7), *time*
6310 peh (2), *mouth; opening*
1437 ĕan (2), *indefiniteness*
1875 ĕpan (3), *whenever*
1893 ĕpĕi (1), *since*
2259 hēnika (2), *at which time, whenever*
2531 kathōs (1), *just or inasmuch as, that*
3326 mĕta (2), *with, among; after, later*
3698 hŏpŏtĕ (1), *as soon as, when*
3704 hŏpōs (1), *in the manner that*
3752 hŏtan (123), *inasmuch as, at once*
3753 hŏtĕ (99), *when; as*
3756 ŏu (1), *no or not*
4218 pŏtĕ (13), *at some time, ever*
5613 hōs (40), *which, how, i.e. in that manner*
5618 hōspĕr (2), *exactly like*

WHENCE
335 'ay (1), *where?*
370 'ayin (19), *where from?, whence?*
1992 hêm (1), *they*
3606 hŏthên (4), *from which place or source*
3739 hŏs (2), *who, which, what, that*
4159 pŏthên (28), *from which; what*

WHENSOEVER
3605 kôl (1), *all, any or every*
3752 hŏtan (1), *inasmuch as, at once*
5613+1437 hōs (1), *which, how, i.e. in that manner*

WHERE
335 'ay (16), *where?*
346 'ayêh (45), *where?*
349 'êyk (1), *where?*
351 'êykôh (1), *where*
370 'ayin (2), *where from?, whence?*
375 'êyphôh (9), *where?*
413 'êl (2), *to, toward*
575 'ân (2), *where from?*
645 'êphôw (5), *then*
657 'epheç (1), *end; no further*
834 'ăsher (58), *where*
1768 dîy (Ch.) (1), *that; of*
3027 yâd (1), *hand; power*
5921 'al (2), *above, over, upon, or against*
8033 shâm (20), *where*
8478 tachath (1), *bottom; underneath; in lieu of*
8536 tâm (Ch.) (1), *there in the road*
296 amphŏdŏn (1), *fork in the road*
1330 diĕrchŏmai (1), *to traverse, travel through*
1337 dithalassŏs (1), *having two seas*
2596 kata (1), *down; according to*
3606 hŏthĕn (2), *from which place or source*
3699 hŏpŏu (58), *at whichever spot*
3757 hŏu (21), *at which place, i.e. where*
3837 pantachŏu (5), *universally, everywhere*
3838 pantĕlēs (1), *entire; completion*
4226 pŏu (37), *at what locality?*
5101 tis (1), *who?, which? or what?*

WHEREABOUT
834 'ăsher (1), *where, how, because*

WHEREAS
518 'îm (1), *whether?; if, although; Oh that!*
834 'ăsher (2), *because, in order that*
1768 dîy (Ch.) (4), *that; of*
3588 kîy (5), *for, that because*
6258 'attâh (2), *at this time, now*
8478 tachath (1), *bottom; underneath; in lieu of*
3699 hŏpŏu (2), *at whichever spot*
3748 hŏstis (1), *whoever*

WHEREBY
834 'ăsher (17), *because, in order that*
4100 mâh (1), *whatever; that which*
4482 mên (1), *part; musical chord*
3588 hŏ (1), *"the," i.e. the definite article*
3739 hŏs (1), *who, which, what, that*

WHEREFORE
199 'ûwlâm (1), *however or on the contrary*
3651 kên (18), *just; right; correct*

3861 lâhên (Ch.) (1), *therefore; except*
4069 maddûwa' (28), *why?, what?*
4100 mâh (86), *what?, how?, why?, when?*
686 ara (1), *therefore*
1161 dĕ (2), *but, yet*
1302 diati (4), *why?*
1352 diŏ (41), *consequently, therefore*
1355 diŏpĕr (3), *on which very account*
3606 hŏthĕn (4), *from which place or source*
3767 ŏun (7), *certainly; accordingly*
5101 tis (3), *who?, which? or what?*
5105 tŏigarŏun (1), *consequently, then*
5620 hōstĕ (17), *thus, therefore*

WHEREIN
834 'ăsher (70), *when, where, how, because*
1459 gav (Ch.) (1), *middle*
2098 zûw (2), *this or that*
4100 mâh (15), *what?, how?, why?, when?*
8033 shâm (1), *where*
3739 hŏs (1), *what, that*
3757 hŏu (3), *where*

WHEREINSOEVER
1722+3739+302 ĕn (1), *in; during; because of*

WHEREINTO
824+8432 'Esh'ân (1), *support*
834+413+8432 'ăsher (1), *when, where, how*
1519+3739 ĕis (1), *to or into*

WHEREOF
834 'ăsher (24), *where*
3739 hŏs (11), *who, which, what, that*

WHEREON
834 'ăsher (2), *where, how, because*
834+5921 'ăsher (13), *where, how, because*
5921 'al (2), *above, over, upon, or against*
5921+4100 'al (1), *above, over, upon, or against*
1909+3739 ĕpi (4), *on, upon*
3739 hŏs (1), *who, which, what, that*

WHERESOEVER
834 'ăsher (1), *where, how, because*
3605 kôl (1), *all, any*
3699 hŏpŏu (1), *at whichever spot*

WHERETO
834 'ăsher (1), *where, how, because*
4100 mâh (1), *what?, how?, why?, when?*
1519+3739 ĕis (1), *to or into*

WHEREUNTO
834 'ăsher (6), *where, how, because*

3739 hŏs (6), *who, which, what, that*
5101 tis (7), *who?, which? or what?*

WHEREUPON
413 'êl (2), *to, toward*
5921 'al (1), *above, over, upon, or against*
3606 hŏthĕn (3), *from which place or source*

WHEREWITH
834 'ăsher (68), *when, where, how, because*
1697 dâbâr (1), *word; matter; thing*
4100 mâh (9), *what?, how?, why?, when?*
1722+3739 ĕn (2), *in; during; because of*
1722+5101 ĕn (3), *in; during; because of*
3739 hŏs (9), *who, which*
3745 hŏsŏs (1), *as much as*
5101 tis (1), *who?, which? or what?*

WHEREWITHAL
5101 tis (1), *who?, which? or what?*

WHET
3913 lâṭash (1), *to sharpen; to pierce*
7043 qâlal (1), *to be, make light (sharp)*
8150 shânan (2), *to pierce; to inculcate*

WHETHER
176 'ôw (8), *or, whether*
335 'ay (1), *where?*
518 'îm (27), *whether?*
996 bêyn (4), *"either...or"*
2006 hên (Ch.) (2), *whether, but, if*
3588 kîy (1), *for, that because*
4100 mâh (1), *what?, how?, why?, when?*
4480 min (3), *from, out of*
5704 'ad (1), *as far (long) as; during; while; until*
5750 'ôwd (2), *again; repeatedly; still; more*
1487 ĕi (22), *if, whether*
1535 ĕitĕ (31), *if too*
2273 ētŏi (1), *either...or*
3379 mēpŏtĕ (1), *not ever; if, or lest ever*
4220 pŏtĕrŏn (1), *which*
5037 tĕ (1), *both or also*
5101 tis (8), *who?, which? or what?*

WHILE
518 'îm (1), *whether?; if, although; Oh that!*
834 'ăsher (1), *when, where, how, because*
3117 yôwm (7), *day; time*
3541 kôh (1), *thus*
3588 kîy (3), *for, that because*
4705 mits'âr (1), *little; short time*
5704 'ad (9), *during; while*
5750 'ôwd (7), *again; repeatedly; still; more*
5751 'ôwd (Ch.) (1), *again; repeatedly; still*

WHILES

7350 râchôwq (1), *remote, far*
2193 hĕôs (8), *until*
2250 hēmĕra (2), *day; period of time*
2540 kairôs (1), *occasion, i.e. set time*
3153 mataiŏtēs (1), *transientness; depravity*
3397 mikrŏn (2), *small space of time or degree*
3641 ŏligŏs (2), *puny, small*
3752 hŏtan (1), *inasmuch as, at once*
3753 hŏtĕ (1), *when; as*
3819 palai (1), *formerly; sometime since*
4340 prŏskairŏs (1), *temporary*
5550 chrŏnŏs (3), *time*
5613 hôs (4), *which, how, i.e. in that manner*

WHILES

5750 'ôwd (1), *again; repeatedly; still; more*
2193+3755 hĕôs (1), *until*

WHILST

834 'ăsher (1), *when, where, how, because*
5704 'ad (4), *as far (long) as; during; while; until*

WHIP

7752 shôwṭ (2), *lash*

WHIPS

7752 shôwṭ (4), *lash*

WHIRLETH

1980 hâlak (1), *to walk; live a certain way*

WHIRLWIND

5492 çûwphâh (10), *hurricane wind*
5590 çâ'ar (3), *to rush upon; to toss about*
5591 ça'ar (11), *hurricane wind*
7307+5591 rûwach (1), *breath; wind; life-spirit*
8175 sâ'ar (2), *to storm; to shiver, i.e. fear*

WHIRLWINDS

5492 çûwphâh (1), *hurricane wind*
5591 ça'ar (1), *hurricane*

WHISPER

3907 lâchash (1), *to whisper a magic spell*
6850 tsâphaph (1), *to coo or chirp as a bird*

WHISPERED

3907 lâchash (1), *to whisper a magic spell*

WHISPERER

5372 nirgân (1), *slanderer, gossip*

WHISPERERS

5588 psithuristēs (1), *maligning gossip*

WHISPERINGS

5587 psithurismŏs (1), *whispering, detraction*

WHIT

1697 dâbâr (1), *word; matter; thing*

3632 kâlîyl (1), *whole, entire; complete; whole*
3367 mĕdĕis (1), *not even*
3650 hŏlŏs (2), *whole or all, i.e. complete*

WHITE

1858 dar (1), *mother-of-pearl or alabaster*
2353 chûwr (2), *white linen*
2751 chôrîy (1), *white bread*
3835 lâban (4), *to be, become white*
3836 lâbân (29), *white*
6703 tsach (1), *dazzling*
6713 tsachar (1), *whiteness*
6715 tsâchôr (1), *white*
7388 rîyr (1), *saliva; broth*
2986 lamprŏs (2), *radiant; clear*
3021 lĕukainō (2), *to whiten*
3022 lĕukŏs (24), *bright white*

WHITED

2867 kŏniaō (2), *to whitewash*

WHITER

3835 lâban (1), *to be, become white*
6705 tsâchach (1), *to be dazzling white*

WHITHER

413 'êl (2), *to, toward*
575 'ân (20), *where from?, when?*
834 'ăsher (6), *when, where, how, because*
8033 shâm (3), *where*
3699 hŏpŏu (9), *at whichever spot*
3757 hŏu (2), *where*
4226 pŏu (10), *at what?*

WHITHERSOEVER

413+3605+834 'êl (1), *to, toward*
413+3605+834+8033 'êl (1), *to, toward*
575 'ân (1), *where from?*
834 'ăsher (2), *where, how, because*
1870+834 derek (1), *road; course of life*
3605+834 kôl (13), *all, any or every*
3605+834+8033 kôl (1), *all, any or every*
4725+834 mâqôwm (1), *general locality, place*
5921+834+8033 'al (1), *above, over, upon*
5921+3605+834 'al (1), *above, over, upon*
3699+302 hŏpŏu (4), *at whichever spot*
3699+1437 hŏpŏu (1), *at whichever spot*
3757+1437 hŏu (1), *at which place, i.e. where*

WHOLE

854+3605 'êth (13), *with; by; at; among*
2421 châyâh (1), *to live; to revive*

3117 yôwm (4), *day; time*
3605 kôl (115), *all, any*
3606 kôl (Ch.) (6), *all, any*
3632 kâlîyl (2), *whole*
4749 miqshâh (1), *work molded by hammering*
7495 râphâ' (2), *to heal*
8003 shâlêm (4), *complete; friendly; safe*
8549 tâmîym (4), *entire*
8552 tâmam (1), *to complete, finish*
537 hapas (3), *whole*
1295 diasōzō (1), *to cure*
2390 iaŏmai (1), *to heal*
2480 ischuō (2), *to have or exercise force*
3390 mētrŏpŏlis (1), *main city, metropolis*
3646 hŏlŏkautōma (1), *wholly-consumed*
3648 hŏlŏklērŏs (1), *sound in the entire body*
3650 hŏlŏs (43), *whole*
3956 pas (3), *all, any*
3958 paschō (2), *to experience pain*
4982 sōzō (11), *to deliver; to protect*
5198 hugiainō (2), *to have sound health*
5199 hugiēs (13), *well, healthy; true*

WHOLESOME

4832 marpê' (1), *cure; deliverance; placidity*
5198 hugiainō (1), *to have sound health*

WHOLLY

3605 kôl (9), *all, any*
3615 kâlâh (1), *to complete, prepare*
3632 kâlîyl (1), *whole*
4390 mâlê' (6), *to fill*
5352 nâqâh (1), *to be, make clean; to be bare*
6942 qâdâsh (1), *to be, make clean*
7760 sûwm (1), *to put*
7965 shâlôwm (1), *safe; well; health, prosperity*
1510+1722 ĕimi (1), *I exist, I am*
3651 hŏlŏtĕlēs (1), *absolutely perfect*

WHORE

2181 zânâh (9), *to commit adultery*
6948 qĕdêshâh (1), *sacred female prostitute*
4204 pŏrnē (4), *prostitute*

WHORE'S

2181 zânâh (1), *to commit adultery*

WHOREDOM

2181 zânâh (11), *to commit adultery*
2183 zânûwn (1), *adultery; idolatry*
2184 zᵉnûwth (7), *adultery, infidelity*
8457 taznûwth (3), *harlotry*

WHOREDOMS

2181 zânâh (2), *to commit adultery*
2183 zânûwn (11), *adultery; idolatry*
2184 zᵉnûwth (2), *adultery, infidelity*
8457 taznûwth (15), *harlotry, physical or spiritual*

WHOREMONGER

4205 pŏrnŏs (1), *debauchee, immoral*

WHOREMONGERS

4205 pŏrnŏs (4), *debauchee, immoral*

WHORES

2181 zânâh (2), *to commit adultery*

WHORING

2181 zânâh (19), *to commit adultery*

WHORISH

2181 zânâh (3), *to commit adultery*

WHY

4060 middâh (1), *measure*
4069 maddûwa' (41), *why?, what?*
4100 mâh (119), *what?, how?, why?, when?*
4101 mâh (Ch.) (2), *what?, how?, why?*
1063 gar (4), *for, indeed, but, because*
1302 diati (23), *why?*
2444 hinati (4), *why?*
3754 hŏti (2), *that; because; since*
5101 tis (66), *who?, which? or what?*

WICKED

205 'âven (6), *trouble, vanity, wickedness*
605 'ânash (1), *to be frail, feeble*
1100 bᵉlîya'al (5), *wickedness, trouble*
2154 zimmâh (2), *bad plan*
2162 zâmâm (1), *plot*
2617 cheçed (1), *kindness, favor*
4209 mᵉzimmâh (3), *plan; sagacity*
4849 mirsha'ath (1), *female wicked-doer*
5766 'evel (1), *evil*
5767 'avvâl (3), *evil*
6001 'âmêl (1), *toiling; laborer; sorrowful*
6090 'ôtseb (1), *idol; pain*
7451 ra' (26), *bad; evil*
7489 râ'a' (5), *to be good for nothing*
7561 râsha' (4), *to be, do, declare wrong*
7562 resha (4), *wrong*
7563 râshâ' (252), *wrong; bad person*
113 athĕsmŏs (2), *criminal*
459 anŏmŏs (2), *without Jewish law*
2556 kakŏs (1), *wrong*

4190 pŏnērŏs (17),
malice, wicked, bad
4191 pŏnērŏtĕrŏs (2),
more evil

WICKEDLY
4209 mᵉzimmâh (1),
plan; sagacity
5753 'âvâh (1), to be
crooked
5766 'evel (1), moral evil
7451 ra' (1), bad; evil
7489 râ'a' (5), to be good
for nothing
7561 râsha' (13), to be,
do, declare wrong
7564 rish'âh (1), moral
wrong

WICKEDNESS
205 'âven (2), trouble,
vanity, wickedness
1942 havvâh (3), desire;
craving
2154 zimmâh (4), bad
plan
5766 'evel (7), moral evil
5999 'âmâl (1), wearing
effort; worry
7451 ra' (59), bad; evil
7455 rôa' (3), badness
7561 râsha' (1), to be, do,
declare wrong
7562 resha' (25), wrong
7564 rish'âh (13), wrong
2549 kakia (1),
depravity; malignity;
trouble
4189 pŏnēria (6), malice,
evil, wickedness
4190 pŏnērŏs (1), malice,
wicked, bad; crime
5129+824 tŏutŏᵢ (1), in
this person or thing

WIDE
2267 cheber (2), society,
group; magic spell;
4060 middâh (1),
measure; portion
6605 pâthach (3), to open
wide; to loosen, begin
7337 râchab (3), to
broaden
7342 râchâb (1), roomy
7342+3027 râchâb (2),
roomy, spacious
4116 platus (1), wide

WIDENESS
7341 rôchab (1), width

WIDOW
490 'almânâh (37), widow
5503 chêra (13), widow

WIDOW'S
490 'almânâh (4), widow
491 'almânûwth (1),
widow; widowhood

WIDOWHOOD
489 'almôn (1),
widowhood
491 'almânûwth (3),
widow; widowhood

WIDOWS
490 'almânâh (12), widow
5503 chêra (10), widow

WIDOWS'
5503 chêra (3), widow

WIFE
802 'ishshâh (301),
woman, wife
1166 bâ'al (1), to be
master; to marry
1753 dûwr (Ch.) (1), to
reside, live in
2994 yᵉbêmeth (3),
sister-in-law
1134 gunaikĕiŏs (1),
feminine
1135 gunē (80), wife

WIFE'S
802 'ishshâh (8), woman,
wife; women, wives
3994 pĕnthĕra (3), wife's
mother

WILD
338 'îy (3), solitary wild
creature that howls
689 'aqqôw (1), ibex
891 bᵉ'ûshîym (2), rotten
fruit
2123 zîyz (2), fulness
2416 chay (1), alive; raw
3277 yâ'êl (3), ibex
6167 'ărâd (Ch.) (1),
onager or wild donkey
6171 'ârôwd (1), onager
or wild donkey
6501 pere' (10), onager,
wild donkey
6728 tsîyîy (3), wild beast
7704 sâdeh (8), field
8377 tᵉ'ôw (2), antelope
65 agriĕlaiŏs (2), wild
olive tree
66 agriŏs (2), wild
2342 thēriŏn (3),
dangerous animal

WILDERNESS
3452 yᵉshîymôwn (2),
desolation
4057 midbâr (255),
desert; also speech
6160 'ărâbâh (4), desert,
wasteland
6166 'Ărâd (1), fugitive
6723 tsîyâh (2), desert
6728 tsîyîy (3), wild beast
8414 tôhûw (2), waste,
desolation, formless
2047 ĕrēmia (3), place of
solitude, remoteness
2048 ĕrēmŏs (32), remote
place, deserted place

WILES
5231 nêkel (1), deceit
3180 mĕthŏdĕia (1),
trickery, scheming

WILFULLY
1596 hĕkŏusiŏs (1),
voluntarily, willingly

WILILY
6195 'ormâh (1), trickery;
discretion

WILL
14 'âbâh (5), to be
acquiescent
165 'êhîy (3), Where?
2654 châphêts (2), to be
pleased with, desire
3045 yâda' (1), to know
5314 nâphash (1), to be
refreshed
5315 nephesh (3), life;
breath; soul; wind

6634 tsᵉbâ' (Ch.) (5), to
please
7470 rᵉ'ûwth (Ch.) (1),
desire
7522 râtsôwn (15), delight
210 akŏn (1), unwilling
1012 bŏulē (1), purpose,
plan, decision
1013 bŏulēma (1),
resolve, willful choice
1014 bŏulŏmai (12), to be
willing, desire
1106 gnŏmē (1), opinion,
resolve
1479 ĕthĕlŏthrēskĕia (1),
voluntary piety
2107 ĕudŏkia (2),
delight, kindness, wish
2133 ĕunŏia (1), eagerly,
with a whole heart
2307 thĕlēma (62),
purpose; decree
2308 thĕlēsis (1),
determination
2309 thĕlō (70), to will; to
desire; to choose
3195 mĕllō (6), to intend,
i.e. be about to

WILLETH
2309 thĕlō (1), to will; to
desire; to choose

WILLING
14 'âbâh (4), to be
acquiescent
2655 châphêts (1),
pleased with
5068 nâdab (3), to
volunteer
5071 nᵉdâbâh (2),
spontaneous gift
5081 nâdîyb (3),
magnanimous
830 authairĕtŏs (1),
self-chosen, voluntary
1014 bŏulŏmai (5), to be
willing, desire
2106 ĕudŏkĕŏ (2), to
think well, i.e. approve
2309 thĕlō (8), to will; to
desire; to choose
2843 kŏinōnikŏs (1),
liberal
4288 prŏthumia (1),
alacrity, eagerness
4289 prŏthumŏs (1),
alacrity, eagerness

WILLINGLY
2656 chêphets (1),
pleasure; desire
2974 yâ'al (1), to assent;
to undertake, begin
3820 lêb (1), heart
5068 nâdab (13), to
volunteer
5071 nᵉdâbâh (1),
spontaneous gift
5414 nâthan (1), to give
1596 hĕkŏusiŏs (1),
voluntarily, willingly
1635 hĕkōn (2), voluntary
2309 thĕlō (2), to will

WILLOW
6851 tsaphtsâphâh (1),
willow tree

WILLOWS
6155 'ârâb (5), willow

WILT
2309 thĕlō (21), to will

WIMPLES
4304 mitpachath (1),
cloak, shawl

WIN
1234 bâqa' (1), to cleave
2770 kĕrdainō (1), to
gain; to spare

WIND
7307 rûwach (82),
breath; wind; life-spirit
7308 rûwach (Ch.) (1),
breath; wind; life-spirit
416 anemizō (1), to toss
with the wind
417 anĕmŏs (20), wind
4151 pnĕuma (1), spirit
4154 pnĕō (1), to breeze
4157 pnŏē (1), breeze;
breath

WINDING
3583 kâchal (1), to paint
4141 mûwçâb (1), circuit
5437 çâbab (1), to
surround

WINDOW
2474 challôwn (13),
window; opening
6672 tsôhar (1), window
2376 thuris (2), window

WINDOWS
699 'ărubbâh (8),
window; chimney
2474 challôwn (18),
window; opening
3551 kav (Ch.) (1),
window
8121 shemesh (1), sun
8260 sheqeph (1),
loophole
8261 shâqûph (1),
opening

WINDS
7307 rûwach (11),
breath; wind; life-spirit
7308 rûwach (Ch.) (1),
breath; wind; life-spirit
417 anĕmŏs (11), wind

WINDY
7307 rûwach (1), breath;
wind; life-spirit

WINE
2561 chemer (1),
fermenting wine
2562 chămar (Ch.) (6),
wine
3196 yayin (135), wine
3342 yeqeb (1), wine-vat
4469 mamçâk (1),
mixed-wine
5435 çôbe' (1), wine
6025 'ênâb (1), grape
6071 'âçîyç (4), expressed
fresh grape-juice
7491 râ'aph (1), to drip
8492 tîyrôwsh (40), wine,
squeezed grape-juice
1098 glĕukŏs (1), sweet
wine
3631 ŏinŏs (32), wine
3632 ŏinŏphlugia (1),
drunkenness
3943 parŏinŏs (2),
tippling

WINEBIBBER
3630 ŏinŏpŏtēs (1), *tippler*

WINEBIBBERS
5433+3196 çâbâ' (1), to *become tipsy*

WINEFAT
1660 gath (1), wine-*press* or *vat*
5276 hupŏlēniŏn (1), lower *wine vat*

WINEPRESS
1660 gath (2), wine-*press* or *vat*
3342 yeqeb (7), wine-*vat*, wine-*press*
6333 pûwrâh (1), *wine-press* trough
3025 lēnŏs (4), *trough*, i.e. wine-*vat*
3025+3631 lēnŏs (1), *trough*, i.e. wine-*vat*

WINEPRESSES
1660 gath (1), wine-*press*
3342 yeqeb (3), wine-*press*

WINES
8105 shemer (2), *settlings* of wine, *dregs*

WING
3671 kânâph (13), *edge* or *extremity; wing*

WINGED
3671 kânâph (2), *edge* or *extremity; wing*

WINGS
34 'ebyôwn (1), *destitute; poor*
83 'êber (2), *pinion*
84 'ebrâh (1), *pinion*
1611 gaph (Ch.) (3), *wing*
3671 kânâph (60), *edge* or *extremity; wing*
6731 tsîyts (1), *wing*
4420 ptĕrux (5), *wing*

WINK
7169 qârats (1), to *blink*
7335 râzam (1), to *twinkle* the eye

WINKED
5237 hupĕrĕidŏ (1), to *not punish*

WINKETH
7169 qârats (2), to *blink*

WINNETH
3947 lâqach (1), to *take*

WINNOWED
2219 zârâh (1), to *winnow*

WINNOWETH
2219 zârâh (1), to *winnow*

WINTER
2778 châraph (2), to spend the *winter*
2779 chôreph (3), *autumn, ripeness* of age
5638 çethâv (1), *winter*
3914 parachĕimazŏ (3), to *spend the winter*
3915 parachĕimasia (1), *wintering* over
5494 chĕimôn (4), *winter*

WINTERED
3916 parachrēma (1), *instantly, immediately*

WINTERHOUSE
2779 chôreph (1), *autumn* (and winter)

WIPE
4229 mâchâh (3), to *erase;* to *grease*
631 apŏmassŏmai (1), to *scrape away, wipe off*
1591 ĕkmassŏ (2), to *wipe dry*
1813 ĕxalĕiphŏ (2), to *obliterate*

WIPED
4229 mâchâh (1), to *erase;* to *grease*
1591 ĕkmassŏ (3), to *wipe dry*

WIPETH
4229 mâchâh (2), to *erase;* to *grease*

WIPING
4229 mâchâh (1), to *erase;* to *grease*

WIRES
6616 pâthîyl (1), *twine, cord*

WISDOM
998 bîynâh (2), *understanding*
2449 châkam (1), to *be wise*
2451 chokmâh (144), *wisdom*
2452 chokmâh (Ch.) (8), *wisdom*
2454 chokmôwth (4), *wisdom*
2942 ṭeʿêm (Ch.) (1), *judgment; account*
3820 lêb (6), *heart*
6195 'ormâh (1), *trickery; discretion*
7919 sâkal (2), to *be* or *act circumspect*
7922 sekel (3), *intelligence; success*
8394 tâbûwn (1), *intelligence; argument*
8454 tûwshîyâh (7), *undertaking*
4678 sŏphia (51), *wisdom*
5428 phrŏnēsis (1), *moral insight, understanding*

WISE
995 bîyn (3), to *understand; discern*
2445 chakkîym (Ch.) (14), *wise one*
2449 châkam (19), to *be wise*
2450 châkâm (122), *wise, intelligent, skillful*
2454 chokmôwth (1), *wisdom*
3198 yâkach (1), to *be correct;* to *argue*
3823 lâbab (1), *transport* with love; to *stultify*
6031 'ânâh (1), to *afflict, be afflicted*
6493 piqqêach (1), *clear-sighted*
7919 sâkal (12), to *be* or *act circumspect*
7922 sekel (1), *intelligence; success*

3097 magŏs (4), Oriental scientist, i.e. *magician*
3364 ŏu mē (1), *not* at all, *absolutely not*
3588+3838 hŏ (1), *"the,"* i.e. the definite article
3779 hŏutŏ (6), *in this way; likewise*
3843 pantŏs (1), *entirely; at all events*
4679 sŏphizŏ (1), to *make wise*
4680 sŏphŏs (21), *wise*
4920 suniēmi (1), to *comprehend*
5429 phrŏnimŏs (13), *sagacious* or *discreet*

WISELY
995 bîyn (1), to *understand; discern*
2449 châkam (2), to *be wise*
2451 chokmâh (2), *wisdom*
7919 sâkal (8), to *be* or *act circumspect*
5430 phrŏnimŏs (1), *prudently, shrewdly*

WISER
2449 châkam (4), to *be wise*
2450 châkâm (2), *wise, intelligent, skillful*
4680 sŏphŏs (1), *wise*
5429 phrŏnimŏs (1), *sagacious* or *discreet*

WISH
2655 châphêts (1), *pleased with*
4906 maskîyth (1), *carved figure*
6310 peh (1), *mouth*
2172 ĕuchŏmai (3), to *wish for;* to *pray*

WISHED
7592 shâ'al (1), to *ask*
2172 ĕuchŏmai (1), to *wish for;* to *pray*

WISHING
7592 shâ'al (1), to *ask*

WIST
3045 yâda' (7), to *know*
1492 ĕidŏ (6), to *know*

WIT
3045 yâda' (2), to *know*
1107 gnŏrizŏ (1), to *make known, reveal*
5613 hŏs (1), *which, how*

WIT'S
2451 chokmâh (1), *wisdom*

WITCH
3784 kâshaph (2), to *enchant*

WITCHCRAFT
3784 kâshaph (1), to *enchant*
7081 qeçem (1), *divination*
5331 pharmakĕia (1), *magic, witchcraft*

WITCHCRAFTS
3785 kesheph (4), *magic, sorcery*

WITHAL
834+3605 'âsher (1), *who, which, what, that*
1992 hêm (1), *they*
2004 hên (3), *they*
3162 yachad (2), *unitedly*
5973 'îm (1), *with*
260 hama (3), *at the same time, together*

WITHDRAW
622 'âçaph (4), to *gather, collect*
3240 yânach (1), to *allow to stay*
3365 yâqar (1), to *be valuable;* to *make rare*
5493 çûwr (1), to *turn off*
7368 râchaq (1), to *recede*
7725 shûwb (1), to *turn back;* to *return*
868 aphistēmi (1), to *desist, desert*
4724 stĕllŏ (1), to *repress*

WITHDRAWEST
7725 shûwb (1), to *turn back;* to *return*

WITHDRAWETH
1639 gâra' (1), to *shave, remove, lessen*

WITHDRAWN
2502 châlats (1), to *pull off;* to *strip;* to *depart*
2559 châmaq (1), to *depart,* i.e. turn about
5080 nâdach (1), to *push off, scattered*
7725 shûwb (2), to *turn back;* to *return*
645 apŏspaŏ (1), *withdraw* with force

WITHDREW
5414+5437 nâthan (1), to *give*
7725 shûwb (1), to *turn back;* to *return*
402 anachŏrĕŏ (2), to *retire, withdraw*
5288 hupŏstĕllŏ (1), to *cower* or *shrink*
5298 hupŏchŏrĕŏ (1), to *vacate down,* i.e. *retire*

WITHER
3001 yâbêsh (8), to *wither*
5034 nâbêl (2), to *wilt*
7060 qâmal (1), to *wither*

WITHERED
3001 yâbêsh (11), to *wither*
6798 tsânam (1), to *blast*
3583 xērainŏ (9), to *shrivel,* to *mature*
3584 xērŏs (4), *withered*

WITHERETH
3001 yâbêsh (5), to *wither*
3583 xērainŏ (2), to *shrivel,* to *mature*
5352 phthinŏpŏrinŏs (1), *autumnal*

WITHHELD
2820 châsak (3), to *restrain* or *refrain*
4513 mâna' (3), to *deny, refuse*

WITHHELDEST
4513 mâna' (1), to *deny, refuse*

V

WITHHOLD
3240 yânach (1), to *allow to stay*
3607 kâlâ' (2), to *hold*
4513 mâna' (5), to *deny*
6113 'âtsar (1), to *hold*

WITHHOLDEN
1219 bâtsar (1), to *be inaccessible*
2254 châbal (1), to *bind by a pledge; to pervert*
4513 mâna' (8), to *deny, refuse*

WITHHOLDETH
2820 châsak (1), to *restrain or refrain*
4513 mâna' (1), to *deny, refuse*
6113 'âtsar (1), to *hold back; to maintain*
2722 katěchō (1), to *hold down fast*

WITHIN
413 'êl (2), *to, toward*
990 bețen (2), *belly; womb; body*
996 bêyn (1), *between*
1004 bayith (23), *house; temple; family, tribe*
1157 be'ad (3), *up to or over against*
2315 cheder (1), *apartment, chamber*
2436 chêyq (1), *bosom, heart*
4481 min (Ch.) (1), *from or out of*
5704 'ad (2), *as far (long) as; during; while; until*
5705 'ad (Ch.) (1), *as far (long) as; during*
5750 'ôwd (4), *again; repeatedly; still; more*
5921 'al (8), *above, over, upon, or against*
5978 'immâd (1), *along with*
6440 pânîym (1), *face; front*
6441 pe'nîymâh (10), *indoors, inside*
6442 pe'nîymîy (1), *interior, inner*
7130 qereb (26), *nearest part, i.e. the center*
7146 qârachath (1), *bald spot; threadbare spot*
8432 tâvek (20), *center, middle*
8537 tôm (1), *completeness*
1223 dia (1), *through, by means of; because of*
1722 ĕn (13), *in; during; because of*
1737 ĕndidukō (1), to *clothe*
1787 ĕntŏs (1), *inside, within*
2080 ĕsō (3), *inside, inner, in*
2081 ĕsōthĕn (10), *from inside; inside*
2082 ĕsōtĕrŏs (1), *interior, inner*
4314 prŏs (1), *for; on, at; to, toward; against*

WITHOUT
268 'âchôwr (1), *behind, backward; west*
369 'ayin (42), *there is no, i.e., not exist, none*
657 'epheç (3), *end; no further*
1097 be'lîy (16), *without, not yet; lacking;*
1107 bil'ădêy (4), *except, without, besides*
1115 biltîy (4), *not, except, without, unless*
1372 gabbachath (1), *baldness on forehead*
2351 chûwts (71), *outside, outdoors*
2435 chîytsôwn (5), *outer wall side; exterior*
2600 chinnâm (17), *gratis, free*
2963 țâraph (1), to *pluck off or pull to pieces*
3808 lô' (29), *no, not*
3809 lâ' (Ch.) (1), *as nothing*
4682 matstsâh (1), *unfermented cake*
5493 çûwr (1), to *turn off*
7387 rêyqâm (2), *emptily; ineffectually*
8267 sheqer (1), *untruth; sham*
8414 tôhûw (2), *waste, desolation, formless*
8549 tâmîym (50), *entire, complete; integrity*
35 agĕnĕalŏgĕtŏs (1), *unregistered as to birth*
77 adapanŏs (1), *free of charge*
87 adiakritŏs (1), *impartial*
88 adialĕiptŏs (1), *permanent, constant*
89 adialĕiptŏs (4), *without omission*
112 athĕŏs (1), *godless*
175 akarpŏs (1), *barren, unfruitful*
186 aklinĕs (1), *firm, unswerving*
194 akratŏs (1), *undiluted*
267 amarturŏs (1), *without witness*
275 amĕrimnŏs (1), *not anxious, free of care*
278 amĕtamĕlĕtŏs (1), *irrevocable*
280 amĕtrŏs (2), *immoderate*
282 amĕtōr (1), *of unknown maternity*
298 amōmĕtŏs (1), *unblemished*
299 amōmŏs (5), *unblemished, blameless*
361 anamartĕtŏs (1), *sinless*
369 anantirrhĕtŏs (1), *without raising objection*
379 anapŏlŏgĕtŏs (1), *without excuse*
427 anĕu (3), *without, apart from*
448 anilĕŏs (1), *inexorable, merciless*

459 anŏmŏs (4), *without Jewish law*
460 anŏmŏs (2), *lawlessly, i.e. apart from Jewish Law*
504 anudrŏs (2), *dry, arid*
505 anupŏkritŏs (2), *sincere, genuine*
540 apatōr (1), *of unrecorded paternity*
563 apĕrispastŏs (1), *undistractedly*
677 aprŏskŏpŏs (1), *faultless*
678 aprŏsōpŏlĕptōs (1), *without prejudice*
729 arrhaphŏs (1), *of a single piece, without seam*
772 asthĕnĕs (1), *strengthless, weak*
784 aspilŏs (3), *unblemished*
794 astŏrgŏs (2), *hard-hearted*
801 asunĕtŏs (3), *senseless, dull; wicked*
815 atĕknŏs (2), *childless*
817 atĕr (1), *apart from, without*
820 atimŏs (2), *without honor*
866 aphilargurŏs (1), *not greedy*
870 aphŏbŏs (4), *fearlessly*
880 aphōnŏs (1), *mute, silent; unmeaning*
886 achĕirŏpŏiĕtŏs (2), *unmanufactured*
895 apsuchŏs (1), *lifeless, i.e. inanimate*
1432 dōrĕan (1), *gratuitously, freely*
1500 ĕikē (1), *idly, i.e. without reason or effect*
1618 ĕktĕnĕs (1), *intent, earnest*
1622 ĕktŏs (1), *aside from, besides; except*
1854 ĕxō (23), *out, outside*
1855 ĕxōthĕn (6), *outside, external (-ly)*
2673 katargĕō (1), to *be, render entirely useless*
3361 mē (1), *not; lest*
3672 hŏmŏlŏgŏumĕnōs (1), *confessedly*
3924 parĕktŏs (1), *besides; apart from*
5565 chōris (36), *at a space, i.e. separately*

WITHS
3499 yether (3), *remainder; small rope*

WITHSTAND
2388 châzaq (2), to *bind, restrain, conquer*
3320 yâtsab (1), to *station, offer, continue*
5975 'âmad (4), to *stand*
7854 sâțân (1), *opponent*
436 anthistĕmi (1), *oppose, rebel*
2967 kōluō (1), to *stop*

WITHSTOOD
5975 'âmad (2), to *stand*

436 anthistĕmi (4), *oppose, rebel*

WITNESS
5707 'êd (45), *witness; testimony*
5711 'Ădâh (1), *ornament*
5713 'êdâh (3), *testimony*
5715 'êdûwth (4), *testimony*
5749 'ûwd (5), to *protest, testify; to encompass*
6030 'ânâh (2), to *respond, answer*
8085 shâma' (1), to *hear intelligently*
267 amarturŏs (1), *without witness*
2649 katamartureō (4), to *testify against*
3140 martureō (28), to *testify; to commend*
3141 marturia (15), *evidence given*
3142 marturiŏn (4), *something evidential; the Decalogue*
3144 martus (8), *witness*
4828 summartureō (3), to *testify jointly*
4901 sunĕpimartureō (1), to *testify further jointly*
5576 psĕudŏmartureō (6), to *be an untrue testifier*
5577 psĕudŏmarturia (2), *untrue testimony*

WITNESSED
5749 'ûwd (1), to *protest, testify; to encompass*
3140 martureō (3), to *testify; to commend*

WITNESSES
5707 'êd (23), *witness; testimony*
3140 martureō (1), to *testify; to commend*
3144 martus (21), *witness*
5575 psĕudŏmartur (3), *bearer of untrue testimony*

WITNESSETH
1263 diamarturŏmai (1), to *attest or protest*
3140 martureō (1), to *testify; to commend*

WITNESSING
3140 martureō (1), to *testify; to commend*

WITTINGLY
7919 sâkal (1), to *be or act circumspect*

WIVES
802 'ishshâh (115), *woman, wife*
5389 nâshîyn (Ch.) (1), *women, wives*
7695 shêgâl (Ch.) (3), *queen*
1135 gunē (12), *woman; wife*

WIVES'
1126 graŏdēs (1), *old lady-like, i.e. silly*

WIZARD
3049 yidde'ônîy (2), *conjurer; ghost*

WIZARDS
3049 yidd^e'ônîy (9), conjurer; ghost

WOE
188 'ôwy (22), Oh!, Woe!
190 'ôwyâh (1), Oh!, Woe!
337 'îy (2), alas!
480 'al^{e}lay (2), alas!; woe!
1929 hâhh (1), ah!; woe!
1945 hôwy (36), oh!, woe!
1958 hîy (1), lamentation, woe
3759 ŏuai (39), woe!; woe

WOEFUL
605 'ânash (1), to be frail, feeble

WOES
3759 ŏuai (1), woe!; woe

WOLF
2061 z^e'êb (4), wolf
3074 lukŏs (2), wolf

WOLVES
2061 z^e'êb (3), wolf
3074 lukŏs (4), wolf

WOMAN
802 'ishshâh (211), woman, wife
5291 na'ărâh (1), female child; servant
5347 n^{e}qêbâh (2), female, woman
1135 gunē (96), woman; wife
1658 ĕlĕuthĕrŏs (1), not a slave
2338 thēlus (1), female

WOMAN'S
802 'ishshâh (7), woman

WOMANKIND
802 'ishshâh (1), woman, wife; women, wives

WOMB
990 beţen (31), belly; womb; body
4578 mê'âh (1), viscera; anguish, tenderness
7356 racham (4), compassion; womb
7358 rechem (20), womb
1064 gastēr (1), stomach; womb; gourmand
2836 kŏilia (11), abdomen, womb, heart
3388 mētra (2), womb

WOMBS
7358 rechem (1), womb
2836 kŏilia (1), abdomen, womb, heart

WOMEN
802 'ishshâh (104), woman, wife
5347 n^{e}qêbâh (1), female
1133 gunaikariŏn (1), little woman
1135 gunē (33), woman
2338 thēlus (1), female
4247 prĕsbutis (1), old woman

WOMEN'S
802 'ishshâh (1), woman

WOMENSERVANTS
8198 shiphchâh (3), household female slave

WON
2770 kĕrdainō (1), to gain; to spare

WONDER
4159 môwphêth (6), miracle; token or omen
6382 pele' (1), miracle
8539 tâmahh (3), to be astounded
2285 thambŏs (1), astonishment
2296 thaumazō (2), to wonder; to admire
4592 sēmĕiŏn (2), indication, sign, signal

WONDERED
4159 môwphêth (1), miracle; token or omen
8074 shâmêm (2), to devastate; to stupefy
1839 ĕxistēmi (1), to astound
2296 thaumazō (11), to wonder; to admire

WONDERFUL
6381 pâlâ' (13), to be, make great
6382 pele' (3), miracle
6383 pil'îy (1), remarkable
8047 shammâh (1), ruin; consternation
1411 dunamis (1), force, power, miracle
2297 thaumasiŏs (1), miracle, wondrous act
3167 mĕgalĕiŏs (1), great things, wonderful works

WONDERFULLY
5953 'âlal (1), to glean; to overdo
6381 pâlâ' (1), to be, make wonderful
6382 pele' (1), miracle
6395 pâlâh (1), to distinguish

WONDERING
7583 shâ'âh (1), to be astonished
1569 ĕkthambŏs (1), utterly astounded
2296 thaumazō (1), to wonder; to admire

WONDEROUSLY
6381 pâlâ' (1), to be, make wonderful

WONDERS
4159 môwphêth (19), miracle; token or omen
6381 pâlâ' (9), to be, make wonderful
6382 pele' (7), miracle
8540 t^{e}mahh (Ch.) (3), miracle
4592 sēmĕiŏn (1), indication, sign, signal
5059 tĕras (16), omen or miracle sign

WONDROUS
4652 miphlâ'âh (1), miracle
6381 pâlâ' (14), to be, make wonderful

WONDROUSLY
6381 pâlâ' (1), to be, make wonderful

WONT
1696 dâbar (1), to speak, say; to subdue
1980 hâlak (1), to walk; live a certain way
2370 châzâ' (Ch.) (1), to gaze upon; to dream
5056 naggâch (1), act of butting
5532 çâkan (1), to be serviceable to
1486 ĕthō (2), to be used by habit
2596+1485 kata (1), down; according to
3543 nŏmizō (1), to deem

WOOD
636 'â' (Ch.) (2), tree; wood; plank
2793 chôresh (4), wooded forest
3293 ya'ar (18), honey in the comb
6086 'êts (106), wood
3585 xulinŏs (2), made of wood
3586 xulŏn (3), timber and its products

WOODS
3264 yâ'ôwr (1), forest

WOOF
6154 'êreb (9), mixed or woven things

WOOL
6015 'ămar (Ch.) (1), wool
6785 tsemer (11), wool
2053 ĕriŏn (2), wool

WOOLLEN
6785 tsemer (5), wool
8162 sha'aţnêz (1), linen and woolen

WORD
562 'ômer (2), something said
565 'imrâh (26), something said
1697 dâbâr (433), word; matter; thing
1699 dôber (2), grazing pasture
3983 mê'mar (Ch.) (1), edict, command
4405 millâh (2), word; discourse; speech
4406 millâh (Ch.) (2), word, command
6310 peh (15), mouth; opening
6600 pithgâm (Ch.) (1), decree; report
518 apaggĕllō (2), to announce, proclaim
2036 ĕpō (1), to speak
3050 lŏgikŏs (1), rational, logical
3056 lŏgŏs (173), word, matter, thing; Word
4487 rhēma (28), utterance; matter

WORD'S
1697 dâbâr (1), word; matter; thing
3056 lŏgŏs (1), word, matter, thing; Word

WORDS
561 'êmer (42), something said
565 'imrâh (3), something said
1697 dâbâr (373), word; matter; thing
1703 dabbârâh (1), word, instruction
4405 millâh (21), word; discourse; speech
4406 millâh (Ch.) (5), word, command
3054 lŏgŏmachĕō (1), to be disputatious
3055 lŏgŏmachia (1), disputation
3056 lŏgŏs (48), word, matter, thing; Word
4086 pithanŏlŏgia (1), persuasive language
4487 rhēma (31), utterance; matter
5542 chrēstŏlŏgia (1), fair speech

WORK
731 'arzâh (1), cedar paneling
1697 dâbâr (1), word; matter; thing
3018 y^{e}gîya' (1), toil, work; produce, property
3027 yâd (1), hand; power
3336 yêtser (1), form
4399 m^{e}lâ'kâh (125), work; property
4639 ma'ăseh (113), action; labor
4640 Ma'say (1), operative
4649 Muppîym (1), wavings
4749 miqshâh (5), work molded by hammering
5627 çârâh (1), apostasy; crime; remission
5647 'âbad (4), to do, work, serve
5656 'ăbôdâh (10), work
5673 'ăbîydâh (Ch.) (3), labor or business
5950 'ălîylîyâh (2), execution, deed
6213 'âsâh (23), to do
6381 pâlâ' (2), to be, make wonderful
6466 pâ'al (5), to do, make or practice
6467 pô'al (28), act or work, deed
6468 p^e'ullâh (8), work
6603 pittûwach (1), sculpture; engraving
7553 riqmâh (1), variegation of color
7639 s^{e}bâkâh (2), reticulated ornament
1411 dunamis (1), force, power, miracle
1754 ĕnĕrgĕō (2), to be active, efficient, work
2038 ĕrgazŏmai (12), to toil
2039 ĕrgasia (1), occupation; profit
2040 ĕrgatēs (1), toiler, worker
2041 ĕrgŏn (45), work

W

2716 katĕrgazŏmai (1),
to finish; to accomplish
3056 lŏgŏs (2), word,
matter, thing; Word
3433+2480 mŏlis (1), with
difficulty
4229 pragma (1), matter,
deed, affair
4903 sunĕrgĕŏ (1), to be
a fellow-worker

WORK'S
2041 ĕrgŏn (1), work

WORKER
2790 chârash (1), to
engrave; to plow

WORKERS
2796 chârâsh (1), skilled
fabricator or worker
6213 'âsâh (1), to do
6466 pâ'al (1), to do,
make or practice
1411 dunamis (1), force,
power, miracle
2040 ĕrgatēs (3), toiler,
worker
4903 sunĕrgĕŏ (1), to be
a fellow-worker

WORKETH
5648 'âbad (Ch.) (1), to
work, serve
6213 'âsâh (6), to do or
make
6466 pâ'al (4), to do,
make or practice
1754 ĕnĕrgĕŏ (11), to be
active, efficient, work
2038 ĕrgazŏmai (7), to
toil
2716 katĕrgazŏmai (7),
to finish; to accomplish
4160 pŏiĕŏ (1), to make
or do

WORKFELLOW
4904 sunĕrgŏs (1),
fellow-worker

WORKING
4639 ma'ăseh (1), action;
labor
6213 'âsâh (1), to do or
make
6466 pâ'al (1), to do,
make or practice
8454 tûwshîyâh (1),
ability, i.e. direct help
1753 ĕnĕrgĕia (6),
efficiency, energy
1755 ĕnĕrgēma (1),
effect, activity
2038 ĕrgazŏmai (4), to
toil
2716 katĕrgazŏmai (2),
to finish; to accomplish
4160 pŏiĕŏ (2), to make
or do
4903 sunĕrgĕŏ (1), to be
a fellow-worker

WORKMAN
542 'âmân (1), expert
artisan, craftsman
2796 chârâsh (5), skilled
fabricator or worker
2803 châshab (2), to
weave, fabricate
2040 ĕrgatēs (2), toiler,
worker

WORKMANSHIP
4399 mᵉlâ'kâh (5), work;
property
4639 ma'ăseh (1), action;
labor
4161 pŏiēma (1), what is
made, product

WORKMEN
582+4399 'ĕnôwsh (1),
man; person, human
2796 chârâsh (1), skilled
fabricator or worker
6213+4399 'âsâh (7), to
do or make
2040 ĕrgatēs (1), toiler,
worker

WORKMEN'S
6001 'âmêl (1), toiling;
laborer; sorrowful

WORKS
1697 dâbâr (1), word;
matter; thing
4399 mᵉlâ'kâh (3), work;
property
4566 ma'bâd (1), act,
deed
4567 ma'bâd (Ch.) (1),
act, deed
4611 ma'ălâl (3), act,
deed
4639 ma'ăseh (70),
action; labor
4640 Ma'say (2),
operative
4659 miph'âl (3),
performance, deed
5652 'ăbâd (1), deed
5949 'ălîylâh (3),
opportunity, action
6467 pô'al (2), act or
work, deed
6468 pᵉ'ullâh (1), work,
deed
2041 ĕrgŏn (104), work
4234 praxis (1), act;
function

WORKS'
2041 ĕrgŏn (1), work

WORLD
776 'erets (4), earth,
land, soil; country
2309 chedel (1), state of
the dead, deceased
2465 cheled (2), fleeting
time; this world
5769 'ôwlâm (4), eternity;
ancient; always
8398 têbêl (35), earth;
world; inhabitants
165 aiōn (37), perpetuity,
ever; world
166 aiōniŏs (3),
perpetual, long ago
1093 gē (1), soil, region,
whole earth
2889 kŏsmŏs (183), world
3625 ŏikŏuměnē (14),
Roman empire

WORLD'S
2889 kŏsmŏs (1), world

WORLDLY
2886 kŏsmikŏs (2),
earthly, worldly

WORLDS
165 aiōn (2), perpetuity,
ever; world

WORM
5580 çâç (1), garment
moth
7415 rimmâh (5), maggot
8438 tôwlâ' (5), maggot
worm; crimson-grub
4663 skōlĕx (3), grub,
maggot or earth-worm

WORMS
2119 zâchal (1), to crawl;
glide
7415 rimmâh (2), maggot
8438 tôwlâ' (3), maggot
worm; crimson-grub
4662 skōlĕkŏbrōtŏs (1),
diseased with maggots

WORMWOOD
3939 la'ănâh (7),
poisonous wormwood
894 apsinthŏs (2),
wormwood, bitterness

WORSE
2196 zâ'aph (1), to be
angry
5062 nâgaph (5), to
inflict a disease
7451 ra' (1), bad; evil
7489 râ'a' (5), to be good
for nothing
1640 ĕlasson (1), smaller
2276 hēttŏn (1), worse
5302 hustĕrĕŏ (1), to be
inferior; to fall short
5501 chĕirōn (10), more
evil or aggravated

WORSHIP
5457 çᵉgîd (Ch.) (8), to
prostrate oneself
6087 'âtsab (1), to
fabricate or fashion
7812 shâchâh (54), to
prostrate in homage
1391 dŏxa (1), glory;
brilliance
1479 ĕthĕlŏthrēskĕia (1),
voluntary piety
2151 ĕusĕbĕŏ (1), to put
religion into practice
3000 latrĕuŏ (3), to
minister to God
4352 prŏskunĕŏ (34), to
prostrate oneself
4352+1799 prŏskunĕŏ (1),
to prostrate oneself
4576 sĕbŏmai (3), to
revere, i.e. adore

WORSHIPPED
5457 çᵉgîd (Ch.) (2), to
prostrate oneself
7812 shâchâh (39), to
prostrate in homage
2323 thĕrapĕuŏ (1), to
adore God
4352 prŏskunĕŏ (24), to
prostrate oneself
4573 sĕbazŏmai (1), to
venerate, worship
4574 sĕbasma (1), object
of worship
4576 sĕbŏmai (2), to
revere, i.e. adore

WORSHIPPER
2318 thĕŏsĕbēs (1), pious,
devout, God-fearing
3511 nĕŏkŏrŏs (1),
temple servant

WORSHIPPERS
5647 'âbad (5), to serve
3000 latrĕuŏ (1), to
minister to God
4353 prŏskunētēs (1),
adorer

WORSHIPPETH
5457 çᵉgîd (Ch.) (2), to
prostrate oneself
7812 shâchâh (3), to
prostrate in homage
4576 sĕbŏmai (1), to
revere, i.e. adore

WORSHIPPING
7812 shâchâh (3), to
prostrate in homage
2356 thrēskĕia (1),
observance, religion
4352 prŏskunĕŏ (1), to
prostrate oneself

WORST
7451 ra' (1), bad; evil

WORTH
3644 kᵉmôw (1), like, as;
for; with
4242 mᵉchîyr (1), price,
payment, wages
4373 mikçâh (1),
valuation of a thing
4392 mâlê' (1), full;
filling; fulness; fully
7939 sâkâr (1), payment,
salary; compensation

WORTHIES
117 'addîyr (1), powerful;
majestic

WORTHILY
2428 chayil (1), army;
wealth; virtue; valor

WORTHY
376 'îysh (1), man; male;
someone
639 'aph (1), nose or
nostril; face; person
1121 bên (2), son,
descendant; people
2428 chayil (1), army;
wealth; virtue; valor
6994 qâtôn (1), to be,
make diminutive
514 axiŏs (35), deserving,
comparable or suitable
515 axiŏŏ (5), to deem
entitled or fit, worthy
516 axiŏs (3),
appropriately, suitable
2425 hikanŏs (5), ample;
fit
2570 kalŏs (1), good;
beautiful; valuable
2661 kataxiŏŏ (4), to
deem entirely deserving
2735 katŏrthōma (1),
made fully upright

WOT
3045 yâda' (6), to know
1107 gnōrizō (1), to
make known, reveal
1492 ĕidō (3), to know

WOTTETH
3045 yâda' (1), to know

WOULD
14 'âbâh (41), to be
acquiescent
305 'achălay (1), would
that!, Oh that!, If Only!

2654 châphêts (1), to be pleased with, desire
2655 châphêts (1), pleased with
2974 yâ'al (3), to assent; to undertake, begin
3863 lûw' (6), would that!
5315 nephesh (1), life; breath; soul; wind
6634 ts°bâ' (Ch.) (5), to please
1096 ginŏmai (1), to be, become
2172 ĕuchŏmai (1), to wish for; to pray
2309 thělō (73), to will; to desire; to choose
3195 mĕllō (9), to intend, i.e. be about to
3785 ŏphělŏn (4), I wish

WOULDEST
3426 yêsh (1), there is
2309 thělō (4), to will; to desire; to choose

WOUND
2671 chêts (1), arrow; wound; thunder-bolt
4204 mâzôwr (1), ambush
4205 mâzôwr (2), sore
4272 mâchats (3), to crush; to subdue
4347 makkâh (8), blow; wound; pestilence
5061 nega' (1), infliction, affliction; leprous spot
6482 petsa' (2), wound
1210 děŏ (1), to bind
4127 plēgē (3), stroke; wound; calamity
4958 sustěllō (1), to draw together, i.e. enwrap or enshroud a corpse
5180 tuptō (1), to strike, beat, wound

WOUNDED
1214 bâtsa' (1), to plunder; to finish
1795 dakkâh (1), mutilated by crushing
1856 dâqar (1), to stab, pierce; to starve
2342 chûwl (2), to dance, whirl; to writhe in pain
2470 châlâh (3), to be weak, sick, afflicted
2490 châlal (3), to profane, defile
2491 châlâl (10), pierced to death, one slain
4272 mâchats (2), to crush; to subdue
4347 makkâh (1), blow; wound; pestilence
5218 nâkê' (1), smitten; afflicted
5221 nâkâh (3), to strike, kill
6481 pâtsa' (2), to wound
4127+2007 plēgē (1), stroke; wound
4969 sphazō (1), to slaughter or to maim
5135 traumatizō (2), to inflict a wound

WOUNDEDST
4272 mâchats (1), to crush; to subdue

WOUNDETH
4272 mâchats (1), to crush; to subdue

WOUNDING
6482 petsa' (1), wound

WOUNDS
2250 chabbûwrâh (1), weal, bruise
3859 lâham (2), to rankle
4347 makkâh (6), blow; wound; pestilence
6094 'atstsebeth (1), pain or wound, sorrow
6482 petsa' (4), wound
5134 trauma (1), wound

WOVE
707 'ârag (1), to plait or weave

WOVEN
707 'ârag (3), to plait or weave
5307 huphantŏs (1), knitted, woven

WRAP
3664 kânaç (1), to collect; to enfold
5686 'âbath (1), to pervert

WRAPPED
1563 gâlam (1), to fold
2280 châbash (1), to wrap firmly, bind
3874 lûwṭ (2), to wrap up
4593 mâ'ôṭ (1), sharp, thin-edged
5440 çâbak (1), to entwine
5968 'âlaph (1), to be languid, faint
8276 sârag (1), to entwine
1750 ĕnĕilĕō (1), to enwrap
1794 ĕntulissō (3), wind up in, enwrap
4683 sparganŏō (2), to strap or wrap

WRATH
639 'aph (42), nose or nostril; face; person
2197 za'aph (1), anger, rage
2534 chêmâh (34), heat; anger; poison
2740 chârôwn (6), burning of anger
3707 kâ'aç (1), to grieve, rage, be indignant
3708 ka'aç (4), vexation, grief
5678 'ebrâh (31), outburst of passion
7107 qâtsaph (5), to burst out in rage
7109 q°tsaph (Ch.) (1), rage
7110 qetseph (23), rage or strife
7265 r°gaz (Ch.) (1), to quiver
7267 rôgez (1), disquiet; anger
2372 thumŏs (14), passion, anger
3709 ŏrgē (31), ire; punishment
3949 parŏrgizō (1), to enrage, exasperate

3950 parŏrgismŏs (1), rage

WRATHFUL
2534 chêmâh (1), heat; anger; poison
2740 chârôwn (1), burning of anger

WRATHS
2372 thumŏs (1), passion, anger

WREATH
7639 s°bâkâh (1), reticulated ornament

WREATHED
8276 sârag (1), to entwine

WREATHEN
5688 'âbôth (8), entwined things: a string, wreath
7639 s°bâkâh (2), reticulated ornament

WREATHS
1434 g°dîl (1), tassel; festoon
7639 s°bâkâh (2), reticulated ornament

WREST
5186 nâṭâh (3), to stretch or spread out
6087 'âtsab (1), to fabricate or fashion
4761 strĕblŏō (1), to pervert, twist

WRESTLE
2076+3823 ĕsti (1), he (she or it) is; they are

WRESTLED
79 'âbaq (2), grapple, wrestle
6617 pâthal (1), to struggle; to be tortuous

WRESTLINGS
5319 naphtûwl (1), struggle

WRETCHED
5005 talaipŏrŏs (2), miserable, wretched

WRETCHEDNESS
7451 ra' (1), bad; evil

WRING
4454 mâlaq (2), to wring a bird's neck
4680 mâtsâh (1), to drain; to squeeze out

WRINGED
4680 mâtsâh (1), to drain; to squeeze out

WRINGING
4330 mîyts (1), pressure

WRINKLE
4512 rhutis (1), face wrinkle

WRINKLES
7059 qâmaṭ (1), to pluck, i.e. destroy

WRITE
3789 kâthab (35), to write
3790 k°thab (Ch.) (1), to write
1125 graphō (50), to write
1924 ĕpigraphō (2), inscribe, write upon
1989 ĕpistěllō (1), to communicate by letter

WRITER
5608 çâphar (2), to inscribe; to enumerate

WRITER'S
5608 çâphar (2), to inscribe; to enumerate

WRITEST
3789 kâthab (2), to write

WRITETH
3789 kâthab (1), to write

WRITING
3789 kâthab (1), to write
3791 kâthâb (14), writing, record or book
3792 k°thâb (Ch.) (10), writing, record or book
4385 miktâb (8), written thing
975 bibliŏn (1), scroll; certificate
1125 graphō (1), to write
4093 pinakidiŏn (1), wooden writing tablet

WRITINGS
1121 gramma (1), writing; education

WRITTEN
3789 kâthab (138), to write
3790 k°thab (Ch.) (2), to write
3792 k°thâb (Ch.) (1), writing, record or book
7560 r°sham (Ch.) (2), to record
583 apŏgraphō (1), enroll, take a census
1123 graptŏs (1), inscribed, written
1125 graphō (134), to write
1449 ĕggraphō (2), inscribe, write
1722+1121 ĕn (1), in; during; because of
1924 ĕpigraphō (2), to inscribe, write upon
1989 ĕpistěllō (1), to communicate by letter
4270 prŏgraphō (2), to write previously; to announce, prescribe

WRONG
2555 châmâç (3), violence; malice
3238 yânâh (1), to suppress; to maltreat
3808+4941 lō' (1), no, not
5627 çârâh (1), apostasy; crime; remission
5753 'âvâh (1), to be crooked
5792 'avvâthâh (1), oppression
6127 'âqal (1), to wrest, be crooked
6231 'âshaq (2), to violate; to overflow
7451 ra' (1), bad; evil
7563 râshâ' (1), morally wrong; bad person
91 adikĕō (11), to do wrong
92 adikēma (1), wrong
93 adikia (1), wrongfulness

W

WRONGED
91 adikĕō (2), to do wrong

WRONGETH
2554 châmaç (1), to be violent; to maltreat

WRONGFULLY
2554 châmaç (1), to be violent; to maltreat
3808+4941 lô' (1), no, not
8267 sheqer (4), untruth; sham
95 adikōs (1), unjustly

WROTE
3789 kâthab (34), to write
3790 kᵉthab (Ch.) (5), to write
1125 graphō (21), to write
4270 prōgraphō (1), to write previously; to announce, prescribe

WROTH
2196 zâ'aph (2), to be angry
2534 chêmâh (1), heat; anger; poison
2734 chârâh (13), to blaze up
3707 kâ'aç (1), to grieve, rage, be indignant
5674 'âbar (5), to cross over; to transition
7107 qâtsaph (22), to burst out in rage
7264 râgaz (1), to quiver
2373 thumŏō (1), to enrage
3710 ŏrgizō (3), to become exasperated

WROUGHT
1496 gâzîyth (1), dressed stone
1980 hâlak (2), to walk; live a certain way
2790 chârash (1), to engrave; to plow
4639 ma'ăseh (3), action; labor
4865 mishbᵉtsâh (1), reticulated setting
5647 'âbad (1), to do, work, serve
5648 'ăbad (Ch.) (1), to work, serve
5656 'ăbôdâh (1), work
5927 'âlâh (1), to ascend, be high, mount
5953 'âlal (2), to glean; to overdo
6213 'âsâh (52), to do
6466 pâ'al (7), to do, make or practice
7194 qâshar (1), to tie, bind
7551 râqam (1), variegation; embroider
7760 sûwm (1), to put, place
1096 ginōmai (2), to be, become
1754 ĕnĕrgĕō (2), to be active, efficient, work
2038 ĕrgazŏmai (7), to toil
2716 katĕrgazŏmai (6), to finish; to accomplish

4160 pŏiĕō (5), to make or do
4903 sunĕrgĕō (1), to be a fellow-worker

WROUGHTEST
6213 'âsâh (1), to make

WRUNG
4680 mâtsâh (4), to drain; to squeeze out

YARN
4723 miqveh (4), confidence; collection

YEA
432 'illûw (1), if
637 'aph (39), also or yea; though
834 'ăsher (1), who, which, what, that
1571 gam (66), also; even; yea; though
3588 kîy (7), for, that because
235 alla (15), but, yet, except, instead
1161 dĕ (13), but, yet; and then
2089 ĕti (1), yet, still
2228 ē (1), or; than
2532 kai (5), and; or; even; also
3304 mĕnŏungĕ (1), so then at least
3483 nai (22), yes

YEAR
3117 yôwm (6), day; time period
8140 shᵉnâh (Ch.) (5), year
8141 shâneh (323), year
1763 ĕniautŏs (13), year
2094 ĕtŏs (3), year
4070 pĕrusi (2), last year; from last year

YEAR'S
3117 yôwm (1), day; time period
8141 shâneh (1), year

YEARLY
3117 yôwm (6), day; time period
8141 shâneh (3), year

YEARN
3648 kâmar (1), to shrivel with heat

YEARNED
3648 kâmar (1), to shrivel with heat

YEARS
3027 yâd (1), hand; power
3117 yôwm (3), day; time period
8027 shâlash (2), to be, triplicate
8140 shᵉnâh (Ch.) (2), year
8141 shâneh (466), year
1096+3173 ginōmai (1), to be, become
1332 diĕtēs (1), of two years in age
1333 diĕtia (2), interval of two years
1541 hĕkatŏntaĕtēs (1), centenarian
1763 ĕniautŏs (2), year
2094 ĕtŏs (46), year

2250 hēmĕra (2), day; period of time
5063 tĕssarakŏntaĕtēs (2), of forty years of age
5148 triĕtia (1), triennium, three years

YEARS'
8141 shâneh (2), year

YELL
5286 nâ'ar (1), to growl

YELLED
5414+6963 nâthan (1), to give

YELLOW
3422 yᵉraqraq (1), yellowishness
6669 tsâhôb (3), golden in color

YES
3304 mĕnŏungĕ (1), so then at least
3483 nai (3), yes

YESTERDAY
570 'emesh (1), yesterday evening
865 'ethmôwl (1), heretofore, formerly
8543 tᵉmôwl (4), yesterday
5504 chthĕs (3), yesterday; in time past

YESTERNIGHT
570 'emesh (3), yesterday evening

YET
227 'âz (1), at that time or place; therefore
389 'ak (13), surely; only, however
559 'âmar (1), to say
637 'aph (1), also or yea
1297 bᵉram (Ch.) (2), however, but
1571 gam (14), also; even; yea; though
2962 ţerem (4), not yet or before
3588 kîy (14), for, that because
5704 'ad (4), as far (long) as; during; while; until
5728 'ăden (2), till now, yet
5750 'ôwd (142), again; repeatedly; still; more
7535 raq (2), merely; although
188 akmĕn (1), just now, still
235 alla (11), but, yet, except, instead
1063 gar (3), for, indeed, but, because
1065 gĕ (2), particle of emphasis
1161 dĕ (19), but, yet; and then
2089 ĕti (54), yet, still
2236 hēdista (2), with great pleasure
2532 kai (7), and; or; even; also
2539 kaipĕr (1), nevertheless
2579 kan (1), and (or even) if

2596 kata (2), down; according to
3195 mĕllō (1), to intend, i.e. be about to
3305 mĕntŏi (2), however
3364 ŏu mĕ (1), not at all, absolutely not
3369 mĕdĕpō (1), not even yet
3380 mēpō (1), not yet
3764 ŏudĕpō (4), not even yet
3765 ŏukĕti (3), not yet, no longer
3768 ŏupō (21), not yet

YIELD
3254 yâçaph (1), to add or augment
5186 nâţâh (1), to stretch or spread out
5375 nâsâ' (1), to lift up
5414 nâthan (13), to give
5414+3027 nâthan (1), to give
6213 'âsâh (6), to do or make
1325 didōmi (1), to give
3936 paristēmi (4), to stand beside, present
3982 pĕithō (1), to assent to authority
4160 pŏiĕō (1), to make or do

YIELDED
1478 gâva' (1), to expire, die
1580 gâmal (1), to benefit or requite; to wean
3052 yᵉhab (Ch.) (1), to give
591 apŏdidōmi (1), to give away
863 aphiēmi (1), to leave; to pardon, forgive
1325 didōmi (1), to give
1634 ĕkpsuchō (1), to expire, die
3936 paristēmi (1), to stand beside, present

YIELDETH
5414 nâthan (1), to give
7235 râbâh (1), to increase
591 apŏdidōmi (1), to give away

YIELDING
2232 zâra' (3), to sow seed; to disseminate
4832 marpê' (1), cure; deliverance; placidity
6213 'âsâh (3), to do or make

YOKE
4132 môwţ (1), pole; yoke
4133 môwţâh (4), pole; ox-bow; yoke
5923 'ôl (39), neck yoke
6776 tsemed (7), paired yoke
2201 zĕugŏs (1), team
2218 zugŏs (5), coupling, yoke

YOKED
2086 hĕtĕrŏzugĕō (1), to associate discordantly

YOKEFELLOW
4805 suzugŏs (1), colleague

YOKES
4133 môwṭâh (4), pole; ox-bow; yoke

YONDER
1973 hâlᵉâh (1), far away; thus far
3541 kôh (2), thus
5676 'êber (1), opposite side; east
5704+3541 'ad (1), as far (long) as; during; while; until
1563 ĕkĕi (2), there, thither

YOUNG
667 'ephrôach (4), brood of a bird
970 bâchûwr (42), male youth; bridegroom
979 bᵉchûrôwth (1), youth
1121 bên (20), son, descendant; people
1121+1241 bên (34), son, descendant; people
1123 bên (Ch.) (1), son
1241 bâqâr (1), plowing ox; herd
1469 gôwzâl (2), young of a bird
1482 gûwr (1), cub
3127 yôwneqeth (1), sprout, new shoot
3206 yeled (10), young male
3242 yᵉnîqâh (1), sucker or sapling
3715 kᵉphîyr (25), walled village; young lion
3833 lâbîy' (1), lion, lioness
5288 na'ar (92), male child; servant
5288+970 na'ar (1), male child; servant
5291 na'ărâh (6), female child; servant
5763 'ûwl (3), to suckle, i.e. give milk
5958 'elem (1), lad, young man
6082 'ôpher (5), dusty-colored fawn
6499 par (1), bullock
6810+3117 tsâ'îyr (1), young in value
6996 qâṭân (2), small, least, youngest
7988 shilyâh (1), fetus or infant baby
1025 brĕphŏs (1), infant
2365 thugatriŏn (1), little daughter
3494 nĕanias (5), youth, up to about forty years
3495 nĕaniskŏs (10), youth under forty
3501 nĕŏs (4), new
3502 nĕŏssŏs (1), young
3678 ŏnariŏn (1), little donkey
3813 paidiŏn (10), child; immature
3816 pais (1), child; slave or servant

YOUNGER
6810 tsâ'îyr (7), little, young
6810+3117 tsâ'îyr (1), little, young
6996 qâṭân (14), small, least, youngest
1640 ĕlassŏn (1), smaller
3501 nĕŏs (8), new

YOUNGEST
6810 tsâ'îyr (3), little, young
6996 qâṭân (15), small, least, youngest

YOUTH
979 bᵉchûrôwth (2), youth
2779 chôreph (1), autumn (and winter)
3208 yaldûwth (2), boyhood or girlhood
5271 nâ'ûwr (46), youth; juvenility; young people
5288 na'ar (5), male child; servant
5290 nô'ar (2), boyhood
5934 'âlûwm (4), adolescence; vigor
6526 pirchach (1), progeny, i.e. a brood
6812 tsᵉ'îyrâh (1), juvenility
7839 shachărûwth (1), juvenescence, youth
3503 nĕŏtēs (5), youthfulness

YOUTHFUL
3512 nĕŏtĕrikŏs (1), juvenile, youthful

YOUTHS
1121 bên (1), son, descendant; people
5288 na'ar (1), male child; servant

ZAANAIM
6815 Tsa'ănannîym (1), removals

ZAANAN
6630 Tsa'ănân (1), sheep pasture

ZAANANNIM
6815 Tsa'ănannîym (1), removals

ZAAVAN
2190 Za'ăvân (1), disquiet

ZABAD
2066 Zâbâd (8), giver

ZABBAI
2079 Zabbay (2), Zabbai

ZABBUD
2072 Zabbûwd (1), given

ZABDI
2067 Zabdîy (6), giving

ZABDIEL
2068 Zabdîy'êl (2), gift of God

ZABUD
2071 Zâbûwd (1), given

ZABULON
2194 Zabŏulŏn (3), habitation

ZACCAI
2140 Zakkay (2), pure

ZACCHAEUS
2195 Zakchaiŏs (3), Zacchæus

ZACCHUR
2139 Zakkûwr (1), mindful

ZACCUR
2139 Zakkûwr (8), mindful

ZACHARIAH
2148 Zᵉkaryâh (4), Jehovah has remembered

ZACHARIAS
2197 Zacharias (11), Jehovah has remembered

ZACHER
2144 Zeker (1), recollection; commemoration

ZADOK
6659 Tsâdôwq (52), just

ZADOK'S
6659 Tsâdôwq (1), just

ZAHAM
2093 Zaham (1), loathing

ZAIR
6811 Tsâ'îyr (1), little

ZALAPH
6764 Tsâlâph (1), Tsalaph

ZALMON
6756 Tsalmôwn (2), shady

ZALMONAH
6758 Tsalmônâh (2), shadiness

ZALMUNNA
6759 Tsalmunnâ' (12), shade has been denied

ZAMZUMMIMS
2157 Zamzôm (1), intriguing

ZANOAH
2182 Zânôwach (5), rejected

ZAPHNATH-PAANEAH
6847 Tsophnath Pa'nêach (1), Tsophnath-Paneäch

ZAPHON
6829 Tsâphôwn (1), boreal, northern

ZARA
2196 Zara (1), rising of light, dawning

ZARAH
2226 Zerach (2), rising of light, dawning

ZAREAH
6881 Tsor'âh (1), stinging wasp

ZAREATHITES
6882 Tsor'îy (1), Tsorite or Tsorathite

ZARED
2218 Zered (1), lined with shrubbery

ZAREPHATH
6886 Tsârᵉphath (3), refinement

ZARETAN
6891 Tsârᵉthân (1), Tsarethan

ZARETH-SHAHAR
6890 Tsereth hash-Shachar (1), splendor of the dawn

ZARHITES
2227 Zarchîy (6), Zarchite

ZARTANAH
6891 Tsârᵉthân (1), Tsarethan

ZARTHAN
6891 Tsârᵉthân (1), Tsarethan

ZATTHU
2240 Zattûw' (1), Zattu

ZATTU
2240 Zattûw' (3), Zattu

ZAVAN
2190 Za'ăvân (1), disquiet

ZAZA
2117 Zâzâ' (1), prominent

ZEAL
7065 qânâ' (1), to be, make zealous, jealous or envious
7068 qin'âh (9), jealousy or envy
2205 zēlŏs (6), zeal, ardor; jealousy, malice

ZEALOUS
7065 qânâ' (2), to be, make zealous
2206 zēlŏŏ (1), to have warmth of feeling for
2207 zēlôtēs (5), zealot

ZEALOUSLY
2206 zēlŏŏ (2), to have warmth of feeling for

ZEBADIAH
2069 Zᵉbadyâh (9), Jehovah has given

ZEBAH
2078 Zebach (12), sacrifice

ZEBAIM
6380 Pôkereth Tsᵉbâyîym (2), trap of gazelles

ZEBEDEE
2199 Zĕbĕdaiŏs (10), Zebedæus

ZEBEDEE'S
2199 Zĕbĕdaiŏs (2), Zebedæus

ZEBINA
2081 Zᵉbîynâ' (1), gainfulness

ZEBOIIM
6636 Tsᵉbô'iym (2), gazelles

ZEBOIM
6636 Tsᵉbô'iym (3), gazelles
6650 Tsᵉbô'îym (2), hyenas

ZEBUDAH
2081 Zᵉbîynâ' (1), gainfulness

ZEBUL
2083 Zᵉbûl (6), dwelling

Z

The Strong's Family of Products

CONCORDANCES

1. Classic Edition

Our Flagship volume, this edition sets the standard for all other concordances. Our number one best-selling reference book. This edition is truly exhaustive, with *Strong's* numbering system, easy-to-read modern type, a 200-page topical index, the famous Greek and Hebrew dictionaries, pronunciation guides, words of Christ highlighted, and Nelson's Fan-Tab Thumb Index system.
Hardcover / 1,824 pages / 0-7852-6750-1

2. Comfort Print Edition

Our Comfort Print Edition is the only truly enlarged-type exhaustive edition available! Newly typeset and updated, with corrected text throughout, this volume is a sight for sore eyes. Includes the famous Greek and Hebrew dictionaries, and Fan-Tab reference system.
Hardcover / 1,968 pages / 0-7852-2072-6

3. Portable/Super Value Edition

Same contents as our Comfort Print Edition, only in a smaller more portable size! Perfect for the classroom, Bible study group, or just to keep around the house, this edition has everything you want in a *Strong's Concordance,* in an easy-to-carry size!
Hardcover / 1,920 pages / 0-7852-1155-1

4. Concise Edition

A slightly trimmed-down version of the Classic Edition, both in size and content. It contains most of the word entries from the full-size edition, without the Greek and Hebrew dictionaries and *Strong's* numbering system. It does include Fan-Tab Thumb index reference system, easy-to-read typeface, and brief definitions and pronunciation guides for all proper names.
Paperback / 768 pages / 0-7852-1166-7

WORD STUDIES

5. Complete Dictionary of Bible Words

The famous *Strong's* dictionaries are now available in a fully corrected, updated version as a separate volume, in an enlarged, easy-to-read format. Includes a completely new and exclusive

English word index showing which Greek and Hebrew words are translated into specific English words, how often each translation occurs, and brief definitions.
Hardcover / 736 pages / 0-7852-1147-0

6. New Strong's Guide to Bible Words

Helps you get the full benefit of your current Bible study resources. This exclusive guide gives quick access to over 14,000 biblical words, showing Hebrew and Greek words that lie behind each English word, along with the number of times each occurs, Strong's numbers, and brief definitions. It belongs in the library of every owner of a *Strong's Exhaustive Concordance*.
Hardcover / 292 pages / 0-7852-1197-7

The Vine's Family
of Products

Collected Writings of W. E. Vine—5-vol. set

All of W. E. Vine's writings are available in this 5-volume set. His writings on biblical studies and theology, his commentaries on selected Bible books and other topics, and his self-study Greek grammar are all here. Also available as individual volumes.

5-volume hardcover set / 0-7852-1159-4

Vine's Complete Expository Dictionary

This classic edition combines *Vine's Expository Dictionary of New Testament Words* with the *Expository Dictionary of the Old Testament* by M. F. Unger and W. White. Entries are coded to *Strong's Concordance,* to the *B-D-B Hebrew Lexicon* and the *Bauer-Arndt-Gingrich Greek Lexicon.*

Hardcover / 1,128 pages / 0-7852-7559-8

Vine's Complete Expository Dictionary with Topical Index

In addition to the features of the classic edition, above, a new Topical Index has been created to aid Bible study. It is organized so it can become at once a dictionary, a commentary, and a concordance.

Hardcover / 1,184 pages / 0-7852-1160-8

Vine's Expository Dictionary of Old and New
Testament Words—Super Value Edition

This Super Value Edition offers the combination of Vine's *original* Old Testament dictionary and his New Testament dictionary. This is the most affordable edition of the famous dictionaries.

Hardcover / 912 pages / 0-7852-1181-0

Vine's Expository Commentary on Galatians
Vine's Expository Commentary on 1 & 2 Thessalonians

These small but thorough commentaries use an approach that takes into consideration ev reference to particular words in the Bible—and their uses in ancient Greek—the language c New Testament. The verse-by-verse word studies are in-depth commentaries on Galatia the two epistles to the Thessalonians.

Hardcover / 224 pages / 0-7852-1172-1 (Galatians)
0-7852-1171-3 (1 & 2 Thessalonians)

Vine's Learn New Testament Greek

Designed especially for the layperson, this book is an easy "teach yourself" c
have no previous knowledge of Greek. Start by learning the Greek alphabe

lesson read directly from the Greek New Testament. Includes grammar, lessons, charts, tables, and diagrams—all created for self-study.

Paperback / 128 pages / 0-7852-1232-9

NQR Vine's Dictionary of Bible Words

Covers both Old and New Testament words in one easy-to-use A—Z listing, this compact size *Vine's* has the most-theologically significant and most-often consulted entries in the ultimate quick-reference resource. Keyed to *Strong's* reference numbers, each entry includes how the word is used, key Bible occurrences, English transliteration, and definitions. An exceptional value for studying the meaning of biblical words.

Paperback / 800 pages / 0-7852-1169-1

Printed in the USA
CPSIA information can be obtained
at www.ICGtesting.com
LVHW010832210724
785408LV00002B/3